D1710400

THE CIVIC MUSE

THE
CIVIC
MUSE

Music and Musicians in Siena
during the Middle Ages
and the Renaissance

FRANK A. D'ACCONE

The University of Chicago Press ⚬ Chicago ⚬ London

Frank A. D'Accone is professor emeritus in the Department of Musicology at the University of California, Los Angeles. He is author of *The History of a Baroque Opera: Alessandro Scarlatti's* Gli equivoci nel sembiante, and is editor of the series *Music of the Florentine Renaissance*.

The University of Chicago Press gratefully acknowledges the assistance of the Guggenheim Foundation in the publication of this book.

The University of Chicago Press, Chicago 60637
The University of Chicago Press, Ltd., London
©1997 by The University of Chicago
All rights reserved. Published 1997
Printed in the United States of America
06   05   04   03   02   01   00   99   98   97   1   2   3   4   5
ISBN: 0-226-13366-4 (cloth)

Library of Congress Cataloging-in-Publication Data

D'Accone, Frank A.
    The civic muse : music and musicians in Siena during the Middle
Ages and the Renaissance / Frank A. D'Accone.
        p.   cm.
    Includes bibliographical references (p.   ) and index.
    ISBN 0-226-13366-4 (cloth)
    1. Music—Italy—Siena—History and criticism.   I. Title.
ML290.8.S43D33   1997
780'.945'580902—dc21   96-46888
                                                         CIP
                                                         MN

To William C. Holmes

CONTENTS

ILLUSTRATIONS

FIGURES

PLATES
(following page 472)

TABLES

MUSICAL EXAMPLES

Examples are grouped at ends of chapters.

PREFACE

RESEARCH FOR THIS BOOK was carried out over a number of years in Siena, Florence, and Los Angeles. I first became interested in Sienese musical history in 1970, when Edward E. Lowinsky invited me to read a paper at an international festival-conference honoring Josquin des Prez and suggested that I write about performance practices in Italian chapels during the composer's lifetime. While searching for pertinent materials I read Martin Staehelin's study about Pierre de la Rue in Italy and the composer's possible presence in Siena in the 1480s. I was intrigued because La Rue had not previously been documented in Italy and it occurred to me that Siena might have played a far greater role than was then known in the cultural exchange that characterized late fifteenth-century European music. But apart from a few isolated reports, mentioned below in the Introduction, there was little in musicological literature, or elsewhere for that matter, that hinted, as Staehelin's study did, at any significant musical activity in the city at that time. In spring 1970 it proved possible during a brief trip to Siena to gather information in cathedral archives that was later incorporated into my study presented at the Josquin Festival-Conference. As valuable as the information was, I was painfully aware that I had only skimmed the surface of available documentation. I use the word "available" advisedly because at the time, owing to a lack of personnel and a proper reading area, access to cathedral archives was sporadic and limited. But in the next decade it was possible, during brief trips to Italy, to conduct a systematic examination of many fifteenth- and sixteenth-century documents. By 1980 I had gathered enough material to begin writing a book about music at Siena cathedral during the Renaissance.

The project was well along when, as a result of a generous grant from the Guggenheim Foundation during the 1980–81 academic year, I had an unbroken stretch of time in Siena and uncovered additional materials in cathedral archives and in the city's Biblioteca Comunale degli Intronati. At the same time I became aware of the wealth of documentation, most of it unpublished, concerning musicians and musical performance at Siena's Palazzo Pubblico and other places that was kept in the Sienese State Archives. My initial interest in these materials was kindled by my old friend and mentor Gino Corti of Florence, who was himself engaged on a research project in Siena at the time. Thanks to him I was able to gain daily access to cathedral archives, and it was then that I became aware of new avenues of research that still awaited exploration and of the rich materials they demonstrably contained. The result was that I changed the scope of my project to encompass what I now present in this book. Gino Corti, however, did far more than induce me to gain a broader perspective of Sienese music in earlier times and of musical developments elsewhere in the city. Without his help I should never have been able to examine and read as many documents as I have, and I would have been unable to publish with such assurance those included here. He has not only reread and corrected most of my transcriptions but also transcribed from start to finish those that I could not do myself. I acknowledge his assistance with gratitude and affection.

Though I was aware that enlarging the scope of the book would necessarily prolong its completion, I never dreamed that fifteen years would pass before I was able to finish my work. In a sense, I use the word "finish" with some reservation because I am aware that there are other sources, particularly chant books, in Sienese archives still awaiting examination. But to have attempted more detailed study than I was able to give them and other materials would probably have taken another fifteen years, and I thought it wise to leave these sources for another time or to other scholars. Meanwhile, since starting this Sienese project, I have completed an edition of the extant works of Andrea Feliciani and a number of other Sienese polyphonic pieces, and all of the extant music for the feast of Sant'Ansano, Siena's patron saint. Though I would have liked to include more of the music here, I have heeded the advice of my editors and reserved publication for another time.

It gives me great pleasure to express my gratitude to the many people who assisted me during the preparation of this book. In the first place I should like to remember the late Howard Mayer Brown, who encouraged my initial concept of *The Civic Muse* and gave, as only he could, a thorough and critical reading to some of the early chapters. These chapters were likewise read by Gabriel Dotto, who not only supported the project in its initial stages but also accompanied me to Siena to solicit the support of the Accademia degli Intronati. Later, Colleen Reardon, H. Colin Slim, Keith Polk, Lewis Lockwood, Barbara Sparti, and Leofranc Holford-Strevens read all or portions of the text and made many valuable suggestions. Agostino Ziino, William F. Prizer, Stefano Mengozzi, Allan Atlas, Andrew Hughes, and Gilbert Reaney gave me information on specific points, and Robert Judd, Gail Aronow, Nicholas Adams, Samuel K. Cohn, Jr., and Franco Pavan called my attention to materials I might otherwise have overlooked. Maria Grazia Ciardi Dupré, Richard Sherr, James Westby, Tommaso Urso, John Kmetz, Enzo Settesoldi, Victor Coelho, Kathryn Bosi-Monteath, Carmela Speroni, Jeffrey Dean, and Giuliano Baroncelli assisted me in various ways, as did Andrew Maz, who copied the musical examples with dispatch and accuracy. I wish also to thank Enzo Carli, past president of the cathedral Opera, the late Sonia Fineschi, Carla Zarrilli, director of the Sienese State Archives, Curzio Bastianoni, director of the Biblioteca Comunale degli Intronati, and the staffs at these institutions for their many kindnesses and for facilitating my research. From afar Stefano Moscadelli came to my rescue a number of times, and Nello Barbieri kept a critical and informed eye on aspects of the text relating to musical performance spaces at the Palazzo Pubblico and to things Sienese in general. I owe special thanks to my editor, Bonnie J. Blackburn, who gave generously of her time, knowledge, and invaluable advice as I prepared the final reading of the text. Without her wise counsel I should have been less successful in present-ing archival materials in what I hope is a concise and logical manner and in confronting the organizational problems that inevitably arise in a documentary study such as this.

Finally, I wish to record my gratitude to the UCLA Committee on Research for its continuing support over the years and to the John Simon Guggenheim Memorial Foundation, both for its early assistance and later, as the book was going to press, for a timely subvention to assist in publication costs.

NOTE ON SOURCES, CITATIONS, AND TRANSCRIPTIONS

MOST OF THE DOCUMENTARY MATERIAL in this book comes from two archives, the Archivio di Stato, Siena, and the Archivio dell'Opera Metropolitana, Siena. I have also made extensive use of holdings in Siena's Biblioteca Comunale degli Intronati and in Siena's Archivio Arcivescovile, which contains the surviving papers of the cathedral's Archivio Capitolare. Additional source materials are from the Biblioteca Nazionale Centrale, Florence, the Archivio di Stato, Florence, and the Vatican Library, Rome.

From the cathedral come records of decisions taken by the overseer and the governing board of the Opera and of the myriad payments made on their behalf to various artists, artisans, workmen, and musicians in the service of the Opera. These survive in several series of volumes, which, though neither complete nor continuous, allow a reconstruction of the day-to-day workings of the great fabric and the many activities that occurred within its walls. The records were compiled for internal, administrative purposes and were meant primarily to give an accurate accounting of the names and duties of people officially employed by the Opera, how much they were to be paid, when and how much they actually received for their services; they also list monies accruing to the Opera from its various holdings. Principal among the volumes I consulted are those compiled annually listing in double-entry bookkeeping income received and salaries and other obligations paid out each month (*Entrata & Uscita*); records of daily expenses and income received (*Giornali*); the large registers in double-entry bookkeeping of payments made and received for various reasons to and from individuals over a period of several years (*Debitori & Creditori*); reports of decisions taken at meetings of the overseer and his counselors (*Deliberazioni*); monthly reports of tardiness and absences at Divine Offices compiled by the sacristans (called *Scritte* in contemporary sources, formerly described as *Puntature di messe* and *Salariati* and now classified under the general heading *Salari, "puntature" e pagamenti al clero e a musici e cantori*); yearly and monthly reports compiled for the sacristy of salaries due and disbursed to officially employed clerics and others serving in the choir (formerly listed as *Maestranze,* now as *Ore canoniche*); reports of income received and expenditures made by the camerlenghi or treasurers and stewards (*Memoriali*); inventories of cathedral holdings (*Inventari di beni immobili e mobili*); and letters written to and by the overseer and others on matters regarding cathedral administration (*Carteggio*). Today these and other records as well as musical manuscripts and prints that belonged to the cathedral and its dependencies are kept in the Opera's offices in the small museum adjacent to the church.

For my account of music at the Palazzo Pubblico I have relied mainly on the records of discussions and deliberations of the ruling signory, these compiled into bimonthly volumes, the whole spanning a period of several centuries (Concistoro); on records of payment similar to those described above (*Entrata & Uscita, Debitori & Creditori*) maintained by the state treasury, though not so systematically preserved as at the cathedral (Biccherna), and on the records of a few other government officials and bodies (Balìa, Consiglio Generale, Regolatori). These are all kept at the Archivio di Stato, as are records of deliberations and expenditures from various churches and monasteries (Patrimonio resti, Ospedale di Santa Maria della Scala), records of various notaries (Notarile antecosimiano, Notarile postcosimiano), reports filed for tax authorities (Lira), and a few other sources mentioned in the course of my narrative.

In general most of the manuscript materials I consulted are gathered in bound volumes whose folios are numbered, as is customary, on the right-hand (recto) side. References in my citations are accordingly made to a recto (r) or verso (v) side of each folio. There are, however, many account books whose pages are numbered so that the facing sides of an opening, that is, a verso of the preceding folio and a recto of the next one, share the same number. I refer to these by a single number that I designate "left" and "right." A few of the sources I consulted, particularly the *Salari, "puntature" e pagamenti al clero e a musici e cantori,* consist of collections of looseleaf sheets, generally unnumbered, gathered into packets that are tied with short lengths of string. I refer to them by volume number, month, and year.

The only available guide to cathedral holdings while I was conducting my research was Giovanni Cecchini's still quite useful, though summary, inventory that is appended to his "L'Archivio dell'Opera Metropolitana." As I prepared the final draft of my manuscript Stefano Moscadelli very kindly made his computerized inventory of cathedral holdings available to me so that I was able to renumber my references to conform to his. Moscadelli has synchronized his numbering system with Cecchini's, so readers should have no trouble locating volumes in cathedral archives cited in this study or in previous ones citing Cecchini's. Both inventories are listed in the Bibliography together with the most recent general guides to the various Sienese archives just mentioned.

Apart from the addition of minimal punctuation and the resolution of abbreviations, my transcriptions of documents reproduce texts as they appear in the original sources. I do the same in many footnotes, where, when making brief references, I quote names and dates directly from documents. In the course of my narrative, however, I have changed the orthography of given and family names to conform to modern Italian usage. Thus I have omitted superfluous letters, such as the "h" in Charlo, though in several instances I have retained unusual spellings or others that reflect local usage, such as, for example, Barzalomeo and Meio. In some instances several forms of the same name—Michelangelo/Michelagnolo, Giovanbattista/Giovambattista—appear regularly and I have chosen the one most frequently encountered in a given period or set of documents, again omitting redundant vowels, such as the "i" in Michelagniolo, or supplying a missing consonant, such as the second "t" in Giovanbatista. (The names, however, are indexed under Giovanbattista.) The names of foreign musicians were always given in Italian or in Latin, and I have rendered these, as I have all Latin forms of names, into modern Italian equivalents.

Documentary evidence concerning individual musicians appears under the relevant name in the Register of Musicians.

NOTE ON SIENESE DATING AND MONEY

THE SIENESE NEW YEAR, like the Florentine, began on the feast of the Annunciation, on 25 March. As a result, documents recorded between 1 January and 24 March carry the date of the previous year. I have emended such dates to conform to modern usage during the course of my narrative, though I have retained the original dating (followed by a slash and the modern date) in my transcriptions of documents. When it was necessary to add a date to the text of a document, this has been placed within brackets, as have been the few editorial emendations I have made. Generally, these latter have been confined to occasional though egregious errors in the original, signaled by [*sic*]. The fiscal year for cathedral documents runs from May through April.

The Sienese florin (Fl.) fluctuated in value during the early fifteenth century, containing around 4 or slightly fewer lire (L.) to the 1, depending on the gold content. I have indicated its worth, when such information appears in relevant sources. Later in the century the value of the gold florin rose as high as 7 lire and more. In cathedral payments from the late fifteenth century the ducat (Du.) appears to have been equivalent or nearly equivalent to the florin and, from the early sixteenth century onward, worth slightly more than the scudo (Sc.). The lira contained 20 soldi (s.), each worth 12 denari (d.). In the text, when referring to payments made in lira, soldi, and denari, I often separate the denominations by periods; thus L. 2. 3. 4 means 2 lire, 3 soldi, 4 denari.

ABBREVIATIONS

AAS	Archivio Arcivescovile, Siena
AOMS	Archivio dell'Opera della Metropolitana di Siena
ASF	Archivio di Stato, Florence
ASS	Archivio di Stato, Siena
BCIS	Biblioteca Comunale degli Intronati di Siena
BSSP	*Bullettino Senese di Storia Patria*
Constitutiones	*Constitutiones Sacri Capituli Metropolitanae Senensis Ecclesiae* (Siena: Luca Bonetto, 1579)
D&C	Debitori & Creditori
E&U	Entrata & Uscita
EMH	*Early Music History*
fasc.	fascicolo
FBNC	Florence, Biblioteca Nazionale Centrale
JAMS	*Journal of the American Musicological Society*
MGG	*Die Musik in Geschichte und Gegenwart*
New Grove	*The New Grove Dictionary of Music and Musicians,* ed. Stanley Sadie, 20 vols. (London, 1980)
OO	*Ordo Officiorum Ecclesiae Senensis ab Oderico eiusdem Ecclesiae Canonico Anno MCCXIII Compositus,* ed. Giovanni Crisostomo Trombelli (Bologna, 1766)
Pacta . . . nova	*Pacta et capitula nova,* in *Constitutiones,* 70–79
Pacta . . . vetera	*Pacta et capitula vetera,* in *Constitutiones,* 57–69
PR	ASS, Patrimonio Resti
RISM	Répertoire international des sources musicales
RMI	*Rivista Musicale Italiana*

INTRODUCTION

THE *CIVIC MUSE* as the title of a history of music in Siena from 1200 to 1600 has its origins in the premise that patronage policies developed by the state to favor the common good largely determined the course of Sienese music during most of that time. A legacy of the government of the Nine, whose rule (1287–1355) saw the establishment of ideals of collective achievement and public support of the arts, these policies continued to affect the city's three principal performing groups throughout the last centuries of Siena's republic, in spite of the increasing importance of patronage by private families and individuals in the other arts. Somewhat surprisingly, they remained in effect even in the later sixteenth century, after Siena had lost its independence and was incorporated into the Medici state, and at a time when the private musical patron began assuming a more visible role in society. It was their very existence and the traditions they perpetuated that furnished the financial means and organizational structures ensuring the survival of publicly supported ensembles in a once proud city now reduced to provincial status. In this book I shall trace the development of policies of civic, or state, patronage of music and discuss the manner in which they were shaped to meet the needs of church and state in a typically Sienese fashion, thus providing a framework within which all major developments in Sienese music occurred from later medieval times through the end of the Renaissance.

Lurking in the background throughout those centuries was the spectre of Florence, Siena's feared neighbor to the north, whose territorial and economic ambitions had been on a collision course with Siena's almost from time immemorial. The Sienese military victory over Florentine forces at the battle of Montaperti in 1260, arguably the most important event in the tortured history of Tuscan rivalries, loomed large throughout subsequent centuries as Siena drifted into the role of a secondary power. Yet the qualities that defined the fiercely independent spirit of the Sienese—their love of liberty, their religious piety, their devotion to their advocate, the Virgin Mary, their passion for beauty, their civic pride—never burned so brightly as they did in those times. By the late fourteenth century, however, internal political differences appeared almost irreconcilable as one faction battled another for control of the state. Despite a seemingly chronic inability to govern itself, Siena displayed a remarkable instinct for survival during the next hundred and fifty years and found an important place in the flowering of arts, letters, and music that defined the civilization of Renaissance Italy. It was then, even as mythic tales of Siena's origins and its ancient grandeur gained currency, that its scholars assumed places among the leading ranks of humanists, its university drew students from throughout Europe, its sons and daughters found their niches in the Christian hierarchy in heaven and on earth, and its artists and architects enriched the repository of Italian and the world's art. And it was during those years that the city's principal

performing groups, long the recipients of various forms of public patronage, continued
the development that placed them on a level with some of the best that could be found
in Italy. Siena's artistic heritage continues to draw visitors to the city, which, despite the
restorations, if not the recreations, of an over-zealous citizenry yearning for affirmation
of the town's former glory, presents as do few others an unrivaled and unparalleled
panorama of the European experience of centuries past. But not even a distant echo
calls forth the sounds heard within Siena's walls, little trace of them remaining except
for a few musical sources and a voluminous written record of where and when they
were made and by whom.

A few remarks about the city's history and its institutions furnish the background
for my discussion of civic patronage in the development of Sienese music. After aban-
doning the remnants of feudalism and consular rule at the turn of the thirteenth century,
the Sienese, like others in Tuscany, gradually adopted a democratic system of government that placed political power in the hands of the citizenry. Though "freedom" and
"liberty" proudly proclaimed the aspirations of the Sienese city-state, in the following
centuries the struggle of various classes to gain or retain supremacy inevitably led to
fierce factionalism and endemic rivalries that more than once brought the city to the
brink of disaster. But Siena remained a republic, true to democratic institutions that
were refined and modernized over the centuries to meet its own needs and those of its
dependencies. As the system evolved, many powers of the purse and of determining
economic and foreign policy were assigned to the signory, or Concistoro, as it was
called in Siena. It was the town's supreme executive organ. Comprising a group of
bimestrially elected priors, who were members of the then ascendant party or coalitions
of parties, and of representatives of various government bureaus and others, who served
somewhat longer terms of six months, the Concistoro was directly responsible for
choosing the commune's highest appointed officials.

Principal among them was the podestà, or chief magistrate, in whom was vested
jurisdiction over a broad array of civic and criminal matters as well as leadership in
military operations and diplomatic missions. He also initiated legislative matters and
convened meetings of the General Council, or Council of the Bell, the city's major
legislative assembly. By law, the podestà was a foreigner, obliged to reside in the city
during his six-month term of office, after which he remained ineligible for reappointment until five years had passed. His salary, including expenses for maintaining a
large personal entourage of judges, notaries, knights, infantrymen, and trumpeters, was
set by the Concistoro and paid by the state treasury, the Biccherna. So, too, with the
captain of the people, at first a foreigner, but later drawn from the ranks of Siena's most
eminent citizens. His most conspicuous duties lay in safeguarding the rights of the poor
and the powerless and in maintaining order in the city. Other major officials in the
service of the state, among them the major syndic, who acted as guardian of the constitution, and the captain of war, were similarly dependent upon the approval of the
Concistoro, which thus retained the ability to safeguard its own party interests as well
as those of the state. The parties, called *monti* in Siena, originated in response to the
aims and needs of various classes, though with the passing of time, social status, wealth,
and other ideological lines dividing them were often blurred.

In the last century of Siena's republic, in response to social and economic developments and to the changing needs of government and of the citizenry, new offices and assemblies, as, for example, the Council of the People, were created and existing ones were reinforced or given new mandates. Though the Concistoro retained many of its prerogatives and responsibilities as well as the outward semblance of power, by the later fifteenth century an appointed commission composed generally of elder statesmen, the Balìa, emerged to become the most authoritative policy-maker in the government, exercising both legislative and executive power in ways that the larger, constantly revolving Concistoro never could. Throughout the first half of the sixteenth century, all these institutions found a place in a political structure that despite the rapacious designs of larger states and the sometimes self-destructive policies of its own leaders, served the Sienese well until their dominion fell prey to overwhelming external forces.

Siena knew great prosperity and political stability under the government of the Nine. So named for the nine members who represented its interests on the Concistoro, this regime of merchants, bankers, and businessmen brought efficient management policies and farsighted measures to running the state as they sought to fulfill their expertly promoted ideal of good government. Hand in hand with the development of trade and commerce went the international successes of a dynamic banking industry. Agriculture likewise flourished, and exploitation of rich mineral deposits in the lands of Siena's dominion—for the republic was no less assiduous in bringing its countryside and the lesser cities and towns nearby within its political orbit than it was in fostering its own democratic aspirations—contributed to an economic expansion without precedent. In the mid-fourteenth century, before the advent of the Black Death, Siena's population soared to more than 40,000, making it one of the largest cities in Europe. It was surrounded, moreover, not by desolate, uninhabited countryside but by other prosperous and well-populated urban centers that owed it their political allegiance. But hard times followed the ouster of the government of the Nine in 1355, and the socio-economic crisis of the following decades was reflected in the decline of the city's population, to about 17,000 inhabitants in the early fifteenth century and then to 14,000 by the mid-fifteenth century, less than a third of what it had been a hundred years earlier. Though Siena would never again regain its former wealth, economic revival in later decades saw its population increase to about 20,000, where it remained until experiencing new growth in the decades before the fall of the republic. All the more wonder, then, that despite declining wealth and population, Siena would sustain musical establishments comparable in standards of performance and often in numbers of personnel to those maintained by the largest and wealthiest cities on the peninsula. But this is to anticipate.

The social and financial havoc brought on by the plague and collapse of Siena's banking houses, the failure of successive regimes to bring stability to government, an ill-advised alliance that threatened the sovereignty of the city and its dominion—all contributed to the turbulence of Sienese life in the fifteenth century. In 1459 a formula for resolution of age-old rivalries forced on warring factions by the Sienese pope Pius II Piccolomini brought the noble party into the government and with it a respite that lasted only briefly after his death. Renewed tension was seemingly put to rest with the grand reconciliation of various parties in 1483, but feelings still ran high among exiles, who within four years staged a coup d'état that brought Pandolfo Petrucci to power. From that time until his death in 1512, Petrucci, as the uncontested head of the new ruling coalition, was generally successful in keeping the reins of the state in his own hands, a talent notoriously lacking in his heirs, who were less fortunate than he in responding to both internal and external threats to the regime. The short-lived government headed by Alessandro Bichi, assassinated at the moment of his investiture as the city's ruler in 1525, led to continuing agitation, fueled by the ambitions of various foreign rulers. Repeated admonitions from Siena's imperial overlord, the emperor Charles V, failed to calm the troubled waters. In the end expulsion of a Spanish garrison sent by Charles to maintain order within the city led to full-scale revolt and alliances with the French and Florentine rebels, the siege of Siena, and the loss of Siena's cherished independence in 1555. Within a few years Siena was incorporated into the greater Tuscan realm of the Medici. There it remained for centuries, a secondary, provincial town, whose artistic legacy and monuments, visible at every turn, provided a constant reminder of its glorious, if troubled, past to even the most casual visitor.[1]

Sienese civic patronage found its most visible and lasting expression in the architecture, decoration, and furnishings of the city's cathedral and Palazzo Pubblico, focal points of most of the major events in Sienese life. It followed almost as a matter of course that policies regarding musical groups associated with those places, the Palace trumpeters and wind band, and the cathedral chapel of singers, would be governed by similar attitudes. Employing the most highly trained and talented musicians available, these publicly supported ensembles were necessarily in the forefront of Sienese musical life both because of the people they employed and by virtue of where and for whom these people performed.

As the seat of government, the Palazzo Pubblico, or Palace, as I shall often refer to it, was where Siena's rulers lived and worked and in whose magnificently decorated great hall and rooms distinguished visitors were received and entertained. Completed in the early years of the fourteenth century during the government of the Nine, the Palace was situated in an area where the city's terzi or three major districts met, on the site of the old marketplace, subsequently to become the beautifully paved shell-shaped Campo. A brief walk uphill through the narrow winding streets of the Terzo di Città, the city's ancient core, led to the cathedral and the surrounding bishop's palace, canons' residence, and hospital of Santa Maria Nuova. As the principal place of worship in the city and the most visible expression of Sienese piety and wealth, the cathedral furnished the backdrop for many of the significant moments in the city's history. It was both the seat of the bishop and the site where government leaders inaugurated their terms of office with special ceremonies. Victories, proclamations of peace, and political treaties were all observed there amid pomp and splendor, as were the arrivals and departures of popes, emperors, cardinals, ambassadors, and others. Not least of all, it was there that daily services were celebrated by a full complement of canons, chaplains, and clerks,

---

1. The best recent books on Siena in this period are William M. Bowsky, *A Medieval Italian Commune: Siena under the Nine, 1287–1355* (Berkeley and Los Angeles, 1981) and Judith Hook, *Siena: A City and its History* (London, 1979); Italian trans., with an introductory essay by Roberto Barzanti, *Siena: Una città e la sua storia* (Siena, 1985). I have also relied on several articles by David Hicks, Anne Katherine Chiancone Isaacs, Maria Giantempo, Valerie Wainwright, and Giuliano Catoni and Gabriella Piccini, listed in the Bibliography.

and it was there that Sundays and other major feast days were marked from very early times by the performance of both plainchant and polyphony.

The cathedral and the Palace thus provided the settings where music, in all of its varied forms, enhanced the many solemn ceremonies, whether religious, civic, political, or patriotic, that were witnessed by citizens from every walk of life. Tracing the activities of the musicians employed in these places forms the principal part of this book, which also seeks to place music and musical performance within both the Sienese cultural experience and the broader context of Italian musical history.

Civic, or state, patronage of music in Siena meant that decisions regarding music were made by political parties, acting through legally constituted branches of government such as the Concistoro, as Siena's ruling body of priors was called, and the General Council or Council of the Bell, Siena's principal legislative body. At the Palazzo Pubblico it was the priors, or their surrogates, who authorized musical programs and made decisions that directly affected the music performed there: who and how many musicians would be employed, where and when they would play, what they would be paid, and what privileges they would enjoy. Regardless of the faction in power, the Palace's two musical ensembles, many of whose duties were designed to emphasize the stability and legitimacy of the government, functioned according to a system defined by custom and practical need. A notable feature of the system was its permanence. Successive governments might come and go, but the musical groups, once established, continued to enjoy uninterrupted state support throughout the period of the republic.

At the cathedral decisions regarding building, decoration, and musical programs and their financing were the responsibility of a secular administration presided over by an overseer and an advisory board, all elected and appointed with government approval. There, too, though circumstances were quite different, it was a group deriving its authority from the state—and acting also with the consent of church authorities—that determined what kinds of musical performance would best enhance the liturgy, how much cathedral revenue would be spent on them, and who would be hired to realize them. Since cathedral music programs depended on the commitment of individual overseers, their willingness to provide funds sufficient to maintain musical forces beyond those that met the basic requirements of the liturgy was essential. At times, as happened particularly at the end of the fifteenth century, an overseer's personal predilections might result in increased expenditures for the larger forces necessary for performance of the latest forms of polyphony. His actions, however, were presumably made in accord with prevailing sentiments favoring the common good.

The role of the state, as I show throughout this book, lies at the heart of almost all aspects of musical culture in Siena, whether through its support of performing groups at the cathedral and the Palace or, as will be seen, through its encouragement and subvention of teaching programs initiated in those places. Certainly, the tastes and sensibilities of individuals or small groups of them influenced decisions taken and implemented in the name of the state, but these were generally directed by tradition, custom, and the needs of the institutions they served. People in such positions, of course, were not immune to pressure from outside influence, as an occasional glimpse of behind-the-scenes activities indicates. A cardinal's word here, a governor general's suggestion there, all were obviously bound to affect decision making. On the whole, however, outside intervention appears to have been concerned more with personnel matters than with lofty issues. In music's case cultural policies that promoted the prestige of the city and its institutions clearly took precedence over any display of individual preferences.

The precise role of private patronage in musical matters, nevertheless, remains inconclusive due to the loss of many personal and family records. Siena, of course, had its share of noble and wealthy families whose background, connections, and interests would have allowed one or more of them also to assume roles as principal patrons of music. But every indication is that politics and the rules of society discouraged private patronage of music on the same scale as that practiced by public institutions. There is, indeed, little reason to believe that private patronage, however influential or modest it might have been, significantly affected the course of Sienese music during the period of the republic and even immediately after its fall. In the early fifteenth century the German and French instrumentalists who played at the Palace were first and foremost government employees, whether or not they were able to supplement their incomes by performing at private occasions. The Franco-Flemish musicians who sang in Siena during the late fifteenth century were first and foremost cathedral employees, whether or not they received any additional support from private individuals. Similarly, foreign composers who lived and worked in the city during the sixteenth century did so because they were employed at the cathedral. All of the most renowned local instrumentalists were associated at one time or another with the Palace. Siena's own composers also earned their livings at public institutions. The earliest of them, a cathedral singer and a Palace woodwind player, contributed the lion's share of pieces to the first known printed book of music in Siena, and in the later sixteenth century it was again performers employed at the cathedral and the Palace who through their compositions helped spread knowledge of Sienese music throughout Italy and Europe, even though publication costs of their works might be borne by private patrons.

In tracing the history of Siena's leading musical groups, one point that emerges with great clarity is that Sienese music flourished best when it was able to draw on its own resources. This was as true in the early fourteenth century, during the heyday of the republic, as it was in the late sixteenth century, when city fathers, under the rule of a foreign prince, scrambled to find the formulas and means necessary to assure the survival of centuries-old musical programs. From very early times self-sufficiency as a means of achieving success was evident in the Palace trumpeters' corps. It came about in part because of town statutes, which favored the employment of local musicians, and in part because of employment policies favoring ties of kinship and familial systems of musical instruction. Almost the opposite situation was true of the Palace wind band. There were few if any local musicians capable of serving in the group when it was first established in the early fifteenth century, and foreigners, particularly the renowned German wind players, continued to fill its ranks for many decades afterwards. Lacking familial ties and any incentives for remaining in the city other than financial ones, foreign performers came and went with dizzying regularity. It was only later in the century, after the government implemented a policy requiring foreign appointees to bring their families to Siena, that a measure of stability was gained, and with it the beginnings of a distinctively Sienese wind ensemble tradition. Results were visible within a generation, and by the turn of the sixteenth century all of the wind band members were not only Sienese but also children of former employees. Familial systems of education and government employment policies were thus again at the root of a program that ensured sufficient numbers of trained musicians ready to fulfill the needs of the group. Later in the sixteenth century, when traditional employment policies proved inadequate, the government itself began sponsoring teaching programs at the Palace that were aimed at encouraging and training the most promising young instrumentalists in the city.

Developments in the cathedral chapel paralleled in many respects those in the Palace wind band, though with some important differences. Cathedral musicians needed training in chant and in the liturgy, training that could only be had at a cathedral school, where instruction in polyphonic music might also be available. Cathedral singers and organists were generally clerics, though this was not always the case in later times. As long as improvised polyphony or simpler forms of written part music prevailed, Siena's cathedral school was able to train sufficient numbers of musicians to meet local needs. But this was obviously no longer true when, in the early fifteenth century, the government sought to strengthen the school's program by mandating the establishment of permanent posts for the teaching of plainchant, polyphony, and organ playing. It was a decision whose effect was not immediately apparent, though eventually it would prove to have lasting results. Later, as knowledge of newer and more sophisticated forms of written polyphony and performance practices reached Siena, the demand grew for musicians trained in the centers of production from which the new styles emanated. These were the legendary Franco-Flemings, who dominated many if not all Italian musical establishments during the last decades of the fifteenth century and well into the next. In the long run Sienese efforts to attract and retain northern musicians were unsuccessful, and for a number of years the chapel remained an unstable institution, subject to the erratic presence of itinerant singers.

Gradually, conditions improved, as native-born singers assumed a greater role in the chapel, though at a slower rate than those in the Palace wind band. There, ties of kinship and familial training hastened the process of transforming the group into one with local personnel, whereas at the cathedral it was support of the teaching program and the effectiveness of individual masters of the chapel that largely determined the pace of the transformation. From the end of the fifteenth century onwards cathedral-trained choirboys formed an indispensable and integral part of the chapel's makeup. Several of them subsequently rejoined the chapel as adult singers, though it was only toward the end of the sixteenth century that their number significantly increased. By that time all of the city's major musical ensembles, as a result of teaching programs and residency requirements instituted decades earlier, were training sufficient numbers of musicians to meet their own needs and those of society at large.

Outside musical influences, however, provided the stimulus that hastened the development of polyphony in Siena. Those emanating from Florence were among the most important and affected developments in Siena both positively—when Siena actively embraced musical practices that were fashionable there—and negatively, when Florentine musicians were barred because of a perceived threat to Siena's cultural independence. Despite periods of intense political hostility, the two cities maintained a lively musical exchange throughout the fifteenth century and much of the sixteenth. By far the most frequently traveled route was from north to south, with Florentine instrumentalists journeying to Siena at least once a year for the Assumption Day celebrations in August. Though not as frequently, Florentine chapel singers also traveled there. A ceremonial motet in honor of Siena composed by a Florentine singer was in all probability given its first performance on one such visit. Musical contacts, however, were not limited to these occasions, nor were itineraries only in one direction. Sienese instrumental groups and chapel singers were frequently in Florence for the annual St. John's Day celebrations. Individual Sienese instrumentalists often went for personal reasons and one of them even found permanent employment there. Nevertheless, Florence, by virtue of its more cosmopolitan outlook, its size, its wealth, its cultural and political ambitions, and a well-established tradition in polyphonic music, was the major Tuscan musical center of the fifteenth century, as it had been earlier and would continue to be in the future. It was also Florence that took the lead in embracing new developments in polyphony and performance practices originating in the Franco-Flemish regions of northern Europe. Siena's acceptance of the new northern music was slow at first, but quickened in the late fifteenth century when programs initiated in Florence and other major musical centers were consciously emulated.

Florentine practices were known in Siena long before that time, however. In earlier times, when improvisational and simpler forms of written polyphony were the norm at Siena cathedral, local musicians pursued traditional practices, though musical innovations, particularly as they occurred in Florence, were not long in reaching Siena. Chapel singers were the principal purveyors of Florentine models in fifteenth-century Siena before the beginning of the great northern migrations. A Florentine singer was at Siena cathedral as early as 1401 and others followed. Florentines continued to arrive even after northern musicians began appearing in Siena at mid-century. One group of singers who brought much needed stability to the catheral's music program in the 1460s originated in Florence and was led by a Florentine. To a certain extent an analogous situation is evident earlier in the century when German woodwind players journeyed between the two cities, ensuring access to similar repertories and performance practices. Many of the Franco-Flemish singers at Siena cathedral during the 1470s and 1480s had already been employed in Florence or were en route there after having sung in Rome and Naples. Florentine singers or others with connections to both cities could be found at Siena cathedral well into the sixteenth century. Several of Siena cathedral's organists were Florentine, including the first known one, hired shortly after the earliest known organ was built in 1375. In subsequent years Florentine-based organ builders found a ready welcome in Siena, as did Florentine organists called in to assess various Sienese instruments. Clearly, these examples underscore a lively, unself-conscious musical exchange between the two cities, with no hint of Sienese fears of Florentine cultural domination, or of Sienese reluctance to emulate musical models successfully adopted in Florence.

Familiar patterns of exchange ceased with the fall of the republic and Siena's absorption into the Medici dominion in 1557. From that time onward Florentine singers were never again employed at the cathedral. Nor, despite the new political ties, were Florentine musicians considered for the post of *maestro di cappella* in the 1560s, when qualified Sienese were unavailable. Instead recourse was had to musicians from Modena, with which Siena maintained close musical ties for some time. Only later in the sixteenth century, long after Medici rule was firmly established and the Sienese chapel itself securely anchored under the direction of a native son, were Florentine singers once again welcomed to Siena's Assumption Day festivities. Perhaps this was the result of a new parochialism, which saw most major Italian musical centers achieving self-sufficiency in matters of musical personnel at that time and may explain why the Florentines, likewise, seem to have lost interest in Sienese developments. Nevertheless, the situation in Siena developed as it did primarily because of a cultural policy that sought to keep things as Sienese as possible. It was one that fit in well with the political programs of Cosimo I and his successors, who allowed the Sienese to retain and administer many of their traditional institutions so long as their activities did not threaten Medici rule. Thus, while Sienese musicians might look to and learn from Florence, their institutions continued to function on paths of their own, proudly maintaining the traditions of Siena's own independent musical world.

The history of Siena's musical world has remained largely terra incognita, despite the pioneering efforts of Rinaldo Morrocchi more than a century ago. In *La musica in Siena* (1886) Morrocchi alluded to many of the riches that awaited exploration, though the brevity of his presentation precluded detailed illustration. Music at popular and political festivities, music in the academies, music's place in the thirteenth-century cathedral liturgy as reported by the canon Oderigo, the city's major musical institutions, its leading musical personalities and their works during a period of some 800 years— all were mentioned, often with reference to contemporaneous events in Italian and European musical history. To this Morrocchi added brief biographical sketches of 129 Sienese musicians, professionals and dilettantes, active from the fourteenth through the mid-nineteenth century. Though his information was not always complete or accurate, Morrocchi's work outlined issues essential to an understanding of Sienese musical achievements in those centuries. In my own work I have traversed many of the paths he indicated, always to my great reward.

In the early twentieth century Luigia Cellesi made an outstanding contribution to the study of Sienese musical history with her *Storia della più antica banda musicale senese* (1906). In a work that conformed to the highest standards of musical scholarship Cellesi traced the development of the two instrumental ensembles employed at the Palazzo Pubblico from their beginnings to her own day. Some of Cellesi's conclusions are no longer tenable, but her mastery of source materials, her analytical skills, and her musical insights make her book as profitable to read today as it was when it was first published. Several of the approaches I have pursued owe their origin to Cellesi's work, which, in view of its wider chronological scope, was necessarily less comprehensive than mine.

In *La musica in Siena* (1942) Sebastiano A. Luciani revisited some familiar topics and examined others previously unmentioned. To a substantial general introductory essay on Sienese musical history he added a series of shorter ones devoted to such diverse subjects as *Sena vetus,* the just-mentioned ceremonial motet in honor of Siena by the fifteenth-century composer Arnolfo Giliardi, Agostino Agazzari's treatise on the performing orchestra, and the life and works of Claudio Saracini. Luciani enriched his work with a very useful bibliography of printed works by Sienese composers. Like that of his predecessors, his study proved invaluable for the information it brought to bear on little-explored topics, and it remains, more than half a century later, one of the few books available devoted exclusively to the history of music in Siena.

Little research was directed toward Sienese musical history for some time after the appearance of Luciani's book, but recent years have seen the publication of a number of specialized studies whose subject matter runs the gamut from Oderigo's *Ordo Officiorum* through biographical sketches and musical editions of selections of music by Sienese composers of the early Baroque. These are cited, where pertinent, during the course of the book, but here I shall call attention to a recent book on Agostino Agazzari's life and works by my former student, Colleen Reardon, which is mentioned a number of times in the following pages. Agazzari, Siena's most famous musician, was employed at the cathedral on several different occasions in the early seventeenth century, and Reardon's study of the chapel during his time there continues several of the themes I have explored. In a few instances we share materials relating to late sixteenth-century personnel and repertories, and I hope that the resulting continuity will compensate for any redundancy of information.

In this book I have been concerned mainly with musicians and musical practices at Siena's cathedral and Palazzo Pubblico from the beginning of the thirteenth century through the end of the sixteenth. I have also considered musical practices at a number of other Sienese churches and religious foundations, for which in some cases very little documentation survives. Extant records, however, make it clear that, apart from one or two exceptions, musical programs in these other places were limited in scope and often dependent upon the services of musicians employed at the cathedral and the Palazzo Pubblico from whom they took their lead. In addition, I have attempted a general overview of music in the life of the town during the centuries under consideration. In illustrating various aspects of musical performance in Siena I have paid particular attention to public festivals and celebrations, state receptions, and government-sponsored festivities in which musicians from within and outside the city participated. Obviously, other musicians besides those associated with the two main institutions lived and worked in Siena, as did instrument makers and repairmen, music teachers, dancing masters, and independently employed musicians. I have included some information about them, though records of their activities have not come down to us in any great number. In any case I do not believe that these records and those from other religious establishments, even if more were available, would significantly alter an assessment of Sienese musical history as it can be reconstructed from data provided by the institutions responsible for the city's major musical programs.

With regard to these latter, I have documented, thoroughly I hope, though not tediously, the numbers and activities of personnel they employed. I have related the data to policies regarding the place and function of musical performance at the cathedral and the Palace, to the conventions and peculiarities of Sienese performance practices, and to Sienese repertories, both documented and undocumented, viewing them, when it seemed pertinent, within the context of events in the city's political and social life. In the few cases where it proved possible to do so, I have included information about the social and economic status of Sienese musicians and shown how official employment policies at the Palace, and to a lesser extent at the cathedral, affected both employers and employees and consequently the development of local musical traditions and practices. I have compared performing ensembles at the cathedral and the Palace with similar ones in other Italian cities for which data are available, noting similarities and differences in their numbers, compensation, repertories, and performance practices, and I have done this principally for the purpose of evaluating Sienese achievements within the broader context of Italian and European musical developments. I have analyzed and discussed, at times all too briefly, music by Sienese composers and others who worked in the city. I have limited my remarks about Sienese plainchant and its sources to those relating directly to my objectives, and I have treated only briefly, if at all, the works of several composers whose names appear in my narrative but whose production lies outside the chronological or geographical confines of my book.

In reconstructing Siena's musical history on the basis of surviving archival, literary, and musical documents, I am aware that I have run the risk of presenting an unbalanced account of music's true place in the life of the city. In concentrating on the "official" music performed at the cathedral and the Palace, the twin pillars of church and state, I have considered only the "high art" music, as it is called in today's parlance, of privileged classes. The reader should bear in mind, however, that in Siena, as in other cities of comparable size and wealth during the period under consideration, ordinary citizens, too, had many opportunities to experience and enjoy this music. Cathedral services featuring performances by the chapel of polyphonic music and the organist were open to, and frequented by, all classes of society. While private performances within the Palace by the trumpeters' corps and the wind band were, necessarily, not accessible to private citizens, both groups gave daily concerts for the public at large from the Palace balcony and both groups made many appearances at other places in the city. Then, too, there were frequent public ceremonies, receptions, and processions, as well as the renowned annual festivals on Assumption Day, in which music performed by these musicians and others played a prominent part. "Official" music was quite literally in the air everywhere in the city on many days throughout the year and was heard by all, regardless of social station.

What music ordinary people themselves sang, played, and danced to is another matter. In Siena's case the social music of all classes remains largely unknown, especially before the early sixteenth century, because of the lack of sources and a paucity of precise references to specific musical works. For the upper classes occasional reports from late medieval times point to possible repertories within the larger European context, and by the later sixteenth century attitudes favoring musical training for the young and music publications by Sienese composers and dilettantes alike indicate repertories shared by literate classes in cities throughout Italy and many other European countries. But for the less privileged members of society no such records exist. The music they heard and played—the music, whether improvised or written, of dance musicians, ballad singers, story tellers, and others, the only kind of music that may truly be described as popular—has disappeared altogether in Siena, its only traces preserved in the fleeting allusions of chroniclers and others. How fortunate for us, then, that the record of Siena's place in the glorious experience of European polyphony has survived largely intact to our own day and that we can now begin to assess its achievements.

THE CATHEDRAL

Chapter One

THE CATHEDRAL AND ITS ADMINISTRATION, PERSONNEL, AND LITURGICAL CALENDAR

D ESPITE CHANGES and alterations to its original plan, the cathedral of Siena stands today among the most inspired and harmonious of Italy's major churches. From inception it was one of the grandest buildings of medieval Italy, and the decoration that was bestowed upon it in later periods offers remarkable testimony to the collective Sienese passion for beauty, to Sienese civic pride, which transcended all political factionalism, and to Sienese reverence for the Virgin Mary, whose name for most townspeople was inextricably linked with that of the city itself: "Sena vetus civitas Virginis." As a prelude to this account of music and musicians at Siena's cathedral, it will be helpful to fill in the background with a discussion of various aspects of the cathedral and its functions, all of which were bound to affect musical matters: the building's history and architecture, the places within it where music was performed, its secular administration, the number of its clergy and regulations governing their duties and behavior, the governance of the choir they performed in, and the liturgical calendar they followed.

THE BUILDING

The prehistory of the cathedral is shrouded in obscurity. In early medieval times the site of Siena's bishopric was within the old Roman fortress, and it was there that the first Duomo probably arose. By the ninth century, however, the cathedral was located outside the fortress, on a spot close to the site occupied by the present building. At least four structures have occupied the area since then, among them two earlier churches that were subsequently demolished, the present church, which has been modified and enlarged, and parts of a projected new church. Construction of the last was abandoned not long after it began, though some highly visible traces of what was to have been remain to this day. Despite the various building programs, religious services have been held continuously on the site throughout the centuries, even as various phases of alteration and new construction were undertaken.

Work on the building that replaced an earlier one of the ninth and tenth centuries was sufficiently advanced by the third quarter of the twelfth century to allow a consecration ceremony. Tradition placed this event on 18 November 1179, with the Sienese Pope Alexander III Bandinelli presiding. The papal presence has long been debated, but recently solid arguments have been advanced in favor of the traditional consecration date, which was mentioned as early as 1215 by the Sienese canon Oderigo in his description of liturgical practices at the cathedral, the *Ordo Officiorum*.[1] The twelfth-

---

1. The original, or a coeval copy, of Oderigo's customary survives in BCIS, MS G. V. 8. It was edited and published by Giovanni Crisostomo Trombelli under the title *Ordo Officiorum Ecclesiae Se-*

century church was an elevated structure with three naves and three main doors on the west side that gave on to a porticoed courtyard. From this it was but a few steps down into the piazza. To the right of the church was the bishop's palace, to the left the canons' cloister, one of the focal points of the many processions described by Oderigo.[2]

Inside the cathedral the principal destinations of processions were the tomb of the bishops in the middle of the church and the crypt, apparently situated beneath the choir, which was above the floor level of the nave.[3] The high altar, dedicated like the cathedral to the Virgin Assumptive, was on a platform four steps high at the entrance of the elevated choir.[4] From Oderigo's time onwards it was there that solemn high Mass and the people's Mass were celebrated on Sundays and many feast days. Next to the altar was the bishop's throne and behind, facing each other on either side, two rows of choir stalls, where the canons said Divine Offices.[5] A lectern, from which the cantor and his associates sang, was apparently in the middle of this space. Two pulpits, a larger one of stone, the other of wood, stood in front of the choir, perhaps on the left and right sides. It was from the stone pulpit, Oderigo tells us, that polyphony was performed on solemn occasions. Altars in the upper part of the church were dedicated to St. John Evangelist, St. Michael the Archangel, St. Ansanus (Sant'Ansano as he was called in Siena), and to the three remaining members of the town's quadrumvirate of heavenly protectors, St. Crescentius (San Crescenzio) and SS. Savinus (San Savino) and Victor, whose feasts, Oderigo says, were celebrated as major ones with elaborate musical services. Altars in the lower part of the church were dedicated to several other saints, whose feasts were marked with similar observances.[6] These included St. Bartholomew, St. Lucy, St. Nicholas, St. Sylvester, and SS. Fabian and Sebastian. There were other altars,

---

nensis ab Oderico eiusdem Ecclesiae Canonico Anno MCCXIII Compositus in 1766. References to the *Ordo Officiorum* (*OO*) are from this edition. See p. 383 of Trombelli's volume for the consecration date. The *OO* has been discussed by Enzo Carli in a number of studies, including *Il Duomo di Siena* (Siena, 1979), 11–13, where recent arguments regarding the consecration date are summarized. A comprehensive description and analysis of the *OO* as well as the list of feasts in the calendar preceding the main body of the work are given by Kees van der Ploeg, *Art, Architecture and Liturgy: Siena Cathedral in the Middle Ages* (Groningen, 1993), 121–45, 147–58. Italian translations of several chapters of the *OO* are given by Mino Marchetti in *La chiesa madre e la madre della chiesa* (Siena, 1979).

2. Access to the bishop's and canons' residences could also be had from within the church. See Carli, *Il Duomo di Siena*, 14–16.

3. Kees van der Ploeg, "Architectural and Liturgical Aspects of Siena Cathedral in the Middle Ages," in Henk van Os, *Sienese Altarpieces, 1215–1460,* vol. 1 (Groningen, 1984), 131–33; see also his *Art, Architecture and Liturgy,* 69–71, 81.

4. Van der Ploeg, *Art, Architecture and Liturgy,* 69, 71, 81, revising an earlier view in "Architectural and Liturgical Aspects," 133. He postulates the existence of a second altar in the presbitery, situated behind the area occupied by canons, which he believes was used for conventual Masses (ibid., 69 and 73, also revising an earlier view stated in "Architectural and Liturgical Aspects," 134). He notes that the high altar clearly divided the church into two parts, with the choir area behind it reserved for the clergy and the nave and transept for the public (*Art, Architecture and Liturgy,* 72).

5. Van der Ploeg, "Architectural and Liturgical Aspects," 133, 135; *Art, Architecture and Liturgy,* 71, 81.

6. The exact location of the lower altars is still a matter of some discussion. Van der Ploeg, "Architectural and Liturgical Aspects," 132 summarizes his own views regarding the problem.

among them ones dedicated to St. Boniface, an early patron saint of the cathedral, and to the Holy Cross, a fragment of which was kept in the church. Oderigo, however, does not say that these were celebrated as major feasts.

Few traces remain of the building that figures so prominently in Oderigo's account. After 1220 the structure was gradually demolished and entirely rebuilt so that by the beginning of the fourteenth century it had largely assumed the shape it has today.[7] It seems that the thirteenth-century church, like its predecessor, originally had an elevated choir at the crossing, above the crypt.[8] New choir stalls are mentioned in November 1259, and the reconstructed high altar was in place before the eve of the historic battle of Montaperti in November 1260, when the solemn ceremony in which the Sienese dedicated their city to the Virgin took place before it. The high altar was the site of a different kind of ceremony in June 1311, when amid great rejoicing Duccio's *Maestà* was placed on it. Music was not lacking on that occasion, for the altarpiece was accompanied from the painter's workshop to the cathedral by a throng of clerics, laymen, and members of the government, who marched to the sounds of bells pealing and of trumpets, shawms, and nakers.[9] Though the altar was moved once and perhaps twice in later years, the painting remained on it for almost two centuries. From the mid-fourteenth century onwards Mass was celebrated at the high altar on Sundays and major feast days by the bishop or his surrogate and occasionally by other high-ranking clerics and cathedral canons who had been invited to do so.

Basic changes to the church's structure date from 1317, when an enlargement of the transept and an extension of the choir area were initiated. Soon afterwards a plan to expand the entire edifice was adopted, and construction of the "duomo nuovo" began in 1339. Within a decade, however, the unsuitability of the terrain and recurrent structural problems forced abandonment of the grandiose project. Consequently, after 1357 the Sienese turned their attention to completing and refining previously conceived plans. Subsequent programs involved furnishing and decorating the church. From the end of the fourteenth century onwards major efforts within the building were directed toward installation of the pavement—which to this day remains one of the glories of Italian and European art—the high altar, the choir and choir stalls, various chapels, the organs, and the celebrated Piccolomini Library.[10]

The enlarged presbytery was the scene of continuous construction in the last decades of the fourteenth century, which saw the installation, among other things, of new choir stalls, new segments of pavement, and an organ, and the relocation of the high altar. Though abundant documentation regarding the choir survives, there is little to help reconstruct the original, which was redone during the sixteenth century. Work

---

7. Various dates around this time have been advanced by van der Ploeg, ibid., 109, 135; *Art, Architecture and Liturgy,* 38.

8. Van der Ploeg, "Architectural and Liturgical Aspects," 113. A more recent discussion is in his *Art, Architecture and Liturgy,* 38–40.

9. See chapter 14.

10. Gail Aronow, "A Description of the Altars in Siena Cathedral in 1420," in Henk van Os, *Sienese altarpieces 1215–1460,* vol. 2 (Groningen, 1990), 225–42. See also van der Ploeg, *Art, Architecture and Liturgy,* 61, 85.

was begun around 1362 by Francesco del Tonghio, who, with several others, was associated with the project for the next thirty-five years.[11] One section with forty-eight new stalls was in place by 1370, when those from a century earlier were removed. Five years later the reconstructed high altar was relocated to the top of the steps in the forward part of the apse, having apparently been moved once before a dozen years earlier.[12] Additional stalls called for in a newly adopted design were commissioned in 1378. Completed before the end of the century, the elaborately carved intarsiated structure contained eighty-eight stalls in two rows, one above the other, and stood behind and around the high altar.[13] Early fifteenth-century inventories describe the section under the dome behind the high altar as the place where the daily office was said, and the cathedral's Constitutions of 1459 note that during services canons were required to sit in the upper stalls, chaplains in the lower ones.[14] When they sang, the chaplains stood before a lectern, completed by Francesco del Tonghio in 1374, in the middle of the choir.[15] During the last decades of the fifteenth century, and probably earlier, the chapel singers also performed in the choir at Masses and Vespers on Sundays and feast days. The general public heard these performances from below the steps leading up to the presbytery because that area, at least until the early sixteenth century, was closed off by a choir screen.[16]

The Organs

The choir was bounded on one side by the door to the sacristy and on the other by the organ, built in 1372 by the Florentine monk Frate Domenico degli Ermini.[17] Many

---

11. Vittorio Lusini, *Il Duomo di Siena* (Siena 1911, 1939), 1:265; Carli, *Il Duomo di Siena,* 91.

12. Gail Aronow, "A Documentary History of the Pavement Decoration in Siena Cathedral, 1362 through 1506" (Ph.D. diss., Columbia University, 1985), 48. Aronow has made many useful observations regarding the choir on the basis of her study of sections of the pavement installed during the late fourteenth century. I have incorporated several of them into the present discussion.

13. The new choir had two sections, which were apparently constructed in phases, the part beneath the dome, built first, and the part surrounding the high altar, which, according to Aronow, was begun only in the later 1370s (ibid., 37ff.) Aronow notes that the development of this new choir has not been satisfactorily explained and that its overall plan remains elusive.

14. Ibid., 38, 114; see also Rubric 16 of the *Constitutiones,* discussed more fully below.

15. Ibid., 46; Lusini, *Il Duomo di Siena,* 1:265.

16. As Aronow notes, the composition of the choir screen has yet to be studied in detail, and its placement is still a matter of conjecture ("Documentary History," 187). Lusini, however, says that it was "in front of the altar in the presbytery, closed from behind by the master wood carver with two sides of the new choir" and that it was faced "with a marble rood screen (enclosure) furnished with a beautiful grating" (*Il Duomo di Siena,* 1:265). Aronow cites a 1420 inventory of cathedral holdings that mentions some benches "where the women stay" situated around the circumference of the choir, probably leaning against its marble enclosures ("Description of the Altars," 232).

17. Lusini, *Il Duomo di Siena,* 1:277, mentions the work of Frate Domenico and others in the construction and decoration of the instrument; Aronow, "Documentary History," 49, cites a record from 16 February 1397 giving this location. Lusini, ibid., notes that even before this time an organ was used to accompany the chant and that changes to the altar and choir necessitated its rebuilding. Documents recording the earlier instrument, however, seem to be lacking. With regard to Frate Do-

records concerning the instrument's construction survive—for casting the pipes, for glue, for tin, for various kinds of wood, for iron rods for the doors, for leather for the bellows, for cutting into the stone wall, and for constructing a loft where the organ was to be placed—but nothing regarding its specifications or the size of its keyboard.[18] Another organ builder, Fra Benedetto de' Servi from Lucca, was brought in to assess Domenico's work, and on receipt of his favorable report, the instrument was formally inaugurated in March 1373 in the presence of city officials, ambassadors from Florence, and other notables.[19] Located to the right of the high altar, the organ was in use for more than eighty years.[20]

A second organ was ordered in October 1452, and was apparently completed by the following June, when it was placed opposite the existing one, on the wall above the sacristy door.[21] Changes and improvements to the new instrument were begun within a few years, and on 2 April 1457 a formal contract was drawn up with the

---

menico, Franco Baggiani notes that he was a friar of the Basilian Order who restored the organs at Pisa cathedral in 1387 (he was said to be from Orvieto on that occasion), at Santa Felicita in Florence in 1387, and at San Piero Maggiore in Florence in 1388. He also constructed a new instrument at Florence cathedral in 1388. See Baggiani, *Monumenti di arte organaria toscana* (Pisa, 1985), 10.

18. The earliest record regarding the instrument comes from shortly before March 1372, when L. 8. 4 were reimbursed to the overseer Andrea di Minuccio for expenses when he went to Florence to sign a contract with an organ builder: "A me Andrea, quando andai a Fiorenza per fare e' patto co' maestro degli orghani, otto lire e quattro soldi" (AOMS, vol. 198, *E&U, 1371–72*, fol. 48ᵛ). Most of the records of expenses for the organ's construction were published by Lusini, *Il Duomo di Siena*, 1:331–33, where expenses for the *palco degli organi*, or organ loft, are also mentioned. Frate Domenico is cited in an entry from December 1372 that shows him receiving L. 326. 8 for his own work and a few other payments for small pipes that he had had made in Florence and sent to Siena (vol. 199, *E&U, 1372–73*, fol. 63ʳ). On the basis of these few surviving records, Baggiani, *Monumenti di arte organaria toscana*, 11–12, speculates that the instrument may have had forty-seven keys, an incomplete pedal board, and eleven bolts that controlled the registers.

19. They were all entertained by the overseer at a reception afterwards: "A Guido di Domenicho Ghidaregli, espetiale, diecie lire e sedici soldi e nove denari, per fogli reagli e per biriqhuocogli e ragieia per fare onore agli a[m]basciadori fiorentini e a' suoi chonselglieri e ad altre persone che si raunaro[no] per ponare gli organi" (vol. 199, *E&U, 1372–73*, fol. 77ʳ, dated March 1373).

20. Lusini, *Il Duomo di Siena*, 1:277; Aronow, "Documentary History," 64, says: "in the penultimate bay on the side of the chapel of St. Victor, on the right side of the apse, directly across from the sacristy."

21. Summaries of pertinent deliberations are given by Lusini, *Il Duomo di Siena*, 2:153, n. 3. The first, dated 11 October 1452, reports that the overseer was authorized to spend "infino a la quantità di fiorini dugento de' danari d'essa Huopera in fare fare e di nuovo edificare um paio d'organi oltre a quelli che al presente sonno in essa chiesa" (AOMS, vol. 13, *Deliberazioni dell'operaio e dei consiglieri, 1434–55*, fol. 115ʳ, dated 11 October 1452: [margin: Che si faccino di nuovo um paio d'organi]). The second gives the exact location of the instrument: "E veduto e considerato in che luogo del duomo possino meglio stare li organi nuovamente facti, non vedendo si possino più adattamente ponere che a capo l'uscio de la sagrestia, che vengono riscontra ali altri, concordevolmente delibera-ro[no] che si ponghino ine a' piei la finestra, con quello ornato di legname che al decto misser l'operaio parrà conveniente sichè stia bene, come tale materia e anco e' luogo richiede" (ibid., fol. 127ʳ, dated 18 June 1453 [margin: Per lo luogo degli organi nuovi]).

Hungarian organ builder Maestro Pietro Scotto, who was instructed to use as many of the instrument's existing pipes as possible.[22] Information about this organ is also lacking, except for a report from February 1458 that Scotto was paid more than the price originally agreed upon because he made additions to his design, because he had put in more time and labor than envisaged in making new tin pipes to replace the old lead ones, and because his work was judged perfect in every respect by a jury of citizens and organists.[23] At that time Scotto was asked to restore the older, now called smaller, organ, but he was unable to do so.[24]

The restoration was eventually undertaken by Maestro Lorenzo di Jacopo da Prato, who was awarded a contract in July 1459 and finished his work in 1461 (see Doc. 1.1).[25] In 1510 Sigismondo Tizio, the Sienese historian and chronicler, wrote that the instrument was to the right of the main altar next to the chapel of St. Victor, and that it was used while the principal organ was being rebuilt.[26] In 1548 it was transferred to the chapel of the Magi in the north aisle, across from the altar of the Madonna delle Grazie or Madonna del Voto. The instrument had an important function, for as a contract from 1563 shows, it was the one played by the organist whenever the chapel singers performed before the revered image of the Madonna delle Grazie.[27] It was mentioned in September 1582, when decorations were commissioned for the altar "below the organ, opposite the altar of the Madonna."[28] It remained in place until well into

---

22. The contract (AOMS, vol. 14, *Deliberazioni dell'operaio e dei consiglieri, 1454–59,* fols. 35ᵛ–36ʳ) is published by Lusini, *Il Duomo di Siena,* 2:153, n. 4. In the same note Lusini publishes a payment to Scotto from August 1459 for his work in tempering the new instrument.

23. The document in AOMS, vol. 14, *Deliberazioni dell'operaio e dei consiglieri, 1454–59,* fols. 44ᵛ–45ʳ, dated 3 February 1457/58, is published in Scipione Borghesi and Luciano Banchi, *Nuovi documenti per la storia dell'arte senese* (Siena, 1898; repr. Soest, 1970), 197.

24. "Decreverunt quod sit et esse intelligatur plene remissum et commissum in operarium . . . qui possit et ei liceat facere conductam et locationem organorum parvorum existentium circumcirca nova organa, videlicet magistro Petro" (ibid., fol. 48ᵛ, dated 8 July 1458; in margin: "pro organis parvis"). A document dated 1 August 1458 notes that the overseer was empowered to negotiate the cost of the work with Pietro "pro organis parvis fiendis" (ibid., fol. 49ʳ). Earlier, on 18 August 1456, Francesco Landi, an organ builder and priest from Lucignano, had written to say that he would come to Siena to restore the old organ, but there is nothing in the record to show that he did. His letter is mentioned ibid., fol. 25ʳ.

25. Lusini, *Il Duomo di Siena,* 2:154, has published summaries of this and of documents pertaining to the decoration of both instruments in the 1480s made by Guidoccio Cozzarelli and others. The organ builder Lorenzo di Jacopo da Prato was also responsible for constructing the instruments in two other Sienese churches, Sant'Agostino and the Santissima Annunziata, before beginning work at the cathedral. See Baggiani, *Monumenti di arte organaria toscana,* 15, 44.

26. See note 31.

27. "con questo che detto Mariano sia obligato sonare . . . sempre che si canti alla Madonna, sonare l'organo rincontro a quella e non quello sopra la sagrestia" (cited in Doc. 7.4).

28. "di fare e fabricare uno ornato all'altare che è nella chiesa chattedral sotto alli organi li quali vengano di rincontra a l'altare della Madonna" are the words used in the document, dated 3 September 1582, published by Gaetano Milanesi, *Documenti per la storia dell'arte senese* (Siena, 1854–56), 3:252–55. The organ was again mentioned in 1587, when Pietro Sorri was commissioned to paint a picture of the Magi bearing gifts that was intended "for the altar under the organ in the duomo, opposite the altar of the Madonna" ("per illaltare [*sic*] che viene sotto gli organi in Duomo, rincontro all'altare de

the seventeenth century, when it was cited by Alfonso Landi in his well-known description of the cathedral's furnishings and it was only in 1679 that it was transferred back to its original site, in the loft that had lately served as a singing gallery.[29]

The principal organ, to the left of the high altar above the sacristy door, was completely rebuilt in the early sixteenth century. The new instrument was commissioned on 26 September 1508 from Maestro Domenico di Lorenzo degli Organi of Lucca (see Doc. 1.2).[30] According to the specifications, the longest pipe was to be nine Venetian feet (approximately the same as today); the external pipes were to be made of tin, and those within of lead. The manual was to have twenty-nine white keys and eighteen black ones, for a total of forty-seven keys. There were to be six stops, the tenor (fundamental or principal), an octave, a quintadecima (superoctave), a decimanona (quint), a vigesimaseconda (3 octaves), and flute. The instrument was inaugurated on the feast of St. Mary Magdalene, 22 July 1510,[31] but it did not live up to expectations. A subsequent evaluation made by Fra Alessandro de' Servi, the Florentine organist and composer, noted that the organ builder had not fulfilled his obligations and recommended the addition of thirty pipes. Tizio reports that after Domenico did this, the Sienese government imprisoned him for thirty days. The organ was reinaugurated on 9 November 1511.[32] Though modified in later centuries, the instrument remains in place to this day,

la Madonna"). This document, too, is published ibid., 262–63. Also see Colleen Reardon, *Agostino Agazzari and Music at Siena Cathedral, 1597–1641* (Oxford, 1993), 70, for quotation from a cathedral report of July 1627 noting the completion of a new balustrade "of carved, gilded iron for the organ across from the Most Holy Madonna delle Grazie . . . made especially to provide for concertizing and singing the litanies of the Madonna on Sundays after Vespers, a devotional practice that received overwhelming approval by the citizenry who came in large numbers."

29. Alfonso Landi, *Racconto di pitture, sculture e architetture eccellenti che si trovano nel Duomo di Siena* (1655) (BCIS, MS C. II. 30), 53–54; Baggiani, *Monumenti di arte organaria toscana*, 44.

30. The document is summarized in Lusini, *Il Duomo di Siena*, 2:154, where reference is made to other reports in the same volume, fol. 15^v, regarding payment of 100 ducats, or L. 700, for the instrument. A payment summarizing Maestro Domenico's work is in vol. 512, *D&C, 1521–29*, fol. 89 right: "Maestro Domenico degli Organi di Luca . . . E de' avere adì II di setembre [1521] . . . ducati 600 per manifatura del'organo nuovo sopra ala sagrestia, ducati 300 sonno per l'organo vechio rischontra al detto, e ducati 90 sonno per temparatura di tutti e due elgli organi, che fa la somma di detto ducati 900, el quale precio fu giudichato per Mons. Rafaello reverendissimo cardenale de' Petrucci che fu rimesso da ungniuno della patria in Sua Reverendissima Signoria, chome di tutto ne fu rogato ser Renaldo di Iacopo Cinbecchi, nostro notaro . . . L. $\overset{M}{VI}$ DCCCCXXX."

31. "Organis interea, quae supra sacrarii ostium in Aede maiori sita erant destructis, quae ad aram Sancti Victori erant, penitus refecta in destructorum locum ad dexteram maioris arae reponuntur. Hac vero die, quae Divae Mariae Magdalenae dicata est, sonare coepere. Nova vero organo, elegantiora et ditiora, a Lucensi fabro peritissimo formantur, supra ostii sacrarium reponenda" (Sigismondo Tizio, *Historiarum Senensium ab initio urbis Senarum usque ad annum MDXXVIII*, 7:184, dated July 1510).

32. "Novembris subinde nona die, organa denuo supra sacrarii ostium constituta Pandulphi opera, pulsari coepere. Erat ea dies Salvatori dicata, ut autem periculum ipsorum fieret religiosus quidam Florentinus ordinis Servorum Divae Mariae eiusdem opificii peritus, accitus est, qui organis pulsatis Dominico Lucensi, qui illa fabricaverat, contradixit rationibus illum convincens: organis itaque cannas triginta addere Dominicum oportuit. Verum cunctis peractis, Dominicum ipsum circiter diem vigesimam publico in Palatio detinuere Senenses" (ibid., 7:260, dated 1511). Although Tizio does not mention the name of the person who evaluated the instrument, Landi quotes cathedral payments indicating his

above the sacristy door, adorned with the beautiful wooden case and loft begun in 1506 by Antonio Barili and Giovanni Castelnuovo.[33] The loft was mentioned by Tizio as one of the places where singers stood when they performed polyphony at services on Pentecost Sunday in 1522.[34]

The Singers' Gallery and Other Places for Performance

Barili was also commissioned to execute a design for a new choir necessitated by the removal in 1506 of the stalls under the dome.[35] A general reorganization of the area was effected in the following decades, with the installation of new pavement under the dome and, in 1532, of the high altar designed by Bartolomeo Peruzzi. The addition of the musicians' singing gallery to a design by Bartolomeo Neroni, called Il Riccio, was completed in 1552 by Lorenzo di Bartolomeo, who also carved the wooden case of the small organ (see Fig. 1).[36] This latter, as mentioned, had been moved four years earlier to the wall above the chapel of the Magi in the north aisle. A report of services held during the siege of Siena in 1555 notes that government officials were seated below the singers' gallery, but the singers did not perform on that occasion. Still in use a century later, when it was described by Alfonso Landi, the gallery must have served as one of the cathedral's principal performance sites, though sixteenth-century documents say nothing about this.[37] Though the small organ was subsequently returned to the space occupied by the singers, the gallery's beautifully sculptured wooden frame still remains in its original place in the right side of the apse, opposite the organ above the sacristy. The present-day choir structure, which retains only thirty-six of the stalls carved by Francesco del Tonghio, was in place by the early 1570s (see Fig. 2). The new stalls, with their magnificent marquetry and elaborate carvings, were all designed by Il Riccio, who was also responsible for the splendidly decorated lectern and bishop's throne.

At least two other areas in the cathedral served as sites for performances by the plainchant choir and the chapel singers. The chapel of Sant'Ansano was mentioned in 1367 as one the principal places for the daily celebration of the Chapter, or canons', Mass. It was located just below the door to the sacristy at the left of the high altar, in the northeast corner of the transept, and essentially occupied the same position it has today.[38] Its decoration was completed early in the fifteenth century, by which time it was furnished with a stained-glass window and intarsiated choir stalls, where the canons and chaplains sat during services. On the altar stood Simone Martini's incomparable

---

name was Alessandro, and a somewhat later document regarding construction of an organ for Santa Maria della Scala confirms that it was the Servite organist and composer Alessandro Coppini of Florence. See chapter 13 below.

33. Lusini, *Il Duomo di Siena*, 2:154.

34. Tizio's report is discussed below in chapter 6.

35. Aronow, "Documentary History," 114–15, points out that "along with the choir stalls themselves, most of the 'choir floor' must have been removed in 1506 to make way for a whole new pavement program subsequently designed by Domenico Beccafumi." She also notes that "remnants of the older paving below the dome that were not destroyed . . . were removed to the Opera del Duomo in the 1870's and replaced with modern works of Alessandro Franchi."

36. Pèleo Bacci, *Fonti e commenti per la storia dell'arte* (Siena, 1944), 163.

37. Landi, *Racconto di pitture*, 51.

38. Aronow, "A Description of the Altars," 230, 232.

FIGURE 1. View of the sixteenth-century singers' gallery, with organ case. Siena, cathedral.
Courtesy Opera della Metropolitana di Siena; photograph from Foto Lensini

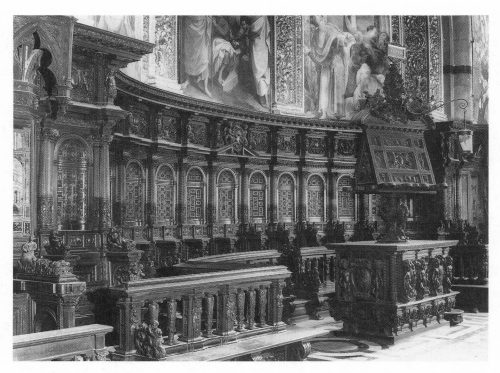

FIGURE 2. View of the sixteenth-century choir stalls and lectern. Siena, cathedral. Courtesy
Opera della Metropolitana di Siena; photograph from Foto Lensini

Annunciation. This was kept behind a red curtain that was opened during Mass and on
holidays. The painting was so well known to the general public that Bernardino Albiz-
zeschi, Siena's fiery reformist preacher, later to become saint, alluded to it in one of his
Lenten sermons in 1427.[39] San Bernardino's remark is of assistance in assessing the role
of the arts in everyday life of the time. For just as a painting formed part of the collective
experience of Sienese worshippers and could be expected to evoke a response, so, too,
must the music heard at services have resonated in the congregants' minds.

From as early as 1367, but probably even earlier, the Mass of Our Lady was celebrated at Siena cathedral as the third Mass of the day on Mondays. There is little information about where the Mass was sung, though the well-known cover of a Biccherna
volume from 1483 depicting a service in the chapel of Santa Maria delle Grazie suggests

39. Keith Christiansen, Laurence B. Kanter, and Carl Brandon Strehlke, *Painting in Renaissance
Siena, 1420–1500* (exhibition catalogue, The Metropolitan Museum, New York, 1988), 108, in remarks about another painting, no. 10a of the catalogue, Saint Anthony at Mass by the Master of the
Osservanza. Christiansen, citing van der Ploeg, "Architectural and Liturgical Aspects," 147, notes that
the St. Anthony painting preserves a glimpse of the post–1375 cathedral and that it was not until 1483
that another view of the interior of Siena cathedral was depicted with greater accuracy and boldness.

that it was done there (see Pl. 1).[40] The chapel is mentioned in 1420 as being on the south side of the church, next to the now demolished Porta del Perdono.[41] Reports from the late 1430s make it appear that the singers of polyphony performed there at Vespers on feast days, though the site itself is not mentioned. Plans to enlarge and redecorate the chapel in marble were discussed as early as 1448, and by 1452 the commission to do so was awarded to Urbano and Bartolomeo di Pietro da Cortona.[42] As the site of a much revered votive painting of the Madonna, the chapel was one of the most frequented places in the city.[43] The 1483 depiction of the chapel shows singers standing before a lectern to the left of the altar during one of the many services held there. A late sixteenth-century view of the chapel from the school of Ventura Salimbeni captured the moment during communion at Mass when the Palace instrumentalists played, a practice corroborated by many documents (see Fig. 3).[44] Although the chapel was demolished in the later seventeenth century to make way for the grand Baroque edifice that replaced it, several of its panels and bas reliefs were salvaged, and these are now scattered throughout the cathedral.[45] The painting of the Madonna, of course, remains to this day as the centerpiece of the chapel, now known as the Cappella della Madonna del Voto.

The chapel of St. John the Baptist, located at the east end of the Piccolomini Library on the north aisle, was one of the principal building projects of the late fifteenth century. Reports regarding musical performances in the chapel are lacking, though the nineteen magnificently decorated choir stalls executed in 1482 by Antonio Barili indicate that it must have served as the site of musical performances on feast days dedicated to St. John the Baptist as well as at votive Masses throughout the year. Barili's work, which included nineteen inlaid panels, was removed during the course of a seventeenth-century restoration of the chapel. Seven of the panels survive, however, and of these, two feature musical illustrations, one of a man enjoying the sound of an organ and another of a lutenist performing.

---

40. The Biccherna was the name of the building that originally housed officials of the Sienese treasury. From early in the thirteenth century it became customary to decorate with designs and paintings the wooden covers of the volumes in which accounts were kept. Many of these covers have been preserved and are highly prized, both for their artistic value and for the intimate glimpses they afford of Sienese life. The 1483 cover, titled "L'unione delle classi e l'offerta delle chiavi della città alla Vergine," is reproduced with commentary in *Le Biccherne: Tavole, dipinte delle Magistrature Senesi (Secoli XIII–XVII),* ed. L. Borgia, E. Carli, M. A. Ceppari, U. Morandi, P. Sinibaldi, and C. Zanetti (Rome, 1984); and in Ubaldo Morandi, ed., *Le Biccherne Senesi* (Siena, 1964), 112.

41. The Porta del Perdono was the principal lateral entrance of the cathedral until the mid-seventeenth century, when it was incorporated into the entrance of the newly constructed Chigi chapel, which replaced the chapel of the Madonna delle Grazie. For a recent discussion see Aronow, "Documentary History," 177–78.

42. Lusini, *Il Duomo di Siena,* 1:68–70; Carli, *Il Duomo di Siena,* 108.

43. On the tortured question of which of two disputed paintings was the original Madonna del Voto see Edward B. Garrison, "Towards a New History of the Siena Cathedral Madonnas," in *Studies in the History of Medieval Italian Painting* (Florence, 1960), 4/1:5–22.

44. The painting is in the Opera's Museum. This is reproduced, as is the Biccherna cover, in Carli, *Il Duomo di Siena,* 106–7.

45. Ibid., 108.

FIGURE 3. A late-sixteenth-century painting of the interior of the cathedral and the chapel
of Santa Maria delle Grazie. Siena, cathedral. Courtesy Opera della Metropolitana di Siena; photograph from Foto Lensini

As precious as these are, there were two others, no longer extant, that still claim
attention because of their references to unknown pieces of polyphony performed in
Siena in the later fifteenth century.[46] One lost panel, the ninth in the series, depicted a
half-open cabinet. Placed above this was a sheet containing a musical setting of the
words "Qui post me venit, ante me factus est cuius non sum dignus calceamenta
solvere" (He who comes after me was created before me, He whose shoes I am not
worthy of untying; John 1: 27).[47] The text was set as a canon, for two or more parts,
although Landi, who was not very well versed in music, said the piece was notated in
plainchant. He made a similar mistake in his description of another panel, the eleventh,
whose loss is all the more regrettable because it contained the music of a piece by the
famous Flemish composer Alexander Agricola that has not otherwise survived. This
panel depicted a half-open writing-desk with musical instruments and a sheet of music
bearing several stanzas of the text of the well-known hymn to St. John the Baptist.
Inscribed above was the name of the composer, Alexander Agricola. The inclusion of
Agricola's music for St. John in a marquetry panel situated within the chapel is doubly
significant, both because it suggests that the piece was performed there by the chapel
singers and because it offers tangible evidence of the refined musical tastes of the overseer Alberto Aringhieri, at whose instance the chapel was built. In matters pertaining
to music, Aringhieri, as will be mentioned below, was without doubt the most active
patron ever to hold the high administrative post of overseer of the cathedral Opera.

---

46. The two panels are cited along with those that have survived by Stefano Landi in his 1655
description of cathedral holdings, mentioned above, *Racconto di pitture*. For a description of these see
Enzo Carli, *Scultura lignea senese* (Milan, 1951), 94–96, and tables 172 and 175 for illustrations of the
organ and the lute.

47. The inscription was also used by Costanzo Festa in the Sicut erat of his *Magnificat tertii toni*.

THE ADMINISTRATION
The Opera

The Opera was the institution charged with supervising the cathedral's building works. It was also responsible for administering the cathedral's considerable financial resources—income received from public and private donations—and with disbursing funds, largely furnished by the state, necessary for the construction, decoration, and maintenance of the building and its dependencies. Exactly when this administrative body came into existence is a matter of conjecture, though a record from 1190 suggests that it was functioning long before then.[48] At first subject to ecclesiastical control, the Opera subsequently came under the direction of the state, which was responsible for financing the construction work and all of the subsequent decorations and furnishings. From that time forward its operations were run by a government-appointed commission, whose principal member was the *operaio,* or overseer. In the early fourteenth century the overseers were drawn from the monks of the monastery of San Galgano, who enjoyed legendary reputations as honest and able administrators, but they were subsequently replaced by laymen.

Statutes from the fourteenth century decreed that the overseer's office would be elective and annual. Owing to the complexities involved in overseeing the many undertakings involved in construction and decoration within the church, the office was transformed during the following century into a lifetime appointment.[49] As the person solely in charge of operations, the overseer assumed the weighty obligation of paying out of his own pocket any debts incurred by the Opera that it might be unable to cover. The overseer was assisted by a group of counselors, whose number varied from the six prescribed in earlier statutes to three during the fifteenth century, and then to two in the early sixteenth century.[50] The overseer's decisions were subject to the board's approval. In addition to the weekly meetings where normal matters were reviewed, the overseer and his counselors met once a month to discuss new projects and biannually for an accounting of the books. Working under the overseer's direction, administering the day-to-day functions of the Opera, was a group of regularly salaried employees, including a chamberlain, a notary, and an accountant.

The Opera was also responsible for paying the salaries of all of the clerics who officiated at cathedral services. Clerics, of course, were under the jurisdiction of the cathedral Chapter, whose relations with the Opera were rigidly defined by agreements concluded between the government, the bishop, and the Chapter.[51] The earliest set of

---

48. Carli, *Il Duomo di Siena,* 13.

49. Bernardina Sani, "Artisti e committenti a Siena nella prima metà del Quattrocento," in *I ceti dirigenti nella Toscana del Quattrocento* (Florence, 1987), 499, for reference to the fourteenth-century statutes. She also notes (p. 500) that until 1417 there was an uninterrupted series of *capimaestri,* or building works manager/architects, the last of whom was the sculptor Jacopo della Quercia, who held the office from 1408 to 1416.

50. Ibid., 500.

51. There are some references to clergy and to their relations with the state in Siena's earliest constitution, but apart from prescribing the number of wax offerings made on the feast of the Assumption, there is little of substance.

such agreements to survive intact, one that describes the duties, rights, and privileges of both the overseer and the Chapter, was drawn up at the instance of the Sienese government of the Twelve, with the consent of Bishop Azzolino de' Malavolti, on 18 April 1364.[52] Its twenty-five chapters were ratified by the Chapter twelve days later. Twenty-three additional chapters were issued on 9 October 1367, again with the approval of the same parties. Subsequently called the *Pacta et capitula nova* to distinguish them from the earlier *Pacta et capitula vetera,* the later chapters were not intended to supersede the previous ones but rather to supplement them.[53] Both sets were reconfirmed by the Chapter on 11 August 1433, an indication that their provisions continued to be observed throughout the intervening period.[54] As will become apparent, a good deal of information about ecclesiastical personnel during the fourteenth and fifteenth centuries is furnished by these sources. For the moment suffice it to cite passages regarding the overseer in order to illustrate the kinds of agreements that were struck between church and state, as each of the parties sought to regulate the duties and obligations of the one to the other.

The *Pacta* specify that Siena's principal legislative body, the Consiglio Generale, had the right to nominate the overseer, though they also granted the cathedral canons a voice in the matter (*Pacta . . . vetera,* chap. 25). Before taking office, the overseer was obliged to swear under oath that he would observe the agreements concluded between civil and ecclesiastical authorities, as set forth in the 1364 *Pacta* (chap. 20). By that time the overseer had complete control over the disbursal of the sacristy's income, although he was obliged to render an annual accounting of his stewardship to the Chapter and to assign a part of that income to the bishop (chaps. 2, 12, 13). The overseer was charged with practical matters, such as furnishing the chaplains and clerks with housing and with a cook, as well as with more symbolic acts, such as providing each of the canons with ten pounds of candles on the annual feast of the Assumption (chaps. 7, 8, 14). He was responsible for all of the valuable objects and books that formed part of the sacristy's holdings. He was also required "to maintain and augment the church's decoration" and he was directed to use the remainder of the sacristy's income "for the good of the church." Should such income prove insufficient, he was to supply whatever was lacking with funds from the Opera's own holdings (chaps. 9, 21). Though the later *Pacta* give few particulars about the overseer's prerogatives, they sum up the situation with a statement that is as informative as it is succinct. They note that the overseer and his counselors had full authority to spend and distribute the sacristy's income for the

---

52. A contemporary copy is in AAS, vol. 368, *Pacta et Capituli,* fols. 1ᵛ–6ᵛ. Another copy is in AOMS, Appendice Documentaria, no. 46. The text was subsequently published at Siena in 1579 by Luca Bonetto in his edition of the *Constitutiones,* mentioned more fully below. References here are to Bonetto's edition, *Pacta et capitula vetera,* unless otherwise noted.

53. A contemporary copy is in AAS, vol. 368, *Pacta et Capituli,* fols. 7ʳ–13ʳ. Another copy is in AOMS, Appendice Documentaria, No. 47. This set of regulations was also published in 1579 by Bonetto in his edition of the *Constitutiones,* mentioned below. References are again to Bonetto's edition, *Pacta et capitula nova,* unless otherwise noted. Pertinent here is the information in chap. 23, p. 78: "Quòd pacta vetera per nova non intelligantur derogata."

54. The revalidation is found in AAS, vol. 368, fol. 13ᵛ of the manuscript copy, and on p. 83 of Bonetto's edition.

primicerius, subsequently disappeared. A new office, that of the decanus or dean, was instituted at Siena cathedral in 1511 by Pope Julius II Della Rovere.[63] The names of canons who held the dean's office, together with those of the provost, the archdeacon, and the archpriest, appear occasionally in Chapter account books after that time. In 1585 the office of primicerius was reintroduced by Papal decree.[64] Chapter records indicate that the post was eventually filled by one of the canons.[65] His duties, however, must have been largely ceremonial because by then the cathedral was employing professional chaplain-singers who also performed chant in the choir.

THE CANONS

A good deal of information about the canons' duties and prerogatives and their relationship to the cathedral Opera comes from the already mentioned *Pacta* of 1364 and 1367, which were reconfirmed by the Chapter in 1433. These were subsequently superseded by a new group of regulations, the *Constitutiones Sacri Capituli Metropolitanae Senensis Ecclesiae,* which were drawn up at the behest of Siena's Pope Pius II Piccolomini. It was the pope himself who sanctioned the new regulations, on 21 April 1459, after they had been ratified by the Chapter.[66] A special provision forbade annulments, cancellations, or additions to them under penalty of a fine (*Constitutiones,* rub. 52). To judge from subsequent events, the Constitutions continued in force through most of the sixteenth century. They were in fact approved for publication by the cathedral's canons and Chapter on 9 April 1578 and printed by Luca Bonetti of Siena in the following year together

---

refers to a privilege issued on 24 November 1228 by Pope Gregory IX dei conti di Segni that confirms the number of Sienese canons as twelve. Further, see Paul Fridolin Kehr, "Le bolle pontifiche che si conservano negli archivi senesi," *BSSP* 6 (1899): 51–102, and his *Italia Pontificia* (Berlin, 1906–35), 3:196–206.

63. V. Lusini, *Capitolo della Metropolitana di Siena,* 45: "Bolla di papa Giulio II all'arcivescovo di Siena, con la quale erige la Dignità del Decanato, come la prima dopo la episcopale, nella chiesa senese; per fondazione di m. Bartolommeo de Bolis, canonico della Basilica di S. Pietro in Roma, notaro apostolico e familiare del Papa. Da Roma."

64. Ibid., 46: "Bolla di papa Sisto V, per la erezione della dignità di Primiceriato nella Metropolitana, per fondazione di m. Francesco Maria Piccolomini vescovo di Pienza. Da Roma." Reasons for reinstituting the office were presented to the Chapter on 19 March 1584/85: "Convocato etc. fuit intromissus magnificus eques dominus Gerundius Piccolomineus qui suo et domini Clementis ipsius fratris nomine, exposuit qualiter cupientes erigere in ecclesia cathedrali primiceriatus dignitatem, tria principaliter exoptant et expetunt a Capitulo; primum, ut consentiat erectioni dictae dignitatis; secundum, ut novo primicerio concedat in choro et in Capitulo secundum locum immediate post quatuor dignitates presentes, et super omnes canonicos, cum voce activa et passiva etc.; tertium, ut eidem dent posse participare ex mensa capitulari et coeteris sicut alii canonici; et porrexit supplicem libellum dictas preces, desiderium et postulationem expresse continentem" (AAS, Capitolo Capitolare di Siena, vol. 1138, *Deliberazioni del Capitolo, 1584–1605,* fol. 6ʳ; in margin: "Super erigenda nova dignitate Primiceriatus").

65. See, for example, AAS, Capitolo Capitolare di Siena, Serie I, vol. 72, *E&U, 1600,* fol. 22ʳ, which names Scipione Bandini in the post.

66. A contemporary copy is in AAS, *Costituzioni ed ordinamenti,* vol. 352, fols. 2ʳ–30ʳ. Several later documents follow this in the manuscript volume, and these were also printed in the edition of the *Constitutiones,* mentioned in the following note.

with both sets of the *Pacta* and with subsequent corrections, ratifications, and a number of other documents pertaining to the Chapter from as late as 1512.[67] Altogether, the details set forth in these documents paint a vivid picture of the spiritual, social, and economic milieu in which the priestly community at Siena cathedral lived and worked for some two and a half centuries.[68]

The *Pacta* and the Constitutions of almost a century later are unanimous in entrusting the canons with responsibility for preserving and maintaining the traditions of the cathedral's liturgy and with ensuring that services be conducted according to the prescribed rites (*Pacta . . . vetera,* chaps. 11, 10). All matters regarding services, as well as any others concerned with the church, the canonicate, and the well-being of the Chapter, were brought before the canons by the provost, who presided over the Chapter's obligatory monthly meetings (*Constitutiones,* rub. 1). As head of the Chapter, the provost had the authority to impose fines on those who did not attend the meetings. The archdeacon, second in the hierarchy, was empowered to act for him in case of illness or absence and was also authorized to assign canons their places in the choir and in the Chapter (rub. 2). The Constitutions declare that the provost or his surrogate was to notify the canons a day in advance of monthly meetings or of any others that he and his counselors deemed necessary (rub. 31, 32). Only canons who held prebends were invited to the meetings. Attendance was mandatory for those who were in the city or within twenty miles of it, unless they were excused because of personal illness or illness in the immediate family, because of imprisonment, or because of absence in the service of the church, the bishop, or the Chapter. Each canon had the right to express his opinion about the subject under consideration before a vote was called for, although only those who had taken holy orders could vote. Less important matters required a quorum of two-thirds, and the votes of two-thirds of those present were needed for passage of a motion. All discussions and decisions were to be kept secret, and failure to observe this rule could result in the loss of emoluments for two years (rub. 33, 34). When an individual was being judged by his peers, he stood apart on a raised platform, in full view of the entire Chapter, and he could not be interrupted or silenced while

---

67. In the preface to the 1579 edition, canons Sansedoni and Preziani, who oversaw publication of the text, do not say whether all of the provisions of the Constitutions were still in effect in their time, though they note that their task, following the Chapter's advice, was to publish and make them more generally available because they were almost unknown and preserved in only one worn copy of the document.

68. To this group of documents may be added general information regarding the code of behavior of Sienese clergy found in the 1335 Constitutions of the diocese of Siena. These both incorporated and superseded earlier regulations introduced between 1232 and 1307. Although several of the provisions set forth in the 1335 Constitutions subsequently took second place to canon law and to laws enacted by the Sienese government—for example, the rubric forbidding taxation of the clergy was ignored on many occasions by the government—there is ample evidence to show that many of these regulations remained in force throughout the fourteenth century and well into the next one. The Constitutions were published by Vincenzo Ricchioni, "Le costituzioni del Vescovado Senese di 1336," *Studi Senesi* 30 (seconda serie, 5, 1914): 100–67. See also Lodovico Zdekauer, "Statuti criminali nel foro ecclesiastico nei secoli XIII–XIV," *BSSP* 7 (1900): 231–64.

pleading his cause except by the provost and two of the most senior members. Canons were always referred to and addressed by the title "Messer," which usually appears before their names in records.[69]

The canons also determined the duties of the chaplains and clerks, who were required to maintain proper deference toward them in all matters. The 1367 *Pacta* and the Constitutions stipulate that canons had to be at least fifteen years of age, and the later document adds that they had to know how to speak Latin and have competency in grammatical rules as well, if they wished to be recompensed for serving in the choir (*Pacta . . . nova,* chap. 11; *Constitutiones,* rub. 45). Since an ability to read music is not mentioned, it is probable that canons learned by rote many of the chants they sang in the offices, that is, unless they had been trained in a cathedral school or had come from a social class in which musical instruction formed part of their studies, as many of them did.

Canons were forbidden to wear indecorous clothing or to dress in colors deemed inappropriate (*Constitutiones,* rub. 9). In church they were obliged to wear a surplice and a biretta and to walk two by two in silence from the sacristy to the choir and back, "their minds intent only on the Divine Offices" (rub. 10). When they celebrated Masses or offices they wore copes or dalmatics (rub. 27).[70] Canons were obliged to wear birettas whenever the Chapter participated in processions, litanies, and funerals, except in summertime, when they could hang them from their shoulders or carry them (rub. 10). A biretta was evidently an immediately recognizable indication of status and station. Canons were accordingly prohibited from wearing them over the hoods of their cloaks in the fashion favored by laymen. They were, however, required to have them at all times so that they would be recognized by the lower clergy and given the honor due them and their office (rub. 27).[71] Even the places they occupied during services were assigned according to their exalted rank, as was customary throughout Christendom. They alone were allowed to sit in the upper stalls of the choir and they were forbidden to stand or sit in the lower stalls unless they were ill or because it was necessary for them to do so (rub. 16).

The Constitutions prohibit the canons, as well as the chaplains and clerks, from bearing arms, except in cases of evident necessity. Canons were forbidden to go to taverns or to "dishonest places," to play dice, or to have suspicious women in their own dwelling places (rub. 9). These regulations were the same as those governing the behavior of all Sienese clergy that were codified in an earlier episcopal decree of 1336. Among the regulations in that decree was one that prohibited the clergy from writing or composing songs, sonnets, or poems that were injurious to others, under penalty of a heavy

---

69. An alternate form, "misser," appears as frequently in the documents as the one I have adopted throughout my text.

70. Another rubric (18) states that when canons wished to celebrate Mass personally, the sacristan was to furnish them with clean vestments appropriate to the season, with a chalice, a missal, and other necessary things.

71. Other clergy were forbidden to wear a biretta under pain of excommunication and a heavy fine.

fine. Singing or reciting such materials was similarly proscribed.[72] Whether this latter regulation was enforced is another matter. Evidently, there were no restrictions against writing love stories or amorous poetry, as did Siena's bishop Aeneas Sylvius Piccolomini, who later became pope. When it came to setting secular texts to music, at least one Sienese canon in the early sixteenth century, the cathedral provost Niccolò Piccolomini, felt no compunctions about proclaiming himself in a music print of 1515 as a composer of frottole.[73]

The Constitutions of 1459 note that in accordance with the cathedral's stature—it had recently been elevated to metropolitan rank by Pius II—solemn high Mass was to be celebrated at the main altar only by the bishop or by prelates who had received permission from the bishop and the Sienese Chapter (rub. 14). This prerogative could be extended to canons if the need arose, but only on Sundays and certain specified feast days. Since the feasts mentioned were among the principal ones celebrated at the cathedral, it is understandable why exceptions were permitted on those occasions. On other days the Chapter, or canons', Mass could be celebrated at the altar of Sant'Ansano and at other altars by the chaplains. These requirements indicate that from the mid-fifteenth century onwards when polyphony was performed at Masses on important feast days, it was sung in the choir behind the main altar, or even in front of it, whereas if it was called for on ferial days or feasts of lesser importance or for votive Masses, it was sung at one of the chapels, such as those of Sant'Ansano or the Madonna delle Grazie, or later of St. John the Baptist. These places are referred to in a document regarding the musical chapel's duties, discussed below.

Sunday Masses and Vespers were, as elsewhere, the most important services because of the large public attendance. Recognizing this, the terms of a bequest made to the Chapter in 1511 stipulated that the annual income of 126 florins earned by the endowment would be used to pay an additional sum on a pro-rated basis to those canons who personally participated at Masses and Vespers on fifty Sundays during the year, on all of the feasts of Our Lord, and on Assumption Day and the day following it, when they were to march in the procession.[74] The canons were required to take part in Sunday processions and a number of others throughout the year, a tradition amply documented as early as 1215 in the *Ordo Officiorum*. They were also obliged to assist at litanies, burials, and Requiem Masses. These duties, mentioned in the earlier documents, are described in some detail in the Constitutions of 1459 (rub. 11, 15, 30, 24). The Constitutions make a point of noting that canons were obliged to prepare privately everything

---

72. Ricchioni, "Le costituzioni del Vescovado Senese del 1336," rub. 116, p. 162.

73. On Niccolò Piccolomini, see Luigia Cellesi, "Il lirismo musicale religioso in Siena nel Trecento e quello profano nel Cinquecento," *BSSP* 41 (1934): 107–8. Niccolò Piccolomini is listed as provost in Chapter accounts that record income from his prebend (AAS, Serie I, vol. 1, *Libro del Camerlengo, 1520,* fol. 40[r], and vol. 3, *Libro del Camerlengo, 1522,* fol. 34[r]). On his music, see chapter 14 below.

74. *Constitutiones,* p. 98. The bequest was made by the Rev. Bartolomeo de Bolis, a citizen of Padua and canon of St. Peter's in Rome, who donated property with a number of shops in Siena to the Chapter. This is the same Bartolomeo de Bolis who was appointed dean of Siena Cathedral in 1510. See note 63.

they read or sang in public and state that if someone was unsure about how things were to be done, it was his duty to learn from the others (rub. 18). This latter statement implies that the canons were at least minimally trained in the performance of chant. The Constitutions also affirm that just as the cathedral was at the head of all of the other churches in the city and in the diocese, so the canons—after the bishop—were to be treated with honor and reverence by all those in the service of the church (rub. 18).

Income from Prebends and Distributions

A significant part of the canons' income was derived from their shares of the earnings of the Chapter's communal possessions.[75] These had been accruing since the second half of the eleventh century, when Sienese bishops and others began donating vineyards, farmlands, orchards, woods, houses, and similar assets to the Chapter.[76] The Constitutions required that all of the Chapter's possessions be listed and described in a volume that would be kept in a secure place in order to avoid "irreparable" alienation of properties, as had occurred in the past (*Constitutiones,* rub. 49). Although the overseer could not interfere in any way with the Chapter's possessions, the canons were obliged every year to account for their expenses, as the 1367 *Pacta* state, and they were responsible for paying their own tithes (*Pacta . . . vetera,* chaps. 16, 18). Canons and chaplains, like other Sienese clergy, were recompensed for the taxes they paid to the commune, although those who held rectorships in other churches in the city received only one refund.[77] All of the Chapter's financial matters were handled by its own administrator, a "camerlingo," or chamberlain, who was elected to the post annually from among the ranks of the canons. A notary was also elected on an annual basis (*Constitutiones,* rub. 4, 6).

The 1367 *Pacta* fixed the number of canons and prebends at fourteen, in addition to the provost and archdeacon (*Pacta . . . nova,* chap. 11). The Constitutions of 1459 assigned a letter to each of the sixteen prebends, reserving A and B for the provost and the archdeacon, and required that an accurate record be kept of the possessions belonging to each prebend (*Constitutiones,* rub. 44, 49). Another prebend was added in the later sixteenth century, bringing the total to seventeen.[78] (Supernumeraries are mentioned at that time, but they had no prebends and received no income from the Chapter's communal possessions.) Although canons kept personal accounts of income received from their prebends, business transactions were overseen by the Chapter.[79] Chapter regulations, for example, forbade canons to lease farms and vineyards to people who were not qualified to work the land or to assign churches attached to their prebends to priests

---

75. Canons' incomes from Chapter holdings are registered in a series of accounts at AAS, mentioned in note 73. The archive and its holdings are described and cataloged in Giuliano Catoni and Sonia Fineschi, eds., *L'Archivio Arcivescovile di Siena* (Rome, 1970).

76. Nanni, "La canonica della cattedrale," 253–55.

77. *Constitutiones,* "Distributioni ordinati ai clerici in ricompensa delle gabelle," 52–53.

78. Seventeen canons were in residence in 1573. Their names are listed in AAS, Serie I, vol. 49, *Libro del Camarlengo dell'anno 1573–76,* fols. 52ᵛ–53ʳ.

79. An undated, mutilated description of the holdings of each prebend, probably from the turn of the fifteenth century, is kept among the "uninventoried papers" at AOMS, scattola I. K.

who did not officiate in them (rub. 47). In this way the Chapter could continue to assert its authority over individual benefices and prebends, the income from which, should they fall vacant or be suppressed in the first year, reverted to the Chapter (rub. 43).

Some prebends were more lucrative than others, and provisions were made to assure that canons currently serving had first right of refusal. Thus if a vacancy occurred because of a death, the Chapter's chamberlain was required within twenty days to ask whether any canon wished to have that prebend in place of his own (rub. 7). "So as to avoid the detestable crime of simony," however, prebends could be exchanged only for others of equal or larger income (rub. 39). Since no one could be appointed a canon unless his nomination was first discussed and approved by the Chapter, it was the canons themselves, together with the bishop, who determined who would receive a prebend (rub. 40, 13). The close family connections between the Sienese ruling classes and the cathedral canons in the fourteenth century, illustrated by William Bowsky, is indicative of the ambience—one that might aptly be described as a kind of closed corporation—that characterized the Sienese Chapter during that period.[80]

Though the situation seems to have been somewhat less parochial in later times, ties of kinship continued to have an important bearing in obtaining a canonry at Siena cathedral. Most telling in this respect is a roster of cathedral canons from 1573. Among its eighteen names is a veritable who's who of Siena's leading families, including a Bandini, two Petrucci, two Borghesi, two Piccolomini, an Ugurgieri, a Pretiani, a Malavolti, and a Cittadini.[81] From this, and countless other examples that could be cited, it is easy to understand how political and social considerations affected the eligibility of those who gained admittance to the cathedral's most lucrative posts, and it becomes obvious why these resources were rarely, if ever, used for the advancement of music. There was, to put it bluntly, simply too much at stake, socially, politically, and financially, for a canonry to be awarded to any but the privileged scions of Siena's upper classes and others with recommendations from popes, emperors, and peninsular potentates. From the end of the fourteenth century through the end of the sixteenth, in fact, there were only two canons who had any professional connections with musical performance. The earlier was the archdeacon Messer Piero di Pasqua, who, as will be illustrated below, apparently performed polyphony for a number of years during the course of his long association with the cathedral. The other was the already cited Messer Niccolò Piccolomini, cathedral provost, scholar, poet, and composer of frottole.

Another source of a canon's income was the monthly distribution he was paid by the Opera for daily participation at Chapter Mass and Divine Offices. At cathedrals, monasteries, and churches where clergy shared a communal life, all members of the establishment were required to gather together daily and celebrate Mass and the canonical hours of Lauds, Matins, Prime, Terce, Sext, None, Vespers, and Compline. At Siena cathedral these services were held, with few exceptions, in the choir. The Constitutions

---

80. William M. Bowsky, *A Medieval Italian Commune: Siena under the Nine, 1287–1355* (Berkeley and Los Angeles, 1981), 267–69.

81. AAS, Serie I, Capitolo Cattedrale di Siena, vol. 49, *Libro del Camarlengo dell'anno 1573–76*, unnumbered folio [2ᵛ], dated 1573.

of 1459 stipulate that in order to receive the distribution for singing in the choir, a canon must have obtained one of the cathedral's sixteen prebends, and that he had to have been in residence for a year and have personally officiated at services (*Constitutiones,* rub. 45). Perfect attendance at all services was required in order to receive the full amount of the distribution; otherwise fines, imposed for absences and tardiness, were subtracted from the monthly payments. Endowments, bequests, and donations, many of them mentioned in papal bulls, episcopal letters, and notarial records, provided supplementary funds that were distributed among the members of the Chapter. The Constitutions state that no one could receive these unless he was in residence for at least two-thirds of the year, although exceptions were made for illness or for absence in the service of the church or of the Chapter (rub. 42). All in all, the Sienese canons were handsomely provided for, and a measure of their satisfaction with conditions at the cathedral is reflected in the knowledge that during the fifteenth and sixteenth centuries several of them are recorded for periods of service in excess of twenty-five years.

Besides participating in required services, canons could say Mass whenever they wished and received extra compensation for doing so.[82] The canons' right to say Mass at a time of their own choosing, as the Constitutions make clear, even superseded the cathedral's requirement that daily Masses said by the chaplains must follow one another at specific intervals. Matins, Vespers, and Compline are specifically mentioned in the earlier *Pacta,* which say that on feast days canons receive twice as much as they do on ferial days for being present at these and other services.[83] The *Pacta* of 1367 enjoin the canons to be punctual and state that the sacristans charged with noting down tardiness would consider them as being absent from services should they arrive later than certain appointed times, as, for example, after the beginning of the psalm *Memor esto* at Terce, after the end of the second psalm at Vespers and at Compline, and after the ninth Kyrie at Mass (*Pacta . . . nova,* chap. 9).[84] Documents from the 1430s show that up to that time only the canons and perpetual chaplains sang the hours of Sext and None.[85] The

---

82. This right is referred to in passing in the *Constitutiones,* rub. 24, pp. 18–19: "De modo celebrationis missarum in ecclesia senensi . . . tamen ordo canonicos non habet ligare missam celebrare volentes, cum illas dicere possint, & legere pro libito voluntatis. . . ." Canons' rights in this regard are explained more fully in *Pacta . . . nova,* chap. 4. Later account books also list extra compensation for Masses. See, for example, AAS, Serie I, Capitolo Cattedrale di Siena, vol. 1, *Libro del Camerlengo, 1520,* fol. 33ʳ, which records a payment to Messer Marcho Pasquali of "s. 11 per lle sue messe chantacte . . . cioè messe quatro dopie e tre singole."

83. Chaps. 4 and 5 of the *Pacta . . . vetera* specify required attendance of chaplains at these services. That the same was required of canons is evident from chap. 6.

84. Required attendance at Matins is mentioned in the previous chapter.

85. The initial decision to compensate chaplains for participating in all of the offices was made by the overseer and his counselors. After acknowledging that customarily the offices of Sext and None were not sung in the choir and that chaplains were not obliged to say them unless they wished to, the board decided "that it would be to the greater glory and honor of God and of the Church," if the bishop were willing, to have the chaplains participate in those services for an additional s. 10 each per month. The board further stipulated that the chaplains were to be in the choir at the required hours if they wished to receive the extra stipend. The decree thus reveals that prior to December 1437 full-time chaplains, and probably the sacristy clerks, were not obliged to be present at all of the offices, but that from that time forward they would be, as befitted the major church of an important city.

1367 *Pacta* also list, month by month, all of the feasts for which the canons would receive a double distribution when they participated at certain Divine Offices. The list includes virtually all of the major feasts celebrated at the cathedral and is discussed below.

Whether fourteen canons were actually in residence at the time the 1367 *Pacta* were drawn up is not altogether certain (*Pacta . . . nova,* chap. 11).[86] Eleven, including the provost and archdeacon, participated in offices during September 1372.[87] Twelve are listed in an account book for the fiscal year May 1376–April 1377 and again in 1396. Fourteen canons, among them the provost and archdeacon, are mentioned in fiscal 1402–3. Sixteen canons—the entire Chapter—were in residence for most of fiscal 1418–19. The number of canons listed in sacristans' monthly reports continued to fluctuate throughout the remainder of the fifteenth century, an indication that not all of them were fulfilling residency requirements and that they were thus ineligible to receive regular distributions. Fifteen canons in all were in attendance for the month of July 1437, and sixteen, including the provost and the archdeacon, signified their approval of the 1459 Constitutions, with sixteen names appearing in the list of those for whom prebends were then authorized. From 1520 onwards information provided by the Opera's records of those who received the monthly distributions is augmented by data from the Chapter's own account books, which, among other things, specify the amount each canon received from his share of Chapter income.[88] The number of canons was increased by one in the sixteenth century. Seventeen of them, in fact, including provost, archdeacon, and archpriest, subscribed to the printed set of the Constitutions on 9 April 1578, when an additional five who were on authorized leave of absence were named, as were five absent supernumeraries.[89]

Information gained from such statistics is useful not only because it enables us to

---

AOMS, vol. 13, *Deliberazioni dell'operaio e dei consiglieri, 1434–55,* fol. 28ʳ, dated 20 December 1437: [margin: Salario de' capellani per dire Sesta e Nona] "Et veduto che ne la detta chiesa cathedrale non è usato per lo passato dirsi lo officio di Sesta e Nona in coro, né e capellani d'essa sonno obligati a dirlo più che si voglino, et pure sarebbe laude et honore di Dio e della chiesa che detti officii vi si dicessero: deliberarono di concordia che sia pienamente rimesso in misser lo Operaio e misser Conte, uno de' detti conseglieri, e quali avuto di questo colloquio e parere del Reverendo padre misser lo Vescovo, se al detto misser lo vescovo pare possion accresciare el salario de' cappellani predetti soldi dieci per ciascuno mese e per ciascuno di loro, con questo che detti capellani et ciascuno di loro sieno tenuti ritrovarsi in coro a dire e detti officii, et qualunche non vi si trovasse, perda el salario per rata."

86. Their number was smaller in earlier times. Nanni, "La canonica della cattedrale," 257–58, cites a privilege granted the Sienese Chapter by Pope Gregory IX dei conti di Segni on 24 November 1228 that confirms the number of canons at twelve.

87. They are listed in the series *E&U* under the relevant year.

88. AAS, Capitolo Cattedrale di Siena, Serie 1, vol. 1, *Libro del Camerlengo, 1520,* fols. 33ʳ–49ʳ, with distributions in two or more payments, list fourteen canons for the entire year, from May 1520 through April 1521: Messer Federigo Petrucci arcidiacono, Messer Giovanni Tolomei, Messer Giovanni Pecci, Messer Marco Pasquali, Messer Federigo Brunelli, Messer Francesco di Nanni, Messer Giovanni Battista di Messer Girolamo, Messer Marco Antonio Ugurgieri, Messer Girolamo Gabrielli, Messer Antonio Benzi, Messer Bandino di Niccolò decano, Messer Niccolò Piccolomini proposto, Messer Girolamo vescovo di Pienza, Messer Giovanni Pecci.

89. *Constitutiones,* p. aiiii.

measure longevity of service and ties of kinship but also because it provides unimpeachable evidence about the number of clergy who participated in services. Absentee holders of prebends were virtually unknown at Siena cathedral throughout these centuries, undoubtedly because the Chapter's Constitutions specifically forbade any disbursal of income for four years to canons who were not resident for two-thirds of a given year (*Constitutiones,* rub. 42). The Opera's records also leave no doubt that regulations regarding distributions were scrupulously observed, particularly because the administration stood to gain from monies not so disbursed.

CHAPLAINS

Income from sacristy revenues, endowed chaplaincies, and other donations provided the means of support for the chaplains, ordained priests who assisted the canons in celebrating the hours and Chapter Mass. They also said daily and votive Masses at one or another of the cathedral's altars, according to the requirements of their appointments. Chaplaincies could not be held in absentia (*Constitutiones,* rub. 53).[90] The Constitutions specify that chaplains were required to take the tonsure and to wear clerical dress, and that they, too, were forbidden, as were the clerks, to adopt any of the fashions favored by laymen (rub. 27). The chaplains were customarily addressed as "Ser," although on occasion a few were called "Don," an indication that they had attained a higher ecclesiastical rank than the ordinary priest.

Eight chaplaincies, established with funds provided by the bishop and private citizens, were attached to the cathedral by 1364. Their incumbents, called "perpetual chaplains," were obliged to assist at all services in which the canons participated. These chaplains officiated at several of the cathedral's dependent churches or at certain altars within the church. In later centuries a few musicians, among them the singer Ser Biagio di Tomè and the organist Ser Francesco di Nanni, are occasionally found within their ranks. The 1364 *Pacta* specified that the canons and Chapter were to appoint eight additional chaplains and four clerks to officiate at Masses for the souls of benefactors who had endowed chaplaincies or made other kinds of endowments and donations to the church (*Pacta . . . vetera,* chaps. 3, 10). At the time salaries for these eight chaplains were fixed at L. 60 each per annum, and it was agreed that they would be paid by the overseer from sacristy revenues. This provision, "made by the Commune of Siena and the overseer of the Opera on the one side and the canons and Chapter on the other," was reaffirmed three years later with the further stipulation that henceforth the eight chaplains and four clerks, the number of which was not to be diminished, would be appointed by the overseer and his counselors, at whose pleasure they would serve (*Pacta . . . nova,* chaps. 6, 1). Any other chaplains, present and future, were to remain under the Chapter's jurisdiction, as was customary (chap. 2). One result of the decision empowering the overseer to appoint chaplains was that musicians who were ordained priests could also be engaged to say additional Masses, as the need arose, a policy that was subsequently at the heart of employment practices regarding musicians. Later rec-

---

90. See also ASS, vol. 3395, a "Book of tithes and ecclesiastical benefices of the city and diocese of Siena" cited by Bowsky, *A Medieval Italian Commune,* 269, and Catoni and Fineschi, *L'Archivio Arcivescovile,* 200.

ords indicate that although sixteen chaplains and more were occasionally employed, particularly toward the end of the sixteenth century, their number more usually hovered around twelve.

The Constitutions make no reference to the education of chaplains or to what was required of them in the way of musical background, perhaps because it was understood that all who aspired to priestly rank would have received, in accordance with canon law, the necessary instruction in the subjects that qualified them for ordination. In Siena, in fact, such instruction was specifically mentioned as early as 1336 by Bishop Donusdeo Malavolti, who issued a set of revised regulations regarding the training of priests in the diocese. These state that no one could receive sacred orders or be appointed as curate of a church in Siena unless he knew how to read competently, could compose a sermon, knew how to sing the chant, and had been examined for competency by the bishop or his surrogate. It was further stipulated that musical instruction, offered gratis, was to be obtained only from church-approved teachers because, in the bishop's words, "if [the chant] is taught by ignorant people, it is received by listeners in an empty and inane way." Teachers who dared "to establish or conduct schools of music in the art of song" without episcopal approval were subject to a fine of L. 10 and were to be turned over to an episcopal tribunal.[91] How strictly this latter was enforced is difficult to say, but the regulations clearly point to the existence of a cathedral school where all Sienese aspirants to an ecclesiastical career were able to obtain a proper musical education free of charge.

Duties and Compensation

The overseer provided living quarters for all chaplains, the perpetual ones as well as the eight whom he appointed, and for four of the clerks (*Pacta . . . vetera,* chap. 7). In addition to paying the cook's salary, he furnished whatever was necessary for the refectory (chap. 8).[92] Like the perpetual chaplains, the eight chaplains and four clerks appointed by the overseer received monthly distributions for assisting in the choir. They were not obliged to participate in all of the canonical hours during the late fourteenth century. The 1364 *Pacta* state that they were to be present at Matins, Vespers, and Compline as well as at the daily Chapter Mass and that absences from services without

---

91. Ricchioni, "Le costituzioni del vescovado senese del 1336," rub. 84, p. 152: "De magistris. Dominus Donosdeus episcopus. Inter sollicitudines nostris umeris incumbentes perpeti curare volumus ut subiectos nostros ignorantes et non intelligentes ad scientiam et intelligentiam inducamus, gratia cooperante divina, diligenti studio et studiosa diligentia laborantes, dantes magistros qui gratis doceant et quantum in nobis est materiam habeant ad discenda; sed non ignoramus quod si scientia ab ignorantibus proferatur vacua et inaniter ab audientibus reportatur; ideo statuerunt et ordinaverunt quod nullus in civitate Sen. audeat scolas in musica seu arte cantus erigere vel tenere nisi prius fuerit domino episcopo approbatus et eius habuerit licentiam retinendi, si quis autem contrafecerit puniatur in decem libras den. sen. minutis [sic] camere domini episcopi applicandas."

92. Chap. 12 states that the house serving as the Chapter's kitchen, the refectory, and the chaplain's dormitory belonged to the sacristy and to the Opera; chap. 15 notes that except for the entrance leading into the house of Messer Meo Parri, the house and little houses leading to the cloister on the side of the canons' Chapter house also belonged to the Opera. These latter may have been used to house singers.

permission from the Chapter and the overseer would be punished with a fine (*Pacta . . . vetera,* chaps. 4, 5). The 1459 Constitutions reaffirm these injunctions and further stipulate that chaplains were forbidden to leave the choir or the church or to celebrate Masses or offices in any other place without first having obtained permission from the appropriate officials (*Constitutiones,* rub. 18). Chaplains and clerks were particularly admonished not to be absent from Matins, although they were permitted one day's respite every week (rub. 55).

By 1459 the duties of the perpetual chaplains were considerably augmented, for the Constitutions further specified that they were obliged to participate in all of the offices, both at night and during the daytime, and that failure to do so without just cause would incur a fine (rub. 54). Conversely, other chaplains, especially those who were engaged as singers of polyphony, were given, as will be shown below, a certain amount of leeway with regard to the number of Masses and Divine Offices they were obliged to celebrate or attend. The Constitutions make a point of noting that at the introit of the Mass and at the start of the canonical hours all of the chaplains were required to stand with their heads bared in front of the lectern and sing the "introits, antiphons, verses, responsories, alleluias, graduals, offertories, Sanctus, Agnus, postcommunions, commemorations and similar things" that were customarily performed at services (rub. 26).

As was the case with the canons, tardiness at services was punishable with a fine. Two instances are cited as examples in the Constitutions, which say that any chaplain who was not at Vespers from the first *Alleluia* through the *Deo gratias* would incur a fine of s. 5, whereas tardiness was not permitted at Compline for any reason (rub. 55).[93] Two chaplains, one chosen by the Chapter, another by the overseer, were charged with noting down absences and tardiness, and at the end of each year the accumulated fines were to be divided between the Chapter and the Opera (*Pacta . . . nova,* chap. 5). These duties were eventually taken over by the sacristans, whose extant rolls, or monthly reports, the "Scritte," furnish exact information about the number of clergy (and lay musicians) who participated in cathedral services. It was the sacristan's duty every week to display prominently in the sacristy a tablet listing all of the services that chaplains and clerks were required to participate in during that week (*Constitutiones,* rub. 19). In addition, he was to post a tablet on which were written the canonical statutes regarding chaplains' dress, conduct, and behavior.

Laughter, yelling, the use of obscenities, and any conversation not pertaining to the service were forbidden in the choir, in the sacristy, and in the church. Chaplains and clerks who contravened this regulation were subject to a fine of s. 10. These were apparently frequent abuses, for the injunction against such disturbances and the prescribed fines are repeated in rubrics concerning the Monday morning Masses for the dead and the processions that followed such Masses once a month (rub. 23, 24, 30). Chaplains were required to sit in the lower choir stalls, the first two seats of which on either side were reserved for cantors, succentors, and officiating weekly priests. During the offices, whether read or sung, chaplains wore surplices (rub. 22, 55). In processions,

---

93. Lauds is also mentioned in the Constitutions, but only to the effect that the sacristan was to administer the sacrament of confession to the people after the service.

of which there were any number both within and outside the church, they were obliged to wear a cope or other appropriate vestment as well as a small biretta.

The Constitutions explain that all chaplains were to say Masses on the days required of them by the terms of their appointments (rub. 55). They were obliged, in addition, to take weekly turns officiating at one or another of the cathedral's regularly scheduled daily votive or low Masses. The 1367 *Pacta* stipulate that chaplains who did not fulfill their obligations to the cathedral in this respect could not say or celebrate other Masses in the cathedral until all of the other chaplains who had complied with the regulation had said theirs (*Pacta . . . nova,* chap. 3). In other words, they might not say Masses required of them by the terms of their chaplaincies, or any other votive Masses for which they received extra remuneration, until they had taken their turn officiating as hebdomadal, or weekly, priests.

There were, quite obviously, exceptions to these rules made on behalf of individuals whose appointments required other services. In the late fourteenth century, for example, the organist-chaplain was obliged to say a few Masses and to be at Terce every day, though not at Matins. His principal duties, of course, entailed playing the organ, which he did at Saturday Vespers and at Vespers and Masses on Sundays and principal feast days throughout the year. During the fifteenth century chaplain-singers of polyphony were obliged personally to celebrate a number of Masses and to be present at certain offices every week, these in addition to the services where they normally sang polyphony. A number of records from the time indicate that some itinerant singers were not always scrupulous about observing the requirements of their appointments. Rather less appears in this regard during the later sixteenth century, as the singers' ranks tended to be filled more and more by chaplains who were from Siena or its territories.

In addition to the daily Chapter Masses and high Masses on Sundays and feast days in which the full Chapter participated, any number of other Masses were celebrated at the cathedral every day of the week. These were votive Masses or Masses with special intentions, many of them for the souls of benefactors and of the faithful departed. They were usually celebrated as low Masses, which meant that they were said rather than sung and did not call for musical embellishment of any kind. The 1367 *Pacta,* as mentioned, say that all chaplains were to take turns as hebdomadal priests in celebrating these regularly scheduled daily Masses. Their obligations are spelled out more fully in the 1459 Constitutions, which show that the order of daily Masses was strictly regulated (*Constitutiones,* rub. 24). The first Mass of the day was said by a hebdomadal priest who was directed to be vested and ready to begin his service as soon as the bell sounded the Ave Maria. After the first priest elevated the Host, the most solemn moment of the Mass, the hebdomadal priest who was to say the second Mass of the day might then begin his service, and so on through the third, fourth, and following Masses. Canons could celebrate Mass whenever they wished and were not bound to follow this sequence of Masses or of other low Masses that were said during the week. Strictly simultaneous celebration of such low Masses was forbidden, but a chaplain could begin to celebrate one at any time after the reading of the Epistle of another previously begun. The only exception in the order of regularly scheduled daily Masses was the conventual or canons' Mass. On feast days Terce was customarily done before this Mass, which was a solemn high Mass, but as the new Constitutions of 1459 state, it might be said before or afterwards, according to the season and the solemnity of the feast (rub. 24).[94]

The Mass of Our Lady was celebrated as the third Mass of the day, especially on feast days (rub. 24).[95] There were a few exceptions to this rule as well. On Mondays, obligations regarding daily Masses having otherwise been fulfilled, the third Mass was sung instead for the souls of the faithful departed, especially for the souls of those benefactors who had left properties and endowments for permanent chaplaincies to the Sienese church. Similarly, on feast days of the Virgin Mary, when solemn high Mass was dedicated to her, the third Mass was sung instead in honor of the Holy Spirit or of the Trinity. The place where the Lady Mass was celebrated is not mentioned in this or in any record regarding performance, but instructions given in another of the Constitution's chapters say that it was sung at the main altar on principal feast days. On other days it may have been done in the chapel of Santa Maria delle Grazie. Pictorial evidence, as mentioned above, shows in one case singers performing there at an unspecified service and in another instrumentalists playing during a Mass. No records are extant, however, that speak of endowments for musical performances at Lady Masses by the chapel singers. Since the Palace trumpeters' duties included weekly performances before the revered image, it is possible that these took place during Lady Masses on Saturdays.

Eight chaplains are mentioned in a set of payments disbursed by the sacristy for the month of March 1365[96] and in a similar set for September 1371. Another set of sacristy records from 1 May 1380 names nine of them. An account book for the fiscal year 1388–89 has the names of sixteen chaplains who served for shorter or longer periods during that time. All but one of them is called "our chaplain," though several also had additional duties, notably two who served as rectors of parish churches, another who acted as the bishop's vicar, and yet another, Ser Bartolomeo di Ser Laio, who was cathedral organist.

Fifteenth- and sixteenth-century records reveal that the number of chaplains fluctuated constantly over the course of the years, though it was a rare occasion when fewer than eight were present. Twelve were present during the 1402–3 fiscal year, but two of them were replacements for others who left during the year.[97] Sacristans' lists for December 1435 and July 1437 name nine and fifteen chaplains, respectively. A similar list from February 1455 names eight chaplains, among whom were two singers and the cathedral organist. Various records of appointment from the middle decades of the century leave no doubt that the overseer and his counselors were always ready to welcome new singers, teachers, and organists who could also serve as chaplains. How

---

94. See also the relevant passage in the 1367 *Pacta,* which states that Terce was said before the canons' or Chapter Mass on feast days, but was said quickly afterwards on ferial days (*Pacta . . . nova,* chap. 9).

95. See also rub. 55, item 15, enjoining priests to be on time for the Lady Mass.

96. The figures are taken from the following registers: AOMS, vol. 515, *Memoriale, 1364–65;* vol. 198, *E&U, 1371–72;* vol. 576, *Memoriale, 1380;* and vol. 520, *Memoriale, 1388.*

97. The figures for the fifteenth century come from vol. 230, *E&U, 1402–3;* vols. 1074–75, 1076, *Note di salari . . . ,* and volumes from the *Ore canoniche* series, by year.

successful they were, at least for brief periods, is revealed by the figures for 1472, when seventeen chaplains are recorded, among whom were included five singers of polyphony and the organist. A low point was recorded in February 1501, when six chaplains were present, though the number rose to nine in April 1503 and twelve in March 1515. There were eleven in May 1520 and in October and December 1535. In 1553 ten chaplains were mentioned, a number also recorded in 1565 and in 1590. By the end of the sixteenth century, when the number of singers reached an all-time high, at least three among the chaplains sang in the chapel, as personnel lists from 1598 through 1603 demonstrate. By that time funding for chaplaincies had apparently stabilized, and this, in fact, may account for the ease with which new singers were added to the roster in those years.

THE CLERKS

Four clerks are mentioned in connection with eight chaplains in the *Pacta* from 1364 and 1367. Their positions were funded by the Opera from sacristy revenues, an arrangement often referred to in later documents that call them "clerks of the sacristy."[98] The *Pacta* impose the same conditions regarding participation at canonical hours and Masses on the clerks as they do on the chaplains. They also state that the overseer was to provide living quarters for the four clerks whom he and his counselors appointed, but make no mention of living arrangements for any others. The Constitutions of 1459 are silent on this matter, too, although accommodations must have been made in later times, when greater numbers of clerks were employed. Like chaplains, clerks were forbidden to serve in other churches. They wore surplices at services and were fined if they were tardy.[99] They were also obliged to participate at Matins, from which they might be exempted once a week. The Constitutions forbid clerks and boys "to intone introits, antiphons, graduals, offertories, postcommunions, and other similar items that occur in the divine services" and state that during services in the choir unordained clerks were to stand in front of the lectern with heads bared. They were, at all times, to receive direction from their superiors with modesty, under penalty of a fine (*Constitutiones,* rub. 26, 16).

The boys mentioned in the 1459 Constitutions were students who were enrolled in the cathedral school. Although the school's origins went back to the earliest centuries of the cathedral's existence, there is little information about teachers employed there before 1419. In that year a governmental decree formally charged the overseer with ensuring that a chaplain-teacher of grammar, a chaplain-teacher of chant and polyphony, and a chaplain-organist be continuously employed at the cathedral.[100] This is, as

---

98. The number of clerks was considerably larger in the following century, though it seems that only four of them had long-term appointments and received steady salaries.

99. The very young clerks doubtless lived at home with their parents, as was probably the case with those in their early teens.

100. A copy of the relevant passage is in AOMS, vol. 1, *Diplomatico,* no. 52, dated 15 November 1419: "Item che lo Operaio sia tenuto continuamente tenere nella detta chiesa uno cappellano maestro di gramaticha, uno cappellano maestro di canto et di bischanto, et uno cappellano maestro d'orghani, acciò che essa chiesa ne sia honorata. Et con pacto che essi maestri sieno tenuti di insegnare a tutti e

mentioned, a certain indication that by that time the office of master of the school was no longer considered one of the cathedral's dignitaries. The statute stipulated that teachers were required to instruct cathedral clerks and priests and all other Sienese clerks who wished "to learn those sciences from them," words which practically echo the sentiments expressed by Bishop Donusdeo Malavolti in his regulations concerning the musical education of Sienese clergy issued in 1335. In practice, however, the student body was not restricted to youths studying for the priesthood, for as in other Italian church schools—St. Mark's in Venice and Santa Maria del Fiore in Florence, to cite two of the better-known institutions—there were many instances of students who who did not take holy orders after completing their training. Notable among such students in Siena were Galgano d'Enea and Ascanio Marri, both of whom pursued professional careers as instrumentalists.

None of the extant documents speaks of the number of students enrolled in the school, perhaps because this varied from year to year. Some idea of how many students there were, however, can be had from the sacristans' monthly lists of those eligible for the distribution, even though it is not certain that all of the students sang in the choir. Records often refer to these youths according to their age and status in the school. *Cherico minore* or *cherico piccolo* are the terms used to describe the youngest ones; *cherico mezzano* those who were somewhat older, perhaps in their early teens; and *cherico grande* the eldest.[101] The names of many former clerks, preceded by the title "Ser," are on occasion found listed along with those of the cathedral chaplains, an indication that they were given appointments at the cathedral soon after they were ordained. From time to time, even after they became priests, a few of them continued to serve as clerks of the sacristy before moving on to posts outside the cathedral.

Records of payments to personnel for March 1365 give the names of five clerks, one more than the number specified in the *Pacta* of the previous year.[102] Five are also mentioned in a similar document for the month of September 1371, and again in a list of "all of the priests and clerks who serve in the Duomo" dated 1 May 1380. The names of eighteen clerks are registered in a volume from 1388, though, as in the case of Jacomo di Benedetto Bellanduccio, who was later to serve as a singer-chaplain, many of them are listed for only a few months. Nevertheless, the figure is significant because it points to a considerably larger number of students in the cathedral school than is indicated by extant employment records. Greater numbers of clerks are consistently

---

cherici della detta chiesa et preti che volessero imparare tali scientie, et similmente a tutti altri cherici di Siena che da lloro imparare volessero."

101. In its broadest sense "cherico" means (and meant, as other contemporary Sienese documents attest) "cleric." But in cathedral documents from the centuries under consideration in this book the term "cherico" is used for the most part to identify boys or young men in minor orders who were not yet ordained. In the course of my text I have translated it in several ways, according to the context in which these boys and young men were employed at the cathedral, namely, as "clerk," "middle clerk" (*cherico mezzano*), "older clerk" (*cherico grande, cherico maggiore*), "young clerk" (*cherico piccolo, cherico minore*), "chorister," or "choirboy." I use the latter particularly in referring to those who sang in the chapel of polyphonic music.

102. The personnel are listed in AOMS, vol. 515, *Memoriale, 1364–65;* vol. 351, *E&U, 1371–72;* vol. 576, *Memoriale, 1380;* and vol. 520, *Memoriale, 1388.*

cited in fifteenth- and sixteenth-century records. To cite two instances only: a sacristan's roll for January 1508, which names twenty-five clerks, among them seven older youths, nine in their middle teens and nine younger ones; and accounts from May 1564 through the end of April 1566, which name thirty-six of them, including eight older, five in their middle teens, and the remainder younger. Similar numbers in similar proportions are found through the remaining decades of the century, with the numbers fluctuating between twenty-four and forty-four.

THE PLAINCHANT CHOIR

A few sporadically preserved records from the late fourteenth century indicate that Divine Offices were celebrated at the cathedral throughout the time of the reconstruction of the choir. Eight canons, eight chaplains, and five clerks were present in March 1365, with one canon and one clerk fewer in the following month of April.[103] Numbers were not substantially changed by September 1371, when eleven canons, including the provost and archdeacon, eight chaplains, and five clerks were cited. In addition to the bishop and two preachers, eleven canons, including the provost and archdeacon, thirteen chaplains, and nineteen clerks were listed among "all of those who serve in the Duomo" in 1388. The names of twelve canons, ten chaplains, including the organist, and six clerks appear in an accounts for fiscal 1396–97. Although lists of this kind from before the turn of the fifteenth century are rare, several different sources from the following decades preserve complete records of personnel who sang in the choir. These, as mentioned earlier, leave no doubt that canons, chaplains, and clerks were paid on a monthly basis for singing the daily office in the choir and that they were fined for tardiness or absences. Fines subtracted from their base salaries thus account for the slight discrepancies occasionally found in the distributions paid to choir members. The number of clergy who sang at offices, as is apparent from figures already cited, was considerably enlarged after the turn of the fifteenth century, reaching forty within the next hundred years and even more in the following decades (see Table 1.1).

At the turn of the thirteenth century it was the cathedral's archpriest who had the principal role in leading the daily offices and Masses. Oderigo has a good deal to say about the archpriest's duties, and he also makes it clear that these could be assigned just as well to a hebdomadal priest, a canon appointed on a weekly basis, who could fulfill the functions of the archpriest in the event of his absence.[104] Oderigo begins his account by noting that early on Saturday afternoons the hebdomadal priest who celebrated the Mass began Vespers. This was dedicated to the Virgin Mary and included prayers for Vespers of whatever feast was specified for that day.[105] During the service the hebdomadal priest read the chapter after the psalms and at the end he said the prayer. His role was no less conspicuous at Matins, which he also began with the customary prayers.

---

103. Figures come from vol. 515, *Memoriale; 1364–65,* vol. 198, *E&U, 1371–72;* vol. 520, *Memoriale, 1388;* and vol. 225, *E&U, 1396–97.*

104. *OO,* part 2, chap. 7, 408–9.

105. An explanation of the order and content of Vespers and other services is given in the following chapter.

TABLE 1.1.   A representative sampling of clergy
participating in the choir

Time	Canons	Chaplains	Clerks	Total
December 1412	13	11	7	31
May 1423	12	12	7	31
July 1437	15	15	10	40
March 1447	15	12	11	38
May 1455	14	10	16	40
June 1482	15	13	15	43
June 1492	13	14	15	42
February 1501	12	6	14	32
March 1515	16	12	20	48
January 1535	16	9	21	46
May 1553	18	10	16	44
May 1565	18	10	22	50
May 1588	18	10	30	58
May 1593	20	11	23	54
May 1600	17	13	23	53

NOTE: The data are drawn from AOMS, vols. 1074–75, *Note di salari
e liste di canonici, chierici, cantori, suonatori, sagrestani e cappellani (1412–
1535)*, for 1412, 1423, 1437, 1446/47, 1482, 1500/1, 1514/15,
1534/35; vol. 1076, *Note di salari . . . Secc. XV–XVIII*, for 1455; SA
155, *Ore canoniche, 1553–54*; SA 165, *Ore canoniche, 1565–66*; SA
185, *Ore canoniche, 1588–89*; SA 190, *Ore canoniche, 1593–94*; SA
197, *Ore canoniche, 1600–1*.

On Sundays he blessed the holy water, blessed those who read lessons, and read the penultimate one or the last one himself if it was not read by the archpriest or the provost. After Matins, if the provost or archpriest were not present, it was the weekly priest who dismissed the Chapter. At Lauds he began the verse and said the *Deus in adjutorium meum* as well as the chapter and the prayer. He did the same at Prime and all the other canonical hours.

Before the beginning of the Mass for the people on Sundays the hebdomadal priest heard confessions. At that Mass (which was usually said before major, or solemn high, Mass) he announced forthcoming feasts and said the prayers for peace and other customary prayers. On feast days of the saints he gave the sermon or invited one of the deacons to give it, if no other prelate was scheduled to do so. He sprinkled holy water during processions, and when they were concluded, he said the verse and prayer in front of the church doors. After this, assisted by the deacon and the subdeacon, he celebrated the major Mass of the day at the high altar, unless a special feast was being commemorated at another altar. It was also his prerogative to purify women who returned to church after giving birth, to say votive Masses, and to give absolution to the infirm who called for a priest. If the archpriest was absent, the hebdomadal priest blessed the altar at the beginning and end of communion, and after leaving the church, if the provost or archpriest were not present, he dismissed the Chapter by saying *Benedicite*.

When the same officials were not present at Requiem Masses, he began the service and said all of the necessary prayers, after which, in the company of the parish priest, he accompanied the coffin to its burial place.

When the bishop presided at services, it was the archpriest or the hebdomadal priest who was always at his side. This was the case, for instance, at Matins, where the penultimate lesson was read by the archpriest, the last one by the bishop. At Lauds, when the bishop said the *Deus in adjutorium meum,* the archpriest said the verse, and later in the service the archpriest read the chapter and the bishop said the prayer. Similarly, at Vespers when the bishop said the *Deus in adjutorium meum,* it was the archpriest or the weekly priest who said the chapter. One or the other of them, wearing a cope, also assisted the bishop whenever he celebrated Mass.

The 1459 Constitutions show that there was little change in the hebdomadal priest's duties after Oderigo's time, though the passages in which these are listed do not mention an archpriest. This was undoubtedly because the office had been discontinued temporarily. Instructions concerning services "in the choir or in the church" stipulate that "introits, antiphons, graduals, offertories, or postcommunions and other similar things that are done at services" could be begun only by the canon who was serving as hebdomadal priest or by his surrogate, or on ferial days by a chaplain, but never by clerks in minor orders or by boys (*Constitutiones,* rub. 26). This, as will be seen presently, is a distant, though audible echo of the same sentiment expressed by Oderigo centuries earlier, when he noted that "in our church only a cleric can officiate at offices." The Constitutions further specify that when the officiating priest intoned these chants, he was to rise to his feet, with his head bared, and begin them in the usual way. He was also obliged to be in the choir at the appropriate time so that he might begin Matins, Vespers, and Compline (rub. 55). Similarly, he was expected to begin Terce as soon as the bell was sounded, at which service he would be assisted by the clerk–organist. This, incidentally, is the only instance in the 1459 Constitutions where the organist is cited, and it may be an indication that his presence at Terce was required because he was to perform at high Mass, which usually followed immediately (rub. 55).

The 1459 Constitutions speak at some length about the duties of the prefect of the choir, an office unmentioned at the cathedral before this time (rub. 3). The prefect was chosen from among a group of three resident canons nominated by the provost, the chamberlain, and the outgoing incumbent, none of whom was thus eligible for the position. His term of office was an annual one that began in May, on the first day of the cathedral's fiscal year. The post called for administrative skill and a thorough knowledge of the liturgy. The prefect determined how services were to be celebrated during the different seasons of the year, he decided when funeral Masses might be held, and he was responsible for fixing the order of litanies and of processions. All of his decisions regarding cathedral rites were accepted without question unless the Chapter decided otherwise. He had, in fact, absolute control of every aspect of worship at liturgical functions, whether these were held in the choir or in some other part of the church, and all were obliged to obey his decisions. During offices, furthermore, chaplains and clerks were subject to punishment and fines should they leave the choir without his permission. The prefect's duties, which were disciplinary as well as administrative, car-

ried no extra stipend. This explains why incumbents are rarely if ever named the Opera's account books.

Among records testifying to the continuing presence of the prefect of the choir in
the following century is one from 24 April 1512 that reports the election of the Chapter's new administrators, among whom were Messer Bartolomeo Lazoli, prefect of the
choir; Messer Giovanni Tolomei, chamberlain; and Messer Giovanni Pecci, scrivener.[106]
Another record from 25 November 1552 reports that at the Chapter meeting held that
day it was decided, on the recommendation of the prefect of the choir, with the dean
and the provost acquiescing, to celebrate the upcoming feasts of St. Matthew and of St.
Dominic as duplex feasts, if the archbishop were in agreement.[107] In the past both days
had been named among the cathedral's principal feast days, though it appears that for a
century or more the latter was celebrated with less solemnity than previously.

THE CATHEDRAL'S PRINCIPAL FEAST DAYS

Though not very numerous, cathedral records from the fifteenth and sixteenth centuries are unanimous in assigning the performance of polyphony at Masses and Vespers to
Sundays and principal feast days throughout the year. This was an ancient practice,
already established by 1215, when Oderigo wrote his account of cathedral rites. Subsequent reports are not as complete or as comprehensive as his, but the information they
provide serves to corroborate, amplify, and update the lists of principal feasts observed
at the cathedral through the end of the sixteenth century. They also chronicle the
emergence of new feasts dedicated to relative newcomers, such as Siena's own San
Bernardino, as well as the decline of others. That the rank of some feast days changed
during the course of centuries is, of course, not surprising, and the same may be said of
the prayers and chants that were sung in polyphony at services on many of them, if, in
fact, polyphony was always performed during the period for which personnel records
are lacking. In any case it is clear that from the early thirteenth century onwards there
was a core of feast days celebrated at Siena cathedral, whose services included polyphony whenever trained singers were present.

This core of feast days was already well established by the end of the twelfth century,
as demonstrated by the terms of an accord signed on 21 April 1190 between Siena's
bishop and the cathedral canons regarding the division of offerings made by the faithful.
The text includes a list of occasions when the largest donations of the year were received, and these were plainly the feast days that were regarded as especially significant
by both laity and clergy:[108]

Christmas (25 December)
Circumcision (1 January)

---

106. AAS, vol. 1136, *Deliberazioni del Capitolo, 1508–49,* fol. 9ʳ.

107. Vol. 1137, *Deliberazioni del Capitolo, 1550–54,* fol. 20ʳ. Records such as this suggest that it
was the prefect of the choir who approved the texts of motets and other polyphonic pieces that were
proposed by the *maestro di cappella* for performance at services.

108. Nanni, "La canonica della cattedrale," 258. The document is in the ASS, Diplomatico, Opera
Metropolitana, 1190, aprile 21.

Epiphany (6 January)
Easter
Ascension
Pentecost
Purification of the Blessed Virgin Mary (2 February)
Annunciation of the Blessed Virgin Mary (25 March)
Assumption of the Blessed Virgin Mary (15 August)
Nativity of the Blessed Virgin Mary (8 September)
All Saints (1 November)
Maundy Thursday
Consecration of the Sienese cathedral (18 November)
St. Ansanus (1 December)
St. Crescentius (14 September)
St. Savinus (30 October)
St. Victor (14 May)

None of these feast days can be considered unusual for the period and place. Apart from five local feasts, the list includes some of the oldest ones from the Proper of the Time and the principal ones of the Virgin Mary, in addition to All Saints and Maundy Thursday. These had been celebrated by the universal church for centuries and, with the exception of Maundy Thursday, were ranked as doubles of the first or second class, the most solemnly observed feasts of the Christian calendar. It was a group which, with very few exceptions and several additions, was to remain at the core of all of the lists of principal feasts celebrated at Siena cathedral throughout the next three centuries. And since these same days were mentioned some two decades later, in 1215, by Oderigo as feasts at which organum was sung at one service or another, it is likely that some form of polyphony was being performed even at this early time.

Important feast days at the cathedral are mentioned again only a few years afterwards in a bull issued by Pope Celestine III Orsini on 17 April 1194.[109] At that time the pope stipulated that all chaplains residing in Siena and its suburbs were required to be present at the cathedral on a number of specified days so that they might participate in the processions that took place on those occasions. Some of the feasts cited in the document of 1190 are lacking, but several new ones appear. This is doubtless because processions were not prescribed for all of Siena's major feast days. Thus, Circumcision, Nativity of the Virgin, All Saints, and the four patron saints of Siena are not mentioned, although others such as St. John the Baptist, the Rogation days (Monday, Tuesday, and Wednesday before Ascension), and all Sundays during the year are now included. The papal bull also directed all chaplains to be present at services in the cathedral on Ash Wednesday, on Maundy Thursday, and on the days of the Scrutinium, as well as at the baptismal ceremonies that took place on Holy Saturday and on the Saturday preceding Pente-

---

109. A copy is at ASS, Transunto delle cose, vol. B 39, no. 93; another copy in AAS, no. 3, antica segnal. 74; see Nanni, "La canonica della cattedrale," 257; the document is also published by Kehr, *Italia Pontificia*, 3:207, no. 10.

cost.[110] These requirements were eventually renewed by Pope Gregory IX dei conti di Segni, who reissued the bull without any changes on 8 December 1228.[111]

Feast Days in the Ordo Officiorum

While it is clear that not all of the cathedral's major feast days are mentioned in these early documents—which were, admittedly, drawn up for different purposes—they are important because they serve to corroborate information given by Oderigo, who gives detailed accounts of how all of the feasts of the church year—the Proper of the Time, the Proper and Common of Saints, and Sundays—were observed shortly after the turn of the thirteenth century. In turn they serve to strengthen Kees van der Ploeg's contention that a customary such as Oderigo's Ordo Officiorum did not originate overnight and that it was probably a compilation of previously uncodified or only partially codified practices.[112] The large number of feasts cited in the Sienese customary, many of them of duplex rank and with nine lessons, points to derivation from monastic models, which may have been adopted as a result of canonical reforms instituted earlier.[113] The ever-increasing tendency toward uniformity in liturgical books sanctioned by the papacy may also have played a part in the compilation.

Although Oderigo mentions a great number of feast days, his descriptions make it clear that some feasts were celebrated less elaborately than others and that more often than not a simple commemoration was the rule for many of them.[114] A calendar of the

---

110. The seven scrutinies incorporated into Lenten Masses or occurring between Terce and Sext of Wednesdays and Saturdays after the third Sunday of Lent took the form of public exorcism and exhortation to progress toward baptism. See Andrew Hughes, *Medieval Manuscripts for Mass and Office: A Guide to Their Organization and Terminology* (Toronto, 1982), 908–9. Hughes notes that the most important were those occuring on Wednesday of Laetare Sunday, "the Day of Great Scrutiny," and the seventh and final one on Holy Saturday.

111. Pecci, *Storia del vescovado Senese,* 201–5, published the documents from AAS, no. 7, antica segnal. 6 e 103; and no. 6, antica segnal. 3 e 63.

112. Van der Ploeg, *Art, Architecture and Liturgy,* 63.

113. Van der Ploeg, ibid., 148, makes this point and says that the sheer quantity of feasts mentioned by Oderigo would suggest a monastic congregation rather than a foundation of secular clergy. He notes further that the use of a liturgy deriving from monastic observance fits in well with "the image of a second reform" of the Sienese liturgy, which he believes "was accomplished around 1200."

114. As Garrison pointed out, the hagiology of the *Ordo Officiorum* comprises prescriptions for the celebration of a number of saints who are connected with Siena, such as Virgilio, bishop of Trent, Desiderius, bishop of Vienne, and the Roman martyr Mustiola, to whom churches were dedicated within the city; to others such as Antimo, a widely venerated saint in the Tusco-Umbro-Sabine region; and to a number of others who are unmentioned in other Sienese liturgical books ("Twelfth-Century Initial Styles of Central Italy: Indices for the Dating of Manuscripts," in *Studies in the History of Medieval Italian Painting,* 4/4:346–52). Van der Ploeg mentions saints such as Boniface and Severinus who were especially revered in northern Europe and notes that these may have been introduced by German bishops or as a result of imperial influence and Siena's Ghibelline politics (*Art, Architecture, and Liturgy,* 148–49). But most of these were celebrated with simple commemorations and have no distinguishing rituals as do those saints particularly associated with Siena or with the Cathedral. Whatever the reasons, it is clear that the Sanctorale section of the *Ordo Officiorum* contains a good many saints, not all of whose feasts were celebrated with the same degree of solemnity.

cathedral's feasts precedes Oderigo's account in the manuscript that preserves his work, and despite erasures and some inconsistencies and omissions, its contents generally agree with the degree of importance accorded the feasts in the main body of the text.[115] Following Oderigo's criteria, the feasts celebrated as major ones at the cathedral during his time can be grouped into three categories. Though all of them had one or two features in common, the most important were marked by more elaborate services that often included the performance of polyphony. Most of them had nine lessons read at Matins, though nine lessons were also prescribed for many other feasts of lesser importance and only three were read on Easter, the most solemn feast of the year. Processions, as has been mentioned, also distinguished many of these feast days, and they, too, are described at some length by Oderigo.

In addition to Sundays, there were over two dozen major feasts that were celebrated with special observances, feasts constituting what may be called the primary category (see Table 1.2, feasts labeled I). They were distinguished, above all, by having antiphons sung in their entirety both before and after psalms—"doubled," as Oderigo put it—at Vespers, Matins, and Lauds (OO, part 1, chap. 435).[116] Nine of the feasts are of saints to whom altars were dedicated in the cathedral (marked with an asterisk in Table 1.2). The similarities between Oderigo's primary feasts and the earlier list from 1190 are immediately apparent. Common to both are the six feasts from the Proper of the Time, the near universal ones of the Virgin Mary and of All Saints, and the specifically Sienese ones dedicated to the town's patron saints and the cathedral's consecration day. New are the Octave of the Assumption, the two feasts honoring St. Michael the Archangel, the feasts of the translations of two of Siena's patron saints, and the feasts of several saints who were especially venerated in the city—saints, with the possible exception of St. Thomas, to whom altars were dedicated in the cathedral. Significantly, at the time there was no altar dedicated to St. Victor, one of the city's four patrons, even though his relics were preserved in the altar of St. Savinus, and as a result, his feast day was not observed in quite the same manner as the others. For all of these feasts, except St. Lucy, nine lessons were read at Matins, a usage Oderigo explains by noting that saints thus honored were those whose "histories we have in our lectionaries."

At Vespers and Matins of these feasts with doubled antiphons the archpriest or the officiating priest, or the bishop if he were present, put on a cope at the beginning of the service (chap. 436). The officiants censed the altar, the clergy, and the congregation at various times throughout the ceremonies. In addition, the cathedral's two large bells were rung at the beginning of Matins, at the beginning of the major Mass of the day,

---

115. The calendar, on fols. 1ʳ–6ᵛ of BCIS, MS G. V. 8, was not included by Trombelli in his edition of the OO. Listings for a few months are incomplete because the lower parts of several folios were cropped during rebinding. Later entries, mainly obituaries, were added to the monthly lists of feasts. The calendar has recently been published by van der Ploeg, *Art, Architecture and Liturgy*, 151–58.

116. The exceptions to the use of plainsong were the feasts of the Assumption and Consecration of the cathedral, when polyphony was adopted, as noted below. Oderigo also remarks that if one of the feasts fell on a Sunday and if the Sunday antiphon was said, then it was not repeated. Elsewhere, Oderigo shows that on Christmas Day and on Epiphany, among others, antiphons were also repeated "wherever they fall" within the psalms (*intra psalmos, ubi tanguntur, cantentur*).

TABLE 1.2. Principal feast days at the cathedral of Siena

Date and feast	1190 accord	Ordo Officiorum[a]	Pacta of 1367[b]	1459 Constitutions
Movable feasts				
Ash Wednesday				x
Maundy Thursday	x		x	x
Good Friday			x	x
Holy Saturday			x	x
Easter	x	I	x	x
Easter Monday			x	x
Easter Tuesday				x
Ascension	x	I	F.V.	x
Pentecost	x	I	x[c]	x
Greater Litanies			x	
Corpus Christi			F.V., Matins	x
January				
1 Circumcision (Octave of Christmas)	x	I	F.V.	x (and vigil)
8 Octave of Circumcision			x	
6 Epiphany	x	I	F.V.	x (and vigil)
18 St. Peter's Chair				x
20 SS. Fabian and Sebastian		I★		
25 Conversion of St. Paul	x	I	x	x
February				
1 St. Bridget		II		
2 Purification of the B.V.M.	x	I	F.V.	x (and vigil)
6 Translation of St. Ansanus		I★		
24 St. Matthias Apostle		III	F.V.	x
March				
12 St. Gregory Pope		III	x	x
21 St. Benedict Abbot		III		
25 Annunciation of the B.V.M.	x	I	F.V.	x (and vigil)
April				
25 St. Mark Evangelist		III	x	x (and vigil)

TABLE 1.2 continued

Date and feast	1190 accord	Ordo Officiorum[a]	Pacta of 1367[b]	1459 Constitutions
May				
1 SS. Philip and James		III	F.V.	x
3 Invention of the Holy Cross			x	
6 St. John before the Latin Gate			F.V.	
8 Apparition of St. Michael the Archangel		I	x	x
14 St. Victor	x	II	F.V.	x
20 Blessed Confessor Bernardino of Siena				x
June				
11 St. Barnabas Apostle		III	F.V.	x
14 SS. Cantius, Cantian, and Cantianilla		II		
24 St. John the Baptist			F.V.	x
29 SS. Peter and Paul		II	F.V.	x
July				
2 Visitation of the B.V.M.			F.V.	x (and vigil)
9 Octave of the Visitation			x	
10 Seven Brothers and St. Felicity		II		
25 St. James Apostle		III	F.V.	
August				
1 St. Peter's Chains			x	
5 Dedication of the Church of Our Lady of the Snow				
10 St. Lawrence			x	x
15 Assumption of the B.V.M.	x	I	F.V.	x (and vigil)
22 Octave of the Assumption		I	F.V.	
24 St. Bartholomew		I*	F.V.	x
28 St. Augustine Bishop		III	x	x
29 Beheading of St. John Baptist			x	
September				
8 Nativity of the B.V.M.	x	I	F.V.	x (and vigil)
15 Octave of the Nativity			F.V.	
14 Exaltation of the Holy Cross		I	x	
14 St. Crescentius	x	I*		
20 St. Matthew Apostle and Evangelist		III	F.V.	x (and vigil)
29 Dedication of the church of St. Michael the Archangel		I	x	x
30 St. Jerome		III		

Table 1.2 *continued*

Date and feast	1190 accord	Ordo Officiorum[a]	Pacta of 1367[b]	1459 Constitutions
October				
1 St. Remigius		III		
6 St. Balbina		II		
12 St. Crescentius		I★d	F.V.	x
18 St. Luke Evangelist		II	F.V.	x (and vigil)
23 St. Severinus	II			
28 SS. Simon and Jude		III	F.V.	x
30 St. Savinus	x	I	F.V.	x
November				
1 All Saints Day	x	I	F.V.	x (and vigil)
2 All Souls Day			x	x
11 St. Martin			x	
18 Consecration of Sienese Cathedral	x	I	F.V.	x
30 St. Andrew Apostle		II	F.V.	
December				
1 St. Ansanus	x	I★	F.V.	x
6 St. Nicholas		I★	x	
7 St. Ambrose		III		x
8 Conception of the B.V.M.			F.V.	x (and vigil)
13 St. Lucy		I★	F.V.	
21 St. Thomas Apostle		I★	F.V.	
25 Christmas	x	I	F.V.	x
26 St. Stephen			x	x
27 St. John Evangelist			x	x (and vigil)
28 Holy Innocents			x	x
29 St. Thomas à Becket		III		
31 St. Sylvester			x	x

[a]Roman numerals indicate first, second, and third categories; ★ indicates altar dedicated to the saint.
[b]The *Constitutiones* of 1579 list the same feasts, except for St. Savinus and St. Martin. F.V. = First Vespers.
[c]And two days following.
[d]Translation of St. Crescentius.

and at the beginning of Vespers, as well as when the *Te Deum* was sung.[117] And on these same days, as on all Sundays during the year, the first two in August excepted, the officiant at the major Mass was assisted by a deacon and a subdeacon.[118]

The performance of polyphony at one service or another also distinguished the feasts of this primary group. Polyphony and polyphonic repertories in Oderigo's day will be discussed in the following chapter, so suffice it to note here its place in services on principal feast days. At First Vespers, except on Holy Saturday, the responsory of the following day was always sung in organum while the archpriest and sacristan together did the censing (chap. 436).[119] As will be explained below, organum was a manner of improvising polyphony which might be done in a simple note-against-note style or with a more florid part, or parts, sung above the chant in a slower-moving lower voice, in measured or in unmeasured rhythms. On these same feasts a jubilus, or extended melisma, was sung at the end of the Magnificat antiphon, at the end of the Benedictus antiphon, and at the end of the concluding antiphon of each Nocturn (chap. 437). The Magnificat antiphon, furthermore, was sung in organum. Christmas, Epiphany, Easter, Ascension, and Pentecost were particularly distinguished by having the Alleluia of the major Mass of the day sung in organum from the stone pulpit, as it was on Sundays (chap. 437). On Assumption day and the feast of the Consecration of the cathedral antiphons repeated after the psalms were sung in organum.[120] On the evenings preceding the ten feasts that honored saints to whom altars were dedicated there was an abbreviated Matins service, which included three Lessons, the Benedictus canticle with its antiphon, and the *Benedicamus Domino*.[121] One or more of these items was sung in organum. As for other feasts that featured polyphony but were not included within the primary group, Oderigo notes that the feasts of St. John Apostle and Evangelist and St. Sylvester, to whom altars were dedicated in the cathedral, were also celebrated with an abbreviated Matins service in which organum was performed, even though antiphons were not doubled on these days.[122]

117. Oderigo also specifies that on these days the large bell alone was sounded at Prime and at the Mass of the people and that the same was true for St. Stephen and for St. John Evangelist, even though antiphons were not doubled for these latter (*OO,* part 1, chap. 437).

118. Sext was sung later if the feast occurred during Advent or during Lent, when the clergy normally fasted.

119. This responsory, a chant placed between the chapter and the hymn, was suppressed in the post-Tridentine liturgy. See Craig Wright, *Music and Ceremony at Notre Dame of Paris, 500–1550* (Cambridge, 1989), 246, who notes that this responsory was sung in polyphony at the Parisian cathedral.

120. The days comprising the octave, that is the week following some of these major feasts, such as Christmas, Pentecost, Assumption of the Virgin, and Consecration of the cathedral, were also distinguished by the use of polyphony at one service or another, as were the two days following Easter and Low Sunday.

121. One of these services is described in detail below in conjunction with music for the feast of Sant'Ansano.

122. Polyphony was also performed at a few other services: on St. John's Day (sequence, Alleluia, R *Qui vicerit,* and responsory in the evening after Vespers), on St. Stephen's (Epistle, Alleluia), on Holy Innocents (Alleluia), and on all of the days within the Octave of Christmas (the Magnificat anthem at Vespers and the antiphon at Lauds (*OO,* 50, 47, 48). Oderigo further notes that for St. Sylvester it was customary to sing the responsory of the day at First Vespers and to sound both bells

A second category of feasts comprised several that were not celebrated so elaborately, having neither doubled antiphons nor a major Mass on the day (see Table 1.2, feasts labeled II). They did, however, share a number of features with those of the primary group. These included singing the responsory proper to the day at First Vespers and an elaborate pattern of bell ringing, although only the smaller of the two bells was struck at the third sounding at Vespers, at Matins, and at the *Te Deum* (chap. 437). Of the saints in this category, it appears that only Andrew, Bridget, and Peter and Paul had no special connection with the cathedral at this time.[123] Two altars dedicated to other saints (Savinus and Bartholomew) are designated as being under the patronage of Luke and Severinus, which explains their inclusion, and the remaining saints were ones whose relics were kept at the cathedral. For the feasts of these latter Oderigo states that neither Vigils nor the major Mass of the day were said unless the feast fell on a Sunday. He also specifies that if the responsory proper to the feast was sung at Vespers, then the *Benedicamus Domino* was sung in organum. His remarks thus indicate that polyphony was performed on all of these feasts, except for Bridget, Luke, and Severinus. Although St. Agnes is not mentioned in this group, Oderigo's remarks show that the *Benedicamus Domino* was sung polyphonically at First Vespers on her feast (chap. 314).

Singing the major Mass of the day, at which one of the large bells was sounded, distinguishes the final category of Oderigo's special feasts (see Table 1.2, feasts labeled III). It includes apostles, evangelists, and other saints "whose histories we have in our antiphonary and are sung in our church."[124] These, as his descriptions show, included feasts of apostles and evangelists not previously mentioned. Oderigo also mentions a number of other feasts which he says were celebrated with the same degree of solemnity because of "the privilege and merit" of the saints so honored. They included several church fathers and one famous martyr.[125] It was customary on these days to sing the responsory proper to the feast at First Vespers, although Oderigo does not specify whether the *Benedicamus Domino* was done in organum, as it was on other occasions when it was sung. In fact, polyphony is not indicated at any feasts in this third category. The only other saints' days for which it is prescribed besides those within the Octave

---

at Vespers, at Matins, and at the *Te Deum,* even though the major Mass of the day was not said if the feast did not fall on a Sunday. Other days on which polyphony was sung included the second, third, and fourth days after Low Sunday (ibid., 187, 188, 189).

123. The feasts are discussed, in the order listed here, in the *OO,* 273, 296, 325, 326, 331, 337, 370, 373, 374. The rubrics for each of these feasts also specify the items sung in polyphony, as, for example, on the feast of SS. Peter and Paul, where the Magnificat antiphon and *Benedicamus Domino* at First Vespers and *Benedicamus Domino* at Second Vespers were sung in polyphony (*OO,* 332–33). For St. Felicity and the Seven Brothers Oderigo specifies that the *Benedicamus Domino* at First Vespers was sung in organum (*OO,* 337).

124. By this he means antiphons, versicles, and responsories whose texts are based on episodes in the saints' lives (*OO,* part 1, chap. 438, p. 393: "Item in omnibus festivitatibus Apostolorum, & Evangelistarum, & illorum Sanctorum, de quibus propriae habentur Historiae in Antiphonario").

125. Already mentioned were Peter and Paul, Andrew, Bartholomew (Nathanael), Thomas, John the Apostle and Evangelist, and Luke, thus completing the list of twelve apostles (thirteen including Barnabas) and four evangelists. The feasts of saints named here are found on pp. 318, 341, 366, 375, 306, 326, 314, 53, 307, 307, 358, 369, 369, 282 of the *OO.*

of Christmas are St. John the Baptist, St. Lawrence, and St. George, none of which, inexplicably, finds a place in Oderigo's three categories of major feasts.[126]

Notwithstanding the lack of polyphony at services on this latter group of feasts, the three categories were equivalent to what eventually came to be called major duplex, minor duplex, and duplex feasts, the latter subdivided into two classes. Thus, in Oderigo's day, as in later times, polyphony was performed on Sundays and feast days of major duplex rank, though it was also sung on lesser feasts that had special significance for Siena.

Another Sienese *Ordo Officiorum,* which I view as a condensed version of Oderigo's work, is of interest for the information it brings to bear on feasts that were specially observed in the later thirteenth and early fourteenth centuries.[127] It is preceded by a calendar that is somewhat different from the one in Oderigo's work, though it does list most of the feasts cited by him. Within the main body of the text all but three of the feasts cited by Oderigo are discussed, namely, Translation of St. Ansanus, Translation of St. Crescentius, and Consecration of the cathedral, all from Oderigo's primary group. The omission of this last was undoubtedly an oversight, for subsequent records continue to list it as a feast day celebrated with great solemnity. Feasts of lesser categories remain unchanged, and no new ones are added. The greatest difference between Oderigo's *Ordo* and the later text, in fact, lies not so much in the listing of feast days as it does in its description of how services were celebrated on those days. Feasts of second and third categories are generally dismissed with a single sentence, such as: "For the sainted martyrs Cantius, Cantian, and Cantianilla, 9 Lessons," or "for St. Augustine, bishop and confessor, 9 Lessons are read from his life." Rubrics for the feast days of Oderigo's primary category are also somewhat abbreviated, those for Ansano furnishing a case in point: the abbreviated Matins service is only briefly alluded to and there follows a short list of items sung at Matins and Lauds, with no mention whatsoever of polyphony.

Indeed, the only extensive descriptions furnished by the later *Ordo* are those for Sundays in Advent, for Christmas and the week following, and for Epiphany, Easter, Ascension, Pentecost, and Assumption. These, furthermore, are the only ones that specify the performance of organum. Whether this is because by then polyphony was not being performed so frequently at services or because the abbreviated rubrics generally adopted for the later volume did not allow for longer and more detailed descriptions is a matter of conjecture. In any case what the later *Ordo* does show is that, with very minor changes, the feasts specified by Oderigo in 1215 were still being observed at the cathedral by the turn of the fourteenth century and that no major ones had yet been added.

126. For St. John the Baptist, see *OO,* 328–30; for St. Lawrence, 346; this latter, as mentioned, featured organum at the procession. Oderigo says that for the St. George's Day procession, which went from the cathedral to the church of San Giorgio, the responsories *Laetitia sempiterna, Beatus vir,* and *Pretiosa* were sung in organum, as were their verses (p. 314). For St. John the Evangelist, the sequence was sung in organum (50).

127. BCIS, MS G. V. 9. See van der Ploeg, *Art, Architecture and Liturgy,* 135–37, for a detailed description of the manuscript.

Fourteenth-Century Feasts

A definitive list of principal feast days observed at the cathedral around the middle of the fourteenth century is appended to both the manuscript and printed versions of the *Pacta et capitula nova* of 1367.[128] They comprised all of the days when Sienese canons would receive a double distribution for participating in daily offices and, as later reports show, most of the days when Mass was celebrated at the main altar (see Table 1.2). The list begins with feasts occurring in the month of May, when the cathedral's fiscal year began. Because special financial compensation was at issue and the required days and services when it was to be made were so clearly spelled out, there is no reason to doubt that the feasts enumerated here were considered to be the cathedral's principal ones at the time. The publication of the list in 1579 suggests that they still represented the cathedral's principal feast days two centuries later. The 1579 version lacks two feasts, St. Savinus and St. Martin, found in the manuscript version from 1367. Although this may be the result of an editorial or printing error, it may also be that the two feasts were omitted because they had ceased to be celebrated with the same degree of solemnity during the intervening centuries; this is, however, rather difficult to imagine. Lacking in both sources are any mention of the feasts of St. Bernardino and of St. Catherine of Siena, canonized in 1450 and 1461, respectively. Their exclusion from the earlier list is understandable, though one wonders why they were not appended to the published list, if indeed changes were made before printing. In manuscript and printed versions alike, only First Vespers are specified for certain feasts, an indication that though attendance was required at both First and Second Vespers and other offices and Masses on the days listed, extra compensation was to be provided only for those services so specified.

Several feasts not mentioned in Oderigo's various groups are recorded here for the first time, although others are now lacking. Figuring prominently, as might be expected, are all of the feasts of the Proper of the Time and the principal ones of the Virgin Mary, the same days that are cited in cathedral documents from the end of the twelfth century onwards, which also include All Saints, Consecration of the cathedral, and the town's four patron saints. But five feasts from Oderigo's primary group—those with doubled antiphons—are now missing. They are: SS. Sebastian and Fabian, Translation of St. Ansanus, Translation of St. Crescentius, St. Nicholas, and St. Lucy. Five of the ten in Oderigo's second group are also lacking, namely, St. Bridget, SS. Cantius, Cantian, and Cantianilla, Seven Brothers and St. Felicity, St. Balbina, and St. Severinus. Only three of those in Oderigo's last group are not named, notably, St. Thomas à Becket, St. Benedict, and St. Remigius.

As opposed to the loss of these thirteen feasts, twenty-three new ones are now added to the list of the most solemnly observed feast days. The most important of these are Corpus Christi and Conception of the Virgin Mary, the celebration of which had obviously gained in importance throughout Christendom in the century and a half since Oderigo's time.[129] Apart from the Visitation of the Virgin Mary, the Dedication of the Church of Our Lady of the Snow, All Souls, and the Conversion of St. Paul, the

---

128. The published version is in the *Constitutiones*, 80–82.
129. Corpus Christi was in fact authorized for universal use in 1264.

remaining feasts all appear in Oderigo's narrative and in the calendar preceding his work. Some feasts, such as those of St. Stephen, St. John the Evangelist, Holy Innocents, St. Sylvester, St. John the Baptist, and St. Lawrence, were even celebrated with polyphony in Oderigo's time, though they were clearly distinguished from those of the primary group. Others, including Invention of the Holy Cross, St John at the Latin Gate, St. Peter's Chains, Exaltation of the Holy Cross, and St. Martin, are described by Oderigo, although he attaches no special significance to them. The remaining ones, such as the last three days of Holy Week and the three days of the litanies, are also mentioned by Oderigo, who, however, does not include them in any of his special categories, though he does describe the elaborate rituals associated with those days.

Feast Days in Later Sources

Immediately following the manuscript copy of the *Pacta* and the list of feasts in which double distributions were awarded to participating clergy is a codicil, dated 11 August 1433, witnessed and signed by a number of people acting on behalf of the cathedral canons and Chapter. This not only attests to the authenticity of the *Pacta*'s contents but also indicates that they were still in force more than half a century later.[130] The codicil was signed by Giovanni de Ruffaldi, bishop of Siena, and the cathedral canon Pietro di Tommè, acting on behalf of the canons and Chapter.

Apart from codifying revisions concerning governance, duties, prerogatives, and remuneration of the clergy, the 1459 Constitutions also reflected the new status of the cathedral, which Pius II had recently raised to metropolitan rank. One provision, mentioned above, notes that in keeping with this honor, it had recently been decided that solemn high Mass could be celebrated at the high altar only by the bishop or by someone who had permission from the bishop and the Chapter to do so (*Constitutiones,* rub. 14). On certain feast days this restriction could be relaxed, if the need arose, and canons were authorized to celebrate high Mass at other altars. There follows a list of the principal feasts celebrated at Siena cathedral at mid-century, when high Mass was celebrated with all of the appropriate accoutrements, including polyphony, that befitted the see of an archbishop (see Table 1.2). Though not as specific as the list given in the *Pacta,* the feasts were essentially the same. New are St. Peter's Chair and Ash Wednesday. Saturdays and Sundays are also mentioned. Lacking are Invention of the Holy Cross, St. John at the Latin Gate, the days of the litanies, Beheading of St. John the Baptist, and Exaltation of the Holy Cross. Perhaps the final rubric "all other duplex feasts" refers to these feasts or possibly to these and yet other feasts adopted by the Roman curia, which, given the papal impetus behind the framing of the new Constitutions, would seem to be the case. Furthermore, it was, as mentioned, the prerogative of the prefect of the choir to recommend to the Chapter how certain feasts might be celebrated, and such decisions may also account for the flexibility implied by the rubric. The text outlining the new regulations concludes with the stipulation that "on all other days chaplains can and must celebrate conventual Mass at the altar of St. Ansanus and

---

130. AAS, vol. 368, fol. 13ᵛ, wherein are inscribed the additional feasts mentioned above and following these, and the date, 11 August 1433, of the revalidation of the list and its provisions.

at other altars." A final clause stipulates that anyone who contravened orders regarding the celebration of Mass at the high altar would be fined s. 20 for each infringement. Since St. Catherine was not canonized until 1461, it is understandable why her feast day does not appear on this list.

A third document relating to the cathedral's principal feast days was published in the 1579 edition of the *Pacta* and the Constitutions. Dated 22 November 1511, it records a gift made to the Sienese canons and Chapter by the Paduan priest Bartolomeo de Bolis, a canon of St. Peter's in Rome who was the newly named dean of Siena cathedral.[131] He had established an endowment, the annual income from which was to be used to augment the canons' prebends, for the purpose of enhancing celebration of various services at the cathedral. Income from the endowment, which yielded 126 florins (each worth L. 4), was to be distributed every year among those canons who participated at the principal Mass of the day and at Vespers on fifty Sundays throughout the year (Fl. 100) and at the same services on Christmas (Fl. 4), Circumcision (Fl. 2), Epiphany (Fl. 2), Easter (Fl. 4), Pentecost (Fl. 4), Ascension (Fl. 2), Corpus Christi, including the procession (Fl. 4), and Assumption of the Virgin, including the procession on the day following (Fl. 4). Once again, the days named are, with few exceptions, those that formed the earliest core of feast days celebrated at Siena cathedral with special reverence since the end of the twelfth century.

DOCUMENTS

Doc. 1.1. Contract with the organ builder Maestro Lorenzo di Jacopo da Prato to restore the organ, 20 July 1459. AOMS, vol. 14, *Deliberazioni dell'operaio e dei consiglieri, 1454–59,* fol. 59[r]

Domini Operarius et consiliarii . . . locaverunt magistro Laurentio Iacobi de Prato, presenti et conducenti ad fabricandum et de novo faciendum organa vetera dicte ecclesie secundum de-signum ut eidem magistro Laurentio melius videbitur convenire. Et debet illa facere ad perfectio-nem et bona du[l]cia et meliora illa Sancti Augustini de Senis, ad dictum boni magistri. Et dicta Opera teneatur et debeat dare eidem magistro Laurentio stagnium, lignamina et ferramenta que remanent in dictis organis, et omnibus aliis necessariis dictis organis et in eis remanentibus. Et quod dicta Opera debeat ei dare illum salarium ut dictis dominis Operario et consiliariis videbitur expedire. Et debeat incipere predicta facere immediate post festum S. Marie de medio mensis Augusti proximi. . . . Actum ut supra, coram ser Aiuto sacrestano et Bartholomeo [gap] de Poppi clerico, testibus etc. [margin: Orghani vecchi pro magistro Laurentio]

Doc. 1.2. Contract with the organ builder Maestro Domenico di Lorenzo degli Organi for a new instrument, 26 September 1508. Vol. 27, *Contratti, atti notarili e memorie, 1438–1599,* fols. 4[v]–5[r]

Anno Domini MDVIII, Inditione XII, die vero XXVI Settembris [in margin: 1508. Aloghatione de l'orghano nuovo in duomo a maestro Domenico da Lucha, maestro d'orghani, per ducati 500 d'oro]. Magnificus Pandolphus Bartolomei de Petruciis, Iohannes Baptista Francisci de Gu-glielmis et Paulus Vannocii de Beringucciis, tres operarii et commissarii Opere cathedralis ecclesie civitatis Senarum, electi et deputati per spectatissimos offitiales Balie civitatis Senarum, vice et nomine dicte Opere, titulo et causa locationis ad faciendum per se et vice et nomine dicte opere locaverunt Magistro Dominico olim magistri Laurentii de Organis, Lucensi, presenti et

---

131. *Constitutiones,* 98–102, mentioned above in note 74.

conducenti, unum organum positum in ecclesia cathedralis civitatis Senarum, super hostium Sacrestie dicte ecclesie et pro usu dicte ecclesie, cum infrascriptis pactis, modis et conditionibus, videlicet. Un organo che la maggiore canna sia piei nove vinitiani da la bocha in su, et le canne principali di fuore hanno a essare di stagnio e 'l ripieno di drento di piombo. Et debba havere tasti vintinove bianchi et semituono dic[i]otto, che sonno in tutto fra bianchi et neri tasti quaran-tasette. Et die havere registri sei: tinore, ottava, quintadecima, decimanona, vigesima seconda; et uno registro di fiuti [sic], che fanno la somma di registri sei. Et decto organo el sopradecto maestro Domenico die dare facto sonante et accordato in nella decta chiesa senza chiudende et ornamento, et tutte le altre cose debba fare a tutte sue spese et buono fra il termine di anni due da oggi, et secondo la forma del'organo et disegnio lassato senza chiudende et ornamento, come di sopra. Del quale organo lo dieno dare detti operarii al decto maestro Domenico ducati cinque-cento d'oro in oro larghi, et quello più per insino alla somma di ducati settecento d'oro che parrà al magnifico Pandolfo Petrucci. Et che ora al presente solo debbi dare al decto maestro Domenico ducati cento d'oro in oro di decta somma, da scomputarsi in decta somma. Et de tempo in tempo se li paghino el resto delli denari per lavorare per insino alla somma di ducati cinquecento. Que omnia et singula suprascripta partes supradicte promiserunt ad invicem atten-dere et observare et contra non facere vel venire, sub pena. . . .

Chapter Two

CHANT AND IMPROVISED POLYPHONY
IN LATER MEDIEVAL TIMES

DESPITE THE ABSENCE of records regarding musicians prior to the end of the fourteenth century, a considerable amount of information survives about the music performed in the cathedral during later medieval times. Much of it is furnished by Oderigo in his descriptions of daily rituals and his remarks concerning the office of the cantor, and some can be gleaned from the second Sienese *Ordo Officiorum* of the early fourteenth century. Sienese plainchant manuscripts from the twelfth, thirteenth, and fourteenth centuries also attest to a flourishing musical culture, though the oldest of these have yet to be studied in detail and thus cannot always be linked with absolute certainty to Oderigo's descriptions. Other cathedral manuscripts from the late fourteenth and fifteenth centuries transmit the chant as it was then being performed, probably in readings that derive from earlier Sienese sources, and several contain, in whole or in part, a body of music in honor of the town's patron saint created expressly for the Sienese liturgy.[1] Lacking, however, are sources illustrating the kinds of improvised polyphony mentioned by Oderigo and the music that must have gradually supplanted extemporized practices, as written polyphony came more and more to the fore. To a certain extent these lacunae in Sienese sources can be filled with a few fortuitously preserved examples of liturgical music as it must have been improvised in nearby towns. From Siena itself comes a version of a widely diffused polyphonic piece whose roots lay in late medieval improvisational practices. Given the very nature of improvisation, it is obvious that the few examples cited here can provide only a hint of what Sienese practices must have been like, though together with the cycle of monophonic pieces composed for the feast of Sant'Ansano, they can help provide the basis for a reconstruction of certain aspects of musical repertories at the cathedral in the thirteenth and fourteenth centuries.

CATHEDRAL CHANT BOOKS

Oderigo leaves little doubt that by the turn of the thirteenth century, apart from the celebration of feasts of local saints such as Ansano and a few others, the cathedral's liturgy was essentially that of the Roman church, or, in the words of colophons of later Sienese liturgical books, it was celebrated "according to the usage of the Roman curia." Oderigo provides incipits and, on occasion, several lines or whole stanzas of text, but the only music he furnishes is a setting of the first stanza of the hymn *Jam lucis orto sidere,* copied in the newer forms of square notation—punctum, virga, climacus, and others—

---

1. Apart from a few isolated pieces, the earliest Sienese sources of polyphony are from the fifteenth century and are discussed in chapter 3.

FIGURE 4. *Ordo Officiorum*, fols. 46^v–47^r, with manuscript addition of the hymn *Jam lucis orto sidere*. BCIS, MS G. V. 8. Courtesy Biblioteca Comunale degli Intronati di Siena; photograph from Foto Testi

then coming into use in Italy, but without a staff (see Fig. 4).[2] He explains, probably in reference to the notation, that the hymn was sung "more Francigenarum," in the French manner, every day at Prime from Septuagesima Sunday through Wednesday in Holy Week, except on Palm Sunday and on feasts celebrated with nine lessons occurring during that period. In discussing prayers and chants used for the procession on Palm Sunday Oderigo notes that the music could be found in the "little processional book," a volume which, as it happens, survives to this day. Although this is a rarity—few such Sienese chant books from Oderigo's time or earlier are known—a considerable number of volumes of plainchant made for the cathedral during the fourteenth and fifteenth centuries are extant and are still in Siena, in the museum and archives of the Opera, in the church itself, in the archiepiscopal library, and in the Biblioteca Comunale degli Intronati. Though their musical contents have yet to be studied comprehensively,

---

2. On fol. 47^r of BCIS, MS G. V. 8. *Jam lucis orto sidere* is notated in the right-hand margin on the lower part of the page, next to the written text. Dry-point lines used for the text are extended into the right-hand margin in a few places, but were used only occasionally by the scribe. Most neumes fall between the lines to the left of the chant; to the right of the text there appear to be several "F" clefs.

they have been the object of much attention because of the generally high quality of their illuminations, the work of some of Siena's leading artists. A few of these chant books will be considered here.

Vittorio Lusini, whose remarks on the chronology of liturgical books and chant books in the cathedral's historical collection remain fundamental, if not totally accurate, grouped them into three series on the basis of information provided by cathedral inventories of the late fourteenth century.[3] With regard to the earliest extant volumes, those he placed in his first series, Lusini reasoned that the cathedral would naturally have owned books from the time of its foundation and that they must have been the ones that were described as "all'antica" or "d'antica scrittura" in the inventories.[4] He assigned chant books notated in square notation, the later neumes of Gregorian music, to his second series and described them as replacements for the earlier ones, whose notation had made them difficult to use.[5] The inventories list a total of thirteen volumes, including graduals, antiphonaries, a book of invitatories and other pieces, and a book of sequences, that fit into his second series.[6] Lusini noted that nine of the thirteen volumes remained in use through the last century and are still on cathedral premises. Inexplicably, he did not take into account a few older volumes that went unlisted in the earliest inventories but appeared in others after the turn of the fifteenth century and several chant books added to the collection during the late fourteenth and early fifteenth centuries. The chant books in the third series, which comprises the celebrated collection of graduals and antiphonaries now on display in the cathedral's Libreria Piccolomini, were completed during the second half of the fifteenth century.

Three musical manuscripts cited by Lusini in his first series are now in the Biblioteca Comunale. The oldest, MS F. VI. 15, is a twelfth-century gradual and troparium with music notated in heighted, or Beneventan, neumes.[7] These are written on a dry-point staff, with a single line in red labeled "F." Generous markings in the right-hand margin indicate pitches of lines, for example, "a" for one dry-point line above the red "F."[8]

---

3. Surviving inventories of cathedral holdings, including the earliest ones examined by Lusini, are bound into single volumes, many containing a number of fascicles. A few unbound folios, mentioned below and in later chapters, also preserve inventories of volumes of music owned by the cathedral. Lusini naturally did not take into account a number of chant books now in the Opera's archives that were transferred there—probably during the nineteenth century—from other churches within and outside Siena. These have recently been catalogued, though they have yet to be studied comprehensively. Also housed in the Opera's archives is the better-known collection of chant books from the hospital of Santa Maria Nuova. A catalogue of these is published by Ubaldo Morandi and Aldo Cairoli, "Dall'inventario del 1900. I Libri corali," in *Lo spedale di Santa Maria della Scala* (Siena, 1975), 168–75.

4. Lusini, *Il Duomo di Siena,* 2:242, 253.

5. Ibid., 2:246.

6. Inventories from 1397, 1409, 1420, 1429, 1435, and later continue to list the chant books just cited as well as others not mentioned by Lusini. These are mentioned below and in the following chapters.

7. Lusini, *Il Duomo di Siena,* 2:241, n. 1. Henry Bannister appended a note to the cover of the manuscript volume which says that it was copied after 1050 for a Benedictine monastery. This latter does not preclude the volume's having been in use at the cathedral.

8. "c" is one and a half lines below a red line. When scribes insert these letters in the margin, the red line is left unlabeled.

The volume, in two sections, has been mutilated both at the beginning and at the end. Various feasts from the Proper of the Time and the Proper of the Saints arranged in chronological order make up the first section. This now begins with the verse *Eructavit cor meum* of the introit *Gaudeamus omnes* for the feast of St. Agatha, on 5 February, a probable sign that its original opening pages contained propers for Advent Sundays and feasts in December. Following St. Agatha are propers for the feasts of various saints, including St. Valentine, St. Benedict, the Annunciation, St. John the Baptist, St. Lawrence, the Assumption, and St. Andrew Apostle, on 30 November, interspersed with others for the four Sundays before Lent, Ash Wednesday, Palm Sunday, Easter, Sundays after Easter, Pentecost, and Ascension. The second section (beginning on fol. 100ᵛ) contains propers for the Common of Saints, for Sundays after Pentecost, and for the Requiem Mass. Appended to it (beginning on fol. 132) are a group of tropes for the feasts of St. John the Evangelist, Epiphany, Easter, and Ascension and a group of sequences for Advent Sundays, Christmas, Epiphany, Easter, and Pentecost, at which point the manuscript breaks off.

A notable feature of the propers is their inclusion of texts and music of tracts for many feasts. Since Oderigo does not always specify tracts on these same feasts, it is impossible to link all of those given in the chant book to the Sienese liturgy of his time. However, a few of the tracts that he lists, such as *De profundis clamavi ad te* for Septuagesima Sunday and the four sung on Holy Saturday morning, also appear in the chant book. A similar situation arises with the tropes and the sequences because Oderigo rarely gives the titles of those that were sung on major feasts. Many of the other texts of propers in the chant book, on the other hand, are the same as those mentioned by Oderigo, as, for example, the introit *Statuit ei* for St. Peter's Chair and the introit *Sancti tui* for St. Tiburtius.[9]

The second chant book, MS I. I. 7, an early thirteenth-century antiphonary, was copied by the Sienese cathedral canon Gratia di San Donato.[10] It, too, is notated in Beneventan neumes, written on a staff with a red line labeled "F" and a yellow line, above or below it, labeled "C," the remaining lines in dry point. This manuscript is also in two sections, the first beginning with offices for Sundays in Advent and December feasts and continuing through Palm Sunday, the second with offices for the paschal season through Ascension, followed by feasts of saints ending with St. Nicholas on 6 December. Appended to each section are offices for the Common of Saints and the dedication of a church. Many of the antiphonary's texts correspond to Oderigo's incipits, as do, for example, those for Sundays in Advent, St. Lucy, and St. Thomas. But some, such as the great or "O" antiphons sung before and after the Magnificat on the

---

9. *OO,* part 1, chap. 330, pp. 305–6: "In Cathedra Sancti Petri Apostoli," and on fol. 2ᵛ of the MS; chap. 385, p. 347: "De Sancto Tiburtio Martyre, & S. Susanna," and on fol. 89ʳ of the MS.

10. He signed his work on fol. 160ᵛ, at the beginning of the part for summer: "Presbiter Gratia Sancti Donati Senensi Canonicus hunc librum scripsit manibus suis ad honorem dei et beati Donati episcopi et martiris. Deo Gratias." The notation is consistent throughout except for places such as fol. 161ʳ, where it is clear that a later hand made additions on an originally blank folio. The manuscript is discussed briefly by Garrison, "Twelfth-Century Initial Styles of Central Italy," in *Studies,* 1/1:27 and 3/1:64.

nine days leading to Christmas, do not, for the incipits of the last two differ in the two sources. Nevertheless, it seems logical to assume that the antiphonary was in use during Oderigo's time, an assumption shared by Giovanni Crisostomo Trombelli, the eighteenth-century editor of the *Ordo Officiorum,* who published its texts for the office of SS. Fabian and Sebastian, texts to which Oderigo, in his usual manner, had only briefly alluded.[11]

The third chant book, MS F. VI. 11, is a twelfth-century hymnary and processional, again written in the Beneventan style of notation but with a varicolored staff of four lines—red, yellow, red, and black.[12] Its opening pages are also lacking and it now begins with Vespers of Epiphany, an indication that music and texts for the month of December have been lost. Following this is music for processions on the feasts of St. Anthony Abbot on 17 January, the Purification of the Virgin on 2 February, and many others through the end of November, including the extensive itinerary of the procession held on Palm Sunday, discussed below. These texts, as well as others from the same volume, were also used by Trombelli to supplement Oderigo's descriptions. From the many concordances with incipits cited by Oderigo, it seems reasonable to believe that the volume contains music that was performed at Siena cathedral during his time.

Lusini believed that the chant books of the second series originated after 1259, when work on the cathedral's new choir was begun. His remarks about the dates of their illuminations—the work, he said, of a number of unknown artists from the late thirteenth and early fourteenth centuries—have not been accepted by more recent art historians, who assign the decoration of seven of the nine volumes to a more restricted time frame between 1290 and 1295.[13] Lusini also noted that few of the remaining chant books of the series were in their original state, for they were restored over the course of centuries and suffered the loss of some pages and the addition of others. The result was that folios from the thirteenth, fourteenth, and fifteenth centuries can now be found in one and the same volume.[14] His remarks are certainly applicable to MS 42-N, a book of invitatories and sequences he considered to be the oldest in the second series. The volume is of considerable interest because it contains the music of an early Sienese proper for the feast of Sant'Ansano, to be considered presently.[15]

---

11. *OO,* 289–90, n. [a]; Trombelli says that the texts were from an ancient Sienese antiphonary and that they were sent to him by Abbate Joseph Ciaccheri.

12. Lusini, *Il Duomo di Siena,* 2:241, n. 1. The notation is set in dry point throughout, although the lines seem lightly sketched in black with red lines labeled "F." Fainter yellow lines for "c" are usually two lines above the red, or at times one and a half lines below; they are labeled "c" in the margin. On the present fol. 1, after the guard sheet, is an inscription that reads: "Idibus Maii 1539 in die ascensionis et victoris martyris fuit beati Francisci pititerre {conversio *added above*} qui dum predicaretur a Schappucinis in vox {chatedrali ecclesa [sic] *inserted*} qui in pergamo coram populo veniam petiit, hec Bastianus scripsit. Regnanti Carolo imperatore et Paulo pontefice maximo etc."

13. See Anna Maria Giusti's remarks in "Libri Corali per il Duomo di Siena" and her analyses of several of these volumes in *Il Gotico a Siena* (Florence, 1982), 47–58.

14. Lusini, *Il Duomo di Siena,* 253, note.

15. In a manuscript inventory compiled by Lusini in 1911 (AOMS, vol. 1526, *Inventario artistico*), MS 42-N is described as a book of invitatories and sequences, in a modern black leather binding, with five brass studs on each side, consisting of 176 leaves, numbered relatively recently in place of

The first part of MS 42-N opens with a collection of invitatories, beginning with
Regem venturum for the first Sunday of Advent, followed by a collection of sequences,
copied by the same hand, that starts with the Christmas sequence *Laetabuntur exultet.*
This section breaks off in the middle of the penultimate strophe of *Nobili prosapia,* the
sequence for the feast of Sant'Ansano. Unfortunately, an illumination of the saint has
been cut out of the opening page of the sequence. After this comes a fragmented
portion of a second part, contemporaneous with the preceding one, which contains,
among other things, a Requiem Mass and a Mass for Sant'Ansano. The latter is incomplete because the manuscript has been mutilated after the Alleluia. A short section,
copied in a much later hand, was appended to the two principal parts when the volume
was rebound in the seventeenth or eighteenth centuries.

MS 42-N was in the cathedral's possession as early as the middle of the fourteenth
century, and probably for several decades before then. A "sequenziale," or book of
sequences, is mentioned in a list of "all of the furniture, books, vestments, chalices,
missals in the duomo's sacristy" compiled in May 1364.[16] The same volume is cited in
the late fourteenth-century inventories referred to by Lusini and in others from 1408,
1409, 1420, and later.[17] Inventories from 1429 and later also list a second book of
sequences with music, said to be "beautiful, covered in yellow leather" (see Table 3.1).[18]

As it turns out, the second book of sequences has also survived and is now at the
Biblioteca Comunale, where it carries the call number MS G. III. 2. This volume was
also mentioned by Lusini, who noted that it came from the cathedral, without connect-
ing it with the volume mentioned for the first time in the 1429 inventory.[19] Recent
scholarship has assigned its illuminations to an unknown Sienese artist, working between 1285 and 1290, whose style is evident in several volumes in Lusini's second series
of cathedral chant books, and to Pietro Lorenzetti and to the painter known as Ugolino
Lorenzetti, both working around 1335. As opposed to the earlier chant book, which
was misnamed but still begins, as it did originally, with invitatories rather than sequences, this volume is essentially a collection of sequences that begins, as the old

the old foliation, which disappeared when the volume was last rebound. Lusini also pointed out that
several illuminations had been cut out of the volume, notably one for the Assumption on fol. 107 and
another of Sant'Ansano on fol. 139, and that interpolations in the main body of the volume were
made in the eighteenth century, notably between fols. 82 and 83, 143 and 148, 158 and 165, and 167
and 176, which is the last folio. Lusini described the state of the volume's preservation as very poor,
which unfortunately is still the case.

16. The list, dating from 2 May 1364, was overlooked by Lusini. Among the missals, psalters, and
antiphonaries and other liturgical books is "uno sequenziale," a book of sequences. AOMS, vol. 1535,
Elenchi, note e inventari di beni mobili e immobili, datati (1364–1711), fasc. 1, doc. 1.

17. AOMS, vol. 1491, *Inventari, 1397–1409* [Inventario . . . cominciato al tempo di Pavolo di
Fuccio operaio] [1408], fol. 63ᵛ: "Seghuenziale da chantare, uno"; [1409], fol. 78ʳ: "Uno seghue[n]-
ziale"; vol. 867, *Inventari, 1420–post 1488,* fasc. 1, 1420–24 [Inventario . . . al tenpo delo egregio e
famoso chavaliere misser Turino di Mateio operaio], fol. 9ᵛ: "Uno seguenziale."

18. For the inventories of 1458 and ca. 1517 see Tables 4.1 and 5.2.

19. See Giusti, "Libri corali," *Il Gotico a Siena,* no. 55, *Sequentiae missarum,* pp. 160–63, where an
up-to-date bibliography is given.

inventories note, with the Christmas sequence *Laetabuntur.* The sequence for Sant'Ansano, discussed below, is found here.

By far the most famous of all Sienese chant manuscripts are those comprising Lusini's third series, now on display in the cathedral's Libreria Piccolomini and in the church choir. In all there are twenty-nine of them, the result of a decision to furnish the cathedral with a complete set of graduals and antiphonaries made in the late 1450s, during Cristoforo Felici's first term as overseer.[20] Felici himself commissioned the earliest of these from the music copyist Fra Gabriello Mattei, a Servite friar, in 1457. At least twelve volumes were completed by 1464, when the music copying was taken over by Don Andrea d'Alemagna, a German monk and canon at the Sienese church of San Martino. The music copying of an additional six volumes was finished between 1464 and 1468 and two others come from the years immediately afterwards. Seven more, the majority of them copied by Fra Benedetto Rinaldi da Siena, were completed in the early 1480s.[21] Decoration and illumination of the volumes began in 1466, when Cipriano Corti was briefly overseer. But major contributions of artistic significance come from a few years later, during the tenure of two of the Opera's most culturally conscious overseers, Savino Savini and Alberto Aringhieri, particularly through 1475, the year of Savini's death.[22] A vast literature exists on the decoration and illumination of these volumes, the work of artists such as Girolamo da Cremona, Liberale da Verona, Pellegrino da Mariano, and Guidoccio Cozzarelli, among others.[23] No less than the numerous sculptures, paintings, furniture, wood carving, stained glass windows, and pavement decorations that adorn the fabric of the church, the illuminations of these volumes, collectively, form one of the cathedral's greatest treasures, a legacy testifying to Sienese reverence for an art of transcendental grace and impeccable workmanship whose noblest aspirations found focus in the glorification and exaltation of the Christian faith.

Altogether, there are thirteen graduals in the third series, including eight for the Proper of the Time, from the first Sunday of Advent through the 23rd Sunday after

20. Maria Grazia Ciardi Dupré, *I corali del duomo di Siena* (Milan, 1972), 5. This is the most recent and most comprehensive study of the illuminations and contains magnificent color reproductions, a bibliography, and a short essay on the musical contents, "Aspetti musicologici dei corali Piccolomini," by Clemente Terni on pp. 23–28.

21. Two other chant books are grouped with the collection, both graduals for the feast of the Transfiguration, the first probably copied in the 1480s, the second assuredly copied just before it was decorated, in 1519. See Ciardi Dupré, *I corali del Duomo di Siena,* 7.

22. Lusini, *Il Duomo di Siena,* 2:269–71. Earlier volumes not mentioned above include a psalter (AOMS, Cathedral Museum, MS 106, 13) copied by the Servite friar Fra Gabriello di Mattei and a martyrology copied by the cathedral organist Ser Francesco di Nanni ("per sua fadigha di facitura d'uno libro che si chiama Martirologio"). Also mentioned are Messer Martino da Cola dall'Aquila, paid on 11 September 1439 for copying music ("à servito in duomo a scrivere il canto"), and after 1450, several volumes copied by the monks Don Niccolò di Antonio da Genova, Don Arrigo di Andrea della Magna, and Don Bernardo de' Riesi da Genova (ibid., 2:261–62).

23. The list of art historians and critics who have contributed to our knowledge of the volumes is long and illustrious and includes names such as Gaetano Milanesi, Vittorio Lusini, Bernard Berenson, and Enzo Carli. Ciardi Dupré, *I corali del Duomo di Siena,* cites them all in her bibliography.

Pentecost, one for the feast of the Transfiguration, two for the Proper of the Saints, from St. Andrew through St. Clement, and two for the Common of Saints. The antiphonaries number sixteen and encompass the same cycles of propers of the time and propers and commons of the saints as the graduals. The contents of this vast repertory still await detailed study, though preliminary research suggests that while there are occasional melodic variants, Sienese readings of the chant repertory present few major differences from versions in general use at Rome and elsewhere in Italy at the time.[24]

Of particular interest here are a pair of volumes whose histories are emblematic of the series as a whole. The first, MS 27. 11, a gradual with propers and commons of saints from St. Andrew to the eve of SS. Peter and Paul, was copied during one of Cristoforo Felici's two terms as overseer, 1456–57 or 1459–63. It was illuminated by Sano di Pietro during 1471–72, when Savino Savini was at the Opera's helm, the last payment for the artist's work on the volume having been issued on 25 January 1472.[25] The volume contains music for the new proper of the Mass of Sant'Ansano, discussed below, and among its prominent illuminations is one that adorns the introit for that feast (see Pl. 2). The second volume, MS 11. M, is an antiphonary with offices for four feasts from St. Andrew through St. Lucy, including Sant'Ansano and the Conception of the Virgin. It was copied shortly after August 1480 by Benedetto Rinaldi and illuminated in 1481–82 at the instance of Alberto Aringhieri, whose coat of arms is on the frontispiece and in one of the decorated initials.[26] It contains the complete rhymed office for the feast of Sant'Ansano, also discussed below.

THE CANTOR AND THE PLAINCHANT CHOIR IN THE EARLY THIRTEENTH CENTURY

Oderigo's remarks in the *Ordo Officiorum* leave no doubt that the plainchant choir was an effective performing body by the turn of the thirteenth century, though he gives no particulars regarding the number of canons, chaplains, and clerks from the *schola* who participated in the daily rounds of offices and Masses. Throughout his narrative Oderigo also makes it clear that all musical performances were under the direction of the cantor. Moreover, he devotes a lengthy chapter to the cantor's duties and his role in the plainchant choir, and makes frequent references throughout his account to the many chants that the cantor intoned, sang alone, or performed with others in polyphony at various services on Sundays and feast days. On major feast days it was the cantor who guided the choir and on those occasions he had the authority to designate others whom he might wish either to sing with him or to sing in his place. When nonmembers of the Chapter were to read lessons, the cantor chose them. He alone was responsible for selecting those who would sing organum whenever it was required and for ensuring

---

24. See the examples furnished by Terni, p. 26, in Ciardi Dupré's *I corali del duomo di Siena*.

25. Cathedral, Piccolomini Library, MS 27. 11 is described by Ciardi Dupré, ibid., 37–38.

26. Cathedral, Piccolomini Library, MS 11. M is discussed, as part of the series initiated by the overseer Savino Savini and continued by the overseer Alberto Aringhieri, in Lusini, *Il Duomo di Siena,* 2:322–25, where relevant documents are also printed. A recent assessment of the volume is given by Ciardi Dupré, *I corali del Duomo di Siena,* 43, who posits an ascription to Pellegrino di Mariano of the 163 small decorated initials.

high standards in the performance of both chant and polyphony, factors strongly suggesting that he also had charge of the cathedral's singing school. He was, furthermore, entrusted with maintaining order and decorum in the choir. In this latter capacity he must have been rather like an athletic coach in the service of the Lord. For as Oderigo explains, "he awakens those who fall asleep, he stimulates those who are lazy, he restrains those who are tempestuous, he sets an example for all those who are less expert," and "like the trumpet of the Lord, which sounds loud or soft at the right time, he seeks to bring all together into a well-tempered whole."[27]

Oderigo reports that it was customary for the cantor, appropriately vested, to assume a prominent position in the choir during services. After the officiating priest began the service, the cantor, wearing a cowl or a robe, went to the middle of the choir in front of the altar—where the lectern must have been placed—and sang or recited from that spot. "In our church," adds Oderigo, "not only the cantor but whoever sings in the choir or reads the lesson or the epistle must be a cleric and must always be dressed in a cope or a robe." On major feasts and during Eastertide the cantor always wore a cope when he was in the choir, and when the bishop was present, it was the cantor who held the pastoral staff.

During the course of this discussion Oderigo provides an outline of the cantor's duties at everyday services as well as on special feast days, when some modification of the norm was required. Vespers, occurring around sundown and often attended by a large public, can serve as an example. At Siena cathedral in the early thirteenth century a Vespers service consisted of an opening versicle, *Deus in adjutorium meum,* and its response, five psalms and their antiphons, a short reading (chapter), a hymn, the Magnificat and its antiphon, and various prayers, versicles, and responses. At Saturday Vespers, Oderigo tell us, the cantor intoned and sang the first antiphon and then sang through the end of the first verse of the psalm that followed, "according to the tone of the antiphon." In addition, he intoned the response that followed the chapter and the Magnificat antiphon. If a feast fell on a Saturday, however, he either sang the closing versicle, *Benedicamus Domino,* in organum with two additional singers or he appointed

---

27. "Officium autem Cantoris in Ecclesia nostra tale est. Quod Cantor in magnis solemnitatibus Chorum regit, & tanquam bonus exhortator in castris Domini, dormientes excitat, pigros stimulat, effraenatos retinet, omnibus minus peritis modum imponit, & velut tuba Dei pro congrua opportunitate quandoque submisse, quandoque alte, temperate omnes studet insimul concordare. Beatus namque Augustinus de concordi modulatione cantantium, in libro de Civitate Dei sic dicit. *Diversorum sonorum rationabilis, modulatusque concentus concordi varietate compactus bene ordinatae Civitatis insinuat unitatem.* Postquam igitur Sacerdos inceperit suum Officium, Cantor qui Officiare debet, semper in *Cappa* vel in Toga, vadens in medium Chori ante Altare, Sabbato ad Vesperum incipit primam Antiphonam super Psalmos, & primum Versiculum Psalmi secundum tonum Antiphonae finit. Verum notandum est quod non solum ipse Cantor, sed quicumque aliquid cantat in Choro, aut in Ecclesia nostra legit Lectionem, vel Epistolam, debet esse Clericus, semper inductus *Cappam* vel togam, & idem Cantor in solemnitatibus precipuis, & Paschalibus diebus, semper in Choro incipit cum Pluviali, praecipue praesente Episcopo, & tunc tenet Virgam Pastoralem" (*OO,* part 2, chap. 17, pp. 417–19). Despite remarks such as these, Oderigo does not say that the cantor was charged with noting down absences and tardiness or that he was empowered to take disciplinary action against choir members who were remiss in their duties.

others to sing it without him.[28] Organum required the participation of trained singers, and the businesslike manner in which Oderigo speaks of the cantor's right to name those who might sing in his place or to call others to assist him must surely mean that there were a number of musically qualified clergy in the *schola* at the time.[29]

Matins, divided into three parts called Nocturns, was sung during the middle of the night.[30] It opened with the verse *Domine labia mea aperies* and its response and the verse *Deus in adjutorium meum* and its response, after which came the invitatory antiphon and psalm and a hymn. These were followed by psalms with their antiphons, prayers, lessons, and responsories. The number of lessons varied according to how the feast was ranked, though Oderigo also notes that nine lessons were said for those "saints whose histories we have in our books." After the opening prayers, verses, and responses the cantor intoned the invitatory antiphon proper to the day and sang the invitatory psalm, *Venite exsultemus,* either alone or with others. Oderigo specifies that for a feast of nine lessons the cantor was to go to the middle of the choir with two others and sing the invitatory antiphon and all of the *Venite* psalm in organum. This procedure was followed even during the periods from Easter Sunday through its octave and from Pentecost through its octave when only three lessons were sung. On these occasions the last responsory was always sung in organum. At each of the nocturns the cantor was responsible for intoning the antiphon that framed the first psalm, and he sang the first responsory, either alone or in organum with those who had earlier sung the *Venite* with him. If someone other than a member of the cathedral Chapter were to read the lessons, it was the cantor who signified whom he wished to have read, unless the bishop was present, in which case the cantor "with his reverent counsel shall decide about what was to be read or sung" (part 2, chap. 17).[31] Lauds, which was customarily celebrated at sunrise, began with the usual *Deus in adjutorium meum* verse and its response and continued with five psalms and their antiphons, the Benedictus canticle and its antiphon, the *Te Deum laudamus,* and lessons, responsories, and a hymn. On ordinary days the cantor intoned the first antiphon, the Benedictus antiphon, and the *Te Deum laudamus.* On feast days, when the bishop was present and gave his consent beforehand or nodded his head in a sign of assent at the appropriate moment, the cantor could begin

---

28. Ibid. Elsewhere in his account, Oderigo mentions that at Sunday Vespers, whenever the hymn *Lucis creator* was sung, it was always performed in organum, though he does not mention the cantor in this regard (ibid., chap. 263, p. 252).

29. For instance, Oderigo mentions the *schola* in connection with services on Maundy Thursday: "Deinde Cantor cum Schola, mox ut jussum fuerit, incipit ad Missam Introitum. *Nos autem gloriari.* V. *Deus misereatur*" (*OO,* part 1, chap. 145, p. 127). He never mentions more than three singers in the performance of organum except for a few occasions when he speaks of the choir divided in two for certain feasts and on Sunday processions, when his vague wording makes it appear that all who took part in the procession sang organum. See remarks about his discussion of the Palm Sunday processions below.

30. Oderigo explains that the canons arose at midnight and prepared for the beginning of the day's offices by saying the Lord's Prayer three times and the Credo (*OO,* part 2, chap. 2, p. 404).

31. "Si tamen Episcopus fuerit praesens in Choro cum ejus consilio, & reverentia disponit legenda, vel cantanda."

the Benedictus antiphon and the _Te Deum laudamus._ In such circumstances it was also appropriate for him to begin the Magnificat antiphon at Vespers.[32]

The lesser canonical hours of Prime, Terce, Sext, and None also called for verses and responses, psalms, prayers, lessons, antiphons, hymns, canticles, and responsories, and the cantor's duties at these services were no less demanding. At Prime and the other hours he, or someone he assigned in his stead, intoned the first antiphon, the hymn, and the responsory and its verse. More specifically, at Terce he intoned the hymn _Nunc sancte,_ which was sung in organum on Sundays and feast days, as were the antiphon and the responsory and its verse.[33] At Prime it was also his duty to announce to his colleagues the phase of the moon and the name of the feast that was to occur on the following day, if there was one (ibid.).

Mass, the celebration of the Eucharist, was the principal service of each day. By the later Middle Ages its most important musical parts consisted of settings of five fixed texts—the ordinary—and another five, the proper, the texts of which changed from day to day. During Oderigo's time three Masses were normally celebrated at Siena cathedral on Sundays and feast days, matutinal Mass, sung after Prime,[34] Mass of the people, in which the congregation took communion,[35] and major or solemn high Mass, celebrated immediately after Terce. At high Mass and at Mass of the people the cantor began the introit in the choir and sang all "those other things that must be sung," including the Alleluia in organum on Sundays and feast days. For this latter he designated beforehand those whom he wished to have assist him in performance, which was executed from the large stone pulpit.[36] On principal feast days he also sang, chanting in unison with the others, three items of the ordinary, the Kyrie eleison, the Sanctus, and the Agnus Dei (part 2, chap. 17).

---

32. Ibid. The _Te Deum laudamus_ was sung in organum on a few occasions during the year, notably Easter, the two days after Low Sunday, and the feast of Sant'Ansano (_OO,_ 174, 187, 274).

33. In an earlier chapter devoted to Sundays throughout the year (part 1, chap. 263, p. 252) Oderigo reports that after the customary procession the clergy returned to the choir, where Terce was begun by the officiating priest, and that the cantor began the hymn _Nunc sancte._ This, he is at pains to make clear, was always sung in organum on Sundays at Terce before the principal Mass.

34. _OO,_ part 2, chap. 12, p. 413. Oderigo specifies that after Prime, the introit antiphon was _Salve sancta parens_ for the Mass of the Virgin that followed and he notes that "just as we say _Te Deum laudamus_ daily at Matins of the B.V.M., so in her Mass do we sing Gloria in excelsis." He also explains that offices and Mass of the B.V.M. were not said during certain periods, such as Advent through the octave of Epiphany, Palm Sunday, Holy Thursday through the octave of Pentecost, All Saints, Dedication of the cathedral through its octave, and Assumption Day through its octave, "but in all the other feasts of the B.V.M. we do the offices as noted."

35. Oderigo notes the differences, as, for example, at high Mass when the bishop presided, after the Agnus Dei, the subdeacon went into the choir and gave the kiss of peace to the leading person on one side, the provost, and to the archdeacon on the other, whereas at the people's Mass on Sundays and feast days, the priest who sang the Epistle received the kiss of peace from the priest who celebrated Mass and brought it outside to the people, particularly to the magistrates (_OO,_ part 2, chap. 9, p. 410). The passage is cited by van der Ploeg, _Art, Architecture and Liturgy,_ p. 73.

36. _OO,_ part 2, chap. 17. In an earlier discussion regarding the major Mass on Sundays Oderigo says that the cantor began the service, that is, the introit, in plainchant, together with two others

At Siena cathedral during Oderigo's time processions customarily preceded the office of Terce on Sundays and many feast days, with high Mass following directly. Before the procession began the cantor always intoned the *Asperges me* or another appropriate antiphon in the choir (part 2, chap. 17, and part 1, chap. 262). After the customary blessings and sprinkling of holy water, the cantor, together with the officiating priest and the crucifer, then led the clergy in singing the *Benedictus Dominus* responsory in organum as they walked in procession through the church and the cloister of the canons' residence. After more blessings and prayers outside the church, the group returned to the choir singing the antiphon *Specialis Virgo* in organum, again led by the cantor.

This general account of the cantor's duties hardly does justice to the actual number of times Oderigo says he was called upon to sing, in both chant and polyphony, during the course of the church year. Although there were a good many services that did not require him to participate in some special way, there were just as many that did, and the list of the occasions on which he was to sing polyphony with others covers all of the previously cited major feasts celebrated at Siena cathedral around the turn of the thirteenth century (see above, Table 1.2, feasts labeled "I").

LITURGY AND RITUAL IN THE EARLY THIRTEENTH CENTURY
Sunday Mass

For those who recall the post-Tridentine solemn high Mass as it was celebrated in Roman Catholic churches until Vatican II, Oderigo's description of that service at Siena cathedral around the turn of the thirteenth century offers few surprises. Though major Mass, as it was then called, was primarily celebrated for the canons and Chapter, Oderigo makes it clear that the public was also present at this service, notwithstanding the people's Mass that preceded it.[37] A number of details of this major Mass have changed over the centuries, but even by then the order and sequence of events and prayers had assumed the form that was to endure through the mid-twentieth century. Oderigo explains that when the priest who was to say high Mass had vested, Terce was sung in the choir. Terce was no sooner finished than Mass began. The priest, with the deacon on his right and the subdeacon on his left, went toward the altar and standing before it began the service by saying the antiphon *Introibo ad altare Dei,* the psalm *Judica me Deus,* the lesser Doxology or *Gloria Patri,* and a repetition of the *Introibo,* after which he made a silent confession. The ministers followed with the *Misereatur,* and they, too, made their confessions (part 2, chap. 42). The celebrant then said other prayers, among them *Parce Domine,* and at the end of these the ministers responded with Amen, *Dominus vobiscum,* and *Benedicamus Domino.*

---

in the choir and that this was repeated by the chorus, after which the cantor sang the psalm verse and the lesser Doxology in organum. He again specifies that afterwards, throughout the entire Mass, only the Alleluia and its verse were sung in organum (part 1, chap. 263, pp. 252–53).

37. On the evolution of the major Mass in later medieval times see Joseph A. Jungmann, *The Mass of the Roman Rite: Its Origins and Development,* trans. Francis A. Brunner (New York, 1951–54), 1:202ff.

For the people's Mass and major Mass on Sundays and feast days the cathedral's silver cross was placed on the altar and candles were lighted (part 2, chap. 43). The priest made the sign of the cross, climbed the steps to the altar, kissed the altar, and said a prayer, after which he placed the missal on the right side of the altar and kissed it. Then he went to the other side of the altar and embraced the ministers, who thereupon embraced each other. Then, while the introit and the Kyrie eleison, both of which were begun by the cantor, were being sung in the choir, the subdeacon received the thurible from an acolyte and kindled the incense before giving it to the priest, who then censed the altar as he said "Dirigatur Oratio mea, sicut incensum in conspectu tuo." Oderigo notes that these prayers were "read and not sung," because at this point the chorus, led by the cantor, was singing the introit (chaps. 43, 44).[38] The priest alone, in a loud voice, intoned the Gloria in excelsis Deo, with the ministers, in a low voice, and the choir joining him for its continuation (chap. 45).[39] When this was finished the priest moved to the right and turning towards the people said "Dominus vobiscum," to which the clergy responded "Et cum spiritu tuo."

The priest then turned to the altar, raised his hands, and said "Oremus." The collect and its response followed, and as the latter came to a close, the subdeacon, preceded by an acolyte, went toward the pulpit carrying the missal with him, and then standing at the altar on the right side, facing east, he read the epistle (chap. 49).[40] (Oderigo noted in chap. 36 that the priest placed the missal on the right side of the altar, where it remained until the gospel was to be read, when it was moved to the left side, where it remained until the postcommunion, when it was returned to the right side.) When the subdeacon finished reading the epistle, the acolyte returned the missal to the altar and if the bishop was present, the deacon kissed his hand and received his blessing. The gradual and the Alleluia with its verse, its *neuma,* and a sequence—if one were called for—followed (chap. 50). Oderigo is careful to point out that the gradual was sung in unison in the choir and that it was done only rarely by two voices—presumably in organum. When it was finished, the cantor joined the others or the two soloists and together they sang the Alleluia in organum, on Sundays and feast days. The sequence, Oderigo explains, was so named because it followed the *neuma,* or melisma, of the jubilus, a vocalized passage on the concluding vowel, "a," of the repeated alleluia that came after the verse. Oderigo says that the jubilus represents ineffable joy, a joy that cannot be expressed with words, nor passed over in silence. Those who sing it with full

---

38. Oderigo explains that the introit consists of three parts, an antiphon, a psalm verse, and the Gloria Patri. He notes that on solemn feasts tropes, containing words of praise in keeping with the text of the introit, were inserted (*OO,* p. 446). Elsewhere, he mentions that the cantor did the Introit on Sundays and feast days, meaning he led the choir.

39. In this same chapter Oderigo explains that whenever the Gloria was said in all feasts of nine lessons, *Te Deum laudamus* was said at Matins, except during Lent and Advent. He specifies further that whenever *Te Deum laudamus* was said at Matins, the Gloria was sung at the Mass, except on the vigils of Apostles, and that both prayers were said every day from Christmas Day through the Octave of Epiphany and from Easter through the Octave of Pentecost.

40. He did not read the Epistle from the raised pulpit, but rather stood below the altar steps.

voice, he adds, "signify the rectors of the church, who praise God with a loud voice and invite others to praise Him by their example. The others, who sing the Alleluia in the pulpit," he adds, "are perfect and contemplative, their conversation being in heaven."[41]

Preparations for the singing of the gospel then began, with an acolyte handing the thurible to the subdeacon, who censed the bishop or the officiating priest, after which the deacon picked up the missal and kissed both it and the altar before going to the bishop or the priest, from whom he asked a blessing by saying "Jube Domne benedicere" (chap. 51). This was given with the words "Dominus sit in corde tuo" and was acknowledged by the deacon who kissed the bishop's, or the priest's, hand. Then, holding the missal before him, with the acolyte bearing lighted candles, and the subdeacon holding the thurible, the deacon proceeded to the pulpit, from where he sang the gospel (chap. 52). Before he did this the subdeacon greeted the people so as to prepare them to hear the word of the Lord and then, turning to the deacon, he said "Et cum Spiritu tuo." Following this the deacon said "sequentia Sancti Evangelii," kissed the missal, and sang the passage appropriate to the day, apparently in one of the then current gospel tones. When the gospel was finished, the subdeacon returned the missal to the altar and the officiating priest began the Credo in unum Deum in a full voice (chap. 66). The choir sang the rest of the text, which was also completed by the ministers at the altar.

With regard to the intonation of the Credo, Oderigo specifies that if the officiating priest remained at the altar, he began the Credo at once, and when the deacon and subdeacon returned with the missal, the deacon kissed the missal and censed the priest. If the priest himself sang the gospel from the altar, the acolyte censed the priest. If the bishop was present, the acolytes brought him the missal, which he kissed, and censed him. Oderigo also explains that the Credo was not sung at every Mass, especially at Masses on Christmas, Circumcision, or Epiphany, though at Siena cathedral it was done on a considerable number of days, including, among others, those during the periods from St. Stephen's Day through the octave of Epiphany, from Easter through its octave, from the cathedral's consecration day through its octave, and on all the feasts of the

---

41. "Post Epistolam Chorus canit Gradualia, Alleluja, cum Versibus, Pneumis, & Sequentiis . . . Cantatur autem Graduale aequaliter, & raro, a duobus in Choro, & eo cantato jungitur eis, vel aliis duobus Cantor, & cantant Alleluja cum Organo, in Dominicis, & Festis . . . Sequentia dicitur, quia neuma jubili sequitur . . . Jubilus ineffabile gaudium representat; quod nec verbis exprimi, nec potest omnino taceri. Qui alte cantant, significant Rectores Ecclesiae: qui magna voce Deum laudant, & alios verbo, & exemplo ad laudandum invitant, qui summisse, illos qui in activa conversatione, virtutum gradibus ad altiora conscendunt. Alii sunt perfecti, & contemplativi, qui Alleluja in pulpitis concinunt, quorum conversatio est in Celis" (*OO*, part 2, chap. 50, pp. 451–52). Oderigo's words were perhaps inspired by Augustine's explanation of "jubilatio" in his commentary on Ps. 46, a commentary that was apparently also known to Gregory the Great, who wrote in much the same vein about the effect experienced in expressing in joyful song what cannot be said with words. Quotation of pertinent passages by both Church fathers and full references are given by Bonnie J. Blackburn, "Music and Festivities at the Court of Leo X: A Venetian View," *Early Music History* 11 (1992), 15, n. 53.

Virgin and of the Apostles and Evangelists (chap. 66).[42] Oderigo also notes that during the Credo, when the words "Et homo factus est" were sung, all knelt, and that at the end, as at the end of the Gloria in excelsis, the gospel, the Sanctus, the Pater noster, and several other prayers, everybody made the sign of the cross.

The Credo having been sung, the priest turned to the people and said "Dominus vobiscum" and after the response he turned to the altar and said "Oremus," whereupon the choir immediately sang the offertory in chant (chap. 57). Meanwhile, the deacon, the subdeacon, and the acolyte prepared the corporal, the chalice, the paten, the wine, the water, and the bread for the sacrifice of the Mass, and these were then censed as were the altar, the celebrants, and the clergy in the choir (chap. 59). The celebrant then turned to the congregation and said "Orate fratres," after which he said the secret and the preface. This latter changed according to the season (chap. 59). The Sanctus followed, and as it was being sung in the choir, the deacon and subdeacon joined the celebrant and said the prayer with him (chap. 62). With regard to the origins and meaning of the words of the Sanctus, Oderigo notes that the Hosanna was repeated so as to signify that both body and soul, both male and female, both clergy and laity, all are welcomed by the angels. And, he says, at this angelic concert, as all raise their voices to God in the highest, they are accompanied at times by the organ or other musical instruments ordained by David. This is the only place in his account where Oderigo mentions instruments, and while his allusion appears to have symbolic meaning rather than any practical intent, it may be an indication that the cathedral had an organ at the time and that it was played at services.

The prayers said, the deacon and subdeacon came and stood behind the priest, who, after making the sign of the cross and bowing his head, his arms outstretched and his hands open, began the canon of the Mass with the words "Te igitur" (chap. 63). The canon, including the elevation, was said in silence, but toward the end of it the priest interrupted the silence at the words "Nobis quoque peccatoribus," whereupon those in the congregation beat their breasts three times. The Lord's Prayer, the "Pax Domini," and the threefold Agnus Dei followed. At the end of the third exclamation of the Agnus Dei, at the words "Dona nobis pacem," the priest gave the kiss of peace to the deacon and to the subdeacon, who then passed it on to the clergy in the choir. Meanwhile the priest took communion. When the host was taken from the altar for distribution to the faithful, the clergy in the choir bowed their heads and said the prayers *Hujus Sacramenti susceptio* and *Omnipotens sempiterne Deus* (chap. 65).

For times when the bishop was present the rituals were somewhat more elaborate. Oderigo specifies that after the bishop said the Agnus Dei and gave the kiss of peace to the ministers, he himself took communion, and while he did this, the choir sang the Agnus Dei three times (chap. 67). On occasions when the bishop was not present, after the priest and the other ministers received communion, and after replacing the corporal, washing the chalice, and completing the remaining rituals, the deacon and subdeacon

---

42. He also notes that normally the Credo was not said on a feast of nine lessons unless it fell on a Sunday.

returned to their places behind the priest. Meanwhile the communion was being sung in plainchant in the choir, and when this was finished the priest returned the missal to the right side of the altar, after which the postcommunion followed (chap. 68). At the close of this last the priest turned to the people and said "Dominus vobiscum." After the choir responded with "Et cum spiritu tuo," the deacon, who was also facing the congregation, said in a loud voice *Ite missa est,* the words used when the Gloria in excelsis was sung. When Gloria in excelsis was omitted, *Benedicamus Domino* was said instead, and the choir in both cases responded with the words "Deo gratias" (chap. 69).

Christmas Eve and Midnight Mass

Siena cathedral celebrated the Advent and Christmas seasons with special services. The most elaborate of these were reserved for Christmas Eve and Christmas Day, when polyphony was used, as was customary, both to enhance the joy of the occasion and underline the extraordinary importance of the feast. Oderigo begins his description by noting that some observances were changed when the day before Christmas fell on a Saturday (part 1, chap. 36). Thus the traditional fasting period of the *quatuor Tempora* (Ember days) began in the previous week so that Advent would have four full weeks and the antiphons at morning Lauds were sung daily during the fourth week except on the feast of St. Thomas Apostle, when they were sung as though this were a day occurring in the previous week. Oderigo also says that on whatever day of the week Christmas Eve fell, all of the offices of the Virgin and the vigils of the dead were omitted, and indeed that this was true for the rest of the season through the Octave of Epiphany.

If Christmas Eve fell on a Sunday, at Matins the invitatory *Rex noster adveniet Christus* was sung "in a respectful manner" by three singers—presumably in organum—with the choir responding "Venite adoremus," after which the entire psalm *Venite exultemus* was also sung in organum (chap. 36). Oderigo observes that it was traditional every year to sing the hymn *Verbum superno* in organum, regardless of the day on which Christmas Eve fell. Otherwise, Matins was done as on the second Sunday of Advent, with nine lessons and nine responsories. Six of the responsories were from Sunday and three were proper to Christmas Eve. Customarily the cantor and two "brothers," or canons, began the third responsory, *De illa occulta,* in unison, from behind the high altar. At the words "Descendit Jesus" the entire choir joined in and sang in unison through to the end. Afterwards the verse, *Omnes,* and the *Gloria Patri* were sung in organum before a return was made to "Descendit." This done, the cantor once again began the responsory, which he and the other soloists now sang in organum through to "Descendit," when the choir entered and finished the rest of the piece in unison.

At Lauds the first antiphon was *Judaea et Jerusalem* and the following ones were from Sunday Lauds except for the Benedictus antiphon, *Orietur.* The chapter was *Paulus servus,* the hymn *Vox clara,* the verse *Crastina die,* and the prayer for Christmas Eve, *Deus qui nos redemptionis,* preceded the Sunday prayer. The antiphon and prayer were used at all offices throughout the day except at morning Mass, where the gospel from the preceding Saturday, *Anno quintodecimo,* was read. At the major Mass, which was that of Christmas Eve Day, the introit was *Hodie scietis* and though the Gloria was omitted, the Credo was not. Following the prayer came the prophecy *Haec dicit Dominus, propter Sion non tacebo,* and then the gradual *Hodie scietis* and its verse *Qui regis,* the epistle *Paulus servus Jesu Christi,* the Alleluia and its verse, *Erunt prava,* and the gospel *Cum esset desponsata Mater.* Although Oderigo does not say so here, he mentions in another place that the Alleluia was sung in organum at major Mass on Sundays. What he does say is that when a major Mass was sung on Christmas Eve Day, the response, *Constantes estote,* was sung in the procession and that the preface of the Mass, *Quia per incarnati,* was then said at daily Masses through Epiphany eve. Furthermore, from Christmas through the octave of Epiphany nine lessons were said every day, as were the Gloria in excelsis and the Credo. The antiphon from Lauds was sung at all of the other canonical hours, which also made use of many of the responsories and verses just mentioned.

If Christmas Eve fell on a day other than Sunday, "as often happens," services began on the evening before with a short vigil service (chap. 37).[43] The invitatory and the *Venite* psalm were sung in organum by three singers, and the hymn *Verbum supernum* was sung by the choir. The remaining prayers for this service were taken from the first nocturn of Matins and Lauds of the day. Oderigo mentions the verse *Hodie scietis* and the lessons from the homily of St. Remigius which begins with the words "Cum esset desponsata." He also notes that responsories were sung with the "history proper" to the day and he cites *Sanctificamini hodie,*[44] and the third responsory, *De illa,* "as was mentioned for Lauds," and the verse *Crastina.* The other ferial psalms such as *Miserere mei Deus* were not done, but the Benedictus antiphon *Orietur* and the hymn *Vox clara* were both now sung in organum.

When Christmas Eve Day fell on weekdays, the Kyrie eleison was not said at any of the canonical hours, and the commemoration of the Virgin Mary was omitted until the octave of St. Stephen, which was true also of the vigils prayer. The *Benedicamus Domino* was sung in organum. At Prime, the antiphon was *Hodie scietis,* and the hymn *Jam lucis* was sung in the tone usually adopted out of Advent time, as were the other hymns sung at the other hours. The chapter *Omnis enim* and the responsory *Christe Filii Dei vivi* were followed by the prayer *Dominus Deus Omnipotens Pater qui ad principium.* When Prime was finished, the canons gathered together with the bishop, if he was present, and when the bell sounded and after the phase of the moon and the future birth of the Lord were announced, all knelt and prayed and "*Pretioso* was recited, finishing in the usual way." After they were dismissed, the canons went into the refectory, where the warmth of "a worthy fire" awaited them, and there they received the order of offices on the following day (chap. 37).

At the Mass of the people the introit was *Hodie scietis,* the prayer *Deus qui nos redemptionis,* and after this latter the prophecy was read. The epistle and gradual were followed by the tract *O Judaea et Jerusalem* and the gospel. The Gloria in excelsis Deo was not sung at this Mass of the people on Christmas Eve Day, even if it fell on a Sunday.

---

43. The following remarks about Matins, Lauds, and the major Mass are also from this chapter.

44. *Sanctificamini hodie* appears in two well-known medieval antiphonaries from Lucca and Worcester. Its verse is *Hodie scietis.* See *Antiphonaire monastique: XIIe siècle: Codex 601 de la Bibliothèque Capitulaire de Lucques* (Paléographie musicale 9; Tournai, 1906), 29; and *Antiphonaire monastique: XIIIe siècle: Codex F. 160 de la bibliothèque de la cathédrale de Worcester* (Paléographie musicale 12; Tournai, 1922), 25.

Oderigo says little more about this service except to note that the preface was *Quia per incarnati* and that it was followed by a Mass for souls of the faithful departed. He again notes that at the other canonical hours, the antiphons of Lauds, the responsories, and verses were those he named earlier.

Vespers on Christmas Eve were celebrated before the canons dined (chap. 38). The antiphons and psalms were *Rex pacificus* and *Laudate pueri; Magnificatus est* and *Laudate Dominum; Scitote* and *Lauda anima; Completi sunt* and *Laudate Dominum quoniam;* and *Ecce completa sunt* and *Lauda Jerusalem.* The chapter *Apparuit gratia Dei* was followed by the responsory *Judaea et Jerusalem,* the latter sung by the soloists from behind the main altar alternating with the choir in this way: the responsory was sung first in unison and the verse, *Constantes estote,* and the *Gloria Patri* followed in organum; the repetition of the responsory was sung in organum up to the words "Cras egredietur," when unison singing was resumed,[45] and this held through the new verse that followed, "Benedictus qui venit." The Magnificat antiphon was *Dum ortus fuerit sol* and the prayer *Concede.* Afterwards either *Benedicamus Domino* or *Verbum Patris* was sung in unison. Oderigo makes a point of noting that his church customarily sang no hymns at Vespers, Matins, and Lauds until the feast of Holy Innocents.

After Vespers the canons repaired to the refectory. At the beginning of dinner they said *Verbum caro factum est, Gloria Patri,* Kyrie Eleison, Pater noster, and a number of other prayers, and when they left the refectory, *Benedictus qui venit, Gratias agimus,* and the psalm *Benedixisti,* which was recited as they made their way back into the church. Having finished the psalm with *Gloria Patri,* they said the Kyrie, the Lord's Prayer, and the verse *Verbum caro factum est,* as well as other verses and prayers for Christmas, *Benedicamus Domino,* and finished with *Benedicat nos qui creavit.* These rituals of benediction were observed at table from Christmas Eve through Epiphany. The prayers and chants sung at Compline, which again included *Verbum caro factum est,* the antiphon *Natus est nobis,* and the *Nunc dimittis* canticle, were also retained throughout this same period.

Oderigo begins his description of Matins by noting that the clergy arose at midnight to sing the office because the church believed that that was the hour when Christ was born, when the angels appeared to the shepherds, and when, in place of "the songs, that is, the lullabies nurses usually sang to babies, they sang Gloria in excelsis Deo to the Child."[46] While the Sienese liturgy for Christmas Matins had its share of pieces sung in organum, it contained none of the incidental dramatic touches, such as the *Officium Pastorum,* used in other medieval churches to reenact the events surrounding Christ's birth, these being reserved instead for morning services.[47] Before Matins began, all of the canons, holding lighted tapers in each hand and led by the provost, the arch-

---

45. Contrary to modern practice, where the repetition of the responsory is resumed at "Cras egrediemini," Oderigo specifically indicates a return to the opening: "R. *Judaea et Jerusalem.* Quod Responsorium post Altare B. Mariae Virginis hoc ordine cantatur. Primo R. equaliter canitur; v. & *Gloria* cum Organo. Item repetatur R. cum Organo usque: *Cras egredietur.* V. *Benedictus qui venit.*"

46. "& pro sescenninis (idest Cantilenis quas Nutrices Pueris cantare consueverant) *Gloria in Excelsis Deo* illi Puero alto decantasse" (*OO,* part 1, chap. 40, p. 33).

47. The phrase is from Karl Young, who furnishes an excellent account of dramatic reenactments of the *Officium Pastorum* at Matins in *The Drama of the Medieval Church* (Oxford, 1933), 2:9–20.

priest, and the cantor, who carried the bishop's staff, walked from the church to the bishop's residence. There they were received by the bishop, who said "Verbum caro factum est" to each of the canons as he gave them his blessing. Each of them responded with "Deo gratias." The group then returned to the choir of the church with the bishop, who began the office by saying *Domine labia mea aperies* and *Deus in adjutorium meum intende* in front of the main altar. Immediately afterwards the cantor and three others, standing to one side of the bishop, began the invitatory antiphon *Christus natus est nobis: Venite adoremus,* which they sang through completely in organum. The choir, singing in unison, repeated the antiphon, and the *Venite* psalm followed (chap. 40).

Although Oderigo is not altogether clear, his remarks suggest that various verses of the psalm were sung by the cantor and his group, with interjections of the "Christus natus est" by the choir in unison. Still standing in the same place to the side of the bishop, the cantor and his group then began the antiphon *Dominus dixit ad me,* which the choir picked up at the words "Filius meus," and this led to the psalm *Quare fremuerunt.* The antiphon was repeated when the psalm was finished and Oderigo notes that all subsequent antiphons were sung through in their entirety both before and after the psalms as well as in between psalm verses wherever they were called for. The second antiphon, *Tanquam sponsus,* and psalm, *Caeli enarrant,* and the third antiphon, *Diffusa est,* and psalm, *Eructavit,* followed, and after them the first three lessons from Isaiah and three responsories and their verses. The first responsory, *Hodie nobis caelorum,* and the second, *Hodie nobis de caelo,* were sung in unison, but the third, *Descendit,* was sung in organum. The performance of this latter was quite elaborate, calling for passages in three-part organum by the cantor and the other soloists, unison singing by the chorus, and virtuoso passages for one or all of the soloists. The performance was also defined spatially, as were so many others at Siena cathedral, by having the soloists stand in one place and the chorus in another. For this third responsory Oderigo says that the cantor and two others stood behind the main altar and sang its first half in unison, up to the words "Et exivit," and then finished the remainder in organum. The verse and the *Gloria Patri* were also sung in organum, though not completely because the verse was troped, musically and textually, and called for the participation of both soloists and chorus. Oderigo describes the performance further by noting that "the beginning of the verse, that is, *Tamquam,* which has a jubilus (melisma), is sung by those behind the altar" and after this "the chorus sings the prosas in unison, that is, *Quem Gabriel.*" The remainder of the verse and the *Gloria Patri* were similarly treated: "Thus they respond to the jubilus (melisma) with prosas [both] in the verse and in the *Gloria* until all of the responsory is finished." The psalm, furthermore, was "always repeated," as were "the verse and afterwards the *Gloria* and [the second half of the responsory from the words] "Et exivit." Another prosa, *Ante saecula,* was begun by the cantor and was sung in organum up to the words "psalmavit Adam," whereupon the chorus responded with "Et spiritu Sancto," and in this manner "one part is said behind the altar, the other in the choir, until all is finished."[48] Afterwards the cantor recommenced the responsory, *Descendit,* and sang it through to the end in organum with the other soloists.

---

48. "Tertium ℞ *Descendit.* Cantor cum duobus Fratribus post Altare Beatae Mariae Virginis canit aequali voce usque *Et exivit,* hoc ℞; & ℣, & *Gloria* cantantur cum Organo. Principium Versiculi:

The second and third nocturns of Matins also had their share of spatially defined performances featuring unison singing and organum. Oderigo names three psalms and their antiphons, three lessons, and three responsories for each. With regard to the performance of the remaining responsories, he notes simply that all nine responsories of Christmas Matins were sung in unison, except for the third, sixth, and ninth, and that the versus and the *Gloria Patri* of all were sung in organum (chap. 42). More informative are his remarks about the third lesson of the second nocturn, taken from the sermon of St. Augustine, which began *Vos inquam, Convenio, Judaei*. This, he notes, "according to ancient usage was customarily sung in our church by two canons" up to the verse, *Judicii Signum,* at which point the cantor and two others immediately began singing in organum. The following verses were said in pairs, with the choir always repeating the verse *Judicii Signum* in organum until all the verses were finished (chap. 41).[49] This is one of the few places where Oderigo says that the choir also performed organum, though he fails to specify whether its music differed in style from that of the soloists.

As the ninth lesson of Matins was being read, the bishop, or archpriest, began preparing for the midnight Mass. Oderigo explains that this was one of three Masses said on Christmas Day and that the others occurred at dawn and at the hour of Terce. (In reality, the Chapter participated in four Masses on Christmas Day because there was also the customary Mass of the people.) The midnight Mass was celebrated with the assistance of a deacon and a subdeacon. Oderigo reports that as soon as the ninth lesson was finished the cantor and two others began the trope, though he fails to give its name and to say whether it was sung polyphonically (chap. 43). He prescribes organum for the Kyrie, the Sanctus, and the Agnus Dei, but again he does not specify the number of voices required for the performance. Nor does he speak of those who performed the Alleluia and its verse, *Dominus dixit,* and the sequence, *Natus ante saecula*. When this Mass was concluded with *Ite missa est,* the deacon, standing in the large pulpit, recited the "Genealogy of Christ" from the Gospel according to St. Matthew, after which he began the *Te Deum laudamus.*

Christmas Day

At Lauds, which preceded the Mass at dawn, only the closing *Benedicamus Domino* was performed in organum (chap. 44). Otherwise, the chant was sung in unison, but again, in one instance, with the physical separation of singers, who, through the simple repetition of phrases in dialogue form from texts within the liturgy, reenacted the wondrous events experienced by the shepherds. Though Oderigo's description can hardly be said

---

scilicet *Tam,* in quo sunt notae jubili, ab his qui sunt post Altare canitur cum Organo: & post notas jubili, Chorus canit prosas aequali voce: Scilicet *Quem Gabriel* etc., & sic semper ad jubilum respondentur prosae in versu, & *in Gloria,* donec totum ℞ finiatur, & semper repetitur Psalmus: ℣ & post *Gloria,* & *exivit per.*" (*OO,* part 1, chap. 40, pp. 35–36).

49. The only other lesson mentioned by Oderigo as being sung in organum was the third lesson from the Lamentations of Jeremiah, *Recordare Domine,* in the third nocturn of Holy Saturday. Oderigo says it was customary to have it performed by three singers and that these lamentations were sung so as to provoke grief and tears, "such being the nature of music," which makes those who are happy more happy, those who are sad more sad (part 1, chap. 167).

to represent a model of clarity with regard to the dialogue's placement within the service, he does furnish enough information to permit a reconstruction of how it was performed. He begins matter of factly by stating that the psalm, *Laudate Dominum de caelis,* followed the antiphon *Quem vidistis, pastores, dicite.* Since this traditionally was the first antiphon of the service, it seems fair to assume that the psalm was also the first one, though it is the fifth psalm in present-day liturgy. Towards the end of the psalm another antiphon from Lauds was introduced. This was *Pastores, dicite, quidnam vidistis . . . Infantem vidimus pannis involutum,* a text which in some medieval churches was sung singly or in several repetitions during the singing of the first or of the fifth psalm of Christmas Lauds.[50]

At Siena cathedral the antiphon was done after every verse of the psalm, for Oderigo says that *Laudate Dominum de caelis* was first sung through to the words "in sanctis ejus," that is, through the middle of its last verse, whereupon the chorus, apparently from the choir area, interjected with the opening words of the antiphon "Pastores, dicite." Then, from behind the main altar, singing in unison, two boys replied with the second part of the antiphon, "Infantem vidimus." The chorus responded to this with the words "Laudate Dominum in sanctis ejus," and subsequently each verse of the psalm was sung "in this order" until it was completed. Although it is impossible to say where this special dialogue occurred in this Sienese service, as Karl Young pointed out in connection with its use in other liturgies, whatever its place, the normal liturgical arrangement of Lauds was otherwise undisturbed.[51]

The pealing of the cathedral's large bell signaled the beginning of the Mass at Dawn. Here, the introit, *Lux fulgebit,* was preceded by an unnamed trope sung in organum (chap. 45). Except for the Alleluia and its verse, *Dominus regnavit,* polyphonic performance is not otherwise mentioned, not even for the sequence, *Cunctum orbem.* Prime was sung as soon as Mass was finished. Oderigo names the hymn, *Enixa est Puerpera,* the antiphon, *Genuit Puerpera,* the chapter, *Apparuit,* the responsory, *Christe Filii Dei vivi,* the verse, *Verbum caro,* and the prayer, *Concede quaesumus,* and says that the same chapter, responsory, verse, and prayer were sung at Lauds every day until Epiphany eve. He also notes that at Prime, Terce, Sext, and None the responsory and verse were sung with an "alleluia, which represents the great joy that comes to us in this time of goodwill." At the conclusion of Prime the canons assembled in Chapter, where the phase of the moon and the feast on the morrow were announced. Afterwards the archpriest or the weekly priest said the verse *Verbum caro factum est . . . Et habitavit* and other prayers and dismissed the canons, who responded with *Pretiosa* and *De profundis,* this latter being said again after they had eaten.

The Mass of the people was held at a "convenient hour" sometime before Terce (chap. 46). It was at this service that the populace made their confessions and took communion. Oderigo says that in his sermon the officiating priest exhorted the congregation to attend the major Mass and to hear the bishop's sermon. Otherwise, apart from noting that at this Mass, as at the other three on Christmas, two lessons, the first from

---

50. Young, *The Drama of the Medieval Church,* 2:20–22.
51. Ibid., 2:22.

the prophet Isaiah, the second from the apostle Paul, were read, he has very little to say about the service, presumably because its chants and prayers were the same as those of the major Mass.

The large bells were rung at length after the people's Mass in anticipation of major Mass. No procession was held on Christmas Day, even if it fell on a Sunday, and the same was true of the three following days, St. Stephen's, St. John's, and Holy Innocents (chap. 47). All of the bells were sounded at Terce, which was sung in the choir (ibid.). Oderigo makes no mention of polyphony at this service, though he does note that the hymn, *Enixa est puerpera,* was sung in unison in a loud voice. As Terce was being sung, the bishop, the archpriest, deacon, and subdeacon were dressing in their most solemn raiment in the sacristy or behind the main altar, and as soon as it was finished, the cantor and two canons proceeded to the choir and intoned the trope *Ecce,* which they sang through completely in organum. The introit, *Puer natus est,* followed and then the Kyrie eleison. Parts of the latter, "that is, where there are the prosas, *Lux et origo,*" were sung in organum. The Gloria in excelsis, the prayer, *Concede quaesumus,* the prophecy, *Propter hoc sciet,* an unspecified gradual, and the epistle, *Multifariam,* came in due order and then the cantor and three others ascended the large pulpit from where "they solemnly sang the Alleluia *Dies Sanctificatus* in organum."

As they were singing, the subdeacon brought incense to the bishop, who placed it in the thurible, while the deacon removed the missal from the altar and went and stood to the bishop's side to receive his benediction. Then, a small procession consisting of the bishop, the archpriest, the deacon carrying the missal, the subdeacon carrying the thurible, preceded by sacristans holding lighted candles, made its way to the large pulpit, whereupon the cantor, the Alleluia being finished, in a loud voice intoned the antiphon, *Gloria in excelsis,* which "those who were with him finished in organum."[52] The deacon read the gospel, *In principio erat Verbum,* from the large pulpit, which was where the bishop delivered "a solemn sermon to the clergy and the people." Confession was administered to the people by the deacon and an indulgence and benediction were pronounced by the bishop. The Credo was said after the bishop and his ministers returned to the altar. Apart from noting that the Sanctus, sung with its prosas, *Verbum quod erat,* and the Agnus Dei were sung in organum and that after the *Ite missa est* the bishop gave another solemn benediction, Oderigo says little else about this third Mass of the Day. Nevertheless, his remarks are sufficient to show that with its tropes and numerous chants sung polyphonically, it was one of the most musically opulent Masses celebrated at Siena cathedral throughout the entire year, rivaling even that of Easter Sunday.

Easter Sunday

Easter, too, was not without some dramatic embellishment of the liturgy, this occurring at Matins rather than before the introit of the Mass, as was customary in many medieval churches. In anticipation of Matins the cathedral's large bells were sounded and the entire church was illuminated, as the Chapter assembled for the beginning of services.

---

52. This is apparently the same antiphon that is sung at Christmas Lauds today; see the *Liber Usualis,* 402. It was also in use in other places such as Lucca and Worcester during the Middle Ages. See *Antiphonaire monastique . . . de Lucques,* 38, and *Antiphonaire monastique . . . de Worcester,* 32*.

Then, led by the archpriest and the cantor, the canons proceeded with lighted candles in hand to the bishop's palace (part 1, chap. 191). There they were received by the bishop, who greeted them with the words "Resurrexit Dominus," to which they responded "Deo gratias." Afterwards, the canons escorted the bishop back to church, where he began Matins, which on this occasion was limited to one nocturn. The cantor and three others then climbed to the fourth step in front of the main altar and sang the invitatory antiphon, *Alleluia,* and the *Venite* psalm in unison, repeating the invitatory in organum. Standing in the same place, the cantor began the antiphon *Ego sum qui sum,* and the choir responded in unison with *Sed in lege Domini* and followed this with the psalm *Beatus vir.* The same order was used for the other two psalms and their antiphons, which Oderigo notes were sung in their entirety before and after the psalm. The lessons were read from the large pulpit, and while they were being said the altars, the clergy, and the congregation were censed. The *Gloria Patri* was said after each responsory.

Organum was not used again at Matins until the third and final responsory, *Dum transisset sabbatum* (chap. 192). Its text tells how on Easter Sunday morning the three women went to the tomb to annoint the body of Jesus, and its music was performed with the same kind of spatial separation of singers used at Christmas, which of course added a dramatic touch to the momentous event recounted by the scriptures. For this performance Oderigo says it was customary for the cantor and two others to go behind the main altar and sing the responsory in unison, but to sing the verse, *Et valde,* in organum. The choir quickly responded to this latter by singing "the prosas in organum, that is, *Christus ab Inferis* and others in the antiphonary," while after every single prosa the cantor and his group sang "the notes in organum, each in its own place, until the end of the responsory." Then the cantor and the soloists recommenced the responsory and sang it in organum through the word *Aromata,* and "the choir responded similarly in organum" with the words that followed, *Ut venientes ungerent Jesum.*[53] Though Oderigo's description lacks any suggestion that the troped texts were distributed between soloists and choir so as to assume the kind of dialogue form characteristic of the famous Easter trope *Quem quaeritis,* it is clear that the placement of the two groups served in the simplest way to heighten the dramatic effect of the text.

Adding to the intensity of the moment was another theatrical touch that was supplied by the actions of the cantor and the other soloists. Immediately after the responsory was finished, they walked to the front of the main altar and there the cantor, standing in the middle and the other two standing on each side of him, "holding in his hand the shroud where the painting of the Savior is,"[54] began the antiphon *Surrexit*

---

53. "Consueto nostrae Ecclesiae talis est, quod Cantor cum duobus Fratribus, hac nocte tertium ℞ post Altare Beatae Mariae Virginis aequali voce incipit: *Dum transisset Sabbatum.* ℣ *Et valde,* cum Organo, & statim Chorus respondet, & dicit prosas semper cum Organo, scilicet *Christus ab Inferis,* & alias sicut sunt in Antiphonario, & post prosas singulas Cantor cum Sociis cantat notas cum Organo, quisque in suo loco, & sic usque ad finem Responsorii. Quo finito, & Cantor reincipiat ℞ cum Organo usque *Aromata,* & Chorus similiter cum Organo respondet ab eo loco ubi dicit: *Ut venientes ungerent Jesum*" (*OO,* part 1, chap. 192, p. 174).

54. "& tenent linteum in manibus, ubi est pictura Salvatoris" (ibid.). Whether Siena claimed to have a relic of the Holy Face, as did Lucca, is not attested, but the mention of a "pictura Salvatoris"

Christus, to which the choir responded *Alleluia.* Though Oderigo does not say that the cantor unveiled the painting, this must have been what occurred, given the text of the antiphon and the symbolism of such an action. As the antiphon came to a close the bells began to peal and the crosses were uncovered and then the *Te Deum* was sung in organum, after which the verse, *Haec dies,* was also sung.[55]

The bishop also presided at Lauds, which he began in the usual manner (chaps. 192 and 194). The cantor intoned the antiphon, *Et valde mane,* and the remaining prayers followed in order. The Benedictus antiphon was *Angelus autem Domini,* and after the prayer the *Crucifixum in carne* was sung standing before the cross. Oderigo says that throughout the following Easter Week the antiphon *Surrexit Christus* was sung in organum and then the verse *Dicite in nationibus alleluia* was sung before the cross. The service concluded with the two final stanzas, beginning *In hoc Paschali jubilo,* of the Easter hymn *Rex Christe Clementissime.* At the close of this, Prime was immediately begun by the bishop, who again began the service with the usual prayers. The cantor then intoned the opening stanza of the Easter hymn sung a few minutes earlier, which was now sung through to the end in organum. The hymn was performed throughout Easter Week at Prime, Terce, Sext, and None, apparently in this same way. No other performances in organum are mentioned at this service, which was followed by a re-gathering of the canons in the chapter house, where additional verses and responses were said, after which the canons embraced each other and were dismissed. The people's Mass was sung "at a convenient hour after Prime," apparently replacing the usual matutinal Mass, which is not mentioned on Easter Sunday. Oderigo says little about this service, except to note that it was here that the people were reminded of their obligation to take holy communion and that it was also when their offerings were received.

After the people's Mass the cathedral's large bells sounded the call for the major Mass (chap. 195). All of the city's clergy made their way to the bishop's palace, where the bishop, the deacon, and the subdeacon were vesting for Mass. When everyone was in place, the procession began, led by the crucifer, followed by a priest wearing a cope, who sprinkled holy water as he walked, and choirboys, dressed in surplices, with lighted tapers in hand. As the crucifer took his first step the cantor intoned the antiphon *Vidi aquam* in a loud voice and this was followed by the verse *Salvum me fac* and the antiphon *Surrexit Christus.* Afterwards, he began the *Crucifixum in carne* and marched with all of the clergy, walking two by two, in procession. Oderigo furnishes an alternate beginning for the service if the bishop was not present. In that case, Oderigo says that the arch-priest, deacon, and subdeacon were to don their vestments in the sacristy or behind the main altar and, leaving the choir with the assembled clergy, they were to march in order to the church of St. James, next to the bishop's palace, whence they would return to the stairway in front of the cathedral. There, they gathered in the formation of a choir, standing around the bishop, or the archpriest, together with the deacon and subdeacon,

---

is an early reference to the cult of St. Veronica and her veil, and antedates the earliest mention of the Holy Shroud of Turin.

55. Similar troped performances of this third responsory at Easter Matins are discussed by Young in *The Drama of the Medieval Church,* 1:234–36, to which this discussion is much indebted.

the crucifer, and the candle bearers. At that point the cantor and two others went and stood on the stairs by the cathedral doors and in a loud voice sang the verse *Salve festa dies* and *Qua Deus* in organum, which the choir repeated, singing in unison, as the procession, led by the crucifer and the others, began to move forward.[56] In this way, with the cantor and his group singing the other verses, and the choir responding with *Salve festa dies,* they climbed the stairs to the doors. When the bishop, or the archpriest, passed through the doors and entered the church, the antiphon *Regina caeli* was begun and was sung by all in organum as the clergy returned to the choir.

When all were back in their places, the officiating priest began Terce with *Deus in adjutorium,* and this was followed by the hymns *Rex Christe Clementissime, Quaesumus ave,* and *Gloria tibi Domine,* the antiphon *Et respicientes,* and the psalm *Legem pone.* Oderigo explains that in place of the customary verse after the psalm, the gradual *Haec dies,* without its verse, was sung, and he says that afterwards the cantor and two others sang an unspecified trope in organum in the choir (chap. 196). At the close of the trope, the same singers intoned the introit *Resurrexi* and performed it in alternation with the choir in this way: the introit was picked up at once by the canons and the other clergy standing next to the choir stalls, who sang it through to the verse, which was then sung in organum by the cantor and his group. The *Resurrexi* was then repeated by the choir, after which the soloists sang the *Gloria Patri* in organum and the choir sang the *Resurrexi* for the last time. The cantor, still in the choir, then began the Kyrie eleison, "that is, the one which has the prosas *Cantemus cuncti,*" which he and the soloists sang in organum, and afterwards this was sung by "the others, from the other side of the choir," presumably in unison.

The bishop and his group, having meanwhile said Terce, went before the main altar and made their confessions before ascending the steps. After the usual rituals and blessings, the bishop seated himself in his throne and facing the altar said "Gloria in excelsis," after which he turned to the congregation and said "Pax vobis," to which the people responded "Et cum spiritu tuo." The prayer *Deus qui hodierna die* preceded the epistle, *Expurgate.* This, Oderigo says, "according to long and ancient custom, is traditionally sung at major Mass in our church by three people," and he goes on to recount how three singers dressed in copes, or two singers and the subdeacon, ascended the pulpit and sang each verse of the epistle first in Hebrew, then in Greek, and then in Latin through to the last verse, "Sed in Azymis," which they all sang together in organum. When this was finished, they went to the bishop's side, whereupon the cantor had the gradual *Haec dies* and its verse *Confitemini* sung by two in the choir. Then he and the other three went up into the large pulpit, from where they sang exultantly in organum the Alleluia *Pascha nostrum,* the prosa *Epulemur,* and a repetition of the Alleluia in organum, before singing the antiphon *Angelus autem Domini,* also in organum. Mean-

---

56. The complete text of this, together with other texts, music, and rubrics for the procession, Terce, and major Mass, are found in the already mentioned Sienese processional, BCIS, MS F. VI. 11, the volume Oderigo refers to later in connection with the procession on Pentecost Sunday. Some of the texts were published by Trombelli in his edition of the *OO,* 178–79. Of immediate interest here is corroboration of Oderigo's remark that the versus *Salve festa dies* was sung in organum by three soloists in front of the church doors.

while, the bishop and the others were completing the various rituals preceding the reading of the gospel, which was then read by the bishop, who also preached a sermon. The people then made their confessions and received the bishop's indulgence and benediction. The bishop subsequently returned to the altar and recited the Credo and afterwards the cantor with the other soloists, standing in the choir, solemnly sang the Sanctus and the Agnus Dei in organum. The remainder of the Mass followed in due course, but no other prayers or chants were sung in polyphony.

The Procession on Palm Sunday

In addition to Sunday and Easter processions, Oderigo describes a number of others held on principal feast days, including Ascension, Pentecost, St. Anthony Abbot, Purification of the Virgin, St. Lawrence, and the second day after Low Sunday, when the litanies were said and the cathedral Chapter visited a large number of churches. It is his description of the Palm Sunday procession, however, that claims attention because it is unique in its prescriptions for the performance of polyphony (chap. 132). Many of the texts and plainchant melodies used in the service are also preserved in MS F. VI. 11, the twelfth-century hymnary-processional described above on p. 67.[57] Oderigo explains that after morning Mass was celebrated and the large bell sounded, it was customary for the bishop, the clergy, and the people to gather in the duomo and march in procession to the church of St. Martin. Along the way they sang three pairs of responsories and verses, *In die qua invocavi* and *Deus Deus meus; Fratres mei* and *Amici mei; Eripe me* and *Accurrunt linguas;* and two other verses, *Circumdederunt* and *Quoniam tribulatio.*[58] The responsories were sung in unison by all and the verses were sung in organum by an unspecified number of singers (see Fig. 5). It is unusual for Oderigo not to specify the number of soloists involved in the performance of organum, and his failure to do so here must mean that the choir was divided into groups—probably not more than two—when the verses were sung in organum. He likewise fails to mention whether the choir and soloists sang as they walked along or stood in one spot.

Having arrived at their destination, the bishop, the archpriest, the deacon, the subdeacon, and the clergy were received in front of the church doors by the canons of St. Martin's, who censed them and sprinkled them with holy water. Then the bishop and the others went to the doors and blessed the palm fronds and olive branches with incense and holy water. Meanwhile, the canons and other clergy who had remained outside the church sang Terce, with the cantor leading the *Deus in adjutorium meum* and later the hymn *Nunc sancte,* which was sung "festively in organum." The musical source also prescribes a "festive" rendition of the hymn in organum, but gives only the chant. This doubtless indicates that the cantor and the other soloists sang "from the book," which is to say that those who improvised the new melodies had the chant before them as they did so. The antiphon, *Pueri Hebraeorum,* and psalm, *Legem pone,* were then sung

---

57. Fol. 36[r]: "Ad processionem in dominica palmarum," followed by the music and text of the responsory *In die qua invocavi te, Domine*. The processional is cited by Michel Huglo in "A propos de la Summa artis musicae attribuée à Guglielmo Roffredi," *Revue de Musicologie* 58 (1972): 93–94, n. 15.

58. Oderigo fails to mention the last two verses, which are found, together with all of the others, in BCIS, MS F. VI. 11, fols. 36[r]–37[v].

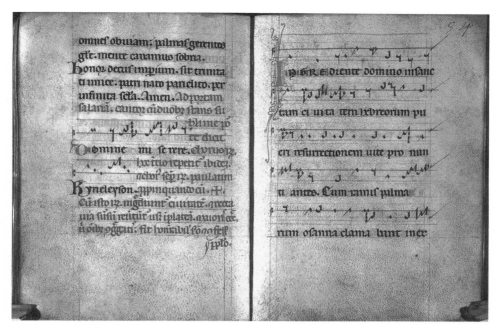

FIGURE 5. Cathedral hymnary/processional (twelfth century), fols. 53ᵛ–54ʳ, with music and instructions for singing organum in the Palm Sunday Procession. BCIS, MS F. VI. II. Courtesy Biblioteca Comunale degli Intronati di Siena; photograph from Foto Testi

in unison by the choir and after the chapter, *Hoc enim sentite,* was read, the responsory, *In Monte Oliveti,* and verses, *Veruntamen* with the *Gloria Patri* and *De ore Leonis,* followed, these, too, in unison. Exceptionally, the *Benedicamus Domino* was not said after the prayer, *Deus qui pro nobis Filium tuum,* and instead the subdeacon immediately read the lesson from Exodus, *In diebus illis venerunt filii Israel,* the final verse of which was done "in modum Epistolae," which probably means it was chanted in one of the epistle tones then in use.

Additional antiphons followed, all sung in unison, *Collegerunt, Quid faciemus,* and *Unus autem ex ipsis,* and afterwards the deacon read the Gospel according to St. Matthew, *Cum appropinquasset Jesus.*[59] The bishop and archpriest again blessed the palms and olive branches and sprinkled them with holy water, and then the clergy and the people, preceded by the crucifer, made their way back to the cathedral square. As they walked, they sang three antiphons, *Cum appropinquaret, Cum audisset,* and *Multa turba,* and a hymn, *Magno salutis,* all the way through in organum.[60] When they reached the city's Porta Salaria, the clergy halted and, together with the crucifer and the people, "formed

59. MS F. VI. 11 gives another antiphon not mentioned by Oderigo, *Ne forte veniant,* before the last named.

60. MS F. VI. 11 replaces *Cum audisset* with *Si quis vos interrogaverit.*

a choir," whereupon the cantor and two clerks went to the threshold of the door at the gate's entrance and sang *Domine miserere*. This piece, Oderigo explains, "is found in the little processional book," as indeed it is.[61] The choir responded with Kyrie eleison to the trio's *Domine miserere*, and this was done three times in all, each time "altiori voce cantando," singing in a louder voice, as the group drew nearer the door. When they had passed through it, the cantor began the responsory *Ingrediente Domino*, which was also in the little book of processionals; this, like the verse, *Cumque audisset*, and the *Gloria Patri*, was sung entirely in organum.

The group reentered the city singing this responsory and retraced its steps to the cathedral square. En route they sang two other responsories in organum, *Civitatem istam* and *Beatam me dicent*. Upon arriving at the cathedral all stood silently as the bishop or one of the other dignitaries stood at the top of the stairs in front of the church doors and delivered a "worthy sermon" to the canons and the people, who made a general confession afterwards. Following this, standing on the stairs above the crowd, the cantor and two clerics began to sing in unison, "with great reverence," *Gloria, laus, et honor* and *Cui puerile decus*. The choir, on bended knee, responded singing the same verses in the same way. Then the cantor and the two others, singing in rhythmically measured organum ("modulando" is Oderigo's term), performed two more verses, *Israel es tu*, and *Nomine qui*, the choir repeated *Gloria laus*, and again the cantor and two others sang two more verses, with the choir again responding in unison and ending with all singing a repetition of *Gloria, laus, et honor*.[62] When this was finished the bishop or the archpriest began the antiphon *Occurunt Turbae*, which was continued by the canons and clergy as they returned to the choir of the church amid the pealing of the bells. This is the only time that Oderigo hints at singing in measured rhythms, and precisely what he meant by the term he used is impossible to know, though it seems logical to assume that it was not the avant-garde mensural practices of Notre Dame cathedral in Paris.

Oderigo's meticulous account, corroborated by the instructions and music found in the processional MS F. VI. 11, is rendered all the more informative by his statement that all of the clergy sang organum on this occasion, not just the cantor and a few of his chosen associates. They, of course, were responsible for most of the polyphony that

---

61. At this point, in fact, MS F. VI. 11, fol. 53ᵛ, uses almost identical wording: "Ad Portam Salariam cantor cum duobus stans sublimine porte dicit: [music] Domine Miserere. Chorus respondit: [music] Kyrie eleison. Hoc tertio repetitur ibidem. Et chorus semper respondit paulatim appropinquando cum †. Cum isto ℞ ingrediuntur civitatem et recta via sursum revertuntur usque in plateam maioris ecclesie ubi omnibus congregatis fit honorabilis sermo et confessio populo." Fol. 54ʳ: [music] "Ingrediente Domino, ℣ Cumque audisset, [fol. 55ʳ] ℞ quae retro, Civitatem istam, ℣ Avertantur . . . ℞ Beatam me dicent, ℣ Et misericordia eius: Versus qui ante ianuis ecclesie super gradum, cantor cum duobus dicit equali voce duos primos versos. Et chorus respondit similiter. Alios dicunt cum organo et chorus usque ad finem [music] Gloria laus et honor [through fol. 58ʳ]. [fol. 58v] Cum hac antiphona repetuntur in choro. Et tunc debent omnia signa pulsari. antiphona [music] Occurunt turbe" (through fol. 59ᵛ).

62. Oderigo does not mention the titles of several subsequent verses given in MS F. VI. 11, fols. 55ᵛ–57ᵛ, all of which alternate with *Gloria, laus, et honor* in that source.

was sung, including at least one piece in measured organum. Exceptionally, the choir—and perhaps even the people, who may have joined in singing the melody of the chant—sang organum as the procession moved through the city. This polyphony of massed voices marching through the streets must have produced an extraordinary effect and was an altogether fitting aural accompaniment to the extensive itinerary, which itself served to symbolize Christ's entry into Jerusalem. Enriched as it was with performances of organum on a scale reserved only for the most solemn days in the Sienese liturgy, the Palm Sunday procession stands out as one of the outstanding examples of how polyphony could be used to enhance the importance as well as the joy of a special occasion.

Assumption Day

Assumption Day was the most Sienese of all religious holidays, celebrating as it did the Assumption of the Virgin, to whom the cathedral was dedicated. Even by the turn of the thirteenth century it had become customary for citizens and representatives of the town's dependencies to bring offerings of wax candles to the cathedral as an act of devotion to the Virgin and of fealty to the state. As will be noted in some detail below, various festivities involving music and dance as well as the Palio were among the many secular entertainments offered the crowds who thronged the city for the event. Oderigo, of course, says little about these secular festivities, though in introducing his subject, he explains that Assumption Day was the greatest of the five feasts dedicated to the Virgin Mary and was celebrated in Siena with the highest devotion, like Christmas Day (part 1, chap. 387). He also notes that since the concourse of people attending services on this day was larger than at any other time during the year, it was necessary for the canons to recite the office with even greater ardor and to be sure that they were prepared musically. He particularly admonishes them to restrain those among their ranks who might be inclined to hurry, so that the office would be conducted decorously to the end.

Oderigo says that at First Vespers all five of the antiphons were sung both before and after the psalms without organum, except for the last, which was done with organum and concluded with an extended melisma (chap. 388). The responsory, *Veni electa mea,* was sung throughout in organum by two choirs in this way: one half of the responsory and the verse by one choir, apparently standing at the side of the bishop, and the other half by the other, apparently in the choir. When the verse was finished, "those who remained in the choir stalls sang the repetition of the responsory in organum." At the end of this all stood together in the same place in the choir and sang the first stanza of the hymn, *Ave maris stella,* in organum and then went and stood at the side of the bishop, if he was present, where they sang the remaining stanzas, again in organum. Then came the verse, *Assumpta est Maria,* and the antiphon, *Virgo prudentissima,* which was sung both before and after the Magnificat in organum, and finished with a melisma. There followed the prayer, *Veneranda nobis,* and the *Benedicamus Domino,* which, as noted, Oderigo says was sung in organum on feasts of this class. *Hodierna fulget die* was then sung by the cantor and two others on one side of the choir, and the response was made, apparently by a group of canons, from the other side. When this was concluded, those who had just finished singing went to the bishop's side, if he was present.[63]

Immediately after the *Benedicamus Domino* and the end of Vespers, the cantor intoned the responsory for the dead, *Libera me, Domine,* while the sacristans draped the pallium over the tomb of the bishops in the middle of the church. Then, preceded by priests bearing candelabra blazing with the light of many candles, the crucifer, and all of the clergy, the presiding bishop, the canons, and the other clerics proceeded to the tomb, all the while singing the responsory in organum. There they formed a choir and when the responsory was finished, the bishop or the archpriest censed the tomb and said the prayer *Deus qui inter Apostolicos Sacerdotes.* After this the procession returned to the choir in the same order, and after receiving benediction from the bishop, if he was present, and having said *Benedicite,* everyone was respectfully invited to the refectory to drink, since, as Oderigo explains, "by ancient custom on the evening of these Vespers all of the city's clergy came to the duomo."

Polyphony was also used extensively at Matins. The invitatory, *In honore beatissime,* was sung, as was the Venite psalm, by the divided choir in organum, though it was repeated in unison. Afterwards, the first stanza of the hymn, *Quem terra,* was sung in organum, though Oderigo does not specify whether it was one part of the choir or a group of soloists who performed. This done, the singers went and stood at the side of the bishop, if he was present. At the first nocturn the three antiphons, *Specialis, Caeli Regina,* and *Virgo Creatoris,* were sung in their entirety in organum, both before and after the psalms, and the third antiphon was finished with a melisma. Oderigo does not comment on the performance of the antiphons at the second and third nocturns. He does, however, name all of them, as he does the three responsories and verses for each nocturn. He specifies, moreover, that the *Gloria Patri* was said for all nine responsories and that every *Gloria Patri* and all nine of the verses were sung in organum. Organum is likewise prescribed for the third responsory of each of the nocturns. Three lessons were read at each of the nocturns and after the fourth lesson the altar, the clergy, and the people were censed. The presence of the public at this service, which must have taken place long after nightfall, may in part account for the prominent place of polyphony in all of the nocturns.

At Lauds the first antiphon, *Assumpta est Maria,* was chanted before and after the psalm in unison, as were the other antiphons. The only piece sung in organum was the hymn, *O gloriosa Domina,* which was then done in the same manner at Prime. *O gloriosa Domina* was also sung at Terce, Sext, and None, but Oderigo makes no mention of organum at those hours (part 1, chaps. 389 and 490). Nor does he speak of organum at the major Mass, though from his earlier remarks it is clear that the Alleluia was sung by the cantor and two others. Organum reappears at Second Vespers, both in the hymn, *Ave Maria,* and in the Magnificat antiphon, *Hodie Maria.* This latter was subsequently sung in organum at all Vespers throughout the Octave of the feast. Oderigo barely mentions the major Mass of the day, which was celebrated after the Mass of the people

---

63. Oderigo notes that the collect for St. Lawrence was said neither at this service nor at Matins and Mass on the following day.

by the bishop or archpriest, the deacon, and the subdeacon, and he says nothing about polyphony at either service. From his earlier remarks, however, it appears that at the major Mass the Alleluia was sung by the cantor and two others, and this was also the case if the feast fell on a Sunday. The procession marking the feast was reserved for the following day.

ORGANUM AND IMPROVISED POLYPHONY

Though Oderigo says nothing about musical styles or techniques, his description of how organum was performed within the prevailing monophonic context of liturgical services is, as can be seen, quite informative. As a rule the choir sang the chant in unison, though at times, such as when psalms were sung, it was divided into two groups that sang antiphonally (part 2, chap. 20). Boys from the *schola* are occasionally mentioned as performers, but in general the adult singers were the mainstays of the choir. Polyphony was performed by an ensemble of two, three, or four soloists, including the cantor, and only exceptionally by the choir. The latter, in fact, is mentioned as singing organum only at processions on Sundays and on a few major feast days. The cantor, as the principal singer, intoned the chant melody and set the pitch for the improvised part or parts that were to be sung with it. The soloists sang entire sections of pieces in organum or they sang the opening portions of pieces that were then continued by the choir singing in unison. The choir also sang repeated sections of the chant in unison, as, for example, the return of the alleluia or the return of the antiphon after a psalm or canticle. Certain chants sung at the end of services, such as *Gloria Patri* and *Benedicamus Domino,* were at times performed by the soloists in organum, though these were more often done by the choir in unison. The polyphonic sections were varied by having different numbers of soloists in the ensemble or, on rare occasions, by having two ensembles of soloists responding to one other, as on the feast of the cathedral's consecration. By using phrases such as "and we customarily do this every year" ("et sic omni anno facere consuevimus") and "the custom of our church is such" ("consuetudo nostrae Ecclesiae talis est") during the course of his narrative, Oderigo makes it clear that the organal practices he describes were neither new nor unusual at the cathedral in his time.[64] The repertory sung in organum at Masses and at various canonical hours on Sundays and principal feast days was, as must be evident by now, a large and varied one and embraced a number of chants including Kyries, Glorias, introits, Alleluias, sequences, tracts, epistles, litanies, lessons, psalms, antiphons, responsories, verses, invitatories, hymns, and a few others, such as *Benedicamus Domino* and *Te Deum laudamus,* which were done at different services on more than one occasion. Almost any melody, it seems, could serve as the basis for extempore performance.[65] In this respect Sienese practice closely resembled that of another Tuscan cathedral, San Martino at Lucca,

---

64. *OO,* 30, 174, 248.

65. A point made by Gemma Gonzato, "Alcune considerazioni sull'Ordo Officiorum Ecclesiae Senensis," in *Le polifonie primitive in Friuli e in Europa: Atti del congresso internazionale, Cividale del Friuli, 22–24 agosto 1980,* ed. Cesare Corsi and Pierluigi Petrobelli (Rome, 1989), 254. Gonzato's very useful study contains a list of the occasions when Oderigo says organum was performed as well as references to specific chants.

where the extensive use of organum performed by two, three, four, and as many as eight singers is documented in a customary from the late thirteenth century.[66] The vastness and variety of both Tuscan repertories, as Agostino Ziino observed, differs enormously from the contemporaneous production of the cathedral of Notre Dame in Paris, the leading center of polyphony in the early thirteenth century, where polyphonic elaborations were directed mainly toward certain responsorial chants for Vespers and Matins and the gradual and Alleluia of the Mass.[67]

In discussing the variety of forms that Oderigo says were sung in organum as well as the absence of others, such as graduals, Kurt von Fischer argued that the unwritten Sienese repertory could be linked to all of those notated repertories emanating from various parts of medieval Europe that lay outside the mainstream of musical developments.[68] Doubtless this is true, though how closely Italian improvisational practices approximated those of northern Europe is impossible to know. What is certain, as Ziino and others have noted, is that improvised polyphony prevailed in the majority of churches and convents in Europe during later medieval times and that though it required the participation of trained singers, it was normally a simple affair, distinctly different from the high art polyphony of the Notre Dame repertory. The Parisian achievement, exceptional even within France, was the work of a musical-cultural elite that by the turn of the thirteenth century had embarked on a course that would take European written polyphony on a voyage unique in the annals of world music. By then Parisian composers had refined concepts of melody, rhythm, and meter and had invented or adopted a system of notation that enabled them to indicate the desired duration of the notes of a given melody, thus ensuring greater control over the newly added part or parts as well as of the chant—in other words, of the entire polyphonic ensemble. Only gradually did these innovations make their way to other musical centers, which continued with earlier practices, whether improvised or written, practices a later age would describe as retrospective or peripheral.

In view of the absence of Sienese sources of sacred polyphony from before the end of the fifteenth century, it is difficult to offer more than the most general remarks about the kinds of music that were performed at the cathedral in medieval times. In Oderigo's

---

66. References to organum in the Lucca customary have been analyzed, discussed, and to a certain extent compared with Oderigo's remarks by Agostino Ziino in "Polifonia nella cattedrale di Lucca durante il XIII secolo," *Acta Musicologica* 47 (1975): 16–30. Though fragmentary, the Lucca customary points to an even wider use of organum, especially on saints' days, than does Siena's, and this may be because it comes from a later time. Ziino (p. 17) notes that despite the later date (1289 or later), the Lucca customary could reflect earlier practices, for it seems that it was compiled from an earlier customary, as demonstrated by some passages that refer to certain churches as outside the city walls, though by 1289 they were within the city walls. Yet another Tuscan customary, from the cathedral of Volterra, can be mentioned here, though it makes no mention of organum. It has been published in modern edition in *De Sancti Hugonis actis liturgicis,* ed. M. Bocci (Florence, 1984).

67. See Wright, *Music and Ceremony at Notre Dame of Paris,* 246 for this particular point and pp. 247–58 for an excellent discussion of the Notre Dame legacy and its indisputable ties to the Parisian cathedral.

68. Kurt von Fischer, "Die Rolle der Mehrstimmigkeit am Dome von Siena zu Beginn des 13. Jahrhunderts," *Archiv für Musikwissenchaft* 18 (1961): 177–78.

day older, traditional, forms of organum may have been the norm, ones in which the chant was accompanied by a second voice singing in parallel motion at the interval of a fourth or a fifth, with one or the other or both parts being doubled at the octave when three or four singers participated in the performance. Another form of improvisation may have featured a melody or added part sung in oblique and contrary motion to the chant, producing a number of intervals such as unisons, fourths, fifths, octaves, and even occasional seconds and thirds. Melodic formulas and certain types of vocal ornamentation may also have played a larger part in performance than is suggested by theorists' reports and surviving examples. Other practices, in which the added part or parts were sung in a more florid style against slower moving notes of the chant in measured or unmeasured rhythms, may also have reached Siena cathedral by Oderigo's time. Still later, the characteristically simple techniques of *cantus planus binatim* described by fifteenth-century theorists may have been introduced. These entailed little more than having a second voice improvise a countermelody comprised of concordant intervals against the plainchant of the tenor in note-against-note style.[69] Here, too, the prevailing rules of "good counterpoint" were observed, and both parts were probably embellished by occasional ornamental flourishes. All of these practices required a certain skill on the part of singers. Whatever the preferred style, improvisational practices continued at Siena cathedral throughout the remainder of the thirteenth century, if the few references to organum in the later *Ordo Officiorum* are any indication, and it is probable that they were still in use through the end of the fourteenth century, when written polyphony must have begun making inroads.

From among a number of examples preserved in various sources, three have been chosen to illustrate the kinds of polyphony that might have been heard at Siena cathedral during Oderigo's time and later in the thirteenth and fourteenth centuries. Though they share textual incipits with chants that he says were performed in organum and are of Italian origin, there is little possibility of knowing—given the nature of improvisation as well as the wide chasm between extempore performance and performance from a written source—how closely they approximate Sienese practices. The earliest example, a twelfth-century setting for two voices of a *Benedicamus Domino* trope, *Regi regum glorioso,* for the feast of SS. Peter and Paul, appears in a manuscript from Lucca, where, as mentioned, organum was also performed on a large number of occasions (see Ex. 2.1).[70] The four rhyming lines of the troped text, each of eight syllables, are set to three short phrases, the first, repeated, for the first two lines, the second for the next, the third for the closing "Benedicamus Domino." Both parts—chant and added voice—are unmeasured and sing the text simultaneously in a note-against-note style that is distinguished

---

69. For a description and illustration of the practice see Alberto Gallo, "'Cantus planus binatim': Polifonia primitiva in fonti tardivi," *Quadrivium* 7 (1966): 79–89.

70. A facsimile and transcription of the piece were published by R. Baralli, "Un frammento inedito di *discantus,*" *Rassegna Gregoriana* 11 (1912), cols. 5–10; see also Dom Anselm Hughes, "The Birth of Polyphony," in *The New Oxford History of Music,* vol. 2: *Early Medieval Music up to 1300,* ed. Dom Anselm Hughes (London, 1954), 281. Although Oderigo notes that the *Benedicamus Domino* chant was sung in organum at Siena cathedral on the feast of SS. Peter and Paul, he says nothing about a trope.

by contrary motion and a variety of intervals, including the octave, fifth, fourth, third, sixth, unison, and even a second.

Later written examples of *Benedicamus Domino* tropes that preserve vestiges of improvised practice come from two other nearby Italian cities, Bologna and Florence. The Bologna trope, for the *Benedicamus* at None in the office of Pierre de Corbeil, is taken from a fourteenth-century manuscript, probably of Italian origin, that once belonged to a monastic establishment.[71] The chant melody, slightly varied, is embellished with another melody distinctive in its own right (see Ex. 2.2). Mensuration signs are lacking in the manuscript, though Giuseppe Vecchi, who edited the piece, has made a convincing case for transcribing both the added part and the original melody in duple meter. With a few minor exceptions, the texture is, once again, note-against-note, and the organal voice forms consonances of unisons, fifths, fourths, and an occasional third as it moves in contrary motion, for the most part, against the melody. Though the music is later than that of the Lucca trope, the improvisational technique remains essentially the same. This is true also of the Florentine *Benedicamus* trope, which is found in a fourteenth-century manuscript collection of laudi and motets compiled for the use of one of the city's religious companies (Ex. 2.3).[72] Although it, too, lacks a mensuration sign, the appearance of longs, breves, and occasional groups of semibreves, now in iambic, now in trochaic rhythms, undoubtedly signifies a setting in triple meter, which is the one chosen by Johannes Wolf in his transcription of the piece almost a century ago.

The three examples, though originating from different cities and encompassing a period of a century or more, demonstrate the continuity of the improvisational techniques that characterized retrospective polyphony, techniques that also appear in written pieces from the time. Only one of these has been preserved in Siena, a two-part setting of the fourth Credo in the modern Roman liturgy, the so-called *Credo Cardinalis*. This is found in a chant book from the Palazzo Pubblico.[73] A gradual containing the music of Masses for the Proper of the Time and the Proper of Saints as well as a number of troped Glorias, it has magnificent illuminations executed by Memmo di Filipuccio between 1295 and 1300.[74] The *Credo Cardinalis,* in a reading that differs only slightly from other Italian sources, is appended to the main body of music.[75] In the Sienese version

71. The piece is discussed and transcribed by Giuseppe Vecchi in "Tra monodia e polifonia: Appunti da servire alla storia della melica sacra in Italia nel secolo XIII e al principio del XIV," *Collectanea Historiae Musicae* 2 (1956): 460–63.

72. The example here is after the transcription by Johannes Wolf, *Handbuch der Notationskunde* (Leipzig, 1913), 1:267–68.

73. The volume is now in BCIS, where it carries the signature MS H. I. 10. Its illuminations have been most recently discussed by Anna Maria Giusti in *Il Gotico a Siena,* no. 18, p. 73. A mensural version of the chant melody alone appears in vol. 20, fols. 128ᵛ–132ʳ, of AOMS.

74. It also contains a Mass proper for Corpus Christi, a feast authorized for universal celebration in 1264. Among the troped Glorias are those for the Mass "In minoribus festis duplicatis," on fol. 239ʳ; for the Mass "In maioribus semiduplicibus," on fol. 297ᵛ; and for the Mass on all feasts of the Virgin Mary, on fol. 306ʳ.

75. On fols. 321ᵛ–323ʳ. On the various sources preserving this version of the piece, as well as other polyphonic settings of the Credo IV melody, see Giulio Cattin, Oscar Mischiati, and Agostino Ziino, "Composizioni polifoniche del primo Quattrocento nei libri corali di Guardiagrele," *Rivista*

the original Gregorian melody, presented in measured phrases, is occasionally embellished by recurrent ornamental figures, especially at the frequent cadences, and the newly composed melody is set below the chant in a predominantly note-against-note style (see Ex. 2.4). The varied succession of perfect and imperfect consonances that results is not unlike the effect produced by the settings of the *Benedicamus* trope just cited, though here the harmony is more ordered and is clearly centered around the D mode of the original chant. The frequent halts at cadences undoubtedly derive from traditional improvisatory practices, to which the piece seems so closely allied. An essential difference, however, is that consonances in the written Credo were predetermined by the composer, who also sought to impose a certain unity—by repeating some phrases—as well as a certain variety, through the use of embellished cadences and changing harmonies. Although there is nothing to prove that the piece ever formed part of the cathedral's repertory, its presence in a manuscript from the Palace at the very least argues in favor of its having been performed in Siena.

THE FEAST OF SANT'ANSANO

In late medieval times an impressive body of text and music was created in honor of Siena's patron saint, Ansano. It consists of a rhymed office with antiphons, responsories, and hymns for Vespers, Matins, and Lauds as well as settings of the introit, gradual, Alleluia, offertory, and communion for the proper of the Mass on his feast day.[76] Little is known of the origins of these works, although internal evidence and other circumstances make it appear that they were put together long after the time that Ansano's feast day was elevated to major status at Siena cathedral. Neither the rhymed office nor the proper of the Mass was cited by Oderigo in the thirteenth century and they also went unmentioned in the later Sienese customary.[77] The earliest sources of both music and texts are all from more than a century after Oderigo's life. Compositional methods evident in many of the works as well as melodic idiosyncrasies and structural similarities indicate that they were conceived fairly closely in time and that some if not all of their materials were derived from previously composed pieces. The pieces of the rhymed office follow no set pattern in their modal order, yet another indication that they may have been taken from earlier works. Complementing the evidence of a later date is a governmental edict from 1325 that in effect made the feast of Sant'Ansano a national holiday, a move that found its parallel in the renovation and decoration of the chapel of

---

italiana di musicologia 7 (1962): 160–63 and 174–79, for a transcription which differs in a few respects from the one presented here. For late medieval Italian polyphonic settings of the Credo see Galliano Ciliberti, "Diffusione e trasmissione del Credo nelle fonti mensurali del tardomedioeveo (Nuove evidenze in Italia centrale)," *Musica Disciplina* 44 (1990): 57–97. Another setting of the *Credo Cardinalis* in *cantus planus binatim* is found at the end of a twelve-page manuscript addition to a copy of the *Graduale Romanum* published at Venice in 1515 by Giunta, now in the British Library, where it carries the shelf mark C. 35. 1. 2.

76. Some of the material presented here first appeared in D'Accone, "The Sienese Rhymed Office for the Feast of Sant'Ansano," *L'Ars Nova italiana del Trecento* 6 (1992): 21–40.

77. The later customary, BCIS, MS G. V. 9, omits the short Vigils service, but gives, in somewhat abbreviated fashion and with a slight change, the longer version of Matins, with six lessons from Ansano's *legenda* and the three from the homily of St. Remigius.

Sant'Ansano at the cathedral.[78] All of these factors suggest that the rhymed office and the Mass of Sant'Ansano were the products of a time when there was a resurgence of pride in Siena and its accomplishments and a desire to reaffirm the city's links to a golden past. In seeking a subject that glorified Siena's antiquity and its early embrace of Christianity, there was no better candidate than the noble Roman youth who had willingly given his life so that Christ's message might triumph, the saint for whose very relics Siena's sons had warred with neighboring Arezzo.

The Lessons and Ansano's Vita

Ansano and Siena's Roman origins are indissolubly linked in all of the traditional accounts of the city's early history.[79] These give the date of his martyrdom as 1 December 296, during the time of the Roman proconsul Lysius. The classical martyrologies make no mention of Ansano. His cult, however, is attested in Siena from very early times, and a church dedicated to him within city walls was already in existence in the mid-seventh century.[80] A fourteenth-century Sienese source preserves the earliest known *Vita* of Ansano.[81] It may have been based on the life of some other saint or saints, but no specific models have yet been unearthed. While Ansano's *Vita* is rather brief, the principal events of his life and martyrdom are vividly and dramatically narrated in the nine lessons read at Matins on his feast day. These tell how Ansanus, son of the noble Roman Tranquilinus, desired to be baptized at age twelve; how when he was baptized by Prothasius the room was filled with a sweet odor and the baptismal font flowed of its own accord; how at age seventeen, when he and his godmother Maxima[82] were brought before the emperors Diocletian and Maximian, he refused to acknowledge Jupiter and abjure Christ; how Maxima was martyred but Ansanus, with divine assistance, fled to Bagnorea, where he accomplished many miracles before removing to

------

78. Van der Ploeg, "Architectural and Liturgical Aspects," 143. He notes that from the thirteenth century Siena had begun to attach increasing importance to its patron saints, which led to the erection of altarpieces on the four patronal altars, the first commissioned from Simone Martini in 1329 for the altar of Sant'Ansano.

79. See, for example, Orlando Malavolti, *Dell'Historia di Siena* (Venice, 1594; repr. Bologna, 1982), 13.

80. *Prophylaeum ad Acta Sanctorum,* ed. Socii Bollandini, vol. 76: *Martyrologium Romanum* (Brussels, 1940), 558. See also Francesco Lanzoni, *Le diocesi d'Italia dalle origine al principio del sec. VII* (Faenza, 1927; repr. 1963), 1:564–65.

81. This is MS F. VI. 2 of the BCIS, which preserves the account of the saint's life on fols. 128ᵛ–129ʳ. Lusini places it in the fourteenth century. The manuscript, like most of the others from BCIS cited here, is listed by Lorenzo Ilari in his catalogue of the library's holdings, *La Biblioteca Pubblica di Siena* (Siena, 1844–48), 5:65. Here, two successive volumes are listed as MS F. VI. 2, but it is the second, described as a "Martyrologium per anni circulum. Sec. XIV. Ms in 4to di fog. 100 memb.," that contains the text in question. The same text was published by Étienne Beluze, *Stephani Baluzii Tutilensis Miscellanea nova ordine digesta* (Lucca, 1761–64), 4:63. A shorter *Vita* of Ansano is preserved in another Sienese manuscript from the fourteenth century, MS B. VII. 22 of the Biblioteca Queriniana in Brescia, fol. 158ᵛ. This source, once thought to have originated in the Augustinian monastery at Lecceto, is now believed to be of Franciscan origin. See Paolo Guerrini, "Un martirologo senese del Trecento nella Biblioteca Queriniana di Brescia," *BSSP* 40 (1940): 57–63.

82. The account of Maxima's martyrdom names Ansano.

Siena; how when the emperors were apprised of his having converted many of the Sienese, they ordered the Roman governor Lysius to have him put to death; how when Ansanus was placed in a burning oven, the flames were miraculously extinguished; and how he met his end when he was decapitated by Roman soldiers at a spot near the river Arbia.

All of the earliest sources preserving the texts of the lessons are now at the Biblioteca Comunale in Siena. The most complete and authoritative version is found in MS F. VIII. 12, a fourteenth-century breviary of Franciscan origin.[83] This has nine lessons and begins with the words "Refertur in divinis scripturis." Its text was published in 1764, with one notable error, in the fourth volume of Étienne Beluze's *Miscellanea novo ordine digesta*.[84] The same text appears also in a late thirteenth- or early fourteenth-century book of homilies and passions from the cathedral, MS G. I. 2.[85] Although the cathedral manuscript is the earliest of the known sources, it lacks a crucial passage in the ninth and final lesson. A shorter version of the text appears in another Franciscan breviary, MS X. IV. 2. This once belonged to the Poor Clares' convent in Siena and has illuminations by Sano di Pietro that have been dated variously from 1443 to 1480.[86] Its nine lessons contain the text of only the first five and one-half lessons of the principal source, and these, too, are not given in their entirety. It alone, moreover, lacks the opening words of the principal source.[87] An even more abbreviated version of the text is in an Augustinian breviary that carries a date of 1406, MS F. VII. 4.[88] Only six lessons are given here and they draw their materials, with omissions and variations, from the texts of the first three lessons in the principal source, the Franciscan breviary. An eighteenth-century copy of the complete text, apparently derived from the Franciscan breviary, is in MS B. X. 8.[89] There are, in addition, several translations of the lessons into Italian. The earliest is an eighteenth-century copy, MS C. VI. 8, which is said to have been

83. Ilari, *La Biblioteca Pubblica di Siena*, 5:67, where it is described as "Ordo Breviarii Fratrum Minorum etc. Cod. membranaceo in piccolo 4to del Secolo XIV. di carte residue 588; malconcio dall'uso e con qualche mancanza; nondimeno le Lezioni dell'Officio della Traslazione di S. Ansano M., posto a fog. 577, credo che possono essere di qualche interesse per la Storia sacra e profana nella nostra Città." The Office for the feast of Sant'Ansano is on fols. 573ᵛ–576ʳ, and the first two sets of lessons for the feast of his Translation begin on fol. 577ʳ, the second one ending on fol. 581ᵛ.

84. Vol. 4, pp. 60–67.

85. Lusini, *Il Duomo di Siena*, 2:257, assigns it to the first or oldest series of cathedral volumes.

86. Ilari, *La Biblioteca Pubblica di Siena*, 5:68; Gino Garosi, *Inventario dei manoscritti della Biblioteca Comunale di Siena* (Florence, 1978–86), 1:23–33. The manuscript is also discussed by Daniele Benati, no. 145, *Breviarium fratrum minorum*, in *Il Gotico a Siena*, 403–4, where an up-to-date bibliography is given.

87. All but one of the known Latin sources of the text begin with these words. The exception is BCIS, MS. X. IV. 2, which begins with the fifth sentence of the principal source, BCIS, F. VIII. 12, and of BCIS, G. I. 2, "Imperante Diocletiano et Maximiano in urbe. . . ."

88. Ilari, *La Biblioteca Pubblica di Siena*, 5:67–68.

89. Ibid., 5:76, says it is a collection of documents, records, and copies from the sixteenth through eighteenth centuries; the title of BCIS, MS B. X. 8 is: *Opusculi e Memorie di molto rilievo*. The section with Ansano's lessons begins on fol. 233ʳ and is headed: "Ex Breviario Miniato sec XIV in Arch. Metr. Ecc. Sen."; in the upper left-hand corner is the annotation: "Correctiones et Additiones sunt ex Passionali magno Ms sec XIII ibidem." It begins: "Lectio prima; Refertur in scripturis Divinis,"

taken from a fourteenth-century original in the library of the Chigi family.[90] Another Italian translation, virtually indistinguishable from the eighteenth-century copy, is one that was used by the members of the Sienese Company of Sant'Ansano for their services, MS A. XI. 25. This evidently dates from 1474, the date appended to the Company's Statutes which precede the lessons in the manuscript.[91]

The text of the ninth lesson, as presented in the main source, MS F. VIII. 12, is of great importance because it helps to establish when the liturgy for Sant'Ansano took definitive form. After recounting details of the saint's martyrdom on 1 December "in the year of Our Lord 296" it ends with the statement that "984 years have gone by since Ansano received the martyr's crown in Siena's fortress."[92] This leaves no doubt that the last lesson, or at least its conclusion, was written in the year 1280. And since the events of the saint's life and martyrdom as they are recounted in the nine lessons furnish the basis of the texts for the antiphons, hymns, and responsories of the rhymed office on his feast day, it is likely that the music was composed or compiled after that time.

Information provided by Oderigo supports the later date. He mentions the lessons twice in his description of the liturgy for Ansano's feast day, first when he notes that three lessons from the saint's *legenda* were read at a Vigils service on the evening before and then when he reports that at Matins six lessons from Ansano's *passio* were read. He says these began with the words "Refertur in scripturis divinis," and that they were followed by three lessons from the homilies of St. Remigius on *Nihil opertum,* the gospel of the day (part 1, chap. 296). Since no readings of the lessons from Oderigo's time are extant, it is impossible to ascertain whether the six he mentions were the same as those found in later manuscripts, although—allowing for minor discrepancies—it seems reasonable to assume that they were. In any case knowledge that Oderigo cites six rather than nine lessons suggests that the saint's *legenda* was enlarged and elaborated upon

---

and on fol. 236ᵛ says, at the crucial dating passage, "et hic sunt C/VIIII anni quibus Ansanus corona martiri suscepit in oppido Senensi."

90. The lessons, preceded by the rubric "Incomincia la Leggenda di Sancto Ansano martire nella Città di Siena," are on pp. 191–202 of BCIS, MS C. VI. 8. A note at the bottom of p. 202, in a different hand, says "Questa leggenda sembra estratta da un codice della Chigiana segnato Mo Misc. del secolo XIV postillata dal Celso Cittadini." The translation follows the Latin version of BCIS, MS. F. VIII. 12 quite closely and the only major difference is the ending of the ninth lesson. This makes no mention of the year in which Ansano was martyred. Another Italian version of Ansano's life, highly elaborated, is in a volume entitled *Leggende de' Santi,* in the Vatican Library, Rome, MS Barb. Lat. 4065, fols. 10ʳ–12ᵛ. Various eighteenth-century copies of the *Vita* in BCIS are of lesser importance.

91. Described in Garosi, *Inventario dei manoscritti,* 3:278–81. *Capitoli della Compagnia di S. Ansano,* written in a hand different from the previous ones; on fol. 38ʳ, the *Vita,* preceded by a short preamble, begins: "Questa è la vita del nostro padre S. Ansano: Se gli huomini che in questa vita con militari o literali exerciti si sono affatichati per lassar dopo di loro una caduca fama, sono stati dali scriptori celebrati . . . Dico adunque che Imperanti i Diocletiano et Maximiliano imperatori ne la cipta di Roma."

92. The whole passage in MS F. VIII. 12 of BCIS reads as follows: "Currebant autem tunc anni Domini a Nativitate CCLXXXXVI, et sic sunt VIIIILXXXIIII anni quibus beatus Ansanus coronam martirii suscepit in oppido Senensi." Both eighteenth-century sources, Beluze, *Miscellanea novo ordine digesta,* 4:63, and MS B. X. 8, mistranscribed the date, as 9 and 900 years, respectively.

during the course of the thirteenth century and that it assumed definitive form around or after 1280, the date mentioned in the ninth lesson of the principal source.

The Early Thirteenth-Century Liturgy

Oderigo's account of the feast of Sant'Ansano is noteworthy also for the light it throws on the development and date of the liturgy for the saint's day as it appears in later sources. He begins by noting that the cathedral gloried in its possession of the saint's relics and that his feast day had been celebrated there with great devotion since ancient times (chap. 295). It was, of course, one of the cathedral's major feasts and was observed with all of the special honors accorded such occasions, among them multiple bell ringings, doubled antiphons, and performances of polyphony at Vespers, Matins, and Lauds.[93] In addition, a short Vigils service, or service of one nocturn, as Oderigo called it in another place, was held on the evening before the feast day, as was customary for saints whose relics were kept at the cathedral.[94] Polyphony was also prescribed for that service. Despite this, there were as yet very few texts dedicated to Ansano in the Sienese liturgy. At First Vespers, for example, the psalms and antiphons were drawn from the previous day's feast of St. Andrew, while the hymn and the Magnificat antiphon were those of the feast of the Common of One Martyr. The invitatory, antiphons, psalms, and responsories for the short Vigils service, where the three lessons from Ansano's *legenda* were read, were also from the feast of One Martyr, and the only text with specific reference to the saint was the verse *Ora pro nobis beate Ansane* that was said after the *Te Deum laudamus*.[95]

The same situation held for the longer services when Matins and Lauds were celebrated in their entirety at the normal hours. At Matins, where six lessons from the saint's *legenda* were read, the responsories and verses were those from the Common of One Martyr. At Lauds texts from One Martyr and from St. Andrew's feast predominated, though the verse after the hymn, which was also from the Common of One Martyr, was the just mentioned *Ora pro nobis beate Ansane*. The antiphons at Prime and

---

93. From Oderigo's account of the liturgy for Sant'Ansano and remarks elsewhere in the *OO*, it appears that the following items were sung in polyphony at services on that day: At First Vespers the hymn *Deus tuorum militum;* the Magnificat antiphon *Iste est, qui pro lege Dei sui,* both before and afterwards, ending with a melisma (p. 273); the responsory *Domine praevenisti,* after the chapter *Juxtum deduxit* (p. 391, feasts with doubled antiphons); *Benedicamus Domino* (p. 393, feasts of saints whose relics we have in our church). At Matins, *Te Deum laudamus* (p. 274); at Lauds the antiphon *Iste est,* before the *Benedictus,* finished with a melisma (p. 274). Elsewhere (p. 390), Oderigo cites the feast of Sant'Ansano among those with antiphons sung in their entirety both before and after psalms (doubled) at Vespers, Matins, and Lauds that were sung without organum; furthermore, if the feast fell on a Sunday, the antiphon was not repeated because the Sunday antiphon was said instead.

94. At the short Vigils service, the invitatory, *Aeterni Patris,* and the psalm, *Venite,* were done throughout in organum by the cantor and two others, as were the responsories, *Iste Sanctus* and *Domine praevenisti,* sung after the first two lessons; the repetition of the antiphon *Iste est* after the Benedictus and the *Benedicamus Domino* were also sung in organum (*OO,* 274).

95. The text of the verse and its response are prescribed for the commemoration of Sant'Ansano in a fifteenth-century volume that once belonged to one of Siena's religious companies. See note 99, item (2), below.

the remaining canonical hours as well as at Second Vespers were those of Lauds, and again, no texts addressed to the saint were prescribed. In fact, Oderigo mentions only two additional prayers in which the saint is named, both occurring as commemorations during the week leading to the octave of his feast (chap. 291). These are the antiphons *Sancte Ansane, Martyr Christi pretiose, adesto nostris precibus pius, ac propitius* for Lauds and *Ora pro nobis Beate Ansane* for Second Vespers.[96] In summary, though it seems strange in view of the importance accorded the feast, there were very few texts in the cathedral's liturgy at the turn of the thirteenth century that made special reference to Ansano. What few there were, moreover, have survived without their musical settings, a circumstance implying that they went into complete disuse when the old liturgy for Sant'Ansano was superseded by a newer one.

The later Sienese customary, in many respects an abbreviated redaction of Oderigo's work, indicates that the liturgy for Ansano's feast described by Oderigo in 1215 prevailed throughout the rest of the thirteenth century and perhaps well into the next.[97] Although it omits the short Vigils service, it gives in a somewhat perfunctory fashion, and with a slight change, the longer version of Matins, with six lessons from Ansano's *legenda* and the three from the homily of St. Remigius specified by Oderigo. Clearly, the last three lessons, codified in 1280, had yet to be incorporated into the service by the early fourteenth century, the presumed date of this later customary.

The New Fourteenth-Century Liturgy

A decree issued on 24 October 1325 by the Consiglio Generale, Siena's principal lawmaking body, represents a move on the part of the government to transform the feast of Sant'Ansano into a major civic holiday. Henceforth, all citizens were to refrain from working on that day, and government officials would be obliged to attend services at the cathedral, where they were to make offerings of wax candles, apparently in ceremonies modeled on those of Assumption Day. The symbolism of the ceremony and its political

---

96. Oderigo also explains that if the octave were to occur on the first Sunday of Advent, the texts of the season were to be given precedence, as he had already specified for the feast of St. Andrew.

97. BCIS, MS G. V. 9 contains the text of the later Ordo. The volume is listed in Ilari, *La Biblioteca Pubblica di Siena,* 5:74, where it is described as a fourteenth-century copy, lacking certain sections, of Oderigo's customary. I view the contents somewhat differently, though I believe an early fourteenth-century date to be correct. Van der Ploeg, *Art, Architecture and Liturgy,* 121, 135–45, dates the manuscript from the beginning of the fourteenth century. He gives a physical description and analysis of it and demonstrates that it is a volume mentioned in Cathedral inventories from 1409 onwards, the third of three customaries, including Oderigo's and a second one that does not survive. Van der Ploeg notes (p. 137) that while the script allows for a dating no earlier than the second half of the thirteenth century, the decoration and especially the decorated initial point to the period 1300–10. The passage in MS G. V. 9 regarding the feast of Sant'Ansano, on fol. 55ʳ, reads as follows: "In Kalendis decembris festum beati Ampsani celebratur in vigilia ad Vesperum Antiphona super psalmo de Apostolo, Salve crux et cetera. Capitulum: Iuxta deduxit. Responsorium: Dominum prevenisti. Ynnus: Deus tuorum. Versiculus: Gloria et honor. Antiphona ad Magnificat: Iste est qui pro lege. Oratio: Propitiare. Postea Antiphona et Oratio De Apostolo. Ad Matutinum Invitatorium: Regem martirum. Ynnus: Deus tuorum. Vi lectiones de Passione eius que sic Incipit: Refertur. III ultime de Omelia: Nihil opertum. Antiphona, Versiculum et Responsorium: De Uno martire cantetur."

overtones would, of course, have been understood by all. For though it was ostensibly an act of devotion made to a heavenly protector, as on Assumption Day, in reality it was an act of fealty to the Sienese state. There is no reason to believe that the government's decree was meant to detract from the importance accorded Assumption Day festivities, which indeed would assume even grander dimensions with the passing of time. Rather, the party of the Nine was seeking to institute another national holiday whose exclusively Sienese origins would instill a sense of patriotism among the citizenry, paying tribute as it did to the city's venerable Christian heritage, to its antiquity, and to its indisputable links to Rome. The text of the opening of the decree reads as follows:

> For the celebration of the feast of the blessed Ansano
> each year in perpetuity
> In honor of the blessed Ansano and in exaltation of his most holy name, his holy feast shall be celebrated with great devotion each year in perpetuity in the city of Siena, with all Sienese citizens being obliged to abstain from any form of manual labor whatsoever. And the podestà or his vicar, the captains, the Nine Lords, and the other officials of the same city who serve at the pleasure of the Nine Lords are obliged to go and venerate the blessed Ansano on his feast day with appropriate candles. The offerings that are made by the abovesaid government and officials must then be handed over to whomever is overseer of the Opera of the glorious Virgin at that time.[98]

Although the groundwork was thus laid for the saint's feast day to become another of the city's major holidays, this was not to be the case. The December festivities in honor of Ansano never assumed a position in Sienese life comparable to those of the Assumption Day celebrations in August. Part of the reason for this may have been the weather—December is a cold month in Siena, hardly conducive to the reception of throngs of visitors, processions, pageants, and the entertainments out of doors that marked observance of the August feast. Then, too, festivities dedicated to a saint of purely local significance may not have had the same appeal as those devoted to the more universally venerated Virgin Mother of God. There are, as will be noted below, reports showing that some groups, such as the cathedral's confraternity of laudesi, responded to the edict by instituting special services, but these were done primarily for members rather than for the townspeople or for visitors. In any case the new program

---

98. ASS, Consiglio Generale, vol. 103, fols. 95ʳ–95ᵛ: "Pro festivitate Beati Ansani annuatim in perpetuum veneranda. Ad reverentiam Beati Ansani et exaltationem sui nominis sanctissimi, anno quolibet in perpetuum eius sancta solempnitas in civitate Senarum devotissime celebretur, omnibus civibus Senarum ab omni opere servili cessantibus. Et quod teneantur dominus potestas seu vicarius, capitanei, domini Novem et alii ordines civitatis Senarum et alii officiales forenses civitatis predicte, qui videbuntur et placebunt offitio dominorum Novem, in die festivitatis eiusdem Beatum Ansanum cum luminariis decentibus venerari. Oblationes vero que tunc deferentur per regimina et officiales predictos perveniant et pervenire debeant ad manus operarii opere Virginis gloriose qui pro tempore fuerit." The document is referred to by Bowsky, *A Medieval Italian Commune*, 263. See pp. 275–77 of the same study for Bowsky's report of earlier efforts by the government of the Nine to endow Assumption Day festivities with greater importance, particularly a decree of 30 October 1309 ordering the closure of the city's shops on that day.

for Ansano's feast day—even though it eventually did not live up to the expectations of its promotors—would have called for musical services at the cathedral befitting a holiday of major importance.

The Rhymed Office

Perhaps the new liturgy in Sant'Ansano's honor took final and definitive form in response to the government's action. Based on the saint's *legenda,* which by then had nine lessons, it included a complete rhymed office for Vespers, Matins, and Lauds and a Mass proper. Extant sources suggest that although the new liturgy was adopted at the cathedral and a few other places, it was never very widely diffused and that it was put aside after the mid-sixteenth century, perhaps in response to liturgical reforms enacted by the Council of Trent. The earliest and most complete textual source of the rhymed office is the fourteenth-century Franciscan breviary, MS F. VIII. 12, mentioned above.[99] This presents in ordered succession all of the hymns, antiphons, psalms, and responsories for Vespers, Matins, and Lauds.[100] Two volumes of Sienese origin preserve musical settings of these items. The earlier of the two is Ospedale MS 9 (olim 89-I), a mid-fifteenth-

---

99. Among volumes that preserve parts of the office are the following, all in BCIS:

(1) MS F. VII. 1, Breviarium romanum, sec. XIV, discussed by Lusini, *Il Duomo di Siena,* 2:257, who says the volume once belonged to the cathedral. The principal prayer to Sant'Ansano, though added to the margin at the bottom of fol. 60^r, is also written in a fourteenth-century hand: "Celestis gratie quas Domine largire nobis dignare suffragium ut qui fidei lumen beato Ansano martire devote ministrante percepimus apud tuam clementiam ipso intercedente salvemur." The second prayer is on fol. 112^r: "In festo beati Ansani Martiris Oratio: Propitiare nobis quis domine famulis tuis per huius sancti martiris tui Ansani qui in presente requiescit ecclesie mente gloriosa ut eius pia intercessione ab omnibus semper protegamur adversis." This is probably the prayer mentioned by Oderigo as occurring after the *Benedictus* canticle at Lauds, which, he says, began: *Propitiare.* Another prayer, not from MS F. VII. 1: "Mentibus nostris, quaesumus Domine, caelestis gratie tribue largitatem: ut, qui fidelium beati Ansanis martiris tui praedicatione susecepimus; ipso pro nobis intercedente, aeterna gaudia consequamur."

(2) MS F. VII. 12, Libro di compagnia, sec. XV, fol. 62^v: "Commemoratione di Santo Sano: V Ora pro nobis beate Ansane R Ut digni efficiamur promissionibus Christi. Oratio: Celestis gratie quas Domine. . . ."

(3) MS F. VII. 10, Libro di compagnia, sec. XV, fol. 69^v: "Incominciano le commemorationi delle feste . . . [fol. 70^r]: Di Sancto Ansano martire: Antiphona Qui vult venire post me . . . et sequatur me. V Iustus ut palma florebit. R Sicut cedrus libani multiplicatitur. Oratio: Celestis gratie . . . intercedente salvemur."

(4) MS F. VI. 13, a fifteenth-century antiphonary, has Ansano's feast added to the calendar by a later hand; a later hand also added the text of the prayer *Celestis gratie* to the original guard sheet.

A number of breviaries from the cathedral now preserved in BCIS are of interest because Ansano's feast is listed in their calendars, though none of them has texts of the office. They are listed by Lusini, *Il Duomo di Siena,* 2:257. Among them are four fourteenth-century Roman breviaries: MSS F. VII. 2 (fol. 7^v), F. VII. 7, F. VIII. 2, and F. VIII. 11. A fragment of another volume in BCIS, whose provenance is unknown, also lists Ansano's feast in its calendar. This is MS F. VII. 6, Breviarium romanum, sec. XIV, fol. 6^r.

100. The texts of the rhymed office are printed in Beluze's *Miscellanea novo ordine digesta,* 4:60–67; the texts of the antiphons, responsories, and hymns are published by Clemens Blume and Guido M. Dreves, eds., *Analecta Hymnica Medii Aevi* (Leipzig, 1886–1922), 22:36–38.

century antiphonary from the hospital of Santa Maria della Scala now at the cathedral Opera.[101] It has illuminations by Fra Benedetto da Siena that are said to date from 1473; if this is so, the music must have been copied no more than a decade or two earlier. A somewhat later source is Cathedral, MS 11. M (olim 25), the antiphonary mentioned in Lusini's third series which is on permanent display in the cathedral's Libreria Piccolomini. As noted above, this was copied shortly after August 1480 by Don Benedetto di Maestro Paolo Rinaldi and has illuminations by Pellegrino di Mariano from less than two years later.[102] The hospital antiphonary is mutilated and lacks the music of the first two antiphons and a part of the third antiphon for First Vespers. Its fourth and fifth antiphons, furthermore, are different from those found in the cathedral antiphonary, an indication, evidently, of the unsettled state of the liturgy even in its last phase. A less important, though earlier, musical source is MS I. I. 6 of the Biblioteca Comunale, an antiphonary compiled for a Sienese convent in the late thirteenth century with some early fourteenth-century additions.[103] Among the latter are the three hymns to Sant'Ansano from Vespers, Matins, and Lauds. The same works appear in a hymnary from Santa Maria della Scala, Ospedale MS 25 (olim 105–11), another volume now at the cathedral Opera. It, too, has illuminations by Pellegrino da Mariano, these dating from 1475. A third hospital volume at the Opera is Ospedale MS 14 (olim 94-P), a fourteenth-century antiphonary that contains the Matins invitatory antiphon *Regi nobiscum Senis advocatum Ansanum*.[104]

The sources suggest that the hymns and the invitatory are among the oldest items of the rhymed office for Sant'Ansano. While their brevity and the restricted ranges of their melodies are typical of much of the music in the cycle, they do not share the frequent repetition of motives and phrases that is a hallmark of the more numerous antiphons and responsories. The hymns, as was customary, are set strophically, the music of the first stanza serving for all subsequent ones. *Martyr Ansane,* for First Vespers, consists of seven stanzas in Sapphic adonic meter (see Ex. 2.5). Its melody, in an F mode with strong Ionian tendencies, is simple but attractive and closely follows the structure of the text. The first three lines, set to phrases of almost similar length, are closed off by a short final phrase employing the interval of a descending fifth to the tonic, which recalls the descent previously heard in the first phrase. *Aeterna nutu baiulans,* for Matins, has four stanzas, each of four lines, in iambic dimeter (see Ex. 2.6). The phrase that sets the first line, firmly establishing the D Dorian mode, is only slightly longer than the three following, though all are predominantly syllabic, marked by an occasional brief

101. Listed by Morandi and Cairoli, "Dall'inventario del 1900. I libri corali," 168–69.

102. The manuscript is discussed as one of those in the series initiated by the overseer Savino Savini and continued by the overseer Alberto Aringhieri by Lusini, *Il Duomo di Siena,* 2:322–25, where relevant documents are also printed. A recent description of the volume is in Ciardi Dupré, *I corali del Duomo di Siena,* 43.

103. *Il gotico a Siena,* 75 notes that the last three additions to MS I. I. 6—among which are the hymns to Sant'Ansano—are in different hands, but gives the date of the illuminations as from ca. 1285–90.

104. Ospedale MS 25 is listed in Morandi and Cairoli, "Dall'inventario del 1900," 172–73; Ospedale MS 14 is cited on pp. 170–71 of the same volume.

melisma. The melodic high point on B-flat, a sixth above the final, is reached early on by stepwise motion, at the beginning of the second phrase. Subsequently, the remaining phrases hover around the A dominant of the mode before beginning a descent to the conclusion on the D final.

The most attractive and musically ambitious of the hymns is *Ansani vita* for Lauds (see Ex. 2.7). This has four stanzas of four lines, which are actually two divided Sapphic lines. The setting is primarily syllabic, though brief melismas appear in each of the four phrases. These are again of almost nearly equal length, the first firmly establishing the F mode on which the piece concludes. The four phrases that set the four lines of the somewhat more florid invitatory, *Regi nobiscum,* are less well balanced but more varied tonally, as the music moves from an initial C to successive phrase endings on D, E, and C before settling on the D final of the mode (see Ex. 2.8). Not even the slightest recall of a motive is apparent here. As with the hymns, the absence of repetition as a unifying element of structure serves to set these pieces apart from others in the rhymed office for Sant'Ansano and suggests that they were composed separately, if not beforehand, thus supporting the evidence of the sources.

Appearing as they do throughout the office, antiphons are the most prominent of the pieces in honor of Sant'Ansano. There are twenty-four of them in all: five for the psalms at First Vespers and a sixth for the Magnificat; nine in all for Matins, three for as many psalms in each of the three nocturns; five for the psalms and a sixth for the Benedictus canticle at Lauds; another for the Magnificat at Second Vespers; and two additional works, alternate settings for the fourth and fifth antiphons for First Vespers. (These latter, as mentioned, offer another indication of the unsettled state of the rhymed office for Sant'Ansano, even in what was presumably its last phase.) The text for all but three of the antiphons consists of a single stanza of four lines, with the rhyme occurring between the second and fourth lines. Similar rhyme schemes are found in the antiphons for the Magnificat and the Benedictus, but these have two stanzas instead of one. As a group, the antiphons have a number of features in common and they share some of these with the less numerous responsories. In all pieces, antiphons and responsories alike, a phrase of music normally corresponds to a line of text.

The antiphons are characterized by simplicity of structure and clarity of mode. Of the twenty-four, eight are in mode 1, one in mode 2, one in mode 3, two in mode 4, four in mode 5, two in mode 6, and six in mode 7. This unequal distribution, resulting from the prominence of modes 1 and 7, obviates the possibility that the cycle of pieces in the rhymed office for Sant'Ansano was composed in an ordered sequence of modes. This was the more usual procedure during the earliest centuries of rhymed office composition, when such pieces were set successively to one of the church modes beginning with the first, to which a return was made after the eighth. Taken in the order in which they appear, all of the pieces for Sant'Ansano—invitatory, antiphons, hymns, responsories—have no semblance of modal order, which is perhaps the most convincing argument for supposing that they are late medieval reworkings of earlier pieces, altered and reshaped so as to accommodate the new texts in honor of the Sienese saint. It is possible, however, that failure to observe strict adherence to modal order was not simply a matter of contrafacture and recomposition, but rather represented another approach to creating a rhymed office. Many of the pieces make use of a compositional process known as centonization, whereby stock melodic formulas and phrases were strung together to create an entirely new work, and it may be that herein lies one possible explanation of their origins.

In general, the antiphons for Sant'Ansano use incipits and modal formulas that are as modally distinct as those of the standard repertory, a typical feature of chants of the thirteenth-century rhymed office.[105] Other features of the latter, including strong internal cadences, phrase endings marked by textual rhyme, and transferral of whole sections or of individual phrases from one piece to another, are also apparent on a number of occasions. Prominent as well are cadential patterns in which the last note of a phrase, generally the final or another important tone, is approached from above and then repeated. This is in contrast to other late rhymed office antiphons, where the last note is more often reached from below. Likewise, the wide ranges, chromatic alterations, and temporary or permanent modulations from one mode to another that are also found in late antiphons are altogether lacking in the Sienese pieces.

The antiphons for Sant'Ansano begin like chants in the standard Gregorian repertory, though they continue differently. The majority of them are short, balanced compositions, distinguished structurally by the repetition of brief motives or entire phrases. Melodies unfold within a limited range, often less than an octave, and have a tendency to hover around a central tone, normally the final of the mode. The antiphons are always designed so as to fit gracefully with the psalms they frame. Intonations of the standard psalm formulas of the Gregorian repertory appear frequently—the second and the fifth are favorites—sometimes at the beginning of the antiphon, but more often internally. The first antiphon for First Vespers, *Ansanus Romae,* offers a good example of the compositional procedure evident in a number of others (see Ex. 2.9). Here, the first two phrases, alternately melismatic and syllabic, flow imperceptibly one into the other. Beginning on the D final of the mode, the melody rises to the dominant A, while stating twice a short motive that recalls the intonation formula of the first psalm tone. After reiterating the dominant, a stepwise descent to the final concludes the setting of the first couplet. The melody of the second couplet stresses D and F before ascending by step to the high point of an arch on B, and as it does so, it makes use of the same intonation formula. The piece closes with the phrase previously used to conclude the first couplet, thus emphasizing the textual rhyme. As might be expected, the psalm following, *Dixit Dominus,* is in the first mode.

Actually, *Ansanus Romae* is less typical than many of the others because it is somewhat longer and has fewer repetitions. A more representative example of the procedure is furnished by *Ansanus cum Maxima,* the fourth of the Matins antiphons (see Ex. 2.10).

---

105. Much of this material originally appeared in D'Accone, "The Sienese Rhymed Office for the Feast of Sant'Ansano," 21–40. Two studies by Andrew Hughes, "Modal Order and Disorder in 13th-century Rhymed Offices," *Musica Disciplina* 38 (1983): 29–51, and "Chants in the Rhymed Office of St. Thomas of Canterbury," *Early Music* 16 (1988): 185–201, have proved most useful to me, and I take this opportunity to thank Prof. Hughes for having shared his wide knowledge of the repertory with me and for searching through his computerized files of thirteenth-century rhymed offices for possible contrafacta or prototypes of these Sienese pieces, none of which can yet be linked to earlier works.

The final is G of mode 7 and the melody encompasses the range of a sixth, though in truth it does little more than flutter around the D dominant except for the ending on G at "fideles" and "crudeles." This exemplifies a kind of antecedent–consequent effect, strengthened here by a slight variation in the repeated phrase, that is characteristic of phrase structure in several pieces in the set. Another representative antiphon is the second one at Matins, *Imperantes respuens* (see Ex. 2.11). It has a final on D, the range of an octave from A to A, and, predictably, it frames the psalm, *Quare fremuerunt,* in tone 2. Here the intonation of the psalm formula for tone 2, which begins the first phrase, appears only incidentally in the second phrase and then recurs in the fourth. Although the latter is not an outright repetition of the second phrase, enough is there to recall it.

Exaudi nos, the fourth antiphon at Lauds, has a G final and encompasses the interval of a seventh (see Ex. 2.12). A leap of a fourth—unusual in these works, but here clearly derived from the intonation formula of tone 8—introduces the first phrase, which ends with an appoggiatura-like figure on the notes F, A, A, G. The next phrase begins with this figure transposed up a third to end on B, and with a slight modification the same figure is then stated twice, the second time so that the word "autor" ends on the dominant note D, the melodic high point on E having meantime been attained. The opening of the second couplet retraces the high point on E and then descends to the G final before proceeding to the last phrase, whose close is a slightly altered version of the appoggiatura figure on G, previously used to end the first phrase.

The antiphons with two stanzas exhibit similar compositional methods. *Ad civitatem balneum,* which frames the Magnificat at Second Vespers and is thus the last piece in the set, is a model of economy of construction, despite its greater length (see Ex. 2.13). Its first two phrases establish the first mode on D and include the first of two ascents to a high point on the dominant A. The two phrases also contain most of the materials that appear throughout the rest of the piece. The third phrase begins with a reference to the latter part of the second before proceeding on its own, and though the fourth phrase begins independently enough, it soon recalls materials from the first and second; likewise the fifth phrase, which, after its initial note, picks up most of the material of the third. The sixth—though reaching a high point on C—and the seventh phrases borrow heavily from portions of the fourth, itself derived from the first two phrases, and the eighth is simply the second with one new note substituting for the two opening notes of the original phrase. Notable in *Ad civitatem balneum* is the appearance of material previously used in the very first antiphon, *Ansanus Romae,* whose second phrase, but for one note, and whose closing phrase are the same as those heard in the last antiphon. Transferral of materials from piece to piece, of course, serves as a unifying factor for the set and lends credence to the idea that most, if not all, of the pieces in the rhymed office for Sant'Ansano were composed at the same time.

The process of phrase transferral finds full expression in *Sub mandatis angeli,* the Magnificat antiphon for First Vespers (see Exs. 2.14a and b). Like its prototype *Exaudi nos,* it is in a G mode, has the range of a seventh, and reaches a high point on E twice during the course of its development. Its first phrase reproduces exactly the first phrase of the shorter piece, which itself was characterized by internal repetition. Internal repetition, however, is even more substantial in *Sub mandatis angeli,* for its third and last phrases derive from its first phrase and this also furnishes materials for most of its second phrase. Some variety is provided by the fourth phrase, which begins independently before turning in on itself. With a few minor adjustments, the next four phrases are direct, though differently ordered, quotations of the first four. The piece thus gains a kind of aural unity that is immediately appealing and the unpredictable repetition of materials demonstrates that whatever borrowings there may be in this music, they have been thoroughly assimilated into the compositional process, melodically as well as structurally. In the accompanying examples *Sub mandatis angeli* is illustrated twice, the music of the second example arranged to show the irregular repetition patterns, which occur without regard to phrase structure or to rhyme.

Each of the nine responsories follows one of the lessons, which are read in groups of three at the three nocturns of Matins. The texts of the responsories are in two sections, a longer respond comprised of six lines, with the rhyme occurring on the even lines, followed by the shorter verse of four lines, with a different rhyme, again occurring on the even lines. As was customary, the musical score indicates a return at the end of the verse to the text and music of the last two lines of the responsory. The first mode on D and the seventh on G are again favored, with three settings in each, while the fifth on F appears twice, and the third on E once. This last is the mode of the opening responsory, *Ansanus cum Maxima*, which displays the same technique of repetition evident in many of the antiphons (see Ex. 2.15). The first and second phrases are set to new materials, but the third partakes of both before proceeding independently. The fourth is drawn from the second and the fifth is derived from the first, though it has a different cadence. The sixth makes reference to the second, whose cadence it reproduces. Thus in the respond the phrases that set the rhyming lines all share similar materials, though the fourth ends differently than the second and sixth. Repetition of phrases also reinforces the rhyme scheme of the verse. Both the first and third phrases have completely new material. But the second phrase, based to a certain extent on the first, twice furnishes the materials that make up the fourth.

A different approach to the use of repeated materials is evident in the second responsory of the first nocturn, *Vir iniquos intuens* (see Ex. 2.16). Here each of the six lines of the respond has its own phrase of music and there is no notable repetition except at the very end, where the closing notes of the fourth phrase appear as the last part of the last phrase, which closes on the G final of mode 7. The phrases that set the four lines of the verse, however, tell a different story. The first three embroider on parts or on the whole of the second and third phrases of the respond and only the last is independent, though this is illusory because it, too, refers, however fleetingly, to the same phrases of the respond.

Not all of the responsories exhibit such cohesive structures, though transferral of materials between pairs of pieces occurs twice. In each instance, as might be expected, the pieces are in the same mode. Both *Nostros deos colite,* the first responsory of the second nocturn, and *Non vos huc adduximus,* the first responsory of the third nocturn, are in mode 1 and end on D (see Exs. 2.17 and 2.18). All four phrases of their verses are identical, as are several of those of their responds. *Nostros deos colite,* however, has a few more melismatic passages and reaches its high point on C only toward the end of respond, whereas the climax of *Non vos huc adduximus* occurs very near the beginning, when the melody soars to the D an octave above the opening note. It is virtually impossible to tell which was composed first and this is true as well of the second pair of pieces, both in the seventh mode on G, *Nostra vox instrepuit,* the second responsory of the second nocturn, and *Tu probasti, Domine,* the third responsory of the third nocturn (see Exs. 2.19 and 2.20). These, too, have virtually identical verses. There are fewer corresponding passages between their responds, though some phrases of *Nostra vox instrepuit* give the impression of being distillations of those in the more expansive *Tu probasti, Domine.* The recurrence of blocks of materials in both pairs of pieces offers yet another reason for believing that the rhymed office for Sant'Ansano was created in a single place and at the same time.

The Mass

Oderigo furnishes very little information about Masses celebrated at Siena cathedral on the feast of Sant'Ansano. He notes that the introit, *Laetabitur justus,* the epistle, *Beatus vir,* and the gospel, *Nihil opertum,* were said at one of the earlier ones and that the major Mass "of the Martyr" was celebrated later, at the usual hour, by the officiating priest with the deacon and subdeacon (chap. 296). Elsewhere, he reports that the proper of the Mass for the feast of "One Martyr in nine lessons," as Ansano's was designated, included the introit *Laetabitur justus,* the epistle *Beatus vir,* the gradual *Justus ut palma,* the Alleluia with its verse *Posuisti,* and the gospel *Nihil opertum* (chap. 446). At this service, as was customary on feasts of such high rank, the cantor and two others performed the Alleluia in organum. Oderigo's failure to mention the incipits of the offertory and the communion is probably an indication that they, too, were drawn from the Mass for the Common of One Martyr. More important, his remarks point to an obvious parallel with the office for Sant'Ansano and suggest there were few if any texts in the proper that were specifically addressed to the saint at that time.

Extant musical sources for the proper of the Mass of Sant'Ansano illustrate the changeover in Siena from an earlier form to a later one. The earlier form, perhaps a replacement for Oderigo's that I shall call "the old proper," is found in the chant book from the cathedral mentioned earlier, MS 42-N.[106] An illumination of the saint kneeling as he adores the Redeemer appears at the beginning of the section that presents the music for the introit *Laetabitur justus,* the gradual *Gloria et honore,* the Alleluia and its verse *O Ansane gloriose,* and the offertory *In virtute tua.* As noted above, the manuscript has been mutilated after the opening passage of this last piece, and the communion, which normally follows, is also lacking. Except for the Alleluia, the same texts and music are prescribed as suitable for the Common of One Martyr in several contemporaneous or near contemporaneous Sienese sources, among them MS G. I. 9 of the Biblioteca Comunale,[107] whose readings are virtually identical to those of MS 42-N. In addi-

---

106. Lusini, *Il Duomo di Siena,* 2:246.

107. MS G. I. 9, fols. CXX^r–CXXXVIII^r includes each of these as choices from among several that may be sung on the feast of One Martyr. The manuscript also gives a choice of a number of communions, but since the communion is lacking in AOMS, MS 42-N, it is impossible to determine which of them was used with the others. The Sienese readings of these chants vary only slightly from readings found in near contemporary Roman sources, specifically the *Graduale secundum morem sancte romane ecclesie . . . Correctum per fratrem Franciscum de Brugis ordinis minorum de observantia,* printed at

tion to the Alleluia and its verse, *O Ansane gloriose,* MS 42-N preserves a "Sequentia de beato Ansano" beginning with the words *Nobili prosapia.* The same sequence appears, together with another dedicated to the quadrumvirate of Siena's patron saints, *Cum ingenti iubilo,* in MS G. III. 2 of the Biblioteca Comunale, the second book of sequences from the cathedral. This has illuminations that have been dated from 1295 through the mid-1330s.[108] It seems, then, that up to the beginning of the fourteenth century, and perhaps later, the proper for the feast of Sant' Ansano was still essentially that of One Martyr, but with the important difference that the Alleluia verse and a sequence now made specific reference to the saint.

The music of the Alleluia and its verse employs the same compositional methods found in the antiphons and the responsories (see Ex. 2.21). A melody, limited to the range of an octave and proceeding mainly in stepwise motion, is organized into a number of discrete phrases, often featuring the intervals of the major triad. Characteristically, phrases are repeated and recombined so as to form a pleasing and easily remembered whole. Frequent reference to the central tone of the mode, on F, with a B-flat in the signature in this instance, is also typical.[109] A six-note passage outlining two interlocking thirds forms the underlying structure. The passage first appears in the setting of the penultimate syllable "lu" of alleluia. Subsequently, it begins the melismatic section on the last syllable known as the jubilus, where it is followed by two other prominent passages that feature thirds. It returns once again before the close of the jubilus, which itself contains material heard before on the syllable "le."

The verse has two pairs of rhyming couplets, each of whose lines has eight syllables, and a closing line of seven syllables. Its language vividly evokes the exuberance and fervor of medieval Christianity as it calls upon the town's protector to intercede with the Lord for the salvation of his Sienese people. As is typical of many Alleluia settings, the jubilus, in whole or in part, recurs in the verse. Here, the repetition with some variation begins on the first syllable of "prece" and the end of the phrase is extended to include new as well as old material. The frequent recurrences of melodic motives in asymmetrical patterns, both in the syllabic and melismatic sections of the piece, and the wholesale repetition in the verse recall the compositional process discernible in the antiphons and responsories of the rhymed office and may indicate that the Alleluia originated under similar circumstances.

The text of *Nobili prosapia* has ten stanzas grouped in pairs, one of the usual forms taken by the late medieval sequence. The stanzas consist of six alternately rhyming lines

---

Venice in 1515 by Antonio Giunta. This is not surprising in view of the fact that Sienese liturgical sources often reflect current Roman usage, as the incipits of several volumes proudly state, "secundum consuetudine curiae Romane." (A copy of this *Graduale* with manuscript additions containing, among others, the two-voice setting of the *Credo Cardinalis,* is mentioned above in note 75.)

108. MS G. III. 2 is discussed by Giusti in *Il gotico a Siena,* 160, who notes that its illuminations are the work of the same person responsible for those in a series of cathedral chant books. Lusini, *Il Duomo di Siena,* 1:110, also says that the volume belonged to the duomo. Ilari, *La Biblioteca Pubblica di Siena,* 5:72, dated it in the fifteenth century. As noted above, I believe the volume is the same as the one mentioned in cathedral inventories in 1439.

109. The melody moves decidedly within the interval of a fifth below and a fourth above C, the midpoint.

of seven and six syllables that recount in capsulized form the story of the saint's life, martyrdom, and miracles. At the end there is an invocation to him to grant grace to those who venerate his memory and praise for the Creator of all things who is asked, through his son Jesus Christ, to make a place among the elect for the Commune of Siena. The music has five sections, each of which serves for a pair of the stanzas. The uniformly constructed sections contain three main phrases, one for each group of the alternately rhyming lines (see Ex. 2.22). Within the main phrases there are shorter, irregular subphrases that set the individual lines of the poetry. These flow unpredictably into one another to create a balanced whole. The piece is in an F Ionian mode and the range of the octave is exceeded only a few times by a momentary dip below the final. Even more pronounced is the limited range of the phrases, for their melodies generally proceed in stepwise motion within the range of the lower fifth and the upper fourth of the octave, with C as the dividing point. The text is set syllabically, although brief melismas appear occasionally and sometimes unexpectedly during the course of the phrases.

The frequent repetition of melodic motives and phrases, encountered in so much of the music for the feast of Sant'Ansano, is even more pronounced here, a hint perhaps that the piece was composed around the same time as the antiphons of the rhymed office. All five sections and the Amen end with a similar melodic formula, except for a minor variant in the fourth. Another cadential formula appears at the close of the second phrase of the first, second, third, and fifth sections, with a minor variant in the first. A third cadential formula appears in the first phrase of the first, second, and fourth sections, this latter with a minor variant, and yet another formula is used to end the first phrase of the third and fifth sections as well as the second phrase of the fourth section. The quest for unity goes beyond cadential formulas, for other brief melodic passages are repeated within the course of the phrases and in a few other places, such as the opening of the third phrase of the first section and of the Amen, and the opening of the second phrase of second and third sections and of the third phrase of the second section. It is difficult to avoid thinking that the composer deliberately set out to create a piece whose repetitive structure would both facilitate memorization for the singers and make it directly appealing to the large audience that might hear and remember it.

Another sequence in MS G. III. 2, *Cum ingenti iubilo,* is of interest both because of its text, which is addressed to all four of Siena's patron saints, and because of its unusual mensural setting. This latter was first noticed by Agostino Ziino, whose transcription of the first stanza of the piece provides the basis for my remarks (see Ex. 2.23).[110] The text, like the sequence for Sant'Ansano, consists of five pairs of stanzas and an Amen:

1a) Cum ingenti iubilo
  canticum eructet,
  devotoque modulo
  cetuis decantet

1b) Ansano Christicole
  primo melodia
  Senarum agricole
  iussione dia

---

110. See his "Testi religiosi medioevale in notazione mensurale," *L'Ars Nova italiana del Trecento* 4 (1978): 469–72. Another mensural setting in the same manuscript, *Ave virgo mater Christi,* is also transcribed and discussed on p. 468 of the same study.

            sanctorum radiolo   metrum honorabile
            Sena quo reluctet.   det votaque pia.

2a) Tibi grates reddimus,   2b) Exempli mirifici
    inclite patrone,   vigilem pastorem
    nam per te qui credimus,   Savinum, veridici
    dabuntur corone,   sermonis doctorem,
    bona si egerimus   honoret dominici
    in celi palcone.   gregis bellatorem.

3a) Savine doctissime   3b) Sit memor martirii
    tribue doctrinam,   pueri beati
    vitandi cautissime   undeni Crescentii,
    mundanam ruinam   urbe alma, nati
    servandi tutissime,   pro penis supplicii
    fidei carinam.   celo coronati.

4a) Te quem novo ordine   4b) Militis fortissimas
    misit Deus Senas   Siculi Victoris
    precamur hoc carmine,   penas inclitissimas
    aufer nobis penas,   penset cordis coris,
    Crescenti, cum lumine   quas tulit asperrimas
    gratie da venas.   zelo creatoris.

5a) Largire potentiam,   5b) Summa Dei bonitas
    Victor, ut serpentis   laude veneretur
    possimus proterviam   qua quaterna sanctitas
    delere mordentis,   Senis retinetur
    qui ad tis custodiam   ut eius auctoritas
    sumus defendentis.   semper invocetur. Amen.

The stanzas are again comprised of three pairs of rhyming couplets with alternating lines of seven and six syllables. But the music of *Cum ingenti iubilo* proceeds in precisely defined note values rather than in the unmeasured neumes of *Nobili prosapia* that are so typical of the Gregorian repertory. Although it seems that the scribe who copied *Cum ingenti iubilo* was uncertain at times about the significance of some of the note forms he was writing down, particularly longs and breves, the work was clearly copied in a form of notation that has come to be called post-Franconian. Its most striking aspect—one that sets it apart from normal chant notation—is the use of semibreves in ligature or as single notes in groups of two, three, and four. These are occasionally set off by dots of division.[111] The appearance of a form of mensural notation in a volume that belonged to the cathedral around the turn of the fourteenth century suggests that the singers employed there at that time were capable not only of improvising vocal counterpoint but also of performing mensural music. They must, as a consequence, also have been able to improvise certain parts of the chant repertory in a measured style similar to that

---

111. The use of the dot of division in conjunction with semibreves is explained in an anonymous Tuscan treatise of the early fourteenth century. See F. Alberto Gallo, "Due trattatelli sulla notazione del primo Trecento," in *Memorie e contributi . . . offerti a Federico Ghisi* (Bologna, 1971), 1:119–30.

found in the Florentine *Benedicamus Domino* trope and in the *Credo Cardinalis,* mentioned above. Similarly, it could be argued that Oderigo's use of the word "measured" in reference to one performance of organum was indeed an indication that Sienese singers were even then acquainted with some kind of rudimentary mensural system.

Like *Nobili prosapia, Cum ingenti iubilo* is in an F Ionian mode and its text is set to melodies of limited range and movement. Once again five main sections of music are devoted to as many pairs of stanzas. But now the sections are subdivided into six short and for the most part regular phrases of similar length, each set to one line of the rhyming couplets. Despite the somewhat florid appearance of the piece, melismas are used sparingly and are reserved for the penultimate syllable of each line of text. Held notes at the end of every phrase impart a somewhat static quality to the music and produce an effect that is quite unlike that of the flowing Gregorian-style melody of *Nobili prosapia.* Lacking also is the repetition of small melodic phrases and motives. Notable instead is the regular recurrence of an iambic rhythmic pattern, which appears on average three times in every stanza, usually just before the end of a phrase. Its prominence suggests that the composer eschewed unifying devices such as melodic rhyme and repetition in favor of similar rhythms and metrical regularity.[112]

---

112. Other music in honor of the Sienese pantheon of heavenly protectors includes two antiphons at the end of a late sixteenth-century antiphonary from the cathedral, MS 31-A, where they were added by a hand other than the principal one, on fol. 278^{r-v}. Above the music, written in pencil, is the rubric: "In Dominicis ad Vesperas." The text reads:

Sabinus et Crescentius	Crescenti, auge gratiam
Ansanus cum Victore	Ansane, da salutem.
Triumphant excellentius	Sabine, sapientiam
Sacro sparso cruore.	Victor, dona virtutem.
Victor, dona virtutem.	[S]e[cul]o[rum.] [Am]e[n].
[S]e[cul]o[rum. [Am]e[n].	

The texts are suitable for the feasts of any one of the four saints. Each of the stanzas is set separately, though it is possible that they were meant to be sung one after the other, perhaps on Sundays, as suggested by a relatively recent annotation that appears above the music. The poetic meter and structure of the texts recall those of several antiphons and hymns of the rhymed office. But the musical settings are not of similar quality and betray a conscientious, though not altogether successful, attempt to emulate the style of traditional plainchant. This is particularly true of the first antiphon. Its opening line of text is set to two phrases, the first of which furnishes material for the fourth and fifth phrases, these, too, ending on the D final of the mode. A high point on D is reached at the beginning of the third phrase and afterwards there is a stepwise descent to the final, an octave below. Despite the contrast provided by this, the rest of the piece has a static quality about it that is reinforced rather than relieved by the variation and repetition of previous material in the two concluding phrases.

The second antiphon, in an F mode and lacking the intended B-flat in the signature, more nearly captures the spirit of earlier Gregorian music. Its first phrase rises to a fifth above the opening F, while its second makes a gradual ascent to the climax on the F an octave above. The third phrase begins like the second before proceeding independently down a fifth to the final, which is where the last phrase begins. The material here recalls that of the opening phrase before it, too, closes on the F final. The setting again betrays the hand of a later composer who had a good knowledge of the chant and who had little trouble in stringing together melodic phrases committed to memory. In this case, however, the composer was somewhat more successful, for in their simplicity the neatly balanced and slightly more melismatic phrases offer a memorable contrast to the shorter syllabic ones that follow.

The new proper was apparently composed during the first quarter of the fourteenth century. Its principal musical items, introit, gradual, Alleluia, offertory, and communion, are preserved complete in two volumes now at the cathedral. The first, Ospedale MS 17 (olim 97–3), is a late fourteenth-century manuscript from the Hospital of Santa Maria della Scala.[113] The second, cathedral, MS 27. 11 (olim 15), was copied almost a century later and, as noted, was illuminated by Sano di Pietro between 1471 and 1472.[114] There is no sequence in either of these volumes, as is also the case in the two oldest textual sources of the new proper, which are also the most reliable ones. These are MS G. III. 7, a late fourteenth-century Roman missal which is said variously to have been illuminated in or around 1400 by Andrea di Bartolo or by an unknown Sienese painter who worked under the influence of Lippo Vanni,[115] and MS X. II. 3, a fifteenth-century Roman missal with illuminations attributed to Liberale da Verona that once belonged to the cathedral.[116] Both volumes are now in the Biblioteca Comunale. In addition to the items already mentioned, the missals contain texts of the collect, the epistle, the gospel, the secret, and the post-communion.[117] All of these texts also appear in MS G. III. 14, a late fifteenth-century missal which may have once belonged to the Sienese church of San Maurizio.[118]

---

113. Listed by Morandi and Cairoli in "Dall'inventario di 1900," 170–71.

114. Described by Ciardi Dupré, *I Corali,* 37–38. She says that it was written during Cristoforo Felici's tenure as overseer, 1456–57 and 1458–63, and that it was decorated by Sano at Savino Savini's instance in 1471–72. The final payment for Sano's work is dated 25 January 1472.

115. The attribution to Andrea di Bartolo is from *Il gotico a Siena,* 317. See also Grazia Schoenberg-Waldenburg, "I codici miniati senesi liturgici della Biblioteca Comunale di Siena dalla fine del sec. XIV alla fine del sec. XV" (Tesi di laurea, Università degli Studi di Firenze, Facoltà di Lettere e Filosofia, anno academico 1973/74), 1:17–23; 2:15–30, who attributes the illuminations to Lippo di Vanni and says that the volume is from the early years of the fifteenth century.

116. Described by Ilari, *La Biblioteca Pubblica di Siena,* 5:73. Lusini, *Il Duomo di Siena,* 2:258, also says that it comes from the duomo. He describes it as "ricco di miniature, Sec. XV," and notes that it has the Opera's coat of arms on fol. 180ᵛ. The calendar, in the hand of the principal copyist, on fol. 6ᵛ at the beginning of the volume, lists Sant'Ansano's feast. The beautifully illuminated proper for Sant'Ansano begins on fol. 244ʳ: "In Sancti Ansani Martiris."

117. The collect, the secret, and the post-communion also make specific reference to Sant' Ansano:

collect: "Celestis gratie quas domine largiri nobis dignare suffragium ut que fidei lumen beato Ansano martire devote ministrante percepimus apud tuam clementiam ipso intercedente salvemur."

epistle: "Beatus vir qui in sapientia morabitur et qui in militia . . . proximos suos. Et nomine eterno hereditabit illum dominus deus noster" (from Liber Sapientiae)

gospel: "In illo tempore dixit I. D. S. Nichil opertum quod non revelabitur . . . Omnis ergo qui confitebitur me coram . . . meo qui est in celis" (Matt. 10:26–32).

secret: "Accipe pater luminum sacrifitii presentis misterium quod Ansani tui gloriosi misteriis precibus animarum nostrarum et corporum auxilium tribuat ad salutem."

post-communion: "In mense tue caritatis deus opus salutifera sacramenta quem sumpsimus intercedent fidelissimo martire tuo Ansano ad eterne refectionis convivia nos perducas."

The collect "Celestis gratie" and another prayer also appear in BCIS, MS F. VII. 1; see note 99 above. The collect appears as well in MS F. VII. 12; see note 99 above.

118. Described as an "Ordo missalis" by Ilari, *La Biblioteca Pubblica di Siena,* 5:73; the manuscript is discussed by Schoenberg-Waldenburg, "I codici miniati senesi liturgici," 1:148–50; 2:386–96, who

Each of the five items of the Mass is characteristic of its type and exhibits features inherent to its function. Thus the melodies of the introit, the offertory, and the communion are predominantly neumatic and relatively short, whereas those of the gradual and the Alleluia and its verse are ecstatically melismatic and of grander dimensions. On the whole, the music for the new proper is quite different from that of the rhymed office, its settings at once more expansive and more ambitiously conceived. Absent are the phrase repetitions and transferral of materials that so aptly reflect the schematic narration of the antiphons and responsories, replaced here by a compositional method that melds function and form with an apparent quest for originality and expressivity. Just as the texts of the proper speak of Siena's everlasting devotion to Ansano, of the strength of his faith, of the purity of his life, of the profundity of his sacrifice, and of the heavenly rewards of his martyrdom, so the music reflects an aesthetic that stresses a more imaginative and independent approach to the problems of structural unity and melodic variety. It is a fitting companion to Simone Martini's depiction of the saint that decorated the altar where the proper would have been sung.

The introit, *Exultet hodie collegium,* consists of the customary antiphon framing a single psalm verse and the lesser doxology (see Pl. 2 and Ex. 2.24). It is in an F mode, with B-flats occurring throughout, and both psalm and doxology begin with an elaborated intonation of tone 6. The antiphon's text proclaims that on this day all of Siena joyously celebrates Ansano's martyrdom, a sentiment complemented by the following verse from Ps. 91, which says that it is good to give thanks to the Lord and sing psalms to his name. In the musical setting joy and elation are signified by the rapid ascent to the D an octave above the opening note on the word "collegium," regained again on "Ansani." A cadential pattern on F is reintroduced as a means of emphasizing the rhyme ("Senesium," "tripudium"). (This is one of the few times the device is used in the settings of the proper.)

True to its kind, the gradual, *Beatus es Ansane,* is melismatic throughout both its respond and verse (see Ex. 2.25). Set in the first mode, its range extended by one note on either end of the D octave, the melody of the respond proceeds by step and with an occasional skip of a third from the opening D to the note an octave above, just as a blessing is invoked on Ansano and his love for the Lord. The verse moves upward to a climax on the high E, at the point where the text begins its promise to the saint that his glory will not be diminished in eternity.

Similarly expressive melodic ascents characterize the setting of the Alleluia and its verse, *Egregie fortitudinis,* both in the sixth mode on F (see Ex. 2.26). In the brief but rapturous Alleluia a climax on D appears almost at midpoint. The high points and goals here are clearly the same as those of the introit antiphon, but they are achieved differently, for now the melody soars to the high D on a single syllable, unencumbered by textual demands, and the effect is even more striking. The extended verse following the Alleluia comprises entirely new material. This reaches its highest note on E twice,

says its provenance is unknown but that it is from the second half of the fifteenth century. With regard to its provenance, the following references to the church of San Maurizio are notable: A calendar at the beginning of the volume, on fol. 4ᵛ, for August, notes the feast on "XVII b XII Consecratio ecclesie Sci Mauritii de Senis" and on fol. 5ʳ, for September, "f. X. Kl. Sci Mauritii cum sociis eius."

at "adolescens" and "radiantis," emphasizing the key words of the text, which assures the youthful saint, so full of strength, that the ruler of heaven crowns him with the diadem of the radiant army of martyrs.

The melody of the offertory, *Obtulisti tu,* breaks out into a melisma almost immediately on the word "tu," though such effusions are rare in what is essentially a neumatic setting of a brief four-line text (see Ex. 2.27). Each of the four newly composed phrases eschews repetition, even at the internal rhymes on "venustatem" and "puritatem." A different cadential pattern on the G final of the seventh mode concludes all of the phrases. These proceed mostly by step except for the third, where skips of thirds and a fourth lead quickly from G to the F a seventh above for the climax of the piece, at the point where Ansano's virtues are likened to those of St. John in their purity.

The communion, *Martyrii calicem sitivisti,* again addresses Ansano directly, this time with the assurance that he is welcome at the banquet of the angels because he drank of the cup of martyrdom. Function, text, and musical setting beautifully meld in this shortest piece of the proper, where simplicity of structure matches gracefulness of melody in an artful blending of motivic interplay and melismatic expressivity. Three phrases of nearly equal length, each moving within the ambitus of an octave, are in the first mode on D (see Ex. 2.28). The opening passage introduces the interval of a third, which will be so prominent throughout the first phrase and in much of the rest of the piece. At the beginning of the second phrase the skip of a third moves directly to the high point on C, after which a descent, also incorporating a third, is made to the C an octave below. Two consecutive thirds occur at the outset of the third and last phrase, which concludes with a melisma rising to A on the word "angelorum," before making its descent to the D final.

Altogether, the music for the proper of the Mass complements the earlier settings of the rhymed office for the feast of Sant'Ansano. Both indicate that for at least a century and a half and perhaps more, from the end of fourteenth century through the beginning of the sixteenth, the cathedral's liturgy, as well as that of the hospital of Santa Maria della Scala and of various Franciscan convents, was embellished with texts and music that paid singular homage to the saint on his feast day. While the feast itself never attained the status accorded Assumption Day, it did give rise to a body of music that, whatever its origins, captures more than any historical document ever could the affection and fervor with which the people of this medieval town regarded their patron saint and the trust they placed in his mediation and powers to earn Siena and its citizens a place at the heavenly banquet over which God's angels presided.

Example 2.1. Benedicamus trope, *Regi regum* (Lucca, Biblioteca Capitolare, MS 603, fol. 256ʳ, after Baralli and Hughes)

Example 2.2. Benedicamus trope, *Verbum patris hodie* (Bologna, Civico Museo Bibliografico Musicale, MS Q 11, fol. 8ᵛ, after Vecchi)

Example 2.3. Benedicamus trope, *Verbum patris hodie* (FNBC, MS Banco rari 19, fol. 73ʳ, after Wolf)

1. Ver - bum   pa - tris   ho - di - e   pro - ces - sit   ex____   vir   -   gi - ne
2. Na - to   no - bis   ho - di - e   de   Ma - ri - a____   vir   -   gi - ne

vir - tu   -   tes   an - ge - li - ce   cum   ca - no - re   iu - bi -
ae - ter - no   re - gi   glo - ri - ae   cum   su - a - vi   iu - bi -

-lo   Be - ne - di - ca - mus   Do - mi - no.
-lo   De - o   di - ca - mus   gra - ti - as.

Example 2.4. Credo IV (Credo Cardinalis) (BCIS, MS H. I. 10, fols. 321ᵛ–322ᵛ)

Example 2.4 continued

† lacking in MS

Example 2.4 continued

Example 2.5. Hymn, *Martyr Ansane* (AOMS, Ospedale, MS 9, fols. 27ʳ–30ᵛ)

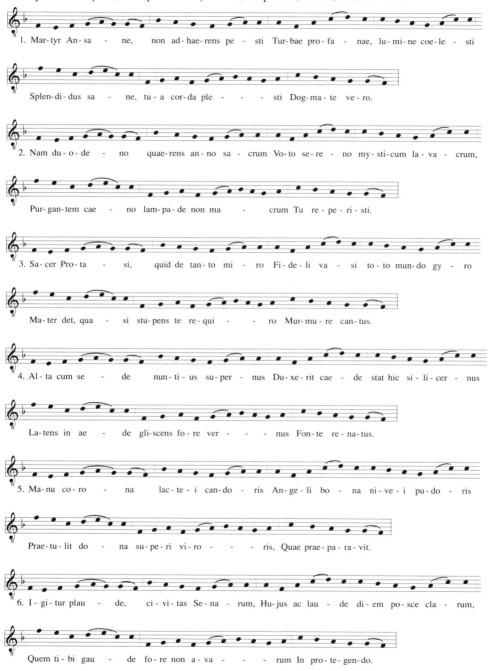

1. Mar-tyr An-sa - ne, non ad-hae-rens pe - sti Tur-bae pro-fa - nae, lu-mi-ne coe-le - sti
Splen-di-dus sa - ne, tu-a cor-da ple - - - sti Dog-ma-te ve-ro.

2. Nam du-o-de - no quae-rens an-no sa-crum Vo-to se-re - no my-sti-cum la-va - crum,
Pur-gan-tem cae - no lam-pa-de non ma - crum Tu re-pe-ri-sti.

3. Sa-cer Pro-ta - si, quid de tan-to mi - ro Fi-de-li va - si to-to mun-do gy - ro
Ma-ter det, qua - si stu-pens te re-qui - - ro Mur-mu-re can-tus.

4. Al-ta cum se - de nun-ti-us su-per - nus Du-xe-rit cae - de stat hic si-li-cer - nus
La-tens in ae - de gli-scens fo-re ver - - - nus Fon-te re-na-tus.

5. Ma-nu co-ro - na lac-te-i can-do - ris An-ge-li bo - na ni-ve-i pu-do - ris
Prae-tu-lit do - na su-pe-ri vi-ro - - - ris, Quae prae-pa-ra-vit.

6. I-gi-tur plau - de, ci-vi-tas Se-na - rum, Hu-jus ac lau - de di-em po-sce cla - rum,
Quem ti-bi gau - de fo-re non a-va - - - rum In pro-te-gen-do.

Example 2.5 continued

7. Laus cre - a - to - ri   sit non ge - ne - ra - to Sit re - dem - pto - ri vir - gi - ne pla - sma - to,

Con - so - la - to - ri fla - mi - ni - que gra - - - to cun - cta re - gen - ti.

A - - - men.

Example 2.6. Hymn, *Aeterna nutu baiulans* (AOMS, Ospedale, MS 9, fols. 32ᵛ–35ʳ)

1. Ae - ter - na   nu - tu ba - iu - lans An - sa - ne Mar - tyr, prae - mi - um Vo - to - que mi - ti po - stu - lans

Quae - si - sti coe - li gre - mi - um.

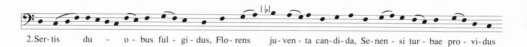

2. Ser - tis   du - o - bus ful - gi - dus, Flo - rens ju - ven - ta can - di - da, Se - nen - si tur - bae pro - vi - dus

Ut stel - la lu - cens splen - di - da

3. No - stras   su - per - no fla - mi - ne Men - tes fi - de - les im - bu - i Fac te pre - ca - mur lu - mi - ne

Cor - dis   ca - nen - do cer - nu - i.

4. Laus di - gna   Chri - stum con - ci - nat, Pa - trem si - mul - que spi - ri - tum, Qui san - ctus or - bes or - di - nat

Vi - tae - que pan - dit me - ri - tum. A - - - men.

Example 2.7. Hymn, *Ansani vita* (AOMS, Ospedale, MS 9, fols. 55^r–56^v)

Example 2.8. Invitatory, *Regis nobiscum* (AOMS, Ospedale, MS 9, fol. 32^r–^{v})

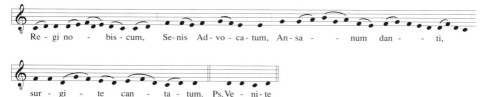

Example 2.9. Antiphon, *Ansanus Romae* (Cathedral, Libreria Piccolomini, MS 11. M, fol. 25^v)

Example 2.10. Antiphon, *Ansanus cum Maxima* (AOMS, Ospedale, MS 9, fol. 40ᵛ)

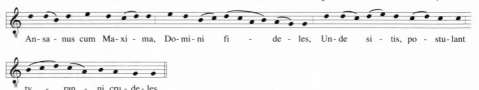

An- sa- nus cum Ma- xi- ma, Do- mi- ni fi - de - les, Un- de si - tis, po - stu- lant

ty - ran - ni cru- de- les.

Example 2.11. Antiphon, *Imperantes respuens* (AOMS, Ospedale, MS 9, fol. 36ʳ)

Im- pe- ran - tes re- spu - ens cu - cur- rit ad ma - tri- nam, Cum qua si- mul si - ne - ret

hanc vi - tam pe - re - gri - nam. Ps. Qua - re fre - mu - e - runt gen - tes: et po- pu - li

me- di - ta - ti sunt in - a - ni- a?

Example 2.12. Antiphon, *Exaudi nos* (AOMS, Ospedale, MS 9, fol. 54ʳ⁻ᵛ)

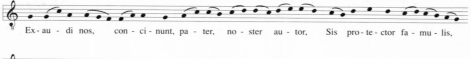

Ex- au - di nos, con - ci - nunt, pa - ter, no - ster au - tor, Sis pro- te- ctor fa - mu- lis,

ve - re ju- stis fau - tor.

Example 2.13. Antiphon, *Ad civitatem balneum* (AOMS, Ospedale, MS 9, fol. 58ʳ⁻ᵛ)

Ad ci- vi- ta - tem bal- ne- um Re - gen- se Cum re- fu - gis- ses, spi- ri - tus

ac - cen - sae Sub vi- si- o - ne Do- mi - nus te vo - cat Et te co- lum - nam

tem - plo su- o lo- cat.

Example 2.14. Antiphon, *Sub mandatis angeli* (AOMS, Ospedale, MS 9, fols. 31ᵛ–32ʳ)

(a) antiphon

Sub man - da - tis   an - ge - li cum   sa - cer - dos pe - tit Fo - res san - ctu - a - ri - i,

mi - rus   o - dor_ ste - tit,   Spi - ri - ta - lis   Ma - xi - ma   ma - ter mi - re da - tur

Et   fons   a - quae lim - pi - dae, pu - er   ut   ter - ga - tur   Ma - gni - fi - cat

a - ni - ma me - a Do - mi - num

(b) motivic similarities

Sub man - da - tis   an - ge - li   cum sa - cer - dos

pe - tit Fo - res san - ctu - a - ri - i,

mi - rus   o - dor

ste - tit,   Spi - ri - ta - lis   Ma - xi - ma ma-ter

mi - re   da - tur

Et fons a - quae   lim - pi - dae,

pu-er   ut   ter - ga-tur.

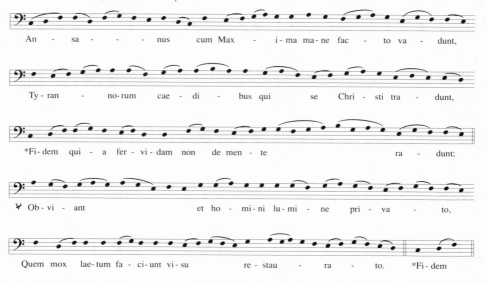

Example 2.15. Responsory, *Ansanus cum Maxima* (Cathedral, Libreria Piccolomini, MS 11. M, fols. 37ᵛ–39ʳ)

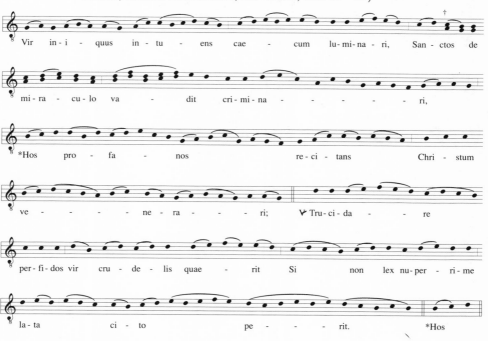

Example 2.16. Responsory, *Vir iniquos intuens* (AOMS, Ospedale, MS 9, fols. 37ᵛ–39ʳ; Cathedral, Libreria Piccolomini, MS 11. M, fols. 39ʳ–40ʳ)

† At this point, the two manuscript versions give different readings

Example 2.17. Responsory, *Nostros deos colite* (AOMS, Ospedale, MS 9, fols. 41ʳ–43ᵛ)

† Omitted: "ip-sos" on *a*, *g*

Example 2.18. Responsory, *Non vos huc adduximus* (AOMS, Ospedale, MS 9, fols. 48ʳ–49ᵛ)

Example 2.19. Responsory, *Nostra vox instrepuit* (AOMS, Ospedale, MS 9, fols. 43ᵛ–44ʳ)

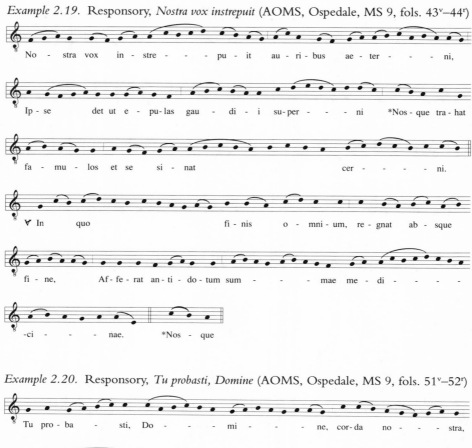

Example 2.20. Responsory, *Tu probasti, Domine* (AOMS, Ospedale, MS 9, fols. 51ᵛ–52ʳ)

Example 2.21. Alleluia and verse, *O Ansane gloriose* (AOMS, MS 42-N, fols. 167ᵛ–168ᵛ)

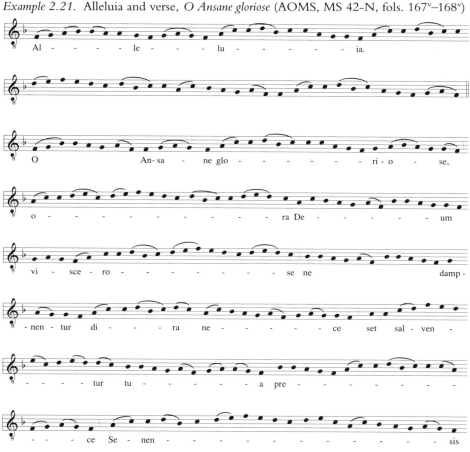

THE CATHEDRAL

Example 2.22. Sequence, *Nobili prosapia* (AOMS, MS 42-N, fols. 139ʳ–142ᵛ; BCIS, MS G. III. 2, fols. 51ᵛ–56ᵛ)

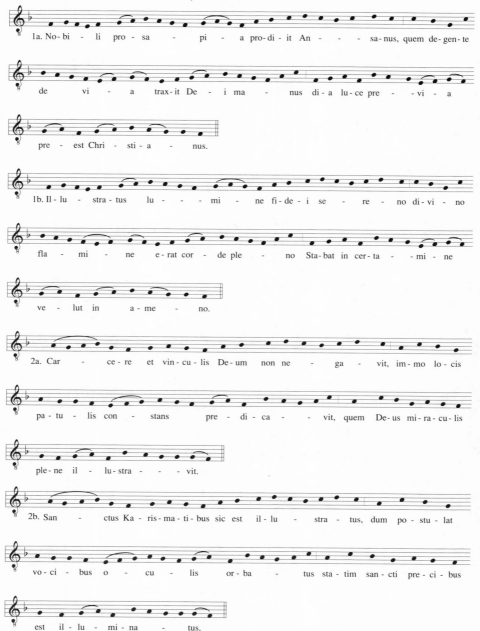

Example 2.22 continued

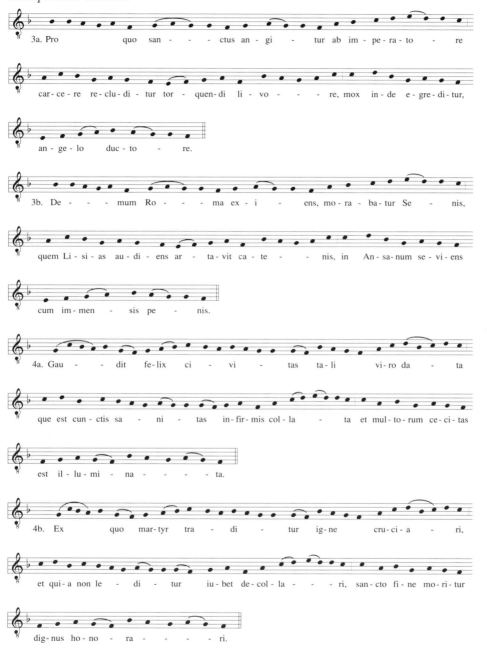

3a. Pro quo san - - - ctus an - gi - tur ab im - pe - ra - to - re

car - ce - re re - clu - di - tur tor - quen-di li - vo - - - re, mox in - de e - gre - di - tur,

an - ge - lo duc - to - re.

3b. De - - - mum Ro - - - ma ex - i - ens, mo - ra - ba - tur Se - nis,

quem Li - si - as au - di - ens ar - ta - vit ca - te - nis, in An - sa-num se - vi - ens

cum im - men - sis pe - nis.

4a. Gau - - dit fe - lix ci - vi - tas ta - li vi - ro da - ta

que est cun - ctis sa - ni - tas in - fir-mis col - la - ta et mul - to - rum ce - ci - tas

est il - lu - mi - na - - - ta.

4b. Ex quo mar - tyr tra - di - tur ig - ne cru - ci - a - ri,

et qui - a non le - di - tur iu - bet de - col - la - - - ri, sanc - to fi - ne mo - ri - tur

dig - nus ho - no - ra - - - ri.

Example 2.22 continued

Example 2.23. Sequence, *Cum ingenti iubilo* (BCIS, MS G. III. 2, fols. 86ᵛ–91ʳ, after Ziino)

Example 2.24. Introit, *Exultet hodie collegium* (Cathedral, Libreria Piccolomini, MS 27. 11, fols. 10ᵛ–11ᵛ; AOMS, Ospedale, MS 17, fols. 13ᵛ–14ᵛ)

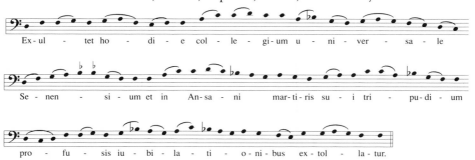

Ex - ul – tet ho – di – e col – le – gi - um u – ni – ver – sa – le

Se - nen – si - um et in An - sa – ni mar - ti - ris su – i tri – pu - di - um

pro – fu – sis iu – bi – la – ti – o – ni - bus ex - tol – la - tur.

Ps. Bo – num est con - fi - te - ri Do - mi - no et psal – le - re no - mi - ni tu - o, Al – tis - si - me.

Glo – ri – a Pa - tri

Example 2.25. Gradual, *Beatus es Ansane* (Cathedral, Libreria Piccolomini, MS 27. 11, fols. 12ʳ–13ᵛ)

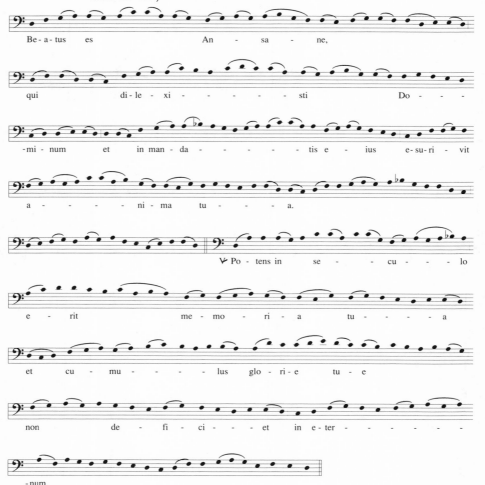

Example 2.26. Alleluia and verse, *Egregie fortitudinis* (Cathedral, Libreria Piccolomini, MS 27. 11, fols. 13ᵛ–14ᵛ)

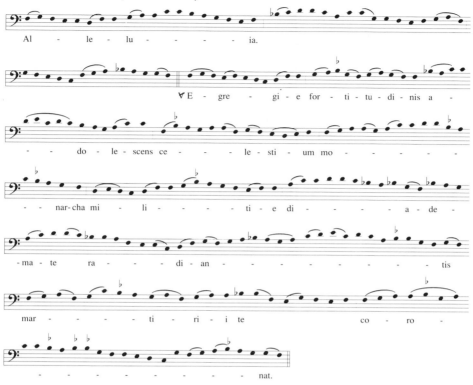

Example 2.27. Offertory, *Obtulisti tu* (Cathedral, Libreria Piccolomini, MS 27. 11, fols. 14ᵛ–15ʳ)

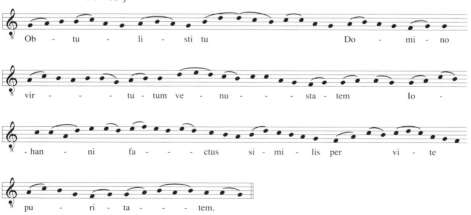

Example 2.28. Communion, *Martyrii calicem sitivisti* (Cathedral, Libreria Piccolomini, MS 27. 11, fol. 15ʳ–ᵛ)

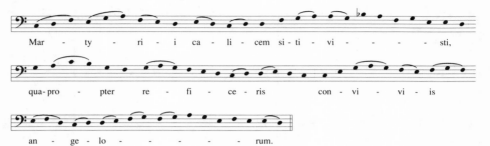

Mar - ty - ri - i ca - li - cem si - ti - vi - - - - sti,

qua- pro - pter re - fi - ce - ris con - vi - vi - is

an - ge - lo - - - - - rum.

Chapter Three

SINGERS AND ORGANISTS, 1380–1448

A LL MENTION OF improvised polyphony, so meticulously described by Oderigo in the early thirteenth century, disappears from the cathedral records in the next two centuries. Personnel records, which might have furnished information about musical practices, are altogether lacking for most of the period in question. The few that survive from the late fourteenth century are of little assistance because of their failure in general to acknowledge the presence of singers. But in view of what is known, it seems reasonable to assume, as I have in the preceding chapter, that some kind of vocal part music was being performed at the cathedral during the thirteenth and early fourteenth centuries, particularly because records regarding chaplain-singers from after the turn of the fifteenth century give the impression that there was no break with past practices. These same records suggest that improvised polyphony such as *cantus planus binatim* and its many offshoots, written as well as improvised, may have continued to have some currency at Siena cathedral well into the fifteenth century, though most of the evidence points to growing inroads of performance from written music and, after the 1430s, especially, the most recent types of high art polyphony.

This was consistent with developments in other major Italian cities, where, particularly after the Council of Constance in 1418 and the return of the papacy from Avignon, northern European practices began to appear with increasing frequency. Repertories had changed profoundly during the two centuries since Oderigo's time. Evolving from the notated organa, clausulae, and motets of the Parisian school and its successors, and culminating in the innovations of the fourteenth century, Continental music was enriched during the early decades of the fifteenth century with new sound ideals from England that emphasized the intervals of thirds and sixths and with new concepts governing melodic and formal structure. High art polyphony had come to be characterized by a refined and sometimes elaborate contrapuntal style whose melodic and rhythmic subtleties placed new demands on performers. An improvised art and its simplest written offshoots, hitherto within the capabilities of most cathedral-trained musicians, were superseded by a written one that required a comprehensive and specialized knowledge of complex mensural systems. In nearby Florence high art polyphony was slow to gain acceptance because of episcopal opposition to its use in church services. But how thoroughly the aesthetic sensibilities and practical aspects of its notation were absorbed is evidenced by the extraordinary body of secular song composed there from the mid-fourteenth century onwards, when the works of a school of native composers transformed a local art into a truly universal one.[1]

---

1. A recently discovered Florentine manuscript demonstrates that by the turn of the fifteenth century Florentine musicians were well aware of the latest developments in the French motet. See

Although Siena did not boast similar developments, its ongoing preoccupation with its powerful neighbor to the north makes it improbable that Florentine musical achievements went unnoticed. Nor were written compositions representative of contemporary trends and developments in transalpine Europe, particularly after the end of the fourteenth century, unknown. Siena's geographical position on the road to Rome and its political and economic interests made it an obvious point for the reception of musical influences emanating from centers far beyond the confines of Tuscany. Sienese churchmen, statesmen, and merchants, furthermore, assuredly heard performances of the newest music on their business ventures and travels, which took them to Avignon and to the farthest reaches of the Empire, and their experiences led them to seek ways in which to adorn the rituals of their major church with performances of similar kinds of music.

THE TRANSITION TO WRITTEN POLYPHONY

It was clearly only a matter of time before changes in musical styles and forms and in performance requirements affected Siena cathedral. But until the changeover from older modes of performance to newer ones was completed, a flexible hiring policy was necessary, especially during the period of transition, when earlier practices were giving way to a growing preference for northern polyphonic models. This, to judge from surviving records, was precisely the solution adopted by the Opera. By the end of the fourteenth century, singers who were expert in newer forms of written polyphony gradually began replacing those whose strengths lay primarily in traditional practices such as *cantus planus binatim* or in the more elaborate forms of improvised counterpoint, though in the interim singers who were proficient in all kinds of performance were welcomed. Northern musicians, as might be expected, led the way during the transitional period, although gifted Italians were often found alongside them. By the middle of the fifteenth century, when northern polyphony triumphed at Siena cathedral, improvisational vocal practices had been relegated to minor status involving occasional ornamentation, while extempore performance became the almost exclusive province of the organist.

With the passage of time the cantor's duties, as described by Oderigo, underwent significant changes, though exactly when these occurred is not mentioned in any extant documents. Given the conservative nature of liturgical practices, modifications undoubtedly came about gradually and in various stages. Perhaps changes occurred because of a lack of qualified personnel, which is to say that, in the case of the cantor, duties may have been modified because of the unavailability of clerics who could lead the chant and improvise new countermelodies to the traditional ones. But changes may also have ensued because of the widespread adoption of written forms of polyphony that called for clerics with different kinds of musical training. As a consequence, the improvised polyphony required on so many occasions by the early thirteenth-century liturgy was abandoned and with it the need for cantors trained in various modes of improvisation. Another factor, contemporary attitudes toward the use of polyphony,

---

D'Accone, "Una nuova fonte dell'Ars Nova italiana: Il codice di San Lorenzo 2211," *Studi musicali* 13 (1984): 3–31, and John Nádas, "Manuscript San Lorenzo 2211: Some Further Observations," *L'Ars Nova italiana del Trecento* 6 (1992): 145–68.

may also have had some bearing in the matter, although this seems not to have been an issue in Siena, as it was in Florence, where the bishop Ardingo simply forbade its use.[2] Whatever the case, by the mid-fifteenth century, as the Constitutions indicate, many of the duties previously assumed by the cantor were radically different. No longer was he entrusted with assigning tasks to various participants or responsible for their conduct during services. He was, to be sure, still the principal singer in the plainchant choir, but he no longer improvised polyphony.

The Constitutions of 1459 speak only briefly of the cantor, in keeping with his diminished role. They note that he was to be in the choir and begin the introit at Mass as soon as the bell rang and that he was to be there to intone the office when the bell sounded the start of Matins, Vespers, and Compline.[3] The succentor, likewise, was to be ready to intone the second psalm. No mention is made of the cantor's singing solo portions of the chant or of leading the others in the portions that were sung by all, probably because this practice was so well established that it needed no explanation. But neither is any mention made of the cantor performing polyphony or of selecting others who would do so, with or without him. The Constitutions, moreover, do not specify whether the cantor's office was to be held by a canon or by a chaplain, though they do indicate that the office could be assigned on a weekly basis, which is a good reason for believing that the incumbents were chaplains. In support of this is a further stipulation in the Constitutions, that during services the hebdomadal cantor and succentor were obliged to sit in the first and second rows of the lower stalls on either side of the choir and to dedicate themselves entirely to the celebration of offices. Like the others, the cantor and succentor were fined for failure to do their jobs properly. By this time Siena cathedral was employing professional chaplain-singers of polyphony, and perhaps some of them were assigned the cantor's duties on a weekly basis. A cantor with a pleasing voice who could sing in tune, after all, was clearly preferable to one with lesser musical gifts.

Funding Performances of Polyphony: The Sienese Solution

For the overseers and their counselors at Siena cathedral the problems of funding performances of polyphony were quite different from those encountered by secular rulers, by papal administrators, and even by the governing board of the cathedral in nominally republican Florence. Chapels of singers maintained by princes such as Leonello and Ercole d'Este in Ferrara, Galeazzo Maria Sforza in Milan, and the kings of Naples were funded from state treasuries or from the personal revenues of the ruler—the two were often inseparable—and these were enlarged or diminished according to the prince's taste and to the financial resources available to him. In those places the singers' principal

---

2. Robert Davidsohn reports that in 1234 Florence cathedral had singers who were proficient in polyphony (*canto figurato, canto rotto*) but that Bishop Ardingo (1231–49) prohibited its use, decreeing that only chant could be sung during divine services because it alone was worthy and because it was traditional. See Davidsohn, *Storia di Firenze,* 7 vols. (Florence, 1956–65; Italian trans. of *Geschichte von Florenz,* 1896–1927), 7:572.

3. *Constitutiones Sacri Capituli Metropolitanae Senensis Ecclesiae,* rub. 55. (For particulars, see chapter 2.)

duties were connected with court activities, whether at public or private religious services or at formal and informal social functions. Early on, several of the music-loving Italian princes, emulating the Dukes of Burgundy and other northern sovereigns, learned to take advantage of the system of ecclesiastical benefices as a means of supplementing the salaries of favored musicians. The popes, of course, had long made use of benefices as well as of unlimited funds from the papal treasury to support their retainers and to maintain a chapel of singers which, even before the permanent return of the papacy to Rome, was the most stable and generally the largest one in Italy.[4]

The situation at Siena cathedral also differed substantially from similar institutions in Florence, Milan, and Ferrara, to cite a few places for which some documentation is available. In Florence, even before the advent of Medici rule, the Opere of the cathedral and the Baptistry, enriched through private and public gifts, were under the aegis of two powerful and wealthy guilds, whose control was ensured through governing boards drawn from their memberships. At various times after the establishment of the chapel the guilds and their governing boards devised a system of subvention that allowed the two churches to share the singers' services.[5] Medici involvement, initially covert so that republican sentiments might not be aroused, became more and more acknowledged, as the far-flung resources of their banking empire were utilized for recruiting purposes and sometimes for support of singers. By the late fifteenth century a complex system of musical patronage had evolved, one which saw the Opere, the Medici, and even the cathedral canons on occasion, financing the singers' performances. Although the conferral of ecclesiastical benefices on singers was a practice that was almost completely unknown in Florence, at times Lorenzo the Magnificent, like other Italian princes, did not hesitate to seek them for his favored musicians.[6]

At Milan cathedral there was apparently little state subvention of musicians during the final decades of the Visconti reign, but after 1450, when Francesco Sforza became duke, the chapel grew from four to eleven singers. Several of them were foreigners who on average, perhaps because of ducal intervention, earned a higher salary than native musicians.[7] The chapel's transformation, however, was shortlived. Francesco's son Galeazzo Maria established two singing ensembles at court, and the foreign singers were soon transferred to them, leaving the cathedral with a smaller group of Italian singer-

---

4. Useful studies of musicians' benefices in this period are Christopher Reynolds, "Musical Careers, Ecclesiastical Benefices, and the Example of Johannes Brunet," *JAMS* 37 (1984): 49–97, and Pamela Starr, "Rome as the Centre of the Universe: Papal Grace and Musical Patronage," *Early Music History* 11 (1992): 223–62.

5. These arrangements and the Medici's role in recruiting and helping maintain the chapels are discussed in D'Accone, "The Singers of San Giovanni in Florence during the Fifteenth Century," *JAMS* 14 (1961): 307–58, and "The Musical Chapels at the Florentine Cathedral and Baptistry during the First Half of the 16th Century," *JAMS* 24 (1971): 3–50.

6. See D'Accone, "Lorenzo il Magnifico e la musica," in *La musica a Firenze al tempo di Lorenzo il Magnifico,* ed. Piero Gargiulo (Florence, 1993), 237–39.

7. Claudio Sartori, "Josquin des Près, cantore del Duomo di Milano (1459–1472)," *Annales Musicologiques* 4 (1950): 67. Information for the years following, cited here, is from the same article, pp. 69, 73, 77, and 81.

chaplains. Links between the two groups remained, and on major feast days the cathedral musicians were assisted by the ducal singers.[8] In Ferrara, whose rulers were no less fervent in their cultivation of music, the cathedral apparently maintained a more modest number of singers, but they too were frequently assisted by singers employed at the court.[9]

Few, if any, of these arrangements were possible at Siena cathedral. The overseer of the Opera and his counselors alone were responsible for financing and maintaining the cathedral's musical programs, funds for which could only be drawn from revenues under their control. Government-employed instrumentalists—the trumpeters and woodwind players—who were brought in to perform at the cathedral throughout the year were paid for these extraordinary services not from Palace coffers but from the Opera's own funds. Nor did the cathedral Chapter contribute to the support of cathedral singers and organists, many of whom were chaplains. There is, in fact, no evidence to suggest that any of the cathedral's canonries or "perpetual" chaplaincies were awarded especially to singers during this period, even though one of the canons joined the singing ensemble for a while in the early fifteenth century and several musicians later held permanent chaplaincies. Furthermore, Sienese officials, unlike church administrators and secular princes elsewhere, did not actively seek benefices in the city and its territories or from a wider area for cathedral musicians. Thus, in the absence of outside support and of specific bequests and endowments specifically earmarked for performers of polyphony, the Opera was forced to provide for them from its own income. This was not inconsiderable, but there were other claims on the Opera, principal among them the ambitious building and decoration programs. How the overseer and his counselors met the challenge of funding the singers' performances is an ever-recurring theme in the history of the cathedral's musical establishment.

For most of the fifteenth and sixteenth centuries recourse was had to employing singers and organists who could also serve as full- or part-time chaplains, a solution apparently made possible by the terms of the *Pacta* of 1368, by which the Opera agreed to pay for eight chaplaincies with its own funds. Many of the Opera's chaplains were, in fact, hired precisely because they could sing polyphony, take part in offices, and officiate at votive and other Masses with special intent. This kind of arrangement may already have been in effect by the late fourteenth century, for when records become available after the turn of the fifteenth century, they give the impression of continuation of an established practice. The case for continuity is strengthened by other reports regarding another group of singers employed at the cathedral at this time. These show that singers of laudi, or laudesi, as they were often called, performed there from the mid-fourteenth century through the first several decades of the following one without interruption and with few, if any, changes in their programmed activities.

---

8. Claudio Sartori, "La cappella del Duomo," in "La musica nel Duomo e alla corte sino alla seconda metà del '500," in *Storia di Milano*, 9: *L'epoca di Carlo V (1535–1559)* (Milan, 1961), 737.

9. See Enrico Peverada, *Vita musicale nella chiesa ferrarese del Quattrocento* (Ferrara, 1991), 24–26, regarding the assistance of ducal musicians. Unfortunately, the numbers employed are not mentioned.

Patterns of Practice

Three records among the few extant regarding cathedral personnel in the late four-teenth century point to the presence of singers of polyphony. One lists a payment to Ser Isidoro di Francia, "a *chantatore,* who served the duomo as a chaplain," from 17 May through 15 August 1383. Isidoro is the earliest known of a succession of itinerant clergymen, many of them of French origin, who, as reports from the following century indicate, served the cathedral both as chaplains and singers of polyphony. This much is evident from a statement in his account noting that he received "L. 90 per annum for his salary and his expenses, and because he was a singer, he had L. 5 more than the other chaplains." Although the exact nature of his duties was not specified, it is probable that he earned the extra stipend because he was able to perform some kind of music that was beyond the abilities of others in the choir. Also significant in this regard is the use of the word *cantatore,* or *cantore,* to describe Isidoro's status. It is, quite obviously, an Italian translation of the Latin word *cantor,* that is, the person who led and sang the solo portions of the chant in the choir, though there is no question that here, as in all subsequent Sienese records regarding *cantores* or *cantori,* the term refers to a singer who was employed primarily to perform polyphony.

Ambiguities also surround the status of another singer employed at the cathedral while Isidoro was there, Frate Anselmo of the Dominican "monks of Santo Spirito." He "sang in the choir in the duomo" for two years, from May 1383 through April 1385. While the record clearly indicates that Anselmo was not a cathedral chaplain and thus not a regular participant in services requiring the presence of Chapter members, it does not say what kind of music he sang. But he must have been hired because he had performing abilities the cathedral's chaplains did not have. Very likely, then, these few records preserve the only traces from this time of the practice of employing two singers of polyphony—singers, moreover, who could perform written polyphony. This is con-sistent with practices recorded in Siena, in Florence, and in Milan after the turn of the fifteenth century.

In Milan cathedral two biscantori, or singers of polyphony, were reported from 1414 onwards, when Ambrosino da Pessano joined Matteo da Perugia, a composer employed there as a biscantor and teacher since 1402.[10] Matteo's duties called for him to give public lectures on music and also to teach three boys chosen by church authorities. These latter, presumably, were to perform polyphony with him in the choir, though it is not certain that they ever did. Because of a dispute with church authorities Matteo was away from 1407 through 1414, when two priests and then Ambrosino alone substi-tuted for him. After Matteo's return in 1414 he and Ambrosino sang together as a pair until the time of his departure in 1416. In the following years another singer joined Ambrosino from time to time. Despite these inconsistent employment patterns, it seems that the ideal practice at Milan cathedral was to have two singers, who could perform either improvised or written polyphony. The case for the latter is strengthened by

---

10. Claudio Sartori, "Matteo da Perugia e Bertrand Ferragut, i primi due maestri di cappella del Duomo di Milano," *Acta Musicologica* 28 (1956): 12–27; also Sartori, "La cappella del Duomo," 728–29.

Matteo's presence, and then by the appointment of the Avignonese composer Bertrand de Feragut to the second singer's post in 1425. He sang alongside Ambrosino until his departure in 1430, when a new group, consisting of Ambrosino and three other singer-chaplains, took over. This four-man ensemble, typifying the groups who sang written polyphony in Italian cathedrals in the following decades, was associated with Milan cathedral for the next twenty years.

During the early decades of the fifteenth century the practice at the Florentine cathedral of Santa Maria del Fiore was to employ two singers of polyphony among the chaplains who sang in the plainchant choir.[11] Apart from whatever improvisational skills the singers might have had and however these might have been utilized, there is no doubt that they were performers of written polyphony. Several of them, like Corrado da Pistoia and Ugolino da Orvieto, were also composers. Florentine records indicate that it was no easy task to recruit and retain qualified performers, and the cathedral was forced to do without them on a number of occasions. Nevertheless, two singers consti-tuted a normal complement through the late 1430s, when a chapel of four singers was inaugurated under Medici supervision in time for the transferral to Florence in 1438 of the Council for reunion of the Greek and Roman churches.[12] Among the new singers was Bertrand de Feragut, the erstwhile Avignonese singer.

Although no known composers sang at Siena cathedral in the first four decades of the fifteenth century, several factors point to a parallel situation there. Two singers were simultaneously employed from shortly after the turn of the fifteenth century until the late 1430s, when the Sienese group, too, was enlarged to include four or five singers. More significant is the knowledge that despite the paucity of information about early fifteenth-century Sienese singers, no changes are evident regarding their duties and those of later singers. Indeed, during the 1430s and the 1440s the names of chaplains, who were clearly singers of written polyphony, appear on the rolls with not so much as a hint that their presence represented a break with tradition.[13] A few later records suggest that some singers might have been adept both at improvising and at performing written polyphony, and this was probably true of singers in the earlier part of the cen-tury as well. Perhaps, then, it was only in later decades that, imperceptibly, the term *cantore* in Siena took on the exclusive meaning of singer of written polyphony.

SINGER-CHAPLAINS TO 1430

Ser Bartolomeo di Mariano, the earliest of the fifteenth-century singer-chaplains, was a native of Florence, where he probably trained. Awarded a chaplaincy at Siena cathe-dral in August 1401, he held the post through July 1414. Payment records from the beginning of his tenure, consistently referring to him as a chaplain, show him earning an annual salary of L. 80; they do little more than list his monthly distributions for

---

11. In Florentine documents the singers are referred to as *cantores* or *cantori,* depending on whether Latin or Italian was used. See D'Accone, "Music and Musicians at Santa Maria del Fiore in the Early Quattrocento," in *Scritti in onore di Luigi Ronga* (Milan, 1973), 99–126.

12. D'Accone, "The Singers of San Giovanni," 308–10.

13. Interestingly, the singing teacher, invariably referred to as a cantore, was usually a singer of polyphony.

participating in offices. An entry in one account from the fiscal year 1406–7, however, credits him with an additional payment of L. 8. 4 "for his work singing in the choir," an unnecessary explanation, had he merely been performing his normal duties. Another record covering the period May 1407–April 1412 is more informative. It specifies that during that time he received Fl. 6 each year "for serving in the choir singing the tenor part of the music and for keeping the clocks in order."

Perhaps the belated raise in salary indicates that Bartolomeo was not originally hired to sing polyphony and that he began doing so only after he had been at the cathedral for some time. Similar situations occurred on occasion in the following decades, when clerics, employed only as chaplains, were subsequently paid for singing. This suggests that at times there were chaplains and others among cathedral personnel capable of performing polyphony but that they were not called upon to do so formally. In Bartolomeo's case, it could also mean that he replaced another singer–chaplain, though extant records are silent in this regard. In any case if he sang tenor, during his tenure at least one other singer of polyphony must have performed the upper part in two-voice pieces.

Two other singers, Ser Jacomo di Bellanduccio da San Quirico and Bartolomeo di Luti, were at the cathedral when Bartolomeo di Mariano was first designated a tenorista. Jacomo, called a "chaplain and singer" in his earliest payments, was present from December 1406 through April 1408, and then, after a year's absence, from May 1409 through April 1411. Bartolomeo di Luti, called a "singer and clerk" in his first payment, also appears on two separate occasions, from May 1408 through April 1410, and during the months of May, June, and July 1411. One or another of them was thus employed with Bartolomeo di Mariano through April 1409, and all three served simultaneously from May 1409 through April 1410. Clearly, some kind of polyphony, improvised or written, was the order of the day.

Two chaplain-singers also appear occasionally in the following decade, although the sporadic nature of their employment suggests that the Opera was experiencing difficulty in retaining qualified performers. Cited together for six months from November 1415 through April 1416 were Ser Jacomo di Bellanduccio, once again identified as a "singer in the duomo," and the singer Ser Leonardo di Bartolomeo.[14] Ser Giovanni di Matteo da Perugia, a chaplain for a number of years, was first listed as a singer from February through April 1418 and then again from July 1419 through April 1420 as a "chaplain and singer in the duomo." For part of that time, from July through October 1419, the second singer was another chaplain, Ser Agnolo di Domenico. Ser Giovanni di Matteo da Perugia continued as a chaplain in the early 1420s, but was called "our singer" only in payments from May 1425 to April 1426. Ser Giovanni di Tommaso da Bologna, a chaplain in May 1424, was likewise designated "our singer" in payments from May 1425 through April 1426.

After an absence of many years Ser Jacomo di Bellanduccio returned to cathedral

---

14. Ser Jacomo may be the same person as the "Ser Iacobo chantore" mentioned in an undated letter written to the overseer Caterino Corsini by Maestro Bartolomeo d'Arezzo, a preacher in that city, who says that he had heard that Iacobo was returning to Siena on the same day he was writing: "adì 22 del presente mese ser Iacobo chantore me rechò una vostra lettera per la quale me dite che io vengha a cominciare le mie prediche per l'Avento . . . Anche vi pregho che ringratiate ser Iacopo

service in 1430 as a chaplain and singer of laudi. He was one of several laudesi employed at the cathedral in the early fifteenth century who on occasion were also identified by the term cantore. Distinguishing between the two kinds of singers is relatively easy because several of the laudesi were not otherwise employed at the cathedral and their names usually appeared separately under the heading laudesi in the sacristans' monthly rolls.

Several others, like Ser Jacomo, came from the ranks of the cathedral's own chaplains and clerks. Principal among these latter were Ser Leonardo di Bartolomeo, Ser Giovanni di Matteo da Perugia, and Ser Mariano di Giovanni. Leonardo, initially recorded as a singer-chaplain from November 1415 through April 1416, subsequently served as one of the two singers of laudi from September to December 1417 and then again from April 1422 to July 1424, all the while receiving his usual monthly distributions as a chaplain. Ser Giovanni di Matteo da Perugia's career followed a parallel path. First mentioned as a chaplain-singer in February 1418, he served in both capacities for the next several years. An account for May 1420, however, credits him with an additional s. 10 for singing laudi. Similar payments are listed to him, along with his usual monthly distributions, from that time through the end of July 1424. In his case the two separate sets of payments, corroborated by various sacristans' reports, demonstrate that he served simultaneously as a singer in the choir and as a singer of laudi.

Ser Mariano di Giovanni called Trafiere was one of the principal figures in the cathedral's musical establishment during the first quarter of the fifteenth century. A summary of his forty-year career provides a good deal of information both about his many talents and about the cathedral's flexible hiring policies. It also reflects the continuing interaction at this time between singers who performed polyphony in the choir and those who sang what was essentially a monophonic repertory in the vernacular with decidedly popular roots, the laude.

Ser Mariano was cited as a clerk as early as May 1396, while he was studying for the priesthood. Ordained around the turn of the fifteenth century, he served as both chaplain and sacristan during the fiscal year 1401–2, when he earned a salary of L. 97. 10. One record of payment from the following year credits him with the same salary; another registers an additional L. 1 that he received for "singing laudi in the duomo, that is, the Passion." His account from the fiscal year 1403–4 again refers to him as chaplain and sacristan and lists, in addition to his regular salary, payments "for singing laudi from January through April" and "for singing the Passion during Lent," 1404. He received monthly distributions for the next thirty years. During that time he became the cathedral's principal singer of laudi and was probably the teacher of many younger singers who eventually assisted him in the program.

Toward the end of his career Mariano also assumed a leading role in the choir, as is evident from a deliberation of 30 October 1434. After noting that Ser Mariano di Trafiere "is an honor to the choir and to the church and that he attends to his duties with more diligence than any of the others," the Opera's governing board decided to recognize his many merits by authorizing the overseer to give him an increase in salary.

---

chantore che me rechò la vostra lettera . . . m'è stato ditto che oggi esso è partito e tornato a voi" (AOMS, vol. 67, *Carteggio, Sec. XV,* fasc. 1, doc. 22).

Confirmation of this action comes from a few months later when it was reported that as of the past 30 October, Ser Mariano was "to have an additional Fl. 4 per annum, each valued at L. 4." Beginning in December 1435 the sacristans' monthly rolls record his service "as a chaplain and tenorista" and continue to do so until January 1440, when his name disappears from cathedral records. The later documents, all of which call him tenorista, offer the first indication from throughout his many years of service that he sang polyphony in the choir as well as laudi. But before discussing further developments in the choir during the 1430s, some remarks about companies of laudesi in Siena and an account of their activities at the cathedral will be useful to our understanding of the different kinds of music that were performed at services during these years.

THE LAUDESI

Soon after the death of St. Francis of Assisi in 1226 societies of laymen, inspired by his teachings and devotional practices instituted by him, sprang up in Tuscany. In the following centuries confraternities or companies, dedicated to a saint or to some holy relic, and embracing two distinct groups, the flagellants (called *disciplinati*) and those whose meetings were dedicated to prayer and song (called laudesi), could be found throughout Italy. Siena has the distinction of having had the earliest known company of laudesi, founded in 1267 by the blessed Ambrogio Sansedoni at the Dominican church in Camporegio.[15] The company's statutes, preserved in a letter from Siena's bishop Tommaso Fusconi, set forth procedures for elections of officers, meetings, processions, charitable activities, appointment of clergy as spiritual advisors, and members' obligations. Principal among the latter was attendance at meetings at the hour of Compline, where singing and hearing laudi, recitation of prayers, particularly the Pater noster and the Ave Maria, and a brief sermon formed the daily programs. Also required were bimonthly attendance at Sunday Mass and, on the following Monday, at commemorative Masses for deceased members and their families, as well as annual processions on twelve feasts. In 1273, when another Sienese bishop, Bernardo Gallerani, granted the company's members an indulgence, he noted that they sang laudi to the Blessed Virgin Mary every day. An important aspect of the company's activities, one adopted by the Dominicans in general, was the provision it made for boarding young boys who were trained to sing laudi.[16]

Singers of laudi were already performing at Siena cathedral in the mid-fourteenth century, though they may have started doing so decades earlier. Their continuing presence during the next century reflects a widespread form of popular devotion and lay expression in religious life that took root and flourished not only in the city but also throughout Tuscany and much of Italy at this time. The singers were members of the

---

15. This discussion is much indebted to Blake Wilson, *Music and Merchants: The Laudesi Companies of Republican Florence* (Oxford, 1992), 39–42. For the date see G. Meerseman, "Note sull'origine delle compagnie dei Laudesi (a Siena, 1267)," *Rivista di storia delle chiese in Italia* 17 (1963): 395–405.

16. As reported by Fra Recupero d'Arezzo, who gives an account of Sienese laude singing, ca. 1288, in his biography of the blessed Ambrogio Sansedoni. The passage has been most recently quoted by Wilson in *Music and Merchants,* 40–41.

Confraternity or Company of San Pietro, or San Pietro nel Duomo, which had ties to the cathedral dating from as early as the beginning of the fourteenth century. The confraternity held services at the altar of St. Peter, of which it was principal patron; its membership may initially have been limited to cathedral priests. But in later centuries it counted both clergy and lay men and women among its members.[17] Unlike its flagellant counterparts at the hospital of Santa Maria della Scala, across the square from the cathedral, the confraternity's principal activities were dedicated to prayer and singing laudi. Exactly when laudi were sung at the cathedral is not specified in surviving documents, though several references to daytime services and another to Lauds indicate a flexible performing schedule. Operating expenses were covered by members' annual dues and from income from endowments and bequests from deceased members, though cathedral records from the late fourteenth century through the mid-fifteenth indicate that the sacristy provided for some of the group's needs and supported a good many, if not all, of its activities.

Among the earliest references to laudesi at the cathedral are those found in a record from 1365, which lists payment for 10 pounds of large candles that were used when "the laudi of the confraternity were sung," and in another from 1367, which cites the cost of having "a new book made for the laudesi of the confraternity."[18] This may have been one of the three books of laudi listed in a cathedral inventory of 1429, but if so, there is no mention of it in the earlier inventories of 1390 and 1391.[19] Maestro Michele di Nello, a foreman in the cathedral's building program, has the distinction of being the first singer of record, although it is possible that there were others before him who were cited in documents no longer extant. A payment of Fl. 2 to him for his annual salary, registered in September 1372, is followed by a number of others in the following years. As these and other reports reveal, paid performers of laudi at this time were laymen rather than clerics, which suggests that their repertory was an essentially monophonic one sung to predominantly vernacular texts. During 1375 several payments for various purposes were issued to the confraternity's administrator, Crescenzio di Meo Benucci, among them one from September listing an honorarium of L. 7 "for the

---

17. Some information about the confraternity in the fourteenth century is given by Lusini, *Il Duomo di Siena,* 1:229, 336, 341, 361. Several of the confraternity's account books from later centuries have survived and are now in ASS among the holdings of PR, Compagnia di San Pietro nel Duomo di Siena. Among these may be cited vol. 1360, *E&U, 1513–24,* which shows that several cathedral chaplain-singers of the early sixteenth century were among its members, as were lay men and women such as Maestro Vincentio, medico di Lucca, Ser Feliciano di Ser Neri, notario, Camillo di Bartolomeo Petrucci (fol. 37 l–r); Monna Magdalena di Domenico da Rampaglia, Monna Niccola, sorella di Ser Aenea, Monna Lisabetta di Francesca (fol. 40 l–r); Pierotto Spagnuolo, familiare delli Spannocchi (fol. 58 l–r); and Andrea trombetto (fol. 86 l–r). The singer-chaplains are mentioned below in chapter 7.

18. "A Ghido di Viero, pizichaiuolo, quatro lire, quindici soldi per diece libre di chandele grosse da cantare len [*sic*] lade della fraternita" (September 1365); "A Michele di Nello . . . per fare uno libro nuovo pe' laudesi della fraternità" (August 1367) (AOMS, vol. 1227, *E&U della Sagrestia, 1365–67,* fols. 19ʳ and 46ʳ).

19. On these books, see chapter 2, notes 16–17, and Tables 3.1 and 4.1.

laudesi so that they will come more willingly to lauds." Another from November cites expenses for the customary meal the singers enjoyed on the feast of Sant'Ansano.[20]

The feast of Sant'Ansano is mentioned again in 1381, when Michele di Nello was given L. 4. 10 "to honor those singers who help him sing laudi" on that day.[21] Records such as these point to the presence of several performers at some services, though they also suggest that Michele di Nello was the only regularly salaried singer in the early 1380s. Perhaps he led the congregation in singing monophonic laudi on ferial days and performed polyphonic laudi on feast days with singers who were brought in for the occasion. Records from 1388, 1389, and 1390 indicate that it became customary to employ two singers at a time.[22] Laudesi cited during the last decade of the century include Niccolò di Berto, who also served as the company's administrator in 1392, and a number of others who invariably appear as the second singer, among them, Agostino di Vannuccio, Frate Ambrogio di Giovanni, Antonio di Cirello, and Brandaglia, several of whom appear to have been laymen.[23]

Cathedral Laudesi, 1400–1440

The practice of employing two singers of laudi at the cathedral continued with only an occasional interruption throughout the first four decades of the fifteenth century. Many of the laudesi were now clerics or youths in training for the priesthood. Perhaps they learned to sing laudi under the guidance of Ser Mariano, who may have had a larger role in the program than is suggested by payment records. Some laudesi were employed as cathedral chaplains. All were from Siena or from places nearby. These factors likely contributed to the stability of the program and to the relative ease with which singers replaced one another. The nature of the repertory itself may also have contributed to continuity, for it was a genuinely "popular" one that must have lain within the capabilities of most people. During this period, as has been noted, the Opera was often hard put to maintain a steady number of chaplain-singers of polyphony in the choir. Perhaps this was because singers of written polyphony were still relatively rare and their services were priced accordingly, whereas singers of laudi required little if any training and were generally available.

The two singers listed for the fiscal year May 1401 through April 1402 were Gu-

---

20. "Uscita di settenbre 1375 . . . A Crese[n]zio di Meio Benucci chamarlengho della fraternità di duomo per fare onore a' laldesi aciochè venissero più volentieri a le lalde, sette s., VII s." (AOMS, vol. 207, *E&U, 1375–76,* fol. 56ᵛ); "Uscita di novembre 1375 . . . A Crescienzio di Meio Benucci chamarlingo de la fraternità di duomo per lo mangiare per la festa di Santo Sano chome usanza a' laldesi, per la spese desse mangiare" (ibid., fol. 61ʳ); "Uscita del deto mese d'aprile 1377 . . . A Crese[n]zo sagrestano de' laldesi del duomo uno fl. ebe fino d'otobre per [gap] mesi servì al detto uffizio" (vol. 208, *E&U, 1376–77,* fol. 64ʳ).

21. "L. 4. 10 per fare onore a cholor che gli aitano a chantare le lade" (vol. 1231, *E&U della Sagrestia, 1380–81,* fol. 16ʳ).

22. A typical payment reads: "e laldesi che chantano le lade in duomo dieno avere per lo chantare dele lalde a ragion di 40 soldi el mese. L. 2" (vol. 1242, *E&U della Sagrestia, 1392–93,* fol. 45ʳ).

23. Vol. 1243, *E&U della Sagrestia, 1393–94,* fol. 64ʳ, mentions a payment "a quegli che chantano le lalde in duomo." Payments to Niccolò di Berto and the others cited here are in vols. 980–82, *E&U della Sagrestia* for 1398–99, 1399–1400, and 1400–1.

glielmo di Martino, a clerk at the hospital of Santa Maria della Scala, and Antonio di Cirello. Guglielmo subsequently became a priest and a mainstay among the performers of laudi, sharing an almost continuous role in the group with Ser Mariano. As chaplain at the hospital of Santa Maria della Scala, across the square from the cathedral, Guglielmo doubtless had charge of laudi singing there, though there is no record of this. One entry in this early account from the cathedral notes that he was paid for having sung the gospel during May and June of 1401 and for having sung the "Passion" in March 1402. Records from the fiscal year 1402–3 are somewhat more informative about these practices. They note that the gospel was sung throughout the year by two of the hospital's clerks and that the "Passion" was sung on the evenings of Lent, 1403 by four different people, Guglielmo di Martino, Lorenzo di Menico, Matteo di Guido, and Mariano di Giovanni. There is no record of whether this was the *Passione del Signore,* composed in 1364 by the Sienese Niccolò di Mino Cicerchia, though possibly it was.[24] Additional payments to laudesi for performing the same duties are registered in the years immediately following, but the absence of payments in later records suggests that they were eventually taken over by other cathedral personnel.[25]

Three laudesi were employed intermittently through December 1403, but after that time two became the norm. Ser Mariano di Giovanni and Guglielmo are routinely listed at a monthly salary of L. 1 (s. 20) each from January 1404 through September 1411, when Mariano ceded his duties to others. After that one of three singers sang intermittently with the now ordained Ser Guglielmo. Among them was Ser Francesco di Nanni, then a chaplain at the hospital of Santa Maria della Scala, who later became cathedral organist, his presence among the laudesi thus providing another link to laudi performances at that institution. Ser Mariano was back in his old post by March 1416 and was again assisted by another singer. Despite a temporary gap in records, listings in the fiscal year 1417–18 show that he was still employed with a second singer. Financial problems had apparently arisen, for both were now on a monthly salary of only s. 5. The same salary is registered during the fiscal year 1418–1419, but was raised to s. 10 in the following year.

The participation of chaplain-singers in the early 1420s, as remarked, suggests that some Sienese singers of laudi were also capable of singing part music and that some of the Sienese laude repertory, like that of Florence, may have included polyphonic pieces. Ser Mariano di Giovanni reappeared among the laudesi in May 1424 and, but for the period between May 1427 and April 1428, is recorded with one or another of three singers through April 1434. During the 1430s several previously recorded chaplains again assisted him, among them Guglielmo di Martino, who subsequently sang through the end of November 1434. One payment to Guglielmo from September 1433 notes

---

24. Modern edition in Giorgio Varanini, ed., *Cantari religiosi senesi del Trecento: Neri Pagliaresi, Fra Felice Tancredi da Massa, Niccolò Cicerchia* (Bari, 1965), 309–79. It is in ottava rima.

25. Interesting in this regard is a report from 1403 of expenditures for Holy Week services: "A misser Antonio da Pisa chanonicho che chantò la messa venerdì santo la messa [*sic*] a dì XIII d'aprile, s. vinti; a ser Giovanni prete che chantò l'evangielo, s. diecie; e Antonio d'Alesso chericho chantò deto dì la 'pistola, s. cinque; in tutto s. trentacinque chontanti in mano di ser Mariano sagrestano" (vol. 230, *E&U, 1402–3,* fol. 51ʳ).

that he was also employed as music teacher in the cathedral school. No better argument could be put forth for his having been a singer of polyphony as well as a singer of laudi. Records from the next few years fail to mention the laudesi, though they do list singers of polyphony, perhaps indicating that laudi performances were temporarily suspended. Most of the laudesi were well along in years by now and retirement or death may have thinned their ranks. In any case it is clear that the tradition of employing two or more laudesi on Sunday and feast-day evenings continued through the mid-1430s and that from the 1420s onwards most, if not all, of the singers were chaplains associated with the cathedral. As a result, interaction between "popular" and high art polyphony must have been as frequent, and perhaps as fruitful, in Siena as it was in Florence.

Repertories of the Laudesi

Sienese sources yield no trace of the polyphonic pieces in the repertory of the cathedral's laudesi, though it could be that, like their Florentine brethren, when they sang part music, they adapted ballatas and other secular pieces then in vogue by substituting devotional texts for secular ones. They might also have performed hymns, sequences, and two- and three-part motets of the type preserved in the famous laudario FBNC, Banco Rari 18, prepared in the early fourteenth century for the Florentine Company of Santo Spirito. Certainly, the presence among the laudesi of singers who performed polyphony at cathedral services argues in favor of some kind of polyphony, however limited in scope. But monophony was probably more the norm. Evidence regarding at least one of the monophonic laudi performed by the Sienese singers in the early decades of the fifteenth century appears in cathedral inventories. Three books of laudi were listed in an inventory of 1429, though the number dropped to one in an inventory of 1439, which reported that the book began with a piece entitled *Ave, donna santissima.* Since a similar description is found as well in later inventories from 1449, 1458, and 1467, there is no reason to doubt that *Ave, donna santissima* was, in fact, the name of the book's opening piece (see Table 3.1). As it turns out, a monophonic laude by that name, appropriate for the feast of the Assumption, survives in two famous collections of laudi, the one at Florence, the other in Cortona.[26] This suggests that some portion

26. They are MS Banco Rari 18 of the Biblioteca Nazionale Centrale, Florence, and MS 91 of the Biblioteca Comunale, Cortona. The manuscripts have been discussed in a number of places, most notably by Wilson, *Music and Merchants,* 150–60. The music of *Ave, donna santissima* was transcribed and published by Ferdinando Liuzzi, *La lauda e i primordi della melodia italiana* (Rome, 1935), vol. 1, no. 3; a modern edition of its text is in Giorgio Varanini, Luigi Banfi, and Anna Ceruti Burgio, eds., *Laude cortonesi dal secolo XIII al XV* (Florence, 1981–85), 1/i, 93–101. Wilson, *Music and Merchants,* 23, 156, 158, gives a comparison of the Florence and Cortona versions. Wilson has recently reexamined the Florence manuscript in light of his findings that its leaves were trimmed during the course of a sixteenth- or seventeenth-century restoration, with the resultant loss or mutilation of the top staff of nearly every folio. In the case of *Ave, donna santissima,* apart from the obvious mistake of entering the clef a third too high for the music of the first seven notes that set the incipit, the only questionable section is the one at the top of fol. 49ʳ, which begins on the syllable "tia" of "gratia" in line 4 and continues through the setting of the first seven notes of line 5, "in te, virgo." He notes that this latter is the only part of the melody to depart significantly from the Cortona version. See the Introduction to his edition, Blake Wilson and Nello Barbieri, eds., *The Florence Laudario,* Recent Researches in the

TABLE 3.1.   Inventories of selected music manuscripts, 1429–1449

1429: Inventario . . . al tempo del'egregio kavaliere missere Bartalomeo di Giovanni Ciechi operaio (vol. 1492, *Inventari, 1420–post 1488*, fasc. 2)

      fol. 3ʳ: In sagrestia la cappella de la libraria. Armarii intorno a la detta cappella . . .

      fol. 4ʳ: Uno libro di vilume piccolo, chimasi Musica di Bogio [Boetio], con tavole e cuoio rosso e fondelli

      fol. 5ʳ: Tre libri di laude, di mezano vilume, lettara di testo, solfati, coverti di tavole e cuoio parte nero e parte rosso, con coppe e ciovi

1435: Inventario . . . scripto ala presentia . . . di messer Iacomo di Piero hoperaio (ibid., fasc. 3; the three books of laudi are not mentioned)

      fol. 5ʳ: Uno libro antico chiamato seguentiale coverte di legnio con nove chiovi di ottone per lato e v'è ne cinque per lato

1439: In questo libro e inventario apparranno scripte tucte le cose le quali sono dell'Opera (ibid., fasc. 4, 1439–46)

      fol. 3ᵛ: [18]   Uno seguentiale coperto di biancho, singnato XVIII, Regiem venturum

      fol. 4ᵛ: [46]   Una musicha di Boetio con uno fondello rosso, sengnato XLVI, comincia Omnium quidem

      fol. 5ʳ: [60]   Uno libro de lalde per volgare cuperto di nero, sengnato LX, comincia Ave donna sanctissima

             [61]   Uno seguentiale cuperto di nero, sengnato LXI, comincia Letabuntur

1449: Inventario . . . al tempo dello spettabile et mangnifico chavaliere misser Mariano di Pavolo de' Bargagli dingnissimo et benemerito oparaio di detta chiesa (ibid., fasc. 7)

      fols. 5ᵛ, 6ʳ, 7ᵛ: lists the same items as in the 1439 inventory

---

of the Sienese repertory was drawn from other Tuscan sources and helps place Sienese practices within a regional orbit.

The melody of *Ave, donna santissima,* as it appears in the oldest layer of the Cortona manuscript, does not differ significantly from the version found in the Florentine codex (see Exs. 3.1a and b). This is somewhat surprising, given the wide amount of latitude in the preservation of what was essentially an oral art. The older Cortona reading, representative of an Umbrian tradition distinctive though not independent of the Tuscan one, presents a somewhat less florid version of the melody, whereas the Florentine version expands melismas on important syllables and decorates the tune, typifying a Florentine tendency toward melodic arabesque. The Florence version has only eight stanzas of text as opposed to Cortona's twenty-one stanzas. Blake Wilson suggests that the reduced scope of the poetry was due to the greater emphasis on music in the Florentine collection, which he associates with the increased virtuosic character of the Florentine melodic versions in general. A corollary of this was the professionalization

---

Music of the Middle Ages and Early Renaissance 29 (Madison, 1995), esp. pp. xxiv and 40 for critical notes and a new edition of the piece.

of laudi singers in Florence, evident at Orsanmichele from as early as the 1360s, and the growing tendency toward distancing the congregation from participating in some of the more elaborate music done at services.[27] But the emergence of trained singers and solo virtuosity in the traditional repertory also eased the path leading toward the adoption by the laudesi of certain forms of part music.[28] Eventually, the process of assimilating polyphonic pieces into the laude repertory contributed toward a break-down of traditional barriers between the elaborate style of church music and the popular melodies (and harmonies) sung by an essentially untrained laity, a process I defined some years ago as a "democratization" of polyphonic practices in Florence.[29] The same situation apparently occurred at Siena cathedral after 1400, when all of the singers were chaplains or young clerks, several of whom subsequently became professional singers of polyphony.

Cathedral Laudesi, 1440–1455

The presence of two new singers, the cathedral clerks Francesco di Antonio di Boccone d'Asciano and Giuliano, from April through December 1440, signals a new generation of laudesi and a return to the earlier practice of hiring youths.[30] After a break in the records, two are again registered in payments covering the period May 1446 through September 1450. Francesco's companion was now Simone di Mariano, also a clerk. A record from 1446 notes that they they were paid "for singing the gospel from the pulpit during Lent, just past, and laudi in the duomo during Holy Week, and also because they sang laudi in the duomo on Sundays several months ago." A similar payment to them from the following year reports that "Francesco d'Asciano was staying with the archdeacon," Messer Piero di Pasqua, and that Simone "was staying with Ser Francesco the priest who plays the organ." Piero di Pasqua, canon and cathedral archdeacon, himself had a significant role in the choir at this time, and Francesco di Nanni, a some-time singer of laudi, was then cathedral organist and a teacher in the cathedral school. Connections between the laudesi and performers of polyphony, even at this late date, were thus as close as they ever had been and indeed were to become even closer within a few years, when both Francesco and Simone were hired to sing polyphony in the choir.

Payments to Francesco and Simone for singing laudi continue without interruption from December 1448 through September 1450, after which references to laudesi rarely

---

27. See D'Accone, "Le compagnie dei laudesi in Firenze durante l'Ars Nova," *L'Ars Nova italiana del Trecento* 3 (1970), 253–80, esp. 267, for Orsanmichele, and p. 264 for evidence regarding biscantori from the Florentine church of San Lorenzo who performed at services for the duomo's Company of San Zenobi.

28. Wilson, *Music and Merchants,* 158–59.

29. D'Accone, "Le compagnie dei laudesi," 280.

30. Sacristans' reports for the months in question indicate that Giuliano was temporarily replaced by Ser Angelo in August 1440; Francesco was absent in September; additionally, several similar reports show Giuliano laudese alone in January and February 1440. Both Ser Angelo and Giuliano were previously unmentioned among the laudesi.

appear in the Opera's account books.[31] This may mean that funding for their services was henceforth provided by another source. It could also mean that singing laudi now became the province of professional musicians in the confraternity who, serving without salary, either performed together in small ensembles or led their associates in group singing, or perhaps did a bit of both. It could also mean that from time to time laudesi were brought in to sing on a temporary basis. This latter is a distinct possibility in view of a later report from February 1473 in which three singers, Ser Agostino, Ser Francesco di Barnaba, and Antonio di Troiano, were paid L. 12 "for having sung laudi for three months in the duomo." It is unlikely, in any case, that laude performances at the cathedral were dispensed with, for other documents attest to San Pietro's flourishing state in the following century, as it maintained a place alongside several other companies that had developed elaborate programs in venues of their own.[32]

A letter from a distant quarter also attests to the importance of the performing tradition of laude in Siena in the mid-fifteenth century, while illustrating one of the ways in which the repertories of the Sienese confraternities were enriched with new works. The letter, dated Rimini, 22 December 1454, is from Tracalo da Rimini to his compatriot Pandolfo Malatesta, who was in Siena at the time, serving as Captain General of the Sienese army (see Doc. 3.1). Tracalo says that a few days previously a certain Bernardo cantore (not otherwise known) had asked him to compose "a laude to Our Lady to be sung on the first Sunday of the month of January."[33] Tracalo then goes on to say how he had fulfilled the singer's request. First, he had obtained the text and music of a song, apparently a well-known one, and after studying them, he had composed a new poem of his own that could be sung to the same music. Tracalo also says he was sending his new poem, which he had purposely made brief so as not to bore his listeners, along with his letter. Though no trace of the poem or of the tune to which it was sung survives in Sienese libraries, the letter is important because it offers another affirmation of the widespread practice of setting new laude texts to preexistent music and new information about people who wrote them.

SINGERS AND SINGING TEACHERS

A few chaplains not identified as laudesi also served as singers in the cathedral choir during the 1420s. They included two singing teachers, both of whom were appointed in 1426. But apart from a pair of itinerant French singers who stayed for only a month, no other chaplain-singers besides the teachers are mentioned in the years immediately

---

31. Simone's patronymic is mistakenly given as di Bartolomeo in some records, doubtless a slip of the pen on the sacristan's part. In the 1450s, when he began singing in the choir, he was correctly referred to as Simone di Mariano.

32. In addition to the volume cited above in note 17, mention may be made of the following: ASS, PR, Compagnia di San Pietro nel Duomo di Siena, vol. 1369, *Capitoli, Elenchi dei fratelli, Debitori & Creditori, Entrata & Uscita*, containing later statutes and membership lists from the sixteenth century; and vol. 1364, *Raccolta delle notizie spettanti alle fondazioni, erezioni, dotazioni et obblighi delle cappellanie perpetue . . . e de altri benefizi ecclesiastici de la venerabile congregazione di San Pietro nella Metropolitana di Siena gode il patronato, fatta e compilata in quest'anno 1730 d'ordine de' Signori*.

33. Since laudi were traditionally sung at the cathedral on Sunday evenings, the piece may possibly have entered the confraternity's repertory.

following. The teachers were engaged in response to the previously noted governmental decree of 1419, which obliged the overseer to maintain a chaplain-teacher of grammar, a chaplain-teacher of singing, and a chaplain-organist. Since the directive specifically mentioned that the singing teacher was to be expert in figural music as well as in chant, all of those who held the post in years to come must have been singers of polyphony.

The first of the new singing teachers, Ser Giustiniano di Ser Francesco da Todi, was appointed on 20 April 1426 at an annual salary of Fl. 30. The terms of his contract called, among other things, for him "to say Mass every day, like the other chaplains," to sing in the choir, and to teach singing "to our people who wish to learn." He is recorded through the end of June 1432 and then again from mid-August through the end of November 1435. During his first stint in cathedral service, which lasted through the end of November 1435, he was inevitably referred to as a cantore, and this, coupled with the knowledge that he sang polyphony in later years, suggests that he did the same at this time. Ser Giustiniano, a man of many talents, was also employed by the Opera as a maker of stained glass windows.[34]

The other singing teacher, Messer Battista di Ser Francesco da Todi, was appointed on 27 April 1426, just a week after Ser Giustiniano, who must have been his brother. The terms of his contract show that he was hired primarily to serve as a chaplain. He was obliged, for example, "to do everything the other chaplains and priests do," which meant that he was not exempt from attending the canonical hours or from saying his share of hebdomadal Masses. In addition, he was to teach singing "to all those of ours who would like to learn to sing, without salary" and as the need arose, he was to substitute for the organist. Though he had no extra stipend for teaching, his annual salary of Fl. 35, or L. 140, was higher by L. 20 than Giustiniano's. Perhaps this was because he was also expected to sing polyphony, which he must have been able to do as a result of his training as an organist. Payments to Battista are recorded for the following two years, through the end of April 1428.

There was another singer who figured prominently in the cathedral's musical establishment during the early fifteenth century, though he was identified as a cantore on very few occasions. This was the canon and archdeacon Messer Piero di Pasqua, whose career spanned more than six decades. He began his long tenure at the church in mid-October 1406, when he assumed the office of archdeacon, and for the next twenty years monthly distributions for his participation in offices were regularly recorded without comment. But an entry in his account for the 1425–26 fiscal year indicates that he had taken on other duties, for his annual salary of L. 146. 4 now included a payment of L. 40 for singing in the choir, "per lo canto del coro," an apparently new occupation he began in November 1425. A record from August 1437 is more explicit, calling him "a cathedral canon and singer." Payments in the amount of L. 40 per annum for these additional duties, often described as "for singing" or "for singing in the choir," appear in his accounts during all but a few years of the next two decades through May 1445.

---

34. Documents regarding his work in stained glass, the first dated 12 February 1434, have been published by Borghesi and Banchi, *Nuovi documenti per la storia dell'arte Senese,* 101.

But after that time and until his last month of service in December 1472, he received only the usual monthly distributions.

For some twenty years Piero thus took an active, though unspecified, role in the choir, for which he received an additional salary. His position as a canon and archdeacon would not have precluded his assuming the office of prefect of the choir, as it was described in the 1459 Constitutions. But this seems improbable because the prefect was elected on an annual basis and customarily served for only a year at at a time. Furthermore, no canon before or after him is mentioned in the Opera's accounts as receiving an additional salary for serving in that office, which certainly would have been the case had it been a paying one. There is nothing in the record to suggest that Piero assumed the role of cantor or leader of the choir during that time, for as the 1459 Constitutions make clear, the post was held by canons or chaplains who served, without extra compensation, on a weekly basis. It seems, then, that Messer Piero's twenty-year career as a singer represents the one instance in the cathedral's musical history when a canon actually performed alongside the chaplain-singers of polyphony.

ORGANISTS, 1375–1454

Mention has already been made of Ser Francesco di Nanni, the one-time singer of laudi and organist at the hospital, who became cathedral organist. He assumed the post on 15 October 1424, when he was still associated with the monks of San Martino. He was to remain cathedral organist for the next three decades, serving, in addition, as teacher of organ and on occasion as singing teacher. He was also one of the few musicians at this time to hold one of the cathedral's perpetual chaplaincies, that attached to the altar of San Crescenzio. Francesco's place in the cathedral's musical program is difficult to illustrate, given the lack of records regarding his official duties. But he must have had a good deal of influence because occasionally his name figures among those consulted when major decisions regarding the chapel singers were made. His continuing presence throughout a period when written polyphony made such great inroads into the cathedral's liturgy is a sure sign of his ability to keep abreast of contemporary trends and of his superior gifts as a musician. Though none of his predecessors appears ever to have had the authority he had, there was a long line of them stretching back half a century to the time shortly after the cathedral's first documented organ was finished. An account of their activities will furnish some idea of Francesco's duties, while demonstrating that the Opera often took great pains in seeking the services of the best musicians available for the post.

It is doubtful that the cathedral was employing an organist during the early 1370s because no names appear in any of the extant records concerning the organ's construction, installation, and evaluation. This surely would have been the case had there been one. More than two years, in fact, were to pass after the inauguration of the new instrument before an organist, Benedetto di Jacomo da Firenze, was engaged. His annual salary, fixed at Fl. 8, was lower than what would be offered in the future and may account for his brief stay. Benedetto arrived in Siena from Florence—his travel expenses courtesy of the Opera—in September 1375 and monthly payments to him, at the rate of L. 2. 11. 4, are registered from November 1375 through April 1376. None of these mentions the days and services when he performed.

Another musician was auditioned for the organist's post only a few months after Benedetto's arrival. This was Maestro Matteo di Martino, a Sienese organist employed at the cathedral of San Martino in Lucca since 1357.[35] His name first appears in Sienese records in January 1376, when he was reimbursed Fl. 2 for his expenses in traveling from Lucca to Siena and back, "as was promised him in our letter." Additional expenses for refreshments "to honor Matteo on several occasions" indicate that the audition process included a number of performances. Evidently, the overseer and his counselors were so pleased with Matteo's playing that he was offered a five-year contract on the spot. Dated 12 January 1376, this states that his tenure would begin in the following March and that he was to play on "all solemn days, as is customary, and any other days that were necessary for the honor of the church of Santa Maria." In return Matteo was to receive an annual salary of Fl. 30, "a bedroom, a small room, and a bedstead for his abode" and "all of the expenses needed for his clothing and his shoes." It is difficult to judge how advantageous these terms were in comparison with what Matteo had at Lucca, where he earned an annual salary of Fl. 12 in cash and was given a house and yearly supplies of bread, wine, and oil.[36] But he clearly had second thoughts about accepting the Sienese invitation once he returned to his old post, for a note appended to the contract by the overseer Pietro Venturini says that he "didn't do what he had promised." Matteo, in fact, was so satisfied with his situation in Lucca that he remained there until his death in 1401.

In the annotation to the contract just mentioned Venturini also noted that the Opera had hired an organist named Monte instead of Matteo. Monte di Lillo da Prato, to give him his full name, began his tenure on 15 September 1376. His contract called for him to receive a monthly salary of Fl. 2—six less per annum than Matteo had been promised—as well as his meals "in the rectory with the duomo's other priests." If he wished instead to dine alone, he would receive "bread and wine due him from the sacristy." And should he decide to buy a house, he was to have "a bed, and furniture to his taste" (see Doc. 3.2). These terms suggest that musicians, whether organists or singers, laymen or priests, received the same kinds of perquisites given to cathedral chaplains. Although Monte's duties are not enumerated, the contract states that he was to play every Saturday afternoon (presumably at Vespers) and on Sundays and feast days (undoubtedly at Masses), as well as when he was requested to do so by the overseer or the sacristan. The terms were essentially those echoed through the ages, whenever a new organist was hired.

As later events show, Monte, like Matteo, was an organist of some renown. How his particular talents came to the attention of cathedral officials is a matter of speculation; however, as suggested by a later situation involving recruitment of cathedral musicians that will be recounted below, it seems that it was through one of the usual channels, that is, through reports from Sienese musicians, merchants, diplomats, or clergymen traveling outside the city who had heard him play or knew others who recommended

---

35. Luigi Nerici, *Storia della musica in Lucca* (Lucca, 1879; repr. Bologna, 1969), 42, 149–50. Matteo became a citizen of Lucca in 1381 and sold a house there in 1384. One of his sons succeeded him as organist at San Martino.

36. Ibid., 150.

him. Similarly, potential candidates for the organist's post at Siena cathedral may have had news about the new instrument and about working conditions from other organists and organ builders who knew the situation there, either first-hand or through interme- diaries. There may, in other words, have been support systems, unknown to us, that provided organists and other musicians, well-established ones as well as newcomers, with information about openings, working conditions, and the possibilities of employ- ment in cities throughout the peninsula. Such a network, however informal it may have been, as well as what appear to have been loosely established migratory patterns, might help explain the appearance in the decades—and centuries—to come of out-of-town musicians with no previously known ties to Siena.

Monte was cathedral organist through September 1379, at which time he refused to accept a new contract with revised terms of employment (see Doc. 3.3). These called for him to play only on Sundays and feast days, but at a reduced annual salary of Fl. 20 and with a new food allowance of four loaves of bread a day, a measure of wine, and ten pounds of meat a month. His whereabouts immediately after he left Siena are unknown, but subsequently he was organist at the cathedral of Milan, from 1394 through August 1416, where he became a colleague of the composer Matteo da Peru- gia.[37] Monte's later career suggests that, as before, the Opera set its sights high in the matter of hiring organists.

Monte's immediate successor was Messer Matteo di San Giorgio, cited from Sep- tember through mid-October 1379, when Messer Francesco di Vanni, a canon of Cor- tona, took over the post. The terms of Francesco's contract obliged him "to play the organ for one year and to officiate in the choir and to say Mass," though he was ex- empted from attending Matins. He received an annual salary of Fl. 30 for himself and one of his student assistants and both were invited to have their meals in the refectory. A note appended to his contract says that he remained at the cathedral "officiating and playing" through 15 October 1380, as stipulated in his contract.

Francesco was succeded by Don Bartalomeo di Ser Laio, whose annual salary was fixed at Fl. 25. A number of payments issued to him through December 1383 indicate that he played at Vespers on certain days and that on others he played "in the night at Matins and in the morning at Mass and the evening at Vespers." In December of that same year he was also paid for playing on the feast of San Frediano, which was also the feast of the cathedral's consecration, and the feast of St. Sebastian, a certain indication that these were celebrated as major feast days at the time. Beginning service in May 1384 at an annual salary of Fl. 30 was Ser Paolo, "a chaplain in the duomo who plays the organ." He was employed through 23 October 1385. Paolo's appointment may have come about as a result of a misunderstanding with the previous organist, for within a week of his departure Bartalomeo was back at his old post, this time at a salary of 8 gold florins per annum. Bartalomeo began serving as a chaplain once again on 1 May 1386 and thereafter he received a combined annual salary of L. 100 for serving in both

---

37. Sartori, "Matteo da Perugia e Bertrand Feragut," 12, n. 1; p. 22. Sartori shows that in 1406–7 Monte's monthly salary of L. 6. 13. 4 was augmented by a subsidy of L. 2. 18. 8, bringing it to a total of L. 9. 11. 8. This was only a few denari lower than the L. 9. 12. 0 paid to the singer-composer Matteo da Perugia.

capacities. In the following years through April 1392 he was paid a somewhat lower salary because he was exempted from attending Matins.[38] Though there is no mention of his duties, records of payments to the three men who pumped the bellows reveal that Bartalomeo normally played at Masses and Vespers on Sundays and feast days and, additionally, at other services on feasts that were celebrated with more than the usual pomp. On Corpus Christi, for example, he played at first Vespers and Compline on the evening before and then on the following day at Matins, at Mass, at Second Vespers, and at Compline. Two other organists are mentioned in the following decade, the cathedral chaplain, Ser Michelino di Nanni, from June 1392 through August 1393, and Frate Colo, a Carmelite friar from Pisa, from January 1394 through April 1396. Subsequently, the post was held alternately by Frate Colo and Don Bartalomeo. This latter served for two years, from August 1396 through August 1398, at the rate of Fl. 30 per annum. Frate Colo reappeared in February 1399 and was employed at his usual salary of Fl. 24 per annum through July 1400. In October of the same year Bartalomeo returned to the cathedral for the last time and remained through the end of April 1401. As before, he was obliged to say Mass every morning and he was accordingly paid the same salary he had previously received.

Ser Michelino di Nanni also returned for a final stint in his old post. This began on 22 December 1401 and lasted through the spring of 1404. On one occasion during that time he was also called *maestro* in a record specifying that he, too, was obliged to say a daily Mass and that his annual salary was pegged at Fl. 30. His successor was Don Agostino di Pietro, a canon of San Martino, who began serving with a two-year contract in July 1404 at an annual salary of Fl. 16. Though initially hired to play the organ only, he later took on additional duties as a chaplain. Except for the period from May 1414 through April 1415, when he took a leave and was replaced by Maestro Nanni di Jacomo di Firenze, the Dominican monk Fra Ugolino, and Don Matteo di Antonio, he served as organist for the next two decades, through summer of 1424. He was apparently fired shortly afterwards, serving perhaps within a few weeks before mid-October of that year, when Ser Francesco di Nanni assumed the post.

THE ADVENT OF ITINERANT SINGERS

The important role played by foreign musicians in the Sienese chapel during the latter part of the fifteenth century was foreshadowed by the arrival in 1431 of a pair of itinerant French singers, the tenorista Riccardo, also called Gherardo, and Ser Giovanni Ragione cantore. The former, cited from February through May, received a monthly salary of L. 6. 13. 4, the usual one paid chaplains, an indication that he was a cleric. He is probably the same person as Gherardo LeFay (Leay), who served in the chapels of Pope Eugene IV, from 1436 to 1443, and of Marquis Leonello d'Este of Ferrara, from 1443 to 1446, before returning, in 1447, to papal service in Rome, where he died in 1453.[39] Ser Giovanni Ragione may be identical with Johannes Reson, composer of a

---

38. The payment records indicate that the gold florin at this time was worth L. 3. 10.

39. F. X. Haberl, "Die römische 'schola cantorum' und die päpstlichen Kapellsänger bis zur Mitte des 16. Jahrhunderts," *Bausteine für Musikgeschichte* 3 (Leipzig, 1888), 221; Lewis Lockwood, *Music in Renaissance Ferrara 1400–1505: The Creation of a Musical Center in the Fifteenth Century* (Cambridge,

cyclic Mass and a few other sacred and secular French pieces.[40] He is mentioned for ten days in April and for all of May 1431, during which he was paid at the rate of L. 10 per month. After this time half a dozen years were to pass before French singers of polyphony would again appear. Meanwhile, as mentioned, the cathedral continued its usual practice of employing chaplain-singers and performers of laudi.

The first Frenchman to have a more permanent appointment as a singer-chaplain was Ser Giovanni di Jacopo biscantore.[41] Though his name is lacking in sacristans' rolls and accounts from the spring of 1437, when he began his tenure, a record of an unusual sort fixes precisely the date he entered cathedral service. This is a payment for s. 40, made to a secondhand dealer, Chimento di Pavolo, "for the rental of a pair of sheets . . . used by Ser Giovanni di Jacopo biscantore Francioso" for the period 14 May through 23 October 1437. Giovanni's name subsequently appears on sacristans' rolls from July through December 1437. Though he is not cited in extant records from the months immediately following, he was present from April through October 1438. His monthly salary of L. 8. 2 also included compensation for his services as a chaplain. Regarding these, an annotation in attendance records for September 1438 says that he missed Vespers on the 2nd and did not return until the 7th, while another for October states that he was away on the 6th. The sacristan's roll for August 1438 calls him "Giovanni di Jacopo Francioso alias Messer Violetta," which probably means that he was an instrumentalist as well as a singer of polyphony.

The other singer-chaplain of French origin associated with the cathedral at this time was also named Giovanni. This was Messer Giovanni di Giovanni Francioso, who is generally referred to as cantore or tenorista in surviving records. Mentioned for the first time on 27 July 1437, when he received L. 4. 13. 6 for a half-month's salary, there are payments to him for the next year and a half through the first week of February 1439. His appointment record is lost, but salary payments show that he initially earned L. 10 per month. A deliberation from 20 December 1437 notes that the board discussed the terms of Messer Giovanni's original contract, which did not oblige him to say Mass, as well as his reported willingness to sing four Masses a week "for a small salary." Since this would be "less costly" than hiring another chaplain, it was decided to increase his annual salary by 6 florins, or L. 24, beyond the usual amount he received "for singing the tenor," on condition that he say at least four Masses each week. A later document, quoted below, shows that he accepted the offer but that he was somewhat negligent about honoring his new commitments. He, too, had a spotty record of service in the plainchant choir. Attendance reports note that in October 1438 he was absent from Vespers and Compline on the 3rd and from Vespers on the 4th, that he missed Terce

---

Mass., 1984), 48–49; a summary of his career is given by Pamela Starr, "Music and Music Patronage at the Papal Court, 1447–1464" (Ph.D. diss., Yale University, 1987), 127.

40. Nothing is known of his life, unless he is the Johannes Re(e)son listed as a member of the London Gild of Parish Clerks from 1448/9 who died between Ascension Day 1459 and Ascension Day 1460. See the entry for Johannes Reson by Richard Loyan in *New Grove*, 15:756.

41. A biscantore, as noted above, was a singer of polyphony, and, more specifically, the person who sang a second, higher, part against the tenor. Sartori defines the term as an adult singer of polyphony. See his "Josquin des Près, cantore del Duomo di Milano," 57.

on the 12th and 19th of November, and that he was away for ten days beginning 20 December.

The Opera also rented bedding for this Giovanni. Yet another payment to Chimento di Pavolo notes that Messer Giovanni had a pair of sheets for some eighteen months, beginning in August 1437. The record of a decision made by the board on 11 February 1439 directed the overseer and the chamberlain to come to an agreement with Messer Giovanni Francioso, "a singer in the duomo who today took his leave," about "the Mass he missed each week" and about "the rental of some sheets he has from the secondhand dealer." If necessary, the overseer was authorized to pay all or part of the debt with the Opera's funds. This he did, although there is no note showing that the singer's salary was docked.

The few records concerning these itinerant professional singers reveal that they were able, even at this early date, to secure highly favorable working conditions for themselves. Both Messer Giovanni and his compatriot Ser Giovanni had negotiated the number of services they were obliged to attend in the choir and both had been exempted from saying hebdomadal Masses. This contrasts sharply with employment terms offered to the majority of chaplain-singers, who were often assigned the same duties as regular chaplains. It is doubtful, furthermore, that Messer Giovanni sang polyphony at the few daily offices he did attend—Vespers, Compline, and Terce are mentioned in the records—because all indications are that at this time polyphony was sung principally at Masses and Vespers on Sundays and feast days. Like the other chaplains he had his meals and lodging at the Opera's expense, and as the rental of sheets suggests, an extra effort was made to ensure his comfort. All in all, it seems that itinerant professional musicians, especially those with exceptional voices and a command of the latest repertories, were already beginning to assume the privileged status that so many of them enjoyed in the later fifteenth century, when Franco-Flemish singers were all the rage and the music they performed was eagerly received by their Italian employers.

EXPANSION OF THE ENSEMBLE IN THE LATER 1430S

The French biscantore, cited from May 1437 through October 1438, and the French tenorista, mentioned from July 1437 through February 1439, performed together from July 1437 though October 1438. At least three other singers were present during that time, bringing to five the number of polyphonic singers. Apart from the venerable archdeacon Messer Piero di Pasqua, they included the chaplain-tenorista Ser Mariano di Giovanni di Trafiere, from January 1437 through January 1440; the clerk Pavolo di Ser Agnolo, from May through July 1437; and Messer Marino di Niccolò da l'Aquila, a new singing teacher, who took up his post in December 1436.

These numbers indicate that after more than three decades a break with past practices occurred around this time. Rather than having a normal complement of two singers, the Opera would now seek to employ an ensemble of four or five, the number that was to become standard in mid-fifteenth-century performing practices. Significantly, this change occurred in the late 1430s, when a move in the same direction was made in Florence, where the Medici, relying on the recruiting skills of their representatives in northern Europe, spared no effort during the next four decades to keep the Florentine chapel at a normal complement of five or six singers.[42] At Milan cathedral, as noted above, four adult singers, all of them from the city or its environs, were employed after 1430, and the same number was maintained through 1450, when three singers were added to the group.[43]

In the mid-1430s Messer Marino was brought in to replace the singing teacher Don Pietro di Francesco da Perugia. Records of appointments of both men are lost, although the terms of Marino's contract appear in abbreviated form in a pay register. His tenure was to run from December 1436 through December 1437 and in addition to his "ordinary salary" for serving as a singer, he was to have a salary of L. 40 per annum for teaching "the clerks and the boys in the duomo." The same terms are reiterated in the record of his reappointment from 21 December 1438, which notes that his annual salary of Fl. 40, at L. 4 per florin, was calculated at "Fl. 30 for singing and Fl. 10 for teaching the clerks."

Another tenorista, Frate Guglielmo di Francia, began serving on 1 June 1438, and five singers were subsequently employed through the end of the following October. Among them were three Frenchmen, including three tenoristas and a biscantore, and two Italians, including a tenorista and an unspecified cantore. Four were present from November 1438 through January 1439, when the sacristan listed the tenorista Ser Mariano at a salary of L. 8, Messer Marino at L. 10, the biscantore Ser Giovanni Francioso at L. 10, and Frate Guglielmo tenorista at L. 10. Performance practices in Italian cathedrals at this time generally saw two or more singers on the highest part and one each on the lower parts in music for three voices. For four-voice music an additional singer was needed to perform the fourth or lowest part. Practically speaking, the Sienese ensemble was able to do four-voice music in the best of times, though three-voice works, to judge from the personnel records, must have been more the norm. And on many occasions, when only three singers were employed, it is clear that such works were sung one to a part.

The just cited tenorista Frate Guglielmo was first mentioned, though not by name, in a deliberation from 23 April 1438, when the council gave overseer Jacopo della Quercia permission to hire "the French singer . . . newly arrived in Siena." Negotiations were successful and the musican's full name, Frate Guglielmo di Francia, tenorista, subsequently appears in various accounts from June 1438 through 21 March 1440. During that time he stopped serving for a few months—from May through July 1439—because of a salary dispute with his employers. The incident is of interest because of the light it sheds on the Opera's need to hire clergy who could also fulfill other functions at the cathedral.

Frate Guglielmo was initially hired at a monthly salary of L. 10. But at a meeting on 6 March 1439, after affirming the importance of having "a tenorista in the major church, for the honor of the city and of its citizens," the overseer and his counselors decided that "the person who presently sings the tenor" could have a monthly salary of

42. D'Accone, "The Singers of San Giovanni," 315–16.
43. Sartori, "Josquin des Près, cantore del Duomo di Milano," 67–68.

L. 12, on condition that he say one Mass a week at the sacristan's request. Although Guglielmo was paid L. 12 for the month of April 1439, he stopped coming to the cathedral at the end of the month, evidently because he decided that his compensation was inadequate. His actions prompted the Opera to rethink its position, too, and as a result, on 17 July the board authorized the overseer to spend up to the sum of 40 florins per annum in order to secure "the appointment of Frate Guglielmo di Giovanni di Francia of the Carmelite Order for a year or two," as he saw fit. A decree from 4 August 1439 records Guglielmo's appointment as a tenorista for a period of two years at Fl. 40 per annum. The same amount is confirmed by one of the sacristan's rolls, where his monthly salary was calculated as L. 13. 6. 8. The contract says nothing about his duties as a singer of polyphony, though it does specify that he had to attend the major Mass every morning and Vespers, "just like the other chaplains paid by the Opera." He was in debt to his employers to the amount of L. 15. 8 when he left cathedral service, and in order to cover this, a breviary he had put up as security for the loan was subsequently sold to a monk of the Order of St. Gregory for L. 17. 5.

Reports of few other singers during Frate Guglielmo's tenure demonstrate that every effort was being made to keep the ensemble at full strength. Messer Marino was reappointed in March 1439 for another year as a singer and teacher with the same salary. In the following June Messer Giustiniano da Todi, last recorded at the cathedral in November 1435, was reappointed as chaplain and singer for one year, at an annual salary of 40 florins. He was obliged "to be at offices in the choir and to do all the things the other chaplains do." A few weeks later he was forgiven a debt of Fl. 4 previously incurred in connection with glass windows he had made for the church. Giustiniano evidently did not accept the contract because there are no immediate payments to him after this time.

A replacement was found within two months, and in early August 1439 Messer Bartolomeo di Marino da Fermo was appointed as a singer for one year at an annual salary of 24 florins, valued at 4 lire each. The terms of his contract state that he was "to say Mass and to sing on all of the cathedral's solemn days and all of the feasts commanded by Holy Mother Church, like the other chaplains." Further, "on other days should there be no solemnities or feasts, he is not obliged to come unless he wants to, except that on Thursdays, if no feast occurs during the week, he must come and officiate and sing because classes are not held on that day at the university." Finally, he was required "to play the organ whenever the need arises." At first glance the reference to university classes suggests that Bartolomeo was associated with Siena's Studio, as a teacher—given his rank—or as a student, though there is no other evidence to this effect. Bartolomeo did not finish the entire year; payments to him are listed for only seven months, to the end of February 1440. Appearing with Bartolomeo in sacristans' reports from April through December 1439 were the venerable chaplain-singer Ser Mariano di Giovanni di Trafiere, Messer Marino, and, after the salary dispute was settled, Frate Guglielmo.

EARLY SIENESE SOURCES OF POLYPHONY

Sienese sources of medieval and early Renaissance polyphony are not as plentiful as those of many other Italian cities, and the few that have survived in the town's libraries cannot always be linked with certainty to Siena or to the cathedral. Among them are two fragments now preserved in the Sienese State Archives, which represent all that remain of a lost volume of fifteenth-century polyphony. The first, Fragment 326, is a double folio with remnants as well as complete readings of diverse pieces: a single voice part from an unidentified motet; the mutilated superius, tenor, and contratenor parts of a three-voice Gloria and trope, *Gloria, laus, honor,* and of a three-voice Gloria; and two Italian-texted ballatas for two voices, *Yvi neglecta rosa* and *Adio, adio, amore mio sostegno.*[44] The second, Fragment 327, is a single folio also containing incomplete parts, in this case those of two three-voice Credos and a complete two-voice ballata, *Amor amaro.*[45] Both Glorias and Credos are works by Antonius Zacharias de Teramo, complete in other sources; the ballatas are apparently unique to the Sienese fragments.[46] Zacharias, a musician in papal service from 1391 to 1407, is presumed to have passed through Siena in the entourage of Pope Gregory XII Correr.[47] If this is so, it might help explain the presence of his works in the Sienese manuscript. It appears that Zacharias's Mass compositions formed part of a fascicle dedicated to his works alone and that the ballatas, which are copied in a different hand and may represent pieces that were current in Siena, were added at a slightly later date, perhaps in the 1420s.[48] The presence of both sacred and secular pieces in a single volume suggests that the volume belonged to a nobleman or an important clerical personage, or to a wealthy monastery, or perhaps even to the Palazzo Pubblico, but in any case to a household or establishment where polyphony was performed by trained singers on social occasions as well as at Masses. Presumably such works would also have been available to cathedral singers.

A second group of fifteenth-century pieces is found appended to MS L. V. 36 of the Biblioteca Comunale degli Intronati, a volume containing several anonymous tracts on plainchant as well as abbreviated versions of celebrated theoretical treatises by Franco of Cologne and Philippe de Vitry and a brief introduction to counterpoint by the Florentine composer Don Paolo Tenorista. The polyphonic pieces comprise a four-

44. Federico Ghisi, "A Second Sienese Fragment of Italian Ars Nova," *Musica Disciplina* 2 (1948): 173–77, with a supplement containing partial transcriptions of the two Italian ballate.

45. Federico Ghisi, "Italian *Ars Nova* Music," *Musica Disciplina* 1 (1946): 182; a transcription of the piece in the supplement, pp. 19–20.

46. For a description of the sacred works in the fragments see Kurt von Fischer, "Una ballata trecentesca sconosciuta: Aggiunti per i frammenti di Siena," *L'Ars Nova italiana del Trecento* 2 (1968): 39–47. One of the Glorias is based on Antonius Zacharias's ballata *Un fior gentil m'apparse.* The second Credo, called Patrem *Scabroso* in a Bolognese source, is also apparently based on a previously composed piece, now lost. All four works are published in modern edition by Gilbert Reaney, in Early Fifteenth-Century Music, 6:48–57, 58–63, 72–73, and 103–112; the Gloria trope is also published in Andrew Hughes and Margaret Bent, eds., *The Old Hall Manuscript,* 4 vols. (American Institute of Musicology, 1969–73), 1:105–11.

47. The Pope was en route to a church council in Pisa in 1408. On the problem of early fifteenth-century composers named Zacharias, see Nino Pirrotta, "Zacharus musicus," *Quadrivium* 12 (1971): 153–75; Agostino Ziino, "Magister Antonius dictus Zacharias de Teramo: Alcune date e molte ipotesi," *Rivista italiana di musicologia* 14 (1979): 311–48; Gilbert Reaney, "Zacharias," *New Grove,* 20:609–10; John Nádas, "Further Notes on Magister Antonius dictus Zacharias de Teramo," *Studi musicali* 15 (1986): 167–82.

48. Von Fischer, "Una ballata trecentesca sconosciuta," 43, 46–47.

voice motet by the Italianized Johannes Ciconia of Liège, *O virum omnimoda veneratione digne/O lux et decus tranensium/O beatae Nicole,* and three French rondeaux, only one of which, *Belle que rose vermeille,* is complete.[49] Another fifteenth-century collection of theoretical treatises now at the Biblioteca Comunale, MS L. V. 30, includes works by Johannes de Muris, Marchettus of Padua, Philippe de Vitry, and others.[50] This preserves a single polyphonic work complete, a ballata for three voices, *Io veggio,* by Antonio da Cividale.[51] Together with the fragments just mentioned, the presence of these few works in the theoretical treatises suggests that Sienese musicians—whether laymen, members of religious orders, or cathedral singers—were aware of developments in contemporary polyphony in France and in Italy and that there were several places in the city, besides the cathedral and the Palazzo Pubblico, where polyphony was performed. The presence, moreover, of works by famous theorists as well as of the *De musica* of Boethius, cited in fifteenth-century inventories of cathedral holdings, leave little doubt that the classic treatises of late medieval musical theory were known and read in Siena.[52]

RECRUITING AND RETAINING SINGERS IN THE 1440S

The Frenchman Giovanni de' Ricci, who was apparently passing through Siena, sang at the cathedral for a few days around Christmas in 1439. When Frate Guglielmo left Siena at the end of March 1440, he was immediately replaced by the Florentine tenorista Ser Agnolo di Nanni. He was living at the bishop's palace, where he may also have been employed, and since he would not be serving as a chaplain, his monthly salary was fixed at L. 5. New at the cathedral on 1 April 1440 was another Frenchman, Ser Jacomo di Fosco da San Germano, who was engaged as a singer and chaplain at a salary of L. 10 per month. An addendum to his account notes that L. 20 were loaned to him at the overseer's request so that he could buy a cloak to wear when he sang in the choir.

Only three singers, Ser Jacomo di Fosco, Ser Agnolo di Nanni, and Messer Marino,

---

49. The pieces are mentioned by F. Alberto Gallo, "Alcune fonti poco note di musica teorica e pratica," *L'Ars Nova italiana del Trecento* 2 (1968): 74–75. The motet, in honor of St. Nicholas of Trani, is published in *The Works of Johannes Ciconia,* ed. Margaret Bent and Anne Hallmark (Monaco, 1985), 81–84. For a recent study about Ciconia in papal Rome and the diffusion of his music, see Giuliano Di Bacco and John Nádas, "Verso uno 'stile internazionale' della musica nelle cappelle papali e cardinalizie durante il Grande Scisma (1378–1417): Il caso di Johannes Ciconia da Liège," *Collectanea* 1 (1994): 7–74, particularly pp. 33–34, n. 64, for the Sienese sources of Ciconia's music and of the music by others associated with Roman popes that may have its origins in papal meanderings during the great schism.

50. The volume is described by Chris Maas, *The Theory of Music from the Carolingian Era up to 1400,* vol. 2 (Munich-Duisberg, 1968), 120–23.

51. The piece is found as an insertion, on fols. 47^v–48^r, in the middle of a treatise ascribed to Johannes de Muris that begins on fol. 33^r of the manuscript: "Incipit practica cantus mensurabilis secundum magistrum Johannem de Muris. Quolibet in arte pratica mensurabilis cantus erudiri." Other musical items in ASS include No. A 176 (Miscellanea 193), a collection of several fragments taken from book bindings, among them a piece of chant in Beneventan notation. For descriptions of musical items on display at one time or another at SSA see *Le sale della mostra dell'Archivio di Stato Siena* (Rome, 1956), nos. 306–22, p. 90; no. 325, p. 91; nos. 326–27, p. 91; nos. 328–29, p. 91; no. 330, p. 92.

52. Boethius' treatise is listed in various inventories; see Tables 3.1 and 4.1.

are named along with the organist in sacristans' monthly rolls from April 1440 through March 1441, when they were joined by a fourth, Ser Antonio di Gabrielo da Montepulciano. Antonio was to be associated with the cathedral off and on for many years to come. The terms of his initial appointment, dated 16 March 1441, say little except that he was to serve as a chaplain and singer and, should he be asked, as an organist. He served through the end of September, leaving a month after Jacomo di Fosco. Earlier, in May of the same year, the young clerk Biagio di Tomè, who would also become a permanent cathedral employee, began the first of his many appointments in the chapel. In October 1441 Biagio, Agnolo, and Marino were joined by Don Pietro di Francesco da Perugia, last recorded at the cathedral in 1436. His formal appointment, dated 8 November 1441, notes that two singers, Jacomo da San Germano and Antonio da Montepulciano, had recently left the cathedral's service and that he was being appointed as a chaplain and singer for one year at an annual salary of 40 florins (see Doc. 3.4). Clearly, the departure of these other singers was embarrassing and convinced the board that more flexible hiring policies were needed if the singing group was to be maintained at full strength. This much is evident from the closing statement of the record, which notes that the overseer and one of his counselors could appoint other singers and chaplains as they thought necessary "for the honor of God and of the said church and choir." Despite the generous terms of employment, Pietro left in April 1442, after having served only seven months of his new contract.

In an attempt to facilitate appointments of qualified singers, the board made another ruling on 2 July 1442 that empowered the overseer "for the rest of the present counselors' term of office" to fire or engage singers, chaplains, clerks, and bell ringers "at whatever salary he sees fit." The overseer was also authorized to order the chamberlain to pay such salaries, "without any prejudice or damage to himself personally."[53] In other words, if, in order to hire competent personnel, it should prove necessary for the overseer to spend more than what had been allocated for salaries, he would not be obliged to make up the difference out of his own pocket. The freedom of action granted the overseer and the flexible employment terms offered to several musicians during the 1440s provide further proof that the Opera was seeking to maintain a full complement of singers, even though at times unsuccessfully.

The remainder of the 1440s, in fact, reveals a consistent pattern of appointments

---

53. "Similmente e per simil modo fu rimisso e commisso in misser lo Operaio predetto che questo anno due [*recte* dove] siamo e mentre dura el tempo de' presenti conseglieri, possa e a llui sia licito condurre a honore di Dio e de la gloriosa sua madre Madonna Santa Maria, camptori, cappellani, cherici e sonatori di campane con quegli salarii e prezi che a llui parrà e piacerà, e essi cassare e di nuovo condurre come a llui parrà e piacerà, e così essi fare al camarlingo dell'opera de' detti salarii pagare, la qual cosa fare possa senza suo preiudicio overo danno" (AOMS, vol. 13, *Deliberazioni, 1434–55,* fol. 70ᵛ, dated 2 July 1442 [margin: camptori e cappellani]).

With regard to bell ringers, suffice it to note that payments are regularly recorded to people who held the post throughout the fifteenth and sixteenth centuries. Particularly interesting are a group of payments documenting the presence of German bell ringers (vol. 272, *E&U, 1444–45,* fol. 86ʳ, for payment of L. 5 to Iachomo Tedescho sonatore champanaio for May 1444; fol. 87ʳ, for payment of L. 6 to Pietro Tedescho sonatore for June; and fol. 88ʳ, for payment of L. 5. 10 to Matio Tedescho sonatore de le champane for August).

and reappointments of foreign musicians, most of them of brief duration. This situation may have resulted from geographical as well as financial reasons. Siena, the principal town on the Via Francigena that connected Rome to the north, traditionally had been the natural and the most convenient stopping-off place for travelers; after September 1443, when the seat of the papacy returned to Rome, it once again assumed its role as a primary way station. Princes, potentates, bishops, and diplomats all made their way to the city as eagerly as did merchants, pilgrims, itinerant musicians, and others of less exalted rank. For northern singers, particularly, who journeyed throughout the peninsula in search of preferments and a place on the world's stage, Siena offered ideal conditions for temporary employment. A cathedral church with a resident bishop, a sophisticated and well-to-do bourgeoisie, a thriving artisan class, and a university with an international student body all contributed to creating the atmosphere of a cosmopolitan and vibrant urban center where performers of the new northern polyphony were not only appreciated but actively welcomed.

As attractive as living conditions might be, however, Siena could not hope to vie on a large scale with other places in Italy when it came to engaging star performers on a more permanent basis. The cathedral was unable to offer the higher salaries and perquisites found at princely courts and other major Italian musical institutions. The town itself offered few possibilities for advancement. Committed as it was to one of the most elaborate building and decorative programs in Italy, the Opera was unable to cover the costs of maintaining a group of resident northern singers employed for the sole purpose of performing polyphony. Thus, in an effort to meet obligations of votive Masses, processions, and other commemorative services imposed by the terms of bequests and endowments, the Opera was constantly seeking singers of polyphony who could serve as chaplains, if not full-time, at least on a part-time basis. These chaplains were required to officiate at certain services without extra compensation, and this must have been considered a drawback by many of them. A few, as has been noted, simply refused to comply and left Sienese service without having fulfilled their obligations. Unfortunately, such occurrences were to be repeated many times in the future.

There were also other drawbacks to serving in Siena. There was apparently little supplementary work for itinerant singers within the city. Other Sienese institutions— the smaller conventual churches and religious companies—either lacked the endowments necessary to introduce the new polyphony into services or were content to continue with forces they traditionally employed. Whether the grand Sienese families supported any of the itinerant musicians is unknown, owing to the disappearance of many private papers and archives.

Lacking endowed posts or other revenues that could be used specifically to attract singers, and dependent upon the income from donations, from restricted endowments, and from its own possessions, the Opera could not compete with princely chapels in Naples, Ferrara, Milan, with the papal chapel in Rome, and even with the ostensibly public chapels in Florence, Milan, and Venice. Unlike its counterparts at the Florentine Baptistry and cathedral, the Opera had no major guilds at hand to which it could turn when additional support for music was needed. Siena, moreover, had no single ruling family—such as the Aragonese kings of Naples, the Medici in republican Florence, the Este lords in Ferrara, and the Sforza dukes of Milan—that could draw upon its own resources as well as those of the state to enhance the glory of its musical institutions. How seriously Italian rulers took the business of recruiting and retaining star singers is reflected in part by their efforts to tap into the elaborate system of benefices which the popes at Rome themselves used to bolster their musical forces.[54] Siena, as far as can be ascertained, did not enter into the fray and played no part in the hunt for benefices. In short, throughout Siena's history as an independent commune and despite the best intentions of individual overseers and different ruling factions at various times, the various means that would have allowed the cathedral to compete for very long with major institutions were unavailable.

Itinerant northern singers, particularly clerics, would continue to come to the city for the rest of the century, attracted by the beauty of the surroundings, the pleasant living conditions, and salaries that must have been considered acceptable on a short-term basis. But inevitably, the northerners and even many of the Italians would leave as the lure of preferments, higher salaries, and the possibilities of obtaining benefices in their native land through service to a powerful Italian lord beckoned them to Rome or the north Italian cities and even beyond the Alps. Compounding the problem for the Opera was the ever-present need of securing singers who could also serve as chaplains. This was one way of guaranteeing a suitable income to gifted singers while fulfilling the legitimate needs of cathedral donors and the Opera's obligations. But the primary vocation of many of the northern clerics was musical performance, and this solution was unsatisfactory if exclusive preference was given to foreign rather than to native singers.

Despite its inability to retain northern singers for long periods of time, Siena cathedral played a significant role in the cultural exchange that characterized European music in the fifteenth century. Sienese patterns of patronage were disjunct and unsteady, but there was an attempt, however flawed, to make use of the musicians from beyond the Alps who began arriving in Italy in ever increasing numbers as the century progressed. Siena's place in the web of peninsular musical patronage was not crucial, but it was conspicuous. For the town's geographical position, as I have noted, made it almost inevitable that it would be a stopping-off place for musicians who had come to Italy seeking employment in Rome and Naples to the south, or conversely in Florence and points northeast and northwest.

The Sienese documents of the 1440s and 1450s demonstrate that the migration of northern singers began much earlier than previously acknowledged. In Florence, where the Medici began seeking singers through agents in their banking offices in the North, a network of recruiters engaged in identifying and hiring qualified musicians was already in place by the late 1440s, even though the names of most of the musicians who actually served in Florence are unknown because of the loss of records. Shortly after Marquis Leonello d'Este of Ferrara established his chapel in 1443, he not only brought in singers from the papal chapel but also sent one of his singers to recruit others in Burgundy.[55] The Sforza policy, which also relied primarily on its own trusted singers as recruiters in Rome and in the north, went into high gear in the early 1470s, when large

---

54. See Reynolds, "Musical Careers, Ecclesiastical Benefices," 50–51, nn. 3–4, for a list of works regarding personnel and benefices in various places. Others are cited in the following notes.

55. Lockwood, *Music in Renaissance Ferrara*, 48, n. 13.

numbers of musicians were hired.[56] But the Sienese documents indicate that northern singers, most of them clerics, had already begun the trip south—many on their own initiative—a decade and even more before some of the courts initiated their policies of active recruitment.[57] And although the analogy remains a cliché, Sienese records nonetheless show that what was a trickle in the later 1430s did indeed become a flood in the next half century.

Italians, particularly clerics from nearby regions, continued to dominate the singers' rolls during the next few years, as the number employed continued to fluctuate. Messer Marino, chaplain and singer, and Ser Agnolo di Nanni, tenorista, were present through the mid-1440s. A number of singers joined them in that time, among them the venerable Don Giustiniano di Ser Francesco da Todi, now called a singer of polyphony, from July 1442 through 30 September 1443 at a salary of L. 13 per month. Biagio di Tomè was present from May 1441 through April 1446, although it is uncertain whether he served as a singer for the entire time. Niccolò Francioso, *cantore in duomo,* named in September and October 1442, was perhaps the same person as Ser Niccolaio, recorded in March and April 1445. Messer Lorenzo da Orvieto was one of five singers currently employed in October 1442. His monthly salary of L. 11. 18, like that of the others, included payment for his services as a chaplain.

Ser Giovanni da Bologna, who may be the same singer employed at the cathedral fifteen years earlier, appeared on the sacristans' roll at L. 10 in December 1442, when five singers were again listed.[58] Several Frenchmen took up temporary service during the next few years. Giulietto Francioso cantore was present only for the month of September 1444. Rubino cantore stayed somewhat longer, from April through July 1445. Overlapping service with him were Colinetto Francioso, from May through early September 1445, and Jannesi Francioso, for May and part of June, 1445. The sacristans' roll for May 1445 lists seven singers of polyphony: Ser Jacomo di Antonio, Biagio, Ser Agnolo di Nanni tenorista, Messer Marino, Ser Colinetto Francioso, Rubino Fran-

---

56. Emilio Motta, "Musici alla corte degli Sforza: Ricerche e documenti milanesi," *Archivio Storico Lombardo,* 2 ser., 14 (1887): 311–12. Two recent studies of the Milanese court chapel are William F. Prizer, "Music at the Court of the Sforza: The Birth and Death of a Musical Center," *Musica Disciplina* 43 (1989): 141–93, and Evelyn S. Welch, "Sight, Sound and Ceremony in the Chapel of Galeazzo Maria Sforza," *Early Music History* 12 (1993): 151–90.

57. Further on musical migration see Christopher Reynolds, "Southern Pull or Northern Push?: Motives for Migration in the Renaissance," in *Trasmissione e recezione delle forme di cultura musicale,* ed. L. Bianconi, F. A. Gallo, A. Pompilio, and D. Restani, *Atti del XIV Congresso della Società Internazionale di Musicologia (Bologna, 1987)* (Turin, 1990), 155–61; Barbara Haggh, "Itinerancy to Residency: Professional Careers and Performance Practices in 15th-Century Sacred Music," *Early Music* 17 (1989): 358–66; Alejandro E. Planchart, "Guillaume Du Fay's Benefices and his Relationship to the Court of Burgundy," *Early Music History* 8 (1988): 117–71.

58. It would be tempting to identify this latter with the priest Johannes Bononiensis, the tenor of whose isorhythmic motet *Certa salutis,* dated 1440, is quoted in a letter from Giovanni del Lago to Giovanni Spataro dated 8 October 1529; see Bonnie J. Blackburn, Edward E. Lowinsky, and Clement A. Miller, eds., *A Correspondence of Renaissance Musicians* (Oxford, 1991), 385. Blackburn tentatively identifies him with Giovanni d'Andrea di Bazo, singer and "maestro dell'organetto" at San Petronio in Bologna from 1443 to 1452.

cioso, and Jannes cantore. For June, however, Colinetto alone of the Frenchmen was present, and he, too, departed by the end of September, leaving only the Italians. Perhaps Rubino left for Rome, where from at least April 1447 a singer called Maestro Rubino was in the chapel of St. Peter's.[59]

Although the series of monthly rolls compiled by cathedral sacristans is incomplete for the following years, the few there are show that the problem of retaining a steady corps of singers was not a thing of the past. Marino was the only one present throughout all of 1446, for Biagio was gone after May and Agnolo di Nanni left in October. Itinerant musicians recorded during that year included Ser Antonio da Viterbo, in February; a Frenchman called Ser Jacomo da Sancto Vierno, in May; the returning Giulietto Francioso, from October through the end of November; and Guglielmo di Michele da Francia, from August through the following March 1447. The two latter musicians and Marino were thus the only singers employed during November 1446. A Florentine tenorista, Ser Goro di Pavolo, for whom a special payment was approved by the overseer and his counselors on 27 December, joined them for Christmas festivities. Goro must have made a lasting impression on his hosts, for within the decade he was invited to return to Siena as a permanent member of the chapel.

By spring of 1447 the number of singers had dwindled to a new low. Marino and Guglielmo di Michele da Francia were on the rolls through the beginning of February, when the chaplain-tenorista Don Girolamo appeared, but all of them left by the end of March. It was probably in response to this situation, communicated to him in correspondence no longer extant, that the Sienese envoy in Genoa began interviewing singers who might be engaged for the cathedral.[60] He reported the results of his efforts to the overseer in a letter written from Genoa on 20 June 1447 (see Doc. 3.5). This not only provides information about recruitment procedures but also reveals a good deal about the musical criteria applied to prospective singers at Siena cathedral.

> Because you asked me to see if it was possible to find singers and because my
> desire is to see our major church provided with all the necessary things, I'm

---

59. Haberl, "Die römische 'schola cantorum' und die päpstlichen Kapellsänger," 236 n. The fluctuating number of singers at this time may indicate that the Sienese were attempting to enlarge the ensemble on a more permanent basis. Lockwood points out that under Marquis Leonello the numbers of singers employed at the Ferrarese court jumped from four in 1443 to nine in 1445 and ten shortly afterwards (*Music in Renaissance Ferrara,* 48). In Milan, thanks to the interest of the Sforza, the number of singers in the cathedral choir was raised to seven in 1459 (Sartori, "Josquin des Près," 67).

60. Little is known about musicians employed at the cathedral of San Lorenzo and at the doge's palace in Genoa during this period, though singers and instrumentalists are said to have arrived there from other Italian courts, from France, and from Flanders during the period 1450–1530. See Remo Giazotto, *La musica a Genova* (Genoa, 1951), 102. In 1437 construction of a new large organ was begun at the cathedral. Testifying to the existence of a native school of composition in the mid-fifteenth century are a few extant works by two Genoese composers, Johannes de Janua and Antonio de Janua. This latter is named in a list of musicians employed at the doge's palace in a record from 14 October 1456. At the time the group counted four Flemish musicians, probably part of a group of five who arrived in Genoa on 2 June 1448 (ibid., 103–4). The information about Genoese cathedral musicians given below is consistent with the notion of foreign musicians arriving and finding employment in the port city.

writing to say that here I've found Guglielmo Francioso who's at the duomo, and that I believe he'll come under my guarantee. But because there's need for a good tenor, and he tells me that there's one at Florence who has a very substantial voice, you must try to get him, for he'll come willingly when he learns that Guglielmo is coming. Also there's another excellent singer in Florence who will do the same. In Genoa, working with Guglielmo, is another good singer, who would also come with Guglielmo. But this tenor's voice seems too small to me for our church. As things now stand, I've agreed that once I'm back there, I'll write him and he'll do as I say. And because I've just now come across another tenor who has been in the doge's service and who says he's also a good singing teacher—I've had him sing a few ballatas and I think he sings well, but I don't know whether his voice is suitable for plainchant—I'll send him there to you, and you can try him out for yourselves. I recommend him to you, and he's willing to come to Siena rather than to any other place. But I doubt that he's a stable person.

The letter offers vivid testimony to the competitive spirit and politicking that characterized recruitment efforts in mid-fifteenth-century Italy, as cities and institutions vied with one another to obtain the services of outstanding singers. Obviously, an ability to judge vocal performance and a knowledge of the kinds of voices best suited to certain repertories were essential for those who engaged in such efforts. The Sienese envoy was quite competent in both respects, as revealed by his comments about whether one tenor's voice might be too small for Siena cathedral and whether the singing teacher, who sang ballatas well, had the kind of voice that was suitable for plainchant. How we wish the writer had elucidated this latter point! Did he mean the voice was too rich or that it had too much vibrato or not enough? Character and attitude were also important considerations. The singing teacher, according to the writer, was not a stable person, a remark that was probably intended to convey the impression that he could be expected to leave Siena even after serving only a month, if a better offer were to come along.

The writer also reveals his knowledge of contemporary practice when he implies that four singers—two from Genoa, including a tenor, and two from Florence, one of whom was also a tenor—would furnish a normal complement of singers. To this nucleus, others, such as the tenor who was a singing teacher, could be added. Not surprisingly, this assessment of the forces needed for a first-rate performing ensemble fits in well with immediate past practice in Siena and with information about performing practices elsewhere in Italy at this time.

Obtaining the services of the best singers involved more than offering salaries and certain privileges—issues that were, of course, of interest to all concerned, although the envoy hardly bothered to mention them in his letter. The singers' perceptions of whom they would be working with were also important factors. Here was a tenor who might be persuaded to leave Florence for Siena because he knew another good singer, Guglielmo, then in Genoa, would be there. A second singer in Florence might do the same. Evidently, a communications network of sorts was operating among itinerant singers, to the mutual advantage of both employees and employers. It was, to put it another way, not merely a question of singers communicating with one another about such basic considerations as the availability of work or the advantages of certain situations but also about more elusive matters such as the musical sensibilities and experience of their prospective colleagues.

The envoy directed his efforts toward seeking musicians who could be offered long-term appointments at the cathedral, but a more immediate need was securing a sufficient number of singers to perform at the upcoming Assumption Day festivities. This was accomplished—extant records say nothing about how, when, or where they were engaged—and six singers were on hand when the holiday arrived. Most of them, however, were employed only during the weeks immediately surrounding the mid–August celebration. A Frenchman, Riccardo di Viviano Francioso, for example, was paid Fl. 1 for a few days service on 17 August, while an Italian, Guglielmo da Pavia, was paid for twenty days he had previously served on 15 September. Two Spanish singers, perhaps from Elche in Alicante province, were also employed during the month of August, Ser Gonsalvo de Nuvalis tenorista and Frate Raimondo Bianco da Elci cantore.[61] Another newcomer in August, Ser Giovanni di Martino da Massa, a chaplain and singer, was the only one of the newcomers to serve for a longer period. He remained through the end of November. Joining him in his last month were three French singers, Jacomo di Longo, Giovanni Fanti (Frutti, Furtti, and other forms are also given), and Pietro Domarlla. Whether any or all of them came to Siena as a result of the envoy's efforts in Genoa cannot be determined, although it is noteworthy that they arrived as a group at the same time.

The three Frenchmen, who may have been laymen, were joined in January 1448 by another northerner called Eustachius di Binolio. The new group did not perform together for very long, however, because Pietro Domarlla left at the end of the month. (If, as seems likely, this musician was the same person as Petrus de Domarto, composer of at least two polyphonic Masses and two chansons, there is yet another connection between musicians employed in Siena and the Ferrarese musical repertory.[62]) Jacomo,

---

61. Although the name is an extraordinarily rare one among singers employed in Italy, it is doubtful that this Gonsalvo is to be identified with Gonsalvo de Cordova, who was associated with the Neapolitan court from 1437 to 1470 and mentioned in other Neapolitan records as late as 1481; see Allan Atlas, *Music at the Aragonese Court of Naples* (Cambridge, 1985), 106–7.

62. His three-voice *Missa quinti toni irregularis* and his four-voice *Missa Spiritus almus,* criticized several times by Johannes Tinctoris in three theoretical treatises, are preserved in Italian and Polish manuscripts. The four-voice Mass is found, among others, in Modena, Biblioteca Estense, MS α M. 1. 13, a parchment codex, dated 1481, containing works by Martini, Caron, Dufay, Faugues, Weerbecke, and Vincenet (Lockwood, *Music in Renaissance Ferrara,* 217). Siena's connections with Rome and Naples should also be taken into account in Domarto's case, for an earlier source of the same Mass is MS Cappella Sistina 14 of the Vatican library, a volume thought to have been copied in Naples between July 1473 and January 1475 and brought to Rome by Ferdinand I on a pilgrimage at the end of January 1475; see Adalbert Roth, *Studien zum frühen Repertoire der Päpstlichen Kapelle unter dem Pontifikat Sixtus' IV. (1471–1484): Die Chorbücher 14 und 51 des Fondo Cappella Sistina der Biblioteca Apostolica Vaticana,* Capellae Apostolicae Sixtinaeque Collectanea Acta Monumenta 1 (Vatican City, 1991), 328–88. The work has recently been studied by Rob C. Wegman, "Petrus de Domarto's *Missa Spiritus Almus* and the Early History of the Four-Voice Mass in the Fifteenth Century," *Early Music History* 10 (1991): 235–303.

Giovanni, and Eustachius were subsequently employed through the end of April.[63] A record from 3 May 1448 says that the singers Jacomo, Giovanni, and Vincentio—this latter apparently a replacement for Pietro—took their leave on that day "with our permission." Since Vincentio is not mentioned in sacristans' reports before this time, he must have arrived toward the end of April, on the eve of the others' departure. Whether Vincentio is to be identified with one or another of the two known singers with similar names is moot. The earlier, Johannes Vicenetti (or Vincenot), was in the papal chapel from 1424 through 1429, whereas the later Vincenet was in Neapolitan service for more than a decade from perhaps as early as the mid-1460s. The latter visited Florence, and it is possible that, like so many others, he stopped off in Siena as he traveled north.[64] Eustachius, called Eustachio di Giovanni Francioso in some records, continued to receive a monthly salary through the end of August 1448. Two new singers, Rasso di Lorenzo and Maestro Giovanni, performed with him during his last month, but after that no other adults appear on the rolls for the remainder of the year. Maestro Giovanni's surname is given as Calot in another record, which says that he began serving on 10 August. He is the same person as the Johannes Calot, a cleric of Arras, who was employed in the papal chapel from November 1448 to July 1450.[65] Foreign singers at Siena cathedral during this period are listed in Table 3.2, and a chronological list of cathedral musicians is in Table 3.3.

DOCUMENTS

Doc. 3.1. Letter from Tracalo da Rimini of of 22 December 1454 concerning the composition of a laude. ASS, Particolari, Carte Malatestiane, MS N° 1

Illustrissimus princeps et Excellens domine meo, post recommendationem.

Dicendomi ali dì passati Bernardo cantore che io facesse certa laude ala Nostra Donna per cantare la prima domenica del mese di Genaro, io mi feci dare il canto et consyderata la sua rima conveniente, feci la interchiusa laude la quale mando ala Vostra Illustrissima Signoria, et se ho lla facta brieve è per non attediare li audienti. . . .

Arimini die XXII^a Decembris 1454

Servulus Trachalus

---

63. Two entries from 16 April 1448 record the return, perhaps after a few days' illness, of Eustachio and the illness of Giovanni.

64. For these two musicians see Atlas, *Music at the Aragonese Court,* 69–71. For Vincenet in the papal chapel, see Manfred Schuler, "Zur Geschichte der Kapelle Papst Martin V," *Archiv für Musikwissenschaft* 25 (1968): 30–45; Haberl, "Die römische 'schola cantorum' und die päpstlichen Kapellsänger," 220. It is interesting to note that Vincenet's surviving works, considerably greater in number than Domarto's, have been preserved in several manuscripts and prints now in Bologna, Florence, Berlin, Munich, Prague, Trent etc., including volumes of Ferrarese and Neapolitan origin (Rome, Biblioteca Casanatense, MS 2856; Vatican City, MS Cappella Sistina 14 and MS Cappella Sistina 51). For the former, see Lockwood, *Music in Renaissance Ferrara;* for the latter, Roth, *Studien zur frühen Repertoire. The Collected Works of Vincenet* have been edited by Bertran E. Davis, Recent Researches in the Music of the Middle Ages and Early Renaissance 9–10 (Madison, 1978).

65. See Starr, "Music and Music Patronage at the Papal Court, 1447–1464," 133–34 and 269–86 for chapel rosters from this period. Also see her "The Ferrara Connection: A Case Study of Musical Recruitment in the Renaissance," *Studi musicali* 18 (1989): 4.

Table 3.2.   Foreign singers at Siena cathedral, 1383–1448

Name	Place of origin	Period of service
Ser Isidoro di Francia	France	17 May–15 August 1383
Riccardo (Gherardo) di Francia, *tenorista*[a]	France	February–May 1431
Ser Giovanni Ragione di Francia[b]	France	April–May 1431
Ser Giovanni di Jacopo Francioso, alias Messer	France	14 May–December 1437;
Violetta, *biscantore*		April–October 1438
Messer Giovanni di Giovanni Francioso, *tenorista*	France	27 July 1437–11 February 1439
Frate Guglielmo di Giovanni di Francia,		
O.Carm., *tenorista*	France	1 June 1438–21 March 1440
Giovanni de Ricci (Derici) di Francia	France	Christmas 1439
Ser Jacomo di Fosco da San Germano	France(?)	April 1440–August 1441
Niccolò Francioso[c]	France	September–October 1442
Giulietto Francioso		September 1444;
	France	October–November 1446
Rubino Francioso[d]	France	April 1445–July 1445
Ser Colinetto Francioso	France	May–September 1445
Jannesi (Jannes) Francioso	France	May–June 1445
Ser Jacomo da Sancto Vierno	France	May 1446
Guglielmo di Michele da Francia	France	August 1446–March 1447
Riccardo di Viviano Francioso	France	August 1447
Ser Gonsalvo de Nuvalis (Nurvalis), *tenorista*	Spain	August 1447
Frate Raimondo Bianco da Elci	Spain	August 1447
Jacomo di Longo Francioso	France	November 1447–April 1448
Giovanni Fanti (Frutti, Furtti) Francioso	France	November 1447–April 1448
Pietro Domarlla Francioso[e]	France	November 1447–January 1448
Eustachio di Giovanni Binolio (Brulio) Francioso	France	January–August 1448
Maestro Giovanni Calot[f]	Arras	10 August 1448

[a]Probably identical with Gherardo LeFay (Leay)
[b]Possibly identical with Johannes Reson
[c]Possibly identical with Ser Niccolaio, March–April 1445
[d]Possibly Maestro Rubino, singer in St. Peter's, April 1447–February 1448
[e]Possibly Petrus de Domarto
[f]In papal chapel, November 1448–July 1450

[front: Signor Pandolfo de' Malatesti, Mag[co] Capitano Generale del Comune di Siena]

(Elsewhere in these papers the writer signs his name as Tracalo da Rimini.)

Doc. 3.2. Record of a contract with the organist Monte di Lillo, 15 September 1376. AOMS, vol. 498, *Memoriale, 1359–1415,* fol. 48[r]

[margin: Postura di Monte che suona gli organi] Anco sia manifesto come noi Pietro Venturini, con consiglio de' miei consiglieri, facciemo patto e compusizione co' Monte di [gap] da Prato, sonatore e maestro d'organi, per uno anno, i' questo modo:

    Ch'esso promette di sonare eli organi di duomo il detto tempo, ogni sabato sera e ogni domenica e ogni dì solenne e dì di festa, e tante e quante volte ne sarà richiesto da l'operaio o dal sagrestano.

    Debba avere da la sagrestia ogni mese per suo salaro due fiorini e più ch'esso possa ma[n]giare i' refetoro cho' gli altri preti di duomo; e se volesse per caso ma[n]giare per sè, abbi el vino e 'l pane de la sagrestia li tocha. Ed esso si debba sue spese acatare casa, letto masarizio, come sarà di suo piacere. Comi[n]ci il deto tempo adì XV di settembre MCCCLXXVI.

Compì il detto tempo e rifermò sì come si vede i' questo libro inanzi, a carta 52.

Doc. 3.3. Contract offered to the organist Monte di Lillo, 20 September 1377. AOMS, vol. 498, *Memoriale, 1359–1415,* fol. 52ʳ dated 20 September 1377

[margin: Postura di Monte che suona gli organi] Sia manifesto a chiunque vedarà questa ischrita, come io Pietro di Migliore ispeziale, operaio de la Opara Sante Marie, m'òne rifermato Monte di Lilo da Prato, sonatore de li organi per tempo d'uno anno, per prezo di vinti fiorini l'anno e le spese cioè, quatro pani i' dì, una metadella di vino il dì, diecie libre di carne il mese. Ed egli deba sonare li organi ad ongni richiesta de l'oparario e del sagrestano ch'è e che fuse per inanzi, di domeniche, solenità, pasque, apostoli e qualunque altra festa fuse.

Chominciando l'anno in calende octobre 1378. Fata presente Lorenzo di Michele e di Checo di Ghoro adì 20 di settembre.

Rifermòssi il detto Monte di stare choll'Uopara per tempo d'uno anno cio[è], da chalende otobre anno 1379 e seghuendo insino a chalende otobre 1380, cho' sopradetti patti e modi e chondizioni che per l'anno passato fe'.

El detto Monte non seghuì di stare ancho' se n'andò sanza farne sentire nulla. E ischontò il tempo che servì di denari che aveva avuti, restò a dare a la sagrestia lire vinti e d. otto.

Doc. 3.4. Appointment of Don Pietro di Francesco da Perugia as chaplain-singer, 4 November 1441. AOMS, vol. 13, *Deliberazioni, 1434–55,* fols. 66ᵛ–67ʳ

[margin: condotta d'uno cantore o più] Misser l'operaio et conseglieri suoi soprascritti . . . veduto e considerato che a questi dì proximi passati sia [*sic*] della chiesa nostra due cantori, cioè ser Iacomo da San Germano e ser Antonio da Montepulciano, per la qual cosa la chiesa ne viene assai nel choro a essare manchata, e per questo sia necessario provedere d'altri cantori che a la detta chiesa e coro servino per honore di Dio e de la Chiesa . . . e così rimissero e commissero nello spectabile cavaliere misse l'operaio predecto e nel venerabile huomo misser Giorgio di misser Giovanni, consegliere, che possino e debbino condurre dom Pietro di Francesco da Perugia in cantore e cappellano, per quello tempo e per quello salario lo' parrà e piacerà, confermando però et aprovando la condotta e salario già factogli per lo spectabile cavaliere misser Giovanni operaio, che è per uno anno con salario di Fl. quaranta, di lire quatro [per] fiorino. Et anche ogni altro cappellano e camtore condurre possino e debbino in quel modo e forma l' parrà, a honore di Dio e de la chiesa e coro predetti.

Doc. 3.5. Letter from the Sienese envoy in Genoa concerning the recruitment of singers, 20 June 1447. AOMS, vol. 53, *Carteggio,* by date

Spettabile e gieneroso chavaliere e magior mio honorando etc.

Perché m'imponeste ch'io cierchasse se trovare si potesse trovare [*sic*] cantori, e perché io so' disideroso che la chiesa nostra sia bene hornata di tutto quello si richiede etc., e però v'aviso che qui ò trovato Ghuglielmo frangioso che sta in duomo, il quale più volte ò fatto venire a me e credo fare lui tornarà sotto la mia promessa. Ma perché bisognia uno buono tenore, e lui dice essere uno a Firenze il quale è vantagiato, e però date modo d'averlo che verrà volentieri quando saprà che Guglielmo vengha lui, e ancho là è uno bravo cantore che farà il simile. Vero è che qui a chonpagnia d'esso Ghuglielmo è uno altro chantore assai buono e uno tenore che ancho a chonpagnia di Ghuglielmo verebero. Ma questo tenore a me pare piccholo ala nostra chiesa. Chome si sia, io so' rimasto d'acordo con lui che quando sarà costì e io li scriva, chè lui farà quello li scrivarò.

E perché in questa ora mi è chapitato uno tenore ale mani, il quale è stato famiglio del duge, il quale dice essere buono maestro di canto, ed è vero ch'io l'ò fatto cantare alchune ballate e parmi dicha assai bene, ma non so chome s'adatti a chanto di chiesa, io lo mando costì a voi e potrete provare sed è chosa da voi. Ve lo racomando: lui mostra avere volontà di stare piutosto costì che in altro luogho, ma dubito sia persona stabile.

Né più vegho per questa dovere dire, se non che a voi mi racomando.

Iddio vi conservi in buono stato. Data a Genova, adì XX di giugno 1447.

Vostro Cristofano de' Montucci

anbasciadore etc.

[front: Nobile e gienoroso chavalieri

Misser Giovanni Borghesi, honorevole

Hoperaio della chiesa chattredale [*sic*] di Siena,

magior mio honorando, etc.]

TABLE 3.3. Chronological list of cathedral musicians to 1448

The list includes only those mentioned specifically as singers at some point in the calendar year; records are sketchy for the early years, when some of the chaplains may have sung polyphonic music as well. An asterisk under a year indicates that the cathedral singer was also paid for singing laudi. Laudesi are listed through 1450. Note that the fiscal year runs from May through April; a singer listed under two consecutive years may have served no more than a few months (for exact months see Register of Musicians).

	1383	1384–85	1401	1402–5	1406–7	1408–11	1412	1413–14	1415	1416	1417	1418	1419
SINGERS, 1383–1419													
Isidoro di Francia	x												
Anselmo	x	x											
Bartolomeo di Mariano			x	x	x	x	x	x					
Mariano di Giovanni				x*	x*	x*	x*			x*	x*	x*	x*
Jacomo di Bellanduccio					x	x			x	x			
Bartolomeo di Luti						x							
Leonardo di Bartolomeo									x	x*	x*	x*	x*
Giovanni di Matteo											x	x	x
Agnolo di Domenico													x

	1420	1421–23	1424	1425	1426	1427	1428	1429	1430	1431	1432	1433	1434	1435
SINGERS, 1420–35														
Jacomo di Bellanduccio									x*	x*	x*	x*		
Leonardo di Bartolomeo	x*	x*												
Mariano di Giovanni	x*	x*	x*	x*	x*	x*	x*	x*	x*	x*	x*	x*	x*	x*
Giovanni di Matteo	x*	x*	x*	x*	x*	x*	x*	x	x	x	x	x	x	x
Guglielmo di Martino	x													
Piero di Pasqua[a]				x	x	x	x	x	x	x	x	x	x	x
Giovanni di Tommaso da Bologna				x										
Giustiniano di Ser Francesco[b]					x	x	x	x	x	x	x	x		
Battista di Ser Francesco					x	x	x							
Riccardo (Gherardo) di Francia													x	
Giovanni Ragione di Francia													x	

SINGERS, 1436–48

	1436	1437	1438	1439	1440	1441	1442	1443	1444	1445	1446	1447	1448
Piero di Pasqua	x	x	x	x	x	x	x	x	x	x			
Mariano di Giovanni	x	x	x	x	x								
Giustiniano di Ser Francesco							x	x					
Marino di Niccolò[b]	x	x	x	x	x	x	x	x	x	x	x	x	
Giovanni di Jacopo Francioso		x	x										
Giovanni di Giovanni Francioso		x	x	x									
Pavolo di ser Agnolo		x											
Guglielmo di Giovanni di Francia			x	x	x								
Bartolomeo di Marino				x	x								
Giovanni de' Ricci Francioso				x									
Agnolo di Nanni					x	x	x	x	x	x	x		
Jacomo di Fosco					x	x							
Antonio di Gabriello						x							
Biagio di Tomè						x	x	x	x	x	x		
Pietro di Francesco						x	x						
Niccolò Francioso							x						
Giovanni da Bologna							x						
Lorenzo da Orvieto							x						
Giulietto Francioso									x		x		
Ser Niccolaio										x			

TABLE 3.3 *continued*

	1436	1437	1438	1439	1440	1441	1442	1443	1444	1445	1446	1447	1448
Rubino Francioso										x			
Colinetto Francioso										x			
Jannesi Francioso										x			
Jacomo di Antonio										x			
Antonio da Viterbo											x		
Jacomo da Sancto Vierno Francioso											x		
Guglielmo di Michele da Francia											x	x	
Goro di Pavolo											x		
Don Girolamo												x	
Riccardo di Viviano Francioso												x	
Guglielmo da Pavia												x	
Gonsalvo de Nuvalis												x	
Raimondo Bianco da Elci												x	
Giovanni di Martino												x	
Jacomo di Longo Francioso												x	x
Giovanni Fanti Francioso												x	x
Pietro Domarlla												x	x
Eustachius di Binolio Francioso													x
Vincentio													x
Rasso di Lorenzo													x
Giovanni Calot													x

LAUDESI, 1401–18

	1401	1402	1403	1404	1405–6	1407	1408–9	1410	1412	1413	1414–15	1416	1417	1418
Guglielmo di Martino	x	x	x	x	x	x	x	x	x	x				
Antonio di Cirello	x	x	x					x	x	x	x			
Niccolò di Berto	x	x	x											
Lorenzo di Menico		x	x											
Matteo di Guido			x											
Michelino di Nanni					x									
Donato di Lodovico						x								
Giovanni di Tommaso							x							
Arcolano di Nanni									x					
Baldassare di Antonio										x				
Antonio di Matteo										x				
Francesco di Nanni[c]										x	x			
Jacomo di Andrea												x		
Leonardo di Francesco													x	x
Antonio di Biagio													x	

LAUDESI, 1419–50

	1419	1420	1421–23	1424	1425–26	1427	1428	1429	1430–31	1432	1433	1434	1440	1446–50
Guglielmo di Martino		x					x	x						
Leonardo di Francesco		x	x									x	x	
Antonio di Biagio	x	x		x										
Francesco di Nanni							x							
Jacomo di Rico				x	x									
Pietro di Luigi						x	x		x		x			
Francesco di Antonio														
Giuliano													x	x★
Angelo													x★	x
Simone di Mariano														x

TABLE 3.3 *continued*

ORGANISTS, 1375–98

	1375	1376	1377–78	1379	1380	1381–83	1384	1385	1386–91	1392	1393	1394–95	1396	1397–98
Benedetto di Jacomo	x	x												
Matteo di Martino[d]		x												
Monte di Lillo	x		x	x										
Matteo di San Giorgio				x										
Francesco di Vanni				x	x									
Bartalomeo di Ser Laio					x	x		x	x	x			x	x
Pavolo di Giovanni							x	x						
Michelino di Nanni										x	x			
Colo da Pisa											x	x	x	

ORGANISTS, 1399–1424

	1399	1400	1401	1402–3	1404	1405–13	1414	1415	1416–23	1424
Bartalomeo di Ser Laio		x	x							
Michelino di Nanni		x	x	x	x					
Colo da Pisa	x									
Agostino di Pietro					x	x			x	
Nanni di Jacomo[e]							x	x		
Fra Ugolino[e]								x		
Matteo di Antonio[e]								x		
Francesco di Nanni										x (to 1470)

[a] archdeacon since 1406
[b] singing teacher
[c] cathedral organist from 1424
[d] offered appointment; did not accept
[e] temporary replacements for Agostino di Pietro during fiscal year 1414–15

Example 3.1. Lauda, *Ave, donna santissima:* (a) Cortona, Biblioteca Comunale, MS 91, fols. 5ᵛ–6ʳ; (b) FBNC, MS Banco rari 18, fols. 48ᵛ–49ᵛ (after Liuzzi and Wilson)

Chapter Four

BUILDING A CHAPEL, 1448–1480

I T MUST HAVE been obvious to the overseer and his counselors by the summer of 1448 that the time had come to take more vigorous measures if the cathedral were to continue to have any kind of musical program at all. For reasons unmentioned in extant documents, chaplains, clerks, and teachers, such as Marino and Biagio, were no longer employed, and it was proving impossible to retain itinerant musicians for more than a month or two at a time. Clearly, another approach was needed. It was with this thought in mind that at a meeting of 6 August 1448 the Opera's governing board decided to move in a new direction. After noting that "the church lacks singers because it cannot find any to hire" and after expressing "the hope of ensuring that there will be some in future," the board decreed that in future the overseer would be empowered "to appoint a singing teacher to instruct the boys and the clerks," and "similarly to appoint those boys whom he thinks are qualified at a salary and for the period of time he deems appropriate."[1] Since a singing teacher had been on the Opera's payrolls for almost three decades, such an action hardly represented a change in policy and merely facilitated the reappointment of a replacement for Marino. More momentous was the decision regarding the boys.

TRAINING THE BOYS

By authorizing the appointment of a group of boys to primary positions in the ensemble the board was seeking to alleviate the recurrent problem of staffing while giving, at the same time, fresh impetus to the cathedral's training program. Though in the past clerks had on occasion sung with the group or joined its ranks after being ordained as priests, this was the first time the overseer was directed to draw singers from the cathedral school. It was one of some consequence because in the future, though their number might vary, boys would generally be associated with the group regardless of the strength of adult forces. In fact, the few subsequent attempts to build a chapel without including boys from the school came to naught. The board's action at this time was thus one that had far-reaching implications for Sienese cathedral music. Henceforth, boys would sing

---

1. "Misser lo Operaio e suoi consiglieri prefati . . . considerati quanto la chiesa catredale [*sic*] à mancamento di cantori per non poterne trovare da conducerne, et volendo dare opera che per l'avenire ce ne sieno, deliberarono di rimettere e rimissero in misser lo Operaio che possi conducere uno maestro di canto per insegnare a li fanciulli e cherici, e similmente conducere delli detti fanciulli e quali cognosciarà essere atti a tale exercitio, per quello tempo e con quello salario che a lui parrà" (AOMS, vol. 13, *Deliberazioni, 1434–55,* fol. 98, dated 6 August 1448 [margin: Conducasi uno cantore per insegnare a' fanciuli]).

the upper part or parts alone, or they would supplement adult singers, so that the sounds produced by the ensemble would be quite different from anything previously heard.

Some time was to pass before the decree was fully implemented—probably because of an outbreak of plague in the fall of 1448.[2] But it was clearly in response to it that Messer Marino resumed his association with the cathedral in January 1449. The sacristan's roll for February says that he was then receiving a monthly salary of L. 2. 6. 8 as a singer and an additional L. 4 "for teaching the boys." His work as a teacher was again mentioned in March, when the sacristan made a note to the effect that with the overseer's approval he agreed to give Marino L. 4 every month "for his work in teaching four boys." Whether the boys were actually performing at the time is not stated. Marino's name appears in various accounts through May of the same year, when he once again left cathedral service.[3]

No immediate attempt was made to replace him. It was, in fact, not until 18 February 1450 that the appointment of Maestro Guglielmo Francioso as "a singer and teacher of chant and polyphony to the priests and clerks" was proposed. The board accordingly authorized the overseer to offer him an annual salary of between 30 and 40 florins, as might be necessary. Evidently, the proffered amount was not acceptable to the Frenchman, for a month later the overseer was given permission to hire, at whatever salary he thought appropriate, "a teacher of singing and organ playing" who would give instruction to "those Sienese clerks who showed talent and wished to learn." Maestro Guglielmo apparently declined a second invitation and disappeared from the records. Perhaps he is the tenor-composer-scribe Guillelmus da Francia who served alternately at St. Peter's in Rome and at Padua cathedral from October 1455 through 1467.[4] The Opera had better luck in keeping the post of teacher of grammar filled, for Don Niccolò d'Antonio, _maestro di scuola,_ is mentioned frequently during this period. Meanwhile, on 2 March 1450, another resolution aimed at shoring up forces was passed by the board, this one authorizing the overseer and one of his counselors, the cathedral provost Messer Giorgio, to hire singers for the church on whatever terms they deemed appropriate.[5]

Various records indicate that the teacher's position was next offered to Antonio di Gabriello da Montepulciano. He had returned to cathedral service as a chaplain in

---

2. Tommaso Fecini, a Sienese chronicler, reported that a solemn procession took place on 23 October 1448 to beg the Virgin's intercession. The image of the Madonna delle Grazie was taken from the duomo and carried through the streets, and as the populace marched, with lighted tapers in hand "praying God and our Lady to liberate us from the plague," they cried out "Misericordia, Madre Nostra" ("Cronaca Senese," in Muratori, ed., _Rerum italicarum scriptores,_ vol. 15, pt. 6/2, p. 860).

3. For all biographical information quoted without source, documentation will be found in the Register of Musicians under the name of the individual.

4. For this Guillelmus, see Christopher A. Reynolds, _Papal Patronage and the Music of St. Peter's, 1380–1513_ (Berkeley and Los Angeles, 1995), 199–201; and Raffaele Casimiri, "Musica e musicisti nella Cattedrale di Padova nei secoli XIV, XV, XVI," _Note d'archivio_ 18 (1941): 8–11, 152–56.

5. "E similemente deliberarono che sia e essere s'intenda pienamente rimesso in esso misser l'operaio e in misser Giorgio proposto, uno de' suoi conseglieri, potere provedere che cantori s'abbino a cantare in duomo, e quali loro abbino a condurre per quello tempo e tempi, e con quelli salari, modi, pacti e conditioni che a loro parrà, a più honore e utile de la chiesa che fare potranno" (vol. 13, _Deliberazioni, 1434–55,_ fol. 104ᵛ, dated 2 March 1449/50 [margin: pro cantoribus conducendis]).

March 1449 and appeared as a singer in the sacristan's roll for August of the same year and in records from 1450. A sacristan's roll for August 1451 lists him as "Ser Antonio da Montepulciano who teaches singing," as do several later ones. A record from 2 October 1451 notes that L. 5. 4 were paid to him at the overseer's command for a monochord "for teaching several of the duomo's clerks to play." (Within the week another monochord was bought from a Catalan called Messer Raffaello for the same purpose.[6]) Like the other chaplains, Antonio was housed at the Opera's expense, and a report from 1451 even mentions his having been loaned a blanket. He was at the cathedral through the end of May 1452, though he may have relinquished his teaching post to Marino in the previous November.

Payment records to Marino from that month through May 1452 refer to him only as a singer. But he probably resumed his old teaching duties because no other teacher is named at this time. Marino's appointment was reconfirmed on 27 May 1452 and on 2 May 1453. An addendum to a record of appointment dating from 3 June 1454 notes that he turned down a new contract that had been offered him and four other singers. He is not heard of again. Several months passed before a replacement for him was found. This was none other than Antonio da Montepulciano, who on 30 December 1454 agreed to return to cathedral service as a singer, organ player, and teacher at a salary of Fl. 32 per annum. His name appears in sacristans' lists from November 1455 through March 1456. On 30 December of that year, together with two other singers, he was awarded a new contract whose terms called for him to receive Fl. 40 per annum. He did not serve the full term specified, however, for he was fired for unknown reasons on 11 August 1457.

PROFESSIONALIZING THE CHOIR

Beginning service as a singer on 1 January 1449 was Ser Luca di Giovanni da Pisa, previously recorded as a chaplain from 1446 through 1448. His new appointment, formalized by an agreement with the overseer, called for him "to serve in the choir and particularly to take the tenorista's part at all times and to be at Mass by the beginning of the introit and at Vespers by the beginning of the first antiphon." (As with the other chaplains, he would be fined if he were tardy at services, greater penalties being imposed for feast days.) Luca served in this new capacity until the end of April 1457. A record of reappointment from 27 May 1452 and a similar one from a year later report that he was to be paid an annual salary of Fl. 9, or L. 36, for singing polyphony only, "per la cantoria solamente." Biagio di Tomè, having meanwhile been ordained a priest and now referred to as Ser Biagio, reappears in the accounts in May 1449 and is named as a singer from February 1451 through February 1454. He was subsequently associated with the cathedral in various capacities, which invariably included singing, until the mid-1480s, when he achieved the longest record of service of any of the fifteenth-century singers.

---

6. "E adì VIIII d'ottobre lire cinque soldi dieci, dè contanti Nicholò nostro a misser Raffaello chatelano, per uno monachordo si comprò da lui per li cherici, per detto di missere Mariano, L. V. s. X d. —'" (vol. 564, *Memoriale, 1451–52*, fol. 24ᵛ, dated 9 October 1451).

Singers from Poland

1449 saw the arrival of a contingent of Polish singers in Siena. This is the only time that musicians from that distant land are mentioned in cathedral records, and while they do not represent a unique case in the annals of Italian fifteenth-century music, as yet few other Polish singers have been reported at peninsular courts and chapels during this period.[7] Their appearance in Siena is significant in itself, for it attests further to the existence of musical centers in northeastern Europe able to train sufficient numbers of singers who could fill the needs both of local institutions and of others in faraway places. The lure of Italy, of the wealth and favor that men of talent could gain there, particularly at the papal court in Rome, was, of course, the principal reason why the more adventurous foreign singers made their way to the peninsula. The majority of those who went, at least at that time, were clerics, men who could hope to supplement their incomes, as so many of them did, by serving as chaplains wherever their travels might take them in their quest for benefices and other preferments. This was not the case with the Polish singers mentioned in Siena, who were all laymen. Nor were they students, like so many of the northern Europeans, particularly Germans, who journeyed to Italian university cities, where they remained, often for years at a time, as emissaries of northern culture. The Polish singers at Siena's cathedral were, in fact, itinerant professional musicians.

The Poles first appeared in the sacristan's roll for May 1449. It names Andrea, Giovanni, Jacomo, and Vito under the heading "cantori," in addition to Ser Antonio da Montepulciano at L. 8, Ser Biagio di Tomè at L. 8, and another new singer, Ser Giovanni di Michele da Radicondoli, at L. 7. 3. 8. The Polish group was paid the sum total of L. 8, apparently for one week's service. Subsequent rolls for June, July, and August show them receiving L. 32 per month and indicate that of that amount L. 16 were for Giovanni and L. 4 for Vito. Both these musicians were present from September through December 1449, though Andrea and Jacomo left at the end of August.

The sacristan's roll from January 1450 reports that Giovanni, "cantore di Polonia," and Vito cantore were joined by "Matteo and two companions from Poland." These latter, named in another record, were Andrea and Jacomo, the same musicians cited during the previous summer. The five Polish singers are mentioned in two decrees from 21 January 1450, both of which furnish some information about their ages and their relationships. The first confirms the salaries and working conditions already granted to Giovanni Polacchio and to his son Vito (see Doc. 4.1).[8] The second records the appointments of the other three, an adult, who was clearly Matteo, and two boys, Andrea and Jacomo, now referred to as "garzonetti." Altogether, the group was to have an annual salary of Fl. 80 and continuation of the appointment was subject to confirmation every month by the overseer and his counselors.

---

7. Reinhard Strohm, "European Politics and the Distribution of Music in the Early Fifteenth Century," *Early Music History* 1 (1981): 311–12, for references to Polish, Silesian, and Czech canons in the Trent cathedral Chapter during the 1440s and to Othmar Opilionis, a graduate of Cracow University and cantor of the bishop of Trent in 1441, whose music appears in Trent Codex 93.

8. Vito is called "suo garzone" in this document, but "fanciullo suo" in the sacristan's report for March 1450.

The new provisions, however, were no more successful than those previously awarded other singers. Matteo and the two boys were gone by March and Giovanni served only through the beginning of April 1450. Another record from this time shows that Giovanni left "a book of songs on fine rag paper" as security for a loan of L. 12 that he had received from the Opera. (The volume eventually found its way into the cathedral library, where it was mentioned in inventories for many years to come; see below, Table 4.1.) Perhaps Giovanni's intention was to return to Siena because his son Vito, cantore, is cited among the clerks until the middle of February 1451. But nothing in the official record shows that he did.

The tenure of the Polish musicians, however brief, invites a few observations about their repertories and performing practices. Giovanni's possession of a book of music indicates that they sang written polyphony and that they traveled with a repertory of their own, which they performed with or without the assistance of additional singers. Their repertory, which allowed them to move into a new situation such as Siena cathedral's with a minimum of effort, must have been an international one consisting of polyphonic Mass movements, motets, antiphons, hymns, Magnificats, and other items that were customarily done in polyphony at Masses and Vespers. The makeup of the group—two adults and three youths—suggests that the boys sang the top part in three-voice music and that each of the men took one of the lower parts when they performed as a group. In music for four voices one of the youths may have taken over the additional part, usually an altus. These were fairly standard performing practices in mid-fifteenth-century Italy and do not represent any significant departure from the norm. Soloists, as remarked earlier, would generally sing all parts but the uppermost one, which might be done by as many as three or four singers. How this disposition of voices might have been modified when the Poles performed with other singers, as they did for a few months in Siena, is a matter of speculation. But the presence of two or three additional singers would not have posed many problems if such singers could read music and had adequate rehearsal time with the group. Rather, accommodating additional voices might have posed more of a problem in terms of vocal balance, which would have called for some variation in the distribution of singers on each part. In any event the salaries the Polish singers were paid at Siena cathedral leave little doubt about their professionalism and the quality of their performances. Giovanni earned L. 8 per month, double the amount paid to Italian clergymen such as Marino, Biagio, and Luca, whose salaries were the same as that paid to Giovanni's son Vito.

Boy Singers

Despite the continuing scarcity of singers, the board's decision to hire students from the cathedral school had yet to be implemented. Sacristans' rolls from May and June 1450, for example, list Ser Antonio da Montepulciano, Ser Biagio di Tomè, the Polish youth named Vito, the chaplain Ser Francesco di Antonio di Boccone, who formerly served as a laudese, and a singer-chaplain called Ser Giovanni. Beginning in November the new policy was at last put into effect with the appointment of three local youths from the cathedral's school, Simone di Mariano, tenorista, Menico di Matteo, and Michelagnolo di Daniello. By now, Simone, previously recorded as a singer of laudi, must have been in his late teens because he was taking the tenorista's part. How old the others were is difficult to gauge, although if they were singing higher parts, it is probable that their voices had not yet broken. With their appointments, the plan to train local youths for eventual service in the chapel was finally realized. It was a group such as this, including the boys, that performed at the ceremony held in the cathedral on 21 January 1451, when Siena's newly appointed bishop, Aeneas Sylvius Piccolomini, received the red biretta.[9]

The youths' performances evidently lived up to everyone's expectations, at least initially, for on 11 February 1451, only a few months after they began serving, the board gave the overseer and cathedral archdeacon Messer Piero di Pasqua permission to appoint any or all of "those three boys and their tenor and contratenor who are presently singing in the duomo at whatever salary and terms they think appropriate" (see Doc. 4.2). Three boys and Biagio di Tomè appear on the rolls in the next few months. Continuing satisfaction with the boys' work led to another favorable action on the part of the board in the following October. This again empowered the overseer to appoint or confirm "those three boys presently singing there to posts in the duomo's choir" and also approved monthly salaries of L. 4 for two of them and of L. 4. 10 for the tenorista (see Doc. 4.3). Sacristans' rolls from December 1451 through April 1452 show that the personnel now comprised the two boys and their tenorista as well as Ser Luca di Giovanni tenorista, Ser Biagio cantore, Messer Marino, and the singing teacher, Ser Antonio da Montepulciano. Again, as with the Polish singers, there is no indication of how the older singers worked with the others, especially since the youths had their own tenorista. But since they were performing with experienced clerics, two of whom had probably been their teachers, it is likely that there was a single ensemble, which perhaps may have been grouped and regrouped according to the requirements of the music that was being performed, rather than two groups, each of which had its own repertory.

VISITING MUSICIANS: THE PAPAL AND NEAPOLITAN CHAPELS

In 1443 Siena played host to Pope Eugene IV and his court for several months. Eugene, who had resided in Florence and elsewhere for a number of years, was finally making his way back to a pacified Rome. In Florence, he had entered fully into the city's political and cultural life, presiding at the consecration of the Florentine duomo on 25 March 1436—a ceremony celebrated with the performance of a motet especially written for the occasion by the then papal singer Guillaume Du Fay.[10] During the time he and his court were in Siena, from mid-March through mid-September 1443, Eugene's

---

9. Fecini, "Cronaca Senese," 862.

10. Haberl, "Die römische 'schola cantorum'," 221. The motet, *Nuper rosarum flores,* was published in Guillaume Dufay, *Opera Omnia,* ed. Heinrich Besseler, 1:70–75. Alejandro Planchart, "The Early Career of Guillaume Du Fay," 351, suggests that the motet's text was written by Du Fay himself and says that a number of such texts set to music by the composer "rise well above the standards of mere competence." Further on *Nuper rosarum flores* and Du Fay's music for Florence, see David Fallows, *Dufay* (New York, 1982), 9, 44–47, 112, 117–19, 212, 291, and Craig Wright, "Dufay's *Nuper rosarum flores,* King Solomon's Temple, and the Veneration of the Virgin," *JAMS* 47 (1994), 395–439.

chapel counted about a dozen singers, most of them of Franco-Flemish origin.[11] The extent to which the papal singers performed at public ceremonies in Siena is not given in any surviving reports, but they would have done so at services whenever the pope officiated. Although Du Fay had long since left the chapel, some of his music must assuredly have been in the papal repertory.

One of Eugene's lasting contributions to Florentine musical life was his issuance of a papal bull establishing the cathedral school of chant and grammar, an action he also took in some other Italian cities.[12] Eventually, the school had a profound effect on the course of polyphony in Florence. Eugene did not take similar action in Siena for the simple reason that as early as 1419, the Sienese themselves, in the form of a governmental decree, had decided that the Opera's overseers would be responsible for providing instruction in chant, grammar, and organ playing for students in the cathedral school from the Opera's own funds. Some of the fruits of that action were, of course, realized with the appointment of the boy singers in November 1450.

An unexpected visit from the largest and one of the most renowned musical groups on the peninsula occurred at the end of June 1451, during the tenure of the boy singers at the cathedral. This was the chapel of the Aragonese King of Naples, Alfonso I, with whom Siena was then allied politically. Alfonso's chapel, which numbered at least twenty-one singers and perhaps more, was comprised of a majority of Spaniards, as one might expect, considering the king's origins, and a sprinkling of Italians.[13] The Neapolitan singers must have made quite an impression on the Sienese, accustomed as they were to small ensemble polyphonic performances. None of the documents mentions exactly where the Neapolitan group performed in Siena, though the cathedral and the Palazzo Pubblico would have been the most suitable places. In any event the singers were handsomely rewarded for their performances by the Sienese government. On 30 June 1451 they and the king's heralds received L. 47. 10 or 10 ducats for their services, "out of consideration," as the report puts it, "for the sacred majesty of the king of Aragon."[14] Since the monthly expenses of the cathedral's entire singing establishment did not amount to more than L. 28 at this time, it was very generous consideration indeed. Earlier, the Neapolitan chapel had been in Florence, where, as part of a cultural exchange program that was no doubt intended to improve relations between the two

----

11. Haberl, "Die römische 'schola cantorum'," 223.

12. On the establishment of the school in Florence, see Albert Seay, "The 15th-Century Cappella at Santa Maria del Fiore in Florence," *JAMS* 11 (1958): 46–48. On the establishment of a school in Torino (March 1435), see Gino Borghezio, "La fondazione del Collegio Nuovo 'Puerorum Innocentium' del Duomo di Torino," *Note d'archivio* 1 (1924): 211–12; for a similar action at Urbino, see B. Ligi, "La cappella musicale del Duomo d'Urbino," *Note d'archivio* 2 (1925): 6, 18–20. For a general assessment of cathedral music schools in light of the new humanism of the time see Nino Pirrotta, "Music and Cultural Tendencies in 15th-Century Italy," *JAMS* 19 (1966): 127–61.

13. Atlas, *Music at the Aragonese Court of Naples,* 29–30.

14. "A' chantori e araldi della sacra Maestà dello Re di Raghona, adì detto duchati dieci larghi, paghamo per pulitia [*recte* polizza] di Chonciestoro . . . di mano di ser Ranicci Biringhucci, et quali se li donaro[no] per chomtempratione della sacra Maestà del Re di Raghona . . . L. XLVII s. X" (ASS, Biccherna, vol. 319, fol. 81ᵛ, dated 30 June 1451).

states, the group performed on Pentecost Sunday (13 June) at the cathedral and later in the week at the church of the Santissima Annunziata.[15]

The visit of the Neapolitans, like that of the papal chapel eight years earlier, must have been of inestimable value to the Sienese singers both in terms of acqusition of repertory and of the latest trends in performance practices.[16]

CATHEDRAL SINGERS IN THE 1450s

A record from 27 May 1452 of reappointments and confirmation of salaries for the singing group, "per la cantoria," names all of the previously mentioned musicians except Ser Antonio da Montepulciano (see Doc. 4.4). Their annual salaries were as follows: Messer Marino, L. 48; the two boys, Menico di Matteo and Michelagnolo di Daniello, L. 48 each; Simone di Mariano, their tenorista, L. 54; Ser Luca da Pisa, for singing only, "per la cantoria solamente," L. 36; and Ser Biagio di Tomè, for singing only, L. 36. A distinction was made in the case of the latter two adults because their services as chaplains were being paid from a different account. Nevertheless, the boys were receiving higher salaries as singers than the adults, perhaps because this was the only salary they received and because they were not being given room and board. A deliberation of 9 June 1452 notes that even though the youths were not clerics, they were obliged to stay in the choir throughout Masses and Vespers, whenever they sang.[17] Presumably, such regulations also applied to adult singers who were not clergymen. Noteworthy also is the affirmation that Masses and Vespers were the services at which polyphony was being performed at this time.

Reconfirmation of appointments and salary increases for all of the same singers were registered on 2 May 1453 (see Doc. 4.5). Two other youths, Giovanni di Santi and Meo di Maestro Giovanni, began singing with the group that same month. All of the singers were present through April 1454, except for Biagio and Marino, who left after January 1454. A new arrangement was apparently made at that time whereby the organist, Ser Francesco di Nanni, was to be solely responsible for training, rehearsing, and perhaps even accompanying the young singers, who now constituted the entire "cantoria." This much is indicated in the annual record of reappointments and confirmation of salaries from May 1454, which under the heading "singers" cites the organist and the five "cherici," Simone, Michelangelo, Giovanni, Menico, and Francesco di Lorino, a new singer (see Doc. 4.6). A separate provision was made at this time for a sixth singer, Meo, who, like the others, was to receive a monthly salary of L. 5. Paylists confirm the presence of the youths throughout the rest of the year. No adults other than the organist are mentioned with the boys in these and in later records, a clear

---

15. The visit to Florence is well documented. See D'Accone, "The Singers of San Giovanni," 317–18; Atlas, *Music at the Aragonese court of Naples,* 34.

16. The Neapolitans' visit was also recorded by Fecini, "Cronaca Senese," 854–55.

17. "A tre giovanetti cantano e già più tempo ànno cantato in duomo, soldi dieci per ciascuno di loro e ciascuno mese, sì veramente debbino stare compitamente a tutti li offici dela messa e del Vespero quando cantaranno" (AOMS, vol. 13, *Deliberazioni, 1434–55,* fol. 118ʳ, dated 9 June 1452 [margin: Salarii di certi preti e cantori del duomo]).

indication that they performed as a group by themselves, that is, with their own tenor and contratenor, and perhaps with the assistance of the organist.

There was some dissatisfaction with this arrangement, however, for a record from 3 June 1454 indicates that the overseer and his counselors were seeking another solution to the problem of engaging and retaining adult singers of polyphony (see Doc. 4.7). This took the form of a one-month trial appointment in the chapel offered to five adults, three of whom, as part-time chaplains, would also be obliged to "be at Matins." They included Messer Marino, Ser Biagio, Ser Luca, Don Antonio, who was a parish priest from the town of Chiusdino, and a German singer identified simply as "Teotonicus." This latter was to receive a salary that was almost double that of the others. An addendum to the record notes that on the following day the offer was turned down by both Biagio and Marino and that it was therefore withdrawn. A deliberation from the end of December 1454 shows that another attempt was made to shore up musical forces, this time by reappointing Antonio da Montepulciano as a singer, organist, and teacher at an annual salary of 32 florins (see Doc. 4.8). (Despite this, the regular organist, Francesco di Nanni, was reaffirmed in his position with his usual salary.) After this time, as has been mentioned, Antonio is listed through the end of August 1457, and the four youths, Simone di Mariano, Menico di Matteo, Giovanni di Santi, and Meo di Giovanni, are recorded in a number of accounts through the end of October 1456.

Events in 1456 indicate that even though five years had passed since local youths had been hired, ways were still being sought to engage clerics who were professionally trained musicians. The youths—some of whom, like Simone, by now were young men—had obviously acquired a great deal of experience as well as a larger repertory. But the Opera was not satisfied with things as they stood. Perhaps some of the discontent had to do with the quality of the boys' voices. Perhaps it stemmed from an attitude that considered having only young singers as unworthy of a great cathedral. Or perhaps, as performers of written music, their repertory was limited to what they could master. It may also have had to do with their lack of knowledge of liturgical matters or an inability to participate fully in the plainchant choir's activities. In any event, on 3 May of that year the board decided that the overseer and one of his associates could have full authority to hire singers who could sing counterpoint, "cantores a contraponto," without delay.[18]

One result of their decision was the proposed appointment on the following 5 July of Ser Antonio di Niccolò "of the Chancellors' [Palace] of Rome," who also held the parish priest's post at Suvereto in the Sienese Maremma. He was hired as a chaplain at an annual salary of Fl. 10 on condition that he say Mass three days a week and on feast days, that he be present at Matins on feast days, that he be in the choir to sing at Mass and Vespers on feast days, and that "during the Studio's vacation time he continue to

---

18. "Et deliberaverunt quod sit remissum in dominum Tonium et Andream domini Cristofori qui possint et eis liceat conducere in cantores a contraponto in ecclesia catredale [*sic*], ut melius noverint expedire, et in predictis habeant plenam autoritatem" (vol. 14, *Deliberazioni, 1454–59,* fol. 20ᵛ, dated 3 May 1456 [margin: Cantores conducantur]).

be in the choir and sing music of all kinds, that is, plainchant, counterpoint, and figural music, to the best of his abilities." The schedule of classes at Siena University thus figures once again in a singer's contract. Perhaps this indicates that some singers came to Siena in order to pursue their studies. Or it could mean that scholars and students normally attended Masses and Vespers at the cathedral and that polyphonic performances would be not dispensed with simply because they were on vacation. Whether there were closer connections between the cathedral chapel and the Studio is difficult to say, though it is tempting to think that some among Siena's large foreign student population might have been responsible for transmission of musical repertory in ways that went unrecorded.[19]

A report from 12 August 1456 notes that Antonio did not accept the position and that the board authorized the overseer to make him another offer, this time with the promise of an annual salary not to exceed Fl. 12, but with the same pacts and conditions previously mentioned. The new salary apparently met the singer's expectations, for payments are subsequently registered to "our chaplain," Ser Antonio di Niccolò di Trecerchi, through April 1457.[20]

"Music of All Kinds"

The types of singing mentioned in the first two records regarding Antonio Trecerchi are of interest because of the questions they raise regarding the use of written, and perhaps improvised, polyphony at the cathedral at this time. Figural music, or *canto figurato,* refers to music written in florid counterpoint, the high art music of the day. "Counterpoint," however, as used here and in the previous record could refer either to simple written compositions of the note-against-note variety or to improvised polyphony, which might be simple or considerably more elaborate.[21] If the latter were intended, it would mean that even at mid-century, extemporized polyphony was considered a perfectly acceptable way of embellishing certain sections of the cathedral's liturgy; it was perhaps introduced by the many northern singers who make their appearance in Siena; however, written polyphony was by then becoming the norm.

---

19. On Siena's University, in addition to Lodovico Zdekauer's *Lo studio di Siena nel Rinascimento* (Milan, 1894), see the recently published *L'Università di Siena: 750 Anni di Storia* (Siena, 1991).

20. Whether the singer had previous ties to Siena is unknown, but his surname is found often in Sienese documents of the time.

21. For a lucid explanation of the term "counterpoint" as used by Johannes Tinctoris, the most authoritative of late fifteenth-century theorists, see Bonnie J. Blackburn, "On Compositional Process in the Fifteenth Century," *JAMS* 40 (1987): 246–60. As Blackburn has observed, Tinctoris defined counterpoint as "successive composition, whether note-against-note in the same time values, or diminished, in which several notes, of different or the same value, can be placed against one note. It could be accomplished in writing or in the mind," meaning that it could be improvised. She further notes that Tinctoris's definition of counterpoint that was achieved "mentaliter is no different in terminology or in execution than in the 16th century, where it is called *contrappunto alla mente* in Italian sources." For recent commentary and illustration of "counterpoint" and the improvising tradition, see Keith Polk, *German Instrumental Music of the Late Middle Ages* (Cambridge, 1992), 166–69.

TABLE 4.1. Inventories of music manuscripts, 1458–1467

1458: Inventario . . . al tempo dello spectabile e mangnifico chavaliere misser Cristofano di Filigi (AOMS, vol. 1492, *Inventari, 1420–post 1488,* fasc. 8)

fol. 6^r:	[18]	Uno seguentiale coperto di biancho, comincia Regem venturum, segnia XVIII
fol. 7^r:	[46]	Una musicha di Boetio con un fondello rosso, comincia Omnium quidem, segnia XLVI
	[60]	Uno libro di laude per volgare coperto di nero, comincia Ave donna sanctissima, segnia LX
	[61]	Uno seguentiale coperto di nero, comincia Letabuntur, segnia LXI
fol. 8^r:	[100]	Uno libro di charta banbagina, di contra [gap], con tavole mezze coperte di bianco, segnia C
	[113]	Duo libri di canto di contrapunto: uno legato in tavole, in carta banbagina, et l'altro conn una fodara di chapretto

1467–70: Inventario . . . al tempo del . . . chavaliere misser Savino di Matteo d'Antonio di Ghuido [Savini] dengnissimo hoperaio (ibid., fasc. 9)

fols. 4^r, 5^r list items 18, 46, 60, and 61 as above		
fol. 6^r:	[100]	Uno libro di charta banbagina con tavole, mezzo coperto di biancho, solfato da canto et figurato, [segnato] C
	[113]	Due libri di canto di contrapunto, uno legato in coverte di carta et l'altra con coverte di pecora, tutti in charta banbagina, sengniano tutti e due CXIII

Some explanation about what these terms may have meant in Siena around mid-century is furnished by successive inventories of the cathedral's possessions. One from 1458, the first to mention music other than chant, notes the presence of three books of polyphony, one of which must have been the volume left to the Opera as a security by the Polish singer Giovanni in 1450 (see Table 4.1). The first, cited as item no. 100 in the inventory, is described as "a book of counter[point] on fine rag paper, with boards half covered in white." Two other items, numbered together as 113, comprised "two books of contrapuntal song: one on fine rag paper, bound in boards, and the other with a loose kidskin cover." In both instances "counterpoint" and "contrapuntal song" clearly refer to written polyphony, without specifying its exact nature. In an inventory of 1467, however, item no. 100, is said to be "a book of fine rag paper with boards, half covered in white, notated in song and figured," whereas the two items of no. 113 are still called books of "contrapuntal song." This designation was abandoned by ca. 1488, when the next inventory was compiled (see Table 5.2). Item no. 100 is now described as "a book of figural music, on fine rag paper," and while only one of the items previously grouped together as no. 113 was still in use, it was now reported as "a book of figural music, on fine rag paper, with paper covers and the Opera's coat of arms." Perhaps by this time distinctions were no longer being made between simpler note-against-note music, in counterpoint, and the more complicated figural music, although it could also be that earlier the two terms were synonymous in Siena. Whether or not that was the case, all of these terms were used by compilers of cathedral inventories to indicate written polyphony. In all probability it was also written rather than improvised polyphony that was referred to in the records regarding Antonio Trecerchi's appointment in 1456.[22]

A New Professional Group and Their Duties

The major decision affecting the course of musical events during 1456 was taken at a meeting on 27 October, when the board decreed that "if the newly chosen singers should come to serve," the boys were to be dismissed, and indeed, that if the singers should arrive before the end of the month, the boys were to be let go at that time.[23] (The possibility of hiring new singers from out of town had obviously been discussed at a previous meeting, records of which are no longer extant.) The boys' names, as noted, disappear from the sacristans' rolls after the end of October, and a contract dated 1 November 1456 reveals that the new singers, Ser Goro di Pavolo da Firenze, a tenorista, and two sopranos, the Frenchman Ser Giovanni di Stefano di Piccardia and Ser Antonio di Matteo da Prato, did in fact arrive on time (see Doc. 4.9). They were priests as well as singers, some of them with considerable experience. Goro and Antonio both served in the Florentine chapel prior to coming to Siena.[24] Goro, who sang in Siena as early as Christmas 1446, was apparently a great favorite of the Sienese. More recently, he had returned to the city in August 1456 to sing at Assumption Day festivities, perhaps in the company of the others. Maybe his coming to Siena on a more permanent basis was first discussed at that time.

Goro's appointment, however, was made possible because of the direct intervention of Siena's bishop, Cardinal Aeneas Sylvius Piccolomini. The cardinal's role in the matter is revealed in his letter of 10 November 1457 to the cathedral overseer Cristoforo Felici.[25] This regards a missal that the cardinal had been authorized to take from the Opera by the former overseer Antonio di Luca, who was now being threatened with legal action by city authorities unless the missal was returned. After stating in no uncertain terms that as head of the Sienese church he believed it was his right to take what-

---

22. In one respect the situation is analogous to the terms used to describe the cathedral's singers of polyphony. Throughout this time the word *cantoria* is the only one used, whereas the more usual *cappella di canto figurato,* the chapel of figural music, does not appear in documents until later in the century.

23. "Deliberaverunt etiam quod si cantores noviter electos venient ad serviendum, quod statim intelligantur cassi clerici cantores; et si venirent ante finem presentis mensis, quod clerici illi intelligantur cassi in fine huius mensis" (vol. 14, *Deliberazioni, 1454–59,* fol. 30^r, dated 27 October 1456 [margin: Cantores clericos]).

24. Goro's patronymic is mistakenly given as Maso in the few Florentine payments (after 6 March 1445) that mention him. Both singers' length of service is unknown because Florentine salary records usually preserve the name of the *maestro di cappella* only, in this case Maestro Benotto di Giovanni, sometimes said to be "de Ferrara." See D'Accone, "The Singers of San Giovanni," 313. Starr has established that Maestro Benotto was the same person as the French composer Benoit (Benedictus Sirede), who served in Ferrara. See "The Ferrara Connection: A Case Study of Musical Recruitment in the Renaissance," 8–12.

25. MS Lat 298 of the Houghton Library, Harvard University. An English summary of its contents is published on pp. 9–10 of *Italian Humanists in Ten Manuscripts from The Houghton Library: An Exhibition on the Occasion of the Annual National Meeting of the Renaissance Society of America, 30 March–1 April 1989,* Catalogue by John Hankins.

ever he pleased from the cathedral library, the cardinal asked that no reprisals be made against the former overseer. He promised in return to arrange matters with the archbishop of Florence so that Ser Goro would be given permission to accept a post in Siena.[26] None of this, of course, appears in cathedral records, and were it not for the survival of Piccolomini's letter, his part in the matter might never have been known. The letter also suggests that many other appointments at the cathedral, particularly of foreign musicians, came about through such informal conversations and recommendations. Perhaps Piccolomini himself was responsible for the presence of some of the foreign singers. He was, after all, a man of the world—a brilliant scholar and seasoned diplomat who had assuredly heard performances by some of the leading singing groups in northern Europe, where his travels repeatedly took him.

The contract signed by Goro, Antonio, and Giovanni di Piccardia was to be in effect for a year. It stipulated that they were each to have a room in the canons' residence furnished with a bed—but not with a sheet—a chest, and a dining table, and that each was to receive 50 florins per annum. The salary, equivalent to L. 16. 3. 4 a month, was more than had ever been paid to any of the previous chaplain-singers and is indicative of the reputations of these "Florentine" singers and of the expectations they had aroused. Their duties, on the other hand, were more numerous in some respects than those of their predecessors. With regard to their performing polyphony, they were "obliged to be at Mass and at Vespers on all feast days and to sing the said Mass and Vespers honorably, as required." The feast days were undoubtedly those enumerated in the Constitutions of 1459, and included, in addition to Sundays, all of the major feasts of Our Lord, of the Virgin Mary, of Siena's patron saints, and a number of others. On non-feast, or ferial, days the newly appointed singers were "obliged to be at Mass and Vespers and to sing the Alleluia, the offertory, and the Sanctus, as is customary, [and] at Vespers."[27] As chaplains, each of them personally was "to say Mass at the cathedral on all feast days" and also "during the week, should the necessity arise." In addition, they were to be present at Matins on Christmas and Assumption Day and at a number of other Masses throughout the year, notably at midnight on Christmas and "on the days when the Magnificent Lords [Priors of the Republic] assume office," as well as when there were processions or when extraordinary services were celebrated.

Several important aspects of the singers' duties can be gleaned from these few statements. Principal among them is the frequency with which polyphony was performed at the cathedral at this time. Masses and Vespers were specified for Sundays and all feast days, which, as the Constitutions show, were now quite numerous (see above, Table 1.2). What they sang in polyphony at Masses on these days may be inferred from what

---

26. Earlier that summer Piccolomini, who had recently been created a cardinal, was in Siena negotiating an alliance between the papacy and Milan against the Turks. Ser Goro had sung at the celebrations marking the successful conclusion of the alliance, in August 1456, and it is possible that he was invited to Siena at the request of Piccolomini himself.

27. See Doc. 4.9. The wording is unclear here, but it is apparent that the singers were required to perform one or more items in polyphony at Vespers as well, a practice corroborated by documents and musical sources from later in the century.

they did not sing on ferial days. Evidently, the Alleluia, the offertory, and the Sanctus were specified for the latter because these were the only items that were sung in polyphony, as opposed to the entire ordinary and selected items from the proper that were sung on feast days. The 1459 Constitutions offer some information in this regard as well as about performing practices at this time. They explain that in times of war, plague, famine, and other universal afflictions, the "Benedictus qui venit in nomine Domini" (of the Sanctus) and the "Et incarnatus est" (of the Credo) were sung with devotion by unison voices and "not with the sound of the organ because the sound of the organ diminishes devotion somewhat."[28] This must mean that these items of the Mass were normally performed in polyphony with organ accompaniment or in alternatim style with the organ. Although Vespers on ferial days are cited in the singers' contract of 1456, the item or items that were to be done in polyphony went unmentioned. Perhaps, it was again a question of having fewer items done with polyphony than at Vespers on feast days. In any event their repertory would have comprised hymns, psalms, and Magnificats, the kinds of pieces represented in a volume of Vespers music compiled for the cathedral a quarter of a century later. Whether the singers performed polyphony at Christmas Matins and midnight Mass, as well as at those other services when their presence was required, is a matter of conjecture, but they likely did, given the importance of those occasions. As for the repertory they sang, in addition to the pieces in the three books owned by the cathedral, it seems reasonable to assume in view of their previous employment that Goro and his companions would have known, or brought with them, works by Du Fay—whose music at this time was highly esteemed in Florence, as it was throughout Italy.[29]

The duties of Sienese chapel singers seem compatible with those of singers employed in other major Italian churches around this time. A Milanese cathedral statute outlining singers' duties from January 1463 required them to sing polyphony at Masses, Vespers, and other offices on all major as well as less important feast days, and on a number of occasions elsewhere, such as Vespers at the church of Sant'Ambrogio, the city's patron saint, on his feast day.[30] Specific items that were to be sung in polyphony

---

28. "Quibus temporibus in ecclesia dici debeant Litaniae . . . Totum ponentes conatum ad augendam populi devotionem . . . statuerunt ut temporibus guerrae, pestis, famis, vel alterius notoriae afflictionis universalis, vel quadragesimae, & adventus Domini in principio maioris missae litaniae cum omnibus requisitis, & consuetis orationibus cum summa cordis devotione, & corporis modestia flexis genibus per canonicos, & caeteros de ecclesia cappellanos & clericos (canonico cessante impedimento) debeant humiliter decantari. Et causa simili etiam adijcientes quòd Benedictus qui venit in nomine domini &c. & versus ille in Credo contentus scilicet; & Incarnatus est &c. diebus solemnibus in cantu vocis idoneorum cantorum devotissimè dici debeant, & non per organorum sonoritatem, per quorum organorum sonum devotio quodammodo evanescit" (*Constitutiones,* rub. 15).

29. For Du Fay's relations with Florence see D'Accone, "The Singers of San Giovanni," 318–19, 322; for his relations with Ferrara, see Lockwood, *Music in Renaissance Ferrara,* 48.

30. See Sartori, "Josquin des Près cantore del Duomo di Milano," 70–71, for the text of the document. Note that the second item specifies: "pro maiori parte honore Ecclesie teneantur aliquem cantum per contrapunctum cantare ingressum vel lucernarium vel alium cantum: prout cantoribus videbitur: et maxime in confractorio vel transitorio."

included the Ambrosian equivalents of the introit, communion, and Agnus Dei of the Roman rite, as well as the responsory sung during the lighting of the lamp at Vespers.[31] The Florentine chapel, from its inception in 1439, was obliged to sing Vespers at the cathedral and Masses at the Baptistry on Sundays and major feast days, as well as Masses at the Baptistry four times during the year, as each new group of priors assumed office.[32] For Vespers, at least one full psalm was done in polyphony, and probably hymns and antiphons were also performed. In the absence of evidence to the contrary, we can only assume that the entire ordinary as well as selected items of the proper were sung polyphonically. In the 1460s the Florentine singers' duties were expanded to include singing polyphonic Masses on Saturday mornings at the church of the Santissima Annunziata.

The overseer and his counselors were so pleased with the new arrivals that within the month they agreed to compensate them for their moving expenses.[33] Nor were the cathedral's other musicians forgotten in this burst of generosity. On 30 December 1456 new monthly stipends of L. 4 "for singing according to the custom of the singers" were voted for Ser Antonio di Trecerchi and Ser Biagio di Tomè. At the same time a yearly salary of Fl. 40, or L. 160, was awarded to Ser Antonio da Montepulciano (see Doc. 4.10). These musicians, together with Ser Luca da Pisa, are recorded through April 1457, after which only Biagio and Antonio da Montepulciano are mentioned in connection with the three newly arrived singers. Antonio, however, was summarily dismissed on the following 11 August and from then until the end of November only four singers were present. Joining them for the month of December was Ser Francesco da Sancta Reina, who received L. 3 for his services. A record from 30 December 1457 reports that the contract of the three "Florentine" musicians was renewed immediately upon the expiration of the previous one (see Doc. 4.11).

The spotty records for 1458 show that Antonio da Prato left after January; that because of illness Goro was absent for the month of July, though he was paid his full salary while he was away; and that the three continuing singers were joined by a newcomer, Antonio di Antonio. The latter's appointment on 28 November states that his monthly salary is not to exceed 10 lire, a figure confirmed by the overseer a few weeks later. Although Antonio is called Teutonico in the record of appointment, subsequent documents are unanimous in referring to him as Ser Antonio di Antonio Ongaro or Ser Antonio Ongaretto, and it is quite clear that precise information about his Hungarian origins was initially lacking. Like the Polish singers almost a decade earlier, Antonio's appointment represents a first in the chapel's musical annals, though a Hungarian organ builder, Pietro Scotto, had been engaged earlier to construct a new instrument. Another newcomer to the chapel, Ser Giovanni di Jacopo da Francia, appointed on 7 February

31. Prizer, "Music at the Court of the Sforza," 150.

32. D'Accone, "The Singers of San Giovanni," 311–13.

33. "Domini operarius et consiliarii . . . auditis cantoribus de libris 12 habitis in eorum a[d]ventum Senis . . . decreverunt quod camerarium, sive suo preiudicio aut damno, accendat tres novos cantores in libris 4 denariorum pro quolibet, qui denarii danti [sic] eis quando venerunt Senis, pro spensis factis, et sic deinde solvat sine suo preiudicio aut damno" (vol. 14, *Deliberazioni, 1454–59,* fol. 31ᵛ, dated 7 December 1456: [margin: pro cantoribus]).

1459, at a salary not to exceed what was being paid to Ser Goro and to Ser Giovanni di Piccardia, was required to "serve at Divine Offices the way the Opera's other chaplains do." Within the month his salary was fixed at 50 florins per annum. He is mentioned, however, only through the middle of the following September.

THE PAPAL VISIT OF 1458

A year earlier, on 3 September 1458, Siena's Cardinal Aeneas Sylvius Piccolomini succeeded to the papacy as Pius II. Grand festivities featuring triumphs and bonfires marked the occasion in the Pope's native city.[34] Solemn Masses of thanksgiving were sung in churches throughout Siena at the time, particularly at the cathedral, though there is no mention of the chapel participating in any of the ceremonies. Piccolomini was the scion of one of the city's most ancient clans. As a young man, he served various ecclesiastical personages at the Council of Basel. Later he traveled the length and breadth of Europe as a papal emissary and as counselor and friend of the Emperor Frederick, before becoming bishop, cardinal, and, finally, pope. Piccolomini has often been called the "apostle of humanism to the north." And it is no exaggeration to say that his accomplishments as historian, novelist, and chronicler of his own life and times were no less distinguished than his remarkable career as a diplomat and clergyman.[35] Although we know little about his musical abilities and tastes—he included a witty account of a Mass that was poorly performed at the coronation of the antipope Felix V—he is thought to have acquired on his travels the well-known Aosta Codex, a collection of English and Continental repertories from the earlier decades of the century.[36] If this is so, possibly some of this music was passed on to his Sienese compatriots, though nothing of this sort is mentioned in contemporary reports.

During his pontificate Pius visited his native city a number of times. On one such occasion the Sienese honored him with an extraordinary musical performance that had decidedly humanistic overtones. Few details are extant about the performance, which took place on the last day of January 1460, though the chroniclers carefully reported that the city had arranged a magnificent tableau with stage machinery representing a "chorus of angels or a paradiso" and that from it "an angel descended, singing certain stanzas."[37] Perhaps it was one of the cathedral singers who sang the stanzas, which surely

---

34. See Tommaso Fecini, "Cronaca Senese," 868.

35. There is a vast literature on Pius II and his works. Accessible biographies are by Gioacchino Paparelli, *Enea Silvio Piccolomini, Pio II* (Bari, 1950) and Curzio Ugurgieri della Berardenga, *Pio II Piccolomini, con notizie su Pio III e altri membri della famiglia* (Florence, 1973). A recent edition of the Pope's autobiography is *I commentarii. Enea Silvio Piccolomini, Papa Pio II*, ed. Luigi Totaro (Milan, 1984); an English translation is *Memoirs of a Renaissance Pope: The Commentaries of Pius II*, translated by Florence A. Gragg, ed. Leona C. Gabel (New York, 1959). See also Luigi Totaro, *Pio II nei suoi Commentarii: Un contributo alla lettura della autobiografia di Enea Silvio de Piccolomini* (Bologna, 1978).

36. Marian Cobin, "The Compilation of the Aosta Manuscript: A Working Hypothesis," in *Papers Read at the Dufay Quincentenary Conference*, ed. Allan Atlas (Brooklyn, 1976), 83–85.

37. Allegretto de Allegrettis, "Ephemerides Senenses ab Anno MCCCL usque ad MCCCXCVI. Italico Sermone scriptae ab Allegretto de Allegrettis," in Muratori, ed., *Rerum Italicarum Scriptores*, 23:722: "apparato a guisa d'un coro d'angeli over un paradiso . . . poi . . . un angel discese di quel coro più a basso cantando certe stanze."

celebrated the pope and his family in the most elegant Latin phrases Siena's humanists could muster. The performance must have included accompaniment by a lyra, a viol, or a lute, indispensable instruments in the then fashionable manner of solo singing, which took its cue from the *cantimpanche* of the public squares and the courtly poet-improvisors. Like many other humanists of his time, Piccolomini enjoyed not only listening to classical verse sung to the accompaniment of a lyra but also performing it himself.[38] The chroniclers also report that Pius celebrated Mass in the cathedral a number of times. The pope's singers would have performed at those services, either as an independent group or with the cathedral singers, but extant records are silent in this regard. During Pius's reign the papal chapel counted on average sixteen singers, most of whom were of French or Franco-Flemish origin. Among them was the former cathedral singer Ser Antonio di Gabrielo da Montepulciano.[39]

Despite problems with his employers at the Opera, Antonio had clearly remained in the good graces of Siena's bishop. In November 1458, just two months after Piccolomini became pope, Antonio was called to Rome to become a member of the papal chapel. There, like the other singers in papal service, he would earn a monthly salary of Fl. 8, a sum that was more than double the annual salary of Fl. 40 he earned during his last period of employment in Siena.[40] He held the post throughout Pius's reign and well into that of Pius's successor, Paul II, who assigned a subvention of Fl. 8 to him in November 1470, when he was ill. He was retained on the papal roster through July 1471, though he received no salary. His name disappears from Roman records altogether by 1473, by which time he must have died.[41] Antonio's presence in the papal chapel reveals a good deal about his own capabilities as well as those of the singers with whom he served during the years of his employment in Siena. It also lends support to the supposition that during the 1440s and 1450s the Sienese cathedral repertory had points of similarity with cathedral repertories in places such as Ferrara and Florence as well as with the papal chapel.

Antonio was the only Sienese musician and one of the few Italians to serve in the papal chapel in the fifteenth century. He holds the further distinction of being the only papal musician of his day who received no ecclesiastical preferments, in marked contrast to several of his colleagues, one of whom, Johannes Pulloys, was the recipient of a notable number of benefices.[42] Pamela Starr, who has documented the fortunes of various members of the papal chapel at this time, suggested that Antonio was disqualified from holding benefices because he may have been married. It is, of course, possible that

---

38. This according to the testimony of Raffaele Brandolini, *De musica et poetica opusculum* (Rome, Biblioteca Casanatense, MS 805, fol. 16ᵛ), as reported by F. Alberto Gallo, "Orpheus christianus," in *Musica nel castello* (Bologna, 1992), 104; now also in English as *Music in the Castle,* trans. Anna Herklotz and Kathryn Krug (Chicago, 1995), 78. Further on Brandolini, see Pirrotta, "Music and Cultural Tendencies."

39. Starr, "Music and Music Patronage at the Papal Court, 1447–1464," 281–83. Among the musicians were Johannes Hurtault, Johannes de Monte, Johannes Pulloys, and Antonio Cernier da Montepulciano, hired by Pius in November 1458, serving through July 1470 (117–18).

40. See ibid., 282–86, for tables showing monthly salaries paid papal singers from 1458 to 1464.

41. Ibid., 117–19.

42. See ibid., 167–68 and 287–88, for a list of the benefices.

he did take a wife after leaving Siena, but he was unmarried during the time he served as cathedral chaplain. Rather, it may be that Pius arranged other kinds of assistance for him because there were few benefices within the Sienese diocese to award him. Such arrangements would fit in well with an apparently close relationship between the singer and his papal patron. Pius, in fact, entrusted Antonio with supervising the preparation of chant books and for overseeing the construction of an organ ordered for the newly built cathedral at Pienza.[43]

The Core Group, 1459–1469

Sacristans' rolls and other accounts from June 1459 through March 1469 show that the four musicians, Goro di Pavolo, Giovanni di Stefano Francioso, Antonio di Antonio Ongaro, and Biagio di Tomè, had the longest tenure of any one group of singers recorded during the entire century. All of them served as chaplains as well, which enabled the Opera to draw support for their positions from the funds set aside for that purpose, according to provisions agreed upon almost a century earlier. During this decade the group came to constitute a nucleus—comprised of two sopranos, a tenor, and another low voice. From time to time it was augmented by as many as three adults, as well as by a few youths from the cathedral school. The group thus had the opportunity to develop and refine a stable repertory, to which new music could be added as it became available to them. An inventory from 1458, as mentioned, indicates that there were at least three volumes of polyphony in the cathedral's library at this time, among them the one left by Giovanni Polacco (see above, Table 4.1). Precisely what was in these volumes is not known. But since the singers were performing at Masses and at Vespers, it seems likely, as I have said before, that they contained items appropriate to those services, such as settings of the Mass ordinary, motets, hymns, Magnificats, and psalms—in other words, the same kinds of pieces that would be copied for the Opera a few decades later, when new volumes of polyphonic music were commissioned.

Transmission of Repertories

Various records mentioned thus far, and others yet to be cited, leave little doubt about the frequent international inroads that were made into what was essentially a parochial musical establishment. Quality of performance must have been considerably enhanced as a result of sojourns, however brief, of the numerous itinerant French singers, such as Gherardo Le Fay, Johannes Calot, Jachetto di Marvilla, Giletto, Remigio, and others with connections to singers in the Ferrarese, Florentine, Neapolitan, and papal chapels, as well as of the Polish contingent and of Goro and his French and Hungarian confreres. Performances given by visiting groups such as the chapels of the king of Naples, the pope, and the Florentines must also have provided models of the kinds of performances offered by elite cosmopolitan ensembles and set a standard for Sienese musicians to emulate. What the presence of all of these musicians means in terms of transmission of repertory, a theme reiterated throughout the course of this chapter, cannot be underes-

---

43. The document was published by Eugenio Casanova, "Un anno della vita privata di Pio II," *BSSP* 38 (1931): 23 and is cited by Starr, "Music and Music Patronage," 118.

timated. Though we lack any traces of the music performed or copied there prior to the last two decades of the century, Siena's experience with visitors and itinerant musicians as well as with others who came to stay for longer periods complements Reinhard Strohm's remarks to the effect that a city or place need not necessarily have been a major center of musical production in order for it to have played a noteworthy role in the reception, dissemination, and distribution of music.[44]

Some idea of the contents of the three volumes mentioned in the 1458 inventory may be had by looking at one of the central sources of mid-fifteenth-century sacred polyphony, the manuscript Modena B of the Estense Library. This is a collection of Vespers music by John Dunstable, Lionel Power, Guillaume Du Fay, Gilles Binchois, and other English and Continental composers compiled for use by the chapel of Marquis Leonello d'Este of Ferrara.[45] Though lacking some of its original contents, the manuscript still preserves a considerable number (131) of settings of motets, hymns, Magnificats, antiphons, and other liturgical pieces. Lewis Lockwood has put forth convincing reasons for believing that the music in Modena B was "accumulated from sources outside Ferrara, not written there, nor written specifically for Leonello's chapel."[46] In support of his argument Lockwood hypothesizes five main lines of transmission, none of them mutually exclusive. He cites circumstances such as Du Fay's more than casual relations with the Ferrarese nobleman, his visit to Ferrara in 1437, the presence there, from 1438 to 1439, of the papal chapel of Eugene IV during the Council, the pope's residence in Florence, and cross-employment among all three chapels—papal, Ferrarese, and Florentine. In addition, at this time there were more intensified cultural relations between the papacy and both Ferrara and Florence, contacts between the Ferrarese and Burgundian courts, and English students present at Ferrara's university.

All of these lines of transmission find correspondences in Siena's situation. Chief among them were Siena's strong, if at times strained, cultural ties with Florence, its constant contacts with the papacy and Rome, and its political dependence on Milan and on Naples, which resulted in never-ending exchanges at all levels with the most powerful forces on the peninsula. Siena had commercial and diplomatic relations with all of Europe, as exemplified by the recruitment efforts of its Genoese envoy and the employment decades earlier of a group of Avignonese wind players at the Palazzo Pubblico. Its university housed a strong northern European contingent, and its most famous son, Aeneas Sylvius Piccolomini, had extensive European-wide connections. Further, there were encounters on its own soil with other visiting dignitaries, among whom in later decades would be the duke of Ferrara. And there were the transient singers and the occasional visiting singing groups, who surely must be accounted among the principal purveyors of new music to Siena.

The Modena manuscript may serve as a guideline, if not an actual model, for hy-

44. Strohm, "European Politics and the Distribution of Music," 305–6, 312.

45. Charles Hamm and Ann Besser Scott, "A Study and Inventory of the Manuscript Modena, Biblioteca Estense, α.X.1.11 (ModB)," *Musica Disciplina* 26 (1972): 101–43; Scott, "English Music in Modena, Biblioteca Estense, α. X. 1, 11 and other Italian Manuscripts," *Musica Disciplina* 26 (1972): 145–60.

46. This discussion owes much to Lockwood, *Music in Renaissance Ferrara,* 51–63.

pothesizing what Siena's musical repertory might have been at mid-century and later, keeping in mind, of course, that the cultural outlook and aspirations of Leonello's court chapel were decidedly different than the aims of a musical institution in a religious foundation such as the cathedral. Modena includes twenty-four hymn settings, most of them by Du Fay, seven Magnificats in various tones, ten antiphons, numerous motets, and two offertories, among which is a setting of the text *Virgo Maria, non est tibi similis,* by Benedictus Benoit.[47] Another setting of the same text is found in one of the first extant Sienese cathedral volumes of polyphony, surely a coincidence, but also one that implies a place for such a text in the Sienese liturgy. Many of Modena's settings of hymns for the feasts of Our Lord, the Virgin Mary, St. John the Baptist, St. Michael, and SS. Peter and Paul, of also its motets, Marian antiphons, and settings of other Marian texts were part of a larger international repertory, as witnessed by the many concordances it shares with manuscripts in Florence, Trent, Aosta, Bologna, and Rome, among other places. In light of various routes of transmission evident in Siena it makes sense to suppose that some of these very works found their way there as well. Also favoring such a supposition is the knowledge that other settings of many of the same texts formed part of the new Sienese repertory copied in 1480.

Attracting New Singers and Organists in the 1460s and 1470s

Several records reveal the Opera's desire to make conditions as attractive as possible for these singer-chaplains. Antonio's monthly salary rose to L. 12 in mid-July 1459, and at the same time Goro received permission to be absent for six days. Goro was also granted a loan of Fl. 6 on the following 5 September. A decree issued by the Sienese government on the last day of June 1460 states that all of the singers were to earn their usual salary for the month, even though they had been absent for several days, when they went to Florence to assist in St. John's Day celebrations.[48] Occasional individual absences are noted in these years, as are the names of a few other singers who remained for shorter or longer periods of time. Claudio, whose patronymic is not given, is recorded only for the month of July 1460. He was probably a young clerk, to judge from his monthly salary of L. 3 and the absence of a title before his name. Antonio Ongaretto was absent from July through October 1461. His replacement may have been Ser Piero Baiardi, who joined the group in September of that year and remained through May 1462.[49] He was followed by Maestro Guglielmo Francioso, who was paid L. 8 for forty days' service on the following 16 July. Given the brevity of the latter's stay, it may be that he is the same person as the Guillelmo da Francia who served around this time at St. Peter's in Rome, where he was on leave of absence from his post in Padua cathedral.[50] Another

47. Published in modern edition by Gilbert Reaney, *Early Fifteenth-Century Music,* 2 (American Institute of Musicology, 1966), 102–3.

48. See Doc. 4.13.

49. It is doubtful that he is the same person as the singer named Pietro Alardi del Boys (Dominus Bovis), who was employed in the Milanese court chapel in July 1474. That musician, a tenor and priest from Lyons, was in Milan from as early as 1472. See Motta, "Musici alla corte degli Sforza," 519–20.

50. See note 4.

young clerk, Agostino d'Antonio, is recorded for the first time as a singer for the period April 1463–March 1464.

In a letter to the overseer dated 23 November 1462 Goro reported that a young man who "is a singer and a priest" had recently arrived in Siena and that "he would willingly remain as a chaplain and singer." Goro added that the newcomer "has sung with us and the group liked him very much." For this reason they were recommending his appointment, particularly since he could serve in "two capacities," as a singer and chaplain (see Doc. 4.12). The latter consideration, as Goro rightly surmised, could be expected to carry great weight because the Opera was ever alert to the possibility of using some of the funds allocated for its eight chaplaincies to strengthen the musical ensemble. Goro's remarks that the new singer had sung with the core group and that he had passed muster with them are significant because they reveal that the singers' opinions may on occasion have influenced personnel decisions. It also offers evidence that Siena's musical ensemble was finally gaining some much needed stability and colle- giality, factors that necessarily influenced the choice of repertory as well as the quality of performance. All too often in the past, musicians had been brought together more by chance than by design, a circumstance that could hardly have provided the best ambience for good ensemble singing. In this particular instance, despite Ser Goro's approbation, there is no indication that the Frenchman was invited to stay.

A successful try-out period and the singers' approval, however, is indicated a year later in the case of a Frenchman named Carlo. He is cited in a deliberation from 20 November 1463, which authorized his provisional appointment for six months at a monthly salary of L. 8, to take effect the day he began service. He must have pleased authorities and colleagues alike, for within two months he was granted a one-year appointment at a monthly salary of L. 12, with the stipulation that his stipend for Febru- ary would be determined by the overseer. Monthly payments of L. 12 appear under his name from March 1464 through April 1465, his contract having meanwhile been re- newed in February 1465. His name is lacking in the sacristan's list for May of that year, which instead cites a new singer, Giovanni Francioso, whose appointment, at an annual salary of Fl. 30, was registered a month earlier. Whether this Giovanni is Johannes Cornuel, a contratenor and music copyist who served at St. Peter's in Rome from 15 March through April 1465 before leaving and then returning in November of that same year, cannot be ascertained.[51] But it may be more than coincidence that the Sienese Giovanni left just as suddenly as he appeared and is not heard of again for a few years. Carlo too left Siena for a post at St. Peter's in Rome, where a soprano called Carulo

---

51. On Johannes Cornuel, see Reynolds, *Papal Patronage,* 333, which shows that he served in Rome from March 15 to April 1465; from part of November 1465 to February 1466; and, after a break in the records, from March 1467 to February 1468. Another possible person with whom the Sienese Giovanni might be identified, Johannes Guillant, was at St. Peter's in Rome from March to September 1467, December 1467 to July 1471, and May 1472 to February 1473 (ibid.). Interestingly, Guillant was replaced by the singer Guillelmus Des Mares at St. Peter's in 1471 and he returned after Guillelmus joined the papal chapel in 1472. At that time he was called a *tenorista antiquus* (ibid., 48, n. 42).

Britonio served from mid-May through June 1465 and then from the following September through January 1466.[52]

The four adult singers of the core group, Goro, Antonio Ongaretto, Biagio, and Giovanni di Stefano Francioso, were joined in early July 1465 by two Frenchmen, the returning Carlo di Guglielmo and Guglielmo di Lodovico, whose appointments as singers were approved that same month. Each received Fl. 3, or L. 12, per month. Carlo di Guglielmo, previously called Ser Carlo Francioso when he was also serving as a chaplain, was at his post only during the months of July and August 1465. This was reason enough for his dismissal to be registered without comment in the following February.[53] Guglielmo, however, performed with the four other adult singers for the next fourteen months, through September 1466. His name also appears in a set of extraordinary payments issued at the overseer's command in May and June—when he received L. 2 for having journeyed to Florence to sing at the St. John's Day festival—and July. Evidently, every effort was made to keep him in Siena, including an increase to L. 15 in his monthly salary. In spite of these efforts he left. Perhaps he is the same person as Guillelmus Des Mares, the former teacher from Chartres cathedral recorded at St. Peter's in Rome in July 1471 and later as a papal singer.[54]

Politics permitting, Florentine instrumentalists had for some time been coming to Siena to participate in the annual Assumption Day festivities and their Sienese counterparts often reciprocated by performing at Florence's annual St. John's Day celebrations. With the establishment of stable singing groups in both cities, singers also were included in these exchanges of musical personnel. Five of the seven Florentine chapel singers recorded at Siena's Palazzo Pubblico on Assumption Day, 1456 were there in the following year.[55] In 1458 the Florentine singers also sang at the cathedral.[56] The Sienese returned the compliment in 1457, 1459, and 1460, when the cathedral chapel journeyed to Florence for St. John's Day. The Sienese singers were absent for several days as a result of these trips. In 1457 the Balìa itself decided that, despite any previous decision to the contrary, the singers were not to suffer a loss of salary, a sentiment echoed in a decree from 1460 stating that the government had decided that the singers should receive their full salary for the time they had missed because they brought

---

52. Ibid., 143.

53. July and August 1465 were the months that Carlo was absent from his post at St. Peter's in Rome.

54. On Guillelmus Des Mares (Des Maris) see Reynolds, *Papal Patronage,* 194–99. As mentioned above (see note 51), the connection between him and Johannes Guillant, whom he replaced at St. Peter's in 1471 and who then returned to St. Peter's when Guillelmus joined the papal chapel in 1472, may offer a clue to the identity of both as singers in Siena.

55. For the record from 1456, see Luigia Cellesi, *Storia della più antica banda musicale senese* (Siena, 1906), 31, 70; this lists them as "sette cantori di Santo Giovanni" who received 280 grossi. A payment of 50 grossi to five Florentine singers who participated in Assumption Day festivities in 1457 is in ASS, Concistoro, vol. 545, fol. 58ᵛ, dated 19 August 1457: "V cantori fiorentini—grossi 50."

56. "Domini operarius, consiliarii et camerarius . . . decreverunt quod camerarius sine suo preiudicio aut damno det et solvat cantoribus florentenis [*sic*] qui venerunt ad honorandum festum S. Marie de Augusto in Absuntione" (AOMS, vol. 14, *Deliberazioni, 1454–59,* fol. 49ᵛ: [1458] [cantoribus]).

"honor to the city" and "especially because they were paid their full expenses when they went the previous year" (see Doc. 4.13). Later in 1460, the government again gave the singers permission to leave town, this time in order to perform in Lucca for the feast of the Holy Cross.[57] A return visit from the members of the Lucca cathedral chapel, however, is not mentioned until 16 August 1471, when the government awarded them a gratuity of L. 16 for singing at Assumption Day services at the cathedral.[58]

The tangible results of such visits are impossible to gauge, although it is clear that, besides the goodwill they generated, they offered occasions to exchange or gather repertories and to judge singers from elsewhere with an eye to possible employment. Certainly, singers from Florence, other than Goro, continued to be recruited for Siena, as can be seen from later records. One entry from 7 November 1467 states that L. 2. 10 were paid to Benedetto, an employee of the counselor Francesco Luti, for having gone to Florence "for singers for the duomo," that is, to escort new singers to Siena.[59] There is some doubt as to whether any of the musicians in question remained, however, because only one new arrival is reported in 1467, several months before this time.

The venerable organist Ser Francesco di Nanni remained at his post throughout all of the changes that occurred in the cathedral's singing establishment during this time.[60] He himself probably had been actively involved in some of them, though surviving records say very little in this regard. His advice, for instance, must surely have been sought when the decision was made to have a new organ constructed by the Hungarian builder Pietro Scotto. The instrument was not located in the usual place above the sacristy door, opposite the other organ, but rather on the part of the wall below the window (on this organ and its location, see Ch. 1). Francesco had the satisfaction of inaugurating the new organ and seeing its builder warmly commended by the Opera's

---

57. "Magnifici domini . . . deliberaverunt concedere et concesserunt licentiam cantoribus ecclesie chaptedralis [*sic*] Senensis eundi Lucce ad festum S. Crucis, sine aliquo eorum preiuditio vel admissione [*recte* amissione] salarii, per totam diem Martis proxime venturam. Et hoc in quantum sapientes Opere dent eis bonam licentiam" (ASS, *Concistoro*, vol. 564, fol. 8ʳ, dated 10 September 1460).

58. "Spese fatte per la festa di Santa Maria d'Aghosto de l'anno 1471 de' dare . . . E de' dare a dì XVI d'aghosto lire xedici, i quali demo a' chantori di Lucha, xi chome apare a la mia uscita di me Iacomo d'Andrea Pasquali Kamalingo, fo. 39. L. XVI s. XVI" (AOMS, vol. 507, *D&C, 1466–75*, fol. 161 left). The record is of particular interest because nothing is known about the Lucca chapel in these years.

59. "Benedetto, fameglio di misser Francesco Luti, per sua fadiga d'andare a Firenze per cantori per lo Duomo" (vol. 505, *D&C, 1461–81*, fol. 303 left).

60. Francesco undoubtedly received lodging and meals at the Opera's expense, as had several of his predecessors. Rather late in his career, however, he decided to take a house on his own and bought one, opposite the canons' residence in the precincts of the cathedral, from the hospital of Santa Maria della Scala, which sold it to him for use during his lifetime. The price of the house was fixed at only 25 florins because Francesco agreed to write and decorate a missal for the hospital free of charge: "1464. A dì XVI di Marzo. Remisero in esso Rectore di potere vendare ad vita a ser Francesco degl'organi la casa fu di madona Urbana, riscontra ad la canonica, per fiorini vinticinque, et debbi scrivare ad lo spedale uno messale fornito, senza alchuno pagamento" (ASS, Ospedale vol. 24, *Deliberazioni, 1485–87*, fol. 154ᵛ). The document is of great interest because it confirms his continuing work as a copyist, mentioned above in chapter 2.

board on 3 February 1458. Annual reappointments, such as one registered on 11 August 1457, indicate that he continued to enjoy his employers' highest esteem.

This same year a decision was taken to employ a second organist. Whether it was because Francesco decided to go into semi-retirement or because conditions now favored having two organists is not explained in any of the records, which nevertheless show that Francesco continued to be active as an organist. The board's first choice for the post was Maestro Piero di Guasparre Guiducci da Pisa. He arrived in Siena around the beginning of February and after a successful audition was offered a formal appointment on 9 February 1458. Although this called for him to begin playing on the following 25 March, an addendum to the record indicates that he actually began on 1 July. His salary was fixed at Fl. 38 annually, but a single record of payment to him for L. 42. 10 indicates that he stayed for only a few months.

Thus, on 5 December 1458 Ser Lazaro di Jacomo, a Sienese organist, was appointed as one of the Opera's chaplains at the usual salary and as organist at an annual salary not to exceed Fl. 16. Both Lazaro's and Francesco's names are in accounts from the following years, Francesco's appearing up to the time of his death in September 1470. Lazaro's success as organist and the increases in salary he received as a result of his good work are reflected in a report from April 1465. This notes that he was to receive a salary of Fl. 48 for the remainder of the fiscal year he was currently serving and that beginning in the following July he was to have a five-year appointment at an annual salary of Fl. 50, each valued at L. 4. He held the post through April 1467, when a new organist, Frate Giovanni di Francesco, replaced him. A month later the overseer was given full authority to appoint an organist for a period of two years, beginning in June, at a monthly salary of Fl. 3 (see Doc. 4.14). Frate Giovanni, identified as a Spaniard from Valencia and as a Servite monk in later accounts, subsequently served as sole organist through the end of June 1479.[61]

Ser Goro meanwhile continued to enjoy the Opera's highest regard, for in February 1466 his salary was raised to Fl. 60 per annum, which amounted to a monthly salary of L. 20, and he was forgiven yet another loan, this time of 10 florins. Ser Biagio's annual salary as a singer also was increased to Fl. 24, in addition to what he earned as a chaplain and occasionally as a sacristan. Ever receptive to the possibility of employing clerics who could serve in a dual capacity, on 1 July 1465 the Opera appointed Ser Domenico di Matteo as a singer and chaplain at an annual salary of Fl. 30, six of them as recompense for his services as a singer. No records of payment indicate that he accepted the position. A decree from the following September mentions two young clerks, Alberto and Gabriello, "who are singing in the cathedral," and says that each would earn a monthly salary of L. 4 beginning in January 1466. (The youths had been performing since August 1460, each earning L. 2 per month.) Accounts from September 1466 to March 1469 record the continuing presence of the four adult singers Goro, Biagio, Antonio Ongaretto, and Giovanni Francioso, though this last was absent for several months during that time. Another adult singer, Giachetto Francioso, appears in pay-

---

61. Frate Giovanni was apparently employed simultaneously as organist at the hospital of Santa Maria della Scala, where he was mentioned as late as January 1481. See chapter 13.

ments from June 1467 through October 1468 at a salary of L. 13. 6. 8. Chances are, given his high salary, that he also performed some of the duties of the Opera's chaplains, although the records fail to mention his clerical status.

Giachetto or Jachetto di Marvilla was one of the most peripatetic singers of the day. He was at the Neapolitan court before coming to Siena and later he was at St. Peter's in Rome before going north, where he served both the Milanese and Ferrarese courts.[62] His presence in Siena offers yet another indication of how easily repertories and performance practices were disseminated, thanks to the peregrinations of itinerant singers. A remark Jachetto made in a letter to Francesco Gonzaga, duke of Mantua, in 1500 is of great interest with regard to performance practices, for Jachetto noted that even at that time he had not lost his voice, "except for the falsetto, which I never had anyway."[63] Presumably, in a four-man ensemble such as the one Jachetto sang in at Siena in the late 1460s, the higher parts were sung by adult falsettists, with or without the assistance of boys from the school.

A significant change in personnel occurred with the departure (or death) of one member of the original core group, Ser Giovanni di Stefano Francioso. He is mentioned in a record from March 1469, but loss of the accounts for the fiscal year 1469–70 make it impossible to know exactly when his employment ceased. Accounts from the following fiscal year, 1470–71, show that only three of the original core were then present: Goro, Antonio Ongaretto, and Biagio. All of them remained in cathedral service for the next seven years and sang together until just after the Assumption Day festivities in August 1478. In the meantime, many new appointments were made, as efforts intensified to recruit more and more of the northern singers who passed through Siena as they made their way up and down the peninsula.

As in the past, very few of the new singers stayed for long. A new appointee, Jacomo, is reported for three months in the summer of 1468. Since accounts for the fiscal year 1469–70 are lacking, there is no official record of when he resumed service. Subsequently he is mentioned from April 1470 to February 1471 at a monthly salary of L. 10. He was probably the same person as the Jacomo di Fiandra, "a new singer in the duomo," who on 14 May 1469 was given at the request of the overseer Messer Savino "the key to the room next to the cistern where Giachetto had stayed." The room contained a bedstead and a feather bed with a new cover, two bolsters or pillows and a blanket, a three-footed table, and three benches. The description of Jacomo's accom-

---

62. Atlas, *Music at the Aragonese Court of Naples,* 37–38, reports that Jachetto's Neapolitan service lasted from approximately 1455–56 to the middle of the next decade. Reynolds, *Papal Patronage,* 48–49 and 119–21, shows that he was at St. Peter's for at least six months in 1471, and investigates Jachetto's claim in his letter to Lorenzo the Magnificent when he was seeking employment in Florence that he had served in the papal chapel. (The letter is published in D'Accone, "The Singers of San Giovanni," 324.) Jachetto referred to his Sienese sojourn in the same letter, but said only that he departed Siena, having heard in November (1468) of Lorenzo's intention to reestablish the Florentine chapel. Lockwood, *Music in Renaissance Ferrara,* 166–67, traces Jachetto's career at the Ferrarese court, where he was mentioned until 1501. Motta, "Musici alla corte degli Sforza," 323, first published the register from 15 July 1474 of Milanese court musicians, which lists Jachetto among the duke's "cantori di cappella."

63. Lockwood, *Music in Renaissance Ferrara,* 167.

modations is valuable because so little is known about how itinerant musicians were housed in Siena.[64] Since the overseer had specifically requested the room for Jacomo, one which had previously been given to another singer, it may be that certain rooms were reserved for singers. The furnishings appear to have been more than adequate, although they may not have been as plentiful as those in quarters assigned to the Opera's more permanent employees, among whom, of course, were singer-chaplains such as Goro and his colleagues. For the three days of Pentecost Jacomo was also lent "a surplice that Giachetto had worn." Chaplains and clerks were required to wear surplices at all services, and the loan to Jacomo demonstrates that singers of polyphony did the same when they performed in the choir. In other accounts listing sporadic payments to him, dated 31 April 1470 and 7 May 1473, he is further identified as Jacomo di Novo Porto. Besides indicating that he again served only for brief periods, they also suggest that he is the same person as the Jacheto de Nemport, cantore, who appeared on Ferrarese court rosters in 1472.[65]

As is apparent from this discussion, greater efforts than ever before were made on behalf of the cathedral's musical program during the stewardship of Savino di Matteo Savini, who was overseer of the cathedral Opera from 1468 to 1480. He was an ardent patron of music and musicians, as indicated by the scope and significance of his activities during the short span of his tenure.[66] By the time Savini assumed office, a number of "libri corali," those grand and elaborate books of chant mentioned earlier, had already been commissioned and the copying of the music and text finished. Overseeing their decoration and illumination, Savini engaged a number of prominent and not so prominent artists, both Sienese and foreign.[67] The results were the famous volumes of plainchant, admired to this day in the cathedral's Libreria Piccolomini, which is itself adorned with frescos by Pinturicchio celebrating the career of Aeneas Sylvius Piccolomini, as bishop, cardinal, and pope. Reference has already been made to several of these volumes, particularly those containing the rhymed office and Mass for the feast of Sant'Ansano.[68] Curiously, Savini made no effort to commission volumes of polyphony for the singers, leaving this task to his successor. He did, however, provide generous terms of employment to many of the northern musicians who began arriving in Siena in ever increasing numbers.

Among the better known singers recorded during Savini's tenure was Giletto can-

---

64. This compares favorably with accommodations offered singers by the Santissima Annunziata in Florence, which in one instance guaranteed singers a bed with sheets, a mattress, a spring, a pillow, and a blanket, presumably in one of the same kind of cell assigned to the convent's friars. The singers were also awarded clothing, shoes, and the weekly services of a barber, as well as a monthly payment in cash. See D'Accone, "The Singers of San Giovanni," 335.

65. Lockwood, *Music in Renaissance Ferrara,* 318.

66. Savino was elected earlier, in 1467, for a brief period, then after Cipriano Corti's death he became overseer in his own right (Ciardi Dupré, *I corali del Duomo di Siena,* mentioned above in chapter 2). Carli, *Il Duomo di Siena,* 159, notes that he was forced out of office in 1480 for political reasons. Aronow, "A Documentary History of the Pavement Decoration," 208, n. 3, gives the date of Savino's ouster as 23 June 1480.

67. Ciardi Dupré, *I corali del Duomo di Siena,* mentioned above in chapter 2.

68. For the Mass of Sant'Ansano and the chant volumes in the Libreria Piccolomini see chapter 2.

tore, who along with Giachetto di Marvilla must be counted among the more peripatetic musicians of the time. Giletto sang in the Neapolitan chapel in 1456,[69] and he is known to have traveled in the company of another singer named Jacotino di Borgogna, with whom he served at St. Peter's in Rome in 1468.[70] In 1474 he was one of the chamber singers employed at the court of Galeazzo Maria Sforza in Milan.[71] Giletto's stay in Siena, where he earned a monthly salary of L. 8 from November 1470 through the middle of March 1472, was one of his longer stops on his way north. His presence offers yet another example of how repertories and performance practices must have been transmitted from one town to another, as well as a reasonable explanation of how major Italian cities came to share a common repertory at this time. Other singers in this period include the northerner Giacopetto cantore, who received L. 10 per month during April, May, and June 1471, and Ser Guglielmo di Cortese, whose origins are difficult to determine, mentioned from September 1471 to March 1472, at a monthly salary of L. 10. A youth from the cathedral school, Francesco di Guido, was present during April, May, and June of 1470, earning a monthly salary of L. 2. 10. Another youth named Bernardino is recorded at L. 2 per month from April to September 1471. A newcomer who stayed for a considerably longer time was another Italian, Ser Benedetto da l'Aquila, first cited in April 1472 at a salary of L. 11 per month. Thereafter, his name appears on sacristans' rolls through March 1478.

Itinerant northerners, however, also continued to find a warm welcome at the cathedral (see Table 4.2 for a list of foreign singers during this period). Antonio Piccardo is mentioned in monthly salary payments of L. 8 from mid-April 1472 through the end of February 1473. Alberto cantore earned L. 6 per month in April and May 1473 and in January and February 1474. He reappeared in Siena more than a year later and was listed as receiving monthly salary payments of L. 8 from April to November 1475. Ruberto di Giovanni Francioso also had a monthly salary of L. 8 during the brief time he sang, from January to March 1474. (He may be the same person as Robertus de Ligin, mentioned in Florence in 1482.[72]) Remigio cantore was credited with L. 5. 12 per month in sacristans' rolls for August, September, and October 1474. He is doubtless the same person as the soprano Remigius Massin, subsequently recorded in Rome at both St. Peter's and the papal chapel.[73] Returning after a long absence was Carlo di Guglielmo Francioso, who at the command of the overseer, Messer Savino, received a gold florin on 26 April 1475 "for serving as a singer in the duomo's choir for one month, after which he left."

69. Allan Atlas, "Alexander Agricola and Ferrante I of Naples," *JAMS* 30 (1977): 319, n. 23.

70. Reynolds, *Papal Patronage,* 48, which brings together the information about Giletto given here.

71. Barblan, "Vita musicale alla corte sforzesca," in *Storia di Milano, 9: L'epoca di Carlo V (1535–1559* (Milan, 1961), 826, 830, 836, where Giletto is identified as Giletus Cossu who had had benefices in Agno and Donzo.

72. See D'Accone, "A Documentary History of Music at the Florentine Cathedral and Baptistry during the Fifteenth Century" (Ph.D. diss., Harvard University, 1960), 1:205.

73. Reynolds, *Papal Patronage,* 335, notes his employment at St. Peter's from December 1475 to February 1477. Haberl, "Die römische 'schola cantorum'," shows that Remigius served as a papal singer through 1509.

TABLE 4.2.   Foreign singers at Siena cathedral, 1448–1480

Name	Place of origin	Period of service
Maestro Guglielmo Francioso[a]	France	18 February 1450
Andrea da Polonia	Poland	May–August 1449; January–March 1450
Giovanni da Polonia (polacchio)	Poland	May 1449–April 1450
Jacomo da Polonia	Poland	May–August 1449; January–March 1450
Vito da Polonia (son of Giovanni)	Poland	May 1449–February 1451
Matteo da Polonia	Poland	January–March 1450
Ser Giovanni di Stefano de Grieve di Piccardia, *sovrano*	Picardy	1 November 1456–March 1469
Antonio di Antonio Ongaro (Ongaretto)	Hungary	28 November 1458–August 1478 (absent July–October 1461)
Ser Giovanni di Jacopo da Francia	France	7 February–September 1459
Maestro Guglielmo Francioso[b]	France	June–July 1462
Carlo di Guglielmo Francioso[c]	France	20 November 1463–April 1465; July–August 1465; April 1475
Giovanni Francioso[d]	France	April 1465
Guglielmo di Lodovico Francioso[e]	France	July 1465–September 1466
Giachetto Francioso[f]	France	June 1467–October 1468
Jacomo di Novo Porto (di Fiandra; Francioso)[g]	Flanders	July–September 1468; April 1470–February 1471, May 1473
Giletto[h]		November 1470–March 1472
Giacopetto		April–June 1471
Ser Guglielmo di Cortese	?	September 1471–March 1472
Antonio Piccardo	Picardy	April 1472–February 1473
Ruberto di Giovanni Francioso[i]	France	January–March 1474
Remigio[j]		August–October 1474
Gottifredi, soprano[k]	Liège	July 1476–December 1477
Niccolò di Lanberto da Bruggia, contratenor	Bruges	July 1476–November 1477
Michele, soprano[l]	Brabant	July–September 1476

[a]Hired as singer and teacher of chant and polyphony, but declined

[b]Possibly same as Guillelmo da Francia, at St. Peter's in Rome and Padua cathedral

[c]Possibly Carulo Britonio, at St. Peter's in Rome, mid-May–June, September–December 1465, January 1466

[d]Possibly Johannes Cornuel, at St. Peter's in Rome, 15 March–April, November 1465, or Johannes Guillant, at St. Peter's March–September 1467, March–mid-July 1471, May 1472–February 1473

[e]Possibly Guillelmus Des Mares, at St. Peter's July 1471 and later

[f]Jachetto di Marvilla

[g]Jacheto de Nemport, singer at Ferrara, 1472

[h]Giletto Cossu, at Naples, St. Peter's, Milan

[i]Possibly Robertus de Ligin, at Florence cathedral, 1482

[j]Probably Remigius Massin, at St. Peter's December 1475–February 1477

[k]Ghottifredo di Thilman de Liegio, singer at San Giovanni, Florence. See Table 5.2 for his later service

[l]Probably Michele di Guglielmo da Ludicha di Brabante, in Florence, 1481

During the summer and early fall of 1476 the Sienese ensemble counted seven adult singers, including Ser Goro, Ser Antonio, Ser Biagio, Ser Benedetto da l'Aquila, and three new northerners, Gottifredi, Niccolò, and Michele, who began serving in July of that year. Michele, probably the same person as the Michele di Guglielmo da Ludicha di Brabante recorded in Florence some five years later,[74] was a soprano, who earned a monthly salary of L. 9. 10 during the three months (July–September) he stayed in Siena. Gottifredi, subsequently employed in Florence around the same time as Michele, was also a soprano.[75] His full name as found in Florentine documents, Ghottifredo di Thilman de Liegio, does not appear in Sienese cathedral documents, which record his presence through December 1477 at a monthly salary of L. 9. 10. Niccolò di Lanberto from Bruges, called a contratenor in some records, earned L. 8 per month. He departed Siena a few weeks before Gottifredi, in November 1477.

By April 1478 the only regularly employed singers were the three who for so long had formed the core of the cathedral's musical establishment. Chances are that a few other chaplains were performing with them, although surviving records do not clarify this point. Ser Austino di Antonio, for example, a cathedral chaplain from as early as April 1464, is listed as a singer only in payments from April–August 1478. Another long-time chaplain, Ser Matteo di Marchione, may also have sung. Perhaps some of the young clerks from the cathedral school were brought in to bolster the adult voices. No mention of them, however, is made in extant records. In any event the decisive blow to the ensemble came only a few days after the Assumption Day festivities in August 1478, when Goro di Pavolo left cathedral service. Antonio Ongaretto was subsequently registered through the end of May 1479 at a lower salary, an indication that he did not serve as a singer in the intervening time. The same was true of Biagio, whose name appears on the rolls sporadically until as late as June 1480. A chronological list of cathedral musicians from 1448 to 1480 appears in Table 4.3.

Although no record says as much, performances of vocal polyphony were suspended. Perhaps this state of affairs was a result of the forced resignation, for political reasons, of the overseer Savino Savini. Savini had found the means to attract some of the leading singers of the time and even to retain a few of them for longer periods than usual. But with the departure of Goro and Antonio Ongaretto, the long-time nucleus of the singing ensemble was completely dispersed and with it the musical practices and traditions of the two previous decades. The situation called for action and perhaps also for some new thinking about the objectives of the cathedral's musical program. As subsequent events show, it was Savini's successor, Alberto di Francesco Aringhieri, who successfully revived Savini's tactics and furnished the leadership and drive that were to move the Sienese chapel, even if only temporarily, into the ranks of the major Italian musical institutions of the time.

74. D'Accone, "The Singers of San Giovanni," 332.

75. Ibid. Gottifredi and Michele were both probably employed in the chapel of San Giovanni, many of whose personnel also served at the Santissima Annunziata and at the cathedral. San Giovanni's records for this period are lost.

DOCUMENTS

Doc. 4.1. Confirmation of contract for two Polish singers, 21 January 1450. AOMS, vol. 13, *Deliberazioni, 1434–55,* fol. 103^r

[margin: riferma e condotta de' cantori] Et confermaro Giovanni polacchio e Vito suo garzone per cantori d'essa chiesa, col salario e modi usati e per lo tempo infrascripto ne' tre sottoscripti:

Et condussero per cantori de la decta chiesa tre polacchii ne' dì proximi venuti, cioè uno grande e due garzonetti, con salario di fiorini ottanta tra tutti e tre, a ragione d'anno. Con questo inteso che ogni mese di loro si faccia proposta tra essi misser l'Operaio, conseglieri e camarlingo, e in questo non s'optenesse loro riferma, s'intendino cassi. E similmente in questo non se ne facesse proposta, per simile modo s'intendino cassi.

Doc. 4.2. Appointment of three boy singers, 11 February 1451. Ibid., fol. 108^r

[margin: di condurre e fanciulli che cantano] Per simile modo e forma rimessero nel prefato Operaio et in misser Pietro arcidiacano del duomo, che possino condurre a cantare in duomo quelli tre fanciulli che al presente vi cantano, e chol tenore e contratenore vi sono al presente, o tutti o parte, come lo' parrà, per quello tempo e con quelli salarii lo' parranno discreti et ragionevoli, e con ogni altro modo e forma che lo' piacerà.

Doc. 4.3. Reappointment of three boy singers, 13 October 1451. Ibid., fol. 112^v

[margin: per li tre cantori del duomo] Et congregati ne la buttiga di Landuccio predecto, absente Cipriano, deliberaro[no] che il decto misser l'Operaio predecto possa condurre o rifermare a l'officio del coro del duomo quelli tre carzoni [*sic*] che al presente vi cantano, per salario di lire IIII ciascuno de' due cantori, e L. IIII s. 10 il tenori[s]ta, in tutto L. 12 s. 10, ciascuno mese, ad beneplacito d'esso operaio.

Doc. 4.4. Reappointment of singers, 27 May 1452. Ibid., fol. 117^v

[margin: Condocte di molti al servigio del duomo e de l'Uopera] Et una cum camerario dicte Opere fecero le condotte infrascripte, con salarii sottoscripti e per l'infrascripti modi, cioè . . .

    Cantori e sonatori
    ser Francesco de li Organi, con salario di L. sexanta l'anno
    misser Marino da l'Aquila per cantore, per L. quarantotto l'anno
    due cantori fanciulli v'ànno cantato l'anno passato per L. 48 per uno, a ragione d'anno, in
        tutto L. 96
    el tenorista usato d'essi fanciulli, per L. 54 l'anno
    ser Luca da Pisa per la cantoria solamente, L. 36 l'anno
    ser Biagio di Tommè prete, per la detta cantoria, L. 36 l'anno

Doc. 4.5. Reappointment of singers, 2 May 1453. Ibid., fol. 125^v

[margin: Condotta de' cappellani]
    Ser Luca da Pisa, cappellano di Sancto Pavolo, per cantore, con salario di Fl. nove di L.
        IIII il fiorino, per la decta cantoria solamente, Fl. 9 l'anno
    Ser Francesco de li Organi, per sonatore, per Fl. 15 l'anno
    Ser Biagio di Tommè, per cantore, per Fl. 9 l'anno
    Ser Marino da l'Aquila, per cantore, Fl. 15 l'anno
  Cantori cherici
    Simone di Mariano tenorista, per Fl. 15 l'anno
    Michelagnolo di Daniello cantore, per Fl. 13 L. 2 l'anno
    Menico di Matteio cantore, per Fl. 13 L. 2 l'anno
    Et questo medesimo s'intenda per lo passato

Doc. 4.6. Reappointment of singers, 3 May 1454. Ibid., fol. 132^{r-v}

Insieme col camarlingo deliberarono conducere e deliberando conduxero in cappellani, cherici, sonatori, cantori et altri a' servitii della chiesa chatredale [*sic*] l'infrascritti per tempo d'uno anno cominciato a dì primo di questo . . .

[fol. 132^{v}] sonatore: ser Francesco di [gap] a sonare gli orghani, à di salario per ciaschuno mese lire cinque

cantori: ser Francesco predetto, con cinque cherici a cantare per ciascheduno mese in tutto lire dic[i]otto in tutto, de' quali cherici questi sonno e nomi: Simone di [gap], Michelagnolo di [gap], Giovanni di [gap], Menico di [gap], Francesco di [gap].

cantore: Et deliberorono conduciare et conduxero Meo di [gap] in cantore per uno anno e in questo mezo e a beneplacito con salario di lire cinque el mese.

Doc. 4.7. Temporary appointment of singers, 3 June 1454. AOMS, vol. 14, *Deliberazioni, 1454–59,* fol. 7^{v}

[margin: pro cantoribus]
Et deliberaverunt conducere et conduxerunt infrascriptos in cantore et pro cantoribus ecclesie, pro uno mense, cum infrascripto salario, cum hoc quod dicta conducta sit valida quando omnes acceptant, alias non:

[gap] Teotonicus, pro libris otto	tenentur
dominus Marinus, pro libris quatuor	ad
ser Blasius, pro libris quatuor	mactutinum
ser Luca, pro libris quatuor	non tenentur
dominus Antonius plebanus Clusdini, pro	ad
soldis viginti	mactutinum

die 4 Iunii ser Blasius non acceptavit et deinde dominus Marinus non aceptavit. Et sic dicta conducta non est valida.

Doc. 4.8. Reappointment of singers, 30 December 1454. Ibid., fol. 18^{v}

[margin: Elettione de' cappellani]
Ser Franciscus de Organis, Fl. 15
Deliberaverunt conducendi et conduxerunt ser Antonium de Montepolitiano in cappellanum Opere et in cantorem et sonatorem organorum in ecclesia et ad docendum cantum et sonum prout fuerit requisitus ab [*sic*] consiliariis et operario, et hoc pro uno anno, cum salario florenorum trigintatrium in dicto anno. Et pro tempore quo servivit solvatur ad rationem 32 florenorum.

[Elettione de' cantori]
Et similiter conduxerunt infrascriptos in cantores Opere pro uno anno, cum infrascripto salario, videlicet:
    Simon Mariani, Fl. 15
    Menicus Mattei, Fl. 12
    Iohannes Sanctis, Fl. 12
    Meino, Fl. 15

Doc. 4.9. Appointment of singers, 1 November 1456. AOMS, vol. 113, *Miscellanea,* fasc. 7, doc. 8

Qui di sotto apparrà manifesto come el magnifico operaio dela maggiore chatedrale chiesa di Siena insieme co' suoi honorevoli consiglieri conducano e venerabili sacerdoti et cantori nela sopradetta chiesa, e quali sonno questi: Ser Goro di Pavolo di Sali da Fiorenza, tenorista, Ser

Antonio di Matteo da Prato, ser Iohanni di Stefano di Piccardia, sovrani, per uno anno da cominciarsi in Kalende novembre proximo avenire, con questi patti et conditioni. In prima.

> Sieno tenuti stare ala messa et vesperi e dì festivi tutti, la detta messa et vesparo honorate-
> mente cantare, come si richiede.
>
> E più sieno obligati tutte le feste dir messa nela detta chiesa.
>
> E più sieno obligati e dì non festivi stare ala messa et vesparo et cantare l'alleluia, offertorio
> et San[c]tus, come si costuma, et così el vesparo.
>
> E più sieno obligati dire messa infra semmana quando bisongniasse.
>
> E più sieno obligati al mattino di pasghua di Natale e messa dela notte e 'l mattino di
> Sancta Maria d'agosto.
>
> E più sieno obligati alla messa quando entrano e magnifici Signori, e quando altre sollem-
> nità si facessero strasordinarie, e quando s'andasse a processione.
>
> E 'l sopradetto operaio et conseglieri s'obligano a dar lo[ro] la stantia in canonica co'
> letto fornito, senza lenzuola, e casse, banche et tavole da mangiare. Et lo salario per
> ciasc[h]eduno de' sopradetti sia fiorini cinquanta di lire quattro per ciascuno fiorino. Et
> a questo detto dì sopra e sopradetti si soscrivaranno di loro mano così essare contenti.
>
> E io ser Ghoro di Pagholo di Sali sopradetto sono contento [a] quanto di sopra si chon-
> tiene.
>
> E io ser Antonio sopradetto s' contento [a] quanto di sopra si contiene in questa scritta.
>
> E io Giovanni di Stefano sopradetto sono contento a quanto in questa scritta si contiene.

[verso: Scritta de' patti de' chantori forestieri che sono achoncii cho' l'opara.]

(Note that Ser Giovanni di Stefano di Piccardia is called "de Grieve" elsewhere.)

Doc. 4.10. Appointment of singers, 30 December 1456. AOMS, vol. 14, *Deliberazioni, 1454–
59,* fol. 32^v

[margin: Ser Blasii, Ser Antonii, Ser Antonii de Montepolitiano, conducta] Et decreverunt facere
et fecerunt salarium infrascriptis cantoribus, ultra salarium per eos alias ordinatum, quod salarium
intelligatur incepisse in Kalendis presentis mensis, et hoc per tempus et usque ad festum Omnium
Sanctorum proxime futurum, et interim ad beneplacitum, cum similibus obligationibus, cum
hoc quod debeant cantare iusta morem cantorum:

| Ser Blasio et | de libris quatuor pro quolibet eorum |
| Ser Antonio de Tricurculis | et quolibet mense, L. 4 per ciascheduno |

Ser Antonii [*sic*] de Montepolitiano, florenos quadraginta, de libris 4 pro floreno, computato
eius salario iam ordinato, cum eisdem obligationibus.

Doc. 4.11. Renewal of contract of three Florentine singers, 30 December 1457. Ibid., fol. 42^v

[margin: Pro cantoribus] Et vista conducta facta de cantoribus pro ordinato et solito salario et ad
beneplacitum, quod intelligatur incepta immediate finita prima, cum modis consuetis, quorum
nomina infra cont[in]entur, ipsam approbaverunt etc. Quorum nomina sunt, videlicet: ser Gorus
Pauli de Florentia, ser Antonius Mattei de Prato, ser Iohannes Stefani de Grieve.

Doc. 4.12. Letter from Goro di Pavolo recommending a singer, 23 November 1462. AOMS,
vol. 65, *Carteggio,* by date

Reverende pater et domine, post humilem et debitam rechomendationem salutem.

Sola questa per avisare la Signoria vostra chome a questi dì è chapitato qui questo giovane,
el quale è prete e cantore e volentieri starebe per chapellano e cantore cholla Signoria vostra. E
perché sapiate egli à cantato chon noi ed è piaciuto asai alla brighata, e chosì credo ve ne scriverrà
messer Domenicho. Ora perché lui non può stare a tedio perché sta in su l'osteria, però diter-
minò venire lui stessi [*sic*] e però ò scritto perché si farebe per la chasa, ché farebe dua ufitii.

Siché se vi pare lo rachomando alla Signoria vostra. E se per me qua si può niente, sono sempre
a' chomandi vostri.

   Christo vi ghuardi. Fatta adì 23 di novembre 1463.

                    Humilus servus Greghorius
                          Pauli tenorista Sene
   [verso:]   Magnificho militi domino
                    Christofano Felicii, dignissimo
                    Hoperario maioris eclesie Senarum
                    in Chastro novo

Doc. 4.13. The singers are given permission to go to Florence for St. John's Day without losing
their salary

15 June 1457: [margin: Pro cantoribus duomi] Cantoribus maioris ecclesie licentiam concesserunt eundi Florentie ad festum Sancti Iohannis sine amissione eorum salarii, non obstantibus
quibuscunque in contrarium facientibus. Mandantes camerario Opere quod dictis cantoribus
solvat, dicta absentia non obstante debitum salarium (ASS, *Balìa,* vol. 4, fol. 50ᵛ).

30 June 1460: Anno Domini MCCCCLX, indictione VIII, die XXX Iunii. Magnifici et potentes domini, domini priores, gubernator Comunis et capitaneus populi magnifice civitatis Senarum, convocati in consistorio . . . deliberaverunt quod Operarius ecclesie catedralis teneatur
et debeat solvere cantoribus dicte ecclesie salarium eis debitum et ordinatum, non obstante quod
steterint per aliquos dies in eundo et redeundo de civitate Florentie ad civitatem Senarum pro
festo Sancti Iohannis proxime preterito, cum sit honor civitatis eorum andata et maxime viso
quod anno preterito iverunt ad dictum festum et fuerunt integraliter soluti non obstante eorum
andata, faciendo dictam solutionem dictus Operarius sine aliquo suo preiudicio aut damno. Et
predictus decreverunt omni modo etc. Galghanus Mei, notarius Consistorii, subscripsit (AOMS,
vol. 64, *Carteggio, 1460–61,* by date)

Doc. 4.14. Authorization to hire a new organist, 24 May 1467. ASS, Notarile antecosimiano
439, no. 59

Pro maioris ecclesie factore, sonatore, miniatore et aliis convocati infrascripti generosus miles
Savinus Mattei Antonii Guidi, Operarius maioris ecclesie Senarum, una cum infrascriptis domino
preposito et consiliariis . . . deliberaverunt ut infra . . . Quod sit plene remissum in dictum Operarium posse conducere sonatorem organorum pro tempore duorum annorum incipiendorum
die primo Iunii proxime futuri, pro mercede ad plus florenorum trium pro quolibet mense, de
libris IIII pro floreno denariorum Senensium, et infra ut melius et utilius facere poterit pro
dicta Opera.

TABLE 4.3. Chronological list of cathedral musicians, 1448–1479

The list includes only those mentioned specifically as singers at some point in the calendar year. Note that the fiscal year runs from May through April; a singer listed under two consecutive years may have served no more than a few months (for exact months, see Register of Musicians). Accounts for fiscal 1469–70 are missing.

A. Singers

	1449	1450	1451	1452	1453	1454	1455	1456	1457	1458	1459	1460	1461	1462	1463–64	1465–66	1467
Marino di Niccolò[a]	x																
Antonio di Gabriello da Montepulciano[b]			x	x	x	x											
Luca di Giovanni da Pisa	x	x	x	x	x	x	x	x	x								
Biagio di Tomè	x	x	x	x	x	x	x	x	x	x	x	x	x	x	x	x	x
Andrea da Polonia	x	x															
Giovanni da Polonia	x	x															
Jacomo da Polonia	x	x															
Vito da Polonia	x	x	x														
Giovanni di Michele	x	x															
Francesco di Antonio	x	x															
Matteo da Polonia		x															
Ser Giovanni		x															
Simone di Mariano		x	x	x	x	x	x	x									
Menico di Matteo		x	x	x	x	x	x	x									
Michelangelo di Daniello						x											
Giovanni di Santi		x	x	x	x	x	x	x									
Meo di Maestro Giovanni				x	x	x	x	x									
Francesco di Lorino						x	x	x									
Antonio da Chiusdino						x											
Antonio di Niccolò Trecerchi								x	x								
Goro di Pavolo								x	x	x	x	x	x	x	x	x	x

218

TABLE 4.3 *continued*

	1449	1450	1451	1452	1453	1454	1455	1456	1457	1458	1459	1460	1461	1462	1463–64	1465–66	1467
Giovanni di Stefano Francioso								x	x	x	x	x	x	x	x	x	x
Antonio di Matteo da Prato								x	x	x							
Bartolomeo di Giovanni								x									
Francesco da Sancta Reina									x								
Antonio di Antonio Ongaro										x	x	x	x	x	x	x	x
Giovanni di Jacopo da Francia											x						
Claudio												x					
Alberto												x	x	x	x	x	
Gabriello												x	x	x	x	x	
Piero Baiardi													x	x			
Guglielmo Francioso														x			
Agostino d'Antonio															x		
Carlo di Guglielmo Francioso															x	x	
Giovanni Francioso																x	x
Guglielmo di Lodovico																x	
Giachetto Francioso																	x

	1468	1469	1470	1471	1472	1473	1474	1475	1476	1477	1478	1479
Biagio di Tomè	x	x	x	x	x	x	x	x	x	x	x	x
Goro di Pavolo	x	x	x	x	x	x	x	x	x	x	x	
Antonio di Antonio	x	x	x	x	x	x	x	x	x	x	x	x
Giovanni di Stefano	x	x										
Agostino d'Antonio											x	
Carlo di Guglielmo								x				
Giovanni Francioso	x	x										
Giachetto Francioso	x											
Jacomo di Novo Porto	x		x	x								
Giletto			x	x		x						
Francesco di Guido			x		x							
Giacopetto				x								
Guglielmo di Cortese				x	x							
Bernardino				x								
Benedetto da l'Aquila					x	x	x	x	x	x		
Antonio Piccardo					x	x					x	
Alberto						x	x	x				
Ruberto di Giovanni Francioso							x					
Remigio							x					
Gottifredi di Thilman									x	x		
Niccolò di Lanberto									x	x		
Michele									x			
Austino di Antonio											x	

B. ORGANISTS	1448–57	1458	1459–66	1467	1468–70	1471–78	1479
Franceso di Nanni	x		x		x		
Piero di Guasparre Guiducci		x					
Lazaro di Jacomo		x	x	x			
Giovanni di Francesco				x	x	x	x
Francesco di Mattia						x	x

a singing teacher
b also singing teacher and organist from 1455

Chapter Five

EXPANSION AND RETRENCHMENT
IN THE CHAPEL, 1480–1507

I N J U L Y 1482 seventeen singers, ten adults and seven boys, were recorded at Siena cathedral, the largest number ever assembled in the history of the chapel. It was one that would not be reached again until almost a century later. Among the adults were several of the leading Franco-Flemings of the time, men who had previously sung or would eventually sing in Rome, Milan, Florence, and Ferrara, the major musical centers on the peninsula. They represented the latest phase of the northern musical invasion of Italy, whose advancing waves, observable in Siena from the 1430s onwards, reached flood proportions in the early 1470s, when Galeazzo Maria Sforza in Milan initiated on a grand scale policies pursued earlier at Naples and Ferrara and, more modestly, by the Medici at Florence. Meanwhile, the reestablished papacy at Rome and its chapel acted as a magnet that beckoned northern musicians south in search of fortune, fame, and benefices. New arrivals continued unabated throughout the 1470s, 1480s, and the early 1490s, when the horrors of war were unleashed on the peninsula by the invading forces of Charles VIII of France. But by the 1490s the groundwork had been laid and the mainstream of European music began a change in course that would eventually place Italian composers in the forefront of musical invention, just as their Franco-Flemish teachers had been in the late fifteenth century. It is perhaps no exaggeration to say that the peaceful Franco–Flemish invasion of Italy's principal musical centers was as momentous for the history of Italian and European music and culture as the subsequent military invasion of Charles VIII and his French armies, which led to changes that forever altered the course of Italian and European politics.

Franco-Flemish composers active in Italy during the last quarter of the fifteenth century constituted a veritable constellation, in Gustave Reese's felicitous phrase, with the incomparable Josquin des Prez as the brightest star among them. Composers of the first rank such as Gaspar van Weerbecke, Johannes Martini, Loyset Compère, Alexander Agricola, Johannes Ghiselin, Heinrich Isaac, and a host of others brought with them their art and knowledge and helped initiate a movement that saw the establishment of forms and techniques that would dominate musical practices throughout Europe for more than a century. A few like Josquin, who arrived at Milan cathedral when he was no more than twenty, truly represented the two cultures, the north in which he was born and nurtured, and the south, where he came to full artistic maturity. These were the musicians who presided over the triumph of northern polyphony in Italy. It was they who introduced to a wider Italian audience than ever before the complexities and glories of the northern polyphonic tradition, and it was they who composed many of the seminal works of the high Renaissance for their Italian patrons in their newly adopted homeland.[1]

By now it is a commonplace of Western musical history to speak of the outstanding achievements of the Franco-Flemings of the post–Du Fay generations and of the merging of their contrapuntal techniques and Italian harmonic practices, of northern artifice and southern sensibility, of the fusion that resulted in the formation of the classical Renaissance style of Josquin and his contemporaries. But this fusion might never have occurred had it not been for the enthusiasm with which Italian patrons and audiences so readily accepted the polyphonic style of the north and so warmly welcomed its practitioners. Nor would it have come about had not the northerners come under the spell of the burgeoning Renaissance, had they been unaffected by the teachings of the humanists, by the refined tastes and predilections of their newfound employers, and by the traditional musical practices of their new environment.[2] One result was the emergence in the early sixteenth century at various centers throughout the peninsula of native schools of composers, who, trained in the rigors of northern counterpoint and imbued with the spirit of peninsular traditions, laid the foundation for the emergence of the madrigal, the late Renaissance style, and an Italian musical hegemony that would captivate all Europe for centuries to come.

Italian Chapels in the Later Fifteenth Century

With his two chapels of singers, the Milanese Duke Galeazzo Maria Sforza, emulating the Burgundian dukes and other northern courts, set an unprecedented standard for

---

1. All of this is not to minimize the importance of northern musical centers in the later development and dissemination of the Renaissance musical style. Ongoing research continues to confirm the seminal role played by northern patrons and the high level of performance and education fostered by musically literate publics north of the Alps.

2. Lowinsky has argued for the fusion of northern artifice and southern sensibilities—the terms are mine—in a number of studies, particularly in his "Music in the Culture of the Renaissance" and his "Humanism in the Music of the Renaissance," both now reprinted in *Music in the Culture of the Renaissance and Other Essays,* ed. Bonnie J. Blackburn (Chicago, 1989). Also see Claude V. Palisca, *Humanism in Italian Renaissance Musical Thought* (New Haven and London, 1985), 1–22, who notes that the musical Renaissance, as with the other arts and learning in general, began in Italy and that "its chief source of inspiration was the revival of antiquity." Palisca further points out that the renewal of learning in Italy led to a rethinking of some fundamental issues in music theory and aesthetics that directly affected practice. Christopher Reynolds, "The Counterpoint of Allusion in Fifteenth-Century Masses," *JAMS* 45 (1992): 252–6, disagrees with the notion that northern musicians of the mid-fifteenth century needed to travel to Italy in order to absorb the ideas of the Italian humanists, which, he says, could have reached them through various channels and people, including Aeneas Sylvius Piccolomini. Be that as it may, reciprocal influences in musical composition, amply illustrated by Gustave Reese in *Music in the Renaissance* (New York, 1954), 10–33, are apparent from the early fifteenth century onwards, culminating during the time of Josquin and his contemporaries, when the nothern presence in Italy reached its apogee. The fusion of northern and southern elements was, as M. Jennifer Bloxam phrased it recently, "a longer and more complicated development than has been previously acknowledged," and many aspects of this development have yet to be fully examined. See her "'La Contenance Italienne': The Motets on *Beata es Maria* by Compère, Obrecht and Brumel," *Early Music History* 11 (1992): 41.

Italy, surpassing even the popes in Rome and the Neapolitan kings in the lavishness of his support and patronage. At the time of his assassination in 1476 Galeazzo's musical entourage included thirty-three singers, after having reached a high point of forty in 1474.[3] These forces were assembled primarily for court activities, though the singers also sang on special occasions at Milan cathedral, where after 1484 a chapel of twelve adult singers and an unspecified number of boys performed throughout the remainder of the century.[4] At Ferrara, Ercole d'Este, Galeazzo's rival in musical matters, also sought to create an elaborate musical establishment. By 1473 he employed twelve adults and a group of German boys, the latter replaced after 1476 by other adults, whose number eventually reached twenty-seven in 1481.[5] Ercole continued to maintain exceptionally large musical forces throughout the 1480s and 1490s, at the time of his death in 1505 employing thirty-one singers, though the number fell as low as twelve at some points.[6] Ercole's chapel in many respects equaled that of the popes, who during the 1460s and 1470s employed between fourteen and twenty singers, and as many as twenty-four in 1483.[7]

Somewhat later, Lorenzo de' Medici in Florence entered the fray, in emulation, according to one writer of the time, of the Aragonese king of Naples.[8] Twenty-one singers are cited at the Neapolitan court in 1480, the same number reported in 1451, and their number probably grew in later years for which records are lacking.[9] In Florence the success of Lorenzo's efforts is revealed by rosters from January 1493, just months after his death, when the chapel reached the unprecedented number of eighteen adults, in addition to the cathedral boys' choir, which performed independently.[10] Similar forces were assembled in Venice, where by the late 1480s as many as seventeen adults

3. Two recent accounts of music at the Sforza court are given by Prizer, "Music at the Court of the Sforza," particularly 158–59, and Welch, "Sight, Sound and Ceremony in the Chapel of Galeazzo Maria Sforza." Fundamental are earlier studies by Motta, "Musici alla corte degli Sforza," and Barblan, "Vita musicale alla corte sforzesca."

4. After Galeazzo's death, however, the Milanese court chapel continued on an uneven course, eventually dwindling to fewer than eight singers.

5. Lockwood, *Music in Renaissance Ferrara,* 134.

6. Ibid., 199–200 and tables for the 1480s.

7. Haberl, "Die römische 'schola cantorum' und die päpstlichen Kapellsänger," 230–32, 241–42; Starr, "Music and Music Patronage at the Papal Court, 1447–1464," passim.

8. This was Raffaele Brandolini in his *De musica et poetica opusculum;* see chapter 4, note 38. See also D'Accone, "The Singers of San Giovanni," 327; Atlas, *Music at the Aragonese Court of Naples,* xi. For the most recent study of musical relations between Naples and Florence in this period see Atlas, "Aragonese Naples and Medicean Florence: Musical Interrelationships and Influence in the Late Fifteenth Century," in *La musica a Firenze al tempo di Lorenzo il Magnifico,* ed. Piero Gargiulo (Florence, 1993), 15–45.

9. Atlas, *Music at the Aragonese Court of Naples,* 45–46, 47, 49; an earlier study by C. M. Riccio also remains fundamental: "Alcuni fatti di Alfonso I di Aragona," *Archivio storico per le provincie napoletane* 6 (1881): 411–61, particularly 411–12 for the 1483 roster.

10. D'Accone, "The Singers of San Giovanni," 346, 330–31; the most recent study of music in Laurentian Florence is D'Accone, "Lorenzo il Magnifico e la musica" and the English version of this, "Lorenzo the Magnificent and Music," in *Lorenzo il Magnifico e il suo mondo,* ed. Gian Carlo Garfagnini (Florence, 1994), 259–90.

and a dozen youths were employed at the church of St. Mark's, seat of the Venetian doges.[11] St. Mark's chapel rivaled that of any major cathedral in Italy. Even cathedrals in smaller cities joined in the general trend: Treviso had eight adults and five boys by the late 1480s and at Padua there were nine adults and an unspecified number of boys by the late 1490s.[12] At that time San Petronio, the principal church in Bologna, was employing eight adult singers.[13]

What did all this mean for Siena? How could its cathedral fit into a system of patronage based on seemingly unlimited purses and easy access to ecclesiastical benefices for favored singers? There was hardly a thought of competing with music-loving princes or popes when it came to seeking benefices for singers within or outside the Sienese dominion. Nor were the Opera's coffers always so overflowing that competitive salaries could be offered on a permanent basis to star singers. Strangely, no recourse was had to tapping government sources, nor was a move made to consolidate cathedral forces with those at the Palazzo Pubblico, whose ensembles continued on an independent course. Even the solution reached in Medicean Florence, which accommodated an elaborate system of patronage involving the city's two principal churches, its guilds, the Medici, and the cathedral chapter, was beyond the reach of the Sienese establishment at this time. Despite such unfavorable odds and an apparent lack of major funding, Alberto Aringhieri, the Opera's new overseer, took the lead in welcoming the representatives of this musical invasion just as his predecessor had done. The results of his efforts form a fascinating chapter in the history of Siena cathedral's musical establishment.

Renaissance of the Chapel under the Overseer Alberto Aringhieri

When Aringhieri assumed the overseer's post in July 1480, the cathedral's musical ensemble was barely functioning. The venerable singer–chaplain Ser Biagio di Tomè was the only adult singer on the roster, and even though a few youths capable of singing polyphony were still enrolled in the school, there is no indication that they actually sang in the chapel. It is difficult to imagine performances of anything more than a few voices singing to the accompaniment of the organist, who probably filled in parts not covered by the available musicians. The repertory of recent decades, if not altogether abandoned, must have been radically modified. The possible causes of this situation are many. Perhaps funds earmarked for music were temporarily diminished. Qualified personnel may not have been available at the time. Perhaps Savino Savini, so distracted by other activities and political considerations in the final years of his stewardship, was unable to attend to the chapel's problems. Maybe all these circumstances converged to create this new crisis in the musical program. In addition, political upheaval within the

---

11. See D'Accone, "The Performance of Sacred Music in Italy during Josquin's Time, c. 1475–1525," in *Josquin des Prez*, ed. Edward E. Lowinsky and Bonnie J. Blackburn (London, 1976), 606–7 for the documents regarding Venice.

12. Giovanni D'Alessi, *La cappella musicale del Duomo di Treviso* (Vedelago, 1954), 55, 62; Casimiri, "Musica e musicisti nella cattedrale di Padova nei sec. XIV, XV, XVI," 149, 158–61.

13. Osvaldo Gambassi, *La cappella musicale di San Petronio: Maestri, organisti, cantori e strumentisti dal 1436 al 1920* (Florence, 1987), 57.

city and unsettled times must also have contributed to the aimless direction and seeming
indifference to musical affairs that marked the last months of Savini's tenure as overseer.

By 1480 the various factions of the popular and noble parties and of the Noveschi,
or party of the Nine, all of whom had been vying for control of the city since the death
of Pius II in 1464, were reconciled and an apparently representative government
formed. The coalition's representatives in the Consiglio Generale and on the Concistoro continued to fulfill traditional roles, though more power was now delegated to
specially formed committees known as the Balìa. In the future, these committees would
continue to influence, if not direct government policies, from behind the scenes. Pandolfo Petrucci, eventually the city's sole ruler, was one of the leaders of the Noveschi
in the new coalition, and in 1482, when his group was excluded from the government
after an internal squabble, he fled the city and became one of the leaders of a new rebel
group. Five years later, in 1487, Petrucci and his cohorts secretly entered the town in
the dead of night and gained control of the Palazzo Pubblico in a bloodless coup d'état.
Political purges and reshuffling of posts were again the order of the day as scores were
evened and the victors went about rewarding their friends and supporters. All of the
city's major factions were ostensibly represented in the government that followed, but
Petrucci was by now de facto lord of the town, a position he further consolidated in
1500, when he had his father-in-law murdered. He ruled Siena with few interruptions
until his death on 21 May 1512, when power passed peacefully to his son.

Alberto Aringhieri was about to begin his seventh year as cathedral overseer when
Petrucci's faction gained control of the state. After 1480, as a member of the Popular
party, Aringhieri had been elected to the governing Balìa on a number of occasions and
had also served several times as captain of the people.[14] As Sienese envoy he traveled to
Florence to negotiate a peace settlement, and a friendship treaty between the two cities
was proclaimed there on 13 June 1483. Service under the previous government apparently did not prejudice Aringhieri's position in the eyes of the Petrucci party, for the
new regime, recognizing his many years of service to the Republic as a brilliant administrator and diplomat, quickly put his talents to its own uses. A measure of the esteem
he enjoyed as an administrator was the very length of his tenure as the Opera's overseer.
Assuming office in 1480, just as the coalition government was being formed, he retained
it for almost a quarter of a century, longer than any other person in the history of Siena
cathedral. It was not until the spring of 1505, when Pandolfo Petrucci, in ailing health
and flanked by two of his closest advisors, forced Aringhieri out of office and personally
took over the post.

Throughout his tenure Aringhieri's position as cathedral overseer was delicate, requiring all of the skills and tact that characterized his work as a politician and diplomat.
He was, as events show, clearly a person who knew how to steer a course in troubled
waters, and his superior administrative gifts obviously made him an asset to the regime.
But if administrative talent and political adroitness were the gifts that enabled him to

---

14. A recent biographical sketch of Aringhieri and an account of his accomplishments at the
cathedral are given by Aronow, "A Documentary History of the Pavement Decoration," 208–10.

continue in his post for so long, it was his personal taste, as well as his knowledge of the arts, particularly music, that made him such an outstanding figure among the fifteenth-century overseers. The extent of his contributions to the musical life of Siena, so long unknown to his countrymen, stands both as a testimony to his own sensibilities as well as to the culture and ambitions of those who supported him in his endeavors to bring the latest repertories and most advanced performance practices to his city's major church.[15]

Aringhieri was apparently the first overseer who had a deep love of music as well as an understanding of the problems inherent in recruiting and maintaining a chapel of polyphonic singers. At the beginning of his stewardship he made a commitment to enlarge the chapel's forces and to put them on a par with those at major churches in other peninsular cities, particularly, we may assume, with those at the Florentine duomo. Like other musically ambitious patrons, Aringhieri also sought to recruit outstanding composers as well as singers, for this would ensure both an appropriate repertory and the highest standards of performance. Many of his predecessors had presided over outstanding events in the cathedral's building program. Some, like Jacopo della Quercia, had given artistic impulse to the decorative programs in a manner that could never be matched by a connoisseur, however well informed and appreciative he might be. Savino Savini, responsible for commissioning the remarkably decorated series of chant books that remain one of the glories of Siena cathedral, possessed a refined taste in artistic matters that had rarely, if ever, been experienced at the cathedral. Yet none of Aringhieri's illustrious predecessors sought to initiate the kind of ambitious musical program that might place Siena on an equal or near equal footing with the most advanced peninsular institutions of its kind.

For Aringhieri to have attempted what he did must mean that he had some musical training and that he was well acquainted with performance practices of contemporary Franco-Flemish music. There are, as yet, no records available concerning the former, but of the latter we can easily imagine that his frequent trips outside Siena gave him opportunities to experience contemporary music in ways that few of his compatriots enjoyed. He probably began studying music as a boy, perhaps when he was in Venice, where his father, Francesco, who had represented Sienese interests there for several years, was knighted by the doge. The record is silent about where he traveled as a young man, though in later life he had himself portrayed in the regalia of the Knights of St. John of Jerusalem and of Rhodes, which suggests a visit to the island or at the least travels within the Venetian empire. He was certainly no stranger to Florence or to Rome. In Florence he was on good terms with Lorenzo de' Medici, whom he met with during his official trips there and with whom he corresponded over the years. Aringhieri was surely aware of Lorenzo's actions on behalf of the Florentine chapel,

---

15. Alberto Aringhieri, Cardinal Francesco Todeschini Piccolomini, and Pandolfo Petrucci have been described as the leading forces in Sienese artistic life in the later fifteenth century, their intervention in artistic matters indicative of a new phase of quasi-private patronage, representing the aspirations of a small cultural elite. See Carl Brandon Strehlke, "Art and Culture in Renaissance Siena," in Christiansen, Kanter, and Strehlke, *Painting in Renaissance Siena, 1420–1500*, 55.

which since the late 1470s had been steadily increasing and attracting many of the most interesting musicians of the day. Aringhieri would have heard the Florentine chapel and been impressed by the quality of its performances and the range of its repertory. He doubtless took a leaf from Lorenzo's book when he moved forward with his own musical program at Siena cathedral.

Book Commissions

One aspect of Aringhieri's program, in fact, called for expanding the Sienese repertory, which would now include recently composed as well as well-known works, music that would find an appropriate place in the cathedral's liturgy. To this end he initiated the policy of commissioning books of polyphony for the chapel's use. When he became overseer, the cathedral owned three such volumes, among them the one left as security for a loan in 1451 by the Polish singer Giovanni and two other "libri di contrappunto." Within a year of taking office, Aringhieri brought the onetime papal singer Mattio Gay to Siena as a copyist and commissioned two books of polyphony from him. Gay's volumes, with additions by others, were subsequently rebound into a single volume now in Siena's Biblioteca Comunale, its pieces offering testimony to Aringhieri's endeavors and to the music performed by the new chapel he so eagerly assembled (on these books, see below, pp. 234–41). Gay's copies of some works represent the earliest known or most complete readings of Masses by, among others, Jacob Obrecht and Heinrich Isaac; many of the Vespers hymns and Magnificats that he copied for Siena are unknown in other sources. It seems unlikely that these latter represent works commissioned by Aringhieri, though he did have new works—Credos and motets—composed expressly for the chapel by the Franco-Fleming Peter Bordon (Pierre Bourdon). Even in his last year as overseer, Aringhieri was still ordering new volumes of music for the chapel from the singer Ser Maddalo d'Arezzo, who later served in Florence.[16]

Aringhieri also continued Savini's work by commissioning illuminations for the new set of chant volumes and by ordering the copying and decoration of a few other volumes.[17] His tenure, furthermore, was distinguished by his commissioning many important works of art. Among them were a number of outstanding pavement panels, one of them in the central nave depicting the personification of Fortuna designed by Pinturicchio.[18] He was also responsible for the construction, decoration, and furnishing of the Piccolomini Library, and for the Pinturicchio frescos for the cathedral's chapel of San Giovanni Battista, whose construction he initiated and whose choir stalls, several with references to performance and polyphony, were carved at his behest. In one of the chapel's frescoed panels, as mentioned, Pinturicchio depicted his patron dressed as a Knight of St. John of Jerusalem. The chapel was clearly a great favorite of Aringhieri, for when he died, he was buried at its entrance and the spot marked with a commemorative plaque. Pinturicchio's paintings, the pavement panels, and the plaque all remain.

---

16. See chapter 7.
17. These are discussed in chapter 2.
18. Carli, *Il Duomo di Siena,* 151; Aronow, "A Documentary History of the Pavement Decoration," 352.

But the sounds of the polyphony performed by the singers Aringhieri engaged were quickly forgotten, as was knowledge of his contributions to the musical life of his city.

The Search for First-Rate Singers

A new account book was begun when Aringhieri took over the overseer's duties in July 1480, and consequently it is possible to trace his initial efforts on behalf of the chapel with little difficulty. The paucity of entries devoted to musicians, indicating that practically nothing was spent on music, reveals how little he was able to do to improve the situation during his first months in office. Even services on Assumption Day, traditionally celebrated with polyphony, seem to have suffered.[19] The only hint of musical performance other than the organist's is an entry citing a payment of L. 11 to the Palace trumpeters "for their services on that day and all of the feasts they assisted at during the year" (see Doc. 5.1). It is possible that singers were furnished the cathedral by the government. As other records show, on 25 August 1480, the Concistoro authorized payment of expenses for instrumentalists, singers, dancers, and others who provided music and entertainment at the Palazzo Pubblico and elsewhere in the city on Assumption Day.[20]

Before the year was out Aringhieri began implementing his plans for revitalizing the chapel by hiring two highly regarded singers, the tenor Ser Niccolò di Lore and the soprano Gottifredi di Liegi, at monthly salaries, respectively, of L. 18 and L. 6. The latter had sung in Siena during Savini's tenure as overseer. Both began serving in December 1480. Niccolò di Lore, identified as a bass in documents from Florence, where he subsequently had a long career, was employed in Siena until the end of June 1481, when, as will be shown below, his failure to return from an authorized leave of absence precipitated a crisis in the chapel.[21] Payment records from early 1481, however, show that even before then Aringhieri's initial efforts to recruit and retain singers were no more successful than those of his predecessors. Gottifredi di Liegi remained only through the end of January.[22] Within weeks he was replaced by Ser Giovanni Cristofani Francioso, who served for an equally short time, departing Siena at the beginning of

---

19. One chronicler reported that on this occasion the festivities were so well ordered and beautiful that never before had there been seen in Siena such a series of games, triumphs, banquets, balls, jousts, tournaments, and other festivities, some of which had even been curtailed because of the sudden departure of the duke of Calabria, who had assisted the new government in regaining power. The festivities clearly did not extend to activities at the cathedral. Cristoforo Cantoni, "Frammento di un Diario di Cristoforo Cantoni (Anno 1479–1483)," in Muratori, ed., *Rerum italicarum scriptores,* vol. 15, pt. 6/2, p. 888.

20. See chapter 14, note 97.

21. On Niccolò di Lore, see D'Accone, "The Singers of San Giovanni," 331. In Florence Niccolò's singing was still remembered decades later and was mentioned favorably by Cosimo Bartoli in the *Ragionamenti accademici . . . sopra alcuni luoghi difficili di Dante,* published in Venice in 1567. James Haar, "Cosimo Bartoli on Music," *Early Music History* 8 (1988): 48, gives the mid-1550s as the probable time of Bartoli's remarks concerning musicians. Haar speculated that Bartoli's Niccolò di Lore might be Niccolò de' Pitti, who served in the papal chapel from 1507 to 1529 (p. 67).

22. Gottifredi also served in Florence and eventually Rome. See chapter 4 above and D'Accone, "The Singers of San Giovanni," 332.

May. New in the chapel in April were Ugo di Gidio Francioso,[23] Roberto Leuder Piccardo, and the cathedral chaplain Ser Domenico di Matteo. The two foreigners were paid L. 8 per month, but the chaplain received half that amount. Pietro di Ghino, also called Pietricchino, a soprano, was present in May, as was Ser Biagio di Tomè, who returned to cathedral service after an absence of several months. Pietricchino's monthly salary of L. 8 was double that of Biagio, who received the L. 4 normally paid him in the past.

Despite the brevity of his stay, Pietricchino's appointment must be viewed as a coup on Aringhieri's part, for Pietricchino was one of those gifted musicians who not only sang but also composed. Like Gottifredi di Liegi and Roberto Leuder, Pietricchino, or Pietrequin Bonnel as he was known to his French-speaking colleagues, was a much traveled musician who eventually entered Florentine service. Later, he returned to northern France, where he sang in the chapel of Anne of Brittany.[24] His presence in Siena indicates that Aringhieri was well informed about the talents, capabilities, and reputations of the itinerant musicians whose services he enlisted for Siena cathedral and that from the very beginning of his tenure he made no secret of his intention to improve the chapel.

A debit entered into one of the account books under Niccolò di Lore's name, dated 8 July 1481, shows six singers performing in the chapel during the previous month of June. The clerk who made the entry explained that Niccolò, granted a leave of absence in order to go to Florence for the St. John's Day festivities, subsequently failed to return to Siena, as promised. On this very day, in fact, it was confirmed that he had taken up service in Florence. Had this been known previously, the clerk continued, the three sopranos and two contras would not have been retained because one cannot sing without the tenor, "senza tenorista non si può cantare." As a result, Niccolò was cited as being in debt to the Opera for L. 48, the total amount paid to the other five singers—Ugo, Pietricchino, Ruberto, Biagio, and Domenico—who had been kept on the payroll but who were apparently unable to perform their normal repertory during his absence (see Doc. 5.2). For some reason the boys were not singing with the adults at this time and the chapel, with its three sopranos and two lower voices, had apparently reverted to the kind of ensemble typical at mid-century.

By early August 1481 only three adults, Pietricchino, Ser Domenico di Matteo, and Ser Biagio di Tomè, remained on the roster. Assumption festivities were little more than two weeks away and for the second year in a row, with the chapel's membership once again extremely small, prospects were poor for having a display of vocal polyphony at cathedral services. The situation called for extraordinary action, which Aringhieri did not hesitate to take. The record of a payment made to him personally on 11 August reveals that, as a result of appointments formally approved on the previous 30 July, he

---

23. He is probably not the same person as Ugo di Parisetto di Champagnia de Reams who sang in the Florentine and papal chapels later in the decade. See D'Accone, "The Singers of San Giovanni," 339, 341–42.

24. For Pietricchino-Pietrequin in Florence, see ibid., 332, 342–43. For his later activities see the entry under Pietrequin Bonnel by Joshua Rifkin in *New Grove*, 14:743.

was being reimbursed L. 28. 13 "for expenses in sending to Rome for the singers newly appointed to our church, that is, sopranos, [a] contra, and [a] tenorista."[25] Perhaps two of the new singers whose names appear on the payroll around this time were among those brought in for the occasion. The first, identified only as Ser Elia, cantore, was on the payroll for the three weeks through 15 August;[26] the second, a tenorista named Messer Alfonso Ferrandi di Castiglia, served from the end of July through mid-March 1482, when "he departed and went to Rome."[27]

Six other singers are recorded with Ferrandi during the remaining months of 1481. Notable among them were the Frenchman Giovanni di Giovanni, called by the surname Pintelli in Florence, the one-time music copyist Jacomo Francioso,[28] Ugo di Gidio, and Ruberto cantore, otherwise known as Robinetto, another Frenchman with Florentine connections.[29] There was little change at the beginning of 1482, although this year ultimately proved to be the greatest period of expansion during Aringhieri's stewardship. Biagio was present throughout the year except for June. Ugo di Gidio left at the end of July, though he later returned. Messer Alfonso Ferrandi was replaced by another tenorista, Frate Giovanni di San Francesco, who joined the chapel in March. A second Frate Giovanni, this one designated as "da San Giorgio," began service a month later. The first-named earned L. 12 per month, the second L. 10. The salaries of both were considerably higher than the L. 4 received by a third Giovanni, Giovanni Farinella, who also began in April. Farinella, whose surname suggests Italian origins, is probably the same musician who sang at Palio festivities a few years earlier. Frate Chimenti de' Servi is recorded in his initial appearance only during May.

Joining the chapel on the first of May was a group of four singers, who together with those already present brought the number of adult singers in the chapel to ten, a number never reached before this time. The four singers were the tenorista Ser Piero

25. "1481. Le spese straxordinarie de l'Opera nostra . . . E adì XI d'aghosto L. vintinove s. tredici li paghamo questte a misser Alberto nostro operaio, furo' per mandare a Roma per la condotta nuovamente fatta de' cantori, cioè sobrani, contra e tenorista per la nostra chiesa cattedrale come n'appare deliberazione de' savi de l'opera, roghato ser Giovanni Danielli nostro notaio, sotto il dì XXX di luglio a libro de le deliberationi in fo. 106, a uscita d'Antonio Paccinelli nostro camarlingo, ffo. 26" (AOMS, vol. 507, *D&C, 1466–75,* fol. 305 left). (A practically identical entry is found in vol. 304, *E&U, 1481–82,* fol. 26ᵛ.)

26. AOMS, vol. 304, *E&U, 1481–82,* fol. 27ʳ also lists payment of L. 2. 5 to an unnamed singer on 23 August for having sung for several days for the feast.

27. A tenor named Ferrando, who was also an organist, was employed at St. Peter's in Rome from November 1478 through February 1479. See Reynolds, *Papal Patronage,* 331.

28. For his work as music copyist, see below.

29. This Ruberto (Robinetto) may be the person (Rubinet) to whom the chanson *Ha traistre Amours* is attributed in Bologna, Civico Museo Bibliografico Musicale, MS Q 18. The chanson is ascribed to Johannes Stochem in a number of sources, an ascription accepted on the basis of codicological and stylistic evidence by the two most recent editors of the piece. See Allan Atlas, *The Cappella Giulia Chansonnier: Rome, Bibl. Apostolica Vaticana C. G. XIII. 27,* 2 vols. (Brooklyn, 1975), esp. 1:106, and Howard Mayer Brown, *A Florentine Chansonnier from the Time of Lorenzo the Magnificent. Florence, Biblioteca Nazionale Centrale, MS Banco Rari 229,* 2 vols., Monuments of Renaissance Music 7 (Chicago and London, 1983), esp. 1:109.

de la Piazza (de Platea), the contra[bass] Bartolomeo de Castris,[30] and the two sopranos Quintino di Martino and the previously recorded Giovanni di Giovanni Pintelli.[31] At L. 24. 11. 8 Piero was the highest paid cathedral singer of the fifteenth century and the salaries given the others, L. 15 for Bartolomeo and L. 12 each for Quintino and Giovanni, though not lavish perhaps by the standards of the Neapolitan or Ferrarese courts, were at the top level of salaries normally paid to northern singers in Siena and compare favorably with the two florins (L. 12. 6. 8) per month the last three received later when they were employed at Florence cathedral.[32] In sacristans' reports these singers usually appear as a group, separated from the other adult singers by the names of boy sopranos. I designate them the second group.

Thus by May of 1482 the chapel had reached the unprecedented number of seventeen singers—ten adults and seven youths, a number that dipped to nine adults in June with Biagio's absence but was then registered again in July with his return. Slight variations in the chapel's makeup also occurred during the following months, as singers came and went. In August 1482 Ugo di Gidio was absent from the first group and Bartolomeo de Castris from the second, so that only eight adults were present. Seven adults were present in September, with Farinella absent from the first group and with the contrabass Giovanni Vichin replacing Quintino di Martino in the second.[33] How difficult it was to keep singers in Siena, despite fairly decent salaries and Aringhieri's

---

30. On Bartolomeo de Castris in Florence, see D'Accone, "The Singers of San Giovanni," 333–34, 338–41. Bartolomeo was also at St. Peter's in Rome, in October 1482. See Reynolds, *Papal Patronage,* 45.

31. Giovanni Pintelli was called a soprano in Siena but a contralto in Florence. See D'Accone, "The Singers of San Giovanni," 336, 341–42. A Mass by "Pintelli" survives in a Sistine Chapel manuscript, perhaps composed by Giovanni rather than by his brother Tommaso, who seems to have traveled much less and not to have settled in Rome. Arguing in favor of Giovanni's authorship is his prolonged stay in Italy, and more particularly at the Vatican. The piece, *Missa Gentilz gallans,* is in Cappella Sistina MS 41, fols. 2–14 (J. M. Llorens, *Capellae Sixtinae Codices musicis notis instructi sive manuscripti sive praelo excussi* [Vatican City, 1960], 81).

As for Giovanni's presence in Rome, possibly he was the contratenor, cited only as Johannes, in St. Peter's from March through June 1495 (Reynolds, *Papal Patronage,* 333). Since papal chapel records for this period are lost, there is no account of when he first joined the group. But he probably went to Rome after leaving Florence in the early 1490s. Richard Sherr has uncovered documents in Vatican archives showing that Johannes Pintelli, described as a cleric of Avignon and singer in the papal chapel, was granted a benefice on 22 July 1504 (RS 1188, fol. 1ᵛ). Pintelli, still described as a cleric of Avignon and papal singer, received two other benefices on 19 March 1505 and requested a third a few days earlier (RS 1198, fols. 92ᵛ–93ʳ; fol. 178ʳ⁻ᵛ). But another report from 26 May of the same year, 1505, notes that three chaplaincies had become vacant because of the death of Johannes Pintelli. I thank Professor Sherr for his generosity in sharing this material with me and for many other kindnesses during the course of my work.

32. For salaries in Florence at this time see D'Accone, "The Singers of San Giovanni," passim. Salaries and benefits, as I shall note presently, are notoriously difficult to compare.

33. The name Vichin is exceedingly difficult to decipher and could perhaps also be read as "Quintin." He may be the same person as Johannes Vitine (?) who signed a contract on 1 May 1482 with the Santissima Annunziata in Florence. See ibid., 333. The boys were paid between L. 2 and L. 4 monthly, an indication that some were older youths.

good will! On the sacristan's roll for October the names of three adults, Frate Giovanni da San Giorgio, Giovanni Farinella, and Ser Biagio, precede the names of eight boys and those of the three adults in the second group, Messer Piero tenorista, Giovanni di Giovanni soprano, and the just-mentioned Giovanni Vichin, contra, another singer with Florentine connections. Two other singers, Fra Chimenti de' Servi and Fra Andrea de' Servi, joined the second group for the month of November, when a total of eight adults was again reached, but the December roll lists only the six adults named in October, now assisted by nine choristers.[34] The two Servite monks, Chimenti Tedesco and Andrea Francioso, were among the musicians employed at the church of the Santissima Annunziata in Florence, and their presence at Siena cathedral suggests that they were resident during this period at the Servite convent church in Siena, where they probably also sang in the choir.

Although sacristans' reports and individual accounts are not always complete for the next few years, there is sufficient evidence to show that several of the singers remained in Siena longer than the itinerant musicians of previous years. Messer Piero de Platea— sometimes called de la Piazza, the Italian translation of his surname—began his tenure in May 1482 and sang in the chapel for the next three years, through June 1485. Martin Staehelin has suggested that this musician was none other than the famous Franco-Flemish composer Pierre de la Rue, who is otherwise unmentioned in Italian musical annals of the time.[35] I tend to doubt the identification, though it is clear that Messer Piero's high salary of L. 24. 11. 8 per month, as well as favorable treatment from Alberto Aringhieri, point to a musician of some stature who enjoyed the overseer's highest regard.[36] Giovanni di Matteo Farinella, who likewise began his career at Siena cathedral in April 1482, also served continuously in the chapel until the end of June 1485. Ser Biagio di Tomè, the long-time cathedral chaplain, was present throughout these years as well, and he, too, disappears after June 1485. Fra Chimenti de' Servi, however, was there from January 1483 through May 1486.

Four adult singers, Piero, Biagio, Farinella, and Chimenti, together with a group

---

34. The new chorister in December was Federigo di Pietro chantore at L. 1. 10 per month. Like several of the other boys and youths in the chapel at this time, he is registered for several years, changes in his salary reflecting not only experience but perhaps also a change in vocal range. For Andrea Francioso and Chimente Tedesco in Florence see ibid., 334.

35. Staehelin, "Pierre de la Rue in Italien," *Archiv für Musikwissenschaft* 27 (1970): 128–37.

36. If the musician in question was Pierre de la Rue, it seems strange that he would been dubbed with the Italianized "de la Piazza" rather than the more obvious "de la Strada." With regard to the special treatment accorded Messer Piero, one entry shows that Aringhieri had a priest's beret bought for him in January 1484: "MCCCCLXXXIII. Le spese strasordinare de l'opera deono dare . . . E de' dare adì detto [XVI di gienaio 1484] s. cinquantacinque paghamo per detto di misser Alberto nostro a Usino di Vieri merciaio per una biretta dopia da prete, la quale donò misser detto a misser Pietro tenorista di duomo e quali portò Ghuasparre nostro [sagrestano] insino adì 9 di gienaio, portì chontanti, L. II s. XV" (AOMS, vol. 306, *E&U, 1483–84,* fol. 98 left). On another occasion, the Opera advanced Messer Piero money for a cloak: "XPO MCCCCLXXXIIII. Misser Pietro de Platea tenorista in duomo di dare adì V d'aprile L. ventotto e s.—, e quali li prestiamo per comprare uno mantello" (vol. 509, *D&C, 1482–1527,* fol. 35 left).

that averaged eight choristers, thus formed the core of the chapel for all of 1483, all of
1484, and through the first six months of 1485.[37] Though complete records are unavailable for these years, surviving pay lists and other accounts indicate that several new as
well as previously employed singers joined the group for longer or shorter periods.
Giovanni Vichin was present from September 1482 through March 1483. Ugo di Gidio
is listed for an unspecified time in 1483 as is Bartolomeo de Castris. The soprano Giovanni di Giovanni Pintelli reappeared in October 1483 and remained through August
1484. Ser Agnolo di Pietro, who eventually became one of the mainstays of the group,
joined the adult singers for April, May, and June 1485. All in all the chapel, despite
these changes, enjoyed a stability not seen since the previous decade, when smaller
numbers were employed. Evidently expanded choral polyphony was held as an ideal,
for otherwise, with a stable nucleus of thirteen singers, there would have been little or
no need to continue to augment the group, as happened whenever the opportunity
arose.

ENSEMBLES AND PERFORMANCE PRACTICES

The sacristans' rolls for June and July 1482 name the four singers of the just-mentioned
second group along with a fifth, Giovanni Comitis, who is likewise recorded later in
Florence and Rome.[38] The way in which their names appear on sacristans' rolls suggests
that these singers constituted a special group, perhaps one accustomed to performing,
or hired especially to perform, as an independent ensemble. The roll from June, for
example (see Doc. 5.3), begins by listing one group of singers, followed by the names
of the seven youths, who are called *cherico* or *cantorino* in other documents. After this
several young clerks who apparently did not sing in the chapel are listed; the roll concludes with the five foreign singers. Although one might argue that I have read too
much into the placement of names on this and similar monthly rolls, it is clear that the
newly hired foreign singers constituted a separate group in the eyes of the sacristans
who kept attendance records. And for this reason one might argue that the placement
of names on these rosters had something to do with performance, perhaps even performance by a special group of soloists. Much later evidence from the papal chapel, mentioned below, suggests performance during the sixteenth century by groups of soloists
of certain passages for two, three, or four voices within a given work or even of performances of entire works by soloists.[39] If this is so, perhaps the practice had its roots in
the late fifteenth century, when Italian chapels first began their record expansion of
forces. At issue is whether the expanded forces, numbering between eighteen and

37. The choristers are listed in the sacristans' monthly reports for 1485, AOMS, vol. 1076, *Note
di salari . . . Secc. XV–XVIII,* and for 1482, AOMS, vols. 1074–75, *Note di salari . . . 1412–1535.* The
number of choristers again reached a high of nine in April and May 1485, though it went to seven in
June and eight in July and August.

38. For Comitis in Florence, where he is mentioned in February 1482 with Bartolomeo de Castris
and Johannes Vichin, see D'Accone, "The Singers of San Giovanni," 333. For his service at St. Peter's
in Rome, where he is listed as Johannes Piccardo, a soprano, see Reynolds, *Papal Patronage,* 334.

39. See also chapter 7, where reference is especially made to Richard Sherr's provocative study,
"Performance Practice in the Papal Chapel in the 16th Century," *Early Music* 15 (1987): 453–62.

twenty-four singers at some places by the end of the fifteenth century and as many as thirty-two singers during the early decades of the sixteenth century at others, were actually used en masse in performances of choral polyphony, with three, four, five, or even more singers to a part, or whether solo ensembles selected from the larger group performed on alternate days rather than at all services. To put it simply, was choral polyphony really practiced in these times?

Choral polyphony, to be sure, is a relative term, and we must acknowledge a world of difference between the behemoth choirs of modern times and the modestly ex-panded church choirs of the Renaissance. When I speak of choral polyphony in the late fifteenth century, I mean that the choirs were relatively small by present-day stan-dards. In general three or four singers were on each of the lower parts, though these may have varied at times, depending on the desired distribution and the strength of the voices within a given group.[40] The presence of boy sopranos was also a mitigating factor. Florentine records indicate a preponderance of sopranos and no more than two or three singers to a part for the lower voices—assuming, of course, that all of the singers were obliged to perform at the same time. This kind of distribution must have been typical of the Sienese chapel, with its large numbers of boys.

Sienese singers, like their Florentine counterparts, had to be present at the appointed times wherever a particular service was being celebrated, and they were required to remain in that place until the service was concluded. Nothing suggests that large num-bers of singers were hired at both Siena cathedral and at Florence cathedral so that smaller ensembles might be drawn from a larger group. This is not to say that for reasons of preference in tone color or because of external circumstances, such as illness and absences, that groups of soloists might not have been used. Nor does it mean that some passages sung by soloists might not have been interspersed among sections sung by the full choir. But such deviations from the norm happened for specific reasons, not as a matter of course. It is difficult, indeed, to imagine the Sienese chapel, where singers and funds for maintaining them were often in short supply, espousing a policy that called for supporting singers who did not perform at all of the required services. Lacking eyewitness accounts or any other precise documentation, such as can sometimes be had from Sistine Chapel diaries, one can only speculate as to what may have occurred in Siena cathedral. It is clear, however, that during these years, as I shall note again in another place, Sienese performance practices clearly kept abreast of those in the churches of Italy's major cities and courts.

With regard to the distribution of voices within the group, records from 1482 and later show that Aringhieri wanted a chapel of eight or nine adults, assisted by as many choristers, the older ones of whom, as suggested by their higher salaries, might also sing lower parts. At least two of the adults were tenors and two were sopranos. Several of

---

40. Pertinent in this regard is some information regarding the Florentine chapel from more than a half century after this time, also cited below in chapter 7. When the group was reorganized in January 1540, it comprised seven sopranos, seven altos, four tenors, and five basses. A report from March 1541 notes that "it seems nothing is lacking in the chapel, except that the contrabasses are so weak they are little heard." Consequently, another bass was hired. See D'Accone, "The Musical Chap-els at the Florentine Cathedral and Baptistry," 25–26, 30.

the remaining singers are sometimes listed as contras, but whether basses or altos is difficult to determine. From records of other cities, especially Florence, it is possible to identify the voice ranges of a number of singers who otherwise remain unclassified in Sienese documents. But even this information is not always reliable because sometimes the designations differ from place to place. Ser Niccolò di Lore, for example, is called a tenor in Siena but a contrabass in Florence, while Giovanni Pintelli is designated as a contralto in Florence and as a soprano in Siena.[41] This may mean that they sang different parts in the two cities, but it also points to the difficulty in distinguishing the disposition of voices on the basis of available information.

With so many other musicians appearing and reappearing on the rolls of the Florentine and papal chapels during this period, it seems clear that the Italian institutions were dealing with a singers' market, one which saw these peripatetic performers changing allegiances and moving about with an ease that seems remarkable to us today, given what we imagine to be primitive means of transportation and perhaps the difficulties of leaving one princely employer for another. The peregrinations of these musicians, as I have repeatedly stressed, illustrate how easily musical repertories and performance practices were transmitted.[42] While allowances must be made for the variety in sound that inevitably resulted from local practices and traditions as well as from the availability of singers trained in the new northern styles, evidently the major centers on the Italian peninsula were now moving toward more universalized practices and forming a truly international style, not only with regard to musical composition but performance as well.[43] Siena, though hardly able to compete with the ambitious plans of its more powerful neighbors, was to share in this musical evolution and would eventually produce its own school of composers.

THE SIENESE REPERTORY AFTER 1481

The volumes of polyphony commissioned by Aringhieri and copied by Mattio Gay in Siena between February and July 1481 (see Table 5.1) amply demonstrate the interconnections between these new practices and repertories.[44] It was possible to identify two volumes with MS K. I. 2 on the basis of an inventory of cathedral holdings from after

41. Similar confusion is recorded in late sixteenth-century documents from Siena. See chapter 7.

42. See chapter 4, where particular reference is made to Strohm, "European Politics and the Distribution of Music in the Early Fifteenth Century," 305–23, passim. See also Lockwood, *Music in Renaissance Ferrara,* 51–63, regarding the contents of Modena B.

43. See Palisca, *Humanism in Italian Renaissance Musical Thought,* passim, with regard to the work of Italian musical theorists of the time who, under the influence of their humanist colleagues, formulated and promulgated stylistic criteria and prescriptions for use of the modes on the basis of their readings of the "ancients."

44. The copyist's name is normally given as "Ghai" in Sienese documents, but here I have adopted the form found in other scholarly literature. Although Mattio Gay was a singer in Rome, there is, surprisingly, no record of his having done anything in Siena other than copy music manuscripts. A description of the manuscript and remarks on its history are in D'Accone, "A Late 15th-Century Sienese Sacred Repertory: MS K. I. 2 of the Biblioteca Comunale, Siena," *Musica Disciplina* 37 (1983): 121–70. A facsimile edition is in my *Siena, Biblioteca Comunale degli Intronati, MS K. I. 2,* Renaissance Music in Facsimile 18 (New York, 1987).

TABLE 5.1.   Payments for copying music books, 1481–1484

---

22 March 1481

Matio ghai francioso, scritore de' libri di canto fighurato, adì XXII detto lire quattro s. 0 chontanti a lui, per detto di misser Alberto operaio, e so' a' libro di 3 rosse, f. 276. L. IIII s.—d.—
(AOMS, vol. 303, *E&U, 1480–81*, fol. 37ᵛ)ᵃ

5 April 1481

A Matio Ghai francioso, scritore de' libri dela musicha, adì detto, lire quatro s. 0 chontanti a lui,
per detto di misser Alberto operaio, e so' a' libro di 3 rosse, f. 276. L. IIII s.—d.—(fol. 38ʳ)

Ser Domenicho di Matteo prete die dare a dì V d'aprile L. quatro e s.—, chonttanti in sua mano
per detto di misser Alberto nostro operaro per rigature di libri de la chantoria di canto figurato
(vol. 508, *D&C, 1475–82*, fol. 279 left)

21 April 1481

A Matio ghai, scritore de' libro di chanto, adì XXI d'aprille, lire quatro s. 0 chontanti a lui, per
detto di missere Alberto operaio, e so' a' libro di 3 rosse, f. 276. L. IIII s.—d.—(vol. 303, *E&U,
1480–81*, fol. 40ᵛ)

6 July 1481

A Mattio Gai francioxo, adì VI di lulglio, lire undici s. cinque contanti in suo mano, sono per
resto di scripttura di libri di canto figurato, pagamo per detto di messer Alberto nostro, a llui al
libro di III roxe, fo. 276. L. XI s. V (vol. 304, *E&U, 1481–82*, fol. 23ᵛ)

24 December 1481

A Jacomo cantore a dì detto L. dieci s. 0 contanti a llui per parte di scrittura per un libro per la sagrestia a llib. di 3 roxe, fol. 341. L. XXI s. VI. d. 8 (fol. 35ᵛ)

after December 1481

A Jacomo di Francesco cantore L. ventuna s. sei d. otto contanti al lui per resto di scripttura di
più libri di canto no[n] fighurato e per regatura à fatto in fino questo dì et sonno allui a llibro di
III roxe, fo. 341. L. XXI s. VI. d. 8 (fol. 36ᵛ)

2 August 1484

Maestro Pietro Bordo' di Fiandra adì detto, lire dodici s. 0 chontanti in sua mano, chome m'ordinò messer Alberto in nela sua partita, per parte di chomposizione e scrittura d'ogni apartenenti
al chanto figurato e sono a libro rosso di uno lione a fol. 107. L. XII s.—(vol. 307, *E&U, 1484–
85*, fol. 35ᵛ)

1 September 1484

Maestro {messer, crossed out} Pietro Bordone chonpositore di chanto figurato adì primo di settenbre, lire dodici per parte si suo servito e sono a lui a libro rosso d'uno lione a fol. 107. L. XII
s.—(fol. 38ʳ)

15 September 1484

Maestro Piero Bordone chonpositore di chanto figurato adì 15 di detto, lire sei chontanti per lui
a messer Pietro di Platera [*recte* Platea], chome disser' detto misser Pietro e Londardo di Crysto-
fano [e] Francesco chericho di duomo, e sono a lui a libro rosso d'uno lione a fol. 107. L. VI
(fol. 38ᵛ)

A more detailed notice is in vol. 509, *D&C, 1482–1527* (fol. 107ʳ): Maestro Pietro Bordone di
Fiandra die avere adì XV di settenbre lire trenta, soldi—, sonno per conponitura di mottetti,
credi e altri chanti fighurati per la chiesa, per detto di messer Alberto nostro operaio, e ssono a le
spese in questo, fol. 135. L. XXX s.—

ᵃThe corresponding entries in the *Debitori & Creditori* ledgers (AOMS, vol. 508, fol. 27 left) for payments
to Gay, in similar wording, are given in D'Accone, "A Late 15th-Century Sienese Sacred Repertory," 127,
n. 19.

TABLE 5.2.   Inventories of music manuscripts, ca. 1488–ca. 1517

ca. 1488 (AOMS, vol. 1492, *Inventarii, 1420–post 1488,* fasc. 11)

fol. 4ᵛ:	[18]	Uno seguentiale cuperto di pavonazo, comincia Regem venturum, segna XVIII
	[46]	Una musica d'Aristotile [*recte* Boetio] cuperta mezo di rosso, comincia Omnium quidem, segna 46
fol. 5ʳ:	[60]	Uno libro di laude vulgare, cuperto di nero, comincia Ave domina, segna LX
	[61]	Uno seguentiale con tavole bianche, comincia Letabuntur, segna LXI
fol. 5ᵛ:	[100]	Uno libro di carta bambagina, di canto figurato, segna 100
fol. 6ʳ:	[113]	Uno libro di canto figurato, in carta bambagina, con tavole di carta, con arme dell'Opera, segna 113
	[126]	Uno libro di canto figurato di nota grossa, per li Vespri, legato e covertato di cuoio pavonazzo con coppe grandi e canti d'ottone, comincia Dixit Dominus, Domino meo. Fece fare messer Alberto, segna 126
	[127]	Uno libro di canto figurato per le messe, di nota grossa, legato e coperto di cuoio pavonazo con coppe grandi e canti d'ottone, comincia Asperges me. Fece fare messer Alberto, segna 127

ca. 1517 (vol. 1493, *Inventarii, 1517?–1590,* fasc. 1, 1517?, without title)

       fols. 7ʳ, 7ᵛ, 8ʳ, 8ᵛ, 9ʳ: all of the items in the previous inventory appear, with the same numeration and without any significant change in description

---

1488, which reports that one volume containing Vespers music began with a setting of Ps. 109, *Dixit Dominus Domino meo,* and that another, containing Masses, began with the *Asperges me* antiphon (see Table 5.2).[45] The volumes were later rebound, together with fascicles from other manuscripts, into a single volume. As it now stands, the single volume contains twenty-nine gatherings.[46]

---

45. No sample of Gay's musical handwriting survives that might confirm his hand in these manuscripts. Christopher Reynolds, in *Papal Patronage,* includes an illustration of a receipt dated 1475 written and signed by Nicholaus Ausquier, copyist of San Pietro B 80 (fig. 8); underneath it is another receipt signed by Gay. The handwriting, certainly that of a northerner, does not appear to match any of those in the Siena manuscript; but, it might be noted, the hand of the two receipts and signatures is suspiciously similar.

46. The first twelve gatherings and traces of another one between fols. 71ᵛ–72ʳ, now lost, must have formed the nucleus of Gay's original Vespers collection, a total of thirteen gatherings in all, from present fols. 1 to 104. Gay completed seven of these gatherings (nos. 1, 2, 3, 6, 10, 11, 12) and about a half of two others (nos. 7, 8). A second copyist filled in many of the blank folios in the two latter fascicles and also copied the major part of three others (nos. 4, 5, 13). A number of different hands copied a few pieces that are interspersed among these and the remaining gatherings. Just before the Mass collection are three gatherings (nos. 14, 15, 16), done for the most part by Gay, whose position in one or another of the original volumes is unclear, though the Marian motets in two of them suggest they were appropriate for Vespers. Gay's Mass collection now occupies folios 130ʳ–185ʳ, fascicles 17 through 22, and folios 199ʳ–207ᵛ.

By a strange twist of fate Gay's volumes preserve some of the earliest known copies of their contents, although these originated in more advanced musical centers in northern Italy such as Milan and Ferrara or possibly even Rome, his last place of employment before arriving in Siena. The Masses copied by Gay, all without ascription, offer perhaps the best illustration of this, though they no longer form a volume in their own right. When Gay's two volumes were rebound into one, apparently after many years of use, some of the original fascicles were discarded, ignoring the proper order of many of the remaining ones. The remains of Masses copied by Gay now comprise fascicles 17–22 and the first few folios of fascicle 26. This latter opens with the *Asperges me* antiphon sung before the beginning of Mass, which the compiler of the first inventory to mention the volume said was its initial item.[47] Included in the Mass fascicles are Isaac's *Missa Quant j'ai,* in what is perhaps its earliest known source, Martini's *Missa Coda de Pavon,* which survives in Milanese and Modenese manuscripts, and Obrecht's *Missa Beata viscera,* in a version that preserves all sections of the Gloria and of the Credo, movements that are incomplete in its only other known source.[48] Some of these Masses were assuredly part of the Milanese repertory, for their composers were associated with the

---

47. This is followed by a second setting of the same text and by a setting of *Vidi aquam,* a text substituted for the *Asperges* during Paschal time. A third *Asperges,* copied by the second hand, is in the last of the Vespers' fascicles (13). A fourth setting of the *Asperges* was copied by a later hand in one of the gatherings appended to Gay's fascicles, now at the end of the volume. The piece is ascribed to "Simonis," who may be the Ferrarese composer active in Loreto several decades later, though this is uncertain.

48. Recently, Rob Wegman, in his examination of Obrecht's *Missa Beata viscera,* has expressed mild doubts about the 1481 dating of MS K. I. 2 that I proposed in my earlier study, mentioned above; see his *Born for the Muses: The Life and Masses of Jacob Obrecht* (Oxford, 1994), 100, n. 12. Citing Briquet's classic, useful but limited, work on watermarks, Wegman notes that the paper in the manuscript bears a type of watermark "not documented anywhere in Europe before 1491" and that "in Siena where the choirbook must have been compiled, paper of this type has been found only in the period 1495–1524." (Agostino Ziino, in his article on MS K. I. 2, "Appunti su una nuova fonte di musica polifonica intorno al 1500," *Nuova rivista musicale italiana* 10 (1976): 437–41, first reported the dates of these watermarks.) Since I was unable to take tracings from the manuscript when I studied it, given the poor state of its binding and many of its pages, I am unable to respond to Wegman's reservations directly, except to note that as I pointed out in my essay, the opening pieces of the two main parts and their contents correspond to the descriptions of the two volumes copied by Gay at Aringhieri's command in 1481. Wegman also notes that the script and spelling variations of the main scribe appear to be Italian and contrasts this with the knowledge that Gay was a Frenchman. While Wegman's reservations may be valid, there is no reason to doubt that a Frenchman or any non–Italian, especially one working in Italy, could have learned then-current forms of calligraphy. And if the contents of the Siena manuscript were copied from a Milanese or other Italian source, as I propose, the Italian cast of the spelling variations could clearly have come from that source. I should also express my misgivings about being too dependent on Briquet's tracings, which, as is well known, only approximate the originals and do not take into account chain lines, twin watermarks, and other refinements of the modern bibliographer's accomplishments. (For these latter, see H. Colin Slim, ed., *A Gift of Madrigals and Motets* [Chicago and London, 1972], 1:20–22; Alan Tyson, "The Problem of Beethoven's 'First' *Leonore* Overture," *JAMS* 28 [1975]: 309, 332–34, and his "The Mozart Fragments," *JAMS* 34 [1981]: 480–81.) Perhaps, assigning a 1481 dating to the pieces copied by Gay may be problematic, but I believe the arguments against doing so are not strong enough to stand up against available documentary evidence as it relates to the contents of the manuscript.

Sforza chapel. Two Masses are, in fact, preserved in volumes compiled for Franchino Gaffurio and the Milanese duomo about a decade after the Sienese source, though these are probably from even earlier copies now lost.[49] The high quality of the works—each of them representing the latest trends in composition, wherein composers such as Isaac and Obrecht, probably following Martini's lead, borrowed from two or more voices of a preexistent polyphonic model—perhaps reflects Aringhieri's quest for the best and the newest.[50] It also provides a clue to the kind of performing forces he hoped to assemble, singers who would be able to negotiate with ease and artistry the complexities of the most modern music to be had on the peninsula.

Following Gay's Mass fascicles is another with fragments of two other advanced works of the time, an incomplete Gloria from Compère's *Missa brevis sine nomine* (fols. 185^v–186^v) and the second half of the Credo of Martini's *Missa Orsus, orsus* (fols. 187^r– 188). Both were copied by a second scribe, who not only filled in some of the folios left blank by Gay but also copied the major part of three other fascicles.[51] All but one of the works he entered, like all of those copied by Gay, are unascribed. It has proven difficult to identity the second copyist, who seems to have worked hard on Gay's heels, but he was probably another Franco-Fleming employed by Aringhieri a few years later. The most likely candidate is the composer Peter Bordon (Pierre Bourdon), to whom payments were issued at Aringhieri's command in August 1484, "for part of the composition and copying" of figural music, and six weeks later, "for the composition of motets, Credos and other figural songs for the church" (see Table 5.1). None of Bordon's

---

49. D'Accone, "A Late 15th-Century Sienese Sacred Repertory," 145–46, 163–66. An as yet unidentified Mass, also for four voices, based on Hayne van Ghizeghem's *De tous biens playne,* completes this group of Mass fascicles copied by Gay (fols. 168^v–181). Added in the midst of eight blank folios at the end of the last fascicle by a second hand is Loyset Compère's four-voice motet *O genitrix gloriosa,* and its *secunda pars, Ave Virgo gloriosa* (fols. 182^v–184). Three other gatherings, added at the end of the volume, contain fragmentary sections of Masses, all anonymous and without title. These are movements from Philippe Basiron's *Missa de Franza* (fols. 208^r–209), the first part of the Gloria of Josquin's *Missa L'ami baudichon* (fols. 212^v–214), Martini's *Missa Dio te salvi* (fols. 214^v–221^v), and at the very end, in a mutilated gathering of music copied perhaps earlier than Gay's Masses, portions of Du Fay's *Missa Se la face ay pale* (fols. 222^r, 223^{r-v}), one of his masterpieces and certainly among the most important works of the second half of the fifteenth century. With regard to the question of why the Sienese volume preserves earlier readings of Masses performed by the Milanese court singers in the 1470s than currently known Milanese manuscripts such as the Gaffurio codices (copied from the 1490s onwards), the obvious answer must be that earlier Milanese sources have disappeared. The existence of such sources is verifed by a letter, dated 30 November 1477, to Lorenzo the Magnificent from Lodovico Sforza, Galeazzo's de facto successor, which accompanied Lodovico's gift of copies of "alcune messe in canto figurato" requested by Lorenzo, no longer existing. (The letter is transcribed in D'Accone, "Lorenzo il Magnifico e la musica," 239.)

50. On Martini's seminal role in the development of the imitation Mass of the late fifteenth century and his links to composers who also drew on the cantus firmus and one or more voices of a polyphonic model, see J. Peter Burkholder, "Johannes Martini and the Imitation Mass of the Late Fifteenth Century," *JAMS* 38 (1985): 470–523, and the more recent study by Murray Steib, "Imitation and Elaboration: The Use of Borrowed Material in Masses from the Late Fifteenth and Early Sixteenth Centuries" (Ph.D. diss., University of Chicago, 1992).

51. D'Accone, "A Late 15th-Century Sienese Sacred Repertory," 135–36.

own compositions is found under his name in the surviving portions of the volume, and if the Mass fragments put in by the second scribe—which include a single Credo by Martini—were not copied by him, then no trace at all remains of his efforts. Although Sienese records are quite clear about Bordon's status—he was paid for composing and copying, not for performing—shortly before his arrival there he was employed as a singer at Treviso cathedral, where some of his sacred music was preserved until the Second World War.[52]

The motets copied by Gay and the second scribe now occupy three fascicles between the opening Vespers materials and the Masses. They are also of high quality. Those that have been identified from other sources belong to composers such as Compère, Weerbecke, and Johannes Mouton.[53] The placement of the three gatherings of motets in the rebound volume makes it difficult to ascertain which of the two volumes they may have belonged to, a situation exacerbated by the mutilated state of the first and last of these gatherings.[54] The texts are predominantly Marian, although a few addressing All Saints, Christ, and SS. Peter and John are appropriate for feasts celebrated as duplex ones at the cathedral. The Marian motets, particularly, would have been much used, notably, in place of antiphons at Saturday Vespers, at Monday morning Masses dedicated to the Virgin, at services on the many feast days celebrated in her honor, and on special occasions venerating the miraculous image of the Madonna del Voto.

Vespers music copied by Gay is now found in three fascicles at the beginning of the volume and several others through the twelfth. Interspersed with these are two fascicles and an added thirteenth copied completely by the second scribe, who also filled in some of the pages left blank by Gay. Apart from an *Asperges me* antiphon at the end, psalm settings, hymns, and Magnificats fill the pages here. In various combinations the psalms are appropriate for all Sundays and feasts of Our Lord as well as for a number of

---

52. Giovanni D'Alessi, "Maestri e cantori fiamminghi nella cappella musicale del Duomo di Treviso, 1411–1561," *Tijdschrift der Vereeniging voor Nederlandsche Muziekgeschiedenis* 15 (1939): 147–65, esp. p. 157, and the same author's *La cappella musicale del Duomo di Treviso*, 49. Wegman (*Born for the Muses,* 70–71) has recently brought together biographical information about Bordon that indicates he was born around 1450, that he was a priest by 1473, and that he was last mentioned in his native Ghent in 1478 before he appeared at Treviso in 1479. Bordon's two known works are song arrangements: one, a three-part setting of *De tous biens playne,* based on Hayne's famous tenor (published by Ottaviano Petrucci in 1501 in *Harmonice Musices Odhecaton A* and in modern edition, as no. 73, 373–74, in Helen Hewitt's edition of Petrucci's volume; also ascribed to Agricola in a Segovia manuscript); the other, ascribed to "Borton" in Rome, Casanatense 2856, features the addition of a fourth part to a three-voice chanson, *Il sera pour vous/L'homme armé,* by Robert Morton or maybe Busnoys (Wegman, 71, n. 7).

53. Compère's *Ave Maria gratia plena* has recently been studied by Bloxam, "'La Contenance Italienne'," 50–66. As she points out, though mutilated, the version of the piece transmitted by MS K. I. 2 intentionally omits the final section, based on the lauda *Beata es Maria,* found in other sources. It concludes instead with the invocation "O Christe audi nos," set here to longer note values than elsewhere, which Bloxam describes as a "different, more effective ending for the Litany portion." Perhaps this was so because Siena's version was meant to be used in processions, which would have also been the case with Mouton's litany-like motet *Sancti Dei omnes,* also in MS K. I. 2.

54. D'Accone, "A Late 15th-Century Sienese Sacred Repertory," 138–39, 161–62. A much later hand added one piece in section 14.

other feasts, including the Purification, Annunciation and Assumption of the Blessed Virgin Mary, St. John the Baptist, SS. Peter and Paul, St. Mary Magdalene, All Saints, the Dedication of the Church of St. Michael the Archangel, and the Common of One Martyr, this latter particularly applicable to Siena's patron Sant'Ansano. All of these feast days, of course, were among the cathedral's principal ones and had been celebrated with polyphony, forces permitting, since Oderigo's time. Some of the more frequently used psalm texts are set to more than one tone in order to ensure their adaptability to the modal requirements of the antiphons that frame them on different feasts.

All of the psalm settings copied by Gay and the second scribe are for four voices and are meant to be performed in alternatim style, the even verses in chant, the odd ones in polyphony.[55] Each psalm begins with its traditional Gregorian intonation, written in black mensural notation rather than the traditional neumes of the chant. Following this and in all subsequent verses, the cantus sings the remainder of the chant, at times presented with little or no decoration, at others paraphrased more fancifully. Apart from an occasional melisma, the text is usually set syllabically and all voices share the rhythms of the cantus. The spirit of mid-century fauxbourdon is omnipresent, for in general the three upper parts move in parallel sixths, the effect, however, being mitigated by the bass. This normally has the root of the chord and serves as the progenitor of harmonic progressions that on the whole are clearly oriented toward the tonic final. Typical of these settings is Ps. 110, *Confitebor tibi Domine,* copied by Gay on fols. 3ᵛ–5ʳ, given here as Ex. 5.1.

The hymns likewise were intended to be performed in alternatim style, though in most cases only the second stanza is provided with a polyphonic setting, the texts of additional stanzas sometimes being added at the bottom of the page. In one instance individual settings of stanzas 2, 4, and 6 of the Advent hymn *Conditor alme siderum* appear in sequence. Every hymn in the manuscript—seventeen copied by Gay, eight by the second scribe—is for four voices except for stanza 4 of the hymn just mentioned, which is for three. This, in addition to its being copied on the same pages as stanza 2, may indicate that the two stanzas were part of a single larger work. Inexplicably, none of the familiar hymns for various feasts of the Virgin Mary is present. Maybe settings of them were in a separate fascicle that was lost when the manuscript was dismembered. There are multiple settings of hymns for the Common of Apostles (2), Common of One Martyr (3), Common of Several Martyrs (2), Sundays of Advent (3 or 4, as noted), Easter (3), and Corpus Christi (2). Additionally, there are settings for all Saturdays and Sundays, Christmas, Ascension, Pentecost, Trinity Sunday, All Saints, Common of Confessors, the Dedication of the Church of St. Michael the Archangel, and St. Mary Magdalene. None of this music has yet been found in other sources.

On the whole, the hymns are much more adventurous harmonically—and less perfunctory in their treatment of the text—than the psalm settings. The traditional melodies, sometimes paraphrased in the cantus, sometimes in the tenor, are set within a freely contrapuntal texture, with bits and pieces of the melody occasionally appearing

---

55. This is true also of psalms in fascicle 5, entered by the second and third copyists.

in the other voices. Typical of them is the setting of stanza 2, *Nobis datus nobis natus,* of the hymn for Corpus Christi, *Pange lingua* (Ex. 5.2). Here, all but one of the six phrases of the well-known melody appear in slightly decorated form in the top part.[56] At the opening the melody of the first phrase is anticipated in the tenor and then in the bass in the same even semibreve motion that will characterize the entrance of the cantus, which they eventually accompany in similar rhythms. The altus all the while fills in with a more animated melody. The second phrase is even more homorhythmic, but the melody of the third is once again anticipated by the tenor before it resumes its accompanimental role. Similar procedures appear throughout remainder of the piece, which concludes with an authentic cadence on the tonic.

The Magnificats are for the most part more ambitious musically than all of the other Vespers music. There are nine settings in the fascicles following those devoted to psalms and hymns, seven entered by Gay, the remainder by the second scribe, who also copied the remaining incomplete parts of a Magnificat entitled *Agricola secundi toni,* the only piece in the original volumes with an ascription. This latter is found complete, though anonymous, in a Cividale manuscript, and two other Magnificats have concordant sources in places as far afield as Rome, Verona, and Warsaw.[57] Like the psalms and the hymns, all these works present polyphonic settings of alternate verses, usually the even-numbered ones, and are for four voices, although the number of parts are diminished for some verses and, on one occasion, increased to five. Five works are in tone 1, three in tone 8, and one each in tone 2 and tone 5. Again, the desire to accommodate the mode of the framing antiphons used on different feasts is apparent.

None of the Magnificats presents its traditional Gregorian intonation beforehand, though the melody of the tone is inevitably present in the setting of every verse and is plainly audible in one or another of the voices. Imitation appears consistently, and often effectively, in many settings, and one verse incorporates a canon. Homophonic textures also emerge occasionally, thus ensuring clearer presentation of the text. Among the most interesting of the Magnificats is one in the first tone, copied by Gay at the end of the series on fols. 78ᵛ–83ʳ. In several of its movements the tone formula is sometimes prominent in longer note values, suggesting cantus-firmus treatment, though more usually the lightly decorated phrases of the Gregorian melody pass imitatively from voice to voice. Standing somewhat apart from the others is the sixth movement, *Fecit potentiam,* where the tone is paraphrased extensively and serves as the basis of a spirited three-voice contrapuntal fantasy. Generally, the harmony moves clearly toward the final of the mode, with the bass taking the lead (Ex. 5.3.). All in all, as demonstrated by the various movements of this anonymous piece, the Magnificats provide excellent examples of the kind of service music that was the mainstay of many a cathedral chapel in the late fifteenth century, and their musical craftsmanship makes them worthy companions of the more musically advanced Masses.

---

56. On folios 47ᵛ–48ʳ. Phrase 5, as it appears in modern chant and in various editions of the sixteenth-century *Cantorinus,* is replaced by another, which I have not yet located in Sienese sources.

57. The first two Magnificats in the Sienese manuscript are mutilated and have missing parts or lack settings of entire verses.

ORGANISTS

As mentioned above, the Servite monk Giovanni held the organist's post through the end of June 1479. The reason for his departure went unstated; possibly he lost favor with his employers, though it is probable that he left of his own volition. His immediate successor was Ser Francesco di Mattia, a chaplain since April 1476, who played the organ in May 1479. Monthly payments of L. 2 in his name appear through mid-December 1480. Meanwhile, Frate Giovanni decided that he wanted to have his old post back. In January 1480 Siena's Cardinal Francesco Todeschini Piccolomini (the future Pius III) wrote to the Opera's board recommending the monk's reappointment, noting that he had also been Frate Giovanni's staunchest supporter in the past (see Doc. 5.4).[58] But the Cardinal's recommendation was not taken to heart and a local musician was appointed instead. This was Francesco di Guido called Petruccio, an organist, organ builder, and repairman, to whom monthly payments of L. 12 were registered for the first time in January 1481. He was the first layman to hold the post in almost a century. To judge from his property holdings and his last will and testament, even though he did not have the usual perquisites enjoyed by cathedral clerics, his professional activities enabled him to earn a very comfortable living.[59] Records are lacking that tell exactly when Francesco took on additional duties as teacher in the cathedral school, but accounts for the fiscal years April 1493 through March 1495 show him serving in both capacities by that time. He must have been in ill health and unable to serve in August of 1500, when his name disappeared from the sacristan's report for that month, as it did in the two months following. A new organist, Maestro Guasparre, named for the first time in November 1500 with a monthly salary of L. 8, held the post through June 1502. His successor, Ser Antonio, mentioned from August 1502 through March 1503, was replaced by Ser Francesco di Tommaso, a student of Francesco Petruccio recorded more than a decade earlier among the boy singers in the chapel. Francesco di Tommaso subsequently served as organist at a monthly salary of L. 8 through May 1508.

---

58. The cardinal's reference to his previous support of the organist Giovanni is verified by an earlier letter he wrote to the Opera's governing board, dated 7 December 1477, published by Borghesi and Banchi, *Nuovi documenti per la storia dell'arte Senese,* no. 152, 249.

59. In a tax report from 1491 he declared that he lived in a house that he owned in the parish of San Salvadore, where many other musicians lived, and that he had an orchard behind his house, a vineyard outside the city walls, and another house in the parish of Sant'Andrea. At the time he had one child, a daughter of marriageable age (ASS, Lira, vol. 224, Terzo di Città, 1491, fol. 111'). The last will and testament of "Franciscus Guidonis alias el Petrucio, musicus de Senis . . . corpore infirmus," dated Siena, 8 January 1504/5, is in ASS, Notarile antecosimiano, 1015, unnumbered folio. In it Francesco names his wife Lucrezia as usufructuary of all of his earthly possessions, which included a house. A codicil to the will, dated 10 January 1504/5, is in ASS, Notarile antecosimiano, 1015, unnumbered folio. This indicates that Francesco's wife was dead by that time, for he now named his daughter Ursina, wife of Ser Mariani Barletti, as his heir. Although Barletti's profession is not mentioned, it is clear that he was a person of some social standing because he was referred to by the title "Ser." This, in turn, indicates that Francesco di Guido also had some social standing. For a record of his work as an organ builder at the church of Santa Maria del Carmine, see chapter 13, note 46.

ASSUMPTION DAY 1484 AND *SENA VETUS*

Assumption Day festivities of 1484 saw a special allocation of eight ducats made for "eight singers of the Florentine Signoria who sang in the duomo on that feast day."[60] This is another of the several surviving records that show Florentine singers participating at Siena's most important feast day. It was a reciprocal situation, for Sienese singers, as noted above, journeyed to Florence for the St. John's Day festivities on several occasions in earlier years. Florentine records make it possible to give an identity to the eight singers mentioned in the 1484 Sienese report: Ser Arnolfo d'Arnolfo, contratenor; Ser Bartolomeo de Castris, contralto; Ser Niccolò di Giovanni, bass; Girolamo d'Antonio; Antonio Gabassoli, bass; Francesco di Martino Migliotti; Cornelio di Lorenzo, soprano; and Guglielmo de Steynsel.[61]

Heading this list was the Franco-Fleming Arnolfo Giliardi, a great favorite of Lorenzo de' Medici and composer of the only known ceremonial motet from the fifteenth century in honor of Siena, the four-part *Sena vetus* (see Fig. 6 and Ex. 5.4).[62] No records relating to the commissioning of the motet have come to light, and the circumstances surrounding its first performance still remain undocumented. Arnolfo, who sang in the Florentine chapel sporadically from 1479 to 1492, had no formal connections with Siena, never having been employed at either the cathedral or the Palazzo Pubblico. Nor is there any record of his having served one of the grand Sienese families. It was, in any event, unnecessary for him to have lived in Siena in order to receive the commission and compose the piece. More important are the reasons for commissioning the piece and the identity of the person responsible. Alberto Aringhieri, by virtue of his Florentine connections and his role as overseer, stands as one of the prime candidates for the honor, although several other prominent Sienese might also be considered, among them two members of the Bichi family, who owned the only known copy of the motet from at least the end of the eighteenth century.

Arnolfo's text apostrophizes the freedom and wealth enjoyed by Siena's citizens, the

---

Isidoro Ugurgieri-Azzolini, *Le pompe senesi o'vero huomini illustri di Siena* (Pistoia, 1649), 2:4, reports that Francesco died on 12 January 1504/5 and that he was buried in the church of the Carmine.

60. "1484 [30 Agosto]. Le spese de la festa di Santa Maria d'aghosto a dì detto lire quarantotto s. 0 chontanti in duchati otto larghi paghati a otto chantori de la Signoria di Fiorenze chantaro[no] in duomo per detta festa" (AOMS, vol. 307, *E&U, 1484–85,* fol. 37 left). The buildup of musical forces was moving into high gear in Florence just around this time and there were other singers besides those mentioned here who did not make the trip to Siena. Thus, if the Florentine visitors performed as a discrete group, rather than joining in with their Sienese colleagues, they may have performed two to a part in four-voice music, since two basses and at least one soprano are mentioned among them.

61. Details about the careers of some of these musicians, who also sang in Milan and Rome, are in D'Accone, "The Singers of San Giovanni," passim. On the identity of Piovano Girolamo d'Antonio, see Atlas, *Music at the Aragonese Court of Naples,* 44.

62. At the bottom of the parchment sheet an inscription in hexameters reveals the composer's name:

Principibus placeant Arnulphi carmina summis
    Ne inter mortalis ultima laus sit ei
(May the songs of Arnulphus please the highest leaders

charm of its women, the beauty of the town, and the fecundity of its surrounding countryside:[63]

> Sena vetus que diceris urbs o virginis alme
> Italiae cuncte, lux honor atque decus:
> Muneris immensi tibi est et innata libertas,
> Et tibi perpetua est et diuturna quies
> Virtutum studio polles, te gloria fama
> Illustrant, populos ingenio superas.
> Copia magna tibi cereris magnaque liei
> Nec tibi deficiunt splendor et eris opes.
> Quid taceam pulcras mundo toto mulieres?
> Aereas turris, quis numerare queat?
> Vive diu felix cedant tibi cuncta secunda!
> Sis felix semper, urbs veneranda, precor
>   o virginis alme.

> Ancient Siena, called city of the life-giving Virgin
> Light, honor and lustre of all Italy:
> Yours is the precious gift of innate liberty,
> And yours is continuing and unceasing peace.
> You excel by your zeal for virtue; glory and renown
> Make you illustrious; you are above all others in intelligence.
> You have great abundance of grain and wine,
> Nor do you lack splendor and a plenitude of riches.
> How shall I be silent about your beautiful women, famous throughout the world?
> Who can count the number of your airy towers?
> Live a long, happy life, and may all things be favorable for you!
> I pray that you be happy, venerable city of the life-giving Virgin.

The expansive structure of the music, though neither based on an isorhythmic plan nor
on a previously composed melody, recalls the ceremonial motets of an age already past,
particularly those composed by Du Fay during the 1430s and 1440s. The six distichs of
the text are evenly divided between two large *partes,* or sections. Arnolfo unified the
structure and gave it cohesiveness and balance by setting up a network of cadences at
key points that emphasize the tonic F mode of the piece. Diversity within the larger
framework is achieved by well-prepared excursions to the dominant C, by a few cadences to closely related tones, and by a few deceptive cadences. Principal points of
articulation usually occur at the end of each distich as well as at the end of each line.
At times they even occur in the middle of a line, as at measure 10, just before the
setting of the words "o virginis alme," and at the close, where the same words are set
to a series of block chords, serving as a coda to the entire piece. In general, the texture

---

so that his shall not be the last praise amongst mortals.)

This recalls a line in Horace's Epistles 1. 17. 35: "Principibus placuisse viris non ultima laus est."

63. The music was first published by Sebastiano A. Luciani, *La musica in Siena* (Siena, 1942),
38–41.

FIGURE 6. A motet in honor of Siena: *Sena vetus* by Arnolfo Giliardi, ca. 1483–84, parchment. Siena, Archivio di Stato. Reproduced by permission of the Ministero per i Beni Culturali e Ambientali. Further reproduction prohibited

is freely contrapuntal, with only occasional imitation, such as occurs at the beginning of the second section. The music's solemn utterances and its resonances of a bygone era point to its having been conceived in response to the expectations of a society steeped in the traditions of high culture and in the belief of its own myths, exemplified, of course, by the text, which unequivocally establishes its function as a *Staatsmotette*.[64]

There were numerous occasions when *Sena vetus* might have received its first performance, though none can be definitively linked to the piece. They include several Assumption Day festivals that were celebrated with more than the usual entertainments and a few grand political ceremonies, such as the one that crowned the momentous reconciliation of Siena's fractious parties on 24 August 1483. As the celebrated painting on the cover of the Biccherna volume shows, the keys to city were offered at the altar of the Madonna delle Grazie, with the singers in attendance (see Pl. 1). But there were other equally compelling moments, such as the visit of the Florentine singers, Arnolfo among them, on Assumption Day in 1484. If *Sena vetus* was commissioned from him some time earlier, in anticipation of his arrival in Siena with the group, there would have been no better occasion than an Assumption Day celebration for a first performance of his piece.

PLAGUE AND POLITICS

The chapel was once again plunged into a crisis at the end of June 1485, when, for unexplained reasons, four of the five adult singers left. Perhaps revenues were low, necessitating a cutback, or maybe Piero de la Piazza was lured away to another position, his departure precipitating that of the others. Whatever the reasons, by July only Chimenti de' Servi of the original group of adults remained, at his usual monthly salary of L. 7. 10. Lonardo di Cristofano, a clerk, earned the rather high salary of L. 10 per month, a clear indication that he had assumed an important role in the chapel. Subsequently described as a tenorista, he probably took the part previously sung by Piero. Jacomo di Salvadore, another higher-paid youth at L. 3 per month, may also have been singing one of the lower parts. These three singers and a group of choristers, whose numbers fluctuated between five and eight, performed from July 1485 through March 1486. Sano di Goro, who was later to become master of the chapel, joined the choristers in October 1485.

External events undoubtedly contributed to the failure to reinforce the chapel in any significant way after this time. The plague struck in June 1486 and continued throughout the summer months. Many people perished, rich and poor alike. One chronicler reports that those who were able left town and the city was practically deserted.[65] As a result, the traditional Palio was suspended and instead there were fireworks in the Campo and a service at the cathedral, where an offering was made to the Virgin

---

64. The classic work on such music is Albert Dunning's *Die Staatsmotette 1480–1555* (Utrecht, 1970).

65. Giovanni Antonio Pecci, *Memorie storico-critiche della città di Siena fino agli anni MDLIX* (Siena, 1755–60), 1:37, for the quotation from Allegretti's diary, which notes that the plague began in June 1486 and that many people left the city for their villas in the countryside. As a consequence, special provision had to be made to bring in troops from the countryside to patrol the city.

together with a supplication begging her intercession with the Lord for deliverance "from the pest, from war, from our insidious enemies and from every harm."[66] The plague was still raging on 15 August, when word came of the peace treaty signed at Rome by representatives of Florence, the duke of Milan, the king of Naples, and the pope. Despite the welcome news, unsettled conditions continued, and less than a year later the government changed again, when the Petrucci forces gained the upper hand. Apparently, the times were too unsettled for appointing new foreign singers. Thus, the general reduction in chapel forces, noted at the end of June 1485, prevailed for several years, with only a few minor changes in personnel. These included the reappointment of Ser Agnolo di Piero in April 1486, two months before the departure of Fra Chimenti, and the temporary appointment of the contrabass Simone Francioso, who served during the month of August 1489. Otherwise, Agnolo and Lonardo di Cristofano, also called "Ser" after March 1487, and the choristers are registered for the rest of 1486, 1487, 1488, 1489, and through December 1490. During these years the number of choristers, some of them occasionally referred to as cantorino, again fluctuated from as many as nine to as few as five.

In the following decade external circumstances must again have played a large part in the decision not to augment the chapel's forces. These years witnessed the inauguration of yet another period of political upheaval and financial instability. In 1494, Charles VIII of France, at the head of an army such as had never before been seen on the peninsula, invaded northern Italy on his way to claim a dubious Neapolitan inheritance. Political unrest and changes of government inevitably followed the French monarch's unimpeded march south. Piero de' Medici's ignominious surrender of Florentine fortresses led to the downfall of the Medici party and a temporary French presence in Florence. Next, it was Siena's turn. Charles entered the city on 2 December 1494, and after extracting gifts and loans from a fearful government, he resumed his march to Naples. Upon the successful completion of his campaign in the south, Charles returned to Siena, where he once again received a royal welcome.

During his second Sienese sojourn, as will be recounted more fully below, the king attended a ball at the Palazzo Pubblico and heard Mass at the cathedral on the morning of 17 June. The French royal chapel, which accompanied him on his Italian campaign, may have performed on that occasion, though surviving records do not mention gratuities given to French singers. Charles's departure from Italy was followed by several years of political uncertainty, from which Siena was generally spared, even though the government was ever fearful of its tenure. Clearly, in such troubled times little thought, let alone money, could be directed toward improving or upgrading the musical chapel. The chapel made do with what it had had for the past several years. Bad as this situation was, it was better than that in neighboring Florence, where, as a result of Savonarola's insistent preaching, the chapel was suspended and not reinstated at the cathedral until 1510.

Although records for the 1490s are incomplete, those surviving indicate that the

---

66. Giovanni Cecchini, "Palio e contrade nella loro evoluzione storica," in Alessandro Falassi, Giuliano Catoni, Giovanni Cecchini, and Pepi Merisio, *Palio* (Milan, 1982), 325, quoting from ASS, Balìa, vol. 34, fol. 97^r, dated 11 August 1486.

Sienese chapel continued with a reduced number of adults into the turn of the new century. The number of choristers was at eight in February 1491, when Ser Lonardo was replaced by another tenor, Fra Lorenzo. The latter and Ser Agnolo also appear in a sacristan's roll from the following month. Sacristans' rolls from February and March 1492 name five boys, in addition to Agnolo and Lorenzo. Called a tenor in many documents, Lorenzo remained with the group through 17 September 1492, when he received L. 9. 15 "for the rest of his service and as a gratuity when he left, as ordered by our overseer Messer Alberto." Evidently, Lorenzo had been brought in to substitute for Lonardo, whose name reappears in the accounts at the beginning of the same month. Ser Lonardo di Cristofano, Ser Agnolo di Pietro, and the boys are mentioned in a few lists through March 1495 and then again in the next surviving ones from the latter part of 1500, when the newly ordained Ser Sano di Goro was earning L. 6 per month.[67]

The opening years of the new century witnessed only a few changes in the chapel's makeup. The three adults, Lonardo, Agnolo di Pietro, and Sano, and eight choristers appear under the heading *cantori* in sacristans' rolls for January and February 1501 and again in March 1502. Lorenzo di Giovanni, another chorister cited among the chapel singers from as early as August 1500, is also called "Ser" during the period May through August 1503, after which he disappears. Evidence thus continues to point to the presence among the boy singers of several older youths, who may have performed parts other than soprano. Ser Sano di Goro left after June 1504, not to return until December 1505. Messer Maddalo di Lorenzo d'Arezzo, identified in later records also as the *maestro de la scuola del canto,* became a chapel singer in September 1503. He apparently replaced the previous incumbent, the deceased organist Ser Francesco. Maddalo's work was so highly regarded that a special payment of L. 24 was later "given to him at the command of our Messer Alberto on account of his excellent service and worthiness." Maddalo sang with Lonardo, Agnolo, Sano, and the boys through February 1507. He was in Florence by the following August, employed as an alto in the cathedral chapel.[68] It was probably a group of singers such as this that inspired the painter Giovanni Antonio Bazzi, "Il Sodoma," in one of a series of frescoes he executed between 1505 and 1508 for the nearby abbey of Monte Oliveto Maggiore.[69] In the fresco nine singers, four of the five in front adults, the other a youngster, behind whom are standing four others whose age cannot be determined, are performing from a book of polyphony placed on a lectern (see Pl. 3). In Siena, where the painter spent several years before he began his work at Monte Oliveto Maggiore, Sodoma could have witnessed this kind of performance only at the cathedral.

THE END OF AN ERA

With Maddalo's departure the chapter in the history of the Sienese chapel inaugurated by Alberto Aringhieri came to an end; within a few months Aringhieri himself was

---

67. Sacristans' rolls for January and February 1493 name five boys; in 1500 three choristers are listed from August to October, four in November, and seven in December.

68. D'Accone, "The Musical Chapels at the Florentine Cathedral and Baptistry," 9.

69. For the frescoes by Il Sodoma see Andrée Hayum, *Giovanni Antonio Bazzi— "Il Sodoma"* (New York, 1976). The scene has also been reproduced on the cover of *Early Music,* 15/4 (1987).

forced out of office and fled to Rome.[70] The commemorative plaque placed at the entrance of the chapel where Aringhieri was interred reports that he served as cathedral overseer for twenty-four years, information corroborated by rubrics in account books from 1505, which name Pandolfo Petrucci and two of his lieutenants as Aringhieri's successors. That Aringhieri succeeded in maintaining his position for so many years testifies both to his own talents and to Petrucci's astuteness. Although Aringhieri had had to accommodate himself to the wishes of the new government, when it came to the cathedral's various decorative and musical programs, he was clearly in command. He also knew how to temper his ambitious plans when forced by circumstances. He had attempted to increase the chapel's role, and for a while he succeeded in building a musical edifice at Siena cathedral that none of his illustrious predecessors had ever envisioned. But no sooner had he put his plan into action and begun to obtain results than he was forced to retreat.

There were a number of factors that contributed to Aringhieri's failure to realize his ambitious program. Politics, of course, were among them, but not overwhelmingly so. When Aringhieri assumed office in 1480, political stability had returned not only to the city but also to the peninsula as a result of Lorenzo the Magnificent's reconciliation with King Ferrante of Naples and the pope at Rome. Siena, at first prey to the duke of Calabria's political ambitions, was spared another crisis when the duke was called south to defend Neapolitan lands from Turkish incursions. All of Italy now entered into the new musical renaissance, as princes, merchants, popes, and overseers vied with one other in securing the services of outstanding singers. Siena, thanks to Savino Savini and then to Alberto Aringhieri, did not remain outside the ring. Aringhieri went several steps beyond those taken by his predecessor, however. At first, his attempts were successful, but then, apparently hampered by the plague and the uncertainty that followed in the wake of the Petruccian coup d'état, he was forced to temper his ambitious scheme. And even though internal politics were eventually stabilized after Petrucci consolidated his control of the government, the overseer made no move to resume his original program. Between the coup and the French invasion of Italy in 1494 there were a dozen years in which the chapel could have maintained the expanded role that Aringhieri had envisioned for it, when it could have followed lines of development that occurred in Florence—where the new music was enjoyed in three major churches practically to the eve of the French invasion. Politics assuredly played a major role in the demise of the Florentine chapel, and while they may also have influenced the future of the Sienese group, in the end they had only a minor impact.

Instead, two other problems were at the root of the Aringhieri's inability to sustain an expanded musical program at Siena cathedral, the one financial, the other best described as social. Sienese officials apparently made no great efforts to procure the benefices and similar ecclesiastical blandishments that attracted northern singers to the papal chapel in Rome. Others in the service of the courts could seek preferments through a prince's intervention, as so many did. Suffice it to recall the efforts of the duke of Milan and the duke of Ferrara to secure benefices for favored musicians, or Lorenzo

---

70. Aronow, "A Documentary History of the Pavement Decoration," 353, quoting Sigismondo Tizio, who reports that Aringhieri left Siena on 30 June 1506.

the Magnificent's intervention in obtaining a prebend in Verdun for a singer he wished
to retain in the Florentine chapel. Options such as these were not open to the Sienese
overseer. As a private citizen without any particular political base and lacking a fortune
of his own, Aringhieri was hardly in a position to seek preferential treatment for favored
musicians as could a Sforza, an Este, or a Medici. It is possible, of course, that he
attempted to do so or that he enlisted the aid of an influential person such as Pandolfo
Petrucci or Cardinal Francesco Piccolomini Todeschini in efforts that were ultimately
fruitless. But records regarding any such actions are nowhere to be found in Sienese archives.

As far as prebends and benefices from the cathedral itself were concerned, here, too,
the overseer was restricted because of the limitations placed on such preferments by
civic, social, and political traditions. The cathedral's canonries were reserved for members of Siena's most powerful families, their friends, and their clients. Similarly, there
were no endowments specifically committed to singers. Chaplaincies funded by the
sacristy, though they might be used to supplement musicians' salaries, were nevertheless
designed for very specific purposes and had always to be held by resident chaplains. As
for income that might be derived from perpetual chaplaincies within the cathedral or
from other churches in Siena or its dominions, there were only a few instances during
the later fifteenth century when musicians were so favored, notably the organist Ser
Francesco di Nanni, who officiated at the altar of San Crescenzio, and Ser Biagio di
Tomè, who officiated at the altar of St. Catherine. Ecclesiastical preferments for musicians, in short, were rarely if ever used in Siena as a means of recruitment and retention.

The amount of money from cathedral revenues available for musical performances
was the most important factor in the chapel's ever-changing fortunes. Clearly, funds
were more readily available for building and decoration programs than for musical performance. The former, by tradition and as a mattter of civic and social expediency, had
top priority. Apparently, income had increased when Aringhieri launched the chapel's
expansion, and it may be that he also momentarily diverted funds from other projects
to music.[71] As overseer, he could set musicians' salaries as he saw fit. But when the
Opera's funds were insufficient, there were no other means at his disposal with which
to reward favored musicians. He had no power, as did a prince, to grant tax exemptions
or to assign mining rights or income from state-owned—or, in this case, cathedral-
owned—properties. Singers could thus expect very few fringe benefits unless, if they
were clerics, they also accepted appointments as chaplains or agreed to sing Masses and
to participate in the plainchant choir.

Nevertheless, Siena cathedral's salaries appear to have been on a par with those

---

71. The overseer, says Aronow, "had access to extensive funds drawn from a number of sources,
e. g., rents on lands and buildings the Opera owned and also donations made through wills and
testaments or through collection boxes on the altars in the church" (ibid., 17). She also notes (p. 210)
that in the early 1480s the Cathedral's ambitious building program was facilitated by "the extensive
financial resources of the Opera" and remarks that "the Opera was absorbing huge sums of money
around this time, prompting the Commune itself to borrow from it." In support of her remarks she
cites a document showing a forced loan of 500 ducati larghi made by the Opera to the Commune on
12 October 1481, for which the Commune in exchange donated 60 lire to the Opera.

offered singers in Florence, although such evaluations are risky and subject to a host of factors such as the value of coin in which the singers were paid. Suffice it to note here that when the Florentine singers visited Siena in 1484 they each received a ducato largo, calculated in the account as being worth L. 6. In 1489 Simone Francioso earned a fiorino d'oro largo, calculated as L. 6. 4. Piero de Platea's monthly salary of L. 24. 11. 8 is reported as 6 ducats in one account. Sienese and Florentine exchange rates were essentially compatible in this period, thus affording some basis for comparison, but precious little information describes differing cost-of-living expenses in the two cities. And even such information would only be of limited value in assessing the economic advantages enjoyed by itinerant singers, often without family and in totally different kinds of situations than ordinary citizens or long-time residents. Many musicians, for example, enjoyed perquisites—often unrecorded—such as room and board and gratuities received for performances at private entertainments. Florentine cathedral singers were officially paid one or two florins per month, and those who sang at the Baptistry, whose accounts are lost, may have earned similar amounts there. Some of the Florentine singers were also employed at the convent church of the Santissima Annunziata, where one florin per month was the usual salary. A few singers were given room, board, and, occasionally, clothing by the convent, in addition to or in lieu of salary. Earlier Sienese records indicate that some musicians were provided with living quarters by the overseer and it may be that Aringhieri did the same for many, if not all, of those he hired. It is possible that he also made arrangements with local convents on behalf of some singers who received room and board in return for certain services such as singing or teaching, though records on this count are lacking.

Well-known singers or composers, as might be expected, earned above the norm. Instructive in this respect is the salary paid to Messer Piero de Platea. His monthly stipend of six ducats, though somewhat lower than the eight florins per month Heinrich Isaac was said to have earned in Florence, was still high by Sienese standards.[72] Aringhieri, as noted, made occasional gifts of clothing to Piero and may also have provided him with lodging. Both Piero and Isaac, of course, must have received additional funds from individual patrons, as Isaac assuredly did when he served the Medici privately.[73]

Determining the relative values of salaries among cities is a notoriously difficult matter, however, and the following remarks must be considered preliminary, given our imprecise knowledge of exactly the kind of coin paid to some singers. But even

---

72. Niccolò Pitti claimed, in a letter he wrote in 1514, that during Lorenzo the Magnificent's time, some twenty years earlier, Isaac earned 5 ducats a month from the Baptistry, 2 from the cathedral, and 1 from the Santissima Annunziata. It is impossible to verify Baptistry salaries because records are lost, but the figures for the cathedral and the Annunziata, where Isaac began working much later, are correct. Isaac was a composer, however, and he was also the Medici's favorite musician, so it would be hazardous to posit the same amount of salary at the Baptistry for other singers. For Isaac's salary see D'Accone, "Heinrich Isaac in Florence: New and Unpublished Documents," *Musical Quarterly* 49 (1963): 473–74.

73. Isaac was one of three Florentine chapel singers, apparently employed privately by the Medici, who accompanied Piero de' Medici on an official visit to Rome in 1493; see D'Accone, "Some Neglected Composers in the Florentine Chapels, ca. 1475–1525," *Viator* 1 (1970): 273. The other singers were Colinet de Lannoy and Pietrequin Bonnel, the last also employed at Siena cathedral.

allowing for this and apart from ecclesiastical benefices and other intangibles such as unofficial wages and tips, salaries in Siena and to some extent in Florence during the 1480s and early 1490s were lower than those offered earlier in major centers such as Naples, Milan, and Ferrara and contemporaneously in Rome. The Milanese group was extravagantly paid, with annual expenditures reaching almost 4,000 ducats (L. 12,127) paid out to singers in 1473, during the reign of Galeazzo Maria Sforza.[74] More specifically, a court record from 1474 shows that the monthly salaries of the twenty-one chapel singers ranged from a low of 5 and 6 ducats to a high of 14, with others earning 8, 10, and 12, whereas the thirteen chamber singers averaged 10 ducats per month, with a few earning a high between 12 and 15, and one a low of 8.[75] A few decades earlier salaries were somewhat less lavish in Naples, though by no means low. In the 1450s singers in the Neapolitan court chapel perhaps averaged 45.5 ducats per annum, or just under 4 ducats per month, though in 1455 one star singer, Cornago, was earning 300 ducats annually and in 1471 another singer earned 10 ducats per month.[76] Allan Atlas has calculated that the Florentine chapel, which was about half the size of the Neapolitan court chapel, cost about a quarter of the amount spent on the southern group.[77]

From the mid-1450s onwards papal singers, with eight cameral florins a month, perquisites of clothing, horses, and transportation expenses as well as the possibilities of benefices, were also among the elect.[78] On the other hand, Ferrarese salaries, after an initial high point, came down considerably over the course of fifteen years, though Ferrarese incomes were generally augmented by benefices. In 1476 monthly salaries in Ferrara ranged from a low of between LM 8 and 9 paid to young sopranos to LM 24. 19. 6 for the highest paid singers, with others in between earning from LM 13. 17. 6 to LM 19. 8. 6.[79] Benefices and other perquisites, including expenses for housing,

---

74. Milanese expenditures are summarized by Prizer, "Music at the Court of the Sforza," 146–47.

75. Barblan, "Vita musicale alla corte Sforzesca," 826. Josquin des Prez, at the beginning of his Italian career, was on the low end of the scale with 5 ducats monthly, though one chapel singer, "uno secreto," earned only 2 ducats.

76. Atlas, *Music at the Aragonese Court*, 62ff., 67. On p. 68, n. 50, he also notes that the 1:1 relationship between florin and ducat at Milan also held for Florence.

77. Ibid., 68.

78. Starr, "Music and Music Patronage at the Papal Court," 88, reports that Pope Nicholas V raised singers' salaries from 5 to 8 florins and that papal singers' earnings remained stable at 8 cameral florins throughout the fifteenth century, and well into the sixteenth. On p. 92 she has taken the salaries paid singers in various European chapels and converted them into a single currency, "the one in which Papal singers were paid," and points out that the ducat was exactly equivalent to the cameral florin (p. 94, n. 62). She notes, with regard to Italian institutions, that the 5–14 ducats paid Milanese singers in the 1470s equaled the 5–14 florins paid papal singers. Similarly, the 3–4 ducats paid Neapolitan singers equaled the 3–4 florins paid papal singers. On the other hand, the 7–25 LM paid Ferrarese singers in 1476 equaled 2. 19–7. 5 florins paid papal singers. (Citing no figures or dates, she calculates Florentine salaries as coming in as under 2 cameral florins.) On pp. 92–93 she says that, in view of perquisites, "many of the necessities of life were actually provided" for papal musicians.

79. Lockwood, *Music in Renaissance Ferrara*, 181–82. On p. 176 he shows that in 1479 one singer, Victor Tarquin of Bruges, whom Duke Ercole was particularly anxious to engage, was offered a monthly salary of 10 ducats (= 32 LM, or LM 384 annually), in addition to benefices that reached 50 ducats per annum (= 160 LM), a travel supplement of 2 ducats per month (= 5. 4. 0 LM) and

horses, and clothing, could add considerably to these figures. Lewis Lockwood, quoting findings made by Werner Gundersheimer, shows that in Ferrara in the 1470s by scrambling a man could just about get by on 2 LM per month, while 25 LM sufficed to keep a gentleman in style.[80] Salaries were considerably lower in Ferrara during the period 1488–91, when nine singers earned LM 72 annually, double the amount paid five singer-chaplains.[81] It is difficult to assess the later Ferrarese salaries in terms of the buying power of Siena's. But they have several points in common. Sienese chaplains were also consistently paid lower wages than itinerant singers. Ferrarese singers of all stripes, furthermore, consistently received lower salaries than instrumental musicians at the court, which was true also of Siena, as will be noted below in chapter 11.

Social factors must also be taken into account when considering the recruitment and retention of musicians. Apart from well-known singers, not one of the major Franco-Flemish composers in Italy during the last quarter of the fifteenth century—Martini, Compère, Josquin, Isaac, Obrecht, Agricola, Ghiselin—ever took up residence in Siena. In the absence of a princely court, or even of a less formal—though no less lucrative—situation as might be found with the Medici in Florence, there were few, if any, grand families in Siena, including the town's new ruler Petrucci, who fostered the kind of musical, intellectual, and social ambience found in the courts and palaces of Italy's major cities. Though Aringhieri personally may have had the intellectual and artistic sensibilites to create such an ambience, he lacked the political and financial power to do so. Some of the prime conditions needed to attract and retain creative musicians of the highest caliber were thus lacking and in this sense Aringhieri's predicament is emblematic of the situation in Siena. Siena, it is true, had its university and produced its own share of humanists, particularly in the last half of the fifteenth century, when scholars, philosophers, and historians emerged from its patrician ranks. Its painters, sculptors, and architects, inheritors of an artistic and intellectual tradition that went back to Duccio, continued on an independent and highly rewarding course throughout the fifteenth century. But the intellectual ferment, the social interplay, and the deliberately nurtured creativity that were to be found in an Aragonese, a Sforza, or a Medici palace and even the cosmopolitan aspirations characterizing the attitudes of some of the smaller courts seem to have been lacking in Siena. When coupled with the lack of financial rewards and preferments that could be had in papal Rome, ducal Milan, ducal Ferrara, or even Medicean Florence, the absence of this kind of milieu ultimately proved to be an equally serious drawback.

As remarked earlier, Siena was an ideal stopping-off place for most singers who traveled the international circuit (see Table 5.3 for a list of foreign singers during this

---

other perquisites, totaling 652. 8. 0 LM per annum. Later, Ercole improved the terms offered so that the yearly salary was 888 LM. Apparently, Tarquin did not accept the offer. Although he may have been offered more than singers were receiving in 1476, the figure is still astronomical when compared with what Siena was able to offer. "LM" refers to the lira marchegiana.

80. Lockwood, 182, quoting Werner Gundersheimer, *Ferrara*, 295. Starr also cites Lockwood's remarks regarding Ferrara in the 1470s and concludes that papal singers' salaries provided considerable comfort ("Music and Music Patronage at the Papal Court," 94).

81. Lockwood, *Music in Renaissance Ferrara*, 183–84.

TABLE 5.3.   Foreign singers at Siena cathedral, 1480–1507

Name	Place of origin	Period of service
Gottifredi di Liegi[a]	Liège	December 1480–February 1481
Ser Giovanni Cristofani Francioso	France	February–May 1481
Ugo di Gidio Francioso	France	April–July 1481; December 1481–July 1482; one month in 1483
Roberto Leuder Piccardo	Picardy	April–July 1481
Pietricchino (Pietro) di Ghino, soprano[b]		May–August 1481
Messer Alfonso Ferrandi di Castiglia, *tenorista*[c]	Spain	July 1481–mid-March 1482
Giovanni di Giovanni (Pintelli), soprano	Avignon	September–December 1481; May 1482–January 1483; October 1483–August 1484
Jacomo Francioso	France	September–November 1481
Ruberto (Robinetto)	France	October 1481–10 January 1482
Piero de la Piazza (de Platea)	?	May 1482–June 1485
Bartolomeo de Castris	?	May–September 1482; one month in 1483
Chimenti de' Servi	Germany	May, November 1482–May 1486
Giovanni Comitis[d]	Picardy	June–August 1482
Giovanni Vichin (Quintin)	?	September 1482–March 1483
Fra Andrea de' Servi Francioso[e]	France	November 1482
Simone Francioso, contrabass	France	August 1489

[a]See Table 4.2 for his previous service
[b]Pietrequin Bonnel
[c]Possibly the tenor and organist at St. Peter's, November 1478–February 1479
[d]Also in Florence, February 1482, and at St. Peter's (Johannes Piccardo)
[e]Also in Florence at the Santissima Annunziata

period). It was a pleasant town with a university, a cathedral, a number of large convent churches, and with more than its share of a wealthy upper class that maintained a high standard of living. Siena was no longer a leading economic power on the peninsula, but the town still retained some portion of its former wealth and its citizens still profited from the fecundity and productivity of its countryside. The general air of prosperity was enhanced by its perfect geographical position and its salubrious air. But none of these factors was enough to attract the leading composers of the day, especially when official salaries were not as high as elsewhere. There was no focal point, no court or palace—it bears repeating—that provided the financial rewards and promise of future benefits as well as the aesthetic stimulus and intellectual ambience that creative artists found so irresistible. A chronic inability to retain singers of international fame for any length of time exacerbated the situation. In short, the city lacked all of the other re-sources needed to make a success of Aringhieri's initial program to expand musical forces. Aringhieri's failure, indeed, showed that Siena could never be successful when forced to rely upon singers from outside its own walls and especially upon singers who made acquisition of benefices or supplemental income from private patrons a prerequi-site for remaining in the city (see Table 5.4 for a chronological list of musicians during this period). Several decades would pass before the chapel once again regained the forces he assembled and then many more before his ambitious program for a chapel equal to those in other major Italian cities would finally be fulfilled. But, as the inventories from more than half a century after his death reveal, the music in the volumes that "Messer Alberto had caused to be made" continued to be performed, even as the seeds of new developments were being sown.

DOCUMENTS

Doc. 5.1. Cathedral payments to trumpeters

The trumpeters normally performed at the cathedral on the principal feast days and at processions on feasts of the Virgin. Their duties are documented in three representative records for the years 1479, 1480, and 1482:

20 November 1479: A le spese della festa d'aghosto passato a dì detto lire nove s. diciasette d. quattro a otto trombetti de' nostri magnifici signori per tutte le feste dell'anno per detto di misser Savino, a lib. 3 rose c. 307. L. 9 s, 17 d. 4 (AOMS, vol. 301, *E&U, 1479–80,* fol. 39^r)

1480: La festa di Santa Maria d'aghosto a dì VII detto lire undici s.—a' tronbetti di Palazo chontanti a Giovanni Martini tronbeto per aver sonato tutte le feste de l'ano et in duomo tuti e tronbetti di palazo e son a libro di 3 rose f. 251. L. XI (vol. 303, *E&U, 1480–81,* fol. 31^v)

1482: La spesa de la festa di Santa Maria di mezo aghosto di questo anno 1482 de' dare in fino adì XX di settenbre L. undici e S.—contanti a tronbetti de' nostri magnifici Signori per la fatica loro di sonare tutto uno anno, dal'una festa d'aghosto all'altra, a sonare in duomo per tutte le feste dell'anno e ala madonna in processione, contanti a Giovanni Martini lor kamarlengo, a uscita di Domenicho Menghin, camerlengo nostro a ff. 43. L. XI S.—(vol. 508, *D&C, 1475–82,* fol. 399 left)

Doc. 5.2. Niccolò di Lore is fined for failing to return to Siena, causing disruption in the chapel, 8 July 1481. Ibid., fol. 304 left

MCCCCLXXXI. Nicholò di Lore da Firenze tenorista die dare adì XVIII di luglio L. quarantaquattro e sol. [blank], e quali sonno per salario abbiamo pagato a Ugo, Petraccino e Ruberto Franciosi cantori, e a sser Biagio di Sansalvadore e a sser Domenicho di Mattio chantori tutti, e questi abiamo tenuti istimando che decto Nicholò tornasse da Firenze che aveva chiesto licenza a lo spect. cavaliere e degnissimo nostro operaro misser Alberto Aringhieri per quatro giorni per andare a la festa a Firenze e questo fu a dì XX di luglio [*sic*] che andò stimando tornasse di dì in dì come ci dava sentire e per non diviare la cappella abbiamo tenuti e detti sovrani e contri, che sapendo non fusse tornato (ché senza tenorista non si può cantare) aremmo dato licenza a detti cantori.

Ora avendo piena informatione come lui s'è acconcciò in Firenze questo dì detto, essendoci chosì detto e affermato, assai conveniente è che avendoci fatta tenere questa spesa senza alcuno nostro frutto, è paruto, e così è l'onesto che la paghi lui. E però per comandamento del sopradetto misser Alberto l'abiamo qui acieso nelo vero debitore perché a qualche temppo ce ne possiamo valere contra di lui o sue cose, acciò che la chiesa nostra non perda ma che sia conservata come è detto. L. XLIII.

Doc. 5.3. Monthly salary list for June 1482. Vols. 1074–75, *Note di salari e liste di canonici, chierici, cantori, suonatori, sagrestani e cappellani,* unnumbered folio

> Frate Giovanni tenorista die avere L. dodici, L. 12
> Frate Giovanni di Sancto Giorgio die avere L. dieci, L. 10
> Francesco Petrucci die avere L. quattordici, L. 14
> Ugho cantore die avere L. dodici, L. 12

Giovanni Farinella cantore die avere L. quatro, L. 4
Pietro di Francesco die avere L. quatro, L. 4
Jacomo di Lorenzo die avere L. quatro, L. 4
Giacoppo di Francesco die avere L. quatro, L. 4
Benedetto di Luca die avere L. uno, L. 1
Bartalomeo di Lonado die avere L. due, L. 2
Domenicho di maestro Angelo die avere L. due, L. 2
Enea di Pietro die avere L. due, L. 2
[following are several young clerks with no known connections to the chapel, then:]
Misser Pietro tenorista die avere lire vintiquatro s. 11 d. 8
Giovanni Comitis cantore die avere lire quatro, L. 4
Bartalomeo contra die avere lire quindici, L. 15
Quintino cantore die avere lire dodici, L. 12
Giovanni cantore die avere lire dodici, L. 12

Doc. 5.4. Cardinal Francesco Todeschini Piccolomini recommends Frate Giovanni as organist, 15 January 1480. AOMS, vol. 66, *Carteggio, 1469–97,* by date

Spectabiles viri Amici nostri carisssimi, Salute.

Amamo singularmente per le virtù sue et bontà frate Giovanni organista stato già tanti anni ad sonare nel Duomo vostro et nostro, et per la nota sufficitientia [*sic*] ad tale exercitio ci pare che voy et ciaschuno ciptadino el debia amare come noy amamo. Più volte lo habiamo recomandato all'offitio vostro et alla Magnificientia dell'Operario ali tempi passati ad tale effecto, cioè per la sua condocta ad sonare, perché ci pare che quella chyesa ne sia assay honorata di luy. Desideraremo grandemente et così vi pregamo che havendosi ad tractare di condurre sonatori d'organi, sì per rispecto dele virtù sue et ancho ad nostra consideratione, haveste per recomendato el prefato fra Giovanni di condurlo allo exercitio predecto. Del che ce ne farete piacere singularissimo. Bene valete.

Rome die XV Ianuarii 1480.

[verso:] Spectabilibus viris, Amicis nostri carissimis Sapientibus Opere ecclesie nostre Senensis Sancti Eustachii Cardinalis Senensis

TABLE 5.4. Chronological list of cathedral musicians, 1480–1507

The list includes only those mentioned specifically as singers at some point in the calendar year. Note that the fiscal year runs from May through April; a singer listed under two consecutive years may have served no more than a few months (for exact months, see Register of Musicians). Lists between April 1495 and the end of 1500 are missing.

	1480	1481	1482	1483	1484	1485	1486	1487–88	1489	1490	1491–92	1493	1494	1495
A. Singers														
Niccolò di Lore	x	x												
Gottifredi di Liegi	x	x												
Biagio di Tomè		x	x	x	x	x	x							
Giovanni Cristofani Francioso		x	x											
Ugo [di Gidio] Francioso		x	x	x										
Ruberto (Leuder) Francioso		x	x											
Domenico di Matteo		x												
Pietro di Ghino (Pietricchino)		x												
Elia		x												
Alfonso Ferrandi		x	x											
Giovanni di Giovanni [Pintelli]		x	x	x	x									
Jacomo Francioso		x												
Ruberto (Robinetto) Francioso		x	x											
Giovanni di San Francesco			x											
Giovanni da San Giorgio			x	x	x	x								
Giovanni Farinella			x	x	x									
Chimenti de' Servi			x	x	x	x	x							
Piero de la Piazza (de Platea)			x	x	x	x								
Bartolomeo di Castris			x	x										
Quintino di Martino			x											
Giovanni Comitis			x											
Giovanni Vichin/Quintin			x	x										
Andrea de' Servi			x											
Federigo di Pietro			x		x	x								
Agnolo di Pietro						x	x	x	x	x	x	x	x	x
Lonardo di Cristofano						x	x	x	x	x	x	x	x	x
Jacomo di Salvadore						x	x							
Ansano di Goro						x	x	x	x	x	x	x	x	x

Table 5.4 *continued*

	1480	1481	1482	1483	1484	1485	1486	1487–88	1489	1490	1491–92	1493	1494	1495
Domenico di Giovanni								x						
Francesco di Antonio Griffolo								x						
Francesco di Antonio tessitore								x	x					
Francesco di Tommaso								x	x	x		x	x	
Pietro di Mattia								x						
Tommaso di Jacomo								x	x	x		x	x	x
Simone Francioso									x					
Arcangelo di Maestro Antonio										x	x	x	x	x
Calixto di Maestro Guglielmo										x		x		
Niccolò di Bernardino										x				
Fra Lorenzo											x			
Bernardino di Cenni												x	x	
Bernardino di Lorenzo												x		
Pietro di Gano												x	x	
Quirico di Luphari												x		

	1500–2	1503	1504–5	1506–7
Agnolo di Pietro	x	x	x	x
Lonardo di Cristofano	x	x	x	x
Ansano di Goro	x	x	x	x
Lorenzo di Giovanni	x	x		
Maddalo di Lorenzo[a]	x	x	x	x
Biagio di Fuccio	x	x	x	

	1479–80	1481–99	1500	1501	1502	1503	1504–8
B. ORGANISTS							
Francesco di Mattia	x						
Francesco di Guido (Petruccio)		x	x				
Maestro Guasparre			x	x	x		
Ser Antonio						x	
Francesco di Tommaso						x	x

[a] also singing teacher

Example 5.1. Anon., *Confitebor tibi Domine* (BCIS, MS K. I. 2, fols. 3ᵛ–5ʳ)

Example 5.1 continued

Example 5.1 continued

Example 5.1 continued

Example 5.2. Anon., *Pange lingua,* second stanza (BCIS, MS K. I. 2, fols. 29ᵛ–30ʳ)

Example 5.2 continued

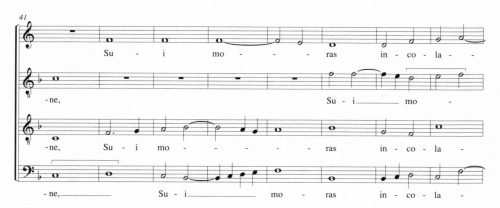

† section erased in MS

†† MS gives an extra sb on *f*

Example 5.2 continued

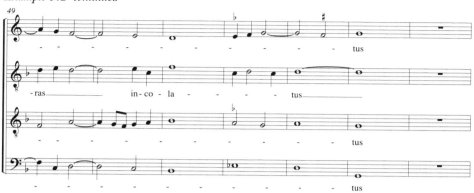

Example 5.3. Anon., Magnificat in the first tone, sixth verse (BCIS, MS K. I. 2, fols. 79ᵛ–80ʳ)

Example 5.3 continued

Example 5.3 continued

Example 5.4. Arnolfo Giliardi, *Sena vetus* (ASS, Diplomatico Bichi–Borghesi, Sec. XV)

Example 5.4 continued

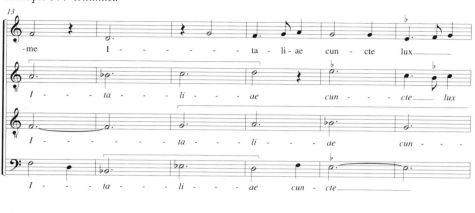

Example 5.4 continued

Example 5.4 continued

272

Example 5.4 continued

Example 5.4 continued

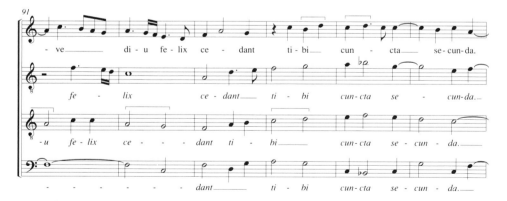

Example 5.4 continued

Chapter Six

THE DEVELOPMENT OF A STABLE CHAPEL, 1507–1555

Aﬅer Alberto Aringhieri fled Siena in 1505, Pandolfo Petrucci assumed the overseer's post, enlisting two of his political allies, Giovanbattista Guglielmi and Paolo Beringucci, as his counselors. At first, the new administration made no policy changes in the governance of the chapel, which thus continued to operate in much the same way it had since the turn of the new century. Adult singers were as difficult to come by as ever and the situation was further exacerbated when, only a few months after Messer Maddalo's departure early in 1507, Ser Sano di Goro fell into the governing board's bad graces and was dismissed. There were now only two adults in the chapel, and what was worse, failure to replace Maddalo left the school without a singing teacher. The problems besetting the chapel quite obviously called for the appointment of an experienced musician who could give new life to the cathedral's teaching program and set new standards of performance for the singers. But finding such a person was not easy.

More than a decade had passed since the French invasion, but all Italy was still in a state of political unrest and continuing economic uncertainty. French, Spanish, and imperial forces could intervene in peninsular affairs on the slightest pretext. In Rome the pope schemed to rid Italy of her oppressors while plotting the isolation of Venice and the restoration of the Medici to Florence. Ironically, this new age of northern interference in Italian politics occurred just as the great era of northern musical migration to Italy was ending. The outstanding singer-composers of earlier generations, figures such as Johannes Martini, Gaspar van Weerbecke, Loyset Compère, Heinrich Isaac, Alexander Agricola, Jacob Obrecht, and Josquin des Prez, were either in retirement, near retirement, or deceased. For the moment, times were less propitious for younger northerners, though conditions would improve within a few years, and another generation of composers, among them Elzéar Carpentras, Adrian Willaert, and Philippe Verdelot, would soon arrive. Siena cathedral's overseers were in the vanguard of those once again seeking to employ northern musicians. No particulars show how Pandolfo Petrucci and his associates went about their search, although personal knowledge of candidates or strong recommendations from others most likely influenced them in making their choice. Whatever the case, the appointment of the musician known in Siena simply as Maestro Eustachio on 1 September 1507 suggests that the cathedral's governors went to some lengths to find a person they believed could revitalize the chapel.

THE FIRST *MAESTRO DI CAPPELLA*,
EUSTACHIUS DE MONTE REGALI

Establishing Maestro Eustachio's identity is relatively easy, even though extant Sienese documents fail to mention both his patronymic and his place of origin.[1] Eustachio was not a very common name, however, and as it turns out, there were two musicians of some prominence called Eustachio who were active in early sixteenth-century Italy. One of them, Eustachio Romano, a gentleman composer, published a book of duos at Rome in 1521. Evidently, he did not hold any professional posts.[2] The other, Eustachius de Monte Regali, was a Frenchman, hitherto reported in Italy for the first time in 1514, when he sang in the Cappella Giulia at St. Peter's in Rome. He was at the papal court in 1519, but in the next year he went to Modena as *maestro di cappella* at the cathedral and music copyist.[3] Most of his extant works, the bulk of them sacred, are, in fact, in a Modenese manuscript. Available data from Siena leave little doubt that it was the French musician who began serving at the cathedral in the fall of 1507. Accordingly, the earliest known date of his activities in Italy may now be pushed back seven years.

Eustachio is the first person called *maestro di cappella,* or master of the chapel, in Sienese documents. Whether this means that he assumed duties other than those traditionally assigned to the *maestro di scuola,* the only title by which his predecessor Messer Maddalo was known, is difficult to ascertain. One record notes that Eustachio received part of the "eighty quinternions of large folio Venetian paper, lined with staves, for making music books," that the cathedral had acquired for Ser Ambrogio di Battista da Cremona, a cleric regularly employed to copy chant.[4] This could mean simply that Eustachio was responsible, as his predecessor had been, for copying some much needed polyphonic music, which he had perhaps assisted the prefect of the choir in choosing.

---

1. Although Eustachio's later career at churches in Rome and Modena makes it appear that he was a cleric, Sienese documents refer to him as "Maestro" rather than as "Ser."

2. For biographical information about this musician see Eustachio Romano, *Musica duorum,* ed. Hans T. David, Howard M. Brown, and Edward E. Lowinsky (Chicago and London, 1975), 9–12.

3. Information about Eustachius de Monte Regali, in David, Brown, and Lowinsky, *Musica Duorum,* 9–12; the entry by Brown on Eustachius Gallus [de Monte Regali Gallus] in *New Grove,* 6:316; Gino Roncaglia, *La cappella musicale del duomo di Modena* (Florence, 1957), 21–22, 81, 309; David Crawford, "Vespers Polyphony at Modena's Cathedral in the First Half of the Sixteenth Century" (Ph.D. diss., University of Illinois, 1967), 73–74, 340–45, 365–380; Richard Sherr, "Notes on Some Papal Documents in Paris," *Studi musicali* 12 (1983): 13, showing that Eustachius was a member of the papal chapel in 1519. Eustachius left Modena in 1524 and returned to Rome before 1526, when he was again reported among the papal singers. See also Sherr, "New Archival Data concerning the Chapel of Clement VII," *JAMS* 29 (1976): 472–78.

4. "MDVII. Ser Ambruogio di Batista de Chermona [*sic*], prette i' Santo Martino, scritore, de' dare . . . L. CCLXXIX S. VI" (AOMS, vol. 510, *D&C, 1506–11,* fol. 169 left); "Ser Ambruogio di Batista da Chermona de' avere L. vinti s.—, sonno per quinterni ottanta di carta righata, reale, viniziana per fare libri di musicha, la quale s'è datta parte a maestro Eustachio, maestro di chapella, per fare libri di musicha, per detto degl'operai, L. XX . . . E de' avere s. quarantatre, sonno per quinterni dieci di cartta, ci[o]è righatta, d'acordo co' lui, L. II s. III . . . E de' avere infino adì VIII di dicembre 1508 L. dugientocinquanta due s.—, sonno per averci scritto uno libro chiamato el Manuale, di quinterni trentasei, L. CCLII . . . E de' avere L. sette s.—, sonno per uno quinterno del detto libro, nel quale si ci è scritto el calendario, L. VII" (fol. 169 right).

It could also mean, however, that he himself composed new works for the singers. For like many a *maestro di cappella* before and after him, he would have been cognizant of their abilities and provided them with suitable, up-to-date settings of texts required by the Sienese liturgy, just as he apparently did later in Modena. This remains a matter of speculation, given the ambiguous wording of the document.

THE OFFICE AND DUTIES OF THE *MAESTRO DI CAPPELLA*

Originating largely as an administrative post in the papal chapel, the title of *magister capellae,* or *maestro di cappella,* was initially assigned to a cleric who was not necessarily a musician.[5] By the time it was adopted in Siena, the post embraced teaching and some kind of conducting duties, in addition to administrative tasks. These latter were mainly running the school and furnishing appropriate repertory for the singers, since book-keeping aspects of the chapel's administration—noting down tardiness and absences—were the sacristan's responsibility. Extant cathedral documents only hint at other duties connected with the post, though it is possible to have an idea of what they were by referring to reports from other Italian cathedrals and to later records from Siena's Palazzo Pubblico.

Instruction in polyphony was formally introduced into the school's curriculum in 1419, but basic principles of chant and musical theory had been taught at the cathedral for centuries. Part of the new curriculum probably consisted of rudiments of musical notation and vocal production as well as exercises in solfège and writing simple counter-point in two and three parts.[6] Results of the new emphasis on polyphony in the teaching program at Siena cathedral were apparent from as early as the mid-1450s, when a group of youths was appointed to sing in the chapel in place of adult singers. Even after

---

5. See Pirrotta, "Music and Cultural Tendencies in 15th-Century Italy," 133–34 and nn. 20–23, for the background and early use of the term in the papal chapel, where it was given to musicians and non-musicians alike. Lockwood, *Music in Renaissance Ferrara,* 154–56, describes the post as it evolved in Rome as that of a non-musician administrator and notes that none seems to have been needed at first in the court chapel at Ferrara. Lockwood also reports that in the early years of Duke Ercole's reign "the title denoted the singers whose job it was to manage and teach the boys." In later years, however, after Martini's death, "Ercole seems to have made the title of *maestro de cappella* a badge of leadership in the chapel itself; the first singer to be so named is Josquin Desprez when he arrives in 1503."

6. This kind of program formed the basis of musical instruction given to young Guido Machia-velli, son of the famous statesman, by the Florentine cathedral organist Bartolomeo degli Organi in the early years of the sixteenth century. See D'Accone, "Alessandro Coppini and Bartolomeo degli Organi—Two Florentine Composers of the Renaissance," *Analecta Musicologica* 4 (1967): 53. Lockwood, *Music in Renaissance Ferrara,* 125, mentions the musical training given the children of Duke Ercole, and Welch, "The Chapel of Galeazzo Maria Sforza," 154–55, speaks of training given to the Sforza children. On the musical education of Lorenzo the Magnificent and his children see D'Accone, "Lorenzo il Magnifico e la musica," 234. An idea of the instruction program in musical theory at the Santissima Annunziata in Florence in the 1540s can be had from Fra Mauro's treatise *Dell'una e l'altra musica,* a good deal of which was based on Giovanni Maria Lanfranco's *Scintille di musica* of 1533. Lanfranco was *maestro di cappella* at Brescia cathedral's music school. Peter Bergquist calls the *Scintille di musica* a textbook well suited to beginners, differing in this respect from most other sixteenth-century treatises. See his entry on Lanfranco in *New Grove,* 10:441.

the reinstatement of the adults, boy singers continued to perform in the chapel, and during the period of its greatest expansion in the 1480s as many as nine of them performed alongside the adults. The need for a person who could coordinate the increased forces probably became apparent then.[7]

The new art of the Franco-Flemings was introduced into Siena cathedral and elsewhere by northern singers, many of whom not only trained in the same schools but also knew each other personally and often traveled about in small groups. When they performed together—given their experience and intimate knowledge of the repertory, their small numbers, and in some instances their friendship with each other—they had little or no need for a leader.[8] In most situations, after prior consultation or rehearsal, it was evidently possible for them to agree on matters such as tempo, balance, and interpretation and to resolve any other problems apt to be raised in performance, such as those posed by the addition of *musica ficta*.[9] Their rehearsals, to make an analogy closer to our own day, resembled those of a string quartet, which is after all a meeting of equals. A record of May 1482 from the Santissima Annunziata in Florence illustrates the aptness of the analogy. It notes that three newly hired northern singers were required to rehearse, presumably with others already employed there, whatever music they were to perform at services, whether a Mass, a motet, or a Magnificat, and does not mention their having to obey a *maestro di cappella*.[10]

From the moment that diverse and larger forces were brought together, whether they included other adults trained in Italy or abroad, or boys trained in cathedral schools, a leader who could coordinate the particulars of performance became a necessity. At Siena cathedral, as at Florence cathedral and other Italian churches with musical establishments of any size, the person who was in charge of directing the chapel's performances was the music teacher. This was a natural extension of the duties originally associated with his post because when he taught the boys to sing polyphony, the master also prepared them, in effect, to perform alongside adults. His role as a teacher thus made him the logical person responsible for directing rehearsals and performances of the entire group, in other words, for leading the singers. The evidence from most

---

7. The cathedral organist Francesco Petruccio is called *maestro di canto* in an account book covering the period May 1493–April 1495. He was earning L. 14 per month at the time (AOMS, vol. 312, *E&U, 1493–95,* fol. 179ʳ). The same volume also lists payments to several students who later became adult members of the chapel, including Sano di Goro, Piero di Domenico d'Asciano, and Filippo di Nicholò Calapaccini; others mentioned in the volume include the adults Ser Lonardo Tenorista, Agnolo di Pietro, and seven other boys who are called "cantori."

8. Instructive in this respect is the often cited letter of Jachetto di Marvilla to the Medici recommending a chapel of three sopranos, a tenor, and himself as contratenor. Jachetto promised to bring the singers, with whom he had worked and knew personally, to Florence and said that once arrived, they could send to France for a bass. Jachetto had been in Siena a short while before he wrote the letter. See D'Accone, "The Singers of San Giovanni," 324.

9. For a recent work on the subject see Karol Berger, *Musica ficta: Theories of Accidental Inflections in Vocal Polyphony from Marchetto of Padova to Gioseffo Zarlino* (Cambridge, 1987). A particularly informative account of how performing musicians approached the problem of added accidentals is Lewis Lockwood, "A Dispute on Accidentals in Sixteenth-Century Rome," *Analecta Musicologica* 2 (1965): 24–40.

10. D'Accone, "The Singers of San Giovanni," 333.

Italian churches, however, is that the title "master of the chapel" was adopted only gradually, as the duties of the incumbent became more defined, owing to the complexities brought about by coordinating greater numbers of singers.

Siena cathedral was rather late in adopting the title to designate the person in charge of its singing establishment. At the cathedral of Santa Maria Maggiore in Milan the title was resurrected after almost a half century of disuse in 1477, when it was bestowed on the newly appointed Giovanni Molli. At the time he was apparently given greater disciplinary and administrative powers over both the adult singers and the boys enrolled in the cathedral school.[11] The title was also conferred on Franchino Gaffurio in January 1484, when he succeeded Molli, and on Gaffurio's immediate sixteenth-century successors, Hermann Matthias Werrecore and Simon Boyleau. At St. Mark's in Venice Pietro de Fossis was designated as "master of the chapel and of the boys" in the decree authorizing his appointment in 1491.[12] Teaching was still required of the incumbent when Adrian Willaert succeeded to the post in 1527, though he was called "master of the chapel," in contrast to his immediate predecessor who was referred to as "singing master."[13] *Magister cantus,* or singing teacher, was the title given to the many musicians who sang and taught at Padua cathedral in the fifteenth century, among them the composer Crispin de Stappen, who twice held the post in the 1490s. It was not until 1520 that one of his successors, Giordano Passetto, was called "master of the chapel."[14]

At Santa Maria del Fiore in Florence the title appeared in a decree authorizing the appointment of a group of singers in 1438 and in a payment to the leader of the group in the following year. But it found little official use after that time, and was not to reappear until 1479, when it was given to Ser Antonio da Montughi, an organist and singer who taught singing and figural music to the young clerks and directed their performances of polyphony at Saturday morning Masses.[15] "Master of the chapel" was the title held by all of Ser Antonio's successors as teachers in the Florentine school. Among them were the leading composers in Florence in the first half of the sixteenth century, including Bernardo Pisano, Mattia Rampollini, Philippe Verdelot, and Francesco Corteccia. Most of these men composed music expressly for the Florentine singers, although in the absence of specific documents regarding their duties, it is uncertain whether the terms of their appointments expressly called for them to do so. Similarly, no information is available about the extent of their obligations as teachers, obligations

---

11. Sartori, "La cappella del Duomo," 738. Sartori also says that in the first decades of the century Matteo di Perugia and Bertrand de Feragut were both named as *maestri di cappella,* but the data he gives show that only one or at most two singers of polyphony were employed at Milan cathedral in those years.

12. Francesco Caffi, *Storia della musica sacra nella già cappella ducale di San Marco in Venezia dal 1318 al 1797* (Venice, 1854), 39. The singing school attached to St. Mark's was established in 1403 and provided for eight boys, each paid a ducat a month, who "would learn to sing well."

13. Giulio Maria Ongaro, "The Chapel of St. Mark's at the Time of Adrian Willaert (1527–1562): A Documentary Study" (Ph.D. diss., University of North Carolina at Chapel Hill, 1986), 76–78, 284–85. Willaert relinquished his teaching duties in 1532; Ongaro, "Sixteenth-Century Patronage at St Mark's, Venice," *Early Music History* 8 (1988): 85–86.

14. Casimiri, "Musica e musicisti nella Cattedrale di Padova," 11, 14, 16, 189, 190.

15. Seay, "The 15th-Century Cappella at Santa Maria del Fiore," 49.

which in Florence by the turn of the seventeenth century were taken over by the vice *maestro di cappella*.[16]

In Siena, sixteenth-century records suggest that the *maestro di cappella*, in consultation with the prefect of the choir or some other dignitary, selected and provided polyphonic settings of texts appropriate to the cathedral liturgy. This was perhaps not as easy a task as it sounds because settings of such texts were not always readily available. Noteworthy in this respect are remarks by the Florentine *maestro di cappella* Francesco Corteccia, who claimed on more than one occasion that he composed and later published his responsories, motets, and hymns because suitable, up-to-date settings of texts required by the Florentine liturgy were unavailable.[17] There was also the problem of finding music that suited the voices of currently employed singers. Again, Francesco Corteccia furnishes valuable information, when, in connection with his own responsories, he mentions the responsories composed years earlier by his teacher, Bernardo Pisano. Pisano, Corteccia tells us, took into account the vocal ranges and musical abilities of the singers he was working with when he made his settings for the Florentine chapel, though by Corteccia's time these pieces were considered too low and too repetitious. Similarly, almost a century later Marco da Gagliano recomposed many of the same texts set by Corteccia, and both the singers' capabilities and a desire to have works in a more up-to-date style clearly furnished the impetus for him to do so.

The same situation applied to Siena in the last quarter of the sixteenth century, when Andrea Feliciani and his successor Francesco Bianciardi composed Masses, Magnificats, and motets for the Sienese singers. Surviving inventories list a good deal of sacred music in the cathedral library at the time, some of it very new indeed. Yet Feliciani and Bianciardi, like Gagliano in Florence, also made noteworthy contributions to the repertory with works of their own. Whether they were required to do so or were motivated by their own artistic needs is another matter. Perhaps it was a little of both. Then, too, there would have been the desire to compose music that showed off the capabilities of singers working under their direction. Telling in this respect are several of Bianciardi's motets, which require virtuoso singing on the part of the sopranos and altos, most of whom studied in the cathedral school.

Evidence from Milan cathedral throws light on some aspects of a *maestro di cappella*'s duties in the second half of the sixteenth century. It comes from a contract the composer Vincenzo Ruffo signed shortly after his appointment there as *maestro di cappella* in 1572. The contract, among other things, required him to "teach the usual number of boys" twice a day, "to compose a Mass and a Magnificat and such hymns as shall be necessary every month," to keep attendance records, and to note down tardiness.[18] At Padua, on

---

16. D'Accone, "The Musical Chapels at the Florentine Cathedral," passim.

17. See the dedicatory letter to his *Responsoria omnia* of 1571, published in facsimile and in English translation on pp. xxxv–xxxvi of the Introduction of my edition of Francesco Corteccia, *Collected Sacred Works: Music for the Triduum Sacrum*, Music of the Florentine Renaissance 11.

18. The terms of the document in the original language are given by Federico Mompellio, "La cappella del Duomo da Matthias Hermann di Vercore a Vincenzo Ruffo," in *Storia di Milano*, 9:777–78. The document is quoted in English by Lewis Lockwood in *The Counter-Reformation and the Masses of Vincenzo Ruffo* (Venice, 1970), 57–59.

the other hand, Costanzo Porta was not required to compose music when he became "master of the chapel" at the Santo in 1565, though he was obliged to teach two hours a day on weekdays.[19] Various records from St. Mark's in Venice indicate that composing new works for the chapel formed an important part of Willaert's duties.[20] None specifies, however, the number or type of works expected of him, nor how often he was to furnish the singers with new music.

Though no records from Siena cathedral stipulate teaching schedules and composing, the situation there was essentially the same as at Milan. Many of the requirements must have been standard throughout Italy, with individual responsibilities defining particular programs. The Sienese *maestro di cappella* was not responsible for keeping attendance records, though he was in charge of manuscripts and printed books of polyphony, many of them purchased or commissioned at his requisition. These were stored in a room in the canon's residence to which he had a key. Music was distributed to the singers by him or under his supervision at the appropriate times, and he could take music books home with him, presumably for study. Obviously, nobody knew better than he what repertory was available and what might be needed in order to accommodate liturgical requirements. And nobody knew the singers' capabilities better than he.

Just as there is no written evidence from Siena cathedral concerning the *maestro di cappella*'s teaching and composing duties, so is there none regarding his role in conducting and regulating aspects of performance. Assigning parts, setting the tempo, keeping the singers together, furnishing the opening pitch, settling disputes of whatever nature, deciding which parts were to be assigned to the performers—all of these were part and parcel of a *maestro di cappella*'s duties in the later sixteenth century.[21] A record from the Palazzo Pubblico, the other principal place for musical performance in Siena, spells out such duties precisely in reference to the leader of the wind band.[22] Presumably, similar things were expected of the *maestro di cappella* at the cathedral, especially when, as happened on at least two occasions during the sixteenth century, the same person held both posts simultaneously.

In Siena, even before Eustachio's time, selection of the polyphonic repertory was probably made by a responsible person in the chapel in consultation with the prefect of the choir. Beginning in the early sixteenth century this person seems to have been the music teacher, since it was he who was generally charged with copying music or arranging for its purchase. In Eustachio's case specific documentation is lacking, but it appears that his primary duties were to teach the choristers, just as his predecessors had

---

19. The same set of regulations obliged the chapel singers to sing Masses and Vespers at specified times and forbade them to sing elsewhere without permission. A division of offerings for singing votive Masses in polyphony was also approved for all concerned. See Jessie Ann Owens, "Il Cinquecento," in *Storia della musica al Santo di Padova* (Padua, 1990), 43–44.

20. Ongaro, "The Chapel at St. Mark's," 88–89.

21. These aspects of the *maestro di cappella*'s duties are not mentioned either in the regulations from Milan cathedral and the church of the Santo in Padua. At the latter, however, outside singers—those who did not live in the convent—were obliged to be present on Saturdays "per provar le cose necessarie al canto," that is, to rehearse the music that was to be performed. See Owens, "Il Cinquecento," 44.

22. See chapter 12.

done. They did not hold Eustachio's title of *maestro di cappella,* however. Perhaps this means that during his tenure the music teacher was given the task of composing music and conducting it, in addition to whatever other responsibilities he had in copying works appropriate to the liturgy. Or perhaps he was called *maestro di cappella* in his previous job, and insisted on the title as conferring more prestige. Either reason, or others unknown to us, would explain why Eustachio was called by a title hitherto unknown at Siena cathedral.

EUSTACHIO'S SACRED MUSIC

Eustachio's extant sacred compositions, preserved in manuscript in a number of Italian libraries and in a printed collection from 1519, include settings of ten hymns, fourteen psalms, three motets, and a Magnificat, though more undoubtedly await discovery. Possibly some of these pieces once formed part of the Sienese chapel's repertory, for most if not all of them are for Vespers on Sundays and other feast days, services that were also celebrated with polyphony at Siena cathedral. Even more significant is the presentation of twenty-two of Eustachio's sacred works in a Modena manuscript, Modena III, copied by the same hand responsible for forty-two of the sixty-seven items in the volume.[23] Modenese records note that in 1520 Eustachio copied a book of music for the cathedral there. Whether or not these are one and the same, twelve years earlier he copied music for Siena cathedral, thus strengthening the possibility that some of his works found their way into one of the Opera's volumes, all traces of which, however, are now lost.

Eustachio set psalm texts appropriate for Sundays and the principal feasts of Our Lord as well as a few for Marian feasts and those of other saints—settings, in other words, that had the same function as those in the Vespers collection copied by Mattio Gay. Like the composers of those works, Eustachio usually sets the psalm-tone formula or a slightly decorated version of it in the cantus and assigns an accompanimental role to the lower parts. Typical is his setting, in Tone 8, of the odd-numbered verses of Ps. 115, *Credidi propter quod locutus sum* (Ex. 6.1).[24] Each verse, as well as the lesser Doxology, cadences authentically on the tonic G. The first half of the first verse uses the Gregorian intonation through the mediation point, after which the remaining text, "Ego autem humiliatus sum," moves quickly to the cadence. Eustachio sought to vary the procedure somewhat in his setting of verse 3, where the Gregorian melody appears in the cantus only for the first half of the setting before migrating to the tenor for the second half. Though the accompanying parts are rhythmically varied, the texture is conceived so that the Gregorian melody predominates. Verse 5 opens with a short imitative passage in all parts, its subject somewhat reminiscent of the termination formula of the tone. There follows a presentation of the Gregorian melody, from beginning to end, now in

---

23. On ModD 3 (Modena, Duomo, Biblioteca e Archivio Capitolare, MS Mus. III), see Crawford, "Vespers Polyphony at Modena's Cathedral," 73; also *Census-Catalogue of Manuscript Sources of Polyphonic Music, 1400–1550,* compiled by the University of Illinois Musicological Archives for Renaissance Manuscript Studies (American Institute of Musicology–Hänssler-Verlag, 1979–88), 2:156.

24. The example, from Modena III, no. 7, is after Crawford, "Vespers Polyphony at Modena's Cathedral," 340–45.

the tenor, now in the cantus. Though ornamented, the melody is still recognizable within and above the predominantly chordal texture, which becomes more animated only as the cadence approaches. Verse 7 is a lively contrapuntal duo for cantus and altus, whose principal melodic material is based on a freely embellished version of the chant. For the concluding *Gloria Patri,* the melody of Tone 8 reappears in the cantus, again rhythmicized and decorated, while the lower voices occasionally furnish counterpoint within the basically homophonic texture. As noted in regard to earlier pieces copied by Gay, Eustachio's setting is very much of the kind of Vespers music favored by Siena's chapel for well over a century: straightforward, effective, and not terribly difficult to sing.

Eustachio's printed works, found in the second volume of the *Motetti della corona* printed by Ottaviano Petrucci at Fossombrone in 1519 (RISM 1519[1]), are another matter. Two four-voice motets of huge proportions, *Omnes gentes plaudite,* in two *partes,* or sections, and *Benedic anima mea domino,* in three sections, display Eustachio's mastery of the conventions and clichés of late fifteenth-century Franco-Flemish style. *Omnes gentes plaudite,* a setting of the entire text of Ps. 46, is in the best motet tradition (Ex. 6.2). Unlike the psalm settings described above, it makes no reference to psalm-tone formulas and the divisions between verses are eschewed in favor of a more continuous setting that seeks to convey the meaning and the spirit of the text through various combinations of voices and textures—now imitative, now freely contrapuntal, now homophonic.[25] Eustachio divided the psalm text so that each section has its share of exhortations to praise the Lord, the opening words of the second section, "Psallite Deo nostro, psallite," aptly complementing those of the first. Each section, moreover, concludes with an "Alleluia" not present in the original psalm text. The closing measures of both "Alleluias" share similar musical materials and thus impart a certain unity to the huge setting of more than two hundred breves. Despite the length and complexity of structure, discrete phrases of limited range are characteristic of the individual voice parts and awkward moments, such as the one in the altus at measures 153–54, are on the whole rather rare. Though the piece remains essentially within the Dorian mode on D—the *prima pars* ends on the dominant A, which becomes a reference point for the beginning of the *secunda pars*—it effectively presents the joyous text exalting the children of Abraham and Jacob. Various verses of the psalm appear as texts of the introit, offertory, and Alleluia verse for Sundays after Ascension and Pentecost and were suitable for any number of occasions within the Sienese liturgy. There is, however, no record of this volume by Petrucci in the cathedral's library, which housed instead the first volume of his *Motetti della corona* series.

EUSTACHIO'S IMMEDIATE SUCCESSORS

Whatever changes might have come about in the cathedral's musical establishment as a result of Eustachio's appointment, his tenure as *maestro di cappella* was exceedingly short. A final entry in his account states that he took his leave on 30 September 1508, after

---

25. For a recent discussion of the psalm motet see John Brobeck, "Some 'Liturgical Motets' for the French Royal Court: A Reconsideration of Genre in the Sixteenth-Century Motet," *Musica Disciplina* 47 (1993): 143–80.

reaching an amicable agreement with Pandolfo Petrucci and the governing board about the salary due him. In all he was paid L. 165. 19. 2 "for the thirteen months he served as *maestro di cappella* at the duomo, that is, for five months, and for eight months that he served as a contralto at L. 12 per month." Thus Eustachio was *maestro di cappella* for only five months—at a salary of L. 14 per month—although he continued his association with the cathedral as a singer for another eight months after relinquishing the post. Clearly, this first attempt to hire a distinguished foreigner must be accounted a failure, as it was undoubtedly considered at the time. No wonder the overseers now turned to a native Sienese, in this case a musician from one of the religious orders!

The Franciscan monk Fra Giovanni Pagliarini is recorded as *maestro di cappella in duomo* from 1 December 1507 through 15 May 1509, which means that his first two months in office overlapped with Eustachio's last two. In all Pagliarini served, as the final reckoning of his account notes, for one year and five and a half months, "not counting the half month he lost." He received a monthly salary of L. 14 for the full time. A sacristan's roll from March 1509 lists him together with the chapel singers, but with no salary, an indication perhaps that he was away at the time. He, too, supplied the chapel with music. Just a few days after he left cathedral service, on 19 May 1509, he received a payment of L. 30 "for a book of music in large folio, of seven Masses and other psalms, which he copied for our Opera" (see Table 6.1). There is no other record of Fra Giovanni's book, but possibly fragments of it survive in the volume, now at the Biblioteca Comunale degli Intronati, that contains the bulk of Mattio Gay's work from 1481.

The half month Pagliarini was paid for but did not serve probably included the first two weeks of May 1509, when a new *maestro di cappella,* Giovanni di Maestro Antonio, began his tenure.[26] In appointing him to the post the overseers took an unusual step, one perhaps dictated by their inability to find a qualified singer. For Giovanni, described in cathedral records as "a piffero and our master of the chapel in charge of the school," was the first woodwind player to be entrusted with the job. Giovanni, employed in the wind band at the Palazzo Pubblico since 1496, was not only a player of various instruments, including shawm, cornett, and recorder, but also a teacher and organ builder. Apart from the novelty of having a professional instrumentalist at the chapel's helm, his appointment at the cathedral is significant for another reason. It indicates that qualified instrumentalists were now being accorded the same kind of consideration previously reserved for musicians trained in cathedral schools. Such consideration is all the more remarkable because Giovanni was not a cleric, which was unusual for Siena cathedral. He was, in fact, the first of three laymen who would hold the *maestro di cappella*'s post during the course of the sixteenth century.

That Giovanni had the necessary qualifications for the post is perhaps the most

---

26. Cathedral records from this period do not survive in any great number. In the few entries that report Giovanni's presence, his father's name is mistakenly given as Jacomo rather than Antonio. Either this was a mistake on the part of the person who copied the entries, or the copyist's information was faulty to begin with. In any case the documents cited here and particularly in chapter 12 leave no doubt that the person in question is Giovanni di Maestro Antonio, Palace woodwind player, organ builder, and teacher.

TABLE 6.1.   Payments for copying and purchasing music, 1509–1548

---

19 May 1509

Frate Giovanni Pagliarini, frate di Santo Francesco, nostro maestro di capella, de' avere adì XVIIII di maggio L. trenta, s. —, sonno per uno libro di musicha, di fogli reali, di 7 messe e altri salmi el quale ci à scritto per l'Opera nostra, e so' a spese in questo a ffoglio 283. L. XXX s. — (AOMS, vol. 510, *D&C, 1506–11,* fol. 284ʳ)

15 July 1521

Maestro Ianni di Michele di Turri, scritore di musicha, de' avere sino questo dì 15 di luglio . . . perché ci à scrito quinterni XXVI½ di musicha . . . per bisongnio della capella del duomo L. LX s. XV (vol. 512, *D&C, 1521–29,* fol. 51 right)

9 September 1524

A Ser Giovanni di Galeazo Golppini, el dì [9 settembre] lire quattordici s. —, se li danno perché scrive uno libro di note per la chappella del chantto (vol. 321, *E&U, 1523–25,* fol. 43ʳ)

23 November 1524

A ser Giovanni di Galeazo, el dì [23 novembre] L. cinquantasei s. — chonttanti, per resto d'avere scritto 29 quaderni di uno libro di musicha per la chapella (ibid., fol. 48ᵛ)

21 June 1526

Bernardino di Matteo, libraio, addì XXI di Giugnio L. 3 s. 5 se li dànno per nove libri di chartta rigata, per schrivere l'inni in solfa per la schuola, L. III s. V (vol. 323, *E&U, 1526–27,* fol. 74ʳ)

5 May 1535

Bernardino cartaio el dì [5 Maggio] L. sette s. — sono per uno libro di canto con dieci messe figurato per la 'scita del canto, contanti al detto Bernardino, L. VII (vol. 330, *E&U, 1534–39,* fol. 236ᵛ)

26 May 1535

Bernardino cartaio el dì [26 Maggio] lire sette, sono per uno libro di canto, undici messe, figurato, per la scuola del canto, contanti a detto Bernardino, L. VII (ibid., fol. 226ᵛ)

24 December 1546

Spese strordenarie adì 24 di dicembre lire tre soldi 0, a Giovambattista di Bartolomeo, maestro di cappella, per due libretti di mottetti di canto (vol. 338, *E&U, 1546–47,* fol. 74ᵛ)

6 October 1547

Massarizie della chiesa deno dare adì VI d'ottobre L. settanta quattro x. —, paghati a ser Niccolò, prete dele monache di Santa Marta, per scrittura di um libro di chamto fermo in charta pechora, di diversi salmi e inni e antifane, che sonno quinterni diciotto e mezo, a L. 4 s. — il quinterno (vol. 514, *D&C, 1542–58,* first part, fol. 233 left)

17 March 1548

El di [17 marzo] . . . L. tre s. — per paghare um libro di chamto fighurato per dare a ser Scipione organista, e s. quaranta per dare a uno chamtore franzese che chamtò in chappella, e sso' a iscita del detto, a fol. 57. L. (ibid., fol. 268 left)

---

remarkable aspect of his appointment. As the son of a "piffero," or shawm player, who
followed in his father's profession, he had been trained in a familial situation rather than
at the cathedral school. Yet he apparently had a musical education comparable in every
respect to what he might have had at the cathedral, perhaps an even broader one, if his
knowledge of instruments is taken into account. Eventually, he became a master organ
builder, entrusted with constructing the instrument in the Palazzo Pubblico that is still
played.[27] A record from many years after his appointment to the cathedral shows that
Giovanni also taught the basic elements of chant, musical theory, and counterpoint.
Early in life he had apparently learned the principles of a system of notation that gave
him access to all of the great polyphonic repertories of the present and the immediate
past.

   Entries in various accounts show that Giovanni held the office of *maestro di cappella*
for fourteen months, through the end of June 1510, earning a monthly salary of L. 12.
Though this was L. 2 less than what his predecessors received, Giovanni's earnings were
considerably greater than those of his immediate successors and were, in fact, quite
high, considering that as a layman he had no clerical duties and, further, that he was
not obliged to compose or copy music. One record suggests that he performed with
the singers in the chapel, even though his name does not appear on the few monthly
rolls extant from that time.[28] If he did participate in the chapel's performances, he could
very well have sung, though he more likely played cornett or another wind instrument.
Perhaps it was during his tenure that the first tentative steps were taken toward employing instruments as a means of bolstering the chapel's vocal forces. Instrumentalists
are, in fact, recorded at the cathedral just a few years after he left.

   Whatever Giovanni's role in the chapel, during one of his absences his place as
maestro della cappella del canto was taken by the chaplain-singer Ser Piero di Domenico
d'Asciano. Piero must have been quite young when he came to Siena from his native
Asciano, a small town southeast of the city, situated in one of the most fertile and
picturesque countrysides in Tuscany. As a student at the cathedral school, Piero was
recorded among the chapel's choristers from August 1493 through March 1495.[29] After

---

27. One cathedral record from many years later, in fact, mentions him in connection with his
buying pipes of the old organ that was being replaced by a newer instrument: "[1521]. Giovanni di
Iacomo, pifaro, de' dare per la monta di libre 180 di stangnio in channe del'orghano vechio" (AOMS,
vol. 512, *D&C, 1521–29,* fol. 4 left). This payment furnished the definitive clue that led to identifying
Giovanni di Maestro Antonio Piffero as the person mistakenly called Giovanni di Maestro Jacomo
Piffaro in this and in earlier documents. Another document regarding Giovanni and the cathedral's
organ is cited by R. Giorgetti, "Nota biografica su Giovanni Piffero e documenti inediti," 23, quoted
below in chapter 12.

28. These, however, may have been compiled during the months he was on leave. More telling
is the entry on fol. 335 left, the debit side, of vol. 510, *D&C, 1506–11,* which calls him "Giovanni
di maestro Iachomo, piffaro et maestro della chapella de' chantori di duomo." The inference is that
he directed or performed with the singers. See also the document quoted in the previous note, which
reports that the singer Ser Piero di Domenico performed in place of Giovanni during his several absences.

29. It appears that the cathedral organist, Francesco Petruccio, was his teacher.

his ordination, he found a post at a parish church and was not mentioned at the cathedral for some time. An account registering the sum of L. 28 he earned while he substituted for or replaced Giovanni calls him "a priest who sings in the chapel."[30] Piero subsequently assumed the master's position in his own right. Another record identifies him both as *maestro di cappella* and *maestro di scuola* and credits him with a salary of L. 104. 5 for service through the end of March 1514. Evidently, he began serving officially in mid-January 1512 because a decree from a few months later specifies that L. 4 were due him for his work as *maestro della scuola di musica*.[31] Piero was a member of the cathedral's laudesi company of San Pietro, as were a few of the other chapel singers at this time. An entry in one of the company's volumes from May 1513 identifies him as a chaplain of the cathedral's chapel of St. Anthony.

A decree from the end of April 1514 says that Ser Piero di Domenico d'Asciano, *maestro della cappella del canto del duomo,* was to have L. 40 for his work up to that time and that beginning on the same day he would receive L. 4 per month as *maestro di cappella.* Subsequent payments to him run through December 1516. He was away from the cathedral for the next thirteen months. Ser Ansano di Goro substituted for him during at least nine of them, from March through November 1517. Piero resumed the *maestro di cappella*'s post in February 1518 and received a monthly salary of L. 8 through the end of February 1520, when he once again departed Siena. As on the previous occasion, his place was taken by Ansano, now cited as *maestro di cappella* in various payments through February 1524.

Ser Ansano, or as he is more frequently called, Ser Sano di Goro, reappeared at the cathedral in 1511 after an absence of almost four years. Sano, the son of a Sienese wool shearer, originally came to the cathedral as a young clerk in March 1484. In 1488 he joined the choristers' ranks, and continued singing in the chapel even after his ordination, as has been mentioned above. But then, in 1507, his tenure came to an abrupt and bitter end as a result of a dispute with the Opera about financial matters and singers' rights. A letter he wrote on 2 September 1507, one of the few extant written by a cathedral musician, gives only some of the particulars, though its tone and wording leave little doubt about how incensed he was because of the way he had been treated (see Doc. 6.1). Sano began by berating a certain Girolamo, one of the Opera's administrators, for his ignorance of the singers' "constitutions" and for having paid one of his

---

30. This entry may indicate he took over the post, without being officially confirmed in it, shortly after Giovanni's departure in June 1510. Rinaldo Morrocchi, quoting Giulio Piccolomini's *Notandi,* mentions "Ser Pietro, maestro di Cappella del Duomo di Siena nell'anno 1505" in *La musica in Siena* (Siena, 1886), 82.

31. The Sienese bibliophile Filippo Montebuoni-Buondelmonti erroneously reports that Ser Pietro became the cathedral's *maestro di cappella* in 1505, which casts some doubt on the accuracy of his charming anecdote about Piero's having taught music so well to a "conversa," a servant girl, that she was eventually able to become a nun, Suor Gismonda d'Agostino Ceraiuolo, in the convent of Saints Abbondio and Abbondanzio; Montebuoni-Buondelmonti also makes reference to that convent's organist in 1576, Suor Orsola Silvestri (BCIS, MS A. IX. 10, Filippo Montebuoni-Buondelmonti, *Mescolanze di cose diverse appartenenti a Siena,* fol. 238ʳ). The anecdote is also reported by Morrocchi, *La musica in Siena,* 86.

creditors without his permission.[32] After admonishing Girolamo to send him what he was owed and not to pay his debts, Ansano observed that Girolamo shouldn't wonder that he was indignant. He had, after all, worked for the whole month of July and the first few days of August and was then fired, and clearly, his "labors were not held in any regard." It is rare to glimpse the personal lives of Sienese musicians, the letter being as remarkable for what it reveals about Sano's independent spirit as for what it says about cathedral policies regarding singers. The letter also leaves no doubt that there were "constitutions" or statutes regulating singers' duties and behavior, and from what Sano says they had rights and privileges, which in his particular case had been violated.

Four years later Sano resumed service, at least temporarily. An account in his name covering payments from April 1511 through the following March puts his monthly salary at L. 6, which may mean that he was serving only as a chaplain and not singing in the chapel. His name disappears again after that time, not to appear again in cathedral records until April 1515, when a new account lists him as Ser Sano di Goro, cantore.[33] Perhaps outside factors influenced his return to the singers' ranks on this occasion, for in August of that year Pietro Sambonetto published a number of Sano's compositions in a volume entitled *Canzone sonetti strambotti et frottole libro primo,* the first collection of music ever printed in Siena.[34] Two pieces by another member of the cathedral establishment, the provost Ser Niccolò Piccolomini, were also included in the collection, and possibly it was through Piccolomini's good offices that Sano was readmitted to his old post with an increase in salary.[35]

The first of a series of entries in the above-mentioned account records a salary payment of L. 40 to Ser Sano di Goro for the four months from April through August 1515. A decree from that same month specifies that he was to have a salary of L. 10 per month, "starting the day he begins to serve in the chapel," and this is confirmed by subsequent entries in the account, which runs through November 1517. But the amount was still not to his liking and he began a campaign to change it. A later account covering the period through November 1519 shows his salary raised retroactively to L. 12 per month on 12 December 1517 by order of the overseer Guido Palmieri, and from that time forward he earned that amount for serving as both chaplain and singer. A payment of an additional L. 36 for the nine months from March through November 1517, "at the rate of L. 4 per month, just as Ser Piero d'Asciano had as master of the chapel," records the first of his terms as a replacement for his long-time colleague and

---

32. By which he certainly meant statutes governing the singers' behavior and obligations, all traces of which are lost.

33. Sano, too, was a member of the Compagnia di San Pietro nel Duomo; he is called "Ser Ansano cantore prete" in an entry dated 22 October 1515. ASS, PR, Compagnia di San Pietro nel Duomo di Siena, vol. 1370, *E&U, 1513–24,* fol. 60 l–r.

34. For a discussion of his music see chapter 14.

35. One of Piccolomini's pieces, *Mentre lo sdegno,* has been published in modern edition by Cellesi in "Il lirismo musicale religioso in Siena." Piccolomini, cathedral provost from 1521 to 1532, was an expert in canon and civil law and taught at Siena's university. Cellesi gives a thumbnail sketch of his life in the article. Payments to Messer Niccolò Piccolomini as proposto (provost) of the cathedral Chapter, January 1513–March 1521, are found in AOMS, vol. 511, *D&C, 1511–21,* fol. 156 left and right, in addition to other documentation in AAS, cited in chapter 2.

friend. Sano's second term was even longer, covering the period from March 1520 through February 1524. Throughout those years his monthly salary was fixed at L. 16. Ailing and in ill health during the spring and summer of 1524, he died shortly before the end of that year.

Ser Piero had, in the meantime, returned to cathedral service and monthly payments of L. 14 list him as chaplain and *maestro di cappella* from March through June 1524. But this was clearly a stopgap measure designed to replace the ailing Ser Sano. During the next two years at least two other singers in the chapel assumed the post. Both were Sienese and locally trained: Ser Marcello di Francesco da Montalcino, cited as *maestro di cappella* from November 1524 through April 1525, and Ser Antonio di Ser Cristoforo Diligente, mentioned from September 1525 through June 1526. Piero was back again shortly after that time. Named as *maestro di cappella* in a set of payments from November 1526 through July 1527, he began another leave of absence in early November of that year. On this occasion he planned to be away for some time because on the third of the same month the cathedral chamberlain reported that he had returned to Ser Piero some musical partbooks of his that were in the school room, that is, "four books in quarto bound in cardboard," entitled *el primo libro de' mottetti de la corona*.[36] Piero, in turn, gave the chamberlain a large folio-size book of the Opera's "containing psalms and hymns," which he had "borrowed for teaching."[37]

The new *maestro di cappella* beginning in mid-December 1527 was the chaplain-singer Ser Ulivieri di Jacomo from Radicondoli, another town in the Sienese dominion. Ulivieri, who, as will be mentioned, had sung in the chapel sporadically during the two previous decades and was to become one of the group's mainstays in later years, served as *maestro di cappella* through the end of May 1530.[38] Ser Piero resumed his dual post as chaplain and *maestro di cappella* shortly after that time. Payments at the rate of L. 14 per month are subsequently registered to him from October 1530 through September 1539, the longest uninterrupted segment of his decades-long career at the cathedral. Ser Piero's salary for serving as *maestro di cappella,* like that of the others recorded during this period, was fixed at L. 4 per month, irrespective of whatever else he earned as a chaplain and singer.

Notwithstanding his many leaves of absence, Piero d'Asciano's various terms as *maestro di cappella,* from 1514 to 1539, spanned more years than any of the others who preceded or followed him, an extraordinary record of service. Although he was neither a composer nor apparently possessed an exceptional voice—his salary was lower than that of several of the other singers—he was a thoroughly professional musician who understood the chapel's needs and the singers' capabilities. To judge from the many

36. "XPO 1527. [margin: Ser Pietro d'Asciano] Ricordo questo dì 3 di novembre ho dato certi libretti di canto quali sonno e' suoi che erano ne la schuola del canto, cioè 4 libri di 4° foglio leghati in cartoni, 4 libri, cioè el primo libro de' mottetti de la corona; e più uno libro di foglio reale scriptovi dentro salmi e inni quale è dell'opera dixe exergli prestati per insegnare" (AOMS, vol. 1047, *Salari, puntature e pagamenti alle maestranze, 1527–28,* fol. 20ʳ).

37. This may be the volume copied by Mattio Gay some forty years earlier, discussed in chapter 5.

38. See also, Table 6.2 and Doc. 6.2 for the inventory of the books of the school of figural music that were consigned to Ser Vieri (Ulivieri), master of the school, in 1527.

times he was called upon to fill the post, he accomplished with skill and tact his primary tasks: to train sufficient numbers of boys who could perform with the adults and to provide the chapel with an appropriate and up-to-date repertory. The true measure of his pedagogical success is illustrated by the frequent leaves granted him and by the administration's apparent willingness to reappoint him every time he chose to return to the post. As cathedral inventories show, the singers' repertory significantly increased during his tenure thanks to the commissioning of several volumes of polyphony and the purchase of a number of volumes of printed music. Unremembered and unsung until now, Piero must nevertheless be considered as one of the principal architects of Siena's musical renascence in the sixteenth century, for it was under his leadership that the chapel regained a sense of continuity and accomplishment, as older traditions were reinvigorated and new ones established.

THE CHAPEL IN THE EARLY YEARS
OF THE SIXTEENTH CENTURY

Changes in personnel were as frequent during the early years of the sixteenth century as in the past. There were, nevertheless, a few singers who compiled lengthy records of service, and one or two who are even recorded for longer periods than the various *maestri di cappella,* except for Piero d'Asciano. The small number of adult singers employed at the time of Eustachio's appointment gradually increased to six within a decade of his departure. Despite occasional variations, the normal complement remained at that figure for some time to come. The number of boys assisting in the chapel also grew during this period, which speaks well for the success of the teaching program under Piero. All in all, developments within the Sienese chapel in these years compared favorably with those in Florence and other major centers, and the overseers' continued support clearly helped Siena regain its place as an active, if minor, center of peninsular musical culture.

The sacristans' rolls for November and December 1507 cite two adults recorded earlier that year, Ser Lonardo di Cristofano, tenorista, and Ser Agnolo di Piero. Like the *maestro di cappella,* Ser Piero, the two singers held perpetual chaplaincies or their equivalents, and the inference is that by now the Opera had adopted a policy of awarding such posts to qualified local singers it wished to retain. Lonardo, chaplain in the chapel of Sant'Ansano, was also a member of the cathedral's confraternity of San Pietro, as was Agnolo, who was prior of the church of the Sapienza.[39] Both were to remain in cathedral service for more than a decade, retiring within a month of each other in July and August of 1519. The alto Messer Maddalo d'Arezzo returned to Siena from Florence in mid-September 1508, having been sent for expressly so that "he might come

---

39. Entries in one of the confraternity's account books name them as members and also furnish their death dates, 1520 for Ser Lonardo, 22 October 1528 for Ser Agnolo. ASS, PR, Compagnia di San Pietro nel Duomo di Siena, vol. 1370, *E&U, 1513–24,* fols. 7ʳ, 32ʳ. Ser Lonardo ("ser Leonardus Cristofori barbitonsoris, presbiter de Senis, corpore languens") made his last will and testament a year before his death. In it he expressed his wish to be buried in front of the cathedral's altar of the Madonna delle Grazie and named his brother's children, Cristoforo and Matteo, as his heirs. ASS, Notarile antecosimiano, vol. 1140, unnumbered folio, dated 10 August 1519.

to serve in the duomo's chapel." Although he was associated with the cathedral from this time through the end of October 1520, he was never again mentioned in connection with the music school. New in the chapel in June 1509 was the previously mentioned Ser Ulivieri (or Vieri, as he is often called) di Jacomo da Radicondoli, described as a bass in later documents. He, too, served for many years to come, his first appointment lasting through mid-February 1526.

But for occasional absences—duly noted in the monthly reports and other accounts—these four adults were employed together for more than a decade, from 1509 through 1519. They thus constituted a core group, which, under the direction of the *maestro di cappella,* who was also a singer, brought much-needed stability to the cathedral's musical program. Throughout this time the core group was assisted by a number of boys and by one and sometimes two other adults. Judging from later records, it is doubtful that all of the boys sang soprano, for occasionally older ones received higher salaries, indicating lower parts. In any case the basic makeup of the chapel remained essentially unchanged, performances typically featuring a small group of sopranos, supported by one or sometimes two adult singers on each of the lower parts.

The earliest newcomer during this period was the singer-chaplain Ser Giovanfrancesco di Antonio, recorded from mid-September 1511 through the end of September 1512. Mentioned for the first time at the end of January 1514 was a Dominican monk named Fra Innocentio. A decree from a few months later states that he was to be paid L. 30 for his services up to that time and that as of 1 April he was to have an appointment as a singer in the chapel at a salary of L. 10 per month.[40] He appears with Piero, Lonardo, Agnolo, and Ulivieri in a sacristan's roll from August 1514, but is lacking in rolls from the first half of 1515, which cite the other four singers and Maddalo. Ansano was the sixth singer in September of that year, and all six adults were also named in the monthly roll for March 1516, which included nine boys.

Only four adults were present, together with eight boys, during June 1517, though five adults and six boys were cited in August of the same year. That certain adult singers were occasionally absent is shown by the monthly roll from August 1518, which names the six regularly employed adults, as well as a seventh, the returning Fra Innocentio, and nine boys. Ten boys are listed in the following month, when, with the departure of Ser Agnolo, the adults once again numbered six. The fluctuations in the number of youths are more difficult to explain, though factors such as the departure of some who had finished their course of studies, the absence of others who stopped attending classes because of illness or for other reasons, and even the season, when many of them went to the countryside with their families, probably explain the varied attendance. New in the chapel in February 1519 was Messer Niccolò Francioso, tenorista, who sang with the group through December of that year.

The sacristan's roll for September 1515 is typical of the reports from this period. Under the heading "cantori" it lists six adults and seven boys, with the monthly salary due each person appearing after his name. The adults were Ser Piero at L. 4, Ser Lo-

---

40. He is called Innocentio in the record of his appointment, though some payments call him Vincentio.

nardo at L. 13, Ser Agnolo at L. 6, Ser Maddalo at L. 10, Ser Ulivieri at L. 8, and Ser
Ansano at L. 10. Among the youths, each earning between L. 1 and L. 2, was Galgano
d'Enea, son of the Palace trumpeter Enea di Senzanome. Galgano, or Gano, as he is
also called in cathedral records, eventually became a tenured member of the Palace
wind band, but before that he had a long career at the cathedral. His presence among
the boy singers at this time reveals that the cathedral school admitted all qualified
Sienese youths, even those not destined for careers in the church. His presence also
indicates that in addition to receiving instruction in a familial situation, some Sienese
instrumentalists were now being given a formal musical education as well. A few of
these students were as adept at singing as they were at playing instruments, and, as later
records reveal, they were employed to do both in the city's major musical institutions.
Their careers thus testify to the contribution the cathedral's teaching program made to
all sectors of the city's musical life.

Gano, like a few others who came after him, may have served both as a singer and
an instrumentalist in the chapel, although the accounts recording his seven-year career
at the cathedral are vague. He had a longer tenure than most of the younger singers
employed during this period, and it was marked by a number of salary increases that
perhaps reflected his versatility as well as his experience. An early account shows that
his initial monthly salary of L. 1 in August 1514 was raised to L. 2 in February 1517
and then to L. 2. 10 in April 1518. By August 1519 he was receiving L. 3 per month,
his salary when he left cathedral service at the end of July 1522. The higher salary, to
be sure, was what many of the older clerks, particularly those about to enter the priesthood and with several years' experience, earned for singing in the chapel and discharg-
ing duties required of clerks. But, considered along with his unusually lengthy record
of service and his training as an instrumentalist, it may also point to his having doubled
as a cornettist.

Some support in favor of Gano's having played the cornett in these years comes from
employment records of two other instrumentalists, mentioned below, whose careers in
the chapel resembled his. Additional support is provided by a later document reporting
a payment of L. 17. 6 to Gano for an unspecified period of service. Originally, a payment in the same amount was entered into an account that recorded his last few months
of employment, ending in July 1522. The later document, dated 1 October 1529, cites
the sum mentioned earlier, but this time entered under the name of Galgano d'Enea,
piffero. Perhaps the later copy is more specific because Gano was a member of the
Palace wind band by then. But it could also mean that the person who copied the
earlier record simply failed to distinguish his special role as an instrumentalist.

Gano's abilities as a cornettist during the time he served in the chapel, perhaps more
than any other argument, have the most direct bearing on the matter. In July 1522,
when he left the cathedral, he was recommended for, and granted, an expectative, or
promise of the next post available in the Palace wind band. Obviously, he was already
considered a highly qualified musician, which is borne out by the events of four years
later, when he succeeded to the coveted tenure position recently held by his teacher,
the former *maestro di cappella* Giovanni di Maestro Antonio. In view of Gano's experience and reputation, it would have been unusual had his talents as an instrumentalist
not been used while he was at the cathedral, especially in his later years.

Other evidence in favor of a cornettist in the chapel at this time comes from an acute contemporary observer of Sienese life, the historian Sigismondo Tizio. In one passage describing a cathedral service on Pentecost, 8 June 1522, Tizio complains that instead of the usual incense, another one was used, and that many present, including himself, found the new odor offensive. Tizio begins his anecdote by saying that the service, undoubtedly Mass, was "celebrated in a most extraordinary manner," and elaborates further with the remark that while the boys and adult singers of figural music were singing, "uniting, as usual, their voices to the accompaniment of cornets, up in the organ loft a boy was sweetly singing the lascivious words of a love song."[41] Apart from its many implications regarding repertory and other aspects of performance practice, Tizio's remark tells us that at this time cornets customarily accompanied the singers.[42] Gano is the only known cornettist mentioned in sacristans' rolls from the early 1520s, though possibly others among the boys also served as instrumentalists, as was the case in the later 1530s. Tizio's remark lends additional support to the thesis that instruments, in this case cornetts, were introduced into the chapel's performances as early as the tenure of Giovanni di Maestro Antonio in 1509. Such information, furthermore, accords well with other data recently brought to light regarding the use of instruments in Italian chapels in this period (see below, pp. 306–8).

THE CHAPEL IN THE 1520s

Recorded for the first time in December 1519 was Ardilasso d'Astore from Pistoia. He sang with the group through April 1521 and is described both as a tenorista and as a contrabasso in various accounts. Perhaps he replaced the temporarily absent Fra Innocentio. A new bass, Ser Marcello di Francesco, began the first of two periods of service in April 1520, remaining this time through the end of 1521. A Frenchman, Ser Lanzelotto di Nanse cantore, was present in February and March 1520. Sacristans' rolls for May, August, and October of the same year list seven adults and seven boys. The adults included Ser Sano, also acting as *maestro di cappella,* Ser Maddalo, Ser Ulivieri, Ardilasso, and two newcomers, Ser Francesco Gerini and Ser Fruosino di Lodovico Tancredi.[43]

Salaries were now on the rise, as revealed by a comparison of figures from this time with those recorded just five years earlier. A few singers were earning salaries far greater than those of the rank and file. Perhaps they had better voices than the others, or their vocal ranges were more sought after, or they were more experienced. Ardilasso, a layman, must have qualified on all counts and perhaps on others unknown to us. At L. 21

---

41. *Historiarum Senensium,* 9:216, dated 8 June 1522: "Die subinde Iunii octava, in celebritate Pentecostes, monstrifera officia divina in Senensi Aede conspiciuntur. Nam cum et pueri et cantores figurato cantu, ut moris est, illi concinerent, admiscebant cornua voces comitantia, super organis autem puer canens melliflue, lascivas amoris cantilenas immiscuit. Tum loco thuris, ut iam diu haec superstitio incoepit, storacem aliosque odores ministraverunt, et arae et civium naribus obtulere, ut iam omittere valeamus nec ulterius dicere "Dirigatur, Domine, oratio mea sicut incensum in conspectu tuo."

42. The reference is undoubtedly to a Mass setting based on a secular cantus firmus, a usage more widespread in the Renaissance than acknowledged. If this is so, then Tizio was referring to the celebration of Mass, although he failed to say so.

43. Ser Fruosino di Lodovico Tancredi, at L. 3 per month, appears only in these reports (see note 44 below).

per month, his salary was more than twice that of Ser Ulivieri's L. 10, more than three times that of Ser Francesco Gerini's L. 6 and seven times the L. 3 paid Ser Fruosino Tancredi.[44] It was even greater than the L. 16 earned by the *maestro di cappella* Ser Sano, who was also serving as a chaplain, which accounted for L. 6 of his monthly salary. This is not to say, however, that the remaining singers were not paid well. Ser Marcello, a bass, and Ser Maddalo, an alto, both of whom also served as chaplains, received, respectively, monthly salaries of L. 18 and L. 14.

A northerner, the contralto Daniello di Simone Lupi Fiamengo, is recorded at L. 7 per month from December 1520 through the following September 1521. With the addition of Daniello, variously identified as Tedesco and Inglese as well as Fiamengo, the chapel continued to maintain its new complement of eight adults for several months, despite the departure of Ser Maddalo. New in April 1521 was Ser Fruosino d'Antonio da Pisa, subsequently employed through June 1523. Ser Andrea d'Andrea de' Rami da Mantova, called a contrabasso in one set of payments, was present from November 1521 through October 1524. The Mantuan was obviously a singer of great ability with a voice to match, for like other basses before him, he earned a higher salary than the others. This is illustrated by the sacristan's roll from September 1522, which names seven men, including Ser Sano di Goro at L. 16, Ser Biagio di Fuccio at L. 5, Ser Fruosino d'Antonio da Pisa at L. 4, Ser Antonio Diligente at L. 8,[45] Lonardo di Lonardo at L. 7, Mariano di Ser Turco at L. 7, and Ser Andrea at L. 18. In contrast to this latter, Ser Biagio di Fuccio, who joined the chapel in February of that year and was subsequently employed through August 1527, never earned more than L. 6 per month.[46] Curiously, Lonardo di Lonardo Franzese, cantore, whose account shows him earning a monthly salary of L. 7 for the time he served, from May through October 1522, appears among the boys in the September roll.

The 1520s, it soon becomes apparent, witnessed a great many comings and goings

---

44. There were apparently two singers named Fruosino around this time, Fruosino Tancredi, mentioned above, and Fruosino d'Antonio. The latter is doubtless the same as the choirboy called Fruosino del Pisano, who appeared as early as May 1513. Later rolls call him Fruosino di Antonio or Fruosino Fiorentino, and he is recorded among the choirboys through September 1518. The later Fruosino is the same person who served as chaplain of the altar of San Bernardino. His chaplaincy is referred to in entries dated 1518 and 1520 in an account book from the cathedral's Confraternity of San Pietro: "1518. Ser Fruosino cappellano di Sancto Benardino de' dare questo dì 22 di g[i]ugno L. quatro per limosina che di tanti s'è obligato per restare nel numero de' nostri fratelli. [opposite] . . . de' avere adì 15 d'aprile 1520, L. 4" (ASS, PR, Compagnia di San Pietro nel Duomo, vol. 1370, E&U, 1513–24, fol. 75 l–r).

45. In 1513 Ser Antonio Diligente is identified as rector of the church of San Donato in an account from the Confraternity of San Pietro nel Duomo: "MDXIII. Ser Cristofano di Antonio [*recte* Antonio di Cristofano] alias el Diligente, rectore di San Donato, die dare persino questo dì 18 di octobre lire quatro, L. 4" (ASS, PR, Compagnia di San Pietro nel Duomo, vol. 1370, E&U, 1513–24, fol. 30 left).

46. Biagio di Fuccio is listed among the cherici in 1506 and was thus a student in the cathedral school. He is called Ser Biagio di Fuccio da Pientia (Pienza) in an account book from the cathedral's Confraternity of San Pietro in 1514, an indication that he was ordained by that time (ibid., fol. 32 left). Later he succeeded Ser Fruosino as chaplain at the cathedral's chapel of San Bernardino and held that post until his death in June 1528. His presence furnishes yet another example of trained singers

in the chapel. Only a few singers, who not coincidentally also served as chaplains, were present for more than three or four years at a time. Employment policies that drew singers from all parts of the Italian peninsula and beyond the Alps continued unabated throughout the decade, even as native Sienese gained admittance to the chapel. The list of new personnel registered during this time continues with a singer from Bruges called Arrigo Tibello di Giovanni. A payment to him for L. 4 on 24 November 1524, however, indicates that his stay was very brief. The contralto Ser Pietro di Maestro Lonardo is recorded for a considerably longer period. Entries in his name from 10 September 1524 through 1 April 1527 show that he earned L. 7 per month. A German singer, Ser Agnolo Ciper of Cologne, called both contrabasso and tenorista, received monthly payments of L. 7 from September 1524 through mid-June 1526. Another singer named Agnolo was a layman. His full name, Agnolo di Bartolomeo, is in various accounts from December 1525 through February 1530, which show him earning L. 7 per month.

The name of yet another layman, the contralto Jacomo di Giovanbattista da Verona, appears in pay registers for the first time on 23 November 1524, when he received L. 7 "for having sung since All Saints Day." Jacomo, as later documents suggest, was associated with the Chigi family, and may have come to Siena at their behest.[47] Successive payments show him receiving salary increases from L. 10 to L. 17 per month through August 1526, and then to L. 18, which is what he was earning in November 1527, when he temporarily left cathedral service. Although possessing a similar name and voice range, he is not the same singer engaged by the chapel of St. Mark's Venice in 1549.[48] Messer Andrea di Baldassarre da Montepulciano, whose voice range is not specified in any document, is recorded at L. 9 per month from August 1524 through July 1525. Mention has already been made of the singer-chaplains Ser Marcello di Francesco and Ser Antonio Diligente, both of whom served as substitute *maestri di cappella* from November 1524 through June 1526. They are also recorded as singers in those years. Don Mariano di Gherardo da Bologna, a tenor, earned a monthly salary of L. 7 from August 1525 through June 1529.

New in the chapel in the closing months of 1527 was Ivo di Giovanni Francese. In the following April he received L. 60 for several months' salary, "partly at the rate of L. 6 and partly at the rate of L. 10 per month." Monthly salary payments of L. 10 through December 1528 are in the same account, though other records for the period ending in May 1529 indicate that he was receiving L. 7 per month. Salary adjustments were evidently made at a later time, for an entry from 17 November 1530 states that he was given L. 80 "for his services as a singer and as a composer through all of June 1530, in settlement of a bill agreed upon with Messer Francesco, our most worthy overseer." Despite the similarity of names and mention of his being a composer, this Ivo presumably is not Ivo Barry, the French singer and composer recruited for papal

associated with the cathedral, who for whatever reasons were not always formally employed in the chapel.

47. See Doc. 6.5.

48. The other Jacomo da Verona was employed at St. Mark's from 1549 through 1562 and perhaps later. See Ongaro, "The Chapel of St. Mark's at the Time of Adrian Willaert," 132, 141, 145, 161, 163, 165.

service by Jean Conseil in 1528. The latter was apparently already in Rome at the time and is said to have remained there until 1550. Should this turn out not to be the case, then his presence in Siena would fall into a pattern—observed earlier in Maestro Eustachio's case and presently to be noted with Bartolomeo Il Conte—of several sixteenth-century papal musicians serving for brief periods in Siena. Barry's extant works include five motets, eight madrigals, a canon, and a treatise on counterpoint.[49] These latter are in manuscript in Perugia, where, interestingly enough, a musician named Maestro Ivo was awarded a one-year contract as *maestro di cappella* at the cathedral of San Lorenzo on 12 September 1535.[50] If this is Ivo Barry—and the presence of his works in Perugia certainly point to such a conclusion—then the composer had other associations besides the papal chapel during the time he supposedly was in Rome and he could also have been employed in Siena. There is, however, no record of the kinds of works the Sienese Ivo composed for his colleagues in the chapel, nor any trace of them in cathedral archives.

Several boys had rather long tenures during the 1520s. Noteworthy in this respect was Camillo di Marco, identified as a pupil of Ser Sano in 1522. He received a monthly salary of L. 2 from August 1524 through May 1528.[51] Domenico di Giovanbattista, first registered in May 1521 at a monthly salary of L. 1. 10, sang with the group through the end of May 1530. He was then earning L. 3 per month, which perhaps indicates that he sang one of the lower parts rather than soprano. Giovanbattista di Bartolomeo, who eventually became an adult member of the chapel, appears for the first time in payments from November 1520 through June 1523 at a monthly salary of L. 1. 10. Among the eight youths named in the sacristan's report from September 1522 were Amore di Francesco Franzese, the son of a Frenchman resident in Siena, at L. 4; and Vincentio di Mattia at L. 3.10. Vincentio, whose accounts run from April 1521 through August 1526, was still a student when he was first cited, but was ordained within a few years. He is, in fact, listed as Ser Vincentio di Mattia among the six adults in the monthly roll from January 1523. Eight boys are also listed. Generally, it is difficult to determine how many other older youths were counted among the boys at any given time, unless, as in Vincentio's case, there is evidence of this sort.

---

49. For a recent biography of Ivo Barry see James Haar's entry in *New Grove,* 9:430. The five motets, all printed, are preserved in (1) *Moteti de la Simia (Liber primus vocum quinque),* published at Ferrara in 1539 by J. de Buglhat, with 2 motets (RISM 1539⁷); (2) *Nicolai Gomberti musici excellentissimi, et inventione in hac arte facile principis. . . musica quatuor vocum (vulgo motecta nuncupatur),* published by Girolamo Scotto at Venice in 1541, with 2 motets (RISM 1541⁴); and (3) *Musica quatuor vocum que materna lingua moteta vocantur ab optimis & variis autoribus elaborata, paribus vocibus decantanda,* also published at Venice by Scotto, in 1549, with one work (RISM 1549⁹).

50. A. Rossi, "Documenti per la storia dell'arte musicale," *Giornale di erudizione artistica* 3 (1874): 164, for the document, dated 25 September 1535, showing that he was hired "pro uno anno a die xij presentis mensis septembris Magistrum yvum pro magistro Cappella ecclesie sancti laurentij presentem etc. cum salario et emolumento xxiiij scutori auri solvendorum de pecunijs fabrice eiusdem ecclesie et eminas xij grani et bariles xij vini solvendos de mense in mensem."

51. Vol. 512, *D&C, 1521–29,* fol. 153 left, one payment to Ser Ansano di Goro, "maestro di chapella del chanto," notes it was taken to him by his student Camillo ("gli portò Camillo suo scolaro").

Also recorded among the boys in the 1520s was Bernardino di Matteo Cartolaio. His monthly salary of L. 5, from May 1524 through 30 April 1526, was almost double that of the other young singers. This could mean that he sang one of the lower parts rather than soprano, though subsequent events in his career—which paralleled Gano's—suggest otherwise and point instead to service in the chapel as an instrumentalist. When he was appointed a supernumerary in the Sienese wind band in October 1524, he was described as "assiduous in playing both within and outside the Palace" but was nevertheless "obliged to perform just as the other Palace musicians do." Bernardino apparently had no difficulty in scheduling his performances at both places because he continued to serve in the chapel for some years after that time. Palace records, which mention him as late as 1538, indicate that he was employed there primarily as an instrumentalist. It is curious that cathedral records fail to identify him as such, though it is true that during the early decades of the century instrumentalists who assisted in the chapel were mostly younger musicians generally listed among the boys. In later times, when professionally established musicians were appointed to the chapel, they were properly identified by the instruments they played.

New Music

Bernardino's father, as the name Cartolaio indicates, dealt in paper and books, and the youth apparently worked in the family business even while he was serving at the cathedral. A record from 18 May 1525 notes that he was paid L. 41 "for a book that was made," but does not specify whether it contained music.[52] Another payment to him from 21 June 1526 mentions "nine books of lined paper for writing hymns in solfa, for the school" (see above, Table 6.1, for this and further payments). In all probability the reference is to Gregorian chants that all of the school's students were obliged to learn. Bernardino also supplied the chapel with polyphony. Almost a decade later, on 5 May 1535, he received L. 7 "for a songbook with ten figural Masses, in cash." And less than two weeks later he was was paid L. 7 in cash "for a book of figural music, eleven Masses, for the singing school." Possibly both references are to a volume whose contents were later expanded to include an additional Mass. But it may also be that the first payment refers to Jacques Moderne's *Liber decem missarum* (first published at Lyons in 1532), which a subsequent inventory shows the school owned.

Bernardino was not the only person who supplied the singers with music during this period. Earlier, on 15 July 1521, Maestro Ianni di Michele di Turri, a music copyist, was paid L. 65. 15 because "he copied 27 and a half quinternions of music, at the rate of S. 45 the quinternion, for the chapel's needs."[53] A few years later, on 9 September 1524, Ser Giovanni di Galeazo Golppini received L. 14 because "he is writing a book of notes for the chapel." A payment from the following 23 November credits him with L. 56, "the remainder [due him] for having copied 29 quaternions of a book of music for the chapel." References to the chapel in both cases indicate that these were books of polyphony rather than of chant, which normally would have been copied for the

---

52. "Bernardino di Matteo cartaro, cantore, el dì [18 Maggio 1525] L. 41 per conto di un libro fatto, L. 41" (vol. 322, *E&U, 1525–26,* fol. 30ᵛ).
53. Turri was also an instrument maker. See chapter 13.

choir's use. Most chant books were eventually illuminated and assumed their rightful places among the sacristy's prized possessions, though others that were used for teaching purposes, such as the hymns just mentioned, were not particularly treasured.

It is difficult to determine if either or both of the manuscripts copied by Turri and Golppini were among those mentioned in inventories of the music school's belongings consigned to Ser Piero in 1524 and to Ser Ulivieri in 1527 and in two official inventories of cathedral holdings from 1525 and 1536, the last two virtually identical in wording and order (see Table 6.2). A prime candidate could be the "large book of motets, in pen," listed among the school's holdings in 1524 and in 1527, when it is further specified that the contents were "new motets." This may be the volume of motets described as "covered in red leather" in the inventories of 1525 and 1536, which also speak of a book of Magnificats and hymns. This latter is the large folio-size volume that Ser Piero was studying at home in 1527 and it appears among the school's belongings in 1524 and 1527. (It may be identical with the volume of Vespers music copied by Mattio Gay in 1481, listed in the inventory of 1500.) Also lacking in the 1525 and 1536 inventories are the "five small partbooks, bound in four volumes," two sets of partbooks, one comprised of ten partbooks, the other of four, of music for processions, mentioned in 1524, and "eight partbooks used in processions, bound in parchment" mentioned in 1527. On the other hand, listed in 1525 and 1536 are "four books in octavo of motets with two Masses, covered in parchment" that are not cited in 1524 and 1527. The inventories evidently do not always list all volumes used by the chapel, perhaps because the *maestro di cappella* had some at home when they were compiled. They also list school furniture (see Doc. 6.2).

Naturally, books owned by the *maestro di cappella* do not figure in any of these listings, though the singers also used them in performance. Notable in this regard is the set of four partbooks in quarto that the sacristan returned to Piero d'Asciano in 1527, the *Motetti de la corona. Libro primo,* printed at Venice in 1514 by Ottaviano Petrucci and reprinted at Rome in 1526 by Pasoti and Dorico (RISM 1516[1], 1526[1]). This print contains works by Févin, Josquin, Mouton, Carpentras, and Brumel, among others, works by some of the leading masters of the day and of a previous generation. It speaks well for Siena's *maestro di cappella* and singers that works of such high caliber could be found in their repertory and suggests that they performed a psalm motet such as the one by Eustachio, mentioned earlier, from Petrucci's second volume of the *Corona* series.

Among the volumes included in all four inventories were two manuscript books of Masses covered in leather, the one red, the other purple. These are described as "medium sized, in pen, old" in 1524 and as "old books" containing "old Masses" in 1527. A third manuscript book of Masses, defined as "very old" in 1524 and as "old, covered in green, containing very old Masses" in 1527, was listed simply as "bound in green leather" in 1525 and 1536. (One of these was the volume copied by Mattio Gay in 1481.) A fourth manuscript volume, described as "large" in 1524 and 1527, is not mentioned in 1525 and 1536, although these latter speak of "four books of Masses in quarto, covered in white parchment" that are lacking in the others. A book of printed Masses, described as medium-sized in 1524, may be the same as the "printed book with fifteen Masses" covered with boards listed in 1527, though it is described as "covered in white parchment" in 1525 and 1536. Perhaps this last is Andrea Antico's 1516 *Liber*

Table 6.2.   Inventories of music manuscripts, 1524–1547

1524: Inventario in chalonica (AOMS, vol. 1494, *Inventario di quanto contenuto delle stanze di cappellani e cherici e note di amministrazione, 1519–1529,* unnumbered folio)

La schuola del chanto fermo, tiene ser Pietro chantore, cho' le sotto iscritte chose:
   uno libro mezano di messe in istampa, figurato
   due libri mezani di messe, in penna, vechi
   uno libro grande di Mangnifichato e inni, in penna
   uno libro grande di mottetti, in penna
   uno libro grande di messe, in penna
   uno libro vechio vechio
   5 libretti picholi, leghati in 4 vilumi
   10 libretti da p[r]ocissioni
   4 libretti picholini da p[r]ocissioni

1525: Inventario . . . al tempo del magnifico et generoso cavaliero missere Antonio di Augustino del Vescovo dignissimo operaio (vol. 1493, *Inventari, 1517?–1590,* fasc. 2)

fol. 5ᵛ:	Segue la libraria di sagrestia . . .
	[18] Uno seguentiale chuperto di pavonazo, chomincia Regem venturum, segnato XVIII
fol. 6ʳ:	[46] Una musicha d'Aristotile [*recte* Boetio]
	[60] Uno libro di laude vulgare, chuperto di nero, chomincia Ave domina, segnato LX
fol. 6ᵛ:	[100] Un libro di charta banbagina di chanto figurato, segnato C
	[113] Uno libro di canto figurato in charta bammbagina chon tavole l'arme dell' Opera, segnato 113
fol. 21ʳ:	La scuola del chanto figurato
	Uno libro di messe chovertato di choiame verde con tre chanti et due choppe
	Uno libro di messe chovertato di choiame rosso con septe choppe d'ottone
	Uno libro di messe chovertato choiame pavonazo
	Uno libro di messe in stampa chovertato di charta pechora
	Quattro libri di messa in quarto foglio chovertato di charta pechora
	Uno libro di hymni psalmi et magnifiche chovertato di choiame rosse con VIII chanti e due choppe
	Uno libro de motetti chovertato di choiame rosso chon VIII chanti e 2 choppe
	Quattro libri di mottetti chon due messa insieme in ottavo foglio chovertato di charta pechora

1527 (vol. 1494, *Inventario . . . 1519–1529,* unnumbered folio)

† XPO 1527. La schuola del canto fighurato i' ne le mani di ser Vieri, maestro d'exa schola, in la quale sonno le infrascritte maxarizie e robbe, cioè libri. E prima . . .
   2 libri vechi, uno covertato di pavonazo suvi mexe antiche, l'altro covertato di roxo con mexe antiche
   3 libri grandi, uno di mexe, uno di Magnifiche e inni, uno di mottetti nuovi
   Uno libro con 15 mexe in stanpa, leghato in tavole
   8 libretti da portare a la procixione, covertati di cartapecora
   Uno libro antico, covertato di verde, scripttovi mexe antiquixime

TABLE 6.2 *continued*

1536: Inventario . . . scritto al tempo del magnifico cavalier messer Francesco di Carlo Tholomei dignissimo operaio (vol. 1493, *Inventari, 1517?–1590*, fasc. 3, fol. 17ᵛ)

as 1525 inventory, but "cuoio" is used instead of "choiame," the "Quattro libri di messa in quarto foglio" are "chovertato di charta pechora," and the penultimate entry of the book of motets bound in red leather is missing

1547: Inventario di libri di canto fighurato (vol. 1535, *Elenchi, note e inventari di beni mobili e immobili, datati [1364–1711]*, doc. 27)

Inventario di libri di canto fighurato:
Addì X . . . di dicembre 1547. Libri di canto rice[v]uti per inventario da Giovanni Battista di Bartolomeo

> Uno libro di messe, scritto a mano, figurato, con coverta di quoio lionato, di foglio reale
> Uno libro di mottetti, di foglio reale, coverta di quoio, in tavole
> Uno libro di Salmi e magnificat, in tavole, di foglio reale
> Uno libro di magnificat e inni, in tavole, di foglio mezano
> Uno libro di messe Morales, in istanpa, con coverta di quoi azzuro
> Uno libro di messe in istanpa, dalla Magna, con coverta di quoi nero
> Uno libro di 5 messe di Carpentras, in tavole
> Uno libro delle XV messe, di vari autori, in tavole
> Uno libro di X messe, in tavole
> Uno altro libro, in tavole
> VIII libri delle processioni, pichuli coverta di carta pechora, N° otto
> Uno corpo di libri di mottetti della divinità, a cinque
> Un altro corpo di mottetti di Ghonberto, a cinque
> Uno libro di messe, scritto a mano, a meza chove[r]ta di rosso

quindecim missarum (RISM 1516¹), with works by Brumel, Févin, Josquin, and Mouton, among others. If so, then the high quality of repertory observed in at least one of the motet volumes found its parallel among the Mass volumes. Unmentioned in the latest inventory of 1536 are any of the works composed for the chapel by Ivo di Giovanni.

THE CHAPEL IN THE 1530S

In Siena the political situation, never stable in the best of times, had once again deteriorated. After Pandolfo Petrucci's death in 1512, power passed peacefully enough to his son Borghese. But Borghese lacked popular support and was forced to flee the city with his younger brother Fabio only three years later as a result of the machinations of the Medici Pope Leo X and his Sienese allies. The scandal-ridden regime of Cardinal Raffaele Petrucci, Borghese's cousin, was equally short-lived, for he died in 1522. Following the brief government of Francesco Petrucci, Pandolfo's direct heirs resumed power with the return of Fabio Petrucci. Fabio also lacked strong support within the city and he, too, was forced to flee from office in mid-September 1524 after a popular uprising. Throughout the rest of his life he schemed with the aid of his Medici in-laws to return to power, but his death at the early age of twenty-four put an end both to his supporters' aspirations and the Petrucci dynasty.

Meanwhile, within Siena age-old rivalries between various factions continued even as the parties of the Nine and the Libertini formed an uneasy coalition government. The Nine, seeking to renew old alliances with Clement VII and the Medici, subsequently allowed a column of French soldiers into the city. Tensions ran high, and when news of the French defeat at Pavia on 24 February 1525 reached Siena, the Libertini used the occasion to force the withdrawal of the troops. In the wake of this, the Noveschi, who had previously secured the support of Emperor Charles V after advancing him a payment of 25,000 ducats, were once again toppled from government. Alessandro Bichi, head of their faction, was killed, as were many of his supporters. The stage was thus set for the invasion of Siena by papal forces and their subsequent defeat in the battle of Camollia on 26 July 1526. Victory, however, did not bring reconciliation to the opposing forces within the city. Neither did the subsequent call to restore order within the city given to Alfonso Piccolomini of Aragon, Duke of Amalfi. Charles V, on the first of his visits in 1529, made it plain that he would not tolerate continued political instability, which was further exacerbated after the emperor's second visit in 1536, when Spanish guards were stationed at the Palace and the Noveschi returned from exile. Siena was proving unreliable, it was feared, and contributing to instability in central Italy. Political events, however, had no apparent effect on the cathedral's governance in general and on the chapel's performances in particular, for policies regarding employment of singers were retained without change.

During the 1530s the chapel continued on the course established in the previous decade, with foreigners and Italians alike appearing on the rolls alongside a steady contingent of students from the cathedral school. Ivo Franzese and Agnolo di Bartolomeo are on the sacristans' rolls from June and August 1530, the only ones extant for that year. Also cited are four other adults and five boys, whose names appear in a volume of accounts begun in the closing months of 1529. Having returned to cathedral service in December 1527 after a brief absence, Ser Ulivieri di Jacomo was now acting as *maestro di cappella*. New were the Frenchman Messer Giovanni da San Germano, who is listed from January through November 1530; Ser Bernardo (or Bernardino) di Jacomo da Pontremoli, who was to remain in the chapel for many years to come; and Ser Pietro (or Pietrino) di Maestro Bernardo, who on this occasion is recorded through September 1530, though he, too, was associated with the chapel in future years. Among the boys was Luzio di Pavolo, son of one the Palace woodwind players. Luzio, recorded in the chapel through May 1533, officially assumed his father's post in the Palace wind band in 1545, although he had been substituting for him for many years before that time. His talent and experience suggest that he was another of the younger instrumentalists whose true role in the chapel remains somewhat ambiguous.

Sacristans' rolls are lacking for 1531, but several accounts record the continued presence of Bernardo Pontremoli, of Antonio Diligente, mentioned from June 1531 onwards, and of the instrumentalist Bernardino di Matteo Cartolaio, now listed among the adults beginning in December 1531. These three are on a sacristan's roll from March 1532 together with the *maestro di cappella* Piero d'Asciano. Jacomo da Verona, also known as Jacometto, rejoined the group in April 1532. The names of the five singers appear in various records from the remainder of the 1530s and the early 1540s. On occasion a few of them were temporarily absent and replaced by other adults; at times new singers joined them. Despite slight fluctuations, however, the presence of a minimal number of four men and an equal number of boys is confirmed by the sporadically preserved sacristans' rolls of the time. And since Luzio di Pavolo is also listed during some of these years, perhaps he and Bernardino di Matteo Cartolaio provided the kind of cornett accompaniment that was described a decade earlier by Sigismondo Tizio.

Ser Pietrino, together with the five men just mentioned, is listed as the sixth adult in December 1534. He was gone by the beginning of the next month, when only four adults, Piero di Domenico, Bernardino Pontremoli, Antonio Diligente, and Jacometto, and three boys, Agnolino, Scipione, and Bastiano del Nica, were present. The report for February 1535 has the same names, and an annotation to the effect that "the singers did not sing at Vespers on the 7th and the organist was absent at the Madonna services on the 6th and at Vespers on the 7th."[54] There were no changes in the chapel until July 1535, when the bass Frate Paulo of the Servite Order appeared as the fifth adult. Five adults were again present during the following October, November, and December, when Bernardino Cartolaio replaced Antonio Diligente. Also named on these sacristans' rolls, just before the boys, was Niccolò da San Gimignano, at L. 12 per month. These were apparently the singers who performed the *Te Deum laudamus* in honor of Emperor Charles V when he visited the city in April 1536.[55] Charles, en route to Bologna to formalize his recent rapprochement with Pope Clement VII, was accompanied by a large retinue that included his own chapel singers. In Bologna the imperial musicians joined the papal chapel in performance at ceremonies in San Petronio and it is possible they did the same when they were in Siena.

A sacristan's roll from a few months later, August 1536, reports a number of absences from required services and notes that the singers did not sing at Vespers on the day of the Assumption nor in the morning and afternoon on the day of its Octave. On that particular feast, as the sacristan wrote, "Pontremoli appeared, but the others did not."[56] Remarks such as this lend substance to the argument that only those who were designated as singers and who were paid as singers actually sang polyphony, regardless of how many other chaplains there were in the choir who may also have been capable performers. Lacking more definitive information regarding the chapel singers' duties in this period, bits and pieces of information such as this and the previously mentioned record of absences are of inestimable value in confirming the days and services when they performed.

They also furnish valuable information about the chapel's performances at the altar of the Madonna delle Grazie. Of course, "Madonna" in the report just mentioned could refer to an evening service such as Vespers or Compline, though that seems not to

---

54. "Scritta del mese di Ferraio 1534/35: Li cantori non cantorno a dì 7 al Vesparo; et l'organista a dì 6 mancò alle Madonne, a dì 7 mancò al Vesparo" (vols. 1074–75, *Note di salari*, fasc. 37, fol. 43).

55. Pietro Vigo, ed., *Carlo Quinto in Siena nell'aprile del 1536* (Bologna, 1884), 28: "[24 April 1536] Et tutto un tempo li cantori della Cappella intonorno Te Deum laudamus, e' l clero seguì: cantando tutto quel cantico."

56. "Nota che li cantori non cantorno el dì della Assumptione ad Vesparo, nè ancora el giorno della ottava, nè la mattina nè la sera. El Pontremoli comparse ma li altri no" (vol. 1076, *Note di salari, Secc. XV–XVIII,* unnumbered folio, Scripta del mese di Agosto A. D. MD XXXVI).

be the case, for Vespers is mentioned separately and specifically. Perhaps the "Madonna services" were Lady Masses held at the altar of the Madonna delle Grazie, or the Saturday morning Mass dedicated to the Madonna, mentioned in some reports. Or perhaps they were devotional services such as the "Salve" services that were so popular throughout Europe during the Renaissance.[57] "Madonna services" are also mentioned around this time in a payment from 11 September 1526 of L. 11 to the Palace trumpeters "for having played at the Madonna this year." Similar payments are registered to trumpeters in 1534, 1537, and 1546, to cite but a few of the pertinent records (see Doc. 6.3). Records from the 1480s specify that the trumpeters were to play to the Madonna on Saturday evenings and Sunday mornings and other feasts, when the image was unveiled.[58] Yet other records, as will be noted more fully below, show that the wind band played at the altar of Santa Maria delle Grazie on certain other occasions.[59] This information, together with the pictorial evidence furnished by the Biccherna cover of some fifty years earlier and the painting from the school of Ventura Salimbeni of several decades later, suggests that the chapel singers regularly performed at services held before the icon, even though such performances are rarely alluded to in extant records and at that, ambiguously.

The sacristan's roll for January 1538 lists five adults and five boys, including Scipione at L. 4, Vastiano (Bastiano) at L. 2, Andrea at L. 2, Benvenuto, at L. 1. 10, and Niccolò Cornetta, for whom no salary is given. Scipione, called a "cantorino" in earlier rolls from November 1533 through July 1535, was the son of another native of Asciano, Pavolo Jacomini, and as such may have had some connection with the *maestro di cappella* Ser Piero. Scipione, enrolled in the school for at least six years, was one the four lower-paid singers as late as September 1539. Subsequently he became cathedral organist, a clear indication that he received his keyboard training in situ from various people who held the post during his formative years. In addition to the boys, the sacristan's roll for that month cites six adults, among them the *maestro di cappella* Ser Piero d'Asciano, Ser Antonio Diligente at L. 17. 10, Ser Bernardino Pontremoli at L. 24. 10, Bernardino

---

57. See the entry "Salve regina" by Jeannine S. Ingram in *New Grove*, 16:435–6. Significantly, a cathedral document from almost a century later notes that "twice a week after Compline the clergy go in procession to the altar of the Madonna, honored with the organ and with music, singing the hymn and the *Salve*" (AOMS, vol. 1459, *Ricordi, 1608–9*, fols. 27ᵛ–28ʳ: "due volte la settimana il clero la sera dopo compieta va in processione honorato dall'organo e dalla musica a cantare l'hynno e la *Salve* all'altare della Madonna"). I have chosen to give a literal translation of the word "musica," though in most instances when it appears in a context such as this, it is better translated as "figural" or "polyphonic" music. Since liturgical practices remained fairly constant at Siena cathedral throughout the period in question, one might argue, given this information, that these references were, in fact, to "Salve" services after Compline.

58. See chapter 10.

59. See chapter 12; see also chapter 1, Pl. 1, and Fig. 3 for reference to the Biccherna cover and to the painting by the school of Ventura Salimbeni of the cathedral's interior from the later sixteenth century, which particularly shows the chapel of the Madonna del Voto and the icon it held. On the extreme right of the picture armored men kneel before a priest, who stands at the front of the chapel. On the left side of the picture, between two of the grand columns of the nave, perhaps the third and fourth from the central section, three instrumentalists, doubtless cornettists, are playing.

Cartolaio at L. 12, Jacometto da Verona at L. 12, and Ser Pietrino at L. 6. Also listed is Niccolò da San Gimignano, whose salary is not recorded this time either.

A New Departure:
Professional Cornettists in the Chapel

Niccolò, first called Niccolò Cornetta in a sacristan's roll from January 1537, first appeared in a similar roll from December 1534. There he was identified as Niccolò da San Gimignano and credited with L. 1 for the month. Although the small amount he was paid might indicate that, like Gano d'Enea, he entered the chapel as a boy singer, the later designation "cornetta" leaves no doubt that by then he was a cornettist, performing in the chapel. This is confirmed by sacristans' rolls from 1535, which show him earning the relatively large monthly salary of L. 12, even though he is still listed among the boys. Further corroboration of his status comes from an account crediting monthly payments of L. 12, from December 1536 through May 1537, to Niccolò di Giuliano da San Gimignano, "who plays the cornett." Clearly, Niccolò's role changed substantially during the two and a half years from the time he first began serving in the chapel, and the salary increase reflects the rite of passage of a youth of limited experience to an adult of professional standing.

Having a professional cornettist in the chapel was now established policy, as shown by the alacrity with which Niccolò's successor was engaged. He was Guasparre di Baldassarre, to whom monthly payments of L. 12 are registered from July 1537 through June 1538. Within a month of Guasparre's departure Gano d'Enea returned to cathedral service. Now called Galgano d'Enea, "who plays the cornett in the duomo," he was employed at a monthly salary of L. 12 from August 1538 through January 1540. His appointment, in a sense, may be said to have completed a cycle begun almost a quarter of a century earlier, for after he left three years were to pass before a professional instrumentalist was again brought in to assist the singers, and this time it would be a trombonist.

Sigismondo Tizio's remark about the use of cornetts in services bears reexamination in view of these and other cathedral records that testify to the successful reception of the instrument in the chapel's performances. Tizio, it will be recalled, referred to cornetts in the plural. Records from the early 1530s, when Bernardino Cartolaio and Luzio di Pavolo were simultaneously employed, support his statement, even though they make no direct references to either musician being an instrumentalist. Bernardino, in fact, continued to be employed during the years when Guasparre and then Galgano were mentioned, but he was still not identified as an instrumentalist. More direct evidence instead comes from records from later in the same decade. Niccolò, for example, was still on sacristans' rolls in January 1538 and September 1539, during the time when another, regularly salaried, cornettist played in the chapel. But because Niccolò is mentioned so infrequently and Bernardino is not called a cornettist, it is difficult to ascertain whether two cornettists were always employed throughout this time. The second cornettist, on the other hand, need not have been a professional adult musician; perhaps one of the youths in the chapel was called in or one of the salaried cornettists' private students assisted his teacher, without benefit of salary. This was a common enough occurrence among instrumentalists at the Palazzo Pubblico. Indeed, probably these very reasons make tracing pairs of cornettists in the chapel during the first four decades of the century so difficult.

Another of Tizio's observations regarding the chapel's performances bears closer scrutiny, namely, that while the singers were performing figural music with cornetts accompanying them, a youth was in the organ loft "sweetly singing the lascivious words of a love song." Clearly, the ensemble was performing a movement from a setting of the ordinary of the Mass based on previously composed music, whose original words the youth was singing as the others sang the liturgically appropriate text. Polyphonic Mass settings derived from pre-existent materials, whether of the cantus-firmus type that used a simple tune or of the "imitation" type that drew on all of the parts of a particular song, formed the bulk of the repertory at this time and would normally have elicited little or no comment. The unusual retention of the original words during the service, however, did not go unnoticed by Tizio, and doubtless by others present.[60] The youth's presence in the organ loft, away from the chapel singers, perhaps indicates that on occasion the organist also played with the vocal and instrumental ensemble. Organ accompaniment was more prevalent than demonstrated by surviving records. This much is implied by a bit of negative evidence, a report from thirty years later, cited below. It speaks of a solemn moment in the history of republican Siena, made extraordinary because in that instance Mass was celebrated without vocal polyphony and the sounds of the organ.[61]

The participation of professional cornettists in the chapel's performances during the 1530s placed Siena cathedral in the vanguard of new and innovative practices that were slowly gaining currency in the performance of sacred music. Though the town's corps of trumpeters and wind band had been performing for years before this on various occasions within and outside the cathedral, as will be amply illustrated in the following chapters, there is no indication that they performed with the singers. They appear instead to have functioned independently, as purely instrumental ensembles whose duties included playing at the Elevation during Mass and at other unspecified services in the Chapel of the Madonna delle Grazie, at processions or other services on major feast days, and at out-of-doors concerts in the cathedral square. The use of instruments other than the organ to accompany chapel singers, while not unknown in Italy before this time, was restricted to rather special occasions, though it may have been more widespread outside the peninsula.[62] Notable among late fifteenth-century occasions in

---

60. For evidence from contemporary or near contemporary sources that point to the retention of the original texts of sacred melodies used as cantus firmi in some Mass settings, see Alejandro Planchart, "Guillaume Dufay's Masses: A View of the Manuscript Tradition," in *Papers Read at the Dufay Quincentenary Conference,* ed. Allan Atlas (New York, 1976), 26–60, esp. 47–48; Gareth R. K. Curtis, "Brussels, Bibliothèque Royale MS. 5557, and the Texting of Dufay's 'Ecce ancilla Domini' and 'Ave regina celorum' Masses," *Acta Musicologica* 51 (1979): 73–86. Tizio's report offers support for Jaap van Benthem's proposal that even the words of secular tunes should be sung; see van Benthem, "Was 'Une Mousse de Biscaye' Really Appreciated by L'ami Baudichon?" *Muziek & Wetenschap* 1 (1991): 175–94.

61. See the passage quoted from Alessandro Sozzini's chronicle, mentioned below in note 110.

62. The situation outside Italy has recently been summarized by Richard Sherr, "Questions Concerning Instrumental Ensemble Music in Sacred Contexts in the Early Sixteenth Century," in *Le Concert des voix et des instruments à la Renaissance: Actes du XXXIVe Colloque International d'Études Su-*

which voices were blended with groups of instruments and the organ was the nuptial Mass celebrating the wedding of Bianca Maria Sforza to Emperor Maximilian I at Milan cathedral on 30 November 1493. Beatrice d'Este Sforza described the ceremony in a letter to her sister Isabella d'Este Gonzaga shortly after the event. "When we were all in our places," she wrote, "the Most Reverend Archbishop of Milan entered in full vestments, with the priests in ordinary, and began to celebrate Mass with the greatest pomp and solemnity, to the sound of trumpets, flutes and organ music, together with the voices of the chapel choir, who adapted their singing to Monsignore's time."[63] But such events were exceptional, perhaps because most Italian cathedrals resorted to the practical solution of having the organist accompany the few singers they employed, while those wealthy enough to employ greater numbers of singers favored an a cappella performance, in emulation of the papal chapel.

Records from Italian churches suggest that instruments other than the organ did not make an appearance in many of Italy's major chapels until the later sixteenth century.[64] To be sure, a trombonist played on two occasions during December 1546 in the Cappella Giulia at St. Peter's in Rome, but no other instrumentalist is mentioned there until 1564, when a cornettist played in the month of May.[65] At Orvieto cathedral one of the four singers employed from 1544 to 1550 was also a cornettist, and other instrumentalists were employed later in the century, among them a trombonist in 1582–83.[66] At Bologna's San Petronio, whose musicians were to be in the forefront of mid-seventeenth-century instrumental music, a trombonist was hired only in 1560. This was the trombone virtuoso Alfonso Viola, whose salary was L. 5 per month. A cornett was not added to the Bolognese group until 1574.[67] A trombonist appeared in the records of Modena cathedral for the first time during the period 1562–83, whereas the Mantuan cathedral registers do not speak of one until 1588.[68]

Instruments were present at services at Padua's church of the Santo on two feast days in the early sixteenth century—trombones and organ at Vespers on the Vigil of the Assumption in 1519 and cornetts, trombones, nakers, and flutes at Vespers on St. Anthony's Day in 1524—but these were more in the fifteenth-century tradition of employing diverse instruments for special occasions.[69] At the Santo cornettists and other instrumentalists are reported sporadically in the following decades until 1553, when a

---

périeures de la Renaissance, 1–11 juillet 1991, ed. Jean-Michel Vaccaro (Paris, 1995), 145–56, esp. 145–47.

63. Quoted in Julia Cartwright, *Beatrice d'Este* (New York and London, 1926), 214.

64. See D'Accone, "The Performance of Sacred Music in Italy during Josquin's Time," 616.

65. See Ariane Ducrot, "Histoire de la Cappella Giulia au XVIe siècle," in *Mélanges d'Archéologie et d'Histoire de l'École Française de Rome* 75 (1963): 506.

66. Biancamaria Brumana and Galliano Ciliberti, *Orvieto: Una cattedrale e la sua musica (1480– 1610),* Historiae Musicae Cultores Biblioteca 58 (Florence, 1990), 32, 34, 56.

67. Gambassi, *La cappella musicale di San Petronio,* 13, 15, 76, 83.

68. Roncaglia, *La cappella musicale del Duomo di Modena,* 26; Pierre M. Tagmann, *Archivalische Studien zur Musikpflege am Dom von Mantua* (Bern and Stuttgart, 1967), 72–84.

69. Antonio Sartori, *Documenti per la storia della musica al Santo e nel Veneto,* ed. Elisa Grossato (Vicenza, 1977), 10–11; Giulio Cattin, "Rivisitati alcuni maestri e cantori cinquecenteschi della cattedrale di Vicenza," in *Scritti e memorie in onore di Mons. Carlo Fanton Vescovo ausiliare di Vicenza nel Cin-*

cornettist was awarded a two-year contract. Later, in 1566, a trombonist who was to supplement the bass part was added to the rolls permanently. This was the composer Bartolomeo Sorte, who served for the following two decades. Padua, within the Venetian orbit, eventually emulated its parent city, and beginning in 1582 a wind ensemble of three trombones and a cornett was added permanently to the Santo's musical forces. A violinist joined the group in 1568.[70] At St. Mark's in Venice, the cornettist Girolamo della Casa (ca. 1543–1601) and an ensemble including two of his brothers and other musicians was hired to assist at services only in 1568. There are reports of as many as twelve instruments at concerts during Girolamo's tenure. Eleanor Selfridge-Field notes that "some (perhaps most) of their playing probably had the purpose of reinforcing vocal parts or of substituting for absent singers."[71] This was certainly the case at Siena cathedral in the later sixteenth century, when a trombonist was usually employed in the chapel, but that situation, as with all of those mentioned here, was considerably after the 1530s, when cornettists first appeared among the singers.

In Siena the practice of employing two cornettists in the chapel was perhaps anticipated by earlier experiments involving unspecified woodwind instruments during the tenure of Giovanni di Maestro Antonio in 1510 and was surely established during the years 1515–1525, when Gano, Bernardino, and Luzio were employed. In view of what we currently know about other Italian chapels at the time, Sienese practice seems exceptional because it was not until the 1560s that instruments can be said to have been used with any degree of regularity in chapel music, and at that, only in a few places. The archival reports find correspondences in data regarding sacred music publications whose titles indicate the suitability of their contents for performance by voices and instruments, recently compiled and analyzed by Stephen Bonta.[72] A few such collections were issued before the mid-sixteenth century. But it was only in the early 1560s,

---

quantesimo di Sacerdozio (Vicenza, 1982), 188. The 1524 report is also cited by Owens, "Il Cinquecento," 30, n. 12.

70. Owens, "Il Cinquecento," 36, 50, 67.

71. See *Venetian Instrumental Music from Gabrieli to Vivaldi* (New York, 1965), 14–15; see also Denis Arnold, "Brass Instruments in Italian Church Music of the Sixteenth and Early Seventeenth Centuries," *The Brass Quarterly* 1 (1957): 85.

72. Stephen Bonta, "The Use of Instruments in Sacred Music in Italy 1560–1700," *Early Music* 18 (1990): 519–35. See particularly p. 521, where he cites Nicholas Gombert's collection of four-voice motets, *Musica quatuor vocum, (vulgo motetcta nuncupatur), lyris maioribus, ac tibijs imparibus accommodata . . . liber primus* (Venice, Girolamo Scotto, 1539; reprinted in 1541 and 1551, RISM G 2977), as an early print whose title advertises its contents as suitable for performance with or by strings and woodwinds. Bonta shows that after 1562, with the publication of Lassus's first book of five-voice motets, whose title bore the instruction that the motets could be performed "tum viva voce, tum omnis generis instrumentis," a number of sacred music prints appeared containing works suitable for performance by voices and instruments. Bonta characterizes his findings, based on a statistical sampling of 320 Italian prints from the period 1560 to 1700, as representative of "roughly 50 per cent of all Italian prints of the time that might be presumed to call for the use of instruments." He notes, moreover, that his sampling is proportionally representative of the repertory as a whole in the types of sacred works published during the period. For the sixteenth century there were eighteen such prints in the decade 1561–70; seven in the decade 1571–80; thirteen in the decade 1581–90; twenty-four in the period 1591–1600. The figure rose dramatically to sixty-five, as might be expected, in the first decade

when, beginning with the publication of Orlando di Lasso's first book of five-voice motets, Venetian publishers and others brought out a spate of volumes of motets and music for Vespers that emphasized instrumental participation in vocal performances. While it is likely that the idea of using instruments was initially conceived more as a means of supplementing the lower parts or substituting for one or more of them, the result was an enrichment of a sound that was still essentially solo polyphony or modified ensemble polyphony. The colors produced by the blending of voices and one or two solo instruments quickly found favor with performers and listeners alike. The upshot of this development in Siena was that professional cornettists were finally hired on a more formal basis and that instrumental accompaniment became a characteristic feature of Sienese chapel music in the later 1530s.

PERFORMANCE PRACTICES IN ITALIAN MUSICAL CHAPELS, CA. 1500–1540

A brief survey of the number of musicians in a few Italian chapels through the 1540s reveals that Siena cathedral compared favorably with some and that it surpassed or lagged behind others. While the territorial possessions, power, and wealth of a city were not the sole determinants of the size and stability of its chapel, the presence of a court, local politics, and economic prosperity certainly played a role. Other factors, such as the number of local singers on hand, the availability of ecclesiastical and other preferments, tradition, and even civic pride, were influential. Large numbers and prestigious performers, of course, did not necessarily guarantee high-quality performance, nor did they furnish absolute indicators of the range and variety of a group's repertory, though they obviously accounted for differences in sound and in performing practices. How *maestri di cappella,* including those at Siena, coped with the fluctuating numbers of adults in these groups is conjectural. Whether all groups always performed at their full strength is also a matter of conjecture. But it stands to reason that considerations of balance and dynamic contrast in any performance were also influenced by the acoustics of a particular ambiance—a side altar or chapel, a choir, a singing gallery, to name the places used in Siena cathedral—as well as by the number of singers and instrumentalists employed.

At Modena cathedral, nine adults were employed between 1505 and 1513, eleven between 1513 and 1520. But only seven adults, among them the *maestro di cappella,* were named in 1548.[73] Bologna's church of San Petronio, as renowned within the city as its cathedral, had a chapel of seven adult singers, including the *maestro di cappella,* in 1505 and 1506. Their number reached eight in 1512, a figure more or less retained for several years before increasing to ten in 1520, and to twelve in 1535.[74] By 1540 there were fourteen adults, in addition to the "old *maestro di cappella*" Giovanni Spataro, who had been in charge since 1512.[75] At Rieti a chapel of four adult singers was established

---

of the seventeenth century, as newer styles demanding the use of basso continuo and obligato instruments took hold.

73. Roncaglia, *La cappella musicale del Duomo di Modena,* 21, 25.
74. Gambassi, *La cappella musicale di S. Petronio,* 59, 61, 63, 67.
75. Ibid., 68–69.

in 1517 and by 1529 the group reached its maximum complement of seven.[76] Mantua cathedral averaged between four and eight adult singers in the period during the first fifteen years of the century, but their number grew to fifteen in 1523 and to eighteen in 1528.[77] As in all of the churches cited here, unspecified numbers of boys from their singing schools also performed with the adults.

Padua cathedral counted five adults in 1511, six in 1523 and 1529, and seven in 1532 and 1533.[78] At Padua's other major church, the Santo, a small group of adult singers, usually three and on occasion four, in addition to the *maestro di cappella* and an unspecified number of young friars, were sporadically employed during the first half of the sixteenth century.[79] Five adult singers served Treviso cathedral between 1509 and 1513 and their number grew to thirteen by 1532. But Verona cathedral's chapel, which counted seven adults in 1524 and eleven in 1527, dropped to nine in 1533. All of these figures pale by comparison with the number of singers at St. Mark's in Venice. Though official lists are lacking after the 1490s, when seventeen adults were present, other documents indicate that there were at least sixteen adult singers in 1527 and eighteen in 1545.[80] The presence of boy singers at St. Mark's is difficult to determine, though a few appear in the records.[81]

St. Peter's singers in Rome, later reconstituted as the Cappella Giulia by Pope Julius II, had seven adults in 1501, eight adults and two boys in 1502, and five adults and three boys in 1514. The number of personnel grew to eleven singers in 1525, before declining to seven in 1534 and then rising to thirteen by 1549.[82] Like St. Peter's, the chapel at Loreto's famed Santa Casa, instituted in 1507, also at the instance of Pope Julius II, had a see-saw existence in the three decades after its establishment.[83] From a low of two singers, mentioned in 1512, 1534, and 1537, there were as many as nine in 1533, although the seven recorded in 1512, and at various times from 1529 to 1540, represent the norm. In 1540 eleven adult singers were present. Instrumentalists, other than organists, are never cited in connection with the chapel singers.

Milan and Florence cathedrals, the two institutions with which it has been possible to compare the Sienese chapel from its very beginnings, reveal a far different situation, one that indicates the less ambitious program and more provincial character of Siena's musical establishment, occasioned perhaps by the unsettled politics of the first four decades of the sixteenth century. Like Siena, both the Milanese and the Florentine chapels relied primarily on local singers, with a sprinkling of foreigners, but with the difference that composers were usually at the helm. Despite political turmoil and eco-

---

76. A. Sacchetti-Sassetti, "La cappella musicale del Duomo di Rieti," *Note d'Archivio* 17 (1940): 126, 129; (1941): 63–64.

77. Tagmann, *Archivalische Studien zur Musikpflege am Dom von Mantua,* 35.

78. Casimiri, "Musica e musicisti nella cattedrale di Padova," 185, 192, 195.

79. Owens, "Il Cinquecento," 31–34, 78.

80. Ongaro, "The Chapel at St. Mark's," 229.

81. Ongaro, "Sixteenth-Century Patronage at St Mark's," 86–87.

82. Ducrot, "Histoire de la Cappella Giulia," 189–90, 192, 195.

83. The figures preserved in its registers, however, may not indicate the actual numbers employed, both because of gaps in the records and because chaplains were no longer listed as singers after they became prebendaries. See Edera Alfieri, *La cappella musicale di Loreto* (Bologna, 1970), 25.

nomic uncertainty, the cathedral chapel in Milan pursued a steady course throughout this period, when the city and its dominions were initially ruled by the last Sforza dukes and then by Habsburg viceroys. The chapel, under the direction of the renowned theorist and composer Franchino Gaffurio from 1484 through 1521, retained twelve adult singers, assisted by an unspecified number of boys.[84] The reverse prevailed at Siena, where the chapel rarely numbered more than six adults, although six, eight, and eleven boys often assisted them.

In 1522, when the Flemish composer Hermann Matthias Werrecore assumed the *maestro di cappella*'s post in Milan, the group comprised eleven adult singers and seven boys. Their numbers fluctuated between eleven and fourteen adults and four and six boys in the following decade, but a more stable group was ensured in December 1534, after administrative and financial changes.[85] At that time, besides the *maestro di cappella,* who earned L. 12 per month, the fully paid singers included eleven adults, among whom were four altos (one also designated as a falsetto), three tenors, four basses, at L. 6 per month, and six boy sopranos, at s. 20. Salaries were, on the whole, lower than Siena's, though other perquisites may have compensated for the apparent differences. Two undesignated singers who received half pay also performed with the group. In this same period Siena's chapel sometimes employed as many as eight adults—though six were the norm—and eight boys, with the difference that instrumentalists began to appear, whereas none are mentioned in Milanese annals. In other words, the Milanese chapel, with a somewhat larger complement of singers, retained the a cappella tradition of which the papal chapel remained a bastion throughout the sixteenth century.

How closely Florence adhered to the ideal of unaccompanied polyphony is illustrated by personnel policies that characterized the chapel there throughout the first forty years of the century.[86] Reestablished after the Savonarolan interregnum, first at the cathedral in 1501 and then a few years later at the Baptistry, the Florentine group, like its Sienese counterpart, comprised primarily local singers. Initially, the cathedral chapel was slated to have seven boys, who would perform with the adult singers under the direction of their teacher. But usually between four and six boys were present, just as in Siena during this period. On the other hand, the number of adults in Florence was greater. Eleven of them, including two sopranos, two altos, two tenors, two basses, and two teachers (one of whom was a tenor), were employed, as were four boys, in February 1502. Similar forces were more or less maintained during the following years. In May 1507, when Ser Maddalo was at Florence cathedral, there were ten adults, in addition to the boys. Nine adults and the boys are mentioned in a decree from August 1510 authorizing the chapel's reestablishment at the Baptistry. Eight adults and six boys sang there in 1512, and within the year the number of adults reached thirteen. Among

---

84. There were twelve boys in Milan cathedral school in 1507 and sixteen in 1520, but there is no indication that all of them sang with the adults. See Sartori, "La cappella del Duomo dalle origini a Franchino Gaffurio," 723–49, esp. 746, 748.

85. Christine Getz, "The Milanese Cathedral Choir under Hermann Matthias Werrecore, Maestro di Cappella 1522–1550," *Musica Disciplina* 46 (1992): 177–83. The Milanese group was further strengthened in 1547 with the addition of four boy sopranos (at half pay) and two new tenors in 1549.

86. D'Accone, "The Musical Chapels at the Florentine Cathedral and Baptistry," passim.

them were two altos, five tenors, and two basses. On average, the singers earned between two and three ducats per month. With larger revenues and the combined resources of two churches to draw on, it is understandable that the Florentine group could support a greater number of adults at higher salaries than Siena cathedral, which at this time rarely counted more than six.

The Florentine chapel continued to maintain a full complement of adults up to the time of its dissolution in 1527. In the meantime several composers, Giovanni Serragli, Bernardo Pisano, Philippe Verdelot, and Mattia Rampollini, served as *maestri di cappella,* and a number of foreign singers, among them the Frenchmen Charles Argenteuil, joined the group. Plague and then siege brought about the complete disbanding of the chapel, but hard times and an uncertain political climate were the principal reasons behind the absence of polyphonic singers at the cathedral and at the Baptistry in the following years.

The discontinuity of the chapel's operations in Florence offers quite a contrast to Siena's continued stability. Although both groups relied increasingly on local singers and *maestri di cappella* and both had an active teaching program, the Florentine chapel, owing to the disruptive forces of internal politics, followed a somewhat irregular course, whereas Siena's chapel, despite the problems caused by similar rifts in domestic politics and frequent changes in personnel, continued to function without interruption. This was particularly true during the 1530s, when the Florentine chapel ceased performing altogether. It was, in fact, only in 1540 that the Florentine chapel, reestablished at the cathedral and Baptistry at the instance of Duke Cosimo de' Medici, achieved a long overdue measure of stability. Under Francesco Corteccia's direction the group, which, in addition to seven boy sopranos, now consisted of sixteen adults, including five basses, four tenors, and seven contraltos, soon joined the ranks of the most progressive and well-staffed musical establishments in Italy.

Florence had strong ties to Rome, where two Medici popes held sway, with a brief interruption, from 1513 through 1534. Thus, it is not surprising to learn that several singers served in both cities and that much of the Florentine repertory in these years derived from Roman usage. Nor is it suprising to find that Florentine performance practices reflected contemporary Roman ideals, at least those of the papal chapel, which at one point during the reign of the first Medici Pope, Leo X (1513–21), counted thirty-one singers in its ranks, and a more normal complement of twenty-four during the reign of his cousin, Pope Clement VII (1523–34).[87] The papal chapel emphasized

---

87. Herman-Walter Frey, "Regesten zur päpstlichen Kapelle unter Leo X. und zu seiner Privatkapelle," *Musikforschung* 8 (1955): 198–99; also his "Klemens VII und der Prior der päpstlichen Kapelle Nicholo de Pitti," *Musikforschung* 4 (1951): 180. During Clement's time the twenty-four singers included seven sopranos, seven contraltos, four tenors, and six basses. As it had in the past, the Sistine Chapel led the way in maintaining a large number of personnel. Records for the first decade of the century indicate that it employed between sixteen and twenty-one singers. See Haberl, "Die römische 'schola cantorum'," 247–49. Sherr has observed that by the middle of the sixteenth century a complement of twenty-four singers seems to have been established as the ideal number in the Sistine Chapel, though he also notes that the chapel apparently never achieved this ideal. See his "Competence and Incompetence in the Papal Choir in the Age of Palestrina," *Early Music* 22 (1994): 620–1.

Although not germane to this discussion of church chapels, it is interesting to note that in Ferrara

a cappella performance and usually admitted no instrumental accompaniment, including that of the organ, which in any case was lacking in the Sistine Chapel where services were usually conducted.[88] But in Florence, which boasted organs and organists at both the cathedral and the Baptistry, there is no mention of instrumentalists in the chapel and the organist's role at this time seems to have been limited to solo performance.

In the papal chapel, furthermore, even though the concept of choral polyphony, that is, of polyphony sung by several singers to a part, seems to have been well established by this time, there is evidence of practices that called for portions of pieces, if not entire pieces, to be sung by soloists.[89] No evidence of performance by soloists exists for Florence—except, of course, in the period when only four adults were employed. When larger forces were employed, all singers performed at the required services at the cathedral and the Baptistry. Indeed, in 1541 another bass was added to the five already present among the Florentine singers because as one report put it, "it seems nothing is lacking in the chapel except the contrabasses are so weak, they are little heard."[90] But it is

---

Duke Ercole's chapel ranked alongside that of the pope and of some major European courts, employing nineteen or twenty singers from 1491 to 1504, twenty-nine in 1499 and 1503, and thirty-one singers and three organists in 1504. After Ercole's death, his successor, Alfonso, "at first maintained similar numbers, but after the collapse of the chapel in 1510, he reconstituted it in 1512 with six and kept thereafter an average of six or eight musicians on a permanent basis" (Lockwood, *Music in Renaissance Ferrara,* 199–200).

88. Patrizio Barbieri has presented evidence indicating that the chapel performed with organ at Vespers in the private apartments of the Pope during the reign of Sixtus V (1585–90), thus anticipating by two decades Lionnet's evidence that similar practices occurred during the first four decades of seventeenth century. See Barbieri, "On a Continuo Organ Part Attributed to Palestrina," *Early Music* 22 (1994): 587–605. Graham Dixon, "The Performance of Palestrina: Some Questions, but fewer Answers," ibid., 667–75, discusses the use of the organ and other instruments with voices at various places in Rome, particularly the German College in the later 1580s. See also Jean Lionnet, "Performance Practice in the Papal Chapel during the 17th Century," *Early Music* 15 (1987): 4–5; id., "Palestrina e la Cappella pontificia," in *Atti del II convegno internazionale di studi palestriniani,* ed. J. Bianchi and G. C. Rostirolla (Palestrina, 1991), 130; and id., "The Borghese Family and Music during the First Half of the Seventeenth Century," *Music and Letters* 74 (1993): 519–22. With regard to Roman practices, at St. Peter's Cappella Giulia performances of polyphony with organ accompaniment, in this case motets, are mentioned only in the last years of the sixteenth century, as noted by G. C. Rostirolla, "La Cappella Giulia in San Pietro negli anni del magistero di Giovanni Pierluigi da Palestrina," in *Atti del Convegno di studi palestriniani,* ed. F. Luisi (Palestrina, 1977), 137.

89. See my remarks regarding choral polyphony in chapter 5. See also Sherr, "Performance Practice in the Papal Chapel in the 16th Century," 453–62. Among the instances cited by Sherr are two occasions in 1583 pointing to the use of soloists, and another from 1596. Sherr also notes that a 1507 report of a Credo sung by sixteen voices indicates that such numbers were unusual. More recently he has published a report by Johannes Burkhard, the late fifteenth-century papal master of ceremonies, who mentioned twelve singers (two tenors, four countertenors, and six high voices) as an ideal complement, though he noted that in the past there were more than that number and as few as eight. Sherr remarks that this runs counter to his own argument that all members of the choir rarely sang together. See his "Competence and Incompetence," 622–23. See also Dixon's summary of the evidence in "The Performance of Palestrina," 673–74.

90. D'Accone, "The Musical Chapels," 30. At the time the chapel was employing sixteen adults and eight boys. This report also offers evidence in favor of the entire Florentine chapel performing at any given time.

possible that similar experiments in sound colors were tried there, in view of the close contacts Florentine musicians maintained with the papal chapel.

In contrast, small ensemble polyphony, with a preponderance of boy sopranos—of whom there were none in the papal chapel—was more usual at Siena cathedral at this time. In addition, there were performances with the accompaniment of cornetts, and perhaps other woodwind instruments and the organ, which further emphasized the different colors in sound produced by the Sienese group. By employing instrumentalists in the chapel Siena moved away from contemporary Florentine and Roman practices. There were, to be sure, resonances of this newly established vocal-instrumental ideal in chapels elsewhere on the peninsula, which, as mentioned, publishers quickly exploited. But since it was to Florence and to Rome that the Sienese had traditionally looked, not only for performers and performance practices, but, in the case of Rome, for liturgy as well, it is clear that Sienese musicians embarked on an independent course in this period. Not that a cappella or unaccompanied performances of part music were totally abandoned at Siena during the time cornettists were associated with the chapel. Lacking any documentation regarding their duties, we can only speculate that instrumentalists played on certain Sundays and feast days such as Pentecost, though not necessarily on all of the days when vocal polyphony might have been performed. Problems regarding precisely what kinds of music were suitable for a group of singers and one or two cornettists and how pieces in the existing repertory were arranged or adjusted in order to accommodate the instrumentalists need to be more fully investigated, though further research will surely provide conclusions valid not only for Siena but for other chapels in Italy and in Europe. In any event, for the moment it seems logical to suppose that some polyphonic pieces were still being done by voices alone, that others were performed in alternation with, or accompanied by, the organ and that yet others were done with cornetts, together perhaps with the organ, should we wish to give the widest possible interpretation to Tizio's remarks.

ORGANISTS, 1503–1563

Local as well as foreign organists participated in these developments in Sienese performing practices. Ser Francesco di Tommaso, a former student in the cathedral school who became organist in May 1503, remained at his post through May 1508, when he was succeeded by the Franciscan friar Fra Lorenzo di Niccolò di Magnio. A contract awarded Lorenzo on 11 June 1508 notes that he was to serve "with the usual obligations, salary, and conditions and at the pleasure of the said overseers." Though Lorenzo was recorded through March 1515, a few records from 1512 indicate some dissatisfaction with his work and show that at least one other musician was auditioned for the organist's post during his incumbency. The musician in question was Don Lodovico di Milano called Zoppino, otherwise known as Lodovico Milanese, a composer of frottole whose works Petrucci published. Lodovico was barely installed as organist at the cathedral of Lucca, when Siena beckoned him.[91]

---

91. For a recent summary of Lodovico's career and a list of his extant works see William Prizer's article in *New Grove,* 11:306.

Siena had traditionally maintained musical ties with Lucca, as frequent visits of the Palace instrumentalists there attest, and more than a century earlier it had even sent one of its sons as organist to Lucca cathedral. When Zoppino arrived in Siena in August 1512, at the express invitation of the overseers who were paying his travel expenses, it appeared that the time might be ripe for another such exchange. Zoppino was received with the customary generosity befitting his noble status, and a contract was drawn up that promised him an unheard of salary of Fl. 100 per annum, thirty of which were guaranteed by Borghese Petrucci, now the Opera's overseer.[92] In return Zoppino was required to perform personally on Sundays and feast days. But either his playing was judged unsatisfactory or it proved impossible to award him the agreed upon sum, for a record from the beginning of September says that L. 5 were spent on a horse to send him back to Lucca.

Fra Lorenzo's immediate successor, Maestro Cristoforo di Vivaldo da Modena, took up his post on 4 July 1515. The terms of his contract granted him a two-year appointment at an annual salary of Fl. 30 and required him to serve "with the same conditions and obligations that Fra Lorenzo had."[93] Cristoforo was the first of the Modenese musicians who played such an important role in the chapel's development later in the century. He bought a harpsichord for the Opera in April 1526, an indication perhaps that he, too, was involved in the teaching program or that the harpsichord served as a rehearsal instrument. Although his tenure lasted for almost twelve years—monthly payments of L. 21 are recorded to him through the end of April 1527—he was away on several occasions. The one-time *maestro di cappella* Ser Antonio Diligente substituted for him for an entire year, from December 1518 to December 1519. Among Cristoforo's temporary replacements were Jacomo da Modena (May 1520), Bartolomeo di Monna Betta (December 1523, February–March 1524), and Giovannandrea d'Alessandro (January–March 1524), some of the latter undoubtedly students of his. Although there are no particulars about the organist named Jacomo, perhaps he was the Modenese composer Jacomo Fogliano, who had strong Roman connections around this time, connections that might have taken him through Siena.[94]

Records of contracts are lacking from this time, but account books register payments to Ser Antonio di Galgano, a cathedral chaplain, from July 1527 through May 1530, indicating that he was Cristoforo's successor. An otherwise unknown organist named Jacomo da Palermo played from September 1530 to the following March. Maestro Pietro di Bartolomeo Corradini, the next tenured organist, is mentioned in several groups of payments from September 1531 through 10 April 1541.[95] He, too,

---

92. A record from the 31st of the month reports that Zoppino was given 2 gold florins for making the trip. The contract, published by Borghesi and Banchi, *Nuovi documenti per la storia dell'arte senese*, 402, is in ASS, Notarile antecosimiano, vol. 1057, unpaginated folio, dated 26 August 1512.

93. Little information survives about Cristoforo, though a document from 11 September 1516 in which he named a Modenese citizen as his procurator indicates that he was a layman (ASS, Notarile antecosimiano, vol. 1058, without pagination, dated 11 September 1516).

94. On Fogliano see the entry by H. Colin Slim in *New Grove*, 6:687–88.

95. See vol. 513, *D&C, 1529–42*, fol. 41ʳ, for payment of L. 140 to Ser Bernardo di Lonardo dal Monte, "che tempara l'organo nuovo," in 1529; fol. 325ʳ, for payment of L. 121. 6 to Ser Girolamo

was away on at least one occasion, in January 1537, when Ser Antonio Moneta served as substitute organist.[96] Both were gone by May and the new organist beginning in June 1541 was the former chorister and student Scipione di Pavolo Jacomini.

With Scipione's appointment the cathedral regained an organist of stature, who brought a knowledge of instrumental practices, talent, and stability to the program. Enjoying the longest tenure of any organist in the century, he held the post through the end of April 1563.[97] Scipione began with a monthly salary of L. 14 and received periodic increments, which doubled it to L. 28 by May 1551. By that time he was living in a house furnished by the Opera, possibly a privilege granted all tenured organists, though this is not mentioned in extant documents. This information comes from a letter Scipione wrote, when he was ill and needed money, to an administrator named Giuseppe. It is signed and dated "from the Opera's house, 27 July 1551" (see Doc. 6.4). A perquisite such as free housing added considerably to Scipione's income, though it is another of those intangibles, such as private teaching and occasional engagements outside official places of employment, that make determing musicians' economic status a difficult task. In Scipione's case, however, there is evidence in later years of additional income derived from a benefice, that of archpriest at the collegiate church in his home town of Asciano. He received the benefice sometime between May 1554, when he filed his first will, and August 1557, when he filed his second one.[98] This—one of the few benefices recorded for a cathedral musician at this time—quite clearly made few demands on his time and allowed him to continue as cathedral organist.[99] Early in his career Scipione was assisted by a second organist, the singer-chaplain Ulivieri di Jacomo, to whom payments are recorded from April 1541 to January 1543. It may be that this was a temporary expedient, for no other organist besides Scipione appears on the books in later years.

THE CHAPEL IN THE 1540S

The history of the chapel in the years before the fall of the Republic reveals a slow but steady expansion of forces. Although the number of adults fluctuated slightly through

---

di Bartolomeo e Nofrio "che fano li organi," "per la temperatura del'organo nuovo," and "per la temperatura del'organo vechio" in October 1537.

96. Pietro eventually became organist of Santa Maria del Fiore in Florence. See chapter 13. Ser Antonio Moneta, sacristan and chaplain of San Paolo, was also a member of the Confraternity of San Pietro nel Duomo. He was elected chamberlain and prior of the confraternity on numerous occasions between 1519 and 1526 (ASS, PR, Compagnia di San Pietro nel Duomo, vol. 1369, *Capitoli, D&C, 1513–76*, fols. 27ʳ, 32ʳ, 33ᵛ, 102ᵛ, 170ʳ).

97. No information survives regarding his apprenticeship at the cathedral or about his having played in some other church before this time, but his emergence as principal organist less than two years after leaving the chapel clearly indicates that he must have been well prepared for the job, perhaps under the tutelage of Pietro Corradini.

98. In the first will he is referred to as "Ser Scipio olim Pauli Iacomini de Sciano, presbiter et organista ecclesie cathedralis Senensis" (ASS, Notarile antecosimiano, vol. 2770, fasc. 1, no. 92). In the second, he is referred to as "Ser Scipio quondam Pauli Iacomini de Asciano, clericus et archipresbiter ecclesie collegiate dicte terre Asciani" (ibid., no. 248).

99. Scipione, however, remained in Siena after leaving his cathedral post. A payment to him for his services as organist at Santa Maria della Scala's church, dated 20 March 1565/66, shows that he

the mid–1540s, at least five adults (names mostly familiar from previous years) and four boys were employed on a regular basis. Tracing the singers' movements from this time forward is facilitated by a number of account books that again list groups of payments issued to individuals throughout the course of an entire fiscal year. (As in the past, the fiscal year ran from the beginning of May through the end of the following April.) Heading the list of the more permanent employees in the 1540s was the former chorister Giovanbattista di Bartolomeo, now described as a tenor. He succeeded Piero d'Asciano as *maestro di cappella* shortly after the latter's departure in late 1539 and held the post through April 1548, earning L. 21 per month throughout most of his tenure. Among the continuing personnel was Bernardino di Matteo Cartolaio, recorded through 1542. New singers in these years included two basses, the Servite friar Gabriello di Giovanni de' Servi, first reported in January 1539, and the Spaniard Gabriello di Ramondo Spagnolo, who began in mid-June 1540. Pietro di Tommaso da Gubbio, an alto, joined the group in mid-December 1542. Cornett players disappear from the official rosters at this time. Trombonists, the first of whom was the Palace musician Ansano Maria di Geronimo, are listed beginning in November 1543. Recorded among the boys during the period January 1542 to February 1548 was a "cantorino" named Ascanio di Andrea. This was Ascanio Marri, in later years a famous trombonist, composer, and director of the Palace wind band, who became master of the same chapel he had once sung in as a chorister.

The Repertory at Mid-Century

During the 1540s the Opera continued to acquire both printed and manuscript music (see Table 6.1 for payments). One record, from 17 March 1548, states that L. 5 were spent that day, "that is, L. 3 to pay for a book of polyphony to give to Ser Scipione the organist, and S. 40 to give to a French singer who sang in the chapel." Apart from registering the presence of an itinerant musician who stayed so briefly that his name did not even appear on the sacristan's roll, the entry is of interest because it shows that music was also purchased for the organist, who by this time was the former choirboy Scipione di Pavolo. While the music in question could have been in manuscript, it is more likely that it was a printed volume, perhaps even one with works composed specifically for the keyboard such as the Venetian publication *Musica nova*.[100] Manuscript music is instead specified in a payment of L. 74, issued some months earlier, on 6 October 1547, to Ser Niccolò, "a priest of the nuns of St. Martha, for having written a book of plainchant on parchment, of different psalms, hymns, and antiphons, which are eighteen and a half quinternions at L. 4 the quinternion." Possibly this is one of the yet-to-be-identified volumes in cathedral archives. Printed music is clearly indicated in a payment dated 24 December 1546, when L. 3 were paid to the *maestro di cappella* Giovanbattista di Bartolomeo for "two sets of partbooks containing motets." Perhaps these partbooks were among the seven items of printed music mentioned in the next

---

was archpriest of the church Sant'Ansano at the time (Ospedale, vol. 28, *Deliberazioni, 1552–72,* fol. 156ʳ, quoted below in chapter 13).

100. *Musica nova* has been edited by Slim, Monuments of Renaissance Music, 1.

extant inventory of the "books of song" that he consigned to the sacristy in December 1547 (see above, Table 6.2).[101]

That inventory is of particular interest because it gives a good idea of what was sung at mid-century, just before and during the siege, which culminated in the loss of Siena's independence. It also shows that Sienese singers were familiar with some of the most recently published music in Italy and abroad and that an international repertory was favored, especially music by the leading composers of the time, Gombert, Willaert, and Morales. The seven printed items in the inventory included:

1. "a book of Masses by Morales"—which could be any one of the volumes for four and five or for four, five, and six voices of that composer's Masses published between 1540 and 1544 (RISM M 3575–3588)

2. "a book of Masses from Germany"—probably J. Petreius' *Liber quindecim missarum, à praestantissimis musicis compositarum* of 1539 (RISM 1539[1]), with works by Josquin, Isaac, Brumel, Layolle, and others

3. "a book of 5 Masses by Carpentras"—published by de Channay in 1532 (RISM G 1571)

4. "a book of XV Masses by various authors"—undoubtedly Antico's publication of 1516, mentioned earlier (RISM 1516[1])

5. "a book of X Masses"—which later inventories suggest was Jacques Moderne's *Liber decem missarum a praeclaris musicis contextus nunquam antehac in lucem editus,* printed in Lyons in 1532, with four-voice works by Layolle, Mouton, Richafort, Jannequin, and others (RISM 1532[8]; reprint, RISM 1540[1])

6. "a set of partbooks of motets *della divinità* a 5,"—that is, Castiglione's *Mutetarum divinitatis liber primus,* containing works by Phinot, Lupi, Willaert, Morales, and others, published at Milan in 1543 (RISM 1543[3])

7. another set of "motets by Gombert a 5"—the collection published by Girolamo Scotto at Venice in 1541, whose title begins: *Nicolai Gomberti musici excellentissimi Pentaphthongos harmonia, que quinque vocum Motetta vulgo nominantur,* and including works by Jachet and Morales (RISM 1541[3]).

At least three of these publications, the first, third, and fourth, were among the four printed volumes of polyphony owned by Orvieto cathedral in 1550, when Jacob de Kerle was hired as singer and *maestro di cappella*.[102] Orvieto, at the time one of the crown jewels of the Papal State, was well within the Roman orbit musically, and it is not surprising that it would have shared its musical tastes with Siena, since both cities took their cues from Rome. Later inventories from both Siena and Orvieto, as I shall note below, indicate that they continued to do so throughout the rest of the century. One final observation regarding the 1547 Sienese inventory is the presence of manuscript copies of masses, motets, psalms, Magnificats, and hymns and the eight partbooks "for processions" listed in earlier inventories, an indication that they were still in use.

---

101. In 1547 furniture owned by the school is listed as: "Uno ghoffano, una tavoletta, 2 banchette, uno leggio, uno telaio da 'npannata, una tavola delle sollenità cantano i cantori." See Doc. 6.2 for school furniture listed in earlier inventories.

102. Brumana and Ciliberti, *Orvieto: Una cattedrale,* 47, 49.

EXPANSION AND ITS CONSEQUENCES

In January 1548 the number of adults serving in the chapel rose to nine with the return of Ser Antonio Diligente, who now assumed the *maestro di cappella*'s post, and with the appointments of two new singers, Ser Serafino di Santi and Alessandro di Masetto. Ser Serafino, a graduate of the cathedral school, sang in the chapel as early as 1534. Later records call him a soprano. Rejoining the group in the following May after an absence of several years was the alto Jacomo da Verona, who, together with the newly appointed older clerk Francesco di Francesco, brought the number of adult singers to eleven during the 1548–49 fiscal year.

Except for Francesco, temporarily absent during fiscal 1549–50, all of the men and five cantorini are listed in accounts from May 1549 through April 1551. A twelfth adult, the Milanese singer Giovambattista di Corvo, sang with the group from May through November 1550, when the French tenor and composer Bartolomeo di Conte took his place. Joining the chapel in April 1551 was the Flemish bass Francesco Fabri, who would eventually become *maestro di cappella*. Although no records so state—reports of the overseers' deliberations from this period are lost—evidently a decision was made to bring the Sienese group up to the level of forces maintained at other major Italian cathedrals. A conscious effort to expand the chapel's forces followed. How this was financed is nowhere mentioned. Either the Opera's revenues increased at this time or funds previously allocated for building and decoration programs were diverted to musical performance.

The summer of 1551 witnessed the culmination of this effort when the number of singers reached twenty-one in May and twenty-two in June. The *maestro di cappella,* three altos, three tenors, and three basses, one adult soprano, and two whose voice ranges are unspecified made up the adult contingent of thirteen singers. Benedetto di Francesco, the tenth boy, as of June, soon became a priest and his later career as a chaplain-singer spanned a quarter of a century. An eleventh boy temporarily brought the number to twenty-three in September, but this began to dwindle by the end of the year. One youth, Giovanni di Francesco, called "our clerk and singer," is identified as an alto in a later document.

Some idea of what these forces mean in terms of contemporary Italian groups may be had from a comparison with the Florentine chapel, under Francesco Corteccia's direction, which around this time (1552) counted sixteen adults and nine boys (four altos, five tenors, three basses, four unspecified), and Willaert's chapel at St. Mark's in Venice, which had eighteen and then twenty-two men (1545, 1556), as well as an unspecified number of boys.[103] At Milan cathedral the chapel continued with its usual complement of thirteen adults and six boys until 1547, when four more boys were brought in, and to these were added two new tenors in 1549.[104] After 1553 a reform of the chapel at the Santo in Padova resulted in the formation of two choirs, each

---

103. D'Accone, "The Musical Chapels," 31; Ongaro, "The Chapel of St. Mark's," 229.

104. Getz, "The Milanese Cathedral Choir," 183–84. Through 1535, thanks to the last of the Sforza dukes, many of the musicians were awarded income from ducal benefices administered by the Milan diocese or income from local chaplaincies.

TABLE 6.3. Foreign singers at Siena cathedral, 1507–1551

Name	Place of origin	Period of service
Maestro Eustachio (de Monte Regali)	France	September 1507–September 1508
Ser Lanzelotto di Nanse Francioso	France	February–March 1520
Daniello di Simone Lupi Fiamengo (Tedesco, Inglese), contralto	Flanders(?)	December 1520–September 1521
Lonardo di Lonardo Franzese	France	May–October 1522
Amore di Francesco Franzese	France	August–November 1522
Arrigo Tibello di Giovanni	Bruges	November 1524
Ser Agnolo Ciper, contrabasso/tenorista	Cologne	September 1524–June 1526
Ivo di Giovanni Francese	France	1527–June 1530, August 1530
Messer Giovanni da San Germano	France	January–November 1530
uno chamtore franzese	France	March 1548
Bartolomeo di Conte Franzese	France	November 1550–January 1554
Francesco di Pietro Fabri Fiamengo, bass	Flanders	April 1551–April 1555
Gienero di Mauritio Luti[a]	Flanders	August 1551

[a]Offered appointment as *maestro di cappella;* did not accept

consisting of four singers.[105] Clearly, the Sienese chapel, with its twenty-one singers, had fully entered the mainstream of contemporary Italian practice.

Not since Alberto Aringhieri's tenure had an attempt been made to maintain such a large number of singers. Unlike the earlier group, however, most of the singers were now native Sienese or from the outlying provinces, and several of them had, with some interruptions, formed the chapel's core group for more than a quarter of a century. The foreign contingent (much reduced for this period; see Table 6.3) once again included a composer, Bartolomeo di Conte. Conte later served in the papal chapel, but his voice, according to one report, was not very good.[106] No extant records say whether Conte composed music expressly for Siena. Nevertheless, some of his music was certainly performed by the chapel because later inventories show that the cathedral owned a printed volume of his works.[107] Just as the inventories show the kinds of works that lay

---

105. Owens, "Il Cinquecento," 35, 78.

106. See James Haar's entry on Bartolomaeus Comes, composer of a book of five-voice motets, in *New Grove,* 4:589. (This was published by Gardane at Venice in 1547 as *Bartholomei El Conte, Motetta quinque vocibus suavissime sonantia.*) Haar reports Eitner's suggestion that Il Conte is the same person as Comes and notes that Il Conte has sometimes been confused with Giovanni Contino. A madrigal by Il Conte was published as late as 1604 at Venice by Francesco Spongia/Usper in *Il primo libro de madrigali a cinque voci di Francesco Spongia* (RISM U 118). Don Harrán, in the entry on Giovanni Contino in *New Grove,* 4:684–5, also notes the confusion but says that Il Conte is perhaps identifiable with Johannes le Cont, papal singer from 1528 to 1548. This confusion about Bartolomeo's identity should now be laid to rest in view of the Sienese documents and those recently published by Sherr, "Competence and Incompetence," 612, 614–15, which show that Bartolomeus Leconte was already singing in the papal chapel by 1555 and that he had left Rome by October 1565, when he was said to be "the worst kind of heretic" in a report concerning the chapel's employees.

107. From the inventory of 1563, where it is listed as "cinque libretti di motetti del Conte, in quarto foglio." It is probably the same volume, mentioned in the previous note, published by Gardane in 1547. See chapter 7 for a discussion of the inventory.

at the heart of the chapel's repertory, so do the accounts with regard to those who performed them. Clearly, the cathedral liturgy was now being embellished with sounds that had not been heard in the city within living memory. Choral polyphony, which I define as an ensemble of three or four singers to a part, resulted principally from an expansion that saw the chapel more than double its membership within a four-year period. The number of men, increased from five to thirteen, now included one soprano, three altos, three tenors, two basses, and four others with unspecified voice ranges. The boy choir, staffed with the largest group of paid singers since the end of the previous century, included at least one alto in its ranks.

Financing the group, as previously, remained a problem, and even at this juncture whatever hoped-for revenues that initially sparked the rapid buildup were insufficient to sustain it. By the end of August 1551 the situation became so critical that the overseers issued a decree prescribing "a reform of the musical chapel" (see Doc. 6.5). In doing so they sought to curtail further growth by limiting the number of adult singers to nine, the level reached in early 1548. Eight of those named were currently employed in the chapel. They included three contraltos: Don Pietro da Gubbio, Jacometto de' Chigi (Jacomo da Verona), and Giannino (Giovanni) di Francesco; three tenors: Ser Bernardo Pontremoli, il Franzese (Bartolomeo di Conte), and Giovanbattista di Bartolomeo; and two basses: Il Fiamengo (Francesco di Pietro Fabri) and Fra Gabriello de' Servi. The decree stipulated that the remaining adult singers could be paid only through the month of September. Newly appointed as the ninth singer and *maestro di cappella* "for the future" was the Flemish musician Gienero di Mauritio Luti. Luti apparently did not accept the appointment, however, and is not cited in subsequent documents, which show instead that the other Flemish singer, Francesco di Pietro Fabri, eventually took over the post. The boy singers, as might be expected, are not mentioned in the decree, although subsequent documents show that their employment continued.

THE CHAPEL DURING THE SIEGE OF SIENA

This decree was never fully implemented, for reasons that are clear when seen in the light of subsequent events. Siena was about to embark upon the final act in the drama of its turbulent republic, one that would witness a major struggle to maintain its independence. The results of years of internal political instability after the ouster of the Petrucci would finally take their toll. During this latest round of factionalism and strife order within the city was maintained at a price, for it depended upon the imperial forces of Charles V and the mediation of his agents. But in July 1552 the construction of a citadel within Siena's walls by Charles's Spanish garrison provoked a popular uprising that resulted in the expulsion of his troops. The seriousness of this action weighed heavily on the government. A formal alliance with the French and the Florentine exiles led by Carlo Strozzi was quickly forged. French troops poured into the city, as antiimperial and anti-Florentine fervor reached new heights. War with the emperor, as even the most impartial observer could have predicted, was inevitable. The siege of Siena, begun in March 1554, came to an end on 17 April 1555, when, despite heroic acts of defense and great sacrifices, the city, now reduced to what has been estimated as a third of its population, agreed to articles of capitulation. These included, among other things, a guarantee of continued independence under Charles's protection, a promise that was never kept.

During the siege of the city several extraordinary religious ceremonies were conducted with great fervor and intensity. On 5 August 1554 celebrations marked the anniversary of the Spanish expulsion.[108] The revered painting of the Madonna del Voto was taken from its chapel and borne through the city's streets in a procession that moved from the cathedral to the church of Sant'Agostino and then back to the cathedral, where Mass was sung. The Madonna del Voto, to whose intercession the Sienese attributed their victory over the Florentines at the battle of Montaperti in 1230, was, as has been noted, revered by citizens of all classes. The icon's miraculous powers were repeatedly invoked in times of plague and disaster, the present crisis being no exception. A chronicler describing the event reports that the procession was headed by "150 pairs of young girls all dressed in white, singing the litanies and crying out in a loud voice, *O Christe audi nos,* which certainly brought tender feelings to those who heard them." Later that year, on 3 December 1554, when the government once again authorized a public ceremony to invoke the Virgin's intercession, the city's priors and other high-ranking officials heard Mass and took holy communion in their private chapel at the Palace, before proceeding to the cathedral, where "the Mass of the Madonna was sung." Afterwards, says the chronicler, there was "a beautiful procession" with the "cathedral's Madonna" taken throughout the city.[109]

The chapel is not mentioned on either of these occasions. There is good reason to believe, however, that it performed at both of them precisely because the chronicler took pains to note its absence at another of the ceremonies he describes. This later one was on the eve of the feast of the Annunciation, 24 March 1555, when all of the priors, the captain of the people, and others in the government, dressed in their purple cloaks, accompanied by a retinue bearing the standard of the Virgin Mary and the keys to the city gates in a silver urn, "went to the duomo without the sound of the trumpets." When they arrived, the members of the government "did not seat themselves in the tribunal," but sat instead, "as an act of humility, in the choir under the *cappella della musica,* and they heard the Mass of the Blessed Virgin without *musica* [polyphony] and the sounds of the organ."[110] After Mass the government made a formal presentation of

---

108. Alessandro Sozzini, *Diario delle cose avvenute in Siena dai 20 luglio 1550 ai 28 giugno 1555,* ed. Gaetano Milanesi (Florence, 1842), 273.

109. Ibid., 328: "La Signoria con tutti gli Ordini udirno messa in Palazzo, e confessi e comunicati andorno alla chiesa catedrale; e dopo che fu cantata la messa della Madonna, si fece per la Città una belissima processione, e si portò la detta Madonna del Duomo."

110. Ibid., 391–92: "Andorno al Duomo li Magnifici Signori, Capitano del Popolo, Gonfalonieri e tutti li Ordini, senza suoni di trombe, con mantelli di pavonazzo, con lo stendardo di nostra donna, ed in un bacino d'argento le chiavi delle porte della Città; e giunti, non sederno nei tribunali, per umiltà, ma in quei cori sotto la cappella della musica; e si udirno la messa della Beata Vergine senza la musica e suoni d'organi." Milanesi, in his edition of the text, explains that "quei cori sotto la cappella della musica" referred to the place "sotto la cantoria, o loggia dove si canta a cappella." The quotation furnishes additional evidence that the organist played at services when the chapel sang, though it does not specify that they performed together.

the city's keys to the Virgin and placed them "on her altar," the main altar, which was dedicated to her. The chronicler also reports that during Mass Alessandro Guglielmi arrived from Florence with the articles of capitulation, which the government was to accept within the month. The importance of this account for the history of Sienese music lies in its making clear that, except for the unadorned chant, music found no place at the cathedral on this occasion, contrary to usual practice. Obviously, the government intended the ceremony to be viewed as a humble act of supplication rather than one of praise or rejoicing.

The chapel continued to function without interruption throughout these troubled times, though with the reduced forces decreed in August 1551 (for a chronological list see Table 6.4). Except for Bartolomeo Conte, who left in January 1554 and was replaced by the returning Ser Ulivieri Gerini, the adults named at that time, assisted by several boys, were employed during the fiscal years 1552 through 1555. This was the group that performed during the worst months of the siege, when famine was rampant and the horrors of war reduced the city's morale to a new low. Continuation of the chapel's performances during this time must thus be considered as part of a larger strategy that sought to preserve pride in Sienese achievements while maintaining a semblance of normality within the city. It was also an act of defiance toward Siena's besiegers, who ultimately triumphed and took possession of the city on 21 April 1555. On that day, after the departure of the last of the French troops aiding in the city's defense, the Sienese government sent two deputies to the camp of the commander of the opposing forces, Giangiacomo de' Medici, marquis of Marignano. There, they made a formal declaration of surrender and presented him with the keys to the city. Later in the day the marquis, preceded by a fanfare of trumpets and drums, made his official entry into the city through the Porta Nuova and rode to the Palace, where he returned the keys to the Concistoro. He then proceeded to the cathedral where he had a Mass of the Holy Spirit sung. The chapel was in attendance even at this solemn moment, its presence noted by one witness who said that the Mass "was concluded with difficulty because the sound of the tears and sobs of those celebrating it and in part of those hearing it was louder than the music being performed by the singing ensemble in a normal tone of voice."[111]

DOCUMENTS

Doc. 6.1. Sano di Goro complains about the Opera's treatment of him, 2 September 1507. AOMS, vol. 69, *Carteggio, 1500–60*, fasc. 1, by date

Girolamo, fattore dell'Opera, parmi intendare che el mio servito de' miei denari ne sodisfate a

---

111. "Havendo nel Palazzo reso le chiavi prescritte alla signoria, entrato nel Duomo si fece solennemente cantare la Messa dello Spirito Santo, la quale con gran fatica condotta a fine, essendo maggiore il suono che facevano i pianti ed i singulti di chi cantava ed in parte di chi sentiva, che il concento della musica, che dall'Ordinarie voci usciva." The anecdote was first published in 1560, presumably from an eyewitness account, by Giovanbattista Cini, *Vita del Serenissimo Signor Cosimo de Medici Primo Gran Duca di Toscana* (Florence, 1611), 334, and was repeated with little change by Pecci, *Memorie storico-critiche della città*, 4:235; and by Lorenzo Cantini, *Vita di Cosimo de' Medici Primo Gran-Duca di Toscana* (Florence, 1805), 235.

chi vi viene a domandare. Per la qual cosa da un canto mi maraviglio, dall'altro no: perché essendo voi nuovamente intrato in cotesto ufitio, non sapete le Costitutioni, massime che veruno può fare integire [= sequestrare] li denari del servito della chiesa, per ben ché quando Pavolo di Vannoccio m'avesse avere non me ne curaria. Ché quando lui ebbe a ffar con esso me, fu sopra-paghato di dodici lire et el suo figliuolo Vanocci pigliava li denari della Opera, e quando fu ischonto el debito si prese più le dette dodici lire. Quando la domandavo per far conto, mai el potetti avere, mi rispondeva non avere i libri. Pur come si sia, non potete pagar delli miei denari li debiti miei. Pregovi che per l'aportatore mi mandiate le fadiche mie. E più mi mandate a dire che da uno ducato in su li avete dato alli mei fratelli e sorelle, e llor mi mandano a dire che non ànno avuto nulla. E li mei denari li voglio io, siché vi pregho che per l'aportatore, che sarà Miser Giovanni di maestro Arcangelo, mi mandiate il mio servito, e non pagate li debiti mei. Non vi maravigliate se el mie scrivare è un poco alterato, ché avendo io servito tutto il mese di luglio, el primo di aghosto che fu la prima domenica poi la medezima [mercoledì] sequente, fui casso, siché le fadig[h]e mie non mi sieno ritenute per nissuno conto. Sonno alli vostri piaceri. Fatti adì 2 di settembre mille 507.

Vostro Ser Sano Cantore agli Altesi

[verso side, outside address: Data a Girolamo, fattore della Opera, in Siena]

Doc. 6.2. School furniture listed in the inventories of 1524, 1525, and 1527 (for sources see Table 6.2)

1524:

La schuola del chanto fermo, tiene ser Pietro chantore, cho' le sotto iscritte chose:
Una tavoletta cho' trepiei
Una bancha. . . .
La schuola de la musicha:
2 banche co' p[i]ei chonfitti
1 bancho chon tre piei
2 banche
1 leggìo nuovo
1 goffano chon serratura
1 telaio da impannata

1525:

Due banchi con piei confitti
Uno bancho a tre piei
Due banche da sedere
Uno leggìo rosso nuovo
Uno goffano chon serratura
Uno telaio da impannate

1527:

Uno ghoffano con la serratura
4 banche, 2 alte, 2 baxe
Una tavola in su 2 treppiey
Una scaletta pichola
Uno telaio a la finestra incartata
Uno leggìo di cuoio roxo, cioè di sovatto roxo

Doc. 6.3. Payments to trumpeters for playing at Madonna services

11 September 1526: Trombetti di Palazo addì detto . . . per la sonatura ala Madonna, di questo anno, L. XI (AOMS, vol. 323, *E&U, 1526–27*, fol. 74ᵛ)

1534: Li trombetti che suonano a la Madonna adì XVIIII di Agosto, L. nove s. dieci contanti a Galira trombetto, L. VIIII s. X (vol. 330, *E&U, 1534–39,* fol. 223ᵛ); similar payment for 1537 on fol. 239ᵛ

1546: Trombetti che suonano a la Madonna, adì 25 di Agosto detto, L. undici s. cinque, a Girolamo di Michelangelo. L. 11 S. V (vol. 330, *E&U, 1546–47,* fol. 74ʳ)

Doc. 6.4. Letter from Scipione di Pavolo Jacomini to an administrator, requesting money, 27 July 1551. AOMS, vol. 74, *Carteggio, 1551–61,* by date

Giuseppe magnifico

Per ritrovarmi nel lecto con pocha di febre e perché io già vi domandai tre scudi, vorrei che vi fusse di piacere fare il mio conto per tutto questo mese e che voi non mi desse più di quello che per tutto questo mese harei d'avere; e quando non vi fussi scommodo da[r]lli all'aportatore di quessta che sarà Giani cherico di duomo, mi farete piacere, e mi vi raccomando.

Di casa del'Opera il dì 27 di luglio 1551.

Vostro Servitore Scipione organista

Doc. 6.5. Decree prescribing the reform of the musical chapel, 31 August 1551. AOMS, vol. 17, *Deliberazioni, 1548–90,* fol. 3ᵛ

[margin: Riforma della Cappella della musica]

Imprima deliberorno che nella Cappella del Canto vi stieno due contrabassi, cioè il fiamengo et frate Gabriello de' Servi, et gl'altri s'intendino cassi con il salario che parrà ala magnificentia di misere [l'operaio].

Item deliberorno che per tenori di detta Cappella sieno il Pontremoli, il franzese et Giovambaptista, et non più.

Item elessero per contralti don Pietro da Gobbio et Iacometto de' Chigi et Giannino di Francesco, con sei carlini il mese.

Item deliberorno d'eleggere per maestro di cappella et così elessero per l'avenire il fiamingo Gienero di Mauritio Luti.

Item deliberono che alli cassi cantando habbino havere il salario [*sic*] o non cantando habbino havere il salario per tutto il mese di Settembre prossimo.

TABLE 6.4. Chronological list of cathedral musicians, 1507–1555

The list includes only those mentioned specifically as singers or instrumentalists at some point in the calendar year; choristers' names are reported selectively. Note that the fiscal year runs from May through April; a singer listed under two consecutive years may have served no more than a few months (for exact months, see Register of Musicians). Lists are missing for 1531, 1550–52.

	1507	1508	1509	1510	1511	1512	1513	1514	1515	1516	1517	1518	1519	1520	1521	1522	1523	1524
SINGERS, 1507–1524																		
Eustachio (de Monte Regali)	x	x																
Giovanni Pagliarini	x	x	x															
Lonardo di Cristofano	x	x	x	x	x	x	x	x	x	x	x	x	x					
Agnolo di Piero	x	x	x	x	x	x	x	x	x	x	x	x	x					
Ansano (Sano) di Goro	x				x	x	x		x	x	x	x		x	x	x	x	x
Maddalo d'Arezzo		x	x	x	x	x	x	x	x	x	x	x	x	x	x	x	x	
Ulivieri di Jacomo			x	x	x	x	x	x	x	x	x	x	x	x	x			
Giovanni di Maestro Antonio			x	x	x	x	x	x	x	x	x	x	x	x				
Piero di Domenico				x														
Giovanfrancesco di Antonio			x		x	x	x	x	x	x	x	x	x	x				x
Fruosino di Antonio da Pisa							x	x	x	x	x	x			x	x	x	
Innocentio di Donato										x	x	x						
Galgano (Gano) d'Enea								x	x	x	x	x	x	x	x	x		
Galgano di Ser Antonio									x	x		x						
Giovanbattista									x	x								
Lorenzo di Andrea									x									
Piero Antonio di Galgano									x									
Ulisse di Girolamo									x	x	x	x						
Jacomo di Francesco										x								
Pietro di Benedetto										x								
Bernardino di Antonio											x							
Dino Ortolano											x							
Giovanbattista di Soriana											x	x						
Niccolò Smeraldi											x	x						
Pietro del Funaio											x	x						

TABLE 6.4 continued

SINGERS, 1507–1524	1507	1508	1509	1510	1511	1512	1513	1514	1515	1516	1517	1518	1519	1520	1521	1522	1523	1524
Niccolò di Ser Lonardo												x						
Pio di Pietro Paoli												x						
Cornelio da Sovana												x	x	x				
Vincentio di Mattia												x	x	x	x	x	x	x
Niccolò Francioso													x	x				
Ardilasso d'Astore													x	x	x			
Marcello di Francesco														x	x			x
Lanzelotto di Nanse														x				
Francesco Gerini														x				
Fruosino di Lodovico														x				
Daniello di Simone Lupi														x	x			
Giovanbattista di Bartolomeo														x	x	x	x	
Andrea d'Andrea de' Rami															x	x	x	x
Domenico di Giovanbattista															x	x	x	x
Biagio di Fuccio																x	x	x
Antonio Diligente																x	x	x
Lonardo di Lonardo Franzese																x		
Amore di Francesco Franzese																x		
Mariano di Giovanni di Ser Turco																x		
Arrigo Tibello da Bruges																		x
Pietro di Maestro Lonardo																		x
Agnolo Ciper of Cologne																		x
Jacomo di Giovanbattista da Verona																		
Camillo di Marco																		x
Andrea di Baldassarre																		x
Bernardino di Matteo Cartolaio																		x

SINGERS, 1525–42

	1525	1526	1527	1528	1529	1530	1531	1532	1533	1534	1535	1536	1537	1538	1539	1540	1541	1542
Ulivieri di Jacomo			x	x	x	x	x	x	x	x	x	x	x	x	x	x	x	x
Piero di Domenico		x	x			x	x	x	x	x	x	x	x	x	x			
Galgano (Gano) d'Enea, cornetta															x	x		
Pietro di Maestro Lonardo	x	x	x															
Agnolo Ciper	x	x																
Jacomo di Giovanbattista da Verona	x	x	x					x		x	x	x	x	x	x	x	x	x
Marcello di Francesco	x	x																
Giovanbattista di Bartolomeo															x	x	x	x
Domenico di Giovanbattista	x	x				x		x	x	x	x							
Biagio di Fuccio	x	x	x															
Antonio Diligente	x	x					x				x				x			
Vincentio di Mattia	x	x																
Camillo di Marco	x	x	x	x	x	x												
Andrea di Baldassarre	x																	
Bernardino di Matteo	x	x					x	x	x	x	x	x	x	x	x	x	x	
Agnolo di Bartolomeo	x	x	x	x	x	x												
Mariano di Gherardo	x	x	x	x	x													
Ivo di Giovanni Francese				x	x	x												
Pietro di Maestro Bernardo					x	x	x	x		x					x			
Bernardino Pontremoli						x	x	x										
Giovanni da San Germano							x	x					x	x		x	x	x
Luzio di Pavolo						x	x	x	x									
Claudio di Stefano						x												

TABLE 6.4 continued

	1525	1526	1527	1528	1529	1530	1531	1532	1533	1534	1535	1536	1537	1538	1539	1540	1541	1542
SINGERS, 1525–42																		
Tullio di Giovanbattista																		
Scipione di Pavolo Jacomini						x												
Niccolò di Giuliano, cornetta									x	x	x	x	x	x	x			
Serafino di Santi										x	x	x	x	x	x			
Bastiano del Nica										x								
Agnolino											x			x				
Fra Paulo											x							
Andrea											x			x				
Guasparre di Baldassare, cornetta														x				
Benvenuto													x	x				
Gabriello di Giovanni de' Servi														x				
Gabriello di Ramondo Spagnolo															x	x	x	x
Bartolomeo di Pietro																x	x	
Pietro di Tommaso da Gubbio																		x
Ascanio di Andrea Marri																		x
Ansano Maria di Geronimo, trombone																		x
Giulio dello spedale																		x

SINGERS, 1543–55

	1543	1544–46	1547	1548	1549	1550	1551	1552	1553	1554	1555
Ulivieri di Jacopo	x	x	x	x	x	x	x	x	x	x	x
Jacomo da Verona	x	x		x	x	x	x	x	x	x	x
Giovanbattista di Bartolomeo	x	x	x	x	x	x	x	x	x	x	x
Antonio Diligente				x	x	x	x	x			
Bernardino da Pontremoli	x	x	x	x	x	x	x	x	x	x	x
Serafino di Santi	x	x	x	x	x	x	x				
Gabriello di Giovanni	x	x	x	x	x	x	x	x	x	x	x
Bartolomeo di Pietro	x	x	x	x	x	x	x	x			
Pietro di Tommaso	x	x	x								
Giulio dello spedale	x	x	x	x	x	x	x	x	x	x	
Ascanio di Andrea Marri	x	x	x	x	x						
Ansano Maria di Geronimo, trombone	x	x		x							
Alessandro di Masetto				x	x	x	x	x			
Francesco di Francesco				x	x	x	x	x			
Girolamo di Ser Annibale					x						
Giovanbattista di Corvo						x					
Bartolomeo di Conte							x	x			
Cesare d'Andrea						x	x	x	x	x	
Giovanbattista di Pasquino						x	x	x			
Giovanbattista di Vincenzio						x	x	x	x	x	x
Lelo di Taddeo						x	x	x			
Mario di Matteo						x	x	x			
Salindio di Ventura						x	x				
Francesco Fabri							x	x			
Benedetto di Francesco							x	x	x	x	
Pietro di Maestro Antonio							x				
Bartolomeo di Tommaso							x	x			
Giovanni di Francesco							x	x			
Girolamo di Ser Antonmaria Mariotti							x	x			
Ascanio Gobbo								x			
Francesco di Bartolomeo								x	x	x	
Bernardo, figlio della cappella								x	x		

TABLE 6.4 continued

	1507	1508	1509–14	1515	1516–17	1518–19	1520	1521–22	1523	1524	1525–26	1527	1528–29	1530
ORGANISTS, 1507–30														
Francesco di Tommaso	x	x												
Lorenzo di Niccolò		x	x	x										
Cristoforo di Vivaldo				x	x	x	x	x			x	x		
Antonio Diligente						x		x	x					
Jacomo da Modena							x							
Bartolomeo di Monna Betta									x	x				
Giovannandrea d'Alessandro										x				
Antonio di Galgano												x	x	x
Jacomo da Palermo													x	x
Pietro di Bartolomeo Corradini														x

	1531	1532–36	1537	1538–40	1541–43
ORGANISTS, 1531–43					
Jacomo da Palermo	x				
Pietro di Bartolomeo Corradini	x	x	x		
Antonio Moneta			x		
Scipione di Pavolo Jacomini				x (to 1563)	
Ulivieri di Jacomo					x

Example 6.1. Eustachius de Monte Regali, *Credidi propter quod locutus sum* (Modena, Biblioteca Capitolare, Mus. Ms. 3, no. 7, after Crawford)

Example 6.1 continued

Example 6.1 continued

Example 6.1 continued

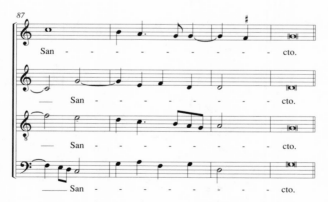

Example 6.2. Eustachius de Monte Regali, *Omnes gentes plaudite manibus* (*Motetti de la corona libro secondo* [Venice: Petrucci, 1519], no. 25)

Example 6.2 continued

Example 6.2 continued

Example 6.2 continued

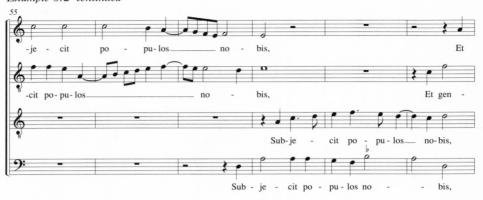

Example 6.2 continued

Example 6.2 continued

Example 6.2 continued

Example 6.2 continued

Example 6.2 continued

Example 6.2 continued

Example 6.2 continued

† print gives *g, a, g*

Chapter Seven

DECLINE AND TRANSFORMATION
OF THE CHAPEL, 1555–1607

W ITH DEFEAT AND ECONOMIC COLLAPSE, the poverty and depression that pervaded civic life were soon reflected in the staffing of the chapel. Inevitably, Sienese cultural institutions, already weakened during the siege, suffered the effects of the prolonged hardships that had been endured and the uncertainty of the times to follow. At the Palazzo Pubblico the immediate result was to scale down musical forces to levels approved earlier in the century and following that, within a few years, to promulgate new statutes reflecting the changed financial circumstances under which the musical establishment would operate in the future. At the cathedral, greatly reduced revenues called for a reduction of forces, and calculated retrenchment, already initiated before the siege, was enacted with alacrity and an unusual severity. In the immediate future was the decline in membership of the chapel and the possible abandonment of polyphonic repertories that had formed the backbone of its performances for more than three-quarters of a century. Almost five years passed before the process of reconstructing the cathedral's musical forces would resume.

Personnel losses occurred as early as the summer of 1555. Accounts for the fiscal year May 1555 through April 1556 list Ser Bernardo Pontremoli, Ser Ulivieri Gerini, Fra Gabriello de' Servi, and a youth, Giovanbattista di Pasquino, soprano, for the entire time but register only a few months' service for three others: Giovanbattista di Bartolomeo, through June 1555; Maestro Francesco Fabri Fiamengo, through October 1555; and Jacomo da Verona, through December 1555. Four singers were thus present during winter and spring, 1556.

After leaving Siena at the end of October 1555, Fabri went to Orvieto, where he was appointed *maestro di cappella,* replacing the incumbent Jacob Kerle, who assumed the organist's post. Fabri's success as a teacher in Siena was apparently well known, for he was specifically brought in to teach the *pueri cantores* in the school.[1]

A tersely worded report from 10 November 1556 shows that the cathedral's financial resources were strained to the breaking point and that its governing board concluded they could no longer afford the luxury of a musical chapel (see Doc. 7.1). The reluctance with which they made their decision is manifest in the opening statement, which says that "after considering the Opera's many needs and the difficulty in finding a way of satisfying its employees and paying its debts" the overseers authorized a suspension of the chapel through the following July and decreed that henceforth, with two exceptions, salaries would no longer be paid to any of the singers. Bernardo Pontremoli was one of the two musicians singled out for exceptional treatment. "Because of the good

---

1. Brumana and Ciliberti, *Orvieto: Una cattedrale,* 49.

service he has given the said chapel for many years," he would receive Sc. 2 per month until such time as the chapel was reinstated, when his salary would be renegotiated. Meanwhile, he would serve in the choir, "at least on solemn feasts." Perhaps he was to sing part music with the choristers, or barring that, to assist in the plainchant choir. The other similarly favored musician was "the venerable priest Ser Vieri," who, as the overseers declared five days later, "has served the chapel for many years, copied books of music, and taught with diligence, as he does at present, teaching music to the boys and to the duomo's choristers." Thus, "the dissolution of the chapel notwithstanding," the board decreed that Ulivieri should be "particularly recognized and that he should have a salary of L. 8 per month, so that he may continue with his good work of teaching." In this way did the overseers seek to reward a long-time employee and at the same time ensure the integrity of the teaching program. In addition, Ulivieri would also continue to train boys capable of singing in the chapel, presumably for little or no salary. In a final bow to economy, the overseers reduced the organist's salary to L. 21 a month.

Despite their resolve and the apparent finality of their decision, there is no evidence that the overseers implemented their action. The accounts for fiscal 1556–57 show that five singers were employed throughout that time: Ser Bernardo Pontremoli, tenor; Ser Ulivieri Gerini, bass; Fra Gabriello de' Servi, bass; the returning Giovanbattista di Bartolomeo, tenor; and the soprano, Giovanbattista di Pasquino, replaced after June 1556 by another boy, Fabio di Francesco Tizzoni. The group apparently performed without the assistance of other adult singers, or at least any who were paid for their services. What this means in terms of performance is not difficult to imagine. One or more of the men must have had wider vocal ranges than those associated nowadays with their respective parts. A tenor with a wide range, for example, could easily have sung most alto parts and a similarly gifted bass could have sung the tenor part, though with differing timbre and quality of sound. Performances with solo voices of repertories that called for the usual ranges of four- and five-part pieces would have been well within the group's capabilities. If this is what actually happened—records are ambiguous about the participation of youths from the school—as late as the mid-sixteenth century sacred polyphony featuring one singer to a part was an acceptable though perhaps not a preferred means of performance.[2] For pieces that the ensemble could not negotiate alone, the organist probably supplemented the vocal parts either by filling in those that were lacking or doubling some or all of them.

A letter from a wholly unexpected quarter reveals that changes in the chapel, planned in the fall of 1556, took effect at the beginning of the new fiscal year, in May 1557. Dated Siena, on the 7th of the same month, the letter was addressed to the overseers by Charles V's lieutenant general and acting governor of Siena, Don Francisco de Mendoza, bishop of Burgos. The bishop's words leave no doubt as to who was in control of the city's religious and cultural institutions as well as its political ones. In a curtly worded rebuke to the board for its decision regarding the chapel, he observed "that matters pertaining to divine worship should be treated with proper reverence and

2. A number of young clerks, "cherici minori," are mentioned in the accounts for fiscal 1556–57, but none is called a singer, apart from Fabio di Francesco Tizzoni.

decorum everywhere, but particularly in cathedral and metropolitan churches such as Siena's duomo." Accordingly, he decreed that the chapel of singers, "which customarily served in the church and which, for certain considerations, was commanded not to serve through a deliberation of this past December," was to resume its duties and "do things in the best possible way, as was customary." The singers, furthermore, were "to be paid as usual because this is in the service of God and in the public honor, and this is our wish" (see Doc. 7.2).

The bishop's brief remarks reveal, more than any tome of learned disquisition ever could, how much importance was attached to cathedral ceremonies and to the chapel's role in them. The incident offers an interesting parallel with events of the immediate past. Just as the Sienese patriots attempted to boost civic morale and foster the appearance of normality throughout the siege by maintaining polyphonic performances at cathedral services, so did the victors now seek to create the impression of a return to the established order by resuming practices associated in the public's mind with the stability and well-being of the state. As it turned out, the Opera was unable to comply with the bishop's request, having at its disposal neither the means nor the personnel required to restore the chapel to its former strength.

The bishop's letter is precious for the light it casts on the political and musical situations in Siena at this time. But it is no less valuable for what it says about the attitudes of some churchmen regarding the use of polyphony. More than half a century had passed since polyphony had been reviled by the Dominican friar Girolamo Savonarola in nearby Florence, and there were many still who were not altogether sympathetic to its intrusive presence in the liturgy.[3] Just then the matter was about to be considered by a council meeting at Trent.[4] Yet, as Bishop Mendoza's directive makes clear, polyphony had also come to be viewed by many other influential clergy as an essential adornment that was "in the service of God and in the public honor." The public honor in this case, of course, was the prestige of the imperial conqueror. But there is no reason to doubt Mendoza's sincerity in his belief that good music redounded to the glory of God. To his way of thinking, derived from an attitude that had traditionally encouraged the development of polyphonic practices, music in public devotions that proclaimed the majesty of the Creator—and not coincidentally the piety and status of those who sponsored them—was both an external expression of profound religiosity

3. On Savonarola's attitude toward music see Seay, "The 15th-Century Cappella at Santa Maria del Fiore in Florence," 55; D'Accone, "The Singers of San Giovanni," 346–49; Giulio Cattin, "Le poesie del Savonarola nelle fonti musicali," *Quadrivium* 12 (1971): 259–80; Salvatore Camporeale, "Giovanni Caroli e le 'Vitae Fratrum S. M. Novellae.' Umanesimo e crisi religiosa (1460–1480)," *Memorie domenicane,* n.s., 12 (1981): 141–267; and three articles by Patrick Macey: "Savonarola and the Sixteenth-Century Motet," *JAMS* 36 (1983): 422–52; "*Infiamma il mio cor:* Savonarolan *Laude* by and for Dominican Nuns in Tuscany," in *The Crannied Wall: Women, Religion, and the Arts in Early Modern Europe,* ed. Craig A. Monson (Ann Arbor, 1992), 161–89; and "The Lauda and the Cult of Savonarola," *Renaissance Quarterly* 45 (1992): 439–83.

4. On music and the Tridentine Council see K. G. Fellerer, "Church Music and the Council of Trent," *Musical Quarterly* 39 (1953): 576–94; Lockwood, *The Counter-Reformation and the Masses of Vincenzo Ruffo,* 74–135, and the introduction of his edition of the *Pope Marcellus Mass* (New York, 1975).

and an affirmation of faith in the efficacy of prayer and ritual. The bishop's thinking was in no way foreign to the position eventually adopted by the Tridentine council that provided the philosophical foundation for Catholic church polyphony in the centuries to come.

The Medicean State and the Cathedral's Cultural Policies

Less than a few months after Mendoza's rebuke to the Opera, Siena's fate was decided, when the political aims of the Habsburgs and the Medici were implemented to the satisfaction of both courts. Siena was formally ceded to Duke Cosimo I de' Medici on 3 July 1557. Within two years, as a result of the treaty of Cateau-Cambrésis, the republican stronghold of Montalcino, which had not capitulated and remained under the protection of a French garrison, was also handed over to the Medici, and thus the last vestiges of the old Sienese republic ceased to exist.[5] Henceforth Siena, although remaining a separately administered entity within the Medici territories, was to share the political and economic destinies of Florence. But not, at least in the late sixteenth century, its musical programs. Although nothing pertaining to Sienese affairs, including periodic reviews of the Opera's accounts and the administration of the cathedral chapel, ever escaped Medici scrutiny, Cosimo and his successors generally adhered to a policy of allowing the Sienese to manage their own cultural institutions without Florentine interference so long as political stability was not threatened. The overseer, or rector as he was now called, though nominated by the ruling Medici, was always a native Sienese. As in the past, he was assisted by a group of counselors, called *savi,* that included the scions of Siena's noblest families as well as a representative from the cathedral Chapter.

Under Medici rule conditions that fostered artistic renewal and economic recovery gradually returned. Within a decade the chapel once again became a flourishing entity, although the process of rebuilding did not occur overnight. New personnel replaced aging members and salaries rose to levels comparable to those of musicians in other Italian chapels. At first, however, the number of adult singers continued at no more than six or seven. And the group's composition remained essentially local, for only occasionally were non-Sienese musicians admitted to its ranks. Perhaps this was part of an unwritten understanding that sought to keep artistic control in the hands of the Sienese themselves or in those of a few outstanding foreigners whose ethnic, cultural, and musical origins could in no way be thought of as representing a bow to Florentine hegemony. Whatever the means of achieving it, it appears to have been a strategy that was kept firmly in place throughout the next century. This is, in fact, the only logical explanation of a policy that in the future accommodated the appointments of several foreign musicians, but never of a Florentine.

Accounts for fiscal 1557–58 paint a bleak picture of the state of the chapel. Two tenors, Bernardo Pontremoli and Giovanbattista di Bartolomeo, were present for the entire period, as were two new youths, Midone di Ser Cesare and Annibale d'Andrea

---

5. For background about the treaty and relations between Charles V and Cosimo de' Medici see Arnaldo D'Addario, *Il problema senese nella storia italiana della prima metà del Cinquecento* (Florence, 1958), 395–99, and Roberto Cantagalli, *La guerra di Siena (1552–1559)* (Siena, 1962), 523–28.

da Radda, each described as "our clerk and a soprano in the chapel." (In later years both would become adult members of the group.) The bass, Ulivieri Gerini, sang only through November 1557, when Giovanbattista di Bartolomeo took over as *maestro di cappella*.[6] Perhaps it was in response to Gerini's departure and because no other bass was available that in January 1558, after a twelve-year hiatus, a trombonist from the Palace wind band was brought in to assist. This was Giovanfrancesco di Benedetto, one of the outstanding Sienese instrumentalists of the day. On this occasion he performed with the group through September 1560. Four singers were also present during fiscal 1558–59, with Fabio di Francesco Tizzoni, "our younger clerk and soprano," replacing Midone. Midone rejoined the group in fiscal 1559–60 so that the chapel now comprised two tenors, three sopranos, and a trombonist, who assuredly played or doubled the bass part in the ensemble. A report from 15 March 1559 recounts how Messer Mario Bronconi, one of the canons, recommended a certain Messer Hercole *musico,* who wished to be appointed master of the chapel. Accordingly, the council authorized a committee to look into the matter and report back on its decision.[7] Evidently, that was the last of it, for nothing further came of the discussion.

Several adults joined the group in the following decade, some of whom had been previously employed. The Flemish bass, Francesco Fabri, resumed his post as singer and *maestro di cappella* in June 1560, after an absence of four and a half years. Also rejoining the chapel in June of that year was the alto Bartolomeo di Pietro dei Farnetani Saracini, who is registered the following April and then again in 1562. A tenor, Austino di Bernardo Magini from nearby Città di Castello, was appointed in July 1560. The tenor Giovanbattista di Bartolomeo and Ser Benedetto di Francesco Franceschi, a chaplain who sang alto, began serving in May 1561, as did the chaplain Ser Alessandro di Domenico, whose voice range is unspecified. The spurt in hiring was accompanied by raises for continuing singers and high salaries for the new ones, an indication that a strong effort was being made to recruit and retain good voices. But expenses soon threatened available revenues and the governing board was forced to take preventive measures. A deliberation from 22 October 1563 notes a number of reductions in salary for the adult singers as well the formal dismissal of one of them, the alto Bartolomeo di Pietro.[8] Francesco Fabri's salary as *maestro di cappella* was lowered from L. 49 to L. 42; Giovanbattista di Bartolomeo's went from L. 21 to L. 10, Bernardo Pontremoli's from

---

6. In a will Ulivieri filed about a year earlier he referred to himself as a priest and master of the Sienese cathedral's chapel of figural music and said that he had served the cathedral for about forty-seven years, both as a singer and as *maestro di cappella,* earning a monthly salary of three and then three and a half gold scudi, though at present he was earning two scudi. He recalled that he had also taught singing, organ playing, and other instruments in the school (ASS, Notarile antecosimiano, 2770, no. 146, dated Siena, 30 October 1556).

Giovanbattista di Bartolomeo was named as the "new master of the chapel" in the inventory of 30 December 1557, quoted in Table 7.1. Payments to him as *maestro di cappella* begin right after this time.

7. AOMS, vol. 17, *Deliberazioni, 1548–1590,* fol. 14ʳ.

8. "Et havendo considerato la grave spesa che ne dà a l'opera la cappella e volendo provedere a quanto conviene, deliberorno solennemente ridurre et ridussero li salari alli sottoscritti e così mandorno eseguirsi" (AOMS, vol. 17, *Deliberazioni, 1548–90,* fol. 29ʳ, dated 22 October 1563 [margin:

L. 28 to L. 18, Austino Magini's from L. 21 to L. 14, Benedetto Franceschi's from L. 14 to L. 4, and Alessandro di Domenico's from L. 12 to L. 6. Pay records indicate, however, that these drastic cuts were not made and that only a few salaries were lowered, and only temporarily, at that. The choristers are not mentioned in the report, an indication that they continued to receive their usual stipends.

Six adults, assisted by as many as five boy sopranos in some years, performed together until May 1565, when the Flemish *maestro di cappella* Francesco Fabri resigned.[9] Once again, Giovanbattista di Bartolomeo, who first held the post almost a quarter of a century earlier and then more recently during Fabri's prolonged absence, stepped in.[10] As on a previous occasion, with the departure of a key figure in the chapel and an apparent inability or perhaps even a certain reluctance to engage a suitable replacement immediately, a decision was made to bring in the Palace trombonist Giovanfrancesco di Benedetto, who began his new term of office in May 1565. Henceforth, but for a few brief years, a trombonist, or a singer who doubled on trombone, was employed in the chapel throughout the rest of the century.[11] Thus, an initial attempt to supplement the sound of the bass in a chapel depleted in numbers became an accepted practice and, indeed, a characteristic feature of Sienese chapel music of the later sixteenth century. In contrast to earlier usage, which bolstered or substituted one or more of the upper parts with cornett accompaniment, the presence of the trombone assured a certain measure of volume to the lowest part and must have amply compensated for any imbalance that might occur with the introduction, as happened later, of additional adult sopranos alongside the choristers.

INVENTORIES AND REPERTORIES AFTER THE SIEGE

An inventory from 1557, the year that witnessed the near dissolution of the chapel, cites three printed works besides the seven mentioned in the inventory of a decade

---

cantori]). (Bartolomeo, in any case, had not been active in the chapel since April 1561 and did not return until the following year.)

9. Fabri, as noted earlier, left Siena in 1555 for a post in Orvieto, where his name remained on the books until July 1560, by which time he was already back at his old post in Siena. After leaving Siena in May 1565, he returned to Orvieto, where he remained as *maestro di cappella* (to October 1583) and bass, until his death on 24 May 1589. But he was in Siena, however briefly, on 16 October 1565, when he acknowledged receiving Fl. 112 from Agostino Bardi. He is referred to as "Dominus Franciscus Petri Fabbri Flandrie, incola Senarum, cantor" in the document (ASS, Notarile antecosimiano, vol. 2732, no. 2188). His children, Pietro and Stefano, were both students at Orvieto cathedral school during his tenure there. Stefano had a particularly successful career, serving as a bass, tenor, organist, and trombonist in Orvieto's chapel before moving as *maestro di cappella* to the Cappella Giulia at St. Peter's in Rome (1599–1601), then to St. John in Lateran (1603–8) and to the Santa Casa in Loreto, where he remained until his death on 28 August 1609. Two of his compositions were printed in anthologies, but it was his son, also named Stefano (d. Rome, 28 August 1658), who achieved greater success as a composer. See Brumana and Ciliberti, *Orvieto: Una cattedrale*, 56–57.

10. Payment records indicate he held the post through April 1568.

11. An interesting parallel is furnished by records from the Santo in Padua, where a trombonist was hired in 1566, a year after the reconstitution of the chapel. In the following years the chapel normally counted seven or eight singers and a trombonist was associated with the group from that point on. See Owens, "Il Cinquecento," 46.

earlier (see Table 7.1).[12] New in the library were a set of partbooks containing four-voice motets by Jachet of Mantua, "un corpo di libretti di mottetti a 4 di Iachett," published at Venice in 1539 by Girolamo Scotto, and two other sets of partbooks, of "motets by diverse authors, a 4 and a 8," whose inadequate description precludes positive identification. Of the works in manuscript, the previously listed books of Masses and motets in large folio, as well as the book of psalms and Magnificats in large folio and "the medium-sized book of Magnificats and hymns," are all mentioned, though the last is described as "uso forte," much used. (This is surely the book copied by Mattio Gay more than three-quarters of a century earlier, in 1481.) "Another book" of Masses, described in the 1547 inventory as "bound in wood," is now called "a book bound in wood, where there is the Mass of the Dead and others, but torn." Also appearing is a book of "5 Masses, copied by hand, bound in wood, half-covered in red leather," that may be new. The "8 partbooks for processions, covered in parchment" are still listed. While it is possible that the Opera acquired some or all of the new items in the years after the siege, more likely it did so earlier, during the time the chapel underwent one of its largest expansions.

So, too, with five new printed items in the next inventory from 1563, purchased during this latest period of renewed growth (see Table 7.1). Three of these are easily identified as sets of partbooks containing motets. The first, "sei libri di Gumbert di mottetti," corresponds to Antonio Gardane's anthology of 1539, *Primus liber cum sex vocibus. Mottetti del frutto,* which contains a large selection of Gombert's motets and others by Jachet Berchem, Loyset Piéton, and Johannes Pionnier.[13] The second new set, "cinque libri di mottetti di Vincenzo Ruffo," must be the first book of his five-voice motets, printed by Giovanni Antonio Castiglione at Milan in 1542. It contains thirty-five works with texts appropriate to Christmas, Corpus Christi, and other feasts of the Lord, the Virgin Mary, and St. Peter, and a number of psalm texts.[14] The third new set, "cinque libri di mottetti del Conte," is a collection of Bartolomeo El Conte's works, *Motetta quinque vocibus suavissime sonantia,* printed at Venice in 1547 by Antonio Gardane.[15] Among its twenty pieces are texts suitable for the just-mentioned feasts and

---

12. The printed items in the 1547 inventory, listed above in Table 6.2, included books of Masses published by Antico (1516), Petreius (1539), and Moderne (1532 and 1540), books of Masses by Morales and Carpentras, and two motet collections containing works by Gombert. For the school furniture in the 1557 and 1563 inventories see Doc. 7.3. The inventory is discussed in D'Accone, "Music at the Sienese Cathedral in the Later 16th Century," in *Trasmissione e recezione delle forme di cultura musicale,* ed. L. Bianconi, F. A. Gallo, A. Pompilio, and D. Restani, *Atti del XIV Congresso della Società Internazionale di Musicologia (Bologna, 1987)* (Turin, 1990), 3:130–31.

13. This is listed in RISM as 1539[3].

14. The contents of the volume, *Il Primo Libro De Motetti A Cinque Voci De L'Egregio Vincentio Ruffo* (RISM R 3047) are listed by Lockwood, *The Counter-Reformation and the Masses of Vincenzo Ruffo,* 250–51.

15. RISM E 596, listed under Bartolomei El Conte. Bartholomaeus Comes and Bartolomeo Conti are the same person, as noted above. The full title: *El Conte/ Bartolomei Comitis Gallici/ Eccellentissimi Musici Moteta/ Quinque vocibus suavissime sonantia, Nunc primum in lucem edita/ Ad Delectationem Canentium;* its contents are listed by Guglielmo Barblan, *Musiche della Cappella di S. Barbara in Mantova* (Florence, 1972), 116–17.

TABLE 7.1.   Inventories of music manuscripts, 1557–1590

Addì 30 di dicembre 1557 (AOMS, vol. 1535, *Elenchi, note e inventari di beni*)

[Lista] de' libri e robbe de la scuola del canto, consegnati a Giovan Battista di Bartolomeo, cantore, nuovo maestro di cappella

> Uno libro di messe, scritto a mano, figurato, con coverta di cuoio lionato, foglio reale
> Uno libro di mottetti, di foglio reale, con coverta di cuoio rosso, in tavole
> Uno libro di salmi e Magnificat, in tavole, in foglio reale
> Uno libro di Magnificat e inni, in tavole, foglio mezano, uso forte
> Uno libro di messe Morales, in stampa, con coverta di cuoio azurro
> Uno libro di messe in stampa, dela Magna, con coverta di cuoio nero
> Uno libro di 5 messe di Carpentras, in tavole, uso
> Uno libro delle 15 messe di vari authori, in tavole, uso
> Uno libro di dieci, in tavole, mezano, uso
> Uno libro in tavole, dove è la messa de' morti et altre, ma stracciate
> Otto libretti della processioni, covertati di carta pecora
> Un corpo di libri di mottetti della divinità a cinque
> Uno libro di 5 messe, scritto a mano, in tavole, a meza coverta di cuoio rosso
> Due corpi di libri di mottetti di diversi authori, a 4 et a 8, senza coverta
> Un corpo di libretti di mottetti a 4, di Iachett

1563: "Inventario . . . scritto al tempo del magnifico cavaliere messer Marcello di Giovanni Tegliacci operaio" (vol. 1493, *Inventari, 1517?–1590,* fasc. 4, fol. 11ʳ)

> Un libro di messe di canto figurato, cuperto di tavole con corame sopra e borchie over affibiatoi d'ottone
> Un altro libro grande di mottetti, parimente figurato, cuperto di tavole et affibbiatoi d'ottone
> Due libri di messe vechi, con tavole di legno sopra, di carta reale, assai tristi, figurati parimenti
> Un libretto piccolo, chiamata le dieci messe, figurato, cuperto di tavole
> Due libri in un volume, di messe di Morales, in stampa, cuperto di corame nero e cartone
> Un libro di messe di Carpentras, cuperto di tavole
> Un libro di messe franzesi, legato in cartone con corame
> Un libro di messe, ditto di quindici messe di Giosquino, legati [*sic*] in tavole
> Un libro di Magnificat figurato, legato in cartone bianco
> Un libro di hinni et salmi, figurato, legato in tavole
> Un libro di quattro messe di Giachetto, legato in tavole
> Otto libretti di processioni in canto figurato di quarto foglio
> Quattro libretti di mottetti, detti i libri di Iacometto
> Quattro libro di Iacometto, in quarto foglio
> Cinque libri di Gumbert di mottetti, in quarto foglio
> Sei libri di Gumbert di mottetti, in quarto foglio
> Cinque libri di mottetti del Conte, in quarto foglio
> Cinque libri di mottetti di Vincenzo Ruffo
> Cinque libri di mottetti senza cuperta, di più autori

TABLE 7.1 *continued*

1578: "Inventario . . . al tempo del . . . messer Giovambattista di Agnolo Piccolomini dignissimo
operaio della detta chiesa et opera" (ibid., fasc. 5, fol. 15^{r-v})

> as above, plus:
> L'introito di tute le domeniche di Gostanzo Porta
> Un libro di responsi di Francesco Corteccia
> Tre libri legati in cartone, cuperti in cartone pavonazzo, della Magnificat et messe del
>   Palestrina et Animuccia con arme del'Opera et del Tegliaccio

1590: "Inventario . . . nuovo signor rettore messer Iugurta Tomasi" (ibid., fasc. 8, fol. 16^{v})
> as above, plus:
>
> Messe del Ruffo a cinque
> Hinni di tutto l'anno del Palestrina
> Hinni e Magnificat del Vittori[a], con arme di Piccolomini in uno, legati in due tomi

others such as All Saints, St. Victor, and Maundy Thursday, days when polyphony was
performed at Siena cathedral. It is tempting to think that Conte donated his book to
the library when he was in the chapel (November 1550–April 1552) or that he himself
had a hand in introducing its contents to the Sienese singers.

The remaining newly acquired printed items include another volume of Masses
by Morales that was bound with the one mentioned in the 1547 inventory, the two
appropriately listed here as "due libri in un volume di messe di Morales in stampa," and
a book of four Masses by Jachet of Mantua, "un libro di quattro messe di Giachetto."
The second volume of Morales' Masses could be any of the volumes for four to five
and four to six voices cited in the previous chapter, printed between 1540 and 1544, as
well as one printed by Antonio Gardane at Venice in 1547, *Quinque missarum harmonia
diapente id est quinque voces referens.*[16] Since four Masses are specified for Jachet's volume,
it is probable that this was either the one printed by Girolamo Scotto at Venice in 1554
under the title *Il primo libro de le messe a cinque voci* or the same publisher's *Messe del fiore,
a cinque voci, libro primo* of 1561. Later inventories, mentioned below, however, describe
it as a book of five Masses by Jachet, in which case it was the second volume printed
by Scotto in 1561, the *Messe del fiore, a cinque voci, libro secondo.*[17] Unidentified further
in this inventory are a set of four partbooks in quarto by Jacometto, "quattro libri di
Iacometto, in quarto foglio," which may be another printed collection of Jachet's mo-

---

16. RISM M 3589. Modern editions of the Masses are in Cristóbal de Morales, *Opera Omnia,* ed.
Higinio Anglés, vol. 1 (*Missarum Liber Primus*), Monumentos de la Música Española, vol. 13 (Barcelona, 1953); vols. 3 and 6 (*Missarum Liber Secundus*), Monumentos, vols. 15, 21 (Barcelona, 1954,
1962). The volumes mentioned earlier are RISM M 3575–3588.

17. RISM J 15, J 18, and J 19, respectively. The second of the *Messe del fiore* series contained only
older works, reprintings of earlier publications, though the first contained four previously unpublished
works. Modern editions of these works are in Jachet of Mantua, *Opera Omnia,* 1: *The Four Masses of
Scotto's Print of 1554,* and 3: *The Masses of the Flower for Five Voices, Book I (1561),* ed. Philip T. Jackson
(American Institute of Musicology, 1971, 1976). A recent summary of Jachet's career is George Nugent, "Jacquet of Mantua," *New Grove,* 9:456–58.

tets.[18] The six manuscript volumes of Masses, Magnificats, hymns, and psalms and the eight partbooks with processional music listed in the 1563 inventory are the same as those mentioned in 1557, as are the furnishings of the school room and "the little notice-board wherein are written the chapel's duties."

With some sixteen printed collections of Masses and motets and a number of manuscript volumes containing Magnificats, hymns, and psalms, the chapel had an adequate supply of music for every occasion on which it was called to participate. Some of the Mass music, such as Antico's 1516 print, identified as Josquin's, "di Giosquino," in the 1563 inventory, and the publications of Moderne and Carpentras were by now decidedly old, but the fairly recent publication dates of some of the other Masses and motets are notable, as is the preponderance of music by Morales, Gombert, and Jachet. By contrast, the hymns, psalms, and Magnificats were still those mentioned in 1536 and even earlier. This may reflect the *maestro di cappella*'s inability or reluctance to acquire new collections of such works. It is impossible to know whether all of the music in these printed (or manuscript) collections was in the singers' repertory. Clearly, the *maestro di cappella* chose only those pieces that were liturgically appropriate. He had to consider also the vocal ranges of available singers and the amount of time needed to learn new parts and rehearse the music. In any case, the collection apparently sufficed the needs of the chapel in 1563, a group that now included at least two adults singing and playing each of the three lower parts and as many as five young sopranos.

ORGANISTS AND *MAESTRI DI CAPPELLA* TO 1575

Scipione di Pavolo ended his long career as cathedral organist on 30 April 1563, the same day his successor, Mariano di Girolamo Pelori, was appointed "to play the two organs," at a monthly salary of L. 12. The terms of Pelori's appointment are vague, as was usual with all such records of contracts; they note simply that he was obliged to play on all the usual days as well as on any extraordinary occasions when his services might be needed, particularly when distinguished personages visited (see Doc. 7.4). The only significant information in the contract, in fact, is the statement that Pelori was obliged "whenever they sing to the Madonna, to play the organ opposite it [the icon] and not the one above the sacristy." It will be recalled that this organ was restored by Lorenzo di Jacopo da Prato and subsequently transferred to the chapel of the Magi in the north aisle, across from the altar of the Madonna delle Grazie. Because the nave separated the singers and the organist, perhaps he played in alternatim with them or merely provided solo pieces. The terms of Pelori's contract specified that he was appointed for a year and that each party was to give the other three months' notice before the end of the year, otherwise his appointment would be extended for the following year with the same duties and salary. A note appended to the record states that on 16 May 1564 the overseer informed him that his contract would not be renewed for the

---

18. I take Jacometto to be a corruption of Giachetto, and thus have identified the "Quattro libretti di mottetti, detti i libri di Iacometto" with the last item of the 1557 inventory, "uno corpo di libretti di mottetti a 4, di Iachett." If this is so, then this poorly identified item may be one of the collections of motets *a 4* published by Gardane in 1545 (RISM J 11) or by Scotto (RISM 1554, reprinted 1565, RISM J 12).

following year and that the three-month obligatory notice was being given far in advance.[19]

A few months before Pelori's departure, the overseer Marcello Tegliacci opened negotiations with friends in the Servite Order in order to secure the services of a promising young musician. This was Fra Arcangelo da Reggio, at the time organist at the cathedral of his native city. Preliminary correspondence regarding this appointment is lost. But in a letter to the overseer, dated 19 February 1565, the General of the Servites spoke of the ties of affection that bound his order "to your magnificent city" and remarked that he had gladly given permission for Arcangelo to become organist at Siena cathedral (see Doc. 7.5). And, he added, "secretly, I am even more happy because the young man will not only study in Siena, but will honor his order and will improve himself." Perhaps he meant by this that Arcangelo would enroll in the university, which continued to maintain excellent faculties throughout this period. Though no evidence at present indicates that the few foreign musicians who served in Siena during the later sixteenth century were attracted to the city because of the university, they presumably took advantage of the educational opportunities available to them once they were there.

Arcangelo began his duties as organist in Siena cathedral on 1 June 1565, at a monthly salary of L. 15. His contract, valid for three years, states that he was to play one or the other of the organs according to cathedral usage on all feast days and on all other special occasions when needed (see Doc. 7.6). He was given permission to preach outside Siena during Lent, on condition that he return at the end of Easter week and that he leave a substitute, approved by the rector, in his place. Arcangelo held the post, as stipulated, until the beginning of May 1568, when he succeeded Giovambattista di Bartolomeo as *maestro di cappella*. His replacement as organist was Messer Bennardo di Salso da Parma. Archangelo's work was well received, for within a few months his initial monthly salary of L. 21 was raised to L. 24. Henceforth he devoted his energies full time to the *maestro di cappella*'s post, which he retained until the end of November 1570. Bennardo di Salso, however, remained only through the end of August 1568, replaced in the following month by the organist Messer Bartolomeo Toscani da Venezia. Toscani held the post through January 1573, when he was succeeded by the returning Mariano Pelori, who would remain as cathedral organist for the next seventeen years.

Archangelo's immediate successor as *maestro di cappella* was his friend and fellow Servite monk, Salvadore Essenga da Modena. Essenga was an experienced teacher and choir director, having served for the decade before his appointment to Siena as *maestro di cappella* at the cathedral of Tortona and at the cathedral of Modena.[20] His Sienese contract, dated 10 February 1571, notes that he was appointed for a three-year period, beginning on the previous December 1st, at a salary of Sc. 42 per annum, that is, L. 24. 10 per month, and that he agreed "to do all of the usual things done by other maestri who held the post." A further provision states that unless one or the other of the parties gave notice six months in advance, the contract would automatically be

---

19. Pelori also played in other Sienese churches. See below, chapter 13.

20. He was mentioned in 1722 by the Servite historian Arcangelo Giani, *Annalium Sacri Ordinis Fratrum Servorum B. Mariae Virginis* (Florence, 1618–22), 1:153. See the entry on Essenga by Iain Fenlon in *New Grove,* 6:253.

renewed for an additional three years. It is regrettable that so little information is given in the document about the *maestro di cappella*'s duties because a list of "the usual things" required of the incumbent does not survive in cathedral records from the sixteenth century.

Teaching, nevertheless, must have still been considered the central, most important aspect of the post. It is, in fact, the only obligation specifically mentioned in Essenga's contract. This states that he was to keep the chapel "furnished with a sufficient number of sopranos" and to give instruction "to the boys and to the duomo's clerks who have promising voices, or to others whom he and the rector might choose." In this regard the contract also notes that Essenga was given the keys to the school "which is in room 3 of the canon's residence." The schoolroom was appropriately furnished with two benches, a table with three legs, three seats, a lectern, a cloth-covered frame, and a "tavolella" on which were written the chapel's duties. Within the schoolroom were "many books of music of various kinds that are for the use of the chapel only," music which, as noted, the *maestro di cappella* was responsible for inventorying and preserving.

Although Essenga was a composer, his contract did not require him to supply the chapel with music. Nor do extant Sienese records state that he composed music for the cathedral. His printed works point to his having been primarily a composer of secular music, although the superius part of a polyphonic Mass ascribed to him is in a Modena cathedral manuscript. Not a trace of his presence survives in Sienese music inventories or in the Opera's library. His extant publications include two books of madrigals from 1561 and 1565 and a scattering of pieces in several collections from as late as 1575.[21] This last, as I note below, has a preponderance of music by Sienese composers from the mid-1570s and the two madrigals by Essenga may date from when he was still at the cathedral.

Essenga served as *maestro di cappella* until the time of his death in May 1575.[22] During his tenure (begun in December 1570) the chapel continued to function on an even keel, the personnel remaining stable with six adults, the trombonist, and two or three choristers. Another singer was hired shortly after Essenga's arrival in Siena. This was his pupil, Orazio Vecchi. Recorded as a tenor in the chapel beginning in February 1571, Vecchi initially received a monthly salary of L. 10, increased to L. 12 by the time of his departure at the end of April 1574. Born in 1550, he was still at a formative stage in his career when he arrived in Siena. His three-year stay in the city, hitherto unrecorded, must have been of inestimable value to his formation as a musician.[23] Perhaps he, too,

21. The two surviving books are: *Il secondo libro di madrigali a cinque voci con alquanti sesti et dui ottavi,* printed by Antonio Gardano at Venice in 1561 (RISM E 827) and *Il primo libro di madrigali a quatro voci,* issued by the same publisher in 1566 (RISM E 828). A third book of madrigals for five voices, though advertised in Giunta's catalogue of 1604, has not survived. Other works appear in *Il secondo libro de le Muse a cinque voci composto da diversi eccellentissimi musici* (Venice, A. Gardano, RISM 1559[16]); *Il primo libro della raccolta di napolitana a tre voci di diversi eccellentissimi musici* (Venice, Scotto, RISM 1570[19]); and *Il quinto libro delle Muse, madrigali a cinque voci con uno a sette novamente composti et dati in luce* (Venice, figliuoli A. Gardano, RISM 1575[12]).

22. Giani, *Annalium Sacri Ordinis Fratrum Servorum,* 1:153, gives his death date and place as Siena.

23. A recent summary of Vecchi's life and works by William R. Martin is in *New Grove,* 19:584–86.

enrolled at the university. More likely, he continued studies, begun in Modena, with Essenga, under whose auspices he published his first work. Whether he composed music for the chapel when he was in Siena is doubtful, since most of his printed sacred works evidently date from long after he left the city. He moved on to Brescia, Bergamo, and Salò before returning as *maestro di cappella* at the cathedral in his native Modena in 1584. After a stint as *maestro di cappella* at the cathedral of Correggio, in 1593 he resumed his old post at Modena, where he died in 1605. Vecchi, who was to become one of the most celebrated musicians of his time thanks to the extraordinary success of his six books of *Canzonette,* later remembered the pleasures of his sojourn in Siena and its amusing pastimes in his delightful madrigal comedy *Le veglie di Siena,* published in 1604.[24]

THE CHAPEL UNDER ASCANIO MARRI AND ANDREA FELICIANI

Vecchi was replaced beginning in June 1574 by another tenor, Ser Alessio Spagnuolo da Valenzia, who in turn was followed in March 1575 by Giovanbattista Tesauro Romano. (Both were initially paid L. 8 per month.) Thus, in June 1575, when Ascanio Marri succeeded Essenga as *maestro di cappella,* the adult singers included two altos (Benedetto Franceschi, Piero Ciotti), two tenors (Annibale Bennardi and Giovanbattista Tesauro), a bass (Jacomo Giusti), and the trombonist (Rivolti). Marri, only the second instrumentalist in more than sixty years to gain the *maestro di cappella*'s post, directed the wind band at the Palazzo Pubblico and had to seek the government's approval before he accepted the new appointment.[25] After assuring the priors that he could discharge his duties effectively at both places, permission was granted, particularly, as was noted in the official decree approving his request, because the extra salary of L. 24. 10 per month paid to him by the cathedral would help support his many children.

Marri's tenure at the cathedral proved to be brief. A report from a quarter of a century later recounts that within a few months of his appointment he journeyed to Rome for the Jubilee year celebrations with members of the Company of St. Catherine of Siena. While attending a service at St. Peter's he was injured when a candlestick fell and struck him on the head. The accident proved to be more serious than first thought and he died several days later at Montefiascone, as he was being taken back to Siena in a litter.[26] Cathedral payments indicate that he remained on the payroll through October 1575.

Marri's appointment is significant for a number of reasons. Perhaps the most obvious is that the overseers decided the time was ripe for appointing a native musician to the

---

24. On Vecchi's madrigal comedy see J. C. Hol, "Le veglie di Siena di Horatio Vecchi," *Rivista musicale italiana* 43 (1939): 17–34; Gino Roncaglia, "Orazio Vecchi e le 'Veglie di Siena'," in *Musicisti della scuola emiliana,* ed. Adelmo Damerini and Gino Roncaglia, Settimana senese XIII (Siena, 1956), 83–89; and especially James Haar, "On Musical Games in the 16th Century," *JAMS* 15 (1962): 32–34, where the connections between the literary content of the first half of Vecchi's comedy and Girolamo Bargagli's 1572 *Dialogo de' Giuochi che nelle vegghie sanesi si usono di fare* are explained.

25. See chapter 12.

26. The report, in BCIS, MS A. IV. 7, has been published by Antonio Mazzeo, *Compositori senesi del 500 e del 600* (Siena, 1981), 13–14.

maestro di cappella's post and that an outstanding candidate was already present in the city. Marri had recently published two books of madrigals in Venice and he had also contributed to another well-known series. He had, in other words, begun acquiring a reputation outside Siena. By virtue of his many years as a performer in the Palace wind band and later as its leader, he was an experienced musician with a wide knowledge of the contemporary repertory. Palace musicians were a versatile lot—Marri himself played the trombone and the cornett—and were accustomed not only to playing music for entertainment in the Palace, but also to singing and playing at Masses in the Palace's private chapel. As a youngster, Marri had trained at the cathedral school and had also sung in the chapel, which meant that he had had a thorough grounding in plainchant and in some of the best music of the high Renaissance. He could thus be expected to bring a first-hand knowledge of the school's traditions and problems to the job as well as several years' experience as the leader of a first-class professional ensemble specializing in a wide variety of repertories.

A report concerning the *maestro di cappella*'s duties at the Palace, to be discussed below in chapter 12, makes it clear that the incumbent (who happened to be Marri at the time the document was drawn up) had complete artistic control over the group's performances and that he alone selected repertory and assigned parts to the musicians. He would have similar responsibilities as *maestro di cappella* at the cathedral, although the repertory he was obliged to conduct there was smaller, since it was restricted to music appropriate to the liturgy. He would also be working with different kinds of musicians and facing different problems, none of them beyond his abilities, as he had already demonstrated at the Palace. Marri clearly was an ideal choice for the position. His appointment can thus be viewed not so much as a departure from the norm as one that confirmed the validity of past practices, one, furthermore, that might even pave the way for a further expansion of the role of instruments within the chapel and for more frequent interchange with the Palace musicians.

One final observation about Marri's tenure as *maestro di cappella* concerns the speed with which his successor, Andrea Feliciani, was identified and appointed. Feliciani, too, was a native Sienese and a layman, although he had no prior association with the cathedral chapel or with the Palace musicians. He is said to have been a pupil of Palestrina, but no documents are extant that show this to have been so. The positions he had occupied before he was awarded the *maestro di cappella*'s post are as yet unknown, though it seems likely that at the time of Marri's death he was in one of the provincial towns in the Sienese dominion, Grosseto, for example. He may have even been in Siena shortly before then because some of his madrigals, together with others by Marri, Essenga, and Vecchi, were published in the just-cited *Il quinto libro delle Muse,* a collection evidently intended as a tribute to composers associated with Siena. Whatever the case, it seems that he was called to Siena from wherever he was employed as soon as news of Marri's death reached the overseers and that he had no hesitation in accepting the post. His appointment confirmed the earlier decision to rely henceforth on Sienese musicians and thereby inaugurated what was to be an established policy throughout the seventeenth and eighteenth centuries.

No record of a contract with Marri survives, which may mean simply that he did not live long enough for one to be drawn up. This much is, in fact, implied in the wording of the agreement Andrea Feliciani signed on 4 November 1575. That document states that Feliciani began serving on the first of the month and notes that he had been given the key to the schoolroom and an inventory of its furnishings and the music books. It then remarks that with regard to his duties "we refer to the contract of Fra Salvadore of Modena, onetime master of the same chapel, on fol. 25 of this [volume], which was read out loud to him in his presence." Clearly, if Marri had had a similar formal agreement, reference would have been made to it instead of to his predecessor's.

Details of Feliciani's biography remain almost as incomplete as the record of his appointment at the cathedral. What little is known of his personal life, apart from his successful career as a *maestro di cappella* and the financial rewards he reaped from his professional activities, can be gleaned from a small number of legal documents. His Sienese origins are verified in a will he filed on 30 May 1583, when he was gravely ill. Though cathedral records make no mention of it, his illness is, in fact, corroborated by a payment from the hospital of Santa Maria della Scala to the cathedral singer Ser Benedetto di Francesco, acting as Feliciani's substitute, for the chapel's performances there on the feast of the Annunciation in March 1583.[27] In the will Feliciani is referred to as "Don Giovanni Andrea, son of the late Feliciano de' Feliciani, Sienese citizen and musician, of infirm body, sick in bed." He had evidently dropped his first name some time earlier, for all subsequent Sienese records, as well as the title pages of his music publications, always identify him as "Andrea Feliciani." A mark of the respect he enjoyed and of his standing in the community is evident in his being called "Don" rather than "Maestro." Feliciani left the rather large sum of Fl. 1,000 to his wife Elisabetta and he named his only daughter, Urania, as his heir. He requested burial in the tomb of the Confraternity of San Pietro nel Duomo, an indication that he, too, was a member of that venerable company to which so many cathedral musicians belonged. Among the witnesses to the will was Jacomo di Antonio Latini, a Palace musician, who is referred to as "musicus Senensis." In a codicil to the will from the following day Feliciani modified the bequest to his daughter by noting that his wife might be pregnant and that should she bear a son, he was to become the principal heir.

Feliciani soon recovered from his illness and resumed his duties in the chapel. Apparently, another illness ten years later caused him to draw up a subsequent will, this one dated 11 October 1593. He was now described as "Don Giovanni Andrea [son of] the late Feliciano de' Feliciani, a Sienese citizen and musician, healthy, though weak in a certain sense." On this occasion he named his eleven-month-old son Francesco as his principal heir. He acknowledged that he had two daughers, Urania and Maddalena, by his beloved wife Elisabetta, to whom he was leaving the sum of Fl. 750, which she had brought as a dowry. Little else is known of his family except that one daughter, probably Urania, became prioress of the Dominican convent of the Mantellate. This was "Sister Hyacinth, daughter of the deceased Andrea Feliciani," who, according to the Dominican necrology, died on 30 April 1649 at the age of sixty-nine.[28] She would thus have been born in Siena in 1580, five years after Feliciani assumed the *maestro di cappella*'s post.

During his tenure as *maestro di cappella* from 1575 to 1596, Feliciani became the

---

27. See chapter 13. The payment is in Ospedale, vol. 811, *Bastardello di cassa, 1582–83,* fol. 38ᵛ.

28. BCIS, MS. C. III. 3, *Necrologio di San Domenico,* fol. 63ʳ: "Soror Hyacintha, filia quondam Andreae Feliciani, celebris musici, una ex sororibus nostris, Priorissa Mantellatarum . . . inter alias

most celebrated Sienese musician of his day through his publications and his work with the chapel. It was in large part due to him that in the last quarter of the sixteenth century the Sienese group assumed a distinct profile, performing works in the standard repertory as well as many others composed expressly for it by its maestro, by his pupils, and by his equally gifted successor. Under his direction the school flourished as never before and the chapel grew in numbers and in prestige. It was a slow but steady growth, one that reflected both a renewed confidence and a renewed sense of cultural identity, which the Medici were content to foster so long as it did not jeopardize political loyalties. Though salaries were initially not as high as previously, reflecting the economically depressed times, they were sufficient to attract the city's best singers, clerics and laymen alike. Feliciani himself began with the modest salary of L. 17. 10 per month, as opposed to the L. 24. 10 offered to his predecessors, Essenga and Marri. He was, however, given several raises over the course of the years and was earning L. 34 per month at the time of his death in 1596, by which time salaries of many of the singers were also at an all-time high.

Chapel Singers to 1588

With the exception of Jacomo Giusti, the same group of adult singers and the trombonist recorded in June 1575 are mentioned through the first five years of Feliciani's tenure. Joining the group from October 1576 through March 1577 was an alto, Ser Piermaria di Tommaso Romano, followed in May 1578 by another alto, Frate Anselmo di Santo Agostino. This latter's successor, in August 1579, was Michelangelo di Giovanni, previously listed as a "young clerk" from 1574 through 1578. Yet another alto, Ser Ventura di Giovanni da Castello, was registered during March and April 1580. Though the opening years of the 1580s witnessed relatively few changes in personnel, the remainder of that decade saw the chapel transformed into a large, stable group which by then counted several of Feliciani's former students among its adult members. As on previous occasions, there are no records of the decisions that led to the expansion of forces and what prompted them or, for that matter, to the new or renewed sources of funding that made the changes possible. A solid financial basis clearly existed or was in the making, for the changes, though modified after a spurt of unrestrained growth, were sustained over a long period of time.

Older students at the school now began to appear more frequently as singers of lower parts, as did, for example, the alto Attilio di Girolamo, cited for a brief four months in 1580, and the previously mentioned Michelangelo di Giovanni, who served for more than five years. Domenico di Maestro Pietro, first listed as a "minor clerk and soprano," was later designated a "clerk in his middle teens and contralto." In 1582 the former choirboy Midone, now called Ser Midone Nannetti, was hired as the third bass, perhaps replacing the trombonist, Tiberio di Girolamo, whose name disappears from the rolls for several years. The choirboys included Bernardino Draghi, first mentioned among the "young clerks" in 1576–78 as a "minor clerk and soprano in the chapel." He would join the adult ranks as an alto within a few years. Benvenuto di Girolamo

---

moniales huius tertii ordinis, aetatis 69 annorum, in sepulcro solito earum contumulatur die 30 Aprilis."

Flori, to give him his full name, would also eventually become an adult member of the chapel, employed off and on as a cathedral singer for well over three decades.[29] Two of the three boy sopranos employed in 1585, Donato di Domenico and Ottavio di Lorenzo Basili, also joined the adult singers in later years, as did Bernardino Cocchi, cited as a clerk and alto in 1587. In November of that same year the long-time alto Ser Piero Ciotti ceased singing and assumed the duties of sacristan. Ser Benedetto Franceschi, a chapel member since 1561, left cathedral service altogether in April 1587, preceded a month earlier by Ser Pietragnolo Nastagi. Other former choirboys returning to service included the tenor Ser Annibale Bennardi and Ser Domenico Lucenti, this latter mentioned both as a bass and as a tenor. The departure in May 1580 and subsequent return in April 1587 of the Palace trombonist, Tiberio Rivolti, is noteworthy because three basses were present throughout the entire time of his last employment, which ran through the end of January 1588. His replacement may have been the bass Giovanni Antonio Napoletano, listed from February 1588 onwards, though more likely he was succeeded by Giovanbattista di Francesco Formichi, who joined the group in December 1587. At the time Formichi, a member of the Palace wind band, was described in cathedral records as a tenor, but later ones state that he played the trombone.[30]

While records from these years generally designate the singers' vocal ranges precisely, occasionally they do not, making it not always possible to determine the exact composition of the chapel. Domenico di Maestro Antonio furnishes a case in point. An account from 1582–84 calls him an "older clerk and tenor in the chapel." For a brief time after he was ordained, from June 1586 through January 1587, records identify him as Ser Domenico d'Antonio Lucenti, "chaplain and bass," though subsequent records from November 1588 through November 1589 again designate him a tenor. This could mean that his range was wide enough to enable him to sing the bass part when the need arose. But it is just as likely that the bookkeeper who called him a bass simply made a mistake. A similar situation occurs with regard to Pietragnolo di Giovanni Nastagi. One account from 1584–86 identifies him as a tenor, another, June 1586–March 1587, as a priest and contralto. Given the similarity of range between alto and tenor parts, even at this late date, one person could have sung either part, though considerations of vocal quality and timbre may also have demanded a stricter separation than similar voice ranges might suggest.

The Repertory

An inventory from 1578, two years after Feliciani assumed the *maestro di cappella*'s post, cites only a few items beyond the manuscript and printed volumes mentioned in previous inventories (see above, Table 7.1).[31] These items, however, reflect a desire to utilize newer music that provided good coverage of musical needs for the entire liturgical year and a predilection for music from the Roman school or other music allied to it in liturgical appropriateness, aesthetic aims, and functional purposes. The newly listed

29. Reardon, *Agostino Agazzari*, 51, n. 60, reports his death in March 1642.

30. He is called Formica in Palace records. See chapter 12.

31. Among the schoolroom's furnishings at this time was a leather-dressed lectern described as "Un leggio di corame per cantare alla Madonna," perhaps used only when the singers performed in the chapel of Santa Maria delle Grazie.

books include Costanzo Porta's collection of settings of introits for Sundays throughout the year, published at Venice in 1566.[32] Also cited is "a book of responsories by Francesco Corteccia," undoubtedly the principal volume of the composer's two-volume set of responsories and other music for Holy Week, published by Gardano at Venice in 1570, but containing a good deal of music written more than a quarter of a century earlier and revised thereafter.[33] The acquisition of this volume points to the use of polyphony at Tenebrae, unmentioned in records as days when the chapel was obliged to sing, though Maundy Thursday had long been designated as one of the cathedral's principal feast days. Since Matins and Lauds were anticipated on the evenings before Maundy Thursday, Good Friday, and Holy Saturday, Corteccia's music, though performed only once a year, was heard by a larger public than might normally be present at those services. Rounding out the list are "three books, bound in cardboard, covered with purple cardboard, of the Magnificats and Masses of Palestrina and Animuccia." These, as later inventories make more clear, comprised Animuccia's *Canticum B. Mariae Virginis,* published at Rome in 1568, and two of the first three books of Palestrina's Masses, published in 1554, 1567, and 1570.[34] The Magnificats were perhaps intended to supplement if not entirely supplant older ones in the chapel's repertory and, like the Masses, would have been repeatedly performed, given the many times during the year the chapel performed at Vespers.

The new emphasis on Palestrina's works in the 1578 repertory is indicative of Feliciani's tastes, which became even more pronouncedly Roman in the following years, as demonstrated by the inventory of cathedral music holdings from 1590 (see Table 7.1). This lists all of the previously mentioned printed volumes and most of those in manuscript as well as four new printed volumes, including one of Vincenzo Ruffo's five-voice Masses, another of Palestrina's hymns from 1589, and two of hymns and Magnificats by Tomás Luis de Victoria, both published in 1581.[35] Apart from Ruffo's

---

32. Porta's introits are in RISM A 1237. They are published in modern edition in C. Porta, *Opera Omnia,* ed. Siro Cisilino, vol. 15.

33. Corteccia's responsories are in RISM C 4153–4154. Modern edition in *Collected Sacred Works: Music for the Triduum Sacrum,* vol. 11 of my Music of the Florentine Renaissance.

34. The Magnificats are in RISM P 655–656, the Masses in RISM P 660 and 664. Palestrina's works in modern edition are in G. P. da Palestrina *Werke,* ed. Franz X. Haberl, vols. 10, 11, 12; and G. P. da Palestrina, *Le opere complete,* ed. Raffaele Casimiri, vols. 1, 4, 6 for the Masses and vol. 16 for Magnificats.

35. It is impossible to determine whether the "Messe del Ruffo a cinque" was the volume first published by Antonio Gardano at Venice in 1557 and subsequently reprinted in 1565 and 1567 (RISM R 3049), or the volume, apparently a reprint of an earlier one, described as *Messe a cinque voci . . . nuovamente composte, secondo la forma del Concilio Tridentino,* issued by Vincenzo Sabbio at Brescia in 1580 (RISM R 3061). Both volumes and their contents are analyzed and discussed by Lockwood in *The Counter-Reformation and the Masses of Vincenzo Ruffo,* 145–213. The remaining volumes correspond to (1) Palestrina's *Hymni totius anni, secundum Sanctae Romanae Ecclesiae consuetudinem, quatuor vocibus concinendi necnon hymni religionum,* published by Giacomo Torniero and Bernardo Donangelo (Francesco Coattino) in 1589 (RISM P 737); modern edition, in *Werke,* vol. 45, and *Opere complete,* vol. 14; and (2) Victoria's *Hymni totius anni, secundum Sanctae Romane Ecclesiae consuetudinem, qui quattuor concinuntur vocibus, una cum quattuor psalmis, pro praecipuis festivitatibus, qui octo vocibus modulantur* (RISM V 1428) and his *Cantica B. Virginis vulgo Magnificat quatuor vocibus. Una cum quatuor antiphonis Beate Virginis per annum: quae quidem, partim quinis, partim octonis vocibus concinuntur* (RISM V 1430), both

Masses, these volumes contained mostly works for four voices, with a sprinkling of others from five to eight voices. Victoria's hymns for four voices must have been highly regarded by Feliciani and his singers, for they were even copied into a manuscript volume that survives to this day in the Opera's archives.[36] In his Masses especially Feliciani emulated these two great masters whose works exemplify in different ways the spirit and ideals of Counter-Reformation polyphony. His harmonies, though rarely venturing beyond simple excursions to tones closely related to the central tonic, are effective and expressive of the general mood he was attempting to depict. So, too, with his textures, which are often varied and effectively contrasted according to the sense of the words. When he writes imitative counterpoint, his motives are generally terse but molded to the text, unfolding within a regulated linear flow of polyphony that is only occasionally marked by a prepared dissonance or fleeting passing tones. Though he was hardly a Palestrina or a Victoria, in his most inspired works a sense of devotion emerges that is as distinctive of Counter-Reformation musical ideals as that of any other composer of the time.

This is most clearly heard in a movement such as the Sanctus from the *Missa Brevis,* published in his first extant collection, the *Missarum cum quatuor, quinque, et octo vocibus, liber primus* of 1584 (RISM F 199) (Ex. 7.1). Here, the initially slow movement of the main motive soon breaks into faster note values as it ascends an octave diatonically, all of this on the word "Sanctus." Having reached its high point, the melody now continues without interruption with a second invocation of "Sanctus" as it begins a downward sweep that will eventually take it back to its opening note, the tonic G. The other voices act accordingly until a cadence is reached on a D minor chord, at measure 11. A new motive, treated in close imitation, is given to the words "Dominus Deus Sabaoth," though in fact its rhythm, if not its exact melodic contour, has been anticipated in the cantus part a few bars earlier. Imitation and free counterpoint characterize the rest of the text through "Gloria tua," which comes to a cadence on G. With the "Hosanna," sweeping ascending and decending scale passages, reminiscent of the opening "Sanctus," return to bring the movement to a close on G. In neat contrast to the more leisurely working out of material in this movement is the succinct treatment of motives in the first Kyrie (Ex. 7.2). Subject and countersubject are sounded simultaneously at the opening between tenor and cantus, with the alto quickly imitating the tenor at the unison, to be followed shortly by the bass imitating the cantus. As the cantus finishes the countersubject (m. 4), it begins the subject and adds to it a lengthy melisma that moves in quicker note values through an octave to the high g″. Below this the other parts now make statements of either the subject or the countersubject. Economy of means to achieve the desired brevity is further emphasized as the altus sings in succession varied versions of the countersubject and subject, this latter anticipating its ultimate presentation in the cantus's high register and with it a quick close to the movement. Though cadences on G and C appear fleetingly, there is no sense of repose until the final cadence (in measure 13) of this brief and beautifully planned movement.

published at Rome by Francisco Zanetto (Dominico Basa) in 1581; modern edition in T. L. de Victoria, *Opera omnia,* ed. Pedrell, vols. 5 and 3.

36. Shelf number MS BB. The hymns are not listed in later inventories.

Feliciani's other sacred music collections include a book of Magnificats for four, eight, and twelve voices, the *Musica in canticum Beatissimae Virginis Mariae* of 1591, and two books of psalms, the *Brevis . . . psalmodia ad vespertinas horas* for eight voices of 1590, and the *Psalmodia vespertinas quatuor canenda vocibus*.[37] It is unfortunate that this last, published posthumously in 1599, survives incomplete, for all traces of the earlier editions are lost. The psalms of the 1590 collection are all for two choirs, each of the standard four parts. They comprise settings of many of the same texts found in the volume copied for the Sienese chapel by Mattio Gay a century earlier, among them all of the psalms for Sundays, for the feasts of Our Lord, of the Virgin Mary, of the Common of Apostles, of the Common of Martyrs, and for the dedication of a church. The style of the psalms shares many features with the Magnificats, particularly the way in which alternation of the two choirs unfolds so as to produce the maximum effect at moments when both groups sing en masse. A Magnificat in the 8th tone may serve as a typical example of his style (Ex. 7.3). Throughout this extended work, the harmony moves within the controlled ambience of the prevailing G mode, whose Ionian leanings are emphasized by the frequently raised leading tone on F (notated F♯). But there are also frequent progressions involving chords on the uninflected seventh of the scale, F, sometimes functioning as subdominant of the subdominant, C, sometimes in conjunction with chords on B-flat, which evoke the lingering echos of an ambiguous modality. Apart from the intonation of the opening word, Feliciani sets all eight verses of the Magnificat and the concluding Gloria Patri without a break. His handling of the two choirs is straightforward but unpredictable, for there is no set pattern that determines how much text one group sings or the juncture at which both will unite. Though the choirs exchange phrases almost imperceptibly with no interruption to the flow of sound, at times there is an underlying nervous quality to the music, brought about by the unexpected appearance of a quick rhythmic figure or by an abrupt momentary change in the prevailing harmonic rhythm. Deviations such as these, however slight, clearly betray the work's late Renaissance origins.

Feliciani's Pupils

Bernardino Draghi was the first of Feliciani's pupils to make his mark as a composer. He was also one of the *maestro di cappella*'s favorites and Feliciani even included one of the young man's works in his collection of Vespers music published in 1590, mentioned above, a setting of Ps. 137, *Confitebor,* for two choirs. In the next year the Venetian publisher Angelo Gardano brought out a volume dedicated exclusively to Draghi's three-voice villanelle. Draghi's promising career, however, was cut short by his untimely death in 1592.[38]

Many other boy sopranos were eventually employed to sing lower parts. Their ser-

---

37. These are listed in RISM as F 201, F 200, and F 202, respectively.

38. Draghi's *Il primo libro delle villanelle a tre voci* was published by Gardano at Venice in 1571 (RISM D 3488). He began studying at the cathedral school at a very young age; he was recorded as a *cherico minore*, June 1578–April 1579, with no indication that he sang (vol. 1082, *Distribuzioni e Salariati, 1578–95,* fol. 23ʳ). Draghi died on 29 June 1592, as reported by Kathryn Bosi Monteath in the entry in *New Grove,* 5:606.

vice records show that Feliciani successfully implemented a policy that assured a pool of well-trained youths and young adults available to serve as the occasion arose, while providing, at the same time, places in the chapel for those of his former pupils who had exceptional voices. Noteworthy in this respect was Domenico Lucenti, who advanced from choirboy to adult singer in the chapel.[39] Like Draghi, he showed signs of a precocious musical talent that was obviously much encouraged by his teacher, so much so that a madrigal by him for six voices, *Se d'ogn'impres'haver bella vittoria,* found its way into Feliciani's *Il primo libro di madrigali a sei voci* of 1586.

Jacomo di Maestro Cesare Panichi, first recorded as a young clerk from 1582 to 1584 and then as an older clerk through the end of fiscal 1588, was another of Feliciani's pupils to make a mark in Siena's musical world. Although Jacomo served for a very brief time as a paid member of the chapel in these years, his subsequent career makes it clear that he received excellent training at the cathedral school and that he had a good deal of experience in performing polyphony. In 1596, after he was ordained and appointed a cathedral chaplain, he became an adult singer in the chapel. Later, he assumed the cathedral organist's post, succeeding no less a musician than Agostino Agazzari on two occasions. He even served as *maestro di cappella* for two years beginning in May 1610.[40] His career was no doubt exceptional. But it is also true that in the last decade of the century the majority of the adult singers who gained admission to the chapel's ranks were, in fact, former students in the cathedral school. There could be, of course, no better testimony to Feliciani's success as a teacher.

Aldobrando Trabocchi of Pienza, recorded as a bass in the chapel in 1590, was yet another of the clerks trained under Feliciani who had a successful career as a performer in later years. By 1598 Trabocchi was in Florence, where his singing was much admired by Emilio de' Cavalieri, and in 1600 he sang the role of Pluto in a performance of Jacopo Peri's *Euridice.* Admitted to the rolls of musicians at the Medici court in 1602, Trabocchi remained in Florence until 1609, when he became a singer in the Sistine Chapel at Rome. He was elected master of that group in 1631 and was living in Rome at the time of his death in 1641.[41]

Not all of Feliciani's most promising students were training for the priesthood nor did they all remain in Siena. His contract called for him to teach the city's youths as well as cathedral clerks and gave him the opportunity to enroll some students of his own choice, just as his predecessors had done. As a result, several of the chapel's adult singers were laymen, like Feliciani himself. Among them was Ottavio Basili, who, as will be noted on several occasions below, had a long and distinguished career at both the Palazzo Pubblico and the cathedral as an instrumentalist and singer. Orindio Bartolini, a contemporary of Basili's, also went through the cathedral school's ranks under Feliciani.

---

39. Lucenti also began studying in the cathedral school at a very early age. He is recorded as a cherico minore, May 1568–April 1576, with no indication that he sang, though he is cited as a cherico minore, soprano, among a group of singers listed from May 1576 to April 1578.

40. On his later service as organist and *maestro di cappella* at the cathedral see Reardon, *Agostino Agazzari,* 34, 36, 37, 40.

41. For Trabocchi's career after leaving Siena see Warren Kirkendale, *The Court Musicians of Florence during the Principate of the Medici* (Florence, 1994), 296–99.

Following in his teacher's footsteps, he was also a prolific composer and published several volumes of sacred and secular music throughout his career after leaving Siena. He became a priest, and after serving for ten years as a singer at St. Mark's in Venice, in 1609 he became *maestro di cappella* at Udine cathedral and held that post until 1635 when he returned in triumph to Siena to direct the chapel where he had begun his career.[42]

THE CHAPEL TO FELICIANI'S DEATH

The last eight years of Feliciani's tenure saw the culmination of his successful teaching program, with more and more students from the school gaining admittance to the chapel as paid singers. Most were sopranos, but several sang lower parts, perhaps many more than are indicated by pay records, which often list middle and older clerks simply as "cantore." Some adults, too, were designated only as "cantore," though their vocal ranges in some instances can be ascertained from other records. The adult personnel remained relatively stable almost as a matter of course, though, as they would in the future, a few left only to return at a later time. Continuing in May 1588 were four basses, the tenor-trombonist, seven sopranos, and two other alto clerks, Draghi and Cocchi, soon to be ordained. The tenor Pieragli rejoined the group at that time, anticipating the return of another former tenor, Lucenti, in the following November.

Discrepancies may be noticed occasionally in these years between the names and number of paid singers and those inscribed on official lists of personnel. Nineteen singers, for example, appear in an official list of employees from May 1589, but only seventeen were paid during fiscal 1589–90, and some of these did not complete the year. Sixteen are on the official list from May 1590, when nine adults were paid, as were nine clerks, seven of whom were new at the time. These eighteen singers were paid through December 1590, their number dropping to fourteen in January 1591. This is one less than the number of singers cited in a report from 22 January 1591, which recounts how the rector convened all of the Opera's personnel in order to remind them of their obligations (see Doc. 7.7). Singers were present at the meeting and took the opportunity to make a polite and, as reported, rather vaguely worded request for higher wages, noting as they did so the large differences in their salaries. Under the heading "chapel" the report cites fifteen singers and their salaries and says that there were "six basses, some of whom have six, others four, and others three carlini a month; four tenors, some of whom have seven, others six, and others three and a half lire a month; and five sopranos who each has three carlini a month." Pay records tell a different story, at least in the number of personnel and the parts they sang. A maximum of five, rather than six, basses was registered up to this time, though at the moment there were only three, unless one of the unspecified singers or the *maestro di cappella* was a bass. As for the tenors, there were now two, though there were as many as four, counting Formichi,

---

42. See Reardon, *Agostino Agazzari,* 44, for an English translation of Azzolini-Ugurgieri's account of Bartolini's return to Siena and his remark that Bartolini left Siena "when he was young, but already reasonably instructed in music (an art which he later perfected)." Bartolini's works, unjustly neglected, await a full-scale study. For an assessment and partial transcription of his motet *Regina caeli,* for two choirs, see Jerome Roche, *North Italian Church Music in the Age of Monteverdi* (Oxford, 1984), 111–12.

in the recent past. Altos are not mentioned at all, but two were present at this time, as were four sopranos, who numbered eight just a month earlier. Perhaps the clerk who composed the minutes of the meeting failed to distinguish between tenors and altos and simply lumped them all together, as the governing board may have done in its deliberations.

No extant documents explain the reasons why there were such disparities. Lower wages, it is evident, did not signify fewer services because this would have been mentioned in the report. Perhaps some chaplains were paid lower wages because they had other sources of income, chaplaincies within the cathedral or elsewhere in the city. But since several of the lay personnel earned additional salaries from the Palace and other places, this kind of consideration could hardly have influenced the amount a musician received from the cathedral. Experience counted for a good deal, as salary raises given to some singers who served over a number of years attest. Several singers, on the other hand, joined the chapel with higher salaries than those paid to musicians already employed for some time. Obviously, both seniority and quality of musicianship affected salary levels. For unknown reasons some singers remained at the same salary throughout their careers at the cathedral. In any event, the singers' request in January 1591 was for higher, or more equitable, salaries and, distinctions of salary and voice range aside, numbers cited in the report possibly represent the actual positions authorized by the Opera at the time.

Tangible results of the discussion with the singers are immediately apparent in accounts for the remainder of the 1590–91 fiscal year, January–April 1591. A number of singers did receive salary raises, several remained at their previous levels, and a few were let go. Those receiving increased salaries included Feliciani himself, whose earnings went from L. 28 to L. 32 per month; the bass Nannetti, from L. 7 to L. 8; the tenor Pieragli, from L. 7 to L. 9; Ser Vincenzo Carli, from L. 6. 10 to L. 7; the soprano Francesco di Matteo, from L. 1. 10 to L. 2. 10; the tenor Flori, from L. 26 to L. 28. Singers whose salaries remained the same were: the tenor-trombonist Formichi, at L. 6; Ser Donato Santini, at L. 6; the boy sopranos Ottavio Basili, at L. 2. 10, Orindio Bartolini and his brother, Teofilo, both at L. 1. 10, and the alto Ser Bernardino Draghi, at L. 8. Two basses, Guglielmo Celli and Giovanni Antonio Napoletano, both of whose salaries remained at L. 4 per month, were gone by the spring of 1591.[43] Three new adults and three new sopranos appear on pay lists beginning in May 1591, though not all remained throughout the rest of the fiscal year. In fact, the names of only eleven singers all told appear regularly in pay lists through November 1593, though fourteen are named in the official list of employees from May 1592.[44]

---

43. Celli left after February, Giovanni Antonio after April. Flori also left at the end of April.

44. Even more curious is a list containing the names of forty-eight "cantori e sonatori" for 1593, found on fol. 325[r–v] of vol. 1082, *Distribuzioni e salariati, 1578–95,* the principal source of pay records from this time. In addition to the adults, boys, and youths mentioned above, it names many other students from the school not otherwise recorded as singers as well as a number of adult clerics whose voice ranges are unspecified. Besides pointing to a wider pool of available musicians than indicated by records specifically referring to chapel singers, inclusion of these names on the list suggests that on special occasions during the course of the year some or all of these others performed with officially

Another reason for occasional discrepancies in the records may lie in the failure of the bookkeepers to identify the student singers properly. Teodoro di Niccolò Morelli, for example, was employed as a soprano from May 1588 to April 1590, and then as a singer with an unspecified range from December 1594 to March 1597. Giovanbattista di Guerrino served as a soprano from May to December 1590; subsequently, his voice range went unmentioned in a payment from December 1594 to November 1595. Both Teodoro and Giovanbattista are cited among the young clerks, May 1591–April 1593, but no mention is made of their singing. Nor is anything said of Giovanbattista in a list of middle clerks, November 1593–October 1594, though Teodoro is described as "still singing." Perhaps in the intervening time they were not performing on a regular basis because their voices had broken. But it is just as likely that on many occasions the information entered by the bookkeepers was simply inadequate.

A renewed effort to build on former strength is evident during 1593 with the appointments of five new adult singers and two new sopranos, who, together with the core formed by Cocchi, Montelauri, Nannetti, Formichi, and others, brought the official number of singers now serving to seventeen. Feliciani's judgment and his ability to produce good results were undoubtedly the operating factors in the renewed buildup. But it is also evident that a discriminating and knowlegeable set of patrons and an appreciative audience were necessary to his successes. The Opera, of course, and particularly its overseer, Giugurta Tommasi, played no small part in providing the ambience that gave Feliciani the means and the opportunity to explore the varied treasures of late sixteenth-century music while maintaining the highest artistic standards of performance. As a result of this official support and encouragement of Feliciani's inspired leadership, the chapel became a renowned Sienese institution, its performances a source of pleasure and pride for all segments of society. Siena might no longer be free, but its cultural achievements were second to none.

All seventeen singers were on the rolls when Grand Duke Ferdinand's "musicians and boys" journeyed to Siena to perform at services on Assumption Day 1594 (see Doc. 7.8). By this time Siena had been in the Medici dominion for almost two generations. Its major musical institutions had survived the shock of Florentine sovereignty and had succeeded in maintaining their own traditions. They could now rely on local musicians such as Marri, Feliciani, and a number of younger men to keep them abreast of musical practices elsewhere, particularly Florence, without suffering any loss of artistic or cultural independence. Flourishing programs in musical instruction at the cathedral and other places ensured sufficient numbers of talented well-trained local musicians to fill coveted posts and there was no need to rely on foreign musicians. Sienese fears of cultural domination, in other words, were now a thing of the past.

Several well-known singers and instrumentalists were at the Florentine court in 1594, but there is no mention of who was in Siena for the festivities nor of music performed. Another record of the event speaks of "li musici di conserto a fiato," the ducal ensemble of wind instruments, and it seems that both singers and instrumentalists

---

employed members of the chapel. Perhaps sporadic payments to them for extraordinary services will be found in their individual accounts.

were involved.[45] Whether they performed together with their Sienese colleagues is likewise not mentioned in any surviving records, though it would be tempting to think that some of the two-choir music composed by Feliciani would have invited such collaboration. The report regarding the Florentines' visit notes that Giugurta Tommasi showed them every kindness and that he authorized payment of L. 196 for their travel expenses—a sum exceeding by some L. 50 what was then being spent each month on the chapel singers' salaries. Many of the Florentine and Sienese musicians were probably more in contact with each other than is suggested by isolated reports such as this. Another visit of Florentine singers that went unmentioned in cathedral registers, for example, occurred eight years earlier, in 1586. At the time eight *musici di Firenze* were in Siena for a fortnight, also during the Assumption Day celebrations. Chances are that they sang at the cathedral as well as at the church of the hospital of Santa Maria della Scala, where they were lodged (see Doc. 7.9). Additional instances of musical interaction between the two cities in the late sixteenth century come from individual cases such as that of the erstwhile cathedral trombonist Giovanfrancesco di Benedetto, who was employed for a number of years by the Medici, and, as will be noted below, by one or two other Sienese instrumentalists who also performed in Florence.

It seems that for the time being personnel policies had once again been brought into line with available finances. But, as demonstrated by records of payment, which are often listed for periods of as many as six or seven months, with November as one of the principal terminal months, the number of singers on official lists was now exceeded. The statistics, necessarily terse and impersonal, nevertheless confirm the scope of Feliciani's achievement and the success of his teaching program and his policies as *maestro di cappella*. For most of the period December 1594–November 1595 fourteen boys and older youths were employed alongside twelve adults, bringing the total number in the chapel to twenty-six, which grew to twenty-seven by November 1596. There were new adult singers and new sopranos, many of whom would remain in the chapel for years to come. Notable among the recent appointees were the returning bass Guglielmo Celli in June 1595 and in the following September, the first castrato ever recorded in the chapel, Girolamo eunuco.[46] Most of the singers were native Sienese or from one of the cities in Siena's old dominion, and though two Romans, an Umbrian, and a Neapolitan had also sung with the group, no Florentines yet appeared on the scene.

This unprecedented number of paid singers was maintained throughout Feliciani's last full year in office, from December 1595 through November 1596. Financial pressures had eased, at least for the moment, and qualified personnel were readily available.

---

45. A record dated 22 August 1594 notes payment of L. 196 "spese in vetture di dieci cavalli da Fiorenza a Siena, et in altri dieci da Siena a Fiorenza, a lire 6 di denari l'uno per l'altro in far venire et rimandare li musici di conserto a fiato per honorare la solennità della festività dell'Assuntione . . . quali musici erano quelli di Sua Altezza Serenissima" (AOMS, vol. 629, *Giornale C,* fol. 317ʳ).

46. His surname, Gulini, is given in later records. Gulini left the chapel in 1602 to accompany Agazzari to Rome, but rejoined the group in 1608. He was the most esteemed and highest paid chapel member for many years, enjoying privileges in later years up to the time of his death in August 1648. See Reardon, *Agostino Agazzari,* 51–52.

Feliciani's success as a teacher and his administrative policies ensured a pool of trained singers in the school, ready to fill in as the occasion demanded. Numbers, of course, did not guarantee the chapel's excellence; the quality of the voices, the precision with which they sang, the maestro's interpretations—all obviously determined the sound and quality of the group's performances. But the numbers indicate diverse forces that made possible a wider range of repertory than was hitherto within reach—double- and perhaps triple-choir music and the newer forms of sacred monody then coming into fashion. The adult core, now melded into a cohesive ensemble under Feliciani's expert direction, performed to universal acclaim traditional and contemporary works, including music composed expressly for them by their celebrated leader. These were doubtless the musicians, together with Feliciani and the cathedral organist Francesco Bianciardi, who were remembered by Adriano Banchieri in the preface to his *Conclusioni nel suono dell'organo,* when he reported that they sang a solemn Mass at the cathedral every year on the 22nd of November in honor of St. Cecilia, in the presence of the archbishop and before a large public.[47]

According to another report, all of the city's musicians customarily performed at First and Second Vespers and at Solemn High Mass at the cathedral on St. Cecilia's Day. Usually, the musicians elected a "king" who was responsible for choosing the music and for arranging the banquet held that evening. An interesting description of the evening's entertainment after one of these banquets in 1600 speaks of presenting "certain most pleasant spectacles in five sections . . . all of them beautifully acted and performed." In the first of them five heroes came on stage, "with as many musical instruments, richly dressed according to their stations." In the second five country people appeared with instruments and performed "very pleasing rustic music." For the third part a personification of Night called upon all to celebrate her domain with "happy and lively musical entertainments." The personification of Day addressed the audience in the fourth section, and the fifth and final section presented the personifications of Glory and Virtue, "the main elements of human actions."[48]

One other account of the chapel singers performing with instruments during Feliciani's tenure comes from a report describing the procession on 21 February 1595 from the cathedral to the quarter where the miraculous statue, the Provenzano Virgin, was located. All of city's hierarchy, clerical and civil, and a large public were present as the bishop's vicar, amid the falling snow, celebrated Mass "with a full choir of singers and all kinds of musical instruments."[49]

---

47. Banchieri's *Conclusioni nel suono dell'organo,* first published at Bologna by the Heredi di Giovanni Rossi in 1608, and in an expanded edition in 1609, was reprinted in 1626 and 1934; reference here is to the 1609 edition and to the English translation by Lee R. Garrett, *Conclusions for Playing the Organ (1609)* (Colorado Springs, 1982), 4. Banchieri says that he was present at the service twelve years earlier, that is, in 1597. But since Feliciani died in 1596, this means it was twelve years from the time Banchieri wrote his account, perhaps in 1595 or 1596.

48. The report, from BCIS, MS C. VI. 9, *Componimeni piacevoli,* has been published by Mazzeo, *Compositori senesi del 500 e del 600,* 10.

49. The pertinent portion of the text, from BCIS, MS A. V. 5, fol. 26ʳ, is given with an English translation by Reardon, *Agostino Agazzari,* 71–72.

THE CHAPEL UNDER FRANCESCO BIANCIARDI

No record of a contract survives for Feliciani's successor, Messer Francesco Bianciardi, who had been cathedral organist since 1591. Instead, an annotation in a payment to Bianciardi from the first day of January 1597 simply describes him as "past organist and now the newly named master of the duomo's chapel," and notes that he was to receive L. 16 for his services of one month as an organist and L. 32 for his first month's salary as *maestro di cappella*. The transition was a smooth one, for, as the payment indicates, Bianciardi took over his new post just a week after Feliciani's death. At the same time the seventeen-year-old Agostino Agazzari, who eventually became the most renowned of all Siena's composers, succeeded to the organist's post.[50] Feliciani's relationship with both these musicians is not explained in available records. Neither one of them attended the cathedral school, though Agazzari could have studied with him privately. Bianciardi probably learned a good deal about the *maestro di cappella*'s job from working under Feliciani, who even included the younger composer's setting of Ps. 127, *Beati omnes,* in his 1590 collection of music for two choirs. Perhaps this indicates a teacher–pupil relationship, as was the case with the other young composers whose works were included in Feliciani's collections. But Bianciardi had at least one other teacher before Feliciani.

Bianciardi was born in or around 1572 in the Tuscan town of Casole d'Elsa, where he apparently received his earliest musical training from a local teacher, the Servite monk Fra Leonardo Morelli. Morelli, whose sacred works were published by Gardano at Venice in 1599, later moved to Volterra to take up the post of *maestro di cappella* and teacher at the seminary.[51] Bianciardi must have followed him, for it was there that he took the first tonsure on 19 September 1587. Within four years, soon after he began serving as organist in Siena, Bianciardi was promoted to subdeacon, and on 14 March 1592 to deacon in the cathedral of Volterra. He was ordained shortly afterwards and appointed a chaplain at Siena cathedral in May 1593, a post he held through 1595. He had meanwhile been composing and published his first book of motets in 1596, with a dedication to Siena's archbishop, Ascanio Piccolomini. The following year saw the publication of his first book of madrigals for five voices. This was dedicated to Giugurta Tommasi, the Opera's rector, to whom Bianciardi said he owed so much for having given him "the opportunity to perform in the service of this metropolitan church," first in appointing him to play the organ and then in giving him the responsibility of guiding the chapel. Bianciardi continued to be a prolific composer throughout the remaining

---

50. Agazzari was cathedral organist through February 1602, when he was succeeded by the chaplain-singer Jacomo Panichi, who held the post from April 1602 to February 1608. For further information on Agazzari's career as organist at the cathedral, which included his serving in that capacity on three other occasions, and of his successors, see Reardon, *Agostino Agazzari,* 13, 34–39.

51. For sources of biographical information see the Introduction to vol. 1 of Bianciardi's *Opera Omnia,* ed. Siro Cisilino and Lodovico Bertazzo (Padua, 1973–78). See also Bernhard Billeter, "Die Vocalkompositionen von Francesco Bianciardi," *Schweizer Beiträge zur Musikwissenschaft,* 3d ser., vol. 1 (1972): 133–41.

ten years of his life and had already published four other volumes of sacred music before he was carried off by the plague in 1607, while still in his thirties.[52]

An attractive picture of Bianciardi's personality emerges from a cathedral report dated 8 March 1602.[53] This notes that Tommasi announced to the governing board that the organist Agazzari had asked to be released from service so that he could pursue a career elsewhere and that the *maestro di cappella* Bianciardi had signified his intentions of leaving to become rector of a church in the town of Colle. This latter news was particularly distressing to the rector, who noted that it would be "very difficult to find someone equal to him, not only because he is among the best and finest musicians in Tuscany and perhaps in Italy and has the highest morals but also because he knows how to keep peace in the chapel." Bianciardi played his hand very close to his vest and bided his time for the inevitable behind-the-scenes discussions that would result in an attractive counter-offer. He did not have long to wait, for steps were immediately taken to ensure his retention. Within the week, with the unanimous approval of the governing board, it was reported that he had agreed to stay on for three more years and that in addition to his monthly salary of L. 32, he would receive an annual increase of Sc. 20, to be distributed monthly, and the use of one of the Opera's houses in Piazza Manetti. Most important, in terms of Bianciardi's artistic goals, was the Opera's agreement that he would be "the superintendent and have the authority of superintendence of the organ and hiring the future organist." Exactly how much authority he was to have in what was essentially a personnel matter traditionally the prerogative of the governing board is not spelled out, but it seems clear that Bianciardi had definite ideas about the kinds of musicians he wished to have working under him and that he wanted a prominent voice in discussions that would determine the future direction of the cathedral's musical program. Though it is clear that Bianciardi's talents were very much appreciated by Giugurta Tommasi and his associates, the board's move was also a practical one. For as the report put it, the Opera was aware that "it would be difficult to identify and appoint someone from outside the city who was his equal, and even if they did, the cost would perhaps be much greater."

Chapel Singers to 1607

Twenty-six singers were on the pay lists by Christmas Eve 1596, the day of Feliciani's death. Though three clerks were gone by the turn of the new year, the Palace trombonist Pietragnolo Maestri began serving at that time so that Bianciardi began his first month in office with a full complement of twenty-three singers and instrumentalists. It was the largest group he would have throughout his tenure. Most, if not all, singers also served as chaplains. The long-time bass Midone Nannetti left after March 1597, though his loss was offset a few months later when Agostino di Francesco became the

---

52. A final volume of spiritual canzonettas was published posthumously by his friend and pupil Marcantonio Tornioli, who succeeded him as *maestro di cappella,* 1607–9; it is in vol. 7 of Bianciardi's *Opera Omnia.*

53. Published by Reardon, *Agostino Agazzari,* 181; the quotation is from Reardon's translation, p. 39.

second eunuch in the group. The alto Bernardino Cocchi left after January 1598, though he returned in 1602. Another singer of long standing, Guglielmo Celli, was gone by October 1598. Familiar employment patterns observed in past years were thus again at work. The Opera was apparently always ready to welcome back singers of proven mettle, especially if they could serve as chaplains. But stability remained the most characteristic feature of the group. Ten singers remained with Bianciardi during the first five years of his tenure, and a core of six adults, Benvenuto Flori, Giovanni Piccioni, Matteo Bondoni, Francesco Franceschi, Fabrizio Martini, and Ottavio Basili, were present throughout the entire time.

Few changes in personnel are recorded during the remaining years of Bianciardi's tenure, which lasted to the time of his death on 29 January 1607.[54] The departure of the trombonist Pietragnolo Maestri at the end of July 1601 is noteworthy because no new replacement is named. Ottavio Basili, who by this time was a valued member of the Palace wind band, must have taken over the post, though he is identified as the official trombonist only in records from 1607 and later.[55] Although the chapel was never again to employ as many musicians as it had in previous years, their number hovered around sixteen, generally ten or more adults and the remainder sopranos. The feature that best characterizes the chapel during the first decade of the new century is its relative stability and its parochialism. With few exceptions, the singers, who were Sienese or from towns in Siena's old dominion, were clerics and served as chaplains at the cathedral. Nine adults, all of them permanent members who formed its core, are recorded from December 1601 through November 1607. They included one alto, Piccioni, four tenors, Flori, Bondoni, Franceschi, and Martini, two basses, Fra Guglielmo di Sant'Agostino and Giovanmaria Cappeletti, and the tenor-trombonist Basili. Singers returning for shorter or longer stays in those years included the alto Cocchi, the bass Chiocciolini, the bass Molandi, and Panichi and Santini, adults whose voice ranges are unknown. With the exception of Cristofano Draghi, a former young clerk, the remaining newcomers were all students from the cathedral school, who stayed for varying amounts of time, as they had in the past.[56] (For a chronological list of singers during this period, see Table 7.2.)

The Repertory

Bianciardi's sacred works reveal the hand of a composer who not only mastered the musical language of his predecessors but was also familiar with the issues that arose as

---

54. The date is given in the Introduction to vol. 7 of Bianciardi's *Opera Omnia.*

55. Reardon, *Agostino Agazzari,* 53, gives the names of his successors as trombonists in the chapel.

56. A number of clerks are recorded after 1600, all cited in AOMS, vol. 1083, *Distribuzioni e salari, 1595–1603,* and vol. 1084, *Distribuzioni e salari, 1603–16.* Though none entered the chapel as adult singers during Bianciardi's tenure, I cite their names and dates of service as an indication of his success as a teacher: Fabio Sozzi (April 1602–November 1606); Girolamo Turchi (December 1602–November 1604); Cesare Tiriassi (November 1603–November 1607); Orfeo (December 1603); Antonio Poli, Fabio Bandini (November 1604–November 1607); Mario Bellini (February 1605–May 1607); Domenico de' Mendici (February–May 1605); Ippolito da Castel Fiorentino (March–July 1605); Augustino del'Orfano (June–November 1605); Alessandro Pasci, Cristofano Piochi (May

the style of the late Renaissance gave way to the experimental practices of the oncoming Baroque. Bianciardi himself was among the first to describe newly emerging performing practices, as is evident from a set of rules he compiled regarding continuo accompaniment. The *Breve regola per imparar a sonare sopra il Basso con ogni sorte d'Instrumento* was printed as a broadsheet in Siena under the auspices of Domenico Falcini on 21 September 1607, shortly after the composer's death.[57] In it Bianciardi gave very elemental rules for harmonizing the bass line, rules obviously representing the thoughts of a man who was confronted with such questions with some degree of regularity. He said, for example, that the lowest sounding voice should be considered the bass, whether or not it was the bass part, showing that the person who accompanied a piece played without interruption. Practical application of this advice is evident in his fourth book of motets for two, three, and four voices, published posthumously in 1608, which features a separate figured bass line for each piece.[58] Here, the figured line of pieces for three and four voices generally reproduces the lowest sounding part as a *basso seguente,* whereas in pieces for two voices, an independent bass line is provided, echoing the practice established by another Italian composer and organist, Lodovico Viadana, in his *Cento concerti ecclesiastici* of 1602. In all probability Bianciardi's primer never reached the wide audience achieved by Agostino Agazzari's well-known treatise of the same year, *Del sonare sopra 'l basso con tutti li stromenti e dell'uso loro nel conserto.* But it seems certain that Bianciardi influenced other younger Sienese musicians such as Mariano Tantucci, who not only saw to the posthumous publication of the fourth book of motets but also included one of his own works in it.

Whether Bianciardi's set of rules may be taken to mean that during his time the organist regularly accompanied the chapel singers in their performances is difficult to say. The few Sienese reports available from before and shortly after his tenure are ambiguous in assigning an accompanimental role to the organist, though it is possible that the organist participated in alternatim performances of psalms, hymns, and Magnificats as a matter of course. There is no hint of such practices, however, in the first three collections of Bianciardi's motets from 1596, 1601, and 1607, published at Venice, like the fourth, under the general title *Sacrarum modulationum.* In general the four-voice settings are typical of their age. Varied textures consisting of imitation, free counterpoint, and familiar style appear in response to the composer's fancy and the needs and moods of the text. Pieces for greater numbers of voices often make much use of homophony, though this is tempered to some extent by contrasting passages featuring motives of

1606–July 1607); Bartolomeo d'Alessandro (December 1606–November 1607); Domenico Franci, Antonio Poli (July–November 1607).

57. It has been republished twice in modern times and reproduced most recently by Dinko Fabris in "Tre composizioni per liuto di Claudio Saracini e la tradizione del liuto a Siena tra Cinque e Seicento," *Il Flauto Dolce* 16 (1987): 16. An English translation is in F. T. Arnold, *The Art of Accompaniment from a Thorough-Bass* (Oxford, 1931), 1:74–80. Also see the entry on Bianciardi by Josef-Horst Lederer in *New Grove,* 2:677.

58. Modern edition in vol. 6 of Bianciardi's *Opera Omnia.* The edition includes all of Bianciardi's music published during his lifetime, referred to below in the course of my text, as well as surviving pieces of a volume of madrigals for five voices from 1597, a volume of three-voice *canzonette spirituali* from 1596, and a few pieces of his organ music surviving in manuscript (these latter in vol. 7).

faster note values more or less evenly distributed among the parts, as in, for example, the opening of the eight-voice *Factus est repente* from Book 1.[59] Bianciardi obviously had some virtuoso singers in his ensemble. A number of his motets, among them the five-voice *Illumina oculos meos* of Book 2,[60] the four-voice *Emitte spiritum tuum,* and the five-voice *Qualis est dilectus* of Book 3,[61] hint at the kinds of ornamentation that may have been applied extemporaneously in performance.

A single volume containing a collection of four-voice psalms and Magnificats by Bianciardi appeared in 1604.[62] As implied by its title, *Vespertina omnium solemnitatum psalmodia,* this contains settings of the same psalm texts suitable for all of the major feasts of the year found in Feliciani's earlier volume and in most of the Opera's collections acquired from the end of the fifteenth century onwards. Unlike Feliciani, however, Bianciardi usually sets only the odd-numbered verses of the texts, and does so in an often perfunctory manner. Homophony is the rule, sometimes incorporating passages in the fashionable *falsobordone* style, and remnants of virtuoso part-writing are glimpsed only occasionally, as in the setting of verse 3 of Ps. 129, *De profundis.* Perhaps it was in pieces such as these that the organist not only accompanied the singers but on occasion substituted instrumental versions for some of the other verses. Several examples of Bianciardi's organ works have survived in a north Italian manuscript, attesting to their diffusion outside Siena. Except for a setting of *Exultate Deo,* however, these are freely composed ricercars and fantasias and have no relationship to his vocal music and the chapel's performances.

Bianciardi's only published collection of Masses, from 1605, contains four works, each providing an exemplar of standard Renaissance compositional procedures in settings of the ordinary. The *Missa Loquebantur,* based on the four-voice motet of the same name for Pentecost by Palestrina, is an "imitation" Mass, a type of composition that, like a similar and perhaps contemporaneous effort by Claudio Monteverdi, was a decided gesture of homage to the past as well as an affirmation of Bianciardi's ability to compose according to the tenets of what was soon to be known as the *stile antico.* Bianciardi's imaginative approach to integrating and transforming the borrowed materials, in this case whole segments of the previously composed work, into a piece of his own is no less noteworthy than that of the composer Palestrina, whom he emulated. In the *Missa Lucis Creator optime,* based on the Gregorian hymn for Sundays in autumn, Bianciardi showed his skills in another traditional type, the paraphrase Mass. The music of the first verse of Gregorian melody appears throughout each movement as a cantus firmus, as do at times phrases from the second, third, and fourth verses. Motives from these are often combined contrapuntally with the music of verse 1, while the remaining voices spin out new melodic lines that occasionally draw their inspiration from various

---

59. Bianciardi, *Opera Omnia,* 1:89–93.

60. Ibid., 2:32–36.

61. Ibid., 3:5–8; 28–34.

62. Published by Angelo Gardano at Venice in 1604 and dedicated to the Sienese patrician and ecclesiastic Ottavio Spannocchi, provost of the collegiate church in Bianciardi's home town of Casole d'Elsa. A modern edition is in Bianciardi, *Opera Omnia,* vol. 5. The piece referred to in this discussion, *De profundis,* is on pp. 46–52.

parts of the original tune. Bianciardi's handling of the material is ingenious and offers a stunning view of his mastery of contrapuntal techniques. The *Missa in diebus Concionum,* for use during the penitential season of Lent when sermons were long, belongs to the *missa brevis* type, its succinct phrases effectively presenting the texts of the various movements of the ordinary in freely composed settings that often share similar motives and harmonies among themselves. The *Missa octum vocum,* for two choirs of the standard four vocal parts, is similar in style to Feliciani's Magnificat discussed above and features true interaction between the parts of both choirs.

The inventory of 1610, compiled three years after Bianciardi's death, indicates that little or no new music was purchased during his tenure as *maestro di cappella.* Indeed, it was not until the second decade of the new century that the Opera began a major acquisitions program, adding a few volumes of his works together with others by Feliciani and Agazzari to its permanent collection.[63] There is no reason to doubt that the works of these Sienese composers were in the chapel's repertory long before they were published, but during Feliciani's and Bianciardi's lifetimes they were probably performed from manuscript copies, most traces of which have now disappeared. The one exception is a manuscript volume of Bianciardi's four Masses still in the Opera's archives, where it is erroneously attributed to Feliciani. In any case, when Bianciardi took over the *maestro di cappella*'s post the cathedral's musical holdings comprised a solid base of conservative works, some modern, some quite old-fashioned, but still suitable for services on all feast days throughout the year when the singers were required to perform.

No records survive from the late sixteenth century regarding the singers' duties, though various reports indicate that, as in the past, they sang at Masses and Vespers on Sundays and principal feast days. There were also many other times when the chapel performed, such as at services held in the chapel of the Madonna del Voto on Saturdays and other days, at services when the town priors entered their bimestrial terms of office, at services on the last three days of Holy Week, and at various processions throughout the year. Inventories of musical holdings from throughout the century provide information about the items sung at those services. During Feliciani's and Bianciardi's time Magnificats and psalm settings, as before, were the principal polyphonic offerings at Vespers. Polyphonic Magnificats, of course, had long been part of the chapel's repertory, as those copied in 1481 by Mattio Gay attest. The acquisition of volumes of Magnificats by Animuccia and Victoria a century later speaks for the continuation of this practice as do the settings composed expressly for the chapel by the two Sienese *maestri.* Polyphonic hymns, too, continued as a staple at Vespers, as evidenced by those copied by Gay and by those of Victoria and Bianciardi. Psalms, mentioned in inventories from 1480s onwards, also figured prominently among works composed by the two Sienese *maestri di cappella.*

Though no evidence exists from the sixteenth century regarding the number of psalms sung in polyphony and the use of motets, there is a set of regulations regarding

---

63. The contents of both inventories, from 1610 and 1620, are in Reardon, *Agostino Agazzari,* 182–84.

singers' duties from 1615 that speaks to the matter in general terms.[64] It undoubtedly echoes usages of the more recent past. One regulation says, for example, that the singers were to intone the first psalm, the *Dixit Dominus,* and to proceed by singing alternate verses with the plainchant choir. Since settings of the most important psalms used throughout the year were available in the Opera's collection, there is a possibility that the four remaining psalms at Vespers were done in a similar manner. More likely, however, such lavish feasts of polyphony were reserved only for very special occasions. The regulation just cited also notes that the singers were to perform a motet after the Magnificat, presumably as a replacement for the antiphon. This was perhaps a traditional practice at Siena cathedral by 1615, and may be one of the reasons why motets figure so prominently among the Opera's acquisitions. The regulation further stipulates that at those times when no motet was used, the singers were to remain in their places until the organist finished playing. With regard to Masses, it seems clear, given the volumes purchased by the Opera and the works of Feliciani and Bianciardi, and of earlier acquisitions, that all five parts of the ordinary were normally sung in polyphony. After the 1570s introits were also sung in polyphony, given the purchase of Costanzo Porta's volume. But what of motets? Were they done at Masses, as they were later in 1624, when the practice was mentioned fleetingly in a letter that also leaves no doubt that all items of the ordinary were sung polyphonically?[65] Siena cathedral in the sixteenth century must have been very much like other Italian churches, where motets were often inserted at the Offertory and the Elevation of the Mass.[66] Apart from the purchases of volumes of motets throughout that time, however, Sienese records remain silent on this matter.

How we should like to know exactly what the singers' obligations were in May 1599, when the rector presented the governing board with an unusual request of theirs! Acting with the canons' consent, the members of the chapel asked to be "excused from singing on some minor feast days" and offered instead "to sing additional things on certain more solemn days" (see Doc. 7.10). Obviously, this would allow some of the singers—though not those who were chaplains—more time away from the cathedral in which to pursue other interests. As has been shown, the list of major feast days celebrated at Siena cathedral was extensive even by the 1360s, when it was compiled in its basic form. It remained current with a few additions and deletions through the mid-fifteenth century and perhaps as late as 1579, when it appeared in the printed edition of the Chapter's Constitutions. The list also made provision for other duplex feasts

---

64. Ibid., 181–82; a summary in English, p. 65. Reardon notes that the 1615 rules were clearly designed to cover the usual services and that musicians could expect to be called for other devotional events.

65. Ibid., 66–67. On p. 71 Reardon also quotes a 1618 report describing the traditional procession held annually on the Sunday after Easter, on this occasion dedicated to Sant'Ansano. After entering and receiving the bishop's blessing, the procession then continued on to the church of Sant'Ansano in Castel Vecchio, where "as at the duomo, it was accompanied by music and particularly beautiful motets."

66. Anthony M. Cummings, "Toward an Interpretation of the Sixteenth-Century Motet," *JAMS* 34 (1981): 47–52.

deemed necessary by church authorities, and many of these, such as St. Cecilia's Day, were added in later times, either permanently or occasionally. Performances of polyphony on ferial days, too, were required of singers in the late fifteenth century, though this was apparently no longer the case in later times. Nevertheless, by the end of the sixteenth century, to judge from the singers' request, the number of feast days—major and minor—requiring polyphonic performances at one service or another must have been considerable.

The singers' request indicates, as do the sacristans' rolls earlier, that all of them were required to be present whenever the chapel performed. Whether all of them always sang as a group is another matter, however, for by this time repertory was often the sole determining factor. All of the singers, or solo ensembles and the entire group, could have performed traditional and current polyphony, works for as few as four or as many as eight parts, works such as those discussed above by Feliciani and Bianciardi, to name the most obvious ones in the chapel's repertory. Double- and triple-choir music, even with one or two singers or singers and instrumentalists to a part, would have required all of the chapel's forces and perhaps even those of a few students from the school brought in especially for the occasion. The newer repertories, as found in Bianciardi's fourth book of motets, called for one, two, or three soloists and keyboard accompaniment. But none of this was apparently taken into consideration at the meeting. Instead, the Opera's governing board, after hearing the singers' request, authorized the rector, the deacon, and two board members to discuss it with two canons representing the Chapter and to settle the matter in whatever way seemed convenient to them. Results would be placed on the "tavolella" in the sacristy, where employees' duties were normally posted. Nothing more regarding the matter appears in surviving records from this time. But it is noteworthy that as late as 1615, when the overseer issued the new set of regulations regarding singers' duties, the matter had evidently not yet been settled to the satisfaction of all. Polyphony must thus have continued to be an integral part of services on a large number of feast days well into the early years of the seventeenth century.

DOCUMENTS

Doc. 7.1. Reports of the governing board's decision to scale down the chapel, 10 and 17 November 1556 (AOMS, vol. 17, *Deliberazioni, 1548–90,* fols. 10ᵛ, 11ᵛ, 12ᵛ)

Considerate le molte necessità del'Opera e la difficultà di trovar modo di satisfare ali stipendiati e debiti suoi, e non vedendo per hora altro minor scommodo del'Opera che alleggierirle qualche spesa, per[ciò] deliberorno sospendere e così sospeseno la cappella del canto per tutto luglio prossimo, nel quale tempo da hoggi ali musici di essa cappella non corga alcun salario. E che a messer Bernardo da Pontremoli, atteso el bon servizio suo di molti anni in detta cappella, s'intendi reservato e così gli riservorno, el salario di scudi due d'oro el mese, da pagarsili secondo 'l solito fin tanto che per mezo e favore e voce del'Opera sia provisto d'una cappella, e in quel caso provisto che ve sarà, non habbia più detto salario, e sia obligato al coro almeno le feste solenni (fol. 10ᵛ).

E attese le buone qualità e opere del venerabile ser Vieri prete, quale ha più tempo servito a la cappella del canto, fatti libri di musica e con diligenzia insegnato come anco al presente insegna di musica a li fanciulli e cherici del duomo, deliberorno che nonostante sia levata la cappella del canto, che esso sia particolarmente sia ricognosciuto et habbia di salario da la detta opera lire otto di denari per ciascun mese, e maxime perseverando lui nela bona opera sua d'insegnare (fol. 12ᵛ).

Deliberorno anco ridurre e così ridusseno el salario del'organista di duomo a lire vintuna el mese, e più per l'advenire haver non possa (fol. 11ᵛ).

Doc. 7.2. Letter to the overseers from the acting governor of Siena, Don Francisco de Mendoza, 7 May 1557. AOMS, vol. 628, *Giornale B, 1554–67,* fol. 57ʳ

Copia di uno precetto mandato dallo Illustrissimo e Reverendissimo Monsignor Cardinal di Burghos al Magnifico messer Azzolino Cerretani, Operaio dignissimo della chiesa cattedral di Siena, che devi rimettar la cappella levata per deliberatione de' Savi.

Don Francisco de Mendoza, Cardinal de la Santità de Roma, obispo de Burghos, Governator y lugoteniente general por su Magesta[d] en la cittade de Sena y su estado.

Perché ragionevol cosa è che le cose partenente al culto divino sieno in ogni luogo trattate con debita reverentia e decoro, e maxime in le chiese cattedrali e metropolitane com'il duomo di questa città di Siena: però per virtù de la presente, con quella maggiore hauthorità che habbiamo e potemo, espressamente diciamo e ordeniamo che la cappella de' cantori, che già era solita tenersi e servire in detta chiesa e duomo e che per certe consideratione fu comandato no' servire per deliberatione fatta nel mese di dicembre proximo passato, non obstante la detta deliberatione et ogni e qualunche altra cosa in contrario, torni a servire e seguitare in quel miglior modo e forma che soleva per innanzi di detta deliberatione e quella non obstante sieno pagati li cantori e persone di detta cappella secondo ch'era solito da ffarsi chè per il servitio di Dio et honor publico è così la nostra voluntade.

    Dato in Siena alli 7 di maggio MDLVII
    Il Cardinal Burgensis

Doc. 7.3. School furniture in the 1557 and 1563 inventories

1557:
    Uno goffano senza serratura
    Una tavoletta quadra, usa
    Due banchette di legno
    Un leggio
    Uno telaio da impannata
    La tavolella dell'oblighi
    Una tavoletta longha con tre piedi

1563:
    Nella tertia camara
    Due banche con piei confitti
    Una tavola con suoi tre piei
    Tre bande da sedere
    Un leggio
    Un telaio da impannata
    Una cassa di legname, senza serratura
    La tavolella dove sono scritti li oblighi de la cappella

Doc. 7.4. Mariano di Girolamo Pelori's contract as organist, 30 April 1563. AOMS, vol. 628, *Giornale B, 1554–67,* fol. 211ʳ

Christo 1563 [margin: Mariano di Girolamo Pelori]
Ricordo come questo dì ultimo d'aprile il magnifico messer Azzolino Cerretani, nostro dignis-

simo operario, l'ha condotto per organista in duomo a sonare li due orghani per uno anno da incominciarsi questo dì e finire come segue, con questo che detto Mariano sia obligato sonare tutte quei giorni che ordinariamente si costuma e di più tutte quelle volte che sarà di bisogno per qualsivoglia festa straordinaria o venuta di qualsivoglia personaggio per la quale la chiesa facesse solenne.

Item che detto Mariano sia obligato, sempre che si canti alla Madonna, sonare l'organo rincontro a quella e non quello sopra la sagrestia.

Item che il detto Mariano habbia per suo stipendio e salario fiorini trentasei l'anno di lire quattro per fiorino di moneta senese e corrente, da doversili pagare per li kamarlinghi dell'Opera ogni tre mesi l'errata che tocha, cioè L. 36 s.—

Item furno d'achordo che in evento che il detto Mariano non volesse sonare detti organi più che uno anno o che il Rettore dell'Opera non volesse che più gli sonasse, si devi significare l'uno all'altro e l'altro all'uno mesi tre avanti spiri detto anno; e non essendo da alcuna dele parti disdetto, si intenda seguire un altr'anno con li medesimi oblighi e salario, e così d'anno in anno finche da una parte tal disdetta sia fatta.

E io Alessandro di Girolamo Sozzini, al presente scrittore dell'Opera, per commissione del prefato signor operario ho fatto il presente ricordo di mia mano, al [sic] quale sarà sottoscritto il detto Mariano affermando quanto di sopra è detto. L. 144 s.—

[below] E io Mario Pelori affermo quanto di sopra. 1564.

Nota chome questo dì 16 di maggio 1564 il Magnifico messer Marcello Tegliacci à fatto la disdetta e data licenzia a detto Mariano per l'anno futuro, la quale dove[va] fare 3 mesi inanzi e l'à disdetto ora per allora.

Doc. 7.5. Letter from the General of the Servite Order in Florence to the overseer Marcello Tegliacci, giving permission for Fra Arcangelo da Reggio to become organist of Siena cathedral, 19 February 1565. AOMS, vol. 75, *Carteggio,* by date

Magnifico Signor Mio Osservando
    La religione de' Servi è legata con un affetto tanto dolce con la vostra Magnifica città che si reputa a gran favore quando gli viene occasione di servirla, come faccio io al presente in concedergli più che volentieri frat'Archangelo da Reggio, organista della sua chattedrale, et io in questo negotio ho più contenti uno che io compiaccio a Vostra Signoria et di questo ne sono contentti tutti i padri del Monasterio nostro che di tanto mi supplicano et mi scrivano che io gli dia licentia come io fo. Ma nel segreto mio m'allegro più, perché el giovane non solamente studierà in Siena, ma honorerà la religione et farà utile a se stesso. Io desidero far maggior cosa in benefitio di Vostra Signoria et della vostra magnifica città alla quale sempre ho desiderato et desider ogni felicità, ogni contento et ogni bene ne essendo questo per altro che per risposta alla sua gratissima gli baccio la mano.
    Di Firenze nel LXIIII il 19 di febraio.
    Di Vostra Signoria Amorevole Servita
      Il Generale de' Servi

Doc. 7.6. Fra Arcangelo da Reggio's contract as organist, 22 February 1565. AOMS, vol. 628, *Giornale B, 1554–67,* fol. 254ʳ

Christo 1564 [margin: Frate Archangiolo da Reggio, frate di Santa Maria de' Servi] Ricordo chome questo dì 22 di febraro [1564/65] il magnifico messer Marcello Tegliacci, Rettore dignissimo dell'Opera nostra, ha condotto per organista a sonare li due orghani del duomo, per anni tre prossimi da chominciare adì primo di maggio prossimo 1565 e finire il dì ultimo d'aprile 1568, dovendo sonare tutti li dì festivi e solenni soliti il sonarsi, e di più tutte quelle volte che occhorrisse per qualche strasordinario di venuta di qualsisia personaggio o per altra chausa che la detta chiesia facessi solennità, dovendo sonare or l'uno or l'altro orghano secondo l'usitario [*recte* l'usitato] della chiesia predetta e che piacerà e li sarà ordinato dal Rettore dell'Opera predetto.

E sonno d'achordo che avendo in questi tempi il prefato frate Archangiolo andare a predichare la quadragesima fuore di Siena, possa a ssuo beneplacito andare et essere di ritorno l'ottava della pasqua seghuente, ma però devi in suo luogho lassare uno a ssonare chome di sopra e sia a sodisfasione del detto Signor Operario nostro.

E per mercede e premio di sue fatighe, sia tenuta l'Opera nostra pagharli lire quindici di denari per ciascheduno mese sempre che sarà finito e doppo, a beneplacito di detto frate Archangiolo, e di tanto è rimasto d'achordo con il detto Signor Operario.

Inoltre sonno rimasti in questa convenzione, che non volendo il suddetto signor nostro Rettore che la detta condotta duri più che li detti tre anni, o veramente non volendo esso frate Archangiolo più servire, si devi significhare l'uno a l'altro almeno tre mesi avanti spiri il detto tempo, e non facendosi da qualsisia delle parti tal disdetta o significhasione, s'intendi chosì seghuire di anno in anno, fino che da una delle parti sarà fatta, con li medesimi obrighi e salari chome di sopra. Della qual condotta chome detto di sopra, del tutto n'è stato consapevole e s'è seghuito con buona grazia del Generale della prefata regligione, chome di tutto ce n'è sua lettera, la quale è appresso del magnifico messer Marcello Tegliacci, nostro dignissimo Operario, sotto il dì 19 detto.

[below] Ego frater Archangelus Regiensis confirmo ut supra.

Doc. 7.7. The singers complain about their salaries, 22 January 1591. AOMS, vol. 18, *Deliberazioni, 1590–1624,* fol. 4^v

Cappella. Messer Giovanni Andrea Feliciani, maestro, Ser Accarigi prete, Ser Midone prete, e Ser Giovanbattista Pagni et altri. Et dissono sono sei bassi, quali hanno chi sei, chi quattro e chi tre carlini il mese; quattro tenori, delli quali alcuni hanno sette, altri sei et altri tre et mezzo lire il mese; et cinque soprano che hanno carlini tre il mese per uno.

Disse loro il Signor Rettore amorevolmente che voglino con modestia et reverenza massime nel tempio servare quello a che sono tenuti; et altre cose disse bene et santamente, ricercando da loro modestia verso Dio, anzi reverenza, modestia in faccia delli homini, assiduità nella carica loro, et obbedienza al maestro di cappella, quale hanno egregio et essemplare. Offerendosi in quello risguardare può egli come Operaio a loro benefitio, et ricercando se loro bisogni cosa alcuna. Detto messer Giovanni Andrea ringratiando araccomandò sè et li altri, quali tutti disse essere di bonissime intentione, et la più parte anco di buona espettatione.

Doc. 7.8. Florentine musicians are paid for performing on Assumption Day, 3 September 1594. Ibid., fol. 37^r

[margin: A' musici di Firenze, per l'Assunta, pagata vettura di cavalli] Disse detto Signor Rettore [Giugurta Tommasi] come per la solennità di S. Maria d'Agosto prossima [passata] et festa principale della detta cathedral chiesa, ci sono stati li musici e fanciulli della musica di Sua Serenissima Altezza, etiam di espressa licentia di Sua Altezza, et li sono state usate cortesie et amorevolezze. Et lui come Rettore dell'Opera avendone conferito, benchè non in Capitolo, poichè difficilmente talvolta si rauna, con più di esso Capitolo: visto il fatto da loro e poichè ci erano per favore fatto da Sua Altezza, li ha satisfatto come Operario la vettura delli cavalli, che importa lire centonovantasei di danari, et a cautela domanda approvarseli tale spesa.

Doc. 7.9. Expenses for lodging the Florentine musicians at Santa Maria della Scala, August 1586. Ospedale, vol. 811, *Bastardello di casa GGG, 1583–84,* fols. 268^v and 272^v

Christo 1586. Spese . . . E addì [3 Settembre] giuli due resi a detto cuoco per spese à ffate in più volte per bisogno dela cucina à fatta in casa del camerlengo nel tempo ci sono stati li 8 musici di Firenze, che sterno giorni 15 . . . L. 1. 6. 8.

Christo 1586. Spese . . . E il dì [5 Settembre] L. dodici. 5 pagati contanti a Tommasso Spagni, li medesimi à pagati per noi in 8 volte che ci sono spesi in comprare melloni 4 volte per il governatore inanzi Santa Maria di Agosto . . . e per più spesi fattosi nel tempo ci sono stati li musici 8 di Firenze in casa del camerlengo e giorni XV . . . L. 12. 5.

Doc. 7.10. The governing board considers the singers' request for a change in their obligations, 13 May 1599. AOMS, vol. 18, *Deliberazioni, 1590–1624,* fol. 54[r]

Propose ancora il Signor Rettore [Giugurta Tommasi] predetto che li Musici della Cappella del Duomo, con consenso delli Signori Canonici, domandano essere sgravati di cantare in alcuni giorni fra l'anno non solemni, et offeriscano di cantare alcune cose di più in certi giorni di solennità maggiori, allegando le ragioni che a ciò li muove. Onde conferito et consultato sopra ciò, deliberorno a consiglio di messer Bernardino Benvoglienti ottenuto per nove lupini bianchi, nessuno nigro in contrario, che il Signor Rettore, il Signor Decano et due delli Savi da eleggersi da esso Rettore habbino piena autorità sopra il fatto di detti musici di trattare con li signori canonici e fare e stabilire quanto li parrà conveniente, e quelle che da loro intorno a ciò sarà fatto valga e tengha come se dall'intero loro Capitolo fusse deliberato e si metta in esecuzione et accomodi nella tavolella. Il detto Signor Rettore poi elesse a quanto sopra: Messer Giovanbattista Placidi et Messer Bernardino Paccinelli.

TABLE 7.2. Chronological list of cathedral musicians, 1555–1607

The list includes only those mentioned specifically as singers at some point in the calendar year. Note that the fiscal year runs from May through April; a singer listed under two consecutive years may have served no more than a few months (for exact months, see Register of Musicians).

	1555	1556	1557	1558	1559	1560	1561	1562–63	1564	1565	1566	1567	1568	1569	1570	1571	1572
A. SINGERS																	
Bernardo Pontremoli	x	x	x	x	x	x	x	x	x	x	x	x	x	x	x		
Ulivieri Gerini	x	x	x														
Gabriello de' Servi	x	x	x														
Giovanbattista di Pasquino	x	x															
Giovanbattista di Bartolomeo	x	x	x	x	x	x	x	x	x	x	x	x	x				
Francesco Fabri	x					x	x	x	x	x							
Jacomo da Verona	x																
Fabio di Francesco Tizzoni		x	x	x	x	x	x	x	x	x	x	x	x	x	x		
Midone di Ser Cesare			x	x	x	x	x	x	x	x	x	x	x	x	x		
Annibale d'Andrea da Radda			x	x			x	x	x	x	x	x	x	x	x	x	x
Giovanfrancesco di Benedetto, trombone				x		x				x	x	x	x	x	x	x	x
Bartolomeo di Pietro dei Farnetani Saracini						x	x	x									
Austino di Bernardo Magini									x	x							
Benedetto di Francesco Franceschi							x	x	x	x	x	x	x	x	x	x	x
Alessandro di Domenico							x	x	x	x	x	x	x	x	x	x	x
Fausto d'Ansano Molandi							x	x	x								
Aurelio Rossi									x	x	x						
Fabrizio Ricci											x	x	x				
Lionardo di Giovanbattista											x	x	x				
Domenico di Maestro Martino														x	x		x
Giovanmaria d'Austino													x	x	x		
Arcangelo da Reggio													x	x	x		
Piero Ciotti															x	x	x
Guglielmo di Antonio Celli															x	x	x
Salvatore Essenga															x	x	
Ottavio di Giovanangelo															x	x	x
Orazio Vecchi																x	x

Name	1573	1574	1575	1576–77	1578	1579	1580	1581	1582	1583	1584	1585	1586	1587	1588
Midone Nannetti															
Annibale d'Andrea	x	x	x	x	x	x	x		x	x	x	x	x	x	x
Giovanfrancesco di Benedetto, trombone	x						x	x	x	x	x	x	x	x	x
Benedetto Franceschi	x	x	x	x											
Alessandro di Domenico	x	x		x	x	x	x	x	x	x	x	x	x	x	
Fausto d'Ansano							x	x							
Domencio di Maestro Martino	x	x					x								
Piero Ciotti	x	x	x	x	x	x	x	x	x	x	x	x			
Guglielmo di Antonio Celli												x	x	x	x
Salvatore Essenga	x	x	x				x	x	x	x	x	x	x		
Ottavio di Giovanangelo	x	x													
Orazio Vecchi	x	x													
Jacomo Giusti	x	x	x	x											
Alessio Spagnuolo	x	x	x												
Tiberio di Girolamo Rivolti, trombone															
Giovanbattista Tesauro	x	x	x	x	x	x	x	x	x	x					x
Andrea Feliciani			x	x	x	x	x	x							
Ascanio Marri			x	x	x	x	x	x	x	x	x	x	x	x	x
Piermaria di Tommaso			x	x											
Domenico di Maestro Antonio Lucenti				x	x	x									
Anselmo di Santo Agostino				x	x				x	x	x		x	x	x
Bernardino Draghi					x	x	x	x	x	x	x	x	x	x	x
Celio d'Ansano Molandi					x	x	x	x	x	x	x	x	x	x	x
Benvenuto Flori						x	x	x	x	x	x	x	x	x	x

TABLE 7.2 continued

	1573	1574	1575	1576–77	1578	1579	1580	1581	1582	1583	1584	1585	1586	1587	1588
Michelangelo di Giovanni						x	x	x	x	x	x				
Ventura di Giovanni da Castello							x								
Attilio di Girolamo							x								
Verio Veri									x	x	x				
Niccolò di Timoteo									x	x	x				
Domenico di Maestro Pietro									x	x	x				
Giovanni di Pasquino										x	x	x	x	x	x
Pietragnolo Nastagi											x	x	x	x	
Ottavio di Lorenzo Basili												x	x	x	x
Giovanbattista Pieragli													x	x	x
Donato Santini													x	x	x
Jacomo di Cesare Panichi														x	x
Giovanbattista Formichi, trombone														x	x
Bernardino di Giovanbattista Cocchi															x
Francesco di Maestro Matteo														x	x
Cosimo de' Mendici														x	x
Giulio dell'Ordine di San Francesco															x
Fausto di Simone Bascarelli															x
Teodoro di Niccolò Morelli															x
Giovanni Antonio Napoletano															x
Ottavio di Cerbone Galli															x
Simone di Domenico															x

	1589	1590	1591	1592	1593	1594	1595	1596	1597	1598	1599	1600	1601	1602	1603	1604	1605	1606–7
Midone Nannetti	x	x	x	x	x	x	x	x	x									
Andrea Feliciani	x	x	x	x	x	x	x	x										
Domenico di Maestro Antonio	x																	
Celio Molandi	x	x																
Bernardino Draghi		x	x															
Giovanbattista Pieragli		x	x															
Guglielmo Celli		x	x				x											
Giovanbattista Formichi, trombone								x	x	x								
Jacomo di Cesare Panichi		x	x	x	x	x		x	x	x			x	x				
Bernardino Cocchi	x	x	x	x	x	x	x	x	x	x				x	x			
Francesco di Maestro Matteo	x	x	x	x	x	x			x	x				x	x			
Giovanni Antonio Napolitano	x	x	x															
Giovanni di Pasquino Sacchi	x	x																
Ottavio di Lorenzo Basili	x	x	x	x	x	x	x	x	x	x	x	x	x	x	x	x	x	x
Cosimo de' Mendici	x									x	x							
Ottavio di Cerbone Galli	x																	
Simone di Domenico	x	x																
Teodoro di Niccolò Morelli	x	x	x	x	x	x	x	x	x									
Donato Santini		x	x	x	x	x	x	x	x					x				
Vincenzo Carli da San Casciano														x	x	x		
Benvenuto Flori		x	x	x		x	x	x										
Aldobrando Trabocchi da Pienza										x	x	x	x	x	x	x	x	x
Simone di Bartolomeo		x																
Orindio di Giovanmaria Bartolini		x						x										
Teofilo di Giovanmaria Bartolini	x		x	x	x	x								x	x	x	x	
Giovanbattista di Guerrino		x	x	x	x	x												

Table 7.2 continued

	1589	1590	1591	1592	1593	1594	1595	1596	1597	1598	1599	1600	1601	1602	1603	1604	1605	1606–7
Onofrio da Gubbio		x																
Attivio Montelauri		x	x		x	x	x	x	x	x	x	x	x	x	x	x	x	x
Michele Scala			x															
Andrea di Giovanni			x															
Fausto di Simone Bascarelli			x															
Antonio di Bartolomeo Fornari	x			x	x	x	x											
Giovanni Piccioni				x	x	x	x	x	x	x	x	x	x	x	x	x	x	x
Frate Andrea da Fossano				x	x	x	x											
Matteo Bondoni					x	x	x	x	x	x	x	x	x	x	x	x	x	x
Silvio d'Anghiari					x													
Carlo Vanni Romano					x	x	x											
Daniello Danielli					x	x												
Scipione Celli					x	x	x	x										
Silvio d'Antonmaria Marzi					x	x	x	x	x	x								
Giovanbattista Mariani								x	x	x	x	x	x	x	x			
Francesco Francheschi						x	x	x	x	x	x	x	x	x	x	x	x	x
Fabrizio di Bartolomeo Martini						x	x	x	x	x	x	x	x	x	x	x	x	x
Piergiovanni di Donato						x	x	x										
Pompilio di Francesco Rossini							x		x	x	x	x	x	x	x			
Girolamo di Maestro Cesare								x	x									
Giovanbattista degli Orfani							x	x										
Antonio Maria di Pasquino [Sacchi]									x	x	x							
Girolamo eunoco [Gulini]									x	x	x	x	x	x				
Giovanbattista Chiocciolini								x	x	x								
Giovanbattista de' Mendici							x	x	x									
Giovanbattista di Michelangelo							x	x	x									

	1589	1590	1591	1592	1593	1594	1595	1596	1597	1598	1599	1600	1601	1602	1603	1604	1605	1606–7
Cristofano Draghi							x							x	x	x	x	x
Pierantonio Formichi								x	x	x	x	x	x					
Giovanbattista Chiocciolini								x	x									x
Pietragnolo Maestri									x	x	x	x	x					
Agostino di Francesco eunoco									x	x	x	x	x					
Michelangelo Grecchi									x									
Francesco Bianciardi									x	x	x	x	x	x	x	x	x	x
Girolamo Fontanini										x	x	x						
Guglielmo di Sant'Agostino										x	x	x	x	x	x	x	x	x
Giovanmaria Cappelletti										x	x	x	x	x	x	x	x	x
Lancilotto Puliti											x							
Michele Pisano											x							
Girolamo Bondoni												x	x	x	x	x		
Annibale dell'Oste												x	x	x	x			
Jacomo di Vergilio												x	x	x	x	x		
Marcantonio Tornioli													x	x				
Celio Molandi													x	x	x	x		

B. ORGANISTS

	1555–62	1563	1564	1565	1566–67	1568	1569–72	1573	1574–90	1591–96	1597–1601	1602	1603–7
Scipione di Pavolo	x												
Mariano di Girolamo Pelori		x	x	x				x	x				
Arcangelo da Reggio				x	x								
Bennardo di Salso da Parma					x								
Bartolomeo Toscani da Venezia						x	x	x					
Francesco Bianciardi										x			
Agostino Agazzari											x	x	
Jacomo Panichi												x	x

Example 7.1. Andrea Feliciani, Sanctus from *Missa brevis* (*Missarum cum quatuor, quinque et octo vocibus liber primus* [Venice: Vincenti & Amadino, 1584])

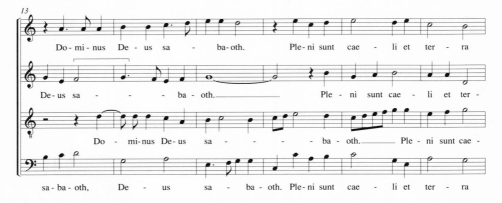

Example 7.1 continued

Example 7.1 continued

Example 7.2. Andrea Feliciani, Kyrie I from *Missa brevis* (*Missarum cum quatuor, quinque et octo vocibus liber primus* [Venice: Vincenti & Amadino, 1584])

Example 7.3. Andrea Feliciani, *Magnificat octavi toni* (*Musica in canticum Beatissimae Virginis Mariae* [Venice: Gardano, 1591])

Example 7.3 continued

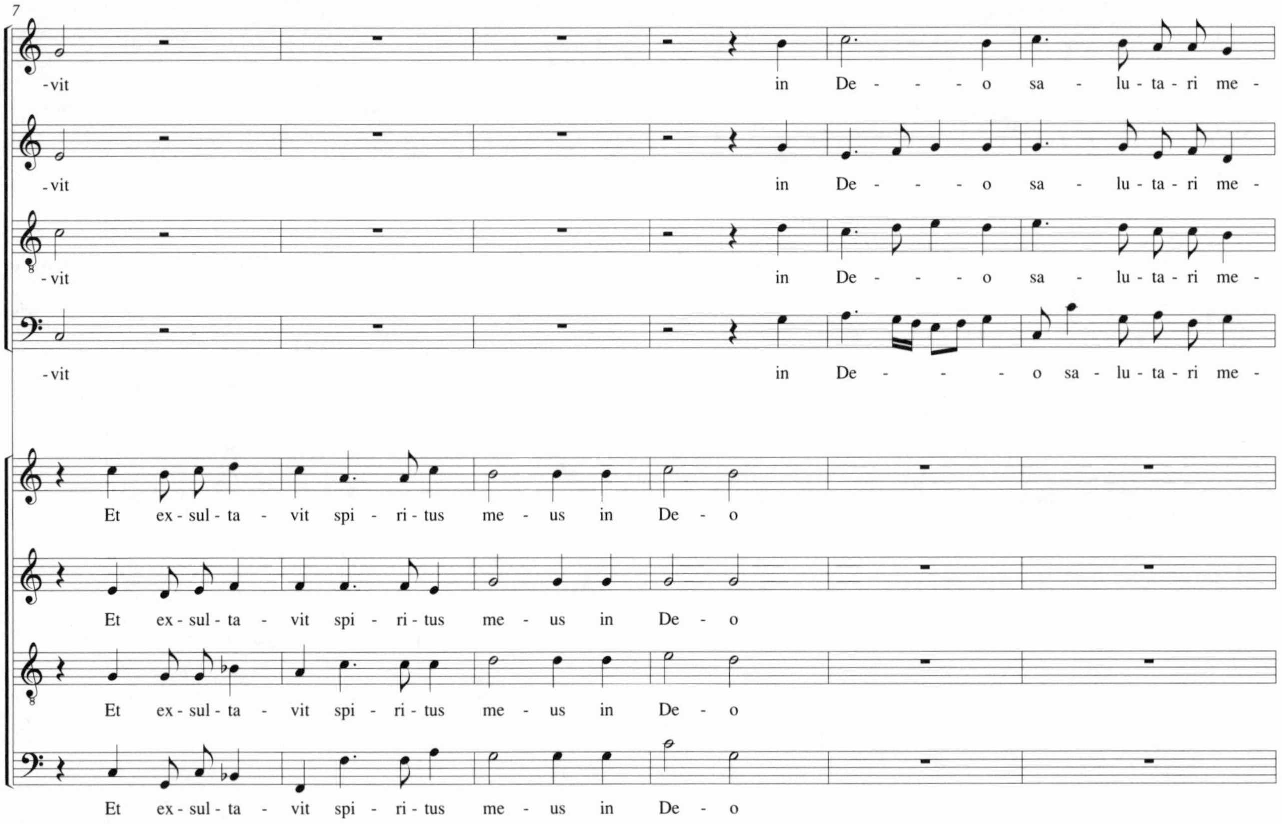

Example 7.3 continued

396

Example 7.3 continued

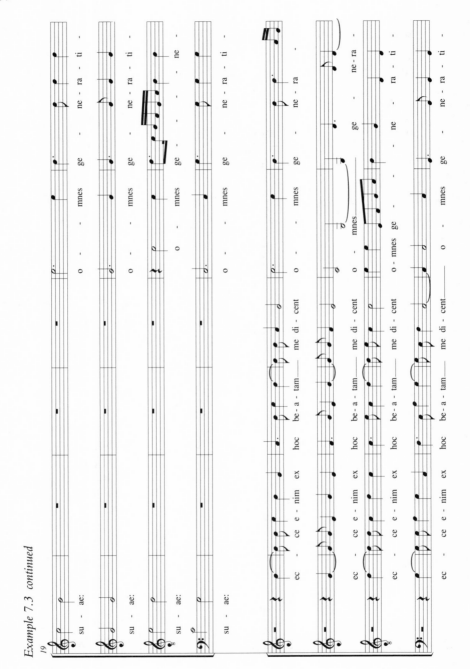

Example 7.3 continued

Example 7.3 continued

Example 7.3 continued

Example 7.3 continued

Example 7.3 continued

Example 7.3 continued

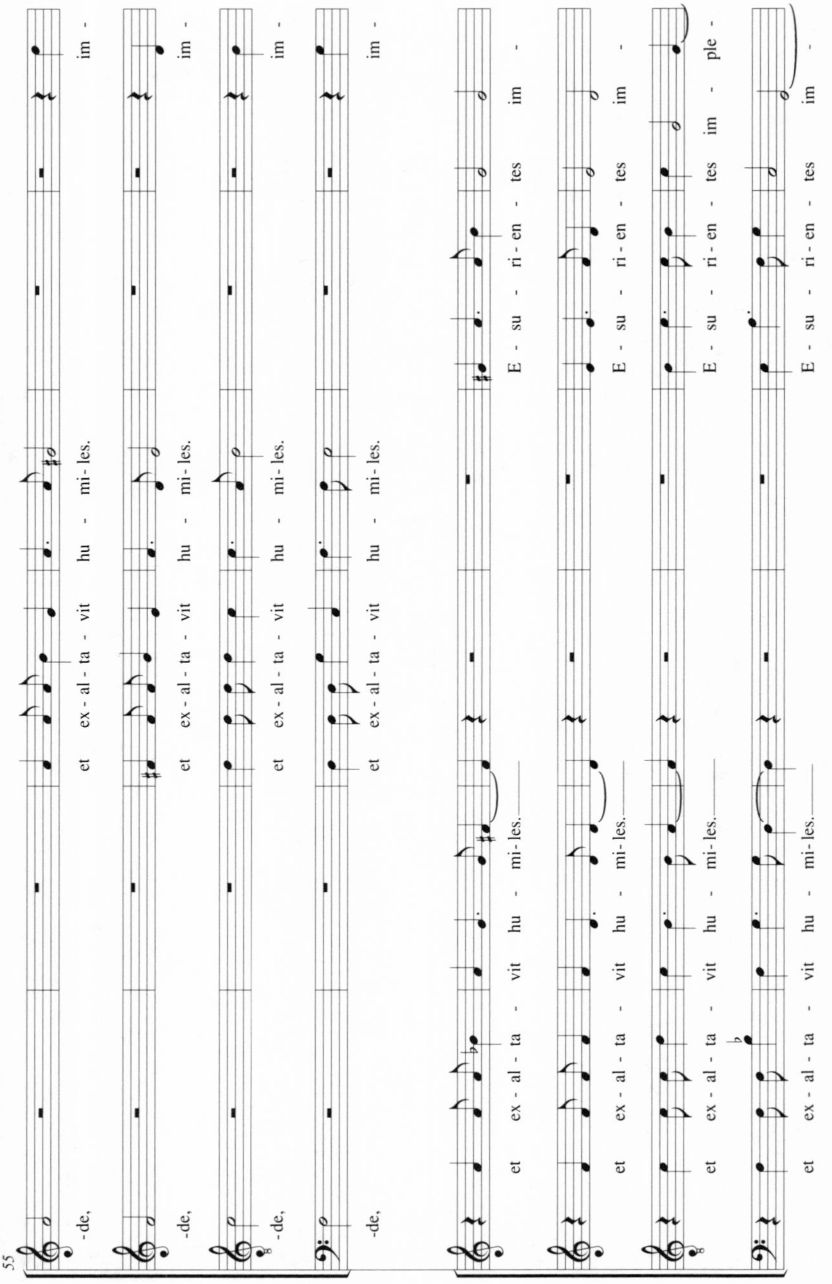

Example 7.3 continued

† lacking in print

Example 7.3 continued

Example 7.3 continued

406

Example 7.3 continued

Example 7.3 continued

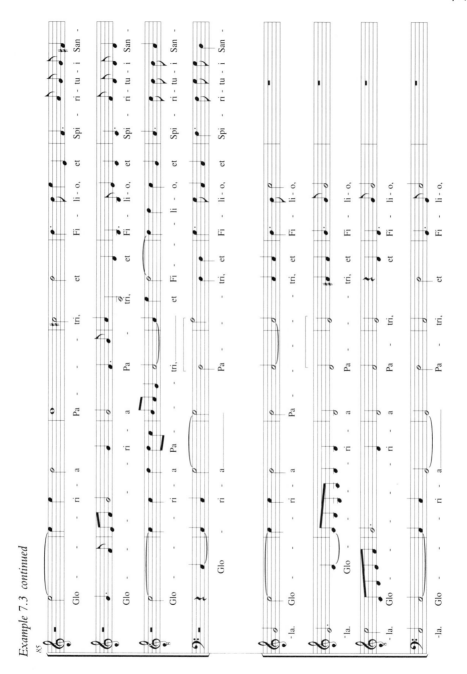

408

Example 7.3 continued

Example 7.3 continued

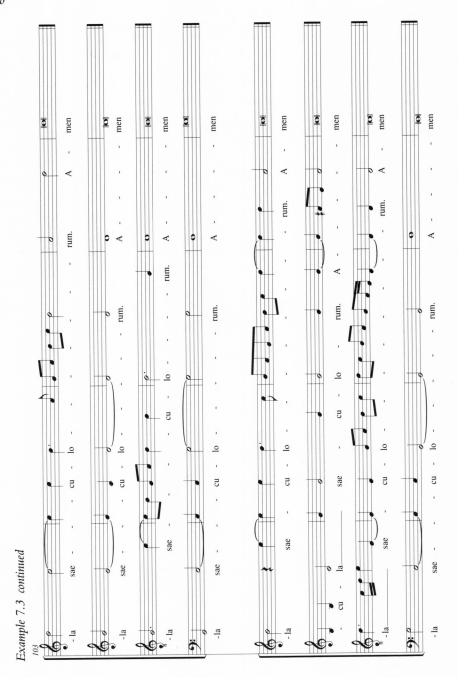

Example 7.3 continued

Part Two

THE PALAZZO PUBBLICO

Chapter Eight

ORIGINS AND ESTABLISHMENT OF THE TRUMPETERS' CORPS, 1230–1399

THE PALAZZO PUBBLICO was the other place in Siena with a long and venerable tradition for musical performance. The official seat of government, the Palace was where the town's highest authorities—the members of the Concistoro, the podestà, the captain of the people, the Balìa, and others—lived and worked and in whose great hall foreign dignitaries were received and entertained. Much of the official bureaucracy as well as groups like the trumpeters existed long before the present-day edifice took shape. Indeed, work began only in 1298 on modifying and enlarging several of the structures that form the nucleus of the present building. Construction was substantially finished by 1310, when officials of the party of the Nine went to live in the new wing that was to serve as their official residence.[1] Among the most visible—and audible—of the Palace employees were the trombetti and naccherini, town trumpeters and drummers, a professional group of state-sponsored musicians that originated in the mid-thirteenth century. Adding the splendor of their sounds to civic and religious ceremonies, riding with the militia into battle, and accompanying the town's rulers in their public appearances constituted the trumpeters' principal duties, duties that made them such a conspicuous element in the complex web of sounds and symbols designed to signify the commune's independence and sovereignty.

Almost from the beginning the trumpeters were regarded as an indispensable part of the government's household, and their duties were regulated as early as the Sienese constitution of 1262. Sharing the roster with them were the equally venerable town criers and, much later, the pifferi, or wind band. The musicians' posts were generally immune to the effects of the many factional upheavals that took place in Siena's often troubled history. Despite changes brought about by successive governments and despite changes every two months in the membership of the Concistoro, nominally the city's principal governing body, the status and role of the musicians, as defined by constitutional statutes, remained fixed and unchanging. It was, in fact, they who provided the image of continuity to the many rituals that enhanced the prestige and magnificence of Siena's ruling elite. The trumpeters, like the later pifferi, represented the commune at all officially sponsored civic, religious, diplomatic, and social events. In effect their presence on such occasions offered a concrete and tangible expression of the stability and legitimacy of the government of those in power. Because musicians were employees of the Palace, they were paid from state coffers and records of their salaries were kept by officials in charge of finances at the Biccherna. Regulations governing musical groups were subject to approval by the General Council, and, later, by the Balìa, though day-

---

1. *Palazzo Pubblico di Siena: Vicende costruttive e decorazione,* ed. Cesare Brandi (Milan, 1983), 34–35.

to-day decisions regarding musicians' terms of employment and livelihood were made by the priors of the Concistoro, Siena's signory. The Concistoro's actions were recorded in volumes that covered each government's bimestrial term of office. These volumes and others recording payments from the Biccherna, as well as a few regarding decisions about music made by the Balìa in the late fifteenth century, are preserved to this day in the Sienese State Archives.

From the many surviving documents concerning the town trumpeters it is clear that their duties paralleled, and in most instances duplicated, those of contemporary groups in other Italian and European cities. Siena's group, though not as large as some of those recorded elsewhere in Italy, maintained personnel of the highest professional caliber. Competition was intense for the limited number of posts within the Palace's organization and admission to the group was gained only upon the recommendation of the Concistoro, which supervised the quality of their work or appointed knowledgeable surrogates to do so. From modest beginnings in the mid-thirteenth century the trumpeters' corps experienced exceptional growth under the government of the Nine and its immediate successors before succumbing to the uncertainties and rigors of Sienese politics in the later fourteenth century. Revivified by the turn of the next century, the trombetti experienced a period of great stability that saw them participating prominently in the splendid panoply of ceremonial life in Renaissance Siena. Later in the sixteenth century their role, already somewhat eclipsed by the more musically progressive pifferi, was diminished considerably under the Medici government, as the aura of republican glory ceased to shine on this ancient Sienese musical institution.

THE EARLIEST RECORDED TRUMPETERS AND TOWN CRIERS

By later medieval times the trombetti constituted the most venerable musical group in Siena. Payments to regularly salaried members of the corps first appear in the Biccherna's account books from the mid-thirteenth century.[2] Before then musicians were employed as the need arose and paid on an irregular basis according to the number and types of services performed. Payments issued in 1230 to several trumpeters note that they accompanied various officials on law-enforcement rounds within and outside the city, that they attended the podestà in public appearances, and that they rode with the militia.[3] A report from the same year gives the names of two players of percussion instruments, Donosdeo and Leonardo da Pisa, who escorted government officers as

---

2. Giugurta Tommasi, an eighteenth-century Sienese historian, maintained that the commune employed trumpeters as early as 1040, when the republic's first consul of justice assumed office. Cellesi, *Storia della più antica banda musicale Senese*, 14–15, justifiably argued in favor of using documentary sources to establish the group's origins, which she assigned to the mid-thirteenth century. She also noted that trumpeters are not mentioned in the earliest volumes of the Biccherna, from 1226; first payments registered to them are from 1257.

3. Their names were Bencivenne, Rusignolo, Andrea, and Altovese. A number of the Biccherna's early volumes have been published in modern edition. See *Libri dell'entrata e dell'uscita della Repubblica di Siena. Libro terzo a 1230* (Siena, 1915), 115; other records of payments issued to musicians in 1230 are on pp. 140, 143, 158, 171, 178, 190, 198, 233.

they went about their business.[4] Also mentioned in 1230 are Barzalomeo, a Pisan trumpeter, and Lottaringo and Ventura, town criers, who made a certain number of public announcements.

The policy of retaining musicians on a regularly salaried basis was instituted within the next decade. In 1246 Altovese Arnolfini and Guido Rosso, "trumpeters of the commune," received payments of s. 15 each for six months' service, an amount increased to s. 20 by 1249.[5] The modest sums involved indicate that these were base salaries, comparable in a certain sense to retainers' fees, which, as other entries show, were augmented from time to time by payments for supplementary services. Except for a few months in 1249, Altovese worked with Guido Rosso through 1251, when he was replaced by Guido's son, Compare. Although Compare's tenure was brief—he died in the following year—it furnishes the earliest known example of the kinship patterns that became so prevalent among Palace musicians in the following centuries.[6]

A payment of L. 12 from 1252 records the salaries of four trumpeters, Guido Rosso, Bonavita, Caroso, and Lombardino, for an unspecified period of time. Six trumpeters were present during 1253. In July of that year Riccio di Palude and Manente each received s. 45, including expenses for horses, whereas Caroso was paid s. 30. Differences in salaries were also registered in the following October, when Caroso again earned s. 30, Riccio, Manente, and Guido Rosso earned s. 45, and Giovanni and Piero s. 50. The higher salaries reflect extra services, probably for heralding. Varying amounts were also paid to the six trumpeters during November and December. Five trumpeters, Giovanni, Guido, Riccio, Manente, and Gabardino, appear in payments from 1255, and five are also cited among government employees who received a beret for the feast of the Assumption in 1257.

In addition to normal salaries—entered into the accounts in monthly, quarterly, or semiannual instalments—other records from these years indicate that musicians' basic incomes were augmented by payments for extraordinary services, including reimbursements for travel and transportation expenses. From 1251, for instance, comes another payment to Caroso and an associate, "who, with cialamella and trumpet, went with the podestà and the army when they rode toward Poggibonsi."[7] The "cialamella" was a predecessor of the shawm. Mention of it at this time indicates that from very early on the Palace employed a "loud band" of the kind imported to Europe from the Near East, about which more will be said below. During the same year Guido Rosso and Altovese, in the company of two others, with pipes and drums, served with the German

4. *Libro terzo a 1230,* 211; the instruments cited are "tamburo et cembalis." Sibyl Marcuse, *Musical Instruments: A Comprehensive Dictionary* (New York, 1964), 85 and 509, describes the cembalo, mentioned by Boccaccio, as a frame drum still in use today in Italy. She notes that the sixteenth-century theorist Gioseffo Zarlino described it as having a parchment head, pellet bells, and jingles. Its modern descendent is the tambourine. Depending on the context, tamburo may be a drum or a kettledrum; a tamburo militare, a snare drum; a tamburo grande, a bass drum.

5. Altovese's surname appears in a document from 1251. Statutes governing the trumpeters' duties were doubtless drawn up at the time, but they are no longer extant.

6. *Dodicesimo libro,* 126; *Tredicesimo libro,* 105, 132.

7. The payment of s. 10 listed to "Caroso et socio cum cialamella et trombecta," is in *Dodicesimo libro a 1251,* 96.

militia.[8] It is difficult for us today to imagine the important role of musicians in medieval military operations. But chronicles and pictorial sources from these and later times provide some idea of the effectiveness of their signal calls and of the dreaded din they provided in the course of battle. Not all of the musicians' extraordinary duties were tied to the military. In 1246 Altovese and Guido were reimbursed for the use of horses "when they went to meet the king as he was approaching Siena and [when] they accompanied the podestà on Assumption Day, *trombando.*"[9] The same musicians are named in another record from 1249–50, which calls them "banditori," an indication that they also served as town criers.[10]

Town criers, as this latter citation and previous ones from 1230 indicate, are also mentioned frequently in early account books. Payments for six months' service, issued in February 1247, to Maffeo Guerrieri, Ventura Tomasini, and Caprone di Cristoforo, show that they were put on a regular salaried basis around the same time as the trumpeters. The same musicians are again named in a payment from eight years later, for their services during July and August 1255. Thereafter, they, too, constituted a discrete group of Palace employees directly responsible to the government. Maffeo, Caprone, and a new employee, Pagno di Marino, are designated banditori and trombatori in payments from 1259, as were Altovese and Guido a decade earlier. Records such as these demonstrate that some of the trumpeters doubled as town criers, an ability to play the instrument being required of holders of both offices. Though not always identifiable—town criers and trumpeters appear together indiscriminately in these early accounts under various headings such as tubatores, trombatori, tubicines, or trombetti—a report from a few years later shows that by then the number of town criers was fixed at three, the same number cited in 1259.

Some of the records just cited occasionally put the trumpeters in the company of the podestà, while others indicate that the group's services were also lent to other public officials such as the captain of the people. An entry from 1253–54, for example, shows that two of the trumpeters went with the podestà and the Sienese army to Pisa,[11] and another from 1257 speaks of their accompanying the captain of the people and the podestà to the cathedral on the evening before Assumption day. But even though trumpeters might be assigned to assist other officials, they still remained directly responsible to the priors of the Concistoro.[12] In later years the podestà and the captain of the people maintained musicians of their own who functioned independently of the town trumpeters. Administrative separation of the various groups, however, did not prevent

---

8. Ibid., 72.

9. *Libro Sesto,* 115.

10. *Decimo liro,* 120.

11. *Libri dell'entrata e dell'uscita della Repubblica di Siena. Quindicesimo libro a 1253–54* (Siena, 1939), 54.

12. The other officials included the sanatore, the captain, and the podestà. Whether the conservadore had trumpeters of his own has yet to be determined. The trombetti apparently played at mealtimes only through the end of the fourteenth century, after which the newly appointed group of pifferi took over this duty. The trumpeters, however, did continue to play for the delectation of the public from the ringhiera, the area in front of the Palace, on or around the same hours. See below.

them from performing together, as is apparent from the rosters of Palio musicians, cited in chapter 14.

The trumpeters were officially recognized as a state-sponsored institution in the constitution of the commune of Siena, drawn up in 1262. The statute devoted to them notes that the podestà, on behalf of the commune, was to retain three pairs of trumpeters and that he should have six eligible players from Siena assigned to the posts.[13] Lacking suitable candidates, the podestà and his advisors were to engage others they deemed capable. The length of the trumpeters' term of office was not specified. Nor were their salaries, which were determined each year during the month of December by a simple majority of the General Council or Council of the Bell, as it was also known. The trumpeters were forbidden to leave Siena with their own instruments or to take any of the commune's musical instruments—specified here as three pairs of trumpets—outside the city without official permission. This was granted only for state business. They were also prohibited from playing at private weddings, in or outside town, even with their own instruments. Similar restrictions applied to others who used the commune's musical instruments. Fines were prescribed for any infractions of contractual obligations. Despite these admonitions, a final sentence specifies that "this article will not be observed in peacetime," which means that these restrictions were infrequently observed or that they were often lifted for long periods of time.

The constitution also devotes a number of chapters to the town criers. The first chapter stipulates the appointments of three town criers (banditores) to three-year terms of office, and fixes a payment of d. 4 for every public announcement made. They were to dress in red or green and to read each announcement three times on horseback in the usual places within the city and its suburbs.[14] They were to provide their own horses and keep the animals well groomed and in good condition. A subsequent chapter calls them heralds or trumpeters (precones sive tubatores) and says that they were required, every time they read a proclamation in public, to sound their trumpets twice before reading the text.[15] Another chapter notes that while holding office, a town crier or herald (bannitor seu preco), could not announce deaths, and that three others should be appointed to do this instead.[16] A final chapter specifies that these trumpeters or town criers (tubatores seu banditores) could not be reappointed within three years of leaving office.[17] While this last stipulation was aimed at preventing any one person from gaining a monopoly on the post, it did not prohibit Palace trumpeters from doubling as town criers or from holding both offices simultaneously, a policy apparently reflecting past practices.[18]

---

13. See Lodovico Zdekauer, Il Constituto del Comune di Siena dell'anno 1262 (Milan, 1897), 117, Distinctio I [CCCI], "De tubatoribus eorum offitio et pena et feudo."

14. Ibid., 115, Distinctio I [CCLXXXXVI], "De tribus banditoribus et eorum officio."

15. Ibid., [CCLXXXXVIII].

16. Ibid., [CCLXXXXVIIII].

17. Ibid., [CCC].

18. In Florence there were four town criers or praecones, one for each quarter of the city. Like their Sienese counterparts, the Florentine heralds were required, with silver trumpets in hand, to read their pronouncements in at least eight places in each quarter. Luigia Cellesi says that the tubatores took their name from the instrument they played, that is, the straight trumpet (tuba), and that their

Town criers, however, did not have to be drawn from among the Palace trumpeters. Successive terms of office were apparently denied them because the government wished to ensure that all qualified people applying for the posts received equal consideration. A system of political patronage, too, may have been at work, for the statute guaranteed that candidates from each of the city's three districts, or *terzi,* be nominated for office triennially. In any case, whether or not the posts were filled by Palace trumpeters or political appointees, the statutes indicate that town criers had to have some ability in playing the trumpet. How much, however, is difficult to assess. Arguably, town criers did not need to be as highly trained as trumpeters because their primary aim when they sounded their instruments was to attract attention before they went about their business of announcing the latest decrees and proclamations. But earlier as well as later records hardly ever bother to distinguish between people who held the two offices, with the implication that all of the commune's employees who played the trumpet possessed some musical skills.[19]

TRUMPETERS IN THE LATER THIRTEENTH CENTURY

The Biccherna's account books from the second half of the thirteenth century list many payments to musicians, though they rarely mention individual names. Exceptional are entries such as the one from December 1277, which cites salaries of s. 6 paid to each of four trumpeters, Conte, Sufilello, Feduccio, and Ghezzo, and a shawm player named Ildino.[20] Names are lacking also in records of expenses of clothing for musicians purchased annually at government expense in time for the gala celebrations held on the feast of the Assumption. Typical is an entry from August 1281. It records L. 20 spent on red cloth for uniforms for the trumpeters and the tabor and shawm players and an additional s. 18 for five pennants, but does not identify the recipients.[21]

Normally, some or all of the Palace musicians participated in extraordinary events

---

function was to attract the crowds' attention before the town criers read their proclamations. Cellesi also notes that in certain cities such as Perugia and Milan, proclamations were read instead by the tubatores, who held both offices simultaneously. See her "Documenti per la storia musicale di Firenze," *Rivista musicale italiana* 34 (1927): 584–85. On the two different groups of trumpeters employed in Florence, see also Keith Polk, "Civic Patronage and Instrumental Ensembles in Renaissance Florence," *Augsburger Jahrbuch für Musikwissenschaft* 3 (1986): 53, who notes that "By 1390 three basic groups were defined; the pifferi (three players), trombetti (trumpets, five or six players), and the trombadori (eight to ten players)."

On Sienese use of the terms tubatore, trombadore, and trombetto see chapter 9. Florentine practice evidently differed from Sienese, which used the words trombadore and tubatore interchangeably. In Florence, at times the two different groups of trumpeters were distinguished by two different words. Thus, tronbadori and tronbetti are listed by the Italian terms in payments from 1402–3 (ASF, Camera del Comune, *Campione,* vol. 18, fols. 36ᵛ, 337ʳ). Six tubicines and two others named individually, together with six trombadores, one naccherinus, and one cembeamellarius [*sic*], are cited in pay lists from 5 April 1494 (ASF, Camera del Comune, Notaio di Camera, *E&U,* vol. 75, fol. 60ᵛ).

19. See Zdekauer, *Il Constituto,* 116, Distinctio I [CCLXXXXVIII]. The statute states that the praecones or tubatores must have a trumpet in perfect condition (*integram*) and that they were to play twice, extensively before reading the proclamation.

20. ASS, Biccherna, vol. 69, fol. 18ʳ.

21. Cecchini, "Palio e Contrade nella loro evoluzione storica," 347.

and received additional compensation for their work. One record of their activities appears among the expenses of the festivities provided by the captain of the people, Pino dei Vernacci da Cremona, on All Saints Day, 1291. On that occasion Ghezzo, Neri, and Vanni Grasso, identified as the commune's trumpeters in other records, were paid s. 3. 4 each for playing at the joust in the main square and for performing at the podestà's palace later in the day. An additional d. 15 were spent on the wine they drank.[22] Names are lacking in a payment from March 1292, which registers d. 8 spent on "four garlands for the commune's trumpeters when they went to the feast of the blessed Ambrose [Sansedoni]."[23] Four trumpeters, Ghezzo Boninsegna, Malfarsetto Boninsegna (apparently Ghezzo's brother), Neri Fava, and Vanni Grasso, were paid for playing at ceremonies in 1298 that marked the change in office of the captain of the people.[24] Names are again lacking in a 1302 record, which lists gratuities to the trumpeters for having played on several occasions, notably, when the wife of Prince Charles of Valois arrived in the city, when the Prince himself returned to the city from Florence en route to Rome, and when the Cardinal of Florence, also en route to Rome, visited Siena.[25]

A revised Sienese constitution compiled between 1288 and 1293 also contains specific statutes regarding the trumpeters' dress, salary, and duties, repeated without change in the vernacular version of the document from 1309–10.[26] Both versions state that the trumpeters and the other musicians—there were now regularly employed players of the shawm and the tabor—would have new uniforms once a year purchased at government expense. (Within a few years the clothing allowance would be made on a semi-annual basis.) All musicians were obliged to wear the commune's arms on their clothing and cloaks, which could not be lined with fur. Each would receive a monthly salary of s. 30. The number of trumpeters was reduced from three to "two pairs" from the city of Siena, "who know how to play well," the shawm and tabor players having apparently been hired to replace the other two. As in the past, musicians would be chosen by the podestà, who was empowered to engage "others who seemed [suitable] to him and his court," if native Sienese were unavailable. Earlier injunctions forbidding musicians to leave the city without official permission and to play at private weddings were restated, and a fine of s. 10 stipulated for each contravention of these restrictions. The trumpeters, the tabor player, and the shawm player were required to have their own horses when they accompanied the podestà in his public appearances.[27]

Three annually appointed town criers are also mentioned in this revised constitu-

---

22. Quoted by Aldo Lusini, "Dante e le sue relazioni con Siena," *La Diana* 3 (1928): 84, n. 11.

23. Biccherna, vol. 107, fol. 154ᵛ, dated 22 March 1292: "in quatuor sertis sive ghirlandis tubatorum comunis quando iverunt ad festum beati Ambrosii."

24. Cited by Cellesi, *Storia della più antica banda,* 16, from ASS, Biccherna, vol. 14, fol. 189.

25. Cited by Lusini, "Dante e le sue relazioni con Siena," 84, n. 12, from ASS, Biccherna, vol. 116, fol. 289ᵛ, dated 8 March 1302.

26. Cellesi, *Storia della più antica banda,* 63, gives the text of the Latin document. The Italian translation of the Constitution of 1309–10 is in Alessandro Lisini, *Il costituto del Comune di Siena volgarizzato nel MCCCIX–MCCCX* (Siena, 1903). The documents referred to here are in vol. 1, pp. 112–13.

27. The player of the tamburino, apparently replacing the cembalo player, was to continue performing with the trumpeters for some time. He was later joined by another percussionist who played

tion, one from each of the city's terzi.[28] Each was obliged to have his own horse, valued at L. 20 or more, and to keep the animal in good condition at his own expense. There were periodic inspections to ensure this latter. The town criers were to read their announcements on horseback (their horses bedecked with red silk pennants) and when they did so, they were to attach white silk pennants to their instruments. Failure to comply with this regulation would incur a fine. Proclamations were read in the usual places within the city and its suburbs, and when the town criers sounded their trumpets before reading, they were to extend them forward to their full length. Penalties were levied against anyone who failed to do so. Representations of the trumpeters in several Sienese paintings and frescoes from around this time show them in characteristic poses.

Town criers earned monthly salaries of s. 40 (L. 2) and, as in the past, they were forbidden to announce deaths, three other criers having been expressly appointed by the commune for this purpose.[29] Town criers' uniforms of red-lined cloth, whose cost was calculated at L. 3. 10 the length, still displayed the commune's arms and were worn throughout the day every day. A final clause in the revised document states that town criers could receive no other salary from the commune—which can only mean that they could no longer be employed simultaneously as trumpeters—though they could accept gratuities for reading various kinds of announcements.

Even in this early period the town trumpeters were engaged in varied activities, some of them regularly scheduled, others changing according to circumstances. None of their duties apparently obliged them to attend members of the government constantly, or later, when construction of the Palazzo Pubblico was completed, to live within its walls. From the thirteenth century onwards records show that the trumpeters' duties—which might be fulfilled while on horseback, on foot, or seated—included accompanying the priors of the Concistoro in their public appearances, playing for their entertainment, playing before and after government audiences, performing at ceremonies when members of the government began and finished their terms of office, performing at state receptions for important visitors, sounding the hours, journeying abroad with government delegations, and accompanying the militia into battle. The very diversity of their assignments and responsibilities demonstrates the indispensable role they performed in an age that valued conspicuous display in sight and in sound.

TRUMPETERS IN THE FOURTEENTH CENTURY

The increasingly important role of the trombetti in the town's life finds some resonance in Sienese poetry and prose of the fourteenth century. Folgore da San Gimignano, Siena's most celebrated poet of the time, alludes to them on several occasions in his celebrated *Sonetti de la semana*. In his sonnet for Tuesday, in particular, he conjures up sights and sounds surely familiar to all his readers when he evokes the excitement of the joust, as knights and others prepare for arms to the sound of "trumpets and drums"

---

the nacchere, that is, nakers, a pair of small kettledrums struck with sticks. A shawm player is mentioned in salary lists and payments throughout the next several decades.

28. Lisini, *Il costituto volgarizzato,* 114.

29. Ibid., 113.

and the pealing of the bells.[30] At the end of the poem Folgore's imagery vividly captures the scene on the field, where steeds with empty saddles drag their lords about, as "the sound of trumpeters, fifes, flutes, and shawms" rally the ranks of the victors.[31] Fourteenth-century Sienese texts, particularly the *cantari,* or religious ballads, make generalized reference to the trumpeters, whose sounds are usually equated with moments of ecstatic glorification, heavenly hosts, and angelic pronouncements.[32] But the frequent mention of trumpets and other instruments at civic and religious functions testifies to their ubiquitous place in Sienese society here on earth, a topic more fully explored in chapter 13.

Names of individual musicians appear more often in various records from the first half of the fourteenth century. Principal among them are the official lists of tenured Palace personnel who received clothing at state expense. In some periods the clothing, which served as an official uniform, was provided twice a year, though eventually it was given only on Assumption Day, 15 August. Compiled with government approval at appropriate times each year, the clothing lists serve as an extremely reliable record of those who served the Republic. Their data enable us to trace the emergence of four themes that assumed prominence in the second half of the fourteenth century and became the dominant characteristics of the group's composition in the following one. These are: (1) ties of kinship and its corollary, (2) persistence of local tradition, (3) continuity of service, and (4) formation of smaller core groups working within the larger ensemble over a period of years. Also evident, though to a lesser extent, was the tendency of some musicians to leave the group only to return to it after a few years' absence. Whether this resulted from the vagaries of political influence and patronage, noted below, which saw some individuals reinstated in their posts by one group of priors after having been deprived of them by a previous group, is difficult to ascertain.

Nine musicians are listed in various records from 1310. The most important of these consist of a payment for two months' salary issued in July and another from August noting the cost of the clothing they received on Assumption Day.[33] The trumpeters were Malfarsetto di Boninsegna, Neri Fava, Vanni Grasso—all three mentioned in 1298—Domenico di Voglia, Pericciuolo Salvucci, and Nicola di Bencivenne. The shawm player was Ciertiere di Guido, the tabor player Marco di Ciereto. Another musician on the list, Marco's brother Ciereto di Ciereto, played the nakers, an instrument mentioned along with trumpets, tabor, and shawm in other records. Siena's trumpeters' corps at this time, at least in terms of numbers, compared quite favorably with

---

30. Folgore da San Gimignano, *I Sonetti,* ed. Ferdinando Neri (Turin, 1917), 57.

31. "El Martedì gli do di novo mondo / udir sonar trombetta e tamburelli, / armar pedon, cavalieri e donzelli, / e campane a martello dicer don do; / e lui prime or e gli altri secondo / armati di loriche e di cappelli, / veder nemici e percoter ad elli, / dando gran colpi e mettendoli a fondo / Destrier veder andare a vote selle / tirando per la campo lor segnori / e strascinando figati e budelli; / e sonar a raccolta i trombatori, / e sufoli e flauti e ciramelle, / e toccar a le schiere i feritori."

32. See Varanini, ed., *Cantari religiosi senesi del Trecento,* passim.

33. Six musicians, trumpeters, tabor, and nakers players, received an extraordinary payment on 4 July 1310 for playing at the inauguration of the new podestà, and eight, now including a shawm, received a similar gratuity on the following 11 July, when they played at a ceremony marking the departure of the previous podestà. ASS, Biccherna, vol. 124, fols. 152ʳ, 156ʳ.

Florence's, where between 1290 and 1300 six trumpeters, a drummer, and a shawmist were employed.[34]

Except for the trumpeter Vanni Grasso, replaced by Petruccio di Tino, and the drummer Ciereto di Ciereto, replaced by another of his brothers, Vanni di Ciereto, the musicians just mentioned are cited in a similar series of records from 1316. One of these lists musicians who received clothing on Assumption Day, another registers salary payments to them on the last day of the year. The nine musicians' names also appear in an Assumption Day clothing list from 1317 and in a payment for six months' salary at the end of December 1318.[35] By this time two of the trumpeters, Malfarsetto di Boninsegna and Neri Fava, had been with the group for two decades, and five of the others—Domenico di Voglia, Pericciuolo Salvucci, Nicola di Bencivenne, Ciertiere di Guido, and Marco di Ciereto—had been working with them for eight years. The presence of three brothers, Ciereto, Marco, and Vanni, all of them percussionists, attests both to families of musicians and to the importance ties of kinship when it came to obtaining a post with the group.

Only three musicians cited in 1318, Marco tamburello, the shawmist Ciertiere, and the trumpeter Domenico di Voglia, were among the eight who received a gratuity for playing at Assumption Day festivities in 1326. The others were the trumpeters Francesco, Romanello, Biagio, and Duccio, and the nakers player Francesco.[36] Except for the last named, replaced by Jacomo di Martino, all of these musicians appear in a salary payment from 1328, which also registers the return of a sixth trumpeter, Petruccio di Tino.[37] Domenico di Voglia completed eighteen years of service with the group that year. His name is absent, as are most of the others, in a salary payment from seven years later, dated 31 December 1335.[38] It includes three musicians mentioned in 1328—the nakers player Jacomo di Martino, and two trumpeters, Francesco Lucchese and Biagio di Neri, this last probably the son of the former trumpeter Neri Fava. The other four trumpeters were Simone di Manno, Simone di Cenno, Giovanni di Petruccio, and Bartolo di Giovanni. The shawmist was Feo di Giovanni della Ciaramella. The tabor player, Galgano di Marco, may have been the son of his predecessor in office, Marco di Ciereto.

Town musicians are mentioned in yet another version of the Sienese constitution from 1337. Apparently the last of its kind from medieval Siena, no other redactions of a complete set are known from before 1544, intervening additions, deletions, and cancellations having been made when necessary.[39] Previously cited records indicate that

34. Cellesi, "Documenti per la storia musicale di Firenze," vol. 34, p. 591, cites documents for the appointments, 1291–98, of "sei tubatores, un suonatore di cembali ed altro di cennamella al servizio del Comune." I translate cennamella and its variants, ceramella, ciaramella, etc., as shawm, though, as mentioned below, it may have been an older version of a kind of wind instrument that was a precursor of the pifferi or shawms introduced by German musicians.

35. Biccherna, vol. 132, fols. 104ᵛ, 144ᵛ.

36. Cecchini, "Palio e contrade," 314, 348.

37. Quoted by Cellesi, *Storia della più antica banda,* 18.

38. Biccherna, vol. 183, fol. 72ʳ.

39. Donatella Ciampoli, *Il Capitano del popolo a Siena nel primo Trecento* (Siena, 1984), 8. She says this is the longest set of statutes from republican Siena and that it is certain that it, too, was translated into Italian, though the translation has not yet been found.

the commune was employing six trumpeters by the late 1330s. This development was accorded official recognition in the new statutes, which now specified that each of them "was to have his own silver trumpet" and would be paid a monthly salary of L. 3.[40] The nakers, shawm, and tabor players were each to receive s. 50, or L. 2. 10, per month.

Many of the privileges and requirements mentioned in earlier statutes were restated, though somewhat more explicitly in a few instances. Musicians would henceforth have two lined suits of clothing and these were to display shields bearing the commune's arms. The cost of each uniform was not to exceed L. 15. Reports from 1334 show that the uniforms were of red material lined with fur, whereas in 1341 two colors, green and blue, were used, again with fur trimmings.[41]

Whether on horseback or on foot, the musicians were obliged to perform their necessary and customary duties at no extra salary. They were to wear their uniforms and bring their instruments on all such occasions. Non-compliance was punishable with fines of up to s. 40. Musicians were sworn to obey the podestà, the captain of the people, and the Concistoro in the conduct of their duties. As in the past, they were not allowed to leave the city except on official business, and even that required the podestà's permission. Similarly, they were forbidden to play, even with their own instruments, at weddings in or out of town, risking a fine of s. 10 every time they failed to observe this restriction.[42] They also had to pay the expenses of maintaining the horses they rode when they accompanied the podestà on official trips within and outside the city. Failure to observe this latter requirement would result in the loss of one month's salary. Musicians' appointments were now to be reconfirmed by the priors of the Concistoro pro tem, at whose pleasure they served.

Town criers are also mentioned in the 1337 statutes. These again fixed their number at three, one for each of the city's terzi.[43] They were, as in the past, appointed for one year at a time with no vacations allowed. Each of the town criers was required to keep a horse valued at Fl. 10 at his own expense. Each would receive annually a suit with

---

40. ASS, *Statuti del Comune di Siena, 26,* fols. 28ᵛ–29ʳ. Reports regarding uniforms and shields worn by trumpeters employed by the Florentine Signoria indicate that Sienese practices were not unique. Their shields, of enameled silver, bore the red Florentine lily and they also had silver trumpets to which pennants bearing the Republic's coat of arms were attached. See Marco Antonio Lastri, *L'Osservatore Fiorentino sugli edifizi della sua patria, Terza editione eseguita sopra quella del 1797, riordinata e compiuta dall'autore, coll'aggiunta di varie annotazioni del professore Giuseppe del Rosso . . . Tomo primo* (Florence, 1821), 124–26. More data regarding Florentine trumpeters appear below in chapters 9 and 10. Unlike their Sienese counterparts, the Florentines were obliged by a decree of the Signoria from 1361 to live in the same quarter, within the precincts of the appropriately named church of San Michele delle Trombe. This information is reported in Lastri, *L'Osservatore Fiorentino,* 124–26.

41. Cecchini, "Palio e contrade," 314–15. The same colors ("verde e sbiadato, cioè azzurro chiaro") are mentioned in expenditures for 1402 (ibid., 318).

42. But as before, this restriction probably applied only during wartime, even though official permission must have been necessary for them to do so.

43. "Eligantur per dominos quolibet anno, infra primos quindecim dies mensis ianuarii, tres boni bannitores dicti Comunis, pro quolibet terzerio unus . . . Teneatur etiam quilibet ipsorum bannire eques cum infolis zendadi rubei, habentibus tubas zendadi albi ex utraque parte capitis . . . super banchis que sunt prope discos tribunales" (ASS, *Statuti del Comune di Siena, 26,* fol. 29ʳ⁻ᵛ, Dist. I, CXIII).

lining of red cloth valued at L. 3. 10 the length. When making their announcements on horseback town criers were required to wear red silk berets and to display white silk pennants on their trumpets. A fine of s. 5 was prescribed for every time they failed to observe this requirement. With their trumpets embannered town criers were to ride through the city and its suburbs and make their announcements in the usual places. If remiss in their duties they would incur fines, and they were still forbidden to announce deaths. They would also be fined should they leave their horses at the Palace when they performed their duties on foot there—the platform near the court is specified as the place where they stood. It was further decreed that town criers and trumpeters could not hold both offices concurrently and that they and their horses were forbidden to ride in other people's entourages. The prohibition against holding two offices simultaneously suggests, as do other statements and situations in the past, that some town criers were experienced musicians, and this is probably the reason why no distinction was made in pay records between them and the trumpeters.

Besides confirming the increase in personnel mentioned in the statutes of 1337, records from the following decades indicate that a number of musicians beyond the nine stipulated in the document—six trumpeters, shawm, tabor, and nakers players—were gradually added to the group. (Town criers remained at the usual number.) No evidence indicates whether the employment of more musicians was sanctioned by later additions to the statutes unknown to us, whether it occurred on a casual basis as revenues and circumstances permitted, or whether some of the additional musicians were appointed as supernumeraries who were given clothing at state expense but no salary—as happened later in the century. Whatever the case, economic conditions were favorable enough that the government of the Nine not only sustained the expansion of forces called for in the statutes but also allowed them to grow beyond what was originally envisioned.

Ten musicians appear in a salary payment from 31 December 1338. Among them were seven trumpeters, a shawm player, and two players of nakers.[44] Four of the trumpeters, Simone di Manno, Simone di Cienno, Bartolo di Giovanni, and Francesco di Biagio, were recorded three years earlier, as were the shawm player Feo di Giovanni and the drummer Jacomo di Martino. New were three trumpeters, Domenico di Vanni, Domenico Petrucci, and Jacomo di Tomasso, and a second player of nakers, Gherardo di Duccio.[45] The names of the last two and Bartolo di Giovanni are lacking in a salary payment to nine musicians from 1340. This lists two new trumpeters, Francesco di Jacomo and the returning Biagio di Neri, and a new shawmist, Matteo di Palmero, in addition to the others mentioned two years earlier. Notable is the citation of Francesco di Biagio, formerly a trumpeter, as the second nakers player. These were surely the same

---

44. Biccherna, vol. 185, fol. 72ʳ.

45. A Sienese nakers player not employed at the Palace at this time is cited in a record from cathedral archives. This was Lorenzo di Giovanni, whose wife Andreuccia sold a house to the cathedral overseer Bendocci di Latino on 13 September 1339 (AOMS, vol. 1487, *Case e possessioni dell'Opera Sante Marie,* fol. 29ᵛ: "1339 [13 settembre]: Bendoccio di Latino operaio compra una casa nel popolo di S. Giovanni da Andreuccia, moglie di Lorenzo [di] Giovanni naccharaio, con approvazione del marito, a prezzo di 57 lire").

musicians recorded in cathedral accounts from February 1340 as receiving s. 10 for "playing the trumpets when the new foundations of the duomo were laid."[46]

Records from 1341 and 1342 name eleven musicians, including seven trumpeters, a shawm player, and three percussionists. The shawm player, Matteo di Palmero, and the two who played nakers, Jacomo di Martino and Francesco di Biagio, earned L. 2. 10 or s. 50 per month, the salary specified by the statutes. Cristoforo di Jacomo, the tabor player, received one third that amount. Six of the seven trumpeters, Simone di Manno, Simone di Cenno, Domenico di Vanni, Francesco di Jacomo, Domenico di Biagio, and Biagio di Neri, each received the stipulated monthly salary of L. 3. The exception, Magio di Petruccio, was paid only two lire a month, perhaps because he was a supernumerary. A few reports from much later times reveal that some musicians began service at half-salary or less, generally because they were young and lacked experience in performing with the group. This, as the present records indicate, was evidently the reason why the third percussionist, Jacomo di Martino's son Cristoforo, received less than L. 1 per month.

New clothing for Assumption Day and payments for six months' salary to eight trumpeters and five others who played shawm, nakers, and tabor are listed in accounts for 1343. The town criers were surely among this group, though they were not designated as such. Thirteen are named in records from 1344.[47] Nine of them were trumpeters: Simone di Manno, Simone di Cenno, Domenico di Vanni, Magio di Petruccio, Francesco di Jacomo, Agostino di Bindo, Giovanni di Azzolino, Paolino di Guccio, and Tommaso di Malfarsetto, son of the trumpeter mentioned earlier. The percussionists were Jacomo di Martino, his son, Cristoforo di Jacomo, and Francesco di Biagio, and the shawm player was Riccio. All but one of these musicians are on a list of employees paid on the last day of 1345, which shows that the trumpeter Agostino di Bindo was replaced by the former percussionist Cristoforo di Jacomo. Cristoforo, however, was still receiving less than L. 1 per month. There was now a new shawm player, Filippo di Ciuccio. For Assumption Day and Christmas 1347 twelve suits of clothing, shields, and pennants were provided for eight trumpeters (among whom were the town criers), the tabor and shawm players, and two players of nakers. At the end of the same year the Concistoro decreed that a silver trumpet, similar to those played by the others, was to be made and consigned by the following July to Francesco di Biagio, "a trumpeter of the commune of Siena" (see Doc. 8.1). Francesco was previously recorded as both a trumpeter and a nakers player.

The plague, which reached Siena in 1348, had little effect at first on the group's composition. Reports from 1349 through 1354 show that the musicians continued to receive their usual uniforms and salaries at the appointed times. No names appear in an entry from August 1349 recording L. 268 spent for twelve suits of clothing for the trumpeters, shawm player, and drummers and in another one from the following 31 December, which notes that nine of them received a total payment of L. 194. 9, their salaries of the past six months.

---

46. AOMS, vol. 175, *E&U, 1339–40*, fol. 103ᵛ.
47. Many of the Assumption Day lists are published in Cecchini, "Palio e contrade," 315–17.

Another indication of the musicians' versatility comes from 27 December 1347, when the Concistoro appointed two of them, Jacomo di Martino and Magio di Petruccio, to play the nakers, a third, Cristoforo di Jacomo, to play the tabor, and a fourth, Riccio, to play the shawm for the following six months (see Doc. 8.2). Since salaries and terms went unmentioned and all concerned were already Palace employees, the action obviously confirmed ongoing appointments. Exceptionally, two musicians were named to posts they had not previously filled. Magio di Petruccio, hitherto known only as a trumpeter, was now designated a player of nakers, and Cristoforo di Jacomo, a former player of the nakers who had since joined the trumpeters' ranks, was named a tabor player.

Clearly, each of these musicians played several instruments and could take on different duties as the situation required. But all four were probably listed together here because they constituted a smaller band within the larger group. Two of them, shawm and tabor, could form a duo, complete in its own right, capable of providing suitable music for all kinds of social occasions. By adding one (or more) trumpeters, the ensemble became a kind of "alta" or "loud" band of the type derived from Near Eastern models found throughout Europe at the time. In these ensembles the melodic, or more active upper part, was played by the flexible double-reeded shawm, the lower, or sustained part, which doubtless consisted of one or two notes in the manner of a drone, by the trumpet, while the percussionist supplied appropriate rhythmic patterns. This kind of ensemble was already in existence in Siena by 1251, when a shawm–trumpet duo was first mentioned. As will be shown, it was eventually succeeded by another kind of "loud" band, which also reflected then current European practices. For now, suffice it to note the apparent ease with which some musicians moved from one instrument to another, a talent that facilitated the formation of this smaller ensemble, not otherwise recorded among the Palace musicians.

The revolution that overthrew the regime of the Nine in March of 1355 caused the loss, at least for that year, of many state documents, among them volumes that contained records regarding the town trumpeters. But evidently the new government of the Twelve not only continued to employ musicians but also sought to maintain the same number reached in the recent past. A deliberation from 19 December 1356 recounts how, in accordance with the town's statutes, the Twelve Lords "had appointed six trumpeters" and that there were others who wished to serve but could not be paid because the statutes prescribed salaries for only six of them.[48] Because the government thought it "useful and honorable for the commune to promote, not reduce" the number of trumpeters—"competent ones tending to be very rare"—it appointed four supernumeraries to serve the commune "as trumpeters" without salary. They were Jacomo Palmerini called Cuccioletta, Niccolò d'Andrea, Giovanni di Meio, and Bartolo di Nicoluccio. In compensation, the supernumeraries were provided twice a year with suits of clothing each worth L. 20, just like the tenured trumpeters. Jacomo was gone by the following year, when on 11 December 1357 the government authorized suits of clothing for the three others.

---

48. ASS, Consiglio Generale, vol. 158, fol. 50, quoted by Cellesi, *Storia della più antica banda,* 65.

Records from 1356 and 1357 signal the resumption of the August festivities and with them disbursements for new uniforms for the musicians. In August 1357 sixteen pennants were ordered for the town criers, trumpeters, shawm player, and percussionists. The supernumeraries, mentioned earlier, were among the group. For Christmas that year the twelve regularly salaried musicians, including six trumpeters, three town criers, one shawmist, one drummer, and another trumpeter, each received a suit of clothing valued at L. 20. A payment in the amount of L. 145. 16 for six months' service, also from December 1357, lists the nine regularly salaried musicians by name. New suits of clothing were approved for fourteen musicians and town criers on Assumption Day 1361. Salaries were disbursed to twelve musicians in November 1364 and the same number received new uniforms on September 1365. The different functions performed by the musicians are reflected in these records, which sometimes name trumpeters as town criers or as drummer and drummers as shawm players.

Annual Performances before the Assumption Day Festivities

From the end of the 1350s come the earliest payments to the trumpeters from the cathedral Opera for performances that heralded the oncoming feast of the Assumption. The performances, in the Campo and in the area in front of the cathedral, were part of a series of deftly orchestrated events that culminated in the sumptuous dinners, thrilling spectacles, and civic and religious ceremonies on the eve of the feast day and the day itself. Palace records, cited below, indicate that the trumpeters' performances were already well established by this time, as does a cathedral payment from August 1359. This latter notes s. 20 given to the trumpeter Biagio and his companions "as is customary for their work when they come and play their trumpets for fifteen days before the feast."[49] These performances doubtless entailed more than fanfares by trumpeters and probably featured the "loud" band playing pieces from its repertory. The performances, of course, served a dual purpose. They entertained townspeople and visitors while alerting them to the significance of the impending festivities, whose lustre, of course, was considerably enhanced by the events leading up to them. The trumpeters' performances on these occasions are also noteworthy within the wider context of similar events in other European cities, for they are among the earliest recorded anywhere on the continent.[50]

Expenses for Assumption Day festivities show little change through 1366, when a revolution swept out the government of the Twelve. Though documents are lacking for that year, records from shortly afterwards indicate that the established order returned by the early 1370s. Salary payments from August and October 1373 name eight musicians, including five trumpeters, a shawm player, and two percussionists, each of whom

---

49. "1359: A Biagio trombatore e compagni vinti soldi chome usanza per loro fadigha quando venghono a trombare XV dì inanzi la festa" (AOMS, vol. 187, E&U, 1359–60, fol. 42ʳ). An entry in an account from August 1363 again records s. 20 paid to the trumpeters (vol. 191, E&U, 1374–75, fol. 68ʳ).

50. For the earliest public concerts in Bruges in the 1480s, see Strohm, *Music in Late Medieval Bruges*, 85; also Polk, *German Instrumental Music of the Late Middle Ages*, 8.

received L. 3 per month.[51] Three of the trumpeters—Ambrogio di Duccio, Luca di Pietro, and Domenico di Michele—and the drummer Giovanni di Domenico had worked together since 1357, and a fourth trumpeter, Bartolo di Nicoluccio, was associated with them since 1365. The shawmist, Cecco di Michele, was listed since 1364. New were the trumpeter Biagio di Meuccio and the nakers player Pietro di Nanni.

These eight musicians appear in similar records from a year later, 1374, though Giovanni di Domenico is now referred to as a shawm player. A payment to Biagio from March 1375 reveals that by then the trumpeters were also performing at religious services held in the outside chapel in front of the Palace, later called the Cappella del Campo. Biagio, as mentioned, was also named in an earlier payment to the trumpeters from the cathedral Opera and he probably acted as leader of the group. On this occasion the musicians received s. 20 for having played on the feast of the Annunciation, "St. Mary of March," as it is called in the document.[52] No mention is made of their duties, but it is likely that they played when an image of the Madonna was unveiled or at the Elevation at Mass, as they were to do in the following century.

Pietro di Nanni's name is lacking in a government decree dated 7 August 1376 authorizing payment for the months of July and August to the others. The remaining seven musicians were present through the end of December 1377. They were also present a year later at Christmas 1378, when they received suits of clothing, along with the town criers and a new trumpeter called Niccolò di Vieri. A decree from 11 August 1379 mentions eight tenured musicians and says that henceforth the six trumpeters, the shawm player, and the drummer were each to have two new uniforms every year but that they would not receive a salary for the months in which the clothing was issued.[53] A seventh trumpeter, the supernumerary, was also to receive two uniforms annually, but no salary. Only six musicians, however, including the four trumpeters, Domenico di Michele, Luca di Pietro, Giovanni di Azzolino, Bartolo di Nicoluccio, the nakers player Giovanni di Viva, and the shawmist Cecco di Michele, are recorded as having been paid their usual monthly stipends for January and February 1381.

There are other indications besides this decree that the state treasury was experiencing difficulty in meeting its obligations. In early August 1381 the Concistoro approved payment of salaries for the months of July and August and the usual Assumption Day clothing and pennants for only three musicians, the trumpeters Bartolo di Nicoluccio and Niccolò di Vieri and the nakers player Giovanni (Nanni) di Domenico (see Doc. 8.3). Apparently, the prohibition against town criers serving simultaneously as trumpeters was now rescinded, for documents from the following years show that one person could and did indeed fill both posts.

---

51. Named with them at the time as a sixth trumpeter was Niccolò d'Andrea, trombetino, who may have been one of the supernumeraries mentioned in 1356, though "trombetino" suggests a younger musician.

52. "A Biagio tronbatore s. vinti, ricievendo per sé e per li chompagni perché feciero onore di trombare alla capella per Santa Maria di Marzo [1375], L. 1" (AOMS, vol. 204, *E&U della Cappella del Campo, 1374–75,* fol. 68ʳ).

53. ASS, Concistoro, vol. 98, fol. 38ᵛ.

Dismissal of the "Loud" Band

It was around this time, between 1382 and 1384, that the shawm and tabor players were dismissed from Palace service. Possibly another result of the need to economize, chang- ing tastes, and a desire to have a band of pifferi—players of the new shawms from Germany recently come into vogue—combined to bring about this turn of events. A band of pifferi had recently been established in Florence and some reports show that they were now also being employed by various Sienese officials.[54] It was clearly only a matter of time before the Concistoro did the same. The pifferi played primarily for entertainment at meals and other social occasions. These functions at the Palace had hitherto been entrusted to the shawm and tabor players and, presumably, to a trumpeter or two. Now the decision was to dispense with the traditional "loud" band. Just as none of the previous documents explain how the duties of the musicians who played in it differed from those of the trumpeters, so do none of the present ones give reasons for their dismissal. For the next few decades shawmists would occasionally be men- tioned among visiting musicians, but the only percussionists listed on Palace rolls would be players of nakers, of whom henceforth there would always be at least one, and at times two.

TRUMPETERS AND TOWN CRIERS THROUGH THE END OF THE CENTURY

In 1385 another revolution overthrew the government of the Fifteen and installed that of the Ten. Normalcy was quickly restored, however, and the town musicians partici- pated in Assumption Day festivities that year as well as in 1386 and 1387. A record from 11 August 1388 lists seven musicians as recipients of new uniforms. New were the trumpeter Jacomo di Corso and a second nakers player, Gabriello di Bencivenni. Returning after an absence of many years was another trumpeter, Balduccio di Angelo, recorded years earlier among the town criers. The remaining trumpeters were all sea- soned musicians, Domenico di Michele, Bartolo di Niccoluccio, and Biagio di Meuc- cio. The principal percussionist was the venerable Giovanni di Domenico. Documents from later in the year list the same musicians except for the second drummer Gabriello di Bencivenni, replaced by another nakers player, Francio di Viva. Francio must have been a brother of the percussionist Giovanni di Viva, mentioned in 1381.

Two new appointments were made in the summer of 1390, though one of the trumpeters cited on 6 July, Jacopo di Leonardo da Colle, apparently never took up his post. Antonio di Ciuccio da Chianciano, mentioned four days later, subsequently served as a trumpeter and town crier. Records from the following month and a Christmas clothing list for the same year name eight musicians: Biagio di Meuccio, Balduccio di Angelo, Domenico di Michele (first mentioned in 1357), Bartolo di Niccoluccio, An- tonio di Ciuccio, Jacomo di Corso, and the drummers Francio di Viva and Giovanni

---

54. Giuseppe Zippel, *I suonatori della Signoria di Firenze* (Trent, 1892), 14, reproduces a document from 22 October 1386 recording the establishment of a group of pifferi consisting of bombard, cor- netta, and cornamusa. See also chapter 11 below.

di Domenico (also cited for the first time in 1357). The same trumpeters, drummers, and town criers appear in an account from December 1392. Seven of them were paid at the rate of Fl. 2 every two months, while Antonio di Ciuccio da Chianciano received an extra florin for the same amount of time.

All of these musicians are in the accounts from 1395, except for Balduccio d'Angelo, replaced by Bertino di Bartolo da Pistoia. Antonio di Ciuccio was again the highest paid musician. Six trumpeters, all but one of them described as doubling as town criers, and the drummer are mentioned in records from 1399. Several changes in personnel had occurred in the intervening years. Those now listed were Antonio di Ciuccio, Jacomo di Corso, Chimenti di Biagio, Matteo di Giovanni da San Gimignano, Giovanni di Antonio da Bologna, and Betto di Giovanni da Prato. The lone nakers player was Francio di Viva.[55] A chronological list of Sienese trumpeters to 1399 appears in Table 8.1.

Traveling to distant places at the behest of the government continued to form part of the musicians' duties throughout the fourteenth century. A record from October 1341, to cite one example from mid-century, registers a payment to two trumpeters for having served abroad with the Florentine army on behalf of the commune of Siena.[56] Later on, a report dated 18 August 1391 says that two trumpeters, Antonio di Ciuccio da Chianciano and Bertino di Bartolo da Pistoia, were delegated to accompany the Sienese envoys sent to confer with Duke Gian Galeazzo Visconti of Milan, otherwise known as the Conte di Virtù (see Doc. 8.4). Though the musicians were not paid a salary while they were away, each received per diem expenses of Fl. 1, the same amount paid to the Sienese envoys. Another report from 1395 states that two trumpeters, Antonio di Ciuccio and Bertino di Bartolo, and the drummer Francio di Viva accompanied Sienese envoys to yet another conference with the Conte di Virtù and that on their return they had to turn in "the flags and pennants of the said trumpets and kettledrums, which bear the arms of the commune and of the count."[57] The Conte di Virtù was by now the virtual ruler of Siena, thanks to a rash invitation from the faction then in power to assume control of the government. He maintained his sway over Siena until his unexpected early death in 1402.

DOCUMENTS

Doc. 8.1. A silver trumpet is ordered to be made for Francesco di Biagio, 30 December 1347. ASS, Concistoro, vol. 2, fol. 89ᵛ

Supradicti domini Novem in consistorio existentes, audito et intellecto a Francischo Blaxii tubatore Comunis Senarum, qualiter ipse Franciscus esset paratus, quando sibi indutieret sive terminum darent, velle facere tubam de argento, secundum quod habent aliqui eorum. Super quibus

---

55. Several of these payments are cited by Cellesi, *Storia della più antica banda,* 22; she also cites Biccherna, vol. 285, fol. 52ʳ, for an earlier payment from June to Betto di Giovanni da Prato.

56. ASS, Biccherna, vol. 208, 115ᵛ, dated 10 October 1341, calling them tubatori.

57. "dien dare alla loro tornata le bendiere e penoni di dette tronbe e nacchare, nelle quali sono l'arme del Comune e del Signore misser lo Conte" (ASS, Concistoro, vol. 2493, fol. 25ʳ). ASS, Biccherna, vol. 282, fol. 41ʳ, notes that Antonio di Ciuccio da Chianciano and Bertino di Bartolo da Pistoia received L. 36 for their salary of thirty-six days when "they went to the Duke."

facta proposita per prudentem virum Antonium Symonis, priorem dictorum dominorum No-vem . . . in plenam concordiam voluerunt et firmaverunt quod dictus Francischus habeat indutias ad faciendum fieri dictam tubam de argento usque ad Kalendas Iulii proxime venturi.

Doc. 8.2. Appointment of four town musicians, 27 December 1347. Ibid., fol. 88^v

[margin: electio naccharariorum, tamburelli et ciaramelle] Item predicti domini Novem in con-sistorio existentes more solito convocati, intendentes ad electionem duorum naccharariorum et unius tamburelli et unius ciaramelli pro sex mensibus incepturis in Kalendis Ianuarii proxime venturi . . . elegerunt et nominaverunt infrascripti . . . Iacobus Martini, Magius Petrucii, nac-chararii, Cristofanus Iacobi, tamburellus, et Riccius, ciaramella.

Doc. 8.3. Payments to musicians, 6 August 1381. Ibid., vol. 109, fol. 48^v

Nos defensores populi civitatis Senarum significamus vobis camerario et IIII provisionibus Bi-cherne Comunis Senarum quod detis et solvatis de pecunia Comunis Senarum infrascriptis banito-ribus et tubatoribus et nacharino Comunis Senarum salarium eis et cuilibet eorum debitum a Comunis Senarum in duobus mensibus, videlicte Iuliis preteriti de proximo et Augusti presentis . . . Item detis et solvatis et tradatur eisdem robbas eis et cuilibet eorum debitas a Comuni Se-narum et dari consuetas, ac etiam pennones pro tubis et narcharis in et pro festo Sancte Marie Virginis mensis Augusti predicti . . . Bartalus Niccoluccii, Nicholaus Verii tubatores, Nannes Dominci, naracharinus.

Doc. 8.4. Two trumpeters and a drummer are deputed to accompany Sienese envoys to Milan, 18 August 1391. Ibid., vol. 162, fols. 19^v–20^r

Preterea solemniter decreverunt quod Antonius Ciucii de Clanciano et Berthinus Bartholi de Pistorio, tubatores Comunes Senarum, ituri cum ambaxiatoribus ad dominum Comitem Vir-tutum etc. habeant unum florenum per diem, secundum modum et formam et prout et sicut habent oratores etc., dum tamen eo tempore nullum aliud salarium recipiant a Comuni Senarum.

TABLE 8.1. Chronological list of Sienese trumpeters, town criers, and drummers, 1230–1399

Names appear only sporadically in the earliest years. Often there is no clear distinction between trumpeters and town criers, the same person occasionally being listed as both.

A. Trumpeters and town criers

	1230	1246–47	1249	1250	1251	1252	1253	1254	1255	1257	1259
Barzalomeo da Pisa	x										
Bencivenne	x										
Rusignolo	x										
Andrea	x										
Altovese Arnolfini		x	x	x	x						
Lottaringo	x										
Ventura Tomasini	x	x	x	x	x	x	x	x	x		
Caprone di Cristoforo		x	x	x	x	x	x	x	x	x	x
Guido Rosso		x	x	x	x	x	x	x	x	x	
Maffeo Guerrieri		x	x	x	x	x	x	x	x	x	x
Lando da Faenza			x								
Compare di Guido[a]											
Caroso					x	x	x				
Bonavita						x					
Lombardino						x					
Riccio di Palude							x	x	x	x	
Manente							x	x	x	x	
Giovanni							x	x	x	x	
Piero							x				
Gabardino									x	x	
Pagno di Marino											x

	1277	1291	1298	1310	1316–18	1326	1328	1335	1338	1339	1340	1341–42
Conte	x											
Sufilello	x											
Feduccio	x											
Ghezzo Boninsegna	x	x	x									
Ildino (shawm)	x											
Neri Fava		x	x	x	x							
Vanni Grasso		x	x	x								
Malfarsetto Boninsegna			x	x	x							
Domenico di Voglia				x	x	x	x					
Periccuiolo Salvucci				x	x							
Nicola di Bencivenne				x	x							
Ciertiere di Guido (shawm)				x	x	x	x					
Petruccio di Tino					x		x					
Romanello						x	x					
Biagio di Neri						x	x	x				x
Duccio						x	x					
Francesco di Biagio★						x	x	x	x	x		
Simone di Manno								x	x	x	x	x
Simone di Cenno								x	x	x	x	x
Giovanni di Petruccio								x				
Bartolo di Giovanni								x	x			
Feo di Giovanni (shawm)								x	x	x	x	
Domenico di Vanni									x	x	x	x
Domenico di Petruccio									x	x	x	
Jacomo di Tomasso									x			
Francesco di Jacomo											x	x
Matteo di Palmero (shawm)											x	x
Domenico di Biagio												x
Magio di Petruccio★												x

TABLE 8.1 *continued*

	1343	1344	1345	1347	1356	1357	1358–61	1362	1363	1364	1365
Biagio di Neri	x										
Francesco di Biagio				x							
Simone di Manno			x			x					
Simone di Cenno		x	x								
Domenico di Vanni		x	x								
Francesco di Jacomo		x	x								
Matteo di Palmero		x	x								
Magio di Petruccio		x	x								
Agostino di Bindo		x									
Giovanni di Azzolino detto Sodo		x	x			x	x	x	x	x	x
Riccio (shawm)		x		x							
Paolo di Guccio		x	x								
Tommaso di Malfarsetto[b]		x	x								
Filippo di Ciuccio (shawm)			x								
Cristoforo di Jacomo★			x								
Matteo di Cenno (shawm)			x								
Jacomo Palmerini detto Cuccioletta					x						
Niccolò d'Andrea					x	x					
Giovanni di Meio					x	x					
Bartolo di Nicoluccio					x	x					
Biagio di Follo detto Mugnaio						x	x	x	x	x	x
Ceccarello di Birretta (shawm)						x	x	x			
Luca di Pietro						x	x	x	x	x	x
Ambrogio di Duccio						x	x	x	x	x	x
Domenico di Michele detto Grillo						x	x	x	x	x	x
Benedetto di Meuccio						x					
Jacomo di Tomasso								x			
Cecco di Michele (shawm)										x	x
Balduccio di Angelo										x	x
Domenico di Nanni										x	
Giovanni detto Mangia										x	x
Niccolao										x	x

	1372	1373	1374	1375–77	1378	1379	1380	1381	1388	1390	1391	1392–94	1395	1396–98	1399
Giovanni di Azzolino															
Niccolò d'Andrea		x													
Bartolo di Niccoluccio			x	x	x	x	x	x	x	x	x	x	x		
Luca di Pietro		x	x	x	x	x	x	x							
Ambrogio di Duccio	x	x	x	x	x	x	x								
Domenico di Michele	x	x	x	x	x	x	x	x	x	x	x	x	x		
Cecco di Michele	x	x	x	x	x	x	x	x							
Balduccio di Angelo									x	x	x	x			
Biagio di Meuccio			x	x	x	x			x	x	x	x	x		
Giovanni di Domenico (shawm)*			x												
Niccolò di Vieri					x			x							
Jacomo di Corso									x	x	x	x	x		x
Antonio di Ciuccio da Chianciano										x	x	x	x		x
Bertino di Bartolo da Pistoia										x	x	x	x	x	x
Chimenti di Biagio											x		x		x
Matteo di Giovanni da San Gimignano															x
Giovanni di Antonio da Bologna															x
Betto di Giovanni da Prato															x

TABLE 8.1 *continued*

B. DRUMMERS

	1230	1310	1316–18	1326	1328	1335	1338	1339	1340	1341–44	1345	1347	1357–63	1364	1365	1373–74	1375–80	1381	1388
Donusdeo	x																		
Leonardo da Pisa	x																		
Marco di Ciereto[c]		x	x	x	x														
Ciereto di Ciereto[d]		x	x																
Vanni di Ciereto[e]			x																
Francesco di Biagio Luchese[†]				x															
Jacomo di Martino					x	x	x	x	x	x	x								
Galgano di Marco[f]						x			x	x	x	x							
Gherardo di Duccio							x												
Lorenzo di Giovanni								x											
Cristoforo di Jacomo[†]										x		x							
Magio di Petruccio[†]												x							
Giovanni di Domenico[†]													x						
Paoluccio di Duccio[g]													x		x	x	x	x	x
Jacomo Nardi[h]														x					
Simone[†]														x	x				
Pietro di Nanni																x			
Giovanni di Viva[i]																		x	
Gabriello di Bencivenni																			x
Francio di Viva[j]																			x

	1390–95	1399
Giovanni di Domenico	x	
Francio di Viva	x	x

*also a drummer
†also a trumpeter or shawm player
[a] son of Guido Rosso
[b] probably son of Malfarsetto Boninsegna
[c] brother of Ciereto and Vanni
[d] brother of Marco and Vanni
[e] brother of Marco and Ciereto
[f] possibly son of Marco di Ciereto
[g] in 1362
[h] shawm in 1374
[i] brother of Francio
[j] brother of Giovanni

Chapter Nine

POMP, CIRCUMSTANCE, AND SECURITY: THE TRUMPETERS' CORPS AS AN ONGOING INSTITUTION IN THE FIFTEENTH CENTURY

A T THE TURN OF THE FIFTEENTH CENTURY the trumpeters' corps was a flourishing group, comprised, as in the past, of sophisticated and experienced musicians. Trumpeters still doubled as town criers, though (as before) only rarely were distinctions made between those who held the two posts, another indication that most if not all of the banditori had some musical skills. Henceforth, the corps enjoyed great stability, for changes in personnel were far less frequent than in the previous century. Group stability and longevity of individual service were inextricably bound and together furnish the first of four concurrent and enduring themes that appear with remarkable consistency throughout the history of the fifteenth-century trombetti. Each of these themes had noteworthy antecedents in the previous century and their origins clearly lay in practices already evident. But only in the fifteenth century did they assume their typical Sienese characteristics.

Longevity of service depended not only upon personal choices made by musicians themselves. Other factors were important, such as the willingness of one ruling faction after another to offer musicians the opportunity for uninterrupted employment and the continuing demand for the services of highly qualified personnel. Still, some individual employment records are remarkable under any circumstances. Among them are those of several trumpeters who served for forty years or more, notably Riccio d'Antonio (53 years, 1402–55), Chimenti di Biagio (48 years, 1399–1447, though absent 1436–38), Tomè di Meio (48 years, 1407–55), the blind Niccolò Turini (48 years, 1454–1502), Giovanni called El Moro (42 years, 1468–1510), Giovanni di Martino (47 years, 1436–83). Less exceptional, though no less notable, were careers of men such as Angelo called Imperadore (35 years of service, 1407–42), Antonio di Ciuccio (29 years, 1390–1419), Santi di Riccarduccio (29 years, 1437–66), and Giovanni da Iesi (28 years, 1450–78).

Admittedly, the careers of these musicians offer examples of a phenomenon not encountered at the cathedral until the close of the sixteenth century, though they seem less remarkable when compared with other musicians employed at the Palace. Several trumpeters and drummers, for example, were tenured more than twenty years and many others stayed for a decade or longer. Musicians who remained with the group for only a few years were a conspicuous minority. Perhaps their brief periods of tenure, far removed from the norm, resulted from extraordinary circumstances. Whatever the hazards of the profession—and there were some, considering the military operations in which the musicians were sometimes involved—a trumpeter's lot was apparently a happy one in fifteenth-century Siena.

The second theme to emerge from a survey of the fifteenth-century personnel is the increasing importance of family relationships in gaining admission to the trumpeters' corp. Occasionally observed in earlier times, ties of kinship now determined the group's formation, perhaps in even more ways than are immediately apparent. Besides illustrating how closely patterns of employment among the trumpeters resemble those in other medieval professions, ties of kinship also point to a mode of private musical education in Siena about which precious little is known. It warrants a momentary digression.

No guild in Siena encouraged and regulated a course of apprenticeship for those who sought to become professional trumpeters—or instrumentalists of any kind, for that matter. But a comparable system, informal and unregulated to be sure, was nevertheless in place, if we may judge from Palace records, which show fathers, sons, brothers, uncles, nephews, and even cousins employed together or succeeding each other to coveted government positions. (A similar situation occurred with players of wind instruments a century later. Remarks here are equally valid for those musicians.) Unlike clerical singers and others trained in written polyphony at cathedral and convent schools, professional instrumental musicians at this time—in Siena, as in many other places—generally learned their art through long years of practice under the tutelage of a family member, a neighbor, or a friend.[1] Instruction began early, like that of the boys in ecclesiastical schools. Records from Siena and elsewhere indicate that a student often learned to play several instruments in addition to his principal one. In earlier times an instrumentalist's training may not have included the fundamentals of musical theory and notation, but it assuredly obliged him to commit to memory fanfares, simple tunes, improvisatory patterns, and other tricks of the trade as he acquired the skill and dexterity on the instrument necessary to use them. The student's progress, in other words, depended upon his having "a good ear," the ability, that is, to imitate the syntax and grammar he heard his teacher and others use, and on his own capacity to produce "a good sound." This latter might reasonably be compared to an ability to speak fluently in the then current pronunciation.[2]

Parental or familial guidance provided a student with even more than the requisite training and coaching, for at the appropriate time his teacher assisted his entrance into the professional ranks. Siena, like other metropolitan centers, though perhaps not to the same extent as larger cities like Florence, Milan, and Venice, offered a number of

---

1. Instruments were expensive and often beyond the reach of most people who might have wished to make professional musicians of their children. This is another reason why kinship was such an important factor in determining who would take up a musical profession requiring the use of instruments. While it is clear that Palace employees owned their own instruments (as revealed by the earlier Constitutions), the instruments they used for their official duties were owned by the state, as will be mentioned below.

The careers of several trumpeters from the town of Chianciano, cited in this chapter, illustrate how this system worked. Though some of them were bound by ties of kinship, others were not. Possibly the others trained with friends or neighbors, who may have helped them obtain posts in Siena.

2. Learning to play brass and percussion instruments was tantamount to becoming a professional musician, unlike the strings, winds, keyboard instruments, and lutes that amateurs could play for their own amusement or in more private social situations. As illustrated in chapter 13, during the later fifteenth century and the following one Siena had teachers of dance, of voice, and of other instruments who catered to the needs of various classes.

possibilities for musicians. In addition to the Concistoro, officials such as the captain of the people and the podestà could offer employment, as could high-ranking prelates and private individuals. Nobody of any consequence, it seems, ventured out in public unless his presence was announced by one or more trumpeters. And if he had none of his own, musicians could always be hired when needed, as the restrictions placed on Palace musicians show. There were assuredly opportunities for employment in Siena, and this was probably true also in smaller towns of the Sienese dominion. Indeed, a number of Palace musicians from the same family coming from such towns demonstrates that familial systems of training existed in those places as well. Not enough data are available to indicate whether all who trained to become professional musicians actually found full-time employment.[3] Records from the 1450s onwards suggest more than enough aspirants for the limited number of trumpeters' posts in government service. By the end of the fifteenth century the majority of those who entered Palace service were relatives of musicians already employed there, a situation that in itself not only testifies to the importance of ties of kinship but also to the effectiveness of the familial system of instruction just described.

The third theme, local tradition, follows logically from links of kinship. Whereas most players of wind instruments in Sienese service during the fifteenth century were foreigners—as the wind band was becoming established—trumpet players were usually from Siena and its dominion, or at the very least, of Italian origin. Records from other Italian municipalities and courts reveal a similar preference for local or domestic talent in their trumpet ensembles. In Florence, where from 1390 onwards two groups of trumpeters were supported by the city, the rosters reveal few, if any, non-Florentine or non-Tuscan names throughout the fifteenth century, as opposed to the wind band, which more often than not comprised primarily Germans.[4] Florentine pay registers from the 1460s and 1470s, in fact, generally list only Italian musicians among the two groups of trumpeters.[5] Though less well documented, a similar situation prevailed in

3. Florentine and Sienese trumpeters, as noted in passing on a number of occasions, often found employment in other parts of Italy.

4. Polk, "Civic Patronage and Instrumental Ensembles in Renaissance Florence," 53. He distinguishes the trombetti, a group of five or six players, who functioned primarily in the same way as their Sienese counterparts, and a group of ten or more trombadori, who were paid less than the others and whose function, though not so clear, "was more often ritualistic rather than musical." (I suspect that the trombadori functioned primarily as town criers, though this does not preclude their being competent trumpeters.) See ibid., 59, for corroboration of the different national origins of the wind players.

Zippel, *I suonatori della Signoria di Firenze,* 16, cites a provision from 1396 in which the number of trumpeters was fixed at five, each with a monthly salary of Fl. 3, the same paid to members of the wind band. He says that "rarely are the names of foreigners found among them." He also notes that Florentine trombetti, after having served at various other Italian courts, where they acquired no small amount of fame, often requested appointments in Florence, where they hoped to spend their declining years (pp. 16–17).

5. ASF, Camera del Comune, Notaio di Camera, *E&U,* vol. 10, fol. 71ʳ, dated 5 May 1462; *E&U,* vol.123, fol. 101ʳ, dated 3 September 1463; *E&U,* vol. 15, dated 7 November 1464; *E&U,* vol. 33, fol. 76ᵛ, dated 27 April 1475.

an another Tuscan city, Lucca. Six trumpeters were employed there in 1377, and by 1496 there were ten.[6] For smaller groups such as the one employed in Bologna, with four trumpeters in 1442—down from a previous high of eight trumpeters and town criers recorded between 1330 and 1399—the evidence overwhelmingly favors Italian, if not always local, musicians.[7]

In Naples the Aragonese kings, as befitted their origins, favored trumpeters of Spanish origin, at least in the dynasty's early years. Three Spaniards were registered at King Alfonso's court in 1437; they were also there in 1441, along with three others, including one or two Neapolitans, or other Italians.[8] The ratio was apparently reversed by the end of the century, for a list from May 1491 names only one Spaniard among the seven, most of whom were from the Neapolitan kingdom.[9] In Ferrara, where under Duke Ercole I the number of trumpeters employed by the court grew from six in 1471 to twelve by 1484, they were, in Lewis Lockwood's words, "mainly or exclusively Italian, with a preponderance of Tuscans."[10]

In Milan, during the reign of the Sforzas in the second half of the fifteenth century, two groups of trumpeters were employed, one by the town, the other by the court. The town traditionally had six trumpeters, a number maintained throughout the following century, and they were all Italians.[11] The court was, of course, more cosmopolitan in its musical aspirations, but even there, though singers and players of wind and string instruments might be foreign, the trumpeters were generally Italian. Among Duke Francesco Sforza's twelve trumpeters in 1450 were eleven Italians, from such diverse places as Siena, Cremona, Soncino, and Milan itself; the sole exception was a German.[12] In the following years the number increased to twenty, and a list of court trumpeters from 1466–67 names several of the same musicians cited in 1450, as well as others from Italian cities such as Correggio, Florence, Verona, and Imola, but no ultramontanes.[13] The same is true of the court trumpeters in 1470.[14] Also telling in this respect are the

---

6. Nerici, *Storia della musica in Lucca*, 183, 185. Though Nerici does not furnish lists of names, those few he gives in nn. 12–25, p. 202, indicate that the trumpeters were all Italian and that the wind players were from Germany or other Italian cities.

7. Osvaldo Gambassi, "Origine, statuti e ordinamenti del Concerto Palatino della Signoria di Bologna, 1250–1600," *Nuova rivista musicale italiana* 18 (1984): 266–67. See also id., *Il Concerto Palatino della Signoria di Bologna: Cinque secoli di vita musicali a corte (1250–1797)* (Florence, 1989), 62, which cites names of the five trumpeters employed in 1439, all of them Italians.

8. Atlas, *Music at the Aragonese Court of Naples*, 100.

9. Ibid.

10. Lockwood, *Music in Renaissance Ferrara*, 140.

11. Barblan, "Vita musicale alla corte sforzesca," 788. He cites Galvano Fiamma (ca. 1283–ca. 1344), who reports that the commune of Milan employed "sex tybicinus sive trumbatores" who were capable of making a "clangor terribilis in nulla alia civitate auditus similis." The Visconti dukes, predecessors of the Sforza, also maintained trumpeters. Joining the Visconti group in 1389 was an Italian, Bertolino da Forlì, who subsequently performed with seven others in 1415. The six town trumpeters' posts were confirmed by the first Sforza duke, Francesco, in March 1450; their names betray their Italian origins (p. 789).

12. Ibid., 789, quoting Motta, "Musici alla corte degli Sforza," 36.

13. Barblan, "Vita musicale," 789–90.

14. Ibid., 795.

origins of the trumpeters, from Milan and elsewhere, who played at the wedding of Galeazzo Maria Sforza and Bona of Savoy. All but one of these musicians, in the service of various princes such as the Duke of Mantua and the Count of Urbino, were Italians.[15]

The persistence of local tradition among all these groups must mean that Italian trumpeters were as technically proficient and as musically advanced as their northern colleagues. Innovations in instrumental construction and design as well as improvements in playing techniques were evidently known and practiced by them as well. Had they not been, foreigners would have been brought in instead, as happened with the German players of wind instruments, who, as will be noted below, became the rage in fifteenth-century Italy, much like the Franco-Flemish singers we have already met at the cathedral. Indeed, fifteenth-century Italian trumpeters made such great strides in their art that by the turn of the sixteenth century, at least, there is reason to believe that the reverse situation obtained. That is, as Peter Downey has pointed out, it was Italian trumpeters who were much sought after by various European courts, a situation that, as will be mentioned below, was still current in the later sixteenth century, particularly in northern Germany and Denmark.[16]

The fourth theme—perhaps not surprising in view of the others—was the presence, noted throughout the fifteenth century, of small numbers of musicians who, grouping and regrouping as changes in personnel occurred, formed nuclei or "core groups" within the larger ensemble. Core groups were not unknown in the previous century—suffice it to recall the four musicians recorded from 1355 through 1365, some of whom subsequently formed part of a group of five employed together from 1365 through 1378. But the plague and perhaps other reasons unknown to us militated against an uninterrupted succession of core groups. Thus they cannot be said to have become characteristic of the trombetti until the early fifteenth century. In general the core groups comprised slightly more than half of the total personnel at any one time. While it was not unusual for a core group to be employed for five years or more, there were periods when the same musicians were together for ten or more years. There was never a time, moreover, without a generational overlap among musicians, so that a direct and unbroken line of succession ran from the earliest of these fifteenth-century core groups through to the latest one, whose members performed well into the following century.

These four themes, of course, were not mutually exclusive and were, in fact, frequently complementary. A few of the trumpeters, fathers and sons alike, served for so many years that they formed part of two, three, and four successive core groups and thus became themselves the principal conduits through which the ensemble's traditions, performance practices, and repertories were handed down from one generation to the next. Continuity and links with the past were inevitably enriched by innovations and changes advanced by younger recruits and others with no ties to the group, who thus contributed to the periodic regeneration essential to maintaining high performance standards and artistic integrity. Employment patterns and practices of the fifteenth-

---

15. Ibid., 794.

16. See Peter Downey, "The Trumpet and its Role in Music of the Renaissance and Early Baroque" (Ph.D. diss., Queen's University of Belfast, 1983), 1:45–54, 66–88, where the author also discusses possible repertories of the time.

century trombetti represent a model of how successful ensembles functioned at a time when performance standards were not yet universal, when the education of professional musicians was not yet formalized, and when changing social and economic conditions had not yet created the climate for the development of organized means of private instruction.[17] As the practices represented by these simultaneously sounding themes became more firmly entrenched, they helped create for the Palace's musical establishment a system of employment and patronage that was eminently successful throughout the fifteenth century and beyond. As in the previous century, Assumption Day clothing lists continue to provide names of officially employed trumpeters. A detailed analysis of the data revealed by them and by other employment records will illustrate the four themes within the broader context of musical life at the Palace, providing at the same time an opportunity to trace the working careers of the musicians.

TRUMPETERS IN THE FIRST HALF OF THE FIFTEENTH CENTURY

In July of 1400 Antonio di Ciuccio, Jacomo di Corso, Chimenti di Biagio, and Giovanni di Antonio, all of them trumpeters cited in the previous year, received a non-taxable payment of L. 16.[18] These four, together with a new trumpeter, Antonio called Riccio, who was Antonio's son, and the drummer Francio di Viva, also appear in a record from December 1402. A payment of Fl. 34 for the months of November and December 1403 shows that except for Riccio, who initially received Fl. 2 a month, all of the musicians, including the newly appointed trumpeter Severino di Bartolomeo called Mancio, were then earning a monthly salary of Fl. 3. The seven musicians were present in July 1404, when Riccio's salary reached Fl. 3. Funds to cover the costs of pennants for the "trumpeters and nakers player of the commune of Siena" and of new suits of clothing for them were allocated in August 1405.[19] Joining the trumpeters on 7 April 1407 was the German musician Angelo d'Arrigo da Alamania called Imperadore, subsequently one of the mainstays of the group.[20] Four months later Angelo di Vanni succeeded Francio di Viva as the nakers player, though pay records indicate that he did not begin serving immediately.

The trumpeters' favored status was not destined to last. On 11 April 1408, as will be recounted in chapter 11, the priors made a long overdue move to engage a band of three pifferi, or woodwind players. To cover some of the costs of maintaining the new group it was decided to drop two of the musicians currently on the rolls, the drummer

---

17. These conditions are evident in Siena only toward the end of the century. The Concistoro began subsidizing trumpet teachers in the sixteenth century.

18. Pay records from January to June 1401 reveal that trumpeters were each earning a monthly salary of Fl. 3, as was the nakers player Francio di Viva. An apprentice, a second nakers player, Antonio, son of Antonio di Ciuccio, earned L. 3 per month.

19. Cecchini, "Palio e Contrade," 318.

20. The record is interesting for its description of the instrument Angelo played: "Prefati Magnifici domini Priore et Capitaneus populi conduxerunt ad servitia Comunis Senarum pro tubetta et cum tuba grossa, cum salario et pro tempore etc. cuius hoc est nome: Angelinus de Alamania, dictus lo 'Mperadore" (ASS, Concistoro, vol. 247, fol. 17ᵛ, dated 7 April 1407).

Francio di Viva and the trumpeter Severino di Bartolomeo.[21] Severino, however, was rehired a few weeks later, when his monthly salary was reduced to Fl. 2, tax free, as were those of four other trumpeters, Antonio di Antonio called Riccio, Chimenti di Biagio, Giovanni di Antonio da Bologna, Angelo called Imperadore, and the drummer Angelo di Vanni (see Doc. 9.1). From this time forward the trumpeters' salaries remained consistently lower than those of the wind players, who would eventually supersede them as the commune's preeminent musical group. But that was in the far distant future. For now the trumpeters, even with their salaries reduced, retained their public position as the most conspicuous element in the periodic stagings of civic pomp and solemn ceremony so necessary to the image of the government's legitimacy and stability.

From September 1409 comes an expenditure of L. 12. 12. 6 for seven pennants "that we had made for the trumpeters and three small ones for the nakers player."[22] For unexplained reasons Tomè di Meio, who joined the group in 1407 and doubled as a town crier, was fired on the previous 26 July and half of his stipend was assigned to Antonio di Ciuccio (see Doc. 9.2). But Tomè regained both posts by February 1410, a payment to him of Fl. 7 for two months' salary showing that the town criers then earned an extra half florin per month. Only Antonio di Ciuccio and Tomè are cited as town criers during this period, an indication that two posts were now the norm.

A list of the musicians who received clothing allowances for Assumption Day 1411 names six trumpeters and the drummer Angelo di Vanni. By this time four of the trumpeters, Antonio di Ciuccio, Chimenti di Biagio, Severino di Bartolomeo called Mancio, and Riccio d'Antonio, had worked together for more than seven years. They thus constituted the earliest of the fifteenth-century core groups. The other two trumpeters listed in 1411, Angelo called Imperadore and Tomè di Meio, subsequently came to form part of the established core, as did two newcomers cited in 1413, Angelo di Biagio (Chimenti's brother) and Bartolomeo di Crescenzio.[23] A new statute redefining some of the expenses made on behalf of musicians by the commune was issued in January 1412. In the future, trumpeters and wind players would receive new pennants

---

21. "Similiter vigore dicte commissionis, concorditer cassaverunt Francium Vive naccharinum et Severinum Bartalomei de Sancto Severino, vocato Manco, tubatorem, a die primo mensis Maii proxime futuri in antea" (Concistoro, vol. 253, fol. 25ᵛ, dated 11 April 1408).

22. "Sette penoni facemo fare per le tronbette e più tre penoncelli per le nachare" (ASS, Biccherna, vol. 294, 58ᵛ, dated 6 September 1409). Three pennants for the nakers indicate that the drummer played more than the one pair of drums usually mentioned in connection with accounts of the instrument. A week earlier, on 31 August, suits of clothing had been approved for six trumpeters (excluding Riccio) and the nakers player.

23. Angelo is identified as Chimenti's brother in a list of eight trumpeters who were authorized to receive clothing for Assumption Day 1413. Riccio (Antonio di Antonio di Ciuccio) is identified as Antonio's son in the same record. As mentioned above, he had served briefly as an apprentice nakers player. The eight trumpeters are also named in 1414. Angelo di Biagio is first mentioned on 21 February 1413, when the government decided that he could serve in place of Severino di Bartolomeo called Mancio while the latter was absent, but not beyond that time (ASS, Concistoro, vol. 282, fol. 53ᵛ). The incident illustrates that there were always musicians in the wings awaiting an opportunity to gain a permanent post at the Palace. Angelo apparently proved himself indispensable, for he was engaged for Palace service soon afterwards.

only once every two years, on Assumption Day. The musicians were now obliged to keep their old pennants and use them on ordinary days, whereas new ones were reserved for feast days and special occasions. Suits of clothing, hitherto authorized twice a year, would be granted only on Assumption Day, and these were to be cut as "tunics, not as cloaks" and not cost more than Fl. 10 each.[24] Another statute from a month later stipulated that the monthly salary of the nakers player was to remain fixed at one gold florin.[25] These were the musicians who received two new silver trumpets with pennants, sounded for the first time on the feast of the Annunciation, 25 March, in 1413, when the relics kept at the hospital of Santa Maria della Scala were exposed to the public amid great solemnities.[26]

Nine trumpeters, among whom were two town criers, received suits of clothing for Assumption Day 1415. The only new name on the list was Guido di Angelo. Bartolomeo di Crescenzio is missing from a similar list of eight trumpeters who received uniforms, "each valued at Fl. 10 according to the statutes," for Assumption Day festivities in August 1416. He was back by 1419 in place of Guido. By that time the group cited in 1413 had been together for six years. In its expanded form this nucleus exemplified all others following it. It included a number of musicians whose tenures overlapped, their periods of service having begun successively in 1390, 1399, 1402, 1403, 1407, and 1413; a percussionist, who maintained a remarkable record of longevity in his own right; and two brothers as well as a father and son, who personified the ties of kinship. And with one or two exceptions, all of the musicians were from Siena or its territories.

Antonio di Ciuccio left after 1419. As subsequent documents show, his son, Riccio, took over his post as town crier. Guido was back by 1420, when he was cited with the other seven trumpeters and the drummer. A deliberation from July 1423 notes that the Concistoro gave the town crier Tomè di Meio permission to use his next clothing allowance of Fl. 10 to buy an enamel shield bearing the commune's arms, which he would wear on his breast when playing with the other trumpeters. Guido di Angelo was granted permission to do the same a year later.

The number of trumpeters hovered around eight during the 1420s. There were, in fact, eight on 5 July 1425, when Alberto di Covaruccio, who replaced Bartolomeo di Crescenzio, was granted a ten-day leave of absence. Although several departed and were replaced during the next decade, this was again a time of relative stability because of the presence of another core of six musicians, recorded through 1435. They were Chimenti di Biagio, Riccio d'Antonio, Tomè di Meio, Angelo called Imperadore, Angelo

---

24. ASS, Statuti, 39, fol. 4ᵛ. The phrase regarding their clothing reads: "tunice seu cioppe et non clamides."

25. Ibid., fol. 15ʳ.

26. "Annales Senensis ab Anno MCCCLXXXV usque ad MCCCCXXII per Anonymum Scriptorem deducti," in Muratori, *Rerum italicarum scriptores,* vol. 19, 424. The order authorizing the silversmith Jacomo d'Andreuccio del Mosca to make the two trumpets has been published by Borghesi and Bianchi, *Nuovi documenti per la storia dell'arte Senese,* 72 and by Cellesi, *Storia della più antica banda musicale Senese,* 66, where the date of consignment is erroneously given as 1422. A year later, on 27 April 1414, Mariano d'Ambrogio and Goro di Ser Neroccio, *orafi,* were ordered to refashion two of the Concistoro's silver trumpets so that they would weigh the same as "those presently owned." This document, too, has been published by Cellesi, *Storia della più antica banda,* 67.

di Biagio—all named in the personnel list of 1420—and Alberto di Covaruccio. Severino called Mancio, with the group since 1403, was gone by 1426, when only seven trumpeters were present.[27] Guido di Angelo left in the following year, as did the drummer Angelo di Vanni. His replacement, Pietro di Giovanni da Chianciano called Petrolino, would subsequently join the trumpeters' ranks. New in 1427 were Gabriel di Tomaso, who stayed for only a year,[28] and a dwarf named Niccolò di Golino, who remained through 1429. Mentioned in 1430 as the seventh trumpeter was another musician whose tenure lasted only a year, Antonio di Niccolò da Urbino. The number of trumpeters was again eight in 1434, with the addition of Giovanni di Antonio and Petrolino. Petrolino's successor as drummer was Francesco di Vanni. The same musicians are mentioned in the following year, when a ninth trumpeter, Agostino di Giovanni da Pavia, joined the group.[29]

Nine trumpeters were also present in 1436, when Giovanni di Martino da Pergola and Pietro di Antonio replaced the brothers Chimenti and Angelo di Biagio. The eight trumpeters listed in 1437 included four from the established core, Riccio d'Antonio, Angelo called Imperadore, Tomè di Meio, and Alberto di Covaruccio, as well as the relative newcomers Giovanni di Antonio, Giovanni di Martino, and Agostino da Pavia, and a recent appointee, Santi di Riccarduccio. Joining them in 1438 as the ninth trumpeter was the returning Chimenti di Biagio. Nine trumpeters are again named in 1439, when Petrolino, absent for a number of years, replaced Giovanni di Antonio.[30] A list of nine trumpeters from four years later, 1443, includes only one new name, Piero di Jacopo, who replaced Angelo called Imperadore.

For reasons unmentioned in surviving records the priors decided to remove Petrolino from his post on 3 August 1444. Hired in his place, with the same salary and duties, was Andrea di Antonio da Urbino. In a parallel move the priors decreed that money earmarked for a suit of clothing for Petrolino would be given to his wife and son "for the love of God and out of pity for them." Petrolino's name, as well as those of the other eight musicians mentioned a year earlier, thus appears in the clothing list for Assumption Day 1444, though not in the list from a year later.

There were few changes in personnel during the late 1440s. Replacing Francesco di Vanni as drummer in 1445 was Maestro Piero di Lantecca Rintere da Cortona.[31] Later records of Palio expenses reveal that Piero was also a lutenist, though this is not evident from clothing lists.[32] He was thus another of those musicians whose versatility

---

27. The musicians are described as "tubatores et tubetti" in the personnel list from this year and the next.

28. The musicians are described as "bannitores et tubetti" in the personnel list from this year.

29. The priors wrote a letter on Agostino's behalf to Florentine authorities on 7 January 1446 asking their help in absolving him from a claim made against him by the convent of St. Martha (Concistoro, vol. 1666, *Copialettere, 1446,* fol. 3ʳ). He was apparently a well-liked musician. The priors wrote another letter of recommendation in his behalf on 10 May 1446 (ibid., fol. 53ᵛ).

30. Published by Cellesi, *Storia della più antica banda,* 28–29. She notes that these names are found for many years after this time.

31. Piero's surname, Rintere, is sometimes given as Rintera, Lantera, or Lantere.

32. See chapter 14 for more records concerning him as a lutenist. Typical is one from 15 August 1450, which registers payment of grossi 20 to "magistro Petro Rintere, pro leuto," that is, for having played the lute at Assumption Day festivities (Concistoro, vol. 506, fol. 32ʳ).

ensured a wider variety of repertories at the Palace than is indicated in official records. One wonders how many more there were like him. Niccolò Teutonico, a German trumpeter resident in Siena, was granted a lifetime appointment with the same salary and privileges enjoyed by the others on 31 July 1446. Perhaps he replaced Andrea di Antonio, missing from the clothing list for Assumption Day that year, but named again in the following one. Niccolò's presence in Siena, which may otherwise have gone undetected had he not received a Palace post, indicates that a good many foreign musicians probably visited or lived in the city at this time. Though the extent of their influence may never be known, in Niccolò's case winning a tenured position at the Palace speaks both to his abilities and to the Palace's policies, which clearly demanded excellence as the principal criterion for employment. On the following 12 December the Concistoro fired Piero di Jacopo called Nibbio for several acts of "dishonest and illicit malfeasance," decreeing that he could never again have a post among the trumpeters. Appointed in his place just over a week later was Giuliano da Chianciano, with the usual salary and privileges. The newcomers and all of the veteran members appear in the Assumption Day clothing list of 1447.

At least one familiar name was registered on 17 February 1448, when Petrolino di Giovanni resumed his old post. Appointed at the same time was Tomè di Meio's son, Antonio, succeeding Chimenti di Biagio, who died that day. Both newcomers are cited in the clothing list for Assumption Day 1448, which lacks both Chimenti and Niccolò de Alamania. Except for Antonio di Tomè, replaced by Tommaso di Cristoforo da Forlì, the same musicians recorded previously appear on the clothing list from 1449. Tommaso actually began serving with the group in October of that year. Earlier, on 4 August, Giovanni di Niccolò da Iesi, who in March had been promised the first vacant post, was also appointed to Palace service, but on condition that he receive no clothing in that year's August allocation. This action, of course, explains the absence of his name from the 1449 clothing list, even though his appointment was a tenured one. Giovanni apparently replaced Andrea di Antonio, whose name, lacking from the 1450 list, now disappears altogether. Present, however, were all other eight trumpeters and the drummer-lutenist maestro Pietro da Cortona.

The trumpeters' ranks remained essentially intact through 1455. Still registered were several of the core's oldest members and one appointed in 1446. They are cited, together with Tommaso da Forlì, Petrolino's son Giovanni di Petrolino,[33] and Giovanni da Iesi, as the nine trumpeters who received clothing on Assumption Day 1451 and, except for Tommaso, again on Assumption Day in 1455. Tommaso was fired in February 1454 and immediately succeeded by the blind trumpeter Niccolò Turini. Niccolò, who received a suit of clothing "for the love of God" in October 1452, once substituted for the ailing Riccio di Antonio and was promised the first available post as early as 18 February 1453. The drummer-lutenist Maestro Piero Rintere continued throughout this time.

Various records indicate that two trumpeters were still doubling as town criers during this period. One, from 26 July 1445 concerning Tomè di Meio, trumpeter and

---

33. Giovanni was promised a post on the last day of 1449: "Conduxeruntque [gap] filium Pietrolini tubicene, loco secundi vacantis, cum officio, salario et modis consuetis" (Concistoro, vol. 503, fol. 37ᵛ, dated 31 December 1449).

town crier, illustrates how a Sienese musician, traveling on his own, could become familiar with the music and musical practices of other lands. Tomè de Meio had returned to Siena four days earlier from a pilgrimage to Santiago de Compostela, whence he had departed on the previous 22 March. After acknowledging that a place had been kept open for him, the Concistoro decided that Tomè could resume his duties as a trumpeter beginning in August, but that he could not return to his other post as town crier. Another record from 5 December of the same year says that Riccio d'Antonio da Chianciano, "a trumpeter and town crier," was given leave for eight days so that he might take a cure at the thermal baths.

Reports of leaves of absence such as these are found throughout the fifteenth century, though none cite destinations as distant as Tomè's. A few from around mid-century typify the situations they record. In May 1446 the priors granted Agostino da Pavia a month's leave of absence at full salary, with the promise that his post would be secure. Some three years later Santi di Riccarduccio, described as a native of Gubbio, was granted a paid leave of absence for twelve days. Agostino da Pavia was allowed an eight-day leave of absence, with no loss of salary, at the end of March 1450. Santi was again excused from service in the following September so that he could go to Rome for fifteen days. He apparently went to seek an indulgence during the jubilee year, as did Giovanni di Martino, who departed Siena on the following 6 December. On 18 January 1453 Riccio d'Antonio once again obtained permission to leave the city, this time for ten days, on condition that he arrange for a substitute. Apart from attesting to the government's liberal policy regarding paid leaves of absences, the records also reveal the continuing travel opportunities that Palace musicians enjoyed, enabling them to keep abreast of developments in their profession elsewhere in Italy, if not in all of Europe.[34] Frequent visits by the entire group to cities such as Florence and Lucca, mentioned below, also provided occasions for the Sienese trumpeters to meet, to exchange repertories, and to discuss questions of mutual interest with foreign musicians, as well as to hear them perform.

INSTRUMENTS AND REPERTORY

Depending upon whether records are in Latin or Italian, Sienese documents from the thirteenth century onwards invariably refer to the players as tubicen (pl. tubicines), tubator (pl. tubatores), trombatore (pl. trombatori), and trombetto (pl. trombetti), and to the instruments they played as tuba (pl. tube), tubetta (pl. tubette), trombetta (pl. trombette), and tromba (pl. trombe). A Latinized form of the Italian, trombator, appears in the earliest of the Biccherna's volumes, though tubator is given in the Sienese Constitution of 1267 and in later payments from 1291. Tubator and tubicen continued as the preferred Latin terms well into the sixteenth century, when the Italianized form tubicena gained currency. Trombatore in its Italian form appears in records from after the

---

34. I have limited my remarks to the period of the decade from the time of Tomè di Meio's journey to Compostela. There are many other records of leaves of absence throughout the century that attest to the continuing opportunities Sienese musicians had to keep abreast of developments elsewhere through personal travel. These occurred, of course, in addition to their frequent trips abroad in larger groups, such as the visits to Florence, Lucca, and other places mentioned below.

turn of the fifteenth century, though trombetto is more frequently found after that time, sometimes Latinized.[35]

Although none of the instruments has survived, in Siena or elsewhere for that matter, a few iconographical and literary sources show that the trumpets of medieval times were long, straight metal instruments, bell-shaped at one end and with a detachable mouthpiece at the other.[36] The music theorist Johannes de Grocheo, writing around 1300, reports that the trumpet could play three consonances, the octave, the fifth, and the fourth, the intervals formed by the first three partials of the harmonic series. The range of the instrument was thus quite low and its available pitches quite restricted. As a consequence, trumpeters' repertories—none of which survive—must have consisted primarily of the simplest of fanfares and signal calls. When playing together, the trumpeters produced unisons or simple chords. In later medieval times two other types of trumpets, the one shaped like an S, the other short and folded, came into more general use. Some of these instruments may have been of variable pitch, capable of playing a good many more notes than the earlier medieval instruments.

Sienese records from these centuries offer few clues about the instruments played by Palace trumpeters. Since most surviving documents deal with personnel and policy matters, appointments, and salaries, it is understandable why they include little or no information about the makeup or design of the instruments. But even those records which preserve details of the purchase or commissioning of new instruments lack specific information about their design and capabilities. For example, several fifteenth-century reports cite the exact amount of silver that was to be used and its cost, though little else.[37] Similarly, fifteenth-century Palace inventories reflect the gradual increase in

---

35. Regarding the spelling of these terms as they appear in Sienese documents, it should be borne in mind that orthography was not yet standardized, as will be apparent from documents already quoted and others cited here and in the following chapters. Thus, for example, "n" is often found in place of "m," as in "tronbe" for "trombe," and "d" frequently replaces "t," as in "trombador" for "trombator." I should also note that the terms denoting players and instruments are often used interchangeably, as illustrated by these two instances: (1) a payment from 31 December 1357, which records disbursement of 300 lire "pro pretio XV robarum novem tubatorum, trium banditorum, unius ciaramelle, unius naccharini et unius trombette, ad rationem XX librarum denariorum pro roba"; (2) a payment from 17 August 1408, which speaks of "pluribus tubettis, piffaris, instrionibus sive giollaribus, cantoribus et aliis pulsatoribus strumentorum plurium comitatum et dominorum" (Concistoro, vol. 10, fol. 91ᵛ; vol. 255, fol. 63ᵛ).

36. For what little is known about medieval trumpets, see Edward Tarr, *The Trumpet* (Portland, Ore., 1988), 38–40, and Don L. Smithers, *The Music and History of the Baroque Trumpet* (2d ed., Carbondale and Edwardsville, 1988), 35ff. Smithers (p. 52) notes that one of the oldest trumpets of European manufacture to have survived until the Second World War was described in 1922 by Curt Sachs, who reported that it bore a printer's mark and the inscription "Vbaldo/Montini/in Siena/ 1523." See Sachs, *Sammlung alter Musikinstrumente bei der Staatlichen Hochschule für Musik zu Berlin* (Berlin, 1922), 222, n. 465. I have thus far been unable to locate anyone by that name in Sienese tax records from the early sixteenth century.

37. The specifications for two silver trumpets that were commissioned from Jacomo d'Andreuccio del Mosca and companions, silversmiths, in 1412 read as follows: "due trombete d'ariento a lega popolino, ben fazionate e bene sonanti e isquelanti e chon buona perfezione a giudicio di buoni tronbeti . . . e farvi l'arme del Chomuno e del popolo ismaltate in que' luoghi dove sarano bisognio."

the number of instruments, but give no descriptions of them.[38] Inventories from November 1413 to June 1414 list two silver trumpets with pennants and two linen covers, whereas four silver trumpets are mentioned from July 1414 to June 1417. Five silver trumpets are reported beginning in July 1417, and six from November 1417 to November 1418. An inventory from May 1436 notes that the trumpet player Riccio had eight silver trumpets in his possession that the trumpeters used when they played, and these instruments continue to appear in inventories through January 1445. Nine silver trumpets for the trumpeters are cited in an inventory from 1467, though only seven, each consisting of three pieces, are reported from March 1506 to July 1518. An inventory from 1525 again speaks of trumpets in three pieces, noting this time that they were without mouthpieces and that they had recently been repaired. Apart from these few remarks, the records are silent.

Sienese iconographical sources, while more plentiful, add few details to our knowledge. Some of them show that trumpeters, at least when they escorted officials on horseback, as in Pinturicchio's *Coronation of Pope Pius III,* played single straight trumpets (see Fig. 7), as did Sienese angel musicians who played at solemn moments such as

---

The instruments were finished on 24 March 1413 and "pesarono libre cinque oncie dieci e quarti 1: per L. 4 s. 10 oncia, monta in tutto L. 316. 2. 6" (Concistoro, vol. 2496, fol. 198ᵛ). As mentioned above, they were played for the first time on the following day at ceremonies in which relics from the hospital of Santa Maria della Scala were exposed to the public.

From 27 April 1414 comes the report of a commission to Mariano d'Anbruogio and Goro di ser Neroccio, *orafi,* for "due trombe, del peso di due che al presente sonno in Concistoro e con quelli smalti e civori che sonno in esse" (Concistoro, vol. 2497, fol. 14ʳ). On 31 August 1415 Nicholò di Treganuccio and Goro di ser Neroccio, *orafi,* were paid L. 52 s. 1 in advance for "due tronbette d'ariento" which they were to make for the commune (ibid., fol. 69ʳ).

Jacomo d'Andreuccio and compagni were again mentioned on 30 April 1417, when they were paid L. 35 s. 17 "per chaparra d'una trombetta, la quale devve fare al pregio consueto e di quello ariento che sonno l'altre" (ibid., fol. 152ʳ). They were paid L. 147. 7. 6 for the finished work on 31 December 1417 (ibid., fol. 170ʳ). Another disbursement of L. 41. 10 shows that two more trumpets were ordered from the same firm on 12 February 1417 (ibid., fol. 176ʳ).

38. The inventories mentioned in the following discussion are in Concistoro, vol. 2497 (for the years 1414–19), fols. 3ʳ, 15ʳ, 24ʳ, 28ʳ, 30ʳ, 118ʳ, 138ʳ, 147ʳ, 150ʳ, 158ʳ, 160ʳ, 169ʳ; vol. 2498 (for the years 1436–45), fols. 3ᵛ, 35ᵛ, 57ᵛ, 59ᵛ, 81ʳ, 101ʳ, 135ʳ, 151ʳ, 362ᵛ, 381ᵛ, 395ʳ, 411ʳ, 419ᵛ; vol. 2505 (for 1467), fol. 245ʳ; vol. 2512 (for the years 1506–9), fols. clxxxiiiʳ, clxxxvʳ, clxxxviiiʳ, and various unnumbered folios; vol. 2513 (for the years 1518–25), fols. 167ᵛ, 178ʳ, 182ᵛ, 206ʳ, 210ʳ, 213ʳ. From these I quote the following:

"Qui appresso saranno scritte per partito tutte le chose chonsegniate . . . per gli due mesi prossimi passati, cioè novembre e dicembre anno detto . . . per gli due mesi prossimi a venire, cioè giennaio e ferraio [1414] . . . ii tronbette d'ariento cho' pennoni et ii invoglie di panolino" (vol. 2497, fol. 3ʳ, 1413).

"Riccio tronbetta de' magnifici nostri signori de' dare a dì primo di maggio otto tronbetti d'ariento li quali tiene per quando bisongniasse trombare" (vol. 2498, fol. 3ᵛ, 1436).

"Inventario delli argenti et a[l]tre robbe . . . Sette trombe d'argento di pezzi tre l'una, quali per essere rotte e la maggior parte storciate si sonno fatte acconciar et rifar, sono di tre pezi senza boccaletti et si sono dati a rifar di novo" (vol. 2513, fol. 210ʳ; May–June 1525).

FIGURE 7. Pinturicchio, *Coronation of Pius III,* with musicians in attendance, fresco on arch above the entrance to the Libreria Piccolomini. Siena, cathedral. Courtesy Opera della Metropolitana di Siena; photograph from Foto Lensini

the Crucifixion in Ambrogio Lorenzetti's Allegory of the Redemption and "Ugolino Lorenzetti"'s Assumption of the Virgin.[39]

Sienese trumpeters undoubtedly had instruments of their own as well as those furnished by the Palace, but just what these were is not mentioned in surviving documents. Perhaps some of them had the kinds of slide trumpets that were coming more and more into use throughout Europe during the mid-fifteenth century. These and the equally new short folded trumpets could sound notes other than those in the natural overtone series, an indication that a repertory wider than fanfares was within their range. Keith Polk has suggested that German trumpeters were playing in the upper harmonics by about 1450, which would have given them access to a more interesting repertory than was possible with older forms of the instrument.[40] Nothing of this sort can be said of Sienese trumpeters, though some reports suggest that they were keeping abreast of all of the latest developments in instrumental construction and that they, too, could play according to the latest techniques. Several Sienese trumpeters, for example, subsequently became trombonists in the wind band, a circumstance that argues in favor both of a wider dissemination of the newer instruments than indicated by Palace records and of musicians capable of playing a wider repertory than might be expected, points that merit further exploration.

Versatility among Palace musicians was, of course, nothing new. The percussionists who joined the trumpeters' and shawm players' ranks in the previous century and the fifteenth-century drummer Piero Rintere, who was also a lutenist, give ample evidence of this. They were no different than other instrumentalists in other periods and places who learned to play a variety of instruments in their apprentice years. With the passing of time, however, versatility came to mean more than having facility on another instrument, in this case the trombone. It also embraced an ability to improvise counterpoint and to read some form of musical notation. These offered the player access to a repertory that was at once more refined and more demanding than what was possible on the straight trumpet with its limited range of notes. Sienese trumpeters who became trombonists in the wind band in the later fifteenth century must have had such ability, otherwise they would hardly have qualified as members of that ensemble. They must, furthermore, have owned instruments—only in the late fifteenth century did the Concistoro provide funds for the purchase of a trombone—and they must have learned to do the things that qualified them to play in the wind band during the time they served as trumpeters or even earlier. The wind band's repertory comprised polyphonic pieces. Playing polyphony presupposes an ability to improvise counterpoint or an ability to read some form of written musical notation, or both. Thus, knowledge that several Palace trumpeters eventually played the trombone (or slide trumpet) in the wind band

---

39. Both paintings are in Siena's Pinacoteca Nazionale and are reproduced as nos. 61 and 92 in Piero Torriti, *La Pinacoteca Nazionale di Siena: I dipinti dal XII al XV secolo* (2d ed., Genoa, 1980). They are also listed as nos. 259 and 316 of Howard Mayer Brown's "Catalogus. A Corpus of Trecento Pictures with Musical Subject Matter," *Imago Musicae* 1 (1984): 189–243; 2 (1985), 179–281; 3 (1986), 103–87; 5 (1988), 167–241; for nos. 259 and 316, see esp. vol. 2, pp. 246–47, 266–67.

40. Polk, *German Instrumental Music,* 50.

leads to the inevitable conclusion that many, if not all, of them had some kind of training that enabled them to do so.

Corroborating evidence in support of this conclusion comes from outside Siena, in the personal account book of an itinerant musician compiled just around this time, more precisely, from between 1444 and 1449.[41] The musician in question was Zorzi trombetta da Modon, a Venetian port in the Peloponnese. Zorzi was a trumpeter on a Venetian galley that made a commercial voyage to northern Europe in 1447–48 and a second one along the Adriatic coast in 1449. His notes indicate that on this latter trip he and a shawmist named Augustin played at weddings and other festivities for local officials, residents, and visitors at various ports of call.[42] They formed, in other words, the kind of duo that was present in the Sienese trumpeters' corps until the end of the fourteenth century. Apart from providing a fascinating glimpse into the personal and professional life of a shipboard musician, Zorzi's diary is of extraordinary interest because it contains music, copied by him and others, that must have formed part of his repertory, namely a few French chansons for three voices, the two lower parts (tenor and contratenor) of John Dunstable's well-known *Puisque m'amour,* and four single tenor parts. Though lacking the superius part here, Dunstable's piece was composed, like the others, in a style typical of the times, featuring a main melody in the highest part and supporting roles for the lower ones.

Surviving evidence indicates that when such pieces were taken over by instrumentalists, their parts were sometimes modified and put into a form easily read by the musicians. In the case of Zorzi's repertory this is exemplified not so much by the highest parts, most of them notated in a slightly varied version of the standard mensural notation of the time, which were probably played by more literate musicians—maybe the shawmist—but by the accompanying lower parts that he himself would have played. These are written in a very simple kind of notation, the duration of the pitches being indicated by one or two note forms that appear either singly or in combination. In Zorzi's notation a single pulse is represented by one note form, two pulses are represented by another, and longer notes are indicated by repeating the two in appropriate combinations. Beyond reading the simple steps of the musical staff that designate the pitch, Zorzi or other musicians who played from these parts only needed to count and perhaps to settle on certain conventions among themselves before they performed. Thus Zorzi, and others like him, though lacking the formal training usual with singers and composers, could gain access to a wide repertory of polyphonic music, rearranged to suit the instrument, by using this alternative system of musical notation.

Any number of similarly simplified systems of notation must have been in use, though our knowledge of them is limited because, being utilitarian and of no value

---

41. Daniel Leech-Wilkinson, "Il libro di appunti di un suonatore di tromba del quindicesimo secolo," *Rivista italiana di musicologia* 16 (1981): 20ff.

42. Wilkinson reports that two other musicians, Girardo and Bortholamio piffari, were also in the same naval squadron.

except to the musicians for whom they were designed, few have survived.[43] As for Sienese trumpeters from this time, information is totally lacking testifying to their performing abilities or to performances by the entire corps of improvised or written polyphony. But knowing that several of them subsequently played part music with the wind band and that there were systems of written notation that gave trumpeters access to polyphonic repertories suggests that many of them could play more than simple fanfares.

THE TRUMPETERS' CORPS IN THE SECOND HALF OF THE FIFTEENTH CENTURY

Major changes in the corps occurred after August 1455. In that month the Concistoro appointed Santi di Paolo da Volterra "as a trumpeter in their Palace" at a monthly salary of Fl. 2, tax free, and with the guarantee of a new suit of clothing, valued at Fl. 10, every year on Assumption Day.[44] Santi di Paolo's name appears on the clothing list for the following year, 1456. By that time Riccio d'Antonio and Tomè di Meio had retired and a new core, comprised of seven trumpeters, was in the process of coalescing. The seven were Petrolino, Santi di Riccarduccio, Giovanni di Martino, Giuliano da Chianciano, Giovanni di Petrolino, Giovanni da Iesi, and Niccolò Turini. Also mentioned in 1456 were the drummer-lutenist Maestro Piero Rintere and the returning Antonio di Tomè, son of the veteran trumpeter Tomè di Meio, previously fired after less than a year's service. Santi di Paolo remained with the group through the end of June 1459, when he evidently left town. Antonio di Tomè soon died and was replaced, first by Niccolò di Piero da Città di Castello and then by Sano di Matteo da Siena.[45] At the beginning of July 1459 the eight trumpeters were joined by a ninth, Monaldo di Bartolomeo. Like several of his colleagues, he was from the town of Chianciano; possibly all of them were bound by ties of kinship not immediately apparent in available documents. Monaldo was appointed in a dual capacity: as trumpeter and as town crier, replacing Petrolino, removed from office for not having fulfilled his duties properly (see Doc. 9.3).[46] All of the trumpeters are mentioned through August 1460. By that time a new drummer, Meio di Maestro Mino, had taken over from Piero Rintere.

The core group formed at this time remained remarkably stable during the next two decades, for only gradually did some of its older members cede their places to younger men, who in turn had equally long careers. A record from these years concerning the blind trumpeter Niccolò Turini is of some importance, for it reveals that annual

---

43. For an explanation and illustration of some of these forms of simplified notation, now more generally known as stroke notation, see Margaret Bent, "New and Little-Known Fragments of English Medieval Polyphony," *JAMS* 21 (1968): 137–56, esp. 149–53; for a more recent account, Margaret Bent and Roger Bowers, "The Saxilby Fragment," *Early Music History* 1 (1981): 1–27.

44. Note the value of the florin here is s. 82.

45. Sano had been appointed to a trumpeter's post on the previous day.

46. As the record makes clear, there was disagreement among two successive groups of priors. Those currently holding office appointed Monaldo in place of Santi di Paolo da Volterra, who had left; at the same time they canceled Petrolino's appointment as a town crier, made by their predecessors, because they thought he was incompetent and the appointment illegally made. Petrolino's appointment was registered only a week earlier, on 30 June 1459.

clothing allowances need not always be spent on new uniforms. Dated 31 July 1465, it reports a decision by the priors allowing Niccolò to exchange the money from his allowance "for grain to meet his family's needs." A salary payment for the months of January and February 1470 reveals that three trumpeters were once again doubling as town criers. Each of them earned L. 13. 7 per month, as opposed to the remaining six trumpeters with monthly salaries of L. 8. 4. The few changes occurring in the 1460s concern primarily Petrolino's son Giovanni.

Giovanni di Petrolino, also known as Barbulia, was apparently as talented and as impetuous as his father. Having run afoul of the government for "many dishonesties committed in days past," he was removed from his post and condemned to torture and six months' imprisonment on 6 June 1463. His name is lacking in the clothing list from that year, but is there again in 1464–66, signifying his apparent rehabilitation. By 1468 two new trumpeters, Bartolomeo di Monaldo and Giovanni called El Moro, appeared in place of Barbulia and Santi di Ricarduccio, this latter having completed twenty-nine years' service. Bartolomeo di Monaldo's talents were much in demand. On 16 June 1469, when the priors appointed him as trombonist in the wind band, they also formally pardoned Giovanni di Petrolino called Barbulia and reinstated him in his old post, the one vacated by Bartolomeo (see Doc. 9.4). Barbulia's latest reappointment points to a network of power linkages and a system of patronage barely hinted at in surviving records. He had been let go twice, apparently for good reasons, and tortured and imprisoned, but he was able, undoubtedly through the good offices of highly placed friends, to regain his post when the bimestrial changes among the priors placed someone sympathetic to his cause on the Concistoro. To be sure, covert, or overt, political pressure is difficult to prove in Barbulia's case, as in several similar instances. But this is as logical an explanation as any other of the many occasions when musicians were punished or fired by one group of priors, only to be pardoned and rehabilitated by another.

No other changes in personnel are recorded until 1473. By that time Giuliano da Chianciano was dead, succeeded by Domenico da Brescia called Voltolina.[47] Enea di Senzanome, as will be noted below, was admitted to the group in the same year, but since no other post was vacant at the time, he was granted only half salary and was not given a uniform. As a result, his name does not appear on any of the Assumption Day lists for several years, even though he performed with the group. In 1475, when Gaddo di Manno succeeded Monaldo di Bartolomeo, six of the core musicians mentioned in 1457 were still present. With his resignation on the first of August 1478, Enea di Senzanome finally gained full admission to the group.[48] The drummer, Meio di Maestro Mino, is recorded throughout this time.

By 1480 this core, whose center had remained stable for more than two decades, began disintegrating as yet another nucleus took shape. A clothing list for Assumption Day that year shows three of the older group, Giovanni di Martino, Niccolò Turini,

---

47. A report from 8 November of that year says that Giuliano's wife had laid claim to the suit of clothing issued for Assumption Day and that the Concistoro countermanded an order given by the Biccherna and awarded it to Voltolina (Concistoro, vol. 637, fol. 6ᵛ).

48. His appointment is discussed below.

and Sano di Matteo, still present.[49] Continuing also were three others, El Moro, the returning Gaddo di Manno, and Enea di Senzanome da Brescia. The three newest musicians were all related to present or former members of the corps. They were Turini's son Michelangelo di Niccolò and the sons of two former trumpeters, Bernardino di Monaldo and Geronimo di Giovanni da Iesi. Meio di Maestro Mino remained as drummer.[50] Bernardino was apparently a much traveled musician. A deliberation from 15 May 1480 notes that he went to Lombardy several months earlier and that since he had yet to return, the Concistoro voted to substitute in his place the son of yet another trumpeter, Britio di Sano (see Doc. 9.5). Though Bernardino's name is lacking in the Assumption Day list from 1482, it appears, together with the names of all of the other musicians just mentioned, in similar lists from 1481 and 1483. Mariano called Mancino, appointed in place of the ailing Giovanni di Martino in mid-November 1483, was the only newcomer to the Assumption Day lists of 1484 and 1485.[51]

Trumpeters, Poets, and Cantarini

By 1485 Britio di Sano became the tenth trumpeter in the group, a number that dropped to nine in 1486 because of Mancino's absence, but was once again at ten by 1487.[52] Previously, on 1 September 1486, the Concistoro fired Britio for his scornful response to "their order forbidding him to talk to Niccolò cieco, who spoke to someone who had the plague." Words attributed to Britio, to the effect that he knew of the order but still intended to speak and practice with his teacher, tell as much about Britio's training as they do about the petty resentments that must have been all too prevalent among a group of people who worked together on a daily basis for years on end. In addition to the training he had at home from his father—Sano was also a Palace trumpeter—Britio was apprenticed to Niccolò, who may have been a superior teacher. But despite Britio's reputed loyalty to Niccolò, it turned out that he had obeyed the order after all. As a result, the priors rescinded their action and reinstated him in his post two

---

49. Concistoro, vol. 683, fols. 26^v–27^r, dated 2 August 1480. Mentioned as a trombonist with the Palace woodwind players at this time is another son of Monaldo, Bartolomeo, previously recorded among the trumpeters. Geronimo, or Girolamo, di Giovanni, listed here as a trumpeter, later became a trombonist in the wind band. See chapter 11, note 144, for a report from 1 September 1489 that calls him a trombonist and says that he had one of the Palace's silver trombones on loan since 14 April 1488 so that he could break it in. The same document identifies him as the son of the former trumpeter Giovanni da Iesi.

50. A report from a year later says that the Concistoro voted to give eight bushels of grain to the drummer Meio, who was impoverished and had had many children. The report is exceptional, the only one I have seen that speaks of an impoverished musician at this time.

51. See Doc. 11.15, Bartolomeo di Monaldo's request of 23 November 1483 to be appointed as town crier in place of Giovanni di Martino, who was ill. For his services as a town crier Bartolomeo was to receive the same salary as Giovanni did with the proviso that Giovanni would receive s. 40 from Bartolomeo's salary every month until he died, at which time the entire salary would be Bartolomeo's. This provision offers another illustration of how the Concistoro sought to provide for elderly or infirm musicians who could no longer serve. See below for a discussion of this point.

52. Mancino's name is lacking in the list for 1486, which otherwise names the remaining nine trumpeters and the drummer. The newcomer on the 1487 list was Niccolò di Meio Naccharini, son of the drummer Meio.

days later. Britio, as subsequent reports show, had a long career as a Palace employee. Nothing in the record suggests that he ever held any other post at the Palace but that of trumpeter, though evidence of his talents as a poet comes from a rare collection of printed items from the early sixteenth century, now in Siena's Biblioteca Comunale degli Intronati.[53] Of particular interest are the second and third of these, which contain two of Britio's works. The second, entitled *Terzina nobilissima della Ave Maria disposta: Composta da Britio trombeto da Siena: Con due altre bellissime Terzine di altri auctori: Ad laude della Vergine Maria,* was printed at Siena by Simone di Niccolò and Giovanni di Alexandro Carrai da Siena on 13 October 1511.

Britio's capitolo, a "laude de la gloriosa Vergine Maria," is in terza rima and is the first of three prayers to the Virgin; the second is by Antonio da Ferrara, the third by the Palace herald Antonio da Fabriano, about whom more presently. Notable is Britio's felicitous gift for rhyming as well as his evident piety, exemplified in the closing tercet:

Ora per me ch'ognor te vo chiamando	Pray for me, for I call on you always;
Ora per tucti e peccator di socto:	Pray for all sinners here below;
Ora per me, tu sai e 'l come e 'l quando.	Pray for me, you know how and when.

Britio's other poem, also a capitolo in terza rima, is in the third item, which lacks a proper title page and begins instead with a *Tavola di ciò che si contiene in questo libretto. Jesus Maria.*[54] The "Terzina di Britio tronbetto da Siena / In laude della Vergine Maria" follows several works by Antonio da Fabriano on fols. 6^v–7^v. This, too, is a devoted prayer to the Virgin. Britio begins by asking the Virgin's intercession with her son:

Clementissima madre immenssa e pura	O most clement Mother, boundless and pure,
Ora per noi, O sancta genitrice:	Pray for us, O holy Mother
Del Redentor de l'humana natura.	Of the Redeemer of mankind.

and in the course of his prayer proudly reminds her and his audience of Siena's ancient devotion to the Holy Mother of God:

Nissuna altra ciptà si può dar vanto	No other city can boast
Esser di te chiamata, O Vergin pia,	Of being named for you, o pious Virgin
Però che Sena vetus, dice el chanto,	For the song says Ancient Siena,

---

53. BCIS, R. 14. IX. R, second item. The first item, "E Septe dolori della Vergine Maria. Con una devota Oratione," was printed at Siena by Michelangelo di Bartolomeo at the instance of Maestro Giovanni di Alixandro, Libraio, on 1 April 1523. It ends with the instruction: "Queste sono le Messe del Confitemini" and lists "Sabbato, la Messa della Madonna, con una candela." Britio's works, in the second and third items, are mentioned briefly by Cosimo Corso, "Araldi e canterini nella repubblica senese del Quattrocento," *BSSP* 62 (1955): 140–60, esp. 153.

54. BCIS, R. IX. R, third item. This, too, was printed at Siena by Simone di Niccolò and Giovanni di Alexando Carrai, on 13 October 1511.

Civitas Virginis,[55] inclita Maria	City of the Virgin, glorious Mary
Alpha et Omega, principium et fine	Alpha and Omega, beginning and end;
O felice colui che 'n te disia.	O happy he who longs for you.
Tardi non furno mai gratie divine	Your divine graces were never late,
Et lo sperare in te no fu ma' i' vano	And hoping in you, never in vain.
El buon perseverante fa buon fine.	He who perseveres will have a good end.

Apart from their intrinsic devotional value, the poems attest to an unsuspected level of culture and literacy on the part of one of the Sienese trumpeters from this time. Whether all of the members of the corps shared Britio's interests or were as gifted is a moot point. More important is that his talents bespeak an education not only of reading and writing, but also of the rudiments of musical theory and perhaps training in reading some form of written notation. Surely, in view of his studies with the blind trumpeter Niccolò, whose son and grandsons eventually succeeded to Palace posts, it must be that others among his peers had similar backgrounds in music.

The just-mentioned Palace herald, Antonio Scapuccini da Fabriano, to give him his full name, was first mentioned in Palace records on 30 June 1444, when he performed for the Concistoro, but it was not until 24 August of the following year that he was officially appointed to the herald's post with a monthly salary of L. 6 and the usual provision of daily meals and new uniforms annually on Assumption Day.[56] From that time until his death on 26 May 1451, Antonio remained a much appreciated and valuable member of the Palace establishment. His principal duties, like those of heralds employed at Florence and other Tuscan communes, were to entertain the members of the Concistoro at mealtimes with songs and histrionics and particularly to recite or sing poems he himself had composed that expressed the government's views and intentions, either at home before the Concistoro and its guests or at courts abroad, as a representative of the state.[57] A herald was clearly a man of parts, an entertainer, a poet, a diplomat, a courtier, and on occasion a musician capable of accompanying himself on the lute or some other instrument. Antonio's surviving works, like the Terzina beginning "Inclita veneranda alma regina" and the "Canzone Bellissima in laude della Assumptione della Vergine," are mostly addressed to or in honor of the Virgin Mary, though one poem that mentions the wolf (Siena) and the lion (Florence) speaks of the horrors of war and the joys of peace, a particularly apt subject in view of relations between the two states.

One of Antonio's best-known predecessors in Siena was the Palace mace bearer Pietro di Viviano (1343–1421), called "Chantarino," a prolific poet and man of letters and author of an extended "novella in versi," *La Bella Camilla*.[58] Pietro, a native Sienese

---

55. This may be a reference to Arnolfo's motet, discussed above in chapter 5, though the motto "Sena vetus, civitas Virginis" was a constant in Sienese life at this time.

56. Details of Antonio's biography and remarks about his poetry and its sources are given by Corso, "Araldi e canterini," esp. 140–48.

57. An overview of heralds in medieval Europe and a detailed account of Florentine heralds in the fifteenth century is given by Richard Trexler, *The Libro Ceremoniale of the Florentine Republic* (Geneva, 1978), 13–52.

58. For remarks about Pietro's life and works, see Corso, "Araldi e canterini," 148–53.

who lived in the Camollia section of the city, is mentioned on many occasions beginning in 1398 and gifts of clothing to him are regularly recorded in the following years. In 1399 he accompanied Sienese ambassadors to Pavia, and he went on a similar mission in 1409 to the court of the anti-pope Alexander at Pisa. A number of "cantori" were employed at the Palace before Pietro, either casually or full time. Among them were Martino, a "cantatore" from Bologna who received L. 48 on 10 October 1341 for his service in military operations; Giovanni Ceccharelli, "cantore," who was paid L. 6. 13 for twenty-one days' salary on 1 August 1354, for similar duties; Tortto, "chantatore," who was given L. 2. 2 on 29 April 1403 for having sung for Sienese officials on several occasions; and three singers, all of whom were present in 1414: Ciecholello Romano, paid L. 4. 2. 6 on 26 February "for his work because he came to the Palace many, many times to play the lute and the guitar (gittern?)"; Tomè, "chantarino," L. 1. 2 on 30 June and L. 2. 15 on 31 December, "for having sung many times"; and an unnamed singer who played the viola, "un chantatore che suona la viuola," who received L. 2. 4 on 31 October "for having sung several evenings."[59] Somewhat later, in October 1422, Niccolò d'Arezzo, "cantatore," was recorded as receiving L. 16 by order of the Concistoro.[60] Records such as these indicate that improvised singing to the accompaniment of string instruments was a venerable form of entertainment at the Palace by the turn of the fifteenth century and that Pietro di Viviano was probably the first to be employed on a regular basis, albeit his official position was that of mace bearer and custodian of books in a government office. Antonio da Fabriano apparently had no official successors in the post, for none is mentioned in annual clothing lists of Palace employees after 1451. Occasionally, however, there were itinerant performers such as the Luchese musician "who played and sang several times before the Magnificent Lords" during March and April 1474 and was rewarded for his services with a payment of L. 5. 12.[61]

The Closing Decade

In October 1486 Enea di Senzanome was granted a ten-day leave of absence to accompany a Sienese envoy to Florence.[62] Two months later the priors gave Sano's son Domenico permission to substitute for his father, who was feeble and well along in years. Domenico, however, was not granted a tenured post. Another change occurred on 9 February 1487, when the Concistoro decreed that Gaddo di Manno could resume the post he had resigned earlier in favor of his brother Lodovico, provided Lodovico received his salary through the month of February. Lodovico was also promised the first vacancy to occur (see Doc. 9.6). The promise, called an "expectative" in the decree,

59. "A dì 31 d'otobre dèi al chantatore che suona la viuola soldi quaranta e quat[r]o, e cho[s]ì ebi da' miei chonpangni, per avere chantato più sere. L. II s. IIII" (Concistoro, vol. 2497, *Proventi, spese e inventari, 1414–19,* fol. 33ʳ). Tomè di Bartolomeo chantarino, as Corso, "Araldi," 154, shows, was a native Sienese who declared assets of L. 200 in a tax report from 1410.

60. The payment is published in Corso, "Araldi e canterini," 155.

61. "1474, ragione di Rasmo di Giovanni spenditore, di marzo e aprile . . . a uno Luchese L. 5 s. XII, che chanta inproviso, el quale sonò et cantò più volte dinanzi a' nostri Magnifici Signori" (ASS, Regolatori, vol. 9, fol. 409ʳ).

62. During his absence he was obliged to send someone to serve in his place.

was honored on 8 August 1489, when Mancino resigned.[63] An earlier decree from 18 March 1488 is important because it shows that some, if not all, of the trumpeters were given meal allowances. At the time the Concistoro declared that Enea di Senzanome was to have "expenses for food in the Palace, with others of the family," that is, others regularly employed there.

Relatively few changes in personnel occurred during the last decade of the century. Nine trumpeters appear in the clothing list for Assumption Day 1490, eight of them continuing, the other a newcomer, Andrea di Giovanni.[64] Niccolò di Meio's name, along with all of the others, appears on the official clothing list from July 1492, though it is lacking in one from 1493, which also lacks Michelangelo di Niccolò (absent again in 1494) and Lodovico di Manno. Niccolò was clearly another of those musicians who had problems with his employers: he was fired in October 1494 and rehired in the following April.[65] On 6 November 1494 Piergiovanni di Niccolò, another son of the blind trumpeter Niccolò Turini, replaced Lodovico di Manno, who had requested release from Palace service two days earlier. The clothing list for 1495 names a ninth trumpeter, Giovanni di Pietro called El Civile, in place of Niccolò di Meio, with the others.

Events leading to the discovery of a thief among the trumpeters are briefly alluded to in the first of two documents from 14 May 1496. This recounts how the Concistoro was informed that a silver dish weighing six ounces, stolen from the Palace some months earlier, had been melted down and sold to a local silversmith by a Palace trumpeter called Meciaro, who subsequently left town. In consequence, the government put a price on the trumpeter's head should he be found in Siena or any of its territories and forbade payment of any salary he might have earned while he was in Palace service. The second document reports that Jacopo di Giuliano was appointed in Meciaro's place, according to the expectative he had already received. Jacopo's name accordingly appears in the clothing list from 1496. Three musicians from this time could have been Meciaro: Lodovico di Gaddo, fired by the Concistoro in November 1494 for daring to ask to be

---

63. That Lodovico had played with the group even before Gaddo turned his post over to him is apparent from the record of a deliberation, dated 30 April 1485, which says that the Concistoro appointed Lodovico Manni to serve in Mancino's place until such time as he should return (Concistoro, vol. 711, fol. 30ʳ). Lodovico is called a trumpeter from Siena in that record. Lodovico was given the pennant formerly used by Mancino on 14 October 1489, when it was returned on Mancino's behalf by his brother (Concistoro, vol. 738, fol. 10ᵛ). Another dismissal, registered on 22 December 1488, against Britio di Sano, was apparently rescinded within a short time (Concistoro, vol. 733, fol. 20ᵛ).

64. Interestingly, only four trumpeters, Lodovico di Manno, Bernardino di Monaldo, Niccolò di Meio, and Giovanni detto El Moro, and the nakers player Meio di Maestro Ghino (recte Mino) are mentioned in Biccherna records (vol. 344, fol. 83ᵛ) as having received new suits of clothing in August 1490, though nine are named on the Concistoro's list (Concistoro, vol. 743, fols. 36ᵛ–37ʳ).

65. Concistoro, vol. 754, fol. 2ʳ, dated 4 May 1494, records a deliberation granting the trumpeter Niccolò di Meio permission to accompany the lords Antonio Venafro and Jacopo Germonia to the thermal baths and to remain there with them until their return. Niccolò was fired on 26 October 1494. When he was rehired on 20 April 1495, the priors decreed that an expectative was to be returned to the person who had replaced him.

released from service, Domenico di Sano, and Niccolò di Meio. Their names are on the clothing list for 1494, but never appear again after that time.[66] There were no further changes in the group until 1498, when Meio di Maestro Mino was succeeded as drummer by his son Geronimo.[67] The same group was present in the last year of the century. By then, Niccolò Turini had been at the Palace for forty-seven years, El Moro for thirty-one, and Enea for more than twenty. A few of the other musicians had also accumulated impressive records of service: Michelangelo, Bernardino, and Britio were each completing twenty years of employment. The relative newcomers, Andrea di Giovanni, El Civile, Jacopo di Giuliano, and Piergiovanni di Niccolò, had all been appointed within the decade.[68] Longevity of service, the core groups, and stability—all offer ample testimony to the success of the government's employment policies, which may now be assessed more fully.

EMPLOYMENT POLICIES AND BENEFITS

Throughout the fifteenth century having a family member in the trumpeters' ranks was generally an asset for those who aspired to join the group. But during the 1480s and 1490s, when almost three-quarters of all new appointments went to children of musicians already employed, the power of such ties was clearly revealed. Employment records point to an increasingly slow rate of turnover among the trumpeters as the century progressed. A consequence of this was that posts at the Palace became even more difficult to obtain. To meet the situation these were now promised to favored candidates long in advance of their conferral in the form of an expectative. This was, as mentioned, nothing less than a guarantee of employment at the time of the next vacancy. In a few instances musicians served without salary, anticipating a formal appointment, so that occasionally the number of trumpeters actually performing with the group exceeded the one cited in payment records or on the annual clothing lists. A place on the clothing lists was generally reserved only for tenured employees, though occasional exceptions were made.

Expectatives testify to the attractiveness of Palace service for Sienese musicians and to the jockeying that went on among them to obtain an obviously favored status. Musical ability, as the records so frequently remind us, was a requirement, without which no aspiring candidate could hope for consideration. But family connections eased many a path on the way to such consideration. Whether other Palace employees were similarly favored has yet to be ascertained. Understandably, aspirants to government service were ready to wait their turn and even served for long periods without obtaining full benefits. A lifetime appointment at the Palace assured a musician a steady salary, extra compensation in the form of tips and occasional gifts, and a certain security available in

---

66. The list for 1497 names an eleventh trumpeter, Leonardo di Taddeo, serving in place of Jacopo di Giuliano, who was on leave and traveling in the company of a Sienese diplomat.

67. Concistoro, vol. 791, fol. 24^r, dated 4 August 1498, shows, in addition, that Piergiovanni was absent that year, though he was on the list.

68. Andrea di Giovanni was fired on 5 January 1499 for having left the city without the Concistoro's permission. He was pardoned and readmitted to his post within the month (Concistoro, vol. 794, fol. 3^v).

few other professions, not to mention the prestige that attached to a post so close to the seat of power. Then, too, one might pass one's job on to one's progeny. But apart from a desire to see their children properly placed, there was another reason why Palace musicians were so eager to have their own children succeed them. It was a simple matter of survival. Records reveal time and again that when a musician became too old, too feeble, or too sick to continue in his post, the state was ready and willing to allow his son, provided he was capable, to replace him. In an age where any kind of social assistance for the elderly was unknown, government service for a musician with well-trained offspring almost certainly guaranteed a more financially secure old age.

From the government's point of view these employment practices were also considered advantageous for the state. By hiring musicians' relatives, or giving hiring preference to them, the government could reasonably expect that competently trained people who already knew a good deal about their jobs would come into the Palace establishment. Such practices obviously bolstered employees' morale and virtually guaranteed their "good and faithful service," as so many records from the time put it. Good and faithful service, as all could see, worked not only to an employee's advantage but also to that of his children. Ultimately, all would be well served, but the state particularly would benefit. The government's employment policy was also a socially conscious one, for it had a direct bearing on the integrity of family structure as well as on the economic status of those affected. By guaranteeing future employment to close relatives, particularly children, of its musicians, the government assured them of a certain measure of financial security, whether they lived out their retirement in sickness or in health.

The case of Antonio di Tomè may serve as an example of the government's policies and actions. His name first appears in a deliberation from 19 April 1447 when he petitioned the priors for a post among the trumpeters. At the time his father, Tomè di Meio, was one of the two senior employees in the Palace's musical establishment. After noting that they were "cognizant of Antonio's musical abilities," the priors decided that he could perform with the group whenever he pleased, "at whatever festivities or places to which the Magnificent Lords go," and that, like the others, he could display the commune's arms on the pennant attached to his trumpet. Although he would receive no salary for his efforts, the Concistoro promised Antonio that he would be assigned to the first vacant position, "with the usual salary and preferments."

Antonio, a rambunctious youth, excelled in music but did rather less well in diplomacy. A document from a little over two years later reports that that he made several "disgraceful" remarks, which the Concistoro for the sake of public decency declined to have entered into the record. As punishment, he was forbidden to play with the trumpeters and deprived of all his Palace privileges for a year. Antonio was eventually rehabilitated and the government's earlier promise was honored when his father retired. His name, as has been noted, appeared in the list of employees given new clothing on Assumption Day, 1456. However, he died shortly afterwards, and on 26 February 1457 his place was awarded to Niccolò di Piero da Città di Castello. The terms of the latter's appointment show that Tomè di Meio was still alive and that the Concistoro decided to provide for him as though his son were still in their service. Accordingly, they decreed that during his lifetime Tomè would continue to receive his usual salary but that the suits of clothing he would normally receive, indicative of a tenured post, were to go to Niccolò di Piero. Upon Tomè's death, Niccolò would then receive both salary and clothing, like the other regularly employed trumpeters (see Doc. 9.7). Niccolò, however, served for only a few months. A deliberation from 21 July 1457 states that Sano di Matteo, appointed as a trumpeter the day before, was to receive part of the clothing allowance that was earmarked for Niccolò, "who served in place of the recently deceased Tomè."

The careers of Tomè and his son, and a large number of Sienese documents concerning such matters, allow much more certainty about trends in musical patronage only hinted at in discussions above. These trends were, in fact, not peculiar to Siena or even to Italy. Well-known German families of musicians—the Schubingers, the Nagels, and the Neuschels—begin to appear in the records at precisely the same time that family connections become predominant in Siena.[69] A tightening of professional family bonds among musicians undoubtedly reflected general economic and social forces. As Richard Goldthwaite and others have observed, the economic situation for artisans became more troubled toward the end of the fifteenth century.[70] Evidently competition for employment increased and wage scales for tradesmen declined. Although they could hardly be called tradesmen, the trumpeters were in a similar market. In the early 1400s they were forced to take a cut in salary so as to make way for the wind band. The cut was never restored, and as the century progressed, their salaries remained fixed while those of the wind players, always in short supply in Siena, increased. As conditions for professionals such as the trumpeters became bleaker, one reaction, as demonstrated by a wide range of Sienese records, was for them to tighten their grip on what they could control. For trumpet players in Siena this meant recourse to a variety of means so as to pass on their positions to their own progeny.

The government's policy of preferring relatives of its employees often extended to its friends and partisans and at times even cut across the narrow confines of any particular profession. Taking advantage of one's connections and influence, of course, is political patronage in its purest and simplest form, and it comes as no surprise to find at least one example of it among the fifteenth-century Sienese trumpeters.[71] In this instance it was the sixteen-year-old Enea di Senzanome, a musician without familial ties among the trumpeters but with important connections at the Palace, who benefited from the government's patronage.

The circumstances relating to Enea's appointment are in a record, copied on 16 July 1473, carrying the text of a petition addressed to the Concistoro by his father, the Palace storekeeper Giuseppe di Giovanni da Brescia, called Senzanome. The boy, in his father's words, "wished very much to be a trumpeter in your Palace," and despite his

69. On the German families, see Polk, *German Instrumental Music,* 76–79. See also id., "The Schubingers of Augsburg: Innovation in Renaissance Instrumental Music," in *Quaestiones in musica: Festschrift für Franz Krautwurst* (Tutzing, 1989), 495–503; and "Augustein Schubinger and the Zink: Innovation in Performance Practice," *Historic Brass Society Journal* 1 (1989): 83–92.

70. Goldthwaite, *The Building of Renaissance Florence* (Baltimore, 1980), 317–80.

71. On the use of influence as a characteristic of Italian patronage at this time, see Ronald Weissman, "Taking Patronage Seriously: Mediterranean Values and Renaissance Society," in *Patronage, Art, and Society in Renaissance Italy,* ed. F. W. Kent and Patricia Simons (Oxford, 1987), 24–45.

youth, "already plays very well and is the equal of the Palace's salaried [musicians]." For this reason Senzanome requested that Enea be appointed a Palace trumpeter and that he given "half-pay like the others, that is, L. 4 a month and a suit of clothing every year," from the day his request was approved. An addendum to the text of Senzanome's petition states that it was read on 13 July and approved by the Concistoro, "with the proviso that Enea . . . not have the said suit of clothing but that he have L. 4 in cash every month" (see Doc. 9.8). In other words, Enea was not granted a tenured appointment and his name, in fact, is not on the 1473 clothing list, even though he received a salary for the remaining months of that year. Later he received other privileges at the Palace, and in the summer of 1477 he was permitted to journey to Naples with the other trumpeters and to share any gifts and gratuities they might receive there. A year later, in August 1478, the Concistoro honored its commitment to Enea by appointing him to substitute in the position recently vacated by Gaddo di Manno. Enea was later confirmed in the post, which he then occupied until his death in August 1511.[72]

Like Niccolò Turini, Enea di Senzanome was the progenitor of a musical family recorded in Palace service for more than half a century. In his case what is more remarkable is the giant step, professionally, economically, and perhaps socially, that his descendents made as a result of his appointment to Palace service, all of it revealed by subsequent tax records. In 1481 Senzanome declared to tax authorities that he had only his salary and no property, but within a few years Enea owned his own house in the contrada di San Salvadore, an area much favored by musicians. The house was inherited by his son Galgano or Gano, who, as will be mentioned below, became a professional cornettist and member of the Palace wind band.[73] In 1548 Gano's daughter, an orphan of marriageable age, reported ownership of the house in which her ancestors had lived and capital in excess of Fl. 900 (500 of which was from her mother's dowry), now administered by the Bolgarini bank of Siena (see Doc. 9.9). It was not a great fortune by any means, but few other Sienese musicians of the time fared as well, testimony both to what a family of talented musicians could achieve in a few generations as well as to the opportunity for advancement and security provided by government service.

The cash payment Enea initially received as an apprentice was only one of the ways the government used to recompense musicians who were not officially inscribed in the list of Palace employees. In the previous century suits of clothing, as mentioned, were given on one occasion to supernumeraries as compensation for serving without salary. But what is noteworthy about Enea's situation is his father's statement in the petition that the son would serve at half-pay, L. 4, "like the other musicians." Because this obviously did not refer to the tenured trumpeters, who were earning a monthly salary of Fl. 2 (L. 8 or more, according to the value of the florin), it can only mean that

---

72. On 21 August 1511 the Concistoro, "actenta morte Enee Senzanome," appointed Silvestro di Pio in his place.

73. In filing a report to tax authorities in 1481, as he had previously in 1473, Giuseppe di Giovanni da Brescia detto Senzanome, "canavaio del palazo," stated that he had nothing but his salary and that he did not own a house (ASS, Lira, vol. 189, Terzo di Città, 1481, fol. 272ʳ). The evidence for Galgano's owning a house, perhaps inherited from his father Enea, was given by Galgano's daughter in her tax report (see Doc. 9.9).

Enea willingly accepted the same salary conditions granted other young or apprentice trumpeters who performed with the group after they received guarantees of future employment.[74] Though rarely mentioned, the practice of awarding half-pay to non-tenured musicians, in fact, prevailed well into the seventeenth century.

OFFICIAL PERFORMANCES OUTSIDE THE PALACE

It is almost impossible for us today, with our reliance on radio, television, sound recordings, and concert going, to imagine how prominent live musical performance was in the everyday life of a medieval town—performance, moreover, that was offered gratis, in Siena's case, by highly trained professional groups working under the auspices of the state or of state-controlled institutions. As has been mentioned, the trumpeters performed every year in the cathedral square for fifteen days before the feast of the Assumption.[75] There were also performances during those two weeks in the Campo; after the formation of the Palace wind band, the trumpeters were joined in these musical events by the other Palace musicians. Some idea of how the two groups may have interacted in public performance can be had from a fresco (1502–8) above the entrance to the Sienese cathedral's Libreria Piccolomini by Pinturicchio commemorating the coronation of Siena's Pope Pius III (see Fig. 7). This depicts a group of pifferi, two cornetts, and a trombone, on foot playing opposite a group of three trumpeters, two of whom are sounding their instruments, on horseback. Performances such as these, public or private, were closely monitored, as shown by a decree from 2 August 1449, when the Concistoro decided to fine "any piffero or trumpeter who fails to perform tomorrow in the Campo or at the cathedral."[76]

Almost forty years later similar penalties were prescribed for failure to participate in other, by then traditional, ceremonies outside the Palace. On 22 February 1484 the Concistoro decreed that trumpeters were to be present with their instruments every Saturday and Sunday, when the image of the Blessed Virgin Mary was unveiled at the cathedral. Failure to attend would incur a fine of s. 10, to be subtracted from their salaries, for each absence. Five days later another decree lowered the fine to s. 5 and specifically mentioned that the trumpeters were "to play when the figure is unveiled, as has been customary" (see Doc. 9.10). One can only speculate about the kind of music they played at such times, though it is likely that simple fanfares or other pieces that signified a solemn moment were the rule.

Participation in Religious Ceremonies

Documents from a decade later attest to yet another civic-religious function in which the trumpeters participated, the Mass celebrated daily in the outdoor chapel in the Campo. A decree from 25 September 1494 notes that the trumpeters designated to play

---

74. See chapter 10 for remarks about Vergilio di Pier Giovanni, who also began service at half-salary.

75. See pp. 427–28.

76. "Et deliberaverunt Magnifici domini quod quicunque ex piffaris vel trombettis non ibit cras ad sonandum per Campum Fori et ad ecclesiam maiorem, ut tenentur, intelligatur et sit puntatus" (Concistoro, vol. 501, fol. 24ᵛ, dated 2 August 1449).

at the Elevation that morning failed to appear and that the government decided to make an example of them so that others would be more diligent in future. Accordingly, the offenders were condemned to four days in prison and deprived of their meals at the Palace (see Doc. 9.11). On the following day, however, it was reported that the order against the blind trumpeter Niccolò Turini and his son, who had been sent to jail because they had not played at the Elevation, was revoked and that they were to be released.[77] Playing at the Elevation of Masses celebrated out of doors in the Campo continued to form part of the trumpeters' duties throughout the century and is mentioned also in a decree from 1524.[78]

Cathedral records also attest to the presence there of the trumpeters, and later the wind band, on a number of occasions throughout the year (see Doc. 9.12). One payment from May 1428 says the trumpeters played in the cathedral on the feast of St. Victor, and another from Christmas of the same year records a gratuity given them and the members of the wind band. From 1434 come reports of expenses incurred for providing dinner for the trumpeters on Assumption Day and for dinners on five additional feasts, namely St. Victor, St. Crescentius, St. Savinus, St. Ansanus, and the Consecration of the cathedral. The same feasts, St. Victor excepted, are mentioned in a 1451 payment to "Santi the trumpeter and his companions for having played at the duomo on those days." In later years such payments are more generally worded. In 1470 the Palace trumpeters received L. 11 "for having played at all of the feasts of the year in the duomo, as is customary." Records from the 1480s, however, specifically mention their playing on Assumption Day as well as "on feasts and processions and to the Madonna on Saturday evening and on Sunday morning and on other feasts, as is usual."

Processions

The ubiquitous place occupied by the trumpeters in the everyday life of fifteenth-century Siena is amply documented in contemporary chronicles. Several types of events always mentioning their presence, particularly the August Palio, are described below in chapter 14. Suffice it here to examine the trumpeters' role in a few of the many civic and religious processions of which they were so conspicuous a part. The Sienese loved a parade and rarely let an opportunity to put one on go by. Even more rare was a procession without trumpeters. Often, townspeople as well as the clergy and members of religious orders and the confraternities were the principal participants in processions, and though many of these were held for religious reasons, just as many marked some significant social or political event. The annual procession for the feast of Corpus Christi offers an example of the one, the procession in 1443 that honored Pope Eugene's gift of a golden rose, of the other.

---

77. Niccolò was apparently an independently minded person who was quick to stand up for his rights. An earlier record, from 19 January 1494, states that he had been sent to prison, where he was to remain at the government's pleasure, because he had spoken disrespectful words to the Lord Tengoccio (Concistoro, vol. 764, fol. 9ᵛ).

78. "Et decreverunt quod tubicines qualibet mane, quando elevatur Corpus Christi ad Cappellam Campo Fori, teneantur sonare, sub pena eis imponendam per priorem una cum consiliarii[s] prioris" (Concistoro, vol. 948, fol. 2ᵛ, dated 1 November 1524).

The official order of the procession for the feast of Corpus Christi occurs in an addition to the Sienese statutes dating from 12 May 1456, though it was probably fixed long before (see Doc. 9.13).[79] Traditionally, the consuls of the Wool Guild, under whose aegis the festivities were organized, proceeded to the Palace with their trumpeters and a baldachin, accompanied by all of their associates. There they were joined by the Concistoro, whom they then accompanied to the duomo, where, at the sounding of the bells, citizens and guild members had assembled for the service. Afterwards all marched in the customary procession: first came the baldachin accompanied by members of various guilds, then the confraternities, followed by the clergy. Next came the Palace trumpeters and the wind band, then the cathedral canons, who walked ahead of the monstrance containing the host. Immediately following were the cardinal and the bishops, and after them the Concistoro and distinguished citizens, all marching according to rank. Bringing up the rear were the consuls of the Wool Guild and their associates. No mention is made of the position in the procession of other trumpeters, such as those in the service of the Wool Guild or of various government officials, but the description leaves little doubt about the prominence accorded the Palace musicians, placed so they could signal with appropriate music the appearance of the monstrance bearing the host, the principal object of veneration.

The procession on 31 March 1443, less well organized though apparently no less imposing, was occasioned by the presentation of a golden rose by the visiting Pope Eugene IV to Renaldo Orsini, commander of the Sienese army. After the ceremony, as one chronicler recounts, a group of two hundred Sienese youths accompanied the rose throughout the city, "to the sound of trumpets."[80] It must have been a grand and inspiring spectacle for the assembled crowds, the solemnity of the occasion reflecting the great joy and pride the Sienese felt at receiving this signal papal honor. Although the chronicler says nothing about where the ceremony was held, it must have been at the cathedral or, weather permitting, in some large outdoor place such as the chapel in the Campo. Neither does he mention the other musicians who must have taken part in the ceremony. The Palace wind band was undoubtedly there and appropriate vocal music must have been sung by the papal chapel, if not by the cathedral musicians. But documentation of these others was perhaps not essential to the chronicler's point. For the procession was the one part of the event that the entire town witnessed and he knew that merely mentioning the trumpeters' presence sufficed to impart to his readers a sense of the splendor and importance of the occasion.

79. Preceding this are rubrics for "S. Bernardini de Senis festo ordo oblationis" (fol. 76ʳ) and following are rubrics for processions on the feast "de S. Caterina Senensi" (fol. 79ᵛ) and "Nella pasqua delo Spirito Sancto" (fol. 80ʳ), all from 1456.

80. Fecini, "Cronaca Senese," 855. The chronicler's report is summarized by Girolamo Macchi, *Memorie,* tomo V (ASS, MS DIII), fol. 266ʳ: "Giorni felici della settimana per la città di Siena" under "Domenica," where he notes that "L'anno 1443 Papa Eugenio IV venne in Siena con numero 24 Cardinali il quale vi dimorò 6 mesi e la quarta Domenica di Quaresima vi benedì la rosa d'oro e ne fece dono a Missere Renaldo Orsini generale dell'Armi della Repubblica di Siena." Under Sunday Macchi also lists: "L'anno 1458 Papa Pio Piccolomini vescovo di Siena già era Cardinale, fu assunto al Pontificato in Roma e si chiamava Enea Silvio e l'anno 1459 trovandosi in Siena fece Arcivescovato."

No less significant though perhaps less well attended were the university-sponsored ceremonies in which the trumpeters participated. A report from 8 April 1440 states that the "university of the scholars of the studio" had two trumpeter's pennants made, one with [an image] of St. Nicholas, the other of St. Catherine, and a silver baton for the university marshals, "which is adopted when doctorates and other honors are conferred."[81] Whether more than two musicians were present on this occasion is difficult to assess. However, several later reports, such as one from 21 September 1538, which says that the priors allowed the trumpeters and the wind band "to go as a group to honor the doctor who received his decree this morning," indicate that the musicians continued to perform at university celebrations throughout the fifteenth and sixteenth centuries (see Doc. 9.14).

EMISSARIES AT HOME AND ABROAD

When the government wished particularly to honor an important occasion either in or out of town, it used its official musical establishment as well as its most trusted orators and honored citizens, acting as its emissaries. The coronation of Pius II typifies one such situation. Chroniclers speak of the jubilation that erupted throughout the city when news arrived that Siena's cardinal, Aeneas Sylvius Piccolomini, had been elected to the papacy. In addition to the usual bonfires and dancing in the streets and public squares, an impromptu procession featured all of the Palace musicians.[82] Later, the city organized a more formal celebration, and Agostino Dati's account of it leaves the impression that music was everywhere, with the sounds of the bells clanging, the trumpeters playing their fanfares, and the wind band supplying music throughout the festivities.[83]

---

81. BCIS, MS A. IV. 2, *Annali di Siena da 1400 al 1500,* fol. 163[r]: "mazza d'argento per le bedelle, la quale s'adopra a far dottor e altre honoranze."

82. Allegretto Allegretti, "Ephemerides Senenses ab Anno MCCCL usque ad MCCCXCVI. Italico Sermone scriptae ab Allegretto de Allegrettis," in Muratori, ed., *Rerum italicarum scriptores,* 23:765. The celebrations were also mentioned by Malavolti, *Dell'Historia di Siena,* Book 4, p. 60.

83. Agostino Dati, *Augustini Dati Senensis Opera* (Siena, 1503), fol. LXXXIIII[v]–LXXXX[r]:
    Augustini Dathi Senensis Orationum Liber Quartus Foeliciter Incipit. Sequitur brevis annotatio eius solemnitas quae a Senensibus celebrata est in assumptione et coronatione summi Pontificis Pii II Senensis . . . Cum faustus et letissimus nuntius allatus est de Summi Pontificis Pii II Senensis assumptione XIII Kal. Septembris: Anno ab Incarnatione dominica. MCCCCLVIII. Haec prodiit Senensis civitas admirabilis gaudii et summae letitiae signa.
    Primum recognita tantum repente civium animos incessit gaudium: cum maioribus incredibili quodam et raro audito a seculis exultarent gaudio . . . Omnia cum festum ara et campane totius civitatis tinnierunt: tubarum clangor: tibicinarum concentus: timpanorum boatus: cymbalorum sonitus mirus exauditur est . . . In ore omnium Pius Pontifex et Pastor sanctissimus versabatur mox vero magnus Magistratis et Balie collegium precinentibus tubicinibus ac tibicine et timpanis curiam ingressi sunt et Senatum frequentatissimum coegerunt. Ubi summa omnium letitia annuntiata est gloriosissima Summi Pontificis assumptio . . . Modulorum omnium et musicorum concentus maior reperitus est fidibus et cytharis et organis campus et vici totius urbis circumsonabant. Plausus et cantus ubique exaudiebantur? Quo densiore ignes collucebant loco: ibi non

The pope's family was also singled out for special attention a few years later, when on 4 January 1459 the Concistoro decided to make an exception to the statute that forbade Palace musicians to participate in private celebrations within the city.[84] As part of the official government delegation, which included "knights, doctors, and others," the government sent the trumpeters and the wind band to accompany the Pope's nieces in the traditional bridal processions that were such an important part of wedding ceremonies.[85] The city's most generous gesture, however, was reserved for the marriage of Eleanor of Aragon, daughter of King Alfonso of Naples, and Ercole d'Este, Duke of Ferrara. The princess was traveling to Ferrara, where her new husband awaited her, and it had been arranged for her to stop off at Siena en route. One payment of L. 63. 12 from May for "when they went to Naples," indicates that all of the Palace musicians, trumpeters as well as woodwind players, were sent south so that they might accompany the princess back to Siena. During her stay, as will be recounted below, the Concistoro staged an elaborate ball in her honor, and when she resumed her journey north, the Sienese musicians were again in her train. Accordingly, a second payment, in the amount of L. 168, records expenses the musicians incurred when they accompanied "the retinue of the marquis [duke] of Ferrara's bride."[86] This was not the first contact between Sienese musicians and the Ferrarese lord, who a decade earlier had taken a former member of the Palace wind band into his service.

Lest it be thought, however, that the Concistoro was willing to relax its rules about musicians playing in other places without their approval, suffice it to cite two instances of the consequences that awaited those who dared to do so. The first concerns the trumpeter Petrolino, who went to the monastery of St. Claire without official permission. He may have even performed while he was there, although the record of deliberation does not say so. In any case as punishment and also as an example to others, the priors sentenced Petrolino to a month in jail beginning in June 1457. (He was, however, let out in time for the feast of Corpus Christi on June 13 so that he could accompany

---

modo puerorum sed etiam gravioris etatis hominum tripudia et saltatus agebant: ut nemo asolutissima letitia temperaret.

See chapter 11, notes 129–30, for a report of the musicians sent to Rome with Sienese emissaries to offer the pope official congratulations. (BCIS, MS B. V. 40, fols. 3ʳ–8ʳ, contains a slightly varied version of Dati's account.)

84. Lodovico Zdekauer, *La vita privata dei Senesi nel Dugento* (Siena, 1896–97), 79, mentions the statute that prohibited town musicians from performing at private weddings, spelled out in the Constitution of 1262. The statute, Distinctio I, [301], is published in Zdekauer, *Il Constituto del Comune di Siena*, 117.

85. Eugenio Casanova, *La donna senese del Quattrocento nella vita privata* (Siena, 1901), 22, quoting a document from ASS, Biccherna, *Provvedimenti, 1450–66*, fol. 54, 145. Casanova also notes that the traditional practice of having trumpeters accompany bridal processions predates the first written Sienese constitutions, which, in fact, prescribe the number of musicians who might be employed for such purposes and exactly where in the order of events they might participate (pp. 22, 65).

86. ASS, Regolatori, vol. 9, fol. 402ᵛ, in the "Uscita di Nicolò da Castel del Piano, spenditore dei Signori," dated May–June, 1474: "Item, per dare a' trombetti e buffoni e piffari quando andorono a Napoli . . . L. 63 s. 12 d—. Item, per dare a' trombetti, piffari, tromboni e tanburini quando andò suso la sposa del Marchese di Ferrara . . . L. 168 s—d—."

the priors when they marched in procession.) A report from June 1464 notes that the government fined the trumpeters and the members of the wind band s. 40 each for having gone to the thermal baths outside the city to visit the Magnificent Taddeo da Imola, when he was passing through Sienese territory (see Doc. 9.15). Musicians, however, were not forbidden to leave the city for personal reasons, as a number of other records already cited demonstrate.[87]

A number of records reveal that from time to time Palace trumpeters and woodwind players went on state-approved trips. Typically, they visited other cities in Tuscany to assist in celebrations of special feast days. The government's contribution consisted mainly of excusing the musicians from their normal duties and keeping them on the payroll while they were absent, though travel subsidies are mentioned on occasion. Normally, however, these were covered by gratuities the musicians received from their hosts. One of the earliest recorded trips occurred on 9 September 1404, when three trumpeters were permitted to go to Lucca for the festivities there marking the feast of the Holy Cross. On the 26th of the same month two trumpeters were dispatched to Cortona to assist in that city's celebration of its patron saint's day.[88] Journeys to Lucca for similar reasons are frequently recorded throughout the fifteenth century. In 1459 and 1462, for example, four trumpeters made the trip, and in 1482 the entire corps went.[89] Six trumpeters, the drummer, and the wind band were authorized to travel to Massa for the feast of St. Corbonus on 6 October 1498.[90] By far the most important and most frequently recorded of the Sienese musicians' trips were those to Florence for the St. John's Day celebrations on 24 June. On such occasions the musicians in effect represented the Sienese government; understandably, in times of war or when relations between the two states were strained, as happened often, there were no exchanges of musicians. One of the earliest recorded trips to Florence was in 1415, when four trumpeters went.[91] Only four trumpeters, together with the members of the wind band,

---

87. In addition to those cited, the following may be noted: Concistoro, vol. 546, fol. 11ʳ, which records permission given to Sano di Matteo on 15 September 1457 to leave the city for four days; vol. 547, fol. 10ᵛ, showing that Santi da Volterra was given three days' leave on 27 November 1457; and vol. 552, fol. 25ʳ, which notes a leave of absence for Giovanni da Iesi so he could go to the thermal baths for twenty days, though he was not to receive any salary during his absence.

88. Concistoro, vol. 234, fol. 10ᵛ, for the trip to Lucca, dated 9 September 1404, and fol. 21ᵛ, for the trip to Cortona, dated 25 September 1404.

89. "Deliberaverunt dare et dederunt et concesserunt licentiam quattuor ex eorum tubicenes Palatii eundi Lucam ad festa Sancti Crucis ut est consuetis" (Concistoro, vol. 558, fol. 8ᵛ, for 1459; vol. 576, fol. 8ʳ, dated 10 September 1462). Vol. 694, fol. 16ᵛ, dated 24 May 1482, gives a similar text.

90. "Concesserunt licentiam sex tubicenis eorum palatii, nacharino, trumbone et piffaris, eundi ad civitatem Masse pro honoranda festivitate Sancti Corboni" (Concistoro, vol. 792, fol. 14ᵛ, dated 6 October 1498). Permission to visit other Italian cities, including places outside Tuscany, was granted to Palace musicians any number of times during the first half of the sixteenth century. A typical record comes from 28 September 1536, when four trumpeters and the nakers player were given permission to go to Bologna: "Et concesserunt licentiam quatuor tubicenis et naccarino eorum palatii eundi Bononiam ad honorandum festum" (Concistoro, vol. 1020, fol. 20ʳ).

91. Concistoro, vol. 296, fol. 35ʳ, dated 21 June 1415.

made the trip in 1457,[92] but the Palace's entire musical establishment went in 1493.[93] These trips formed part of reciprocal exchange programs with other cities, and as noted below in connection with the August Palio, many foreign musicians came to Siena to help celebrate the Assumption Day festivities. More important for the history of Italian instrumental music, these trips provided opportunities for musicians to exchange ideas and to learn what their counterparts in other places were doing. Surely, occasions such as these illustrate how easily repertories and techniques were transmitted.

Visiting Musicians

Just as Sienese musicians went to other cities to lend their sounds to important events, so did foreign musicians journey to Siena. Typical of records concerning visiting musicians is one payment of L. 2. 4 issued to the trumpeters of Count Ugo and others on 31 December 1402 "for the mornings, and for playing when the standards (banners) were given out and at table when the dinner was held for the officials."[94] A few years later, on 10 August 1410, the trumpeters and woodwind players of Duke Louis of Anjou, onetime ruler of Naples, received 10 florins for performing for their Sienese hosts.[95] Florentine musicians appear twice in the following decade. On 24 January 1417 a gratuity of L. 8. 5 was given to trumpeters and woodwind players from Florence who attended the joust.[96] From January 1419 come payments of L. 5. 10 to Florentine trumpeters and woodwind players, "as a courtesy, when they returned from [the head-quarters of the condottiere] Tartaglia and came to visit the lords," and of L. 1. 2 to trumpeters of the podestà for L. 1. 2, "when they came to visit the lords."[97] Sometimes, Palace musicians were not forgotten in these bursts of generosity, as is shown by a payment from the same month of a gratuity of s. 11 to regularly salaried woodwind players, trumpeters, and drummer.[98] Later in the century Siena was engulfed annually on the feast of the Assumption by scores of foreign trumpeters who came to the city

---

92. Concistoro, vol. 544, fol. 20^r.

93. "tubicenibus et tibicenibus, trumbono et timpaniste palatii licentiam concesserunt eundi Florentiam ad festum Sancti Iohannis" (Concistoro, vol. 760, fol. 16^v, dated 21 June 1493).

94. "tronbetti del conte Ugho e altri, per mattinate e sonare la mattina si dero e gonfaloni e a tavola quando si fece el disinare agl'uffiziali" (Concistoro, vol. 2495, fol. 89^v).

95. "Quod operarius Camere solvat tubettis et piffaris regis Lodovici decem florenos senenses novos" (Concistoro, vol. 267, fol. 18^v).

96. "Ai tronbetti e piffari da Firenze che vennero a vedere la giostra, a dì 24 di gienaio dèi trenta grossi d'ariento per mancia, L. 8 s. 5" (Concistoro, vol. 2497, *Proventi, spese e inventari, 1414–19*, fol. 145^r, dated 1416/17).

97. "A' tronbetti et a' piffari fiorentini, di cortesia quando tornaro dal Tartaglia e venero a visitare i signori, grossi vinti d'ariento, vagliano lire cinque soldi dieci, L. V s. X . . . A' tronbetti del Podestà, a dì 5 del detto, grossi quatro di cortesia quando venero a visitare i Signori, L. I s. II" (ibid., fol. 161^v, dated January 1418/19). Other musicians mentioned in this volume include: the trumpeter of Cristofano de' Lavello, who received L. 2. 15 for an unspecified reason on 23 February 1418 (fol. 174^r), and two trumpeters of Signor Braccio da Montone who received L. 8. 5 for an unspecified reason on 28 June 1418 (fol. 126^r).

98. "A' piffari e t[r]onbetti e 'l nacharino, per bene 'scita soldi undici, L. 0 s. XI" (ibid., fol. 162^r, dated January 1418/19).

to assist in the celebrations. Their presence and numbers will be discussed below in chapter 14.

Other City Trumpeters

The just-cited January 1419 payment to the trumpeters of the podestà proves that by this time other Sienese officials maintained their own trumpeters. Further corroboration comes from a record of payment from 16 August 1430, which mentions two trumpeters of the podestà of Siena and one trumpeter of the past podestà of Siena, in addition to the town trumpeters.[99] Sometimes their presence is even noted outside the city, as in a document from nearby San Gimignano, which says that two trumpeters of the podestà of Siena and one of the captain of the people of Siena participated in festivities honoring the town's patron saint on 31 January 1463.[100] More typical are the documents from Siena itself, such as the lists of expenditures for Assumption Day festivities in 1475 and in 1482, which mention two trumpeters of the podestà of Siena and one trumpeter of the captain of the people of Siena among the many musicians who performed on those occasions.[101]

DOCUMENTS

Doc. 9.1. The trumpeters' salaries are reduced, 26 April 1408. ASS, Concistoro, vol. 253, fol. 33^v

Magnifici domini . . . concorditer conduxerunt Severinum Bartalomei de Sancto Severino, vocato Manco, pro tubatore Comunis de consensu cum salario et stipendio duorum florenorum auri Senensium, nitidorum de cabella, pro quolibet mense et cum robbis usitatis et cum aliis condictionibus contentis in stantiamento aliorum tubatorum. Et similiter reduxerunt soldum et stipendium infrascriptorum quatuor tubatorum et infrascripti naccarini ad eandem quantitatem duorum florenorum auri Senensiun nitidorum pro quolibet mense et quolibet eorum, remanentibus firmis aliis contentis in eorum stantiamento. Et ista incipiat in Kalendis Maii proximi . . . Quorum hec sunt nomina, videlicet: Antonius Antonii, vocatus Riccio; Chimentus Blasii; Iohannes Antonii de Bononia; Angelus Arrigi de Alamania, alias vocatus Imperatore; Angelus Vannucii naccarinus.

Doc. 9.2. Tomè di Meio is fired and half his stipend assigned to Antonio di Ciuccio, 26 July 1409. Concistoro, vol. 261, fol. 23^r

Et decreverunt quod scriptor Bicherne tollat et casset a posta Tome tubatoris et ab eius salario illud plus quod sibi fuit additum propter bannire per civitatem, videlicet a die qua Rex Ladizlaus venit super territorium Senense, que fuit XII aprilis proxime preteriti. Item decreverunt quod medietas illius quantitatis que tolletur et cassabitur a posta dicti Tome dicta de causa, addatur salario quod habet ad presens Antonii Ciucii tubatori, pro bannis per eum quotidie mis[s]is.

---

99. ASS, Biccherna, vol. 310, fol. 48^v.

100. "Ai 2 trombetti del Podestà di Siena, s. 20 per uno, L. 2; a 1 trombetto del Capitano di Siena, s. 20, L. 1" (San Gimignano, Biblioteca Comunale, Comune, MS NN 126, fol. 370^r, dated January 1462/63). The other trumpeters included five from the community of Volterra, four from the community of Colle, one from San Miniato, two each from the governors of Certaldo and San Miniato, and one from a private party.

101. See chapter 14, Doc. 14.6 and note 99.

PLATE 1. A service in the chapel of Santa Maria delle Grazie, from the Biccherna cover of 1483. Siena, Archivio di Stato. Reproduced by permission of the Ministero per i Beni Culturali e Ambientali. Further reproduction prohibited

PLATE 2. Sano di Pietro, illumination of Sant'Ansano and the martyrdom of Sant'Ansano, Libreria Piccolomini, MS 27. 11, fol. 10ᵛ. Courtesy Opera della Metropolitana di Siena; photograph from Foto Testi

PLATE 3. "Il Sodoma." Saint Benedict excommunicates two believers. Detail of singers. Abbey, Monte Oliveto Maggiore, outside Siena, 1505–8; photograph from Scala/Art Resource, New York

PLATE 4. Ambrogio Lorenzetti, dancers, detail of fresco of "The Allegory of Good Government." Siena, Palazzo Pubblico. Courtesy Museo Civico, Siena; photograph from Foto Lensini

Doc. 9.3. Monaldo di Bartolomeo replaces Santi di Volterra, and Petrolino is fired, 7 July 1459. Concistoro, vol. 557, fol. 6^v

Magnifici domini . . . deliberaverunt conducere et conduxerunt Monaldum Bartholomei de Clanciano, tubicinam, in tubatorem et banditorem et tubicinam Comunis Senarum . . . loco Santis de Vulterris, olim tubicine et banditis palatii, cum salario ordinato et prout habet idem Santes . . . Annulantes omnem conductam factam de Petrolinum [gap] de Senis per eorum predecessores, eo maxime quia ignorat bandire et quia etiam non fuit iuridice factam.

Doc. 9.4. Bartolomeo di Monaldo is appointed trombonist in the wind band, and Giovanni di Petrolino detto Barbulia is pardoned and reinstated, 16 June 1469. Concistoro, vol. 615, fols. 30^v–31^r

Magnifici domini . . . viso quod locus tromboni palatii vacat ad presens, decreverunt conducere et conduxerunt in trombonum palatii et ad sonandum trombonum . . . Bartholomeum Monaldi, cum salario librarum XII pro quolibet mense . . . incipiendo in Kalendis Maii proxime venturi et deinde ad beneplacitum Consistorii.

Item decreverunt quod ego notarius Cassem de Balzanella amonitionem et condennationem factam alias per Consistorium Iohanni Petrolini tubicini, alias Barbulia, ipsum absolvendo penitus ab omnibus in ea contentis. Et informati quam idoneus tubicen sive tubettus sit Iohannes Petrolini, alias Barbulia, de Senis, et locus unius tubicinis vacat propter Bartholomeum Monaldi assumptum pro trombono, decreverunt conducere et conduxerunt dictum Iohannem pro tubicine seu tubetto palatii, ad beneplacitum Consistorii . . . et cum salario et modis ordinatis et consuetis pro aliis tubettis Comunis Senarum.

Doc. 9.5. Britio di Sano substitutes for Bernardino di Monaldo, absent in Lombardy, 15 May 1480. Concistoro, vol. 682, fol. 12^v

Attento insuper quod Bernardinus Monaldi, tubicena eorum palatii, iam sunt plures menses ivit in Lombardiam et nemo est qui serviat eius loco in dicto palatio, servatis servandis concorditer deliberaverunt substituere et subrogare et substituerunt et subrogaverunt loco ipsius Bernardini, pro tempore quo stabit absens, Britium Sani, tubicenam de Senis, cum salario emolumentis et modi consuetis et quibus serviebat dictus Bernardinus.

Doc. 9.6. Gaddo di Manno resumes the post he resigned in favor of his brother Lodovico, who retains an expectative, 9 February 1487. Concistoro, vol. 722, fol. 12^{r-v}

Magnifici domini . . . decreverunt quod Gaddus Manni tubicen sequatur eius conductam pro tubicene Magnificorum dominorum non obstante quod renunciaverit et loco ipsius fuerit conductus Ludovicus eius frater, cuius conducta intelligatur esse et sit suspensa, non preiudicando gratie expectative ipsius Ludovici, quam voluerunt habere roborem pro primo vacante. Hoc declarato, quod salarium presentis mensis currat pro dicto Lodovico per totum presentem mensem, et restituere ipsi Lodovico tres ducatos, alias conducta ipsius Gaddi sit nulla et Ludovicus predictus sequatur in eius conducta.

Doc. 9.7. Niccolò di Piero assumes the post of Antonio di Tomè, but Antonio's father is to continue to receive his salary, 26 February 1457. Concistoro, vol. 542, fol. 23^v

Antedicti Magnifici domini . . . conduxerunt Nicolaum Pietri Antonii de Civitate Castelli, in tubicenam et pro tubicena Comunis Senarum hoc modo videlicet, quod durante vita Thommei Mei, tubicene Comunis Senarum, dictus Nicolaus serviat cum tuba palatio dicti Comunis pro dicto Thommeo, et habeat omnes vestes quas Comune Senarum in futurum daret dicto Thomme, et dictus Thommas habeat salarium tantum. Post mortem autem dicti Thomme, dictus Nicolaus succedat et remaneat conductus eius loco, cum vestibus et salario ordinato seu ordinando aliis tubicenis dicti palatii.

Doc. 9.8. The Palace storekeeper Senzanome da Brescia petitions for his son to be hired as trumpeter at half-pay, 16 July 1473. ASS, Consiglio Generale, vol. 235, fol. 83^{r-v}

Senzanome da Brescia, vostro devotissimo servidore et al presente vostro canovaio, con reverentia expone come . . . ha el primo figl[i]uolo d'età d'anni XVI et ha gran vogl[i]a d'essere trombetto del vostro palazo, et già suona bene et al pari d'alcuno [altro] che sono salariati al vostro palazo. Unde Magnifici Signori miei . . . vi piaccia . . . deliberare che Enea mio figl[i]uolo sia et esser s'intenda dal dì che si obterrà la decta petitione, essere conducto trombetto del vostro palazzo et habbi meza paga come hanno li altri, cioè lire quattro el mese et la veste ogni anno. . . .

Die XIII dicti mensis lecta et approbata fuit dicta petitio . . . cum hac limitatione, quod Eneas . . . non habeat dictam vestem, sed habeat libras quatuor denariorum quolibet mense.

Doc. 9.9. Tax declaration of the granddaughter of Enea di Senzanome, 1548. ASS, Lira, vol. 243, Terzo di Città, 1548, fasc. 3, fol. 32^r, no. 1790

Dinantia da voi Magnifici Signori Alliratori, Filosina figlia di Galghano piffaro di Palazzo, d'età di anni quattordici, per la presente scritta dà alla nuova lira da farsi l'infrascritti beni e erediti con l'infrascritte gravezze e prima

Una casa posta in Siena, Terzo di Città e contrada di San Salvadore fra suoi confini di valuta di fiorini trecento in circha, quale anticamente fu di detto già Galghano e suoi antenati sopra la quale si ha in parte a rintegrar di fiorini cinquecento per la dote di Monna Battista già suo [*sic*] madre.

Trovasi fiorini trecento nelle mani di Bolgharino Bolgharini banchiere qual già più fa ha retratto d'una metà d'una possessione che detto Galghano haveva, talche oltre alli fiorini cinquecento della dote di sua madre, dette [illegible] può essare d'avanzo intorno a cento fiorini quali già pervenghano di heredità doppo la vita di Monna Francesca, madre di detto Galghano, sua nonna, la quale e vechissima e vive delle poche sustantie di detta Filosina. Li parenti di essa Filosina son tuttavia in pratica di maritarla, ne li rimarrà se non la detta casa peròche li fiorini 300 detti si convertiranno in spese [illegible].

Ha di credito nel monte di sale del Magnifico Comune di Siena in nome di detta Monna Francesca fiorini cinquecento. Dall'altra banda si trova debiti [illegible] la detta casa circa fiorini 25 senza entrata e avuta alchuno et con il charico di governo di detta Monna Francesca. Però si raccomanda quanto più può alle Spettabilità Vostre, Dio le felicita.

Doc. 9.10. The trumpeters are ordered to play at the unveiling of the image of the Virgin every Saturday and Sunday, 22 and 27 February 1484. Concistoro, vol. 704, fols. 39^r and 44^r

Et decreverunt quod trombetti debeant interesse cum tubis et sonare omni die sabati et omni die dominico, quando discoperitur imago Virginis Marie in ecclesia cathedrali, sub pena soldorum decem pro quolibet trombetto quem tangit, de suo salario auferenda.

Decreverunt quod trombetti teneantur et debeant singulis sabbatis et aliis diebus quando discoperitur figura beate Marie Virginis in ecclesia cathedrali interesse cum tubis et sonare quando discoperitur dicta figura, ut est consuetum. Pena illis trombettis quos tanget dictis diebus, soldorum 5 pro quolibet eorum, solvenda seu auferenda per Camerarium Opere. Et sacristanus duomi debeat illos inobedientes denuntiare dicto camerario qualibet vice qua non intererit. Et hec deliberatio ponatur in breve trombettorum. Et fuit scripta hec deliberatio in breve trombettorum per me notarium.

Doc. 9.11. The trumpeters are ordered to prison for failing to perform at the Elevation during Mass in the Cappella del Campo, 25 September 1494. Concistoro, vol. 768, fol. 8^v

Magnifici et potentes domini . . . Viso quod hoc mane tubicenes, qui tenentur sonare tubas in elevatione Corporis Domini in capella Campi Fori, non sonuerunt, et volentes eos punire ut alias sint diligentiores et aliis sint in exemplo: servatis servandis solemniter decreverunt quod illi qui tenentur tuba canere in dicta elevatione, mittantur per barigiellum in carcere et ibi stent per quattuor dies, et durante tempore eorum magistratus non habeant expensas victus in palatio.

Doc. 9.12. Cathedral payments to Palace trumpeters, 1428–87

May 1428: Le spese dela casa del'Uopera . . . E dieno dare a dì 18 di maggio soldi vintiesette denari sei, e quagli paghai . . . a' tronbetti de' Singniori perchè venero a tronbare el dì [di] Santo Vettorio in duomo, L. I s. VII d. VI . . . E dieno dare a dì 28 di dicembre [1428] lire quatro soldi otto, e quagli paghai . . . a' trombetti e a' piffari e a' donzegli e fameglli de la porta de' nostri mangnifici Singniori, e a due ghazonetti de l'Uopera, e quali lo' diei per la pasqua come s'usa, L. IIII s. VIII (AOMS, vol. 545, *Memoriale, 1428–29,* fol. 8 left)

August 1434: Le spese del'Uopara . . . E dien dare . . . insino a dì 15 d'agosto soldi vintiquatro, sono per pane e frutta per la colazione de' tronbetti che venero a onorare la festa, L. I s. IIII . . . E dien dare a dì detto [17 agosto 1434] soldi vintisette denari sei, pagamo alo 'Mperadore tronbetta per la festa di San Vettorio a dì 15 di maggio, contanti in sua mano, L. 1 s. VII d. 6 (vol. 547, *Memoriale, 1434,* fol. 14 left)

October and December 1434: E die dare a dì XV d'ottobre soldi vintisette denari sei, pagamo ad Agniolo di Biagio tronbetta e conpagni perchè venero a tronbare la festa di San Crescienzio, L. 1 s. VII d. 6 . . . E die dare a dì IIII di dicienbre lire quatro soldi due denari sei, pagamo ad Agniolo di Biagio tronbetta, furo' per tronbare la festa di San Savino e dela sagra e di Santo Sano, a grossi cinque per festa, L. IIII s. II d. 6 (ibid., fol. 16 left)

2 December 1451: E de' dare . . . grossi vintiquatro . . . a Santi tronbetta e conpagni, fu per quatro feste sonno venuti in duomo a sonare, per Santo Crescentio e Savino e la sagra e Santo Sano . . . L. VI s. XII d. 0 (vol. 564, *Memoriale, 1451–52,* fol. 29ᵛ)

November 1470: Spese di casa dieno dare . . . E dien dare a dì 8 di novembre lire undici s. 0 per detto di messer Savino a' tronbetti di palazo, per lor salario d'uno anno di tronbare per tutte le feste dell'anno come si costuma, contanti a Giovanni di Nicholò Kamarlengo di deti tronbetti . . . L. XI (vol. 507, *D&C, 1466–75,* fol. 123 left) (payments to trumpeters for 1471, 1473, and 1474 are recorded in the same volume, fols. 172 left, 292 left, and 343 left)

August 1484: Le spese de la festa di Santa Maria di mezo Aghosto de l'anno presente 1484 die dare . . . E adì XXVI di detto [aghosto] L. undici s.—a' tronbetti dei nostri Magnifici Signori, in mano a Nicholò loro camerlengo, sonno per lor fadigha d'uno anno avere sonato per le feste e processioni et a la madonna il sabato sera e la domenica mattina e altre feste come è consueto, a uscita di Tomaxo d'Antonio di Niccolò nostro camerlengo a fo. 37. L. XI (vol. 509, *D&C, 1482–1527,* fol. 109 left)

September 1487: Ghaddo di Manno e chonpagni tronbetti de' nostri Magnifici Signori dieno dare adì VII di settenbre L. undici s. 0 . . . [opposite:] dieno avere L. undici s. 0 per havere sonato tutte le feste e sabati di questo anno presente e sonno alle spese in questo fo. 296. L. XI (ibid., fol. 224 left and right)

Doc. 9.13. Order of the procession on Corpus Christi, 12 May 1456. ASS, *Statuti,* vol. 39, fol. 79ʳ

> L'ordine della processione della festa del sanctissimo Corpo di Christo:
> Doppo il padiglione vadino tucte l'arte sicondo so' state ordinate per lo passato
> Dipoi seghuitino le compagnie
> Dipoi seghuiti il creicato [*sic*]
> Dopo il crero [*sic*], le trombe et piffare

Dapoi, i canonici innanzi al Corpo di Christo
Doppo il Corpo di Christo, il cardinale co' veschovi
Dipoi i Magnifici Signori con i graduati et ordini
Doppo questi, i consoli dell'Arte dela Lana con li lanaiuoli.

Doc. 9.14. The Palace musicians perform at the conferment of a doctoral degree, 21 September 1538. Concistoro, vol. 1038, fol. 11^{r-v}

Excellentissimi et potentissimi domini . . . deliberaverunt quod tubicines habeant licentiam et eant una ad honorandum doctorem qui fit hoc mane et similiter tibicines. Et actento quod quamplurimi tubicines non serviunt palatio debitis temporibus prout solitum est, deliberaverunt precipi dictis tubicinibus haud servientibus, quod infra triduum debeant allegasse causam et quo iure non inserviant, alias cum non sit hec causa, nunc pro tunc et e converso intelligantur privi de ipsorum salario tam preterito quam futuro tempore non servito.

Doc. 9.15. The trumpeters and pifferi are chastised for leaving the city without permission, 18 June 1464. Concistoro, vol. 586, fol. 46^{v}

Advertentes prefati Magnifici domini . . . quod infrascripti tubicene et tibicene et trombonus iverunt, contra precepta eis facta, ad visitandum Magnificum dominum Taddeum de Imola in eius transitu quando rediebat a balneis, deliberaverunt quod dicti et infrascripti . . . sint condenati in solidis 40 pro quolibet eorum.

TABLE 9.1. Chronological list of fifteenth-century trumpeters and drummers

A. TRUMPETERS	1400–1	1402	1403–4	1405–6	1407–10	1411–12	1413–14	1415	1416	1417–18	1419	1420–21	1422–23
Antonio di Ciuccio[a]	x	x	x	x	x	x	x	x	x	x	x		
Jacomo di Corso	x	x	x										
Chimenti di Biagio[b]	x	x	x	x	x	x	x	x	x	x	x	x	x
Giovanni di Antonio da Bologna	x	x	x	x									
Antonio di Antonio detto Riccio[c,d]		x	x	x	x	x	x	x	x	x	x	x	x
Severino di Bartolomeo detto Mancio			x	x	x	x	x	x	x	x	x	x	x
Angelo d'Arrigo da Alamania detto Imperadore					x	x	x	x	x	x	x	x	x
Tomè di Meio[e]					x	x	x	x	x	x	x	x	x
Bartolomeo di Crescenzio							x	x	x	x	x	x	x
Angelo di Biagio[f]							x	x	x	x	x	x	x
Guido di Angelo								x	x	x	x	x	

	1424	1425	1426	1427	1428–29	1430	1431–33	1434	1435	1436	1437	1438	1439–42	1443
Chimenti di Biagio	x	x	x	x	x	x	x	x	x			x	x	x
Antonio di Antonio	x	x	x	x	x	x	x	x	x			x	x	x
Severino di Bartolomeo	x	x	x											
Angelo d'Arrigo	x	x	x	x	x	x	x	x	x	x	x	x	x	
Tomè di Meio	x	x	x	x	x	x	x	x	x	x	x	x	x	x
Bartolomeo di Crescenzio	x													
Angelo di Biagio	x	x	x	x	x	x	x	x	x					
Guido di Angelo	x	x	x											
Alberto di Covaruccio	x	x	x	x	x	x	x	x	x	x	x	x	x	x
Gabriel di Tommaso			x	x										
Niccolò di Golino				x	x									
Antonio di Niccolò da Urbino						x								
Giovanni di Antonio								x	x	x	x	x		
Pietro di Giovanni detto Petrolino*								x	x	x			x	x

TABLE 9.1 *continued*

	1424	1425	1426	1427	1428–29	1430	1431–33	1434	1435	1436	1437	1438	1439–42	1443
Agostino di Giovanni da Pavia									x		x	x	x	x
Giovanni di Martino da Pergola										x	x	x	x	x
Pietro di Antonio										x				
Santi di Riccarduccio											x	x	x	x
Piero di Jacopo detto Nibbio													x	x

	1444	1445	1446	1447	1448	1449	1450	1451–53	1454	1455	1456	1457	1458	1459–62
Chimenti di Biagio	x	x	x	x	x									
Antonio di Antonio	x	x	x	x	x	x	x	x	x	x				
Tomè di Meio	x	x	x	x	x	x	x	x	x	x				
Alberto di Covaruccio	x	x												
Pietro di Giovanni detto Petrolino	x		x	x	x	x	x	x	x	x	x	x	x	x
Agostino di Giovanni da Pavia	x	x	x	x	x	x	x							
Giovanni di Martino da Pergola	x	x	x	x	x	x	x	x	x	x	x	x	x	x
Santi di Riccarduccio	x	x	x	x	x	x	x	x	x	x	x	x	x	x
Piero di Jacopo detto Nibbio	x	x	x											
Andrea di Antonio da Urbino	x	x	x	x	x	x								
Niccolò Teutonico			x	x										
Giuliano da Chianciano	x	x	x	x	x	x	x	x	x	x	x	x	x	x
Antonio di Tomè[g]					x	x					x			
Giovanni di Niccolò da Iesi						x	x	x	x	x	x	x	x	x
Tommaso di Cristoforo da Forlì						x	x	x	x					
Giovanni di Petrolino detto Barbulia[h]									x					
Niccolo Cieco Turini										x	x	x	x	x
Santi di Paolo da Volterra										x	x	x	x	
Niccolo di Piero da Città di Castello												x		
Sano di Matteo da Siena													x	x
Monaldo di Bartolomeo													x	x

	1463	1464–66	1467	1468	1469	1470–72	1473–74	1475–78	1479	1480–81	1482	1483	1484	1485
Pietro di Giovanni detto Petrolino	x	x	x	x	x	x	x	x						
Giovanni di Martino da Pergola	x	x	x	x	x	x	x	x	x	x	x	x	x	x
Santi di Riccarduccio	x	x	x											
Giuliano da Chianciano	x	x	x	x	x	x								
Giovanni di Niccolò da Iesi	x	x	x	x	x	x	x							
Giovanni di Petrolino detto Barbulia		x		x	x	x	x							
Niccolò Cieco Turini	x	x	x	x	x	x	x	x	x	x	x	x	x	x
Sano di Matteo da Siena	x	x	x	x	x	x	x	x	x	x	x	x	x	x
Monaldo di Bartolomeo	x	x	x	x	x	x	x							
Bartolomeo di Monaldo				x	x									
Giovanni detto El Moro				x	x	x	x	x	x	x	x	x	x	x
Domenico da Brescia detto Voltolina							x	x						
Enea di Senzanome							x	x	x	x	x	x	x	x
Gaddo di Manno[i]								x	x	x	x	x	x	x
Bernardino di Monaldo[j]								x		x	x	x	x	x
Britio di Sano										x	x	x	x	x
Michelangelo di Niccolò[k]										x	x	x	x	x
Geronimo di Giovanni da Iesi[l]										x	x	x	x	x
Mariano detto Mancino												x	x	x

	1486	1487	1488	1489	1490–92	1493	1494	1495	1496	1497	1498–99
Niccolò Cieco Turini	x	x	x	x	x	x		x	x	x	x
Sano di Matteo da Siena	x										
Giovanni detto El Moro	x	x	x	x	x	x		x	x	x	x
Enea di Senzanome	x	x	x	x	x	x	x	x	x	x	x
Gaddo di Manno	x	x									
Bernardino di Monaldo	x	x	x	x	x	x	x	x	x	x	x
Britio di Sano	x	x	x	x	x	x	x	x	x	x	x
Michelangelo di Noccolò	x	x	x	x	x			x	x	x	x
Geronimo di Giovanni da Iesi	x							x	x	x	x
Mariano detto Mancino	x	x									
Domenico di Sano[m]	x	x	x	x	x	x	x				
Niccolò di Meio Naccharini		x	x	x	x	x	x				

TABLE 9.1 continued

	1486	1487	1488	1489	1490–92	1493	1494	1495	1496	1497	1498–99
Lodovico di Mammo[n]				x			x		x		
Andrea di Giovanni					x	x	x	x	x	x	x
Giovanni di Pietro detto El Civile								x	x	x	x
Piergiovanni di Niccolò								x	x	x	x
Jacopo di Giuliano da Pistoia									x	x	x
Meciaro									x		
Leonardo di Taddeo										x	

	1400–6	1407	1408–26	1427	1428–33	1434	1435–44	1445–59	1460–79	1480–97	1498–99
B. Drummers											
Francio di Viva	x	x									
Angelo di Vanni		x	x	x							
Pietro di Giovanni detto Petrolino				x	x						
Francesco di Vanni						x	x				
Piero di Lantecca Rintere								x	x		
Meio di Maestro Mino									x	x	
Geronimo di Meio[o]											x

*also as a drummer
[a] also as town crier, 1410–19
[b] brother of Angelo
[c] son of Antonio di Ciuccio
[d] as town crier, 1419
[e] as town crier, 1423
[f] brother of Chimenti
[g] son of Tomè di Meio
[h] son of Pietro di Giovanni detto Petrolino
[i] brother of Lodovico
[j] son of Monaldo di Bartolomeo
[k] son of Niccolò Turini
[l] son of Giovanni da Iesi
[m] son of Sano di Matteo
[n] brother of Gaddo
[o] son of Meio di Maestro Mino

DIMINISHING IMPORTANCE AND NOSTALGIA FOR TIMES PAST: THE TRUMPETERS' CORPS IN THE SIXTEENTH CENTURY

THROUGHOUT THE SIXTEENTH CENTURY, as in the past, it was ability above all that guaranteed appointment to the Palace trumpeters' corps, even though the number of qualified musicians seeking posts diminished somewhat during the course of time. Consequently, the government itself encouraged the training of young musicians by subsidizing the salary of an officially appointed teacher. With family ties as important as ever, the government was no less solicitous about its employees' welfare than previously. Once again, the presence of core groups can be traced, as can the lengthy careers of several of the musicians. The first half of the sixteenth century thus saw a continuation of previously established practices, for a sharp break with the past occurred only after the siege of Siena and the incorporation of the city and its dominion into the Medicean state.

TRUMPETERS IN THE FIRST HALF OF THE SIXTEENTH CENTURY

The nine trumpeters mentioned in 1499 and 1500 were also present in 1501, when Giovanni di Pietro called El Civile resumed service as the tenth trumpeter.[1] The same group appears in records from 1502.[2] But within the decade the core transformed itself once again, as older musicians died or retired and younger ones replaced them. A clothing list for Assumption Day in 1505 shows that the blind musician Niccolò Turini was gone by then, as was the relatively recent employee, Jacopo di Giuliano.[3] Britio, also identified as a town crier in other documents, must have died shortly before the list was compiled because his heirs were named as recipients of his clothing allowance.[4]

---

1. The payments appear under the usual heading "vestes pro familia Palatii" and with the usual sum of L. 31. 4 "pro quolibet" in the volumes recording Concistorial proceedings during July and August each year.

2. Later records, however, indicate that Pier Domenico di Maestro Antonio had not yet been appointed to a permanent post.

3. "Et detis et solvatis infrascriptis servitoribus nostri palatii . . . pro vestibus eis et cuilibet eorum debitis et ordinatis . . . tubiceni pro quolibet eorum, L. 31 s. 4, Iohannes alias Moro, Eneas Senzanome, Bernardinus Monaldi, Michelangelus Nicolai Ceci, Andreas Iohannis, Iohannis alias Civile, Pietrus magistri Antonii; heredibus Britii Sciani trombatori, L. 31 s. 4" (ASS, Concistoro, vol. 833, fols. 28ᵛ–29ʳ).

4. Pier Domenico had previously been employed as an usher in the Palace, as is evident from the approval in April 1506 of a petition he sent the Concistoro requesting an appointment to the trumpeters' corps. He is sometimes called "Petrus magistri Antonii" in the clothing lists. His relationship to Maestro Antonio piffero and to Giovanni is also made clear by a deliberation from the last day of February 1512, which granted him an official leave of absence with the proviso that his duties as town crier would be taken over by the trumpeter Michelangelo di Niccolò. His name was still on the clothing list for 1512, though it may be that someone was substituting for him or that another trumpeter named Piero was serving at the time. See note 9.

The latest member of the group was Pier Domenico di Maestro Antonio called El Capone. He was another son of the woodwind player Maestro Antonio da Venezia, consequently brother of the cathedral *maestro di cappella* Giovanni. Like his brother, he would also make his mark as a teacher.

Joining the eight trumpeters and drummer in August 1510 were Salvestro da Asciano and Carlo di Piero. Salvestro was no stranger to the group, having substituted for Bernardino on at least one previous occasion.[5] Recorded during the next year are two other newcomers, Maso or Tommaso called Briciola, who replaced El Moro on 19 March 1511, and Silvestro di Pio, succeeding the recently deceased Enea di Senzanome on the following 21 August.[6] The four newly hired musicians and Pier Domenico called El Capone are listed in 1512, by which time a new core formed. It consisted of Michelangelo di Niccolò, Bernardino di Monaldo, Andrea di Giovanni, Giovanni called El Civile, and Piergiovanni di Niccolò, all these appointments dating from the mid-1490s.[7] The drummer throughout this time was Geronimo di Meio.

Except for Bernardino, mentioned only through 1522, the musicians in the new core appear in clothing lists through 1523.[8] Also present throughout most of this

---

5. This was in early fall of 1501, when the Concistoro granted Bernardino a four-month leave of absence and decreed that Salvestro da Asciano could serve in his place on condition that he wear the Palace uniform. See Doc. 10.1.

6. This also suggests that Giovanni died on 18 March: "El Moro servì per infino a dì 18 di marzo passato; Masso da Pontremoli cominciò a dì 19 di marzo." The record of Silvestro di Pio's appointment, dated 21 August 1511, says that he had been promised the first vacant post immediately after Maso da Pontremoli, and that the promise was now being honored, in view of Enea di Senzanome's death.

7. Another Sienese trumpeter named Bernardino, "Bernardino di Stefano di Domenico, tubicina de Senis," filed his last will and testament on 19 February 1504 (ASS, Notarile antecosimiano 663, no. 53). He may have been employed by the captain of the people or some other Palace official.

8. Records of expenditures actually made for new clothing are sometimes at odds with the official lists of those authorized to receive them. An account for 1518, for example, reports that suits were bought for five pifferi and the trombonist and for four trumpeters and the drummer (ASS, Biccherna, vol. 352, fol. 33r). A similar discrepancy can be found in 1490, when clothing was bought for two pifferi, the trombonist, five trumpeters, and the drummer (Biccherna, vol. 344, fol. 120v). There are undoubtedly many reasons for these discrepancies, but one of the principal ones was clearly tied up with whether tenured musicians actually served or sent others in their stead. This much is revealed by a record from July 1513, when Michelangelo di Niccolò, acting in his own behalf and in that of the others, petitioned the Concistoro to grant them clothing "according to custom." The request was honored, though the priors stipulated that El Civile, Pietro Cavallo, and Silvestro di Pio, "who neither serve nor play, should [not] have anything" ("Audito Michelangelo Nicolai tubicene palatii, suo proprio et privato nomine ac etiam vice et nomine aliorum tubicenum et nacharini, petenti dictis nominibus vestes sibi concedi secundum consuetudinem . . . deliberaverunt dicto Michelangelo et sociis concedere dictas vestes . . . exceptis tamen Civili, Pietro Cavallo et Silvestro Pii, qui non serviunt neque sonant, neque aliquis pro eis"; Concistoro, vol. 881, fol. 10r–v, dated 28 July 1513). A few days later, after hearing from El Civile that he would wear the Palace uniform should he be granted his clothing allowance, the Concistoro agreed to allocate the necessary funds with the proviso that the treasurer of the Biccherna be instructed to deduct the full price of the uniform, L. 31. 4, should he not have it made.

These discrepancies may mean that new uniforms were not needed by all of the musicians or it

eleven-year period were Carlo di Piero, temporarily replaced by Silvestro di Pio in 1516, and Maso called Briciola, absent in 1521 and 1522. Serving with the group from 1514 to 1518 was Piero Cavallo, whose record of appointment is lost. He must have joined the corps sometime in 1510 because he was given permission to go to Bologna on 8 January 1511 and was still absent in 1513, when the priors refused him clothing.[9] Although his service was extremely sporadic, he was one of the trumpeters favored with meal privileges, as is evident from a 1524 record, which coincidentally notes his death. Salvestro da Asciano and Silvestro di Pio left after 1517. Joining the group in 1519 were Ansano Maria di Geronimo, Giovanni called El Gallina, and the returning Pier Domenico called El Capone. Ansano, who moved over to the wind band as a trombonist in 1521, was a third-generation Palace musician, his father, Geronimo, being the son of Giovanni da Iesi. Pier Domenico's talents were evidently much in demand, for after his return to Palace service he petitioned the Concistoro for more freedom of action in his official duties. The Concistoro responded in August of 1520 by granting him permission to play at his own pleasure and serve as a substitute for others. Like Giovanni called El Gallina, Pier Domenico would remain with the trumpeters for many years to come. Recorded only for 1521 were Geronimo di Giovanni and Giovanni di Lodovico. Dionisio di Geronimo's name appears for the first time in 1522. New in 1523 was Costantino di Bernardino Monaldi, who received an expectative enabling him to succeed his father on 30 August 1520 (see Doc. 10.3). Bernardino, a Palace trumpeter since 1480, was the son of the trumpeter Monaldo di Bartolomeo, who had begun serving in 1459. The drummer from 1517 through 1521 was Ansano di Bartolomeo. His successor, Austino di Jacopo, held the post from 1522 to 1526.

The ten trumpeters cited in the clothing list for 1524 included the oldest members of the corps, others appointed within the last decade, and the two latest appointees, Costantino di Bernardino and Dionisio di Geronimo. These latter were quick to incur the priors' wrath. A report from 15 September 1525 says that both had gone to Lucca for the Holy Cross Day festivities without official permission and that as a consequence the Concistoro fired them (see Doc. 10.4). Two days later Savino di Vincenzo, a trumpeter who had received a promise of employment in July 1522, was granted one of the recently vacated posts. A second one was ceded to Francesco di Mariano di Galgano on 11 November 1525. There is no record showing that either one of these ever received clothing. Constantino, however, was restored to his old position by the next

---

may mean that a policy was in effect which only granted uniforms every second or third year. Being named on the clothing list, however, was the important consideration, for it signified tenure and its attendant privileges.

9. This is a reasonable assumption, given the available information regarding the presence of two trumpeters named Piero in these years. Pier Domenico called El Capone, as mentioned in note 4, was granted permission to leave his post on 29 February 1512, when Michelangelo di Niccolò took over his duties as town crier. Pier Domenico's name, however, is on the clothing list from that year, 1512, unless the "Petrus" mentioned there is the other trumpeter, Pietro called Cavallo, "Petrus Equus" in some lists. On 8 January 1511 the priors granted Pietro Cavallo permission to go to Bologna, and in doing so they specified that Geronimo trombone could serve in Cavallo's place and have the daily meal privileges which he enjoyed (see Doc. 10.2). Pietro Cavallo took an extended leave, as confirmed by the deliberation from July 1513, mentioned in note 8.

Concistoro in the following January, even though "his post had been given to another." Several new musicians joined the group after this time. The clothing list for Assumption day 1526 shows that Michelangelo di Niccolò was replaced by his son, Niccolò di Michelangelo. Andrea di Giovanni, Giovanni called El Civile, and Pier Giovanni di Niccolò were now the only remaining musicians of the core formed more than a quarter of a century earlier. The other older members of the group included Carlo di Piero, Maso called Briciola, and Giovanni called El Gallina. Costantino di Bernardino had recently been reinstated in his post. The only new trumpeter, Bartolomeo di Stefano del Griccia, was substituting temporarily for Pier Domenico called El Capone. The names of all these musicians, and the drummer Austino di Jacopo del Griccia, appear without comment on the list. But some confusion existed about who was to receive the tenth suit of clothing allocated to the trumpeters because the names of two musicians, Silvio di Antonio and Savino di Centi, appear with the explanation that "whoever of them has a better claim" would be given it. Subsequent documents reveal that Silvio d'Antonio remained with the group.

A report from late November 1524 furnishes new information about the trumpeters' meal privileges. It notes that the priors were aware that "two of the trumpeters approved by the Concistoro must continually have their expenses for meals in the Palace" and says that they granted the privilege formerly enjoyed by the deceased Pietro called Cavallo to the long-time employee Andrea di Giovanni, "for life, so long as he stays in service" (see Doc. 10.5). The report suggests that not all trumpeters were guaranteed dining privileges and that some received them at the pleasure of the priors then in office. Perhaps this preferment was determined by whether the musician served full time or part time. Earlier records never specify the exact number of trumpeters with such privileges, though provisions such as those for Enea di Senzanome in 1480 and for Bernardino di Monaldo in 1512 imply that tenured members did have them, regardless of the percentage of their appointments.[10] Later in the century all of the trumpeters had their meal privileges revoked in exchange for a cash payment every two months—an unnecessary action had not the entire group been enjoying them at the time.

The names of nine trumpeters and a drummer in a list from August 1530 indicate the formation of a new core. Still present were two members of the old nucleus, Pier Giovanni di Niccolò and Giovanni di Pietro called El Civile. Pier Domenico called El Capone, first cited with the group in 1505 and reinstated in 1519 after intermittent service, and Giovanni di Alessandro called El Gallina, in his eleventh year, rounded out the list of more seasoned performers. Relatively recent appointees were Niccolò di Michelangelo, son and grandson of former trumpeters, and Silvio di Antonio, both from 1526. One-third of the group now comprised newcomers, two of them related to musicians employed at the Palace. They were Niccolò's brother, Geronimo di Michelangelo,[11] and Orazio del Gallina, Giovanni's son. The third newcomer, Annibale dello Spedale, was apparently an orphan who had been trained at the school run by

---

10. "Magnifici domini . . . concesserunt expensas in tinello eorum familie Bernardino tubicene" (Concistoro, vol. 874, fol. 2ᵛ, dated 4 May 1512).

11. He is identified as Niccolò's brother in a deliberation of 14 February 1538.

Santa Maria della Scala. New also was the drummer Bernardino di Valerio, son of the Palace piffero Valerio.

Except for Silvio and Annibale, the same musicians are cited in 1532.[12] The three new trumpeters that year were Pavolo di Niccolò (also doubling as a town crier), Lo Stiaccia, and Vergilio di Pier Giovanni. The last-named was the son of the core's oldest member, Pier Giovanni di Niccolò, and grandson of the blind Niccolò Turini. Initially, Vergilio was not appointed full time, even though he was granted a suit of clothing. A year and a half earlier, when the priors decided to hire him, they awarded him "one-half of one place for his lifetime," stipulating that he was to receive one-half the regular salary every month. No record survives to show when the priors changed the formal terms of his appointment. But he was clearly earning a full salary by the end of 1537, when monthly salaries of five of the trumpeters, including Vergilio, were reduced to L. 13, those of three others to L. 12, L. 11, and L. 10, and of another to L. 14 (see Doc. 10.6).[13] Clearly, at some time in the not distant past, some trumpeters' salaries had been raised substantially, though when this occurred is not mentioned.

Initial employment of trumpeters at half-pay, already noted in connection with the appointment of Enea di Senzanome, may have been more prevalent than surviving records indicate. It probably accounts for the greater number of trumpeters than the six specified in the statutes. It probably also explains why Orazio del Gallina received clothing, even though the record of his expectative for a full-time post was not registered until eleven years later. Confirmation that all of the musicians who received clothing at this time were not paid the same salary comes from a decree of mid-August 1534. It contains the text of a petition from Annibale saying that he had no other means of support and that his earnings were so low they did not allow him to live properly. How true the latter statement was is difficult to ascertain. But the priors were clearly sympathetic to his request, for after acknowledging that other trumpeters received higher salaries, they decided to increase his salary by d. 4 to a total of L. 14 per month.

The raise was evidently insufficient because Annibale was not among the eight trumpeters authorized to receive clothing on Assumption Day 1535. Neither were Pavolo di Niccolò and Lo Stiaccia. The new trumpeter that year, another Annibale, whose father Tommaso may be identified with the former Palace trumpeter Maso called Briciola, did not stay for very long, however, and on 21 March 1536, after learning that he wished to renounce his post, the Concistoro appointed Austino di Michelangelo in his stead. This latter and two other newcomers, Pavolo di Giovanni and Pavolo dello Spedale, appear on the Assumption Day list for 1536. Rejoining the group was Pavolo di Niccolò, now listed as a town crier. The core, in the form it had assumed six years earlier, still comprised Pier Giovanni di Niccolò, Pier Domenico called El Capone, Giovanni called Gallina, his son Orazio, Niccolò di Michelangelo, Girolamo di Michelangelo, and Vergilio di Pier Giovanni. The drummer throughout these years was Bernardino di Valerio.

---

12. In 1532 the cost of each vestment was still L. 31. 4.

13. See below, with regard to Annibale di Tommaso; the monthly salary of L. 13 listed for him probably records a raise rather than a reduction. Noteworthy also is the reference to Pier Domenico, called El Capone, who was serving rather than Benedetto's son.

A report from 20 November 1537 shows that the priors were aware that they had lost the services of a good musician with the departure of Annibale di Tommaso (see Doc. 10.7). It notes that they had been informed by several trumpeters about Annibale's abilities, talent, and experience and that they were also told that "many trumpeters in their Palace are not up to par." Desirous of making a suitable provision for Annibale, because, as they put it, "all work deserves recompense and the republic wishes to recognize its servants," the priors took the unprecedented step of providing additional funds for his salary by reassigning a subsidy of L. 6 previously awarded to Pier Giovanni di Niccolò for the purpose of keeping a horse. Their justification was that they learned that Pier Giovanni "does not have a horse, nor has he ever had one." The priors' action assured Annibale of a monthly salary of L. 13, sufficient to induce his return; a report of the following December calls him "the new, ninth trumpeter" (see Doc. 10.6). As mentioned, this list names the seven members of the core and Austino, with monthly salaries ranging from L. 14 for Pier Giovanni di Niccolò to L. 10 for Geronimo di Michelangelo.

Town Criers

With Pier Domenico called El Capone, Pier Giovanni di Niccolò, and Pavolo di Niccolò described variously as town criers and trumpeters in many of the records and lists just cited, it is clear that, as in the past, the record keepers often failed to identify properly those who served in this dual capacity. The same situation holds for the following years. A payment for two months' salary from April 1537, for example, speaks of nine trumpeters, two town criers, and a nakers player, but others from later that year put the number at ten trumpeters and one drummer; none of them lists names. Pavolo di Niccolò's name is absent from the list of those whose salaries were reduced in December 1537, which does, however, cite the town crier Pier Giovanni di Niccolò and the eight trumpeters mentioned the previous year (Doc. 10.6). Two town criers and a drummer are cited in payments from 1542 and 1543. The clothing list for Assumption Day 1544 names Pavolo alone as a town crier; Pier Giovanni appears with the other trumpeters, among whom were Giovanni called Gallina, Niccolò di Michelangelo, Geronimo di Michelangelo, Austino, Pavolo, four newcomers called Alessandro, Camillo, Marco, and Piero del Volpino.[14] The drummer was Bernardino. A clothing list from 1549, though describing Pier Giovanni di Niccolò as a town crier and trumpeter, calls Pavolo di Niccolò a town crier and nothing more.[15] These and similar records from subsequent decades thus indicate that two of the trumpeters simultaneously served as town criers, even though they are not always identified as such in the records.

---

14. Pietro, referred to here as "Pietro, figlio del Golpino," was evidently a brother of the more famous Giulio del Volpino, mentioned below. The alternate form of the family name, Golpino, however, continues to appear in some later documents concerning Giulio.

15. Extant are copies of two testaments made by Pier Giovanni di Niccolò, the first dated 28 June 1523, which calls him Pierus olim Niccolai Ceci tubicena de Senis (ASS, Notarile antecosimiano 1091, no. 1321) and a second, dated 13 September 1544, which refers to him as Pier Iohannes Niccolai, tubicini excelse Reipublice Senarum (Notarile antecosimiano 1928, no. 9).

Kinship Ties and Economic Status

One incident from this time involving family ties is significant because it illustrates how the Concistoro maneuvered in order to accommodate its valued employees. All the activity centered around the trombonist Benedetto di Domenico, a member of the wind band, who, as will be noted below, figures prominently in the history of that group. A record dated 7 August 1542 speaks of a petition he addressed to the Concistoro wherein he requested that the trumpeter's post previously awarded to his son Agostino (Austino) be transferred to his son-in-law Camillo di Marcantonio because Agostino himself was unable to fill it (see Doc. 10.8).[16] Although specific information is lacking about what transpired, a report from 17 December 1546 shows that originally Agostino was to share the post with his brother Partenio (see below, Doc. 12.6). A notarial act from a week later also notes that the priors had awarded the post to Benedetto's two sons, Agostino and Partenio, and reports that now, with Benedetto's consent, the priors had ceded it to Camillo. As a result, and as a token of his gratitude, Camillo agreed to pay Partenio L. 5 from his salary every month under certain specified conditions.[17]

Camillo's willingness to give so much of his monthly salary to his brother-in-law reveals a good deal about why trumpeters' posts at the Palace were still so sought after. In addition to salary, clothing allowances, and meal privileges for most of them, all could count on receiving gratuities from visitors as well as extra earnings when the group performed at Assumption Day festivities (see Doc. 10.9) and other officially approved functions or when they accompanied government officials abroad.[18] More could be earned also by playing at private functions. Thus, besides testifying to the Concistoro's continuing concern for its employees' welfare, the incident also confirms that trumpeters' earnings were considerably larger than their nominal salaries. How much more is difficult to assess, for few of these additional sources of income were formally reported.[19] Nevertheless, they must have had considerable bearing on the economic status of musicians, several of whom were well enough off to have houses of their own.

A recurrent problem for Palace administrators was absenteeism on the part of musicians, trumpeters as well as pifferi. Typical in this regard is a report from 8 April 1516

---

16. The record of Agostino's appointment has not been found.

17. The agreement among the parties in question was formalized on 24 December 1546, in a "Compositio et quietantia inter Benedictum tronbone et Camillum Marcii Antonii tronbettum" (Notarile antecosimiano 2528, no. 101).

18. One record from this time shows that the trumpeters and the wind band customarily received a gratuity of L. 32 for their pre–Assumption Day concerts; see Doc. 10.9. Further on the pre–Assumption Day concerts see chapter 9. Another record from 31 December 1542 shows two trumpeters requesting payment of L. 8, the sum customarily disbursed to the group for playing on the feast of the Conception of the B.V.M.: "Auditis duobus ex tubicenis, petentibus eisdem fieri decretum camerario Biccherne quod eis solvat libras octo denariorum pro sono sive canore tubarum in festo Conceptionis Marie Virginis prout consuetum est . . . deliberaverunt quod duo eligendi per priorem videant si ita consuetum est, quo invento faciant fieri decretum iuxta petita" (Concistoro, vol. 1057, fol. 78ʳ, dated 31 December 1542).

19. When the rules regarding outside performances were relaxed later in the century, the priors put a cap on what the Palace musicians might charge for playing at private functions. See chapter 12.

recounting how the trumpeter Silvestro di Pio was given twelve days in which to appear before the Concistoro to explain why he had been away so long from his duties. If he failed to do so within the allotted time, he was to be fired. Silvestro's explanation was evidently accepted because his name is on the clothing list from the following August. On other occasions, however, musicians had no legitimate reasons for absences. Whether many such absences were due to moonlighting cannot be ascertained. But some suspected they were, for the priors reaffirmed the restriction prohibiting employment outside the Palace in a decree of 1 November 1524.[20]

A later admonition to the musicians from the Concistoro regarding absenteeism, from mid-March 1550, is of particular interest because it reiterates earlier information regarding the musicians' duties. At the time the priors were notified that the trumpeters and other instrumentalists were not always present in the cathedral when the image of Virgin was unveiled, at the daily Mass in the Campo, and at certain other times when they were to perform in the Palace. In an attempt to remedy the situation the priors decreed that henceforth if the musicians were not at all the required places and hours, they would lose their meal privileges and would be imprisoned for fifteen days. It is uncertain whether the edict was ever put into effect (see Doc. 10.10).

In economic respects Sienese trumpeters in the early sixteenth century seem to have done somewhat better than their predecessors, few of whom were registered as property owners.[21] Like the pifferi, several of the trumpeters lived in the company of San Salvadore in Terzo di Città.[22] Among them was Andrea di Giovanni, who reported in 1509 that he owned a house, but that he had no income other than his monthly salary from the Palace. Another trumpeter called Pietro, probably Pier Domenico, was also resident in the company of San Salvadore in 1509. At the time he said he owned a vineyard, valued at Fl. 400, which he had recently bought with a down payment of Fl. 80. Michelangelo, Niccolò Turini's son, also reported owning a house in San Salvadore and he, too, said he had nothing more than his monthly income of L. 8 from the Palace. The house was eventually inherited by Michelangelo's son, Niccolò, also a trumpeter.[23]

------

20. "Et decreverunt quod piffari, tubicines, et tubonus non possint sonare extra palatium sine licentia Magnificorum dominorum sub pena ducatorum decem pro quolibet et qualibet vice" (Concistoro, vol. 948, fol. 2ᵛ, dated 1 November 1524).

21. In 1481 Niccolò Turini declared that he owned a house in the Casato di Sopra section of Terzo di Città (ASS, Lira, vol. 185, fol. 230ʳ, Terzo di Città, 1481). A report from seven years later shows that he still had the house. Also in 1481 and from Terzo di Città the by-then retired trumpeter Giovanni Martini declared that he was old and sick and had no salary from the Signoria, though he had a house in the Compagnia di S. Agata and a vineyard as well (Lira, vol. 190, fol. 151ʳ). In that same year, however, Enea's father, Giuseppe di Giovanni da Brescia, called Senzanome, "carnavaio del Palazo," reported that he had nothing beyond his salary (Lira, vol. 189, fol. 27ʳ, Terzo di Città). The family's financial rise is mentioned above in chapter 9.

22. This grouping of musicians in a particular part of town finds its parallel in Florence, where by government decree of 1361 the trumpeters were obliged to live in the same quarter, within the precincts of the parish subsequently known as San Michele delle Trombe. There is no evidence to show that the Sienese government did the same. The Florentine information is reported in Lastri, *L'Osservatore Fiorentino sugli edifizi della sua patria,* 1:124–26.

23. The house was listed in 1548 by Michelangelo's son Niccolò, who said that he was disabled and had a son who was ill.

In 1509 Michelangelo's brother, Pier Giovanni, filed an almost identical report, saying he had a house in San Salvadore and his salary from the Palace. Pier Giovanni outlived his brother, and in 1548 he was still living in his "small house with a bit of an orchard" in San Salvadore. Bernardino di Monaldo, member of a dynasty of Palace musicians, declared that he owned a house and a small orchard next to it in the contrada Val di Rosa in Terzo Camollia, when he filed his report in 1509. Also filing in that same year was Giovanfrancesco called El Moro, by then the oldest member of the trumpeter's corps. He had no children and had arranged matters so that his house in the Piano de' Mantellini district and all of its contents would go to the convent of Santa Maria del Carmine after his and his wife's death.

The significance of this data should not be underestimated. Six of the ten trumpeters employed at the Palace in 1510 owned some kind of property. Whether any or all of the others had done as well has yet to be determined, but information from later years indicates that at least one other was also a property owner. None of the trumpeters mentioned in these tax reports, of course, could be or would have been considered wealthy, their livelihood depending, as they claimed, on their wages from the Palace. Yet having houses and vineyards of their own and the certainty of a monthly salary brought a measure of security not enjoyed by much of the populace at large. Trumpeters, as will be noted in the following chapter, occupied a lower step on the economic scale of Palace employees than the pifferi, who, from all appearances, did quite well. But like the pifferi, many, if not all, of the trumpeters had meal privileges at the Palace and all of them had uniforms and were eligible to share in tips and extra earnings for performing at non-official functions. Thus at the least it appears that in the early decades of the century, and perhaps even up to the end of the republic, most trumpeters enjoyed a fair standard of living, one that enabled them to own property, to support families, and, as a few reports note, to dower their daughters.

The Trumpeters at Mid-Century

A list of the twelve musicians receiving clothing for Assumption Day in 1545 names ten trumpeters, one town crier, and a drummer. The only change from the preceding year is that Partenio appears in place of Camillo. Evidently, there was still some question as to which of them officially held the post, though a report from June of the same year places Camillo in the group. At the time, citing negligence and the need to uphold public honor, the Concistoro deprived Camillo, Pavolo, and "the son of Gallina" of a month's salary, decreeing the money be used instead for new pennants for them.[24] The last-named may have been Orazio, unmentioned since 1537, or another son who is not cited as such in the lists. Pavolo is doubtless Pavolo di Giovanni, first cited in 1536, but then not mentioned among the trumpeters whose salaries were reduced the following

---

24. "Actenta etiam negligentia infrascriptorum in honorantia Vexilliferorum, ex quo minime accesserunt ad loca eorum nec subiverunt onus eis iniunctum . . . decreverunt notum fieri camerario Biccherne qualiter retineat eis salarium unius mensis ordinatum, quod erogari debeat in conficiendo uno pennone quo[d] deficit uni tube, et in nota detur successoribus; Camillus, Paulus, filius Galline, omnes tubicene" (Concistoro 1072, fol. 60^{r-v}, dated 30 June 1545).

year. Patronymics are also lacking in clothing lists from the 1540s, which speak of Pavolo banditore, that is Pavolo di Niccolò, and Pavolo tronbetto.

The clothing list for 1548 again names a total of twelve musicians. A decree from 30 October of the same year reports that Giulio, son of the deceased Giovanbattista Volpino, had departed for Rome sometime earlier. It further notes that though the priors were aware of his intention to return, "as could be seen from a letter of his to the trumpeter Simone, son of the deceased Pavolo da Siena," they nevertheless decided to appoint Simone in his place because "he has been playing in the Palace for a long time" (see Doc. 10.11). Giulio returned to Siena early in the new year and in mid-January 1549 both he and Simone, surnamed Brucia, appeared before the Concistoro seeking a solution to their rival claims. The priors solved the problem, as reported a month later, by restoring Giulio to his old place and creating a new place for Simone (see Doc. 10.12). Both are cited among the twelve musicians in the clothing list for 1549, which now lacks Piero del Volpino. In 1550 the only notable event concerning the trumpeters was the dismissal of Giulio called Volpino for an unspecified offense, and then, after having spent eight days in prison, his return to his post at the beginning of September.[25]

With eight (and sometimes more) members Siena's trumpet corps at mid-century was as plentifully staffed as those in any major city in Italy. In 1537 Milan, now under the Habsburgs and their surrogates, could nevertheless field a group of eight, two of whom were in the private service of the imperial governor.[26] By June of that year the annual salaries of each of the six trumpeters assigned to the Commune of Milan were raised to L. 80, and remained at that for the rest of the century. Six trumpeters are again named in Milan in 1558.[27] Lucca, a city with which Siena traditionally maintained musical ties, counted five trumpeters in 1543.[28] At Bologna, where an ancient tradition of supporting civic musicians still held, there were eight trumpeters in 1537 and in 1559.[29] The viceregal court of the Spanish overlords at Naples had four trumpeters in 1521, five in 1558.[30]

The Palace Trumpet School

Pier Domenico di Maestro Antonio called El Capone was one of the most successful Palace trumpeters of his time and certainly one of the most motivated, as events leading

---

25. A decree from the end of September 1550 prohibited Biccherna officials from paying three months' salary to a number of trumpeters, pifferi, and the drummer, but their names are not given in the record, which also gives no reason for the priors' action.

26. Guglielmo Barblan, "La vita musicale in Milano nella prima metà del Cinquecento," in *Storia di Milano, 9: L'epoca di Carlo V (1535–1559)* (Milan, 1961), 877.

27. Ibid., 879.

28. Nerici, *Storia della musica in Lucca,* 186.

29. Gambassi, *Il Concerto Palatino della Signoria di Bologna,* 144, publishes a record of eight trumpeters and eight pifferi, "per il suo companatico a L. 2. 6 il mese per ciascuno, L. 27. 12 sono l'anno"; p. 155 for 1559.

30. Keith A. Larson, "Condizione sociale dei musicisti e dei loro committenti nella Napoli del Cinque e Seicento," in *Musica e cultura a Napoli dal XV al XIX secolo,* ed. Lorenzo Bianconi and Renato Bossa (Florence, 1983), 67, n. 30.

to his appointment to the group reveal. Although he had no family members in the corps, he had other connections that served him just as well. For years his father's voice was an authoritative one in the wind band and he apparently used his connections to help Pier Domenico obtain a post as a Palace usher. In an undated petition addressed to the Concistoro, Pier Domenico explained that he had practiced and studied diligently for many years to learn to play the trumpet so that he might have a place alongside the others. Since he now felt he was qualified to perform with them, he requested consideration for the next vacant post. A marginal addition to the document dated 16 April 1506 notes that his request was granted. As we have learned, he was named among the musicians who received suits of clothing in August 1505 and was employed intermittently at the Palace for many years afterwards.

His sporadic service was undoubtedly a result of his successful activities outside the Palace. His reputation as a teacher is implied by a decree from 1534 stating that the priors, "aware of the scarcity of trumpeters in our Palace," granted Pier Domenico a supplementary stipend of L. 6 per month on condition that he "teach at least two students."[31] There is no record of how long he continued teaching, but information from three decades later indicates that he not only held the post for some years but that he also had successors. One of them was the widely traveled Palace trumpeter Giulio Volpino, who was granted meal privileges in 1567 for teaching an unspecified number of students. Perhaps it was then, by which time expenditures for music were sharply curtailed, that the practice arose of recompensing trumpeters who taught at the Palace with meal privileges rather than cash. In 1579 another Palace trumpeter, Sacripante di Pavolo Rimbombi, petitioned the priors for the apparently vacant post, noting "that it has always been the use and custom in the Palace of Your Illustrious Lordships to have a teacher of the art and practice of trumpet playing so that the Palace would not lack musicians." Replying affirmatively to his request on 22 June 1579, the priors spoke of "the consideration in which trumpet playing was held in the past and how the statutes provided for twelve players, even though there were now only six," and decreed that Sacripante was to have at least two students at all times in exchange for his "full expenses at the Palace," that is, for meal privileges.[32] The government's active encouragement of young players thereafter is evident in a decree from November 1584. At the time the priors declared that Andrea and Francesco, pupils of the trumpeter Sacripante, should be given pennants in recognition of their abilities, so that other students, emulating them, would wish to learn.[33]

---

31. The document has been partially quoted by Cellesi, *Storia della più antica banda senese,* 34: "Attesa la penuria de' Trombetti del nostro Palazo si è data provvisione a Pierdomenico Cappone di lire sei di danari al mese con obligo di insegnare almeno a duo scolari, altrimenti non goda ma si intenda levata detta provisione."

32. There were, as noted, twelve trumpeters before the fall of the republic and it is possible that there was a later addition to town statutes, unknown to us, which actually called for twelve trumpeters. Twelve is the number mentioned also in the revised regulations regarding trumpeters after the fall of the republic, though this was shortly emended to ten. See below.

33. Concistoro, vol. 1296, unnumbered folio, dated 6 November 1584. The document has been published by Cellesi, *Storia della più antica banda musicale senese,* 80. The same volume of deliberations also has two other documents, both on unnumbered folios, concerning the two students, dated 6 and

Repertory and Performance Practices

Some idea of the trumpeters' repertory can be had from an account of the arrival in Siena on 28 March 1520 of the Spanish envoy Don Giovanni Emanuel who came to announce the election of Charles V as King of the Romans and Emperor.[34] The envoy entered the city in procession through the Porta Camollia, accompanied by numerous Sienese gentlemen who had ridden several miles out of town to greet him. As the cavalcade reached the Croce del Travaglio, the Spaniard was greeted "by many trumpeters playing very beautifully" from the Palace battlements and by seven artillery pieces fired in the Piazza del Campo. After presenting his credentials and reading his letter to the government in the Sala del Concistoro, richly decorated for the occasion with tapestries and velvets, the envoy was escorted to his lodgings at the Palazzo Petrucci near the duomo. As he left the Palace, the trumpeters, from the battlements, and the wind band, from the lower windows, played the *imperiale,* as the artillery and rifles, firing salvos, made appropriate noises in the Piazza.[35] The account, indicating that all the musicians formed a single ensemble on special occasions, implies that by this time they used a particular repertory, either improvised or written down.

The *imperiale* was evidently a special fanfare, played by a prescribed number of performers. It is also mentioned in a document from 1 November 1524. This states that whoever was head prior during the present bimester, and all of his successors as well, must, under penalty of twenty-five ducats, have the trumpeters sound "an *imperiale*" at least once during his term of office "in that place in the Palace which is called 'above the corridor' in the vulgar tongue."[36] Apart from their anecdoctal value, which is considerable, both this and the previous report are significant because they mention a piece that was one of the trumpeters' specialties, which they alone were required to play a minimum of six times annually. The *imperiale* may have been similar to those kinds of written-improvised pieces described by Cesare Bendinelli in his *Tutta l'arte della Trombetta* of 1614.[37] (The dated pieces in this method all come from the 1580s, when the author led the trumpet corps in Munich.) In Bendinelli's sonatas for five parts a principal

7 November of the same year. It is noteworthy that in 1584 the city of Genoa also established a public music school. See Giazotto, *La musica a Genova,* 176.

34. A synopsis of the report, in ASS, Concistoro, vol. 921, fol. 8, was given by Aldo Lusini, "Una curiosità musicale senese," *La Diana* 3 (1928): 303–5.

35. The relevant passage is: "tubicine ad merlos palatii et piffari ad fenistras inferiores fecerunt imperialem sonatam," which Lusini (ibid., 303) translates as "trombetti dai merli del Palazzo e i pifferi dalle finestre inferiori, dettero fiato al loro strumenti e suonarono la Marcia imperiale."

36. "Et decreverunt quod prior qui nunc est et illi qui in futurum erunt durante presenti bimestri sub pena ducatorem vigintiquinque teneatur facere sonare tubicenibus semel ad minus durante tempore sui prioratus, unam imperialem in loco quod vulgariter dicitur sopra el corritoio. Et decreverunt quod tubicines qualibet mane, quando elevatur Corpus Christi ad cappellam Campi Fori, teneantur sonare sub pena eis imponendam per priorem una cum consiliariis prioris" (Concistoro, vol. 948, fol. 2ᵛ, dated 1 November 1524).

37. A facsimile of the original Italian manuscript that the author, a native of Verona, presented to that city's Accademia Filarmonica in 1614 is in Documenta Musicologica, 2d ser., 5 (1975). An English translation is *The Entire Art of Trumpet Playing, 1614,* with critical commentary by Edward H. Tarr (Nashville, 1975).

part, playing a written melody that employed no more than the notes of a single triad, was imitated note for note, one step lower in the harmonic series, by the part immediately below it.[38] Below them, the two lowest parts played single notes, providing the harmonic foundation, the root and fifth of the same chord. Above them all soared the clarino, or highest trumpet, who improvised a new tune, again utilizing the notes of the triad and an occasional passing tone. Bendinelli's method included a number of toccatas for single trumpeters in addition to the 332 sonatas, for which he supplied one or two parts. Trumpeters obviously needed some knowledge of written notation in order to play them, and this was probably true of Sienese trumpeters at the time the *imperiale* was in their repertory.

While Bendinelli's pieces come from more than sixty years after reports of the Sienese *imperiale,* they may nevertheless give an idea of the methods adopted by Italian trumpeters of a generation or two earlier. That such methods were already well established by mid-century is shown by a pair of letters from northern Europe, one from 3 February 1557 written by King Christian III of Denmark to Augustus, Elector of Saxony, and the latter's reply from the following 5 April.[39] In the earlier letter the Danish king spoke regretfully of having lost several of his best trumpeters and wrote of his hope that some of the Saxon trumpeters might be sent to him along with some examples of Italian table music and cavalry signals. In his reply the Saxon Elector reported that all of his Italian trumpeters and most of the other Italian instrumentalists had left his service but said that he was sending the requested signals and a sonata to be "played in six parts according to the Italian trumpeters' method," which, he averred, trumpeters at the Danish court would easily understand. As explained by Peter Downey, who discovered the letters, this must mean that although musicians at the Danish court were not yet using the Italian style, they were aware of the method of playing.[40] By this time the Italian style of trumpet playing was not novel, having begun its spread northward with the migrations of Italian musicians more than fifty years earlier.[41] As a consequence, it is likely that Bendinelli's works represent a century-old practice rather than a development of the late sixteenth century. And if this is so, then there is no reason to doubt that such methods were also the property of Sienese musicians at the time of the *imperiale.*

TRUMPETERS DURING AND AFTER THE SIEGE

Nobody in Siena at the time could have predicted the fate that awaited the city after its expulsion of Charles V's imperial garrison in the summer of 1552. Nor could anyone have envisioned the horrors of the siege, which authorities began preparing for almost immediately after breaking with the Habsburg emperor. The chronicler Alessandro Sozzini recounts that work began on new fortifications at the end of December 1552 and that people from every district assisted in building them. "They did so," he says,

---

38. As illustrated by Tarr, *The Trumpet,* 70–71.

39. Peter Downey, "A Renaissance Correspondence concerning Trumpet Music," *Early Music* 9 (1981): 326–7.

40. Ibid., 329.

41. See chapter 9, note 16.

"with joy, to the sound of trumpets and drums."[42] He also relates how one of the soldiers among the Swiss guards, sent to help defend the city by the king of France, played flute *alla svizzera* very delightfully. "So that those who were digging would be merry," continues the chronicler, the commander of the guards "would have the soldier go to the top of the hill to play his flute and all who heard him deemed it a rare thing."[43]

During the siege the trumpeters are mentioned in connection with delegations sent from one camp to the other as well as in connection with their regular duties, which took them into the field with the troops.[44] Music making during this time, however, was not the sole province of professional musicians. Blaise de Monluc, commander of the French forces assisting in Siena's defense, recounts in his *Commentaries* how in the worst moments of the siege the women of Siena stood by the city's fortifications and sang "a song in honor of France" so as to rally the brave defenders. "I would give the best horse I have if I could but put it down here," he remarks. "And so would I," says Alessandro D'Ancona, who quotes the passage.[45]

After the fall of the republic and its incorporation into the Medicean state the trumpeters' duties underwent changes, as the need for public display of Siena's sovereignty diminished. That the corps itself survived the imposition of a new regime is illustrative of the strategy pursued by Duke Cosimo de' Medici. Cosimo, as has been mentioned, was content to foster the illusion of self-government so long as power remained firmly in his hands. This he did by retaining traditional Sienese institutions and governing bodies such as the Concistoro, although he now made these subservient to his will and to policies pursued by governors acting in his behalf.[46] The trumpeters thus continued to serve the priors, who, as before, held bimestrial terms of office. Working with greatly

---

42. Sozzini, *Diario delle cose avvenute in Siena,* 92–93: "e vi andavano tutte le Contrade a lavorare e far fascinate sempre allegramente, con suoni di trombe e di tamburi."

43. Ibid., 93: "E acciochè quelli che cavavano stessero più allegramente, il detto reverendissimo aveva a uno della sua guardia che sonava un flauto alla svizzera tanto gentilmente, che lo faceva stare alla cima del poggio a capo il Prato, e sonava detto flauto che ognuno lo stava a scoltare per cosa rarissima." It is this same chronicler, Alessandro Sozzini, who reports that the town trumpeters and the cathedral singers did not perform at the solemn service held on 24 March 1555, when in a humble and symbolic act of supplication invoking her aid in deliverance, the keys of the city were presented to the Virgin Mary and placed on her altar in the Cathedral. See chapter 7 above.

44. Both sides used them: on 1 February 1555 it was reported that one of Duke Cosimo's trumpeters had arrived in the city with a message for the government.

45. D'Ancona, *La poesia popolare italiana* (Livorno, 1906), 74 and 87. He quotes another text that was sung at the time of the siege, a "lamento" or ballata with a political cast that begins: "Sono Siena sfortunata / che pensavo di far bene: sono entrata in tante pene, / certo fui mal consigliata." The meter and rhyme scheme of this passage, which was clearly the *ripresa,* or refrain, of the piece, indicate that the music took the typical form of a barzaletta or frottola. The text may have been sung to preexisting music, in the manner of the "cantasi come" laudi.

46. The situation is summarized by Elena Fasano Guarini, "Le istituzioni di Siena e del suo stato nel ducato mediceo," in *I Medici e lo stato senese, 1555–1609, storia e territorio,* ed. Leonardo Rombai (Rome, 1980), 52, who notes that the "Reformazione del governo della Città di Siena e Stato di Siena," promulgated by Cosimo in Siena in February 1561, concentrated power in the hands of Cosimo's governor, while preserving the outward form of the Concistoro and its officers, as well as their honorific and noisy entourage of "Famiglia Donzelli Trombeti Piffari e altri servitori e famigli."

reduced means, the priors henceforth attempted to maintain their musical establishment on the same scale and at the same level established during the time of the republic. Despite their best efforts, however, the trumpeters' corps gradually declined in the latter part of the sixteenth century, as straitened financial circumstances and a drop in the number of qualified musicians seeking to join the group began to take their toll. The trumpeters' situation offered quite a contrast to the flourishing condition of the wind band and should, therefore, not be charged entirely to changes brought about by Medici rule. Times had changed, but so had musical forms and styles. Instrumental ensemble music, featuring a variety of wind and string instruments, began gaining the place it occupied ever afterwards in European music. These factors favored the continued development of the wind band, whose greater repertory and versatility enabled it to serve in a variety of capacities, as opposed to the more limited role of the trumpeters. The trumpeters' function in Siena, though still considered indispensable, was now quite literally ceremonial, their activities confined to repeating the rituals of an expired republic enacted for the edification of a powerless populace.

In the years immediately preceding the siege the trumpeters' corps often included as many as twelve musicians—eleven trumpeters and a drummer—and shortly after the consolidation of Medici rule the new government sought to regularize their positions. This much is evident from an undated addition to the statutes, made shortly after 1556 (see Doc. 10.13). In its first redaction the new passage declares that twelve trumpeters and a drummer were to take turns playing during the priors' mealtimes and when the Concistoro appeared in public in an official capacity. The text specifies that at those times the musicians were to be "elegantly dressed in identical uniforms of two colors, green and azure, as is the ancient custom." An emendation to the passage correcting the number of musicians from twelve to ten says they should be prepared to play at the wish of the most illustrious captain of the people (now Cosimo's representative) and of the lord priors. It also stipulates that the drummer must play with them whenever they performed, under penalty of losing his salary and his post.[47]

Although ten, rather than twelve, trumpeters are mentioned in the revised passage, salary payments and other records from the following decades reveal that their number rarely exceeded six. Because positions within the group became even more difficult to obtain than in the past, incumbents tended to stay for extended periods of time. Thus, longevity of service continued to characterize the group, as did the presence of core groups. But since the possibilities of renewal were limited by the smaller number of posts, a certain amount of atrophy inevitably resulted. Ties of kinship also continued to be important, although, understandably, they were no longer as dominant a factor as previously.

Records from the 1550s show that the six trumpeters employed after the group's reorganization were all long-time employees. Pier Giovanni di Niccolò, who had been

---

47. The date is revealed by another decree concerning the wind band, cited below. Though the text of one passage cited above says that election, or confirmation, of all of the musicians was the senate's prerogative, the documents leave no doubt that the business of appointing, firing, and supervising the musicians in general lay in the hands of the Concistoro, acting under the watchful eye of Cosimo's governor general.

with the group since 1494, is mentioned in three decrees from 1553. The first two, from February and April, speak of his inability to fulfill his duties as a town crier properly because of his great age. Embarrassed because they did not wish to offend a faithful servant, but wishing to rectify the situation, the priors commanded him to find a capable substitute. The third decree, from May, permitted an unnamed person to serve as substitute for him.[48] A report from the end of April 1555 notes that the trumpeter Camillo di Marcantonio, first cited in 1544, had been in prison for several days and that the priors decided to set him free on condition that "he not set foot in the Palace for the rest of the month nor play in any other place." He was, nevertheless, required "to accompany and play when the priors go out from the Palace in public." Failing to do that, he would receive two lashes of the whip. Pavolo di Giovanni was given permission in June 1555 to accompany Signor Chiappino Vitelli on a trip outside the city, on condition that a town crier called Domenico serve as his substitute. What is perhaps more interesting about the report is the description of Pavolo as a trumpeter and a saddler, a clear indication that he had another means of earning a living. This must have been true of other Palace musicians, though only rarely do such references appear in official Palace documents.[49]

Six trumpeters are named in a decree from the end of March 1558, which reveals that absenteeism continued to be a problem at the Palace even after the fall of the Republic (see Doc. 10.14). As a result, the priors now instituted a new system for keeping attendance records and specified that fines would be meted out to those not fulfilling their duties. Giovanni called El Gallina, who began serving in 1519 and is described in the decree as the oldest of the trumpeters, was charged with keeping the records. The five others were Niccolò di Michelangelo, his brother Girolamo di Michelangelo, Pavolo, Camillo, and Simone. Niccolò had been a trumpeter since 1526. Girolamo, or Geronimo as he was often called, was first mentioned in 1530. Simone was appointed in 1548. A later record shows that Giovanni called El Gallina also had other duties at the Palace. In a petition to the Concistoro, dated 27 June 1559, he noted that he was without male issue and requested that at his death his place as the Palace shield bearer be granted to his son-in-law, Gregorio di Savino (see Doc. 10.15). Apparently, Gallina's only son, Orazio, for whom some sixteen years earlier he obtained an expectative in the event of his own death, predeceased him.[50]

New Regulations and Their Consequences

A record from 11 January 1558 contains information about changes made in the trumpeters' privileges, as well as in those of other Palace musicians. It signals the beginnings of a new system designed to yield income that could be used to supplement musicians' salaries. As of 1 January just past, the trumpeters would be given Sc. 3 every other

---

48. Concistoro, vol. 1118, fols. 34^v–35^r, dated 23 February 1553; vol. 1119, fols. 7^v, 23^v, dated 15 April, 12 May 1553.

49. Pavolo's patronymic is lacking in this and in another report from 1558 (Doc. 10.14). I have assumed that this is Pavolo di Giovanni, father of the trumpeter Sacripante, who substituted for him in later years.

50. The expectative is dated 25 August 1543.

month instead of their meal expenses.[51] The money paid out to them was to be taken from an account called the *piatto dei Signori*, "the priors' plate."[52] The change particularly affected the pifferi because all of them did not have meal privileges and the savings thus made were used to increase the number of people in the wind band. It seems not to have benefited the trumpeters' corps, however, for the official number of employees remained at six in the following decades, even though student apprentices and a few supernumeraries and unpaid volunteers often played with the group. The new arrangement also brought a readjustment in the services required of trumpeters. Besides playing every morning throughout the year, they now had to play "only on the evenings of feast days through Easter and every evening after Easter." Other records indicate that these references to mornings and evenings mean that they played on a Palace balcony, called the *ringhiera*, facing the square just before or during the time the priors took their meals.[53] One of the trumpeters' principal duties remained unstated, probably because it was understood that they always accompanied the priors whenever they went out in state from the Palace.

As some older musicians reached retirement age, recourse was had to time-honored

---

51. ASS, Balìa, vol. 109, fol. 142ʳ. The document has been published by Cellesi, *Storia della più antica banda musicale senese*, 77.

52. It is referred to in numerous documents quoted in the course of my narrative. Some of the ways it is referred to include: del piatto, ex plato, ex piatto, and companatico. It was used as a supplementary salary in place of the meals hitherto given musicians and to other Palace employees. The musicians' normal salaries, as is evident in so many of the records mentioned, was paid by Biccherna officials and after the incorporation of Siena into the Medici state by an official of the Grand ducal treasury called the "depositario." A third method of compensation was the distribution of bread and wine, this latter being particularly used to reward supernumeraries among the pifferi. I would have had considerably more trouble interpreting these various means of compensation had it not been for the information provided by Colleen Reardon and Nello Barbieri, who on the basis of several seventeenth-century documents were able to corroborate my findings from sixteenth-century records.

53. I am grateful to Nello Barbieri for his assistance in clearing up this matter. Using currently available published material (*Palazzo Pubblico di Siena. Vicende costruttive e decorazione*), as well as relevant material in Pecci's MS *Raccolta universale di tutte le iscrizioni esistenti in Siena . . . scritto intorno al 1730*, Barbieri shows that there were two areas in the Palace designated as *ringhiera*. In his description of the "Sala del Capitano" Pecci speaks of a *ringhiera del concerto de' musici*, no longer existent today, which was reached by a now-demolished spiral staircase that was next to a still preserved fresco of Sant'Ansano, at the entrance of the Sala. Pecci explains that this *ringhiera* faced the interior of the room, and, as I note below, I presume that this was where the wind band played when the priors were at table. Pecci's description corresponds exactly to two architectural plans of the Palace, one of which Barbieri dates as having been executed before 1783 because it is measured in Sienese *braccia*, the other from after that date because it is measured in Florentine *braccia*. The outside balcony, or *ringhiera*, is not present in Santo di Pietro's almost photographic depiction of the Palace facade in his *Predica di S. Bernardino* of 1444, which shows shutters on two windows of the first floor, but no balcony. This, of course, fits in well with reports of various chroniclers, mentioned in my text, of the trumpeters and pifferi playing from the Palace windows and battlements. A document from 1580 shows that the captain of the people recommended the construction of a canopy or roofing "a l'aringhiera," and this can only refer to an outside *ringhiera*, which was the one used by the trumpeters (Concistoro, vol. 2365, fol. 99ᵛ). As Barbieri has noted, the balcony is unmistakably present in two 1610 depictions of the Palace facade found on Biccherna and Gabella covers for those years, and in a 1655 painting by Deifebo Burbarini.

practices. A record from mid–December 1564 notes that the priors reviewed the request of the trumpeter Giovan Domenico di Camillo, called Il Colonello, together with a favorable recommendation from the governor, and that they elected him to his father's post with the same salary and privileges. Camillo di Marcantonio, it will be recalled, was a son-in-law of the trombonist Benedetto.[54] Another record, dated 10 February 1565, recounts how the priors, after having read the petition sent them by the trumpeter Severo di Simone, agreed that Severo should have the first available vacant post and that he might also substitute for his father, if the latter were unable to serve. Severo, called Silverio in later records, soon succeeded his father. A report from December 1567 calls him a Palace trumpeter and tells how he had "annoyed and disturbed the doctor while he was teaching in the school gymnasium by playing the trumpet and inciting the students to leave" and to go outside "to play ball." Evidently, students and musicians were no different in those times. Punishment was harsher, however, for Silverio was sent to prison for four days and released only by order of the governor Federigo Montauti.

A number of records from this time concern the onetime employee Giulio di Giovambattista called Volpino. They merit consideration because of what they tell us about the musician himself as well as about the situation at the Palace. Giulio had lately applied for and been granted the next vacant post. One record, dated 17 September 1567, notes that after learning of the death of the lame trumpeter Niccolò di Michelangelo, the priors sent for Giulio, who was then absent from the city. From a month later comes a report that the appointment of Giulio, "who is at present in Spalato [Split]," was discussed with the governor, who gave his consent and that a letter from the musician signifying his willingness to accept the post had been received. Successive decrees from the end of October confirm Giulio's appointment to the post, "with the same salary, duties, and honors" the other trumpeters have. Later, at his request a new case for his trumpet was ordered and paid for from the Palace purse. Meal privileges (or money from funds set aside for such expenses) were awarded him in early November 1567 in exchange for his teaching "those who wished to learn to play the trumpet" and the privileges were reconfirmed by successive magistracies on 3 January and 28 May 1568.

Considering his past history and the government's efforts to effect his recall, Giulio was likely one of the outstanding Sienese trumpeters of his day. A certain amount of nationalistic pride must also have informed the government's action. This and his talents and reputation stood him in good stead on more than one occasion, as subsequent records reveal. Since Giulio was in Split at the time of his reappointment, he obviously had learned and observed musical practices both in that Venetian depot and in Venice itself, where he must have stopped before moving on to the Dalmatian coast. All of this suggests, of course, that he returned to Siena with a wealth of musical experience and knowledge of performance practices current in what was assuredly the most advanced center of instrumental music in Italy, if not in all of Europe.

---

54. Camillo remarried after the death of his first wife. Relations between his new wife and his son were apparently not the happiest, for Giovan Domenico was subsequently admonished by the priors for having insulted Madonna Antonia, his stepmother (Concistoro, vol. 1183, fols. 36ᵛ–37ʳ).

Like several other Palace musicians, Giulio had a number of brushes with the law. One episode, reported in a decree from September 1568, involved his sending "certain dishonest and infamous women to the Palace," an offense for which he was admonished and confined to the Palace prison for three days. Another incident, unspecified but perhaps more serious, resulted in his losing his meal privileges until the priors decided otherwise and in being sent to prison on 7 February 1570. He was released four days later and confined to house arrest, which was then lifted a week later thanks to "the intercession of Their Most Serene Highnesses' men-at-arms of the city of Siena." Giulio was back in jail within a few months because of a complaint filed by his wife, Donna Emilia, after a domestic squabble. Records such as these, even though they paint a negative picture of the man, excite our interest because they allow an all too rare glimpse into musicians' private lives. To judge from the sound of it, however, Giulio was as much a rascal as he was a good trumpeter.

The priors were eventually forced to admit the failure of their effort in recalling Giulio called Volpino, whose behavior seemed to worsen with the passing of every day. A decree from 9 August 1570 notes that they had heard testimony and were aware of Giulio's contumacy, and because of his crimes, they had dismissed him from Palace service and banished him forever from the city and from the realm of His Most Serene Highness. From the 27th of the same month comes a petition addressed to the priors by the Palace porter Plinio di Leone. It carried a favorable rescript from the governor with it. After explaining that he had played and was then playing with the Palace trumpeters "day and night and whenever the priors went out and at all the necessary hours and places," Plinio requested his appointment to Giulio's old post. Perhaps because they were unsure of his abilities, the priors granted Plinio the post for one year only, with the proviso that thereafter he would serve at the Concistoro's pleasure. Plinio, who was to remain with the group for many years to come, was thus another of those musicians who used Palace connections rather than ties of kinship as a means of gaining admission to the group.

Unlike the members of the wind band, individual trumpeters are rarely mentioned in extant reports from the later decades of the sixteenth century. The impression, confirmed by the prominent position occupied in Sienese musical life by several of the wind players, is that even though the trumpeters' corps still maintained its conspicuous place in traditional rituals and ceremonies, its importance as a musical group was greatly diminished. Perhaps this was the principal reason why talented Sienese youngsters of this time chose to study wind rather than brass instruments.

DISCONTENT AND DECLINE OF THE CORPS

Several records from 1575 indicate that the trumpeters had long resented the employment terms imposed on them some seventeen years earlier. One of these records, from 26 October, speaks of the lack of modesty and disobedience displayed by Silverio di Simone and Sacripante di Pavolo, who were the spokesmen for what appears to have been a nascent labor union. Acting on their own behalf and that of the others, they presented the Concistoro with a declaration that they no longer wished to play evenings without extra compensation and that if their request for additional salary were refused, they would ask to be released from government service without prejudice. Far from feeling unprejudiced, the priors pointedly ignored the issue at hand and then, after remarking that the trumpeters' arrogance did little honor to the Palace and to the Concistoro and should not go unpunished, they condemned Silverio and Sacripante to spend an unspecified amount of time in the "public prison of the poor" (see Doc. 10.16). More than two weeks passed before the priors decided to release the two musicians from prison, with the admonition that in the future they be on good behavior and that they would be fined a testone (L. 2) every time either one of them was absent from required duties (see Doc. 10.17).[55]

The situation was plainly unacceptable to everyone concerned, for in less than a month, on 6 December 1575, a new set of regulations concerning the trumpeters' duties was published.[56] This, as the preamble states, was issued at the request of the trumpeters and approved by both the priors and the captain of the people. The trumpeters' duties were now officially increased and henceforth they were to perform mornings and evenings throughout the year. Thus during the months of November, December, January, and February, they were to play in the mornings at the sound of the Ave Maria from the duomo, and in the evening as soon as the third hour (after sunset) was sounded. For the month of March and through Easter they were to play in the mornings at the sound of the usual bell and in the evening at the Ave Maria. From Easter through the month of August the morning requirement was the same, but in the evening they were to play at the 22nd hour (second hour before sunset). For September and October the morning requirement was the usual one, whereas evening duties began after the Ave Maria. Neither the annual pre–Assumption Day concerts nor Masses in the Campo are mentioned in the decree, probably because, as before, the only issue in dispute was the requirement of service within the Palace area of the *ringhiera*. Not mentioned either is any increase in salary, but it stands to reason that some extra compensation was provided at this time.

Another new trumpeter, Pompilio, is mentioned in a deliberation from 3 January 1575, when the priors ordered him to vacate a house he had been renting from Barbante's wife within three days. Pompilio appears again in a record from August 1576, which speaks of his supplication and the priors' response that he appear before them at their pleasure, apparently to ask their pardon, under penalty of Sc. 25. A report from the same day notes that Pompilio's brother, Silverio di Simone, came before the priors and personally guaranteed his brother's promise. On 10 June 1578 Plinio di Leone, porter and Palace trumpeter, was found guilty of having carried a dagger at night. He was condemned to pay a fine of Sc. 25 within four days, otherwise he would get two lashes. According to a report from eleven days later, Plinio did not pay the fine within the required time and received the prescribed punishment on the 28th of the month. He was not as fortunate as one of the musicians in the wind band, who, as will be mentioned below, was saved from a similar punishment thanks to the intercession of his

---

55. In 1571 the testone, or riccio, a coin minted in Florence, was worth L. 2; see Carlo M. Cipolla, *Money in Sixteenth-Century Florence* (Berkeley and Los Angeles, 1989), 25.

56. Concistoro, vol. 1247, fols. 15ᵛ–17ʳ, dated 6 December 1575. The document has been published by Cellesi in *Storia della più antica banda musicale senese,* 79.

colleagues. Ever resilient, however, Plinio was among the musical delegation that went to Lucca for the Holy Cross Day festivities just a few months later.[57]

A number of documents record the activities of individual trumpeters in the following years. One, from 25 January 1579, preserves the terms of an agreement made between a new Palace trumpeter, Piero di Domenico called Ciro, and a barber, Giovanni di Domenico called Pisanello, who decided to settle their differences amicably. The ever-contentious Plinio di Leone, imprisoned for malfeasance on 25 July 1579, was subsequently condemned to three months in jail. The previously cited request from Sacripante di Pavolo Rimbombi for the teacher's post from 22 June 1579 confirms the number of trumpeters at six. But a list of musicians ordered imprisoned on 22 March 1580 for having disobeyed the priors regarding an engagement outside the Palace cites seven: Piero di Domenico detto Ciro, Pavolo di Giovanni, Severo di Simone, Plinio di Leone, Sacripante di Pavolo, Austino di Pietro Pavolo, and Dionigi di Pavolo (see below, Doc. 12.19). Of these, four had been with the group for some time, while the last two named, like Ciro, were more recent appointees.

A travel permit to Lucca for Holy Cross Day festivities in September of the same year names Plinio and Austino as well as two other previously unmentioned trumpeters, Austino's brother, Giovanni di Pietro Pavolo, and Cornelio di Goro.[58] These latter perhaps served as supernumeraries. Ciro resigned his post on 8 May 1581 and the priors agreed to his request to appoint Cornelio di Goro in his place (see Doc. 10.18). Sacripante, apparently still in an untenured position though receiving meal privileges, was given permission to substitute for his father during the latter's indisposition on 19 July 1582. A few months later, on 28 September, Plino de Leone, the Palace porter, renounced his post as a trumpeter. His resignation quickly accepted, on the same day the priors appointed Giovanbattista di Pietro Pavolo, who was a bootmaker, in his stead. Plinio, however, remained in Palace service as a porter, and a request for the pennant he had used was later made by Francesco di Giuliano, another of the supernumeraries.[59]

Plinio's continuing service at the Palace is demonstrated by requests he made for permission to leave the city on 5 May and 10 September 1584.[60] He apparently also

---

57. "Et derno licentia alli infrascripti musici del palazzo et altri al servitio loro, poter andare a Lucha a honorar la loro festa di S. Croce, e di ciò farsene fede in forma, cioè: Adriano Manghoni, Tiberio Rivolti, Giovanbattista Formichi, Jacomo Latini, Baldaxar Ponti, Alberto di Francesco, Anibale di Girolamo e Piergiovanni Oderini, musici, et Giovanmaria di Mattio, quoquo, Pietro di Domenico Masini, portiere, Plinio di Leone, trombetto, et Ventura di Giovanni Michele, donzello" (Concistoro, vol. 1264, fol. 7ʳ, dated 10 September 1578).

58. "Et denique prefati Illustrissimi domini Capitaneus populi et priores . . . concesserunt licentiam infrascriptis tubicinis et rutellinis palatii eundi ad civitatem lucensem ad solemnem festivitatem Sancte Crucis . . . Li nomi sono questi, cioè: Plinio di Leone, trombetto, Austino et Giovanni di Pietropavolo, trombetti, Cornelio di Goro, trombetto" (Concistoro, vol. 1276, fols. 8ᵛ–9ʳ, dated 10 September 1580).

59. Concistoro, vol. 1290, without foliation, dated 25 January 1583. On 4 April Sacripante challenged Francesco's right to the pennant, but the priors upheld it (Concistoro 1291, fol. 13ʳ). Plinio was imprisoned on 20 July 1588 for having left the city without official permission (Concistoro 1300, unnumbered folio, dated 20 July 1588).

60. Concistoro, vol. 1296, fol. 40ʳ, and an unnumbered folio.

played with the group from time to time, as shown by a decree, dated 8 September 1584, which authorized the trumpeters' trip to Lucca for Holy Cross Day festivities. Also listed at the time were Austino di Pietro Pavolo, Giovanni (Giovanbattista) di Pietro Pavolo, Mauritio di Pietro Pavolo (this latter undoubtedly a brother of the first two), Francesco di Giuliano, and Arcangelo di Dionisio.[61] The trumpet teacher, Sacripante de' Rimbombi, was cited on 18 July 1591 in a dispute with the monastery of Santa Marta over certain funeral expenses. Francesco di Giuliano still served as a trumpeter in early October 1591, when it was reported that he had been imprisoned in the nearby town of Pienza and subsequently released.[62]

Another travel permit to Lucca, issued to the trumpeters in September 1592, names the two brothers Austino and Giovanni di Pietro Pavolo, Francesco di Giuliano, Giovan Maria di Matteo, and Giovanni di Pietro.[63] Sacripante died shortly before 9 October 1597, the day Giovanni di Pietro succeeded to his post. Later, the post went to Piero di Domenico, whose name, however, is absent in subsequent records concerning the trumpeters. On 30 December 1597, after noting the death of Silverio, the priors assigned the vacant post to the one candidate with the most votes. This turned out to be the Palace usher Giovan Maria di Matteo, whose name was in the travel permit just cited. Clearly, a few supernumeraries or unpaid volunteers, most of whom had other professions, were serving with the group at this time, though there are no formal declarations to this effect. For unknown reasons Giovan Maria did not hold his new post for very long, as shown by a record from the following February 1599. This notes that Annibale, grandson of the deceased Palace food taster, and Aquilio, a cobbler and trumpeter, had petitioned to be appointed in place of the deceased Silverio and that after an extensive discussion in which the Medici governor participated, the priors decided to award the post to Annibale (see Doc. 10.19).

Annibale is, in fact, named in a list from 26 February 1600 of Palace employees who "were prohibited from playing in the games."[64] The five other trumpeters named shows that the official number of musicians established after the fall of the republic was still in force. A deliberation from 15 June 1602 states that the priors, noting how poorly Cornelio di Goro was serving them, fired him and named Bartolomeo di Nicoluccio da Castiglione Fiorentino as his replacement (see Doc. 10.20). Less than a month later the government reversed its decision and reinstated Cornelio in his old position with the same salary and duties. The new priors took this action after having heard arguments in Cornelio's favor and also after learning from trusted people that Bartolomeo "did

---

61. Ibid., unnumbered folio.

62. Concistoro, vol. 1303, unnumbered folios dated respectively 1 October and 5 October 1591.

63. "L'Illustrissimi et excelsi Signori . . . derno . . . licentia . . . d'andare a servire et honorare l'Illustrissima et excelsa Signoria di Lucca nella festività di Santa Croce che viene alli 14 del presente" (Concistoro, vol. 1304, unnumbered folio, dated 10 September 1592).

64. "Relatio significationis illis de familia de prohibitione ludi . . . All'infrascritti musici e trombetti, sotto il dì 25 di Febraio, cioè: Alberto Gregori, Piergiovanni Odorini, Pietragnolo Maestri, Ottavio Basili, Giulio d'Alessandro, Niccolò d'Aurelio Farraoni, Anibale Gregori, musici; Augustino e Giovanni di Pietropaolo, Cornelio di Goro, Pavolo di [gap], Anibale et Francesco, trombetti" (Concistoro, vol. 1312, unnumbered folio, dated 26 February 1599/1600).

not play according to the custom and manner of the said Palace" (see Doc. 10.21) Cornelio, however, resigned his post on 13 July 1603 and Aquilio, denied one five years earlier, was appointed in his stead with the stipulation that "at present he is to have the smaller salary given to new trumpeters, without prejudicing [his chances] for a larger salary in the future, according to the ways of our forebears" (see Doc. 10.22). Surely, no more fitting remark could illustrate the sorry state of the Palace trumpeters, who now more than ever served merely as a reminder of a glorious past, even as citizens scrambled to find funds necessary for the preservation of Siena's hallowed traditions and ancient institutions. A chronological list appears in Table 10.1.

DOCUMENTS

Doc. 10.1. Bernardino Monaldi is given a leave of absence, and Salvestro da Asciano is to replace him, 6 September 1501. ASS, Concistoro, vol. 810, fol. 3^r

Et decreverunt concedere licentiam et concesserunt Be[r]nardino Monaldi, tubicini eorum palatii, pro tempore 4 mensium, et ad eius instantiam in locum suum aprobaverunt Sylvestrum Angeli de Castro Asciani, cartularium, pro dicto tempore ad serviendum, cum hac conditione quod dictus Sylvester ferat vestes ad divisam palatii consuetas: quo tempore durante currat sibi salarium ordinatum, non obstantibus quibuscunque in contrarium.

Doc. 10.2. The trombonist Geronimo replaces the trumpeter Pietro detto Cavallo temporarily, 8 January 1511. Concistoro, vol. 866, fol. 4^r

Excelsi domini . . . visa deliberatione facta per Magnificos precessores quod Hieronymus tubonus serviat pro tubicena loco Pietri Cavalli, cui licentia concessa fuit eundi Bononiam, servatis servandis deliberaverunt quod dictus Hieronymus habeat expensas in palatio singulis diebus prout habebat dictus Pietrus . . . affinis ipsius Hieronymi serviat pro tubono usque ad reditum ipsius Pietri, loco ipsis Hieronymi et habeat expensas tanquam tubonus.

Doc. 10.3. Costantino di Bernardino Monaldi receives an expectative to replace his father, 30 August 1520. Concistoro, vol. 923, fol. 16^v

Audita petitione facta pro parte Bernardini Monaldi tubicene eorum Palatii continente quod ex gratia spetiali deliberari quod eius locus tubicene quem habet ad sonandum sit datus et concessus Constantino eius filio, post mortem dicti Bernardini. Et habita ratione fidelitatis et bone servitutis predicti Bernardini quam semper habuit erga eorum Palatium, et attenta etiam sufficientia dicti Constantini et qualiter ipse est bone indolis . . . dederunt et concesserunt dictum locum tubicene quem dictus Benerardinus in presentiarum obtinet . . . prefato Constantino . . . ad habendum, serviendum et sonandum immediate post mortem dicti Bernardini, cum offitio sonandi, salario et emolumentis consuetis prout habet dictus Bernardinus et alii tubicene eorum Palatii."

Doc. 10.4. Two trumpeters are fired for going to Holy Cross festivities in Lucca without permission, 15 September 1525. Concistoro, vol. 954, fol. 18^{r-v}

Attenta inobedientia Dionisii olim Hyeronimi tubicine et Constantini olim Bernardini Monaldi, tubicenarum, eo quia contra voluntatem domini capitanei populi et eius precepta iverunt ad festum Sancte Crucis ad civitatem Lucensem . . . ipsos Dionisium et Constantinum . . . privaverunt ab eorum conducta pulsandi in palatio et locis et iuribus eorum et cuiuslibet eorum salario.

Doc. 10.5. Trumpeters' meal privileges, 28 November 1524. Concistoro, vol. 948, fol. 34^r

Et attenta sufficientia et bonitate Andree [gap] tubicinis eorum palatii, attenta etiam eius antiqua servitute et attento quod duo ex tubicinibus aprobandis per Consistorium debent continuo habere expensas victus in eorum palatio. Et attenta morte Petri alias di Pietro Cavallo, qui temporibus preteritis habebat dictas expensas in dicto eorum palatio . . . decreverunt dicto Andree dictas expensas aprobare . . . durante tempore sue vite et dum steterit ad servitium dicti palatii.

Doc. 10.6. Reduction of the trumpeters' salaries, 2 December 1537. Concistoro, vol. 1027, fol. 23^{r-v}

Magnifici domini . . . reduxerunt infrascripta salaria pro singulo mense . . . ad infrascriptas summas . . .

> Pierus Iohannes Niccholai, tubicena et bannitor, libr. XIIII
> Virgilius, eius filius, tubicena, libr. XIII
> Nicolaus Michelangeli, tubicena, libr. XIII
> Hieronimus Michelangeli, tubicena, libr. X
> Pierdominicus Capponis [recte Capponus], immo filii Benedicti tubonis, tubicena, libr. XIII
> Hieronimus [recte Johannes] Gallina, tubicena, libr. XIII
> Oratius, eius filius, tubicena, libr. XII
> Augustinus Michelangeli, tubicena, libr. XI
> Anibal Tommasii, novus et nonus tubicena, libr. XIII

Doc. 10.7. Annibale di Tommaso is lured back with a higher salary, 20 November 1537. Concistoro 1027, fol. 17^v

Et habita notitia et informatione a pluribus tubicenis eorum palatii de sufficientia, arte et experientia Hanibalis olim Tomasii in sonando tubam, et qualiter eorum palatium patitur cum sit quod multi ex tubicenis non sunt ita sufficientes, pluribus de causis desiderantibus ipsum Hanibalem eligi ad dictum officium in eorum socium . . . deliberaverunt conducere et eligere et ita conduxerunt et eligerunt dictum Hanibalem in tubicenam et pro tubicena eorum palatii, cum honoribus, oneribus et aliis consuetis. Et quia omnis labor optat premium, et decet rempublicam suos servitores de mercede condigna recognoscere, in primis pro parte sui salarii applicaverunt et ei constituerunt quandam provisionem iam plures sunt anni concessam Pier Ioanni Nicolai dicto Pier trombetto . . . sub die trigesimo Iunii 1524 . . . de qua . . . fuerunt sibi adsignate libre sex pro quolibet mense ad hoc ut teneret unum equum ad servitium publicum pro bannitoribus . . . De qua provisione cum dicta condicione ipsum Pierum tubicenam privaverunt, attento quod ipse non tenuit neque tenet equum iuxta tenorem dicte deliberationis, nec adimplevit ea ad que tenebatur.

Doc. 10.8. Benedetto di Domenico requests that his son's post be transferred to his son-in-law, 7 August 1542. Concistoro 1055, fol. 39^{r-v}

Et visa et lecta petitione Benedicti Dominici, tubonis, super transmutatione loci tubicine Augustini eius filii in personam Camilli Marciantonii Galeazi, eiusdem Benedicti generi, de qua infra . . . decreverunt ipsam petitionem approbare et deliberando unanimiter approbaverunt . . . Cuius [petitionis] tenor talis est, videlicet. Dinanti a voi . . . el vostro servitore Benedecto di Domenico, trombone del vostro palazo, expone come Augustino suo figlio si trova havere un loco del trombetto . . . non può el decto suo loco con la persona sua propria exercitare, ma per lui lo exercita Camillo di Marcantogno di Galeazo, genero del decto Benedecto e cognato di esso Augustino . . . ricorre davanti alli piedi di Vostre Signorie e quelle humilmente suplica si voglino degnare far solennemente deliberare . . . che tal loco per lo advenire s'intendi essere et sia permutato in la persona propria di esso Camillo, con tutti li pesi, salari et emolumenti usuali per fino al presente ha goduto esso suo figlio.

Doc. 10.9. Gratuities for trumpeters and pifferi on Assumption Day 1544. Concistoro 1073, fol. 29^r

Et visa et audita petitione facta pro parte tibicinarum et tubicinorum eorum palatii circa mercedem librarum 32 denariorum, quam soliti sunt habere in festo Assumptionis pro sonando per dies quindecim ante dictum festum in platea et per vias usque ad ecclesiam cathedralem: servatis etc. deliberaverunt quod casu quod demonstrent per vices sex se habuisse a camerario Biccherne dictam mercedem, quod tunc et eo casu ego notarius possim et valeam eidem facere decretum in favore pro dictis libris 32 denariorum.

Doc. 10.10. Palace musicians are cited for absenteeism, 17 March 1550. Concistoro, vol. 1101, fols. 13^v–14^r

[margin: contra sonatores] Et habita notitia quod sepe sepius tubicene et alii sonatores instrumentorum palatii sepe sepius aliquis eorum ex eis deficit quando detergitur pictura Virginis in ecclesia cathedrali ac etiam ad missam platee et in aliis horis quibus tenentur sonare in palatio etc., volentes igitur predictis inconvenientibus et defectibus obviare et remedium imponere, servatis, etc., deliberaverunt quod quilibet sonator palatii debeat interesse omnibus in locis et horis sibi deputatis ad sonandum, declarando quod deficienti non detur pars in tinello vel palatio, et condennatus intelligatur ad carcerem per quindecim dies.

Doc. 10.11. Simone Brucia replaces the absent Giulio di Giovambattista Volpino, 30 October 1548. Concistoro, vol. 1092, fol. 26^r

Attento quod Iulius quondam Iohannis Battiste Vulpini, unus ex tubicenis et servitoribus eorum palatii, se a civitate Senarum diebus preteritis absentavit et Romam versus se contulit animo et intentione amplius redeundi ... prout manifeste constat per litteras suas directas Simoni quondam Pauli de Senis tubicene ... volentes ne propter huiusmodi suum discessum dictum eorum palatium ... aliquod detrimentum patiatur ... considerata itaque sufficientia et ydoneitate supradicti Simonis in dicto exercitio et sono tube, prout longho tempore ipsum in dicto palatio experti sunt ... deliberaverunt dictum Symonem Pauli de Senis eligere ... et ita deliberando eligerunt et deputaverunt in tubicenam et pro tubicena ad dictum locum sic vacantem ... cum officio, exercitio, salario, onere, emolumentis ... actenus consuetis.

Doc. 10.12. Giulio is reinstated and another place is found for Simone, 21 February 1549. Concistoro, vol. 1094, fols. 30^v–31^r

Et cum vexilliferis et consiliaris sub die decimasexta Ianuarii proxime preteriti auditis Iulio Volpino et Simone Brucie tubicinibus, super loco alias dicti Iulii et hodie dicti Simonis ... consideratis omnibus etc. ... imprimis restituerunt et reintegraverunt dictum Iulium ad locum suum qui hodie tenetur a dicto Simone, cum salario, emolumentis et gravedinibus solitis ... Et ipsi Simoni, attento quod numerus tubicinorum non est satis prout decet, concesserunt novum locum pro tubicina ... cum salario librarum octo pro singulo mense.

Doc. 10.13. The Palace musicians' duties, 1556. Concistoro, vol. 2357, *Precedenze, 1514–1755,* fol. 24^{r-v}

Famegli segnati in numero di trentasei ... accompagnino il magno magistrato dove andarà, dilicata et elegantemente vestiti di due colori, verde e cilestro, come è antico costume. ...

Musici cinque piffari con le piffare Sinfoniace sempre apparecchiati a sonare ai Magnifici Signori, Capitano di popolo e Signori Priori.

Trombetti dodici con un tamburino, volgarmente detto naccarino, quali quando il magno magistrato mangerà fuori publicamente saranno pronti a sonare scambievolmente. Questti tutti usino le medesime vesti di due colori. De' quali almeno due sieno publici banditori da dichiararsi dal prefato Ilustrissimo integro Concestoro. L'electione de' cinque musici piffari et de' dodici trombetti predetti appartenga all'amplissimo Senato.

[Vol. 2357, fols. 26^v–27^r for emendations:]
Musici cinque piffari, con li flauti, tromboni e cornetti, qualunche volta ai Magnifici Signori,

Capitano di popolo e Signori Priori parati sonare, sieno tenuti e devino sonare ai debiti et orde-
nati tempi, come sarà parso a essi et al Capitano di popolo. Et il camarlengo di Biccherna oltra i
prefati cinque musici a niuno altro paghi, e se altrimenti pagherà, si dica haver pagato della sua
pecunia e non del fisco.

Trombetti, dove si dice dodici, si dica dieci, et s'aggiunga ivi parati a sonare, cioè a volontà
degl'Illustrissimi Signori Capitano di Popolo e Signori Priori. Et sempre nel suono prefato sia
tenuto intervenire un naccarino, sotto pena della perdita del salario et del tempo.

Doc. 10.14. The trumpeters are reprimanded, 28 March 1558. Concistoro, vol. 1142, fols.
19^v–20^r

Et caso che li trombetti manchino di sonare sicondo il solito, caschino in pena, hora per alhora,
per ciascheduna volta, di un terzo del salario per ciascheduno . . . Et caso che li musici manchino
di sonare ordinariamente quando sonno obligati, la prima volta caschino, hora per alhora, per
ciascheduno et ciascheduna volta, [in pena] di uno terzo del salario . . . la seconda volta caschino
in pena di tutto il salario, et la terza volta caschino in pena di tuto il vivare di detto tempo di
loro Signori et non più: non essendo però quello che mancasse inpedito per legitima causa, da
chiarirsi per loro Illustrissimo Consistorio . . . Dovendo maestro Niccolò piffaro tener contio
[sic] di chi mancharà, come più anticho de' musici; et Giovanni detto il Gallina, come più anticho
de' trombetti, devi tener contio de' trombetti che mancharanno et non faranno quanto di sopra
. . . Li nomi de' musici sonno questi, cioè: maestro Niccolò di maestro Cristofano, piffaro; Giovanfrancesco, trombone; Simone di Domenico, piffaro; Adriano di Luzio, musicho; et Ascanio
d'Andrea piffaro. Li nomi de' trombetti sonno questi, cioè Giovanni detto il Gallina, Niccolò di
Michelagniolo, Girolamo di Michelagniolo, Pavolo di [gap] sellaio, Camillo di [gap], Simone
fabro.

Doc. 10.15. Giovanni di Alessandro petitions to be succeeded by his son-in-law, Gregorio di
Savino, 27 June 1559. Concistoro, vol. 1149, fol. 29^{r-v}

Giovanni d'Alissandro detto 'l Gallina, tronbetto, antico e fedele servidore delle Signorie vostre
magnifiche, ritrovandosi un luogo di fameglio rotellino nel quale egli serve . . . et essendo vechio
et senza figli maschi, desiderarebbe con buona gratia delle medesime lassare nel servitio del detto
suo luogo di rotellino, doppo la vita sua, Gregorio di Savino, suo genero. Però supplica humilmente le eccelse Signorie Vostre che si compiaccino dare et concedere il detto suo luogo di
rotellino, doppo la vita sua, al suddetto Gregorio di Savino.

Doc. 10.16. Two trumpeters demand extra pay for evening service and are sent to prison, 26
October 1575. Concistoro, vol. 1246, fols. 15^v–16^r

Item atteso le parole usate da Silverio et Sacripante trombeti con lor Signorie, visto la poca
modestia e disobbedientia loro et anco la proposta da essi fatta come capi con gli altri trombetti,
di non voler sonare la sera al suono del campanello senza le spese da farsegli dall'Illustrissimo
Concistorio oltre al loro salario, et in caso di recusation di ciò, di voler domandare buona licentia
. . . acciò la loro poca modestia e arrogantia non passi in essempio, in dispregio, poco honore
et pregiuditio del palazzo e degnità dell'Illustrissimo Concistorio . . . condennarono i detti Silverio et Sacripante . . . a dovere stare nelle pubbliche carcere de' poveri, a beneplacito dell'Illustrissimo Concistorio.

Doc. 10.17. The trumpeters are released, 14 November 1575. Concistoro, vol. 1247, fol. 4^r

Item, nella causa di Silverio e Sacripante trombetti, i medesimi trombetti si devino liberare dalle
carcere, con conditione che per l'avvenire trasgredendo e mancando di sonare le trombe al debito
tempo . . . caschino nela pena di un testone per ciascheduno et ciascheduna volta, et dell'arbitrio
delli detti Signori.

Doc. 10.18. Piero di Domenico detto Ciro petitions to be able to resign in favor of Cornelio di Goro, 8 May 1581. Concistoro, vol. 1280, unnumbered folio

Odito maestro Ciro trombetto et letta la supplica da lui fatta all'Illustrissimo Signor Governatore, nella quale domandava che fusse messo in luogo suo Cornelio di Goro trombetto . . . al conseglio del Signor Guido Beringucci che atteso la renuntia per il detto Ciro fatta . . . et la soffiscenza di esso Cornelio, si accetti e metter in luogo del prefato maestro Ciro el sudetto Cornelio, con li soliti salari et pesi.

Doc. 10.19. Annibale di Antonio and Aquilio compete for Silverio di Simone's post, 5 February 1599. Concistoro, vol. 1311, fol. 5$^{\text{r–v}}$

Auditis supplicationibus Anibalis quondam Antonii, filii Francisci impensoris palatii, Aquili sutoris et tibicinae . . . petentium electos esse in locum Silverii tibicinae defuncti, ad presens detentum per Iohannes Mariam rotellinum palatii, habita super eis matura discussione, informatione et discursu . . . Illustrissimus dominus capitaneus acceptavit dictam electionem, et cum participatione Illustrissimi et excellentissimi domini Gubernatoris . . . ellexit in tubicina et pro tubicina dictum Anibalem quondam Antonii de Palatiis, et mandavit sibi fieri decretum in forma.

Doc. 10.20. Cornelio di Goro is fired and Bartolomeo di Nicoluccio hired, 15 June 1602. Concistoro, vol. 1314, fol. 11^{v}

Et statim post prandium, in mantione domini Capitanei populi, habito maturo colloquio inter eos circa malam servitutem Corneli[i] Gori, tubicinae Palatii, demum deliberaverunt viva voce et uno animo, eum cassare et privare, prout cassarunt et privarunt de eius officio tubicinae, cum de eius servitute non sunt bene satisfacti, et loco ipsius deliberaverunt eligere prout elegerunt et deputarunt Bartolomeum Nicoluccium de Castiliono Florentino.

Doc. 10.21. Cornelio is reinstated and Bartolomeo let go, 10 July 1602. Concistoro, vol. 1314, fol. 20^{v}

Audito Cornelio de Goris, tubicina, exponente qualiter sub die 15 Iunii proxime praeteriti fuit ab Illustrissimis praecessoribus privatus, et in eius locum electus Bartolomeus de Nicoluccis de Castilione Florentino, sub praetextu quod non remanebant . . . satisfacti licet semper convenienter inserviverit officiumque suum bene ac diligenter exercuerit, exponente insuper privationem huiusmodi de se factam fuisse et esse nulliter et male factam et praeter et contra formam Constitutionum, quia non intervenerunt in ea omni [sic] vexilliferi et Consiliarii ad quos spectat electio et privatio similium serventium praefato Palatio . . . Visis pluribus fidibus continentibus dictum Bartolomeum non sonare iuxta consuetudines et ad modum tubicinarum dicti Palatii . . . decreverunt dictum Cornelium restituendum et reponendum esse, prout reposuerunt in dicto eius tubicinae officio, cum honeribus et salariis solitis et consuetis. Et praefata quatenus placeat et non aliter Illustrissimo et Excellentissimo nostro Gubernatori, et omni meliori modo etc.

Doc. 10.22. Cornelio di Goro resigns and Aquilio di Giovanbattista is hired, 13 July 1603. Concistoro, vol. 1315, fol. 4^{r}

[margin: Refutatio Cornelii tubicenae. Aquilius electus tubicena Palatii] Audita Cornelii Gori tubic[en]ae refutatione et renuntia loci ipsius in Palatio pro tubicena, libere facta . . . Postea die dicta, statim et incontinenti Aquilius quondam Iohannis Baptistae de Senis, tubicena, habita notitia de repudiatione facta . . . a Cornelio quondam Gori de loco tubicenae huius Palatii . . . porrexit preces Illustrissimis dominis, petens sibi dictum locum dari et concedi, cum honoribus et oneribus solitis et consuetis . . . Illustrissimus dominus Vexillifer pro Terzerio Civitatis consuluit quod officium tubicenae renuntiatum a dicto Corneli, concedatur Aprilio [sic] supradicto, cum oneribus et honoribus solitis, et quod habeat in presenti salarium minore uti tubicenae novitiori, absque preiudicium in futurum pro maiori salario secundum stilum anzianorum . . . Et missum ad scrutinium . . . fuit obtentum pro lupinis albis novem, nemine discrepante.

TABLE 10.1.   Chronological list of sixteenth-century trumpeters and drummers

	1500	1501–4	1505–9	1510	1511	1512–13	1514–15	1516	1517	1518	1519–20	1521	1522	1523–24
A. TRUMPETERS														
Niccolò Turini	x	x												
Giovan Francesco detto El Moro	x	x	x	x	x									
Britio di Sano	x	x	x											
Enea di Senzanome	x	x	x	x	x									
Bernardino Monaldi	x	x	x	x	x	x	x	x	x	x	x	x	x	
Michelangelo di Niccolò	x	x	x	x	x	x	x	x	x	x	x	x	x	x
Piergiovanni di Niccolò	x	x	x	x	x	x	x	x	x	x	x	x	x	x
Andrea di Giovanni	x	x	x	x	x	x	x	x	x	x	x	x	x	x
Jacopo di Giuliano	x	x												
Giovanni di Pietro detto El Civile	x	x	x			x	x	x	x	x	x	x	x	x
Pier Domenico di Maestro Antonio detto El Capone[a]			x	x	x	x	x	x			x	x	x	x
Salvestro da Asciano				x	x	x	x	x	x					
Carlo di Piero da Pontremoli				x	x	x	x	x	x	x	x	x	x	x
Maso detto Briciola					x	x	x	x	x	x	x			x
Pietro Cavallo					x	x	x	x	x	x				
Silvestro di Pio						x	x	x	x					
Giovanni di Alessandro detto El Gallina								x	x	x	x	x	x	x
Ansano Maria di Geronimo[b]											x			
Geronimo di Giovanni												x		
Giovanni di Lodovico												x		
Dionisio di Geronimo													x	x
Costantino di Bernardino Monaldi[c]														x

	1525	1526	1527–29	1530	1531	1532	1533–34	1535	1536	1537	1538–41	1542–43
Michelangelo di Niccolò	x	x	x	x	x	x	x	x	x	x	x	x
Piergiovanni di Niccolò		x	x	x	x	x	x	x	x	x	x	x
Andrea di Giovanni		x		x	x		x	x				
Giovanni di Pietro detto El Civile		x	x	x	x	x	x	x	x			
Pier Domenico di Maestro												
Antonio detto El Capone		x	x	x	x	x	x	x	x	x		
Giovanni di Alessandro detto El												x

	1525	1526	1527–29	1530	1531	1532	1533–34	1535	1536	1537	1538–41	1542–43
Carlo di Piero da Pontremoli	x											
Maso detto Briciola	x	x										
Dionisio di Geronimo	x											
Costantino di Bernardino Monaldi	x	x										
Savino di Vincenzo	x											
Francesco di Mariano di Galgano	x											
Bartolomeo di Stefano del Griccia		x										
Silvio di Antonio		x	x	x								
Niccolò di Michelangelo[d]		x	x		x	x	x	x	x	x	x	x
Orazio del Gallina[e]				x	x	x	x	x	x	x	x	
Geronimo di Michelangelo[f]				x	x	x	x	x	x	x	x	x
Annibale dello Spedale				x	x		x					
Pavolo di Niccolò						x	x		x	x	x	x
Lo Stiaccia						x	x					
Vergilio di Pier Giovanni[g]						x	x	x	x	x		
Annibale di Tommaso[h]								x	x	x		
Austino di Michelangelo									x	x	x	
Pavolo dello Spedale									x			
Pavolo di Giovanni									x			
Austino di Benedetto[i]												x

	1544	1545	1546–47	1548	1549	1550–53	1554	1555	1556–57	1558–59	1560–63	1564	1565
Piergiovanni di Niccolò	x	x	x	x	x	x							
Giovanni di Alessandro detto El Gallina	x	x	x	x	x	x	x	x	x	x			
Niccolò di Michelangelo	x	x	x	x	x	x	x	x	x	x	x	x	x
Geronimo di Michelangelo	x	x	x	x	x	x	x	x	x	x	x	x	
Pavolo di Niccolò	x	x	x	x	x	x	x	x	x				
Pavolo di Giovanni	x	x	x	x	x	x	x	x	x	x	x	x	x
Austino di Benedetto	x	x	x	x	x								
Alessandro	x	x	x	x	x	x	x	x	x				
Camillo di Marcantonio[j]	x	x	x	x	x	x	x	x	x	x	x	x	
Marco	x	x	x	x	x	x	x	x	x	x	x	x	
Piero del Volpino[k]	x	x	x	x	x								

TABLE 10.1 *continued*

	1544	1545	1546–47	1548	1549	1550–53	1554	1555	1556–57	1558–59	1560–63	1564	1565
Partenio[l]													
Giulio di Giovambattista detto El Volpino[m]		x											
Simone di Pavolo Brucia				x	x	x	x		x	x	x	x	x
Domenico				x	x		x	x	x				
Giovan Domenico di Camillo detto Il Colonello[n]												x	x
Severo (Silverio) di Simone[o]												x	x

	1566	1567	1568–69	1570	1571–74	1575–76	1577–78	1579	1580	1581	1582	1583	1584	1585
Niccolò di Michelangelo	x	x												
Pavolo di Giovanni	x	x	x	x	x	x	x	x	x	x	x			
Giulio detto El Volpino		x	x	x										
Severo (Silverio) di Simone	x	x	x	x		x	x	x	x	x	x	x	x	x
Plinio di Leone			x	x										
Sacripante di Pavolo[p]						x	x	x	x	x	x	x	x	x
Pompilio di Simone[q]						x								
Piero di Domenico detto Ciro								x	x	x				
Austino di Pietro Pavolo[r]									x	x	x	x	x	x
Dionigi di Pavolo									x					
Giovanni di Pietro Pavolo[s]									x	x	x	x	x	x
Cornelio di Goro									x	x	x	x	x	x
Francesco di Giuliano													x	x
Arcangelo di Dionisio													x	
Mauritio di Pietro Pavolo[t]														x

	1586–91	1592–97	1598	1599	1600	1601	1602	1603
Severo (Silverio) di Simone	x	x						
Sacripante di Pavolo	x	x						
Austino di Pietro Pavolo	x	x	x	x	x			
Giovanni di Pietro Pavolo	x	x	x	x	x			

	1586–91	1592–97	1598	1599	1600	1601	1602	1603
Cornelio di Goro	x	x	x	x	x	x	x	x
Francesco di Giuliano	x	x	x	x	x	x		
Giovan Maria di Matteo		x	x	x	x			
Giovanni di Pietro		x						
Annibale di Antonio				x	x			
Pavolo					x			
Bartolomeo di Nicoluccio da Castiglione Fiorentino							x	
Aquilio								x

	1500–16	1517–21	1522	1523–26	1530	1544–49
B. Drummers						
Geronimo di Meio	x					
Ansano di Bartolomeo		x	x			
Austino di Jacopo del Griccia			x	x		
Bernardino di Valerio[u]					x	x

[a] son of Maestro Antonio da Venezia, brother of Giovanni
[b] son of Geronimo di Giovanni
[c] son of Bernardino Monaldi
[d] son of Michelangelo di Niccolò, brother of Girolamo
[e] son of Giovanni di Alessandro detto El Gallina
[f] son of Michelangelo di Niccolò, brother of Niccolò
[g] son of Pier Giovanni di Niccolò
[h] son of Maso detto Briciola
[i] son of trombonist Benedetto di Domenico, brother of Partenio
[j] son-in-law of trombonist Benedetto di Domenico
[k] brother of Giulio
[l] son of trombonist Benedetto di Domenico, brother of Austino
[m] brother of Piero
[n] son of Camillo di Marcantonio
[o] son of Simone Brucia, brother of Pompilio
[p] son of Pavolo di Giovanni Rimbombi
[q] son of Simone Brucia, brother of Severo
[r] brother of Giovanni and Mauritio
[s] brother of Austino and Mauritio
[t] brother of Austino and Giovanni
[u] son of Valerio

Chapter Eleven

ESTABLISHMENT AND CONSOLIDATION OF THE PIFFERI IN THE FIFTEENTH CENTURY

S HORTLY AFTER the turn of the fourteenth century, when Folgore da San Gimignano wrote of the joys of April, he evoked the fresh scents of the Sienese countryside in bloom, the playful sound of water trickling from fountains, the ambling palfreys and chargers from Spain, and "the people dressed in the French mode, singing and dancing in the Provençal style, with new instruments from Germany."[1] The poet was referring to newly developed forms of woodwind instruments—shawms, recorders, bombards, and others—that had rarely been seen or heard in Italy before his time and were now being played by musicians freshly arrived from the north and by others emulating them. From the first the music of these pifferi, as the Italians called both the musicians and their instruments, was highly esteemed, so much so that within a few decades pifferi, usually of German origin, were found throughout the peninsula at courts, in the service of the Italian republics, and in the retinues of wealthy laymen and ecclesiastics.[2] The large numbers of foreign musicians, their frequent arrivals, and their ubiquity all constituted a pacific musical invasion of grand dimensions, one that profoundly affected the course of Italian music. It can only be compared with the peaceful onslaught, a century or so later, of Franco-Flemish singers and composers who for a generation and more held a virtual monopoly on vocal polyphony in Italian cathedral chapels.

The effects of the presence in Italy of these latter musicians produced tangible results that the historian can weigh and measure. The enthusiasm for the vocal polyphony of the north in Italy, the subsequent fusion of northern contrapuntal practices with Italian concepts of melody, harmony, and word setting that resulted in the international style of the later Renaissance, the emergence of Italian polyphonists of European reputation, the creation of the madrigal and related forms of secular song, the adaptation of vocal repertories to instrumental practices, and the rise of independent instrumental forms—all of these are themes that have been documented, analyzed, and commented upon by musicologists for well over a century. But the influence of the German pifferi is much more difficult to assess because of the very nature of instrumental music at the time of

---

1. Folgore, *I Sonetti,* ed. Neri, 29: "D'april vi dono la gentil campagna, / tutta fiorita di bell'erba fresca, / fontane d'acqua che non vi rincresca, / donne e donzelle per vostra compagna, / ambianti palafren, destrier di Spagna / e gente costumata a la francesca, / cantar, danzar a la provenzalesca / con istormenti novi d'Alemagna."

2. The modern Italian word is *piffero* (plural, *pifferi*). The Sienese spelling, *piffaro,* is found in many documents of the period and has been retained in my transcriptions, though not in the text.

their arrival in Italy.[3] Their repertories were based primarily on dance tunes and previously composed vocal pieces—chansons and their own songs, or lieder—but apparently few composers of stature were among them whose arrangements and original works were deemed important enough to merit preservation as models for future generations. Practically nothing is known about their performing practices, but their renown must have derived from their ability to produce a smooth tone that blended well with other instruments, their capacity for precise ensemble playing and, above all, their skill as improvisers of counterpoint. Their improvisations, like those of contemporary Italian vocal improvisers, were rarely if ever written down—hence the ephemeral nature of their legacy. Their influence was thus due as much to the great artistry with which they played their novel instruments as to the new sounds and tone colors produced by the characteristic ensembles.[4] Northern instruments and modes of playing were quickly adopted by Italian musicians, so much so that by the turn of the fifteenth century the more gifted ones were performing alongside foreign pifferi in many Italian cities, among them, Siena.

The pifferi, who generally performed in groups of three or four, were often designated by contemporary chroniclers as the "alta cappella," or "loud band," as a means of distinguishing them from musicians who played stringed instruments, the principal components of the "bassa cappella" or "soft band." Customarily, the pifferi ensembles included two shawms, a bombard, and a slide trumpet or trombone.[5] The shawms were a family of double-reed woodwind instruments usually made in one piece with a conical bore. A brass tube, the staple, was placed into the top of the bore and over this a pirouette, or mouthpiece. The reed fitted over the protruding end of the staple. The various instruments of the family were pitched a fifth apart so that, for example, the alto shawm was a fifth below the treble shawm and a fifth above the tenor shawm, or bombard. Finger holes enabled the player to produce various pitches within the range of an octave and a fifth.

---

3. In recent years Keith Polk has been making the case for the German contribution. See his "Instrumental Music in the Urban Centres of Renaissance Germany," *Early Music History* 7 (1987): 159–86, and "Innovation in Instrumental Music, 1450–1510: The Role of German Performers within European Culture," in *Music in the German Renaissance: Sources, Styles and Contexts,* ed. John Kmetz (Cambridge, 1994), 202–14.

4. These concepts of performance practice and instrumentation were not, and perhaps could not, have been written down at the time. The German musicians' performances, like all performances before the age of sound recordings, were ephemeral—admired, prized, and soon emulated by other musicians who heard them, and ultimately forgotten as new styles and influences and new repertories overtook them.

5. Polk, "Municipal Wind Music in Flanders in the Late Middle Ages," *Brass and Woodwind Quarterly* 2 (1969): 1, remarks that the presence of bombards was rarely noted, while mention of the trombone was more frequent. The makeup of wind bands, the numbers and types of players and their instruments, and the written sources of melodies used in their improvisations are among the many topics treated by Polk in *German Instrumental Music of the Late Middle Ages,* 79–86. Also see his remarks (pp. 50–53) about the shawms and bombards used by the prototypical *pfeifen,* a term that he says in a wider sense referred to two instruments, the soprano shawm and its tenor companion, the bombard.

Many of the performers were extraordinarily versatile and played several instruments, as did the music master of Gentile Sermini's tale, cited in chapter 13, who brought a lute, a flute, and a pair of "pifferetti sordi" (perhaps mute cornetts) to the daily lessons. At first the Sienese bands had only two or three pifferi, but within a few decades a trombone joined the ensemble. Although fifteenth-century Palace records rarely if ever specify instruments other than the trombone, documents from the following century show that the pifferi, of whom there were as many as eight at times, were by then playing recorders, transverse flutes, cornetts, and curtals as well as trombones. Reports from other Italian cities also testify to the versatility of instrumentalists and show that Siena was by no means unique in this regard.[6] After the establishment of the Sienese wind band in the early fifteenth century the drummers, who in the past had always appeared with the trumpeters in payment records, now began to be listed with the pifferi. This new grouping suggests that although the drummers continued to assist the trumpeters, they now also performed with the wind band.[7]

The earliest of the fifteenth-century Sienese pifferi were performers of polyphony, musicians, like their peers elsewhere, well versed in the art of improvisation, which doubtless lay at the heart of most of their performances. There is no hint that all of them read music until after the mid-fifteenth century, when, for the first time in Siena, the parts played by individual performers were specified in various records.[8] The case for reliance, at least in part, on a written repertory at Siena gathers strength later in the fifteenth century, when one Sienese player found service in the Ferrara wind band, whose performers, apart from whatever other talents they possessed, used a written repertory. In the sixteenth century there are reports of the purchase of printed partbooks of polyphony for the Sienese band as well as evidence that some of the pifferi themselves taught and composed polyphony. Several of the Palace instrumentalists were employed in the cathedral chapel at various times during the later sixteenth century and this would not have been possible had they been unable to read part music.

---

6. William F. Prizer, "Bernardino Piffaro e i pifferi e tromboni di Mantova: Strumenti a fiato in una corte italiana," *Rivista italiana di musicologia* 16 (1981): 160–1, gives testimony regarding the versatility of musicians in the Manutan wind band. For musicians outside of Italy, see Polk, *German Instrumental Music,* 50, who makes the point that "the medieval German pfeifer was a professional musician" and that "as such, though his primary instrument was the shawm, he was expected to be able to provide whatever music, on a variety of instruments, was demanded at a particular occasion."

7. Thus, though the names of percussionists have been cited in previous chapters in connection with those of the trumpeters, the drummers played an important role, literally and figuratively, in the wind band's performances during the remainder of the fifteenth century and throughout the sixteenth. Several specific instances of drummers playing with the wind band at private functions are recorded in the following pages. Polk, in a private communication, notes that he has found a few references to a player of nakers performing with shawms in the late fourteenth and early fifteenth centuries, but that such citations are rare after 1430. The particular grouping of nakers and wind players in the Sienese documents, however, finds a resonance in records from Ferrara, which also reflect "the practical groupings of the players." See Lockwood, *Music in Renaissance Ferrara,* 140.

8. Polk, *German Instrumental Music,* 163–66, has an excellent discussion about this matter. On p. 165, citing Zippel, *I suonatori della Signoria di Firenze,* 15, he also notes that players of parts are named in Florence as early as 1406.

Initially, only non-Sienese musicians, including northern Italians, Germans, and Frenchmen, served in the band. They alone, it seems, were deemed worthy of the honor, an indication that few if any Sienese pifferi were of professional status at the time. Foreigners, in fact, continued to dominate the pifferi's ranks until the end of the fifteenth century, when native Sienese began to appear among them, eventually to claim the band as their own. Available evidence suggests that this was true for all of Italy, as peninsular musicians not only succeeded to the posts hitherto reserved for the preferred foreigners, but also set standards for instrumental performance and composition universally acknowledged in the later Renaissance. In Siena's case the history of the sixteenth-century pifferi is largely one that documents the rise of native instrumental music and with it the emergence of a school of Sienese composers and performers whose talents and accomplishments gained them recognition throughout Tuscany and all of Italy.

Players of the "ciaramella," a word used in Siena to denote a kind of shawm that was played in earlier times, were employed on an individual basis at the Palace for almost a century before the pifferi were brought in. Although nothing specific about the duties of the fourteenth-century musicians appears in Palace records, they were likely assigned many of the same duties as the later pifferi.[9] As we have seen, bits and pieces of evidence point to ciaramella players as forming part of a smaller ensemble, which also included a drummer and perhaps a trumpeter or two. This type of "loud band," a precursor of the pifferi bands, probably had its origins in Near Eastern practices brought back to Europe after the Crusades. In the earlier ensembles the ciaramella player performed or improvised melodies above the simpler, slower moving part played by the trumpeter, to the rhythmic patterns supplied by the drummer. From what we can gather, however, this ensemble with the ciaramella had quite a different sound from that of the later pifferi, even though both were classified as "loud" bands. The distinction was probably that the range of dynamics produced by the newer German instruments was considerably more flexible and certainly more subtle than anything known before. Designed to emit a volume of sound loud enough to be heard at functions out of doors, the new instruments could also produce a smooth and balanced tone that was more appropriate to the requirements of indoor performances. The pifferi, then, as has been so often said, were quite special and they were assuredly very different from the older ciaramella ensembles.[10] Probably this distinction prompted an Italian transliteration of their German name, itself indicating something new—new instruments, a new manner of performing, and a new concept of ensemble sounds—as Folgore intimated, never before been heard in Italy.

Shawm bands were already flourishing in northern European cities by the latter

9. Polk makes this point regarding northern musicians in "Municipal Wind Music in Flanders," 95.

10. Dietrich Kämper, *La musica strumentale nel Rinascimento* (Turin, 1976), 67, speaks of a cialamello and a cenamella in reference to a performance in Mantua in 1505 by the Venetian wind band, which played arrangements of two motets scored for four trombones and two pifferi, but the original document refers to pifferi. For corrections to the document, see Prizer, "Bernardino Piffaro," 161, n. 39.

half of the fourteenth century.[11] Despite the hazards of travel and the uncertainties of employment, German musicians soon began arriving in Italy, where, sometimes as groups, sometimes mingling with local players, they quickly established a new standard of wind instrument performance. They were regularly employed in Florence from 1383 onwards.[12] In Bologna, which was to become one of the principal centers for the dissemination of these new standards, a stable group of pifferi was established by 1399.[13] Siena knew them in the fourteenth century, too, even though the government made no move to appoint a group of them to Palace service until after the turn of the fifteenth century, perhaps because qualified players were in short supply. Pifferi, at any rate, are named in the entourages of at least two government officials, of the *conservatore* on 31 October 1361[14] and of the *sanatore* in 1382.[15] Pifferi are even recorded at the Palace several times before the wind band was formally constituted. A payment from 15 August 1401 registers L. 2 s. 4 paid to the two pifferi of the *sanatore* "because they came to play for us this morning."[16] Another cites the gratuities given to the pifferi of the Guelf party of Florence and the pifferi of the Lord of Cortona for having played respectively on the 25th and 27th of December 1405.[17] As mentioned earlier, the trumpeters and pifferi of Duke Louis of Anjou were also recompensed for performing in early August 1410.[18]

PIFFERI IN THE FIRST HALF OF THE FIFTEENTH CENTURY

The first steps toward employing a wind band at the Palace were taken on 10 April 1408, when, "for the honor of the entire city," the priors voted to discharge two of their musicians and appointed three pifferi in their stead (see Doc. 11.1). At the same time a four-man commission was delegated to recommend how best to proceed. But this was evidently a formality because a report from the following day notes the dismissal of two long-time employees, the trumpeter Severino di Bartolomeo and the nakers

---

11. Polk, *German Instrumental Music,* 110–12.

12. Polk, "Civic Patronage and Instrumental Ensembles in Renaissance Florence," 67, gives data showing that a three-man group was employed in Florence from 1383 to 1395 and cites a German piffero who was employed from 1401 through the 1430s.

13. Gambassi, "Origine, statuti e ordinamenti del Concerto Palatino," 267, and *Il Concerto Palatino,* 7.

14. The payment also names minstrels, a singer, a player, trumpeters, and drummers: "A Bunifazio giolaro e non di chorte, istà chol Chonservadore, fiorini quatro d'oro . . . A missere Pavolucio, sonatore, fiorini due d'oro . . . A' pifari, nacharini, tornbatori [*sic*] del Chonservadore, fiorini sei d'oro . . . A missere Bargino giolaro fiorini due d'oro . . . a Tomaso cantatore fiorini quatro" (ASS, Biccherna, vol. 241, fol. 9ʳ, dated 31 October 1361).

15. Cellesi, *Storia della più antica banda musicale senese,* 27.

16. "A due pifari del Sanatore a dì XV d'aghosto soldi quaranta quatro, i q[u]ali lo' diei per deliberazione del Chonciestoro perché ci venono a fare matinata questa matina . . . L. II s. III" (Concistoro, vol. 2495, *Proventi, spese e inventari, 1399–1407,* fol. 46ʳ, dated 1401).

17. "A' piffari da fFirenze di Parte Ghuelfa fiorini due senesi paghai insin a dì 26 di dicienbre per deliberazione del Chonciestoro, F. — L. 8 s. 4 . . . A' piffari del singniore di chortona lire cinque s. quattordici, diei insin a dì 27 di dicienbre per deliberazione del chonciestoro, F. — L. 5. s. 14" (ibid., fol. 154ʳ, dated 1405).

18. See chapter 9, note 95.

player Francio di Viva, and the nomination to a one-year appointment of three pifferi, Filippo di Polo da Venezia, Renaldo di Michele da Cesena, and Antonio di Giovanni da Bologna (see Doc. 11.2).[19] Antonio's father was Giovanni di Antonio da Bologna, a Palace trumpeter since 1399. Giovanni probably had a hand in recruiting the newcomers. This much is implied by an advance payment of Fl. 10 for the three pifferi issued to him a few weeks after their appointment.[20] Their contract called for each piffero player to receive a monthly stipend of Fl. 3. Only two, Filippo and Antonio, appear in pay records for May and June, an indication that Renaldo did not serve beyond the end of April.

None of the pifferi is named in the clothing list for Assumption Day in 1408. That the Palace administration experienced some problem with the musicians at the time is confirmed by a report two months later. This states that the priors fired Filippo and his associates because of their dishonesty and that a German piffero named Corrado da Alamania was appointed with the same salary and privileges in place of them. Corrado was also given authority to bring in two other musicians and told that in the interim he would be assisted by the piffero player called Imperadore (see Doc. 11.3). The musician in question was Angelo d'Arrigo, the German trumpeter who had been appointed to Palace service a year earlier.[21] Versatility, a recurrent theme throughout the history of Siena's instrumental ensembles, can thus be documented among the wind band's members from its very beginnings. In this case it also demonstrates that some musicians employed in the trumpeters' corps could improvise polyphony and perhaps even read some form of written notation. The instrument that Imperadore played with the shawms may have been an S-shaped or folded form of the trumpet fitted with a slide mechanism, one that enabled the player to sound many more notes within a wider range than the straight trumpet.[22]

The new arrangement with Corrado was so satisfactory, and Corrado himself so admirable, that his salary was raised by one florin in July 1409. Meanwhile, another piffero named Gherardo had been hired, and his name, together with Corrado's and Imperadore's, appears in the clothing list for the following Assumption Day. Whatever

---

19. As mentioned in chapter 9, the trumpeter Severino di Bartolomeo was subsequently reinstated with a monthly salary of Fl. 2. Funds for his salary were raised by the simple expedient of reducing the stipends of the other trumpeters.

20. ASS, Biccherna, vol. 444, fol. 26^r, states that money was picked up on 21 April 1408. Another record in the same volume says that Giovanni di Antonio da Bologna received Fl. 6 S. 56 "at the command of the priors" for fourteen days' service in one payment, Fl. 6 in a second payment, and L. 4 in a final payment dated 3 April 1408 (fol. 131^r). These may record expenses incurred while he was on a recruitment trip.

21. See chapter 8.

22. Or it may have been a trombone; in Angelo d'Arrigo's case at the time of his appointment he was said to have a "tuba grossa," which may have been a clerk's way of describing a trombone. See chapter 9. Interesting in this regard also is the description of the trombone as a "tubicinone," or large trumpet, "commonly called a trombone" (Doc. 11.5). See Polk, *German Instrumental Music,* 57 and 60–68, for further information about the slide trumpet and shawm ensembles in Germany. See also id., "The Trombone, the Slide Trumpet and the Ensemble Tradition of the Early Renaissance," *Early Music* 17 (1989): 389–97.

Imperadore's instrument, he surely took the cantus firmus or tenor part in the ensemble. This would have been consistent with contemporary iconographical evidence, often showing a trumpeter or bagpiper as the third member of the shawm band.[23]

Personnel problems continued to plague the band for more than a decade after its establishment. Indeed, although there were times in future years when relatively stable conditions prevailed, difficulties in recruiting and retaining suitable musicians became all too common throughout the first half-century and later of the group's existence. The two pifferi just mentioned were gone by the end of May 1410, when another German piffero, Niccolò di Niccolò da Strasburgo, appeared. The terms of Niccolò's appointment state that he was to receive "the same salary as the other trumpeters," an indication that other Palace musicians were once again in the shawm band. The identity of the trumpeters in question is revealed in a set of payments for the last six months of 1410, where Angelo called Imperadore and Giovanni di Antonio are described as pifferi. Giovanni's new role in the band furnishes yet another reason for believing that he was connected in some way with the initial formation of the group.

A list of Palace employees on the clothing list for Assumption Day in 1411 names two pifferi, Nicolaus and Nicola, and a similar list from 1413 refers to them more specifically as Niccolò di Giorgio and Niccolò di Niccolò. By that time there was a third piffero, Jacopo di Antonio da Bologna, whose patronymic suggests that he was Giovanni di Antonio's brother. Niccolò di Niccolò was gone by Assumption Day 1414, and his apparent replacement was Renaldo da Cesena, who returned to Sienese service at the end of the year at a monthly salary of Fl. 3. Renaldo appears in the clothing list for Assumption Day 1415 together with Jacopo di Antonio and Niccolò di Giorgio. The latter is identifed here and in several subsequent records as a native of Zara (Giara), a town on the Dalmatian coast then under Venetian rule. In some documents Renaldo is said to be from Bologna rather than Cesena, a geographical error easily understood in view of the proximity of the two towns, though it could also mean that his professional life centered in Bologna.

Continuing dissatisfaction with the musicians surfaced at a meeting in late October 1415, when the priors declared that the pifferi presently employed were incapable and brought "no honor to the Commune." For this reason they decided to authorize treasury officials to appoint "three good and capable pifferi" at an appropriate salary.[24] The only change that resulted from their decision, however, was that Renaldo was replaced sometime before the following Assumption Day by a piffero called Angelino. He may be the German musician, Angelino della Magna, employed in Florence between 1406 and 1410. But a positive identification is difficult because his patronymic is lacking in both Sienese and Florentine records. The same is true of several German musicians

23. See the illustrations provided by Polk in "The Trombone, the Slide Trumpet and the Ensemble Tradition," 394–96, and in *German Instrumental Music,* 65.

24. "Viso quod pifferi qui ad presens serviunt Comuni non sunt idonei nec pro Comuni honorabiles, et volentes honori Comuni providere, concorditer decreverunt remittere et remiserunt in quatuor provisores Bicherne quod possint invenire et conducere tres bonos et idoneos pifferos, qui bene et idonee sciant pulsare et ex eorum servitio resultet honor Comunis sicut decet, pro salario de quo eis videbitur, pro utili et honore Comunis" (Concistoro, vol. 298, fol. 33ʳ, dated 22 October 1415).

named Corrado, Gherardo, and Niccolò, all recorded in both cities during the first quarter of the fifteenth century.[25] Nevertheless, as in the case of itinerant singers, it seems likely that many instrumentalists served in the one place before moving on to the other.

In mid-October 1416 Angelino was succeeded by yet another German piffero, Michele di Giovanni da Alamania. Michele's appointment brought a certain degree of stability to the group, as shown by a record from three years later, which names him, Niccolò di Giorgio, and Jacopo da Bologna among those who received new clothing on Assumption Day 1419. Jacopo da Bologna died sometime before 1 February 1420, when the priors appointed Tommaso di Biagio da Ungaria in his place. Only Tommaso and Niccolò were on the Assumption Day clothing list that year. Tommaso was gone by Assumption Day of 1421, for a similar list now cites Niccolò di Giorgio, Niccolò d'Andrea, and Francesco di Piero. The same musicians, each paid L. 12 (Fl. 3) per month, appear together in payments through the end of June 1424.[26]

The Bolognese Musicians

In 1425 Niccolò di Giorgio was temporarily replaced by Dadio di Bartolomeo, cited with Niccolò d'Andrea da Bologna and Francesco di Piero da Bologna in the usual Assumption Day clothing list. Niccolò, however, returned the following year, and subsequently served with his original colleagues through Assumption Day 1428. Two other musicians, Bartolomeo di Piero Bochini da Bologna and the much-traveled Renaldo di Michele, performed with Niccolò di Andrea during 1429 and 1430. Except for Renaldo, three of the musicians already named were employed at the Palace for the next decade and a half. They were Niccolò di Andrea da Bologna, Niccolò di Giorgio da Giara, and Bartolomeo di Piero Bochini da Bologna, all of whom are mentioned in documents from 1434 through the end of 1444.[27] By then Niccolò di Giorgio, first employed in 1411, had played in the wind band, with a few interruptions, for more than three decades. His record of service was unique in a period that witnessed continual changes in personnel, as pifferi came and went, seemingly without prejudice to their chances of reemployment at the Palace.

This policy of casual employment may have resulted from an informal arrangement with one of the pifferi, who undertook to keep the wind band supplied with competent musicians, even though it meant an occasionl shuffling of personnel. Some kind of

---

25. Zippel, *I suonatori della signoria di Firenze,* passim. Two pifferi were employed in Florence in 1405 at a monthly salary of Fl. 4. Polk, "Civic patronage," 67, mentions Cristoforo, Niccolo della Magna, and Agnolino della Magna in 1406.

26. Cellesi, who also quotes this document (*La più antica banda,* 27), says there were four of them, doubtless because the same record credits L. 73 s. 16 for six months' service to "Angniolo d'Aricho detto Imperadore, tronbetta e pifaro di nostro Comune." It is possible that he continued to serve in a dual capacity at this time.

27. The names of the these musicians are not always carefully noted in the accounts. Concistoro, vol. 2498, *Proventi, spese e inventari, 1436–44,* fol. 152ᵛ, with inventories of instruments from various years, shows that Niccolò d'Andrea, Niccolò di Giorgio, and Bartolomeo di Piero had "tre piffari d'ariento" in 1438. A deliberation authorizing funds for musicians' uniforms in the same year calls Bartolomeo Maestro Bartolomeo Bochini (Concistoro, vol. 435, fol. 51ʳ, dated 18 August 1438).

network, in other words, may have been in place, one that allowed both for an uncomplicated reception and an easy transfer of highly recommended musicians. The Bolognese origins of so many of them point to that city as the principal supplier to Siena of pifferi, German as well as Italian.[28] At the time Bologna's musical groups were flourishing, though an ongoing process of reducing the number of trumpeters in order to accommodate a three-man shawm band, a nakers player, and a lutenist suggests that employment possibilities there were becoming more limited.[29] Siena, which had already attempted to lure university professors away from Bologna, had considerably more success in recruiting musicians.[30] From the band's very beginnings there was a connection with Bologna through the trumpeter Giovanni di Antonio. Perhaps it was Giovanni himself, as has been suggested, who served as the initial intermediary. In any case, once established, ties with Bologna remained fairly constant, and certain musicians—the most obvious being Renaldo—seem to have come and gone freely for no apparent reason other than their own convenience or the temporary displeasure of a particular group of priors during their bimestrial term of office.

Bologna, with its international university and large contingent of resident foreigners—students, teachers, and papal administrators—was a natural place for the practices of the German pifferi to take root, so it is hardly surprising that many of the Italian musicians employed in Siena came from there. Nor is it surprising that entrepreneurial Venice, where business and social dealings with large groups of resident foreign merchants were everyday facts of life, was also in the forefront of supplying musicians who were well versed in the latest practices of the north.[31] Siena, with its close commercial ties to Avignon and its position on the road to Rome, was aware of northern developments, as some of the records already cited indicate, but for whatever reasons such developments were not so quickly absorbed by local musicians. Thus, it was to places like Bologna and Venice that Sienese institutions turned when they sought musicians capable of playing music in the northern manner.

Bartolomeo, whose tenure began in 1429, was called *maestro* on several occasions during the following years, and it may be that he was the leader of the tightly knit Bolognese contingent in Siena. The same musicians were still employed on the first of January 1445, when an inventory of Palace belongings notes that Niccolò d'Andrea

---

28. Polk, referring particularly to later fifteenth-century events, has pointed to the "apparent prominence of Bologna as a center for the training of Italian wind players." See his review of Gambassi's *Il Concerto Palatino della Signoria di Bologna* in *JAMS* 44 (1991): 330.

29. Gambassi, *Il Concerto Palatino*, 62, gives the names of five trumpeters, three shawm players, and a nakers player in 1439; in "Origini, statuti e ordinamenti," 267, he cites four trumpeters (down from eight in 1399) in addition to three shawm players, a nakers player, and a lutenist in 1442.

30. The unsuccessful Sienese attempt in 1321–23 to capitalize on the dissatisfaction of Bologna's students and faculty has been summarized by Bowsky, *A Medieval Italian Commune,* 277–78, where important literature on the subject is cited.

31. Documents regarding Venetian practices from this time are scarce. Keith Polk writes in a private communication to me that those that are extant indicate, surprisingly, that few German musicians were active in the city.

piffero had three silver sheathed instruments in his possession.[32] Two months later Niccolò di Giorgio was replaced by the ever-accommodating Renaldo di Michele, who must have been a mature musician by then.[33] Renaldo's previous whereabouts are unknown, though it seems he had been using Siena as a base of operations for some time. A record from Perugia, describing him as "a most perfect master in the art of music," shows he was appointed as the third piffero player there on 25 April 1432.[34] He was in Perugia until the beginning of the following October, when he abruptly resigned, citing personal reasons in Siena.[35] His family, as this incident reveals, was domiciled in Siena, and so it is possible that by 1445 he had been in and out of the city on a number of occasions. His activities were probably typical of those of many professional pifferi of the time and serve to remind us how highly sought after they were. Maestro Bartolomeo received permission to leave Siena for several days on 25 April 1446. Niccolò, Bartolomeo, and Renaldo were also among a group of Palace musicians who were fined d. 5 each in October of that year for having refused to perform at the ceremony when the university's rector was awarded a doctor's degree (see Doc. 11.4). By that time, however, the Concistoro had engaged a new group of musicians who even then were en route to Siena.

The Avignonese Group

No documents explain why the Bolognese group was disbanded, whether it was advancing age and a desire to return to their native city that prompted the musicians to request release from Sienese service, or whether the government itself decided that it was time for a change of personnel. Nor do any documents tell how the priors sought replacements for the Bolognese, how long the recruitment process went on, and how many people were involved in it. Perhaps, in the absence of qualified musicians within

---

32. "MCCCCXLIIII [1445]. Nicholò d'Andrea piffaro de' dare a dì primo di gennaio per questi arienti asegnati a lui proprio, III piffare fornite d'ariento" (Concistoro, vol. 2498, *Proventi, spese e inventari, 1436–44,* fol. 420ʳ). That the instruments were sheathed, or covered, with a thin layer of decorative silver is made clear in a number of other entries recorded for the same purpose in this volume, as, for example, on fol. 395ʳ and fol. 411ʳ, which list "tre pifare fodarate d'ariento" in 1443. See also below regarding the "silver" instruments.

33. The clothing list for the same year mistakenly calls him Renaldus Benedicti and lists him with Bartolomeus Petri and Nicolaus Andree, both designated "de Bononia" (Concistoro, vol. 477, fol. 42ʳ).

34. Rossi, "Memorie di musica civile in Perugia," fasc. 5, 131–32: "Et habentes plenam notitiam et experientiam comprobatam infrascripti Raynaldi magistri in arte musice perfectissimi. Ex omnibus arbitrijs etc. conduxerunt dictum magistrum Raynaldum Michaelis de Cesena in piferum et ad sonandum in dicto palatio fistulam seu ceramellam una cum dictis Nicolao et Petro etc. Cum salario et provisione fl. vigintiseptem cum dimidio de camera pro quolibet anno." The document also indicates that Perugia's wind band had three players at this time.

35. Ibid., 133–34: "Cum magister Ranaldus pifer conductus ad servitia M. D. P. et palatij ipsorum . . . et sibi ob multas eius necessitates sit necesse ad civitatem senarum de qua est redire ad regendam et gubernandam familiam eius nec sit condecens dictis M. D. P. et comuni perusij aliquem contra eius voluntatem ad eorum servitia retinere. Qua de re convenientes ad invicem M. D. P. etc. exibitis consilijs etc. dictum magistrum Ranaldum cassaverunt etc. et annullaverunt ab eius conducta etc."

the city, local auditions were dispensed with altogether and recommendations were made by people in government or their knowledgeable friends. This seems the most logical explanation for an invitation to enter Sienese service that the Concistoro sent to Maestro Garino of Avignon on 30 June 1446. Sienese bankers and merchants had a long history of business dealings in Avignon and initial contacts with the musicians could easily have come through just this kind of communication network. Reports about the musicians' playing, furthermore, must have been favorable, for the priors went so far as to offer the musicians lifetime appointments, without ever having heard them perform. The text of their invitation reads as follows:

> Esteemed friend! Having learned of your talents and of your mastery of wind instruments, and desirous of having you in our service, we have, together with our colleagues, nominated you and two other pifferi and a trombone, whom you will choose, for a lifetime [appointment in our Palace], at the salary which will be appended here in the hand of our government's notary. Thus, if you decide to enter our service at that salary, we ask that you bring two good pifferi and a trombone with you and that you come to Siena as soon as you possibly can. You will be welcomed warmly and will be treated so well by us that you will praise our city to the skies.[36]

The Concistoro's letter resulted from action taken a few days earlier, on 27 June, when the priors decided that "Maestro Garino of Avignon with two associates" and a person who played "a large trumpet, commonly called a trombone" could have lifetime appointments at the Palace as pifferi, subject to continuing governmental approval, at a monthly salary of Fl. 4 for each of them. The musicians were, in addition, to have two suits of clothing every year and "their expenses in the Palace" (see Doc. 11.5). This latter means they would also have privileges entitling them to daily meals in the room set aside for employees within the Palace. There is no record as to whether the Bolognese group enjoyed similar privileges.

Within days of their arrival, on 4 November 1446, the Commune's "silver instruments with their pennants" were presented to the Avignonese musicians in a ceremony at once symbolic and practical.[37] A decree from the end of that month, reaffirming an

---

36. Concistoro, vol. 1666, *Copialettere, 1446*, fol. 76ᵛ. The letter has been published twice by Luigi Bonnelli: "Notizie intorno ad alcuni 'musici di palazzo' al servizio della signoria senese nel secolo XV," *BSSP* 30 (1923): 232; and "Musici d'Avignone al servizio della signoria senese," *La Diana* 3 (1928): 230. It is also possible, as mentioned, that musicians had some sort of communication network among themselves. This, at least, seems to explain why a number of French musicians moved in and out of Siena so easily over the next few years. Noteworthy in the letter is the offer of lifetime appointments, for usually appointments were made for a year or two, but always at the pleasure of the Concistoro. Polk found that many such contracts in northern Europe were for shorter periods (three years, on average), after which it seems to have been fairly common practice to engage an entirely new group. He also noted that in the north during first half of the fifteenth century there seem to have been surprisingly frequent personnel changes in many localities, as there were to be in Siena.

37. "Carolus Laurentii, aromatarius de Senis, in Consistorio et in presentia Magnificorum dominorum . . . promisit . . . se facturum quod magister Carinus et socii, novi piffari, salvabunt instrumenta argentea cum pennonibus sirici, eis consignata, que vulgo le piffare vocantur, et ea presentabunt et reddent camerario Consistorii tam presenti quam futuris, ad omnem voluntatem Consistorii vel ipsius

earlier one concerning the musicians' salaries, states that they were each to be paid 4 Sienese florins a month.[38] Subsequent payments reflect this and specify that the Sienese florin or fiorino largo was valued at L. 4. 15 at the time.[39] The pifferi's salaries were thus double those of the trumpeters. Apart from confirming the differences in wages paid to Palace musicians, evident even at the time of the wind band's foundation, the record shows that Sienese salaries compared favorably with those paid to pifferi in Florence, who in 1444 received four and a half Florentine florins or L. 18 per month.[40] More tangible evidence of the warm reception given the Avignonese comes from December 1446, when they were reimbursed L. 40 for expenses incurred in moving to Siena with their families. Garino (sometimes called Carino or Guerrino), Germano (also called Giordano), and Ferrino da Francia, all designated as pifferi, and Giovanni da Alamania, trombone, were also among Palace employees authorized to receive new suits of clothing for Christmas that same year.

Only two of the new musicians, Ferrino da Francia piffero and Maestro Giovanni trombone, were paid salaries at the end of April 1447. The reason that the others were not mentioned is explained in a deliberation from a month later. This recounts that the pifferi Germano and Garino were granted a two-months' leave of absence so that they might go to France but had overstayed their leave, in consequence of which the Concistoro fired them. The deliberation further notes that another piffero, Lorenzo, had been playing at the Palace for eight days and that the priors, having ascertained that he was an expert and capable musician, decided to grant him a two-month appointment, renewable at their pleasure. He was to receive a salary of L. 12, tax free, per month and a new suit of clothing for Assumption Day (see Doc. 11.6). This latter provision would, of course, apply only if Lorenzo remained in Palace service through that time.

The musician's full name, Lorenzo di Giovanni da Francia, appears in a set of payments from mid-May through the end of June 1447.[41] Mentioned in the same records are Ferrino da Francia and the trombonist, who received their normal salaries. Also cited are two former employees, Bartolomeo di Piero and Niccolò d'Andrea da Bologna, who were paid for twenty-two days' service during May, and the recently returned Germano da Francia, who served for twelve days in June (see Doc. 11.7).[42]

---

camerarii, sin autem promisit Comune Senarum indemne conservare" (Concistoro, vol. 485, fol. 6ᵛ, dated 4 November 1446). The Commune's instruments, described here and in inventories as being made of silver, may have been silver-sheathed.

38. Concistoro, vol. 485, fol. 20ᵛ, dated 23 November 1446.

39. This value is based on reports from February 1448 and following months: ASS, Biccherna, vol. 317, fol. 29ᵛ, where payments to "Maestro Gherino d'Avignone" read: "òne dati a dì V d'aprile [1448] . . . gli ritenemo in uno fiorino largo de la sua paga . . . L. IIII. S. XV. òne dati a dì deto L. quatro s. quindici, dè Germano di Francia pifaro in uno fiorino largo, de la sua paga di marzo . . . L. IIII S. XV."

40. Zippel, *I suonatori della Signoria di Firenze,* 28.

41. Mentioned by Bonelli, "Notizie intorno ad alcuni 'musici di palazzo'," 232; and "Musici d'Avignon," 230.

42. It appears that Niccolò was given a pension of some kind that allowed the Concistoro to recall him when it had need of his services. This, at least, is what is implied in a decree from several years later, which revoked "every provision, past, present, and future, that Niccolò piffero da Bologna

New clothing for Assumption Day was authorized for Germano, Ferrino, Lorenzo, and the trombonist Giovanni della Magna on 22 July 1447. Lorenzo, however, was not mentioned in a December resolution of the same year, when Christmas clothing was approved for the other three musicians. Further evidence that Lorenzo, now called Teutonico ("the German"), neglected his duties comes from the following April, when the priors declared that he was incapable of serving with the group and that he was to be fired at the end of the month. Replacing him on the Assumption Day clothing list in August 1448 was another piffero called Guglielmo,[43] also cited with the others in a similar list from the following year.[44]

Unforeseen events continued to plague the group. Giovanni di Giovanni da Francia succeeded the recently deceased Germano da Francia in September 1449, only to resign and request release from service in the same month. He soon changed his mind, however, and began performing with the group once again. On 23 October, after noting this and acknowledging that "the work of a tenorista was an honor to the Palace," the Concistoro agreed to reappoint him at his former salary of L. 12 per month. Meanwhile, unspecified problems had arisen with a third member of the original group. In a tersely worded deliberation of 29 September 1449 the Concistoro decreed that "Maestro Ians, who plays the trombone, could no longer serve the Palace because he had behaved dishonorably." The order, however, was rescinded within the week. Mention of a trombonist in Siena at this time more or less parallels the first recorded appearance of players of the instrument in Florence and Ferrara.[45] The trombone was a relatively new instrument, having evolved from a trumpet with an added slide mechanism, which made a wider range of notes available.[46]

The clothing list for Christmas 1449 names the pifferi Ferrino, Giovanni, and Guglielmo, the recently fired and rehired trombonist Maestro Giovanni, and a heretofore unmentioned musician, Gualfredo, whose role is unspecified. To judge from the name, Gualfredo, too, must have come from beyond the Alps. Both Giovanni and Gualfredo are missing from the clothing list for Assumption Day 1450, which cites Ferrino, Guglielmo, and a new piffero, Matteo, in addition to Maestro Giovanni, trombone.[47] The

would have from the Commune": "iustis et rationabilibus causis revocaverunt omnem provisionem quam habet seu habere debet vel deberet in futurum a Comuni Senarum Nicholaum piffarum de Bononia . . . non obstantibus quibuscunque reformationibus in contrarium disponentibus" (Concistoro, vol. 524, fol. 55ʳ, dated 23 February 1454).

43. Germano is called Giordano on this list.

44. Additional payments from 1448 and others from 1449, listed under the name of "Maestro Garino d'Avignone and associates," may mean that Garino returned to Sienese service, but they are more like entries carried over from one year to the next, the result of an unresolved bookkeeping problem.

45. Polk, *German Instrumental Music,* 59, cites Ferrara (1439) and Florence (1443).

46. Polk, ibid., 56–60, presents information about the development of the slide trumpet and the trombone.

47. Though it seems improbable, this Mathio may be the same person as Mathio Marian de Tomasi da Siena, listed in 1476 among the "musici" employed by Duke Ercole of Ferrara (Lockwood, *Music in Renaissance Ferrara,* 180). Later connections between musicians in the two cities suggest that Matteo represents an even earlier example of musical exchanges.

Florentine wind band, which included three pifferi and a trombone, visited Siena for the August festivities that year, as did a number of trumpeters and a trombonist from Lucca, encounters that, like so many others, assuredly facilitated an exchange of repertories and performance practices (see chapter 14). So, too, did trips made by the Sienese pifferi, who took turns journeying to Rome in order to seek indulgences during September and November of the same year (see Doc. 11.8).

PIFFERI IN THE 1450s

Three pifferi and a trombone are mentioned in payments through February 1451, after which the trombonist is no longer cited.[48] Three pifferi, Ferrino, Guglielmo, and Arrigo, are on the clothing lists for Assumption Day and Christmas 1451, but these likewise fail to mention a trombonist.[49] Thus the position was officially vacant, since clothing was normally given to tenured employees and granted to others only under exceptional circumstances.[50] This policy, as has been noted, explains why some musicians' names are lacking from clothing lists, even though salary payments to them appear in account books. In general, they were either recent appointees awaiting confirmation to permanent positions or others who were supernumeraries. Occasionally, as with the Bolognese in 1447, a few of them served as substitutes for regularly appointed players.

The Arrigo cited in the clothing list from August 1451 is surely the same musician as Arrigo di Giovanni da Venezia, who was formally appointed as a piffero tenorista on the following 7 September. He was promised two suits of clothing a year and a monthly salary of 4 ducats, tax free, on condition that he bring his wife and family to live in Siena.[51] The tenorista, as mentioned, was the person who sang or, in this case, played the tenor part of a polyphonic composition. Arrigo's designation as a tenorista, a term also used previously to describe Lorenzo di Giovanni's role, suggests that at this time the wind band was improvising rather sophisticated ensemble counterpoint or that it was performing written part music, or even doing both.[52] A new trombonist, Agostino di Piero da Albania, was engaged a few months after Arrigo, in December 1451. Although Agostino was Albanian by birth, he most likely had lived and worked in Venice before arriving in Siena. In March 1452 the priors granted him a one-month's leave of absence, to be taken whenever he wished, so that he might go to Venice. They also stipulated that he would not receive any salary should he overstay his leave. A marginal addition to the record of his leave notes that he was gone from Sienese service by the

----

48. In March and April 1451 the pifferi were each receiving L. 18. 10 per month; for December 1452 the amount is L. 19.

49. The list of July 1451 names only Ferrino, Guglielmo, and Arrigo, pifferi, and lists Fl. 8 for each of their uniforms, rather than the Fl. 10 given to other Palace employees.

50. In the past clothing allotments were occasionally provided to musicians who were not regular members of the Palace's establishment. Suffice it to recall the allocation made to the volunteer trumpeters who served without salary in the later fourteenth century.

51. A subsequent report from 23 September 1451 states that he arrived together with his wife and family in Siena on 23 September 1451 and that his salary of Du. 4 was to begin that day.

52. Polk, *German Instrumental Music,* 166–213, has an excellent account of the improvising tradition, with illustrations of the kinds of improvisations these highly trained musicians were capable of providing.

end of the same year. Meanwhile, as a deliberation from several months earlier reveals, steps had been taken to rehire the previous trombonist, Maestro Giovanni Teutonico. Maestro Giovanni is, in fact, listed together with Arrigo da Venezia, Ferrino, and a new German piffero, Giovanni di Piero da Colonia, among those receiving clothing on Assumption Day and Christmas of 1452.[53]

A fourth piffero, Federigo di Lanberto Francioso, also appears on the 1452 clothing lists.[54] His formal appointment is in a record from July of that year. This recounts how the priors, after noting that Federigo dressed well and had several good suits of clothing, decreed that he could use the clothing allowance he was to receive on Assumption Day for the care of his wife, who was ill. The length of Federigo's stay is uncertain, given the absence of clothing lists from 1453. What is certain, however, is that the priors were making an effort to keep four musicians in the ensemble, and this is reflected in the clothing lists for Assumption Day and Christmas of 1454, which name the three pifferi, Arrigo da Venezia, Ferrino Francioso, Giovanni da Colonia, and the German trombonist Maestro Giovanni, all of whom were mentioned two years previously.[55]

Wind Bands and Their Repertory

A glance at the makeup of wind bands employed in some of the major Italian cities around mid-century and afterwards, particularly those that had some connection with Siena, indicates that most ensembles usually counted four musicians. The Florentine Signoria employed three pifferi and a trombone in 1444, and this same number is recorded when Florentine groups visited Siena for Assumption Day festivities in 1450, 1463, 1468, and 1469.[56] At Naples the court ensemble at first included three pifferi and, after 1450, a trombone, precisely the makeup of the Neapolitan group that visited

---

53. The list of 13 December 1452 calls them Ferrino Francioso, Arrigo da Bologna, Giovanni da Alamania, and Maestro Giovanni trombone. Polk, "Civic Patronage and Instrumental Ensembles," 67, notes that one of the musicians engaged in Florence in 1443 was also from Cologne, Giovanni di Giovanni da Colonia.

54. Federigo may have been Ferrino's brother, for both had the same patronymic. One record shows that a son born to Ferrino di Lanberto di Francia, pifaro, was baptized with the name of Niccolò on 12 April 1454 (ASS, Biccherna vol. 1133, fol. 168^r). A second shows that a son born to Federigo di Lanberto di Francia, pifaro de' Magnifici Signori, also named Niccolò, was baptized on 27 January 1461 (ibid., fol. 235^r). This latter is not necessarily an indication that Federigo was in the city at the time of his son's birth. Federigo is mentioned below.

55. On the list of 22 December 1454 they are called Maestro Giovanni trombone, Ferrino Francioso, Arrigo da Bologna, and Giovanni da Alamania. It may be that in this instance Arrigo's place of origin was erroneously given as Bologna instead of Venice, but it could also be that he was originally from Bologna and living in Venice at the time he was hired (Concistoro, vol. 527, fols. 77^v–78^r).

56. Zippel, I suonatori della Signoria di Firenze, 28. For the Florentine group in Siena in 1450, Concistoro, vol. 506, fol. 32^r; in 1463, vol. 581, fol. 57^r; in 1468, vol. 611, fols. 68^v–69^r; in 1469, vol. 617, fols. 56^v–57^r. Some Florentine organizations such as the Parte Guelfa and the Arte di Mercanzia also sent pifferi during these years, and their groups normally numbered two or three musicians. See chapter 14 for records of these and other visiting groups.

Siena in 1465 for the Assumption Day festivities.[57] A similar situation occurred in Bologna in 1469, when a trombonist joined the three pifferi already employed.[58] The ensemble maintained by the duke of Mantua counted three pifferi and a trombone in 1469, and the same number of musicians was apparently maintained throughout the rest of the century.[59] The duke of Milan's group, which had four pifferi and a trombone when it was in Siena in 1465, was exceptional for the time, but clearly reflects the duke's ambitious musical program, soon to set the standard for all of Italy.[60] Earlier reports indicate that the Milanese group had only four musicians, but by 1466 it had six, among them four pifferi and two trombones.[61] The Ferrarese group had two pifferi and a trombone in 1456, evidently the number maintained by Borso d'Este during his twenty-year reign.[62] But a fourth member, in this case a piffero who may have doubled as a second trombonist, was playing in the ensemble by 1471, when Ercole succeeded Borso as duke.[63] Compared with these, Sienese records indicate a policy aimed at keeping the town abreast of musical practices in other major Italian cities. Sienese cultural aspirations, in sum, were no less fervent and no less aggressive than those elsewhere.

More information about the makeup of the group and additional proof that, whatever other talents they may have possessed, the pifferi were also trained performers of polyphony is in a number of records from 1455. These relate how on 30 July of that year the Concistoro decided to fire one of the three pifferi and to replace him with a new musician. Ferrino was exempted from their ruling, which also stipulated that either the tenorista or the contra[altus] was to go, whoever received the lower number of votes in a secret ballot. The loser would nevertheless remain on the payroll through Assumption Day, when he would receive the usual clothing provision (see Doc. 11.9). After the votes were tallied the *piffaro contra* Giovanni da Colonia was declared the winner, the *piffaro tenorista* Arrigo di Giovanni da Venezia the loser.[64] Appointed imme-

---

57. Atlas, *Music at the Aragonese Court of Naples,* 110. The Neapolitan group's visit to Siena in 1465 is recorded in a list of participants in the Assumption Day festivities (Concistoro, vol. 593, fol. 61^{r-v}, dated 17 August 1465). In addition to "5 tronbetti della Maiestà del Re, 3 piffari et uno trombone della detta Maiestà" and "1 tanburino della detta Maiestà del Re," this cites "7 tronbetti dello Illustrissimo Duca di Milano, 4 piffari et uno trombone d'esso Duca, 1 maestro di liuto della Duchessa," and a host of other trumpeters and instrumentalists from Florence, Salerno, Pistoia, Arezzo, Cortona, and Urbino, among other places. The Assumption Day festivities are discussed below in chapter 14.

58. Gambassi, "Origine, statuti e ordinamenti," 268.

59. Prizer, "Bernardino Piffaro," 159.

60. See note 57.

61. For 1461, see Barblan, "Vita musicale," 789, and Motta, "Musici alla corte degli Sforza," 43, as reported by Prizer, "Music at the Court of the Sforza," 148; for 1469, see Edmond Vander Straten, *La musique au Pays Bas avant le XIXe siècle* (Brussels, 1867–88), 6:26, as reported by Prizer, 151.

62. Lockwood, *Music in Renaissance Ferrara,* 178.

63. The fourth member, Zoanne d'Alemagna, is listed as a piffero and in 1476, perhaps erroneously, as a trombonist (Lockwood, *Music in Renaissance Ferrara,* 180 and 321).

64. Arrigo had apparently been in the Concistoro's bad graces for some time. A deliberation from the previous 30 December 1454 reports that a new piffero, whose name is lacking in the document, was hired that day and that Arrigo was fired at the same time: "Magnifici domini . . . conduxerunt infrascriptum piffarum et pro piffaro palatii, cum salario et modis consuetis, cuius nomen est videlicet

diately in Arrigo's place was Stefano di Piero di Francia, who was assigned the soprano part in the ensemble. His salary was fixed at four ducats a month and, like other Palace musicians, he was promised two new suits of clothing every year. Although Stefano di Piero is called a Frenchman at this time, later records specify Savoy as his birthplace. He must have been a very fine player, one whose talents were very much appreciated, for what else could explain this extraordinary situation, which saw the Concistoro dismissing, after a secret ballot, one musician so that another might be hired in his place?

These first extant records designating the Sienese ensemble by the parts they played—superius, contra [altus], and tenor—offer indisputable evidence of their ability to perform counterpoint. Circumstantial evidence, furthermore, suggests that the musicians could read music as well. Stefano di Piero would later become a member of the Ferrarese court ensemble, and, as mentioned below, he was there when the Casanatense manuscript collection of music for piffero ensemble was copied. The preparation of the collection has been convincingly linked to that ensemble, and the obvious inference is that the Ferrarese musicians, including Stefano, could read music.[65] Supposing that Stefano was musically literate, the same was probably true of his colleagues in the Sienese ensemble, particularly since they were designated by their contrapuntal ranges within the group.

Sienese records also corroborate evidence from other times and places about the ranges of the instruments in a typical fifteenth-century band—generally, one or two high shawms, a bombard, or tenor shawm, and a trombone. Given the circumstances, it appears that the move to employ an ensemble at the Palace, all of whose members were performers of written polyphony as well as skilled improvisers, occurred definitively with the employment of the Avignonese group a few years earlier. The Avignonese were the first to employ a trombonist, and except for very brief intervals, a trombonist was thereafter associated with the Sienese wind band as the fourth member. This does not necessarily mean that the band always played four-part music—there is, after all, a good deal of iconographical evidence from the time showing that often only three players might be performing, even if four members were present.[66] In these illustrations it is usually a shawm player, that is, one of the players of the soprano or alto parts, who is resting. The fairly large number of illustrations of piffero ensembles depicting a group without a brass instrument demonstrate that shawms could perform satisfactorily without a trombone, a situation implicit in remarks about wind ensembles by the famous theorist Johannes Tinctoris, writing about 1480. In short, when the pifferi performed three-part pieces, some flexibility and a greater variety of tone color were available, not only in the choice of shawms (or other instruments) for the upper

---

[blank]. Insuper quibusdam iustis causis moti, cassaverunt et pro cassato haberi voluerunt et mandaverunt Arrigum de Bononia, piffarum" (Concistoro vol. 529, fols. 62ᵛ–63ʳ, dated 30 December 1454). The lack of a name indicates that the newly hired musician did not accept the post. The order against Arrigo was probably rescinded.

65. See Lockwood, *Music in Renaissance Ferrara,* 268–71, for the Casanatense manuscript and 318–21 regarding Stefano in Ferrara, ca. 1471–80. The matter is discussed more fully below.

66. See Polk, "Municipal Wind Music," 2, for references to illustrations of four-part shawm ensembles in which one of the shawmists is resting.

parts but also for the cantus firmus or lower part, which could be assigned to a bombard or to a trombone.[67]

Comings and Goings

A flurry of activities during the early part of August 1455 indicates that the priors had second thoughts about the new arrangement and decided to rectify matters before the influx of visitors on Assumption Day. On the fourth of the month they reinstated Arrigo di Giovanni da Venezia, the *piffero tenorista,* in place of Giovanni da Colonia, the *piffero contra.* The latter was nevertheless obliged to continue playing with the group through Assumption Day, when he would receive a suit of clothing (see Doc. 11.10). A week later, on 11 August, the priors appointed a new trombonist, Arrigo di Giovanni da Francoforte, at a salary of L. 16 per month. Whether he actually played at the upcoming festival is uncertain. It is also unclear whether the other recent nominee, Stefano di Piero, was present, since his name is lacking on the Assumption Day clothing list. Cited instead are the three previously mentioned pifferi, Arrigo, Ferrino, and Giovanni da Colonia, and the veteran trombonist, Maestro Giovanni della Magna.

The same musicians appear in an Assumption Day clothing list from 1456. For Christmas of the same year clothing was authorized instead for the pifferi Ferrino, Arrigo, Stefano di Piero da Francia, and for the Frankfurt trombonist Arrigo da Alamania, named a year earlier. But this elusive trombonist is not on the Assumption Day clothing list from 1457, which cites only the three pifferi, Arrigo, Ferrino, and Giovanni da Colonia. Whether Giovanni left Siena after his dismissal and then returned, or whether he remained in town hoping for reinstatement should Stefano decide not to stay, are matters for speculation because nothing is explained in the records. Certainly, this was not the first nor the last time that musicians disappeared from the payrolls only to reappear a few months or a few years later. In any case it is clear that the government's earlier decision regarding personnel did little to stabilize the group. Nor did a subsequent attempt at the end of April 1458, when the Frenchman Tommaso di Pietro Francisena was given a one-year appointment as a "piffero tenorista" beginning on May 1, at a salary of Fl. 3 per month, tax free, with the usual meal and clothing privileges. Tommaso was apparently using an instrument owned by Palace, for the record of his appointment concludes with the proviso that "he have for himself the instrument he is presently using for the price of L. 12, to be deducted from his salary." Another record from the following 7 May suggests that Tommaso's playing was found wanting and that the next group of priors turned instead to another "piffero tenorista," the German Martino di Corrado Teutonico. Martino must have been a far superior musician because his one-year contract, also slated to begin—or to have begun—on 1 May, stipulated that he would have a monthly salary of Fl. 8, tax free, also with the usual meal and clothing privileges. Tommaso was meanwhile appointed to an usher's post in the Palace.

The clothing list for Assumption Day 1458 names Ferrino, Stefano di Piero, and Martino di Corrado Teutonico as pifferi, and Arrigo di Giovanni da Francoforte as

---

67. Polk, *German Instrumental Music,* 53, 79–83, discusses three-part ensembles of shawms as well as ensembles *a 4* and quotes the text of the pertinent passage from Tinctoris.

trombonist. Stefano di Piero subsequently appears in salary payments only through the first six months of 1459. His departure is confirmed by the clothing list for the following Assumption Day, which lacks his name but cites the other three. Payments through September again mention three musicians, but those through December cite only two pifferi. Perhaps one or more of the Palace trumpeters played the third and fourth parts in the ensemble, or recourse was had to hiring other musicians on a casual basis. This latter solution seems possible because musicians, like the former piffero Federigo, were sometimes described as being in the Concistoro's service, even though their names are not on any official personnel lists.[68] Perhaps two players, a duo consisting of performers of the soprano and tenor parts, played for a while without the others. Although this practice was somewhat old-fashioned, the duo could, as Keith Polk phrased it, still "function as an adequate (if less than 'perfect') performing ensemble."[69]

RECRUITMENT IN THE 1460s

Instability, again illustrated by continual hirings and departures, continued to characterize the wind band in the next few years. From the end of January 1460 comes a report that certain belongings seized from a new trombonist named Federico were returned to him. At the same time the priors reappointed the trombonist Arrigo di Giovanni da Francoforte beginning on 1 February. The next day Federico received a safe conduct valid for the month of February. February salaries for the other pifferi and for Arrigo were approved on the sixteenth of that month.[70] On 19 March 1460 Giovanni di Giovanni da Alamania was appointed to a piffero's post with the proviso that he begin serving in April. His monthly salary fixed at L. 19, he was also promised a suit of clothing. But not even the slightest hint in the records shows that he joined the group at this time and his name does not appear on Assumption Day clothing lists until 1463. The priors condemned an unnamed trombonist, probably Arrigo di Giovanni, for unspecified reasons on 29 April 1460.

   A number of documents from the following months point to the priors' attempts to keep the group at full strength. At the beginning of June 1460 they decreed that two recent appointees, Stefano Rusignuoli da Savoia and Bartolomeo da Castello, presently living in Milan, would each receive L. 10, tax free, per month as well as the same privileges and conditions enjoyed by the long-time piffero Ferrino (see Doc. 11.11). (Stefano Rusignuoli, also called Stefano di Piero, had served in Siena from 1455 to 1459.) The two musicians refused the offer, however, and on the 27th of the same month the priors nominated Antonio di Gregorio and Niccolò di Giorgio, both from Venice, in their stead (see Doc. 11.12). The priors also granted them working conditions and privileges similar to Ferrino's. But the monthly salary of L. 19 now offered was almost double the amount mentioned earlier in the month. The alacrity with which

---

68. See note 54 for the baptism of Niccolò, son of "Federigho di Lanberto di Francia, pifaro de' Magnifici Signori," on 27 January 1461.

69. Polk, *German Instrumental Music*, 80.

70. "Et detis et solvatis tubicenis, naccarino et piffaris nostri palatii salarium eis debitum . . . Et detis et solvatis Arrigo Iohannis, trombono palatii, salarium ei debitum" (Concistoro, vol. 560, fol. 65ʳ, dated 16 February 1460).

the priors decided to raise wages suggests that they were willing to pay whatever price was necessary to bring some stability to the group. A further sign of their desire to attract and retain good musicians comes from the following day, when they decreed that the men, "who were appointed yesterday for a period of three months," would be able to stay in the Palace at the commune's expense and that they were to have "a room with a bed and other necessary things so that they might be as comfortable as the other servants who habitually sleep in the Palace." The record also indicates that normally the wind band did not live at the Palace, a point reconsidered below.

The clothing list for Assumption day 1460 cites the pifferi Ferrino, Martino Teutonico, and Antonio di Gregorio and the trombonist Niccolò di Giorgio. This last received permission to go to Venice for a month a few days after the festivities. He apparently postponed returning to Siena, however, because he is not mentioned again for some time to come. Later that same year Antonio di Gregorio or Giringoro, as many documents of the time give his father's name, was also given leave to spend a month in Venice. Antonio was to become one of the mainstays of the group, and he and Ferrino are, in fact, the only pifferi listed without interruption throughout the 1460s. They appear, together with the newly returned Stefano di Piero, in the clothing list for Assumption Day 1461. The trombonist's name is conspicuously absent from the list, as is that of the piffero tenorista, Martino di Corrado da Alamania, whose death is reported on the following 21 February.[71]

No lists are available for 1462. But Stefano di Piero must have left during that time, probably to enter Ferrarese service, where he remained until as late as 1481.[72] Before leaving Siena Stefano entrusted the trumpeter Tommaso da Cetona,[73] who doubled as the Palace concierge, with one of his books, presumably a music book, for safekeeping. Subsequently, it developed that the book really belonged to Ferrino, and when the matter was brought before the priors, they ordered Tommaso to restore the book to its rightful owner, assuring him he would suffer no consequences for his part in the misdeed.[74] It is tempting to think, if the book in question was a music book, that it contained pieces that the Sienese group performed. Certainly, there is every reason to believe that books containing repertory suitable for the pifferi were as available in Siena as they were elsewhere. At least two such manuscripts, to be mentioned in detail presently, are recorded in the library of the duke of Ferrara, with whose musicians the Sienese had close connections through Stefano di Piero. Since Stefano di Piero played in both groups, one might suppose that the extant Ferrarese repertory contains music

---

71. This information comes from a decision of the Concistoro authorizing payment of L. 13 for candles for his burial. Martino had been reappointed to a six-month term on 30 October 1461. An earlier record of reappointment says that he was to earn L. 19 a month.

72. Lockwood, *Music in Renaissance Ferrara,* 180; p. 322 for the 1481 date.

73. Tomè (Tommaso) da Cetona is identified as "sagrestano di Palazo" in a payment in Biccherna, vol. 333, fol. 320ᵛ, dated 1476.

74. "Deliberaverunt Magnifici Domini quod per Thomeum de Scitonio restituatur Ferrino piffaro quidam liber consignatus ipsi Thomeo sub pretextu bonorum Stephani piffari quem dictus Ferrinus allegat esse suum. Et hoc sine aliquo preiudicio aut danno dicti Thomei. Accepto primo iuramento a dicto piffaro quod ad se pertineat liber predictus" (Concistoro, vol. 576, fol. 16ᵛ, dated 30 September 1462).

similar to what the Sienese musicians were performing. The possibility is strengthened by knowledge of a more direct encounter of the Sienese pifferi with their Ferrarese counterparts in 1473, when the duke visited the city.

The matter of Stefano's possessions did not end with the book. A document from 28 February 1463 mentions a letter from the lord of Ferrara requesting the release of other goods being held for Stefano by Tommaso da Cetona; the Concistoro quickly complied.[75] In 1463 two other musicians, Maestro Giovanni da Alamania, a piffero appointed three years earlier, and Andrea trombone, appear on the Assumption Day clothing list together with Ferrino and Antonio da Venezia. This Maestro Giovanni is evidently not the same musician as the "new trumpeter" Giovanni di Giovanni da Alamania, mentioned in a decree from February 1463, granting him sleeping quarters at the Palace through all of March.[76] The "new" Giovanni di Giovanni da Alamania, as other records show, was a trombonist. On 2 June 1463 an apparently retroactive appointment recognized his service and declared that he was to have a monthly salary of L. 10, tax free, effective on the day he began serving. This, as a report from a few days later shows, was the previous May 1st, at the start of the priors' bimestrial term of office, the nearest time they could be certain he began playing. But Giovanni quickly proved unsuitable for the post and in the following July the Concistoro rehired Niccolò di Giorgio at a monthly salary of 4 gold ducats or L. 21. 4.[77] Niccolò, however, proved as elusive as ever, and as the just-mentioned Assumption Day list for 1463 shows, another trombonist named Andrea received a clothing allowance on that occasion, while Maestro Giovanni de Alamania remained with the pifferi.

The Economic Status of the Pifferi

Although salaries paid to a few individuals were at an all-time high, the consensus among the group was that wages were still too low. A letter from the pifferi to the Concistoro in 1463 addresses the point directly (Doc. 11.13), despite its obsequious tone, and reveals that the musicians had thought of a way to address the problem:

> To our Magnificent and most powerful lords, a humble supplication on behalf
> of your faithful servants, the pifferi and trombone, who having considered their
> great poverty and misery, and the necessity of providing for their poor families,
> and having seen that they have no earnings nor provision other than the one
> they receive from this magnificent Palace, and aware that they have left their
> own countries and all paternal affection so that they might serve your hallowed
> Palace, in the service of which they wish always to live and die, beg that it
> please your most clement lordships to remove the tax [on their salaries], and

---

75. "Magnifici domini . . . audito Stefano piffaro petente sibi restitui certa bona depositata per Consistorium penes Thommas palatii Magnificorum dominorum; ac etiam visis et auditis licteris Illustris Marchionis Ferrarie recomendantis dicti Stefani, deliberaverunt quod dictus [Thommas] de Scitonio, sine suo preiudicio aut damno, restituere debeat dicto Stefano omnia sua bona penes eum depositata" (Concistoro, vol. 578, fol. 39ᵛ, dated 23 February 1462/63). In this and other documents of the time Ferrara's ruler is referred to as a marquis and not a duke.

76. The designation "tubicen" was a slip of the pen.

77. Earlier, this musician was said to be from Venice.

[specifically] the portion that has been imposed for the tower that is to be built,
[just] as your lordships have deigned to exempt your ushers.[78]

This tax was levied on all commune employees in order to raise funds for constructing
a tower planned to complement the existing Torre del Mangia. The tax had been
waived for some of the previously employed pifferi as well as for some of the trumpeters.
Several recently appointed musicians, however, had not been exempted, nor had apparently the long-time employee Ferrino da Francia. Obviously, the tax weighed more
heavily on the lower-paid members of the group, hence the pifferi's request for equal
treatment. Quite apart from taxes, the reference to the musicians' families in the letter
shows that the pifferi normally lived outside the Palace. Temporary lodging at the Palace
for new appointees was made available as needed, but the government's policy was to
encourage, or even require, foreigners to settle in the city with their families. The lack
of subsidized housing for state employees notwithstanding, municipal tax records reveal
that several of the musicians who came to Siena in the later fifteenth century eventually
acquired houses of their own.[79] This indicates sufficient earnings both to maintain a
decent standard of living and to save for the future. Salaries, of course, accounted for
the major part of the pifferi's official earnings, but other privileges such as clothing and
meal allowances at the Palace represented a considerable savings. Exactly where the
pifferi, or other musicians for that matter, stood on the economic scale in Siena is very
difficult to determine, however, because little information is available regarding the cost
of living in Siena at this time and the buying power of Sienese money.

The pifferi made no mention in their letter of the extra monies they received for
playing at special events and during the two weeks before Assumption Day.[80] Their
earnings were also augmented by tips from visiting dignitaries, by tips from the priors'
own purse, and by income from the cathedral for performing there on certain feast
days. Perhaps the pifferi were actually saying that they had not accepted—or were not
allowed to accept—private engagements outside the Palace. Although later documents
indicate that this ancient restriction against Palace musicians taking outside employment
was often ignored and eventually abolished, apparently it was enforced at this time. The
musicians' financial situation, at any rate, was probably not as dire as they claimed.
Their remarks must have struck the right chord because eventually salaries of those who
wrote the letter increased and musicians subsequently appointed were exempted from
the tax.

Frequent changes in personnel among the pifferi in these years illustrate the difficulties encountered by patrons, even those as well placed and financially solvent as the
Sienese government, wishing to employ qualified pifferi for any length of time. They
were, to judge from the evidence, in as much demand as singers of polyphony, many

---

78. Also in Cellesi, *Storia della più antica banda musicale senese,* 28, n. 2.
79. See below for tax reports filed by individual pifferi.
80. In addition to records already cited in connection with the trumpeters, there are records of
payments for playing at other events such as the Palio held on St. Mary Magdalene's Day in 1489:
"Item, a li trombetti et piffari, in tutto, per ogni loro fadigha, lire undici s. sei, da diversi intra loro,
L. XI s. VI" (Biccherna, vol. 2, fols. 336ᵛ–337ʳ, dated 24 July 1489).

of whom were also northerners. Trombonists were no less sought after. Events of these last few years show the very best among them came and went as they pleased, like the singers and many of the pifferi. Although native musicians were quickly joining the ranks of these exalted players, available northerners were still given preference.

The large salaries commanded by experienced pifferi and trombonists are perhaps the ultimate measure of the value contemporary institutions placed on their worth. From their very beginnings in Siena the members of the wind band were given higher stipends than the trumpeters, who indeed suffered salary cuts so that there would be sufficient funds to pay the newcomers. The disparity in salaries remained constant throughout the rest of the century; pifferi and trombonists were consistently paid between one and three florins more per month than trumpeters. Significantly, when musicians moved from one group to the other, their salaries were adjusted accordingly. Santi di Pavolo, whose career will be discussed below, was one such musician. When he entered Palace service as a trumpeter in August 1455, his initial monthly salary was Fl. 2.[81] He also had two suits of clothing a year. But this was considerably lower than both the L. 16 per month offered to the trombonist Arrigo di Giovanni in that same year and to the L. 14 per month that Santi himself was earning a few years later, when he was appointed to the wind band as a trombonist. By the time he left Siena, he was earning L. 19 per month, in addition to daily meals at the Palace and a new suit of clothing annually.

Generally, the pifferi and the trombonist were in a financial stratum even higher than that of the cathedral's singers. In the 1450s the singers' monthly salaries ran between L. 4 and L. 8, though many had additional income as chaplains and also received living quarters at the Opera's expense and meals in the refectory. Occasionally, singers such as Giovanni da Polonia earned more, as did the three singer-chaplains appointed at L. 16. 3. 4 in 1456. By the mid-1460s the highest-paid singer—the venerable Ser Goro—was earning L. 20 per month, while itinerant northerners normally received L. 8, though some were paid L. 12 and even L. 15 per month. Nevertheless, during these years, singers on average earned less in terms of actual salary than wind players and trombonists, a situation that was to prevail throughout the following decades, and it was only in the next century that the salaries of both groups were in general more commensurate.

As with singers, salary differences often occurred within the ranks of instrumentalists. In 1463, when the pifferi wrote requesting exemption from the building tax, the Concistoro paid some musicians an initial monthly salary of L. 10, at the same time offering others L. 19 and L. 21. Such disparities obviously reflected the individual performer's experience and talent, as well as his reputation—this latter of no mean importance, considering that sometimes a musician was hired only on the strength of a recommendation from someone known to the Concistoro. Hiring musicians without benefit of an audition undoubtedly accounts for the policy of giving many of them a

81. The florin was valued here at s. 82, which was L. 4. 2, putting his initial monthly salary as a trumpeter at L. 8. 4 tax free. This document, too, points to the differences in salaries of the trumpeters and the pifferi.

trial period before a formal appointment and, occasionally, salary increases. Siena, in this respect, must have been no different than any other city.

Our imprecise knowledge of the buying power of money and comparative costs of living, not to mention the value of fringe benefits such as meals, lodging, and tips, makes it difficult to know just how competitive Sienese salaries were with those paid to pifferi in other cities.[82] The Florentine pifferi and trombonist each received monthly salaries of L. 18 or four and a half Florentine florins in 1444.[83] In 1463 the three Florentine pifferi each had L. 22. 10 per month, whereas the trombonist was paid L. 30. 10.[84] The pifferi still earned the same salary in 1474, though by then the trombonist, a new one, was receiving L. 24 per month.[85] In 1456 there was a wide range in the monthly salaries of Ferrarese pifferi, one of whom earned LM 30 as opposed to the LM 8 of the other and the LM 10 of the trombone.[86] Similar disparities appear in 1476 when the two Ferrarese pifferi earned LM 26 and LM 15, respectively, and the two trombones LM 18 and LM 12.[87] Sienese salary ranges must have compared favorably with these as well as with those of the Florentines, otherwise Siena would hardly have been able to attract so many musicians in what was clearly a national, if not an international, market.

The value and effectiveness of other kinds of formal compensation are equally difficult to assess. Certainly, the Concistoro could not, as could a prince or an absolute ruler, reward favored musicians with gifts of houses or lands or even with posts with guaranteed incomes that then might be farmed out to surrogates. The Concistoro, moreover, apparently never subsidized housing for its instrumentalists, as did the Florentine Signoria.[88] On rare occasions, Sienese musicians held other posts in the Palace

---

82. Fringe benefits and tips are particularly difficult to assess. Lockwood, *Music in Renaissance Ferrara*, 69, speaks of gifts to the Ferrarese players for playing at special events in 1446 under Leonello d'Este, but he also notes that special payments and gifts were not as lavishly bestowed by Borso d'Este as his biographer would have us believe (p. 178).

83. Zippel, *I suonatori della Signoria di Firenze*, 28. Earlier in 1443 another group of pifferi were earning Fl. 2 a month.

84. ASF, Camera del Comune, Notaio di Camera, *E&U*, vol. 13, fol. 101^r, dated 3 September 1463, with payments to each for two months.

85. Ibid., vol. 33, fol. 76^v, dated 27 April 1474, with payments to each for two months.

86. Lockwood, *Music in Renaissance Ferrara*, 178. The monetary unit referred to is the lira marchegiana.

87. Ibid., 180. Annual salaries for the years 1488–91 are given by Lockwood on p. 183; they range from the LM 120 of the lowest-paid piffero, to the LM 201. 12. 0 for two others and to the LM 240. for the fourth; the two trombonists' salaries also fluctuated from LM 210.12.0 to LM 288 (L. 10 to L. 24 per month).

88. The practice is recorded in Florence, for example, in October of 1487, when the Signoria granted, in addition to usual salaries, an annual allowance of Fl. 12 each to two of its prized performers, Maestro Giovanni trombone and Maestro Iacopo piffero. Both were foreigners and the Signoria hoped by its action to ensure that the musicians would remain in Florentine service. The text of the decision notes that this sort of thing had been done before: "Inteso e Magnifici et excelsi signori . . . come maestro Giovanni della Magna, al presente trombone della Signoria, l'anno passato chiese licentia alla Signoria per acconciarsi in altro luogho, et la Signoria inteso della sua virtù, che vale assai nel suo exercitio, et del continuo miglior musico diventa, ricerchò per vari mezi della cagione, et trovò

and thus had a second salary, though this was more the exception than the rule. Sienese musicians, however, did fare well enough to own their own homes and to leave estates of some value to their children, as will be noted on a number of occasions below.

Competition for Star Players

Difficulties finding a trombonist during the summer of 1463 were finally surmounted when Santi di Pavolo da Volterra, a former Palace trumpeter, was appointed to the post beginning in September. His new monthly salary of L. 14, as mentioned, was considerably higher than his trumpeter's salary of L. 8. 4. Santi's playing obviously met with official approval, for six months later, on 1 March 1464, his salary was raised to L. 19 per month, the whole being declared tax free. Santi was not the first former trumpeter to gain admission to the shawm band as a trombonist; his appointment thus offers additional evidence that some, if not all, of the trumpeters could play polyphony, a point that bears repeating. Santi appears with Ferrino, Antonio da Venezia, and Giovanni da Alamania on the Assumption Day clothing lists for 1464 and 1465.

Giovanni da Alamania was eventually succeeded by another Giovanni, Giovanni di Fruosino Mangoni da Siena, the first local musician ever recorded among the pifferi. Payments to him, at the rate of L. 8 per month, show that he began serving at the Palace in September 1465. A decree of 23 July 1466, noting his increased proficiency and his agreeable disposition, declared that beginning in August his initial monthly salary would be raised to L. 10, tax free. At the same time the priors approved a suit of clothing for him on the next Assumption Day. He is, in fact, named with Ferrino, Antonio, and Santi on the 1466 list. Giovanni received several salary increases in the following years, most notably to L. 15 on 26 January 1468, to L. 17 on 18 April 1469, and to L. 19 per month, tax free, on 14 May 1470, when he was named as a tenorista. That his wages more than doubled in four years offers additional proof that higher salaries were directly proportional to the musicians' experience and knowledge of the repertory as well as to their individual talents. Like Antonio da Venezia, Giovanni became one of the mainstays of the group in the following decades. He was also the

---

che procedeva perché poteva con difficultà vivere col suo salario, et che altri in simile exercitio più salario havevono havuto, et anchora era suto loro pagato la pigione d'una casa . . . che da hora, per virtù della presente, s'intenda data auctorità a' presenti signori di dichiarare quanto a decto maestro Giovanni trombone et maestro Iacopo piffero et a ciascuno di loro dare si debba per pigione d'una casa ciascuno anno durante la loro vita, habitando nella città et servendo la Signoria mentre fare lo potessino" (ASF, *Provvisioni, Registri,* vol. 178, fol. 119^{r-v}, dated 19 October 1487).

Later records again show provision being made for housing certain pifferi. A payment from 23 April 1498 reads as follows: "Dictis pifferis pro eorum pensione domus et pro sex mensibus initorum die primo octobris preteriti ad rationem L. 15 per quolibet eorum . . . L. 45" (ASF, Camera del Comune, Notaio di Camera, *Uscita generale,* vol. 20, fol. 321^v). The practice was still in force in the early decades of the sixteenth century, as revealed by an entry dated 28 November 1518: "A tutti quattro pifferi L. 60 piccioli per loro provisione d'una casa per uno di loro per sei mesi cominciata a dì primo d'aprile, L. 48" (ASF, Camera del Comune, Notaio di Camera, *E&U,* vol. 124, fol. 57^r). A pay list from April 1484 shows that at that time the trombonist was earning L. 28. 10 per month and that each of the three pifferi was paid L. 22. 10 per month (ibid., vol. 53, fol. 64^r).

progenitor of a musical family that was associated with the Palace through the end of the following century.

More and more records brought to light in recent years show that virtuoso instrumentalists were no less prized than star singers by the music-loving princes of Renaissance Italy. From Florence several reports attest to attempts, sometimes successful, sometimes not, by Lorenzo the Magnificent to lure renowned players to the city.[89] Although no evidence suggests that Lorenzo personally intervened in recruiting musicians from Siena, a letter to him from one of his friends from 29 June 1469 affords a glimpse of some behind-the-scenes activities that often characterized recruitment efforts. It also affirms the talents of Antonio di Gregorio da Venezia, whom the Sienese had hired in June 1460 at the high salary of L. 19 per month, tax free (see Doc. 11.14):

> Respected and most honored lord!
> Because I know that you truly delight in men of talent, I am sending Maestro Antonio, piffero player of the Signoria of Siena, to you. As far as my thinking and taste are concerned, I have never seen the equal of his talent. It really seems to me that he would stay willingly with us here in the Palazzo [Vecchio], should there be need of him, because he could [perform] contra or tenor or soprano or with the trombone, as might be required. This seems to me something not to be lost and I would be happy if you would hear him because I am certain that you will be immensely pleased. He has come here to honor you during the celebration of the joust for as long as you require him.
> Nothing else to report. May God watch over you always.
> Written at Florence on the 29th of January 1469.
> Your Mario de' Nobili

No surviving records show whether Lorenzo actually gave Antonio a private audience or that if he did, whether he was sufficiently enough impressed to want to hire him. Whatever transpired in Florence, Antonio remained in Sienese service for the rest of his life and was eventually succeeded in his post by his son, who went on to become one of sixteenth-century Siena's most respected musicians. Still, knowledge that Antonio was so highly regarded by a musically informed person in Lorenzo's circle offers precious information about the talents of at least one individual in the Sienese band and of the caliber of the group in general. Noteworthy, too, is the writer's remark about Antonio's versatility, that he could play any one of the shawm parts in the ensemble and that he would work well in a duo with the trombone. The letter also testifies to how easily musicians moved between the two cities, especially during times of festivities and other events such as the famous tournament put on by Lorenzo and his brother Giuliano, subsequently the subject of Luigi Pulci's celebrated poem.

Though Santi di Pavolo de Volterra had made a successful return to Palace service with a coveted position in the wind band, he proved to be no easier to retain than the foreigners. This time, competition for a Sienese musician's services came from Florence rather than Ferrara, and as before, it was successful. Circumstances of Santi's initial employment in Florence are only imperfectly known. He may have worked there, or

---

89. On Lorenzo's recruiting efforts, see D'Accone, "Lorenzo il Magnifico e la musica."

elsewhere in Tuscany for that matter, as a freelance musician for several years before being granted an official appointment, for he is listed as one of the trumpeters in the Florentine corps who received Fl. 8 for two months' service in September 1463.[90] He subsequently went back to Siena, as mentioned, and it is not until 1470 that his name begins to appear regularly in Florentine records.[91] Santi was initially hired as a trumpeter in Florence. He is described as one in a report from December 1470, which notes that because the Palazzo Vecchio lacked a trombonist, the Florentine Signoria decided that he should serve in both capacities for an additional Fl. 2 each month until such time as a suitable replacement was found.[92] This he did, and after a foreign trombonist was hired, he resumed his official post among the trumpeters. Santi's career is noteworthy because he left his trombonist's post in Siena's elite wind band to serve as a trumpeter in Florence and was perfectly willing to serve in that capacity for the remainder of his life. Perhaps the salary was better and living conditions in Florence were more congenial for a musician of his talents. In Florence he probably had opportunity to play polyphony in both groups, though this is apparent only because of his ability to move between them so easily, as he had at Siena. By 1484, with a monthly salary of L. 20, Santi was among the higher paid trumpeters in the Florentine corps. He was still receiving the same salary in 1498.[93]

At Siena, the trombonist's position, vacant again by the end of 1467, was offered to a Frenchman from Valence, Petro Tristano da Valenza. The terms of his contract, registered on 29 February 1468, granted him a monthly salary of L. 8, although this was later raised to L. 12. He appears together with Ferrino, Antonio, and Giovanni on Assumption Day clothing list for 1468. A year later, on the first anniversary of his appointment, the Concistoro decreed that Petro would henceforth receive L. 16 per month, tax free, on condition that he acquire and wear a uniform like the other Palace pifferi. This he apparently refused to do, for within a few months Bartolomeo di Monaldo, who had served with the Palace trumpeters for the last year, succeeded to his

---

90. ASF, Camera del Comune, Notaio di Camera, *E&U*, vol. 13, fol. 101ʳ, dated 3 September 1463.

91. In a record dated 27 April 1475, he was not cited among the trumpeters (tubicinis) who were each earning Fl. 3 per month, but rather among those (trombatoribus) who were each earning L. 5 per month (ibid., vol. 33, fol. 76ᵛ).

92. "Atteso e Magnifici et excelsi Signori . . . che al servigio della Signoria non è trombone, come è consueto essere, et che egli ànno fatto sonare il trombone a Santi di Pagolo da Volterra, trombetto della Signoria, et per tal faticha a llui aggiunta sono consueti stantiargli ogni due mesi XX lire di certi extraordinarii della camera dell'arme . . . et volendo provedere che tantto che e' s'abbia uno buono rombone, lui faccia l'exercitio del trombetto et del trombone et habbia oltre al suo salario, per tale aggiunta di faticha, fiorini due il mese . . . deliberaverunt che a detto Santi di Pagolo da Volterra s'intenda, per vigore della presente provisione, condotto, oltre al suo exercitio del trombetto, in trombone della Signoria per tempo da durare tanto che uno altro si truovi et elegga nel tale exercitio del trombone" (ASF, *Provisioni, Registri*, vol. 161, fol. 109ʳ⁻ᵛ, dated 10 December 1470).

93. ASF, Camera del Comune, Notaio di Camera, *E&U*, vol. 53, fol. 60ʳ, payments dated 24 April 1484; vol. 75, fol. 60ᵛ, payments dated 5 April 1494; Notaio di Camera, *Uscita generale*, vol. 20, fol. 321ᵛ, dated 23 April 1498; vol. 21, fol. 24ᵛ, gives the last payment to him, for 18 October–18 December 1498.

post. According to Bartolomeo's contract, dated 16 April 1469, he received an initial monthly salary of L. 12. This was raised to L. 14 in July of the same year and to L. 19 tax free in May 1470. Giovanni di Fruosino, described as a tenorista in the same decree, was also raised to L. 19 at this time, so that both he and Bartolomeo now received the same salary as the others. These successive increments complement those received by others in the band and reinforce the perception that experience and accomplishment were prime factors in determining compensation for musicians.

PIFFERI IN THE LAST DECADES OF THE FIFTEENTH CENTURY

The trombonist Bartolomeo and three pifferi, Ferrino da Francia, Antonio di Gregorio, and Giovanni di Fruosino, appear in records through August of 1471, after which Ferrino's name disappears.[94] His tenure among the pifferi, a few months short of twenty-five years, was remarkably long, equaled up to then only by that of Niccolò di Giorgio. Ferrino's replacement was Maestro Cristoforo di Brandino Lombardo, mentioned with the pifferi for the first time on 1 August 1472. With his appointment the wind band finally gained a long overdue measure of stability, and the same four musicians, Antonio di Gregorio da Venezia, Giovanni di Fruosino da Siena, Maestro Cristoforo di Brandino Lombardo, and Bartolomeo di Monaldo remained together for the next fifteen years, through the end of 1486.

Apart from several trips the wind band made outside the city, the only notable occurrences in the group's activities in those years were the temporary replacement of Bartolomeo by his brother Giovanni di Monaldo for a time in 1477 and Bartolomeo's additional appointment as a town crier on 23 November 1483.[95] Following Bartolomeo as trombonist was another former trumpeter, Geronimo di Giovanni. Geronimo, himself the son of the trumpeter Giovanni da Iesi, had been in Palace service since 1480.[96] He is cited as trombonist for the first time, together with Antonio da Venetia, Cristoforo Lombardo, Giovanni di Fruosino, and a fourth piffero, Jacopo di Salvatore, in the clothing list for Assumption Day 1487.[97] The same musicians served, except for a few brief absences, through Assumption Day 1492.

---

94. Bartolomeo was also mentioned in a deliberation of 6 March 1470, when he was was given permission to go to Rome with Francesco Luti for twelve days with salary, but with the proviso that if he overstayed his leave, he would lose his stipend for the whole time.

95. Bartolomeo was appointed to the town crier's post only after the priors were told that the trumpeter Giovanni di Martino, the current incumbent, was unable to leave his house and unlikely to recover from what appeared to be a mortal illness. Accordingly, they decreed that Bartolomeo could have the post but that s. 40 of the stipend attached to it would go to Giovanni until his death (see Doc. 11.15). Bartolomeo is mentioned in two notarial acts from 1482, which show that his future wife, Elisabetta di Francesco di Sano da Siena, brought Fl. 225 as a dowry and that she gave a quarter of this to him on the day the marriage contract was signed. The transaction took place in his home in Val de Rosa (ASS, Notarile antecosimiano, vol. 388, fols. 41ᵛ–42ʳ, dated 25 January 1481/82). The house, probably bought by his father, Monaldo, was still in the family in 1509, when Bernardino di Monaldo filed a tax report (see chapter 10).

96. For Geronimo as a trumpeter, see chapter 9.

97. Geronimo, also called Girolamo in some records, is reported to have had the commune's trumpet on loan for the period 14 April 1488 to 1 September 1489 (see note 144). A deliberation

Economic Status

Though a few of these musicians initially began at salaries as low as L. 8 per month, by this time all of them were earning monthly salaries of L. 19, tax free. In addition, they were receiving suits of clothing valued at L. 31. 10 once a year as well as a certain number of guaranteed gratuities for playing annually at certain state-sponsored events, as has been mentioned in connection with the trumpeters and as will be explained more fully below. There were also the tips and gratuities from visitors who came their way on any number of occasions, as well as what they were paid for playing at private functions. Their meals, at Palace expense, constituted another form of indirect payment, like their uniforms, and some of the instruments they played were likewise supplied by the priors. All in all the Palace pifferi and trombonist were very well treated, and it is small wonder that during these years there are no reports of their requesting raises in salary or other perquisites.

Another indication of the favorable economic status of the Palace pifferi comes from tax reports filed by them and, later, by their children. Most if not all were able to buy houses of their own and even vineyards, which may have produced enough both for their own needs and for bartering for other goods and services or for extra cash. The Venetian expatriate Maestro Antonio, the oldest of the group, settled in Siena in 1460. By 1481 he was able to report to the tax collectors that he had a little house where he lived in the company of San Salvadore in Terzo di Città and that he also had a small vineyard.[98] In 1488, when he described himself as "old and ailing" with three small children, a girl and two boys, he specified that the house was valued at Fl. 100 and the vineyard at Fl. 90. The same house and another vineyard, valued at Fl. 160, are mentioned in 1491, when Antonio was still living. In 1509, after his death, the house was listed as belonging to his son Giovanni, a notable Sienese musician, who said at that time that he was responsible for furnishing his sister with a dowry of Fl. 70.

Another foreign piffero, Maestro Cristoforo di Brandino from Lombardy, who came to Siena in 1472, also achieved a certain measure of prosperity. In a statement for tax officials prepared in 1488 he declared that he had a vineyard outside the city walls in a place called "la volta a Fighille" in San Giorgio Papaiano and that he and his wife, who was pregnant, were the parents of four boys, the eldest of whom was not yet twelve. The property was valued at Fl. 100 in his tax report from 1491, when he said that he had three "small" boys. The property, now valued at Fl. 200, was still in the family in 1509, when a tax report was filed by his sons Niccolò and Antonio, both of whom, as will be mentioned below, were also pifferi. Jacopo di Salvatore, who joined the pifferi in 1487, was no less assiduous in gaining a measure of prosperity for himself and his family. By 1491 he had acquired, at a cost of Fl. 200, a house where he was then living. He had made a down payment of Fl. 50 on the property and was paying off the remainder as rent. In 1509 Jacomo's widow, Monna Frasia, filed a tax report for herself and her three children, the eldest of whom was fifteen. She claimed that the

---

from 2 May 1488 granted a leave of absence of twenty days to Geronimo di Giovanni trombone and the Palace sacristan Petruccio so that they might go to the shrine at Santa Maria di Loreto.

98. ASS, Lira, vol. 189, Terzo di Città, fol. 60^r, where he is listed as "maestro Antonio di Ghiringoro pifaro e servidore del vostro palazo."

house was old and worth about Fl. 160, but she also had another small property outside the city in the commune of Frontignano.

Mona Frasia's declaration is interesting in another regard. Tax reports make it clear that most of the pifferi lived in the company of San Salvadore in the Terzo di Città,[99] but hers shows that at least two of them, Jacopo di Salvatore and Maestro Antonio di Gregorio, were next-door neighbors on a street that fronted the Via del Comune behind the Mercato Vecchio. Some of the trumpeters also lived in the same company, though there is no evidence to suggest that the Sienese government obliged its musicians to live in any one area, as did the Florentine.[100] Other trumpeters, to be sure, lived in the Terzo di Città, but in different parishes, which was true also of the trombonist Girolamo (Geronimo) di Giovanni when he filed his tax report in 1491. At the time he listed a house he had bought that year, at a cost of 100 florins, in the company of Sant'Antonio. Living with him were his mother, his wife, and two children. Though he still owed Fl. 70 on the property and had other debts totaling Fl. 35, he also had a small vineyard in Terrenzano.

Such holdings of real property, of course, do not point to the pifferi's having amassed great wealth, but they do indicate that these musicians enjoyed a comfortable standard of living and that they were able to provide for their progeny. Just how well they were doing is immediately apparent from a comparison of their salaries with those of other officially employed musicians in Siena. At Fl. 2, or L. 8. 4, per month a trumpeter's salary was less than half that of a woodwind player. Even some of the much sought after northern chapel singers with monthly salaries ranging from L. 10 to L. 15 were not as handsomely provided for, though many of them also enjoyed additional perquisites such as room and board. Only one musician in the 1480s, the chapel singer Piero de la Piazza at L. 24. 10 per month, is recorded as having earned more than the members of the wind band, but he was the most highly paid Sienese singer of the fifteenth century and his was clearly an exceptional case. In other words, Siena's pifferi, like their counterparts in other places in Italy, were the highest paid musicians in town and would remain so for several decades to come.

The "Old-Fashioned Way" and Recommendations for Reform

Evidently, stability and economic well-being brought a certain amount of stagnation and slackening of musical standards. Early in August of 1492, increasing dissatisfaction with the group's performances finally came to a head and reached the ears of the Balìa, the behind-the-scenes committee whose decisions set much of government policy. In one of their few decisions regarding music at the Palace, the Balìa responded by ap-

---

99. The exception was Giovanni di Fruosino, mentioned in a 1491 list of citizens residing in the company of Santo Stefano in Terzo Camollia. ASS, Lira, vol. 97, *Compagnie della città di Siena, 1491,* fol. 132ʳ.

100. Regarding the Florentine decree, see chapter 9, where mention is made of the Sienese trumpeters who filed tax reports from San Salvadore in 1509. A later piffero, Gano d'Enea, son of a Palace trumpeter, whose father, Senzanome di Brescia, reported that he had nothing to declare in 1489, also had property in the parish of San Salvadore. A tax report filed by his daughter in 1548 shows that Gano left her very well off (see Doc. 9.9).

pointing a five-man commission to recommend how best to improve matters. In its subsequent report from the 9th of that month the commission was unsparing and showed not the slightest hesitation in naming names and saying what it thought was wrong. It also recommended that a number of immediate steps be taken, as is evident in this transcript of its findings:

> First: your lordships have already ordered that Maestro Antonio piffero should not perform any longer but should [continue to] have his salary. He does not wish to obey, [however,] and since he does not know how to play except in the old-fashioned way nothing good can be done. With the present we recommend that he be made to stop playing, as you see fit, but that he retain his provision.
>
> Item: since you have only two pifferi who are really qualified, that is, the trombone [Girolamo] and Jacopo, and [since] Cristoforo piffero's son Domenico, who equals them in knowledge, is available, the three of them can play together. We are certain they will bring you as much honor as any others in Italy because they'll be able to learn to perform things that your other pifferi can neither play nor are capable of learning. For this reason we believe these three should not be stopped when they wish to perform some of [this other music]. Thus we wish, with your lordships' permission, to be able to tell so and so not to play sometimes, especially when they want to perform things they do not know how to play.
>
> And finally, [we ask] that no one perform without our permission, and should he do so, that we be empowered to fine him as we see fit, except for the three just named.
>
> Item: [we recommend] that the above-mentioned Domenico receive a regular salary from your lordships' palace, any other matters notwithstanding.[101]

Two closely related issues were undoubtedly at the root of the dissatisfaction with the group's performances. One was the generational gap among the musicians; the other, closely interconnected, was the question of repertory and related issues of performance practice.

The older generation was represented by Antonio di Gregorio, whose intransigence the commission singled out. Now nearing sixty, he was already an experienced musician when he entered Palace service in 1460. Though he had recently been granted his full salary as a pension and exempted from playing, he persisted in doing so, probably because he wanted to safeguard his post for his son, who was either not yet old enough or not expert enough to succeed him.[102] Somewhat younger than Antonio were Giovanni di Fruosino, whose appointment in 1465 may very well have been his first professional one, and Cristoforo Lombardo, another experienced musician who joined the group in 1472. Although neither was mentioned, one or both of them were also held responsible for the band's inability to keep up with the times, and for this reason the

---

101. See Doc. 11.16. It has also been published by Cellesi, *La più antica banda senese,* 74.
102. Antonio's is thus far the only known case of a Palace musician receiving full salary as pension.

commission wished, with governmental approval, to prevent them from playing certain kinds of music.

Records already cited leave no doubt that the pifferi of this generation performed polyphony. But the commission's report suggests that they became accustomed to working with a long since learned traditional repertory and relied upon outmoded improvisational skills. They were, in other words, musicians of the "old school," whose repertory was limited by their earlier training and experience. They were either unable or unwilling to learn newer works and to master the concomitantly different demands or techniques these probably required in ensemble playing. Perhaps part of the problem was due to the notation of the newer works. While the older players in the Sienese band surely could read some kind of musical notation, we cannot be certain of their ability to read music written in the system of white mensural notation. This system, an outgrowth of centuries-old practices normally taught to singers and composers in cathedral schools, was now beginning to be adopted by instrumentalists, more and more of whom found their way to cathedral schools.

Up to this time woodwind players, like trumpeters, received their training in the traditional master–apprentice system. In Siena, as there has been occasion to note in conjunction with the trumpeters, this was often through a network of family members or friends.[103] When they learned the pieces that formed their repertory, they relied on their ears and on their memories and, as they enlarged and diversified that repertory, on their ability to improvise counterpoint. The freedom of invention inherent in improvising counterpoint must have greatly delighted audiences as well as performers and while it was never banished from instrumental performance, with the increasing inroads made by written polyphony, it took on a different role, assuming more and more the functions of an art of ornamentation and variation.

After the mid-fifteenth century, Sienese wind players, like players elsewhere, must also have begun to learn to read the music of the individual parts of composed polyphonic pieces. This was an inevitable development. An ability to read polyphony made all of the great vocal music of the time available to instrumentalists, not coincidentally enabling them to adapt it to their own purposes. It also helped spawn the growth of an independent instrumental literature that would soon incorporate the compositional techniques of high-art polyphony. Although the kind of musical notation the Sienese apprentices read remains unknown, possibly the older players in the wind band used one of the many alternate forms adopted by performing musicians not "classically" trained in cathedral schools. Like the one used by the Venetian trumpeter Zorzi (see chapter 9), these alternate forms, though rudimentary by singers' standards, were per-

---

103. See Doc. 12.8 for a later example in 1522, where Maestro Antonio's son and successor, Giovanni, wrote on behalf of his pupil Galgano di Enea. The report indicates that Giovanni had taught his pupil musical theory as well as instruments. Giovanni, in turn, must have been trained by his father Antonio di Gregorio, the Venetian piffero who settled in Siena. Later documents show that Giovanni was an organ builder as well as a piffero and imply that he had had some keyboard training along the way. All of this, of course, points to the fact that the apprentice system and familial modes of music instruction were working quite well in Siena at this time.

fectly adapted to the needs of instrumentalists. A contemporaneous example of one system devised by woodwind players survives in a setting of the ordinary of the Mass performed by Bolognese musicians.[104]

In the system adopted by the Bolognese all of the parts in the five movements use a kind of stroke notation, a single note form, a black semibreve. This represents a constant value, as, say, might a modern eighth note. Values of longer duration are indicated by the requisite number of semibreves on the same pitch, so that a breve, or an equivalent modern quarter note, is represented by two semibreves on the same pitch, a dotted breve, or modern dotted quarter note, by three semibreves on the same pitch, and so on. Clearly, whoever performed this music did not need to know the many rules and conventions that guided singers through the intricacies of the white mensural notation system, with its perfect and imperfect tempus, major and minor prolation, and its rules for alteration, imperfection, and proportions. All he needed was an ability to read lines and spaces and to count up to six. Although this particular method of notating music was used by the Bolognese musicians for a Mass setting apparently conceived as an independent instrumental work, it could just as easily have been adopted for the arrangements of vocal music that then—and later—formed the backbone of instrumentalists' repertory. And even though nothing in written records indicates that this particular system of notation was ever used in Siena, the older generation of pifferi, with a bit of explanation and experience, probably could have read it or one similar to it. Lacking a knowledge of the standard vocal notational practices, they would, in other words, have had some kind of a system that enabled them to read their various parts.

The ability to read music written in the more conventional system of mensural

---

104. Charles Hamm, "Musiche del Quattrocento in S. Petronio," *Rivista italiana di musicologia* 3 (1968): 226–30. The Mass is one of five recovered by Sergio Paganelli from the bindings of other manuscripts in the archives of San Petronio in Bologna and was undoubtedly in the repertory of instrumentalists who performed there. It is the only one of the five not in white mensural notation. While the music is composed in a style that is similar, in Hamm's words, to the most common polyphony of the time, it is distinct in the sense that the melodies of the superius part move in disjunct steps, in chordal figurations, and make use of wider skips such as fourths and fifths, at times consecutively. The vertical structure of its various sections is quite pronounced, with all parts beginning and ending every phrase together. Harmonically, the Mass is constructed almost exclusively on four diatonic chords: tonic and dominant chords, repeatedly used in fundamental position as basic triads, and supertonic and subdominant chords in first inversion. Chords on the third, sixth and seventh degrees of the scale are found rarely, if ever. All of these factors point to instrumental rather than vocal conception. As Hamm puts it, the compositional technique reveals that the composer was perfectly aware of current polyphonic Mass styles, and that within the precise limits he chose to operate, he constructed an able and at times interesting piece. Hamm hypothesizes that the character of the work suggests that it was composed for performance by wind instruments. This in turn would justify the peculiar form of notation, since players of wind instruments were probably not able to read mensural notation, whereas they could certainly distinguish between lines and spaces and count to ten.

The Sienese wind band may have visited Bologna as it did Florence, Lucca, and other cities, to assist in the annual celebrations of the town's patron saint. The earliest recorded visit to Bologna that I have uncovered, however, is from 28 September 1536, and this speaks only of four trumpeters and a drummer. "Et concesserunt licentiam quatuor tubicinis et naccarino eorum palatii eundi Bononiam ad honorandum festum" (Concistoro, vol. 1020, fol. 20[r], dated 28 September 1536).

notation, on the other hand, had clearly been mastered by several young Sienese musicians, as the commission's report implies. Some of these musicians were children of older pifferi who succeeded to their fathers' positions in the wind band. One of them, Niccolò di Cristoforo, composed polyphonic frottole and was an older brother of the Domenico mentioned in the report. Domenico, too, may have been a composer. Another, Giovanni di Maestro Antonio, subsequently became master of the cathedral chapel, as noted above. The ability to perform, let alone compose, written music was not learned overnight but could only be acquired, along with other skills, from long years of training. One must conclude, therefore, that instruction in written notation was available to young performers in Siena by the end of the fifteenth century, whether in a familial situation or in a more formal one such as the cathedral school, where, within a decade or two, the names of young performers began to appear on the rolls.

Repertories and Performance Practices

At the end of the fifteenth century the younger generation of Sienese musicians, doubtless as adept at improvising as their elders, included some players who not only could perform written music, notated in the universal system, but who also knew, through contact with cathedral musicians or others, the latest developments in Franco-Flemish polyphony and the most up-to-date instrumental performing practices.[105] No collections of Sienese instrumental music from this time are extant, but what might have been required of highly qualified contemporary ensembles is suggested by a 1495 inventory of the Ferrarese court's music holdings. These included four volumes of secular music, two of which were intended for use by the duke's instrumentalists.[106] One, a now lost volume of German tenors, undoubtedly contained the kind of melodies that musicians customarily used as a basis for their improvisations.[107] The other, already

---

105. This first fits in with parallel developments in northern Italy. See studies by Prizer and Kämper, cited above in notes 6 and 10, for an account of the Venetian wind ensemble playing arrangements of motets and other polyphonic pieces at Mantua in 1505. Significantly, there is no indication in Siena of string music or of stringed instruments at the Palace, though these were just beginning to come into fashion at the north Italian courts. (Prizer, "Bernardino Piffaro," 163, cites the case of Michele Tedesco, a Ferrarese piffero who was also a viola player; Lockwood, *Music in Renaissance Ferrara,* 144, cites performance on bowed string instruments in Ferrara.) Perhaps the situation in Siena is another example of parallel practices with Florence, where string instruments are also strangely lacking at this time (Polk, "Civic Patronage," 62–63). Nevertheless, little is known about musical instruments owned personally by members of Sienese wind band. It is possible that one or more of them played a string instrument of his own or even a lute, which was certainly the case in the 1540s, when a lute was listed among the Palace's holdings, along with trumpets, trombones, and flutes (see below). Earlier, Maestro Piero Rintere, officially employed as the Palace drummer, was also a lutenist (see chapter 9).

106. Lockwood, *Music in Renaissance Ferrara,* 260, 273. The following discussion leans heavily on Lockwood's conclusions as well as on those of Howard Mayer Brown in *A Florentine Chansonnier,* text vol., 68, 91, 140ff., 193.

107. Recently, four instrumental melodies preserved in the Florentine manuscript London, British Library, Add. 29987 have been associated with the now lost "tenori tedeschi" of the ducal collection. See Giuliano Di Bacco, "Alcune nuove osservazioni sul Codice di Londra (British Library, MS Additional 29987)," *Studi musicali* 20 (1991): 199; and Marco Gozzi, "Alcune postille sul Codice Add.

mentioned several times, was a volume of *Cantiones a la pifarescha* that has been identified with a manuscript now in Rome's Casanatense Library. It was compiled around 1480 and contains additions from the early 1490s. Some of its pieces, notated in the white mensural system, have been adjusted so as to fit the range and requirements of a typical shawm band. This surely indicates the general way in which melodies, cadential phrases, inner parts, and even bass lines were accommodated to the idiomatic possibilities of the instruments involved. The Casanatense manuscript contains "newer" polyphonic pieces by composers such as Johannes Ghiselin, Josquin des Prez, Alexander Agricola, and Loyset Compère as well as chansons by older composers such as Antoine Busnois, Hayne van Ghizeghem, Robert Morton, and Johannes Ockeghem. Questions of notation apart, works by the older composers likely posed few problems for the veterans in the Sienese ensemble when they adapted them to their own purposes, but the newer pieces probably presented difficulties they were ill equipped to handle.

Just what these might have been is speculative, but some aspects of the newer music bear examination in view of the explicit charges made by the commission. Instrumentally conceived pieces of the 1480s written in what has been termed an "advanced style," works such as *Ile fantazies de Joskin* and Johannes Martini's *La Martinella,* depart markedly in conception and structure from vocally conceived chansons of an earlier generation. The newer music, among other things, featured imitative entries and motivic interplay among parts and clearly demanded a different approach in its execution, one in which nuances of dynamics, subtlety of phrasing, exact rhythmic articulation, and extreme clarity in ensemble playing were indispensable. This is not to say that artistry and precision were not required in the older chanson-based repertory, but rather that the requirements were quite obviously different. Mid-fifteenth-century music with its treble-dominated style, generally a lyrical melody with its accompanying lower parts, simply posed a far different set of problems for performers than did the newer music whose instrumentally conceived lines and structural devices were meant to engage the listener's attention and admiration in a different way. The same was probably true of selections from the latest vocal repertories that instrumentalists were adapting for their own use, especially of those works for four parts, where syntatic imitation and homophony commingled within full-voiced ensembles and contrasting duos and trios, the whole governed by an aesthetic that prized a clearly ordered succession of sound and controlled dissonance. The newer music demanded more rehearsal and practice time than performers experienced in playing familiar works of the past were willing to give. Maybe the commission had in mind pieces precisely like the ones by Martini and Josquin just mentioned when it recommended that the three younger players be permitted to perform certain pieces without interference from the others.[108]

All of this, of course, is speculation. But the record shows that the generational gap

29987 della British Library," *Studi musicali* 22 (1993): 264–65. A transcription of the melodies is given on p. 275 of Gozzi's study.

108. The popularity of certain Mass movements, usually sections such as the "Benedictus" set as duos and trios, shows that instrumentalists also appropriated sacred music for their needs. One of the most diffused pieces of this type was the *Benedictus* from Isaac's *Missa Quant j'ai.* Since the Mass was copied for the Sienese cathedral in 1481, the Benedictus was surely available to instrumentalists.

among the Sienese pifferi led to two different approaches with regard to questions of repertory and performance. These, in turn, exacerbated by animosities real or imagined and a desire on the part of some musicians to pass on their posts to their children, surely bred dissension within the group and impaired its ability to function as a truly up-to-date ensemble. For this latter reason the commission recommended that some of the musicians with tenured posts not be allowed to perform with the three musicians it singled out as outstanding and knowledgeable: the relatively recently appointed piffero Jacopo di Salvatore, the trombonist Geronimo di Giovanni, and Cristoforo's son Domenico, who had been serving as a supernumerary since January 1488.[109] This kind of ensemble, which assuredly included treble and tenor shawms and a trombone, represented one of the standard instrumental combinations of the time and was, as mentioned earlier, ideal for performing three-part works. The commission's remark that the younger men would soon be able to vie with the best musicians in Italy should also be noted in view of a consciously determined cultural policy which traditionally sought to keep Siena abreast of developments throughout the peninsula.

Changes in Personnel

The government eventually heeded the commission's principal recommendation, although the implicit call to make immediate changes in personnel was implemented only gradually, as the incumbents' children came of age. Domenico must have been formally appointed shortly after the commission's report because on 17 June 1493 the priors ordered him to spend some time in jail as punishment for having failed to play at the supper hour the day before. Domenico is also named, together with Maestro Antonio, Maestro Cristoforo, Jacopo di Salvatore, and Geronimo, in an Assumption Day clothing list for 1493. The list from 1494 is the same, except that Giovanni di Fruosino appears once again, so that now there were five wood winds and a trombonist. Antonio da Venezia was gone by the following February, and Cristoforo Lombardo left soon afterwards.[110] The clothing list for Assumption Day 1495 thus names only four players.

Next it was the turn of Maestro Antonio's son. A record from 20 July 1496 tells how the priors, desirous as ever of extending their kindness to Palace employees and cognizant of the faithful service Maestro Antonio had given during his lifetime, decided that his fifteen-year-old son Giovanni was to receive the same expenses as the others who took meals at the Palace and that he was to play the contralto part with the other pifferi.[111] This, of course, indicates that four-part pieces once again formed part of the

---

109. This is evident from an order issued on the 17th of that month stating that in future Domenico di Cristofaro piffaro "was to have his expenses at the Palace, as do the other piffari." Another supernumerary, Mariano di Galgano, was also hired around the same time as Domenico. A deliberation from 13 January 1488 says that the Concistoro, noting his "extreme poverty" and that he played with the other pifferi, decreed that Mariano was henceforth "to have his expenses at the Palace."

110. No names are mentioned in the payment issued to four pifferi and a trombonist on 28 February 1495 (ASS, Biccherna, vol. 347, fol. 64ʳ). Antonio was dead by 25 March 1496, when it was reported that the priors had agreed that while the pifferi were in Monte Pulciano, Giovanni, son of the late Maestro Antonio, could serve as a substitute at the Palace.

111. For Giovanni's birth date, see chapter 12.

band's repertory, since, though there were by now instrumentally composed pieces requiring four parts, the altus was generally dispensed with when vocal pieces were adapted for instrumental usage. The decision was reaffirmed in October of the same year, when the priors decreed that Giovanni be given a suit of clothing immediately and that in future he was to receive clothing every August like the others. Shortly afterwards Giovanni di Fruosino Mangoni, the last of the older musicians, relinquished his post to his son Pavolo, whose name appears on the Assumption Day clothing list of 1497. The five tenured musicians are subsequently recorded together in clothing lists from 1498 and 1499. Thus at the end of the century the band had three younger men, Domenico di Cristoforo, Pavolo di Giovanni, and Giovanni di Maestro Antonio, who were children of former employees, and two mature musicians, Jacopo di Salvatore and Geronimo di Giovanni, whom the commission seven years earlier had deemed worthy of Palace employment. (See Table 11.1 for a chronological list.)

PRIVILEGES, DUTIES, AND OBLIGATIONS OF THE PIFFERI

Reference has already been made to the pifferi's duties as well as to some of the privileges they enjoyed. Since these originated in the fifteenth century and remained unchanged through the fall of the Republic, they may be considered here, even though in some instances the examples used in illustration are drawn from sixteenth-century records. Principal among the pifferi's privileges, in addition to their usual salary and clothing, was the provision allowing them meals at government expense in the employees' dining room at the Palace. Other privileges included each employee's right to a fair division of gratuities that the group might receive from visiting dignitaries—this was a usual courtesy practiced in princely courts as well as in public palaces—and from the government itself for playing at municipal festivities and spectacles on holidays. The many officially sponsored balls, both public and private, that were so much a part of Sienese social life also provided extra income. (These will be discussed in chapter 14.) The government was concerned that extra compensation received by the group be shared equally by all and sought to regulate this income with various decrees. One of the earliest, from 28 June 1503, concerns the musicians who had recently played at the St. John's Day festival in Florence (see Doc. 11.17). The pifferi, when permitted, could also reap handsome earnings by playing at private ceremonies and parties in and out of town.[112] Individuals could further supplement their earnings when they accompanied government officials on journeys abroad.

Vacations are not mentioned in fifteenth-century documents, but a deliberation from 28 September 1536 implies that musicians customarily had them every year. This

112. Few of the latter are mentioned in fifteenth-century records, one of the most notable occurring on 8 July 1459, when the Concistoro decreed that the Commune's silver instruments could be lent to the trumpeters and pifferi so that they could play at the wedding of Biagio di Guidone's daughter (Concistoro, vol. 617, fol. 7v).

Also notable was the time the same groups were sent by the government to perform when the pope's nieces were married (see chapter 5). Individual pifferi were sometimes authorized to accompany government officials on out-of-town trips. Bartolomeo trombone, for example, was given paid leave on 6 March 1470 so that he might go with Francesco Luti to Rome.

says that the pifferi and trombone were granted eight days' vacation to begin that very day, "so that they can enjoy the pleasure of the countryside in the usual way." At the same time the Concistoro declared that the two musicians, Niccolò and Valerio, who were remaining in the city could take their meals in the employees' dining room, as they pleased.[113] This latter provision suggests that a few of the tenured musicians, assisted by supernumeraries, took over while the others were away, and that their vacations were deferred to another time.

During the fifteenth century the pifferi's principal duties at the Palace were to play at afternoon and evening meals, both within the Concistoro's private dining room and afterwards from the Palace windows, this latter for the public's delectation. Playing from the Palace windows at the supper hour is specifically mentioned on 17 June 1493, when Domenico di Cristoforo was fined for dereliction of duties. A decree from 9 March 1515 admonished the pifferi to play at the required times, otherwise they would lose their meal privileges as well as their salaries.[114] The entire group was reproved in August 1536 for habitually failing to be on hand at the required times and threatened with dismissal and loss of salary should this laxity continue (see Doc. 11.18). A report from a month later speaks of the musicians' having been fined for not having played the entire time the priors were at table one evening, but notes that the Concistoro absolved them after hearing the reasons for their behavior.[115] Two years later the band was upbraided once again for being derelict in its duties when the priors were at dinner and at supper, the trombonist particularly being singled out for his many absences. On this occasion, after noting that the group had previously been warned and censured, the priors resolved that henceforth any musician who failed to appear at the required times would be fired immediately. Substitutes would no longer be allowed, furthermore, and absences would only be excused because of illness and with prior permission (see Doc. 11.19).[116] This latter condition must mean that sending capable substitutes had long been considered an acceptable alternative.

Precious little information about performances by the pifferi at religious services in the Palace survives from the fifteenth century, though sixteenth-century reports note their playing in the Concistoro's private chapel during the Elevation at Mass. Solemn Masses sung with polyphony were held at the Palace on certain occasions in the later fifteenth century, among them one performed by "excellent singers" in February

---

113. "Et concesserunt vacationem per octo dies piffaris et tubonibus ab eorum officio sonandi, ad hoc ut possint gaudere voluptatibus rusticis more solito, et nichilominus interim Niccolaus et Valerius possint comedere in tinello ad libitum omni modo" (Concistoro, vol. 1020, fol. 21ʳ, dated 29 September 1536).

114. "Similiter deliberaverunt quod pifari debeant sonare ut moris est . . . et si non sonant, quod non habeant expensas in palatio nec salaria" (Concistoro, vol. 891, fol. 4ᵛ, dated 9 March 1515).

115. "Auditis deinde piffaris et tubonibus eorum palatii, se excusantibus eo quod elapsa die non functi sunt eorum officio sonandi ad mensam more solito, propter quod vigore deliberationis precessorum sunt privi a servitio palatii, unde motis iustis causis pro hac vice pepercerunt eisdem piffaris et tubonibus, et declaraverunt eos non incidisse dictam penam privationis" (Concistoro, vol. 1020, fols. 7ᵛ–8ʳ, dated 6 September 1536).

116. Since Valerio and Galgano were expressly informed of the new ruling the day it was published, the inference is that both of them had been sending replacements in their stead.

1473.[117] The Mass was apparently celebrated in conjunction with a banquet honoring the city's various orders at which the same singers performed "a certain song." Whether the pifferi accompanied the singers at Mass and at table is open to question, but they likely played both times, given the importance of the occasion. This would have been consistent with their official duties, which, in addition to escorting the priors when they left the Palace in state and accompanying them in civic and religious processions, included performing at state receptions in and out of doors.

The pifferi were also heard frequently throughout the year at other notable state-sponsored events. Principal among these was the series of daily concerts held in the streets leading to the cathedral and in the Campo during the two weeks before the Assumption festival. The trumpeters had been playing at these concerts for almost a century when the wind band was established in 1408, the pifferi's obligation to share in the public music-making undoubtedly dating from then.[118] They were certainly doing so by the summer of 1449, when the priors decreed that any piffero or trumpeter not performing that day in the Campo and in the cathedral square would be subject to a fine.[119] Several reports from the early decades of the sixteenth century complain of the musicians' failure to honor this obligation and tell of various actions taken by the Concistoro to curb absences.[120] As for remuneration for their services, a record from 26 August 1544 mentions a gratuity in the amount of L. 32 given to the trumpeters and to the wind band for having played, "as is customary," for fifteen days before Assumption Day, "and not only in the piazza but at the cathedral."[121] A pair of records from August 1544 again attest to the musicians' being paid for performing in these places for the same reason (see Doc. 11.20).

A decree from 17 January 1493 shows that by then the pifferi were playing at the Saturday morning Mass in the Cappella del Campo. At the time the Concistoro decided to punish absent musicians by prescribing a fine of s. 40 for each absence.[122] Another

<hr>

117. "Et detis et solvatis . . . Item in alia manu ducatos duos, datos quibusdam optimis cantoribus, qui cantaverunt missam in palatio, et certam cantionem ad mensam quando fuit factum convivium ordinibus civitatis" (Concistoro, vol. 638, fol. 66ᵛ, dated 22 February 1473).

118. See chapter 9; the document is in ASS, Biccherna, vol. 215, fol. 119ʳ.

119. "Et deliberaverunt Magnifici domini quod quicunque ex piffaris vel trombettis non ibit cras ad sonandum per Campum Fori et ad ecclesiam maiorem, ut tenentur, intelligatur et sit puntatus" (Concistoro, vol. 501, fol. 24ᵛ, dated 2 August 1449).

120. A not so specific report from 9 March 1515 complains of their not fulfilling all of their duties and says that if they did not play, they would forfeit their meal allowance: "Similiter deliberaverunt quod pifari debeant sonare ut moris est, et incipiant [illegible word], et si non sonant, quod non habeant expensas in palatio nec salario [sic]" (Concistoro, vol. 891, fol. 4ᵛ, dated 9 March 1514/15 [in margin: Contra piffaros]).

121. ASS, Biccherna, vol. 365, fol. 18ʳ. Earlier, on 31 December 1542, two of the trumpeters asked the priors to approve a payment of L. 8 to them for playing on the feast of the Conception of the Virgin (see chapter 10, note 17), and the inference is that the musicians had extra earnings for other feast days.

122. "Et decreverunt quod tibicines quolibet sabbato teneantur et debeant sonare ante figuram beate Marie Virginis, pictam in cappella turris in Campo Fori, ut hactenus fuit consuetum, sub pena soldorum XL pro quolibet eorum et qualibet vice quod non servaverint predicta, de eorum salario auferenda" (Concistoro, vol. 758, fol. 5ʳ, dated 17 January 1493).

decree from over half a century later addressed the problem once again. Dated 17 March 1550, this noted that trumpeters and some of the other Palace instrumentalists (that is, members of the wind band) were often absent when the image of the Virgin was unveiled at the cathedral, at the Mass in the Campo, and at other times when they were obliged to play in the Palace. Accordingly, the priors declared that no musician was exempt from these duties and that failure to perform them would result in suspension of meal privileges and fifteen days' imprisonment (see Doc. 11.21).[123] The reference to the requirement that all Palace musicians be present at the unveiling of the Virgin's image means that by that time, if not in the previous century, the wind band was also performing at Saturday and Sunday services at the cathedral.

Mid-fifteenth-century records already cited indicate that the restrictions in the town's statutes prohibiting trumpeters from performing at non–government-sponsored events were initially extended to the pifferi. This is particularly noted in a decree of 1 March 1460, which warned the Palace pifferi and trumpeters not to visit other lords or even those who came to Siena without the government's permission.[124] The musicians were expressly forbidden to play outside the Palace, under penalty of a fine, in a decree from two months later.[125] While later reports show that such restrictions were eventually lifted, it is also clear that particularly for those occasions necessitating journeys to distant places, all of the musicians had to seek the priors' permission before accepting any kind of private engagement, as, for example, when one or more of them traveled with Sienese ambassadors or in the entourages of prominent visitors.[126] These restrictions prevailed even when the band was invited to attend the wedding of Pierfrancesco de' Medici and Laudomia Acciaiuoli in Florence in 1456.[127] A quarter of a century later, with the Concistoro's approval, the musicians also traveled to Lucca for the wedding of the town's lord Giovanni de' Franciotti.[128] At times, however, it was the Concistoro itself that sent the musicians abroad, as happened in October 1458,

---

123. A reference to the trumpeters being obliged by custom to play on Saturdays and "other days when the figure of the B.V.M. is unveiled at the Cathedral" comes from 27 February 1484, but the pifferi are not mentioned on that occasion (see Doc. 9.10).

124. "Magnifici domini . . . deliberaverunt quod piffari et tubicene eorum palatii non vadant ad visitandum aliquem dominum nec quem alium qui venerit in civitatem Senarum absque licentie ipsorum Magnificorum dominorum, sub incursu eorum idignationis" (Concistoro, vol. 561, fol. 2ᵛ, dated 1 March 1460).

125. "Magnifici domini . . . deliberaverunt quod tubicines, piffari et naccarinus non possint ire ad sonandum in aliquo loco extra palatium, sub pena privationis et librarum XXV" (Concistoro, vol. 562, fol. 8ᵛ, dated 1 May 1460).

126. Another record shows that the piffero player Jacopo was given permission to travel to Rome with the Sienese envoy Angelo Fundi. Jacopo had arranged for a substitute: "Iacobus tibicen palatii habuit licentiam [a] dicti dominis eundi cum Angelo Fundio oratore Romam, relinquendo tamen loco sui alterum tibicinem" (Concistoro, vol. 786, fol. 8ʳ, dated 19 September 1497).

127. "Magnifici domini et capitaneus populi concesserunt licentiam piffaris et trombono eundi Florentiam ad honorandum nuptias Pieri Francisci de Medicis eundi die XXIᵃ presentis mensis et redeundi a [gap] per totum diem vigilie festi Corporis Christi. Et per eorum absentiam nullum ammitantur salarium" (Concistoro, vol. 538, fol. 3ᵛ, dated Sunday, 2 May 1456).

128. "Excelsi domini . . . concesserunt licentiam piffaris et trombono eundi ad civitatem Lucanam, ad nuptias Iohannis Francisci de Franciottis" (Concistoro, vol. 694, fol. 16ᵛ, dated 24 May 1482).

when the priors decreed that the Sienese envoys who were being sent to Rome to congratulate Aeneas Sylvius Piccolomini on his election to the papacy could have four extra horses on condition that the piffari and trombonist go with them.[129] An appropriation from the following January indicates that the band indeed was there.[130]

Official approval, of course, was a sine qua non when any of the Palace musicians journeyed to other cities to assist at feast-day celebrations.[131] This is understandable since in effect they represented the government, which nevertheless made no extraordinary contributions toward their expenses except to approve continuation of their normal salaries for the days they were away. Failure to secure official approval brought swift punishment in the form of a fine or of deduction of wages for the time musicians were absent. On 28 May 1501, for example, the pifferi and trumpeters were ordered to jail and directed to turn over to government officials tips they had received from Cesare Borgia for having had the temerity to attend him without official permission while he was in Florentine territory (see Doc. 11.22).

Prohibiting the pifferi from playing at private engagements within the city obviously posed a different set of problems. How effectively—and how seriously—such restrictions were enforced is difficult to assess. Frequent admonitions to the musicians because of unauthorized absences and dereliction of duties, already mentioned in connection with the trumpeters, suggest that individual players or small groups were willing to risk the government's displeasure and accept some, if not all, of the opportunities available for private employment. A decree from November 1524 forbidding the pifferi, trumpeters, and trombonist to perform outside the Palace under penalty of incurring a fine of 10 ducats is perhaps the best proof we have that this was just what they were doing.[132]

---

129. "Excelsi domini . . . deliberaverunt dare et dederunt oratoribus qui vadunt Romam Sanctitati pape 4 equos inter omnes ultra eos sibi datos, cum hoc quod piffari et trombonus debeant ire cum eis" (Concistoro, vol. 552, fol. 25^r, dated 4 October 1458).

130. "Excelsi domini . . . deliberaverunt quod camerarius Biccherne solvat Arrigo Iohannis tuboni et piffaris palatii nostri salarium eis . . . debitum pro eorum andata quam fecerunt Romam cum oratoribus missis ad papam" (Concistoro, vol. 554, fol. 21^r, dated 26 January 1458/59).

131. The most important visits were those made to Florence on St. John's Day, as has been mentioned in connection with the trumpeters. A record, typical of many others in the following decades, comes from 21 June 1415, when permission to take the commune's silver instruments with them was also granted the musicians: "Et quod quatuor ex tubatoribus palatii possint in presenti ire Florentiam in festo Sancti Iohannis, et piffari, ita tamen quod portent tubas argenteas, quas camerarius Consistorii eis libere comodare possit" (Concistoro, vol. 296, fol. 35^v).

Also typical are a pair of records from 20 and 21 June 1493, which state that "Piffarino, tubicine nostri palatii, licentiam concesserunt eundi Florentiam ad festivitatem Sancti Iohannis, et discendendi suo libitu impune"; and that "Tubicinibus et tibicinibus, trumbono et timpaniste palatii licentiam concesserunt eundi Florentiam ad festum Sancti Iohannis et redeundi debito tempore, dummodo hic maneant et restent tot ex eis quot restari solent eorum loco, ex quo satisfiat honori palatii" (Concistoro, vol. 760, fols. 15^v, 16^v).

Another record, from 25 March 1496, again shows that substitutes were brought in when the Palace musicians were absent with official approval (see note 110, and in Register of Musicians under Giovanni di Maestro Antonio).

132. "Et decreverunt quod piffari, tubicines et tubonus non possint sonare extra palatium sine licentia Magnificorum dominorum sub pena ducatorum decem pro quolibet et qualibet vice" (Concistoro, vol. 948, fol. 2^v, dated 1 November 1524).

The government's policy regarding outside engagements was ambiguous and permission to accept them was granted on an ad hoc basis until well into the middle of the sixteenth century. This ambiguity is strikingly illustrated by a decree issued on 21 September 1536, less than six years before the one just mentioned, when the government decided that both the trumpeters as a group and the pifferi could honor the doctor who was to receive his degree that morning, while noting in the same breath that those musicians derelict in their official duties would have three days to show cause, otherwise they would be fined (see Doc. 11.23).

THE COMMUNE'S MUSICAL INSTRUMENTS

As it did for the trumpeters, the commune also supplied the pifferi with musical instruments. Palace inventories from 1436 through 1444 list three silver pifferi and a silver bracket used to keep the instruments clean.[133] Since pifferi—shawms—were made of wood, the reference to silver instruments must be to silver casings or sheaths that were placed over them at official ceremonies. The three silver pifferi are cited in an inventory from 1472, which also lists nine silver trumpets and a large lute with its case.[134] Subsequent inventories from 1506 and 1508 add little information about the instruments but note that a silver trombone was "in the hands of Girolamo trombone and that one of the pifferi was "senza buciuolo."[135] Another inventory from 1514 specifies that the seven silver trumpets each had three pieces and that the three silver pifferi were without "buciolo," and that one was wooden, "una era di legnio."[136] No longer mentioned in inventories after this time, the silver casings were evidently consigned to the silversmith for the value of their metal. Pifferi also disappear in inventories from the following decades, which now begin to list "sordine and flauti diritti or flauti all'italiana," among others.[137]

Other fifteenth-century documents record the purchase, repair, and refurbishing of the Palace's instruments. One from 18 July 1447 recounts that a decision was made "to have another silver trombone made for the commune, similar to the one that is played with the pifferi."[138] The instrument was ordered from the Sienese silversmith Simone di Pietro del Panziera, with the stipulation that he use the same weight of silver as that of the Palace's trumpets, that he finish the instrument in time for Assumption Day that

---

133. Concistoro, vol. 2498, *Proventi, spese e inventari, 1436–44,* fol. 2ʳ, dated 1436. Also listed with the "3 piffare d'ariento et una forcella d'ariento per mantenere le piffare nette" are "8 trombette d'ariento, co' pennoni di seta."

134. Concistoro, vol. 2505, *Proventi, spese e inventari, 1466–72,* fol. 245ʳ. See also chapter 9, note 38.

135. "VII trombe d'argiento, una ne le mani del Moro trombetto. III piffari d'argiento, una senza buciuolo uno trombone d'argento ne le mani di Girolamo trombone" (Concistoro, vol. 2512, *Proventi, spese e inventari, 1506–18,* fol. CLXXXVIʳ: 1506 [September and October]). The meaning of "buciuolo" is not clear; it is possibly "mouthpiece," though "boccaletto" is used in some other documents.

136. Ibid., unnumbered folio: dated "MDXIII . . . Marzo et Aprile detto anno [1513/14]."

137. Concistoro, vol. 2516, *Proventi, spese, tratte e inventari, 1546–61,* fol. LIᵛ: 1546/ gennaio–febbraio [1547].

138. Concistoro, vol. 489, fols. 14ᵛ–15ʳ. The document is published in Cellesi, *Storia della più antica banda,* 69.

year, and that he be paid L. 4. 10 per ounce for his work. Before this time trombonists—Giovanni da Alamania, who began serving in November 1446, and perhaps some
of the trumpeters before him—had been using their own instruments. Nothing further
is mentioned about the instrument until 14 July 1470, when it was reported that the
chamberlain sent "the Palace's silver trombone" to Francesco di Antonio and company,
goldsmiths, because "it is lacking certain things."[139] The trombone was to be remade
according to a design retained by the chamberlain and the finished product was to be
judged by experts. Another condition was that the instrument be delivered in time for
the Assumption Day festivities, which is, in fact, what occurred.[140] On 31 August 1470,
however, it was reported that the trombone did not have the agreed upon weight and
L. 6 was accordingly withheld from the original price.[141] Francesco di Antonio subsequently received L. 1. 12 for gilding the trombone.[142]

Another new trombone was ordered some eighteen years later. A document from
11 December 1487 reports that Francesco di Antonio was to make seven silver trumpets, each weighing about two pounds, and a silver trombone. The agreement called
for the goldsmith to be paid s. 19 the ounce for his work and stipulated that the finished
instruments were to be approved by the Palace trumpeters.[143] Nothing more is said
about the trombone. An entry in an account from some time later indicates that the
new instrument was given to the Palace trombonist for his approval on 14 April 1488.
Dated 1 September 1489, this notes that Geronimo di Giovanni returned a silver trombone weighing 3 pounds, 9 ounces, which he had apparently taken home "on several
occasions in order to play it so that it might be improved."[144]

DOCUMENTS

Doc. 11.1. The commune inaugurates a wind band, 10 April 1408. ASS, Concistoro, vol. 253,
fol. 24ʳ

[margin: Conducantur piffari] Domini priores, Capitaneus populi et officiales balie concorditer
et solepniter deliberaverunt quod cassentur unus tubator et unus naccharinus de tubatoribus et
naccarinis Comunis, et debeant conduci tres piffari pro honore totius civitatis.

---

139. Concistoro, vol. 2505, *Proventi, spese e inventari, 1466–72,* fol. 191ᵛ: "per certi mancamenti
che ha." The document is published in Cellesi, *Storia della più antica banda,* 72.

140. It was further stipulated that when the trombone was finished, the goldsmiths were to be
paid s. 19 the ounce for their work, having been given silver from the Palace in the form of the old
trombone, which weighed 39½ ounces, with the understanding that if one or two additional ounces
of silver were needed, the Palace would supply them, as it would any gold that might be needed. The
instrument was delivered on 14 August.

141. Concistoro, vol. 2505, *Proventi, spese e inventori, 1466–72,* fol. 97ᵛ. It lacked "oncie 1, quarri
3 et denari 6" of silver. The document is published in Cellesi, *Storia della più antica banda,* 72–73.

142. Ibid., fol. 98ʳ, dated 31 August 1470: "per doratura del tronbone."

143. "7 trombe d'argento et uno trombone d'argento, di peso l'una delle trombe di libre due
incirca, a soldi dicennove l'oncia per sua fatiga . . . et che debbi fare le decte trombe bene et diligentemente in modo che per li trombetti di palazo sieno aprovate buone" (Concistoro, vol. 2508,
Proventi, spese e inventari, 1482–88, fol. 143ʳ). Payment was made in full by 9 February 1489.

144. "de' dare . . . ha in suo mani per sonarlo alcuna volta perché si vengha migliorando, el quale
ebbe insino adì 14 d'aprile 1488" (Concistoro, vol. 2509, *Proventi, spese e inventari, 1489–96,* fol. 100ᵛ).

Et remiserunt dicti Magnifici domini . . . in infrascriptos quatuor prudentes viros qui possint cassare unum tubatorem et unum naccarinum Comunis, et eligere loco eorum tres piffaros, pro salario, tempore et modis de quibus eis videbitur. . . .

Doc. 11.2. Three pifferi are hired, 11 April 1408. Concistoro, vol. 253, fol. 25ᵛ

[margin: Conductio piffarorum] Magnifici domini . . . conduxerunt Filippum Pauli de Venetiis, Antonium Iohannis de Bononia et Renaldum Michaelis de Cesena pro piffaris et ad sonandum piffaros prout requiritur, pro tempore unius anni incohandi die primo Maii proxime futuri et ab inde in antea ad beneplacitum Concistorii, cum salario et modis de quibus constat manu mei Nicholai Dari notari.

Similiter vigore dicte commissionis, concorditer cassaverunt Francium Vive naccharinum et Severinum Bartalomei de Sancto Severino, vocato Manco, tubatorem, a die primo mensis Maii proxime futuri in antea.

Doc. 11.3. Italian pifferi are fired and German pifferi hired, 17 October 1408. Concistoro, vol. 256, fol. 24ʳ

Magnifici domini prefati, attenta inhoneste Filippi, piffari palatii, et socii, ipsos cassaverunt. Et firmarunt Conradum [blank] piffarium [sic] de Alamania, cum modis predictis et prout erant dicti Filippus et socius. Et quod possit mittere pro duobus sociis, de quibus alias dixit esse sufficientes. Et quod Imperator piffarus societ interum dictum Conradum in sonando, donec illi duo accedant de quibus dixit.

Doc. 11.4. Palace musicians are fined for refusing to play at the awarding of a doctorate, 8 October 1446. Concistoro, vol. 484, fol. 23ʳ

Magnifici domini . . . audito precepto oretenus facto tubicenis et piffaris infrascriptis pro parte, videlicet quod pro honore Comunis Senarum [h]odierna die odierna [recte irent] ad doctoratum rectoris Sapientie Comunis predicti . . . et hoc non fecerunt in vilipendium ipsorum et verecundiam dicti Comunis Senarum et dicte domus Sapientie: decreverunt quod camerarius Biccherne sive scriptor accendat . . . debitores in libris ipsius Biccherne infrascriptos in libris quinque denariorum pro quolibet, pro dicta disubidientia, et deinde ipsas summas excomputent ad salarium ipsorum . . . quorum hec sunt nomina, videlicet: Clemens, Augustinus, Santes, Petrus Nibii et Iohannes Martini, tubatores; Nicholaus Bini, magister Bartolus et Renaldus, piffari.

Doc. 11.5. The Avignonese pifferi are hired, 27 June 1446. Concistoro, vol. 482, fol. 49ᵛ

Magnifici domini . . . deliberaverunt quod ex nunc sit et esse intelligatur conductus magister Carinus de Vignione, partibus Francie, cum duobus sotiis et uno tubicinone, vulgariter detto trombone, in quantum dictus magister habere possit dictum trombonem, in pyffaros et pro pyffaris palatii magnificorum dominorum, cum salario 4 florenorum pro quolibet ipsorum et quolibet mense, et duobus vestitis pro quolibet eorum quolibet anno, et etiam habeant spensas in palatio . . . Et intelligantur et sint conducti ad vitam ipsorum, et interim ad beneplacitum Concistorii. Et quod camerarius Biccherne prestet eis et cuilibet eorum florenos decem pro quolibet eorum, nunc de presenti.

Doc. 11.6. Two of the Avignonese pifferi are fired and Lorenzo da Francia is hired, 22 May 1447. Concistoro, vol. 488, fol. 24ʳ⁻ᵛ

Insuper prefati Magnifici domini . . . viso quod pro honore Comunis Senarum et palatii fuerunt conducti certi francigene in phifari et pro phifari Comunis Senarum et ad servitia dicti Comunis et palatii ipsius, quorum duo abfuerunt a civitate per duos menses et ultra, ut dicitur qui fuerunt cassi per Magnificorum dominos . . . quorum hec sunt nomina videlicet Germanus et Gherinus, phifari de partibus Francie. Et volentes providere pro honore dicti Comunis et palatii, visa cassatione facta de predictis . . . volentes igitur providere honorifice, habita precipueque informatione

. . . de infrascripto Laurentio sonatore iam sunt octo dies vel circa quibus continuo servivit palatio in sonando phifaram, et quantum sit idoneus et expertus ad serviendo dicto palatio . . . concorditer fuerunt in plena et uniforma concordia conducendi et eligendi, et elegerunt et conduxerunt dictum Laurentium [gap] in phifarum et pro phifaro Comunis [et] ipsius palatii, ad sonandum phifarum per duos menses proxime futuros incipiendos die XV mensis presentis . . . et post dictos duos menses pur [sic] ad beneplacitum dicti Consistorii, cum stipendio sive salario duodecim librarum denariorum Senensium, nitidorum cabella, pro quolibet mense . . . Item habeat et habere debeat quolibet anno dum sic serviet, in festo Sancte Marie . . . unam tunicam sive robbam cum divisa sive partita . . . valoris decem florenorum auri.

Doc. 11.7. Payments to pifferi, 30 June 1447. Concistoro, vol. 488, fol. 69^{r-v}

Et detis et solvatis Ferrino de Francia, phifaro nostri palatii, tubuono, tubicinis et naccharino nostri palatii, salarium eis et cuilibet eorum debitum . . .

Et detis et solvatis magistro Bartolomeo Pietri et Nicolao Andree de Bononia, fiphfari [sic] palatii nostri, salarium eis et cuilibet eorum debitum pro 22 diebus mensis Maii . . . ad rationem librarum 12 pro quolibet eorum, nitidorum de cabella . . .

Et detis et solvatis Laurentio [gap] de Francia, phifaro nostri comunis, salarium sibi debitum a die XV mensis Maii proxime preteriti, ad rationem librarum 12 . . . usque per totum mensem Iunii presentis . . .

Et detis et solvatis magistro Germano [blank] de Francia seu de partibus Francie, salarium sibi debitum, videlicet a die XIIII presentis mensis Iunii usque in presentem diem . . . ad ractionem videlicet librarum 12 denariorum nitidorum de cabella.

Doc. 11.8. Pifferi are given leave to pilgrimage to Rome in Jubilee year, 2 September 1450

Concesserunt licentiam magistro Iohanni tromboni, Matheo et Guglielmo tibicenis palatii, eundi Romam pro indulgentia, pro XV diebus (Concistoro, vol. 507, fol. 4^r)

Ferrino piffaro concesserunt licentiam . . . eundi Romam pro XVIII vel XX diebus, cum amissione salarii, ita quod dicto tempore nullum habeat salarium (vol. 508, fol. 11^r, dated 10 November 1450)

Et quia Ferrinus piffarus ivit Romam et redivit cum eorum licentia, decreverunt quod tempore quo stetit non amictat aliquod salarium, ymo sine deminutione idem persolvatur integrum (ibid., fol. 30^r, dated 29 November 1450)

Doc. 11.9. Voting on hiring and firing pifferi, 30 July 1455. Concistoro, vol. 533, fols. 30^v–31^r

Decreverunt etiam cum Vexilliferis magistris capsare unum ex piffaris palatii, excepto Ferrino, hoc modo videlicet, quod tenorista et il contra scruptinentur, et qui plures voces habuerit, remaneat in palatio, et alius qui pauciores voces habuerit intelligatur capsus cum hoc quod sonare debeat usque ad festum S. Marie de mense Augusti proximi, et habeat vestem consuetam sine alique salario. Et statim fuerunt scruptinati infrascripti piffari, videlicet:
    Iohannes de Colonia, qui tenet contra, qui habuit sex voces seu lupinos albos,
    Arrigus Iohannis de Venetiis, tenorista, qui habuit quattuor voces seu lupinos albos, ideo remansit capsus.

Et cum dictis Vexilliferis magistris conduxerunt Stefanum Pieri de Francia ad servitia Magnifici Comunis Senarum in piffarum et pro piffaro palatii Magnificorum dominorum prefatorum ad beneplacitum Concistorii, ad sonandum pifferam canti superioris, omnibus et singulis diebus et horis consuetis et prout sibi comandatum fuerit in actibus, honoribus et cerimoniis Magnifici Comunis Senarum, cum salario quattuor ducatorum pro quolibet mense, nitidorum omni cabella, et duarum vestium quolibet anno; incipiendo in festo Nativitatis Domini Nostri Yesu

Christi pro prima veste, et alia pro festo S. Marie de mense Augusti, prout habent alii piffari dicti palatio et eiusdem valoris.

Doc. 11.10. Arrigo di Giovanni is reinstated and Giovanni da Colonia fired, 4 August 1455. Concistoro, vol. 533, fol. 34^r

Similiter cum dictis Vexilliferis, decreverunt conducere et conduxerunt Arrigum Iohannis de Venetiis in piffarum tenoristam, ad beneplacitum Concistorii, cum salario consueto . . . Et capsaverunt Iohannem de Colonia alterum piffarum, cum hoc quod servat usque ad festum S. Marie presentis mensis sine salario, et habeat vestem ordinatam pro dicto festo ut alii piffari.

Doc. 11.11. Stefano Rusignuoli and Bartolomeo da Castello are offered contracts as pifferi, 1 June 1460. Concistoro, vol. 562, fol. 18^v

Simili modo deliberaverunt conducere et conduxerunt Stefanum Rusignuoli de Savoia, qui alias fuit conductum, et Bartholomeum de Castello, eius socium, qui in presentiarum morantur in civitate Mediolani, ad pulsandum tibicines in palatio Magnificorum dominorum Senensium, cum salario librarum decem denariorum pro quolibet mense et quolibet eorum, nitidorum de cabella, et cum illis emolumentis et conditionibus consuetis et prout ad presens habet Ferinus tibicen palatii.

Doc. 11.12. Salary and perquisites offered to two new pifferi, 27–28 June 1460. Concistoro 562, fol. 39$^{r–v}$, dated 27 and 28 June 1460

Magnifici domini . . . conduxerunt Antonium Gregorii tibicinem et Nicholaum Georgii trombonem, de Venetiis, ad pulsandum in palatio, cum salario decem et novem librarum denariorum Senensium pro quolibet mense et unius vestimenti pro quolibet in anno . . . prout habet Ferinus tibicen.

Magnifici domini . . . deliberaverunt quod Antonius Gregorii tibicen et Nicolaus Georgii trombonus, de Venetiis, qui heri fuerunt conducti ad pulsandum in palatio Magnificorum dominorum pro tempore trium mensium proxime futurorum, possint stare in palatio ad dormiendum expensis Comunis Senarum, dando eis cameram cum cubile et aliis necessariis, ut commode stare possint prout alii domicelli qui dormiunt continuo in palatio.

Doc. 11.13. The pifferi protest against low wages, 1463. Concistoro, vol. 2181, *Scritture concistoriali,* unnumbered folio

Magnifici et potentissimi Signori nostri, supplicasi humilmente a le Magnifiche Signorie Vostre per parte de' vostri fedeli servidori piffari et trombone, che considerata la povertà e miseria loro grande e necessità in reggiere le loro povere famigliuole, e veduto che non ànno altro guadagno né provisione che quella che gli è subministrata da questo magnifico palazzo et atteso che hanno abbandonato le patrie loro proprie e ogni loro tenerezza paterna per servire questo vostro sacro palazzo et in servizio di quello sempre vivere et morire, supplicano a le vostre clementissime Signorie vi piacia di rimuovere la tassa et parte gli è imposta per lo edifitio della torre s'à affare di nuovo come si sono degnate le vostre Magnifiche Signorie rimuovere a' vostri donzelli.

Doc. 11.14. A Sienese piffero is recommended to Lorenzo the Magnificent, 29 January 1469. ASF, Mediceo avanti il Principato, 20, fol. 397

Spectabilis tanquam maior honorande.
Per chagione che io so tu ti diletti degl'uomini virtuosi, mando a tte maestro Antonio, sonatore di piffero della Signoria di Siena, che sechondo il mio intelletto e ghusto, non vidi mai simile di sua virtù. Parmi sia d'animo che volentieri starebbe con noi qui in palagio, ad averne di bisognio, perché soddisfarebbe per contro o per tenore o per sovrano o chol trombone, chom'altri volessi. Parmi sia chosa da non la lasciare, e arei charo ne facessi 'sperienza perché son certo ti piacerebbe

sommamente. Era venuto qui per onorarti in questa festa della giostra fin a tanto quanto gli cho-manderai.

Altro non achade. Iddio si tua ghuardia sempre. Data in Firenze, adì 29 di gennario 1468[69]. Tuo Mario de' Nobili

(on verso: Spettabili viro Laurentio Petri de Medicis ut maiori meo precipuo)

Doc. 11.15. Bartolomeo di Monaldo is appointed a town crier, 23 November 1483. Concistoro, vol. 703, fol. 8^v

Et attento quod Iohannes Martini, unus ex preconibus predictis, a pluribus mensibus citra fuit et hodie est infirmis adeo quod de domo exire non potest, et quasi semi mortuus, et ab omnibus eius infirmitas—attenta eius decrepita etate—iudicatur incurabilis et mortalis, et quod ipse Bartholomeus servivit et servit in locum ipsius Iohannis . . . declaraverunt dictum Iohannem Martini vacasse et vacare, et venisse diem et tempus concessionis et gratie predicte dicti Bartholomei, et ipsum vigore dicte gratie esse unum ex preconibus Comunis Senarum in locum Iohannis predicti vacantis, cum salario et emolumentis consuetis et ordinatis dicto Iohanni, cum hoc quod ipso Iohanne vivente, de salario predicto dentur dicto Iohanni soldi quadraginta denariorum in quolibet mense, et eo mortuo integrum salarium predictum sit dicti Bartholomei ut supra omni modo etc.

Doc. 11.16. A commission is appointed to reform the pifferi, 9 August 1492. ASS, Balìa, 37, fol. 45^{r-v}

Magnifici viri quinque de collegio Balie convocati etc. vigore eorum auctoritates audita infra-scripta petitione super piffaris et musicis palatii magnificorum Dominorum, deliberaverunt ipsam approbare et approvaverunt et quod fiat et exequatur in omnibus et per omnia prout et sicut in ea continetur; cuius quidem tenor talis est:

Dinanzi a voi Signori etc. Misser Pio di Misser Goro Loli, Misser Bartolomeo di Giovanni Pecci, Misser Hieronymo d'Aldobrandino Ptolomei, Maestro Lutio di Misser Baptista Bellanti, Vostri minimi servidori espongo: Conciosiacosaché per lo exercitio havendo preso qualche cura sopra de la musica de li instrumenti del vostro palazo et trovianci qualche disordine el quale non si può corregiare [sic] senza autorità di V. M. S.

Et prima, le S. V. ordenonno già che maestro Antonio piffaro non sonasse et havesse el suo salario; lui non vole obedire et non sa sonare se non all'antica, in modo che non si può fare cosa buona; vorremo che per tenore de le presenti li fusse posto silentio come a voi paresse, non levandoli però la provisione.

Item, vorremo, perché de' piffari vostri soli due ne avete e quali intendino qualche cosa, cioè el trombone et Iacomo et ècci [sic] Domenico, figliuolo di Christofano piffaro, intendente a loro pari, e quali tre, quando suonino senz'altro, siamo certi che vi faranno honore quanto piffari d'Italia, perché loro potranno imparare et sonare cosa che gli altri nostri piffari non possano né sanno imparare; et per questo desiderremo che i predetti tre, quando volessero sonare cosa alcuna, non fussero impediti. Siché vorremo con licentia de le S. V. potere dire tale et tale qualche volta non sonare, maxime volendo sonare di quelle cose che non sanno, et finalmente che niuno possi sonare senza nostra licentia; et contrafacendo, che li potiamo condennare come a noi paresse, da' sopradicti tre infuori di sopra nominati.

Item, che Domenico predecto habi le spese continuamente in palazo di Magnifici Signori, non obstante qualunque cosa.

Doc. 11.17. Decree on outside income of the pifferi, 28 June 1503. Concistoro, vol. 850, fol. 15^v, dated 28 June 1503

[margin: pro tubicinis et piffaris] Magnifici domini etc. convocati ad circulum in sala Mappamundi etc. adtenta quadam differentia vertente inter tubicenes, tubonum, piffaros et naccarinum occasione denariorum seu munusculi percepti ab eis in civitate Florentie a pluribus particularibus personis . . . volentes quod servitores palatii et sonatores vivant pacifice et concordes, declaraverunt et deliberaverunt quod omnia munuscula sive denarii percepti tam a trombettis tubone et piffaris, si quos recepissent in civitate Florentie a quibuscunque personis, exceptis a Comunitate Florentie, quas visitassent, sint et esse intelligantur communes, et ita inter eos debeant distribui comuniter pro rata, videlicet inter tubicenes, naccarinum, tubonem et piffaros. Et predicta deliberaverunt omni meliori modi etc.

Doc. 11.18. The pifferi are reprimanded for dereliction of duties, 4 August 1536. Concistoro, vol. 1019, fol. 21^r

Viso quod tibicene, piffari et tubonus et sonatores male se gerunt non serviendo debitis horis et congruis temporibus, quamquam pluries admoniti, deliberaverunt quod in futurum quod quilibet ipsorum sonatorum qui non aderit, non sonaverit et non fuerit functus officio suo in sonando debito et congruo tempore qualibet vice intelligatur et sit nunc pro tunc privatus ab officio suo, et statim fiat preceptum camerario Bicherne quod non solvat eius salarium sed retineat ad instantiam Concistorii. Et hoc tamen non intelligendo in casu infirmitatis et statim fuerit significatum per me notarium.

Doc. 11.19. The pifferi are reprimanded and threatened with dismissal, 12 July 1538. Concistoro, vol. 1031, fol. 14^r

Insuper, quoniam ut plurimum piffari et tubones, prandentibus et cenantibus magnificis dominis, non faciunt quicquid tenentur in sonando, et precipue Benedictus tubonus sepius iam deficit, licet alias admoniti et reprensi fuerint: igitur ad eorum nimiam licentiam . . . referenandam, servatis etc., decreverunt quod quotiescumque de cetero aliquis ex eis deficiet sonare quando tenetur, neque alium sui loco deputaverit qui effectualiter sonet, nisi tamen iusto impedimento detineretur—ut puta infirmitate aut absentia cum consensu et venia obtenta a magnifico priore, intelligatur ille ex eis qui deficeret, statim amisisse suam locum. Mandantes presentem deliberationem eis notificari etc. Et die dicta fuit notificata Valerio et Galgano.

Doc. 11.20. Payments to pifferi for playing in the first half of August, 14 and 17 August 1544. Concistoro, vol. 1073, fols. 29^r and 57^r

Et visa et audita petitione facta pro parte tibicinarum et tubicinorum eorum palatii circa mercedem librarum 32 denariorum, quam soliti sunt habere in festo Assumptionis pro sonando per dies quindecim ante dictum festum in platea et per vias usque ad ecclesiam cathedralem: servatis etc., deliberaverunt quod casu quod demonstrent per vices sex se habuisse a camerario Biccherne dictam mercedem, quod tunc et eo casu ego notarius possim et valeam ei[s]dem facere decretum in favore pro dictis libris 32 denariorum.

Et che diate et paghiate ali piffari et trombetti di loro palazzo lire trentadue di denari infra di loro convenuti, quali denari se dànno per la loro solita mercè et fadighe de havere sonato avanti per quindici giorni ala festa di Santa Maria d'Agosto intorno ala piazza e a Duomo, et sì come è solito per tale solennità, et così pagarete. Dal Concestoro, il dì XVII d'Agosto MDXLV.

Doc. 11.21. Pifferi remiss in their duties are threatened with fifteen days in jail, 17 March 1550. Concistoro, vol. 1101, fols. 13^v–14^r

Et habita notitia quod sepe sepius tubicene et alii sonatores instrumentorum palatii sepe sepius aliquis eorum ex eis deficit quando detergitur pictura Virginis in ecclesia cathedrali ac etiam ad missam platee et in aliis horis quibus tenentur sonare in palatio etc., volentes igitur predictis inconvenientibus et deffectibus obviare et remedium imponere, servatis etc., deliberaverunt quod quilibet sonator palatii debeat interesse omnibus in locis et horis sibi deputatis ad sonandum, declarando quod deficienti non detur pars in tinello vel palatio et condennatus intelligatur ad carcerem per quindecim dies.

Doc. 11.22. The pifferi are jailed for attending Cesare Borgia without official permission, 28 May 1501. Concistoro, vol. 808, fols. 8^v–9^r

[margin: contra tibicines et piffaros] Magnifici domini . . . visa temeritate et audacia ac etiam parva reverentia tibicinum et piffarorum palatii qua usi sunt istis diebus in eundo ad visitandum Illustrissimum ducam Valentinum in comitata Florentie absque licentia Magnificorum dominorum: unde ne tanta audacia et temeritate in futurum uti debea[n]t, servatis servandis deliberaverunt quod dicti tibicines et piffari qui iverunt, deposuerint per totam hanc presentem diem omne id et totum quod receperunt a dicto Illustrissimo duca, in manibus Capitanei populi aut prioris ac etiam infra dictum tempus teneantur ire in carceribus Comunis Senarum et in eisdem permanere. Et dictum id omne quod receperunt non restituatur donec et quousque per presentem collegium non fuerit aliter deliberatum.

Doc. 11.23. Palace musicians are permitted to play at a doctoral degree ceremony, 21 September 1538. Concistoro, vol. 1038, fol. 11^{r-v}

Excellentissimi et potentissimi domini . . . deliberaverunt quod tubicines habeant licentiam et eant una ad honorandum doctorem qui fit hoc mane, et similiter tibicines. Et actento quod quamplurimi tubicines non serviunt palatio debitis temporibus prout solitum est, deliberaverunt precipi dictis tubicinibus haud servientibus, quod infra triduum debeant allegasse causam et quo iure non inserviant, alias cum non sit hec causa, nunc pro tunc et e converso intelligantur privi de ipsorum salario tam preterito quam futuro tempore non servito.

TABLE 11.1. Chronological list of fifteenth-century pifferi

	1408	1409	1410	1411–12	1413	1414	1415	1416	1417–19	1420	1421	1422–24	1425	1426–27
Filippo di Polo da Venezia	x													
Renaldo di Michele da Cesena	x					x	x							
Antonio di Giovanni da Bologna[a]			x											
Corrado da Alamania		x	x											
Angelo d'Arrigo, detto Imperadore★		x	x											
Gherardo		x	x											
Niccolò di Niccolò da Strasburgo			x	x	x	x								
Giovanni di Antonio da Bologna			x											
Niccolò di Giorgio da Zara				x	x	x	x	x	x	x	x	x	x	x
Jacopo di Antonio da Bologna[b]					x	x	x	x	x	x				
Angelino							x	x						
Michele di Giovanni da Alamania								x	x					
Tommaso di Biagio da Ungaria										x	x			
Niccolò d'Andrea da Bologna											x	x	x	x
Francesco di Piero da Bologna											x	x	x	x
Dadio di Bartolomeo													x	

TABLE 11.1 continued

	1428	1429–30	1431–44	1445	1446	1447	1448	1449	1450	1451	1452	1453–54	1455–56	1457
Renaldo di Michele da Cesena		x		x	x									
Niccolò di Giorgio da Zara	x		x	x										
Niccolò d'Andrea da Bologna	x	x	x	x	x	x								
Maestro Bartolomeo di Piero						x								
Bochini da Bologna		x	x	x	x	x								
Maestro Garino of Avignon					x	x								
Germano da Francia					x	x	x	x						
Ferrino di Lanberto da Francia[c]					x	x	x	x	x	x	x	x	x	x
Maestro Giovanni da Alamania, trombone					x	x	x	x	x	x	x	x	x	
Lorenzo di Giovanni da Francia						x	x							
Guglielmo							x	x	x	x				
Giovanni di Giovanni da Francia								x						
Gualfredo								x						
Matteo									x					
Arrigo di Giovanni da Venezia										x	x	x	x	x
Agostino di Piero da Albania, trombone										x	x			
Giovanni di Piero da Colonia											x	x	x	x
Federigo di Lanberto Francioso[d]											x			
Stefano di Piero Rusignuoli da Francia (Savoia)													x	x
Arrigo di Giovanni da Francoforte, trombone													x	

	1458	1459	1460	1461	1462	1463	1464	1465	1466–67	1468	1469	1470–71	1472–76	1477
Ferrino di Lanberto	x	x	x	x	x	x	x	x	x	x	x	x		
Stefano di Piero Rusignuoli da Francia (Savoia)	x	x		x										
Arrigo di Giovanni da Francoforte, trombone		x	x											
Tommaso di Pietro Francisena	x	x												
Martino di Corrado Teutonico, trombone	x	x	x											
Federico, trombone			x											
Niccolò di Giorgio da Venezia, trombone			x			x								
Antonio di Gregorio da Venezia			x	x	x	x	x	x	x	x	x	x	x	x
Maestro Giovanni di Giovanni da Alamania						x	x	x						
Giovanni di Giovanni da Alamania, trombone						x								
Andrea, trombone						x								
Santi di Pavolo da Volterra*						x	x	x	x					
Giovanni di Fruosino Mangoni da Siena								x	x	x	x	x	x	x
Petro Tristano da Valenza, trombone										x	x			
Bartolomeo di Monaldo,* trombone											x	x	x	x
Maestro Cristoforo di Brandino Lombardo													x	x
Giovanni di Monaldo^e													x	x

Table 11.1 continued

	1478–86	1487	1488	1489	1490	1491	1492	1493	1494	1495	1496	1497–99
Antonio di Gregorio da Venezia	x	x	x	x	x	x	x	x	x			
Giovanni di Fruosino Mangoni	x	x	x	x	x	x	x	x	x	x	x	
Bartolomeo di Monaldo	x											
Maestro Cristoforo di Brandino	x	x	x	x	x	x	x	x	x	x		
Geronimo di Giovanni[f]		x	x	x	x	x	x	x	x	x	x	x
Jacopo di Salvatore		x	x	x	x	x	x	x	x	x	x	x
Domenico di Cristoforo[g]			x	x	x	x	x	x	x	x	x	x
Mariano di Galgano			x									
Andrea di Giovanni					x							
Giovanni di Maestro Antonio[h]											x	x
Pavolo di Giovanni Mangoni[i]												x

*also a trumpeter

[a] son of the trumpeter Giovanni di Antonio da Bologna

[b] perhaps a brother of the trumpeter Giovanni di Antonio

[c] probably a brother of Federigo di Lanberto

[d] probably a brother of Ferrino di Lanberto

[e] brother of Bartolomeo di Monaldo

[f] formerly a trumpeter, son of the trumpeter Giovanni da Iesi

[g] son of Maestro Cristoforo di Brandino

[h] son of Antonio di Gregorio

[i] son of Giovanni di Fruosino

Chapter Twelve

TRIUMPH OF THE WIND BAND
IN THE SIXTEENTH CENTURY

B Y THE TURN OF THE SIXTEENTH CENTURY the wind band had become distinctly Sienese, staffed with native-born musicians trained in the city and for the most part already familiar with the ensemble's traditions and repertories. Similar developments occurred within the cathedral chapel, where, as mentioned earlier, several adult singers trained in the cathedral school were now employed. For some time to come, however, the cathedral chapel continued to employ foreign singers and composers, whereas the wind band would now rely exclusively on local instrumentalists. The new turn of events was exemplified by Valerio di Bartolomeo, son of the drummer Meo di Maestro Mino, who replaced Jacopo di Salvatore as fourth piffero in 1500. As a result of Valerio's appointment the wind band for the first time comprised exclusively children of former Palace employees. Although this was not always the case throughout the rest of the century, ties of kinship now became as important a factor in the group's formation as they had long been among the trumpeters. Clearly, policies that the government had pursued since the 1460s and 1470s—when it began requiring newly appointed foreigners such as Antonio di Gregorio da Venezia and Cristoforo Lombardo to bring their families with them—had borne fruit.

Ties of kinship and familial modes of instruction, however, were not the only reasons why the Palace could now be assured of a pool of qualified musicians. Other factors, economic and social, were also at play, and these combined to produce a kind of classic supply-and-demand situation in which professionally trained musicians found a ready outlet for their talents. Among these factors were an increasingly refined and sophisticated public that required music more than ever as it enacted its religious, civic, and social rituals; an ever more enlightened society that viewed musical ability as a worthy accomplishment; and, as a corollary, a sizeable segment of the population with the means to acquire a musical education. Musical instruction for amateurs, hitherto the preserve of a favored few, became more readily available with the emergence of public and private schools that sprang up to meet the demand. All of these factors spawned a pool of highly qualified musicians who could meet the needs of an increasingly informed musical public as well as of the city's musical institutions.

The cathedral school, up to this time the preserve of musicians in training for the priesthood, now opened its doors to others with non-clerical ambitions. It would soon count some of the city's leading wind players and composers among its graduates. Perhaps inspired by the example of the cathedral school, the state itself, as later records indicate, stepped in by encouraging, if not actually subsidizing, a school within the Palace for students who wished to learn wind instruments, just as it had done for trumpeters. Both the city's principal musical institutions thus pursued policies that not only ensured them qualified personnel but also benefited society at large. In some cases musicians were trained in both cathedral and Palace schools, or at the cathedral and in familial situations. Availability of musical instruction ensured that by the first quarter of the sixteenth century Siena became a self-sustaining musical economy that could boast a corps of professional musicians and composers capable of meeting the official needs of its various institutions and the social needs of its citizenry.

THE WIND BAND IN THE FIRST HALF
OF THE SIXTEENTH CENTURY

The early years of the sixteenth century provide a glimpse of conditions that were to characterize the wind band in the ensuing decades. The four pifferi, Domenico di Maestro Cristoforo, Pavolo di Giovanni, Giovanni di Maestro Antonio, Valerio di Bartolomeo, and the trombonist, Geronimo di Giovanni, named in the clothing list for Assumption Day 1500, are also mentioned in similar lists from 1501 through 1510. All, as mentioned, were native Sienese, and this employment pattern would now continue for the rest of the century, as one generation after another of native-born, Sienese-trained musicians entered Palace service. Domenico di Cristoforo died or left after 1510, when his brother, Niccolò, took over his post. Niccolò, one of the earliest known Sienese composers, served with the musicians just cited from 1512 through 1520 and then for many years afterwards.

In 1521 Geronimo passed on the trombonist's post to his son Ansano Maria, previously a trumpeter in Palace service. During this period Giovanni di Maestro Antonio, as will be illustrated more fully below, began pursuing a career as an organ builder, both in Siena and Cortona. Though he must have been absent a good deal of the time, his name continues to appear on Assumption Day lists, showing that he retained his tenured post while providing a suitable substitute during his absences. He must have done this previously, of course, during the fourteen months in 1509–10 he served as cathedral chapelmaster. The only other personnel change in the wind band during the 1520s, in fact, occurred in 1526, when Giovanni was officially replaced by his pupil Galgano (Gano) d'Enea, the onetime cathedral musician and son of a former Palace trumpeter. The other pifferi, Pavolo di Giovanni, Valerio di Bartolomeo, Niccolò di Cristoforo, and the trombonist, Ansano Maria di Giovanni, appear with Gano in Assumption Day clothing lists from 1526 through 1530. A remarkably stable ensemble, characterized by the continuing presence of pifferi related to former Palace employees, was thus in place during the first thirty years of the sixteenth century. Galgano d'Enea, who was to remain a member of the Palace wind band until 1546, evidently married a woman of some means, as evidenced by the tax declaration filed by his daughter in 1548 (Doc. 9.9). His name appears in the Concistoro's deliberations on only two occasions, first on 5 January 1541, when he was sent to jail because he had borne arms and gone to the home of a private citizen rather than to the Palace during a recent disturbance within the city, and two days later, when the order was given for his release.

The next two decades also witnessed few changes. Benedetto di Domenico replaced Ansano Maria as trombonist in 1532. He appears with the four pifferi just mentioned in clothing lists from August 1535 and August 1536. New clothing was approved for six members of the wind band on Assumption Day in 1543. Though no names are mentioned in the record, subsequent ones indicate that the additional musician was the previous trombonist Ansano Maria di Geronimo, who, in fact, appears with the other five musicians on a list from August 1544. Ansano, as noted in chapter 7, had been performing in the cathedral chapel, where he was employed from November 1543 to January 1546. He doubtless came back to the wind band as a tenured member because in February 1546 the priors, exasperated by his habitual and unexplained absences, replaced him with another trombonist named Tulio. Tulio, as later documents indicate, was untenured at this time, even though he received a clothing allowance. Instead, he apparently had the status of official supernumerary.

The musicians named in the clothing lists, as we know, were generally those who held lifetime posts with guaranteed monthly salaries, at the pleasure of the government. They enjoyed the usual rights and privileges granted Palace employees, the most notable of which were daily meal allowances, a share of tips received from visitors and government guests, and, according to later documents, a share of the group's earnings for work outside the Palace. But there were other musicians who also performed in the wind band on a regular basis. Even though they had neither permanent positions nor any of the accompanying privileges, people in this second group were officially designated as supernumeraries and received appropriate compensation for their services. A third group of performers included still others who occasionally substituted for both tenured musicians and supernumeraries. Though mentioned from time to time, these last are difficult to trace both because of the sporadic nature of their work and because they were, as a rule, paid by the people for whom they substituted. One such musician was Andrea di Giovanni da Siena, a piffero who addressed a petition to the Concistoro on or before 24 October 1524, when it was reported that his request had been approved. Nothing more is said in the report, and since the text of the original petition is lost, the privileges Andrea asked for remain unknown. Given the absence of his name in any other records, he was surely one of the many younger musicians who sought experience and future employment by substituting for tenured and salaried members of the band.

Experienced (and well-connected) musicians were compensated in a more concrete manner, and as supernumeraries they could receive either salary or meal allowances. Some had both, remaining untenured all the while, even though they generally performed at the same times and places as the permanent members. Considerably more information is available about sixteenth-century supernumeraries, perhaps because by then many more qualified people sought to gain experience at the Palace as they augmented their income from other sources. Notable among them was Bernardino di Matteo Cartolaio, also one of the mainstays of the cathedral chapel for many years. A report from the end of October 1524 says that the priors were desirous of having good and perfect musicians assisting in the band and that Bernardino "was assiduous in playing both within and outside the Palace." Although the possibility of granting him a tenured post was not even contemplated, the priors did approve a monthly provision of L. 8 for him, stipulating "that he is obliged to perform just as the other Palace musicians do."

Provisions such as Bernardino's are reflected in the fluctuating amounts paid out each month to Palace employees. Thus, though the wind band officially counted five members—four pifferi and a trombonist—in its ranks until the late 1530s, payroll records—those from 1537, for example—point to six and sometimes seven musicians in any given month. Perhaps by then the number of permanent posts was raised to six. The practice of granting meal privileges at the Palace as a means of compensating supernumeraries was also in effect throughout the following decades, as a record from the end of June 1545 illustrates. This reports that the priors reaffirmed expenditures approved by their predecessors on behalf of Ansano Maria's son, Pamfilo called Tromboncino, and decreed that in the future he was to take his meals in the employees' dining room, as he had in the past.

The increasingly important role of supernumeraries is shown by a deliberation from October 1538. This notes that the piffero Virginio di Pavolo often substituted for the regular Palace supernumeraries, Antonio di Cristoforo, Bernardino di Matteo Cartolaio, and Luzio, Virginio's brother.[1] So that the Palace would be well served and Virginio treated fairly, the Concistoro declared that every time one of the supernumeraries failed to play as required and Virginio performed in his stead, he would receive one carlino, that is, s. 12. 6, for each service, to be deducted from the salary of the absentee (see Doc. 12.1). Virginio, it should be noted, was promised a tenured post some thirteen years earlier, in August 1525, when the Concistoro decreed that his expectative would become effective at the time of his father's death (see Doc. 12.2). There is no further mention of Virginio until 5 February 1535, when it was reported that a cornett was taken away from him.[2]

As has been noted in connection with the trumpeters, absenteeism on the part of Palace musicians was a constant source of irritation for Palace officials, who sought to limit it by imposing fines and restrictions. Notwithstanding such measures, it continued to be a problem. On 4 August 1536 the Concistoro, acknowledging the failure of previous admonitions to pifferi because of absences at the appointed times, decided that in the future anyone who failed to fulfill his obligations would lose his post and his salary would be withheld (see Doc. 11.18). Less than two years later, in July 1538, the group was cited for dereliction of duty a second time. On this occasion, after noting that the musicians were particularly lax about playing during the dinner and supper hours, the Concistoro decreed that henceforth all of them were to be present at all required times or were to provide a substitute, and unless absent for a just cause and with the priors' permission they would be dismissed (see Doc. 12.3).[3] The trombonist

---

1. Both were sons of the piffero Pavolo di Giovanni.

2. "fuit Virginio Pauli piffari subtracta una cornetta" (Concistoro, vol. 1010, fol. 31ʳ).

3. As noted in chapter 10, there were two places, one outside, the other within the Palace, neither existing today, that were called *ringhiera*. These were balconies capable of accommodating a number of people, and were apparently constructed principally for use by the musicians. The indoor *ringhiera*, accessible by a now demolished spiral staircase adjacent to the fresco of Sant'Ansano, overlooked the Sala del Capitano. It was presumably from this place that the pifferi played on formal occasions and perhaps also when the priors dined in state with other members of the government. But one document from later in the century specifically mentions the priors' dining room (see Doc. 12.10) and another slightly later one (Doc. 12.34) clearly states that the musicians played when the lords were at table and distinguishes that duty from their playing in the *ringhiera*, which may thus be a reference to the outside balcony.

Benedetto was singled out especially, perhaps because he more than any of the others had failed to send substitutes in his place. Despite admonitions such as these and the regularization of supernumeraries, problems of absenteeism continued to plague Palace officials, however vigilant they might be.

The growth of the Palace wind ensemble, first with the addition of a sixth player, and later a seventh, probably occurred in response to changing performance requirements of the group's repertory. Additional players not only increased the sonority of the group; they also allowed for the performance of works with a greater number of parts. By the early sixteenth century adaptations of vocal music with as many as six instrumentalists were no longer exceptional and, in fact, such adaptations often formed a significant part of the repertories of leading instrumental ensembles in other cities. Information furnished by the Venetian trombonist Giovanni Alvise to the duke of Mantua in two letters of 1495 and 1505 is highly relevant. In the earlier letter Alvise wrote of sending the duke two new instrumental arrangements, the one a four-voice motet by Obrecht scored to accommodate the six members of the Venetian wind band by the addition of two bass parts for trombones; the other a four-voice motet by Busnois with an additional fifth, contratenor, part. In the latter letter Alvise spoke of arranging motets and other pieces in various combinations for ensembles of four trombones and two cornetts, of eight flutes, and of five trombones.[4] Though no Sienese records address similar matters, presumably the Palace wind band kept abreast of performance practices elsewhere, as it had in the past, and its repertories approximated those of similar organizations in other major musical centers.

Besides the traditional groupings of shawms, bombards, and trombones, used particularly for performing dance music, wind bands after the turn of the sixteenth century also used instruments such as the recorder, the transverse flute, the curtal, the crumhorn, and the cornett.[5] Mastery of one or more of these instruments was part and parcel of a professional wind player's bag of tricks, and it seems likely that many musicians had instruments of their own. Exactly when such instruments began to be used in the Sienese ensemble and who played them is difficult to ascertain, principally because official records continue to refer to the players as pifferi (and later as musici), without specifying which instruments they played. The situation is further clouded by extant inventories of Palace holdings, which as a rule do not normally cite all its instruments. No more striking example of this exists than the just-mentioned record from 1535 regarding the cornett that had been taken from Virginio. Inventories from that time do not mention it. Nor does a Palace inventory from January 1547, which also fails to list a chest of curtals and a chest of recorders, or "flauti all'italiana," described in later documents.[6] An inventory from September 1558 does report the loan of a chest of

4. See Kämper, *La musica strumentale nel Rinascimento*, 66–67, for texts of the documents. The text of the 1505 document is more correctly given by Prizer, "Bernardino Piffaro e i pifferi e tromboni di Mantova," 161.

5. In this respect, see Kämper, *La musica strumentale nel Rinascimento*, 204ff.

6. Concistoro, vol. 2516, *Proventi, spese, tratte e inventari, 1545–61*, fol. LIᵛ, inventory for January–February 1547.

recorders to Niccolò piffero, but says nothing about when he and his colleagues began performing on them.[7]

Because Virginio did not live to claim his expectative, his brother Luzio succeeded to Pavolo's post. A lengthy report from 14 April 1545 tells how Luzio, son of the deceased Pavolo, petitioned the Concistoro, explaining that for many years he substituted for his ailing father, who subsequently renounced his position in favor of his son (see Doc. 12.4). Luzio also reported that previous priors had agreed to the change and appointed him to the post with the same salary as his father. In view of Pavolo's death within the past month and the loss of a notarial record of earlier government approval, Luzio now requested a reconfirmation of his own appointment as well as approval of the eventual transfer of his monthly provision of L. 10 to his natural son, Adriano Imperiale. The transfer had also been sanctioned by an earlier concistorial decree of 31 August 1541. The priors' decision was again favorable and Luzio's appointment as piffero, with the same salary, honors, and privileges his father had enjoyed, was reconfirmed, as was Adriano's expectative and monthly provision of L. 10.[8]

Luzio's was the first of a series of appointments signifying a renewal of the wind band. Another more significant action was taken at the end of July 1546, when the priors awarded the L. 4 they had previously added to the trombonist Pamfilo's salary to that of a young supernumerary called Simone piffero. This was Simone di Domenico Nodi, subsequently leader of the ensemble and a renowned teacher. A decree from a few months later gives a hint of his precocious talent. Dated 17 December 1546, it remarks that Simone previously substituted for the ailing Galgano (Gano) d'Enea, and that since Galgano had died, Simone should now succeed to his post among the pifferi (see Doc. 12.5).[9] The priors also decreed that Simone's previous monthly provision of L. 10 was to be divided among several younger players, "well instructed in the art of music," who would function as supernumeraries. They were Ascanio d'Andrea di Lazaro, L. 5 per month; Agostino and Partenio, two sons of the trombonist Benedetto, sharing L. 3; and the trumpeter Giovanbattista Volpini, L. 2.[10] None of these new players was among the seven who received clothing for Assumption Day in 1548 and in 1549. Named in those years were the four pifferi, Niccolò di Cristoforo, his brother Antonio di Cristoforo, Valerio di Bartolomeo, Simone Nodi, and three trombonists, Benedetto, Tulio, and Giovanfrancesco di Benedetto. The makeup of the band is a sure sign that the Sienese ensemble was performing according to the most advanced practices of the time.

---

7. Ibid., unnumbered folio, for inventory of September–October 1558.

8. The petition, in Luzio's hand, has also survived and is found on an unnumbered folio in Concistoro 2232, *Scritture Concistoriali, 1545,* lettere senza data. Luzio appears on the clothing list for Assumption Day 1545 together with Niccolò, Valerio, Galgano, and the trombonists Benedetto and Ansano Maria (Biccherna, 365, fol. 27ʳ⁻ᵛ).

9. Galgano (Gano) died sometime before 18 October 1546, when an extraordinary payment of L. 21 was issued to him (Concistoro, vol. 1080, fol. 33ʳ).

10. Previously, Benedetto had secured a place among the trumpeters for his sons, but Partenio later transferred his post to his brother-in-law Camillo di Marcantonio for a price. See chapter 10. Giovambattista de Vulganis (*recte* Vulpinis) is the name of a trumpeter who must be the brother or father of Giulio di Giovambattista called Volpino, also a trumpeter.

Antonio's and Tulio's presence on the lists suggests they were holding tenured positions, though, in fact, they were only supernumeraries whom the Concistoro favored with gifts of clothing. How exceptional Tulio's case was is revealed by a report from July 1548, which recounts how the priors went to extraordinary lengths to keep him in the group. These were prompted by the Balìa, who removed Tulio from the payroll, presumably because funds for his post had never been officially allocated. After noting that Tulio had proved himself to be "so useful to music at the Palace," the priors moved to request reconsideration of the Balìa's decree and promised that they would find a way to keep him in their service without increasing expenses. How they proposed to do this is not explained, but a way must have been found, since Tulio's name, as mentioned, appears in clothing lists from that year and the following one. Funds for Antonio di Cristoforo's position were apparently not in question at the time, though he would later be denied a tenured position.

Ascanio d'Andrea gained a permanent post with the group at the end of December 1551, when he was appointed to replace the aged Valerio di Bartolomeo, who died that day. Ascanio, whose surname Marri is not given in this and in most other Palace documents of the time, became known throughout Italy as a composer of madrigals and as leader of the Sienese wind band. Later, as we have learned, he also became *maestro di cappella* at the cathedral. Adriano (Imperiale di Luzio), whose right to succeed his father had been approved in 1545, gained his long-awaited reward on 6 June 1554. A decree from that day refers to the report of a commission appointed to judge the merits of his claim to the post and those of Maestro Antonio di Cristoforo. After noting that Adriano had had a salary and meal privileges for these many years and that he was, in fact, understood to be one of the Palace musicians, the Concistoro declared the number of musicians in the group now increased to seven and decreed that Adriano could "play and share in gifts from visitors, called gratuities and tips in the vulgar tongue, with one of seven shares, just like the others" (see Doc. 12.6).[11]

The decree shows the government's continuing concern that all tenured members of the group receive their fair share of the tips customarily received from visitors and guests. Another report from shortly after this time shows that ensuring fairness was not a short-term concern, even during the worst months of the siege of Siena. On 10 February 1555 Simone di Domenico Nodi was ordered to satisfy all debts owed to some of the other Palace pifferi and the nakers player, apparently because he had not given them their fair share of the group's unofficial income. Simone was dilatory in meeting his obligations and less than a month later the government decreed that the money owed to Maestro Antonio di Cristoforo (L. 19. 1), Ascanio d'Andrea (L. 56), Adriano (Mangoni) (L. 13. 9), and to the nakers player Bernardino di Valerio (L. 13. 6. 6) was to be garnisheed from Simone's salary. The sums involved point to more than one occasion and suggest that the issue here was actually a fair division of fees for playing outside the Palace rather than gratuities. Moreover, individual musicians proba-

---

11. He is mistakenly called Adriano di Pavolo in the 1554 document, when in fact Pavolo was his grandfather. In his father's petition of 1546, he was called Adriano Imperiale, son of Luzio di Pavolo, but later documents give the surname as Mangoni.

bly contracted for the band's services at non-official functions and occasionally behaved less than honorably in their dealings with their colleagues.

Various records indicate that the wind band, like the trumpeters' corps and the cathedral chapel, flourished in the years immediately preceding the fall of the Republic. Personnel problems, as usual, continued to preoccupy the priors, as did a concern for the well-being of trusted employees. One case concerned Agostino, son of the trombonist Benedetto di Domenico, who had previously been appointed to a trumpeter's post thanks to his father's influence. In what must have been unusual circumstances, the father went before the Concistoro on 4 June 1554, apparently to complain about the son, and the priors accordingly ordered Agostino to appear before them within five days to explain why he should not be deprived of his post. Another deliberation from the 30th of the same month reports that the priors, having considered Agostino's culpability as well as the qualifications and good habits of Benedetto's son-in-law, Maestro Vincenzo di Giovanbattista, granted whatever it was that Benedetto had requested. Benedetto, it will be recalled, had earlier petitioned the Concistoro to allow another of his sons-in-law, Camillo di Marcantonio, to accept a post among the trumpeters that was originally assigned to Agostino.[12]

Benedetto was the progenitor of a large musical family, as these and other records indicate. He was also a man of many parts. In an earlier petition addressed to the Concistoro, from 14 April 1545, he requested an exclusive privilege to print broadsides and school texts at a predetermined price for a period of time to be set by the government (see Doc. 12.7). In granting him the privilege the priors also decreed that it could be withdrawn by their successors if Benedetto failed to observe the terms of his proposal.

Two Notable Pifferi

Like their predecessors among fifteenth-century trumpeters, several sixteenth-century pifferi also enjoyed long periods of tenure at the Palace. The longest-serving was Maestro Niccolò, one of three sons of the piffero Cristoforo Brandini. Born in Siena, he was baptized on 15 June 1480.[13] His younger brother Domenico was a member of the wind band for a number of years before him, and another of his brothers, Antonio, also played at the Palace before he left to pursue a career as a freelance musician. There is no record of Niccolò's serving as a supernumerary before his appointment in 1510, though very likely he did. Subsequently he remained in the wind band until January 1565. Among Palace musicians his longevity of service was rivaled only by that of another Niccolò, the blind fifteenth-century trumpeter. Longevity aside, few among his colleagues had as distinguished a career as his. Niccolò is frequently called *maestro* in documents. Although no record of his appointment to the post survives, the title,

---

12. See Doc. 10.8.

13. "Nicholò di Christofano di [blank] piffaro, si battezò addì XV di giugno [1480]" (ASS, Biccherna, 1133, fol. 468ʳ). He was five years older than his brother Domenico, whose birth is also recorded: "Domenico Antonio di Christofano si battezò adì 18 di gennaio 1484 [1485]" (ibid., fol. 506ᵛ).

his many accomplishments, and the favored treatment he received from the Concistoro all point to his having, in fact, led the wind band for many years.

Niccolò was a major contributor to Pietro Sambonetto's 1515 collection of frottolas, his eight pieces outnumbered only by Ansano's twelve.[14] His music, like Ansano's, traveled far beyond Siena's walls to Rome and to Venice, where copies of Sambonetto's publication were purchased on two separate occasions by the great bibliophile Ferdinand Columbus, son of the famed explorer.[15] Sambonetto's volume perhaps also helped to broaden Niccolò's reputation in Siena and to alert potential patrons to his gifts as a composer. But this seems not to have happened. Indeed, the central problem surrounding Niccolò's career as a frottolist is the seeming lack of music from later in his life. As a young composer working within the genre, he was well positioned to profit from the new aesthetics regarding text setting emanating from Florence and Rome that led to the creation of the madrigal. Moreover, he lived long enough to witness the establishment and development of the new genre as it took hold throughout Italy, even in Siena, where his younger colleague Ascanio Marri composed madrigals during his lifetime. But the lack of any documentation whatsoever makes it impossible to know whether Niccolò contributed to the early repertory of the madrigal with either published or unpublished works.

Luigia Cellesi, who first pointed out that the Palace musician and composer were one and the same person, rightly argued that nothing opposed the identification—no other Niccolò piffero was active in Siena at the time—and supported her argument by demonstrating that this Niccolò di Cristoforo was so highly esteemed by the government, presumably because of his abilities as a composer as well as a performer, that the priors relaxed the rules quite a bit for him.[16] The example she cited bears repeating here. The town's statutes required Palace musicians to wear their uniforms at all times, their old ones on ordinary days, their new ones whenever they accompanied the priors on official rounds outside the Palace. Fines and punishment were meted out to those who disobeyed the order. But a decree of 18 August 1522 exempted Niccolò from wearing any uniform at all "except when the Magnificent Lords left the Palace" in state

---

14. The music of both men is discussed in chapter 14. Both composers' works and Sambonetto's volume are discussed in my "Instrumental Resonances in a Sienese Vocal Print of 1515," in *Le Concert des voix et des instruments à la Renaissance: Actes du XXXIVe Colloque International d'Études Supérieures de la Renaissance, 1–11 juillet 1991,* ed. Jean-Michel Vaccaro (Paris, 1995), 333–59. Works by Niccolò published there include three frottolas, *Due virtù el mio cor nutrica, Se 'l t'è grato,* and *Lo splendente tuo bel viso;* a strambotto, *Se la serena;* and a capitolo, *Adio, riman, resta.*

15. Catherine Weeks Chapman, "Printed Collections of Polyphonic Music Owned by Ferdinand Columbus," *JAMS* 21 (1968): 40, 42, 44; the entries indicate that Columbus bought two copies of Sambonetto's print, one in Rome in the early 1520s and another in Venice in 1529, the latter a replacement for the first, apparently lost at sea. Columbus's catalogue contains records of three music books printed in Siena in the early decades of the fifteenth century, now lost, and another volume with a polyphonic Mass by Heinrich Isaac, this, too, no longer extant (44, 50, 72–73).

16. Cellesi, "Il lirismo musicale religioso," 93–112. She notes that Niccolò was employed at the Palace from 1512 to 1532, though in point of fact he served well beyond that time. Cellesi also published a modern edition of Niccolò's barzaletta *Due virtù el mio cor nutrica* in the same study.

with all of their retainers.[17] Surely, at a time when position and social status were largely determined by what a man wore, the government could bestow few higher accolades upon its favored servants.

Another sign of the government's esteem comes from much later in Niccolò's career. This was registered after the siege, on 6 October 1555, when the city was occupied by foreign troops. At the time the priors sought to ensure the seventy-five-year-old Niccolò's well-being and safety by releasing him from his evening duties at the Palace. They did this because they were aware that Niccolò piffero, who "because of his great age sees little light when he plays and especially at night," was accustomed to going home after fulfilling his evening duties "at the third or fourth hour of the night." They knew that he did so "at some peril because of the guards who patrol the city." Having concluded that "the Palace will not suffer should he not come," the priors decided, in view of "the authority they have" and of his long and faithful service, to excuse Niccolò if he did not appear at certain times. They also decided that on such occasions Savino, the son of Cecco Bello, "may play in Niccolò's place," with the understanding, however, that he would receive no salary for doing so.

Niccolò di Maestro Cristoforo, "piffero senese," as he styled himself, made his last will and testament on 13 September 1561, adding a codicil to it on 12 June 1566.[18] In it he asked to be buried in the tomb of his ancestors in the church of San Pietro ad Ovile. He left all of his estate to his brother Antonio, with whom he owned a house and vineyard.[19] Antonio, who had once served among the Palace pifferi, stipulated that he was to be buried in the same place when he filed his last will and testament on 31 March 1571.[20] Apparently, neither of the brothers had any surviving issue, since Antonio's heir was Caterina di Paolo Paolini, widow of Girolamo Chiavarini.

A near contemporary of Niccolò's was Giovanni, son of the Venetian piffero Maestro Antonio di Gregorio. Giovanni, baptized in Siena on 12 May 1481, joined the wind band at the age of fifteen, in 1496, some fifteen years before Niccolò.[21] His appointment, a recognition, no doubt, of his talent and precocity, was nonetheless a calculated move on the Concistoro's part to reward his father, a long-time employee, who indeed had continued in his post for several years after an unfavorable review of his playing until such time as his son was able to succeed him. Giovanni, too, had a long career at the Palace and was, as mentioned, officially associated with the wind band until 1526, even though he did not serve for many months at a time during that period. He was one of the most versatile Sienese musicians of his day. He also has the distinction

---

17. Ibid., 108, citing Concistoro, vol. 953, fols. 11–12.

18. ASS, Notarile antecosimiano 1793, no. 4176.

19. These were possessions apparently inherited from their father, which, as mentioned in chapter 11, they reported in 1509. ASS, Lira, vol. 234, Denunzie, Terzo di Città, unnumbered folio.

20. ASS, Notarile antecosimiano 1794, no. 5297. Maestro Antonio di Maestro Cristofano piffaro made a second will on 20 March 1572. Notarile antecosimiano, N. 1257.

21. The birth date has been published by Renzo Giorgetti, "Nota biografica su Giovanni Piffero e documenti inediti," in P. P. Donati et al., *L'organo di Giovanni Piffero, 1519, del Palazzo Pubblico di Siena* (Siena, 1983), 22. As noted in chapter 11 above, a tax report from 1509 shows that Antonio inherited his father's house in the parish of San Salvatore (ASS, Lira, vol. 234, Terzo di Città, unnumbered folio).

of being the first instrumentalist to hold the post of *maestro di cappella* at the cathedral, serving in that capacity, as noted above, for fourteen months, through June 1510. Perhaps his tenure was as brief as it was because he decided to realize his long-standing desire to pursue a career as a professional organ builder. A cathedral payment shows he had already begun to work in the field as early as 1506.[22] Five years later, in 1511, he furnished lead for an organ that was built at the Sienese church of the Carmine by Michele di Ser Giuliano Turri, the onetime cathedral music copyist, and the cathedral organist Francesco di Guido called Petruccio.[23]

Illustration of how Giovanni went about acquiring the skills necessary to pursue his chosen profession comes from 1512, when he petitioned the Concistoro for permission to study the art of organ building under Maestro Domenico di Lucca. Domenico had recently completed his work on the new organ placed above the door of the cathedral's sacristy and Giovanni likely got to know him at that time. He may have even begun his apprenticeship with Domenico by then. Giovanni's request stressed that it would be both "good and convenient for the Republic to have qualified masters in the city who knew how to construct organs."[24] While the Concistoro approved his request to study both in Siena and abroad, it is likely that Giovanni received the bulk of his training from Domenico in Siena, where Domenico was active for a number of years, perhaps as late as 1521.[25] Giovanni's first major project of record was the organ he built for the chapel at the hospital of Santa Maria della Scala, an instrument finished in 1519 after several delays.[26] In 1517 he began constructing another organ at the cathedral of Cortona, and again this project required a number of years before it was brought to completion.[27] Several later records tell how he bid for the commission to build a new instrument to replace the older one in the Concistoro's private chapel in the Palace. In one of these he recalled having gone to Lucca to study so that he might bring the art of organ building to Siena. His bid was successful and the priors commissioned the organ from him in 1519.[28] It was not finished until 1525, when Giovanni received a final

---

22. A record indicating that he furnished lead to the Cathedral in 1506 is cited by Giorgetti, ibid., 24 (AOMS, vol. 719, *D&C*, fol. 45ʳ).

23. The document, dated 15 June 1511, with an addendum from 15 January 1513, records the settlement of a dispute that arose between the church of the Carmine and the heirs of the organ builders, who had not finished their work. It has been published by Milanesi, *Documenti per la storia dell'arte senese*, 3:51–52. Michele Turri is identified as monk of Vallombrosa here.

24. ASS, Concistoro, vol. 2195, *Scritture concistoriali, 1512–18,* packet dated 1512. The document has been published by Borghesi and Banchi, *Nuovi documenti per la storia dell'arte senese*, no. 204, 404, and is quoted in part by Luigia Cellesi, "L'organo della cappella interna del palazzo comunale di Siena," *BSSP* 37 (1930): 500.

25. Giorgetti, "Nota biografica," 22.

26. The record of the commission, dating from 25 January 1513, has been published by Alessandro Liberati, "Nuovi documenti artistici dello Spedale di S. Maria della Scala in Siena," *BSSP* 33–34 (1926–27): 147–79. Work on this instrument proceeded slowly, however, for in 1517 Giovanni signed a new accord with the hospital promising to finish the work within eighteen months. The commission is discussed more fully below in chapter 13.

27. Giorgetti, "Nota biografica," 22, who also publishes the document in the appendix.

28. Concistoro, vol. 917, fol. 8ᵛ. The document has been published by Cellesi, "L'organo della cappella interna," 505; see p. 500 for a report concerning the older organ.

payment for his work.[29] Recently restored, the instrument has been cited as an outstanding example of Italian organ building techniques of the time.[30] Giovanni's last
documented work as an organ builder comes from 18 November 1522, when he contracted to build an instrument for the Sienese convent church of Sant'Agostino. As
before, he was unable to complete his work in the agreed-upon time and the convent
renewed his contract on 29 March 1526.[31]

Giovanni's activities as a teacher, though less well documented, were equally important. As cathedral *maestro di cappella* in 1509–10, he taught singing and the fundamentals of music to students in the school and to others who wished to learn. A petition
he addressed to the Concistoro in 1522 shows that he continued to teach even after
leaving the cathedral. There he described Galgano d'Enea, the Palace trumpeter's son,
as a pupil to whom he had taught "counterpoint and music and shawm and other
instruments as though he were my own son" (see Doc. 12.8).[32] Whether Galgano was
his only pupil, and whether Giovanni had a school at the Palace or a school of his own
elsewhere are moot points because the document just quoted is incompletely preserved.
In any case the events in Giovanni's varied career as a teacher, performer, and organ
builder all point to his being one of the outstanding Sienese musicians of his time.
Like Niccolò, he was a musician trained in familial circumstances whose talents and
perseverance enabled him to reach the pinnacle of the city's musical establishments and
whose influence on a younger generation of Sienese musicians, though probably more
far-reaching than a few extant documents suggest, can only be surmised.

THE WIND BAND AFTER THE FALL OF THE REPUBLIC

With the demise of the republic and the advent of Medici rule, the focus of power
shifted to Cosimo's governor, even though Siena retained its ancient governing institutions. The priors and other government officials, forced to come to terms with a depleted treasury and the changed circumstances under which they would henceforth live
and govern, gradually established policies approved by the Medici that enabled them to
preserve and maintain the Palace's musical establishment. The wind band, as noted
in connection with the trumpeters, was given priority. New directions in European
instrumental music favored the wind band's repertory and development, but neither
these nor the priors' support alone can account for the significant place the ensemble
came to occupy in Siena's musical life of the later sixteenth century. Also important
were the prestige and fame achieved by several talented Sienese musicians, performers
who were on a par with the best anywhere in Italy. Principal among them was Ascanio

---

29. Concistoro, vol. 927, fol. 3ʳ. The document has been published by Cellesi, ibid., 505, who
also gives other relevant documents.

30. For information on the original specifications of the instrument and its recent restoration, see
the report by P. P. Donati et al., *L'organo di Giovanni Piffero*.

31. Both contracts have been published by Borghesi and Bianchi, *Nuovi documenti,* no. 215,
426–32.

32. Cellesi, "L'organo interno," 500, cites the document. Judging from similar petitions filed by
other musicians, it would appear that Giovanni had come before the priors either to request them to
grant an expectative to Galgano or to request that Galgano be allowed to serve in his stead.

Marri, the first Sienese instrumentalist after Niccolò piffero to gain a reputation as a composer outside the city's walls. Other Sienese instrumentalists would be called to serve in Florence, Rome, and even beyond the Alps. These, however, were future developments. For the moment the problem was how to retain the integrity of the Palace's most important musical group and how best to finance it in the wake of military defeat and near economic collapse.

A report from the beginning of July 1556 reveals that the priors took a practical, if somewhat unsentimental, approach to the situation. After noting that the republic wished to retain as many as, but not more than, five pifferi in Palace service, they voted on "every one of the musicians who at present hold appointments and have their expenses" (dining privileges) in the Palace. They did so with the understanding that the five receiving the most votes could continue in Palace service "with the usual office, salary, and emoluments" (see Doc. 12.9). Although the number of musicians then serving is not mentioned, records already cited show that by this time at least seven held appointments of one kind or another. Clearly, the cost of supporting them, and a few others as well, placed a strain on available resources, and it was inevitable that their number be decreased. The five musicians chosen were three pifferi, Maestro Niccolò di Cristoforo, Simone di Domenico Nodi, and Adriano di Luzio Mangoni, and two trombonists, Ascanio di Andrea Marri and Giovanfrancesco di Benedetto.[33]

A new set of statutes regulating the composition and duties of the two musical ensembles employed at the Palace was drawn up shortly after this time.[34] The wind band, as the revised chapters put it, would now number five musicians who, with their "flutes, trombones, and cornetts," were to be "in constant readiness to play for the captain of the people and the lord priors" at all of the required times and occasions decided upon by those ruling bodies.[35] Lest any other branch of government seek to enlarge the group without official permission, the statutes also forbade the Biccherna's chamberlain to pay for the salaries of more than five musicians, otherwise he would do so at his own expense.[36]

---

33. A cathedral record from 12 December 1555 shows that Giovanfrancesco di Bernardo [sic], trombone in Palazzo Publico di Siena, his wife, Caterina, "figliuola e herede di Niccolò di Luca, oste a la Corona," and his mother-in-law Camilla, "moglie già del detto Niccolò di Luca," rented a shop and part of a house in Siena that belonged to the cathedral Opera. Present at the time the document was drawn up was Vincenzo di Giovambattista, described as a Palace musician and Catherine's nearest male relative, "musico in detto Palazzo, più proximo parente di quelle che si possano havere di detta Monna Caterina" (vol. 725, Giornale B, 1554–67, fols. 30ᵛ–31ʳ). Vincenzo, it will be recalled, was a son-in-law of the trombonist Benedetto di Domenico.

34. See above, Doc. 10.13. Cellesi, Storia della più antica banda musicale senese, 78, cites the same document from a Balìa source. Although it is undated, references to certain government offices make it clear that the document was drawn up after the reorganization of the government under Cosimo I.

35. Cornetts and flutes, as has been apparent, are rarely mentioned in official documents, which generally use only the words piffero and trombone to describe the instruments played by the members of the wind band. Cornetts and flutes are cited, however, in Palace inventories, and two deliberations from September 1564 regarding Simone's disregard of an order from the Captain of the people speak of Simone as a cornett player.

36. Concistoro, vol. 2357, fols. 26ᵛ–27ʳ.

This regulation later led to the practice of dividing up single posts and reallocating meal allowances, with the result that two people might share the salary and duties specified for one permanent position and others might be given meals only or might share a meal allowance in return for full- or part-time services. The number of officially approved meal allowances, expenses for which were sometimes described as being paid "from the priors' plate," that is, from funds allocated for the priors' commissary, subsequently increased, as the priors explored and devised yet other means for maintaining their favored musicians. Later in the century daily rations of bread and wine were also distributed both to tenured members and to supernumeraries and occasional employees.[37] Deaths and resignations of tenured personnel also affected tenured and untenured members' earnings. These were raised or lowered, as the priors, ever mindful of maintaining high artistic standards and the integrity of the Palace's group of musici, as the pifferi were now invariably called, sought to operate with legally approved revenues. In short, permutations, adjustments, and variations of salaries and meal privileges originally set for a limited number of permanent personnel—at first five, then six, and finally seven—were the expediencies that ultimately allowed Palace officials to maintain the wind band as a first-rate ensemble.

Several reports indicate that absenteeism continued to present problems for the priors even after Siena's fall and its incorporation into the Medici state. One, from as early as 13 January 1556, notes that the musicians were not meeting their obligations and says that if they were not in the dining room when the lords were washing their hands before going to table, they would forfeit as many meals as the number of those absent (see Doc. 12.10). As in the past, threat of punishment failed to curb excesses, and a few years later even more severe penalties were enacted. A decree from the end of March 1558 states that henceforth the members of the wind band would lose a third of their salary for failure to appear at one of the required times, their entire salary for not appearing twice, and their dining privileges for failure to appear three times. Penalties meted out would hold for the entire term of office of the priors who pronounced the sentence. The new ruling, which, as mentioned, applied also to the trumpeters, was directed toward the permanent members of the group.[38] They included Simone Nodi, Adriano di Luzio Mangoni, Ascanio Marri, Giovanfrancesco trombone, and Niccolò piffero, the band's oldest member, who was made record keeper.

---

37. "Et deliberorno . . . darsi alli musici del Palazo, oltre alla colatione solita darseli, pani due per mattina, per esser loro maggior numero che non erano prima . . . cioè panni quattro in tutto per mattina" (Concistoro, vol. 1198, fol. 26ʳ, dated 21 October 1567). Another document from 28 June 1588 speaks of increasing one of the musician's bread allotment from two and a half loaves to three: "Custodibus Illustrissimi domini Capitanei populi pro tempore futuris, et Iohanni Baptistae de Chochiis musico eorum Palatii, pertinentibus concesserunt per lupinos 11 albos, medietatem panis pro quolibet, ultra panes duos cum dimidio, et sic in totum panes tres pro quolibet, quolibet die" (Concistoro, 1300, unnumbered folio dated 28 June 1588). The amount of bread and wine given them, however, depended on the times and the person involved. When Ottavio di Lorenzo was appointed a supernumerary on 12 November 1585 he received "due pani grandi et una mezzetta di vino" (Concistoro, 1297, fol. 102ᵛ).

38. See above, Doc. 10.14. This identifies "Maestro Niccolò piffaro" as the son of "Maestro Cristofano piffaro" and says Niccolò was the oldest member of the wind band, "più antico de' musici."

Whether the new ruling was more effective than previous ones is difficult to gauge. A report from 21 November 1559 tells how the priors, aware that Adriano "had failed to join the other musicians in playing the usual music in their chapel at the Elevation of the Eucharist," authorized the captain of the people to ascertain the reason why, and to punish the musician, if he was not legitimately excused. He apparently was, for nothing further is heard of the matter.[39] Another record from the same month recounts that Ascanio Marri did not perform with the others "in making the usual music when the priors were at table" and that he was sent to prison for a day. Marri was also ordered to appear before the priors every day during the remaining weeks of their term of office so that he might beg their forgiveness.

Many of these records indicate that Medici policies regarding governance of local institutions were at work most of the time. On occasion, however, when Cosimo's governor intervened on behalf of an individual musician, the Concistoro quickly accepted his recommendations. In cases of conflicting opinions, a face-saving solution was usually found. One such instance occurred in June 1561 when Ascanio Marri, once again in the priors' bad graces because he had disdained them and the captain of the people by failing "to come and play at the Mass that he is obliged to play with the others," was jailed for ten days and deprived of his meal privileges. But he was released after four days' imprisonment by the next group of priors. They read his supplication for leniency and the governor's rescript favoring it and agreed that "he has paid sufficiently for his error."

Sometimes the governor himself was present when such problems were brought before the priors. One such occasion occurred at the end of June 1565, when the trombonist Giovanfrancesco di Benedetto was condemned to prison for an unnamed offense. This was not the first time that he had angered the priors. Almost three years earlier to the day it was reported that he had left his post for a month, even though he had only been granted an eight-day leave. As punishment, the priors decided that on his return he must serve six months without salary and meal privileges. That time, however, after initially deciding to imprison him, the priors went further and, with the governor's approval, fired Giovanfrancesco "for his presumption and temerity and other bad behavior." Despite the furor, Giovanfrancesco was restored to his post within a few weeks.

Talent did not go unrecognized, as several events in Giovanfrancesco's career reveal. A few years earlier the priors permitted him to perform "at the appropriate times at the cathedral, notwithstanding any restrictions to the contrary," and, as noted, he served

---

39. Little is heard about Adriano in the following years, principally because he rarely got in trouble with the law. An exception to his otherwise exemplary record comes from a report of 9 August 1564, which states that he and Maestro Pietro Calzolari, both of whom were then in jail because of an altercation they had had in the Palace, could be released from prison if they were to be reconciled. Otherwise they were to remain in prison: "Che Adriano, piffaro di palazzo, et maestro Pietro Calzolari, atteso l'esser stati tanto tempo in prigione e il patimento che per ciò hanno fatto, che sieno assoluti et liberati per conto della briga et rissa nata fra di loro in palazzo, dovendo fra lor farsi la pace . . . e chi di essi starà renitente a non voler far detta pace, non sia scarcerato, e quello la vorrà fare sia scarcerato" (Concistoro, vol. 1180, fol. 16$^\text{v}$, dated 9 August 1564).

there for several years before ceding his post to a younger colleague in December of 1573.[40] By 1579 Giovanfrancesco Sanese, as he is called in Florentine documents, was serving at the Medici court, where he remained until the early 1590s.[41] During that period he worked with such luminaries as the composers Luca Marenzio and Cristofano Malvezzi, the cornettist Bernardo Pagani called il Franciosino, the violinist Giovan Battista Jacomelli, and the singer-composers Giulio Caccini and Jacopo Peri.[42] He also performed in the famed Intermedi, staged as part of the festivities celebrating the marriage of Grand Duke Ferdinand to Christine of Lorraine in 1589. As an experienced church musician, Giovanfrancesco was much in demand, and the records of one Florentine church, the Santissima Annunziata, mention his performing there at various times during the period August 1584–May 1594. Despite his successful career in Florence, Giovanfrancesco kept his Sienese connections well oiled. In October 1588 he was granted an official leave of absence from the Palace in Siena and then received back into service a few days later. There is no indication that he returned to Siena at that time, though he subsequently resumed service at the Palace and was elected leader of the wind band.

The Strategy of Hiring Supernumeraries

A number of records from the early 1560s show that the practice of hiring supernumeraries, though unmentioned at the time of the wind band's reorganization in 1556, was never abandoned as a cornerstone of the Palace's employment policies. Subsequent strategies enabled the priors to employ outstanding young musicians, even though the number of permanent positions, and consequently the amount of money for the band, were fixed by law. Obviously, adding personnel on a full- or part-time basis made good sense so long as expenses could be contained. Modest amounts later added to the wind band's budget for bread and wine allocations sufficed to ensure that the best and most talented among the city's musicians were employed. The priors, however, were ever alert to budgetary restrictions. In order to stay within their budget they sometimes, as previously, juggled salaries and left tenured posts unfilled. This was precisely what happened after Ascanio Marri's death.

The first record of supernumeraries in post-republican times is from 19 December 1561. It states simply that the priors had read Fabio di Geronimo's petition and granted him everything he requested. Fabio, it turns out, had asked for and was given meal privileges at the Palace for his services as a supernumerary with the wind band. This much is spelled out in another decree from less than a year later when the priors approved a petition from Alfonso, son of the trumpeter Pavolo, to substitute for Fabio until such time as the latter returned from a leave of absence (see Doc. 12.11).[43] Fabio

---

40. See chapter 7 for his tenure at the cathedral.

41. For Giovanfrancesco's Florentine service, see Warren Kirkendale, *The Court Musicians in Florence during the Principate of the Medici* (Florence, 1994), 49, 118, 277, 648.

42. ASF, Depositeria Generale, vol. 389, *1588 Ruolo della Casa del Serenissimo Ferdinando Medici, Cardinale, Gran Duca di Toscana*, p. 17.

43. The wording of the decree makes it appear that Alfonso played the trumpet as well as wind instruments, but in this case "trumpeter" refers to his father.

apparently never resumed service. Alfonso was still playing at the Palace in October 1563, when the priors, after hearing that he had been charged with a crime, decided to have several of their colleagues speak to the governor. A year later Alfonso was in trouble again and was fined L. 100 for assaulting Maestro Pietro Mazzantini, a tailor. Several weeks passed before the Concistoro voted on 9 March 1564 to rehabilitate him and allow him to play with the other musicians at table and outside in the city, "and this so that he can have the experience and learn to become a good musician in the service of the Palace."

A younger supernumerary, Savino di Francesco, appears in a decree from late October 1563, which reports that the priors read his humble petition and decided to absolve him of the punishment previously imposed on him. Savino was back before the Concistoro a month later requesting that his monthly salary of L. 7, which he claimed was insufficient to support himself and his aged father, be augmented by a meal allowance of L. 6 or L. 7 per month. The priors decided to give him a monthly meal allowance of L. 5 and an expectative for the first vacant post, with the proviso that his monthly salary revert to his present one when he succeeded to a permanent position. Savino was apparently advanced to a permanent post soon afterwards and served under the new conditions through the end of 1564 before leaving. His place was taken by none other than Alfonso di Pavolo, whom the priors decreed would now be allowed to share in the tips the band received for playing at dinners, as had Savino di Francesco Belli, in addition to having a monthly salary of L. 7 (see Doc. 12.12).

No less hot-tempered than most of his colleagues, Alfonso di Pavolo's frequent scrapes with the law form a wide and almost continuous path through the dense thicket of Consistorial pronouncements. One incident should not go unnoticed because it testifies to his abilities as an improviser and perhaps as a singer. The priors were informed on 14 October 1567 that Alfonso had been imprisoned, without their permission, on a complaint filed by Giorgio Bonelli, a haberdasher, "for having sung certain stanzas and verses disparaging said Giorgio." The merits of the complaint were not at issue, but the Concistoro's rights to condemn its own employees were. Accordingly, they went to Federigo Montauto, Cosimo's governor, who said he would order Alfonso's release and put the case in their hands. In the end the priors apparently agreed on some form of punishment, for Alfonso's release from jail was not reported until eight days later.

Another supernumerary, the trombonist Tiberio di Girolamo Rivolti, is mentioned in a decree from 9 March 1564, when the then current priors annulled the meal privileges their predecessors had awarded him. The following day saw a swift change of heart, when the priors decided that Tiberio, described as "a musician of tender age and of much musical promise," should have meal privileges during the two months of their term of office on condition that he perform with the others as a supernumerary at the required times. Some of the priors could clearly recognize promise, for as later reports show, Tiberio was one of the most talented musicians to come out of sixteenth-century Siena.

Tiberio, who became a permanent member of the group on Maestro Niccolò's retirement, incurred the priors' displeasure as often as any of his colleagues. A decree from 10 June 1567 suspended him from service, together with the trombonist Giovanfrancesco di Benedetto and Alfonso di Pavolo, for the remainder of the current government's term of office. A supernumerary, Giovanbattista di Bennardino, was authorized to replace them (see Doc. 12.13).[44] Less than a year later Tiberio was jailed for having written "certain scandalous words" on the wall of the employees' dining room and for having lied to Giovanbattista di Bennardino. He was released from prison within the week and apologized to Giovanbattista in the priors' presence. Tiberio was apparently one of those free spirits who said what he thought regardless of the consequences. A decree issued on 26 May 1570 forbade him to enter the Palace for fifteen days, depriving him of both his salary and meal privileges. Later the same day the priors, "having heard from several gentlemen that Tiberio had made certain disparaging remarks about them," and "wishing to make an example for the others," ordered him to spend fifteen days in the prison called "Le Stinche." Tiberio was released a week later because he had promptly obeyed the Concistoro's orders.

Giovanbattista di Francesco called Formica, yet another of the supernumeraries who eventually gained a permanent post, appears in the records for the first time on 22 November 1568. (The plural form of his name, Formichi, also appears in other Palace records and in cathedral documents.) A petition the youth sent to the governor that he be given the place previously awarded to Flaminio di Maestro Antonio Signorini was forwarded with the governor's approval to the priors, who promptly granted the expectative to him (see Doc. 12.14). Giovanbattista was no less independent-minded than Tiberio. A deliberation from 18 January 1570 notes that he had scorned Signor Achille Donati, one of the current priors, by refusing to go with the others to play in Donati's quarters and that his intransigence earned him an eight-day prison sentence. Three days passed before he was formally released.

Jacomo di Antonio Latini was one of the supernumeraries, who, as he put it in a petition he sent the Concistoro on 16 June 1573, had "served the lords for many years with only a provision of bread and wine." Since filial obligations constrained him to move with his father to the town of Casole, he requested that he might retain his provision should he return to the city, either for a few days or to resume residence. The priors apparently appreciated his work, for they immediately complied with his request. Jacomo was back at his old job within a year and a half, and on 10 January 1575 all of the members of the wind band, the "corpo della musica," made an extraordinary supplication to the government on his behalf. He had been condemned for some unnamed offense to two lashes of the whip, and a month in prison. His colleagues begged for mercy on grounds that such severe corporal punishment would prevent him from ever playing again. The Concistoro was inclined to be lenient, perhaps because of Jacomo's talent, and gave him an extra fifteen days in prison instead, his release being duly reported on the following 30 April.

The five tenured musicians in July 1556 were still serving in the wind band in January 1565, when a commission appointed by the Concistoro to judge the merits of

---

44. Giovanbattista's appointment to serve in place of all three indicates that not all of the musicians were required to be present at the same times, since a single substitute could hardly be expected to fill in for two trombonists at the same time.

a suit brought against Maestro Niccolò, Giovanfrancesco, Simone, Ascanio, and Adriano found in favor of the plaintiffs, the trumpeter Pavolo and his son Alfonso (see Doc. 12.15).[45] A month earlier the Concistoro had declared the pair eligible for a share of the group's gratuities. Evidently, the tenured musicians did not obey the new ruling, and each of them was now ordered to pay one giulio (s. 13. 4) to the plaintiffs within three days or face the consequences. Some five years later, on 21 February 1570, Simone and Giovanfrancesco brought a similar suit against Ascanio Marri, by then the group's leader. Marri was found at fault and had to pay a considerable sum to the others. To Giovanfrancesco he had to pay L. 4, "all the rest of his salary as leader" through the end of the present month, without delay, and to both Giovanfrancesco and Simone the sum of s. 16. 8 each, also from his leader's stipend, beginning on the following 1 March, for as long as he held the post (see Doc. 12.16).

No reason is given for such drastic action. But Marri likely had kept part of the income due other musicians while they were on official leave because the priors also declared that in future Marri need not pay them s. 16. 8 if they were absent without permission from the priors or from their Serene Highnesses. Feelings died hard, however, and on the following 13 March the members of the wind band aired their complaints at a meeting called by the priors, who were "aware of the continuing rancor and wished to avoid scandal." Still later, on 21 March 1570, it is reported that in the presence of the captain of the people differences were resolved and harmony restored between Ascanio on the one side and Giovanfrancesco, Simone, Adriano, and Tiberio on the other (see Doc. 12.17).

Duties and Repertory

A set of provisions dated 17 February 1570 gives a full account of the wind band's duties and obligations in the later sixteenth century (see Doc. 12.18). Most information in this document corroborates earlier data and suggests there were few if any substantial changes in the musicians' duties, even after the consolidation of Medici rule. But several remarks concerning the leader's prerogatives makes this one of the most significant Palace documents concerning the group available. The musicians' duties may be summarized as follows:

1. With regard to their playing at table while the priors dined, they were to play immediately after the first course was served and to continue to do so until the fruit course was brought in or "for that additional bit of time" that the captain of the people might think necessary. This meant, of course, that they were to be ready to begin promptly.

2. Failure on the part of any one of the musicians to fulfill these duties and all others that were listed without a legitimate excuse that was approved by the captain of the people would result in the loss of meal privileges for one day.

3. The musicians were forbidden to make noise or disturbances of any kind during their performances.

---

45. The commission was appointed the previous 8 January: Concistoro 1183, fol. 7ʳ. Pavolo is cited in this report.

4. When the priors left the Palace in state, the musicians had to play at least twice en route to their destination, and the same held when the priors returned to the Palace. Also they were to play in two places when the priors went to the cathedral, in front of Casa Cerretani and in the little square called La Postierla.

5. On holy days of obligation, when Mass was celebrated at the chapel in the Palace, they were to play at the Elevation of the Host.

6. On Saturday morning, according to ancient custom, they were to assemble at the usual hour to play music in the Cappella del Campo in honor of the Blessed Virgin, our Advocate.

7. On all other solemn or joyful public events honoring their Royal Highnesses and the city and for any other reason of state, they were to play appropriate music in the usual places in the Palace from which they could be seen and heard.

8. The Palace steward was obliged on the first or second day of every new magistracy and on the first or second day of the second month of the same magistracy to read these provisions to the musicians under penalty of a fine. The same provisions were also to be posted in the employees' dining room in a place where they could be read by all. They were not to be removed, altered, or defaced in any way under penalty of a fine, and half of the fine was promised as a reward to anyone who reported transgressions of this rule.

The musicians' obligations toward the band's leader received considerably less attention, but a good deal of practical information can nevertheless be gleaned from the few remarks made about him. Every musician had to play or sing the musical part assigned by the maestro, and he was forbidden to give his part, either for playing or singing, to any other person. Nor could he exchange his part with any one else without the maestro's assent. The maestro, on the other hand, was to let the musicians know beforehand where they were to play, what music he had chosen, and which instruments or voices were needed. No one could begin to play before the maestro so ordered, and all must defer to him. The maestro, furthermore, set the tempo as he saw fit.

These remarks show that the leader controlled the repertory, selected what he thought appropriate, and designated those whom he wished to perform particular pieces, whether instruments or voices. In other words, he determined which combinations of instruments alone or of voices and instruments he thought best suited the music as well as where it was performed and who performed it. Musical sources of the time, it has long been acknowledged, preserve only skeletal representations of composers' intentions. They tell us little about the many possibilities that the composer, or others, might have envisioned for performing a particular piece. Renaissance musicians were accustomed to realizing music with whatever forces they had at hand. They performed music as they saw fit, guided, to be sure, by contemporary conventions and standards of good taste as well as by their own capabilities and those of their colleagues. Particulars concerning this, however, are not very plentiful. This Sienese document is one of the few known so far that actually fixes such responsibility on the leader, or *maestro di cappella,* as he is often called. The special restriction against musicians exchanging parts was clearly necessary to help him maintain his authority in these matters. The restriction against musicians beginning without a sign from the maestro also occurs in a few records from the Sistine Chapel, as does the maestro's prerogative to set the tempo—

which probably mean that the maestro gave the downbeat.[46] All in all, these few remarks, though they leave us hungering for more, furnish concrete evidence regarding the actual duties of the *maestro di cappella* at this time. By inference, of course, they can be extended to illustrate those of the cathedral *maestro di cappella* as well.

The 1570 document corroborates earlier information about the musicians' duties and where they played within the Palace. One of the sites, the Concistoro's private chapel, known as the "Cappella dei Signori o Nuova," where Mass was celebrated for the priors and their guests, may still be admired today. Constructed on the first floor of the Palace before 1405 and decorated with frescos by Taddeo di Bartolo during the next two years, it was furnished with magnificently sculpted wooden stalls in 1428 and enclosed with an iron gate in 1455.[47] Whether an older organ owned by the Sienese republic was located in the chapel is a matter of conjecture—that instrument was later sold—but in 1522 the new organ built by Giovanni Piffero was placed in the arch on the wall between the chapel and the grandiose Sala del Mappamundo.[48] Organist-chaplains were employed at the Palace for a few years in the following decades, though there is no mention of their performing with the members of the wind band.[49] It was, in any case, within the chapel's rather small space or just outside its gates that the band's musicians performed when they assisted at Mass. Otherwise, they played and sang at mealtimes in the priors' dining room or, if requested, in the private quarters of individual priors. A reference to this latter requirement appears in the already cited report from 1570 concerning Giovanbattista Formichi. Performing in the priors' dining room is mentioned in a report from 22 November 1563, which shows that Adriano Mangoni lost his meal privileges for eight days because he had not taken part "in singing and playing" the previous evening.

Given the musicians' versatility, they combined voices and instruments in many of their performances indoors and their repertory accordingly included sacred as well as secular music. Some idea of their repertory comes from the record of a payment to Ascanio Marri on 30 April 1564 for L. 6, which he spent on a set of music partbooks called *La Pecorina*.[50] This, the first edition of Adrian Willaert's celebrated *Musica nova*, was a collection of madrigals and motets composed in the most advanced style of the time.[51] It thus provided ideal up-to-date materials for the Palace musicians, who both

46. See Sherr, "Performance Practice in the Papal Chapel," 456.

47. Michele Cordaro, "Le vicende costruttive," in *Palazzo Pubblico di Siena,* ed. Brandi, 83. A color photograph of the chapel is on p. 257 of this volume.

48. Cellesi, "L'organo della cappella interna," 500–1.

49. See chapter 13 for the two organists employed at the Palace.

50. "Et deliberorno farsi decreto al camarlingo . . . che paghi lire 9 a maestro Polito libraio, e per esso a Ascanio musico di Palazzo, per pagamento d'un corpo di libri di musica chiamato la Picorina" (Concistoro, vol. 1178, fol. 29^r, dated 30 April 1564).

51. The most recent study of this celebrated volume is Michèle Fromson's "Themes of Exile in Willaert's *Musica Nova," JAMS* 47 (1994): 442–87. She suggests that the collection was composed for two of Willaert's patrons, Neri Capponi and Ruberto Strozzi, both Florentine exiles, both foes of Cosimo I, and that it had distinctly anti-Medicean political themes, these latter encoded in melodies associated with the fallen Florentine republic and particularly Savonarola (esp. 474–78). In speaking of the work's publication under the aegis of Duke Alfonso II of Ferrara in 1559—the year of the

sang and played at Masses and mealtimes in the normal course of their duties. (*La Pecorina* is also the only set of partbooks known by title purchased for use at the Palace in the sixteenth century.) Marri himself also composed many madrigals and these, too, likely formed part of the wind band's repertory. Again, as with the frottolas of Niccolò piffero and earlier composers, his music was performed by various combinations of voices and instruments as well as in totally instrumental versions.

Later records indicate that no more than six musicians—tenured and supernumeraries alike—had to be at indoor Palace functions at any given time. This arrangement must have encouraged the *maestro di cappella* to experiment and to seek the most effective ways of producing satisfying ensemble sounds with the forces he had at hand. Versatility on the part of the musicians, that is, ability to play a number of instruments, was a prime factor in helping him make choices. By this time, besides shawms and trombones, the Palace owned a case of six cornetts, seven transverse flutes, six recorders, and four curtals or dulcians.[52] The musicians assuredly had instruments of their own, though no record exists of precisely what these were. At least two of the musicians had voices pleasing enough to qualify them for membership in the cathedral chapel, and others like Marri, who as a youth also sang there, and Adriano possessed reasonably good voices or at least could hold their own in a vocal ensemble. In addition, the private chapel in the Palace boasted an organ, built by Giovanni di Maestro Antonio, who himself performed on it, as did one or two other professional organists employed by the Concistoro. In later years a few of the wind players and Palace sacristans were also capable organists.[53] With such a rich array of talent at his disposal the *maestro di cappella* could provide his listeners with a great deal of musical variety as he explored and exploited the various possibilities of combining voices and instruments in performances both in the chapel and in the great dining hall.

Musical Instruments

As in the previous century, the Palace continued to provide instruments for its employees. State-owned instruments, however, are only sporadically referred to in Palace inventories, which are not available for all periods. Inventories from 1506 through 1509 mention three "silver pifferi" and a "silver trombone that Girolamo Trombone has."[54]

---

treaty of Cateau-Cambrésis and the capitulation of the last of the Sienese exiles—the author notes the earlier Ferrarese alliance with Siena's republic and advances a fascinating hypothesis. This, in short, is that while the Este duke may have originally purchased the manuscript of *Musica nova* because of his long-standing rivalry with the Medici, his desire to see it "into print may have reflected his awareness that the political themes commemorated in Willaert's music had again captured the attention of the Italian peninsula" (p. 476). If the collection was indeed perceived by contemporary cognoscenti, those at the Florentine court included, as anti-Medicean, its acquisition by Sienese musicians, who assuredly performed its pieces in the presence of Cosimo's governor, invites speculation about how it was received in Siena.

52. See below concerning Simone Nodi and sixteenth-century inventories.

53. There are few records concerning the Palace organist, but the few there are suggest that he doubled as the priors' chaplain. See chapter 13.

54. See chapter 11, note 135.

The same instruments are recorded in an inventory from July 1514.[55] Listed in inventories from the late 1540s are a trombone, "a case of curtals," and "a case of black flutes," this last also called "a case of flutes all'Italiana."[56] Though inventories of Palace belongings from shortly after the fall of the republic make no reference to the instruments, several later records, beginning with one from 1 July 1556 and continuing through 1 January 1560, list "a silver trombone, broken, with its pieces."[57] "A case of flutes," variously described as on loan to the pifferi or "to Maestro Niccolò piffero," appears from 1 July 1556 through the end of October 1558 in the same volume of inventories.[58] A later inventory of the Palace, from 1573, lists the following items "on loan to the musicians":

  a case of mute cornetts, of six cornetts
  a case of seven transverse flutes
  a case with six recorders
  a case with four curtals
  six sets of worn-out partbooks[59]

Very few instruments were apparently bought after this time, or if they were, they replaced existing ones. An order issued on 9 December 1602 to Simone Nodi's heirs noted that Nodi had certain instruments belonging to the illustrious lords when he died and that these were to be returned to the Palace. The instruments included a case of six mute cornetts; two cases of recorders, one black, the other yellowish; a case of transverse flutes; another case of six curtals; and many sets of musical partbooks.[60] Most of these items were undoubtedly the ones cited in the inventory of 1573.

Engagements outside the Palace

Reports already cited and others yet to be mentioned reveal a policy allowing musicians to accept outside employment that took effect soon after the reorganization of the wind

55. "1 trombone d'argento; 3 pifare d'argento senza bucciolo e una l'à di legnio" (Concistoro 2512, unnumbered folio).

56. "Una cassa di sordini, una cassa di flauti negri, nelle mani de' piffari" (Concistoro, vol. 2516, fol. LI^v, for January–February 1546/47); again listed on fol. 58^r for January–February 1547/48; fol. [61]^v for September 1548: "una cassa di flauti all'italiana"; this also mentions "uno trombone d'argento"; again listed on an unnumbered folio for May–June 1549.

57. "Uno trombone d'argento, rotto con i suoi pezzi, in Concistoro" (Concistoro, vol. 2516, unnumbered folio, verso, for 1 July 1556); and fol. CCLXXIII^r for 1 January 1559/60.

58. Concistoro, vol. 2516, various unnumbered pages list: "una cassa di flauti, in mano de' piffari" or "una cassa di flauti in mano di maestro Niccolò piffaro."

59. "Una cassa di cornetti muti di sei cornetti; una cassa di sette flauti traversi; una cassa co' sei flauti dritti; una cassa con quattro sordini; sei corpi di libri legati insieme, già logri" (Concistoro, vol. 2528, fol. 90^v).

60. "Illustrissimi dominus Capitaneus populi et alii Excelsi domini . . . viso informativo fabricato contra heredes magistris Simonis de Nodis, olim musici et magistri Cappelle Palatii dictorum Illustrissimorum dominorum, occasione inveniendi nonnulla instrumenta musicalia, ut vulgo appellantur cornetti, sordine e flauti . . . ea apud dictum magistrum Simonem et in eius manibus diu extitisse certi essent, mandaverunt igitur . . . quatenus infra biduam debeant remictere . . . infrascripta instrumenta vulgari sermone descripta, quibus dictus magister Simeon usus fuit . . . Una cassa di cornetti muti di sei; Due casse di flauti dritti, una nera e l'altra gialliccia; Una cassa di flauti traversi; Un'altra cassa di

band in the mid–1550s. Some records of appointment speak of a musician's right to his fair share of the group's earnings, and reports of several disputes among members of the wind band prove that earnings from playing at suppers, dinners, banquets, weddings, university ceremonies, and other kinds of festivities constituted a considerable part of the musicians' income. The amounts earned on these occasions are, understandably, not mentioned in Palace accounts, but a document from the last quarter of the sixteenth century gives a good idea of the going rate then charged by the musicians. This recounts how Simone Nodi and the other Palace musicians appeared before the priors on 13 May 1576 and asked their assistance in determining an appropriate fee for the group for performing at private functions. The priors, perhaps basing their decision on what the musicians were already receiving, decreed that in future they should not charge more than L. 10 for each occasion.[61] How this sum was divided among the seven (or more) musicians is not stated, but individuals probably received somewhere in the vicinity of L. 1, with a bit extra earmarked for the group leader and organizer. L. 10 was by no means a paltry amount, considering that at the time the monthly wages of tenured Palace musicians averaged about L. 18, with those of supernumeraries much lower. Outside engagements obviously paid well, constituting a lucrative if not always dependable source of additional income for Palace musicians. The changed attitude toward their accepting such employment clearly came about because the priors realized that to retain the best people available, they had to make an accommodation that allowed the musicians to augment their salaries while ensuring that they did not neglect their duties at the Palace.

In addition to performing at purely secular events, members of the wind band also made themselves available to churches and monasteries, where they played and sang on special feast days. The cathedral singers under Feliciani, of course, were doing the same thing at the time, most notably at the chapel of the hospital of Santa Maria della Scala, where they sang every year at Vespers and Mass on the feast of the Annunciation. A record of the Palace wind band's accepting a similar kind of engagement comes from the convent of the Santissima Concezione in Siena.[62] Dated 9 December 1577, it states that the Palace musicians received L. 10 "for having sung a Mass on the morning of the Conception in our church and at Vespers in the afternoon of the same feast, and a Requiem Mass this morning, everything in figural music with voices and instruments." (L. 10, of course, had been recommended by the priors as appropriate for a single

---

sordine di numero sei; Molti altri corpi di libri di musica" (Concistoro, vol. 1314, fol. 46ʳ, dated 9 December 1602).

61. "Li molti Magnifici Signori . . . uditi Simone musico insieme con più altri musici del Magnifico Palazzo, sopra le mercedi dovute ad essi musici del Palazzo da quelli i quali si vogliono servire et servono dell'opera loro in farli far musica et sonare in cene, conviti et desinari et simili, et del tassarsi secondo che pare giusto et honesto a lor Signorie, deliberorno che per l'advenire sia la mercede et premio de' decti musici . . . lire dieci di denari, et . . . non possino domandare più di decte lire dieci" (Concistoro, vol. 1250, fols. 18ᵛ–19ʳ, dated 13 May 1576).

62. See Doc. 13.4. The document is interesting for what it tells about the group's performance practices, for the inference is that they played instruments and sang but without an organist; this probably means that one of them played some other kind of foundation instrument. It is also possible that one of them was also an organist and made use of the church's organ, if there was one.

engagement, probably interpreted here to mean various services connected with the convent's principal feast day.) Appended to the receipt is an agreement between the nuns and the musicians stipulating that in the future besides these three services, the musicians were "to come every year for the same salary and perform Vespers on the eve of the feast as well." Signing on behalf of the members of the wind band was Simone Nodi, "maestro della cappella del Palazzo."

The priors zealously enforced the new policy regarding outside employment, as shown by a series of reports regarding an incident of 18 March 1580, when all of the musicians, trumpeters and wind players alike, performed at a non-official function without the captain's permission.[63] Their action was apparently considered so grave that three days later, on the 21st, the entire government convened to discuss it. (This in itself indicates how few matters of substance came before the priors and how eagerly they seized upon even the slightest pretext to exercise what little authority they had.) At the meeting it was decided to incarcerate the musicians for two days and to deprive them of their meals for six, although the captain of the people could change or lower the sentences as he saw fit. An order to imprison the musicians was issued the next day, the 22nd. Named were the seven trumpeters: Pavolo di Giovanni, Silvio di Simone, Austino di Pietropavolo, Ciro di Domenico, Dionigi di Pavolo, Plinio di Leone, and Sacripante di Pavolo; and six members of the wind band: Maestro Simone Nodi, Adriano Mangoni, Tiberio Rivolti, Giovanbattista Formichi, Giovanbattista Cocchi, and Alberto di Jacomo Latini (see Doc. 12.19).[64] (The latter was substituting for his father, who was away at the time.)

On the following day Maestro Simone Nodi was cited for having had the audacity to say to the captain and the priors that he would not go to prison and that he would not obey the order. In retaliation the priors increased his prison sentence to a month and ordered that his meals and salary be withheld during that time, although the captain was again given permission to change or lower the sentence. On the same day the captain had all of the musicians released, except for Maestro Simone Nodi, and their fines withdrawn. But since nothing further about Nodi is said in this series of records, it is likely that he was not held to the letter of the law and that the whole incident was allowed to fade into distant memory.

The documents are revealing as much for what they say about the musicians' attitude toward authority as they do about the continuing demand for their services. Their behavior was quite in keeping with reports of imprisonment meted out to some of them, either for failure to appear at the required times or for an often independent-minded response to a situation, and it contrasted with that of the chapel singers, who usually adopted an obsequious tone when they dealt with the cathedral administration. Since Palace musicians could now freely accept outside engagements, provided there

---

63. "Convocati . . . fu deliberato etc. che si intimi per il 21 detto l'integro Concistoro per possere in esso si risolvere quanto convenga per causa dell'eccesso commesso il 18 medesimo dalli musici e trombetti, quali senza alcuna licentia dell'Illustrissimo Signor Capitano conforme alli oblighi de' medesimi, sono andati a suonare fuor di Palazzo" (Concistoro, vol. 1273, fol. 6ʳ, dated 20 March 1579/80).

64. The government's action recalls a similar one taken almost a century previously against the pifferi who had played for Cesare Borgia without official permission. See Doc. 11.22.

were no conflicts of duties, understandably they accepted as many engagements as they could fit into their schedule. In this case the immediate cause of the priors' displeasure was that the seven trumpeters and six of the wind players (or five, if Nodi had had prior permission to go) had all taken the night off at the same time. Outside engagements paid well; earnings for a day's or a night's work on a casual basis were especially attractive when compared with a musician's regular monthly salary from a Palace post. The catch, of course, was that for those lucky enough to get into the wind band, the Palace offered steady employment, a lifelong guaranteed income, and numerous perquisites.

THE WIND BAND IN THE 1570S AND 1580S

A report from 4 May 1575 shows that by then the number of musicians serving in the wind band had been officially raised to seven. And though the roll, or "tavolella," with the names of musicians permanently employed at the Palace listed seven names, there were now actually eight. Since the extra provision burdened Palace finances, the priors appointed a two-man commission to look into the matter.[65] An unexpected turn of events a few months later solved the problem. A deliberation from the end of October 1575 reports that shortly after Ascanio Marri's death, several of his colleagues petitioned the priors for raises in salary, noting that this could be done at no extra expense by dividing Marri's wages among them. At the same time they proposed that two other musicians, who apparently had been serving without any provision whatsoever, be assigned "to the place vacated by Maestro Ascanio" (see Doc. 12.20). Both requests were approved and the L. 16 previously paid to Marri was distributed among Giovanbattista Cocchi and Baldassare Ponti, whose monthly salaries each rose by L. 3, and Giovanbattista Formichi and Jacomo Latini, who each received a monthly addition of L. 5. At the same time the priors decreed that Alberto di Francesco Gregori and Domenico di Bartolomeo Fei "be recognized and admitted to Palace service" with the proviso that they share the daily allotment of bread and wine previously given Ascanio.

Domenico Fei and Alberto Gregori worked for half a daily ration of food and with no other privileges until 18 February 1578, when the priors appointed them to the supernumerary's post previously held by Baldassare di Maestro Domenico Ponti. A petition from the two musicians is summarized below the text of the deliberation. In it they stated that they had served the Palace at half a provision for the last twenty-eight months, that is, since Marri's death, and that they were now willing to share Baldassare's monthly salary of L. 3. 10 (see Doc. 12.21). The modesty of their proposal was only slightly tempered by their suggestion that Baldassare's meal allowance be granted to one of them and the meal allowance they now shared be given to the other. That both musicians would serve for so little compensation is a telling reminder that Palace posts

---

65. "Viso qualiter in tabula denominata la tavolella, in qua sunt descripti musici servientes eorum palatio, tantum reperiuntur septem, et tamen octo sunt illi qui hodie serviunt, et sic ultra numerum debitum adest unus ex eis in damnum et preiudicium palatii, volentes super tali re providere et iustitiam facere, solemniter deliberaverunt quod duo ex Illustrissimis dominis . . . viderunt decreta concessa musicis predictis, deliberationes factas et audiant rationes et iura ipsorum, et plene informati referant excelso Concistorio" (Concistoro, vol. 1244, fol. 4ʳ⁻ᵛ, dated 4 May 1575).

were coveted and difficult to come by. A measure of their talent is that their request was so quickly granted.

Baldassare was still associated with the Palace musicians when a group of them received permission to travel to Lucca for the annual feast of the Holy Cross in September 1578.[66] Joining him were Adriano Mangoni, Tiberio Rivolti, Giovanbattista Formichi, Jacomo Latini, Alberto di Francesco Gregori, Pier Giovanni Odorini, and Annibale di Girolamo, a hitherto unmentioned supernumerary.[67] Others, including Simone Nodi, Giovanbattista Cocchi, and Domenico, must have stayed behind to play for the priors. Formichi and Cocchi, both of whom were also in the cathedral chapel, continued to perform at the Palace for many years to come, presumably as supernumeraries. Their names hardly figure in extant reports except on those occasions, noted below, when their salaries increased or decreased because of deaths and new appointments.[68]

Jacomo Latini was apparently as cunning as he was talented, and only a few years after his last encounter with the law, in 1575, he was once again in the government's bad graces. A lengthy report tells that he was given a one-month's leave of absence at the end of April 1579 so that he might go with the other musicians to the shrine at Loreto and seek an indulgence. While en route, he was to stop off at Foligno "to see if there was a teacher of cornett there," from whom he was "to take some lessons," and during his absence his place would be taken by Annibale di Girolamo. All proceeded according to plan, except that once Jacomo arrived in Foligno, "beyond learning the cornett, he settled down there, took a salary, and prolonged his stay by six or eight months." Thus, "keeping silent" about his activities, he delayed returning to Siena until the fifteenth of December. When the priors learned of this, they were so indignant that they ordered Jacomo to pay a fine of fifteen days' salary and told him that he might never again ask for leave whatever the circumstances under penalty of losing his post permanently (see Doc. 12.23). Obviously the situation resulted from bi-monthly changes of government, precluding strict supervision of the musicians, particularly when they provided competent substitutes during presumably approved leaves of absence. But Jacomo's prolonged absence must also have gone unreported to higher authorities by the *maestro di cappella*.

Jacomo, as noted above, was a friend of the cathedral *maestro di cappella* Andrea Feliciani and was a witness to a will drawn up by Feliciani in 1583. His continuing employment at the Palace was noted in April 1585, when the priors issued a request for his release from prison, where he had been sent because he was carrying a dagger

---

66. See chapter 10, note 57. As noted in connection with the trumpeters, the traditional visits made by Sienese musicians to other cities continued under Medici rule. Lucca was one of the most frequently visited places. Another record concerning one such visit is of interest because it is one of the earliest to name Ascanio Marri as "dux musicorum," or leader of the ensemble (see Doc. 12.22).

67. Only one trumpeter, Plinio di Leone, went with the group on this occasion. The pifferi did not go to the event in Lucca every year and it is not certain in any case that the entire group went when permission was given for them to go. A record from 10 September 1580 names four trumpeters (see chapter 10, note 58); that of 10 September 1587 mentions only one.

68. Noteworthy in this respect is a report from 28 June 1588 that Cocchi's daily allotment of bread was increased to three loaves.

on his person in public. Notwithstanding his past troubles, Jacomo was still in the priors' good graces in the following August, when he and Tiberio Rivolti were permitted to accept an invitation to serve a Doria prince with the assurance that his name would be kept on the roll of permanently employed Palace musicians, even though he could draw no salary while absent (see below, Doc. 12.29). Their departure is affirmed by a decree authorizing the appointment of Ottavio di Lorenzo Basili from 12 November 1585. It is doubtful that Jacomo ever returned to Palace service, since he is not mentioned again in Palace reports.

Giovanbattista Formichi is mentioned in a decree from June 1584, when the priors ordered him to pay an indemnity in a dispute with another Palace employee. He was another of the Palace's musical stars whose services were apparently much in demand. A report from the spring of 1588 tells that the Concistoro, as requested by the cathedral rector, allowed him to play in the chapel there, since this would not compromise the Palace's musical program. Formichi did so for a number of years. He was still serving in the wind band in 1597, when Giovanfrancesco's salary was being negotiated, but he must have died shortly after that time.

Domenico Fei also appears infrequently in later records. He was still in the wind band in January of 1585, when he was taken into custody for bearing arms at night. As punishment, he was put under house arrest in the Palace for two weeks. Domenico was a habitual troublemaker. A report from October 1588 states that he was imprisoned because of a complaint filed by Donna Elisabetta di Francesco. He was released a month later. In November of the following year he was again imprisoned, though this time he was released within five days. In April of 1591 he successfully petitioned the governor to review a decision of the priors that deprived him of a raise in salary, which was then used to increase those of Virgilio and Pietragnolo Maestri. At the governor's request his case was reviewed and in the following month the priors once again approved their previous decision (see Doc. 12.24). Somewhat mollified by their reaffirmation, on 12 August 1591, of his monthly salary and a partial meal allowance, he was still not satisfied and resigned his post within the week.

As mentioned earlier, in granting approval on 27 June 1575 of Ascanio Marri's request for permission to accept the *maestro di cappella*'s post at the cathedral, the priors noted especially that Marri had a large family and that they had received his assurances that he could fulfill his new obligations without neglecting his duties at the Palace. Those concerns became irrelevant when Marri's dual career was cut short by his death in October of that same year.[69] On 23 November 1575 Simone Nodi, his successor, was chosen over two other candidates for the post, Adriano Mangoni and Tiberio Rivolti (see Doc. 12.25). Nodi subsequently led the wind band for more than a quarter of a century with great distinction. He was, in fact, so highly regarded that at the end of his career he was given the same kinds of privileges previously awarded only to Niccolò piffero. These were recorded on Christmas Eve of 1601, when the priors unanimously decided that henceforth he was to retain his full salary and meal allowance but he need no longer perform except on certain days during the year. Those were few

---

69. See chapter 7, note 26.

in number and included the feasts of the Assumption, Easter, Christmas, Pentecost, and others "in honor of the Most Serene Grand Duke." Several months later the priors decided that Giovanbattista Cocchi would substitute for Nodi on all other occasions (see Doc. 12.26).[70]

Simone Nodi and the Palace School

A few reports indicate that during the sixteenth century the Concistoro provided space in the Palace for a school for teaching woodwind instruments, just as it had done earlier and continued to do for trumpeters. The piffero Giovanni di Maestro Antonio was cited as a teacher in a Palace record from 1519, although little was said about where he taught or whether he had students other than Gano d'Enea.[71] A deliberation of 21 November 1565 definitely establishes the existence of a school for wind players within the Palace (see Doc. 12.27). It speaks of a request from Giovanfrancesco, Ascanio, and Alfonso, "acting in behalf of themselves and of the other musicians, that they be given the room where up to the present Simone has held school, so that they can practice." Before rendering a decision the priors themselves went to look the room over and to chat with the parties on both sides. In the end, with a decision worthy of Solomon, they declared that

> the first room, that is, the chamber facing the door to the stairs, be used in common for practice by all Palace musicians, and each can have the key; [and] the other room, which overlooks the market, where Simone has kept and continues to keep school, be free for his use, especially since he has had it up to now and refurbished it at his own expense . . . and no other musician can teach school there.

Simone continued to keep a school at the Palace for many years to come. Giovanfrancesco, his successor as leader of the wind band, was apparently too old or too disinterested to continue Simone's work and the school languished during the brief period of his tenure, not to be revived until Alberto Gregori, a master teacher in his own right, was directed to reopen it when he was named to the leader's post. At the time the priors particularly referred to the students from the school who had been promoted to posts in the Palace, a statement that speaks more eloquently than could any other to the leading role Simone played as a teacher and to the success of his endeavors at the Palace. Simone was active even in old age, as revealed by a decree issued only a few days after his death on 9 December 1602. At the time, as has been mentioned, the priors ordered his heirs to return certain instruments, "called cornetts, curtals, and flutes in the vulgar tongue," and "many sets of printed partbooks" belonging to the Palace that he had at home when he died.[72]

---

70. Cocchi is mentioned in subsequent documents, which indicate that he succeeded to a tenured post in the band.

71. Mentioned above; see Doc. 12.8.

72. See note 60. Simone was still alive on 9 September 1602, when the government set the salary of the six tenured musicians at L. 6. 10 per month and confirmed their daily portions of bread and wine.

Simone Nodi's activities as a teacher outside the Palace are revealed by a notarial act he witnessed on 18 December 1574. At the time he was living in a house belonging to the Marchegiani family in the contrada Fonteblanda of Terzo Camollia, and it was there that he had "his own studio or school where he usually teaches his pupils."[73] Simone must have been an exceptionally devoted teacher. When Maestro Bartolomeo di Domenico Fei, a Sienese barber, filed his last will and testament on 8 August 1576, he left the sum of 50 scudi to Maestro Simone di Domenico Nodi. He did this "in recognition of the many kindnesses shown to Domenico, one of [Bartolomeo's] sons," when Nodi "taught him musical theory and to play instruments."[74] (Domenico had earlier begun serving with the Palace wind band.) Other documents show that Nodi enjoyed a certain measure of material prosperity as well as a reputation as an outstanding teacher and musician. Doubtless the two were bound to each other. By the late 1570s he was prosperous enough to have a house of his own, which he subsequently sold for Fl. 180.[75] He had his last will and testament drawn up on 17 November 1594, and added a codicil to it on 20 January 1595.[76] Having amassed a considerable amount of wealth, he made a number of bequests to charitable institutions at the time of his death.[77]

MUSICIANS THROUGH THE TURN OF THE SEVENTEENTH CENTURY

Adriano di Luzio Mangoni was another long-standing member of the wind band who continued to serve at the Palace until the time of his death, in August 1598. Rather less is known about him for the simple reason that he was one of the few members of the group whose name is lacking in reports concerning musicians' misbehavior or their brushes with the law. An unsuccessful aspirant to Ascanio Marri's post, he apparently accepted the decision with good grace and remained a faithful member of the band. With his death one of the oldest links with Siena's musical past ended, for he was the last scion of a musical family that had served the Palace for a hundred and thirty years. Several instances of appointments illustrating the continuing importance of ties of kin-

---

73. "Actum Senis, in terzeris Camollie, in contrata Fontisblandi in domo . . . de Marchegiani, ad presens solite habitationis Simonis quondam Dominici Narditi [*sic*], musici de Senis, et in eius proprio studio seu scola in qua solet discipulos docere, coram dicto Simone musico" (ASS, Notarile antecosimiano, 2732, N. 2188).

74. Notarile antecosimiano, 2253, N. 1932. Another item of interest in the will is the stipulation that "money realized from the sale of Bartolomeo's wife's necklace was to be used to pay for the trombone that has been bought for the said Domenico." This shows that most musicians had their own instruments, even though the Palace had a collection of instruments for their use.

75. Notarile antecosimiano, 3232, N. 722, where it is reported that Simone Nodi, a Sienese citizen and Palace musician, sold his house in Siena for Fl. 180 on 1 June 1577.

76. Notarile postcosimiano, Originali, vol. 53, no. 170, no. 171. In the will he is referred to as "magister Simon olim Dominici de Nodis, civis et musicus Senarum . . . corpore languens." He named his wife Fausta as his heir and said that he wished to be buried in the Sienese church of San Giovanni, in a tomb he himself had ordered.

77. Simone is the "musician from the city of Nodis but who resided in Siena" mentioned in Samuel K. Cohn, Jr., *Death and Property in Siena, 1205–1800* (Baltimore and London, 1988), 165.

ship in the sixteenth-century wind band have already been cited, but none is more remarkable than that of Adriano and his forebears. Giovanni di Fruosino, the Sienese piffero who entered Palace service as a young man in 1466, was founder of the family's musical fortunes. Pavolo, his son, joined the wind band in 1498 and served as a permanent member of the group until shortly before his death in 1545. Meanwhile, Pavolo assured for two of his sons the right of succession to his post. Virginio, apparently the elder, predeceased his father and at the time of Pavolo's death his position passed to another son, Luzio, who substituted for him in his declining years. Luzio, in turn, was able to secure the position for his son, Adriano, surnamed Mangoni in later documents, who then served at the Palace for the rest of his life.[78]

A report from the end of August 1598 tells how the salary of the recently deceased Adriano Mangoni was redistributed among a number of tenured and non-tenured musicians (see Doc. 12.28). A little more than a quarter of that amount, L. 4. 10, was awarded to Maestro Tiberio Rivolti, who had recently returned to the Palace after an absence of several years. Tiberio was one of sixteenth-century Siena's most famous musical sons. He joined the wind band in 1564 and was awarded a permanent post a few years later, all the while gaining a reputation as one of the best performers and teachers in the city. He was the choice of cathedral authorities to succeed Giovanfrancesco as trombonist in the chapel there, and the priors granted him permission to do so at the end of December 1573.[79] On 26 August 1578, he requested and received permission from the priors for a leave of absence so that he might enter the service of the Habsburg Emperor Rudolph.[80] Tiberio had arranged for his brother to replace him during his absence, so it is difficult to determine when he actually left the city and for how long he might have been gone, since under the circumstances his name remained on the payroll.

More tangible evidence of his employment outside Siena comes from several years later, in August 1585, when he was permitted, together with Jacomo Latini, to leave his Palace post to enter the service of a prince of the Doria family. On that occasion the priors declared that both musicians would not receive salary while they were away, but that they could resume their posts at some future date if the Concistoro were willing.

---

78. The family name was Mangoni, as shown by several documents in Concistoro sources and elsewhere. One of these records the presence of Adriano, son of the deceased Lutio Mangoni, a musician and Sienese citizen, who witnessed a legal document on 17 March 1578 (Notarile antecosimiano, vol. 3292, fol. 82ʳ). Adriano's surname is also given in a deliberation that restored him to his usual privileges: "Et per l'autorità . . . di potere assolvere et condannare Adriano Mangoni musico, mossi da giuste considerationi, detto Adriano liberorno et assolvere della constretta assegnatali di non potere uscire di palazzo" (Concistoro, vol. 1185, unnumbered folio, dated 25 July 1565).

79. "Et derno licentia a Tiberio di Girolamo, musico di palazzo, di andare a sonare al'hore et tempi soliti al Duomo, sicome già haveva Giovanfrancesco trombone, omni modo etc." (Concistoro, vol. 1235, fol. 17ʳ, dated 30 December 1573).

80. "Odito Tiberio di [gap], musico et trombone di Palazzo, lor domandante grata licentia di posser andare a servir il Serenissimo et Invitissimo Ridolfo Imperator de' Romani, lassando in luogo suo [blank], suo fratello, durante la sua absentia, fatta proposta fu consegliato et vento per lupini 15 bianchi" (Concistoro, vol. 1263, fol. 22ᵛ, dated 26 August 1578). In the following month of September his name appears on a list of Palace musicians authorized to travel to Lucca (see Doc. 12.22).

In the meantime, given their many years of service, their names would remain on the official list of permanent Palace musicians, whose privileges they, too, would be entitled to enjoy (see Doc. 12.29). Confirming their departure, as noted, is a decree from November 1585 reporting that the priors, having noted that the Palace was lacking musicians because two of them had already left, sought to rectify the situation by appointing Ottavio Basili as a supernumerary. Tiberio had been playing in the cathedral chapel, where he is recorded without a break from January 1574 through May 1580, and then again from March 1587 through January 1588, when he was replaced by Giovanbattista Formichi.[81] Tiberio had also been employed since the summer of 1580 as a singing teacher in the school maintained by the hospital of Santa Maria della Scala, where he served through mid-August 1585.[82] In this capacity he also led the small ensemble of student clerks that performed in the hospital's chapel. After an absence of several years, he resumed work at the chapel in November 1596.[83] Perhaps he also returned to Palace service at that time. He had, in any event, reclaimed his old post long before the end of February 1597, when he had to take a salary cut. His presence in the city is also confirmed by a legal document that he witnessed in August of the same year. This latter describes him as a *musices magister,* perhaps a reference both to his standing in the profession and to his position at Santa Maria della Scala.[84] His fame both as *maestro di cappella* at the hospital's chapel and as a teacher, as well as his membership in the Accademia dei Filomeli, are mentioned in his obituary, which records his burial on 28 January 1601.[85] No trace of his compositions remains. Filippo Montebuoni-Buondelmonti, writing not many decades after Tiberio's death, reported that his works were held in high esteem, though they were not published.[86]

---

81. As mentioned, Tiberio was sent to jail on 22 March 1580 with the other Palace musicians. His cathedral appointments are noted above in chapter 7. Approval of Formica's appointment to the cathedral on 25 January 1588 is noted below.

82. "Christo, 1580. Maestro Tiberio di Girolamo Rivolti, nostro musico, a dì primo di Agosto L. vinti a lui contanti a conto di sua provisione, L. 20" (Ospedale, vol. 810, *Bastardello di casa FFF, 1576–82,* fol. 207^v). "Christo 1580. Maestro Tiberio trombone nostro addì 15 detto [Settembre] L. diciotto a lui contanti come maestro di canto, L. 18" (fol. 211^r). Thereafter payments were issued to him through the summer of 1585: "Christo 1585. Maestro Tiberio Rivolti, maestro di canto, a dì 12 di detto [Agosto] L. cientoquattordici [s.] 1, a lui per resto, L. 114. 1" (vol. 811, *Bastardello GGG, 1585–86,* fol. 198^r). Further on the hospital's school, see chapter 13.

83. Hospital records indicate that "maestro Tiberio Rivolti, maestro di musicha," received L. 42, his salary for two months, on 3 January 1597 (Ospedale, vol. 914, *E&U, 1596–97,* fol. 69^v). Entries from the following years refer to him variously as *maestro di musicha,* as *musicho,* and as *maestro di cappella.* The final payment to him, for two months' salary, is from 22 January 1601 (vol. 918, *E&U, 1600–1,* fol. 73^v).

84. Notarile postcosimiano, Originali, vol. 164, dated 13 August 1597.

85. Tiberio was buried on 28 January 1601: "Tiberius de Rivoltis, musicus, qui diu rexit cappellam maioris Xenodochii et Tiferni et Ianue publice per aliquot annos musicam docuit et inter Accademiae Phylomatum nostrorum asseclas fuit connumeratus, obiit itaque et humatus est die 28 [Januarii] in sepulchro Societatis Divae Catherinae" (BCIS, MS C. III. 3, *Necrologio di San Domenico,* fol. 5^v [1601]).

86. BCIS, MD A. IX. 10, Filippo Montebuoni-Buondelmonti, *Mescolanze di cose diverse appartenenti a Siena,* fol. 240^r: "le sue opere sono in molta stima benché non stampate."

One of Tiberio's most promising students was Alberto di Francesco Gregori, who eventually succeeded to the leader's post that had eluded Tiberio. On 27 June 1585, a few months before Tiberio requested a leave of absence to enter the service of the Doria prince, he addressed a petition to the Concistoro asking that Alberto be granted a larger salary (see Doc. 12.30). Tiberio prefaced his request by explaining that he had taught Alberto since the time Alberto was a boy, and had recently given him his sister in marriage. Now, in part because of their friendship and family relationship, and in part so that he could finish paying the rest of his sister's dowry, he requested that they exchange posts, "that is, that the post that Tiberio has be transferred to Alberto, with all of its emoluments, honors and duties, and Alberto's post to the said Tiberio, with the same honors and duties." The priors promptly approved the request.[87]

They did not react so quickly to a dispute that arose as a result of Alberto Gregori's new position. A record dated 27 August 1585, apparently from just after Tiberio's departure, recounts how Alberto and Giovanbattista Formichi were at loggerheads over the right to play "the first bass in the musical ensemble, in truth, the basic and most important part" (see Doc. 12.31). Each had appeared before the Concistoro, Alberto asserting that as Tiberio's successor, the part was his, Giovanbattista arguing that "it was an old custom of this chapel that the oldest persons succeeded to this post" and that it belonged to him by seniority. In the end the priors, sympathetic to both points of view and breaking with precedent, decreed that each should have the honor a month at a time, beginning with Alberto in September, and that if one should leave Palace service, the other alone would have the bass part. The priors further specified that if both musicians were to leave, the maestro could name whom he pleased to play the bass part, as he did with all the others, and that their ruling in no way changed the current provisions of both musicians.

The report carries far more interest than its account of a quarrel as to who had the right to play a coveted part in the ensemble. Whether a musician was tenured or untenured, seniority, the maestro's prerogative in assigning ensemble parts, and priors impinging on that right are, to be sure, important issues that command attention, as do contemporaneous attitudes regarding them. But the implications for musical performance are even more noteworthy. At a time when theories were just forming that recognized the significance of the bass in part music, the musicians themselves acknowledged that this was so. The remark in turn raises the question of which instrument played this part. Because Tiberio was generally identified as a trombonist, it is likely that the trombone was the preferred instrument. But since Alberto and Giovan Battista are never called by any name other than musico, indicating they were both primarily woodwind players, perhaps a curtal or dulcian could also perform the bass part. Such speculation is pointless, however, since both musicians probably played a number of instruments well, the

---

87. A record of the marriage contract between Alberto and Tiberio's sister, Ippolita, also survives: "Denunciatum fuit per scriptam factam sub die VIII decembris 1580, manu ser Mactie de Burdonibus notarii, qualiter Albertus magistri Francisci de Gregoriis, musicus palatinus, accepit in uxorem dominam Ipolitam filiam quondam Ieronimi de Rivoltis de Senis, cum dota florenorum quatringentorum, Fl. 400. Solvit Camillo Spannocchio camerario, fo. 28, die 6 februarii 1580[81], L. 26. 13. 4" (ASS, Gabella dei Contratti, vol. 404, fol. 77ᵛ).

trombone included. The same could be said about a later situation when the trombonist Giovanfrancesco returned to the wind band, and all three musicians took turns in playing the first bass part. It should also be noted that because there is no mention of the musicians' ability to play well whatever instrument might have been used, both were equally gifted and quality of performance was never an issue.

Tiberio died shortly before 22 February 1601, the day Alberto Gregori replaced him as a permanent member of the group. Alberto was then substituting for his son, in whose favor he had earlier renounced his own supernumerary's post.[88] In the deliberations preceding Alberto's election the priors agreed to transfer Tiberio's tenured post and the meal allowance attached to it to the person who received the most votes and to divide his salary later (see Doc. 12.32). True to their word, the priors later apportioned Tiberio's L. 4. 10, which had been carved out of Adriano's L. 16, among the musicians who had competed unsuccessfully with Alberto, awarding L. 2 to Piergiovanni Odorini, L. 1. 10 to Ottavio di Basilio, and L. 1 to Giulio di Alessandro.

Alberto was back before the Concistoro at the end of 1601, requesting yet another privilege, so that he might pursue a coveted post outside the Palace. As he explained in his petition, he had replaced the deceased Tiberio Rivolti as *maestro di cappella* at Santa Maria della Scala,[89] and now he wished, with their permission, to take on the post permanently, this, of course, in addition to his work at the Palace. Apparently few if any conflicts in schedule existed because Alberto, like the other musicians, had to perform at the Palace only three days a week. Tiberio had set an excellent precedent and with his example in mind that priors told Alberto that "he could play music and sing in the said church at the usual and customary times."

After Simone Nodi's death his post passed to the trombonist Giovanfrancesco di Benedetto, who was elected leader of the wind band on 29 October 1602. Giovanfrancesco was quite along in years by then. He had reclaimed his old post at the Palace in the fall of 1594, after spending fifteen years at the Medici court. Though he apparently left Florence under a cloud, court officials nevertheless sent him home strongly recommending that he be provided with an adequate income.[90] The priors met the problem of granting him a salary and a meal allowance by decreasing the other musicians' provisions, an action vigorously protested by the parties involved. A report from

---

88. See Doc. 12.40 for the deliberation from 15 April 1599 permitting his son to serve in his stead. Alberto prospered exceedingly in his chosen profession, if one can judge from the value placed on one of his properties. A notarial act dated 30 June 1594, for example, shows that he sold a house in Siena for Fl. 300 (Notarile postcosimiano, Originali, vol. 43, no. 2043). Earlier, on 6 August 1587, he was a witness to a legal transaction (Originali, vol. 48, unnumbered folio). His brother Ruberto di Francesco Gregori was also a musician, as shown by a notarial act of 13 March 1592 (ibid., unnumbered folio: "musico de Senis").

89. Subsequent records show that Alberto earned L. 28 per month at the chapel. His first two payments, of L. 56 each, from 20 October 1601 and 26 January 1602, indicate that he had been working there for four months before that time, that is, from mid-August 1601 (Ospedale, vol. 919, *E&U, 1601–2,* fols. 109ᵛ, 118ᵛ).

90. Kirkendale, *The Court Musicians in Florence,* 118, notes that Giovanfrancesco's appointment at court was terminated before 3 November 1595, the date of a note mentioning a trombone given to him by Grand Duke Ferdinand that he had retained "quando fu licenziato."

21 January 1595 tells that the priors read the petition brought to the captain of the people against the trombonist Giovanfrancesco by his colleagues and then reviewed their own pronouncement in his favor from the previous 16 September (see Doc. 12.33). To satisfy both sides, the Concistoro now decided that Giovanfrancesco could continue with his meal allowance and monthly salary of L. 6 but must be at the Palace three days a week, "like the other musicians." Thus he was "expected to play the first bass part on Sunday, Tuesday, and Thursday and Alberto di Gregorio and Giovan Battista Formichi [were to play] on the other days, as has been customary in the past." In addition, Giovanfrancesco, like the other musicians, had to accompany the priors at official functions and play at church services they attended. As for outside employment, the priors declared that whenever Giovanfrancesco went with the others "to play at Masses, Vespers, weddings, banquets, and in other similar places," he was to receive his fair share of the earnings. In return, the Concistoro restored to the other musicians those portions of their salaries and meal allowances received before the decree of 16 September 1594, with the proviso that their new decision did not apply to the previous months of October and November.[91]

The same scenario replayed a few years later, on 28 February 1597, when the priors had to reconsider the burden imposed on Palace finances by Giovanfrancesco's provision and restoration of what had been taken from the other musicians. There simply were not enough funds for the additional expenses. The Medici governor's recommendation that "Giovanfrancesco be provided for as he asks" was read and the other musicians were once again allowed to speak on their own behalf (see Doc. 12.34). But this time their protests were to no avail and the priors decided to continue to honor Giovanfrancesco's request, which in effect meant a return to the previous reallocation of funds. Thus, the L. 6 required for his salary was raised by reducing those of three musicians, Risquillo, Maestri, and Tiberio, by L. 1 and by cutting Cocchi's by L. 3. Giovanfrancesco's meal privileges were assured by revoking those currently enjoyed by Ottavio di Lorenzo. (Ottavio, however, was to receive a salary of 3 carlini, and henceforth obliged to play only on Sundays, and he was to receive a meal allowance every time he did so. He also retained his right to a share of earnings from any of "the banquets, weddings, and conferments of doctorates festivities" at which the group might play.) In a final gesture of generosity for the Medici favorite the priors stipulated that though Giovanfrancesco was to continue to perform at their table on Sundays, Tuesdays, and Thursdays, he would no longer be obliged to play in the *ringhiera,* this latter perhaps a reference to the balcony outside the Palace. Given his age, experience, and connections, it is no wonder that when Nodi died at the end of October 1602, the priors decided to make Giovanfrancesco leader of the wind band.

But Giovanfrancesco was unable to function in his new post. On 22 April 1603, after noting that it was proper and necessary for the good of the group to have a visible leader, the governor and the priors replaced him with Alberto di Francesco Gregori, "who has been a musician in their Palace for many years" (see Doc. 12.35). In appointing Gregori the government decreed that he was to assume the incumbent's usual duties

---

91. Note that this decree makes reference to previous action taken on 16 September 1594.

and obligations, "above all, because of the great necessity of renewing and maintaining a school of music in the Palace, as was the custom in the past, and of promoting young players from it." The priors also decreed that Alberto was to have "the customary honors, emoluments, and salary that previous maestri had."

The government's deliberations did not end here. They next stipulated that Giovanfrancesco, his health permitting, was to continue in the Palace ensemble. In order to do this they assigned him the place previously occupied by Alberto Gregori, with the proviso, however, that L. 2 of that provision were to be given to Ottavio Basili. The priors also decided to submit a copy of their deliberations with a rescript so that the Medici governor could signify his approval. The next morning, however, the governor issued the following statement, appended to the record of the priors' decision by his secretary Giovanni Battista Bernardini on 26 April 1603 (see Doc. 12.35):

> His Excellency does not wish to interfere in this matter, neither approving nor disapproving it, and thus the Most Illustrious Concistoro should do as it must and should do, as though he were not consulted.

Giovanfrancesco lived only a short while longer. His death is reported in two decrees from late October 1603 reassigning his monthly salary of L. 12. 10 in the following way: L. 4 to Niccolò Faraoni, L. 3 to Piergiovanni Odorini, L. 3 to Ottavio Basili, and L. 2 to Pietragnolo Maestri. Another s. 10, to be distributed by the captain of the people at his discretion, went to Niccolò Faraoni. Giovanfrancesco's allowance of bread and wine was evenly divided between two young musicians, Fulvio di Matteo, son of the Palace cook, and Lorenzo della Scala, who were obliged to assist and be present at all times when the band played, in and outside the Palace (see Doc. 12.36).

During the last two decades of the century positions in the Palace's musical establishment continued to be much coveted and many were those who willingly served in the wind band without pay until they could be formally compensated. This situation accounts for the presence of several musicians who probably played in the ensemble for some time before their names appear in minutes of the priors' meetings. Among them was Tiberio Rivolti's brother Piero di Girolamo Rivolti, who was also known as Risquillo. He may have joined the ensemble during one of Tiberio's absences, as Tiberio had requested in his 1578 petition, mentioned above, or he may have been enrolled in the ranks of the supernumeraries. Little is heard of him until February 1597, when L. 1 was removed from his monthly salary during the renegotiation of Giovanfrancesco's salary (see Doc. 12.34). Piero is next mentioned in a deliberation from 29 May 1599 reporting that Orindio Bartolini had renounced his post and its monthly salary of L. 2 and that Piero, a student of Tiberio, was to succeed him with the same duties and privileges (see Doc. 12.37). Piero enjoyed his new status only briefly. A decree from the following November notes his death and the awarding of his post and monthly salary of L. 2 to Ottavio di Lorenzo Basili (see Doc. 12.38). Both Rivoltis were admired by Ugurgieri-Azzolini, who reported in his *Pompe sanesi* that Risquillo and Tiberio easily triumphed over two talented German cornettists in a celebrated musical contest.[92] As in Risquillo's case, little evidence remains regarding Orindio Bartolini's initial appointment and of his work at the Palace.

---

92. Ugurgieri-Azzolini, *Le pompe sanesi*, 2:7; Cellesi, *Storia della più antica banda musicale senese*, 36.

In contrast to these two musicians, Ottavio di Lorenzo Basili, who also sang and played in the cathedral chapel, had a long career at the Palace. His employment record illustrates the route traveled by several musicians in their quest to become enrolled as tenured members of the group on the Palace "tavolella." A record from 1595 states that by then Ottavio had served at the Palace for fourteen years, that is, since 1581. His participation in the wind band, however, was not recognized until November 1585, when after Tiberio Rivolti and Jacomo Latini departed, the priors chose him from among several young musicians who had applied for compensation of some kind. At the time he was granted "two large loaves of bread and a flask of wine every day." Two and half years passed before he was more amply rewarded with a monthly meal allowance of s. 30, on 27 June 1588. This was increased by an additional s. 30 per month on 28 July 1591. The 1595 record says that the priors decided to double this by 3 carlini because they knew that "besides knowing how to play many instruments that the other musicians play, his singing makes music blossom at the Palace" and that his present monthly salary of 3 carlini was "small recognition in respect to what the other musicians receive." Ottavio subsequently lost his meal allowance as a result of the protracted negotiations of 28 February 1597 with Giovanfrancesco, just mentioned. That action apparently satisfied nobody, however, for the priors voted to restore his allowance in the following May. They added L. 2 per month to this on 31 August 1598, after Adriano Mangoni's death, as well as Adriano's meal allowance. Ottavio finally gained a tenured post on 10 November 1599, when he succeeded Risquillo.

The government's decision regarding the distribution of Adriano Mangoni's salary after his death is of interest for a number of reasons (see Doc. 12.28). Principal among them is the revelation that all tenured musicians no longer received the same salary, which, along with meal privileges, might now be distributed according to longevity or according to what the priors deemed proper. It also furnishes additional evidence that several musicians—musicians whose names are not otherwise noted in the records—served without formal recognition at the time. On this occasion the L. 16 previously allocated for Mangoni's salary were distributed among seven musicians, of whom four were regularly salaried players, the others supernumeraries: L. 4. 10 to Tiberio Rivolti; L. 1 to Giovanbattista Cocchi; L. 2. 5 to Pietragnolo Maestri; L. 1. 15 to Piergiovanni Odorini; the just-mentioned sum of L. 2 and meal allowance to Ottavio Basili; L. 2. 10 to Giulio di Alessandro Muratore; and L. 2 to Orindio Bartolini, who renounced his post within the year (see Doc. 12.37).

The meal allowance granted to Pietragnolo di Bernardino Maestri and Virgilio di Lorenzo Ricci in April 1591 was confirmed by decree the following 30 July. But Virgilio was employed at the Palace for only a short time afterwards. An October 1591 deliberation reports that he was fired because he had left the city without permission and failed to return and that Piergiovanni Odorini was to replace him, presumably as a supernumerary (see Doc. 12.39). Odorini was also a teacher because he was described as a *musices professor* when he witnessed a legal document on 13 August 1597, together with his colleague Tiberio Rivolti, who was called a *musices magister*.[93] Odorini, Cocchi, and Maestri are cited in various reports concerning the redistribution of salaries after

93. See note 84.

the deaths of Mangoni, Giovanfrancesco, and Risquillo. All three were also colleagues in the cathedral chapel well into the new century.

Besides Ottavio Basili, the musicians competing for the salary and meal privileges available at Risquillo's death in November 1599 included Pietragnolo Maestri, Piergio-vanni Oderini, and Niccolò di Aurelio Faraoni. The salary, as noted, was awarded to Ottavio, but the meal allowance, considered later in the day, went to Faraoni, a new name in the records. It seems that he left Siena after that time because in February 1601, when Alberto Gregori was elected to replace the recently deceased Tiberio, Faraoni was not among the recipients of the funds attached to that post (Doc. 12.32).

Faraoni was another Sienese musician with Florentine ties. Ugurgieri-Azzolini, who heard him play and described him as a "dolcissimo sonatore," reports that he often performed at the Medici court.[94] A later record shows that he was also a convivial soul. Dated 30 November 1606, this recounts how the Concistoro intervened on his behalf and had him released from prison. His offense, which he was admonished not to repeat without permission, was playing his cornett in the piazza at the fourth hour of the night.

A list of Palace employees prohibited from playing in the games at the end of that same month, February 1600, includes seven musici, Alberto Gregori, Piergiovanni Odorini, Pietragnolo Maestri, Ottavio Basili, Giulio d'Alessandro, Niccolò Faraoni, and Annibale Gregori.[95] Annibale Gregori, the newest member of the group, subse-quently became one of the most famous Sienese musicians of the early Baroque, pub-lishing several volumes of sacred and secular music and assuming the *maestro di cappella*'s post at the cathedral on two separate occasions.[96] His appointment at the Palace began on 15 April 1599, when his father, Alberto di Francesco Gregori, made a supplication on behalf of his son to the Concistoro (see Doc. 12.40). At the time Alberto, already in government service for twenty-six years, cited the burdens of rearing a large family, and requested that Annibale, who "has received more than an ordinary training in the art of music, as Your Lordships can easily learn," succeed to his post, with the same salary and emoluments that he was presently receiving. Alberto further requested that, once appointed, if for some reason his son could not continue, he himself be reinstated to the post. The priors granted the request, with the proviso, however, that Alberto himself was to continue serving the Palace for the next four years, during which time his son, who would also play with the group, would receive no salary.

Incorrigible behavior on the part of one of the musicians led to a further change in the band's composition early in the seventeenth century. This time punishment was more than the usual imprisonment, when on 10 December 1601 Giulio d'Alessandro was condemned to death on the gallows for having committed numerous crimes, in-cluding theft, beating on doors, stealing trumpets, and cutting the strings of musical instruments. The band played on, however, and within two weeks Niccolò Faraoni

---

94. Ugurgieri-Azzolini, *Le pompe sanesi,* 8; Cellesi, *Storia della più antica banda musicale senese,* 36. A cathedral clerk, Silverio Faraoni, listed from 1591 to 1595, was probably his brother (AOMS, vol. 1082, fols. 325ʳ, 373ʳ, 414ʳ).

95. See chapter 10, note 64.

96. On Annibale Gregori as *maestro di cappella,* see Reardon, *Agostino Agazzari and Music at Siena Cathedral,* 44–47.

requested and was granted "the food provision and the small salary that Giulio had received." On 9 September 1602 Giovanbattista Cocchi, Pietragnolo Maestri, Simone Nodi, Ottavio Basili, Alberto Gregori, Annibale Gregori, and Piergiovanni Odorini were each awarded a monthly meal allowance of L. 6. 10, in addition to their daily allotments of bread and wine (see Doc. 12.41). Faraoni, Odorini, Basili, and Maestri, as mentioned, shared in the distribution of Giovanfrancesco's salary after the latter's death, on 31 October 1603 (Doc. 12.35).

Lorenzo della Scala, who was granted a portion of Giovanfrancesco's bread and wine allotment at that time, served at the Palace for a only few years before gaining a tenured post on 1 July 1606. In decreeing that his name should be placed on the "tavolella," or roll containing the names of permanent members of the band, the priors declared that henceforth he would receive L. 3 in salary and L. 6 for meal expenses every month. Lorenzo must have been an exceptionally talented musician, probably a pupil of one of Palace musicians who were also teachers, notably Tiberio Rivolti, Alberto Gregori, or Piergiovanni Odorini. To judge from his name, he was a foundling, like several previously recorded musicians, reared at the charitable institution maintained by the hospital of Santa Maria della Scala. A number of orphaned youths were also hired by the cathedral chapel around this time, proof of the effectiveness of the hospital's teaching program, mentioned below in chapter 13.

Apart from Lorenzo's appointment in July 1606, no further changes in the status of personnel are reported during the next few years. It was not until August of 1611 that the priors approved two new appointments, sought in time-honored fashion for relatives of two of the band members. In separate actions the priors agreed on the 12th of the month to allow Francesco Gregori to assume his brother Annibale's post on condition that Annibale personally continue to honor his commitments at the Palace for the next three years (see Doc. 12.42).[97] Fifteen days later the priors also agreed that Lorenzo Basili could succeed to the post held by his father Ottavio, who had renounced it in favor of his son (see Doc. 12.43). In a way, these reports provide as fitting a close as one might wish for this account of the Palace musicians. They illustrate as perhaps no other anecdotes could the power that ties of kinship exerted for centuries in the history of Sienese instrumental music. It was, in fact, a force as constant at the beginning of the seventeenth century as in the mid-thirteenth century, when the trumpeter Guido Rosso and his son Compare appeared among the Palace employees. (See Table 12.1 for a chronological list of the sixteenth-century musicians.)

DOCUMENTS

Doc. 12.1. Declaration concerning supernumeraries and their substitutes, 23 October 1538. ASS, Concistoro, vol. 1038, fol. 26[r–v]

Et actento quod Virginius Pauli tibicen multoties debet servire in defectu tibicinum supra numerariorum, qui sunt Antonius tibicen, Bernardinus cartularius et Lutius, frater dicti Virginii, sit declaratum quod omni vice quod erit necesse quod dicti tubicenes supra numerarii debere[n]t venire et non veniunt ad sonandum cum fuerint requisiti, sonante Ginio [Virginio] pro eis,

---

97. Thanks to his father, Annibale was by this time also employed at the chapel of Santa Maria della Scala.

habeat habere unum carulenum pro qualibet vice quod sonaret pro quocumque ipsorum requi-
sito et non veniente. Qui carulenus detrahi debeat de salario huiusmodi deficientis venire, et
interim sit puntatus talis qui defecerit, et de dictis pontaturis teneat computum notarium Consistorii.

Doc. 12.2. Approval of a petition by Pavolo di Giovanni for an expectative for his son, 4 August
1525. Concistoro, vol. 953, fol. 48^{r-v}

Visa petitione Pauli Iohannis piffari, tenoris infrascripti . . . solemniter deliberaverunt quod dicta
petitio intelligatur et sit approbata in omnibus et per omnia prout in ea.

Dinanzi da voi Magnifici et eccelsi Signori . . . Exponsi per lo vostro schiavo e servidore Pavolo
di Giovanni piffaro che havendo consumato tutto el tempo dela vita sua in servitio del vostro
Palazo fedelmente ala piffara, ha allevato Virginio suo figliuolo acciò che continui nella medesima
fedel servitù cola piffara, e lo fa diligentemente attendere ad imparare, e non dubbita verrà ex-
cessivo in tale exercitio e farà honor al vostro Palazo. Per il che humamente prego Vostre Excelse
Signorie lo' piaccia deputare detto Virginio nel loco di detto Pavolo doppo la vita sua. La qual
gratia obtenuto, come spera, dale Signorie Vostre, li sarà una elemosina e gratia singularissima
dale Vostre Signorie, de quali humilmente si rachomanda e prega Dio che quelle feliciti.

Doc. 12.3. Renewed warnings to the wind band, 12 July 1538. Concistoro, vol. 1031, 14^r

Insuper quoniam ut plurimum piffari et tubonis, prandentibus et cenantibus magnificis dominis,
non faciunt quidquid tenentur in sonando, et precipue Benedictus tubonis sepius iam defecit,
licet alias admoniti et reprensi fuerint: igitur ad eorum nimiam licentiam quam sibi assumunt et
inobbedientiam coercendam ac refrenandam, servatis etc., decreverunt quod quotiescumque de
cetero aliquis ex eis deficiet sonare quando tenetur neque alium sui loco deputaverit qui
effectualiter sonet, nisi tamen iusto impedimento detineretur ut puta infirmitate aut absentia cum
consensu et venia obtenta a magnifico priore, intelligatur ille ex eis qui deficeret statim amisisse
suum locum. Mandantes presentem deliberationem eis notificari. Et die dicta fuit notificata Valerio et Galgano.

Doc. 12.4. Luzio di Pavolo petitions to have his son given an expectative, 14 April 1545.
Concistoro, vol. 1071, fols. 41^r–42^r

[margin: Pro Lutio di Pavolo piffaro e Adriano Imperiale suo figlio] Audita petitione in scriptis,
presentata per Lutium olim Pauli piffari de Senis, continente qualiter dictus Paulus eius pater
elapsis annis, cum esset iam in senili etate constitutus et male valitudinis et non posset exercere
offitium suum tibicine in eorum palatio, mediante renuntiatione facta per dictum Paulum de
dicto suo officio tibicine in favorem dicti Lutii sui filii, fuit per excelsum integrum Consistorium
dictus Lutius ad dictum offitium tibicine exercendum in dicto palatio, cum eodem salario quod
habebat dictus Paulus, et sic quamplures annos se exercuit in dicto suo offitio loco patris. Et cum
dictus Paulus de mense proxime preterito vita functus sit, et vellet dictus Lutius habere decretum
dicte electionis et conducture de se facte ad dictum offitium exercendum, non potuit adhuc illud
invenire cum non recordetur a quo notario Consistorii fuit rogatum, ideo petente ad cautelam
dictum decretum confirmari et seu denuo ipsum Lutium eligi conduci et deputari ad dictum
offitium tibicine exercendum . . . Et petente etiam declarari provisionem librarum decem
denariorum quolibet mense concessam dicto Lutio fuisse et esse vacatam et concessam Adriano
Imperiali, asserto filio naturali dicti Lutii, prout de huiusmodi concessione constare ostendidit
decretum Illustrissimi Consistorii sub die ultima Augusti anni 1541 . . . Unde habito inter se
maturo colloquio et examine, actenta diligenti fideli et longa servitute in eorum palatio tam dicti
Pauli quam dicti Lutii eius filii, et actentis bonis moribus ac laudabilibus virtutibus et suffitientia
eiusdem Lutii . . . comprobaverunt dictum assertum decretum electionis et conductionis . . . in
personam dicti Lutii . . . in dicto offitio tibicine . . . cum dicto salario, honoribus et oneribus

quibus serviebat dictus eius pater . . . Declarantes insuper dictam provisionem librarum decem denariorum pro quolibet mense concessam dicto Lutio, vacatam esse et pertinere et expectare ad dictum Adrianum Imperialem, eius assertum filium naturalem.

Doc. 12.5. Three new supernumeraries are appointed, 17 December 1546. Concistoro, vol. 1081, fol. 28^{r-v}

Actento quod insuper Simeon alumnus Dominici Pollastre camerarii eorum palatii, per remunerationem alias sibi factam per Galganum Enee tibicinam, et mortem ipsius, consecutus est locum seu officium unius ex tibicenis dicti palatii, et modo provisio quam obtinebat dictus Simon in dicto palatio librarum decem denariorum quolibet mense vacavit et vacat ad presens pro predictis. Et super premissis visis et auditis petitionibus omnium infrascriptorum adolescentium . . . attentis maxime virtutibus et bonis qualitatibus eorum et cuiuslibet ipsorum, et qualiter sunt bene instructi in arte et exercitio musicali et tube respective, et continuo in eodem exercentur, volentes eos et quemlibet ipsorum in aliquali parte, un bonos principes decet, recognoscere, servatis, etc. deliberaverunt dictis et infrascriptis dari et solvi et assignari de dicta provisione . . . qualibet mense, ut infra . . . Ascanio Andree Lazari, libras 5; Augustino et Partenio, filii Benedicti tuboni, in totum libras 3; Iohanni Battiste de Vulganis, tubicine, libras 2.

Doc. 12.6. Adriano Imperiale gains a permanent post in the wind band, 6 June 1554. Concistoro, vol. 1123, fol. 31^{r}

Audita relatione deputatorum super causa Hadriani et magistri Antonii, tibicinarum palatii, deliberaverunt, actento quod dictus Hadrianus Pauli tybicina continue habet victum et salarium in palatio, intelligatur esse et sit unus de musicis palatii, et sic augeatur numerus musicorum et sint septem, et dictus Hadrianus possit sonare et participet de xeniis, vulgo mancie et magaluffi, pro una ex septem partibus prout alii, et propter hoc non intelligatur auctum salarium suum magis quam habet de presentis.

Doc. 12.7. The Palace trombonist Benedetto di Domenico receives a printing privilege, 14 April 1545. Concistoro, vol. 1071, fol. 42^{r-v}

E odito Benedetto di Domenico trombone e la sua petitione in scriptis presentata, continente che se li conceda privilegio che altri che lui non possa stampare in Siena per quel tempo che parrà a llor Signorie, certe compositioni delle quali in quella: deliberonno che sia data auttorità piena alli Magnifici Signori e Capitano di possere sopra le cose contenute in decta petitione capitulare e concedere a decto Benedetto privilegio come lo' parrà intorno a ciò. Dovendosi porre in detta capitulatione che in caso che decto Benedetto non tenesse fornita la città come in decta sua petitione, s'intenda la gratia e concessione nulla e incorra in pena di scudi dieci. Et se vendesse alcuna cosa più prezzo che non si contiene in decta petitione, incorga [=incorrà] in pena d'uno scudo per volta e per ciascuna compositione e opera che vendesse più che non si contiene in detta sua petitione.

Another document, in Concistoro, vol. 2230, *Scritture concistoriali, 1544–45,* unnumbered insert dated April 1545, presents the full text of the petition and the priors' response, here excerpted:

Die XX Aprilis [1545] Privilegio per Benedetto trombone

Illustrissimi et magnifici priores et capitaneus populi. Odito Benedetto di Domenico trombone, servitore del lor palazzo, esponendo come egli nella sua spesa ha ordinato in casa di sua habitacione alla Sapientia, uno edifitio tutto di bronzo come s'usa in Venetia, per stampare e scrivere tre sorte di lettere per detta stampa, delle quali ne ha presentato gl'essempli dinanti a llor Signorie, e ne dice come del continuo s'attende a stampare opere e compositioni per servitio della città. E per questo domanda humilmente a llor Signorie che nissuna persona possa dentro in la città di Siena stampare né vendare alcuna sorte di compositioni che se ne stanpasse per detto Benedetto, come sonno carte da citti, quaderni, Donati, storie, commedie, leggende e orationi e simili altre compositioncelle. Obligandosi nel vendare dette compositioni a minuto, darle a ragione di uno quattrino il foglio, e in grosso a ragione di venti quattrini salvo le carte da citti e altre compositioni che vanno in mezzo foglio solo, che a minuto le possa vendare un quattrino il mezzo foglio e in grosso a venti quattrini il quinterno. Offerendosi tenere fornita la città e suo dominio di simili opere, né farà di bisogno conducerne delle forestiere, e li denari non si veranno a trarre della città. Onde havuto infra di loro maturo parlamento e discorso sopra la detta domanda . . . hanno deliberato concedare, e in virtù del presente decreto concedono privilegio al decto Benedetto che per cinque anni, da cominciarsi in calende di gennaio prossimo che verrà e da finir come segue, che nissun'altra persona posso né le sia lecito, escetto decto Benedetto, stampare dentro dela città di Siena né stampate vendare alcuna sorta di compositioni et opere delle quali se ne stampasse alla stamparia di decto Benedetto, cioè carte da citti, quaderni, Donati, storie, leggende, commedie e orationi, sotto pena di scudi dieci d'oro per ciascuna compositione e opera, e di perdersi dette compositioni stampate.

Doc. 12.8. Petition of Giovanni di Maestro Antonio concerning his student Galgano d'Enea, 29 April 1522. Concistoro, vol. 933, fol. 17^v

Magnifici et excelsi domini . . . audita petitione Iohannis magistri Antonii de Senis, piffari palatii, moti iustis rationibus, dictam petitionem infrascriptam . . . approbaverunt et confirmaverunt in omnibus et per omnia . . . cuius petitionis supra obtente, tenor talis est, videlicet: Dinanzi da voi Magnificie et excelsi Signori, si espone per me Giovanni di maestro Antonio, al presente piffaro del vostro Palazzo, come havendo uno Galgano di Enea, già trombetto del decto Palazzo, tenuto mio discepulo ad insegnare canto e musica e piffara e altri strumenti como proprio figliuolo [text breaks off here].

Doc. 12.9. Reduction of the wind band, 3 July 1556. Concistoro, vol. 1133, fol. 2^v

Illustrissimi domini . . . deliberaverunt scrutinari omnes et singuli piffari et musici ad presens conducti et expensas habentes in palatio, et quinque habentes plures voces et lupino remaneant et remanere debeant pro piffaris et piffaris [sic] seu musicis dicti palatii, cum eodem officio, salario, emolumentis et aliis consuetis. Et statim factum fuit dictum scrutinium . . . et remanserunt infrascripti per plura vota, videlicet: magister Nicolaus tubicina [sic], Simon Dominici tibicina, Ansanus [recte Ascanius] Andree tubonus, Iohannesfranciscus tubonus, Adrianus Pauli [recte Lutii], tibicine [sic].

Doc. 12.10. Tardy pifferi are threatened with loss of meal privileges, 13 January 1556. Concistoro, vol. 1130, fol. 5^v

Atteso che spesse volte alcun delli piffari manchano nell'hora convenienti e non sonno a sonare come sonno obligati, in detrimento del palazzo, e volendo a questo provedere, mandorno farsi precetto alli detti piffari e musici loro che si [se] per l'avenire alcuno di loro mancharà, che non sia in salotto dove si magna quando li Signori si lavano le mani per intrare a tavola, non se li devi dar da magnare tante volte quante mancharanno alcuni di loro, si [se] già non fussono manchati con buona licentia del magnifico signor priore Illustrissimo Capitano del Popolo. E subbito li fu per me notificato.

Doc. 12.11. Alfonso di Pavolo petitions to substitute for Fabio di Geronimo, 30 October 1562. Concistoro, vol. 1169, fols. 16^v–17^r

Visa et lecta petitione . . . presentata pro parte . . . Alfonsi Pauli tubicine de Senis, tenoris et continentie de qua infra, habita noticia et bona informatione de dicto Alfonso et eius bonis moribus et quod bene et recte incepit se gerere tubando musice et addiscendo et particulariter in sonando instrumenta solita cum aliis musicis . . . deliberaverunt quod dictus Alfonsus durante absentia dicti Fabii a civitate, et serviendo dictum palatium in tubendo musice et sonando instrumenta una cum aliis musicis, quod debeat habere expensas pro suo victu in tinello . . . cum hoc quod quando dictus Fabius redierit ad civitatem et ad serviendum dictum palatium in tubendo musice et sonando instrumenta una cum aliis musicis . . . quod dictum Alfonsum intelligatur ipso facto cassum de dicto loco.

Doc. 12.12. Alfonso di Pavolo succeeds Savino di Francesco, 30 December 1564. Concistoro, vol. 1182, fol. 32^v

Illustrissimi domini . . . audito maestro Paolo tubicina eorum palatii, petente declarari Alfonsium eius filium et musicum in palatium, debere participare de omnibus collationibus, mancis, regalis et ut dicitur magaluffis, prout et sicut participabat et gaudebat Savinus Francisci Belli, loco cuius Savini successit prefatus Alfonsius . . . deliberaverunt quod . . . similiter habeat et gaudeat prefatus Alfonsius, ultra salarium librarum septem pro quolibet mense.

Doc. 12.13. Three musicians are suspended, 10 June 1567. Concistoro, vol. 1196, fol. 8^r

[margin: Trium musicorum suspensio] Magnifici et excelsi domini etc., motis iustis et rationalibus causis, privaverunt Iohannemfranciscum olim Benedicti, tibicenam, Tiberium Hieronimi et Alfonsum Pauli tubicene [sic] musicos a victu et salario ipsorum pro omni residue temporis eorum suppremi magistratus; et in loco eorum, pro dicto tempore, subrogaverunt Iohanbaptistam olim Benedicti, [sic] musicum, omni modo etc.

Doc. 12.14. Giovanbattista Formica pertitions for a post, 22 November 1568. Concistoro, vol. 1205, fol. 9^{r-v}

Li Magnifici et Eccelsi Signori . . . Visto . . . il memoriale di Giovambapttista di Francesco Formica, producto et presentato allo Illustrissimo Signor Governatore nostro sopra il luogo vacante di Flamminio di maestro Antonio Signorini, et il rescripto di detto nostro Illustrissimo Governatore del tenore et continentia infrascripto . . . deliberorno di concedere il detto luogo vacante al detto Giovambaptista in tutto et per tutto sì come esso ne domanda . . . Il tenore del memoriale . . . hè [sic] questo, cioè:

Illustrissimo Signor Governatore etc.

Giovambaptista di Francesco Formica, giovanetto exercitato nella musica, dice a Vostra Signoria Illustrissima come del mese di giugno proximo passato Flamminio di maestro Antonio Signorini si partì dalli servitii del palazzo senza altrimenti domandare licentia, et che per sue lettare si hè anche certezza che esso, essendosi provisto di luogo fuore, non vuole più tornare. Perciò supplica humilmente Vostra Signoria Illustrissima le vogli far gratia di detto luogo, promettendoli liberamente, per quanto il suo sapere si extenda, di fargliene honore . . . Contentandosene il Magnifico Concistoro e giudicando degno il supplicante di quanto domanda, ne le concedino sicondo li ordini, che Sua Signoria Illustrissima ne restarà satisfatto. Filippo And.^{li} de mandato, 12 Novembris '68.

Doc. 12.15. The tenured musicians are fined for not sharing gratuities, 26 January 1565. Concistoro, vol. 1183, fol. 21^r

Li Magnifici Signori . . . per l'autorità data lo' a decidere la causa delle materie de' musici, declarorno che maestro Niccolò, Giovanfrancesco, Simone, Ascanio e Adriano, e ciascuno di loro, sieno obligati dare al decto Alfonso un giulio per uno, dovendoli pagare fra tre giorni al decto Alfonso. Et non pagandoli, hora per alhora concesseno la captura omni modo etc.

Doc. 12.16. Ascanio Marri is fined for not sharing gratuities, 21 February 1570. Concistoro, vol. 1212, fols. 15^v–16^r

Li Magnifici Eccelsi Signori . . . in la causa vertente dinanzi a loro Signori, infra Simone di Domenico e Giovanfrancesco di Benedetto, musici, agenti e domandanti, da una parte, e Ascanio di Andrea musico e maestro di cappella, reo conventuo e sé defendente, dall'altra parte . . . solennemente deliberorno . . . e deliberando declarorno il detto Ascanio essare tenuto e obligato, e così lo condemnorno a dare e pagare al detto Giovanfrancesco, per ogni resto della solita provisione del maestrato di cappella di detto Ascanio fino hoggi decorsa et da decorrare per tutto il presente mese, lire 4 di denari, da pagarseli senza alcuna dilatione di tempo et senza alcuna exceptione. Et di più a dare e pagare per lo advenire alli detti Simone et Giovanfrancesco, incominciando il dì primo di marzo proximo fino che esso terrà detto grado et officio di maestro di cappella, soldi 16 denari 8 per ciascheduno et ciascuno mese, senza alcuna exceptione. Dichiarando che sempre et quando li detti Simone et Giovanfrancesco . . . staranno fuore del servitio del palazzo et di loro Altezze Serenissime senza espresso licentia . . . che durante tale absentia detto Ascanio non sia obligato a pagare alli detti Simone e Giovanfrancesco, a conto delli detti s. 16 d. 8 il mese, cosa alcuna.

Doc. 12.17. Peace is restored among the Palace musicians, 13 March 1570. Concistoro, vol. 1213, fol. 6^r

Attenta differentia et malo animo inter musicos palatii, et volentes scandala evitare et paces inter eos componere, deliberaverunt quod duo ex Illustrissimis dominis . . . componant omnes eorum iniurias et malam voluntatem . . . Die 21 Martii fuit in camera domini Capitanei facta pax inter Ascanium et Iohannemfranciscum, Simonen, Adrianum et Tiberium, osculo pacis hinc inde interveniente in forma.

Doc. 12.18. Duties of the wind band, 17 February 1570. Concistoro, vol. 1212, fols. 13^v–17^v

[margin: Musici, provvisioni] Ancora deliberorno che li musici del loro palazzo sieno tenuti et obligati per lo advenire observare et exequire quanto di sotto sarà scripto. Et prima.

Siano tenuti a cominciare a sonare subbito doppo che sarà posto il primo servitio in tavola, durando infino che saranno portate le frutta e quel più di spatio che parerà alli molto Magnifici Signori Capitano del Populo et priore, sotto la pena, manchando, del perdarsi la parte loro del tinello per uno giorno.

Debbino anchora ritrovarsi tutti nel detto tempo a cominciare sonare, non essendo alcuno ritenuto da giusto et legiptimo impedimento, il quale debbi discernare il molto Magnifico Signor Capitano, altrimenti incorrà ciascuno nella pena dell'essare privato della parte per ciascuna volta.

Nissuno de' musici sia cagione, con parole o con atti, di fare tumulto di sorte niuno mentre suonano dinanzi ai Magnifici Signori, exequendo ciascuno l'uffitio a cui hè tenuto et obligato; et all'auctore et del romore sia tolta la parte per uno giorno.

Sieno obligati anchora a sonare o cantare quella parte della musica che sarà data a ciascuno dal maestro di cappella, né possino dare a sonare o cantare la loro parte ad altri, né meno con altri cambiarla senza buono compacimento di detto mastro di cappella, né possa veruno cominciare a sonare prima che da quello non sia dato l'ordine. Al quale maestro di cappella anchora debbano tutti lasciare portare la misura come si conviene. Et egli similmente potrà et dovrà usar qualche volta con loro questa creanza di farlo sapere avanti che si conduchino al luogo dove si suona, qual sorte di musica habbi disegnato di fare, o di instrumenti o di voci et con quali instrumenti. Cadendo in pena chi contra farà, del perdarsi la parte per ciascuna volta, et del'arbitrio del molto Magnifico Signor Capitano del Populo et priore.

Se alcuno de' musici havrà obtenuto licentia dal molto Magnifico Signor Capitano di non ritrovarsi a sonare con gli altri, debbi avanti che sia il tempo del servire haverlo detto al maestro di cappella, acciò che egli sappia che sorte di musica debba preparare. Et facendo altrimenti, perda la parte sua per tutto lo spatio del tempo che havesse ottenuto licentia.

Ancora sieno tenuti, quando i molto Magnifici Signori escano solennemente fuori del palazzo, sonare dua volte almeno per istrada innanzi che arrivino al luogo dove vanno; per il simile faccino nel ritorno a palazzo. Et andando al duomo, i luoghi dove debbano sonare siano da casa Cerretani et dalla Postierla; sotto la pena di perdarsi la parte d'uno giorno.

Che nei giorni festivi comandati dalla Santa Chiesa, mentre si celebra la messa nella cappella del palazzo, devino fare musica nella consecratione et elevatione del Santissimo sacramento; privando della parte ciascuno che manchasse per ciascuna volta.

La mattina del sabbato devino, sicondo l'uso antico, ritrovarsi unitamente al'hora solita a fare musica nella cappella di piazza, in honore della beata Vergine, nostra advocata. Et qualunche mancasse di tale obligo, non havendo però legiptimo impedimento da approvarsi per il Magnifico Signor Capitano, incorrà nella perdita della parte di uno giorno.

Che per tutte le solennità et allegrezze publiche che si fanno per rispetto di loro Serenissime Altezze, della città e di altra publica cagione, devino fare musica conveniente, nei luoghi soliti et apparenti del palazzo, sotto pena di essare privati della parte per giorni quattro.

Non possino anchora andare a sonare in luogo alcuno né di giorno né di notte, senza espresso licenza del Capitano, al quale debbino dire dove et a richiesta di chi vadano a fare musica; sotto la pena di due giorni di carcere et della perdita della parte di giorni sei.

Che il canavaio sia tenuto, il primo o sicondo giorno di ogni nuova [e]lezione de' Magnifici Signori, di leggiare o fare leggiare tutte le provisione contenute nella presente tavoletta, et il simile il primo o sicondo giorno del secondo mese; sotto pena del perdarsi la parte di giorni dieci per ciascuna volta che egli manchasse di tale obligo.

Che le dette provisioni stiano appicate nel tinello della famiglia, in luogo dove possino essare vedute e lette da ciascuno, né quindi essare rimosse, alterate o cancellate da niuno della famiglia, sotto la pena della privatione del luogo, nella quale incorrà medesimamente chi sapendolo, non lo notificasse; et a ciascuno sia lecito essare accusatore o notificatore de' delinquenti, guadagnando la metà della pena nella quale per la inobbedienza fussero in corsi.

Et così come di sopra deliberorno et decretorno, et non solo come di sopra, ma in ogni miglor modo etc.

Doc. 12.19. Seven Palace musicians are ordered imprisoned for disobeying rules on outside employment, 21–22 March 1580. Concistoro, vol. 1273, fols. 6^{r-v} and 7^{r}

Convocati . . . fu fatto dall'Illustrissimo Capitano proposta sopra dalla disubidientia de' musici e trombetti, et . . . fu deliberato, atteso la confessione d'essi musici e trombetti . . . che li medesimi tutti sieno carcerati per giorni due, et privi per giorni sei del vitto dei medesimi conforme alla tavolella et ordini.

Fu per me notaio fatto precetto all'infrascritti musici e trombetti che infra un'hora prossima devino entrare in carcere, conforme alla deliberatione del 21 detto . . . Et sonno, cioè Pavolo di Giovanni, Silvio di Simone, Augustino di Pietropavolo, Ciro di Domenico, Dionigi di Pavolo, Plinio di Lione e Sacripante di Pavolo, trombetti; maestro Simone Nodi, Adriano Mangoni, Tiberio Rivolti, Giovanbattista Formichi, Giovanbattista Cocchi, Alberto e Iacopo Casini [*recte* Latini], musici. Et dal soprastante delle carcere di Siena fu referto esser tutti li predetti in carcere et sotto la sua custodia.

Doc. 12.20. Redistribution of salaries following Ascanio Marri's death, 31 October 1575. Concistoro, vol. 1246, fol. 18^{r}

[margin: Salario accresciuto et dato a' musici] L'Illustrissimi Signori . . . havendo visto e letto le suppliche dei musici di Palazzo, cioè di Giovambattista Cocchi, di Giovambattista Formichi, di Iacomo Latini, di Baldassare di maestro Domenico, di Domenico figlio di Bartolomeo barbiere, et di Alberto figlio di Francesco Gregori, domandanti quelli accrescesergli il salario, et questi due ultimi farsegliene del luogo vacato di maestro Ascanio . . . aggiunsero al lor salario agli infrascritti l'infrascritte somme di denari, cioè: al detto Giovambattista Cocchi lire tre, a Giovambattista Formichi lire cinque, a Iacomo Latini lire cinque, et al detto Baldassare assegnarono et dettero lire tre di denari, a tutti per ciascun mese; et in quanto al detto Alberto et Domenico deliberarono che siano riconosciuti et ammessi a servire in Palazzo, dovendosi servire ivi continuamente, ma habbiano le spese un giorno per uno.

Doc. 12.21. Alberto di Francesco and Domenico di Bartolomeo petition for more compensation, 18 February 1578. Concistoro, vol. 1260, fol. 13^v

Li Illustrissimi Signori . . . radunati in Consistorio . . . udita la renuntia fatta nel luogo di musico da Baldassarre di maestro Domenico Ponti . . . elesseno Alberto di Francesco et Domenico di Bartolomeo nel detto luogo di musico renuntiato dal detto Baldassarre, con il salario et spese come nella loro domanda si contiene, della quale in filza, il tenore della quale è questo, cioè:

Illustrissimi et Excelsi Signori
Alberto di Francesco e Domenico di Bartolomeo, umilissimi servitori delle Signorie Vostre Illustrissime, essendosi esercitati nella professione della musica et havendo servito questo magnifico Palazzo già 28 mesi solo per mezze spese, et essendo che Baldassarre di maestro Domenico, che già esercitava il musico, habbia domandato più fa licentia e più non serve: di qui è che i detti supplicanti con debita humiltà e reverentia supplicano le Signorie Vostre Illustrissime che per gratia si degnino la provisione che haveva detto Baldassarre, che sono lire tre di denari e le spese in tinello, conciedarle e distribuirle infra di loro due, la metà per uno, che con questo e quello che hanno, haveranno le spese intere e soldi trenta per ciascuno il mese, ubligandosi servire continuamente come li altri musici sì come fino a hoggi hanno servito. Et ottenendolo, come sperano, ne li terranno perpetuo obligho, pregandoli da Iddio ogni felicità.

Doc. 12.22. Some Palace musicians are granted permission to go to Lucca, 11 September 1566. Concistoro, vol. 1192, fol. 12^{r-v}

[margin: Licentia musicis ad eundum civitatem Lucche] Et deliberaverunt licentiam concedere et concesserunt infrascriptis musicis et tubicenis eorum palatii ad eundi civitatem Lucche, ad honorandum festum S. Crucis et Illustrissimos dominos dicte civitatis, et mandaverunt eisdem fieri de predictis fidem in formam omni modo.
Quorum nomina sunt videlicet:
    Ascanius Andree de Marris, dux musicorum
    Iohannesfranciscus Bernardini et Tiberius Hieronimi, musici
    Simon Pauli, Iohannesdominicus Camilli et Siverius et Pompilius, eiusdem filii, tubicene
    Et die dicta, de sero, in lodia eorum palatii, viva voce dederunt etiam licentiam Adriano
        de Marris [*recte* Mangonis] musico, una cum aliis ad eundi Lucham ut supra.

Doc. 12.23. Jacomo Latini is fined for not returning for six months, late 1579. Concistoro, vol. 1268, fol. 17^r, undated

Item, atteso che Iacomo Latini, musicho di palazzo, fino d'Aprile prossimo passato ottenne licentia per un mese . . . d'andare in compagnia d'altri musici a Santa Maria del Loreto, dicente d'andare, oltre al pigliare il perdono, di vedere ancora se in Fuligno fusse stato maestro d'insegnare a sonare di cornetta, lassando sostituto Anibale di Girolamo, et dipoi fermandosi in Fuligno oltre al'imparare [a sonare] di cornetta, si sia allogato pigliando salario, et habbia cercato che gli fusse prorogato il tempo di sei o otto mesi, dando sol nome di volere imparare et tacendo d'essersi allogato et senza prorogatione habbia indugiato il suo ritorno sino alli 15 del presente. Imperò . . . deliberorno che al detto Iacomo siano levate le spese per giorni 15 . . . et inoltre che sotto la perdita del luogo del musico non gli sia lecito domandare licentia in alcun modo o sotto alcuno quesito colore.

Doc. 12.24. Domenico Fei complains on being deprived of a raise in salary, 27 April 1591, and is turned down on 17 May. Concistoro, vol. 1303, fols. 34^v and 43^v–44^r

Et vista la suplica fatta a Sua Eccellenza Illustrissima da Domenico di maestro Bartolomeo, musico del palazzo, per causa di certo augumento di salario levatoli et dato a Virgilio et Pieragnolo, altri musici. Visto il rescritto di Sua Eccellenza Illustrissima in piei d'essa. Uditi in Concistoro questa mattina li detti Domenico, Virgilio et Pieragnolo, et inteso quanto hanno voluto dire etc. Deliberarono che per il Cancelliere suo si veda tutte le scritture et quello che occorre, et da esso si facci l'informatione a Sua Eccellenza Illustrissima, et quella fatta si legga et si approvi in Concistoro.

Ad consilium Illustrissimi domini Ubertini de Ubertinis fuit deliberatum quod informetur preces porrectae per Dominicum musicum . . . exponendo quo prima vice fuit assignatum salarium totum Virgilio et Petro Angelo musicis, postea de eodem salario pars fuit assignato dicto Domenico, et per Concistorium subsequens fuit deliberatum quod dictum salarium pertineret ad dictos Virgilium et Petrum Angelum. Qua informatione facta legatur et approbetur in Concistorio.

Doc. 12.25. Simone Nodi wins election as leader of the wind band, 23 November 1575. Concistoro, vol. 1247, fols. 6^v–7^r

Fu consegliato dal Signor Lattantio Petroni come da basso, che maestro Simone, Adriano et Tiberio musici si scontrino, et quello rimarrà per i più voti s'intenda essere et sia maestro et capo della musica del Palazzo, con li soliti emolumenti, salari, honori et carichi . . . Et così scontrinati singularmente, per i più voti rimase maestro et capo dela musica del Palazzo maestro Simone di Domenico Nodi, musico, et mandorno farsene decreto in forma.

Doc. 12.26. Giovanbattista Cocchi is permitted to substitute for Simone Nodi, 26 February 1602. Concistoro, vol. 1313, unnumbered folio

Illustrissimi domini Capitaneus Populi et Priores . . . approbarunt, nemine discrepante, pro sostituto domini Simeonis Nodi, musico [sic] Palatii, Ioannem Baptistam de Cocchis, musico [sic], cum conditione quod dictus Simeon adsit et inserviat in festivitatibus, prout tenetur et obligatus extitit in deliberatione facta ab antecessoribus sub die vigesima quarta Decembris proximi preteriti.

Doc. 12.27. A school for wind players is established in the Palace, 21 November 1565. Concistoro, vol. 1187, fol. 8$^{r–v}$

[margin: Musicorum palatii] Dipoi udita la domanda di Giovanfrancesco, Ascanio et Alfonso, musici di lor palazzo, tancto [sic] in nome loro quanto delli altri musici, domandanti concedarseli la stansa [sic] dove che Simone musico fino al presente ha tenuto la scuola per potersi exe[r]citare in la decta stansa. Et volendo lor Signorie aiutare sempre li loro servitori maxime nelle exercitationi virtuose: riguardato la decta stansa et udito le parti più e più volte, tancto insieme quanto di per sé . . . deliberorno che la prima stansa, cioè la stansa incontro alla porta della scala, sia comune per exercitio a tutti li musici di palazzo, possendone tenere la chiave ciascheduno di loro . . . L'altra stansa, che risponde nel mercato, dove Simone s'è exercitato et exercita nel tenervi la scuola, resti libera al decto Simone, per haverla fino adesso posseduta et fattovi alcuni aconcimi a spese sue, dichiarandosi che nissuno altro di detti musici vi possa tener scuola.

Doc. 12.28. Redistribution of salaries following the death of Adriano Mangoni, 31 August 1598. Concistoro, vol. 1310, fol. 31^v

[margin: Circa il luogo d'Adriano Mangoni] Denique . . . Illustrissimi Domini . . . circa locum vacatum olim Hadriani de Mangonibus et infrascriptae distributioni de mercede vel salario ipsius . . . ipsum declararunt . . . inter dictos musicos et inter eos distribuerunt ut infra . . . magistro Tiberio de Rivoltis libras quatuor et soldos decem singulo mense, L. 4. 10; Iohannibaptistae de

Cochis libram unam denariorum, L. 1; Petro Angelo de Magistris libras duas et soldos quinque, L. 2. 5; Petro Iohanni de Odorinis libram unam et s. quindecim, L. 1. 15; Octavio de Basilis expensas victus que iam concesse fuere dicto Hadriano, et libras duas denariorum, L. 2; Iulio Alexandri fatori murarii, libras duas et s. decem, L. 2. 10; Orindio de Bartalinis libras duas denariorum, L. 2.

Doc. 12.29. Two pifferi are given permission to serve a Doria prince, 13 August 1585. Concistoro, vol. 1297, fol. 75^r

[margin: Licentia a Tiberio e Iacomo musici] Udito Tiberio Rivolti e Iacomo Latini, due delli musici del Palazzo, i quali domandorno licentia di possere andare a servire l'Illustrissimo Principe Doria . . . desiderando nondimeno restare accesi nel rolo delli musici di Palazzo . . . Il molto Magnifico Signor Gonfaloniere [del Terzo] di Città . . . consigliò che li sia dato la detta licentia libera, né possino havere salario né emolumento alcuno dal Palazzo durante la assentia loro, ma che si per alcuno tempo ritorneranno, possino, piacendo all'Illustrissimo Consistorio che per li tempi sarà, rimetterli a far quel tanto iudicaranno, accettando la detta licentia loro libera et senza alcuna congnitione, ma solo atteso la loro longha servitù si intendino esser e sieno sempre descritti nel rolo de' musici di palazzo et godino quei medesimi privilegi che per il tempo godranno li altri. Andò il partito, fu vinto per lupini 12 bianchi et uno nero in contrario non ostante.

Doc. 12.30. Tiberio Rivolti requests that his student, Alberto di Francesco Gregori, replace him, 27 June 1585. Concistoro, vol. 1297, fols. 58^v–59^r

[margin: Tiberio et Alberto] Et vista et udita una supplica posta da Tiberio di Girolamo Rivolti et quella bene considerata per giuste et ragionevoli cause etc., del'infrascritto tenore, cioè

Illustrissimi Signori et Signori miei osservandissimi

Tiberio di Girolamo Rivolti, humilissimo et antiquo servitore di questo illustrissimo palazzo, havendo fino da fanciulezza instruito nella musica Alberto di Francesco Gori [*recte* Gregori], che anco esso ha servito più anni nel detto magnifico palazzo, et ultimamente datoli una sua sorella per moglie, desiderando hora parte per ricompensa della buona amicitia et parentela fra essi et parte per finire di pagarli un residuo di dota, suplica humilmente le Signorie Vostre Illustrissime si degnino concederli di fare permuta tra loro del luogo che hanno in questo illustrissimo palazzo, cioè che il luogo che ha detto Tiberio si converta in Alberto con tutti i suoi monumenti [*recte* emolumenti], honori et pesi, et il luogo di Alberto al detto Tiberio con li medesimi honori et pesi. . . .

Et servatis servandis etc., al conseglio del molto Magnifico Signor Gonfaloniere del Terzo di Città deliberorno concederli et deliberando gli concessono quanto in essa supplica si contiene, cioè che il detto luogo di Tiberio sia in tutto libero di detto Alberto con tutti li suoi honori, pesi et emolumenti, et il luogo di Alberto sia in tutto libero del detto Tiberio con li soliti honori et emolumenti etc. Et mandorno farsi il decreto in forma.

Doc. 12.31. A dispute over the right to play the first bass part, 27 August 1585. Concistoro, vol. 1297, fols. 82^r–84^r

Il Magnifico Iacomo d'Alessandro Venturi sopra la causa della precedentia fra Alberto di Domenico Gori [*recte* di Francesco Gregori] et Giovan Battista di Francesco Formicchia [*sic*], musici dell'Illustrissimo Palazzo, quali pretendevano ciascuno di loro di dover fare il primo basso nel conserto [*sic*] della musica, parte invero finale et suprema, però ciascun di loro insieme et di per sé intrati dentro in Concistoro domandando li fusse assegnato questo primo lugho: Alberto diceva a esso appartenersi per succedere in luogo di Tiberio con tutti li honori, pesi et emolumenti in virtù di una deliberatione, come al libro delle deliberationi della Signoria passata, a foglio 59; Giovan Battista al' incontro diceva egli è antico costume di questa cappella che li più antichi successivamente succedino in questo lugho; "Io so' più antico di Alberto, però si per-viene a me." Onde udite ambe e due le parti tanto insieme quanto di per sé, l'Illustrissimo Signor ViceCapitano, il Signor Marcantonio Tolomei . . . il Magnifico Signor Gonfaloniere [del Terzo] di Città, servate le sollenità [sic] da osservarsi, uditi li detti musici in Concistoro et vista la remissione da essi voluntariamente al Concistoro fatta, consegliò che per tor via ogni disturbo e differentia infra di essi, che devino ciascun d'essi far le parte del primo basso un mese per ciascuno, cominciando in calende di Settembre prossimo futuro il detto Alberto, e questo per giuste e ragionevoli consideratoni. In calende di Ottobre poi segua il detto Giovan Battista, et così continuando mese per mese si segua, et se per qualsivoglia causa quale si sia de' detti si partisse o renuntiasse il luogo ad altre, si intendi detta parte del basso restare assolutamente di quello che rimarrà. Et mancando ambedue loro, hor per allora si intenda data libera facultà al maestro di cappella che per li tempi sarà, di poter concedere e dar la detta parte del basso insieme con tutte le altre a chi a esso parrà che più meriti et che li si pervengha. Declarando che la presente declaratione non si intenda in alcun modo né sotto qualsiasi quesito colore diminu[i]ta, alterata o accresciuta la provisione a qual si sia di detti musici, ma restino ciascuno di essi nel medesimo termine che al presente si trovino.

Andò il partito, e fu vento [sic] per lupini undici tutti bianchi.

Doc. 12.32. Redistribution of salaries following Tiberio Rivolti's death, 22 February 1601. Concistoro, vol. 1312, unnumbered folio

[margin: Concessio loci Tiberii musici] Et quia proximis diebus decessit Tiberius de Rivoltis, musicus huius Palatii, prefatus dominus Capitaneus fecit propositam de concessione dicti loci, cui concurrendo inter alios Albertus de Gregoriis, unus ex musicis Palatii, qui alias se obligaverat in servire huic Palatio pro eius filio, cui eius locum renunciavit cum consensu Concistorii per annos quatuor non adhuc completos, petens dictus Albertus admitti ad concursum dicti loci . . . Deinde consuluit dictus dominus Vexillifer Terzerii Civitatis . . . quod dictus locus tradatur cum expensis victus tantum, ei qui habeat plura vota; et quod salarium, pro nunc non tradatur, sed fiat super hoc aliud consilium. Super quibus misso scrutinio, fuit per omnia vota 14 alba obtentum. Et postea scrutinati omnes petentes dicum locum, fuit per plura vota traditum dicto Alberto de Gregoriis. Denique facta proposita a dicto domino Capitaneo de distributione dicti salarii dicti loci . . . fuit distributum et concessum ut infra, videlicet: Petro Iohanni Odorino libras duas; Octavio de Basiliis libram unam et solidos X; Iulio Alexandri de Senis libram unam.

Doc. 12.33. Redistribution of salaries and obligations following the return of Giovanfrancesco di Benedetto, 21 January 1595. Concistoro, vol. 1307, fols. 5^v–6^v

[margin: musici] L'Illustrissimi et eccelsi Signori . . . convocati et congregati nel concistoro loro . . . Visto il ricorso fatto dalli musici del Palazzo loro all'Illustrissimo et eccellentissimo Signor Governatore contro Giovan Francesco trombone, parimente musico, et decreto fatto a suo favore dalli Illustrissimi et eccelsi Signori sotto dì 16 di settembre prossimo passato . . . Deliberorno e deliberando ordinorno, per pace e quiete delle dette parti, doversi dare e concedere al detto Giovan Francesco, sì come gli detteno et concesseno, il piatto et lire sei di denari per ciascuno mese come da basso, con obligo al medesimo di sonare e servire come li altri musici di detto Palazzo tre giorni della settimana, cioè la domenica, martedì e giovedì, aspettandoli sonare la parte del basso primo, et nelli altri giorni Alberto Gregori et Giovan Battista Formichi, come è stato solito per il passato, e di più devi il detto Giovan Francesco accompagnare la Signoria in tutte le sue uscite e sonare nelle chiese come è solito delli altri musici. Con dichiarazione che quando andarà con li medesimi a sonare a messe, vesperi, nozze, banchetti et in altri luoghi simili, devi participare delli emolumenti che si acquistano come li altri musici, alli quali volseno et così comandorno sia restituita la lor portione del piatto et salario in tutto e per tutto e come l'havevano per prima e avanti al suddetto decreto del dì 16 di settembre, eccetto però dal dì primo di ottobre per tutto novembre passati, che si doveranno pagare detti salari come in detti decreti, et così comandorno per il maestro di cappella darseli et pagarseli.

Doc. 12.34. Redistribution of salaries and obligations, 28 February 1597. Concistoro, vol. 1309, fols. 8^r–9^r

Viso scripto Sue Eccellentie Illustrissime transmisso Illustrissimo Concistorio, continente substantialiter quod Iohanni Francisco ut dicitur trombone detur provisio librarum sex denariorum pro quolibet mense, et ut dicitur il piatto; ac etiam rescripto citato Sue Altitudinis Serenissime . . . huiusmodi tenoris, idest "Il Governatore proveda che sia mantenuto come domanda." Et visis deliberationibus factis in huiusmodi materia . . . et auditis pluribus musicis palatinis insimul et de per se . . . deliberaverunt et decreverunt detrahi debere ex provisione et mercede infrascriptorum musicorum ratam et partem infrascriptam, eandemque dari et assignari eidem Iohanni Francisco pro eius provisione et salario . . . Declarando insuper quod idem Iohannes Franciscus debeat participare eundo ad convivia, nuptias et doctoratus ad sonandum, de illo munere, regaliis, donatione et ut dicitur magaluffi percipiendis et donandis ab illis civibus qui conducent musicos. Et in die dominico, prout etiam in die Martis et Iovis, debeat sonare ad tabulas Illustrissimorum dominorum, prout tenetur, excepto tamen ut dicitur nella ringhiera. Et circa, ut dicitur, al piatto, quod debet habere idem Iohannes Franciscus, decreverunt et deliberaverunt quod expensae quae ad presens tribuuntur Octavio [blank] musico, dentur eidem Iohanni Francisco. Reservando nihilominus eidem Octavio illos tres carolenos qui sibi dantur, prout etiam voluerunt quod participare debeat de omnibus, ut dicitur, magaluffi qui percipientur ut supra, eundo nihilominus personaliter ad sonandum. Cum declaratione quod idem Octavius non teneatur sonare et canere in palatio nisi in diebus dominicis, in quibus debeat habere expensas a palatio; et quando Illustrissimi domini foras exeunt, debeat illos sociare. Pecuniae vero detrahendae ut supra ex portionibus musicorum sunt videlicet: Iohanni Baptistae Cocchio, libre tres; Bisquilli, libra una; Petro Iohanni, libra una; Tiberio, libra una.

Doc. 12.35. Alberto di Francesco Gregori is appointed the new leader, 22 April 1603. Concistoro, vol. 1314, fols. 72^v–73^r

[margin: Albertus de Gregoriis electus magister cappellae] Illustrissimi dominus Capitaneus Populi et septem domini Priores . . . in eorum Consistorio congregati . . . cum Ioannes Franciscus de Vedis vulgo trombone nuncupatus, die 29 Octobris proxime preteriti fuerit electus magister Cappellae Musicorum eorum Palatii, et propter eius senectutem et malam valetudinem non potuerit neque possit eius incumbere officio, et decens sit Palatio atque necessarium valde dictae Capellae pro ipsius manutentione et conservatione habere caput et rectorem visibilem, habueruntque tam a dicto Ioannefranciso quam etiam ab Alberto infra dicendo liberam voluntatem (ut dixerunt) traditam dicto domino Capitaneo faciendi de eorum locis prout eis libuerit. Iccirco ad propositam domini Capitanei et iuxta consilium domini Vexilliferi obtentum per omnia suffragia alba, decreverunt amovere et amoverunt de magistro Capellae musicorum Palatii dictum Ioannemfranciscum. Et habentes plenam notitiam de peritia et excellentia in arte musices Alberti Francisci de Gregoriis senensis, per multos annos iam musici in eorum Palatio, ipsum Albertum dictae capellae magistrum et rectorem elegerunt et creaverunt, cum omnibus oneribus et obligationibus, et presertim (quod maximum necessarium est) de renovanda et retinenda scola artis musicae in Palatio (prout antiqui moris fuit) et promovendi iuvenes ad eam, ac cum praeminentia, honore, salario et emolumentis quibuscunque solitis et consuetis haberi per alios magistros et rectores capellae praefatae. Et dicto Ioannifrancisco trombone, in vim rescripti Suae Celsitudinis Serenissimae et pro observantia ipsius, ac decreti Illustrissimi Concistorii, de quibus in libro ordinum, folio 35, habetur mentio, restituerunt locum musici benemeriti, cum sua solita provisione extrahenda de salario, esculentis et poculentis loci Alberti ut supra vacantis, ac etiam cum oneribus ipsi loco adiunctis si ad bonam valetudinem ipsum redire contigerit. Et libras duas de provisione eiusdem Alberti restantes assignarunt Octavio de Basiliis, musico eiusdem capellae. Et ut praedicta maiorem et perpetuam roboris firmitatem obtineant, voluerint conferri et appro-bari (si placuerit) a praefata sua Excellentia Illustrissima. Et hoc faciendi provinciam assumpsit praefatus dominus Capitaneus Populi.

Mane sequenti, dominus Capitaneus praefatus dixit mihi notario contulisse cum sua Excellentia Illustrissima et dimisisse in suis manibus exemplum suprascriptae deliberationis, quod inde ad paucos dies venit cum rescripto in pede (cuius exemplar erit aput Reformationes) huiusmodi sub tenore:

Sua Eccellenza non si vuole intromettere in questo negotio né approvando né riprovarlo, e però l'Illustrissimo Concistoro faccia secondo che gli parrà di potere o dovere fare e come se non l'havesse participato. [signed] Gio. Battista Bernardini, Segretario, 26 Aprilis '603.

[The governor's seal is affixed to the left of the signature.]

Doc. 12.36. Reassignment of salaries following the death of Giovanfrancesco di Benedetto, 23 and 31 October 1603. Concistoro, vol. 1315, fols. 23^v–24^v

Et facta proposita a domino Capitaneo Populi super petitionibus plurium musicorum pretenden-tium expensas et salarium Iohannis Francisci trombonis defuncti . . . ad petitionem domini Scipionis Chisi consulentis quod tota pars salarii, victus et totius quod habebat dictus Iohannes Franciscus distribuatur inter musicos petentes. Misso partito, fuit obtentum per lupinos novem.
  Deliberaverunt distributionem supradictam fieri debere ut infra, videlicet: libras 4 Niccholao Farraoni, libras 3 Petro Iohannis Odorino, libras 3 Octavio de Basiliis, libras 2 Petro Angelo de Magistris, solidos 10 ad arbitrum presentis domini Capitanei Populi.
Panis et vinum distribuendum mandavit hoc modo: dimidia pars Fulvio filio magistri Mathei, coquis palatini, et altera dimidia Laurentio, filio hospitalis Santa Mariae Scalarum. Hoc adiecto, quod isti duo debeant assistere et intervenire omnibus factionibus [*recte* functionibus] ad quas est obligata capella musicorum, et tam in palatio quam extra. Et succesive dictus dominus Capi-taneus . . . applicavit dictos solidos decem dicto Niccholao de Farraonibus.

Doc. 12.37. Realignment of salaries following resignation of Orindio Bartolini, 29 May 1599. Concistoro, vol. 1311, unnumbered folio

Et auditis pluribus ex musicis eorum Palatii, petentibus sibi dari et concedi libras duas denariorum quas habebat Orindius Iohannis Mariae de Bartolinis, unus ex dictis musicis, qui renunciavit locum suum; facta proposita et servatis etc. . . . fuit victum et obtentum quod omnes scruti-nentur, et ille qui plura vota habuerit, intelligatur electus in musico et pro musico dicti eorum Palatii, cum dicto salario et cum omnibus aliis utilibus et oneribus quos habebat dictus Orindius . . . Et in executione dicte deliberationis, omnibus scruptinatis habuit plura vota Petrus Iuliani de Rivoltis, discipulus Thiberii de Rivoltis, et mandaverunt sibi fieri decretum in forma.

Doc. 12.38. Ottavio di Lorenzo Basili replaces Pietro Rivolti, 10 November 1599. Concistoro, vol. 1311, unnumbered folio

[margin: Petrusangelus, Petrus Iohannes, Octavius et Niccolaus, musici] Postquam auditis et lectis pluribus supplicationibus ex musicis eorum Palatii, petentibus sibi dari et concedi libras duas denariorum quas habebat Petrus Iuliani de Rivoltis, unus ex dictis musicis, vacatas mediante morte ipsius Petri: facta proposita . . . fuit victum et obtentum quod omnes petentes scrutinentur, et ille qui plura vota habuerit, intelligatur esse et sit electus in musico et pro musico dicti eorum Palatii, cum dicto salario et cum omnibus aliis utilibus et oneribus, quos habebat dictus Petrus. Et in executione dicte deliberationis omnibus scrutinatis, habuit plura vota Octavias olim Lauren-tii de Basiliis, librarius Senensis, et mandaverunt sibi fieri decretum in forma.

Doc. 12.39. Piergiovanni Odorini replaces Virgilio Ricci, 1 October 1591. Concistoro, vol. 1303, unnumbered folio

Atenta vacatione Virgilio olim Laurenti, musici eorum Palatii, eo quia recessit a civitate et dominio Senarum absque ulla licentia. Et facta de huiusmodi proposita a domino Capitaneo populi super electione facienda de alicuius musici [*sic*] loco ipsius Virgilii absentis, quem cassarunt. Visa petitione cuiusdam Petri Ioannis Oderini, petente locum ipsius Virgili . . . fuit victum et obtentum quod scutrinetur [*sic*] dictus Petrus Ioannes et alii petentes si assunt [*sic*], et quis ex eis prevaluerit, intelligatur esse et sit electus loco . . . dicti Virgilii, cum solitis honoribus et oneribus ac salario dicti Virgilii. Et servatis servandis . . . et sic fuit electus in dicto loco Petrus Ioannes Oderinus, musicus de Senis, et mandarunt fieri decretum in forma, omni meliori modo etc.

Doc. 12.40. Petition of Alberto di Francesco Gregori on behalf of his son Annibale, 15 April 1599. Concistoro, vol. 1311, unnumbered folio

Et visa supplicatione Alberti quondam Francisci de Gregoriis, musici eorum palatio, petentis prout in ea infrascripti tenoris:

Illustrissimi et excelsi Signori
Alberto già di Francesco Gregori, uno de' mimimi servidori musici delle Signorie Vostre Illustrissime et Eccelse, reverentemente gl'espone che ritrovandosi haver servito già 26 anni a quelle, aggravato et carico di numerosa fameglia . . . onde ritrovandosi tra gl'altri un figlio chiamato Anibale, instrutto nell'arte musicale più che mediocremente . . . et disiderando egli et insieme il detto proprio suo figlio occasione acciò debbia seguitare animosamente di perfettionarsi nella professione . . . supplica . . . a fargli gratia di concedere il luogo tiene nella loro honoratissima famiglia, anzi cappella di musica, insieme con tutti li honori, pesi et emolumenti, al suddetto Anibale suo figlio; et insiememente le suplica a fargli gratia che, mancando detto suo figlio per morte o qualsivoglia altra occasione, resti nell'istesso luogo il detto supplicante et al medesimo restino gl'honori et privilegii che i musici son soliti godere poiché sì come fin hora, anche per l'avvenire desidera vivere e morire servitore di cotesto Illustrissimo Concistoro . . .

Super quibus precibus fuit fata proposita ab Illustrissimo domino Capitaneo proposita, fuit victum pro omnibus suffragiis albis et decretum ut infra, videlicet vulgari sermone: Che si conceda e s'intenda concesso per il presente Conseglio al detto Alberto suplicante quanto domanda, con questo però che esso sia tenuto et obligato servire al palazzo personalmente et come era tenuto avanti la presente concessione, per tempo e termine di quattro anni, senza alcuna spesa d'esso Palazzo per il detto Anibale suo figlio, in ogni miglio modo.

Doc. 12.41. Realignment of salaries following dismissal of Giulio d'Alessandro, 9 September 1602. Concistoro, vol. 1314, fol. 29^r

Illustrissimi et Eccellentissimi dominus Capitaneus populi ac Priores praedicti ordinaverunt in causa musicorum Palatii ut in futurum debeant habere ab eorum Palatio panem et vinum ordinarium et solitum dari musicis . . . ac pro companaticis ordinaverunt eisdem dari libras 6 et solidos decem pro quolibet mense et pro quolibet eorum. [below:]
    Io Gio. Battista Cocchi . . . so' contento . . .
    Io Pietragnolo Maestri . . . mi contento . . . .
    Io Simone Nodi . . . mi contento . . .
    Io Ottavio di Lorenzo Basili affermo
    Io Alberto Gregorii in nome mio e di Anibale mio figlio mi contento . . .
    Io Piergiovanni Odorini . . . mi contento.

Doc. 12.42. Francesco Gregori succeeds his brother Annibale, 12 August 1611. Concistoro, vol. 1320, fol. 94^{r-v}

[margin: elettione di Francesco Gregori in luogo d'Anibale musico] Audito Hannibale de Gregoriis, musico huius Palatii, petente subrogari et de coetero poni in locum suum Franciscum suum fratrem, praecedente proposita Illustrissimi domini Capitanei, et aliis servatis servandis, dictam petitam subrogationem concedentes et admittentes, in locum dicti Hannibalis posuerunt et constituerunt eundum Franciscum suum fratrem, dummodo per triennium ab hodie continuum ipse Hannibal personaliter serviat prout adhuc obligatus fuit. Qua servitute non facta et illam facere negligens quocumque modo absque ulla mercede, prout etiam ipse se obtulit paratum, hanc concessionem delentes, decreverunt illam pro non facta haberi, prout ex nunc penitus revocaverunt omni meliori modo.

Doc. 12.43. Lorenzo Basili replaces his father Ottavio, 27 August 1611. Concistoro, vol. 1320, fol. 97^{r-v}

[margin: Lorenzo Basili in luogo di Ottavio suo padre] Auditis precibus Octavii de Basiliis, musici huius Palatii, petentis in locum suum poni in eodem munere Laurentium suum filium, offerentis se tamen serviturum absque alia mercede in posterum, prout alias usque hodie fecit. Quam oblationem et renunciationem a dicto Octavio factam in personam dicti sui filii acceptantes, munus alias eidem Octavio concessum et ab eo, ut desuper, reununciatum, contulerunt dicto Laurentio suo filio, non liberantes illum a servitute dicta. Mandantes etiam quatenus opus sit decretum fieri in forma, omni meliori etc.

TABLE 12.1. Chronological list of sixteenth-century pifferi

	1500–9	1510	1511–20	1521	1522–23	1524	1525	1526	1527–31	1532	1533–37	1538–41
Valerio di Bartolomeo[a]	x	x	x	x	x	x	x	x	x	x	x	x
Domenico di Maestro Cristoforo[b]	x	x										
Pavolo di Giovanni[c]	x	x	x	x	x	x	x	x	x	x	x	x
Giovanni di Maestro Antonio[d]	x	x	x	x	x	x	x	x				
Geronimo di Giovanni,[e] trombone	x	x	x	x								
Niccolò di Maestro Cristoforo[f]		x	x	x	x	x	x	x	x	x	x	x
Ansano Maria di Geronimo,[g] trombone				x	x				x	x		
Andrea di Giovanni da Siena						x						
Bernardino di Matteo Cartolaio							x	x	x	x	x	x
Galgano d'Enea[h]								x	x	x	x	x
Benedetto di Domenico, trombone										x	x	x
Virginio di Pavolo[i]												x
Antonio di Maestro Cristoforo[j]												x
Luzio di Pavolo[k]												x

	1542	1543–44	1545	1546	1547	1548–49	1550–51	1552–53	1554	1555	1556–60	1561
Valerio di Bartolomeo	x	x	x	x	x	x	x					
Pavolo di Giovanni	x	x										
Niccolò di Maestro Cristoforo	x	x	x	x	x	x	x	x	x	x	x	x
Ansano Maria di Geronimo		x	x	x	x							
Bernardino di Matteo Cartolaio	x	x	x	x	x	x						
Galgano d'Enea	x	x	x	x	x							
Benedetto di Domenico	x	x	x	x	x	x	x	x	x			
Virginio di Pavolo	x	x	x	x	x	x						
Antonio di Maestro Cristoforo	x	x	x	x	x	x	x	x	x	x		
Luzio di Pavolo	x	x	x	x	x	x						
Pamfilo di Ansano Maria detto Tromboncino,[l] trombone				x								
Adriano Imperiale di Luzio (Mangoni)[m]						x	x	x	x	x	x	x
Tulio, trombone				x	x	x						
Simone di Domenico Nodi				x	x	x	x	x	x	x	x	x

	1542	1543–44	1545	1546	1547	1548–49	1550–51	1552–53	1554	1555	1556–60	1561
Ascanio d'Andrea di Lazaro Marri				x	x	x	x	x	x	x	x	x
Agostino di Benedetto[n]				x								
Partenio di Benedetto[o]				x								
Giovanbattista Volpini[p] (trumpeter)				x								
Giovanfrancesco di Benedetto de' Vedi, trombone						x	x	x	x	x	x	x
Maestro Vincenzo di Giovanbattista,[q] trombone									x			
Bernardino di Valerio, drummer										x		
Savino di Francesco Belli										x		
Fabio di Geronimo												x

	1562	1563	1564	1565–66	1567	1568	1569–72	1573–74	1575	1576–77	1578	1579	1580
Niccolò di Maestro Cristoforo	x	x	x	x									
Adriano Imperiale di Luzio	x	x	x	x	x	x	x	x	x	x	x	x	x
Simone di Domenico Nodi	x	x	x	x	x	x	x	x	x	x	x	x	x
Ascanio d'Andrea di Lazaro Marri	x	x	x	x	x	x	x	x	x				
Giovanfrancesco di Benedetto	x	x	x	x	x	x	x	x	x	x	x	x	
Savino di Francesco Belli	x	x	x										
Alfonso di Pavolo	x	x	x	x	x								
Tiberio di Girolamo Rivolti, trombone			x	x	x	x	x	x	x	x	x	x	x
Giovanbattista di Bennardino					x								
Flaminio di Maestro Antonio Signorini						x							
Giovanbattista di Francesco detto Formica						x	x	x	x	x	x	x	x
Jacomo di Antonio Latini								x	x	x	x	x	x
Giovanbattista Cocchi									x	x	x	x	x
Baldassare di Maestro Domenico Ponti											x		

TABLE 12.1 *continued*

	1562	1563	1564	1565–66	1567	1568	1569–72	1573–74	1575	1576–77	1578	1579	1580
Alberto di Francesco Gregori									x	x	x	x	x
Domenico di Bartolomeo Fei									x	x	x	x	x
Piergiovanni Odorini											x	x	x
Annibale di Girolamo											x	x	
Piero di Girolamo Rivolti (Risquillo)[r]											x		x
Alberto di Jacomo Latini												x	x

	1581–84	1585	1586–90	1591	1592–93	1594	1595–97	1598	1599	1600–1	1602	1603	1604–6
Adriano Imperiale di Luzio	x	x	x	x	x	x	x	x	x				
Simone di Domenico Nodi	x	x	x	x	x	x	x	x	x	x	x		
Giovanfrancesco di Benedetto						x				x	x	x	
Tiberio di Girolamo Rivolti	x	x	x	x			x	x	x	x			
Giovanbattista di Francesco detto Formica							x						
Jacomo di Antonio Latini	x	x	x	x	x	x	x						
Giovanbattista Cocchi	x	x	x	x	x	x	x	x	x	x	x		
Alberto di Francesco Gregori	x	x	x	x	x	x	x	x	x	x	x	x	x
Domenico di Bartolomeo Fei	x	x	x	x	x	x	x	x	x	x			
Piergiovanni Odorini	x	x	x	x	x	x	x	x	x	x	x	x	x
Piero di Girolamo Rivolti	x	x	x	x	x	x	x	x	x	x		x	
Ottavio di Lorenzo Basili	x	x	x	x	x	x	x	x	x	x	x		
Pietragnolo di Bernardino Maestri				x	x	x	x	x	x	x	x	x	
Virgilio di Lorenzo Ricci								x	x		x	x	
Orindio Bartolini								x	x	x			
Giulio di Alessandro Muratore								x	x	x	x	x	
Annibale di Alberto Gregori[s]								x	x	x	x	x	x
Niccolò di Aurelio Faraoni									x	x	x	x	x
Fulvio di Matteo												x	
Lorenzo della Scala												x	x

	1607	1608–10	1611
Alberto di Francesco Gregori	x		
Ottavio di Lorenzo Basili	x	x	x
Annibale di Alberto Gregori	x	x	x
Francesco Gregori[t]			x
Lorenzo di Ottavio Basili[u]			x

[a] son of a drummer Meo di Maestro Mino
[b] son of Maestro Cristoforo di Brandino, brother of Niccolò and Antonio
[c] son of Giovanni di Fruosino
[d] son of Antonio di Gregorio
[e] son of the trumpeter Giovanni da Iesi
[f] son of Maestro Cristoforo di Brandino, brother of Domenico and Antonio
[g] previously a trumpeter, son of Geronimo
[h] son of the trumpeter Enea
[i] son of Pavolo di Giovanni
[j] son of Maestro Cristoforo di Brandino, brother of Domenico and Niccolò
[k] brother of Virginio
[l] son of Ansano Maria
[m] son of Luzio di Pavolo
[n] son of Benedetto di Domenico, brother of Partenio
[o] son of Benedetto di Domenico, brother of Agostino
[p] brother or father of Giulio di Giovambattista detto Volpino
[q] son-in-law of Benedetto di Domenico
[r] brother of Tiberio Rivolti
[s] son of Alberto di Francesco Gregori
[t] brother of Annibale
[u] son of Ottavio

Part Three

MUSIC IN THE LIFE
OF THE TOWN

BEYOND CATHEDRAL AND PALACE WALLS: PROFESSIONAL MUSICIANS AND DANCING MASTERS, AMATEURS, BUILDERS, AND REPAIRMEN, 1300–1607

OTHER MUSICIANS besides those associated with the cathedral and the Palace contributed to the richness and diversity of Siena's musical life. Supporting themselves wholly or in part as organists and singers at smaller religious and secular institutions, as occasional retainers of wealthy families, as performers at private social functions, as teachers of music and dance, and as instrument makers and repairmen, their careers must have been as full and as varied as those of their colleagues in the larger institutions, though perhaps not as financially secure. Many of them were independently employed. In this respect the careers of the teachers, the dancing masters, and the instrument makers form what is perhaps the most elusive chapter in Siena's musical life, given the private nature of their work. Some idea, however, of who they were and how they conducted their affairs does appear in such diverse sources as literary works, chronicles, tax reports, contracts, records of business transactions, and testaments, and from these it is possible to place them and their activities within the broader spectrum of Sienese society.

Though neither as systematically nor as consistently preserved as cathedral and Palace records, surviving papers and documents from other Sienese churches and institutions also attest to the flourishing state of music in the city. Siena, it seems, throughout much of the period considered in this book, was a town where, of a Sunday or a feast day, one could go to a parish or convent church and expect to hear some kind of music—monophonic, polyphonic, unaccompanied, or accompanied by organ or other instruments—being performed by professional musicians as an adjunct to liturgical or paraliturgical services. Despite such activities, however, these places still took their lead from the cathedral and the Palace. Thus, even if more documentation regarding other Sienese musical venues were available, I believe that it would not significantly alter an assessment of Sienese musical history in later medieval and Renaissance times as it can be reconstructed from data provided by the larger institutions. They alone had the means needed to sustain major musical programs in performance and in teaching, in good times and in bad ones, and it was they who took the lead in promoting and nurturing newer repertories and performance practices. Nevertheless, activities in other places contributed in no small way to the general atmosphere of a vibrant musical culture, based on traditions that responded to the needs, aspirations and financial resources of citizens of all classes.

MUSIC AT OTHER SIENESE INSTITUTIONS
Santa Maria della Scala

Typical in this respect was Siena's most renowned charitable organization, the great hospital of Santa Maria della Scala. Founded in the late eleventh century by cathedral canons as a way station for pilgrims, it soon evolved into one of the city's principal institutions, fulfilling its role, under the leadership and ministrations of a brotherhood of laymen, as hospice, orphanage, and hospital. In the process of doing so it became the object of great generosity on the part of pious and patriotic Sienese, who enriched it with continuous donations through the centuries. The hospital maintained a school for the many orphans reared under its auspices. It also had its own church, where Masses and the hours were celebrated daily. The church was transformed during the seventeenth century into the serenely beautiful structure the visitor beholds today.

A good deal of documentation about Santa Maria della Scala's music program is available from the late sixteenth century onwards, though earlier material, except for a number of magnificently decorated chant books, has been less systematically preserved.[1] It is certain, however, that musical performances were being given on its premises by the turn of the fifteenth century, when several of its clerks were performing laudi at the cathedral. Principal among them was the former singer, organist, and future teacher in the cathedral school, Ser Francesco di Nanni, who was the hospital's organist from as early as 1415 (see chapter 3). His successors in the post were the same men who followed in his footsteps at the cathedral: Frate Giovanni di Francesco di Raimondi, mentioned in 1481, his immediate successor, Francesco di Guido, and Ser Francesco di Mattia, cited from 1490 through 1493 (see Doc. 13.1). In view of the close ties between the two institutions and their physical proximity, it stands to reason that they would have shared the services of many of the same musicians throughout the centuries.

A record from 1385 shows that even at that early date the hospital celebrated its principal feast day, the Annunciation, on March 25, with special musical performances.[2] Two hundred years later the feast was still being celebrated with extraordinary performances, as will be noted below, by members of the cathedral chapel. By that time the hospital was supporting an ambitious musical program that employed a music teacher and a few singers and instrumentalists. Principal among them was Tiberio Rivolti, the Palace cornettist who took leave from his duties as the Scala's *maestro di canto* and Palace trombonist in order to enter the service of Habsburg and Doria princes. The teaching program had been in force for more than a century by Rivolti's time, though it was perhaps a more modest operation in the beginning.[3] Musicians such as the just-mentioned laude singers, and others whose names are little known to us, assuredly performed in the hospital's church, where decoration of the organ was reported in 1489.[4] Shortly after the turn of the sixteenth century that instrument was no longer

---

1. A few of these, containing music for the feast of Sant'Ansano, are mentioned in chapter 2, where reference is made to an inventory of surviving hospital holdings by Morandi and Cairoli.

2. "La festa di Santa Maria di Marzo [1385] die dare . . . E die dare adì XXVIII di marzo venti soldi, i quagli denari diei a frate Ciano Tonducci, disse per dare al Viuola e a Richardo, che sonaro' el dì dela vesta [festa]" (Ospedale, vol. 852, E&U, 1385–86, fol. 100ʳ).

3. The organist Francesco di Guido, mentioned above, is referred to as the hospital's music teacher, who used a monochord in teaching (see Doc. 13.1).

4. The names of a few singers appear sporadically in the records, among them Giovanni di Bartolomeo, a clerk-singer, who received L. 2 on 3 January 1481; Rinaldo di Palaviali, who was paid L. 1 on 21 April 1481 (Ospedale, vol. 866, E&U, 1480–81, fols. 61ʳ, 77ᵛ); and Ser Cristofano di Bartolomeo, cited on 24 December 1483 (vol. 869, E&U, 1483–84, fol. 76ᵛ). The organ is mentioned in a

deemed sufficient and plans were made to replace it. This much is evident in the brief record of a decision on 25 January 1514 to entrust the building of a new instrument to Giovanni di Maestro Antonio Piffero, the erstwhile woodwind player, cathedral *maestro di cappella,* teacher, and master organ builder, who was also responsible for constructing the organ that stands to this day in the Concistoro's private chapel in the Palace.[5] A series of payments in the hospital's account books from 1514 through 1517 records the progress of Giovanni's work there, and others from the following year give the organ's specifications and a favorable report of the instrument, finished on 28 August 1518, by two Florentine organists who were brought in to review it, Andrea da Prato and Alessandro Coppini of the Servite Order.[6]

The earliest known of the sixteenth-century organists at Santa Maria della Scala, Ser Bernardo, is mentioned in a record from 1508. Like other chaplains in the hospital's church, he was required to say Masses and serve in the choir. In April 1510 he was offered an annual salary of Fl. 24 on condition that he teach music to several of the hospital's clerks, "that is, that he teach two to play and three to sing."[7] This would imply that the hospital's ordinary singing ensemble was at the very least comprised of three singers, who may have been accompanied by the organist. Bernardo left hospital service in two years' time, though it is possible that he remained in Siena and is the

---

report from 1489: "Sano di maestro Andrea, batteloro, die avere persino dì X di marzo, per pezi millesecento d'oro ci à dato per li nostri organi a Guidoccio di Pietro per lire settanta una . . . L. 71" (vol. 806, *Giornale C, 1486–97,* fol. 104[r], 1488 [1489]).

5. Documents regarding the construction of the Palace organ have been published by Cellesi, "L'organo della cappella interna." Further information about the instrument is the report commemorating the recent restoration of the instrument: Donati et al., *L'Organo di Giovanni Piffero, 1519 del Palazzo Pubblico di Siena.* Elsewhere, Oscar Mischiati notes that "le catenacciature in ferro più antiche giunte sino a noi sono probabilmente quelle degli organi senesi di S. Maria della Scala (1517), del Palazzo Pubblico (1519) e di S. Agostino, opere di Giovanni Piffero"; see "Documenti sull'organaria padana rinascimentale—I: Giovanni Battista Facchetii," *L'Organo* 22 (1984): 51, n. 98.

6. The record of the decision to build the organ and the series of payments to Giovanni di Maestro Antonio from 1513 to 1517 have been published by Alessandro Liberati, "Nuovi documenti artistici dello Spedale di S. Maria della Scala," *BSSP* 33–34 (1926–27): 170–72. A record from 20 July 1518 indicates that each of the parties chose one person to evaluate the new instrument. The hospital named Maestro Alessandro [Coppini], "frate di S. Maria de' Servi di Firenze"; Giovanni's choice was Ser Andrea, "prete sta a Prato, alias el Gallone" (Ospedale, vol. 27, *Deliberazioni, 1513–20,* fol. 209[v]). According to the specifications the organ had seven ranks and forty-eight keys, including chromatic tones in all registers but the lowest. The report and specifications are in ASS, Notarile antecosimiano, 714, dated 25 August 1518; another version of the report is in Ospedale, vol. 57, fol. 16[r]. On the same day Maestro Alessandro de' Servi received the large sum of L. 181 s. 5 for his evaluation of the organ, as reported in Ospedale, vol. 894, *E&U, 1518–19,* fol. 42[r]: "L'organi nostri di casa nuovamente fatto [*sic*] lire cento ottantuna [s. 5] . . . dati e donati a maestro Alisandro fiorentino e frate de' Servi, per la sua fadigha dela stima degli organi . . . L. 181 s. 5 d.—."

7. "Pavolo Azoni et Salustio Bandini due delli savi, per vigore della auctorità a lloro data, declarorno il salario di ser Bernardo organista dovere esse fiorini ventiquattro in uno anno, dovendo insegnare a quattro o cinque di quelli di casa ad sonare e cantare come li sarà ordinato, fu declarato adì sopradecto, cioè insegni a due a sonare et a tre ad cantare" (Ospedale, vol. 26, *Deliberazioni, 1507–12,* fol. 105[r], dated 4 April 1510). The earlier record, dated 16 May 1508, is on fol. 33[r].

same person as Ser Bernardo di Lionardo da Monte San Savino, cited as organist in the Concistoro's chapel at the Palace in 1530.[8]

No mention is made of teaching in the record of appointment registered on 21 January 1512 of a new organist at the Scala named Ser Bernardino. His immediate successors were Ser Marchionne da Colle in 1516, Frate Lorenzo, a monk of the Franciscan Order, cited from 1517 through 1519, and Ser Antonio in 1521.[9] Later organists included Ser Girolamo Bizzarini da Radicondoli in 1543, Ser Giovambattista di Vincentio in 1546, Ser Giovambattista di Matteo in 1552, Ser Guglielmo da Campanatico in 1557, and Frate Marcello from the church of Sant'Agostino in 1559. Two organists associated with the cathedral were on the hospital's rosters in the early 1560s, first Mariano Pelori in 1563 and then in 1565 Scipione di Pavolo, who by then was archpriest of the church of Sant'Ansano.[10] The employment of two such well-known musicians shows that the hospital's administration set its musical sights high and that it sought the best people available, many of whom were associated with the musical establishment just across the square. Maestro Agnolo di Francesco assumed the organist's post before December 1566 and occupied it for the next two decades, through 1586. His successors were Maestro Felice Scala, recorded as late as 1593, and Ser Lutio Signiorini, cited in 1596.[11]

In the early sixteenth century trumpeters played for the hospital on feasts of the Virgin, and this practice continued through the following decades.[12] A number of payments also attest to the flourishing state of the hospital's teaching program in the second half of the sixteenth century. By that time teaching duties had apparently been detached from the organist's post and entrusted to a singing master, who, together with several young clerks in the hospital's school, performed at various services in the church.[13] One

8. The documents concerning Ser Bernardo's employment at the Palace have been published by Cellesi, "L'organo della cappella interna," 507–8. He was given four loaves of bread in February 1531 for playing the organ "when necessary." Bernardo's successor at the Palace was Pietro di Bernardino of Novara, mentioned as having been granted meal privileges there later that same year (ASS, Concistoro, vol. 991, fol. 3ᵛ, dated 3 November 1531).

9. Appointments of or payments to these organists are in Ospedale, vol. 26, *Deliberazioni, 1507–12,* fol. 125ᵛ, for Ser Bernardino; vol. 27, *Deliberazioni, 1512–19,* fol. 176ʳ, for Ser Marchionne "g[i]à organista" and Frate Lorenzo; vol. 895, *E&U, 1520–22,* fol. 104ᵛ, for Ser Antonio.

10. Appointments of or payments to these organists are in Ospedale, vol. 25, *Deliberazioni, 1488–1551,* fol. 389ʳ, for Ser Girolamo; fol. 401ʳ, for Ser Giovambattista di Vincentio; vol. 28, *Deliberazioni, 1552–72,* fol. 10ʳ, for Ser Giovambattista di Matteo; fol. 83ᵛ, for Ser Guglielmo da Campagnatico; fol. 108ʳ, for Frate Marciello di Sancto Augustino; fol. 139ʳ, for Mariano di Girolamo Pelori; fol. 156ʳ, for Ser Scipione, arciprete di Sant'Ansano.

11. Appointments of or payments to these organists are in Ospedale, vol. 28, *Deliberazioni, 1552–72,* fol. 162ʳ, for Maestro Agniolo di Francesco; vol. 29, *Deliberazioni, 1573–87,* fol. 143ᵛ, for Maestro Agnolo fiorentino; vol. 912, *E&U III, 1592–95,* fol. 69ᵛ, for Maestro Felice Scala orghanista; vol. 913, *E&U, 1596–97,* fol. 68ᵛ, for Ser Lutio Signiorini.

12. Ospedale, vol. 26, *Deliberazioni, 1507–12,* fols. 18ʳ, 23ʳ, 68ᵛ. Dated 15 March 1509, this notes: "Et deliberaverunt che li trombetti siano pagati di loro fatigha per sonare per la festa come sono soliti."

13. The organist, however, continued to give instruction at the keyboard, as a report from 1584 indicates. The same report shows the loan of an instrument from the convent of Santa Chiara, in turn suggesting that polyphony played a part in services there as well: "Christo 1584. E adì 26 detto [Set-

or two of these clerks, described as orphans or as coming from the hospital, also sang in the cathedral chapel. Messer Niccolò Marapichi, called "our *maestro del canto*" in June 1577, when he bought "fourteen books of music" for the young clerks, was a chaplain-singer who also taught his charges the basics of counterpoint as part of a course of studies that must have been modeled on that of the cathedral school. He left his post before the end of September 1578 and was succeeded by another chaplain, Padre Alessandro Ciellerini, to whom payments are registered through early May, 1580. Tiberio Rivolti, as noted above, took over shortly thereafter, to be followed by Alberto Gregori, who led the hospital's chapel into the new century and the beginning of the period of its greatest glory. Throughout this time the hospital continued to purchase books of music, as shown by records from 1595, 1596, and 1601 (see Doc. 13.2).

Before its own musicians were able to do so, the hospital of Santa Maria della Scala celebrated its special feast day, the Annunciation of the Virgin on 25 March, with performances by the cathedral chapel singers under the direction of Andrea Feliciani. The earliest extant record of this comes from 1577, though every indication is that it was a long-established practice by then (on all these payments see Doc. 13.3). Annual performances on 25 March were the rule throughout all of Feliciani's years as cathedral *maestro di cappella,* even on those occasions when he was unable to lead the group, and they continued during the tenure of his successor, Francesco Bianciardi. A few reports show that both First and Second Vespers as well as Mass on the feast day were celebrated with polyphony in the hospital's church and that all of the cathedral singers and instrumentalists participated. No mention is made of whether the Scala's own forces joined the visitors, though in view of the close relations among the various musicians, it seems likely they did. In the early decades of the seventeenth century Annunciation Day celebrations at Santa Maria della Scala were held on an even grander scale, with double- and triple-choir pieces composed expressly for services by some of Siena's leading composers.[14]

Religious Companies

Religious companies, too, maintained musicians, many of whom were those employed at churches where the companies held their meetings. Principal among these lay fraternities was the venerable Company of Santa Maria degli Angeli e di San Francesco, later known as the Company of San Bernardino of Siena. It was associated with San Francesco, convent church of the Franciscans. The earliest references to singing laudi at the company's services come from April 1359, when mention is made of expenses "to honor the singers who sang laudi" and "to buy candles to burn at the lectern in the

---

tembre] giuli sei pagati contanti di ordine e parola del Cavaliere [rettore] a maestro Agnolo organista per la pigione di uno istrumento per mesi 6, che à insegnato a 4 di nostri cerici a insegnare a sonare a ordine di Sua Signoria, quale disse essere de le monache di Santa Chiara, L. 4" (Ospedale, vol. 811, *Bastardello GGG, 1583–84,* fol. 80 r–l).

14. The rise of the seventeenth-century musical chapel at Santa Maria della Scala is the subject of a forthcoming study by Colleen Reardon, to whom I am indebted for much of the documentation referred to here.

evening, when laudi are sung."[15] Similar payments appear in 1399, 1400, and 1406, while others from the 1390s and early 1400s speak of trumpeters who played for the company on special occasions. Notable among such events were those of 1406, when four trumpeters played for the feast of St. Francis, and of both 1409 and 1427, when the entire corps of Palace trumpeters played, respectively, on the feast of St. Francis and on Easter Sunday (see Doc. 13.4). The use of the organ at the company's services on the feast of the Annunciation is also noted in a record from March 1415, when payments were made to the convent of San Francesco for the loan of its instrument.[16]

The company owned a book of laudi, which on one occasion in 1410 was pawned with the nuns of the convent of Santa Petronilla.[17] The name of a laudi singer, Ser Jacomo—perhaps the cathedral chaplain-singer Ser Jacomo di Bellanduccio—appears in San Bernardino's records in March 1407. Other singers' names were reported on 11 July 1452, when a payment of L. 8 was made to a duo comprised of Frate Bartolomeo Corso and Frate Antonio da Corsignano "for having sung laudi during Lent."[18] The company's sporadically preserved records from the sixteenth century speak of the kinds of practices mentioned a century earlier. Thus, a payment from 27 May 1516 to Frate Ventura, organist of San Francesco, records his having played the organ at the Company's services on San Bernardino's feast day, while another from 1518 mentions the cost of a dinner for the trumpeters who also performed at the feast that year.[19] From later in the century comes a record of L. 3. 6. 8 paid to the Palace musician Giovanfrancesco trombone, attesting to his having come, undoubtedly with others, "to sing music for the Company on the three nights of Holy Week" in 1565.[20] The nuns at

---

15. "Anno mille 359 del mese d'aprile. Ancho spesi in farere [*sic*] onore a' chantatori che chantavano le laude otto soldi de VIII, s. VIII 8 d. Ancho spesi in due cieretti cholati che chonprai perr ardare la sera al lleggio quando si chantano le lalde, chostaro' cuindici soldi" (PR, Compagnia di San Bernardino di Siena, vol. 200, *E&U, 1358–73*, fol. 53ʳ). (Similar payments for August on fol. 54ʳ.)

16. "1414/15. Appresso saranno scritti tutti i denari che io Francesco di Lorenzo Pichogliuomini spendarò per la festa di Santa Maria di Marzo . . . Item adì XXVI di marzo . . . E per fare riportare li orghani e canapa e 'l tinello, s. VIII. Item a Tofano di Stefano s. 22 per dare a' frati ci prestarono li organi, L. 1 s. 11" (PR, Compagnia di San Bernardino di Siena, vol. 206, *Memoriale, 1414–33*, fol. 8ʳ).

17. "1410. Adì 13 d'aprile s. sedici e quali diei a frate Antonio di ser Francescho de' frati minori, e quali furo' per menda d'uno ugho si perdè per lla festa di Santa Maria di Marzo perché le monache di Santa Petronilla avevano per pegno e' libro delle laude però che quello ugho era loro, e quali danari pagai per detto di Bertoccio di Fuorsino priore" (PR, Compagnia di San Bernardino di Siena, vol. 204, *Capitoli, E&U, 1408–16*, fol. 162ᵛ).

18. "1406/7: A ser Jacomo che chanta le lalde di sotto adì VI di marzo soldi nove per la compagnia, s. VIIII" (PR, compagnia di San Bernardino di Siena, vol. 202, *E&U, 1382–1409*, fol. 244ᵛ); "1452, a dì 11 luglio: A . . . per chantatura de le laude chanttoro' di quaresima" (vol. 208, *E&U, 1452–97*, fol. 286ʳ).

19. "27 maggio 1516: soldi vinti pagati a frate Ventura di Santo Franciescho, per sua fadigha d'avere sonato l'organo el dì della festa; 20 maggio 1518, soldi 12 per la cholatione pe' trombetti che sonorno chol Gesù" (PR, Compagnia di San Bernardino di Siena, vol. 212, *E&U, 1516–20*, fols. 61ʳ, 65ᵛ).

20. "E addì 23 di maggio [1565] lire 3 s. 6. 8, paghati a Giovanfrancesco tronbone, per essere venuto le tre sere dela settimana santa nella conpagnia a cantare la musicha, L. 3. 6. 8" (PR, Compagnia di San Bernardino di Siena, vol. 209, *E&U, 1549–67*, fol. 39ᵛ).

Santa Petronilla, home of the Poor Clares, had done much the same thing in 1559, when they hired "five singers from the duomo and the Palace trombone" for a Good Friday performance of "the Passion in figural music."[21]

Frate Ventura's name also appears in a record dated 20 August 1508 from the Company of Sant'Antonio Abate, when he was engaged to play on all of that group's feast days at a monthly salary of L. 1.[22] Sant'Antonio Abate, which held its services in a building attached to the great Dominican convent church of San Domenico, had a long history of engaging organists, most of them employed elsewhere in the city, often in churches whose records are lost.[23] Ventura's predecessor in the post was Ser Antonio, cited in 1502, and his successors included Frate Pietro di San Domenico, in January 1517; Ser Cesare, in October 1518; Ser Agnolo, who agreed to play every Sunday when he began serving on 15 June 1519; and Maestro Giovanni Andrea Pisano, in July 1524.[24] Subsequent organists included "the organist from the convent church of the Carmine," who received L. 24 in March 1578 "for having played at offices and at Compline in our prayer hall,"[25] and Maestro Agnolo, paid L. 3. 17 for playing on Pentecost Sunday and its Octave in 1589. This latter, Agnolo di Francesco, was organist at Santa Maria della Scala at the time.[26]

The Company of Beato Andrea Gallerani, which held its meetings in the university church of the Sapienza, was rather late in adopting the practice of having polyphony performed on the feast day commemorating its patron, which fell on Easter Monday.

---

21. [1559] "El venardì Santo facemo el Passio figurato, ci fu cinque cantori di Duomo e 'l trombone di Palazo" (PR, Santa Petronilla, vol. 3379, *Libro di spese,* fol. 280ʳ).

22. "Frate Ventura, frate di Santo Fra[n]cesco, sonatore d'organi, de' avere soldi 20 el mese, e lui è obrigato a venire a sonare og[n]i dì di festa comandata, e comincia deto tenpo ogi, questo dì 20 d'agosto 1508, d'acordo con deto fra Ventura, L. 1" (PR, compagnia di Sant'Antonio Abate di Siena, vol. 56, *D&C, 1424–1584,* fol. 50ᵛ).

23. The Company apparently had an even longer history of employing trumpeters for services on its principal feast days. This is revealed by entries in an early account book of payments to trumpeters for having played on various feasts such as Corpus Christi, St. Anthony, and St. Martin in 1388, 1389, and 1390. The volume is in BCIS, MS A. I. 5, Compagnia di Sant'Antonio Abate di Siena, *E&U, 1388–1416,* fols. 28ᵛ, 29ʳ (1388), 30ʳ, 36ʳ (1389), 42ʳ (1390).

24. Payments to them are in PR, Compagnia di Sant'Antonio Abate di Siena, vol. 62, *E&U, 1497–1519,* fol. 71ʳ, for Ser Antonio; fol. 90ʳ, for Frate Pietro di San Domenico; fol. 93ʳ, for Ser Cesare; fol. 97ᵛ, for Ser Agnolo; and in vol. 56, *D&C, 1425–1584,* fol. 88ᵛ, for Maestro Giovanni Andrea Pisano.

25. "E adì 20 detto, tanti pagati all'organista del Carmine per aver sonato più volte il nostro organo a uffizi e compiete nel nostro oratorio, L. 24" (PR, Compagnia di Sant'Antonio Abate di Siena, vol. 63, *Memorie, D&C, 1512–1617,* fol. 257ᵛ, dated March 1577/78).

The organ's place in the prayer hall is noted in a report concerning the rebuilding of the choir by Benedetto Amaroni in 1577. This states that the organ, which was previously on the floor facing the company, was moved to a place above the choir, where it was just as easily played: [1577] "nel medesimo tenpo aviano rimutato li organi, che prima si sonavano di verso la conpagnia stando bassi apresso terra, e si sonno messi sopra il coro sonandoli dalla banda di rento con facilità" (PR, Compagnia di Sant'Antonio Abate di Siena, vol. 56, *D&C, 1424–1577,* fol. 178ʳ).

26. "17 giugno 1579: A maestro Agnolo organista, per avere sonato l'organo per lo Spirito Santo e l'Otava, L. 3. 17" (ibid., fol. 258ᵛ).

But when it began to do so, the Company followed the same route chosen by other groups of its kind. In 1592 a payment of L. 6. 1. 8 was registed to the musicians who performed "on the evening of our feast."[27] Similar payments occur during the following years, but only in 1601 are the performers identified as "Palace musicians."[28] A record from 1602 speaks of paying L. 7 to "the Palace musicians for singing on the night of our feast," and another from 1608 names Alberto Gregori as leader of the group.[29] The Palace musicians, of course, were long accustomed to accepting outside engagements such as this, and the group's repertory for these occasions, both vocal and instrumental music, must have been essentially what the musicians performed in the normal course of their duties at the Palace.

Convent Churches

By the mid-fifteenth century Sant'Agostino, convent church of the Augustinian friars, had an organ that was prized throughout the city and perhaps even the object of some envy.[30] This much is implied in the charge given by cathedral overseers to Maestro Lorenzo di Jacopo da Prato in 1459 that he build an instrument at the cathedral that was sweeter and better than the one at Sant'Agostino.[31] A later generation was not so generous in its appraisal of the instrument and in 1522 the friars commissioned a new one from Giovanni di Maestro Antonio Piffero. Giovanni worked slowly, so much so that a new contract was renegotiated with him in 1533.[32] The organ at the church of Santa Maria del Carmine, nearing completion in 1511, was the work of Michele di Ser Giuliano Turri and Francesco di Guido Petruccio.[33] Little else is known about music there except that the church employed organists, as shown by the just-cited reference from the company of Sant'Antonio Abate.

The organist employed by the Company of Sant'Antonio Abate in 1517, Frate Pietro di San Domenico, was a friar from the Dominican convent church in Camporegio. His name is not found in any of the convent's remaining account books from that time. These offer little testimony to musical activities at San Domenico, which nonetheless must have been appropriately scaled to the needs of such a vibrant and prominent center of piety and learning. This is evident from several reports of the previous century and even earlier, when Sienese Dominicans fostered the singing of laudi and kept a

---

27. "L. sei s. uno d. 8 dati a' musici per la sera della festa della nostra compagnia, L.6. 1. 8" (PR, Compagnia del Beato Andrea Gallerani, vol. 113, E&U, 1587–1616, fol. 86ʳ, dated 30 April 1592).

28. Ibid., fols. 88ʳ, 96ʳ, 99ʳ, 103ᵛ, 106ᵛ, this last dated April 1601: "El dì 5, lire sette sono pagati a' musici di Palazzo per chomisione del nostro priore, L. 7."

29. "El dì detto lire sette sono dati a' musici di Pallazzo per cantare la sera della nostra festa, L. 7" (ibid., fol. 109ᵛ, dated 8 April 1602); fols. 112ʳ, 115ʳ, 118ʳ, 120ᵛ, 124ʳ, dated 30 August 1608: "E adì detto L. sette contanti dati a maestro Alberto musico per ordine di messer Giulio Landucci priore, per la musicha della festa, L. 7"; payments from the following years on fols. 126ᵛ (1609), 128ʳ (1610).

30. One of the convent's friars, Frate Cristofano, was an organ tuner and repairman who worked on the cathedral's instruments in 1485.

31. A summary of the document is published by Lusini, Il Duomo di Siena, 2:154; it is cited in part above in Doc. 1.1.

32. Both documents published by Borghesi and Banchi, Nuovi documenti per la storia dell'arte senese, no. 215, pp. 426–32, dated 18 November 1522–25 August 1533.

33. See chapter 12, note 23.

school where boy singers were trained.[34] Frate Piero di Domenico assumed the organist's post at the convent in September 1454 and was still serving in that capacity in December 1466.[35] A report from 1490 concerning payment of a debt incurred by a priest and singer named Ser Filippo who was staying at the convent implies that he was employed there.[36] But it does not specify whether he sang in the chapel, or indeed whether the convent maintained a chapel. At this time the convent's plainchant choir was presided over by various monks who served on a rotating basis. One of them, Frate Innocenzio, is named in a payment of L. 5 for five months' service between October 1488 and February 1489.[37]

A new organ for San Domenico was commissioned from Lorenzo di Jacopo and Francesco d'Andrea da Cortona on 9 December 1473.[38] The convent's failure in the early years of the sixteenth century to retain a teacher of grammar who also served as organist is reported in two accounts from the time. The first, dated 8 November 1507, records the appointment of one of the convent's friars, Maestro Benedetto Pisano, to the post at a salary of L. 4 per month. The appointment was to last for a period of three years and payment of a fine of Fl. 3 was stipulated should one or another of the parties renege on the agreement before that time. For reasons unexplained, Benedetto was removed from his post within two months, on 2 January 1508, this latter action taken, as had been the previous one, with the consent of both the provincial and convent priors.[39] Later organists at San Domenico included Frate Deodato, in 1554, and the ubiquitous Mariano Pelori, recorded from 1568 and 1573. Toward the end of that period two other organists assisted Pelori, Scipione Melari, in 1572, and Maestro Agnolo, in 1573. Little else remains regarding musicians at San Domenico except for a record suggesting that the convent found a more stable successor to Pelori when it engaged Baccio da Battignano as organist on 6 September 1573.[40]

Sporadically preserved papers from other religious establishments record musical

---

34. See chapter 3 for references to the Dominican school, established by 1273, which had a teaching program that included musical instruction.

35. "1466: Frate Piero di Domenico incominciò l'offit[i]o di sonare gli organi adì primo di Settembre 1454 et el convento gli debba dare l'anno septe fiorini, a quatro libre el fiorino" (PR, Convento di San Domenico, vol. 2204, D&C, 1451–78, fol. 16ʳ); "Frate Piero di Domenico die avere addì primo di dicenbre L. vintisei s. dicessette d. 4, sono per lo suo salario del sonare gli organi, L. 26. 17. 4" (ibid., fol. 47r).

36. PR, Convento di San Domenico di Siena, vol. 2206, D&C, 1481–1563, fol. 28ʳ, dated 8 September 1490.

37. "1489: Frate Innocentio nostro dei avere lire cinque per mesi cinque ane fatto la cantoria in convento de l'anno 1488 del mese d'otobre, novembre, dicembre, genaio e feraio. L. 5" (PR, Convento di San Domenico, vol. 2206, D&C, 1476–1563, fol. 104ᵛ).

38. Borghesi and Banchi, Nuovi documenti, no. 147, p. 243, dated 9 December 1473. A payment to Maestro Francesco d'Andrea da Cortona from two years later shows that work on the new instrument was not completed by that time (PR, Convento di San Domenico, vol. 2204, D&C, 1451–78, fol. 110a). Marrocchi reports that Giovanni di Maestro Antonio built an organ for San Domenico, but he, or rather Banchi, his editor, furnishes no documentation. Marrocchi, La musica in Siena, 27, note.

39. PR, Convento di San Domenico di Siena, vol. 2207, D&C, 1492–1533, fols. 54ʳ, 54ᵛ.

40. Payments to these organists are in PR, Convento di San Domenico di Siena, vol. 2257, E&U, 1549–75, fol. 81ʳ, for Frate Deodato; fol. 109ᵛ for Mariano Pelori; fol. 125ᵛ, for Scipione Melari; fol. 127ᵛ, for Maestro Agnolo organista dello Spedale; fol. 128ᵛ, for Baccio da Battignano.

activities even within the ambience of smaller churches and monasteries outside the walls. From 1 January 1503 comes a contract signed by Don Arsenio, abbot of Sant'Eugenio a Monistero in the Sienese countryside, and Ser Paolo organista.[41] According to the terms of their agreement the organist agreed to play at first or second Vespers and Masses on a number of feasts throughout the year for a salary of L. 22 per annum plus his expenses each time he journeyed to the monastery. The feasts included all of those of Our Lord and of the Virgin Mary, SS. Philip and James, St. John the Baptist, SS. Peter and Paul, St. Lawrence, St. Bartholomew, St. Justina, All Saints, St. Martin, St. Stephen, St. John Evangelist, St. Benedict, St. Eugene, as well as Maundy Thursday, Holy Saturday, and Monday and Tuesday in Easter Week. During the following decade the convent commissioned a new instrument from Ser Paolo. But his work was not well received and on 22 December 1513, in a claim asserting, among other things, that the pipes were badly made, the convent demanded that Ser Paolo di Maestro Pietro, as he is called in the document, should redo the ones next to the keys.[42]

Among other places that celebrated their principal feast days with performances of polyphony was the convent church of the Santissima Concezione. In 1577, as has been mentioned, after having auditioned the ensemble at feast-day services, the convent engaged Simone Nodi and the Palace musicians to perform there annually at Vespers and Mass on 8 December, feast of the Conception of the Virgin (see Doc. 13.5).[43]

MUSIC TEACHERS AND AMATEURS

Contributing in no small way to Siena's flourishing musical life were teachers of voice and instruments who earned their living by giving instruction to the ever growing number of amateurs within the city. Several teachers were cathedral or Palace employees, though, as previously remarked, others were either associated with institutions whose records are not extant or were independently employed. Judging their success is impossible, for few of their students had professional careers. Indeed, for the majority of music students, then as now, an ability to perform was a source of great personal satisfaction, one that brought pleasure as well as knowledge and understanding of the art.[44] Parents and society, too, favored musical instruction for the same reasons and also because learning to play an instrument sharpens the intellect and teaches discipline, requiring as it does long hours of assiduous study and practice. For centuries European philosophy and culture, taking cues first from Boethius and later from Aristotle and Plato, placed music among the quadrivium of university studies, the four liberal arts.

---

41. Conventi, Badia di S. Salvadore e Cerino all'Isola, e di S. Eugenio a Monistero, vol. 1613, *Ricordi E, 1450–1550,* fol. 53[r].

42. The document is published in Borghesi and Banchi, *Nuovi documenti,* no. 205, pp. 405–6.

43. See also chapter 12.

44. Apart from information found in texts set by Sienese composers and in dedications of various madrigal books, information about Sienese amateurs is notoriously difficult to assemble. Knowledge of the musical interests of a prominent fifteenth-century amateur, Bartolo di Tura di Bandino, comes in a roundabout way, from a 1483 inventory of his household items. This lists a monochord lacking strings. Bandini was a physician, lecturer in medicine, and author of medical and philosophical tracts, who also served as a prior and as captain of the people. He was also a friend of Lorenzo the Magnificent. See Curzio Mazzi, "La casa di maestro Bartolo di Tura," *BSSP* 5 (1900): 437, n. 468.

For Renaissance men and women the philosophers' pronouncements found fulfillment both in church approval and societal acceptance of musical instruction for the young.[45]

In Siena, as elsewhere in Italy and throughout Christian Europe, such approval and acceptance are implicit both in the various musical programs offered by the cathedral and the Palace and by the emergence of a class of professional teachers. From the very early fifteenth century, as demonstrated by some of Sermini's novellas discussed below, a certain facility at performing on the lute, on the viola, or the keyboard, singing from a partbook, or dancing a galliard became more and more desirable for people who wished to move in the rarefied world of the courtier and, by extension, in that of the cultured classes who set the tone for society's standards. In Siena by the mid-sixteenth century upper- and in many instances middle-class men and women could perform on an instrument or sing part music for their own delectation and that of their friends. Rinaldo Morrocchi, following Isidoro Ugurgieri-Azzolini, cited a number of musicians from prominent families, among them Tommaso Pecci, Scipione de' Vecchi, Pandolfo Savini, Oreste Biringucci, Camillo Spannocchi degli Scacchi, Fra Sinolfo Saracini, Fabio Buonsignori, and Scipione Chigi.[46] Societal attitudes, of course, encouraged people to learn music, and these attitudes found fulfillment thanks to the professional teachers. Their contributions were fundamental. Musical activities at the cathedral, at the Palace, and elsewhere were supported enthusiastically and generously precisely because of a large and influential class of musically literate people in the town.

Music in Gentile Sermini's Novellas

Gentile Sermini's novellas, written around the first quarter of the fifteenth century, provide a rich mine of information about musical instruction and the place of music in Sienese social life during his time. Musical instruments and music making, to be sure, are not mentioned in every one of his forty-odd stories, although many contain such references. When seen in the light of documentary records and information from other sources, incidents recounted by Sermini reflect actual musical practices in the Siena of his day and perhaps even earlier. Trumpeters actually sounded the hours, "singing, dancing, and the sound of instruments" normally formed part of both public and private festivities, and "instruments and pifferi" accompanied the deceased to his grave and the bride to her bridegroom's house.[47] But besides documenting the presence of music in

---

45. Not everybody, of course, wished to learn to sing for personal or for social reasons. Youths who planned to enter the priesthood and for whatever reasons did not attend the cathedral school needed instruction in the fundamentals of music and there were teachers in Siena who provided it. See below for Bartolomeo di Bertino, who sent his son to study with a Benedictine monk.

46. Morrocchi, *La musica in Siena*, 85, 88, 91. For the last named, see Giovanbattista Bellissima, *Scipione Chigi, illustre senese ignorato, musicista, capitano del popolo, gonfaloniere* (Siena, 1922).

47. Gentile Sermini, *Novelle,* ed. Vettori, novella 6, vol. 1, pp. 186, 189, 212. On instrumentalists accompanying brides to their bridegrooms' houses on their wedding day and restrictions placed on the number who could do so, see Zdekauer, *La vita privata dei senesi nel Dugento,* 79, who notes that a rubric in the Constitution forbade the town's trumpeters from such activities. Other musicians, of course, were free to do so. Casanova cites a chapter in the Sienese Statutes of 28 June 1343 limiting the number of musicians on such occasions to two trumpeters and a drummer, a ciaramella (shawm) or a trumpet: "solum duos tubatores, unum nacchererium vel unum tamburellum, unum ciaramellam

everyday life and providing some very important information about musical performance practices, Sermini's tales are significant because they show that some knowledge of music and dancing was considered essential in Siena and that people accomplished in these areas enjoyed tangible social advantages.

This is notably the case in Sermini's tale of the "teacher of song and instruments," *il maestro di suono e di canto,* Giannino da Lodi, who had a school, where he taught many young men and women to sing and to play instruments.[48] (Though the setting is Florence, it could just as easily have been the author's own Siena.) The main theme is introduced at the outset in a few brief sentences of dialogue, as Messer Bobi di Guccio determines that his daughter Lisa should learn to play an instrument and to sing, reasoning that this will be to her advantage when she marries. His wife, Monna Lapa, disagrees, arguing that an early marriage is best for her and warning him of the perils of having a teacher in the house. Lisa, aware that the maestro teaches many other young women, pleads to be allowed to study and both parents finally give their consent. The maestro, in the company of his assistant Nori, begins coming to the house twice daily to give lessons to his new pupil and brings with him a lute, a harp, and a pair of "pifferetti sordi," probably mute cornetts. Sermini thus tells us that private instruction was not a matter of one or two weekly lessons, but consisted rather of several hours of supervised daily study. These were separated, presumably, by periods in which the student practiced alone. Even with little musical talent, a student could, with such intense preparation, master the rudiments and perform creditably within a short time.

Lisa was apparently more motivated than most young women, and, as the narrator recounts, "was consumed with a desire to learn," both because she was attracted to the music maestro and because she disliked the idea "that the other girls would learn to play better than she." When she asks the maestro how she can progress more quickly, he makes one of those remarks as informative about the maestro's intentions as about performance. "It is true," he tells her, "that you've learned to play this saltarello very well because you can see where and how to place your fingers on the instrument."[49] But he doubts she could do this in the dark of night, when she would have to perform by touch. And so it goes, as a number of allusions to playing an instrument, couched in appropriate double entendres, lead the reader through several entwining episodes of seduction and musical pedagogy. The inevitable denouement occurs when Messer Bobi returns home after a six-month trip outside the city on government business to find both his wife and daughter pregnant, thanks to the tender teaching of the music maestro and his assistant. For Sermini's contemporaries the moral of this deliciously lascivious tale was quite clear. It was perfectly fine, indeed desirable, to give young women music

---

vel trombettam" (see his *La donna senese del Quattrocento,* 22). Nevertheless, exceptional circumstances did occasionally call for exceptions to the rule. As mentioned above in chapter 9, when the nieces of Pope Pius II were married on 4 January 1459, the Commune authorized an official delegation to accompany the brides to their husbands' houses and this included the Palace mace bearers, the trumpeters, and the woodwind players (ibid.).

48. Sermini, *Novelle,* ed. Vettori, novella 24, vol. 2, p. 424.

49. It is significant that amateurs were already being taught to play dance music even at this point, sometime before the mid–fifteenth century.

lessons, but these were best given under the strictest supervision at home or in a class-room with others present.

Two of Sermini's novellas describe vividly performance practices in his time. In the first of these, the avaricious servant Scopone is caught deceiving his master. Forgiven and ultimately redeemed, Scopone and his perfidy are revealed to his master, Bartolomeo Buonsignori of Siena, by the handsome young clerk, Ugo Malescotti.[50] Bartolomeo has been joined by a group of friends for a week of hunting at his lodge outside the city. At dinner, as fruit is served and as planned beforehand, Malescotti, "who was a master at singing and playing," picks up his lute and stands on a bench before the assembled guests. Singing to the lute, he improvises forty stanzas—in ottava rima one would suppose—that recount Scopone's treachery. The episode thus documents the well-known practice of improvised singing, which required accompaniment on the lute, the guitar, or another suitable instrument, played either by the singer himself or by a second person. Equally important is the information about the performer's social status. Ugo Malescotti was not a patrician or a particularly wealthy man but rather an employee of somebody who presumably was, perhaps a person of the middle classes. Nevertheless, the kind of musical instruction he had received befitting a youth of his social standing enabled him to accompany himself as he sang.

In another tale, which like so many of Sermini's has the triumph of love as its central theme, the clever Sismondo, hoping to gain the confidence of a young lady he wishes to seduce by making it appear to her and her companion that he is the friend of a handsome young man-about-town, waits for the youth to pass below the lady's window.[51] After greeting him, Sismondo invites him to sing a ballata with him because, as the narrator says, the youth "was a perfect soprano and Sismondo a good tenor." For the student of performance practices the important information given here is that composed vocal pieces such as ballatas were performed under certain circumstances by soloists without instrumental accompaniment. Of equal significance is the indication that two gentlemen of a certain class—Sismondo is described in the opening sentence as belonging to one of the principal families of Pisa—knew polyphonic ballatas by memory, with the implication that they both received a fairly thorough training in musical theory as well as in singing. This, and other information from various sources, offers convincing evidence that in Siena, at least, people of various classes had many opportunities to learn to sing and to play musical instruments and that to do so well was advantageous. The same, as noted below, can be said of the dance.

Music Schools

Evidence is not plentiful about schools where instruction in vocal and instrumental performance were offered, probably because there were not very many of them. Apparently instrumental and singing teachers did not need large studios, for they taught in their own homes or in those of their pupils, as did Sermini's music maestro. If they were monks, they could teach in their convents. This was the case with Niccolò, son

---

50. Sermini, *Novelle,* ed. Vettori, novella 3, vol. 1, p. 143.
51. Ibid., novella 15, vol. 1, p. 309.

of Bartolomeo di Bertino, who, as his father stated on 7 March 1485, was to study "letters and music and other subjects leading to the priestly orders" with the Benedictine monk Dom Bernardino.[52] As mentioned earlier, the renowned woodwind player Simone Nodi taught both in his own studio and at the Palace. His students at the Palace must have been young musicians who aspired to careers in the wind band there or with other professional groups.[53] There is no record of who Nodi's private pupils were, apart from the earlier mentioned Domenico Fei. But a document dated 18 December 1574 shows that he had a number of them, for it was drawn up "in his own studio, which is the place where he usually teaches his pupils."[54] Another report, also mentioned previously, speaks of the Palace instrumentalist and cathedral singer Piergiovanni Odorini as a teacher, though it does not say where he taught.

Sienese literary sources give some idea of the instruments taught by these musicians. Sermini's music maestro had a school where he taught his students both to sing and to play and he also gave private lessons on the lute, the harp, and the cornett. Similar instruments are mentioned by the Sienese gonfaloniere Giustiniano Nelli in one of his novellas written in the early sixteenth century. Nelli tells the tale of the love-struck youth, Giulio, who left no stone unturned in his quest to ingratiate himself with the beautiful Isabella, a well-brought-up noble lady of eighteen or nineteen years of age. Overwhelmed by his passion for Isabella, Giulio, "as young men often do," began doing the things he thought she might like, "playing the lute, the flute, the cornett, and singing and dancing." "Nor," adds the narrator, were there "dinners, weddings, suppers, or other places where she went that he might not quickly be found."[55] Nelli reports all of this—the young man's musical capabilities and the lengths to which he went in order to gain his beloved's attention—in a matter-of-fact way, as though it were an ordinary kind of situation his readers would have recognized. Singing, dancing, and playing the lute were, of course, not extraordinary activities for gentlemen, though playing the flute and the cornett might have been considered so at the time. When amateurs began taking up these instruments, however, inevitably questions were raised regarding their suitability for people of good family. The matter was treated at length by the Sienese playwright, philosopher, and man of letters Alessandro Piccolomini, bishop of Patros, in the revised edition of his treatise on education, *Della institution morale libri XII* (Venice, 1569).[56]

---

52. ASS, Notarile antecosimiano, vol. 684, fol. 104ʳ, dated 7 March 1484/85, specifies "ad discendum litteras et musicam et alias virtutes usque ad ordinem sacerdotalem."

53. See above for the document already cited in ASS, Notarile antecosimiano 2253, no. 1932.

54. The document, cited above in chapter 12, notes that the studio was in a house belonging to the Marchegiani family in the Contrada Fonteblanda of the Terzo Camollia. Simone's surname is mistakenly given as Narditi. (ASS, Notarile antecosimiano 2732, no. 2188, dated 18 December 1574).

55. Gaetano Poggiali, ed., *Novelle di autori senesi* (Milan, 1815), 2:65–87, Novella 1 del Nelli.

56. Piccolomini's work was originally published in 1542 as *Instituzione dell'huomo nobile;* the revised and enlarged edition, entitled *Della institution morale libri XII,* was published eighteen years later at Venice by Francesco Ziletti. Reference here is to the reprint of the volume bearing the same title, brought out by Giordano Ziletti, also at Venice, in 1569. For music in general, see book 12; chaps. 13 and 14 of book 4 deal with vocal and instrumental music, 150–56, and it is these from which all

Alessandro Piccolomini on Music Education

Piccolomini's views regarding the effects of music were decidedly Aristotelian and did not differ much from those of a host of previous medieval and Renaissance philosophers. While acknowledging that there were many diverse opinions about the utility of teaching music to the young, Piccolomini strongly favored it. He cited Plato and Aristotle as his authorities and recommended formal instruction both for the pleasure and for the intellectual stimulus music provided, not only in students' formative years but in the future, wherever their interests might lead them. He also took issue with those who scoffed at the rewards musical performance brought to its practitioners. He argued that those who learned to play derived even more pleasure from music than those who listened to others play it because "between cause and effect, which is delightful by nature, there is always more intense love, and consequently more intense delight." Music, furthermore, he asserted, "functions as a great ornament to morals and as an improvement to the soul's disposition."

Piccolomini enlarged on this last remark in his treatment of the third category into which medieval philosophers had traditionally placed music, *musica instrumentalis* or practical music, as opposed to the other two categories, *musica mundana* and *musica humana,* music of the spheres and music of the body and mind. He embraced the Aristotelian concept that certain melodies, rhythms, and harmonies could produce affects such as anger, love, piety, and gentleness in the minds and souls of listeners. He confessed that he did not know what the music of ancient times sounded like, though he had no hesitation in making analogies with the music he knew. He believed, for example, that "those musical airs that are prevalent in Lombardy excite the soul to a certain boldness and bravery," to the point where they would affect a person's outward actions. By contrast, "Neapolitan airs assuage and soften the soul, rendering it in part unmanly and weak." He was no less sweeping in judging foreign music, adding that "French airs, because they are so intense, sharpen the intellect and the Spanish ones make it docile." For Piccolomini, good Sienese that he was, indigenous music was preferable above all others, for it instilled those personal qualities that his countrymen hold dear even to this day. As he put it, "Tuscan melodies kindle other peoples' hearts to moderate and temperate emotions."

Piccolomini was no less prejudiced when it came to recommending which kinds of instruments noble youths ought to study. For him certain instruments were "plebeian and worthy of scorn," others "honored and capable of stirring various emotions." As far

---

of the following quotations are taken. For a summary of Piccolomini's views on music and on music education in Siena see D'Accone, "La musica a Siena nel Trecento, Quattrocento e Cinquecento," in *Umanesimo a Siena: Letteratura, Arti Figurative, Musica,* ed. Elisabetta Cioni and Daniela Fausti (Siena, 1994), 455–80. See also Stefano Lorenzetti, "Musica vis in animum. On the Relationship between Vocal and Instrumental Practice in the Pedagogical Treatises of the XVIth Century," in *Le Concert des voix et des instruments à la Renaissance: Actes du XXXIVe Colloque International d'Études Supérieures de la Renaissance, 1–11 juillet 1991,* ed. Jean-Michel Vaccaro (Paris, 1995), 39–50, esp. 42–44, where Piccolomini's views are cited in illustration of Lorenzetti's observation that a Renaissance gentleman sought to acquire a certain musical competence principally for two reasons, to enhance his own public image and for his own private delectation.

as instruments favored by the ancients were concerned, he again confessed that he knew nothing about old instruments such as "fistole, tibie, barbiti, and others." But, taking his cue from Aristotle, he condemned modern instruments such as trumpets, shawms, curtals, bagpipes, cornetts, flutes, and trombones, because, he said, playing them, either by blowing and forcing the breath or by some other similarly servile action, gave the performer "a very ugly, repulsive" face. Warming to his subject, he added that playing such instruments "debilitates a person and leaves him breathless," and "what is worse," this kind of excitement leaves him "less disposed to moderation in his habits."

Whether Piccolomini had some of the Palace musicians in mind when he wrote this passage is impossible to know, even though many of them were often in trouble with the law for a number of reasons, which ran the gamut from family squabbles to introducing ladies of dubious morals into Palace precincts and to carrying concealed weapons in public. In Piccolomini's scheme of things there would have been no trumpeters' corps, no wind band at the Palace, or at least none in which people of the upper classes participated. His was, in fact, an attitude clearly at odds with contemporary practices, which more and more used the very instruments he condemned in concerted sacred music as well as in secular music, practices that in his own time were already traditional at the cathedral and at the Palace. In this respect, Piccolomini was simply not in tune with the course of musical history nor, so to speak, with the temper of the times.

The instruments Piccolomini recommended as worthy of study, on the other hand, clearly bespeak his humanistic training as well as his social background. Putting aside, as he said, instruments such as "harps, tricordi, cetoles, rebecs, and similar instruments," he would be happy for society to take pleasure in "viols, lutes, and harpsichords." And even at that the viol was less to be recommended because it required accompanying instruments in performance, whereas the harpsichord and the lute, being complete instruments in themselves, were ideal because should a man find himself alone, they still gave him the opportunity to cheer himself up. Piccolomini preferred the lute above anything else because it was portable, very convenient, and the player could take it with him wherever he went. The harpsichord instead forced one to stay in one place, to play it wherever it was. For the same reason Piccolomi favored certain lironi, a string instrument, now obsolete, with double courses that could be sounded with one touch of the bow to produce chords.[57] These, as he put it, were very useful for those who wished

---

57. As Lorenzetti has pointed out ("On the Relationship," 44), the lirone was not mentioned in the earlier edition of Piccolomini's treatise from 1542, the 1560 citation showing that it had since come into more general use. For earlier references to the instrument see Blackburn, "Music and Festivities at the Court of Leo X," 9–12, where the use of an instrument called lirone in a musical entertainment at the court of Pope Leo X in August 1520 is shown to refer to the viol. Piccolomini, as noted, also speaks of the viol, but is most explicit in his reference to the lirone, specifying in 1560: "sono hoggi parimente in uso certi Lironi ne' quali sono le corde in modo moltiplicate, & disposte, che, potendosi commodamente piu d'una in un tempo insieme con l'archetto toccare; vien l'huomo à poter far per se stesso il concento di piu voci congiunte: & per conseguentia può, senz'haver bisogno d'altro compagno, produr da se stesso assai perfetta armonia. Et è questa sorte di instrumento molto commoda alla ricreation di color, che in camera soli alcuna volta desiderano di ricrear la mente, il che con gran soavità posson fare, accomodando da se stessi la voce in così fatto instrumento, con cantar

to relax alone in their own quarters, accompanying themselves as they sang "a Horatian ode, a Latin elegy, or some Tuscan stanza." Nevertheless, despite the obvious class distinctions implicit in Piccolomini's rather odd reasoning about what instruments were worthy of cultivation, his espousal of the validity of musical instruction gave ample expression to practices and social mores that the Sienese themselves had honored and sanctioned for centuries.

DANCE AND DANCE MUSIC

Dancing had an important place in Siena's social life, to judge from surviving documents. Some idea of how it was viewed can perhaps be had from one of the most celebrated examples of fourteenth-century Sienese painting, Ambrogio Lorenzetti's monumental fresco depicting the Effects of Good Government in the Palazzo Pubblico. In the foreground of his serenely idyllic scene, Lorenzetti prominently placed a group of nine lovely young maidens who dance a carol out-of-doors, while a tenth sings and beats a tambourine, as she provides the accompaniment for their dance (see Pl. 4). The orderly grace of their movements, one might argue, was meant as a metaphor for the stability of the well-ordered state and the rewards it brought the republic's citizens. Almost any pretext, as Sienese novelists and chroniclers imply, furnished a reason for dancing. Holidays, weddings, private parties, proclamations of peace, all were occasions for celebrations in which dancing inevitably took place, whether in private palaces or public squares. Even religious holidays were not immune from the passion for dancing. One record from 1497 speaks of the government's having paid L. 6. 14 to certain players and dancing masters on the feast of Corpus Christi, apparently because they performed and led the dancing at a public ball that was held that day.[58] From as early as the beginning of the fourteenth century dancing was also included among the formal festivities accorded important state visitors. In October 1310 when King Robert of Naples and his wife arrived in Siena, games and balls were held and bonfires lit for the royal pleasure, all at public expense.[59] Four years later similar events marked the visit of the king's brother.[60] This tradition continued through the fifteenth century and up until the fall

---

qualche Oda di Oratio, ò qualche Elegia Latina, ò Canzone, ò Stanza Toscana, ò simile altre cose di gran diletto" (*Della institution morale,* 155–56).

On the lirone see also Benvenuto Disertori, "L'Arciviolatalira in un quadro del Seicento," *Rivista musicale italiana* 44 (1940): 199–211; Howard Mayer Brown, "Psyche's Lament," 10–13; and id., *Sixteenth-Century Instrumentation: The Music for the Florentine Intermedii* (American Institute of Musicology, 1973), 39–56.

58. Borghesi and Banchi, *Nuovi documenti per la storia dell'arte senese,* 353, for citation of a document from the Libro del Camarlingo del Concistoro (ad annum) [vol. 2510, *Proventi, spese e inventari, 1496–1514*], fol. 69ᵛ: "1497. E a dì L. sei e soldi quatordici pacati la mattina del Corpus Domine per ordine de' Magnifici Signori e Chonfalonieri Maestri e Chonselieri a certi sonatori e maestri di ballo. L. 6 sol. 14." Dancing at Corpus Christi services was widespread throughout the later Middle Ages and Renaissance and persisted in some places until relatively recent times.

59. Agnolo di Tura del Grasso, "Cronaca senese," in Muratori, ed., *Rerum italicarum scriptores,* 15/6, 1:311.

60. "Cronaca Senese . . . di autore anonimo," in Muratori, ed., *Rerum italicarum scriptores,* 15/6, 1:103.

of the Republic, by which time state receptions and the formal entries preceding them had become even more elaborate. Staged to impress visitors with the wealth, refinement and, above all, courtly manners and culture of the Sienese ruling classes, the government surely viewed these activities as a necessary political function. A review of a few of these public festivities and the dancing that formed part of them may serve as a prelude to remarks about dance and dancing in the town's everyday life.

Among the most famous of such events in fifteenth-century Siena was the visit of Eleanor, daughter of the king of Portugal, who came to the city to be wed to the emperor Frederick III.[61] The marriage had been arranged by the emperor's former counselor and friend, Siena's archbishop Aeneas Sylvius Piccolomini, the future Pope Pius II. The event, which furnished the background for Piccolomini's famous novel of unrequited love, *The Story of Two Lovers,* was long remembered in Siena.[62] Indeed, a reenactment of it was even staged in the mid-nineteenth century to greet Siena's Habsburg ruler and his wife when they arrived in this southern outpost of the Austrian empire.[63] In the original scenario the Portuguese princess, Eleanor, accompanied by 200 horsemen and many barons and ladies-in-waiting, arrived in Siena on 24 February 1452. There to greet her under a canopy, amid flowing banners, were her future husband, who had arrived some two weeks earlier, the archbishop, members of the government, and a host of local dignitaries.[64] The couple embraced upon meeting, and after a number of welcoming orations, the princess and her entourage were escorted to their lodgings to the sound of the imperial trumpets, and probably of the Palace musicians as well. On the following day a grand ball honored the royal couple and invited guests, among whom were "more than one hundred of the fairest and most elegantly dressed young women of Siena." After all had been seated in their proper places the chronicler reports that "the Sienese youths began to dance with our young ladies, as did the barons

---

61. The event is described, among other places, in Luigi Fumi and Alessandro Lisini, *L'incontro di Federigo III imperatore con Eleonora di Portogallo sua novella sposa e il loro soggiorno in Siena* (Siena, 1878).

62. *Storia di due amanti di Enea Silvio Piccolomini in seguito Papa Pio Secondo, col testo Latino e la traduzione libera di Alessandro Braccio* (Capolago, 1832). In the novella Eurialo of Franconia, a member of Emperor Sigismund's entourage, first sees Lucrezia when she is presented at court. At one point in the story after the two have fallen in love, Lucrezia confesses to Eurialo that she knows he cannot remain in Siena forever and that should she go to a ball and not see him there, she would not know how to quiet her heart ("Tu hic dui esse non potes; nec ego te, postquam in ludum venerim, possem carere").

63. *L'Ingresso Solenne in Siena dell'Imperatore Federigo III e della Principessa Eleonora di Portogallo sua novella sposa, soggetto storico da rappresentarsi nella Piazza di Siena in occasione delle pubbliche feste d'Agosto di quest'anno 1833 onorate dall'augusta presenza delle altezze loro imperiali e reali Leopoldo II, Arciduca d'Austria, Gran Duca di Toscana, Maria Antonia, real Principessa di Napoli Sua Consorte, e Su. I. E. R. Famiglia* (Siena, 1833), 2: "Questo reingresso trionfale di Federigo colla sua novella sposa forma l'azion principal ed il soggetto della spettacolosa rappresentazione, avendovi fatte quelle semplici variazioni che esigeva la circostanza."

64. The event was depicted by Pinturicchio in one of his frescoes for the cathedral's Libreria Piccolomini. A recent reproduction of the fresco is in Carli, *Il Duomo di Siena,* pl. CCVII.

with their ladies, according to their usage, and it was a beautiful occasion and after the dancing there were excellent refreshments."[65]

Similarly, when Eleanor of Aragon, en route to Ferrara and her new husband Duke Ercole d'Este, accompanied by the duke of Amalfi and the duke of Andria, many barons, and a huge retinue, arrived in Siena on 15 June 1473, the princely party was welcomed by dignitaries of church and state and accompanied to their lodgings with all the appropriate fanfare. For the evening's festivities a platform was erected next to the house of Tommaso Pecci. "There in the open they danced," says the chronicler, and two Sienese ladies, "la Bianca and la Bianchina, danced with the duchess."[66] Unfortunately, here, as is often the case, no information regarding the dance choreographies or accompanying music is provided.

In 1465 the beautiful and accomplished Ippolita, daughter of Duke Francesco Sforza of Milan, stopped in Siena en route to Naples, where she was to wed King Ferrante's son, Alfonso, duke of Calabria.[67] The duchess was accompanied by many Lombard lords and a large group of retainers, and the Sienese, mindful of the power and wealth of their guests and of the sumptuous entertainments that had been offered them at various places as they progressed south, staged an event worthy of the occasion. Again, an outdoor platform was erected, this time in front of the Palazzo Pubblico. One chronicler reports that an elegant dinner was served and that there was a grand ball in which two hundred Sienese young ladies and many youths took part.[68] Another chronicler also includes a brief account of a spectacle staged by the guilds that evening, mentioning the popular—if little understood—dance, the moresca, which on this occasion probably took the form of a pantomimed ballet. He recounts that a large gilded wolf—an animal long since adopted by the Sienese as a symbol of the city's Roman origins—was placed on a platform in the Campo and that at the start of the spectacle twelve persons,

---

65. Fecini, "Cronaca Senese," 864.

66. Ibid., 872. When the Neapolitan princess left Siena, she was accompanied by the town's "trombetti, piffari, tromboni e tamburini," who received a lump sum payment of L. 168 for their expenses (ASS, Regolatori, vol. 9, fol. 402ᵛ). The bridal party's progress from Naples to Ferrara, through Rome, Siena, Florence, and the Romagna, and the lavish entertainments offered them in each place are recounted by Clelia Falletti, "Le feste per Eleonora d'Aragona da Napoli a Ferrara (1473)," in *Spettacoli conviviali dall'antichità classica alle corti italiane del '400*, Centro di Studi sul Teatro Medioevale e Rinascimentale, Atti del VII Convegno di Studio, Viterbo, 27–30 Maggio 1982 (Viterbo, 1983), 269–89, 200–66, esp. 281–82 for the stopover in Siena.

67. The duchess's trip has been the subject of numerous studies, many cited by Eileen Southern, "A Prima Ballerina of the Fifteenth Century," in *Music and Context: Essays for John M. Ward,* ed. Anne Dhu Shapiro (Cambridge, Mass., 1985), 183–97. See particularly Alessandro Lisini, *Le feste fatte in Napoli nel 1465 per il matrimonio di Ippolita Sforza Visconti con Alfonso duca di Calabria* (Siena, 1898), which in addition to recounting the events surrounding the union, also gives the text of a letter written by the two Sienese envoys, Giovanni Bichi and Andrea Cristofori, who reported on the reception of the gift of silver items worth L. 3,200, made to the royal couple by the Sienese government. The relevant passage is reproduced and commented upon by F. Alberto Gallo, "La danza negli spettacoli conviviali nel secondo Quattrocento," in *Spettacoli conviviali,* 262–3.

68. Fecini, "Cronaca Senese," 870.

one of whom was dressed as a nun, emerged from it. Then the company gathered around the nun and danced a moresca to a song with the words, "Non vogl'essere più monica, arsa le sia la tonica, che se la veste più" ("She'll be a nun no longer, let her habit be burnt, who'll ever put it on again").[69] As it happens, a musical setting of the text has come down to us in two versions of a well-known ballata, *Oramai che fora son:* one for two voices, cantus and tenor, the other for four, with the addition of altus and bassus. Perhaps one of these was the one danced, or even sung, in Siena that evening.[70]

The moresca is mentioned once again in a later Sienese chronicle that speaks of a ball held in honor of the duke of Calabria and the duke of Urbino in the Sala del Consiglio of the Palace on 18 December 1479. On this occasion the moresca seems to have been performed as a social dance rather than as spectacle. The retinues of both dukes were also invited, as were "all of the most beautiful women in the city," who, like the men, were richly dressed because the sumptuary laws had been waived for the evening. "They danced," says the chronicler, "for six hours and the duke danced several times," and "they did a most beautiful moresca."[71]

The moresca, as shown also by instruction programs offered by Sienese dancing masters mentioned below, continued as a popular form of entertainment in Siena in the following century. Suffice it to cite a few instances that record its continuing vogue. The earliest annals of the Congrega dei Rozzi, Siena's foremost theatrical academy of the sixteenth century, report that in February 1533 four of the members decided to ask the dancer Maestro Lorenzo di Fuccio to teach them "un assato di moresca co' le spade" that is, a moresca assault with swords, and that the dancer charged L. 9 for his

---

69. Allegretti, "Ephemerides," 722. The moresca, a dance of Moorish origin, is usually said to have spread throughout Europe via Spain. Barbara Sparti, in her edition of *Guglielmo Ebreo of Pesaro, De pratica seu arte tripudii* (Oxford, 1993), 53–57, describes *moresche* as mimed and danced spectacle pieces, performed with costumes, scenery, and special effects, that were quite popular in fifteenth-century Italy, where they were often given during the course of lengthy plays or banquets. This perhaps accounts for references to them also as *intermedi.* (On this latter, see Nino Pirrotta, *Music and Theatre from Poliziano to Monteverdi* [Cambridge, 1975], 37–75, particularly 52, 65, 73.) Sparti also notes that various themes, "allegorical, heroic, exotic, and pastoral," characterized these entertainments, which were danced by amateurs (courtiers, squires) and "professionals," that is, dancing masters, alike. Extant descriptions lack specific choreographic details and make little mention of the accompanying music, often performed by "tamburini," or pipe and tabor players, hence the importance of the Sienese report.

70. The music of the two-part version, which survives as a laude contrafactum, *Oramai son in età,* is given by Knud Jeppesen, "Lauda," *MGG,* 8:319; the four-part version, *Ora may, que fforan ço,* has been published by Atlas, *Music at the Aragonese Court,* 220–21 and by Southern, "A Prima Ballerina," 195, reprinted from her *Anonymous Pieces in the MS El Escorial IV. a. 24* (American Institute of Musicology, 1981), 69.

71. Cantoni, "Frammento di un Diario," 881. With regard to a somewhat later assessment of the moresca as a social dance, Pirrotta, *Music and Theatre,* 55, quotes Baldassare Castiglione in *Il cortegiano,* to the effect that "in private quarters [the courtier] might be permitted . . . to dance *moresche* and *brandi;* but not in public, except when in disguise . . . for the wearing of a costume carries with it a certain freedom and licence." In this respect, note Sparti, *Guglielmo Ebreo of Pesaro,* 61: "The distinction that exists today between theatrical and social dancing cannot be applied to the fifteenth century."

services.[72] A reference to the moresca as "un ballo a uso di Etiopia," or "a dance in the Ethiopian style," appears in one of the Company's initial productions, and another of its earliest endeavors, from 1537, was in fact entitled "Commedia nuova in moresca."[73] Here, one of the characters says: "Oh please let's do a *zucca robba*" ("Deh di gratia, facciamo a zucca robba"), which is perhaps the name of one of the dances, of a game, or of a popular song. A description of a choreographed moresca likewise occurs in this play. The dance is also featured in Alessandro Piccolomini's play *L'amor costante,* composed for a performance in honor of Emperor Charles V's visit in 1536.[74] Here, at the end of Act V, three of the cast, which includes a Spaniard and a German as well as Italians, first dance a "moresca in pietosa" with a kiss ("Qui va La Moresca in Pietosa col Bacio"). This is followed by another, perhaps livelier, one for four dancers, a galliard ("Qui va la Moresca Gagliarda"), and the play concludes with a kind of weaving dance ("Qui va Lo Intrecciato") for all three of the characters.[75]

Another fifteenth-century chronicler's report merits repeating because it indicates that dancing was rarely dispensed with, even in times of war. In this case it was a ball given in honor of Charles VIII of France. A few preliminary words about its circumstances will place it within its proper context. The king arrived in Siena for the first time on Tuesday, 2 December 1494.[76] Leading one of the most ferocious armies ever seen on the peninsula, he was making his way south to claim a dubious right to the Neapolitan throne, devastating much of the countryside as he went and, not coincidentally, precipitating calamitous political changes in the cities unlucky enough to lie in his path. Among the latter was Florence, where the Medici were ousted and a republican

---

72. Curzio Mazzi, *La Congrega dei Rozzi di Siena nel secolo XVI* (Florence, 1882), 1:364, n. 4. Fucci was subsequently inducted into the Academy with the name L'Atteno, in March 1533 (p. 440, no. 36). Pirrotta, *Music and Theatre,* 81–83, gives an excellent summary of what can be gleaned about the use of song, dance, and instruments in some of the earliest known sixteenth-century Sienese plays.

73. Mazzi, *La Congrega dei Rozzi,* 1:206.

74. *L'amor costante. Comedia Del S. Stordito Intronato composta per la venuta dell'Imperatore in Siena L'anno del XXXVI* (Venice: al segno del Pozzo, 1541). References to the dances are on pp. 78, 79; they are mentioned by Pirrotta, *Music and Theatre,* 81, who suggests that "instrumental accompaniment of pipes or bagpipes and drums is hinted at in the words of two of the characters." Pirrotta also notes the use of an "abbattimento" (duelling on stage) in this play.

75. A bassadanza called "Pietosa/Piatosa" composed by Guglielmo Ebreo is included in all of the major redactions of his *De pratica seu arte tripudii,* pp. 131–33 of Sparti's edition. Gagliarda is often used as an adjective, meaning vigorous, lusty, gallant. But the term could, in this case, also be an early reference to the dance type itself, meaning that the music that was danced to was a galliard and used galliard steps. The intrecciato is mentioned both in Giovanni Battista Doni's *Trattato della musica scenica* and in *Il Corago,* as well as in Emilio de' Cavalieri's *Rappresentazione dell'anima e del corpo.* According to Sparti, who furnished this information, the intrecciato, a figure like a chain or key in which the dancers weave in and out of one another, was commonly used with choruses in early seventeenth-century music drama because the performers could sing as they danced. In this regard see below for the social dancing described by Bargagli.

76. Lodovico Zdekauer, "L'Entrata di Carlo VIII Re di Francia, in Siena (1494, 2 Dicembre)," *BSSP* 3 (1896): 248–53; Marin Sanudo, *La spedizione di Carlo VIII in Italia,* ed. Rinaldo Fulin (Venice, 1873), 144–47.

regime installed. In Siena, where he demanded a forced loan from the government, Charles's entry was marked by a more than unusual display of pomp. The Concistoro and a host of noblemen and citizens were on hand to greet him and a number of triumphal arches were raised at the city's gates. Principal among these was the one at the Porta Camollia, which featured a tableau vivant with a young boy dressed as the Virgin Mary, surrounded by angels and the city's four patron saints. According to an eyewitness account, the boy declaimed Latin verses in praise of the king to musical accompaniment.[77] Although the text has survived, no trace remains of the music.[78]

After looting Naples and asserting his claim to the throne, Charles began the long journey back to France. He returned to Siena on 13 June 1495. This time his thoughts appeared to turn to lighter things, for a few days later he let it be known that "he wished to see the ladies of Siena." A ball was hastily arranged for that evening at the Palace in the Sala del Concilio, and fifty or more Sienese ladies were invited. The chronicler recounts that "when the king arrived, without any confusion or scandal, they danced and made merry because the hour was late." The King danced with two noble ladies, "one on each arm, and all departed happily at the 24th hour."[79] On the seventeenth, after hearing Mass in the cathedral, Charles was on his way to Pisa, fearful that his enemies might attempt to block his way.[80]

Dancing in Sermini's Novellas

Not all of the references to dancing in fifteenth-century Siena concern state-sponsored balls and receptions honoring visiting royalty. Nor are they confined exclusively to the chroniclers' reports. Tax records, legal documents, literature, and poetry all furnish information about the importance of dance and its place in Sienese society. Gentile Sermini's novellas, already quoted in regard to singing and playing, also give the impression that dancing was enjoyed by all classes of the citizenry. Take, for example, his tale of the lovers Vannino da Perugia and La Montanina, wife of the jealous Andreoccio, who fake her death and flee to Milan, where they live as man and wife. In the Lombard capital Montanina learns to speak the local patois, and when the couple returns to their native city two years later, she speaks it so well at a dinner honoring Vannino and his new wife that nobody recognizes her, though her resemblance to the presumably deceased Montanina is of course noted. Of particular interest is the description of the

---

77. Zdekauer, "L'Entrata," 249. The Latin verses were first printed by Malavolti in his *Dell'Historia di Siena,* Libro Sesto, fols. 99ᵛ–100ʳ, and are given in a corrected version by Zdekauer.

78. The resemblance between this performance and that of the solo song in honor of Archbishop Piccolomini almost a century later, mentioned in chapter 14, is noteworthy.

79. BCIS, MS B. III. 2, *Storia di Siena di Vari,* "Frammento di Diario Senese d'incerto autore," fol. 219ᵛ (p. 446): "Re di Francia disse Lunedì a dì 15 [giugno, 1495] volea vedere le donne di Siena e così li Senesi ordinoro' per la sera a ore 22 e furo' raunate 50 donne o più nella Sala del Consiglio, di poi vi vene e' Re con grande ordine senza strepito e scandolo si danzò, giocò perché era l'ora tarda. Ste' lo re in mezo fra due, cioè Francesca, figlia di Ristoro Scotti, donna di Sozino di messer Niccolò Severini, e Lucretia, figlia di Bartolomeo Luti, moglie di Roberto fratello di detto Sozino, e ale 24, cioè ore si partiron lo re e suo' baroni ben sodisfati."

80. Malavolti, *Dell'Historia di Siena,* Libro Sesto, fol. 101ʳ; see Allegretti, "Ephemerides," 849, for account of the king at Mass and his departure afterwards.

remaining hours of this first reunion of relatives, neighbors, and friends. "Afterwards," recounts the narrator, "the tables having been removed, they remained for quite some time, with singing, dancing, and the sound of instruments."[81] The matter-of-fact introduction of the allusion to music and dancing gives the impression that this was the normal way for people at a gathering of this sort to pass an evening. The social class of the participants is not mentioned in the story, though, considering the circumstances, they were likely people of some means.

This was decidedly not the case with the fourteen-year-old Neapolitan heroine in another Sermini tale. Isabella was "beautiful, wise, honest, and virtuous," but from a humble background, the daughter of a greengrocer.[82] "Among her other praiseworthy virtues," says the narrator, "she danced so marvelously that it was a wonder to behold, and she was invited to all the social gatherings in Naples." Queen Giovanna of Naples, wishing to see her dance, had her invited to dinner at the palace on May Day, along with many ladies of rank. After dinner "almost all of the nobility of Naples" watched Isabella dance. Among those was Messer Agapito of Perugia, who fell in love with Isabella's beauty and her dancing and married her within a few days, with the queen's blessing. "But this was not his calling," we are told, for Agapito then formed an amorous attachment to a student named Germano. When news of Agapito's infatuation reached Queen Giovanna, Agapito was burnt at the stake and Isabella, his heir, later married Germano, who had meanwhile become one of the queen's knights. The story ends in the royal palace where the queen holds "a magnificent and joyous feast, with singing, dancing, and instruments," after which, she and her party accompany the newlyweds, "with much playing and dancing to the house that used to belong to Messer Agapito" and was now theirs. The questionable morality of the story apart, even poor girls with natural talent, in this case for dancing, were clearly accepted into the higher realms of courtly society, where knowing how to sing and dance were quite obviously important social graces.

Dancing in Scipione Bargagli's Writings

Writing more than a century after Sermini, Scipione Bargagli furnishes additional details relating to the place of dance in Sienese life in one of his tales, a Tuscan Romeo and Juliet story with a happy ending.[83] He recounts how two young people from feuding noble families, Antillia and Uguccione, fall in love at first sight and how, after various heart-rending misfortunes, they obtain permission to marry, thanks to the ingenious assistance of a wise physician. The families, predictably enough, are reconciled. The scene of the couple's first encounter is a celebration in a country village, where Uguccione arrives by chance. Antillia, sitting with friends in a loggia overlooking the square, is watching "the country girls and their suitors as they dance to the sound of country instruments" when her eyes meet his. But neither the hero nor the heroine dances, together or with others, although they enjoy the festivities.

---

81. Sermini, *Novelle,* ed. Vettori, vol. 1, novella 1, 102–3.

82. Ibid., novella 8, p. 225.

83. Poggiali, ed., *Novelle di autori senesi* (Milan, 1815), vol. 2, Novella 1 del Bargali, 151–69; *Le novelle di Scipione Bargagli,* ed. Luciano Banchi (Siena, 1873), 61–91, novella prima.

Dancing is also prominently mentioned by Bargagli in his *I trattenimenti* of 1587. He singles out the round dance, which he refers to as "ballo tondo" or "ballo a canzoni," as "a way of dancing that is the most cheerful, most amorous, and most perfect of all the dances that can be found among cheerful people" and says that it was current "in all of our cities and in the country."[84] (Bargagli, as will noted below, also included a round dance in his *cantata pastorale,* scenario and text published in 1589.) His charming account of how the participants got into position to begin the dance falls short of describing the steps, though he does indicate that in time-honored fashion they sang as well as danced.[85] Thus, as the dance begins, Fulvio bows and invites Clezia to dance, and taking her by the hand, gracefully leads her to the middle of the room; the other youths follow his example, and the couples, close together, their hands joined almost like the links of a noble chain, join him, alternating around a ring. As the dance gathers momentum and moves in a circle, the others fall silent and "Fulvio sings in a delightful voice . . . a canzonetta a ballo tondo," *Se 'n mirar di sua donna,* the music of which unfortunately does not survive.[86]

DANCING MASTERS

Dancing, like trumpet playing and other arts, crafts, and trades of the time, was a profession handed down in families from one generation to the next. And, like those other professions, it required a period of apprenticeship that could best be had under the guidance of a family member. One very famous case of kinship in the history of fifteenth-century Italian dance concerns the Jewish dancing master Guglielmo, who became a Christian with the name Giovanni Ambrogio. His famous dance manual survives in a number of copies, including a Sienese one now classified as MS L. V. 29 in the Biblioteca Comunale.[87] Barbara Sparti describes the Sienese exemplar as the most impressive of all of the extant copies, the only one written on parchment, with illuminated initials and chapter headings, and still in its original binding.[88] Giovanni Ambro-

---

84. *I trattenimenti di Scipion Bargagli; dove da vaghe donne, e da giovani huomini rappresentati sono honesti, e dilettevoli giuochi; narrate novelle; e cantate alcune amorose canzonette* (Venice, 1587), 284; portions of the text and reference to the dance, which closes a discussion of the "Giuoco della caccia" are given by James Haar, "On Musical Games in the 16th Century," 24.

85. On round dances, particularly in the late fifteenth century, see Sparti's commentary in her edition of *Guglielmo Ebreo of Pesaro, De pratica seu arte tripudii,* 59.

86. Bargagli, *I trattenimenti,* 285.

87. The treatise has recently been edited and translated into English, with musical transcriptions, commentaries, and annotations in Sparti's *Guglielmo Ebreo of Pesaro, De pratica seu arte tripudii.* Some biographical information about Giovanni Ambrogio is given by Timothy J. McGee, "Dancing Masters and the Medici Court in the 15th Century," *Studi musicali* 17 (1988): 202–24.

88. Sparti, *Guglielmo Ebreo,* 17. The physical aspects of the Sienese copy suggest that it was made for a princely or noble library, but the coat of arms it carries has yet to be identified. Though the choreographic descriptions of the Sienese copy are the most condensed and vague (for reconstruction purposes today), it contains more choreographies than any other redaction and includes the name of the dancing master/choreographer Phyllipo. Perhaps this latter, author of the bassadanza "Consolata in quatro," is the same person as Filippus Bussus of Biandrate, a dancing master who was in correspondence with Lorenzo the Magnificent in 1469 (McGee, "Dancing Masters and the Medici Court," 205–8).

gio's brother Giuseppe was also a dancing master, and both, though employed principally by the duke of Urbino, had strong ties to the Medici in Florence. There is no
indication that Giovanni Ambrogio ever worked in Siena. Given the passion for dancing
in Siena, however, the presence there of one of the most celebrated manuals of chore-
ography is not surprising. Nor is it surprising that the treatise was written by a converted
Jew who hobnobbed with the nobility, for Jewish dancing masters also taught members
of Siena's leading families. Among them was a certain Moisè, who absconded from
Siena with plate and other valuables belonging to the Pecci family, after having duped
the mistress of this patrician household with promises of teaching her the steps of various fashionable dances.[89]

Along with the copy of Giovanni Ambrogio's treatise, chroniclers' reports, and evidence furnished by literary and pictorial sources, a number of legal documents help to
fill in a picture of Siena as a town where dancing flourished throughout the fifteenth
and sixteenth centuries. In Siena, as in other major centers, knowing how to dance—
apart from the pleasure it brought—was clearly considered an indispensable part of
one's education. And there to teach whoever wished to learn—traditional dances or
the latest and most fashionable steps—were the professional dancers and dancing masters. Names of a few of them appear in various records from these centuries. Among the
earliest known is Giovanni Antonio di Jacomo, a *maestro di ballo* living in the company of
San Pietro in Castelvecchio in Terzo di Città, who filed a report with tax authorities
on 20 April 1478.[90] Giovanni had apparently not been very successful in his profession,
for he declared that he was impoverished to the point where he needed public assistance
and that he had three daughters of marriageable age and no property. He was still alive
in July 1484, when he witnessed a notarial act.[91] Another dancing teacher, Maestro
Mariotto di Marchetto, a native of Perugia resident in Siena, was mentioned in two
similar documents a few years earlier. In one of them, from 23 October 1470, he named
the painter Sano di Pietro as his procurator, an indication perhaps that he had entered
fully into the artistic life of the town.[92]

Mariotto is the author of the "balletto for three called La Fortuna" included in the
version of Guglielmo Ebreo's treatise on dance known as the Giorgio redaction, after
the name of the dancing master who compiled it.[93] Unfortunately, none of the choreographies in that redaction is accompanied by music. Mariotto's balletto is one of the later
choreographies, two of which (anonymous) were great hits at the turn of the sixteenth
century. It is difficult to assess how wide a reputation Mariotto enjoyed in his own time,

89. McGee, "Dancing Masters and the Medici Court," 215–16.

90. "† Al nome di Dio amen. Adì 20 d'aprile 1478. Dinanzi a voi, espetabile scitadini [*sic*] eletti
a fare la nuova lira del magnifico comun di Siena, io Giovanni Antonio d'Iacomo, maestro di ballo,
vi do el mobile e immobile" (ASS, Lira, vol. 174, 1478, Terzo di Città, fol. 228ʳ).

91. ASS, Notarile antecosimiano, 739, no. 189, dated Siena, 8 July 1484. His son, "Magister
Gaspare magistri Ioannis Antonii, magistri tripudiorum," was mentioned as a witness to a notarial act
on 24 March 1506/7. ASS, Notarile antecosimiano 664, no. 81.

92. ASS, Notarile antecosimiano, 385, fol. 159ᵛ, dated 23 October 1470.

93. For the Giorgio redaction, now in the New York Public Library for the Performing Arts, see
Sparti, *Guglielmo Ebreo,* 18.

though it is significant that he is, together with the just-mentioned Phylippo, Guglielmo's brother Giuseppe, and Lorenzo the Magnificent, among the few dancing master/
choreographers named in various fifteenth-century treatises besides Guglielmo Ebreo
and his star pupil Domenico da Piacenza. Certainly, he was successful enough in Siena
to settle down there and raise a family.

Mariotto passed his profession on to his son, who was evidently born in his father's
adopted city. Francesco di Mariotto, *ballarino senese,* appears on tax rolls as early as 1488,
when he reported that he and his wife were impoverished and had no properties to
declare.[94] Records from 1509 tell a somewhat different story. By then Francesco owned
a house on the Piano de' Mantellini in the company of San Quirico in Terzo di Città
and was leasing a vineyard from the archbishopric of Siena. He and his wife had nine
children, three young boys, who were not yet working, and six girls, three of marriageable age.[95] One daughter was already married and Francesco had been forced to pawn
a part of the vineyard with his son-in-law, the barber Matteo di Pilucca, to the amount
of Fl. 50, as part of her dowry. Francesco, according to his statement to tax authorities,
was a poor man, eking out a living on what the citizens paid him, struggling to support
his many children and a sick wife. Yet, as this and subsequent documents show, he was
able to own his own house, rear a large family, and pass his profession on to at least one
of his children. Age and experience also brought him a certain measure of respect.
Seventeen years later, in 1526, when he was mentioned in connection with the sale of
the house in Piano dei Mantellini, the notary referred to him to as "Maestro Francesco,
son of the late Mariotto, Sienese dancer."[96] The names of two of his children, the
dancer "Marco Antonio, son of the late Francesco," and his daughter, Cornelia, appear
in legal records dating from 22 March 1534 and 4 October 1536.[97] A grandson who
was also a dancer, Adriano di Fazio di Francesco, had a house in San Quirico. Following
in his grandfather's footsteps, he, too, cited poverty in his tax report in 1549.[98] Three of

94. "Dinanzi da voi spettabili cittadini eletti et deputati a fare la nuova lira dela Magnifica ciptà
di Siena: Franceschino di Mariotto ballarino senese significa havere li infrascripti bovari [poveri] beni"
(ASS, Lira, vol. 215, Terzo di Città, unn. fol. = 30ʳ).

95. "Dinanzi ad voi, Spettabili alliratori . . . Francesco di Mariotto ballarino, vostro minimo servidore, significa havere l'infrascripti beni con l'infrascritti incariche e graveze . . . Item si ricorda ad le
Vostre Spettabilità come decto Francesco è povero homo et governasi sotto el subsidio de' vostri
cittadini, et ha 9 figlioli infra maschi e femine, cioè maschi 3 piccoli e disutili, e sei femine dele quali
ne è maritata una sola et 3 altre ve ne sono da marito, da anni XIIII in su, et tutti li ha ad governare
con la sua povera industria et fadiga, con la sua donna insieme, mezo inferma et malsana. Racomandasi
ad le vostre Spettabilità" (ASS, Lira 236, unn. folio, 1509).

96. ASS, Notarile antecosimiano 826, no. 3151, dated Siena, 17 April 1526.

97. ASS, Notarile antecosimiano, 2187, unnumbered folio, dated Siena, 22 March 1533/34,
which reports that "Marcus Antonius olim magistri Francisci, ballarinus de Senis" made a wedding
gift to his wife Domenica, daughter of the deceased Giovanni di Angelo da Magliano. Notarile antecosimiano 2187, unnumbered folio, dated Siena, 4 October 1536, reports that "Cornelia, filia quondam magistri Francisci Mariotti, ballarini," wife of Agnolo, son of the late Pavolo, made a gift of a
house in the contrada Laterino in Siena to her brother, Marcantonio.

98. "† Al nome di dio adì 22 di feraio 1548/49. Si dicie a voi Signori sopra la nuova lira gome
Adriano di Fazio di Franciescho balarino mi truovo una meza gasa vegia . . . di poga valuta nel Terzo
di città e ganpagnia di San Quirigo e gontrada de Mantelini, povaro e senza altro bene . . . Trovomi

four generations are thus documented as property owners, and protestations of poverty notwithstanding, it seems that a dancing master's earnings, though dependent on the whims of the public, enabled him to earn a decent enough living.[99]

This certainly was so in the case of two other Sienese dancing masters in the later sixteenth century. One of them, Giovanbattista, son of the deceased Sebastiano, had enough capital to acquire a vineyard in February 1570.[100] The other, Giovanbattista, son of the deceased Buono of Siena, was master of his own dancing school. He did so well in the profession that on 7 May 1576 he was able to give Fl. 250 as a dowry to his adopted daughter Giulia.[101]

Documents from the mid-sixteenth century record two other dancing masters, both of whom were named Niccolò. One was "Niccolò, ballarino, son of the deceased Geronimo of Siena," who in October of 1556 was renting a property owned by the Sienese Company of the Virgin Mary. The other was "Maestro Niccolò, son of the deceased Lodovico of Siena," witness to a notarial act registered on 23 December 1558.[102] Perhaps one of them was Niccolò Bendusi, a musician and possibly a dancer, who published a book of four-part ensemble dance pieces in Venice in 1553.[103] The problem of identity goes beyond matching names, however, because it is not even certain that Bendusi was Sienese. François-Joseph Fétis, the celebrated nineteenth-century music historian, whose information is not always reliable, says that he was. But

---

due filioli al presente e più presto gon gualge debitore gredito" (ASS, Lira, vol. 243, 1548, Terzo di Città, fasc. 2, fol. 23[r], no. 1493).

99. Mention may also be made here of another Sienese dancing master, Girolamo di Giovanni, "detto Ballarino," who was renting half of a house belonging to the convent church of Santo Spirito in Siena in 1548 (PR, Santo Spirito di Siena, vol. 2367, *D&C, 1536–39,* fol. 16[r]).

100. ASS, Notarile antecosimiano, 2993, no. 501, dated 21 February 1569/70, which notes that "Giovanbaptista quondam Pieri, aromatarius de Senis" sold the property, which was in the Commune of Monastero in a place called Acquaviva, to "Iohanni Baptiste quondam Sebastiani, ballarino Senarum" for Fl. 68.

101. "Per la presente si fa noto e si declara a ciascuno qualmente mediante il favore divino e la inspiratione dello Spirito Santo, questo dì sopradecto si è concluso vero e legittimo parentado di matrimonio in fra le infrascritte parti, cioè che il provido homo Giovanbaptista già di Buono da Siena, maestro di squola di ballare, dà e dedica per consorte e legittima sposa la honesta e pudica fanciulla Giulia, sua figlia adottiva et allevata, al discreto giovane Martio già di Vittori Focari, setaiu[o]lo e frangiaro senese presente e accettante . . . Et per dote della medesima Giulia promette e si obliga el decto Giovanbatista dare e pagar al decto Mutio fiorini ducentocinquanta di lire 4 per ciascuno fiorino di denari senesi, quali habbi dha [*sic*] havere a conseguire in una possessione vignata e lavorativa di esso Giovanbatista, posta infra le masse di Siena, nel Comune di Monistero . . . La quale possessione esso Giovanbatista si riterrà a nome di fitto et per fitto di essa fiorini 200 promette dargli ogni anno fiorino 5 per cento et fiorini 50 contanti" (ASS, Notarile antecosimiano, 2085, fol. 59[r–v], dated Siena, 7 May 1576).

102. ASS, Notarile antecosimiano, 1777, no. 890, dated Siena, 10 October 1556; Notarile antecosimiano, 2924, no. 391, fol. 392, dated 23 December 1558.

103. Howard Mayer Brown, *Instrumental Music before 1600: A Bibliography* (Cambridge, Mass., 1965), item 1553[2], 147–88, *Opera Nova de Balli di Francesco Bendusi* (Venice, Antonio Gardane, 1553); Brown points out that all but one of the twenty-four compositions in the volume were reprinted two years later in Paul and Bartholomeus Hessen's collection of 322 ensemble pieces, *Viel Feiner Lieblicher Stücklein* (Breslau, Crispinus Scharffenburg, 1555).

Fétis did not document his claim, and since his time nothing has come to light to reinforce it.[104] Bendusi's volume is important in the history of sixteenth-century instrumental dance music because it was the first of its kind printed in Italy. It contains twenty-four dances in all. Twenty-one of these are of the galliard or saltarello type, and are entitled either by genre, such as *Pass'e mezo dito il Romano, Pass'e mezo ditto il Compasso,* or by reference to popular tunes, such as *E dove vastu o bon solda, Il ben ti vegna,* and *Chi non ha martello.*[105] Although the titles do not have much of a Sienese ring to them, what we know about dancing teachers and the ubiquity of dancing in Renaissance Siena makes it possible that Bendusi was Sienese and that the volume preserves some of the tunes that were sung and danced in the city in the time of the republic.

DANCING SCHOOLS

A few records contain information about how dancers and musicians set up their studios and conducted their affairs. A contract drawn up on 22 October 1493 shows that three foreigners, Maestro Giovanni Cristofani di Messer Jacomo da Brescello of Parma, Maestro Domenico di Marco of Perugia, and Maestro Geronimo di Gostanzo, also of Perugia, formed a partnership in Siena for the purpose of teaching people to dance and to play musical instruments.[106] Like several of the entertainers mentioned at various Palio festivities, these dancing masters also played instruments of one sort or another, which was probably true of many of the other dancing masters/choreographers from this time. The general terms of the 1493 agreement state that the partnership was for ten years and that each was to share in one-third of the expenses and profits resulting from the venture. More specific provisions include a fine of ten ducats to be paid by whoever broke the agreement, unless there were no students, in which case the partnership would be dissolved. It was further provided that if one, or even two, of the partners should fall ill, their fair share of the profits would nevertheless be paid them. If one of the partners left town for fifteen or twenty days, however, he would forfeit any of his earnings.

The kinds of dances taught in schools such as this are described in another Sienese record, an undated handbill said to be from around the same time as the contract or, to judge from the handwriting, perhaps a decade or so later (see Doc. 13.6).[107] Its text reveals that a variety of dances, requiring a number of lessons, were available to the

---

104. Fétis, *Biographie universelle des musiciens* (Paris, 1877), 1:338.

105. For a discussion of Bendusi's volume see Daniel Heartz, "Sources and Forms of the French Instrumental Dance in the Sixteenth Century" (Ph.D. diss., Harvard University, 1957), 75.

106. ASS, MS C 60, published by Borghesi and Banchi, *Nuovi documenti per la storia dell'arte senese,* no. 183, pp. 351–53.

107. Published by Borghesi and Banchi, *Nuovi documenti,* 353, following the just-cited document from 22 October 1493. "Nota: In una pergamena, pervenuta all'Archivio senese per legato del compianto senatore conte Scipione Bichi Borghesi, trovansi alcuni capitoli che dovevano essere osservati da chi voleva imparare a ballare. Questi capitoli non hanno data, e sebbene il carattere con cui sono scritti sia della stessa epoca del documento qui sopra riferito, non osiamo affermare che essi appartengano alla stessa società." The text, written on parchment in a clear hand that seems to me to be later than the 1493 date suggested by Borghesi and Banchi, is of such importance that I give its text in full in Doc. 13.6.

interested student and that newer dances, which fewer people obviously knew, were more expensive than traditional ones. The text also demonstrates enforcement of a rigid code of behavior and observance of all the proprieties.

> *In the names of both God and of the glorious Virgin Mary and of all the saints of the* *magnificent city*
>
> Let no one be so daring as to leave the school before he has finished his dance, under penalty of s. 5.
>
> The calata, which has eight [movements?][108] .... L. 7
> The fioretti, with eight [movements?]............................... L. 10
> The seconda, pays .... L. 7
> The galiarda, pays.. L. 21
> The moresca, pays.. L. 21
> The martorella, pays... L. 21
>
> And because new things usually delight according to students' temperaments, since there is a dance *de fioretti novi,* whoever wants to learn it will pay... L. 14
>
> Next, if the said students wish none of the said dances *a la cho[n]tadina,* that is, he/she is obliged to pay L. 10 for the *calata* and L. 14 for the *fioretti.*
>
> And further, if there should be no one who wants some of the said dances he/she undertakes, that is, the dance is [nonetheless] understood to have 8 movements.
>
> Item, nobody can begin instruction, unless he/she has paid the said sums beforehand, that is, half the cost of the dance he/she will learn first.
>
> Item, let no one be so bold as to take the name of God and of Our Lady in vain, under penalty of paying s. 5 each time.
>
> Item, if [someone] takes the names of other saints in vain, he/she will be obliged to pay s. 2, and the said money is to be put into a purse [and] the master may do what he wishes with it, that is, he may buy shoes and other things as needed.
>
> Each student is obliged to pay the bagpiper monthly, or s. 2 every time he dances.

The names of the dances and dance types appear in other sources of the time and later, though little is known about their steps and accompanying music. "Fioreggiare" is mentioned by Giovanni Ambrogio in his treatise, where it seems to indicate generic ornamentation, while at the beginning of the sixteenth century the playwright Ruzante speaks of doing the dance called "il Gioioso with fioretti," implying, apparently, specially ornamented steps. By Fabritio Caroso's time the "fioretto" was a definite step. Equally obscure is the martorella, which occurs among other places in the title of a 1521 play by Stricca, discussed below in chapter 14. The calata, said to be characterized

---

108. I have translated "g[i]ochi" as movements, though it may very well refer to hours or any other "measure." I should also note that this text is particularly obscure in places and that my translation is exceedingly free and offers only one of several possible interpretations. "Una dansa di fioretti novi," for example, may be translated as "new" or as "nine fioretti," while "fioretti," which I give as the title of a dance, might also refer to "flourishes." On this latter, see Sparti, *Guglielmo Ebreo,* 14, n. 36.

by "quick rhythms," is referred to in the mid-sixteenth century as a "ballo di molto fretta," an exceedingly fast dance. It was still being cited in early seventeenth century, as was the contadina, described as "a kind of popular dance of rural origins."[109]

A contract dated 26 February 1505 preserves details regarding the formation of another dancing school by the Sienese dancing master Maestro Gasparo di Giovanni di Antonio, alias el Tozzo, doubtless the son of the dancing master mentioned above, and Maestro Giovanantonio di Tommaso Piccinelli of Brescia, "ballarinus sive saltator," a choreographer and dancer. Also included in the contract were Piccinelli's sons, Andrea and Raffaello, who were artists as well as dancers, having painted, among other things, a *Baptism of Christ*, now in the Opera's Museum.[110] The terms of the 1505 agreement stipulated that Maestro Gasparo was to provide a place for Giovanantonio and his sons in the school where they could teach and earn their living, in return for which the Brescians were to teach "calatas and gagliardas as well as morescas."[111] The Brescians, furthermore, had to share with the Sienese master a fourth of all of their earnings, both from the school and from teaching in private houses. In return, the Sienese promised to pay the Brescians a fourth of any earnings he might receive from pupils brought in by the Brescians, women as well as their husbands. The agreement was to be in force for ten years and should one of the partners seek to break it without the consent of the other before it expired, he would be obliged to pay a fine of 10 ducats. A final clause stipulates that during the time covered by the contract, Giovanantonio and his sons were forbidden to form other companies or societies and to teach in any school other than Gasparo's. The reasons why terms of the contract were so clearly to the advantage of the Sienese partner are not known but they may have to do with the Brescians' need for employment in Siena at that time.

Two later contracts reveal that dancing schools continued to flourish through the mid-sixteenth century. The first, dated 1 January 1537, records how Maestro Lorenzo and Maestro Marcantonio di Maestro Francesco Fineschi, both described as "ballarini senesi," Sienese dancing masters, decided to form a company and and set up a dancing school that they would jointly administer for the next four years (see Doc. 13.7). (Maestro Lorenzo is probably the same person as the Maestro Lorenzo di Fuccio, mentioned in 1533 in connection with teaching actors the moresca.) Both agreed to teach in the school and outside it, as might be necessary and "as was the custom of diligent masters," and to share the profits equally. They also agreed to share their earnings if some legitimate reason, such as illness, prevented one or the other from meeting his teaching obligations. Another clause stipulates that whoever came to the school was to be consid-

109. For remarks regarding these dances I have relied on entries in the *Grande Dizionario della Lingua Italiana* and on information supplied by Barbara Sparti. Also see her "Da Dante a Leonardo: La danza italiana attraverso le fonti storiche," *La Danza Italiana* 3 (1985): 5–37. In the remarks about the anonymous Sienese *Comedia di Pidinzuolo* of 1517 in Pirrotta, *Music and Theatre*, 83, "ballo alla martorella" is translated as "in the peasant style."

110. Carli, *Il Duomo di Siena*, 135, citing materials published by Milanesi, *Documenti per la storia dell'arte senese*, 3:32–33.

111. ASS, Notarile antecosimiano, 1353, no. 19; the contract has been published by Milanesi, *Documenti per la storia dell'arte senese*, no. 9, 3:31–33.

ered a pupil of both of them, as would be the women in the private homes where they might teach, with the exception of the children of Messer Gismondo Chigi whom Marcantonio was then teaching and, among others, the painter Bartolomeo di David and his daughter, who were pupils of Lorenzo.[112]

A petition Marcantonio addressed to the Concistoro a few months later, on 26 April 1537, implies that he had not reaped great rewards from his chosen profession.[113] At the time Marcantonio was applying for the next available porter's post at the Palace and he explained that because he had spent his earlier years teaching the city's young people how to dance, especially ladies of good family, he now had little means of supporting his family. Although Marcantonio did not belabor the point, it appears that he hoped to supplement his income with a job in government service, one that would provide for him later, when he might no longer be able to dance. Whether he was as badly off as he claimed is another matter, but the Concistoro approved his request without hesitation.

The terms stipulated in another contract from five years later between Lorenzo and a new partner, the above-cited Niccolò di Girolamo di Vico, were basically the same as those he had agreed upon earlier with Marcantonio (see Doc. 13.8). Dated 8 October 1542, this new agreement shows the dancing masters setting up a three-year partnership, renewable for another three years if both were willing, and pledging to share their earnings, either in the school or from teaching young women and others privately. They would share any gratuities they received for teaching instruments. Each promised not to leave Siena without the other's permission so long as the school was in session, and to share their earnings equally, even if one of them could not teach for a valid reason. They also decided to hire Maestro Lorenzo's son Pompeo as an assistant for one year at a salary of between 10 and 14 florins, as judged suitable by two arbitrators.

INSTRUMENT MAKERS AND REPAIRMEN

Other people in the arts also formed business partnerships. Instrument makers had, of course, long been active in Siena, as mid-fifteenth-century records regarding the commissioning of Palace trumpets and trombones make clear.[114] Lute makers appeared around the same time. Two of the earliest known were German residents of Siena, Gilio di Gilio, a woodcarver and master lute maker, and Maestro Giovanni di Tommaso, also a master lute maker. Both had been living in the city for some time when, on 19 December 1465, Gilio agreed to furnish Giovanni with an unspecified number of

---

112. Only one of Bartolomeo di David's three daughters, Giulia, reached adulthood. See Milanesi, *Documenti per la storia dell'arte senese,* 3:46.

113. "Dinansi da voi etc. il vostro minimo et fidelissimo servitore Marchantonio di maestro Francesco, ballarino, espone come esso ha già consumato bona parte dela sua gioventù nel suo exercitio, cercando di servire insegnando a non pure tutti li giovani de questa città, come a cciascuno è noto, ha anchora insegnato ad infinitissime gentildonne. E vedendosi hormai non pure agravare dal tempo, ma anchora—il che più li preme—di fameglia, et trovandosi pochissime substantie da nutrirla . . . ricorre dinansi a vostre Signorie . . . supplicandole . . . fare . . . deliberare che esso Marchantonio habbia uno luogo di portiere del palazo vostro, primo vacante . . . Lecta aprobata fuit supradicta precedente petitio in Concistorio" (ASS, Concistoro, vol. 1023, fol. 34^{r-v}, dated 26 April 1537).

114. See chapter 9 for reference to Sienese brass instrument makers.

lutes and their "covers or cases" for a period of one year (see Doc. 13.9). Gilio was to receive s. 40 per lute and s. 40 per cover, or L. 4 for each lute and case, and Giovanni was to provide him with wood, leather, glue, and "everything else needed to make perfect lutes and cases." So as to safeguard his investment, Giovanni reserved the right to sue for damages and recovery of expenses should Gilio not live up to his end of the bargain. Gilio's wife, Donna Agnese, who was present when the contract was drawn up, promised, with her husband's consent, to assume responsibility in the event it should prove necessary to for her to do so.

Beyond providing a rare glimpse into the business end of lute making and marketing as well as another instance of the German musical presence in Siena, the contract raises a number of questions to which there are at present no firm answers. How long, for example, did it take Gilio working alone to turn out a lute and its cover? If he had help from family members or apprentices, as seems likely, he surely could produce more of them more quickly, though his expenses might be higher. Was he responsible only for carving the instrument, or did he furnish it complete with strings and pegs? How much did basic materials cost and what was the margin of profit that might be expected when Giovanni resold the instruments to the public? Did Giovanni have competitors? How large in general was the demand for lutes and was Gilio's work particularly prized? A wholesale price of L. 4 for a lute and case seems rather low in comparison with most musicians' monthly salaries or with gratuities given to visiting performers at the Palio. But the enterprise must have been advantageous to both parties, guaranteeing Gilio a sufficient wage for his labors and Giovanni a decent return on his investment, otherwise they hardly would have undertaken it.

The contract, drawn up at Maestro Giovanni's house in the contrada Salicotto, was witnessed by two other German expatriates, wool weavers by profession. Both had wives and families living with them and both "had equally the German language and the Latin," that is, Italian, as did Gilio and Agnese. All of them had put down roots in Siena and were thoroughly integrated into the city's life, a situation that points to additional avenues, albeit informal ones, by which German musical practices reached Siena. Giovanni, too, had a wife, whom he had married in the previous year. This was Margarita di Nello di Gilio, who, given her grandfather's name, was either a niece or a cousin of Giovanni's new business partner. In their marriage contract, enacted on 6 May 1464 in Margarita's house in the contrada Salicotto—the same house, apparently, where Giovanni and Gilio signed their agreement—Giovanni acknowledged receiving a dowry of 60 florins from Margarita and both consented to certain terms regarding restitution of the money and interest in the event one predeceased the other.[115] The marriage was apparently a successful one and Giovanni must have prospered in his profession, which

---

115. "Pateat evidenter qualiter Magister Iohannes Thomassi de Allamanea, magister liutorum, titulo et causa donationis . . . et propter nuptias in de et super bonis suis, dedit et donavit domine Margarite Nelli Gilii de Senis, sponse et future uxoris dicti magistri Thomassi, florenos sessaginta de libris IIII pro floreno de Senis, eo pacto et lege et condictione, videlicet quod si dicta domina Margarita supervixerit dicto Magistro Iohanni, lucretur ad rationem decem pro centenario nomine antifatii et lucri donationis propter nuptias, ultra dotes suas de bonis suis predictis" (ASS, Notarile antecosimiano, vol. 454, fols. 73^r–74^r, dated 6 May 1464).

in time-honored fashion he passed on to his progeny. This much is clear from the record of a will filed on 7 October 1517 by the lute maker Maestro Alberto, son of the late Maestro Giovanni da Alamania.[116] Alberto's will says nothing further about his parentage, but in it he named his brother Enrico di Giovanni Teutonico as his heir, the latter's surname an indication that the family was still very conscious of its German heritage. That other German instrument makers were still making their way to Siena is shown by the presence of Enrico di Giorgio da Alamania, *liutaio,* one of the witnesses to the will.

Although nothing is known about the volume or the quality of their work, makers of lutes and stringed instruments continued to find a market for their wares in Siena throughout the sixteenth century. One such "master of making strings for lutes," Antonio di Giovanni di Antonio di Siena, lived in the same contrada as the others just mentioned and may have belonged to the same family. He made his last will and testament on 7 March 1550, naming his wife Tarsia as his heir.[117] Antonio subsequently witnessed a legal document drawn up in Siena on 15 April 1559. On that occasion he was called "Antonio son of the late Giovanni, called il Frate, master of lute strings."[118] Maestro Tommaso, son of the late Domenico Brigantini, a Sienese stringed-instrument maker living in Siena at the Arco de' Rossi, made his last will and testament on 27 March 1550. He left "all of the irons . . . lutes, citterns, guitars, viols and every other kind of instrument in his shop" to an apprentice who was then living with him, Sebastiano called Tano, son of Agostino alias Calcagno.[119] Sebastiano went on to become a successful *liutaio* in his own right, and a few years later, on 11 April 1556, he bought a house in Siena for Fl. 51.[120] Sebastiano, again identified an instrument maker, subsequently witnessed a legal document that was drawn up on 24 September 1565.[121] A record from a few years later, which refers to him as Sebastiano alias Tano, son of the late Agostino, shows him and his wife Lucrezia entering into a real estate transaction

---

116. "Magister Albertus olim magistri Iohannis de Alamania, magister liutorum in civitate Senarum . . . corpore languens . . . voluit sepelliri in ecclesia S. Iohannis de Senis . . . heredem universalem instituit . . . magistrum Henricum Iohannis teutonicum et habitatorem Senis . . . coram Henrigo Georgii . . . de Alamania, liutario, habitatore civitatis Senarum" (ASS, Notarile antecosimiano, vol. 1140, unn. folio, dated 7 October 1517).

117. "Antonius Iohannis Antonii, magister faciendi corda ad usum leutorum, de Senis . . . per hoc testamentum . . . eius heredem universalem instituit eius dilectam uxorem dominam Tarsiam, filiam olim Simonis molendinarii" (ASS, Notarile antecosimiano 2174, no. 135, dated Siena, 7 March 1549/50).

118. ASS, Notarile antecosimiano, 2991, no. 88.

119. "Providus vir magister Thommas quondam Dominici de Brigantinis, leutarius de Senis . . . per hoc presens nuncupativum testamentum . . . iure legati reliquit . . . Sebastiano nuncupato Tano, filio Augustini alias Calcagno, eiusdem testatoris educato et qui ad presens comoratur in domo eiusdem testatoris, tutti li ferri, leuti, citare, chitarre, violini et omne aliud genus instrumentorum quod reperiretur in apoteca ipsius testatoris . . . eius heredem universalem instituit . . . Bartolomeam filiam quondam Nicolai de Capo Selvole . . . ad presens secum comorantem" (ASS, Notarile antecosimiano, 2721, no. 29, dated Siena, 27 March 1550).

120. ASS, Notarile antecosimiano 2723, no. 726, dated 11 April 1556, Siena, where he is called "Sebastianus quondam Agostini leutarius de Senis."

121. ASS, Notarile antecosimiano, vol. 3126, no. 502.

that involved selling and renting a house.[122] He apparently lived a good many years after that time. A report dated 5 May 1590 notes that a house belonging to the heirs of the Sienese nobleman Messer Oratio Ugurgieri was rented by Maestro Andrea Milanese, who had a school of playing and embroidery there—presumably for young ladies of good family—and that living with him was a lady named Virginia, "sister of the instrument maker Tano."[123] Another Sienese stringed-instrument maker, Giulio, son of the late Gaspare de' Menchiaferri, filed his last will and testament on 15 March 1560, requesting that he be buried in the tomb of his ancestors in the Sienese church of St. Mark.[124]

Apart from Maestro Giovanni di Antonio, only a few Sienese organ builders and tuners are known, though the presence of organs in many Sienese churches indicates a good deal of activity in this area as well. For the moment suffice it to note a family of organ builders and organists active during the second half of the sixteenth century. They were Fabio de' Bacci, witness to a notarial act on 23 August 1588, and his brother, Maestro Paulo de' Bacci, cited in a notarial act of 4 January 1594, by which time he was living in Florence.[125] Both are described as sons of the late Maestro Onofrio da Castel Fiorentino, who in an earlier document is called a resident of Siena. Fabio appears on several occasions in records from the Hospital of Santa Maria della Scala, notably in 1583, 1603, and 1605, when he tuned the instruments there and made various repairs.[126] A payment of L. 7 to Messer Fabio Organista from the Company of Sant'Antonio Abate on 16 September 1594 records his restoring the instrument in their prayer hall.[127] Onofrio, or Nofrio as he is called in some documents, was himself responsible for constructing the organ in the church of Santo Stefano at Montepescali.[128] A contract he signed with the church on 5 April 1540 specifies that the new instrument was to have five ranks and thirty-eight keys and cost Sc. 30. Eight scudi, the cost of an organetto that Nofrio promised to buy from the church rector, would in turn be subtracted from the total price of the instrument. Doubtless, records that have not yet been examined from other Sienese and Florentine institutions will add further testimony to the prominent role played by this family of organ builders and repairmen.

SIENESE MUSICIANS OUTSIDE SIENA

As might be expected of a city with so vibrant a musical culture, Siena not only employed foreign musicians but also exported musicians of its own, both to neighboring towns and to large and small cities, near and far. One of the earliest known who

---

122. ASS, Notarile antecosimiano, vol. 2729, no. 1195, dated Siena, 23 August 1568.

123. The record, in AAS, vol. 5619, fol. 9ʳ, is published by F. D. Nardi, "Concubinato e adulterio nella Siena post-tridentina," *BSSP* 96 (1989): 9–171, esp. p. 15.

124. ASS, Notarile antecosimiano, vol. 2992, no. 56, dated 15 March 1559/60, refers to him as "Iulius quondam Gasparis de Menchiaferris, leutarius de Senis."

125. ASS, Notarile postcosimiano, Originali, vol. 50, no. 224; vol. 42, no. 1926.

126. Ospedale, vol. 910, *E&U GGG, 1582–87,* fol. LVIʳ; vol. 920, *E&U, 1601–2,* fol. 112ʳ; vol. 923, *E&U, 1605–6,* fol. 47ᵛ.

127. ASS, PR, Compagnia di Sant'Antonio Abate di Siena, vol. 63, *Memorie, D&C, 1513–1617,* fol. 282ʳ.

128. Borghesi and Banchi, *Nuovi documenti per la storia dell'arte senese,* no. 241, pp. 476–77. For his work at the cathedral see chapter 6.

achieved fame outside the city was the already-mentioned Maestro Matteo di Martino, organist at the cathedral of Lucca from 1357 to 1374.[129] Jacopo di Filippo da Siena, "an expert master in the art of music," was reappointed as Palace *citarista* for a year by the priors of Perugia on 20 September 1407.[130] Frate Gabriello da Siena restored the organ at the cathedral of Orvieto on 27 November 1413.[131] Another Sienese friar, Fra Piero di Niccolò da Siena dell'Ordine de' Predicatori, reconstructed the large organ at the same church in the early summer of 1441.[132]

Reports of Sienese musicians employed in other towns come from the sixteenth century as well. On 29 October 1540 Frate Donato Girolami wrote to his brother Ser Lattanzio Girolami announcing his appointment as organist in Tivoli.[133] A record dated 24 September 1559 records a business transaction between the Sienese organist Maestro Vittorio, son of the deceased Niccolò Cagniacci of Siena, who was then resident in Rome, and his wife Prosilia. In exchange for a house in Rome, which he had received from Prosilia as her dowry and then sold, Vittorio gave Prosilia a house in the contrada di Salicotto in Siena.[134] Pietro di Bartolomeo Corradini, organist at Siena cathedral from 1531 to 1541, later found employment in Florence as organist at the cathedral of Santa Maria del Fiore, where he remained from 1552 until the time of his death in 1571. He was highly thought of by Grand Duke Cosimo I, who wrote to cathedral canons approving a salary subvention for him.[135]

Scipione Vecchi called delle Palle, who may have been a student in the cathedral school, pursued a successful career outside the city, first at Naples, where he acted and sang in productions of Sienese plays (*Gli ingannati*, 1545; *Alessandro*, 1558), and in Florence, where he was in the service of Grand Duke Francesco de' Medici.[136] Remembered today principally as Giulio Caccini's teacher, he was famed as a singer in his own day and was also a composer of some repute. Ugurgieri-Azzolini reports that Andrea Moretti was yet another Sienese musician who achieved distinction outside Siena, having, among other things, participated in the wedding festivities of Ferdinando de' Medici and Christine of Lorraine at Florence in 1589.[137] Later he returned to the city and joined the cathedral chapel as a cittern and viola player.[138] Pompilio Venturi, a Sienese

---

129. Nerici, *Storia della musica in Lucca*, 124.

130. The document has been published by Borghesi and Banchi, *Nuovi documenti per la storia dell'arte senese*, no. 32, p. 65. Jacopo is described as "peritus magister in arte music" in the document.

131. Ibid., no. 39, p. 75.

132. Milanesi, *Documenti per la storia dell'arte senese*, no. 159, 2:203–5, dated 1 May–2 June 1441.

133. Borghesi and Banchi, *Nuovi documenti*, no. 242, p. 478.

134. ASS, Notarile antecosimiano 2864, no. 118, dated 24 September 1559, calls them "Magister Victorius quondam Niccolai de Cagniacciis de Senis, organista in Urbe" and "Prosilia Melchioris Petri Gigli, de Tinello in Sabrina."

135. His name is apparently spelled as Curradini in Florentine documents. See Emilio Sanesi, "Maestri d'Organo in S. Maria del Fiore (1436–1600)," *Note d'Archivio* 14 (1937): 175–77.

136. Kirkendale, *The Court Musicians in Florence During the Principate of the Medici*, 100–1. Scipione was another of the Sienese musicians eulogized by Ugurgieri-Azzolini (*Le pompe senesi*, 2:4).

137. Ugurgieri-Azzolini, *Le pompe senesi*, 2:6–7. Moretti, like most of the musicians mentioned in these pages, is mentioned by Morrocchi in the biographical appendix to *La musica in Siena*, 90.

138. Reardon, *Agostino Agazzari*, 54.

composer active mainly in Rome, published three books of villanellas in 1569, 1571, and 1583.[139] Michele Scala Senese, whose surname betrays his training at the hospital's school, was *maestro di cappella* at Malta cathedral in 1573–74 before moving on to posts at churches in Messina (1576) and Bergamo (1580–84).[140] He probably is the tenor of that same name, mentioned earlier, who sang in the cathedral chapel in 1591. Arcangelo Gherardini, a Servite monk of Sienese birth, who perhaps worked in Ferrara, published a book of five-voice madrigals at Ferrara in 1585 and a volume of eight-voice motets at Milan in 1587.[141] Romano da Siena, an Olivetan monk, published his first book of Masses for five and six voices in Rome in 1596.[142] Little is known of any of these musicians, particularly those in religious orders. But their publications testify to other places of musical instruction in Siena and to other musicians and teachers whose activities escaped the eyes and ears of the lawyers, the tax collectors, and the chroniclers.

DOCUMENTS

Doc. 13.1. Payments to organists at Santa Maria della Scala

30 January 1481: A Frate Giovanni di Francesco di Raimondi nostro sonatore delgli orghani adì XXX di genaio L. undici e s. quatordici contanti a lui per detto di messer nostro. . . L. XI s. XIIII (Ospedale, vol. 866, *E&U, 1480–81,* fol. LXI[r])

30 October 1481: Francesco di Ghu[i]do, sonatore d'organi, adì XXX d'ottobre, lire dicesette s. quatordici contanti. . . E noi abiamo uno suo monacordio per insegniare a' nostri fanciulli di casa, L. XVII s. XIIII d.—(Ospedale, vol. 867, *E&U, 1481–82,* fol. 53[r])

20 November 1490: Ser Francesco di Matio, nostro sonatore dell'organi, adì detto, lire dicenove s. dieci contanti. . . L. XVIIII s. X d.—(Ospedale, vol. 875, *E&U, 1490–91,* fol. 67[r])

31 January 1493: Ser Francesco di Matio, nostro sonatore, el dì [31 gennaio 1492/93], s. trenta contanti, L. 1. s. X d.—(Ospedale, vol. 876, *E&U, 1492–93,* fol. 59[v])

Doc. 13.2. Payments to the singing teacher and for the purchase of music at Santa Maria della Scala

+ Christo MDLXXVII: E addì 19 Giugno L. quatro. 13. 4 a quel libraro del'arco de' Rossi, sonno per libri XIIII di musica di più sorti, levò da lui prete Niccolò nostro maestro del canto per ordine di messer [rettore] per li nostri cerici. L. 4. 13. 4 (Ospedale, vol. 810, *Bastardello FFF, 1576–82,* fol. 42[r])

+ Christo MDLXXVII: E addì 10 detto [Dicembre] L. due a messer Niccolò cantore nostro per cartella di contraponto per i citti musicanti, L. 2 (vol. 810, fol. 64[r])

+ Christo MDLXXVIIII: Frate Alisandro Ciellerini, maestro di canto a dì 13 di detto [luglio] L. dodici a lui contanti, L. 12 (ibid., fol. 149[r])

+ Christo MDLXXVIIII: E il dì [6 di ottobre] L. otto pagate contanti a Vincenzo Bidello libraro

---

139. (RISM V 1186, V 1187, V 1189). What little is known about him is summarized by Donna Cardamone in the entry in *New Grove,* 19:625.

140. Giovanni Azzopardi, "La cappella musicale della cattedrale di Malta e i suoi rapporti con la Sicilia," *Musica sacra in Sicilia tra rinascimento e barocco: Atti del convegno di Caltagirone, 10–12 dicembre 1985,* ed. Daniele Ficola, Istituto di storia della musica di Palermo, 5 (Palermo, 1988), 48–49.

141. (RISM G 1763). See the brief unsigned entry in *New Grove,* 7:338.

142. *D. Romani Senensis Congreg. Olivetanae monachi Missarum cum quinque & sex vocibus, liber primus* (Rome: Muti, 1596) (RISM R 2092).

per libri di musica per la chiesa levò frate Alisandro maestro del canto per comessione del signore Cavaliere, si dorno a Paulo suo garzone fino il dì primo di Settembre, L. 8 (ibid., fol. 165ʳ)

+ Christo MDLXXX: maestro Tiberio trombone nostro addì detto [settembre] L. diciotto a lui contanti come maestro di canto, L. 18 (ibid., fol. 211ʳ)

+ Christo 1595: El dì [15 novembre] L. quatro pagati a messer Fedrigho Scala . . . per tanti aveva pagato a uno libraro a l'Arco de' Rossi per quatro corpi di libri di musicha per li figli di casa che imparano, L. 4 (Ospedale, vol. 913, *E&U, 1595–96,* fol. 68ʳ)

+ Christo 1596: El dì [6 maggio] L. due soldi 6. 8 pagati a messer Federigho Scala per sette pezi di libri di musicha, cioè le vergini a 3 e Orlando a quatro, compri per li figli di casa, L. 2. 6. 8 (ibid., fol. 91ʳ)

+ Christo 1601: Sagrestia di nostra chiesa deve dare . . . A dì 14 di luglio L. sette soldi 13. 4, pagati al reverendo messer Fortunato Scala, sagrestano, per due corpi di libri di musicha detti Introiti della messa, L. 4 (Ospedale, vol. 919, *E&U, 1601–2,* fol. 100ʳ)

+ Christo 1601/2 [26 gennaio]: messer Alberto Gregori maestro di cappella, L. cinquantasei a lui, L. 56 (ibid., fol. 118ᵛ)

Doc. 13.3. Payments to cathedral musicians for singing at the feast days at Santa Maria della Scala

30 March 1577: L. dodici pagati contanti a Andrea Filiciani maestro di cappella del Duomo, sono per la solita limosina e cortesia ch'è solito di dare a quelli che cantorno per la nostra festa dico a ttutta essa capella e a lui come capo, L. 12 (Ospedale, vol. 810, *Bastardello FFF, 1576– 1582,* fol. 34ᵛ)

12 April 1578: L. dodici pagati contanti ai musici e cappella del Duomo e palazzo e per essi a messer Andrea Feliciani maestro di cappella, sono per la solita amorevolezza che è solito dico di darsi ai detti per haverci loro servito per la nostra festa di Marzo, L. 12 (ibid., fol. 72ᵛ). (This report implies that the Palace musicians also performed, but it is more likely that the reference is to instrumentalists in the cathedral chapel who were also in the Palace wind band.)

31 March 1579: L. dodici pagate contanti a maestro Andrea maestro di canto del Duomo per la solita cortesia di questo anno per haverci lui haiutato in questa festa 2 giorni lui con tutt'i cantori e tromboni, L. 12 (ibid., fol. 135bisᵛ)

6 April 1582: L. dodici pagati contanti a maestro Andrea maestro di cappella di Duomo per la cortesia e fadiga che è solito ogni anno per la nostra festa di Santa Maria di Marzo con tutta la sua cappella, L. 12 (ibid., fol. 303ᵛ)

4 April 1583: L. dodici contanti a prete Benedetto maestro di cappella del Duomo per le fadige à dato insieme con detta cappella a la festa nostra a 2 vespari e la messa, come solito, L. 12 (vol. 811, *Bastardello di cassa, 1582–87,* fol. 38ᵛ)

19 April 1597: L. dodici pagati a maestro Francesco Bianciardi maestro di cappella in Duomo per essere venuto a cantare la messa e vespero il giorno della festa, L. 12 (vol. 914, *E&U, 1596–97,* fol. 86ʳ)

Doc. 13.4. Payments to trumpeters by the Company of San Bernardino of Siena. PR, Compagnia di San Bernardino di Siena

1391. Ancho spesi per dare a' tronbatori, IIII s. (vol. 202, *E&U, 1382–1409,* fol. 205ʳ)

Ottobre, 1394. A' tronbadori e'n vino e'n denari ch'ebono tra due volte soldi quatordici e d. quatro (fol. 212ᵛ)

1395. Anco adì 26 di marzo a' tronbadori e al nacharino per la sera e la mattina, vinti soldi, L. 1 (fol. 214ᵛ)

1401. Ancho ispesi per fare onore a' tronbatori quando veneno a tronbare s. 2 per uno mezzo quinto di vino, s. 2 (fol. 234ʳ)

1403. Ancho ispesi adì IIII d'otobre s. dieci d. 6 per dare a tronbatori che tronboro[no] quando noi andamo a oferire a santo Franceschо nostro padre, s. X d. 6 (fol. 237ᵛ)

1405. adì 9 d'otobre per dare a' tronbetti s. oto d. 7 in mano di Francio ala botegha di Jachomo di Masaino, s. VIIII (fol. 204ᵛ)

1406. Adì IIII d'ottobre s. undici demo a quatro tronbetti che feciono honore per la festa, s. undici (fol. 244ʳ)

1409. A' tronbatori del chomune che furonci adì IIII d'otobre s. undici per la fadigha quando si fecie la festa di San Franciescho, contanti a loro, s. XI (vol. 204, *E&U, 1408–16,* fol. 161ʳ)

[1427]. A' trombadori del chomune di Siena s. 22 quando venero a onorare la festa di Jesus per la paschua, portò Cierero di Riccho, L. 1 s. 2 (vol. 205, *E&U, 1416–27,* fol. 196ᵛ)

Doc. 13.5. Payment to the Palace musicians for performing at the Santissima Concezione on 8 December 1577. PR, Conventi, Santissima Concezione di Siena, vol. 1293, *Contratti,* fol. 135 left

Musici di Palazo deno havere fin questo dì 9 di dicembre [1577] lire dieci soldi —, sonno che tanti si li deveno per havere cantata una messa la mattina della Conceptione alla nostra chiesia et il Vespro il dì detto della festa, et questa mattina una messa dei Morti, ungni cosa fighurato con suoni e voci. E per il medesimo salario deveno di più ogni anno cantare il vespro in musica la vigilia della festa nostra: così convenuto maestro Simone Nodi, uno di detti musici, con Guido Santi, uno de' nostri protettori del convento, per esser egli maestro della cappella del Palazzo. Et in fede il detto maestro Simone si sottoscriverà affermando di sopra. L. 10.

[below] Io Simone sopradetto affermo.

Doc. 13.6. A handbill from a Sienese dancing school, ca. 1493–1503. ASS, Diplomatico, Appendice Sec. XVI°, Pergamene a Quaderno, Busta 10 (inserito, Provenienza incerta), ex mostra 233

All nome Sia Dio e de la gloriosa Vergenne Maria di tutti li Santi dela Magnifica Citta.

    Non sia nisunno tanto ardito che atravesi la schuola ifinno non à finita la sua dansa, sotto pena di soldi V.

La calata che sono g[i]ochi otto	lib. vii
Li fioretti cho'g[i]ochi otto	lib. x
La seconda, paga	lib. vij
La gagliarda, paga	lib. xxj
La morescha, paga	lib. xxj
La martorella, paga	lib. xxj

E perché le cose nove soleanno molto dilettare sichondo li animi de li scholari, perché c'è ne una dansa di fioreti novi la quale chi lo vorà imparare pagarà lib. xiiij.

Ancora se li detti scolari volesenno nisuna de le dette danse a la cho[n]tadina, c[i]oè sia obligato pagare lib. X de la calatta e de li fioretti lire xiiij.

E ancora se ci fusse nisuno volese de le dette danse sia obligato, c[i]oè s'i[n]tende la dansa di g[i]occhi otto.

Ite[m], no sia nisuno che si mette a' parare se no da la [metà de'] deti denari innasi, c[i]oè li mesi che paga quella dansa che lui ipara prima.

Item, no sia nisuno tanto ardito di bestemiare Dio e la nostra Dona sotto pena che ogni volta paghi soldi V.

Ite[m], se bastemierà di altri santi sia obligato pagare soldi ij e de li sopra detti devare si debi metare in u' bosolo se ne debi fare quelo che lo maestro vorà, c[i]oè se ne debi co[n]prare ischarpe e altre cose chome achadrà.

Sia obligato ungni scholare il pagare la chornamusa si fa a mese, o vero ungni volta che bala sia obligato a pagare soldi ij.

Doc. 13.7. Maestro Lorenzo and Maestro Marcantonio di Maestro Francesco Fineschi agree to set up a dancing school, 1 January 1537. ASS, Notarile antecosimiano 2196, fasc. 11, unnumbered folio

Al nome di Dio, A dì primo di gennaro 1536 [1537]

A qualunque sarà noto come hoggi, questo dì et anno sopradetto, li honorevoli maestri, maestro Lorenzo di [blank] et maestro Marchantonio di maestro Francesco Fineschi, ballarini senesi, hanno infra di loro fatta et ferma compagnia et società di scuola di ballo, da esercitarsi per ciascheduno di loro liberamente et sanza fraude alcuna per anni quatro proximi avenire e con li infrascritti patti, conditioni et modi, cioè:

In prima, che ciascuno deli sopradetti maestri debbi, in scuola et fuor di scuola, dove sarà necessario, essercitare et durar la debita fadiga in lo insegnare, come ali diligenti maestri si costuma, in caso però non fussero da legittime cause impediti, come per infirmità (quale Idio cessi) et altre giuste cause. Le quali in caso occorrisseno, volseno li sopradetti maestri che quello rimanesse a esercitare la scuola, di tutto quello gli pervenisse alle mani tanto di salari quanto di presenti, fusse tenuto a dargliene liberamente l'errata li toccasse, come se elgi havesse esercitato et durato la solita fadigha.

Item, che tutti li scolari dell'uno et dell'altro, cominciati o non cominciati, habino a esser comuni, et il medesimo le spose et le case dove qualsivogli di loro insegnassero. Excetto però a detto maestro Marchantonio, messer Mario, Pandolfo, Agusto, Alisandro, Alfonso et Gismondo, figli di messer Gismondo Chigi, et Marchantonio figlio di Girolamo Cinughi: de' quali tutto quello se ne havesse, furno d'accordo fusse et aspettasse al detto maestro Marchantonio. Et così parimente il detto maestro Lorenzo si reservò Girolamo Bartalucci, maestro Giovan tentore et Bartolomeo dipentore overo sua figlia: de' quali medesimamente furno d'accordo tutto quello se ne cavasse, fusse et appartenesse al detto maestro Lorenzo. Et tutto quello che dalli altri scolari, tanto dell'uno quanto del'altro, presenti et avenire, se ne havesse tanto di salario quanto di presenti, in qualsivogli altra cosa appartenente o dependente dalo istesso insegnare, s'intendi andare mezzo mezzo, ad uso di buona compagnia. Dele quale cose li sopranominati maestri debbono rendersen l'uno al'altro et l'altro al'uno, buono et leale conto, sanza fraude o malitia alcuna, sotto le infrascritte pena o promissione.

Item che durante il sopradetto tempo de' quatro anni, per qualsivogli causa eccetto che per morte (quale Idio cessi) si possi detta compagnia seperare et finire, ma quella concordemente seguire per fino a detto tempo. Et chi contra a cciò facessi, furno d'accordo cascassi in pena di scudi vinti d'oro, quali si deveno a pagare a colui osserverà le sopradette cose.

Per le quale cose osservare, le sopradette parti l'uno al'altro et l'altro al'uno, obligorono loro stessi et loro heredi et beni presenti et avenire, renuntiando a ugni legge, favore o statuto che per loro in alcun modo facesse o far potesse. Giurando li detti maestri alle sancte di Dio Evangeli, con mano toccando le scritture, tutte le sopradecte cose attendere et osservare.

Et in fede della verità et di consenso di dette parti, io Carlo di Bartolomeo da Piano, notaio sanese, come privata persona ha fatta la presente di mia propria mano, quale sarà soscritta dali sopranominati maestri di mano lor propria, affermando a quanto di sopra.

E io Lorenzo so' chontento quanto di sopra si chontiene, e vogl[i]o che ser Carlo sia rogato.

E io Marcantonio sopradeto afermo q[u]a[n]tto è sopra.

Doc. 13.8. Maestro Lorenzo and Niccolò di Girolamo di Vico Pizzicaiuolo agree to set up a dancing school, 8 October 1542. Notarile antecosimiano 2196, fasc. 11, unnumbered folio

Al nome di Dio MDXLII, il dì VIII di Ottobre.

Sarà noto e manifesto a qualsia persona come hoggi questo dì et anno sopradetto maestro Lorenzo di Fuccio scarpellino e Niccolò di Girolamo di Vico picicaiuolo fanno, contraggano e cominciano buona e sincera compagnia fra di loro al'arte et esercitio d'insegnare a ballare in la città di Siena, con l'infrascritti patti, conventioni, capitoli e modi e non altramente, cioè:

In prima, che la detta compagnia duri e durare devi tre anni da hoggi prossimi avenire; e se nel fine non sarà disdetta tre mesi 'nanzi, duri tre altri anni, e così di tempo in tempo, per fino che da loro non sarà disdetta come di sopra.

Item, che tutti salari, denari di mancie, robbe di qualsivogli sorte, che a qualsia di loro perverrà ale mani, tanto in scuola quanto di fuore, dependenti per qual sia colore dal detto insegnare e compagnia, habbi e s'intenda e sia comune, e qual sia di loro habbi da renderne e darne buono a leal contio al'altro.

Item, che mentre che in schola si insegna, nissuno di loro senza licentia del'altro si possa partire, e che l'un l'altro habbi a durare distributiva fadiga, né nissuno se ne habbi da discostare né fuggirla.

Item, che se alcun di loro occorisse che per legittima cagione non potessi insegnare, come se per malatie (che Dio cessi) o altra giusta cagione, che l'altro devi seguire e darne di quello che li pervenisse ale mani, al'impedito, buono e leal contio.

Item, convennero che di denari comuni che si toccharanno in detta compagnia, se ne habbi da dare fiorini dieci o quel più che per fino a 14 l'anno sarà giudicato per Spinello di Niccolò Piccolomini e Giovambattista dala Vacca, a Pompeo figlio di detto maestro Lorenzo. Il quale Pompeo sia obligato a stare in detta scuola e aiutare in quello che egli può, tanto fuore quanto dentro di scuola; e questo sia per uno anno solo, e non più.

Item, che in detta compagnia ci si intenda compreso spose et altri scolari che alcun di loro insegnasse fuor di scuola, intendendosi ogni cosa comune.

Item, si obligorono stare contenti a tutto quello che per detto Spinello e Giovambattista sarà per salario di detto Pompeo giudicato, et il medesimo pagarlo senza alcuna eccettione ciascuno anno.

Item, che la presente compagnia s'intendi essere e sia fatta con li presenti sopradetti capitoli, sinceramente e senza fraude alcuna. Per le quali cose osservare l'un l'altro e l'altro a l'uno obligorono loro stessi e loro heredi e beni presenti e avenire. E renunciorno a ogni benefitio, favore e statuto, che per loro in alcuno modo facessi, giurando ale Sancte di Dio Evangeli, con mano toccando ambi loro le scritture, il tutto attendere et osservare.

Et in fede io Carlo Forti notaio, come privata persona ho fatta la presente di mano propria, a preghiera dell'uno e l'altro, quali si soscriveranno di lor propria mano, affermando il tutto. Di più sono in compositione che qualsia di loro che venisse a guastare la compagnia detta se non ne' modi come di sopra, hora per alhora s'intendi cascato in pena di scudi trenta d'oro, da pagarsi a chi osservasse; e così volsero e si obligorono come di sopra.

Item, che s'intendino comuni tutti denari et altre robbe che venissero a qualsia di loro in le mani, per detto insegnare, tanto di scolari vecchi quanto de' nuovi, da hoggi inanzi, e così mancie che si dessero per insegnare a sonare.

Item convennero, e detto maestro Lorenzo si obligò, che detto Pompeo durante la detta compagnia non terrà scuola in Siena senza lor licentia, sotto le pene sopradette, né anco insegnarà per premio.

E io Lorenzo sopra a [*sic*] detto affermo quanto di sopra si chont[i]ene
E io Nicolò sopra deto afermo quanto di sopra

Doc. 13.9. Agreement between the German lute makers Gilio di Gilio and Maestro Giovanni di Tommaso, 19 December 1465. Notarile antecosimiano, vol. 437, inserto 272

[margin: pro magistro Iohanne Niccolai Theotonico]
In nomine Domini amen. Anno MCCCCLXV, indictione XIIII, die vero XVIIII mensis Decembris. Gilius Gilii, intagliator lignaminis et magister liutorum de Allamania, habitator civitatis Senarum, eius libera et spontanea voluntate suaque certa scientia et non per aliquem errorem, promisit et convenit magistro Iohanni Niccolai de Allamania, habitatori Senarum, magistro liutorum, presenti, recipienti et stipulanti pro se et suis heredibus, pro tempore unius anni hinc proxime futuri, servire dicto magistro Iohanni pro laborante ad faciendum liutos, [pro] pretio soldorum quadraginta pro quolibet liuto, et pro pretio aliorum solidorum quadraginta pro coverta seu cassa liuti, ita quod in totum pro liuto et cassa habeat libras quatuor denariorum Senensium. Et dictus Magister Iohannes debeat de suo proprio mittere lignamen, corium, collam et omnia alia necessaria ad predictos liutos et eorum cassas perficiendas. Et ubi si non faceret, quod dictus Magister Iohannes possit petere, exigere et recipere a dicto magistro Gilio dampna, expensas et interesse que et quas sustinuisset et substinuere posset propter inobservantia[m] predictorum . . . Domina Agnes, uxor dicti Gilii, presens dicte obligationi et omnibus et singulis contentis in ea, faciens omnia et singula infrascripta in presentia et cum consensu dicti Gilii eius mariti ibidem presentis et eidem consentientis, sciens ad infrascripta non teneri sed volens obligari pro dicto Gilio eius marito, fideiuxit et fideiuxorio nomine interessit et promisit dicto magistro Iohanni . . . quo dictus Giulius eius maritus faciet et observabit omnia et singula supra promissa per eum. Et casu quo predicta non faceret, promisit de suo proprio predicta omnia et singula facere et adimpletere, pro quibus omnibus et singulis observandis obligavit dicto magistro Iohanni ut supra presenti et recipienti, sese et suos heredes et bona omnia, presentia et futura . . . Actum Senis, in domo habitationis dicti magistri Iohannis, posita in contrada Salicotti, coram Alberto Pieri, textore pannorum laneorum, et Iuliano Iuliani etiam textore pannorum laneorum, de Allamanea, habitatoribus assiduis, cum uxore et familia eorum, civitatis Senarum et habentibus linguam teotonicham pariter et latinam optime intelligentibus, dictum Gilium et dominam Agnietam, testibus presentibus vocatis habitis et rogatis. Ego Laurentius Iuse, notarius Senensis, predicta rogatus, propria manu scripsi etc.

Chapter Fourteen

MUSIC AT SOCIAL EVENTS,
PUBLIC AND PRIVATE

MEMORABLE MOMENTS in Siena's musical life occurred at the many public festivals, civic and religious, that took place throughout the year. Employing the talents of both native and out-of-town performers, these extravaganzas brought music and spectacle that might not otherwise be experienced to the attention of connoisseurs as well as of the public at large. Equally public, though perhaps not quite so frequent or predictable, were the grand entrances made by the republic's distinguished visitors, who as a rule were accompanied from the city's gates to their temporary residences to the sounds of the cheering crowds and sometimes the roar of cannons. These, too, required the services of the town's official musicians as well as others. But the most frequent occasions requiring musicians were perhaps private ones, stemming from a tradition that grew out of the well-known Sienese passion for parlor games, dancing, and pastimes of all sorts. Girolamo Bargagli's *Dialogo de' Giuochi che nelle vegghie sanesi si usono di fare* of 1572 carried the fame of many of the Sienese parlor games to the four corners of Italy, while other kinds of entertainment featuring music and dance were described for a wide public by his brother Scipione in the already mentioned *I trattenimenti* of 1587. Music, whether performed by professionals or amateurs or both, was inevitably a part of many of these entertainments.

Frequent, also, were those occasions, whether formal or informal, dedicated to performance of secular music—madrigals, canzonettas, and more elaborate forms, held either in the intimate atmosphere of private palaces or on a grander scale out of doors, to which Siena's own composers often contributed. Apart from fleeting mention in some of Ugurgieri's biographical vignettes, however, such occasions were rarely if ever reported, and were it not for works such as those just cited and a few surviving Sienese musical manuscripts and prints, it would be difficult to gain even a glimpse of music's place in the private social life of sixteenth-century Siena. Some remarks about music provided by Sienese maestri for performance within this ambience or in other situations that also went unreported form the conclusion of this chapter. But before this, a survey of public events and ceremonies will be presented, with particular attention to the pageantry and revelries associated with that greatest of all Sienese public festivals, the Palio, of which music formed such a significant part. Though here, too, the names of most participating musicians and entertainers were rarely mentioned, the frequency of the events offers indisputable evidence of their presence at many of the defining moments in the city's history as well as at the more mundane festivities that brought novelty and enjoyment to the daily life of the average citizen. An account of these events and the role played in them by musicians begins this survey of music at public and private social events.

Public Ceremonies and Royal Entries

Among the most important events in which music inevitably played a role and to which the public had access were the state visits of honored guests of the Republic. Their arrivals, their departures—witnessed at times by almost the entire populace—and the receptions accorded them all furnished frequent occasions for performances by officially employed as well as freelance musicians. Generally, visitors were received outside the walls by delegations of noblemen and other important personages, who accompanied them on horseback to the city's gates. There, they were met by members of the government and, on occasion, members of the clergy, and by throngs of citizens, who accompanied them in procession to the Palace or to the cathedral for further welcoming ceremonies. Later, the visitors were escorted in state to their temporary place of residence. Specific protocols changed according to the visitor and the times, but in general the Sienese knew how to do this kind of thing and they did it well for more than three hundred years. Processions, whether for religious or state purposes, were a feature of everyday life, much enjoyed by the populace, who could thus view at first hand public manifestations of important events occurring within the town.

As the principal town on the road to Rome, Siena was a frequent stopping-off place for emperors, kings, dukes, and bishops as well as for merchants and pilgrims from every walk of life. Chroniclers never failed to record the arrivals and departures of important people, who, more often than not, made solemn stately entries into the city, where they were inevitably received, as more than one writer put it, "con gran festa." From the late thirteenth century onwards the chroniclers often mention the presence of musicians on these occasions, though noting little else, leaving us to imagine the magnificence of the official ceremonies and the gaiety of the banquets and balls at which their performances were so essential.[1] When King Robert of Naples arrived in Siena in October of 1310, for example, great honors and expensive gifts were heaped on him, and games, dances, and bonfires were ordered for his entertainment.[2] Obviously, the town musicians, and perhaps even the king's own band, played at the festivities, but the chronicler neglected to say so. A similar situation occurred a few years later with the arrival on 14 August 1314 of the king's brother, Peter of Anjou. All the Sienese nobility gave the Angevin prince a resounding welcome outside the city gates and honored him later in the day with a huge public celebration that included games and dancing.[3] But again the number and kinds of musicians and what they played little concerned the chronicler and, one must presume, his readers as well.

---

1. More specific information about these occasions can sometimes be gleaned from Palace account books. Those from the spring of 1302, for example, record the visit of Charles of Valois and show that payments were made to the Sienese trumpeters for their services "when Charles's wife arrived from Florence, when Charles arrived from Prato, when he went to the court [of Rome], and when the Cardinal of Florence stopped off en route to Rome." The document is published by Alessandro Lusini in "Dante e le sue relazioni con Siena," 84. Lusini reports that Charles had also visited Siena in the previous year and it was there that his wife Catherine gave birth to a son on 6 November 1301.

2. Del Grasso, "Cronaca Senese," 311.

3. "Cronaca Senese dei fatti riguardanti la città e il su territorio di autore anonimo del secolo XIV," in Muratori, *Rerum italicarum scriptores,* 15/6, 1:103.

The visit of Emperor Sigismund to Siena on 12 July 1432 occasioned one of the most spectacular entries seen up to that time and furnishes a particular instance in which musicians were mentioned.[4] As was the case with so many other ceremonies honoring royal guests, specific protocols were scrupulously observed and the order of events carefully planned, these latter punctuated by musical fanfares and the spontaneous acclamations of the crowds. Awaiting Sigismund outside the city gates was a richly clad delegation of Sienese officials, noblemen, and others, who, on bended knee, presented him with the keys to the city. After greeting his hosts and receiving their welcoming remarks the emperor rode through the town, accompanied by a grand cavalcade of warriors, knights, prelates, and a band consisting of twenty woodwind players, trumpeters, minstrels, and two players of nakers. Formal receptions and ceremonies and more substantial meetings with prominent political figures occupied many hours of the royal visitor's days, though state dinners and private receptions also claimed a share of his time. One of the high points of Sigismund's visit occurred a few weeks later, on 3 August, when at a public ceremony in the Campo, Siena's imperial ties were majestically reconfirmed amid the cheers of the populace and the joyous sounds of instruments and bells. Although rain forced postponement of a ball scheduled for that evening till the following day, the inclement weather did not mar other festivities, accounted among the most grandiose ever staged for a royal visitor.

The visit of another emperor, the Habsburg Charles V, a century later was no less notable for its political implications. Seen through the lens of history, it fatefully portended a policy of imperial intervention that eventually resulted in the loss of the city's independence. Having for the moment disposed of French peninsular ambitions and neutralized the papacy with a new alliance, Charles was well on his way to becoming de facto master of all Italy when he came to Siena on 24 April of 1536 to tidy up the fractious political situation within the city.[5] The government outdid itself to honor the new Caesar. Officials especially appointed for the occasion were charged with arranging the ceremonies appropriate to the reception of the imperial visitor and his court. The order of the procession in which, among others, members of the government, the clergy, and one hundred boys of noble family would march, the decoration of the streets through which it would pass, the standards, banners, and devices it would carry, the dress and colors of the accompanying knights, doctors, and noblemen and of the twenty-four youths who were to carry the golden baldachin with the imperial eagle under which the emperor would ride—all were painstakingly determined beforehand.[6]

---

4. Fecini, "Cronaca Senese," 844–45. Agostino Provedi, *Relazione delle pubbliche feste date in Siena negli ultimi cinque secoli* (Siena, 1791), 23–24, describes the event, quoting from Aldobrandini's and Fecini's chronicles. Carli, *Il Duomo di Siena,* 147, provides a description of the section of pavement in Siena Cathedral depicting Emperor Sigismund of Luxembourg enthroned, surrounded by six ministers, from 1434. The entire documentation is reviewed and discussed by Aronow, "A Documentary History of the Pavement Decoration," 124.

5. A first-hand account of Charles's visit is *Carlo Quinto in Siena nell'aprile del 1536,* ed. Vigo. See particularly Vigo's introductory remarks on p. xii.

6. Ibid., 13.

Charles's formal entry into Siena was, in fact, splendidly choreographed. As he approached the church of Santa Maria degli Angeli on the main road to town, he was greeted by elegantly attired noblemen on horseback and by a contingent of young boys garbed in white shouting "Imperio" and "Ben venga Carlo Imperatore." Outside the city gates, to the sound of cannons and bells, throngs of people also shouted "Imperio," and then from the walls above the trumpeters began to play the *Imperiale*.[7] As the music and the shouting subsided, the members of the government walked forward and knelt before the emperor. Speeches of welcome followed and the keys to the city were presented to him on a silver tray. Acknowledging the government's homage, Charles noted that the keys were in the hands of people faithful to the empire and that he was happy to have them remain there. Other speeches followed, after which the procession began.

A triumphal arch with columns and statues and a gold-lettered banner extolling the emperor had been placed above the city's outer gates. As he passed under it, Charles was met by the bishop and the cathedral canons bearing a golden cross. Offered to him, he kissed it, whereupon "all at once the singers of the cathedral chapel sang *Te Deum laudamus* with the clergy joining in." Entering the city, the procession wound its way amid the cries and shouts of the assembled crowds to the square fronting the cathedral and the hospital of Santa Maria della Scala. There, in honor of the occasion, were the "Carri degli Angeli," usually displayed only for the feasts of the Annunciation and the Assumption of the Virgin, and these were much admired by the emperor. Charles then dismounted and entered the cathedral through the main portal. When he reached the high altar he knelt for a few minutes in silent prayer, after which "a young boy up in the organ loft suavely sang a lovely motet."[8] Other ceremonies at the altar followed and at their conclusion the emperor, preceded by mace bearers, left the church and walked to the Petrucci palace, where he was to stay. Later in the evening he viewed from his windows the government's presents of food, wine, candles, sugar, and provisions of sundry kinds artfully displayed in the square below.

On the following morning, after Mass at the cathedral, government officials were received in state by the emperor, who used the occasion to renew imperial privileges and confer knighthoods on several people. Later that day the Sienese government made its gifts to members of the imperial household. Included in the list of recipients were Charles's twelve trumpeters, who were each given one scudo.[9] "At this time there were so many lights in the streets, in the windows of palaces and churches, and in the towers that the city seemed to be on fire and the noise of the artillery and the sounds of the bells and of the trumpets went on for a good long time."[10] The next day the emperor was the government's guest at the Palace, where he was received with great honor. The

---

7. Ibid., 21. On the imperial sonata see chapter 9 above.

8. Ibid., 32: "et havendo per picciol spatio di tempo adorato con la testa china e ignudo, un fanciullo cantò molto soavemente in su l'organo un leggiadro mottetto, il quale finito, il Vescovo che era all'altare in abito pontificale fatte sue cerimonie et ditte alcune orazioni, finalmente volto a Sua Maestà li diè la benedictione." See p. 686 below for the "Carri."

9. Ibid., 41.

10. Ibid., 37.

Palace had been specially decorated inside and out, and when "His Majesty appeared at the Costarella, the trumpeters and the pifferi played successively from the Palace battlements."[11] Although a play scheduled for performance by the members of the Accademia degli Intronati was not performed, the emperor was delighted with the "giuoco delle pugna," a traditional kind of boxing match, put on especially for him.[12] Siena was long a favorite stopping place for the Roman pontiffs whenever they traveled north of Rome. Reports of thirteenth- and fourteenth-century visits rarely give details of the papal retinues, and when they do, they usually name cardinals, ambassadors, and various officials in the pope's personal entourage. Papal singers were undoubtedly among the latter, but no chronicler bothered to refer to them. From the fifteenth-century come reports about papal visits to Siena more directly bearing on the course of musical history in the city, though, as in the past, music and musicians are rarely if ever mentioned. This was certainly true, as has been noted, of the visit of Pope Eugene IV, who was in Siena during the spring and summer of 1443, before his return to the Vatican.[13] Other sources, particularly those from Florence, where the Pope stayed for several years, indicate that his singers performed at public ceremonies whenever he officiated.[14] That must have been the case also when Eugene was in Siena, even though the chroniclers fail to say so. Reference has already been made to the visits in the early 1460s of Pius II Piccolomini, whose chapel included a former cathedral singer.

A number of prominent Sienese citizens had an opportunity to hear the singers of the papal chapel long before that time. Some forty years earlier, in mid-September 1420, when Pope Martin V and his retinue were making their way south from Florence to the Eternal City, they stopped at Cuna, in the Sienese countryside, rather than at plague-ridden Siena. An official Sienese delegation and many citizens went out to greet the pope on behalf of the commune. At Ponte ad Arbia, Martin's next stop, a magnificently decorated tent, under which he and his party and guests were served dinner, was set up at the instance of the wealthy merchant Jacomo di Marco Pecci.[15] Surely, singers in the papal entourage performed for their Sienese hosts on such a grand occasion, if not at dinner, then at the Mass that the pope and all of his visitors attended that day.

FESTIVITIES TO WELCOME DISTINGUISHED VISITORS
The Church Council of 1423

One notable ecclesiastical event in which the pontiff did not participate occurred in 1423, when the organizers of a General Council of the Church, assembling at Pavia,

---

11. Ibid., 49.

12. Giuliano Catoni, "La faziosa armonia," in Alessandro Falassi, Giuliano Catoni, Giovanni Cecchini, and Pepi Merisio, *Palio* (Milan, 1982), 236–44; see also note 61 below.

13. Fecini, "Cronaca Senese," 854–55.

14. D'Accone, "Music and Musicians at Santa Maria del Fiore," 115–16.

15. Paolo di Tommaso Montauri, "Cronaca Senese conosciuta sotto il nome di Paolo di Tommaso Montauri," in Muratori, *Rerum italicarum scriptores,* 15/6, 1:794. The dinner took place on 11 September 1420. Previously, Martin's singers performed in Florence while he was residing there. (See note 14.)

decided to transfer their meetings to Siena.[16] Despite papal procrastination and the machinations of the Florentines, foreign delegations soon began arriving in the city. Some dignitaries, it seems, made almost royal entries. Principal among them was the Cardinal of Spain, who entered Siena early in September of that year to the sound of trumpets, accompanied by an armed escort. Others came and went less ostentatiously. The archbishop of Poland, who had been to Rome to advise the pope of the Council's imminent opening, returned to Siena at mid-month with word that the pope would soon arrive. Meanwhile, the city bustled with activity. On 18 October the doctors of the Sienese Studio, that is, the university, and their students gave sermons in the great hall of the Council, which many bishops and prelates attended. The town trumpeters and others were surely on hand to signal these events.

As the months passed many more prelates and politicians arrived. The bishop of Cologne and the archbishop of Toledo, who, it was said, sang his first Mass at the cathedral, came, as did "many lords who spoke many languages, and "there was more wealth in Siena than there would have been, were it not for the Council." In view of these reports, it is easy to imagine that musical retainers of these grand lords were also present and that Sienese musicians performed at various religious and social functions, both public and private, attended by them and by less exalted personages. In February of 1424 the French patriarch and six doctors, ambassadors from the University of Paris, arrived in the city, these latest participants warmly received by the Council and "particularly by the Commune of Siena, which gave them great honors." All of this activitiy bore little fruit, for the pope never attended the Council, which was dissolved in the following month. But the presence of so many important people from so many distant lands in Siena during this period is significant because it furnishes another instance of a time when foreign musicians must have come to the city and brought with them their own repertories and performance practices, just as they had done at the great Council of Constance, less than a decade earlier.[17]

The Medici

Apart from official visitors, others, equally distinguished, often came to the city under less formal circumstances. Among the most prominent in the late fifteenth century was Lorenzo the Magnificent. Lorenzo was in Siena in early September 1485, en route to the thermal baths at Vignone. Tizio reports that he arrived on 7 September 1485 and that he was received with great honors by the Concistoro, departing Siena the following day.[18] While there is no mention of a formal ceremony at the city's gates nor of a

---

16. See Montauri, "Cronaca Senese," 798–802, passim, for this and the following quotations.

17. On musicians in Constance at the time of the Council see Manfred Schuler, "Die Musik in Konstanz während des Konzils 1414–1418," *Acta Musicologica* 38 (1966): 150–68.

18. Tizio, *Historiarum Senensium,* 4:138: "Laurentius Petri Medices . . . die 7 Septembris [1485] urbem Senam ingreditur, honorifice a civibus exceptus . . . solitisque muneribus publice est affectus . . . inde vero ad Balnea Aveninonis ac Sancti Philippi est profestus . . . Octobris autem die septima Florentiam rediens, Senis propere transivit, in urbe nihil consistens." Another chronicler reports that Lorenzo arrived a day earlier: "A dì 6 di Settembre venne in Siena Lorenzo di Piero di Cosimo de' Medici, cittadino, e come Signore di Fiorenza, e va al bagno a Vignone" (Allegretti, "Ephemerides," col. 818).

state procession, there were assuredly festivities within the Palace with the Palace's own musicians participating. Whether any of the Medici musicians accompanied Lorenzo at this time is unknown, though when he made similar trips on other occasions, he traveled with an entourage that included both instrumentalists and singers.[19]

Members of Lorenzo's immediate family were also in Siena on several occasions. Prominent among them were the visits throughout the summer and fall of 1515 of Lorenzo's son Giuliano de' Medici, duke of Nemours, and Lorenzo's grandson and namesake, Lorenzo, future duke of Urbino, brother and nephew, respectively, of the ruling pontiff, Leo X.[20] Both dukes attended the annual Palio on Assumption Day, 1515, when a number of the customary musical entertainments were offered.[21] Apparently, musicians in the Medici entourage performed at some of them, for an official record of government expenses for that year's festival lists a payment to the famous Jewish lutenist Giovan Maria, who later took the name of his Medici patrons.[22] Earlier in that same year Siena hosted the foremost musical patroness of the age, Isabella d'Este Gonzaga, marchioness of Mantua, who was traveling to and from Rome, where she was received by another great patron of music, Pope Leo X. In Siena, on the evening of 6 February, Raffaelle Petrucci had a play performed in Isabella's honor. Perhaps it

---

19. On Lorenzo and music, and particularly his and his son Piero's private musicians, see D'Accone, "Lorenzo il Magnifico e la musica," esp. p. 221.

20. Like Lorenzo the Magnificent and his second son Giovanni, later Pope Leo X, these scions of the Medici family also have a minor place in the history of Italian Renaissance music. Giuliano was probably the owner of a chansonnier now in the Vatican Library, Cappella Giulia MS XIII, 27, and Lorenzo, Duke of Urbino, was the recipient, on the occasion of his marriage to Madeleine de la Tour d'Auvergne, of a sumptuous codex of sacred music, now in the Laurentian Library in Florence. See Allan Atlas, *The Cappella Giulia Chansonnier*; Edward E. Lowinsky, *The Medici Codex of 1518: a Choirbook of Motets Dedicated to Lorenzo de' Medici, Duke of Urbino* (Chicago, 1968); Anthony M. Cummings, *The Politicized Muse: Music for Medici Festivals, 1512–1537* (Princeton, 1992); and André Pirro, "Leo X and Music," *Musical Quarterly* 21 (1935): 1–16. Leo X, celebrated even in his own day for his love of music and his discriminating taste, was undoubtedly the most musical of all popes. Reference has been made in previous chapters to musicians employed in the papal chapel during his reign. For an overview of Leo as a musical patron and for an extensive commentary and analysis of several entertainments at his court in 1520, as reported by the Venetian Marcantonio Michiel, of the musicians who took part in them, and of the kinds of music they performed, see Blackburn, "Music and Festivities at the Court of Leo X," which also cites previous pertinent literature about Leo and music.

21. Payments made for various expenses on behalf of the Medici guests are listed from March 1515 through January 1516 in an official government account book (ASS, Balìa, vol. 63, fols. 46ᵛ, 48ʳ, 48ᵛ). Other records in the same volume list expenses totaling Du. 33 L. 0 grossi 16 "a più piffari, trombetti et altri sonatori forestieri per mancie per la festa," that is, for the July Palio (fol. 44ʳ) and the expenditure of L. 153. 6 for the August Palio to "piffari, trombetti et altri sonatori venuti a la festa, per mancia" (fol. 42ᵛ).

22. "E a dì decto L. 30 a Giovanni hoste al hosteria . . . per scotti dati a Giovanmaria, sonatore di leuto, L. 30" (ASS, Balìa, vol. 63. fol. 44ʳ, dated July 1515). On Giovan Maria see H. Colin Slim, "Gian and Gian Maria, Some Fifteenth- and Sixteenth Century Namesakes," *Musical Quarterly* 57 (1971): 563–68, and William Prizer, "The Frottola and the Unwritten Tradition," *Studi musicali* 15 (1986): 8–19. More recent research regarding the lutenist is given by Anthony M. Cummings, "Gian Maria Giudeo, Sonatore del Liuto, and the Medici," *Fontes Artis Musicae* 38 (1991): 312–18.

was the "Egloga pastorale di Iustitia," with the famous Sienese actor and poet Niccolò Campani, called Strascino, acting in it.[23]

Cosimo de' Medici did not delay in making his first official visit as ruler of the city. After the peace treaty of Cateau-Cambrésis and the surrender of Montalcino in 1559, Sovana was taken by Medici forces in 1560 and on 28 October of that year Cosimo, accompanied by his wife, Eleonora of Toledo, and his court, en route to an audience with the pope in Rome, paid his first visit to Siena.[24] Though he remained only a few days, his presence occasioned solemn ceremonies both in the cathedral and in the Palace, enabling the Sienese to greet or to catch a glimpse of their new sovereign.[25] The Florentine diarist Agostino Lapini reports that Cosimo and his party entered the city with great pomp and that as his cavalcade made its way to the Palace, where he was to reside, gold and silver coins were thrown to the welcoming crowds.[26] On hand to greet him were one hundred young boys all dressed in white, olive branches in hand, who, like the populace, shouted joyous cries of welcome amid the roar of artillery and the sounds of trumpets, drums, and pifferi. Cosimo reportedly was moved to tears by the spectacle.[27]

After visiting Rome Cosimo returned in January 1561 for a longer and more demanding stay, during which he promulgated his reform of Siena's government with a new constitution.[28] Huge crowds and the city's magistrates were again on hand to greet him when he arrived on the morning of the 9th, and three days of festivities featuring fireworks and other entertainments followed. One of the latter was a performance in the great hall of the Palazzo Pubblico of Alessandro Piccolomini's *L'Ortensio* in which

------

23. Mazzi, *La Congrega dei Rozzi di Siena,* 1:64. The Egloga, first performance date unknown, was republished in Siena as early as 1513. Mazzi quotes from documentation given by Sigismondo Tizio and also cites Uberto Benvoglienti, who thought the play might be an *Egloga pastorale di Iustitia,* which was republished as early as 1513. For the suggestion that Strascino acted in the play see Raffaela Braghieri, "Il teatro a Siena nei primi anni del Cinquecento: L'esperienza teatrale dei pre-Rozzi," *BSSP* 18 (1986): 115.

24. Cosimo's reception by the Concistoro and members of the clergy at the gate outside the Porta Camollia on 30 October 1560 was depicted in one of the Biccherna covers for 1561. The cover is reproduced with commentary in *Le Biccherne,* 158ff. A contemporary account of the event, *Entrata del Duca et Duchessa di Firenze in Siena,* was composed by Anton Francesco Cirni Corso and printed at Rome in 1560, with a dedication to Cardinal Borromeo.

25. Fasano Guarini, "Le istituzioni di Siena e del suo stato nel ducato Mediceo," 51; Lorenzo Cantini, *Vita di Cosimo de' Medici Primo Gran-Duca di Toscana* (Florence, 1805), 380.

26. Agostino Lapini, *Diario fiorentino di Agostino Lapini dal 292 al 1596,* ed. Giuseppe Odoardo Corazzini (Florence, 1900), 130. A near contemporary report by Baccio Baldini, published at Florence in 1578 by Sermatelli, notes that while Cosimo and Eleonora were in Siena "gli furon fatte da i Sanesi molte gran feste e belle" (*Vita di Cosimo Medici, Primo Gran duca di Toscana,* 65).

27. Cirni Corso, *Entrata del Duca,* fol. A IIᵛ: "furono incontrati da cento bei fanciulli vestiti tutti di bianco in segno della loro purità con rami d'olivo in mano . . . [fol. A IVʳ] Sentivasi il rumor grande d'artigliarie, tamburi, pifari, e trombetti che andavano insino al Cielo a furia di populo gridando Palle, Palle. Il concorso della gente era grandissima, e la corte del Duca doveva essere da mille cavalli."

28. Cantini, *Vita di Cosimo de' Medici,* 386–90, esp. 386.

unspecified musical interludes also figured.[29] Little else is reported about the nature of the festivities during this visit, though the cathedral chapel assuredly performed at services Cosimo attended there, as did the pifferi and trumpeters at ceremonies and banquets within the Palace.

An account of a visit many years later of Cosimo's son, Grand Duke Francesco I and his second wife, the Venetian noblewoman Bianca Cappello, tells a different story, perhaps reflecting Siena's acceptance of its Medici lords. The high point of the royal couple's stay was the presentation during carnival, on 22 February 1583, of an entertainment with a pastoral theme featuring music and dance, when gifts from the city were presented to them.[30] Festivities began with a procession of elaborately costumed shepherds, satyrs, and nymphs on horseback parading around the square in front of the Petrucci palace where the duke and duchess were staying. The shepherds, forty in number, carried lighted torches in hand, and the satyrs came bearing richly decorated vases full of fruits and flowers. Some of the shepherds also carried silver panpipes, within which were trumpets and curtals so artfully concealed that when the musicians played, it seemed they were playing the panpipes.[31] The procession eventually came to a halt under the windows of the royal couple, who awaited them with pleasure. Then "the three nymphs with curtals, who had been playing continuously, performed a noble concerto," and all of the satyrs, with their vases and torches, grouped themselves beneath the windows so they could be viewed by the royal couple.

The principal musical entertainments followed. First, four shepherds, accompanied by a lutenist, sang several stanzas of an "arietta," the last in praise of the grand duchess. (The writer says he was enclosing the text with his letter, but no trace survives of it, nor of any of the others he mentions—this despite a printed edition of a thousand copies distributed to the assembled guests that evening.[32]) Then followed "two beautiful and very substantial madrigals a 6, performed by an ensemble of voices and flutes, with two and sometimes three voices to a part." Afterwards the satyrs and nymphs presented gifts in the Sienese manner, which the royal couple received with much pleasure, and then entering the room where the company was assembled the musicians "sweetly sang a madrigal" before presenting the royal couple with the town's major present, which was in gold and silver. The nymphs then invited three of the ladies present to dance

---

29. Duilio Berti, "La Musica in Siena," in *Atti dell'Accademia del Conservatorio di Musica L. Cherubini di Firenze* (1931): 19. An account of preparations made within the city and of expenses incurred in connection with Cosimo's first visit is given by Antonio Pellegrini, "Per l'arrivo di Cosimo I a Siena (1560)," *BSSP* 10 (1903): 165–82. He believes that it was performed by the members of the Accademia degli Intronati during Cosimo's first visit (180, n. 2).

30. An account of the entertainment was given by Flavio Figliucci in a letter to the grand duchess's secretary; the letter was published with commentary by G. E. Saltini, "Bianca Cappello in Siena," *Miscellanea Storica Senese* 3 (1895): 97–106.

31. Ibid., 102: "era accomodata una tromba con una sordina, inclusaci dentro sì leggiadramente, che non appariva cosa alcuna, se non la siringa sonata da ciascuno dei tre, tanto artificiosamente che pareva la siringa stessa."

32. Ibid., 105, n. 1.

and they did a "Barriera," a circle dance with figurations.[33] When this was finished, the musicians sang another madrigal before the troupe departed, leaving as they had arrived through the square, amid great merriment.[34]

Archbishop Piccolomini's Entrance in 1589

After Siena's incorporation into the Medici state, traditional civic functions such as the priors' two-monthly entrances into office were no longer marked with public processions and festivities. But ecclesiastical functions were another matter, and the lingering desire to celebrate things Sienese found an outlet, at least on one occasion, in the welcome given to Siena's newly elected archbishop Ascanio Piccolomini on 21 November 1589, when he made his formal entrance into the city to claim possession of his bishopric. The date of the festivities was approved beforehand in Florence by the grand duke, though the ceremonies were devised by the Sienese. The archbishop, in the words of Scipione Bargagli, who wrote an account of the event, was received "according to the usual custom and ancient usage of his beloved homeland."[35] And as Bargagli makes clear, it was a reception equal in grandeur to any that might have been given an emperor or a grand duke.

As might be expected, music, vocal and instrumental, sacred as well as secular, played a prominent part in the various events scheduled throughout the day. The pro-

---

33. The barriera was originally a kind of tourney or joust and the dance, a mock recreation of it, was usually done to music based on trumpet calls and flourishes. The barriera mentioned here could have been one of the several then in use. Fabritio Caroso gives four versions in his *Nobiltà di dame* (1600) and in his earlier *Il Ballarino* (1581); two are for one couple and two are for three couples, or six people, as here. Cesare Negri also describes the dance in *Le gratie d'amore* (1602). See Fabritio Caroso, *Nobiltà di Dame,* ed. Julia Sutton (Oxford, 1986), 181–92, 217–19; Mabel Dolmetsch, *Dances of Spain and Italy from 1400 to 1600* (London, 1954), 152–63.

34. Saltini, "Bianca Cappello in Siena," 105:

> una bella e pienissima musica a sei, parte con voci, parte con flauti a la svizzera, e con voci tutte doppie e parte triplicate, che cantorno i due allegati madrigali . . . accostatisi ciascuno alla sua Ninfa, esse cominciarono a tirare leggiadramente, a l'usanza senese, i presenti loro: i quali essendo stati, con loro infinita contentezza, ricevuti gratamente così dal serenissimo principe loro, come dalla serenissima principessa; essi scendendo a piedi . . . salseno nella sala, dove erano loro altezze serenissime con tutte quelle altre nobilissime signore donne e donzelle, e fermatisi in mezzo di essa, i musici che si erano posti appresso di loro cantorno dolcemente un madrigale . . . ciascuno delle ninfe presentò il suo principal presente d'argento e d'oro; che ricevuti gratamente . . . onde tornate a loro luogo, mentre che uno de' suoi pastori, che in tre altri in nappi d'argento, avea portato mille carte di questa stanza per presentare, andò a far riverenza a lor serenissime altezze . . . le ninfe invitorno tre signore dame e feceno una Barriera [sorte di danza figurata allora in usa] e i musici, finita quella, cantorno un altro madrigale; per dare tempo ad alcuni pastori che facesseno.

35. See p. 5 of the *Descrizione dell'entrata dell'Illustriss., e Reverendiss. Monsig. Ascanio Piccolomini, alla possesione del suo Arcivescovado in Siena Il dì XXJ di Novembre. 1589* (Siena: Luca Bonetti, 1599). A copy of the booklet, now in the library of the Kunsthistoriches Institut in Florence, has the following inscription on its title page: "Dono del S' Scipione Bargagli Autore ad Antonio Biessa Negrini."

cession that was to march to the city's gates to greet the archbishop assembled at the cathedral's main portal after the sounding of the bells. Heading it was a huge banner with an image of the Virgin. This was accompanied by thirty pairs of youngsters dressed as angels in long white robes, all of them bearing palm fronds. In their wake, one after the other, were various companies of priests, all dressed in their distinctive robes. Following were a number of individuals costumed to represent personifications of virtues and vices such as Pride, Liberality, Chastity, Patience, Abstinence, Charity, Envy, and Diligence, they too accompanied by a group of angels.[36] Behind them walked another angel, richly garbed in a bishop's cope, "holding the crosier of the glorious saint Ansano in one hand." Escorting him on either side were two young angels and behind were twenty more angels walking two abreast, "who together with the others ahead of them gracefully sang *Iste Confessor*," apparently in plainchant.[37] Then came the confraternities and religious companies of lay people in good number and the monks and brothers, followed by all of the other priests and clerics of the diocese and the cathedral canons. Preceding them was the baldachin under which the new archbishop would be received and behind them the Opera's banner with representations of the city's four patron saints. Bringing up the rear were four youths representing the four moral virtues, and after them, various other groups of marchers.[38]

The baldachin was in place at the city's outside gates when the archbishop arrived and under it he was given a cross to kiss. Then, "with great reverence and devotion he knelt and kissed the ground, whereupon the chapel singers from the duomo were heard joyously singing *Ecce sacerdos magnus*."[39] This was sung a cappella and may very well have been Victoria's setting of the text (1572), a copy of which was in the cathedral library.[40] A Latin oration was pronounced before the procession recommenced. Entering through the city's gates, the procession slowly made its way to the cathedral. En route, the crowd's ovations were such that "one could not sing with words nor describe with pen the great noise and joyous sounds that were heard all at once," as the archbishop walked from place to place, past the Porta Romana under the Arco, past the churches of San Galgano, Santa Maria de' Servi, San Maurizio, and San Giorgio, all of whose facades were adorned with banners bearing Latin mottos and painted canvases.[41]

The decorations at the church of San Giorgio were particularly notable and included a throne adorned with the Piccolomini coat of arms—five half moons forming a cross—below which were depicted the five virgins of biblical lore. The throne was placed in the little piazza and street outside the church. This was covered by a painted canvas depicting the sky that extended from the church roof to the roofs of the houses opposite. The walls surrounding the throne were draped in blue cloth and reached from the roof to the pavement. From the sky above, suspended in air, "the personification of

---

36. Ibid., 8–9.
37. Ibid., 12–13. The text mistakenly refers to the hymn as "Idem Confessor."
38. Ibid., 14–15.
39. Ibid., 18.
40. See above, Table 7.1. Costanzo Porta's setting of 1585 is also a possibility, but the only volume of his mentioned in cathedral inventories is the collection of introits.
41. *Descrizione dell'entrata*, 21–27.

Religion, dressed in white with a mitre in her right hand and a model of the duomo in her left," descended to earth, slowly and imperceptibly, on a round cloud. As she did so, "she sang the hymn *Pontifex noster domini urbem* in a very sweet voice." Bargagli further explains that it was a boy singer who depicted Religion and that "behind [him] were a portable organ, a lute, bass viols, and other musical instruments, which accompanied his singing with very sweet harmony, and to this the echo within the church opposite made some response."[42] Clearly, this was music especially composed for the occasion, perhaps monodic, to judge from the description, though it could just as easily have been written in four or five parts, only one of which was sung. In any case, its similarity to the various kinds of music performed at the renowned Medici wedding festival that same year is certainly worthy of note.

Arriving at the cathedral, the archbishop entered through the middle portal and proceeded to the main altar, which was adorned with the church's most holy reliquaries and richest silver, silk paraments, and cloths of gold, resplendent with the light of a thousand candles. "There the archbishop prayed devotedly to God on behalf of all and devout praises sounded from both the chapel singers and the organ, giving thanks to His divine majesty."[43] The archbishop was then conducted to his throne, whereupon the cathedral provost and all of the priests came and knelt before him. A number of speeches followed, among them one by the archbishop himself. At the conclusion of the ceremony he was accompanied to the doors of the bishop's palace, where more speeches were made. The palace had been richly decorated with paintings of allegorical and historical figures.

Activities continued into the night, and at sunset the little square in front of the palace was illuminated with the light of candles, held by bands of people standing there, and from the glow of tapers placed in the windows of all of the buildings surrounding the square—the hospital, the Opera, the church, and the bishop's palace. Thunderous sounds, almost like cannon fire, were heard, and then from the cathedral's bell tower came "the most solemn and joyous sound of the trumpets." Meanwhile in the square "a joyful *concerto* of trombones, curtals, flutes, cornetts, and other wind instruments filled everyone with pleasure and reawakened, or rather increased, in the souls of all citizens what was there already from the day of the entrance."[44] The crowning moment of the evening's festivities was the lighting of candles in a lantern placed at the top of the bell tower. Rays of various colors streamed forth, amid the joyous sounds of the bells in the tower and of bells elsewhere in the city, and it was a sight "deemed wondrous by all."

CIVIC AND RELIGIOUS CEREMONIES

Civic and religious ceremonies also furnished frequent occasions for public musical performances even in earlier times. From April 1257 comes a payment authorized by

---

42. *Descrizione dell'entrata,* 33–34: "Dietro al cantante fanciullo era organetto, leuto, violoni e altri musicali strumenti, che 'l suo cantare, con molto dolce armonia accompagnava, et a questa faceva l'Eco dentro la chiesa adirimpetto alcuna risposta."

43. Ibid., 47.

44. Ibid., 58.

the General Council to a boy "who represented Christ on the Cross on Good Friday," an indication that the city itself subsidized the performance of mystery plays during Lent.[45] In May 1284, when the foundation stone of the façade of the cathedral facing the hospital of Santa Maria della Scala was laid, the event was solemnly celebrated in the presence of the government and the townspeople by the bishop and all of the clergy "with hymn singing and psalms and prayers in honor of the Virgin Mary and with holy water and incense, to the sound of the bells and of the commune's trumpets."[46] The chroniclers fail to mention musicians on many other occasions of similar import, although they were surely present. Conspicuous in this regard is the account of the festivities on 9 June 1310, when Duccio's newly finished altarpiece was brought to the cathedral and placed on the high altar. The chronicler dutifully reported that the shops were closed and the entire population turned out in festive garb to view the "large and devoted company of monks and priests, escorted by the Nine Lords and all of the government officials and many laymen," who marched in solemn procession through the streets of the town, "as the church bells sounded in glory."[47] The presence of the Concistoro is a clear indication that the town trumpeters, and perhaps other musicians, lent their joyous sounds to the occasion.

Holidays, proclamations of peace, the defeat of enemies, and other political events also furnished occasions for grand celebrations in which musicians participated. In 1255 the government commissioned a now-lost ballata from Guidaloste, a *cantastorie,* or minstrel, from Pistoia, to celebrate the acquisition of the fortress of Torniella from its feudal lords.[48] The Sienese victory at Montaperti in 1260, mythically remembered as the most important event in the city's history, was celebrated over a number of days, according to several reports, which may be fifteenth-century fabrications. Authentic or not, the chroniclers were aware that even at that time the commune employed musicians who would have added to the magnificence of the celebrations. The account of the triumphal return of the Sienese army on Sunday, 5 September 1260, offers a case in point. The victorious forces, we are told, entered the city amid great rejoicing. To the solemn rhythms of pipe and tabors, the various companies and ranks marched to the cathedral, where they rendered praise to Almighty God and thanks to the Virgin for the great victory she had given the people of Siena.[49] Another grand procession, in which all of

45. Zdekauer, "L'entrata di Carlo VIII Re di Francia," 252, citing a document in Consiglio della Campana, 1257, vol. VII, dì 7 Aprile. See also *Miscellanea Storica Senese,* 4 (1898): 23–24, Notizie: "Un antico invito ad una rappresentazione sacra," which cites an incomplete record, dated 7 April 1257, from a volume of deliberations of the Consiglio Generale, Deliberazioni, vol. VII, fol. 58ᵛ: "Item si placet vobis, quod, ob reverentiam Iesu Christi, dentur illi puero, qui fuit positus in cruce, loco Domini, die veneris sancte." Also quoted in this same article are two payments from Biccherna accounts of 1256–57 for expenses "pro ludo Mariarum, quod fuit in Campo fori die veneris sancti."
46. "Cronaca Senese . . . di autore anonimo del secolo XIV," 68.
47. Ibid., 90.
48. Reported by Luciani in *La musica in Siena,* 163, citing D'Ancona in *La poesia popolare italiana,* 9.
49. Montauri, "Cronaca Senese," 216: "entraro in Siena con grande trionfo e alegreza . . . Dopo questa seguiva(no) e' tanburini sonando: dipoi seguiva lo stendardo real de re Manfredi."

the religious orders resident in the city, the bishop, and the cathedral canons participated, took place two days later, with the whole town in attendance.[50]

Religious spectacles, or sacred representations as they later came to be called, that took place in Siena throughout the centuries were as numerous as they were sumptuously staged. For many years—although the chroniclers fail to say how many or exactly when, though perhaps in the early fifteenth century—annual celebrations in the Campo commemorated Siena's absolution on 13 July 1276 from a papal interdiction.[51] The pardon had been obtained by the blessed Ambrogio Sansedoni, one of Siena's most beloved candidates for sainthood, and Ambrogio figured prominently in the spectacle that was enacted on a platform erected in the middle of the square. What a spectacle it must have been! Before the audience's very eyes a flower, touched by the flaming bill of a white dove, opened its petals to reveal a papal apartment, within which were actors representing the pope, his cardinals, high-ranking ambassadors, and the blessed Ambrogio. Immediately, an angel appeared to announce the beginning of the pageant and discourses by both Ambrogio and the pope followed. Then, encircling the entire square, came a cart full of angels, who sang in honor of the Blessed Virgin and in praise of Ambrogio to the accompaniment of musical instruments. Meanwhile, on stage, a cavern opened to reveal devils who were subsequently assaulted and subdued by elegantly armed knights—perhaps to the choreographed steps of a moresca—and following this, another angel announced the end of the spectacle with a sweet song. How we wish that the chronicler had said more about the kinds of music that were sung (or danced) and the instruments that took part in the festivities! But as is so often the case, we are left to wonder and to presume. This particular sacred representation was enacted annually for a number of years before being discontinued. Later, in 1469, so that the day would not go unobserved altogether, the government ordered that a Palio be given in its place, but that, too, ceased with the fall of the republic.[52]

Some of the most spectacular public festivities of the fifteenth century celebrated the canonizations of two Sienese saints, typically Sienese events, it might be added, since the line between religious reverence and civic pride was barely distinguishable, if at all. The earlier of the two events was held in honor of San Bernardino, the fiery evangelist who persuaded so many of his fellow townsmen to seek a more Christian way of life.[53] His preaching had moved the Sienese to proclaim Jesus Christ as their ruler, an action that anticipated by almost half a century a similar one by the Florentines under Savonarola. The symbol adopted by Bernardino to proclaim Christ's jurisdiction—a flaming heart with the name of Jesus emblazoned within—was even placed on

---

50. Ibid., 217–18.

51. Provedi, *Relazione delle pubbliche feste,* 16–19: "Rappresentazione spettacolosa per l'assoluzione ottenuta dal Beato Ambrogio dell'Interdetto." Blessed Ambrogio Sansedoni obtained the pardon from the pope, who issued a brief from Florence on 13 July 1276. See Giulio Sansedoni, *Vita del Beato Ambrogio Sansedoni* (Rome: Mascardi, 1611).

52. Provedi, *Relazione delle pubbliche feste,* 19.

53. The literature on San Bernardino is vast. An accessible account of his life is the biography by Iris Origo, *The World of San Bernardino* (New York, 1962).

the façade of the Palazzo Pubblico. Sano's celebrated painting of the saint preaching to the Sienese from a pulpit erected in the square in front of the Palace is perhaps as immediate and vivid a depiction of the crowds and the enthusiasm Bernardino elicited from his congregation as any photograph could be. Regrettably, his popular meetings had no place in them for instrumental music, though there is reason to believe that familiar chants, religious songs, and laudi were often sung. Regarded as a saint even during his lifetime, Bernardino was canonized in Rome by Pope Nicholas V on 24 May 1450.

When word reached Siena three days later, on the 27th, all the shops quickly closed, as bells began ringing and trumpets sounded the joyous tidings. In the evening bonfires were lit everywhere. After all, Bernardino was Siena's own, and his words had inspired the entire city. A few days later the city mounted a huge celebration in the Campo, its beautiful space furnishing then as now the backdrop for some of the most solemn as well as the most joyous ceremonies staged by the Sienese. The square was decorated with triumphal arches, and the festivities opened with Vespers, sung by the bishop, assisted by many of the clergy and by the cathedral singers, on a platform that had been raised in front of the Palace.[54] The principal part of the celebration then followed.

Its theme, of course, was Bernardino's canonization. To commemorate it a dramatization representing the apotheosis of the the saint was presented on a stage, constructed especially for the occasion, atop the Cappella del Campo, the outdoor chapel at the foot of the Palace. (The stage itself was on a level with the Palace windows known as the "windows of the podestà.") The dramatization featured a "paradiso," or heavenly stage set, constructed of wood and adorned with many tapestries and a wheel of lights, wherein an allegory of San Bernardino ascending to heaven was depicted. The crowning moment of the spectacle was when, in the chronicler's words, "San Bernardino was conducted to the foot of God [to the accompaniment of] all of the instruments that could be had."[55] What music this ensemble, which assuredly included all the Palace

---

54. Whatever prayers were used, it is doubtful that they included any of those found in offices subsequently composed in honor of San Bernardino. Antiphons and responsories of two rhymed offices for the saint, from various European sources including a breviary printed at Venice in 1522, were published by Clemens Blume in *Analecta Hymnica Medii Aevi*, 25 (Leipzig, 1897), nos. 54, *Senarum civis inclitus,* and 55, *Bernardinus vir catholicus,* 152–60. A third rhymed office, by Fra Lorenzo da Montepulciano, also beginning *Bernardinus vir catholicus,* is in MS B. VI. 26 (250) of the Biblioteca Casanatense, Rome. This was listed by Blume among the sources of the second office, but apart from the common incipit for the antiphon of First Vespers, the two differ markedly. A late seventeenth/ early eighteenth-century manuscript folio in the Vatican Library, Miscellanea H. 33, no. 10, contains two hymns for the feast, *Sedis etruscis rutilans ab oris* and *Se Deo totum cupiens dicari,* both probably dating from the same time. A sequence in honor of San Bernardino, *Laetabundus Bernardino psallat mundis Alleluia,* sung to the *Laetabundus* melody, was published by Henry Marriott Bannister in *Analecta Hymnica Medii Aevi,* 40 (Leipzig, 1902), no. 168, 152–53.

55. Fecini, "Cronaca Senese," 861; alternative translation: "an artifice where a likeness of St. Bernardino going to heaven was depicted/enacted." See also Allegretti, "Ephemerides," 767. He reports Bernardino's canonization in Rome on 24 May 1450 and says that on 14 and 15 June "se ne fe' in Siena una bella Festa e rapresentazione de la sua Canonizzazione, e per tutta Siena si faceva festa e dava mangiare e bere a chi ne voleva, e 'l vescovo di Siena cantò la Messa in Piazza."

The reference to "bellissimi canti" appears in one of the surviving account books of the Company

musicians and any number of others recruited especially for the occasion, would have played must remain a matter of conjecture. A report in an account book of the Company of Santa Maria degli Angeli e di San Francesco mentions very beautiful songs, "bellissimi canti," at the moment Bernardino ascended to heaven and perhaps this indicates performance of sacred songs and laudi, with texts composed especially in honor of the saint, sung by members of the companies. The chronicler, however, is silent on this subject.

A "paradiso" is also mentioned in connection with the celebration that marked the canonization of Siena's revered Catherine Benincasa. News of her elevation to sainthood by Pope Pius II reached the city on 1 July 1461. Despite the great euphoria, festivities were wisely deferred until August 16, when large numbers of visitors and representatives of vassal cities and towns were expected for the annual Assumption Day festival. One chronicler reports that all of Siena was gaily decorated for the feast in honor of Catherine and that "a paradiso was done atop the Cappella del Campo."[56] Sigismondo Tizio, the Sienese historian who furnished a number of precious, though sparse, remarks about music at the cathedral, noted that on this day for the "celebration of the blessed Catherine of Siena . . . harmonious part-songs were performed and also the sounds of instruments added to the joyfulness."[57] Although Tizio said nothing about the number of musicians who participated in the ceremony, probably one or another of the ensembles that normally journeyed to Siena each year for Assumption Day festivities, not to mention the Palace pifferi, played. Tizio's remarks, in any case, suggest that many of the visiting musicians took an active role in the spectacle, just as they had on two previous occasions when, even before her canonization, Siena had staged celebrations to honor Catherine.

The second of these, held on 5 June 1446, was the more spectacular and the one that claimed the attention of the chroniclers. Various reports put the number of people who witnessed it at more than 20,000.[58] For the occasion a platform was raised in the

---

of Santa Maria degli Angeli e di San Francesco, later subsumed into the Company of San Bernardino in Siena. The report also mentions that it began to rain as the music was being performed: "Memoria chome il chomune di Siena et per lo chomune Nicholò di messer Agnolo, uno de' signori de la festa di Santo Bernardino, anno dati . . . A dì 13 di giugno si chantò in sul champo di Siena uno solenne Vesparo. A dì 14 in domenicha si chantò in sul champo una solenne messa, dissela il vescovo di Siena chon tutt'i preti e frati di Siena e feci a pie il palazo da la schala del podestà . . . Da la chapella del champo si fe' un palchetto alto infino a le finestre del podestà che in sul detto palcho si fe' il paradiso, suvi molti giovani vestiti in fighura di santi. In sul detto palcho si fe l'assemblamento quando Santo Bernardino andò in c[i]elo chon bellissimi chanti e questo si fe', detta fu la messa. E mentre si facevano questi canti inchominciò a piovere e non si finì, e ogniuno si partì" (ASS, PR, Compagnia di S. Bernardino, vol. 207, *D&C, 1447,* fols. 30ᵛ–31ʳ, dated 1450).

56. Fecini, "Cronaca Senese," 869.

57. Tizio, *Historiarum Senensium,* 5:24: "Senenses interea Augusti die sextadecima [1461] . . . Celebritatem Divae Catherinae Senensis . . . agere cantibus atque rhythmis necnon musicis instrumentis ad laetitiam adhibitis."

58. Fecini, "Cronaca Senese," 857. A slightly different version of the report is in BCIS, MS A. IV. 2, fol. 186ʳ: "1446, A dì 5 di giugno si fe' in Siena la seconda volta la festa di Santa Catherina, 3 di pasqua su la piazza di S. Domenico, fu vi la Signoria a sedere su palchette che erono intorno intorno [*sic*] et fu stimato che vi fusse più di 20 mila persone a vederle."

square in front of the convent church of San Domenico (Catherine belonged to the
Dominican order). Seated on the platform were the Concistoro, other prominent
members of the government, and the organizers of the feast, all of them in costumes
representing "an emperor, a king, lords, doctors of law and of medicine, astrologers,
philosophers, poets, musicians, and learned men of all the sciences." A triumphal cart
carrying a noble Sienese youth and his sister, "dressed as a lord and a lady in the French
style," then entered the square. They were escorted by many youths of honorable family
marching in pairs, to the accompaniment of "trumpets, drums, wind instruments, harps,
lutes, viols, organs, psalteries, drums, and all [kinds of] music." This latter remark implies that many other musicians participated, besides those officially employed at the
Palace and at the cathedral. One chronicler, noting that "they marched to the sound of
sweet songs and in such an orderly way," remarked that never before had Siena witnessed "such a magnificent celebration."[59]

POPULAR FESTIVALS AND PRIVATE ENTERTAINMENTS

From late medieval times popular festivals and private celebrations also called for musicians. Numerous entertainments were customarily offered during Carnival, with dancing both in public squares and noble palaces.[60] On the day of the drunkards during
carnival of 1317, "el dì dello unbrighaiuolo," the traditional matches between squadrons
of boxers were held in the Campo. While many bruises were reported, no mention is
made of the trumpeters, who assuredly signaled the start of the event.[61] More decorous

---

59. Fecini, "Cronaca Senese," 857. There are also a number of prayers composed especially in
honor of St. Catherine. Among them are two hymns for Vespers and Lauds on her feast day in a
fifteenth-century manuscript at Karlsruhe, *Haec tuae virgo monumenta laudis* and *Jam ferox miles tibi saepe
cessit.* These were published by F. J. Mone, *Hymni Latini* (Freiburg im Breisgau, 1855), vol. 3, nos.
1012–13, pp. 379–80, who noted the decidedly humanistic character of the texts and speculated that
the accompanying music was probably composed in Italy. Mone also published a hymn to St. Catherine in Italian from 1749, *Vedi e mira Senese.* Two sequences in honor of Catherine were published in
Analecta Hymnica Medii Aevi, the first, *Christi regi iubilemus,* in vol. 39, ed. C. Blume (Leipzig, 1902),
no. 222, pp. 197–98; the second, *Gaude, mater ecclesia,* in vol. 40, ed. H. M. Bannister (Leipzig, 1902),
no. 20, pp. 231–32. A third sequence, by far the longest, *Lux advenit veneranda,* appears with music
on fols. 51ʳ–55ʳ of MS 4509 of the Biblioteca Casanatense, Rome, a volume copied for the Sienese
convent of Santo Spirito by Fra Pietro da Tramogiani in 1561. It is possible that one or more of these
were composed at the instance of Pope Pius II, who apparently knew some of the music composed
in Catherine's honor. In his autobiography he spoke of sojourning at the monastery of Monte Oliveto
in the summer or autumn of 1462 and of introducing "musicians who sang to them while they ate, a
new song about St. Catherine of Siena so sweetly that they brought tears of joy to all the monks";
Aeneas Sylvius Piccolomini, *I commentarii,* ed. Totaro, 2:1950 for the original Latin; English translation
in *Memoirs of a Renaissance Pope,* 294.
60. Carlo Falletti-Fossati, *Costumi senese nella seconda metà del secolo XIV* (Siena, 1882), 199.
61. "Cronaca Senese . . . di autore anonimo," 112 (12 February 1317); and Del Grasso, "Cronaca
Senese," 396 for another report. This celebrated Sienese pastime took place on the "Sunday of carnival," and a number of players, wearing some form of boxing gloves, formed two sides, each guided
by a captain, who to the sound of a trumpet advanced upon each other as they sought to gain control
of the piazza. A description of this bizarre entertainment is given by Falletti-Fossati, *Costumi senesi,*
199–200. A more recent account of the event and of the "gioco delle pugna" through the ages is
given by Catoni in "La faziosa armonia."

were the festivities given by Messer Sozzo di Bandinello Bandinelli when his son Francesco was knighted on 25 December 1326. One of the great Sienese social events
of the early fourteenth century, it was reported in some detail by the chroniclers.[62]
Tournaments, balls, and banquets were held on five successive days and the names of
the invited guests, noblemen and others, foreigners and Sienese, as well as what they
drank and ate—pheasant, roast capon, boiled veal, roasted eel, white ravioli, candied
pears—were carefully noted, as were the presents that Messer Francesco made to several
persons. Among these were gifts of gold florins to Martino, a singer, who also received
a tunic and a silk pennant.[63] Martino, mentioned in Palace registers of the time, was an
improviser who probably accompanied himself on the lute or a similar instrument as he
recounted tales of old and sang the praises of his hosts and the honored guests.[64] Other
musicians who were rewarded for their services included Cardarello, Triata, Besso da
Firenze, Foretano, and "several other trumpeters and other instrumentalists, who were
given a good deal of money."[65] Although particulars such as these are lacking about
another momentous event a few years later, when water was brought to the fountain
known as the Fonte Gaia in 1343, the chroniclers nevertheless report that a great public
celebration was held with "songs and dance."[66]

THE PALIO

By far the most important festivities in Siena were those held annually to mark the feast
of the Assumption on 15 August. The most famous event associated with these festivals,
the Palio, survives to our day, and has become such a symbol of Sienese culture and of
the city itself that the very word "Palio" evokes an almost instantaneous association
with Siena. The Palio—the name derives from the banner awarded to the victor of a
grueling horse race in which riders from all of Siena's "contrade," or wards, competed—was but one event, though perhaps the most eagerly awaited one, in a series of
civic, religious, and political ceremonies that unfolded throughout the two-day festival.
Colorful processions, which traversed the city on both days, high Mass at the cathedral,
sumptuous banquets, public feasting, and music everywhere—from the Palace to the
duomo and the surrounding squares and distant gates—were the order of the day. Siena,
of course, resembled many other Italian and European cities in staging these annual
festivities in which business and pleasure, the sacred and the secular, the religious and
the political, were so inextricably entwined. Florence had its St. John's Day and Lucca
its Holy Cross Day, to name but two other Tuscan cities that also held extravagant

---

A later chronicler reports that a "giuoco delle pugna" took place during carnival, on Sunday, 1
March 1494, in the presence of a visiting French cardinal. The chronicler notes that it was a "beautiful
game" and that in all, there were ten "schiere," or squadrons, of fighters, each squadron having two
trumpeters of its own. See Allegretti, "Ephemerides," 840.
62. Del Grasso, "Cronaca Senese," 446.
63. Ibid., 450: "una gonella e una bandiera di zendado."
64. Martino was one of several singer-heralds officially employed by the Concistoro. Though not
all of them have yet been traced, evidence regarding a number of them survives. See pp. 458–59.
65. Del Grasso, "Cronaca Senese," 451: "tronbatori e tronbette e altri stromenti più denari assai."
66. Ibid., 547.

celebrations. Nowhere, however, were the festivities so integral a part of the town's very being as in the ancient City of the Virgin, "Sena vetus, Civitas Virginis."[67]

The politically significant acts of the Assumption Day festivities took place at ceremonies in the cathedral, where Sienese citizens and representatives of subject cities of the Sienese dominion paid homage to the state and made symbolic gestures of fealty with offerings of candles to the Virgin Mary, Siena's advocate. The origins of the ceremony are very early, certainly before 1147, when the lords of Montepescali rendered homage in this fashion.[68] Regulations pertaining to the ceremonies, perhaps in force from as early as the turn of the thirteenth century, are documented from 1287 and 1337. These show that all Sienese citizens, whether resident within the walls or not, were obliged to visit the cathedral with their offerings on the evening before the feast. To ensure that everyone would be there—even those who were apparently out of favor with the ruling clique—safe conduct and security of person within the city were guaranteed for fifteen days before and fifteen days after the holiday. Siena's vassals made their offerings on the day of the feast. The cathedral overseer was required to set aside an appropriate place in the church where the candles were to be received. He was also to have the wax from three-quarters of the offerings fashioned into an appropriately decorated candle with leaves and flowers. This was then placed on the main altar, where it remained until the following year, when it was replaced by a new one.

The Palio on Assumption Day became an official civic festivity beginning in 1310.[69] Despite frequent changes of government, and eventually even the loss of Siena's independence, the Assumption Day Palio, with a few notable interruptions, has run every year since that time.[70] It was and continues to characterize the remarkable qualities of the Sienese, the intense loyalties they feel for their contradas, and the fierce factionalism so typical of their history and culture. Judith Hook has described the Palio as a kind of

---

67. For the Florentine festivities see Richard Trexler, *Public Life in Renaissance Florence* (Ithaca and London, 1980).

68. Cecchini's pioneering work, "Palio e Contrade nella loro evoluzione storica," has served as a springboard for my account of the musical groups that participated in the festivities. Originally published in 1958 in Cecchini and Neri, *Il Palio di Siena,* it was reprinted in 1982 in Falassi, Catoni, and Merisio, *Palio.* Reference here is to the later edition. Cecchini quotes a document from 1147 when the rulers of Montepescali offered two candles worth s. 5 to the cathedral, homage that was directed not only to the church but to the bishop and commune. He notes that it was surely not the first such offering.

69. Ibid., "Palio e Contrade," 134.

70. Cecchini notes that the plague rarely interrupted the August festivities and cites expenses from 1348, 1349, and through 1355 to prove his point. He also reports that the revolution that overthrew the government of the Nine on 23 March 1355 resulted in the loss of many state documents for that year. But documents from 1356 and 1357 show that the August festivities returned to normal and the musicians, who now numbered fifteen, were furnished clothing in those years (ibid., 29–30). Expenses for the festivities remained more or less the same through 1366, when a new revolution swept out the Twelve. Documents for that year have also disappeared. But the situation returned to normal within the next decade and expenses for the feast are listed throughout the 1370s. The feast of 1378 is particularly well documented in Biccherna, vol. 260. Festivities occurred also in 1385, when another revolution overthrew the government of the Fifteen and installed the new one of the Ten (ibid., 33–34).

state of mind, one that typifies the mystical qualities of the Sienese psyche, and remarks, perhaps rightly so, that to understand it is to understand Siena.[71] Certainly, this day gave the Sienese an opportunity to display their love of beauty, of color, and of spectacle, and to tell their friends and foes alike who they were, what they cared for, and how they thought one should go about enjoying the life of this world.

The trumpeters and later the wind band, as has already been remarked, are mentioned frequently in connection with the August holiday, when they traditionally received suits of clothing from the commune. One of the earliest reports about musicians participating in the festivities comes from 1253. That year s. 105 were spent for vermillion-colored cloth that was made into "berets for the trumpeters who accompanied the procession."[72] Four years later, in 1257, the commune's trumpeters, Guido Rosso and Riccio Pisano, each received s. 10 for having escorted the podestà and the captain of the people to the cathedral on the eve of Assumption Day.[73] After the Palio was established, the trumpeters' role in the festivities became more prominent. In August 1316 s. 12 were given to six musicians—trumpeters, shawm, and tabor players— for having performed when the Palio was run.[74] A decade later, in 1326, eight musicians, including players of the tabor, the nakers, the shawm, and five trumpeters, "all of them minstrels of the commune," received payment for playing on two occasions, when they accompanied the Palio banner to the bishop's residence and when they accompanied the Palio banner throughout the city in the evening.[75]

Festival expenses from 1343 included payments for repairing a broken trumpet and for hiring a horse for Gianetto the shawm player, "when he played at the feast."[76] The trumpeters' customary performances in the Campo for fifteen days before the Assumption festival are mentioned as early as 1344.[77] Documents from two hundred years later show that by then the trumpeters and the wind band performed in front of the cathedral and in the Campo and that they received a gratuity for their services.[78] From 1395 comes a report that the trumpeters escorted the Palio banner throughout the city and played fanfares to announce the feast, after which they accompanied it to the Palace.[79] Another record from 1405 says that the Palio banner was displayed on a cart as it was

---

71. For an objective view of the Palio through the ages, see her *Siena: A City and its History*; Italian trans., *Siena: Una città e la sua storia,* 171–91.

72. Cecchini, "Palio e contrade," 16–17.

73. The payment from 1257 is in *Libri dell'entrata e dell'uscita della Repubblica di Siena, Diciottesimo libro a 1257.*

74. Cecchini, "Palio e contrade," 137.

75. Ibid., 143.

76. Ibid., 29.

77. "pro expensis factis . . . tibatoribus [*sic*] in vino, quando trombaverunt circa campum XV diebus ante festum, XIII libr. XV sold." (ASS, Biccherna, vol. 215, fol. 119ᵣ).

78. For example, ASS, Biccherna, vol. 365, fol. 18ʳ, dated 26 August 1543: "Li piffari e trombetti del mangnifico Comune di Siena . . . per riconoscimento di lor faticha de' 15 giorni andati atorno a sonare com'è solito . . . e non solo a sonare atorno a la piaza ma a la chiesa chatedrale, L. XXXII."

79. Cecchini, "Palio e contrade," 37. Cecchini believes this is an indication that processions on the evening before as well as on the feast day itself began at the Palace and that the Palio banner was featured prominently in them.

escorted throughout the city. The cart was evidently a forerunner of the later "Carro degli Angeli." This latter had a mechanical device that raised and lowered several youths, dressed as angels, who gave the illusion of flying around an image of the Madonna.[80] An earlier report from 29 August 1397 shows that the winner of the Palio had to give tips to various people connected with the race, among them the trumpeters.[81]

From very early times the festivities drew an extraordinarily large number of out-of-town musicians to Siena. There is no firm evidence to show when the practice began. It is not mentioned, for example, in a document of 1386, which speaks of four deputies appointed by the Concistoro to oversee the progress of the festivities.[82] Payments to foreign musicians who participated in the festivities, however, begin shortly afterwards. Two trumpeters of the Lord of Cortona received L. 26. 13 on 29 August 1395 for "having solemnly honored the feast of Our Lady."[83] Gratuities were given to trumpeters from Florence for the same reason in 1404.[84] In 1398 banquets were held in the Palace on the evening before the feast as well as on the feast day, and in 1403 Pandolfo Malatesta, Lord of Pesaro, attended one of these banquets.[85] His trumpeters received a gratuity for playing that day. "Many people came to Siena and did great honor to the holiday," says one of the chroniclers about the festivities of August 1423.[86] By 1430, when an unusually large number of visiting musicians was in attendance, neighboring and even faraway states were routinely sending musical and diplomatic emissaries to Siena as a sign of respect on this grandest of all its holidays.

The record of expenses for the 1430 festival merits attention because it is the earliest extant to give particulars about visiting musicians and the gratuities they received.[87] Among those cited are the following, the amounts they received carefully recorded in the column to the right of their names by the official record keeper:

2 trumpeters and 2 pifferi of the Magnificent Lords of Florence	L. 60. 4. 6
1 viuola player of the Magnificent Lords of Florence	L. 5. 10. 0
1 trumpet and 1 piffero of the Merchants' Guild of Florence	L. 8. 16. 0
4 trumpets of the Guelph Party of Florence	L. 22. 0. 0
2 trumpets of the community of Pistoia	L. 8. 16. 0
1 trumpet of the vicar of San Miniato	L. 3. 6. 0
1 trumpet of the vicar of Lari	L. 3. 6. 0
2 trumpets of the podestà of Siena	L. 4. 8. 0
1 trumpet of the condottiere Sangelino [in Sienese service]	L. 2. 4. 0
1 trumpet of the former podestà of Siena	L. 2. 4. 0
The total sum given to trumpeters, pifferi, and minstrels:	L. 133. 4. 10

80. Ibid., 41.
81. Ibid., 37.
82. Ibid., 36.
83. Ibid., 37.
84. Ibid., 41.
85. Ibid., 38–39.
86. Montauri, "Cronaca senese," 799.
87. This document, in ASS, Biccherna, vol. 310, fol. 48ᵛ, is on display in the Archivio di Stato, Siena.

A glance at the origins of the nineteen musicians attests to opportunities available for exchanging repertories and performance practices. Musical cross-currents of this sort were, of course, known before the fifteenth century, but henceforth they became even more frequent. On this occasion only four of the musicians—apart from the Palace trumpeters and wind band who participated in the festivities—were Sienese. Eleven of them, the majority, were from Florence, employed by the government and by important political and financial institutions, and four others were from Pistoia, San Miniato, and Lari, all within the Florentine dominion. Since Siena and Florence were allied at the time, the presence of a large contingent of musicians from Siena's powerful neighbor reflects then current political realities. But it is also symptomatic of the frequent cultural exchanges that occurred between the two cities. Reciprocal influences involving art, literature, and politics are a matter of record, but in the case of music, where few or no artifacts remain attesting to similar exchanges, these have been less well documented. One recurrent theme in the history of musical events at the Palio, as will become apparent, was the presence of Florentine instrumentalists, who brought with them current practices and repertories from one of Italy's most cosmopolitan and musically advanced cities. Florentines constantly influenced fifteenth-century Sienese musical life, even in later decades, when northern musicians dominated musical life at the cathedral. This, in fact, is one of the most significant findings to emerge from an examination of musicians at the Palio, for it shows that throughout the fifteenth century, with more frequent performances of polyphonic instrumental music, Siena's instrumentalists also could hear and witness the accomplishments of their colleagues from any number of places in Italy, but above all from Florence.

The festivities in 1430 initiated a series of spectacular gatherings of musicians who came from near and far to help the Sienese celebrate their holiday. In the following decades the number of visiting musicians increased steadily, as did the types of instruments and the kinds of music they played, and successive festival organizers clearly spared neither money nor effort to enhance the splendor of the occasion. Thirty-four musicians and entertainers were present in 1449.[88] Florence, with six trumpeters, a trombonist, a herald, and "one who recited many verses," was again represented by a large contingent, as were two of its subject cities, Pistoia, with six trumpeters, and San Giovanni Valdarno, with two. But Perugia, Viterbo, and Massa also sent representatives, as did the Sienese podestà and captain of the people, each furnishing two. Among the wind instrument players was one "who played several times inside the Palace." Two of the Palace's own employees contributed to the entertainment. Fewer numbers are mentioned in the following year, but notable among the foreigners were four trumpeters and a trombonist from Lucca.[89] Again recorded that year were the actor or mime

---

88. "Solutio piffaris et tubicenis . . . camerarius Bicherne solvat infrascriptis tubicenis et giollaribus infrascriptas quantitates, quas eisdem dari voluerunt quia venerunt ad honorandum festivitatem Sancte Marie . . . quidam qui dixit plures rimas, Florentinus, grossi 20 . . . Antonius Urbani Senensis, grossi 36; unus piffarus qui pluries sonavit in palatio, grossi 20; magister Antonius scapuccinus, grossi 100" (ASS, Concistoro 501, fols. 29ᵛ–30ʳ, dated 16 August 1449).

89. "camerarius Bicherne solvat infrascriptis piffaris, tubatoribus et aliis . . . festum S. Marie augusti . . . quatuor trombetti Comunis Luche, grossi 160; uni tromboni qui venit ex Luche, grossi 20

Maestro Antonio Urbano, the Palace "cantarino" Antonio, and also Maestro Pietro Lantera (known as Rintere), a lutenist who was employed as a nakers player at the Palace. Lantera, though officially on the Palace roster as a percussionist, probably entertained the priors more often with his lute playing than is indicated by ordinary payments, his other duties only surfacing occasionally, as in this record.[90] Antonio, or Antonio da Fabriano, officially employed as the Palace herald and singer for many years, must have accompanied himself on the lute or a similar stringed instrument.[91] Given the presence of two such musicians on the Palace payroll, it seems reasonable to suppose that they would also have performed together throughout the year on other occasions.

1456 was a banner year, with eighty outside musicians present. The record of the huge amount spent on them—a total of 1557 grossi or L. 399. 3. 6—again includes all of their names and shows the diversity of entertainment offered on that occasion. Florence, as usual, furnished the lion's share of musicians. Representing the Florentine government were four trumpeters, a shawmist, four pifferi, and a trombone. In addition, there were four of the Merchants' Guild's trumpeters, four of the Guelph Party's, and seven singers of San Giovanni, that is, the singers of the Florentine chapel. Musicians from Lucca, Piombino, Pistoia, Città di Castello, Colle, Montepulciano, Arezzo, San Gimignano, Perugia, and Rome also came, as did several others in the employ of prominent individuals. Antonio Urbano, the mime, was again present, and for more intimate entertainment, presumably indoors, there were a number of instrumentalists, including a tabor player from the Paduan region "who played the citole," two German lutenists, and a Perugian violist.[92] Similar numbers of visitors appeared in the following year when 1158 grossi were spent on trumpeters from many of these same cities and others such as Pisa and Todi, and on five Florentine singers, a blind lutenist, the mime Antonio, a herald of the king of Hungary, a singer called Guasparre (who was a barber from Siena), and the drummer-lutenist Maestro Piero Rintere, who furnished strings for the lute (see Doc. 14.1).

In 1460 more than ninety visiting performers came to the festival. Eleven of the sixty-three trumpeters, a drummer, three players of wind instruments, and a trombonist made up the Florentine contingent, still the largest group of any of the cities represented. These included Milan, whose duke sent two trumpeters; the Spanish ambassador, who sent two tabor players with whistle flutes; Lucca, which with ten performers was quite prominent; Urbino, whose duke sent three trumpeters; Pistoia, Perugia, Cortona, Arezzo, Montepulciano, and a host of smaller Florentine and Sienese cities. Pope Pius II's nephew sent one of his trumpeters and several of the Pope's own attendents also came. Among the visitors were a blind lutenist and four youths, with their father, who are described as players, dancers, fencers, and singers. A tabor player and two

---

... Antonio Verbani, actitatori, grossi 36; magistro Antonio, cantarino palatii, grossi 80; magistro Petro Lantere, pro leuto, grossi 20" (Concistoro, vol. 506, fol. 32^r, dated 16 August 1450).

90. An earlier record, from before he held an official position at the Palace, also refers to Piero as a lutenist; see chapter 9.

91. See p. 458.

92. ASS, Concistoro, vol. 539, fol. 89^r, published by Cellesi, *Storia della più antica banda musicale senese*, 70.

jugglers, one "de le bagatelle," must have entertained the crowds outside the Palace as well as the honored guests within (see Doc. 14.2).

Many musicians flocked to the August Palio throughout the 1460s, making this one of the most notable decades in the history of the festival. From the celebration in 1462 come reports of performances by an unnamed prelate's bagpiper, a blind lutenist called Angelo di Marciano, a singer called Moro, a *tamburino* called Piero delle Donne, a rebec player, a drummer, and two fencers. There were, additionally, trumpeters from Florence, Lucca, Rome, Ferrara, and Cortona (see Doc. 14.3). In 1463 trumpeters from Florence, Milan, Pistoia, Arezzo, Cortona, and the Florentine wind band participated in festivities. These also featured performances by "a boy who danced with the lute before the lords," "a buffoon who did many things," and "two lute players of the Duke of Bavaria"—perhaps the same German lutenists mentioned several years earlier (see Doc. 14.4). An impressive number of musicians and entertainers also assembled for Assumption Day in 1468. In all there were sixty-five trumpeters, whose expenses came to 1134 grossi of the 1516 total spent on the entire group of participants. Among the other musicians were two groups of Florentine pifferi, a duo of two lutenists, an ensemble of three singers, a singer who improvised, an acrobat, three mimes, and an ensemble consisting of lute, rebec, and flute (see Doc. 14.5). Presumably, groups such as the latter, who played "soft" music, performed indoors for the pleasure of the priors and their guests, if not outdoors for the crowd's delectation.

The visiting trumpeters at these magnificent spectacles may claim our interest for a moment, allowing several observations about the musicians assembled. The first observation concerns the kind of music they must have performed. If, at ringside, after the usual procession had taken place, they all played at once, we can only marvel at such a grand sound. Probably nothing more than the simplest of fanfares or, as seems more likely, a succession of blares and blasts, was heard—the kinds of sounds, in other words, typical of the hubbub surrounding outdoor events and spectacles such as a Palio to this day. On the other hand, if they played in smaller groups or in reasonable variations of their normal numbers, some form of polyphonic music, undoubtedly improvised, was likely heard by the assembled crowds, for whom they also played impromptu dance music, as did visiting wind players. As for their participation in the processions that usually preceded the spectacles, various contingents probably each played their own fanfares as they marched, in much the same way different bands marching in a parade do today.

The political implications of the presence of these out-of-town musicians at the Assumption Day festivities also claims attention. Clearly, musicians were permitted to go Siena, or were even sent there, by their employers—cities, guilds, private individuals—because their presence would be construed as a sign of friendship and respect toward the Sienese republic. It was a goodwill gesture reciprocated by the Sienese, for the Palace musicians, as noted above, were paid their normal salaries whenever they traveled abroad with government permission for similar purposes. Such visits obviously occurred only when the governments concerned were not at war or in a state of incipient hostility. Perhaps this explains why Florentine musicians are mentioned only in certain years, although the recurrence of the plague and other factors may also have prevented their coming. In any case, political considerations surely motivated these

visits of foreign trumpeters and woodwind players, as they did those of the visits of
Neapolitan singers in 1451, of Florentine singers in 1456, 1480, and 1484 and of the
Sienese chapel to Florence in 1481. Not limited to official civic or religious festivals,
such exchanges also occurred at private celebrations, as for example, when the Sienese
wind band played at the wedding festivities on 2 May 1456 of Pierfrancesco de' Medici,
nephew of the all-powerful head of state, Cosimo de' Medici.[93]

Also noteworthy is the Sienese government's active role in encouraging the presence of foreign musicians. The Concistoro determined how much could be spent on
these annual displays of Sienese wealth and sovereignty, and it was keenly aware of the
importance attached to such festivities by the public. From among the many extant
documents attesting to their powers of decision making is one advising "the Magnificent Lords who will be in office during July and August 1443" about their duties. It
states that "for the feast of Saint Mary of August you may spend as much as you think
is reasonable on the minstrels, pifferi, and trumpeters, and pay them cash in hand."[94]

The 1470s witnessed equally grand spectacles[95] as well as numerous celebrations
when the Palio alone was run, without benefit of hordes of visiting musicians. By this
time, however, the fame of Siena's annual celebrations was such that when word went
out that they would be held, musicians from throughout the peninsula flocked to the
city. In 1473 over seventy trumpeters sent by Florence, Pistoia, Cortona, by the duke
of Ferrara, the marquis of Mantua, the duke of Milan, and the governor of Genoa—to
name but a few of the cities and private individuals they represented—participated, as
did a woodwind player from Viterbo, a pipe and tabor player from Pitigliano, a lutenist
named Giovanni, a duo composed of an unnamed lutenist and a boy who sang, two
actors, a blind improviser called Francesco Cieco, and two trios. The first trio comprised a harpist (Maestro Giovanni da Mantua), a lutenist, and a boy who sang. The
second trio, somewhat similar in makeup, included another harpist (Maestro Benedetto), a lutenist (Maestro Francesco), and an unspecified instrumentalist (Maestro Giovanni), all of whom also danced.[96] Festivities were curtailed in 1474 because of military
incursions into Sienese territory.

Political matters improved in 1475, with the result that the number of participants
was as impressive as ever. In addition to seventy-four trumpeters from Florence, Ferrara,
Mantua, Rimini, Urbino, Lucca, Arezzo, Burgundy, and a host of lesser towns and
lordships, there were a number of smaller ensembles, including a group of three wood-

93. See chapter 11, note 127.

94. "Nota ad voi, Magnifici Signori, che dovete resedere di luglio e agosto 1443, di quello havete
ad fare al vostro tenpo . . . Nella festa di S. Maria d'agosto . . . pe' giollari, pifari e trombetti potete
spendare quanto ve pare ragionevole, facendosene pagamento in loro proprie mani" (Concistoro, vol.
2263, unnumbered folio). Virtually the same wording is found in notes for 1444 and 1445.

95. ASS, Biccherna, vol. 329, fol. 252^r, for 1471 shows expenses of L. 570. 13. 5 spent on visiting
"trombetti, piffari, sonatori di leiuti, cantori e giolari che venero a onorare la festa di Santa Maria
d'Aghosto," but gives few other particulars. Considering the expense, this must have been a banner
year.

96. Concistoro 641, fols. 59^v–60^r, dated 19 August 1473. The following discussion is based on
the documents given in Cecchini, "Palio e contrade," 322–31.

wind players and a trombonist from Lucca, a hitherto unmentioned singer-improviser named Maestro Lorenzo Cantarino, a duo consisting of "a harpist and a player of Lorenzo de' Medici," another duo that included the unlikely combination of a lutenist and a bagpiper, and a number of soloists, among whom were a lutenist named Maestro Jacomo da Bologna, another lutenist called Giovanni Tedesco, a rebec player, and a pipe and tabor player. Further entertainment was provided by Maestro Benedetto and Franceschino, the dancers and players cited in 1473. Three actors, two of them Florentine, the other in the service of the duke of Burgundy, and two groups of singers completed the list (see Doc. 14.6). The first group of singers, led by the French musician Ser Giovanni Michele, included three youths, all employed by the duke of Urbino; the other comprised Francesco Mire, Antonio called il Torre, and an unspecified number of their companions. Antonio, who was probably Sienese, performed at the festival in later years.

Festivities were again curtailed in 1476, when Siena's dominion was being ravaged both by the invading forces of Count Nicola Orsini and by plague. Although the Palio was run, the modest sums expended on the race and the banquet and the lack of payments to foreign contingents of musicians provided quite a contrast to the previous year. A silver statue was presented to St. Sebastian on 21 July, however, amid pleas for deliverance from the plague. The continuing horrors of the war again accounted for the curtailment of public rejoicing during the next four years, and it was not until 1480, when peace finally came, that the Palio and a joust were given. Although payments to trumpeters and other instrumentalists seem to be lacking, one surviving record shows that 3 ducats were paid to Farinello and Antonio Pollono, singers, "for songs composed on the feast of August," and that a new suit of clothing was authorized for the Palace improviser (called here only by his nickname, Cantarino), "because he sang several times during the festival."[97] Farinello, as noted above, was a singer of polyphony intermittently employed in the cathedral chapel between 1482 and 1485. Presumably, he and his colleague composed (and performed) polyphonic songs.

The early 1480s reflect the desire to keep celebrations as lavish as possible, the uncertainties of Sienese political life, and the return of the dreaded plague. A grand celebration, for which 500 florins were appropriated, was ordered for 1481, but despite this attempt at courting popular goodwill, the government was overthrown only fifteen

97. Cecchini, 325, reports the payment but implies that the three singers performed together. Among the musicians mentioned were a Palace singer and improviser called Cantarino, who "had sung several times during the festivities," and Farinello and Antonio Pollono, singers, who "composed songs for the feast," music which they themselves apparently performed with others: "Die XXV Augusti [1480]. Magnifici domini . . . deliberaverunt quod camerarius Biccherne solvat Cantarino valorem brachiorum septem panni viridis et celestis, ut possit facere vestem que ei donatur, quoniam in festo pluries cantavit. Et deliberaverunt per camerarium Biccherne solvi ducatos tres Farinello et Antonio Pollono, cantoribus, quos eis donari decreverunt pro cantis factis hoc festo Augustis" (Concistoro, vol. 683, fol. 20ᵛ). Festival payments to these same musicians in later years show that at least three singers were in the ensemble. The Palace singer called Cantarino was apparently Maestro Lorenzo, cited in Palio records for the previous year and later in 1482, these furnishing good reason to believe that he was officially employed throughout these years.

days after the festivities.[98] While the musical forces employed in 1482 were not as impressive as those of a few years earlier—as reflected by the L. 244 s. 16 spent on them—records show that there were the same kinds of activities as reported at past celebrations.[99] In all twenty-seven trumpeters came from various cities, including Lucca, Florence, Cortona, and Arezzo, as did two wind players from the Sienese town of Sovana and a player of the ciaramella from Castel della Pieve. In addition, there were two actors, the harpist-dancers Maestro Benedetto and his companion, a lutenist named Antonio, a pipe and tabor player in the service of Stefanino Doria, and three singers, Antonio Torre, Farinello, and Petruzo, two of whom were mentioned previously.

The Palio was also run in 1483, but fear of plague caused suspension of the joust and in its stead the keys of the city were offered to the Virgin at the altar of the Madonna delle Grazie. Nevertheless, "many trumpeters, woodwind players, heralds, actors, and instrumentalists came to honor the feast," and upwards of 410 lire were spent on them.[100] Expenses were allocated by the new government for the 1484 festival, but detailed lists of participants are again not extant. Some idea of the foreign musicians, however, comes from an entry in a cathedral register, dated 30 August 1484. This notes that on Assumption Day just past, by decree of the Balìa, "48 lire, in the form of 8 gold ducats in cash, were paid to eight singers of the Signoria of Florence, who sang in the duomo for the said feast."[101] These musicians probably gave the first performance of *Sena vetus,* the ceremonial motet honoring Siena composed by the Florentine singer Arnolfo Giliardi, who was himself present (see pp. 243–46). Even more was spent in 1485, the cost alone of the visiting musicians, including "trumpeters, woodwind players, heralds, actors, pipe and tabor players, lutenists, and other minstrels" amounting to over 602 lire.[102]

Cecchini reports that in 1486 a great deal was allocated for the celebration because Siena was to play host to an honored guest, Lorenzo de' Medici, who would be en

---

98. Biccherna, 335, fol. 67[v], lists expenses of L. 1066 s. 1. A detailed list of the participants has not survived.

99. Concistoro, vol. 695, fols. 15[v]–16[r]. The twenty-seven trumpeters recorded in this year included official and unofficial delegations from Lucca, Cortona, Arezzo, San Gimignano, Borgo San Sepolcro, Pitigliano, Colle, Castiglione Aretino, the Mercantia and the podestà of Florence, Sovana, Castel della Pieve, Montepulciano, and a few who were employed by private persons. Other musicians named were Maestro Lorenzo Cantarino, an unnamed Paduan in the service of the Commune of Arezzo, and Meio, nacharino di Palazzo. The three singers, Antonio Torre, Farinello, and Petruzo, who were paid L. 36, may possibly be part of the same group for whom in 1475 a payment of L. 8 was made to "Francesco Mire e Antonio detto el Torre e compagni cantori."

100. "più tronbetti, piffari, araldi, attegiatori di persona e sonatori vennero a onorare la festa di S. Maria d'aghosto . . . se li donoro per venire a onorare la detta festa . . . L. CCCCX s. XIII" (Biccherna, vol. 338, fol. 160[r], dated 29 August 1483).

101. AOMS, vol. 454, *Entrata & Uscita, 1484–85,* fol. 37[v].

102. Cecchini, "Palio e contrade," 325; Biccherna, vol. 339, fol. 162[v], dated 4 November 1485: "Tronbetti, piffari, araldi, g[i]ochatori di persona, tanburini, cimamella [*sic*], sonatori di liuti, et altri buffoni, che vennero a honorare la festa d'aghosto . . . per tanti se lo' dona per essere venuti a honorare la festa di S. Maria di mezo aghosto . . . . L. DCII s. XVIII."

route to the thermal baths at Petriolo. The festival was planned on a grander scale than usual, and the cart that was to bear the Palio was even redecorated for this occasion. But the plague struck, discouraging all visitors, and instead of the Palio there were fireworks and a service at the cathedral, where an offering made to the Virgin also supplicated her intercession for deliverance "from the pest, from war, from our insidious enemies and from every harm."[103] Although Pandolfo Petrucci and his confederates had been in power less than a month at the time of the 1487 festival, the newly installed regime still provided fireworks and a bullfight, in addition to the usual Palio. Visiting musicians, who included "other instrumentalists" as well as the same array mentioned in 1485, were paid a total of 501 lire, indicating that the forces on hand were only somewhat smaller than previously.[104]

The remainder of the 1480s and 1490s reveal similar patterns of celebration or suspension of festivities because of political reasons, plague, and the uncertainty of the times brought about by the French invasion. Celebrations were held in 1488 and in 1489, but detailed lists of those participating are not extant. Because Assumption Day fell on a Sunday in 1490, the festival was postponed for a week, perhaps also because the government feared an uprising on the part of Florentine-supported rebels, but it did not happen. Though celebrations were delayed, they were no less elaborate.[105] Specific names are again lacking, but a large number of visiting musicians obviously attended, since L. 686. 4 were spent for "many trumpeters, pifferi, heralds, actors, buffoons, and other foreign players, who came to honor the feast of Saint Mary of August just past."[106] Equally elaborate festivities, including a particularly lavish banquet, occurred in 1491. But the number of musicians attending dropped and was perhaps not as varied as in past years, for the report of their presence says only that L. 474. 19 were spent "for many trumpeters of many lordships who came to honor the feast of St. Mary

---

103. Cecchini, "Palio e contrade," 325. The following passage sums up the situation: "Et ad laudem et reverentiam gloriosissime Virginis Marie ut dignetur intercedere apud Deum . . . pro salute huius alme civitatis . . . et ut defendat et liberet nos a peste, a bello, ab insidiis inimicorum nostrorum et ab omni malo, dederunt et donaverunt ipsi gloriosissime Virgini Marie et domine nostre, pallium ordinatum pro hac festivitate eius proxime futura, et pro hoc anno non aliter currant cursores pro eo" (ASS, Balìa, vol. 34, fol. 97ʳ, dated 11 August 1486). Some idea of the impact of the plague on the city's life is furnished by Pecci, *Memorie storico-critiche della città di Siena,* 1:37, who, quoting Allegretti's diary, notes that the plague began in June that year and that many people left town and that special provision had to be made to bring in troops from the countryside to guard the city.

104. Cecchini, "Palio e contrade," 325, citing Biccherna, vol. 340, fol. 164ᵛ, dated 15 November 1487: "tro[m]betti, pifary, araldi, giochatory di persona, tanburiny, ciammelle [*sic*], sonatori di liuti e altri stormeti, e altri bufoni, che venero a onorare la festa di S. Maria d'aghosto . . . per tanti se lo' donò . . . L. DI."

105. Expenses are listed in Biccherna, vol. 344, fol. 118ᵛ. Also listed for that year are the expenses for the Palio on St. Mary Magdalene's Day, 22 July, which Petrucci and his associates had recently instituted to commemorate their victory in 1487.

106. "A più tronbetti, piffari, araldi, attegiatori, buffoni e altri sonatori forestieri, li quali ven[n]ero a onorare la festa di S. Maria d'agosto prossima passata, adì XXXI d'agosto, lire secento ottantasei s. quatro, paghamo per diliberazione di Choncistoro . . . . L. DCLXXXVI s. IIII" (Biccherna, vol. 344, fol. 117ᵛ).

of August."[107] The festivals of 1492 and 1493 were also held in the usual manner, and for the Palio in 1493 horses were entered by both Cesare Borgia and the marquis of Mantua, whose horse won. Only summary expenses are cited for both years, with no detailed lists of participating musicians, who in 1493 might have included some of those in the entourages of illustrious guests.[108]

There was no Palio in 1494, perhaps because of the plague, which again struck Siena. An offering, however, was made at the altar of the Virgin. This was also the case in 1495. Apparently, the festivals were suspended altogether in 1496 and 1497, since records of authorization to run the races are lacking, as are reports of expenses. A similar situation likely occurred in 1498. Lists of expenses from 1499 are extant but make no mention of the Palio. It was, in fact, only in 1500 that the more elaborate activities of the past resumed, and in that year a banquet, processions, and a bullfight were given in addition to the Palio. Among the musicians named are nineteen trumpeters representing the pope, the cities of Lucca, Urbino, and Piombino, among other places, and thirty-six other musicians, identified as "sonatores" or woodwind players, from Piombino, Bologna, Viterbo, Arezzo, and several other towns. The woodwind players are listed in groups of two and three, the exceptions being the nine who represented the Guelph Party of Florence and a single one from Volterra. Also mentioned are an otherwise unidentified performer called Padovano, two pipe and tabor players, a harpist, and a dancer and his three sons.[109]

Apart from a few years when political disturbances and unrest forced their cancellation, the Assumption Day festivities and the Palio continued throughout the first half of the sixteenth century. Festivities are recorded in 1512, several months after the death of Pandolfo Petrucci, and in the years immediately following. In 1528 a Palio, replacing the one previously run on St. Mary Magdalene's day that had been suppressed after the fall of the Petrucci regime, was held on 25 July, the feast of St. James and St. Christopher. This Palio was subsequently shifted to 2 July, the titular feast of the church of Santa Maria di Provenzano.[110] The August festivities, however, retained their primacy. A record from 6 August 1533 shows that money was allocated to pay the expenses of the foreign trumpeters who would come to Siena for the feast of Saint Mary, that is,

---

107. "più trombetti di più singniorie, che ven[n]ero a onorare la festa di S. Maria d'aghosto, il dì, lire quattrocientosettantaquatro s. dicienove, paghamo per olizia di Balìa . . . L. CCCCLXXIIII s. XVIIII" (Biccherna, vol. 345, fol. 138ᵛ).

108. Ibid.; Biccherna, vol. 346, fol. 147ʳ reports that in 1492 L. 550. 11 were spent for the visiting musicians; visiting musicians are not mentioned in 1493.

109. Concistoro, vol. 804, fol. 3ᵛ.

110. Santa Maria di Provenzano is perhaps the jewel of Baroque architecture in Siena. It was constructed after 1595 to commemorate the miraculous cures attributed to prayers addressed to a bust of the Virgin Mary displayed on the exterior wall of a house in Provenzano, then one of Siena's red light districts. See Colleen Reardon, "Music and Musicians at Santa Maria di Provenzano, Siena, 1595–1640," *Journal of Musicology* 11 (1993): 106–32, for an account of music in the first half century of the church's existence and for remarks about the significance of the Madonna di Provenzano in Sienese culture. As Reardon notes, Sienese devotion to the Madonna di Provenzano was amply demonstrated when, in the mid-seventeenth century, the town began celebrating the feast with an annual Palio.

Assumption Day.[111] Emperor Charles V and the Genoese ambassadors attended the 1529 celebrations, and the emperor was present again in 1536. Both were sumptuously celebrated, notwithstanding the troubled financial times. Though not so numerous as previously, in 1540 the visiting musicians included at least thirty-five trumpeters, from Florence, Lucca, Bologna, Pistoia, Volterra, Pisa, and other places, as well as two student players (see Doc. 14.7). The Palio was held even throughout the difficult years of the early 1550s, but in 1555, the year of the siege and the fall of Siena, only an offering at the altar of the Madonna was made.[112]

Statutes from 1544 recount the antiquity of the races held on the feasts of the Blessed Ambrogio Sansedoni, of SS. James and Christopher, and on Assumption Day and state that on the eve of this latter, after Vespers, a procession consisting of the Concistoro and other high government officials, marching in order according to rank, and preceded by the trumpeters, was to go to the cathedral to make their offerings of candles and other tributes. Afterwards, offerings were to be made by all Sienese citizens over fifteen years of age.[113] Following Siena's defeat, this aspect of the festivities disappeared. Cosimo de' Medici was lord of the city and acts of political fealty were now directed to the grand duke in Florence on St. John's Day, 24 June. Religious ceremonies honoring the Assumption continued, of course, as did, after a while, the Palio, and from that time onwards the festival became the kind of popular celebration that it has remained to this day.[114]

The Palio of 1546

One of the most celebrated Palios of the sixteenth century was held in 1546. This featured bullfights rather than the familiar horse race. The memory of it and the civic pride felt in its realization were still so vivid some forty years later that an eyewitness account of it by a Sienese bookdealer, Cecchino Libraio, was printed in Siena in 1582, long after Siena's freedom had become a fondly cherished memory.[115] Cecchino's text, dated 20 August 1546, shows that this particular festival was considered exceptional even in its own time, for he remarks that "all of the old people of our city were of the unanimous opinon" that "never before had there been a more beautiful or more orderly feast." He adds that he wrote about it so that it could be "seen in the mind's eye of those who were not present." And this he accomplished with his vivid description of

---

111. "tubicinis forensibus qui veniunt in civitatem in festo S. Marie augusti proximo, quicquid solitum est eis dari annuatim, de denariis Pascuorum" (Balìa, vol. 108, fol. 208ᵛ).

112. The Palio was resumed in 1559 and then held sporadically in the following decades through the new century. Foreign players are mentioned in 1562, 1563, and on a few later occasions, though specific information about them is lacking in surviving accounts. It is possible that Florentines were once again among the instrumentalists welcomed to the city, but little information is given regarding the nationalities of the visitors. Cecchini lists the few sources regarding the festivals in this time, among them Balìa, vol. 174, fols. 51, 80, 83, 142, 144, 145 (p. 78).

113. Cecchini, "Palio e contrade," 69.

114. Ibid., 73.

115. La Magnifica et honorata festa fatta in Siena, per la Madonna d'Agosto, l'anno 1546. Con l'ordine delle livree, & altri giuochi fatti in essa (Siena: Alla Loggia del Papa, 1582). A copy of the work in manuscript is on fols. 29ʳ–43ʳ of BCIS, MS A. VI. 4.

the events, which allows us to imagine, just as he hoped, the excitement and splendor of the festivities and of the time-honored rituals that accompanied them. Though he has little to say about the musicians who participated in the various events or about the kinds of music they performed, the important place music had throughout the festival is implicit all through his account.

Cecchino explains that according to custom, the Concistoro invited the cities and towns in the Sienese dominion to send their representatives to the banquet held in the great Sala del Consiglio of the Palace on the evening before the holiday.[116] For the occasion the room was beautifully decorated with tapestries and the dining tables set with the commune's silver. Cecchino first tells how various officials and representatives were seated at dinner according to protocol and then recounts the prescribed order of the after-dinner ceremonies. Though he does not say so, the wind band performed during the meal, as they did every day when the Concistoro was at table. In addition, as at past festivals, singers, dancers, and other musicians, brought in especially for the occasion, entertained the assembled guests. At about the 20th hour the priors went out into the Campo, just as the processional train that was to march to the cathedral was being formed. Meanwhile, several leaders and their squadrons, in full armour, took turns around the square "to the very honored roar of the harquebusiers, the drums, and the trumpets." As the procession began, the men at arms took their places as the Concistoro's vanguard. Immediately behind them came several artfully decorated carts, one of which held a huge wax candle, ornamented with gold and other colors. This was the candle presented to the cathedral in the name of the Sienese government and people. An "infinity of banners, each representing its own contrada," vied with the sumptuously dressed marchers who accompanied the carts. Behind them came "a multitude of trumpets from the Palace and from other cities" and "pifferi and other musicians, who because of the variety of their instruments made such a marvelous noise that no other sound could be heard." The great standard of Our Lady appeared next, with the members of the government and the *festaioli,* the organizers of the feast, following, all wearing garlands of flowers and herbs, "a thing that was as pleasing to see as it was to smell."

Arriving at the cathedral, the Concistoro and their attendants proceeded to the altar where they presented the state candle. Afterwards, representatives of Siena's countryside and vassal cities made their offerings. This ceremony completed, the Concistoro returned to the Palace in state and no sooner had they entered its precincts than the trumpets and drums sounded the fanfares signaling that it was time for citizens, "old and young, rich and poor," from all forty-eight of the city's parishes to go to the cathedral to make their offerings. The crowded streets made it barely possible to walk, and everyone marveled that "so many foreigners" had come to town for the holiday.

For the next day's festivities a large wooden enclosure was set up in the Campo near

---

116. A deliberation from 20 July 1546 shows that on that day the Concistoro decided to honor the feast with "pugnam ut aiunt vulgo la caccia del toro, nec non prandium magnum omnibus comunitatibus dominii more soliti," and allocated L. 600 denariorum for the purpose (Balìa, vol. 131, fol. 37ᵛ). On 2 August 1546 this sum was provided by the Biccherna (fol. 57ᵛ); materials for fireworks are mentioned in a report from the following 7 August 1546 (fol. 68ᵛ): "Dominis festivitatis Beate Marie augusti dari iusserant libra 60 pulvis crasse et libra 5 subtilis, pro gaudendis radiis."

the Fonte Gaia. This was filled with "various animals such as hares, foxes, porcupines, badgers, deer, wild boars, and a large and frightful bear." At the fourteenth hour members of the government went to Mass at the cathedral, which was thronged with visitors and townspeople. Cecchino unfortunately does not describe that ceremony. But his remarks leave no doubt that it was planned so as to take full advantage of the magnificient surroundings as well as of the splendid musical performances outside the cathedral by the Palace musicians and inside by the chapel singers. Later, after dinner, the Concistoro appeared at the Palace windows, "which was much desired by the multitude that was awaiting them." "Immediately the trumpets sounded from the Palace battlements, while at the same time three beautifully decorated carts appeared at the entrance to the square." One of these had an image of the Assumption of Our Lady "surrounded by angels who ascended and descended by means of an admirable contrivance." "God the Father" was seated on another of the carts, and a third featured "many prophets and sibyls." The festivities began as the carts went round the square and "behind them there came a great number of trumpeters on horseback with the standard of the Selvalta contrada," the chosen symbol of the occasion, followed by twenty mules and "the representatives of all the contradas, dressed in their own colors."

After making their rounds of the square, the men of the contradas retired to their assigned places. As the sounds of their many trumpets and drums subsided, in their stead were heard those of the hunting horns and other hunting instruments, for at that moment the hares, foxes, and "other poor animals" were released from their cages and set upon by dogs who chased them around the square. "And then came the first bull," which Cecchino says was "more beautiful than brave." After he was dispatched, several others followed, including one that was judged fiendish. At nightfall, when the last event ended, "all returned to their homes, praising God and Our Lady."[117]

On the following day the trumpets were heard in various parts of the city inviting the crowds to come witness the "giuoco delle pugna," the traditional boxing match. The festivities concluded with another procession to the cathedral. This was so well ordered and praiseworthy that it made a fitting ending for "a day no less beautiful and pleasing" than the previous one.

SIENESE SECULAR MUSIC OF THE SIXTEENTH CENTURY

Nothing remains of the music performed at the historic Palios. But some idea of the kinds of secular pieces current in Siena during the sixteenth century can be had from a few Sienese manuscripts and prints containing works by Sienese composers and others. Principal among the manuscripts is the collection known as the "Siena Lute Book," a central source of sixteenth-century instrumental music copied toward the close of the sixteenth century.[118] Almost encyclopedic in scope, its 156 works make up a veritable

---

117. The event must have been quite similar to the scene depicted by the sixteenth-century Sienese painter Vincenzo Rustici, "La caccia de' tori," now in the collection of the Monte de' Paschi in Siena. It is reproduced by Alessandro Falassi on p. 24 of his "Festa di Siena," in Falassi et al., *Palio,* 9–88.

118. See the edition by Arthur Ness, *Tablature de luth italienne dit Siena Manuscrit (ca. 1560–1570). Facsimilé du Ms. 28 B 39 (ancienne Bibliothèque Scheurleer) La Haye, Gemeentemuseum* (Geneva, 1988).

compendium of then current and retrospective repertories for the lute, from fantasias, ricercars, and intabulations of vocal music from earlier in the century to toccatas and dance music from around the time the volume was compiled. Principal among the former are works by the celebrated lutenists Francesco da Milano, Alberto de Rippe, and Perino Fiorentino, and among the latter three pieces by Andrea Feliciani.[119] The importance of the anthology, apparently copied by a professional lutenist, lies in the variety and quality of the works it transmits, in its disclosure that such a vast repertory was known and played in Siena, and in its confirmation of Ugurgieri's reports of the presence there of highly gifted musicians, professional and amateur alike. The same copyist was also responsible for the major part of what remains of another, once extensive, collection of lute pieces, the somewhat later Haslemere manuscript. This has concordances with the "Siena Lute Book," among them, one of Feliciani's pieces and others by Francesco da Milano, and had it been preserved in its entirety, it too would rank among the important sources of late sixteenth-century instrumental music.[120]

A third manuscript attesting to musical tastes in sixteenth-century Siena is Basevi 2439, a chansonnier copied at the renowned scriptorium of the Habsburg-Burgundian court toward the end of the first decade of the sixteenth century, apparently for the Agostini Ciardi, a wealthy Sienese family of bankers with international connections.[121] The Agostini Ciardi, like other music enthusiasts of the time, were great admirers of French secular song. Represented among the eighty-seven compositions in the volume

---

See also Ness, "The Siena Lute Book and its Arrangements of Vocal and Instrumental Part-Music," in *Proceedings of the International Lute Symposium, Utrecht 1986,* ed. L. P. Grijp and W. Mook (Utrecht, 1988), 30–49, and two important reviews of the facsimile volume by Victor Coelho (*Notes* 46 [1990]: 1060–630) and Dinko Fabris (*Journal of the Lute Society of America* 20–21 [1987–88]: 165–70). The manuscript is also discussed briefly by Dinko Fabris in "Tre composizioni per liuto," 14–15. The manuscript, according to the title stamped on the spine of the modern binding, was acquired in Siena in 1863; see Ness's introduction to the facsimile volume.

119. Perino Fiorentino, son of the organist-composer Bartolomeo degli Organi and retainer of Pope Paul III in Rome, has long been thought to have had connections with Siena because of a 1538 report that he received a payment from the papal purse "so that he might return to Siena." The nature of Perino's connections with Siena at the time is unknown, but a letter from 4 September 1541 to Cardinal Alessandro Farnese reports that the members of his entourage, among them Perino, stopped off at Siena for a day and a half during the course of a journey to Lucca. Both incidents are of interest because they point to the presence in the city, however briefly, of musicians like Perino who were in and out of Siena as they traveled to and from Rome. For Perino's earlier trip, see Elwyn Wienandt, "Perino Fiorentino and His Lute Pieces," *JAMS* 8 (1955): 5; the letter is in Paolo Giovio, *Lettere,* ed. Giuseppe Guido Ferrero (Rome, 1956), 1:268. I am grateful to Franco Pavan for calling my attention to the letter.

120. For a description of the Haslemere manuscript and its concordances with the "Siena Lute Book," see Victor Coelho, *The Manuscript Sources of Seventeenth-Century Italian Lute Music* (London and New York, 1995), 167–69, 650–53.

121. See the facsimile edition, *Basevi Codex: Florence, Biblioteca del Conservatorio, MS 2439,* with an Introduction by Honey Meconi (Peer, 1990), and for remarks about the contents and provenance, the same author's "The Manuscript Basevi 2439 and Chanson Transmission in Italy," in *Trasmissione e recezione delle forme di cultura musicale,* ed. L. Bianconi, F. A. Gallo, A. Pompilio, and D. Restani, *Atti del XIV Congresso della Società Internazionale di Musicologia, Bologna, 1987* (Turin, 1990), 163–74.

are the chansons of a galaxy of leading contemporary Franco-Flemish composers—
Josquin, Obrecht, La Rue, Agricola, Ghiselin—as well as a few Latin-texted pieces,
some Flemish songs, and a single setting of an Italian text, Compère's *Scaramella fa la
galla*. Many of the pieces are cantus-firmus settings, many are given with only textual
incipits—these two traits evidently indicative of chanson collections circulating in Italy—and many were apparently great favorites with Italian audiences, as suggested by
its thirty-two concordances with other Italian chansonniers. Since very little is known
about the circumstances surrounding the acquistion of the volume, it is a matter of
speculation as to whether the repertory it contains was requested by a patron or whether
the scribe who prepared it used his own knowledge of Italian traditions and tastes in
compiling it. In either case the contents testify to the sophisticated musical interests of
a well-to-do Sienese family and suggest that repertories of contemporary French music
were as well known among Siena's upper classes as they were in other major cities on
the peninsula.

The earliest of the printed volumes, and thus far the only known music print to
survive from Siena, is Pietro Sambonetto's *Canzone, sonetti strambotti et frottole libro primo,*
which appeared on 30 August 1515.[122] This includes works by several composers,
among whom were Jacopo Fogliano of Modena and the cathedral provost Niccolò
Piccolomini, though almost half of its contents are by two of the city's leading musicians
of the time, Sano di Goro and Niccolò di Cristoforo—Ansano Senese and Niccolò
Piffaro, as Sambonetto called them. Ansano was the principal composer in the collection, credited with fourteen of its forty-eight pieces. The texts of all but one of his
settings, an oda by Antonio Tebaldeo, derive from local sources and represent forms
then current in Italy: the barzaletta, the frottola, the strambotto, the canzone, the canzonetta, the oda, and the capitolo. The subject matter of most of the poems concerns
love, whose vagaries, hardships, and cruelties are sung by an unrequited lover. One
canzone, rich in allegory, with associations yet to be deciphered, may have served as a
prologue to a theatrical entertainment, and three pieces are carnival songs. Their incomplete texts—only the refrains are printed—suggest that the ribald and often ob-
scene character of the Florentine carnival song was also known in Siena, perhaps furnishing a reason for the absence in the print of the remainder of their texts.[123]

---

122. The most recent study of Sambonetto's collection is my "Instrumental Resonances in a
Sienese Vocal Print of 1515," in *Le Concert des voix et des instruments à la Renaissance: Actes du XXXIVe
Colloque International d'Études Supérieures de la Renaissance, 1–11 juillet 1991,* ed. Jean-Michel Vaccaro
(Paris, 1995), 333–59, where references to other studies dealing with the volume are given. Principal
among these is Daniele Fusi's "Le frottole nell'edizione di Pietro Sambonetto (Siena 1515)" (Tesi di
laurea, Università degli Studi di Siena, Facoltà di Lettere e Filosofia, Anno Accademico 1976–77),
which contains a transcription of the entire contents of the collection and extensive notes and analyses
of the poetry and music.

123. It is also true, however, that a good many of the works published by Sambonetto, the majority by Ansano, also lack complete texts, which may indicate that they were unavailable at the time of
printing. Even when he does print full texts, Sambonetto gives no indication of the function of the
pieces, as in the case of Ansano's *Volge fortuna,* whose theatrical origins are neatly hypothesized by
Francesco Luisi, *Del cantar a libro . . . o sulla viola: La musica vocale nel Rinascimento* (Turin, 1977), 274–
75, and "Musica in commedia nel primo Cinquecento," in *Origini della commedia nell'Europa del Cinque-*

Though Ansano's musical models were the north Italian frottolists, his voice is clearly that of an original working outside the mainstream of the tradition. Apart from the presumably theatrical canzone, which is through-composed, all of his works are in strophic forms, the music of the first stanza or its various sections sufficing for all subsequent stanzas. Ansano worked within the conventions of partial simultaneity of composition, in which cantus, tenor, and bass parts were conceived in conjunction with one another, the tenor and the bass forming an indispensable contrapuntal and harmonic framework for the unfolding of the cantus, which always carries the principal melody.[124] The altus, inevitably the last part to be composed, betrays its origins in its profusion of repeated note patterns, angularity, wide range, and disjunct movement. These characteristics, present to a certain extent in the tenor and bass as well, together with inserted wordless interludes and codas, offer sure indications that he composed the lower parts of his pieces with instruments in mind.

Typifying these characteristics is the carnival song *Noi siamo galeotti,* whose passages in shifting meters and dancelike character betray the tongue-in-cheek attitude of the carnival's mock galley slaves and scoundrels (Ex. 14.1). Ansano's melodies are engaging at times, and his harmonies are for the most part logically conceived. A clear sense of tonal direction characterizes some of the works, such as the plaintive frottola *El mostrarsi lieto* (Ex. 14.2). Each of its parts is composed within the ambience of the authentic and plagal forms of the central F mode, whose tonic and dominant chords are the cadential goals reached at the principal sections of the piece. Like several of his other secular works, the piece shows the hand of an aspiring and gifted composer and suggests that Ansano composed music for the chapel in which he served, as singer and master, for so many years.

Niccolò, too, adopted the technique of partial simultaneity of composition, adding an alto voice to a three-part structure of treble, tenor, and bass, in his settings of odas, capitolos, and frottolas. In his music, like Ansano's, a smooth, conjunct, though sometimes flowing treble supported by lower parts—which are often disjunct, angular, and full of reiterated notes—points to performance by a vocal soloist with the accompaniment or a lute or an instrumental ensemble. During Niccolò's tenure at the Palace, some, if not all, members of the woodwind ensemble also sang, and his music would doubtless have been included in the ensemble's repertory of vocally accompanied pieces. While this was clearly the intended, and perhaps preferred, mode of performance, both Niccolò's and Ansano's pieces, like many vocally conceived works of the time, were probably also performed in completely instrumental versions by the Palace

---

cento, Centro Studi sul teatro medioevale e rinascimentale, XVII Convegno, Roma 30 settembre–3 ottobre 1993, ed. M. Chiabò and Federico Doglio (Rome, 1994), 277.

124. Further on Ansano's and Niccolò's styles, see my "Instrumental Resonances," passim. Several of their works are published there in modern edition, including, by Ansano: two frottolas, *El mostrarsi lieto fuore* and *Fuggo donna,* a strambotto, *Se fiso miro,* and a portion of a canzone for a presumed theatrical production, *Volge fortuna;* by Niccolò: three frottolas, *Due virtù el mio cor nutrica, Se 'l t'è grato,* and *Lo splendente tuo bel viso,* a strambotto, *Se la serena,* and a capitolo, *Adio, riman, resta.* Ansano's three carnival songs, *Noi siamo galeotti, Chi volessi turchi siamo,* and *Logiamenti noi cerchiamo,* are published in modern edition by Francesco Luisi on pp. 201–2, 195–96, and 119–29 of his *Del cantar a libro.*

wind band and similar groups elsewhere. This must have been particularly true in Niccolò's case, with flutes, cornetts, and trombone, among other instruments, at his disposal
throughout most of his working career, when he or others who might have led the
band were called upon to furnish appropriate music on a daily basis. Typical of Niccolò's
production is his frottola *Di lassar tuo divo aspetto* (Ex. 14.3). Here, the melodic cantus,
moving in oscillating rhythmic phrases, now triple, now duple, is set against an accompaniment in the three lower voices that is decidedly instrumental in character, particularly in the coda that closes the refrain. With its lilting tune, catchy rhythms, and simple
though appropriate harmonies, the music provides an effective setting for the plain-
spoken, but evidently lovelorn, sentiments of the text.

Di lassar il tuo divo aspetto reveals Niccolò as a composer of some accomplishment,
one who, though far removed from major centers of frottola production, successfully
assimilated the spirit and style of contemporary Italian music. Unlike Ansano, he did
not have the benefits of a cathedral school education, but received instead a training
that was completely familial. His experience, similar to Giovanni di Maestro Antonio's,
shows that by the end of the fifteenth century, familial training in some instances, especially when talented youngsters were involved, was as effective—and in many ways as
comprehensive—as instruction offered under more formal circumstances. Niccolò was
a professional cornettist, one of the first known to bridge the gap between performer
and creator. He brought the same approach to his compositions as did Ansano, the
music of both sharing many similarities despite Ansano's tendency on occasion to write
more learned counterpoint. Though neither of them apparently composed in the new
madrigal style, their works gained a place for Siena, no matter how limited, on the
international musical scene, as witnessed by Ferdinand Columbus's purchase of Sambonetto's volume in Rome and in Venice.[125]

MUSIC IN THE SIENESE THEATER

Much has been written about Siena's flourishing Renaissance theater, one of its cultural
glories that continued even after the fall of the republic and the imposition of Medici
rule. The achievements of its Accademia degli Intronati and of its Congrega dei Rozzi
and the prominence of such Sienese playwrights as Alessandro Piccolomini, whose plays
were printed and reprinted throughout the century, and Girolamo Bargagli, whose
play *La Pellegrina* was performed, with the more famous musical intermedi interspersed
between its acts, at the extraordinary Medici wedding festivities in 1589, offer ample
testimony to the city's love of theater and the talents of its playwrights, whose fame
extended well beyond Siena's walls. A survey of a cross section of Sienese plays of the
later sixteenth century establishes music's place in them, though disappointingly, the
few texts referred to have not survived with musical settings.[126] As Nino Pirrotta observed with regard to Sienese plays in the earlier part of the sixteenth century, various
kinds of song, from strambotto to madrigal, as well as dance were used to enliven
literary and non-literary comedies alike, though often the choice of music actually

---

125. See chapter 12, note 15.
126. My remarks stem from a survey of Sienese plays in the collection of the Library of the
University of Chicago.

performed was entrusted to the actors. More recently, Francesco Luisi has classified and illustrated the various ways in which music, preexistent or newly composed, appeared in theatrical productions of the Sienese precursors of the Rozzi Academy. Among the examples he cites is the exceptional polyphonic rendition *a 3* of Jacomo Fogliano's *L'amor donna ch'io ti porto,* sung to a text that begins *L'amor grande che i' me porto,* in Legacci's *Egloga alla martorella intitolata Solfinello* of 1521.[127] But Luisi also points to the paradox surrounding musical performance in the Sienese theater when he notes that though the text of the 1537 edition of *Gli ingannati,* the celebrated play by the Intronati, lacks any references to song and to musical performance, when it was given eight years later in Naples, it resounded with musical additions performed by a number of trained musicians, among them the Sienese composer Scipione delle Palle.[128]

More specific about the use of music in late sixteenth-century Sienese dramatic productions is a report of a *cantata pastorale* for May Day festivities by Scipione Bargagli, with now-lost music by Ascanio Marri. Its text, dedicated to the Sienese noblewoman Isabella Ballati, was published in 1589 by the firm of Luca Bonetti. In the dedication Marco Bonetti spoke of various entertainments—eclogues, dialogues, comedies, mascheratas, and other verses with song—performed in Siena in the past, all written traces of which were now lost, and he noted that when he acquired a copy of Bargagli's work, performed some time earlier in Siena and then put aside, he immediately resolved to publish it.[129] In the scenario that accompanied his pastoral cantata Bargagli described in some detail the dress of the participants and the emblems and devices they carried, though he reserved a full explanation of the meaning and symbolism of these latter for the lengthy addendum he appended to the main body of his text.

Bargagli's scenario includes both the texts and a description of their performance. First, he explains, came a merry band of youths, "dressed as shepherds, some of them in the manner of sylvan creatures and satyrs described by the ancients," who marched through the streets of Siena on the eve of May Day in torchlit procession, accompanied by the sounds of "shawms, bagpipes, and other rustic instruments."[130] They were joined by another group of revelers, dressed in the costumes of those they were impersonating, and by musicians who, Bargagli says, carried in their hands or had strapped to their sides various instruments such as "recorders and flutes, cornetts, curtals, lyres, and lutes."[131] Together, both groups moved down the Via Pantaneto to the entrance of the Via Magalotti, where a little pavilion, made to resemble a country hut, was set up amid trees and other greenery. At its sides could be heard the sweet sounds of murmuring waters and

127. Francesco Luisi, "La frottola nelle rappresentazioni popolaresche coeve," in *Trasmissione e recezione delle forme di cultura musicale,* ed. L. Bianconi, F. A. Gallo, A. Pompilio, and D. Restani, *Atti del XIV Congresso della Società Internazionale di Musicologia, Bologna, 1987* (Turin, 1990), 2:232–35. The play, by the Sienese Pierantoni dello Stricca Legacci, was published at Siena in 1521. See also Luisi's "Musica in commedia nel primo Cinquecento," 271–78.

128. Luisi, "Musica in commedia nel primo Cinquecento," 283, 285.

129. *Cantata pastorale, Fatta per Calen di Maggio in Siena: per Rime, & Imprese nuova, e dilettevole* (Siena: Luca Bonetti, 1589), 3–4.

130. Ibid., 5.

131. Ibid., 5–6.

the chirping of birds and nightingales, the whole depicting "a most pleasant Arcadian scene." There, Mersio, a melancholy youth with downcast eyes, sat with his head in his hand.

The company of shepherds grouped itself around him, and another youth, who took the part of the shepherd Arbio, stepped forward and addressed the opening words of a little eclogue to him. These were sung to "a new and very sweet air," accompanied by a harpsichord, a lute, and a trombone.[132] Afterwards, the doleful youth, Mersio, joined with Arbio in a dialogue, at the end of which they both knelt and sang together. Then, led by a youth holding a shepherd's crook with its own device, came another group dressed as country folk playing "nakers, little triangles, tambourines, and other rustic instruments," followed "by perhaps twelve pairs of graceful young people, all elegantly and richly dressed as nymphs."[133] Behind them, others carried shepherd's staves with emblems in one hand "and in the other, citterns, harps, and violas," all of them making delightful sounds. When the nymphs came face to face with the shepherds, they were invited in song to join in the festivities, and the nymphs responded in like manner.[134] The text of this encounter was a "dialogue of shepherds and nymphs," followed by a madrigal for eight voices, *Ora spiri dolcezza e gioia intorno.*

As the nymphs were singing, they strewed flowers about them and offered garlands and flowery crowns to their chosen shepherds, who fashioned from them beautiful boughs of roses and jasmine and bouquets of flowers and strawberries.[135] Afterwards, the shepherds sang a five-part madrigal, *Oh dolcezza d'Amor soave, e grata,* to the accompaniment of "bowed violas, recorders, lutes, and trombones."[136] Following this, the nymphs and youths took each others' hands in alternating lines and formed a spacious crown; then they danced, each group singing alternately graceful and lively canzonettas: *Oh quali dolcezze* for the nymphs, *Ninfe, vostra mercede* for the shepherds, *Pastor grati, e cortesi* for the nymphs again, and the shepherds ending with *Ninfe saggie honorate.* These songs, too, were for eight voices, and the closing madrigal, *Vaghe, novelle fronde,* was accompanied by violas, curtals, trombones, and recorders. At the end of the madrigal, whose cheerful music, Bargagli says, was well received, the nymphs and shepherds, with their emblems in hand, formed couples, and, accompanied by the sounds of the various groups of instrumentalists, paraded through the city's streets well into the night.[137]

SIENESE COMPOSERS IN THE LATER SIXTEENTH CENTURY

Though none of Marri's music for Bargagli's texts survives, a few pieces with pastoral themes are in his two books of madrigals, one for six voices, the other for five (both printed at Venice by the Gardano firm in 1574 and 1575, respectively). The earlier publication, *Il primo libro de' madrigali a sei voci,* has a dedication to the Sienese nobleman Patritio Patriti, signed and dated by the composer at Siena on 28 May 1574 (RISM M

132. Ibid., 7–8.
133. Ibid., 10.
134. Ibid., 10–11.
135. Ibid., 12.
136. Ibid.
137. Ibid., 13.

726). Only the bass part of the second volume, *Il primo libro de' madrigali a cinque voci,* is extant (RISM M 727). This, too, has a dedication to a Sienese nobleman, Camillo Chigi, written by Marri, again at Siena, on 1 April 1575, only a few months before his death.[138] Marri's modesty is apparent in both dedicatory letters, which, apart from their share of the usual flattering words with which composers addressed patrons, are of interest primarily because they indicate that the scions of some of Siena's leading families were among his patrons and their homes, as Marri remarked to Patriti, places where "rare and sweet concerts" were "often heard."

Marri's book of five-voice madrigals contains settings of a number of poems by Petrarch as well as several contemporary texts in a pastoral vein. Among these are an anonymous madrigal, *Del picciol Reno a le fresch'aque intorno,* which alludes to love denied; an anonymous sonnet, *Nimphe leggiadre et voi saggi pastori,* which invokes the pleasant and fecund Tuscan countryside and Siena's river, the Arbia, while celebrating the wedding day of an unnamed "copia gentil"; and another madrigal in two parts, with allusions to Acis and Galatea, in honor of "Isabella." This is Isabella, wife of the noble amateur composer Orazio Ballati, to whom Bonetti dedicated the *cantata pastorale* mentioned above. Another text mourns the death of "Giulia," whose soul, the anonymous poet asserts, has ascended to heaven and lives happily among the bright stars. A number of Petrarch's poems are also in the collection of six-voice madrigals, which has, in addition, texts by Beccuti and Cassola, and an anonymous canzona in six stanzas. This last, set in the grand tradition of cyclic madrigal settings initiated by Jacques Arcadelt, Matteo Rampollini, and Cipriano de Rore, is an imposing work that testifies to the promise of a productive career cut short by Marri's untimely death.

Marri is also represented in another publication, an anthology of five-voice madrigals entitled *Il quinto libro delle muse a cinque voce,* published at Venice by Antonio Gardano in 1575 (RISM 1575[12]). The contents, described as "newly composed" on the title page, were collected by Marco Antonio Ferrari, who, in his dedicatory letter to the Sienese nobleman Ottavio Saracini, noted that some pieces "were born here" (in Siena), while others "were obtained from outside." Besides Marri, composers with Sienese connections include the recently employed cathedral chapel singer Orazio Vecchi, Salvatore Essenga, Marri's successor as *maestro di cappella,* and Essenga's successor, Andrea Feliciani. Altogether, their works account for fifteen of the twenty-three pieces in the collection. The remaining works are by Alessandro Striggio, musician to Grand Duke Cosimo de' Medici, Costanzo Porta, and Pietro Vinci, these last two well-known composers active in northern Italy, whose music, it can be inferred, was known in Siena.

Marri's three pieces include a setting of Niccolò Machiavelli's *Sì soave è l'inganno,* and a text by an unknown contemporary poet set in two discrete sections, *Per voi copia gentile* and *Già si distrugg'il gielo.*[139] This latter (Ex. 14.4), as befits a poem celebrating the

---

138. Camillo's son was the well-known statesman and musician Scipione. See Bellissima, *Scipione Chigi,* 6, who mentions the musical ambience in which the young Chigi grew up.

139. It may be that Marri's setting of *Sì soave è l'inganno* was used for a Sienese revival of either Machiavelli's *La Mandragola* or his *La Clizia,* though no evidence has yet come to light in this regard. On the other settings of the poem, used for earlier productions of these plays, see H. C. Slim, ed., *A Gift of Madrigals and Motets* (Chicago and London, 1972), 1:85–86; a detailed analysis of Marri's setting

return of spring to Siena—its second line reads "the Arbia's banks shimmer green"—is set homophonically for the most part, though all of the voices, grouped into duos and trios, participate in the brief imitative passages that appear occasionally. Most effective is the motivic play on "Doralice" that follows the chordal announcement that "birds come crying" her name. The diatonic harmony, rarely moving beyond chords closely related to the central G of the transposed Dorian mode, is sufficiently varied to suit the sense of the text, especially near the close where the major form of the tonic triad is used to herald spring's return. The piece, like Marri's other works, helps to establish his place among the ranks of minor Italian composers of the period who knew how to set a line of text, who had a good sense of how to express a particular mood musically, and who knew how to put together a well-crafted work that was a pleasure to perform and a pleasure to listen to.

Feliciani's settings in the same volume, all to poems by Petrarch, include *La bella pargoletta, Erano i capei d'oro* and its second part, *Non era l'andar suo, Vivi chiar'e cocenti altieri lumi* and its second part, *Sarà cenere fatt'alhor*. In its first part *Erano i capei* (Ex. 14.5), with its leisurely imitative entrances of a main theme and countertheme, explores the nether reaches of its central mode, a transposed G Dorian, moving far afield to an A-flat chord before cadencing on the dominant D chord. Feliciani's adroit handling of the harmony, his use of a variety of rhythms and textures, as well as his gift for graceful melodic turns, all illustrate his mastery of some of the most advanced techniques of the day.

Feliciani is also represented by two books of madrigals devoted solely to his works, the *Primo libro de madrigali a cinque voci* (Venice, Gardano, 1579) and the *Primo libro de madrigali a sei voci* (Venice, Vincenzi and Amadino, 1586). The earlier collection is dedicated to Monsignor Claudio Borghesi, bishop of Grosseto, a city in the Sienese Maremma, which may have been where Feliciani worked before assuming the post of *maestro di cappella* at Siena cathedral.[140] The later collection, which does not survive complete, is dedicated to another member of the same family, Monsignor Camillo Borghesi, who among other things was vicar of Santa Maria Maggiore in Rome. Feliciani clearly benefited from the family's generosity, for in the later dedication he recalled that he had dedicated his earlier book of five-voice madrigals to Monsignor Claudio as a sign of his reverence and gratitude.[141] The literary tastes of Feliciani and his patrons are evident throughout both books, which have texts by Petrarch, Tasso, Beccuti, Caporali, and Dragonetto interspersed among pastoral and topical poems by unnamed poets, un-

---

is in Wolfgang Osthoff, *Theatergesang und darstellende Musik in der italienischen Renaissance* (Tutzing, 1969), 1:243–46.

140. *Di Andrea Feliciani maestro di capella del duomo di Siena il Primo Libro de Madrigali a cinque voci nuovamente composti, et dati in luce* (Venice: Angelo Gardano, 1579): "Et se i fiori ch'io indrizzo, non riusciranno soavi incolpisi me pianta tenera ancora, et forsi per natura alquanto sterile . . . Siena. 1. III. 1579" (listed as RISM F 203).

141. *Di Andrea Feliciani senese maestro di cappella del duomo di Siena. Il Primo libro de Madrigali a sei voci, novamente composti, et dati in luce* (Venice: Giacomo Vincenzi, et Ricciardo Amadino, compagni, 1586): "havendo io riverito già più tempo l'Illustre, et Reverendissimo Monsignor Claudio Borghesi Vescovo di Grosseto, et per segno della mia servitù dedicatoli una mia opera de Madrigali a cinque voci . . . Siena, 10. IX 1586" (listed as RISM F 204).

doubtedly Sienese. Strangely, none of the texts recited at a tournament given in Siena on 20 June 1577 appears in either volume.[142] The ease with which Feliciani handles five- and six-part texture and his familiarity with all of the canons and conceits of madrigal writing of the period are evident in many pieces throughout both collections. Though his madrigals were evidently not widely circulated, one of his six-part pieces achieved enduring fame across the channel when it was reprinted in the second volume of Nicholas Yonge's celebrated anthology of Italian madrigals newly refitted with English texts, *Musica Transalpina*.[143] This was the sestina *Io per languir mi sfaccio,* whose pathetic melancholia was now appropriately transformed into doleful Elizabethan verse as *For griefe I dye.*

Francesco Bianciardi's only known secular publication, *Il primo libro de madrigali a cinque voci* (Venice: Gardano, 1597), provides a glimpse of another aspect of his musical personality. Though only the tenor partbook is extant, six of its madrigals for five voices and another for six survive in various German, English, Danish, and Dutch collections, both in manuscript and in print.[144] A few of the settings, to judge from this small sampling, reveal him as a madrigalist of no mean gifts, one who had absorbed the lessons of his predecessors and was at the same time keenly aware of the latest developments in the genre. A lighter and more conventional approach is evident in his setting of Guarini's *Ardemm'insieme,* one of three texts by that poet in the original collection. Its opening passages exploit the use of motive and counter-motive, chordal declamation, and quasi-imitative texture before giving way to a dance-like passage in triple meter and then to the rhythmically animated homophony that ultimately dominates the rest of the piece, the whole set to harmonies that remain well within the diatonic confines of the tonic A minor and its relative C major. Equally charming is the retrospective *Dolce, grave et acuto.* In Rinaldi's text a lover likens the "sweet, low, and high" that produce perfect harmony to his own state and to a sweetness still withheld that, once granted by his beloved, will enable him to sing "ut re mi fa sol la" in faultless tones. Predictably enough, this quotation of the solmization syllables elicits a solemn statement in strict imitation of the tones of the hexachord, here on F and C, in a passage oddly reminiscent of bygone times. But then, in a lively and thoroughly contemporary codetta an outburst of imitative entries on a chromatically altered hexachord, now beginning on F-sharp, leads smoothly and inevitably back to the G minor mode on which the piece began.

The jewel of this small group of Bianciardi's secular works is *Io parto, o mio fedele,* scored for two sopranos, alto, tenor, and bass. Its expressive declamation, varied textural changes, and colorful harmonies suggest a flair for the dramatic only hinted at in the

142. The texts were published at Siena in 1577 by Luca Bonetti: *Stanze cantate al torneo rappresentato in Siena il dì XX. di Giugno. MDLXXVII.*

143. A facsimile edition of both volumes of Yonge's *Musica Transalpina* (London, 1588, 1597), with an introduction by Denis Stevens, was published at Farnborough, England, in 1972. (Feliciani's piece is no. XXII of vol. 2.) The Italian text, the English translation, and a note on the sources is given by Alberto Obertello, *Madrigali italiani in Inghilterra* (Milan, 1949), 308, 476.

144. An edition of the six extant madrigals and notes on the sources are in vol. 7 of Bianciardi's *Opera Omnia,* ed. Cisilino and Bertazzo, 1–39 and iii–v.

few other available pieces. A restrained tone, devoid of bathos, pervades the setting of this plaintive text. At the opening the beloved's parting words are set to sustained chords followed by a more characteristic passage in trio texture for the two highest parts and the bass. Then, as the narrator continues to recount the moment of leave-taking, all five voices shift to slower rhythms. Sections in alternating textures follow, each designed to capture the mood of his sorry state. Again, the mode of the piece is unequivocally G minor. But this time it is varied by excursions to B-flat and D and, just before the end, by a poignant passage for all voices that moves through major chords on E-flat, A-flat, C, F, and B-flat, a tonal depiction of pain turned to "lifeless stone that will build a sepulchre for a dying heart."

Both *Io parto, o mio crudele* and *Dolce, grave et acuto,* together with works by Agostino Agazzari, Tommaso Pecci, and Orindio Bartolini, were among the more than 1,200 madrigals, motets, and instrumental pieces copied by the English recusant Francis Tregian during the years of his confinement in London's Fleet Prison, from 1609 to 1619.[145] Unique in scope, Tregian's anthology stands as the most comprehensive contemporaneous collection of Italian madrigals ever assembled, a monument both to the variety and universality of the genre and to the discriminating taste of its compiler. That Sienese musicians were included in a group in which virtually every later Italian madrigalist of note was represented is notable but perhaps not surprising. Sienese music had clearly come of age and, as the compositions of Feliciani and of his pupils and successors show, Siena now shared in the musical efflorescence that ensured the highest place of honor for peninsular achievements at the turn of the seventeenth century.

DOCUMENTS

Doc. 14.1. Payments to musicians at the Palio of 1457. ASS, Concistoro, vol. 545, fol. 58ᵛ, dated 10 August 1457

Et detis et solvatis infrascriptis tubicenis et giollaris, qui venerunt ad honorandum festum Sancte Marie Augusti . . . IIII fra trombetti e con cimamelle de' Signori di Firenze, grossi 120; IIII fra piffari e trombone dela comunità di Firenze, grossi 120; VI trombetti e uno piffaro di Parte Guelfa, grossi 100; IIII trombetti dela Mercantia di Firenze, grossi 60; IIII trombetti del Comune di Pistoia, grossi 80; uno trombetto del Signore Simonetto, grossi 20; uno araldo del Re d'Ongaria, grossi 16; due trombetti del Comune di Cortona, grossi 20; uno trombetto di Troylo del Conte, grossi 24; due trombetti del Comune d'Arezzo, grossi 16; due trombetti del Comune di Colle, grossi 24; due trombetti del Marchese Spinetta, grossi 24; due trombetti del podestà di Firenze, grossi 20; due trombetti del Capitano di Firenze, grossi 20; due trombetti del Capitano di Cortona, grossi 20; due trombetti del podestà d'Arezzo, grossi 20; due trombetti del Capitano d'Arezzo, grossi 20; due trombetti del Capitano di Pisa, grossi 24; due trombetti del Vicario d'Anghiari, grossi 16; uno trombetto del Comune di Todi, grossi 12; due trombetti di Carlo degli Oddi, grossi 24; due trombetti del Signore Guglielmo, grossi 16; uno trombetto di Ceccone, grossi 8; due trombetti del podestà di Pistoia, grossi 20; due trombetti del Comune di Sancto Geminiano, grossi 16; due trombetti del Vicario di Certaldo, grossi 12; uno trombetto del Comune di Montepulciano, grossi 12; V cantori fiorentini, grossi 50; uno sonatore di leuto,

---

145. For notes on Tregian and the manuscript's contents and a complete list of its pieces, see my introduction to the facsimile edition, *London, British Library MS Egerton 3665 ("The Tregian Manuscript"),* Renaissance Music in Facsimile 7 (New York, 1988).

ciecho, grossi 8; uno tamburino co' suffili, grossi 10; due trombetti del podestà di Siena, grossi 16; uno fanciuletto trombetto, grossi 8; due trombetti del Capitano di Giustizia di Siena, grossi 32; Tonio d'Urbano, grossi 32; Guasparre cantarino, barbiere di Siena, grossi 14; arcidiachono novello, grossi 8; maestro Piero di Rintera, per le corde de leiuto, grossi 8. Somma grossi 1158.

Doc. 14.2. Payments to musicians at the Palio of 1460. Concistoro, vol. 563, fol. 52^v, dated 16 August 1460

Et detis et solvatis infrascriptis tubicenis, piffaris, iollariis et ioculatoribus . . . qui interfuerunt ad honorandum festum gloriosissime Virginis Marie . . . due trombetti del Duca di Milano, grossi 80; quattro trombetti dela comunità di Pistoia, grossi 80; quatro trombetti e uno piffaro di Parte Guelfa di Firenze, grossi 120; quatro trombetti dela comunità di Firenze, grossi 120; tre piffari e uno trombone dela comunità di Firenze, grossi 120; uno nacarino dela comunità di Firenze, grossi 30; tre trombetti dela Mercantia di Firenze, grossi 45; quatro trombetti dela comunità di Lucha, grossi 180; due trombetti fanciulli dela comunità di Lucha, grossi 30; due trombetti fanciulli dela comunità di Lucha, grossi 40; tre piffari dela comunità di Lucha, grossi 180; uno donzello dela comunità di Lucha, grossi 30; due trombetti dela comunità di Cortona, grossi 24; tre trombetti dela comunità di San Gimignano, grossi 24; due piffari dela comunità di Perugia, grossi 40; uno fanciullo che atteggiava, grossi 16; uno trombetto dela comunità di Montefia-scone, grossi 12; tre trombetti dela comunità d'Arezzo, grossi 36; due trombetti del potestà di Perugia, grossi 12; due trombetti dela comunità di Massa di Maremma, grossi 24; uno trombetto del Capitano di Perugia, grossi 12; due trombetti del potestà di Città di Castello, grossi 24; due trombetti dela comunità di Castiglione Aretino, grossi 24; due trombetti del potestà di Montepulciano, grossi 16; due trombetti del Vicario della Scarperia, grossi 16; due trombetti del potestà di Sancto Giovanni di Valdarno, grossi 16; uno trombetto del figliuolo di Simonetto, grossi 10; uno trombetto di Cechone, grossi 10; tre trombetti del Conte d'Urbino, grossi 30; due trombetti del Capitano d'Arezo, grossi 16; tre trombetti dela comunità di Città di Castello, grossi 36; due trombetti del Capitano di Cortona, grossi 16; uno trombetto del potestà di Firen-ze, grossi 8; due tamburini con suffoli, dello ambasciatore del Re di Spagna, grossi 24; quatro fanciulli sonatori, ballatori, schermidori et cantori col padre, grossi 80; uno tamburino e uno giocolatore, grossi 16; uno giocolatore dele bagatelle, grossi 10; due trombetti del potestà di Siena, grossi 16; due trombetti del capitano di Siena, grossi 16; uno ciecho sonatore di leuto, grossi 8; uno che ci donò una lupa, grossi 6; uno trombetto del capitano di Pistoia, grossi 8; uno trombetto del nipote del Papa, grossi 20; mastri uscieri del Papa, grossi 72.

Doc. 14.3. Payments to musicians at the Palio of 1462. Concistoro, vol. 575, fols. 74^v–75^r, dated 16 August 1462

Et detis et solvatis infrascriptis tubicenis, piffaris, sonatoribus et cantoribus qui venerunt et in-terfuerunt ad honorandum festum Assumptionis gloriosissime Virginis . . . otto trombetti di Lu-cha, grossi 220; uni tubicine Camere Appostolice, grossi 25; uni piffaro Marchionis Ferrarie, grossi 30; uni sonatori arpe de Luca, grossi 20; tribus tubicenis de Cortonio, grossi 30; tribus tubicenis Partis Guelfe, grossi 60; tribus tubicenis Mercantie, grossi 36; duobus tubicenis de Massa, grossi 16; uni tubiceni de Castilione Aretino, grossi 8; uni cornamusino Patriarce, grossi 14; duobus tubicenis potestatis Senarum, grossi 16; duobus tubicenis capitanei Senarum, grossi 16; uni cecho sonatori lutine, videlicet Angelo de Marciano, grossi 6; Moro cantatori, grossi 4; uni famulo vocato Olcia, grossi 4; uni sonatori ribechino, grossi 4; Piero dele Donne, grossi 4; uni sonatori gravicembali, grossi 8; uni tubicine filio Simonetti, grossi 12; duobus dimicatoribus, grossi 12.

Doc. 14.4. Payments to musicians at the Palio of 1463. Concistoro, vol. 581, fol. 57^r, dated 16 August 1463

Et detis et solvatis . . . due sonatori di leiuto del Duca di Baviera, grossi 32 . . . uno fanciuletto che ballò collo leiuto innanzi a' Signori, grossi 4 . . . Piero delle Donne, tamburino di messer Mariano, grossi 10; tre tamburini e sonatori di staffe e suffoli, in tutto grossi 18; uno buffone che fece più cose, grossi 8 . . . Somma grossi 1228, che ragiono lire 337 s. 14. 4

Doc. 14.5. Payments to musicians at the Palio of 1468. Concistoro, vol. 611, fols. 68ᵛ–69ʳ, dated 16 August 1468

Et detis et solvatis . . . 2 trombetti del duca di Milano, grossi 60; 4 trombetti della Signoria di Fiorenza, grossi 120; 1 con le cimamelle de' Signori fiorentini, grossi 30; 4 piffari dela Signori di Fiorenza, grossi 120 . . . 3 piffari di Parte Guelfa, grossi 72 . . . 2 sonatori di leiuto, grossi 30; 3 sonatori: 1 di leiuto, 1 di ribechino e 1 di fiuto, grossi 30; Filippo Lapaccini che dice improviso, grossi 40; 1 giocatore con la persona, grossi 20; Antonio d'Urbano, giocò con la persona, grossi 15; 1 altro giocatore con la persona, grossi 8; 1 giocatore di bagattelle, grossi 6; 1 che fe' le tre boci, grossi 8; 3 cantori, grossi 24; 3 maestri di scarmaglia, grossi 16.

Doc. 14.6. Payments to musicians at the Palio of 1475. Concistoro, vol. 653, fol. 59ʳ⁻ᵛ, dated 28 August 1475

Et detis et solvatis infrascriptis tubicinis, piffaris, cantoribus, sonatoribus et ioculatoribus qui venerunt ad honorandum festum S. Marie.

Uno trombetto del Marchese di Ferrara	L. 8 s. 8 d. —
Uno trombetto del Marchese di Mantua	L. 6 s. 16 d. —
Sette trombetti Luchesi	L. 86 s. 12 d. 6
Quattro trombetti del Magnifico Ruberto di Rimini	L. 28
Due trombetti del Duca d'Urbino	L. 22 s. 8
Tre piffari et uno trombone del Comune di Lucha	L. 49 s. 10
Cinque trombetti et uno nacharino di Parte Guelfa di Fiorenza	L. 52
Quattro trombetti et uno nacharino di Pistoia	L. 27 s. 10
Due trombetti di Volterra	L. 5 s. 10
Uno trombetto di Signor Ruberto	L. 7
Tre trombetti di Cortona	L. 8
Uno trombetto di Pontriemoli	L. 3
Tre trombetti di San Gemignano	L. 8
Due trombetti di Città di Castello	L. 8 s. 10
Due trombetti di Colle	L. 6
Due trombetti di Prato	L. 6
Due trombetti d'Arezzo	L. 6
Uno trombetto di San Giorgio	L. 2 s. 8
Uno trombetto di Sforza	L. 5 s. 12
Uno trombetto del Duca di Borgogna	L. 5 s. 12
Uno trombetto dela Mercantia di Fiorenza	L. 2 s. 16
Uno trombetto di Bernardino da Todi	L. 2 s. 4
Uno trombetto del Potestà di Castiglione Aretino	L. 2 s. 16
Uno trombetto del Marchese del Monte	L. 3 s. 8
Uno trombetto de' Signori di Rachanata	L. 2 s. 16
Uno trombetto di Giovanni Francesco da Bagno	L. 3 s. 10
Uno trombetto di Giovanni Francesco da Piano di Meleto	L. 3
Due trombetti del Marchese di Fossonovo	L. 5
Uno trombetto di Misser Iacomo Ambruogio da Lunigiana	L. 3 s. 10
Uno trombetto di San Miniato del Tedesco	L. 2 s. 10
Uno trombetto del Capitano di Serzana	L. 2

Due trombetti da Pescia	L. 4 s. 8
Due trombetti da Massa	L. 5 s. 12
Uno trombetto di San Giovanni di Valdarno	L. 2 s. 12
Uno trombetto di Ventura	L. 2 s. 8
Due trombetti del Borgo a San Sepolcro	L. 5
Uno trombetto del Comune di Castiglione Aretino	L. 2 s. 16
Uno trombetto del Signor Gualterotto	L. 3
Uno trombetto di Merlino	L. 3
Uno trombetto di Francesco da Sassatello	L. 2 s. 4
Uno trombetto di Montepulciano	L. 3
Uno trombetto del podestà di San Gemignano	L. 2 s. 10
Due trombetti del podestà di Massa	L. 4 s. 10
Uno trombetto del podestà di Magliano	L. 2 s. 4
Due trombetti del podestà di Siena	L. 4 s. 8
Uno trombetto del capitano di Siena	L. 2 s. 4
Maestro Benedetto et Franceschino, danzatori et sonatori	L. 11 s. 4
Maestro Iacomo da Bologna, sonatore di leuto	L. 5
Maestro Giovanni tedesco, sonatore di leuto	L. 2 s. 17
Due atteggiatori fiorentini	L. 5 s. 12
Uno attegiatore del Duca di Borgogna	L. 5 s. 12
Uno sonatore di ribechino	L. l s. 13
Uno tamburino	L. 1 s. 13
Due sonatori: uno d'arpa, et uno sonatore di Lorenzo de' Medici	L. 16 s. 16
Maestro Lorenzo cantarino	L. 5 s. 12
Due sonatori: uno di leuto et uno di cornamusa	L. 4
Ser Giovanni Michele et tre fanciulletti, cantori tutti del Duca d' Urbino	L. 44 s. 16
Francesco Mire et Antonio detto el Torce e compagni cantori	L. 8

Doc. 14.7. Payments to musicians at the Palio of 1540. Concistoro, vol. 2219, unnumbered page

2 donzelli di Lucha	scudi 4
8 sonatori di Bologna	scudi 22
5 trombetti di Lucca	scudi 10
6 trombetti di Firenze	scudi 12
[all at rate of L. 7.5 per scudo; total: scudi 48]	
2 trombetti di Parte Guelfa	lire 10
2 trombetti di Pistoia	lire 10
2 trombetti di Volterra	lire 8
2 trombetti di Pisa	lire 16
2 trombetti di San Gimignano	lire 9
2 trombetti di Colle	lire 6
1 trombetti di Montepulciano	lire 6
2 trombetti d'Arezzo	lire 12
PierGiovanni trombetto per la lista	lire 4
2 tronbetti nuovi che inparano, novitii	lire 6
Paulo banditore	lire 1
2 famigli di Bicherna	lire 2
total, lire 90	

Example 14.1. Ansano Senese, *Noi siamo galeotti* (*Canzone sonetti strambotti et frottole libro primo* [Siena: Sambonetto, 1515])

No - i sia - mo ga - le - ot - ti   Che por - tia - - - -mo net - t'a' den - ti;   Con fa - di - ga af - fa - ni e sten - ti   A far que - sto siam dot - ti.

Example 14.1 continued

Example 14.2. Ansano Senese, *El mostrarsi lieto* (*Canzone sonetti strambotti et frottole libro primo* [Siena: Sambonetto, 1515])

Example 14.2 continued

Example 14.3. Niccolò Piffero, *Di lassar tuo divo aspetto* (*Canzone sonetti strambotti et frottole libro primo* [Siena: Sambonetto, 1515])

Example 14.4. Ascanio Marri, *Per voi, copia gentile* (*Il quinto libro delle Muse* [Venice: Gardano, 1575])

Example 14.4 continued

Example 14.4 continued

Example 14.4 continued

Example 14.4 continued

Example 14.5. Andrea Feliciani, *Erano i capei d'oro* (*Il quinto libro delle Muse* [Venice: Gardano, 1575])

Example 14.5 continued

Example 14.5 continued

Example 14.5 continued

Example 14.5 continued

REGISTER OF MUSICIANS

The following register records all musicians mentioned by name in the chapters on cathedral and Palace musicians. It is divided into four sections: cathedral singers and wind players; cathedral organists and organ builders; palace trumpeters and shawm players, town criers, drummers and singers; palace pifferi. The names appear in alphabetical order by first name, in a standardized form. For chronological lists of musicians, see the tables at the ends of chapters 3–12.

For many musicians we know no more than the dates of service and, usually, their salary. Some appear in official documents for various reasons, among them records of appointment and reprimands for bad behavior. Most documents concerning individual musicians have been placed in the register and provide the support for statements otherwise undocumented in the text. Documents concerning more than one musician have usually been placed in appendices to the chapters.

Employment data for the cathedral musicians is based on the following sources in the AOMS (the volume number in Moscadelli's inventory is given in parentheses):

E&U for 1365–67 (1227), 1371–72 (198), 1375–76 (208), 1376–77 (225), 1379–82 (1230–32), 1386–88 (1236–37), 1392–94 (1242–43), 1395–96 (1244), 1396–97 (225), fiscal years 1401–2 through 1448–49 (229–76), 1435–43 (1259), 1444–45 (274), fiscal years 1448–49 through 1479–85 (276–307), 1486–87 through 1488–93 (308–11), 1493–95 (312), 1501–2 (313), 1502–3 (314), 1503–5 (315), 1505–6 (316), 1523–25 (321), 1525–26 (322), 1526–27 (323), 1534–39 (330), 1546–47 (338); *Riepiloghi di E&U, 1435–43* (1259)

D&C for 1423–29 (494), 1359–1413 (498), 1420–45 (500), 1439–57 (501), 1456–61 (504), 1461–81 (505), 1466–75 (507), 1475–82 (508), 1482–1527 (509), 1506–11 (510), 1511–12 (511), 1521–29 (512), 1529–42 (513), 1542–58 (514)

Memoriale for 1385–86 (1222), 1386–87 (519), 1388 (520), 1390 (1223), 1398–1401 (1224–26), 1409–10 (528), 1446–47 (559), 1449–50 (561), 1451–52 (564), 1446–57 (583), 1455–57 (567), 1466–76 (587)

Note di salari e liste di canonici, chierici, cantori, suonatori, sagrestani e cappellani for 1412–1535 (1074–75), "Secc. XV–XVIII" (1076), 1446–49 (1079); *Puntature ai cappellani e ai chierici* for 1446–69 (1079); *Distribuzioni e salari* for 1558–78 (1081), 1578–95 (1082), 1595–1603 (1083), 1603–16 (1084); *Ore canoniche* for 1520–21 (SA 152), fiscal years 1588–89 through 1600–1 (SA 185–97)

Deliberazioni for 1434–55 (13), 1454–59 (14), 1463–70 (15)

Giornale B, 1554–67 (628), *Giornale C, 1567–96* (629)

Employment data for Palace musicians in the early years is based on the volumes of the Biccherna (a number of the early ones have been published; see the bibliography under *Libri dell'entrata e dell'uscita della Repubblica di Siena*), and in later years on the records of the Concistoro; these are kept in the ASS. Service was probably more regular than indicated, but payment records often do not give names.

I. CATHEDRAL SINGERS AND WIND PLAYERS

Agnolino. Clerk-singer, January–February 1535
Monthly payments of L. 3

Agnolo Ciper da Cholonia, Ser. Tenorista and contrabasso singer, September 1524–mid-June 1526
Payment of L. 4. 16 on 28 September 1524; thereafter monthly salary of L. 7

Agnolo di Bartolomeo. Singer, April 1525–
August 1530
Monthly payments of L. 7

Agnolo di Domenico, Ser. Chaplain-singer,
July–October 1419
Monthly salary of L. 5. 5. 10

Agnolo di Nanni, Ser. Tenorista, April 1440–
October 1446
Monthly salary of L. 6

Agnolo di Pietro, Ser. Chaplain-singer,
April–June 1485, April 1486–March 1495;
January 1501–August 1519
Monthly payments of L. 7. 15 in 1485, then
L. 8 in 1486–89; L. 4 thereafter

Agostino, Ser. Laudese, November 1472–
January 1473
Payments to laudesi, 1473: "a dì III di feraio lire
dodici s. 0, demo a sere Aghostino, a sere
Francesco di Barnaba, e Antonio di Troiano,
che chantano le lalde in domo, i quali xono
per loro xalaro d'avere chantato tre mexi le
lalde in domo, che viene lire 4 per uno"
(vol. 507, fol. 187 left)

Agostino di Antonio. Chaplain, May 1463–
August 1478; singer, May 1463–March 1464
and April–August 1478

Agostino di Francesco eunuco. Clerk-
singer, soprano, May–November 1597,
December 1598–November 1601
Monthly payments of L. 2, then L. 4 as "cantore," then "cherico piccolo e cantore"

Agostino di Vannuccio. Laudese, March–
May 1389

Alberto. Clerk-singer, August 1460–66
Initially hired at 40 soldi a month, raised to 4
lire in January 1466

Alberto. Singer, April–June 1473, January–
February 1474, April–November 1475
Salary raised from 6 to 8 lire in April 1475

**Aldobrando di Ser Camillo Trabocchi da
Pienza.** Clerk-singer, bass, January–
December 1590
Monthly payments of L. 4, L. 5, and then L. 12
as "cherico grande e basso"

Alessandro di Domenico, Ser. Chaplain-
singer, May 1561–March 1574
Monthly payments of L. 17, then L. 12, then
L. 14

Alessandro di Masetto. Singer, January 1548–
April 1552

Monthly payments of L. 16

Alessio Spagnuolo da Valenzia, Ser. Tenor
singer, mid-June 1574–February 1575
Monthly payments of L. 4, then L. 8, L. 9

Alfonso Ferrandi di Castiglia, Messer. Tenorista, end July 1481–mid-March 1482
Payments of L. 4 for July, L. 20 for August
1481–February 1482, and L. 7. 6. 8 for 10
days in March ("per 10 dì di marzo . . . di
poi partì e andò a Roma"; vol. 451, fol.
112ʳ)

Ambrogio di Giovanni, Frate. Laudese,
December 1388–January 1389

Amore di Francesco Franzese. Clerk-singer,
August–November 1522
Payment of L. 4

Andrea. Clerk-singer, January 1538
Payment of L. 2

Andrea da Fossano, Frate. Bass singer, January 1592–November 1595
Monthly payments of L. 14, then L. 15

Andrea da Polonia. Singer, May–August
1449, January–March 1450
Paid 8 lire for May 1449; thereafter the four Polish singers paid 34 lire as a group ("Andrea,
Giovanni, Jacomo, Vito, cantori lire trenta-
quattro d'accordo cho'lloro per lo detto
mese di giugno, L. XXXIIII"; sacristan's report for June 1449). For contract of 21 January 1450 see Doc. 4.1

**Andrea d'Andrea de' Rami da Mantova,
Ser.** Contrabass singer, November 1521–
October 1524
Monthly payments of L. 18

Andrea de' Servi, Fra. Singer, November
1482

**Andrea di Baldassarre da Montepulciano,
Messer.** Singer, August 1524–July 1525
Monthly payments of L. 9

Andrea di Giovanni. Clerk-singer, May 1591
Payment of L. 1. 10

Andrea Feliciani. *Maestro di cappella,* 1 November 1575–December 1596
Record of appointment, dated 4 November
1575: "Ricordo questo dì 4 di Novembre
chome il magnifico signor Rettore dell'Opera l'à condotto per maestro di cappella della
chiesa cattedrale. Cominciò a servire il
primo di questo mese e se li consegniò la

chiave della schuola e l'inventario delle robbe
e libri di musica, dovendo l'Opera pagarli per
suo salario e mercè, cioè lire diciasette soldi 10
per ciaschuno mese, sempre alla fine del mese.
E di quanto esse sia obrighato fare in detto
offitio ci riferiamo al ricordo di frate Salvadore
da Modana, già stato maestro della medesima
cappella, appare in questo a c. 25, il quale se li
è letto in sua presenza. Et esso e ll'Opera si
sonno obrighati quanto in quello si dice, eccetto che del salario che se li deve solo quanto
s'è detto di sopra. E per fede si sottoschrivarrà.
Io Andrea sopradetto affermo come di sopra"
(vol. 629, fol. 62ʳ; margin: Maestro Andrea di
Filisiano Filisiani)

Monthly payments of L. 17. 10. Last payment:
"Maestro Andrea Feliziani bona memoria et
già maestro della cappella . . . L. 26. 8 . . .
per tutt'il dì 24 di Dicembre [1596] quanto
visse" (vol. 1083, fol. 70ʳ)

Request for higher salary, 22 January 1591: see
Doc. 7.7

Will dated 30 May 1583: "Dominus Iohannes
Andreas olim Feliciani de Felicianis senensis
civis et musicus . . . corpore infirmus et in
lecto iacens . . . suum ultimum nuncupativum testamentum . . . fecit . . . heredem
suam universalem instituit . . . Uraniam, ipsius testatoris unicam filiam legiptimam et naturalem . . . Presentibus testibus . . . domino
Iacobo olim Antonio Latini, musico senensi"
(ASS, Notarile antecosimiano, vol. 3773,
fasc. 9, no. 57)

Will dated 11 October 1593: "Dominus Iohannes Andreas olim Feliciani de Felicianis, Senensis civis et musicus . . . sanus . . . corpore
licet certo modo valetudinarius . . . ultimam
voluntatem fecit et condidit . . . heredem
suum universalem instituit . . . Franciscum
eius filium, modo etatis mensium circa undecim" (Notarile postcosimiano, Originali, vol.
47, no. 269)

Angelo, Ser. Laudese, August 1440

Annibale d'Andrea Bennardi da Radda (Ser
as of May 1570). Clerk-singer, soprano, May
1557–April 1558, May 1561–March 1567,
May 1570–April 1576; tenor singer, May
1575–April 1588

Monthly payments of L. 2. 10 as "cherico mi-

nore e soprano in cappella"; raised to L. 3
May 1560, L. 4, then L. 6 as adult singer

Annibale dell'Oste. Clerk-singer, soprano, January 1600–November 1603

Monthly payments of L. 2

Ansano (Sano) di Goro (Ser by end of 1500).
Chorister, then singer, October 1485–March
1495; August 1500–July 1507, April 1511–
March 1512 (perhaps only as chaplain), April
1515–February 1520 (with occasional absences); substitute *maestro di cappella,* March–
November 1517, March 1520–February
1524; d. end of 1524

Monthly payments of L. 2 as chorister (cantorino); from December 1489 L. 2. 10; from
April 1492 L. 3. 10; from April 1493 L. 4;
from August 1500 L. 6; from March 1507
L. 10

Complains about the Opera's treatment of him,
2 September 1507: see Doc. 6.1

Salary raised retroactively to L. 12 as of December 1517: "1517. Ser Ansano di Goro chantore da fronte de' avere. L. sessanta quattro
s.—e sono per lo suo salario di mesi trentadue a ragione di L. dodici il mese, e perché
aveva auto lo decreto di L. X el mese e di
tanti n'era stato fatto creditore in questo a c.
263 e non ostante che esso decreto dicesse di
L. X mi sta di manco n'aveva L. XII che re-
stava debitore di questa per virtù di un decreto del rettore [Guido Palmieri] 12 Dicembre 1517 . . . E de' avere L. trentasei S.—e
sono per lo suo salario di mesi nove cominciati a dì primo di marzo 1516 [1517] finito
a dì ultimo di novembre 1517 a ragione di
L. IIII el mese come aveva ser Piero d'Asciano per maestro di capella . . . E de' avere L.
sessanta S. quattro e sono per lo suo salario
di mesi quattro, dicembre, gennaio, febraio,
marzo 1518 . . . E de' avere L. sessanta S.
quattro e sono per lo suo salario di 4 mesi,
agosto, settembre, octtobre, novembre
[1519]" (vol. 511, fol. 403 right)

Ansano Maria di Geronimo. Trombonist,
November 1542–January 1546 (also a Palace
musician)

Monthly payments of L. 10

Anselmo de' frati di Santo Spirito, Frate.
Chaplain-singer, May 1383–April 1385

Annual salary L. 10 ("per suo salario d'uno anno che è stato in duomo a cantare in choro")

Anselmo di Santo Agostino, Frate. Alto singer, May 1578–July 1579

Monthly payments of L. 4

Antonio, piovano of Chiusdino. Singer, June 1454

Hired for one month, 3 June 1454 (see Doc. 4.7)

Antonio da Viterbo, Ser. Singer, February 1446

Paid L. 3. 20 for one month

Antonio di Antonio Ongaro (Ongaretto, teutonico), Ser. Singer, 1458–May 1479 (absent July–October 1461)

Hired at salary of 10 lire on 28 November 1458: "Domini Operarius et consiliarii, convocati etc. . . deliberaverunt et solemniter decreverunt remictere et remiserunt in dominum operarium qui possit et ei liceat conducere Antonium Antonii, teotonicum, in cantorem Opere prout ei videbitur, non excedendo salarium de libris X in mense quolibet, que conducta duret ad beneplacitum Operarii et consiliariorum . . . Die 20 decembris dominus Operarius declaravit salarius esse de libris X denariorum in mense quolibet" (vol. 14, fol. 52^v)

Salary raised to 12 lire on 17 July 1459 (ibid., fol. 58^v), but paid varying amounts

Antonio di Bartolomeo Fornari. Clerk-singer, September 1591–May 1595

Antonio di Biagio, Ser. Laudese, May 1418–April 1420

Monthly salary of s. 5

Antonio di Cirello. Laudese, 1399–December 1403

Monthly payments of L. 1 for singing "le laude la sera in Duomo"

Antonio di Gabriello da Montepulciano, Ser. Chaplain-singer and singing teacher, March–September 1441, March 1449–May 1452, December 1454–August 1457

Hired as chaplain, singer, and substitute organist, 16 March 1441: "Similmente e per lo medesimo modo tutti d'acordo deliberarono di condurre e condussero ser Antonio [gap] da Montepulciano prete, per cappellano, cantore e sonatore d'organi quando gli sarà commisso, per tempo d'uno anno e in questo mezo a lloro beneplacito, con salario di lire dieci el mese e non più" (vol. 13, fol. 64^r)

Had left by November 1441: see Doc. 3.4

Payment for purchase of monochord, 2 October 1451: "E a dì II d'ottobre lire cinque soldi quatro dè contanti Nicholò nostro a ser Antonio di ser Gabriello, prete di duomo, per detto di miser Mariano [Bargagli] operaio, per uno monacordo si comprò da lui per ensegnare a sonare a più cherici di duomo, L. V s. IIII d. —" (vol. 564, fol. 22^r)

Loan of blanket: "1451. Ser Antognio di Ghabriello da Montepulciano, nostro cha[n]tore, ebbe in presta una choltre da dosso, lungha" (vol. 583, fol. 46^r)

As teacher: "Ser Antonio da Monte Pulciano che esegna a cantare" (sacristan's report, August 1451)

Contract of 30 December 1454 at Fl. 32 per annum (see Doc. 4.8); renewed 30 December 1456 at Fl. 40 per annum (see Doc. 4.10)

Dismissed 11 August 1457: "Item deliberaverunt cassare et cassaverunt ser Antonium Gabrielis de Montepolitiano, et quod in futurum non habeat salarium, et de tempore quo servivit habeat salarium secundum suam conductam" (vol. 14, fol. 38^r)

Antonio di Matteo, Ser. Laudese, June–July 1413

Antonio di Matteo da Prato, Ser. Soprano singer, 1456–after January 1458

Hired 1 November 1456 (see Doc. 4.9); contract renewed 30 December 1457 (see Doc. 4.11)

Antonio di Niccolò Trecerchi (de' Canceglieri), Ser. Singer, 1456–57

Hired with yearly salary of Fl. 10 on 5 July 1456: "Et deliberaverunt conducere et conduxerunt ser Antonium Niccolai de Canceglieri de Roma, plebanum Suvareti, in cappellanum ecclesie cum infrascriptis modis et pro uno anno et interim ad beneplacitum, pro florenis X in anno, cum his conditionibus, videlicet: che dì tre della semmana e tutte le feste celebrare, et essare al mattino ttutte le feste, essare in coro a messa e a vespero tutte le feste, et el tempo delle vagationi dello Studio continuo stare in coro et cantare d'ogni ragione canto, cioè canto fermo, contraponto, figurato, come meglio potrà" (vol. 14, fol. 21ʳ)

Declined; salary increased to Fl. 12, 24 August 1456: "Viso quod ser Antonio Niccolai, plebanus Suvareti, qui fuit conductus in cappellanum catredalis [*sic*] ecclesie cum certis pactis pro florenis X in anno (prout patet in presente libro, fo. 21) que conducta per dictum ser Antonium non fuit acceptata: deliberaverunt et solemniter decreverunt quod sit et esse intelligatur plene remissum et commissum in dominum Tonum qui possit et ei liceat conducere dictum ser Antonium in cappellanum dicte ecclesie non excedendo pretium florenum XII in anno, et cum omnibus aliis condictionibus et pactis ut in dicta conducta continetur" (ibid., fol. 24ʳ)

Antonio di Ser Cristoforo Diligente, Ser. Singer, September 1522–November 1524; substitute *maestro di cappella,* 5 September 1525–27 April 1526; singer, 1 June–14 August 1526, June 1531–September 1535, September 1539; *maestro di cappella,* January 1548–April 1552 (also an organist)
Monthly payments of L. 8, L. 10 as singer, of L. 32 as *maestro di cappella*

Antonio di Troiano. Laudese, November 1472–January 1473
See Ser Agostino.

Antonio Maria di Pasquino (Pacino) Sacchi. Clerk-singer, April 1595–December 1599
Monthly payments of L. 4, then L. 2 as "cherico minore e cantore," then "cantore"

Antonio Piccardo. Singer, April 1472–February 1473
Paid L. 4 April 1472, L. 8 monthly thereafter

Arcangelo da Reggio di Santa Maria de' Servi, Frate. *Maestro di cappella,* 31 May 1568–April 1570 (previously organist)
Monthly payments of L. 21

Arcangelo di Maestro Antonio. Clerk-singer, April–May 1490, 20 August 1491–March 1497

Arcolano di Nanni, Ser. Laudese, September 1412–February 1413
Paid s. 20 monthly for substituting for Ser Mariano di Nanni

Ardilasso d'Astore da Pistoia. Tenorista and contrabass singer, December 1519–April 1521
Monthly payments of L. 21

Arrigo Tibello di Giovanni da Bruggia. Singer, November 1524
Paid L. 4 on 24 November 1524

Ascanio d'Andrea Marri. Clerk-singer, January 1542–February 1548; *Maestro di cappella,* June–October 1575 (also a Palace musician)
Monthly payments of L. 1 as "cantarino," then of L. 4

Ascanio Gobbo. Clerk-singer, February–June 1552
Monthly payments of s. 10; called "figlio della cappella"

Attilio di Girolamo. Clerk-singer, alto, April–July 1580
Monthly payments of L. 4

Attivio Montelauri. Alto singer, May 1591–July 1602
Monthly payments of L. 6, then L. 8, L. 9

Aurelio di Ser Febo Rossi. Clerk-singer, soprano, May 1562–August 1566
Monthly payments of L. 1. 10, then L. 2. 10

Austino di Antonio. Singer, April–August 1478; chaplain, April 1464

Austino di Bernardo Magini da Città di Castello, Messer. Tenor singer, July 1560–May 1565
Monthly payments of L. 14, then L. 21, L. 14

Baldassare di Antonio, Ser. Laudese, May, September, 1413

Bartolomeo de Castris. Contrabass singer, May–September 1482; unspecified month in 1483
Monthly salary of L. 15 "per contra di duomo"; payment for unspecified time of L. 4. 8 in 1483

Bartolomeo di Conte Franzese. Tenor singer, November 1550–January 1554
Monthly payments of L. 28 November 1550–April 1551; of L. 21, then L. 24

Bartolomeo di Luti. Singer and cleric, May 1408–April 1410, May–July 1411
Annual salary of L. 24

Bartolomeo (Meo) di Maestro Giovanni. Singer, May 1453–November 1456

Contract 4 April 1454: "Et deliberorono conduciare e deliberando condussero Meo di
[gap] in cantore e per cantore della chiesa
catredale [*sic*] per tempo d'uno anno, et in
questo mezo a beneplacito del loro officio,
con salario e a rragione di lire cinque di denari sanesi per ciascheduno mese" (vol. 13,
fol. 129^r); reappointed 3 May 1454 (see Doc.
4.6), 30 December 1454 (see Doc. 4.8)

Bartolomeo di Mariano da Firenze, Ser.
Chaplain-singer, August 1401–July 1414
Hired 29 August 1401 at L. 80 per year
Paid as tenor and for adjusting clocks: "per suo
salaro di stare in choro a servire a tenere el
tenore del canto e a tenparare gli urioli"
(vol. 499, fol. 210^v)

Bartolomeo di Marino da Fermo. Singer
and substitute organist, 14 August 1439–
February 1440
Hired in August 1439 at Fl. 24 per year: "Misser
l'operaio, conseglieri et camarlingo predetti
. . . deliberarono conduciare e conduxero lo
infrascripto in cantore e per cantore ne la
detta chiesa, con modi, pacti e salario infrascripti. El nome del quale, et modi et pacti
sono questi, cioè, misser Bartolomeo di [gap]
da Fermo [1] Imprima, che s'intenda essare e
sia condotto per cantore per tempo d'uno
anno, da cominciare el dì che comincerà a
servire, e da finire come seguita. [2] Item
che debba avere per suo salario del detto
anno Fl. vinti quattro, di L. quattro l'uno di
denari sanesi. [3] Item che sia tenuto venire,
stare et offitiare nella detta chiesa cathedrale
a dire messa e cantare ogni dì che si cele-
brarà solennità ne la detta chiesa, et tutti e dì
di festa per la Santa Chiesa commandata [*sic*],
come e cappellani d'essa chiesa; et glialtri dì
che non fusse solennità o festa, come detto
è, non sia tenuto venire più che si voglia, excepto che 'l giovedì, che non v'è festa ne la
semana, sia tenuto venire a offitiare e cantare
perchè in quello dì si fa ferie a le lectioni de
lo Studio. [4] Item che sia tenuto sonare gli
orgha[n]i a ogni caso e bisogno che avenisse"
(vol. 13, fol. 51^r)

**Bartolomeo di Pietro dei Farnetani-
Saracini da Asinalonga.** Alto singer, January 1542–April 1552; May 1560–October
1563

Monthly payments of L. 6, then L. 21

Bartolomeo di Tomasso. Clerk-singer, May
1551–February 1552
Monthly payments of L. 1

Bastiano del Nica. Clerk-singer, January–
February 1535; January 1538
Monthly payments of L. 1. 10, then L. 2

Battista di Ser Francesco da Todi, Messer.
Chaplain, singing teacher, and substitute organist, 27 July 1426–April 1428
Hired 27 July 1426, with yearly salary of L. 88.
13. 4: "Misser Battista di ser Franciescho da
Todi s'è chondotto adì XXVII di luglio per
prette e die fare tutto quelo che fano gli a[l]-
tri nostri chapelani e p[r]etti, e die i[n]segnia-
re a chantare a tutti que' che volesono
i[m]parare a chantare, di chasa, senza pagha-
mento, e die sonare orghani se bisongniase.
E s'è chondotto questo dì detto di sopra per
tempo d'uno ano per prezo di fiorini trentacinque di lire quatro fiorino in l'ano che so'
lire cientoquaranta, L. CXL" (vol. 494, fol.
10^r)

Benedetto dall'Aquila, Ser. Singer, April
1472–March 1478
Paid L. 5. 10 for April 1472; monthly payments
of L. 11 thereafter

Benedetto di Francesco Franceschi, Ser.
Clerk-singer, June 1551–July 1553; chaplain-
singer, alto, May 1561–March 1570, May
1570–April 1587
Monthly payments of L. 1; from May 1561
L. 16; from May 1570 L. 24, then L. 12

Benvenuto. Clerk-singer, January 1538
Payment of L. 1. 10

Benvenuto di Girolamo Flori (Ser as of
1590). Clerk-singer, soprano, June 1579–
April 1588, tenor singer, May 1590–April
1591, December 1594–November 1607
Recorded in a list of young clerks, May 1576–
April 1578, though not yet singing in the
chapel. Monthly payments of L. 1. 10, then
L. 2. 10 as "cherico piccolo e soprano," then
as soprano only, June 1580–April 1582; as
"cherico grande e cantore," June 1582–April
1586; of L. 5, then L. 7 as "cherico grande e
soprano," May 1586–April 1588; as "cappellano e cantore," later as "cantore," May
1590–April 1591 of L. 26 to L. 28; of L. 10,
December 1594–November 1607

Bernardino. Singer, April–September 1471
Monthly payments of s. 40

Bernardino di Antonio. Clerk-singer, June 1517

Bernardino di Cenni. Clerk-singer, April 1493–September 1494

Bernardino di Giovanbattista Cocchi (Ser after 1595). Clerk-singer, alto, June 1587–April 1588; alto singer, May 1588–January 1598, December 1602–November 1603
Monthly payments of L. 6, then L. 8, L. 9

Bernardino (Bernardo) di Jacomo da Pontremoli, Ser. Tenor singer, December 1529–April 1558; May 1560–March 1570
Monthly payments of L. 17 to August 1537; of L. 24. 10, then L. 24. 20, then L. 28
Retained despite suspension of the chapel, November 1556: see Doc. 7.1

Bernardino di Lorenzo. Clerk-singer, April–October 1493

Bernardino di Matteo Cartolaio. Clerk-singer, May 1524–April 1526; instrumentalist, December 1531–December 1534; September 1535–October 1542 (also a Palace musician)
Monthly payments of L. 5 initially; payment of L. 14. 10, dated 24 December 1524; in later years monthly payments of L. 12 as instrumentalist

Bernardino di Pietro Draghi (Ser after 1586). Clerk, June 1578–April 1579; clerk-singer, soprano, June 1580–April 1584; alto singer, January 1585–May 1591
Monthly payments of L. 3, then L. 4 as "cherico piccolo e soprano in cappella," June 1580–May 1582; as "cherico minore e soprano," May 1582–April 1584; as "cherico mezzano" and contralto, January 1585–April 1586; as contralto, June 1586–April 1588; of L. 6, then L. 8

Bernardo, figlio della cappella. Clerk-singer, May 1552–January 1553
Monthly payments of s. 10

Biagio di Fuccio da Pienza, Ser. Chorister, June 1503–April 1505; clerk-singer, 1506; singer, February 1522–August 1527 (d. June 1528)
Monthly payments of L. 1, then L. 5, L. 6
Paid L. 4 as member of confraternity of San Pie-

tro, 1514: "MDXIII. Ser Biagio di Fuccio da Pientia die dare perfino questo dì 13 di gennaio [1514] lire quattro, L. 4" (ASS, PR, Compagnia di San Pietro nel Duomo, vol. 1370, *E&U, 1513–24,* fol. 32 left)
Legacy after death to the confraternity: "MDXXVIII [Luglio, in margin] Ser Biagio di Fuccio prete et cappellano istato de San Bernardino in duomo, uno delli nostri confratelli di nostra congregatione, venendo già più settimane a morte come piaggeva all'omnipotente Idio, lassò per sua devotione alla nostra congregatione lire sette s. 0, li quali denari sene debbi ogniun di noi pregar Idio per l'anima sua nelli nostri sachrifitii diurni et nocturni" (ibid., vol. 1369, *Capitoli, D&C, 1513–76,* fol. 127 left)

Biagio di Tomè da San Salvadore, Ser. Singer, May 1441–May 1446; May 1449, February 1451–February 1454, sporadically till June 1480; Chaplain-singer, May 1481–June 1485 (absent June 1482)
Monthly payments varying between 3 and 8 lire; for contracts in 1452–54 see Docs. 4.4, 4.5, 4.7
A 1513 document from the Cathedral's Confraternity of San Pietro notes that he was a member of the group (ASS, PR, Compagnia di San Pietro nel Duomo, vol. 1370, *E&U, 1513–21,* fol. 4r). He lived to a great age, an entry in another of the Confraternity's volumes revealing that he died in 1513 (vol. 1369, *Capitoli, 1513–76,* fol. 5r: "MDXIII: Ser Blasius S. Salvatoris cappellanus Sancte Caterine obijt et requiescat in pace")

Brandaglia. Laudese, September 1388–May 1399

Calixto di Maestro Guglielmo. Clerk-singer, April–May 1490, April 1493
Present April–May 1490, and paid s. 5 for a few days in April 1493

Camillo di Marco Giorgi. Clerk-singer, August 1524–January 1530
Monthly payments of L. 2

Carlo di Guglielmo Francioso. Singer, November 1463–April 1465, July 1465–August 1466, April 1475 (possibly Carulo Britonio)
Hired 20 November 1463 with monthly salary

of 8 lire: "Appresso deliberarono conducere e conduxero Carlo cantore ad cantare nella chiesa catredale [*sic*] come sarà di bisogno, per mesi sei cominciati el dì che venne ad cantare in decta chiesa, per salario di lire otto per ciascuno mese, e che 'l camarlingo senza suo preiudicio o danno possi pagare detto salario di mese in mese secondo servirà" (vol. 15, fol. V^r)

Salary raised to 12 lire, 28 February 1464: "Et deliberarono che el salario di Carlo cantore sia di lire XII ciascuno mese, cominciando el dì proximo seguente che sarà primo di marzo 1463 [1464]. E questo per uno anno, e in questo mezo ad beneplacito" (ibid., fol. VII^r)

Contract renewed 8 February 1465: "Rimisero ancora nel detto spettabilissimo Cavaliere misser l'operaio el quale possa conducere Carlo francioso in cantore de la chiesa catredale [*sic*], da durare a lloro beneplacito" (ibid., fol. XIII^v)

Contract confirmed 9 July 1465 at Fl. 3 per month (ibid., fol. XVII^r)

Contract not renewed 8 February 1466: "Modo et forma predecte deliberarono di cassare et cassarono Carlo cantore de l'Opera, el quale s'intende casso et non più conducto in Kalende di mazo proximo advenire" (ibid., fol. XII^r)

Returns for one month, April 1475: "Charlo di Ghulglielmo francioso chantore stette in duomo deve avere Fl. uno largo per tanti li paghai per detto di misser Savino per aver un mese servito in duomo in choro per chanttore e poi si partì, in questo a fo. 157" (vol. 297, fol. 44^v)

Carlo Vanni Romano. Singer, December 1593–January 1595
Monthly payments of L. 8

Celio d'Ansano Molandi, Messer. Bass singer, August 1579–April 1590, November 1602–August 1604
Monthly payments of L. 4, then L. 8; after 1602 of L. 21 as "musico cantore"

Cesare d'Andrea. Clerk-singer, May 1549–December 1551
Monthly payments of L. 2

Chimenti de' Servi, Frate (called Tedesco in Florentine documents). Singer, May, November 1482; January 1483–May 1486
Payment of L. 5. 18 May 1482; payments of L. 4, L. 6, then of L. 7. 10

Claudio. Singer, July 1460
Paid L. 3

Claudio di Stefano Bartalucci. Clerk-singer, January–October 1530
Monthly payments of L. 1

Colinetto Francioso, Ser. Singer, May–early September 1445
Monthly payments of L. 12

Cornelio da Sovana. Clerk-singer, September 1518–October 1520
Monthly payments of L. 1. 10

Cosimo di Jacomo de' Mendici. Clerk-singer, soprano, June 1587–September 1589
Monthly payments of L. 1. 10

Cristofano Draghi. Clerk-singer, December 1595–August 1597, December 1602–March 1607
Monthly payments of L. 2 as "cherico minore e cantore," L. 5. 10 as "cherico maggiore e cantore," then L. 4 as "cantore"

Daniello Danielli, Messer. Singer, December 1593–November 1594
Monthly payments of L. 5

Daniello di Simone Lupi Fiamengo (Tedesco, Inglese). Contralto singer, December 1520–September 1521
Monthly payments of L. 7; the sacristan's account of May 1521 calls him "Ser Daniello inglese"

Dino Ortolano. Clerk-singer, August 1517
Paid L. 1. 10

Domenico di Giovanbattista. Clerk-singer, May 1521–May 1530
Monthly payments of L. 1. 10 to July 1527, then of L. 3

Domenico di Giovanni. Clerk-singer, May 1487–April 1488
Monthly payments of L. 1. 10

Domenico di Maestro Antonio Lucenti (Ser as of June 1586). Clerk-singer, soprano, May 1576–April 1578; tenor singer, June 1582–April 1584; chaplain and bass singer, June 1586–January 1587; tenor singer, November 1588–November 1589

Monthly payments as "cherico mezzano," with no indication that he sang, May 1578–April 1582; as "cherico grande e tenore," June 1582–April 1584; of L. 20 as "cappellano e basso," June 1586–January 1587, and of L. 4 as "tenore," November 1588–November 1589

Domenico di Maestro Martino. Clerk-singer, soprano, May 1568–April 1570, June 1572–April 1574

Monthly payments of L. 1. 10 as "cherico minore e soprano"

Domenico di Maestro Pietro. Clerk-singer, soprano, June 1582–November 1583; alto singer, December 1583–April 1584

Monthly payments of L. 2 as soprano, the of L. 3. 10 as alto

Domenico (Menico) di Matteo. Singer in choir school, November, 1450–October 1456

Appointed 11 February 1451 (see Doc. 4.2); confirmed 13 October 1451 (see Doc. 4.3); reappointed 2 May 1453 (see Doc. 4.5), 3 May 1454 (see Doc. 4.6), 30 December 1454 (see Doc. 4.8)

Monthly payments of L. 3, then of L. 4

Domenico di Matteo, Ser. Offered contract as chaplain and singer, April 1465

"El salario di ser Domenico di Matano [*sic*] da calende di luglio in là, per cantare, sia di fiorini 6 l'anno, di L. 4 per fiorino, per ciascuno anno, e come cappellano sia di fiorini 24 di L. 4 per fiorino" (vol. 15, fol. XVIᵛ)

Domenico di Matteo, Ser. Chaplain-singer, April–September 1481

Monthly payments of L. 4 "per cantare in canto figurato"

Donato di Domenico Santini (Ser as of 1590). Clerk-singer, soprano, November 1585–April 1588, May 1590–November 1594, August 1602–April 1604

Monthly payments of L. 3. 10 as "cherico mezzano e soprano," June–October 1586, and as "cherico grande e cantore," November 1586–April 1588; of L. 6, then L. 7, L. 9

Donato di Lodovico. Laudese, May–June 1407

Monthly payments of s. 20 for singing "le lalde in duomo"

Elia, Ser. Singer, end July–mid-August 1481

Payments of L. 2. 10 for July and of L. 6 for 15 days in August

Eustachius (de Monte Regali). *Maestro di cappella,* September 1507–January 1508; contralto singer, February–September 1508

Comprehensive payment at end of service, 30 September 1508: "Maestro Eustachio, maestro di chapella . . . de' avere per i[n]fino a dì u[l]timo di settenbre 1508 L. cientosessantacinque s. dicienove d. 2, sonno per tredici mesi à servito per maestro di capella in duomo, cioè per 5 mesi, e per otto à servitto per co[n]tra alto a L. 12 el mese, che questo dì n'à fatto conto col Magnifico Pandolfo e chompagni, nostri dignissimi Operai, d'achordo per tutto el tenpo ci fusse statto; so' a spese, a fol. [blank], L. CLXV s. XVIIII d. 2" (vol. 510, fol. 147ʳ)

Eustachio di Giovanni (di Binolio) Francioso. Singer, January–August 1448

Monthly salary of L. 12, but frequently paid less because of absences

Fabio di Francesco Tizzoni. Clerk-singer, then soprano singer, May 1556–April 1559, May 1560–June 1565

Monthly payments of L. 2. 10 as "cherico minore," then as "cantore in cappella," May 1556–April 1557; of L. 4 as "chericho mezano et soprano in cappella"; of L. 6 as "cherico e cantore in cappella"

Fabrizio di Bartolomeo Martini (Messer as of 1599). Clerk-singer, December 1594–November 1596; tenor, December 1596–November 1607

Monthly payments of L. 4 as "cherico mezzano e cantore"; of L. 8, then L. 9 as "cherico maggiore e cantore"; of L. 26. 10, then L. 4, L. 7 as "cappellano e cantore," then as cantore

Fabrizio Ricci d'Aquapendente. Clerk-singer, soprano, February 1565–April 1568

Monthly payments of L. 1. 10

Fausto d'Ansano Molandi (Ser as of June 1580). Clerk-singer, soprano, February 1561–May 1564; bass singer, June 1580–January 1581

Monthly payments of L. 1. 10 as "soprano in cappella"; of L. 6 as basso

Fausto di Simone Bascarelli. Clerk-singer, soprano, January–April 1588, September 1591

Monthly payments of L. 2. 16. 8, then L. 3. 10 as "cherico piccolo e soprano"; of L. 1. 10 as "cantore"

Federigo di Pietro. Clerk-singer, December 1482, May 1484–March 1485

Monthly payments of L. 1. 10, then L. 2, L. 3

Francesco da Sancta Reina, Ser. Singer, December 1457

Paid L. 3

Francesco di Antonio di Boccone d'Asciano (Ser in 1452). Cleric, laudese, singer, April–August, October–December 1440, May 1446–September 1450, May 1452

Paid L. 1 extra for singing laudi on Sundays and in Lent

Francesco di Antonio di Griffolo. Clerk-singer, May 1487–April 1488

Monthly payments of L. 2

Francesco di Antonio tessitore. Clerk-singer, May 1487–April 1489

Monthly payments of L. 2

Francesco di Barnaba. Laudese, November 1472–January 1473

See Ser Agostino

Francesco di Bartolomeo. Clerk-singer, May 1552–June 1554

Monthly payments of L. 2

Francesco di Francesco. Clerk-singer, April 1548–March 1549; singer, April 1550–April 1552

Monthly payments of L. 8

Francesco di Guido. Clerk-singer, April–June 1470

Paid L. 2. 10 monthly

Francesco di Lorino. Clerk-singer, May–November 1454

Hired May 1454 (see Doc. 4.6)

Francesco di Maestro Matteo. Clerk-singer, soprano, June 1587–December 1593

Monthly payments of L. 1. 10, then L. 2. 10

Francesco di Nanni, Ser. Chaplain at the hospital of Santa Maria della Scala. Laudese, June 1413–August 1415; January–December 1428 (also an organist)

Paid s. 10 per month for singing laudi

Francesco di Piero Bianciardi, Messer. Chaplain, May 1593–1595; *maestro di cappella,* January 1597–January 1607 (also an organist)

Renewal of contract, 16 March 1602: "Convocato et congregato il Capitolo delli signori rettore, canonico e savi sei dell'Opera del Duomo di Siena . . . Il signor rettore Giugurta Tommasi referse quanto fra esso et messer Francesco Bianciardi, maestro di cappella dei duomo, fusse passato secondo che si rimase nell'ultima sessione. Et in resoluzione ch'egli si fermarebbe sempre che con l'emolumento della cappella del canto si gli dia dall'opera tanta provisione, che ascendi alla somma di scudi cento, e che in questo conto accetterebbe la casa dell'opera. Onde discorso a pieno et considerato la suffitienza, costumi et altre buone qualità del detto messer Francesco, e che nella città non vi sonno suggetti habili, e quanto difficile fusse a trovare et condurre di fuori uno pari a lui, et quando ancora si trovasse che saria con spese forse molto maggiore, a conseglio del signor canonico Cosci, approvato per otto lupini tutti bianchi, fu ottenuto et deliberato che si fermi il detto messer Francesco per maestro di cappella in duomo per anni tre da cominciarsi ad aprile prossimo. Et che sii sopraintendente et habbi autorità di sopraintendenza dell'organo, et dell'organista del Duomo che si eleggerà. Et al medesimo oltre al solito et ordenario salario di lire trentadue il mese si diano di più ogn'anno scudi vinti di moneta, distibutivamente però ciascun mese la parte. Et in oltre se gli dia ad habitare e fruttare per detto tempo la casa dell'Opera in Siena in piazza Manetti, quale per essere di presente appigionata, devi in questo mentre tirarne la pigione e di poi entrare a goderla" (vol. 18, fol. 59ʳ)

Beginning in April 1602 monthly payments of L. 43. 13. 4 are regularly registered to Bianciardi until the time of his death

Francesco di Pietro Fabri Fiamengo. Bass singer, April 1551–April 1552; *maestro di cappella,* May 1553–October 1555, June 1560–May 1565

Monthly payments of L. 28, then L. 32, April

1551–April 1552, as singer; of L. 32 as *maestro di cappella,* 1555; of L. 49, May 1561–April 1562; of L. 49 then L. 42 to April 1564; of L. 42 to May 1565

Francesco di Tommaso. Clerk-singer, May 1487–May 1490, April 1493–March 1494
Monthly payments of L. 2, then L. 3, L. 4

Francesco di Tomaso tessitore, Ser. Boy singer, July–August, December 1485–March 1486, February 1492 (also an organist)
Monthly payments of L. 1. 10, then L. 3

Francesco Franceschi (Messer as of 1596). Clerk-singer, tenor, December 1594–November 1595, December 1596–November 1607
Monthly payments of L. 10, L. 11, then L. 13 as "cherico grande e cantore"; of L. 20. 10, L. 30. 10, then L. 19, L. 21 as "cappelano e cantore," then "sagrestano e cantore"

Francesco Gerini, Ser. Singer, May, August, October 1520
Monthly payments of L. 6

Fruosino di Antonio da Pisa (del Pisano, Fiorentino, Fioravanti). Choirboy, May 1513–September 1518; singer, April 1521–June 1523
Monthly payments of L. 2 to April 1521, then of L. 3, L. 4

Fruosino di Lodovico Tancredi, Ser. Singer, May, August, October 1520
Monthly payments of L. 3

Gabriello. Clerk-singer, August 1460–66
Initially hired at 40 soldi a month (vol. 15, fol. XXII^r), raised to 4 lire in January 1466 (fol. XXI^r)

Gabriello di Giovanni de' Servi. Bass singer, January 1539–April 1557
Monthly payments of L. 14

Gabriello di Ramondo Spagnolo. Bass singer, mid-June 1540–December 1541
Monthly payments of L. 7

Galgano di Ser Antonio. Clerk-singer, September 1515–September 1518
Monthly payments of L. 1, then L. 2

Gano (Galgano) d'Enea. Clerk-singer, August 1514–July 1522; cornettist, August 1538–January 1540 (also a Palace musician)
Monthly payments of L. 1, then L. 2, L. 2. 10,

L. 3 as singer, of L. 17. 6. 0 as cornettist ("suona la cornetta in duomo")

Giachetto Francioso. Singer, June 1467–October 1468 (= Jachetto di Marvilla)
Monthly payments of L. 13. 6. 8. Various payments for wood bought for Giachetto kantore on 9 December 1468 (vol. 507, fol. 431^r)

Giacopetto. Singer, April–June 1471
Monthly payments of L. 10

Giannino. *See* Giovanni (Giannino) di Francesco

Gienero di Mauritio Luti Fiamengo Intended as *maestro di cappella,* August 1551, but did not accept; see Doc. 6.5

Giletto. Singer, November 1470–March 1472 (= Giletto Cossu)
Monthly payments of L. 8

Giovanbattista. Clerk-singer, September 1515–March 1516
Monthly payments of L. 1. 10

Giovanbattista Chiocciolini. Clerk-singer, December 1595–August 1596, December 1596–November 1597; bass singer, July 1606–October 1607
Monthly payments of L. 6, then L. 4

Giovanbattista de' Mendici. Clerk-singer, December 1595–August 1597
Monthly payments of L. 2 as "cherico piccolo e cantore"

Giovanbattista degli Orfani. Clerk-singer, April 1595–July 1596
Monthly payments of L. 4, then L. 3, L. 2 as "cherico minore e cantore"

Giovanbattista di Bartolomeo. Clerk-singer, November 1520–June 1523; tenor singer, May 1539–June 1555, May 1556–April 1558; *maestro di cappella,* May 1558–April 1560; singer, May 1561–April 1565, *maestro di cappella,* May 1565–April 1568
Monthly payments of of L. 1. 10 as choirboy; of L. 14, then L. 21 as tenor singer

Giovanbattista di Bartolomeo Pieragli da Colle, Ser. Tenor singer, June 1586–April 1587; May 1588–April 1591
Monthly payments of L. 5, then L. 6, L. 7, L. 8, L. 9

Giovanbattista di Corvo milanese. Singer, May–November 1550

Monthly payments of L. 14

Giovanbattista di Francesco Formichi. Tenor singer, December 1587–August 1596

Monthly payments of L. 3, then L. 4, then L. 6, L. 8, L. 10 as cantore, later as "suona il trombone"

Giovanbattista di Maestro Guerrino. Clerk-singer, soprano, May–December 1590; May 1591–April 1593; singer, December 1594–November 1595

Monthly payments of L. 3. 10, then L. 4 as "cherico piccolo e soprano"; as "cherico mezzano e cantore"

Giovanbattista di Michelangelo. Clerk-singer, December 1595–August 1597

Monthly payments of L. 2 as "cherico minore e cantore"

Giovanbattista di Pasquino. Clerk-singer, soprano, November 1550–March 1555; May 1555–June 1556

Monthly payments of L. 2 and L. 3

Giovanbattista di Soriana. Clerk-singer, June 1517–September 1518

Monthly payments of L. 2

Giovanbattista di Vincenzio. Clerk-singer, November 1550

Giovanbattista Mariani, Messer. Singer, December 1594–November 1603

Monthly payments of L. 13, then L. 15

Giovanbattista Tesauro, Romano. Tenor singer, March 1575–January 1581

Monthly payments of L. 8

Giovanfrancesco di Antonio, Ser. Singer, mid-September 1511–September 1512

Monthly payments of L. 14

Giovanfrancesco di Benedetto. Trombonist, January 1558–September 1560; May 1565–December 1573 (also a Palace musician)

Monthly payments of L. 14 as "trombone in cappella," January 1558–September 1560; of L. 12, May 1565–December 1573

Giovanmaria Cappelletti, Messer. Bass singer, November 1598–November 1607

Monthly payments of L. 4, then L. 5, L. 6, L. 8

Giovanmaria d'Austino. Clerk-singer, soprano, May 1568–April 1570

Monthly payments of L. 1. 10 as "cherico minore e soprano"

Giovanni, Ser. Singer-chaplain, May–June 1450

Giovanni Antonio, Napolitano. Bass singer, May 1588–February 1591

Monthly payments of L. 3, then L. 4

Giovanni Calot, Maestro. Singer, 10–31 August 1448

Paid L. 9

Giovanni Comitis. Singer, June–August 1482

Giovanni Cristofani Francioso, Ser. Singer, February–May 1481

Payments of L. 12

Giovanni da Bologna, Ser. Singer, December 1442 (possibly = Ser Giovanni di Tommaso da Bologna)

Giovanni da Polonia. Singer, May–December 1449, January–April 1450

Paid 8 lire for May 1449; thereafter the four Polish singers paid 34 lire as a group (*see under* Andrea da Polonia). For contract of 21 January 1450 see Doc. 4.1

Other payments in March 1450: "Johannes de Polonia chantore, L. 12; el fanciullo suo [Vito], L. 12; Item per dì dieci serviti di Ferraio passato lire quattro, L. 4; Item debba avere per quattro dì d'Aprile serviti più et così mi disser Misser scrivessi per lui et lo fanciullo in tutto soldi trenta, L. 1 s. 10" (ibid.)

Leaves songbook as security: "1450. Giovanni di Pollonia, chantore, die dare lire dodici, i quali ebe da Lorenzo di Giovanni di Chele camarlingo, come apare al suo Memoriale a fo. 30, e a sua uscita a fo. 35; lassò uno libro di chanto in carta banbagina, L. XII. Posto a' libro rosso de' residui, a fo. 99" (vol. 501, fol. 108r)

Giovanni da San Germano, Messer. Singer, January–November 1530

Monthly payments of L. 10

Giovanni da San Giorgio, Frate. Singer, April 1482–August 1484

Monthly payments of L. 10

Giovanni de' Ricci (di Derici) Francioso. Singer, Christmas 1439

Paid L. 1. 12 on 30 April as a gift for having sung at Christmas: "1439. Giovanni di Derici di Francia die avere a dì 2 di giennaio [1440] grossi 6 e quali sono per una chortesia li fe' misser Giovanni perchè stette i' choro al chanto in pasqua, L. 1 s. 12" (vol. 267, fol. 98 left)

Giovanni (Giannino) di Francesco. Clerk-singer, May 1548–April 1549, contralto singer, April 1551–March 1552

Monthly payments of L. 3, later of L. 10

Giovanni di Giovanni Francioso, Messer. Chaplain and tenorista or cantore, July 1437–11 February 1439

Monthly salary of L. 10; frequent absences are noted in the records ("Ottobre 1438. Ser Giovanni tenorista adì 3 non fu a Vespero e compieta, adì 4 non fu a Vespero"; "Novembre 1438. Ser Giovanni Francioso adì 12 non fu a Terza, adì 19 non fu a Terza"; "Dicembre 1438 Ser Giovanni Francioso andò fuore adì XX, tornò adì XXXI, servì [gap]"; vol. 1259, unnumbered folios)

Paid extra for saying four Masses a week: "Et veduto che ser Giovanni francioso, tenorista, non è obligato a dire alcuna messa ne la detta chiesa, et per qualche piccolo salario si obligarebbe a dire ne la detta chiesa almeno quattro messe la semana, e potrebbesi allegerare la spesa d'uno capellano: deliberaro[no] che sia pienamente rimesso in misser lo Operaio e misser Conte, che possino cresciare, se a loro pare al detto ser Giovanni, oltre al salario che à al presente per tenere el tenore, fiorini sei l'anno e el detto ser Giovanni sia tenuto dire almeno quattro messe la semana ne la detta chiesa" (vol. 13, fol. 28ʳ, dated 20 December 1437)

Payments for rental of his bedding: "1437. Chime[n]tto di Pavolo, ligritiere, die avere ogni mese soldi otto per prestatura d'uno paio di le[n]zuolo prestò a misser Giovani di Giovani, franzoso e chantore in duomo, inchomi[n]ciò eso presto adì primo d'agosto 1437 . . . L.—s. VIII ogni mese. . . . Tenesi le le[n]zuola di misser Giovanni tenorista mesi diciotto, cioè per insino adì 11 di feraio 1438 [1439], d'achordo che si paghi per mesi 18" (vol. 500, fol. 311ᵛ)

Leaves 15 February 1439: "Misser lo operaio e conseglieri predetti . . . deliberarono di concordia rimettare e rimissero pienamente in misser l'Operaio e camarlingo predetti, e quali possino fare conventione con misser

Giovanni francioso, cantore stato in duomo, el quale a questo dì à preso licentia, di quello che lui domanda per una messa che à manchato la semana, et della pigione di certe lenzuola che à tenute da ligrittiere. Et se a loro parrà, pagarne tutto o parte de' denari della Opera, el possino fare" (vol. 13, fol. 36ʳ)

Giovanni di Giovanni (Pintelli). Soprano singer, September–December 1481; May 1482–January 1483; October 1483–August 1484

Monthly payments of L. 6, October–December 1481; payments of L. 6 to Giovanni di Giovanni cantore sovrano, May 1482 to January 1483; payment for "un paio di lenzuola"; monthly payments of L. 6, then of L. 12, October 1483–August 1484

Giovanni di Jacopo da Francia, Ser. Singer, February–mid-September 1459

Hired 7 February 1459 with annual salary of Fl. 50: "Dominus Operarius et consiliarii . . . deliberaverunt et solemniter decreverunt remictere et remiserunt in dominum Operarium qui possit et ei liceat conducere ser Ioannem Iacopi de Francia in cantorem et pro cantore Opere, non excedendo salarium quod ad presens datur ser Iohanni et ser Goro cantoribus, et cum hoc quod ipse teneatur et debeat servire Opere ad divina officia ut serviant alii capellani Opere. Et predicta decreverunt omni modo . . . Qui dominus Operarius declaravit salarium esse de florenis 50, et intelligatur incepisse die 4 martii dicit anni 1458 [59]" (vol. 14, fol. 55ʳ)

Giovanni di Jacopo Francioso, Ser, alias Messer Violetta. Chaplain and biscantore, 14 May–December 1437; April–23 October 1438

Monthly salary of L. 8; absences are noted ("Settembre 1438. Ser Giovanni francioso adì 2 andò fuore, non fu a Vespero, tornò adì VII, servì [gap]"; "Ottobre 1438. Ser Giovanni di Iacomo cantore adì VI andò fuore, tornò a dì [gap]"; vol. 1259, unnumbered folios)

Payments for rental of his bedding: "1437. Chime[n]tto di Pavolo, ligritiere . . . die avere adì 14 di maggio per uno paio di lenzuola che prestò questo dì per sere Giovanni di Iacopo, bischantore francioso, e die avere ogni

mese per pigione soldi otto . . . L.—s. VIII
ogni mese. . . . Tenesi le le[n]zuola di ser Giovanni di Iacopo bischantore insino adì 23
d'ottobre, d'achordo che si paghi per mesi
cinque, che montano d'achordo soldi quaranta" (vol. 500, fol. 311ᵛ)

Giovanni di Maestro Antonio. *Maestro di cap-*
pella, May 1509–June 1510 (also a Palace musician)

Comprehensive payment at end of service, 30
June 1510: "MDVIIII. Giovanni di maestro
Jachomo, piffaro e nostro maestro di chapella
a tenere ischuola [fol. 335 left: et maestro
della chapella de' chantori di duomo], de' a-
vere adì ultimo di giugno L. centosesantaotto
s. 0, sonno per suo servito di mesi XIIII ci à
servito lui proprio o ser Pietro d'Asciano in
suo luogo, a ragione di fiorini dodici el mese
e lire sei, d'achordo chon Pavolo uno de' nostri operari; a spese in questo foglio [blank].
L. CLXVIII" (vol. 510, fol. 335 right)

Giovanni di Martino da Massa, Ser. Chaplain and singer, August–November 1447

Monthly salary of L. 6

Giovanni di Matteo da Perugia, Ser. Chaplain; also listed as singer February–April
1418, July 1419–April 1420; also laudese,
May 1420–April 1426; singer, May 1425–
April 1426

Monthly salary of L. 9. 8. 8, plus s. 10 for singing laude

Giovanni di Matteo Farinella. Singer, April
1482–June 1485

Monthly payments of L. 4, April–October
1482; of L. 6 from February 1483

Giovanni di Michele da Radicondoli, Ser.
Singer, May 1449

Payment of L. 7. 3. 8

Giovanni di Pasquino (Pacino) Sacchi.
Clerk-singer, soprano, August 1583–
December 1590

Monthly payments of L. 1. 10, then L. 3 as
"cherico minore e soprano," of L. 10, then
L. 11 as "cherico grande, cantore"

Giovanni di San Francesco, Frate. Tenorista, March–September 1482

Payment of L. 6, 20 April 1482; monthly payments of L. 12 thereafter

Giovanni di Santi. Singer, May 1453–
October 1456

Hired May 1453; reappointed 3 May 1454 (see
Doc. 4.6) and 30 December 1454 (see Doc.
4.8)

Giovanni di Stefano di Piccardia (Fran-
cioso; de Grieve), Ser. Soprano singer, November 1456–March 1469

Appointed 1 November 1456 at Fl. 50 per annum (see Doc. 4.9); reappointed 30 December 1457 (see Doc. 4.11). Monthly salary L.
16. 14. 3

Giovanni di Tommaso. Clerk and laudese,
July 1408–April 1409

Giovanni di Tommaso da Bologna, Ser.
Chaplain from May 1424; listed as singer
May 1425–April 1426 (possibly = Ser Gio-
vanni da Bologna)

Paid L. 9. 3. 5 per month as a chaplain, L. 9. 16
when also a singer

Giovanni Fanti (Frutti, Furti, Futri) Fran-
cioso. Singer, November 1447–April 1448

The three French singers are paid L. 36
monthly as a group: "1447. Jachomo di Longho e Giovanni Frutti e Pietro domarlla
Franciosi e cantiori di duomo" (vol. 275, fol.
92)

Ill in April 1448: "Aprile, adì 16, infermò Giovanni Fanti francioso, cantore, e non servì
per infino a questo dì 20 del detto mese di
sopra" (vol. 1079, unnumbered folio)

Left on 3 May 1448: "Maggio, adì tre del detto
mese, si partì Iacomo, Giovanni, Vincentio
cantori, con nostra licentia" (vol. 1079, unnumbered folio)

Giovanni Francioso. Singer, May 1465–
March 1469 (absent from the end of August
1467 through the beginning of March 1468)
(possibly Johannes Cornuel)

Hired 1 May 1465 at Fl. 30 per annum: "Et conduxero Giovanni francioso cantore per uno
anno, da incominciare adì primo di maggio
1465 ad fiorini 30 per anno, et interim ad beneplacito de l'operaio e consiglieri" (vol. 15,
fol. XVIʳ)

Leaves temporarily at end of August 1467: "Giovanni francioso e lo compagno cantori
deono avere L. quaranta sono per loro salaro
di mesi uno e dì diciasette ànno servito per
cantori in duomo da dì 14 di luglio in sino a

dì ultimo d'agosto fatto d'acordo con messer Savino operaio. L. 40" (vol. 290, fol. 149ʳ)

Giovanni Pagliarini, Fra. *Maestro di cappella,* December 1507–15 May 1509 (absent March 1509)

Comprehensive payment at end of service, 15 May 1509: "MDVIII. Frate Giovanni Pagliarini, frate di Santo Francesco, maestro di capella in duomo . . . de' avere L. dugientotrentotto s.—sono per lo suo servitto di uno anno e cinque mesi e mezo à servitto l'Opera nostra per maestro di capella, per L. quatordici el mese, non ametendo uno mezo mese perdè; li quali cominciorno per insino adì primo di dicenbre 1507 e finitti adì XV di maggio 1509 . . . L. CCXXXVIII" (vol. 510, fol. 217 right)

Giovanni Piccioni, Messer. Alto singer, January 1592–November 1607

Monthly payments of L. 4

Giovanni Ragione di Francia, Ser. Singer, April–May 1431 (probably Johannes Reson)

Paid L. 3. 6 on 30 April 1431, and L. 10 on 31 May "per lo chanto del presente mese à servito in duomo" (vol. 259, fol. 72ᵛ)

Giovanni Vichin/Quintin. Contrabass singer, September 1482–March 1483

Monthly payments of L. 10

Girolamo, Don. Chaplain and tenorista, February–March 1447

Paid L. 3 in February and L. 2 in March

Girolamo Bondoni. Clerk-singer, soprano, December 1600–February 1604

Monthly payments of L. 2

Girolamo di Maestro Cesare. Clerk-singer, April 1595–December 1596

Monthly payments of L. 2

Girolamo di Ser Annibale. Clerk-singer, February–April 1549

Monthly payments of L. 1

Girolamo di Ser Antonmaria Mariotti. Clerk-singer, September 1551–January 1552

Monthly payments of L. 1

Girolamo Fontanini. Clerk-singer, soprano, March 1598–August 1600

Monthly payments of L. 2

Girolamo Gulini, eunuco. Clerk-singer, musico, soprano, September 1595–March 1602

Monthly payments of L. 2, then L. 3, L. 4, L. 7

Giuliano. Cleric and laudese, April–December 1440, May 1446–September 1450

Temporarily replaced by Ser Angelo in August 1440

Giulietto Francioso. Singer, September 1444, October–November 1446

Paid L. 8 for September 1444, L. 6. 10 per month in October and November 1446

Giulio dello spedale. Clerk-singer, July 1542–July 1545

Monthly payments of L. 4

Giulio dell'Ordine di San Francesco, Frate. Alto singer, February–April 1588

Monthly payments of L. 4

Giustiniano di Ser Francesco da Todi, Ser. Chaplain-singer and singing teacher, 20 April 1426–November 1435, July 1442–30 September 1443; maker of stained glass windows, 12 February 1434–November 1435

Hired 20 April 1426 as chaplain, singer, and singing teacher at annual salary of Fl. 30: "1426. Ser G[i]ustiniano di ser Franciescho da Todi s'è chondotto a dì XX d'aprile cho' noi per prette nostro chapelano et a chantare i' choro et levarsi al matino a fare tuto quelo fano e nostri chapelani e a [in]sengniare il chanto a' nostri di chasa che volesso' i[m]parare, per tenpo d'uno ano, per prezo di fiorini trenta di lire quatro fiorino l'ano, i[n]chominciare a dì detto, chome seghue. L. CXX" (vol. 494, fol. 9ᵛ)

Offered contract on 4 June 1439 but did not accept: "Misser lo operaio, conseglieri e camarlingo predetti . . . Veduto che la detta chiesa à grande bisogno di cantori, deliberarono sollenemente conduciare e condussero el venerabile homo misser Giustiniano di [gap] da Todi, in cantore e cappellano et per cantore e cappellano nella detta chiesa, per tempo d'uno anno da cominciare el dì che comincarà a servire, et da finire come seguitarà, et mentre a beneplacito d'essi misser l'Operaio, conseglieri et camarlingo, con salario di Fl. quaranta per lo detto anno, di L. 4 per ciascuno fiorino. El quale salario el camarlingo della detta Opera sia tenuto dargli di mese in mese per rata come tocha. El quale misser Giustiniano sia tenuto dire le messe e ritrovarsi all'offitio in choro e fare tutte le cose che sono tenuti a li altri cappellani della detta opera" (vol. 13, fol. 47ᵛ)

Paid 17 June 1439 for making stained glass windows: "E prefati misser l'operaio, conseglieri e camarlingo . . . veduto l'accordo facto fra la Opera e misser Giustiniano di certe finestre di vetro che lui fece, et Fl. quattro a lui paghati per lo camarlingo, et lo scontia facto di Fl. quattro che lui era debitore a la detta Opera, deliberarono approvare et approvarono e detti scontio e pagamento per bene facti, e che 'l camarlingo non ne possa essare per alcuno modo molestato, ma acceptinseli per bene facti etc." (ibid.)

Monthly payments of L. 13, July 1442–April 1443 as a chaplain; payments vary from L. 10. 13. 4 to L. 13 in the 1440s

Gonsalvo de Nuvalis (Nurvalis), Ser. Tenorista, August 1447

Hired 1 August 1447 at monthly salary of L. 13. 10: "1447. a dì primo d'agosto si condusse Go[ns]alvo di Nurvalis per tenorista a chantare in coro, per prezo di salario di 3 duchati d'oro e 15 bolognini il mese, per detto di misser Giovanni [Borghesi] operaio" (vol. 1079, unnumbered folio)

Goro di Pavolo di Sali da Fiorenza, Ser. Tenorista, Christmas 1446; 1456–August 1478

Paid L. 4. 16 for singing at Christmas: "E die dare adì 27 di dicienbre L. quatro s. sedici, demo a ser Ghoro, prette da Firenze, tenorista, el quale vene per achonciassi in duomo e servì per la Paschua in duomo, L. IIII s. XVI" (vol. 559, fol. 22ᵛ)

Hired 1 November 1456 at Fl. 50 annual salary (see Doc. 4.9); reappointed 30 December 1457 (see Doc. 4.11)

Paid while ill, 30 December 1458: "Decreverunt in super quod camerarius sine suo preiudicio aut damno solvat ser Goro cantori medietatem salarii sibi debiti pro mense Iulii preteriti quia vis [sic] in totum non serviverit pro eius infirmitate et pro eius absentia dicti mensis" (vol. 14, fol. 53ʳ)

Given six days' leave on 17 July 1459: "In super deliberaverunt concedere et concesserunt licentiam ser Goro cantori se absentare per dies sex" (ibid., fol. 58ᵛ)

Loaned 6 florins on 5 September 1459 (ibid., fol. 60ʳ)

Recommends a singer, 23 November 1462: see Doc. 4.12

Forgiven a debt, 8 February 1466: "Anco deliberarono che per li benemeriti et serviti facti per ser Goro tenorista all'Opera, che esso sia casso e cancellato de' libri de l'Opera di fiorini X o circa, de' quali è debitore e non sia per essi denari più obligato all'Opera e sia di ciò casso per lo camarlingo senz'alcuno suo danno" (vol. 15, fol. XIIʳ)

Salary raise to Fl. 60, from 1 May 1466: "Deliberarono ancora nel modo e forma predetti che el salario d'esso ser Ghoro per l'advenire da incominciarsi in Kalende di maggio proximo, sia et essere si intenda di fiorini 60, di libre 4 per fiorino, e per ciascuno anno. El quale salario si paghi di tempo in tempo, el quale salario el camarlingo paghi senza alcuno suo preiudicio o danno" (ibid., fol. XIIᵛ, dated February 1465/66)

Gottifredi di Liegi. Singer, December 1480–January 1481; July 1476–December 1477 (= Ghottifredo di Thilman de Liegio)

Payment of L. 6. 16 for December 1480, of L. 6 for January 1481; monthly payments of L. 9. 10 for 1476–77

Guasparre di Baldassarre. Cornettist, July 1537–June 1538

Monthly payments of L. 12 ("suona la cornetta")

Guglielmo da Pavia. Singer, September 1447

Paid L. 4 s. 16 on 15 September 1447 for singing for 20 days

Guglielmo di Antonio Celli, Ser. Bass singer, May 1570–April 1572, November 1580–February 1591, June 1595–October 1598

Monthly payments of L. 4

Guglielmo di Cortese, Ser. Singer, September 1471–March 1472

Monthly payments of various sums to Ser Ghuglielmo di Chortexe chantore

Guglielmo di Giovanni da Francia, Frate. Tenorista, 1 June 1438–21 March 1440

Authorization given to hire him at the highest salary, 23 April 1438: "Dominus Iacobus [della Quercia] Operarius prefatus, una cum dictis consiliariis essente Iohanne Compagni, convochati ut supra: viso quod in civitate Senarum acessit unus cantor francigena qui optaret conduci ad canendum in civitate Senarum et petit maximum salarium, solemniter decreverunt quod sit plenum rimissum in dictum dominum Iacobum qui possit conducere ipsum cantorem pro illo tempore, salario et modis ei videntibus et placentibus etc. omni meliori modo etc" (vol. 13, fol. 31ᵛ)

Contract offered at L. 10 per month, including obligation to say one Mass a week, 6 March 1439: "Ancho considerato quanto sia necessario ne la chiesa magior di Siena avere uno tenorista per l'onore de la città e cittadini d'essa, et quanto si facci per essa chiesa quello che al presente tiene il tenore in essa chiesa: solennemente i decti operaio, conseglieri e camarlingo tutti d'acordo deliberorno che il prefato tenorista sia et essere s'intenda condocto al decto servitio a beneplacito loro, a ragione di lire dodici il mese, dicendo a lui ancho una messa la semana nella chiesa predecta, a petitione e richiesta del sagrestano d'esso luogho. E quagli denari, servendo, sia lecito al camarlingo de l'Uopera di paghare come si costuma. Et hoc fecerunt omni etc." (ibid., fol. 37ᵛ)

Accepts revised contract of 17 July 1439: "Misser l'operaio et conseglieri e camarlingo sopradetti ... veduto quanto la detta chiesa à bisogno di cantori, et maxima di tenorista, deliberarono d'accordo che sia et essare s'intenda pienamente rimesso e commesso nel detto misser l'operaio conduciare lo infrascripto per tenorista, per tempo d'uno o due anni come a lui parrà e per quello salario gli piaciarà, non passando di salario più Fl. quaranta, di lire quattro l'uno, per ciascuno anno etc. Et possigli fare di prestanza quello che a llui parrà, la quale el camarlingo paghi senza suo preiudicio etc. El nome del quale è questo, cioè, frate Guglielmo di Giovanni di Francia, dell'Ordine del Carmino" (ibid. fol. 50ʳ). Another record gives the exact date of Frate Guglielmo's return to service as 9 July 1439: "Frate Ghuglielmo francioso venne a servire a dì nove di luglio per tenorista" (vol. 1259, unnumbered folio)

Two-year contract confirmed, 4 August 1439:

"Misser Giovanni operaio predetto, per vigore della remissione di sopra in lui facta, condusse per tenorista a' servitii della detta opera frate Guglielmo di Giovanni francioso dell'Ordine del Carmino, per tempo di due anni incominciati adì primo del presente mese d'agosto, e da finire come seguita, con salario di Fl. quaranta, di L. quattro per fiorino, ciaschuno anno. El quale frate Guglielmo sia tenuto ritrovarsi ogni mattina a la messa maggiore, et el dì al Vesparo, come e cappellani della Opera, se non sia pontato come loro etc." (vol. 13, fol. 50ʳ)

An entry in vol. 501, fol. 6ʳ, dated 20 May 1443, records the sale of Guglielmo's breviary to the "frati Armeni"

Guglielmo di Lodovico Francioso, Ser.
Singer, July 1465–September 1466 (possibly = Guillelmus Des Mares)

Contract offered at 12 lire per month, 9 July 1465: "Et conduxero l'infrascripti cantori per tempo d'uno anno et ad loro beneplacito, cum salario di fiorini 3 per ciascuno mese, di L. 4 per fiorino, et per ciascuno di loro, cioè Carlo di Guglielmo e Guglielmo di Lodovico, franciosi" (vol. 15, fol. XVIIʳ)

Increase up to 15 lire authorized 9 September 1465: "Possi l'operaio conducere Guglielmo cantore, non passando la somma di lire XV el mese" (ibid., fol. XVIIIIᵛ), but not implemented till April 1466

Extra payments for singing in Florence, 1466: "Ghuglielmo di Loigi francioso cantore de' dare adì 24 di maggio s. cinquantasei contantti in sua mano per detto di messer Cipriano [Corti] operaio, L. 2. s. 16" (vol. 587, fol. 4ʳ); "Ghuglielmo di Loigi francioso cantore in duomo die dare adì 12 di giugno L. cinque s. dodici per lui e per detto misser Cipriano nostro operaio a ser Ghoro di Pavolo tenorista contantti in sua mano in uno ducato largo, L. 5 s. 12. E die dare adì 20 di giugno s. 40 contantti in sua mano quando andò alla festa a Fiorenza per detto del camarlingo, L. 2 ... E dei dare adì 3 di luglio L. 4 contantti per detto di misser Cipriano, operaio, L. 4" (ibid., fol. 6ʳ)

Guglielmo di Martino. Clerk at the hospital of Santa Maria della Scala; laudese, May 1401–August 1415; March–April 1420; April

1428; January–August 1429; August 1433–
April 1434; singing teacher, September
1433

Paid L. 1 monthly for singing epistles, laudi, and
Passion ("e va[n]gieli e le laude"; "a chantare
la pasione"; vol. 229, fol. 47 left, 1401–2 and
later years). In September 1433 paid s. 12
"per insegnare a chantare a' cherici" (vol.
409, fol. 85)

Guglielmo di Michele di Francia. Singer,
August 1446–March 1447

Monthly payments at varying amounts, indicating absences

Guglielmo di Sant'Agostino, Fra. Bass
singer, November 1598–November 1607

Monthly payments of L. 14, then L. 28

Guglielmo Francioso, Maestro. Invited as
singer and singing teacher, 1450; declined

Contract offered 18 February 1450: "Et per simile modo conduxero maestro Ghugl[i]elmo
francioso per cantore del duomo et anco ad
insegnare musica e canto a' preti e cherici
del duomo, con quello salario parrà e piacerà
al prefato misser l'Operaio, da trenta a quaranta fiorini a ragione d'anno et a beneplacito d'esso Operaio. Con questo che da' preti
e cherici di duomo non debbi avere alcuno
salario" (vol. 13, fol. 104ʳ)

Authorization to hire, 21 March 1450: [margin:
di potere condurre uno maestro di canto e
d'organi] "Item per simile modo pienamente
e liberamente remissero nel predetto misser
l'Operaio potere condurre a le spese de
l'Uopera uno maestro di canto e di sonare organi, il quale insegni le decte facultà a' cherici di Siena senza alcuno salario, a quelli che
esse apti o alcuna d'esse vorrà imparare. Al
quale maestro esso operaio possa constituire
e fare quello debito e discreto salario che a
lui parrà convenirsi" (ibid., fol. 106ᵛ)

Guglielmo Francioso, Maestro. Singer,
June–July 1462

Paid L. 8 for 40 days as replacement of Piero
Baiardi

Hercole musico, Messer

Considered as *maestro di cappella,* 15 March
1559: "Deliberorno, odito 'l reverendo messer Mario Bronconi canonico, a nome d'uno
messer Hercole musico quale desidera esser
condocto per maestro di cappella nella chiesa

cathedrale, che attesa la qualità della persona
e de' tempi, che il magnifico Rettore elegha
due de' Savi, quali insieme con sua Signoria
vedino, intendino e referischino. Et furno
electi messer Renaldo Tolomei et Fabio Buo-
ninsegni" (vol. 17, fol. 14ʳ)

Innocenzo (Vincentio) di Donato, Fra.
Singer, January–August 1514, March 1516,
August 1518

Monthly payments of L. 10

Paid L. 30 on 29 April 1514 and hired as of 1
April: "Spectabilis viri Magnificus Burghesius Petruccius et Georgius Varius [*recte* Ve-
rius], absente Iohanne Baptista de Guglielmis, Operarii ecclesie cathedralis etc.
convocati etc. deliberaverunt quod scriptor
opere predicte det et solvat frati Innocentio
Donati, ordinis predicatorum, cantori in
ecclesia cathedrali libras XXX soldos 0, pro
suo servitu usque in presentem diem. Item
conduxerunt supra dictum fratrem Innocentium in cantorem ecclesie predicte, cum
salario librarum X s. 0 pro quolibet mense,
incipiendo die prima aprilis MDXIIII. Et interim ad beneplacitum" (vol. 16, fol. 26ʳ)

Isidoro di Francia, Ser. Chaplain-singer, 17
May–15 August 1383

Annual salary as chaplain of L. 90, plus L. 5 for
singing: "an[n]o 1383. Iscita de' danari che
darò a' preti: A ser Isidoro di Francia chantare vintidue lire sei denari per due mesi e
ventotto dì che stette in duomo per chapelano, chominciò adì XVII di magio insino
adì XV d'agosto an[n]o detto, aveva l'an[n]o
per la spese e pe' lo salaro novanta lire, perch'era chantore aveva 5 lire più che gli atri
chapelani, L. XXII s.—d. VI" (vol. 1234,
fol. 36ʳ)

Ivo (Ibo) di Giovanni Francese. Singer, end
1527–August 1530

Paid L. 9 on 21 April 1528 and L. 71 on 30
April 1528 at rate of L. 7, then L. 10 per
month; monthly payments of L. 10 thereafter, with some subtractions. The June 1530
payment was also for composing: "Ibo di
Ianni fra[n]sese, cantore da fronte, de' avere
lire ottanta, sonno per lo suo servito del
chanto e del chompore fino a tutto g[i]ugno
1530, di conto saldo fatto con messer Francesco, nostro dignissimo Operaio, e so' ale

distribuzioni in questo, a ffo. 77. L. LXXXX s. —" (vol. 513, fol. 59 right)

Jacomo da Polonia. Singer, May–August 1449, January–March 1450

Paid 8 lire for May 1449; thereafter the four Polish singers paid 34 lire as a group (*see under* Andrea da Polonia). For contract of 21 January 1450 see Doc. 4.1

Jacomo da Sancto Vierno. Singer, May 1446

Paid L. 4

Jacomo di Andrea. Laudese, March–April 1416

Jacomo di Antonio. Singer, May 1445

Jacomo di Bellanduccio da San Quirico, Ser. Chaplain-singer, December 1406–April 1408, May 1409–April 1411, November 1415–April 1416; laudese, July 1430–April 1433

Monthly payments at L. 3. 18, then L. 6. 13. 4

Jacomo di Fosco da San Germano, Ser. Chaplain and singer, April 1440–August 1441

Monthly salary of L. 10

Loaned L. 20 to buy a coat, 3 April 1440: "Ser Jachomo di Foscho da San Germano die dare L. vintti i quali li prestai per detto di misser Giovanni operaio, disse voleva chomprare uno mantello per suo dos[s]o e quali promise misser Marino da l'Aquila a chui servirebbe al chanto in choro e se no' restituirebbe il denaro ebeli a dì 3 d'aprile anno detto [1440], L. XX" (vol. 267, fol. 102)

Had left by November 1441: see Doc. 3.4

Jacomo di Francesco. Clerk-singer, March 1516

Paid L. 1. 10

Jacomo (Jacometto) di Giovanbattista (de' Chigi) da Verona. Contralto singer, 23 November 1524–November 1527, April 1532–January 1543, January 1548–April 1555

Monthly payments of L. 10, then L. 17, L. 21

Jacomo di Longo (Longi) Francioso. Singer, November 1447–March 1448

See under Giovanni Fanti

Jacomo di Maestro Cesare Panichi (Messer as of 1597). Clerk, 1582–88; clerk-singer, May 1587–April 1588; chaplain and singer, March 1596–March 1598, December 1600–

March 1602; *maestro di cappella,* May 1610–12 (also organist, 1602–7)

Monthly payments of L. 4 as "cherico grande e cantore"; of L. 26. 10, then L. 22. 10, L. 30. 10, then L. 36. 10

Jacomo di Maestro Giovanni de' Giusti, Ser. Bass singer, March 1572–April 1577

Monthly payments of L. 4

Jacomo di Rico, Ser. Laudese, June 1424–April 1426

Monthly payments of s. 10

Jacomo di Salvadore. Clerk-singer, 1485–86

Monthly payments of L. 3

Jacomo di Vergilio (Messer in 1602). Clerk-singer, soprano, January 1600–November 1602; singer, June 1602–February 1604

Monthly payments: L. 2, then L. 6 as soprano, then L. 10

Jacomo Francioso. Singer and music copyist, September–November 1481

Payments of L. 3. 10, L. 12, and L. 12, successively, September–November 1481

Jacomo Francioso (di Fiandra) di Novo Porto. Singer, 8 July–26 September 1468; April 1470–February 1471; other payments on 31 April 1470 and 5 May 1473 (= Jacheto di Nemport)

Monthly salary of L. 10

Given Giachetto's old room, 1469: "Ricordo come oggi questo dì 14 di maggio 1469 demo per detto di misser Savino operaio a Jacomo di Fiandra nuovo cantore in duomo la chiave della camera di sotto presso alla cisterna dove stava Giachetto, con queste cose qui disotto dentrovi, e Prima: una lettiera rossa chol sacchione; uno letto di penna colla federa biancha buona; 2 capezali bianchi buoni; una coltre; 2 goffani buoni, uno al letto, dinanzi, uno ditro; una tavola co' tripiei, alta; 3 banche; una banchetta bassa; e più ebbe in presta per 3 dì della pasqua rosada una cotta di Giachetto. Ritornò e intrò in detta camera colle medesime cose" (vol. 587, fol. 64^r)

Jannesi Francioso. Singer, May–June 1445

Payments at L. 8 per month for May and half of June

Lancilotto Puliti. Singer, March–November 1599

Monthly payments of L. 2

Lanzelotto di Nanse Francioso. Singer, February–March 1520

Two payments of L. 7

Lelo di Taddeo. Clerk-singer, November 1550–January 1552

Monthly payments of L. 1

Leonardo di Bartolomeo, Ser. Chaplain-singer, November 1415–April 1416; sacristan and laudese, 1418–August 1424

Leonardo di Francesco, Ser. Laudese, September 1417–April 1418; May 1420–April 1424

Paid s. 5 monthly, 1417–18, s. 10 monthly afterwards as a "chantore di lalde"

Lionardo di Giovanbattista. Clerk-singer, soprano, May 1566–April 1568

Monthly payments of L. 1. 10

Lonardo di Cristofano (Ser after March 1487). Tenorista, 1485–February 1491, September 1492–4 February 1496; August 1500–July 1519

Monthly payments of L. 10; of L. 12 from April 1490; of L. 13 from September 1492

Lonardo di Lonardo Franzese. Singer, May–October 1522

Monthly salary of L. 7

Lorenzo, Fra. Tenor singer, February 1491–17 September 1492

Monthly payments of L. 16 to 17 September 1492, when he was paid L. 9. 15 at the command of "messer Alberto nostro operaio"

Lorenzo da Orvieto, Messer. Chaplain and singer, October 1442

Lorenzo di Andrea. Clerk-singer, September 1515, March 1516

Monthly salary of L. 1. 10

Lorenzo di Giovanni (Ser after May 1503). Singer, August 1500–August 1503

Monthly payments of L. 2

Lorenzo di Menicho. Clerk of the hospital of Santa Maria della Scala; laudese, 1402–3

Paid s. 20 monthly for seven months for assisting Guglielmo in singing the epistle

Luca di Giovanni da Pisa, Ser. Chaplain, 1446–48; singer, January 1449–April 1457

Monthly payments of L. 8. 10 as chaplain

Paid also as tenorista, beginning January 1449: "Memoria come questo dì, oggi dieci di feraio, rimase d'acordo Ser Luca coll'operaio

di servire el coro e nominatamente tenere el tenorista continuamente ed essere ala messa al comincio dello Introito e così al comincio del Vespro a prima antiphana. E quando a queste ore non fusse, pena per lui e dì festivi soldi cinque e denari quatro per c[i]ascuna ora, e dì ritigli soldi due per c[i]ascuna. Intendendossi incominciato el dì primo di giennaio prossimo passato 1448 [1449]" (vol. 1079, unnumbered folio)

Reappointed 27 May 1452 (see Doc. 4.4), 2 May 1453 (see Doc. 4.5), 3 June 1454 (see Doc. 4.7)

Luzio di Pavolo piffero. Clerk-singer, January 1530–May 1533 (also a Palace musician)

Monthly payments of L. 1. 10

Maddalo di Lorenzo d'Arezzo, Messer. Singer and singing teacher, September 1503–February 1507; chaplain and alto singer, mid-September 1508–October 1520

Monthly payments of L. 17 from September 1503, then L. 8 through April 1505

Special payment 1 December 1503: "MDIII. Messer Madalo d'Arezzo maestro de la schuola del chanto de' avere el dì primo di diciembre L. ventiquattro s. 0 contanti, i quali si li danno per ordine di messer Alberto nostro per suo bene servito e benmerito. L. XXIIII . . . E de' avere L. cinquanta s. 0 per tanti posti dare in questo a fol. 657. L. L s. 0" (vol. 509, fol. 622^r)

Ser Agnolo di Pietro paid to bring him from Florence, 1508: "1508. Ser Angniolo di Pietro, nostro cantore, de' avere S. 40 sono per sua fadigha di avello mandatto a Fiorenza per ser Madalo che venisse a servire in capella in duomo . . . L. 2" (vol. 510, fol. 248)

Monthly payments of L. 10, then L. 14

Marcantonio Tornioli. Singer, August–October 1602

Monthly payments of L. 4

Marcello di Francesco da Montalcino, Ser. Tenorista and contrabass singer, April 1520–November 1521; substitute *maestro di cappella,* November 1524–April 1525; singer, May 1525–15 September 1526

Monthly payments of L. 18 as singer; paid L. 33

as "Ser Marciello di ser Francesco, maestro di capella," on 9 May 1525

Mariano di Gherardo da Bologna, Don.
Tenor singer, August 1525–June 1529
Monthly payments of L. 18

Mariano di Giovanni, Ser, called Trafiere.
Cleric from May 1396; chaplain and sacristan from 1401–2; also laudese, 1402–August 1412, March 1416–April 1420; May 1424–August 1435; chaplain-tenorista from December 1435 to January 1440

Paid L. 8. 2 as chaplain; as laudese paid s. 20 "chà a[iu]tò a chantare la passione in duomo uno mese" (1403 and later) and L. 1 per month

An increase in payments is authorized 30 October 1434: "Anco deliberarono, veduto che ser Mariano di Trafiere è lo honore del coro et della chiesa predicta, et con molta più diligentia che nissumo degli altri atende a fare suo debito, per inanimarlo et confortarlo et lui et gli altri al bene fare . . . che sia rimesso nel decto misser l'Operaio usargli et fargli usare al decto camarlingo quella cortesia più che agli altri che a llui parrà discreto, et il decto camarlingo pagare la possa et debba senza suo pregiuditio o danno" (vol. 13, fol. 5ʳ); an entry of 11 January 1435 sets these at Fl. 4 annually: "Et misser l'Operaio . . . dichiarò che ser Mariano di Trafiero, cappellano nella chiesa cathedral del duomo abbi et avere debbi, oltra a l'usato suo salario, dal camarlingo della detta Opera fiorini quattro, di lire IIII l'uno, per ciascuno anno, incominciando a dì trenta di ottobre prossimo passato" (fol. 10ʳ)

Last payment on 4 January 1440: "E die dare a dì 4 di giennaio L. sette, ebe per lui ser Barna perch'era amalato, L. 7." (vol. 267, fol. 70)

Mariano di Giovanni di Ser Turco. Singer, February–September 1522
Monthly payments of L. 7

Marino di Niccolò da l'Aquila, Messer.
Singer and singing teacher, December 1436–February 1447; January–May 1449, November 1451–June 1454

Paid an additional L. 40 annually beginning in December 1436 because "insegnia a chantare a' cherici e a' fanciulli in duomo" (vol. 500,

fol. 310ʳ). Payments in the 1440s vary from L. 6 to L. 10. 13. 4

Rehired 20 December 1438: "Misser lo operaio e conseglieri . . . deliberarono d'accordo conduciare e rifermare, e conduxero e rifermaro' misser Marino da l'Aquila per cantore a cantare nella detta chiesa cathedrale di Siena, et insegnare a' cherici d'essa chiesa presenti e futuri, per tempo d'uno anno, incominciato immediatamente che finì l'anno prossimo passato della condotta d'esso misser Marino, con salario di fiorini quaranta per lo detto anno, di lire quattro l'uno, cioè fiorini trenta per cantare e fiorini dieci per insegnare a' cherici" (vol. 13, fol. 35ʳ). Contract and salary reconfirmed 13 March 1439 (fol. 39ʳ) and 19 November 1439 (fol. 52ʳ)

Hired to teach boys 14 March 1449: "Memoria come adì quatordici di marzo [1449] rimase d'acordo l'operaio con esso meco di dare lire quatro el mese a sser Marino per lo merito dela fadiga d'i[n]segnare a quatro fanc[i]ugli, e ogni dì sia lecito el pilgliare partito a cciascuno di loro. Io ser Credi sagrestano feci questa posta" (vol. 1079, unnumbered folio)

Monthly payments of L. 2. 6. 8, then L. 3 as a singer, L. 4 for teaching the boys

Reappointed 27 May 1452 (see Doc. 4.4), 2 May 1453 (see Doc. 4.5), 3 June 1454 (see Doc. 4.7)

Mario di Matteo. Clerk-singer, May 1550–December 1551
Monthly payments of L. 1. 4

Matteo Bondoni, Messer. Tenor singer, May 1593–November 1607

Monthly payments of L. 14, L. 16, then L. 7, L. 8 as "sagrestano e cantore," then "cantore e pievano di San Giovanni"; then L. 9, L. 10, L. 11, L. 4

Matteo da Polonia. Singer, January–March 1450

Hired with two Polish companions on 21 January 1450 (see Doc. 4.2); paid L. 13. 7 monthly

Matteo di Guido. Laudese, 1403
Paid s. 20 "chè aiutò a chantare la passione uno mese in duomo" (vol. 380, fol. 90ʳ)

Menico. *See* Domenico
Meo. *See* Bartolomeo

Michelangelo di Daniello. Singer in choir school, November, 1450–August 1451

Appointed 11 February 1451 (see Doc. 4.2), confirmed 13 October 1451 (see Doc. 4.3); reappointed 2 May 1453 (see Doc. 4.5), 3 May 1454 (see Doc. 4.6)

Michelangelo di Giovanni. Clerk-singer, alto, August 1579–April 1584

Monthly payments of L. 2. 10, then L. 4 as contralto, August 1579–April 1580; as "cherico grande e contralto," June 1580–April 1584

Michelangelo Grecchi. Clerk-singer, January 1597

Monthly payments of L. 2 as "cherico minore e cantore"

Michele di Nello, Maestro. Foreman and laudese, 1371–72, 1381–82

Paid Fl. 2 annually in 1371–72 "per provigione de la sua fadigha del duomo del chantare le lade" (vol. 198, fol. 63ᵛ), L. 12 annually in 1381–82

Michele Francioso. Soprano singer, July–September 1476 (probably = Michele di Guglielmo da Ludicha di Brabante)

Paid L. 9. 10 monthly

Michele Pisano, Ser. Singer, April–May 1599

Monthly payments of L. 4

Michele Scala, Ser. Tenor singer, September–December 1591 (prior service elsewhere)

Monthly payments of L. 6

Michelino di Nanni. Laudese, July 1405–February 1406

Monthly payments of L. 1

Midone di Ser Cesare Nannetti (Ser in 1582). Clerk-singer, then soprano singer, May 1557–April 1558; May 1559–April 1570; bass singer, June 1582–March 1597

Monthly payments of L. 2. 10 as "cherico minore e soprano in cappella"; then L. 3. 10 as "cherico e soprano in cappella"; L. 4 as basso, then L. 6, L. 7, L. 8

Request for higher salary, 22 January 1591: see Doc. 7.7

Niccolaio, Ser. Singer, March–April 1445 (possibly = Niccolò Francioso)

Monthly payments of L. 10

Niccolò di Bernardino. Clerk-singer, April–May 1490

Niccolò di Berto. Laudese, May–June 1392–93; 1 May–30 December 1400, May 1402–December 1403

Monthly payments of L. 1

Niccolò di Giovanni di Lore. Tenorista and bass singer, December 1480–June 1481

Monthly payments of L. 18, except for L. 10. 10 in the first month

Fined for failing to return to Siena, leaving the chapel in disarray, 8 July 1481: see Doc. 5.2

Niccolò di Giuliano da San Gimignano (Cornetta). Singer, cornettist, December 1534–September 1539

Monthly payments of L. 12; beginning in January 1537 called a cornettist

Niccolò di Lanberto da Bruggia. Contratenor singer, July 1476–November 1477

Monthly payments of L. 8

Niccolò di Ser Lonardo. Clerk-singer, September 1518

Monthly payments of L. 1. 10

Niccolò di Timoteo. Clerk-singer, tenor, May 1582–April 1584

Monthly payments of L. 1. 10 as "cherico minore e soprano"; as "cherico minore e soprano," June 1582–November 1583; and as "cherico mezzano e contralto in cappella," December 1583–April 1584

Niccolò Francioso. Singer, September–October 1442 (possibly = Ser Niccolaio)

Paid L. 4 for September and October on 6 November 1442

Niccolò Francioso, Messer. Singer, February–December 1519

Monthly payments in amounts ranging from L. 6 to L. 9

Niccolò Smeraldi. Clerk-singer, June, August 1517, August–September 1518

Monthly payments of L. 1. 10, then L. 3

Onofrio da Gubbio, Ser. Chaplain-singer, May 1591

Payment of L. 4

Orazio di Guido. Clerk-singer, 15 December 1542–January 1543

Total payment of L. 12

Orazio Vecchi da Modena, Messer. Tenor singer, February 1571–April 1574

Monthly payments of L. 10, then L. 12

Orindio di Giovanmaria Bartolini. Clerk-singer, soprano, May 1590–December 1596
Monthly payments of L. 1. 10 as soprano, then L. 2 as cantore

Ottavio di Cerbone Galli. Clerk-singer, soprano, May 1588–May 1589
Monthly payments of L. 1. 10

Ottavio di Giovanangelo. Clerk-singer, soprano, May 1570–April 1574
Monthly payments of L. 1. 10

Ottavio di Lorenzo Basili. Clerk-singer, soprano, August 1585–November 1596; tenor and trombonist, December 1596–November 1607 (also a Palace musician)
Monthly payments of L. 1. 10, then L. 2. 10 as soprano; of L. 5, then L. 6, L. 8 as cantore, later as musico

Paulo, Frate. Bass singer, July 1535
Paid L. 12

Pavolo di Ser Agnolo. Cleric and singer, May–July 1437
Paid L. 3. 6. 8 per month in 1437 and is described as a young clerk who sings in the duomo; he appears in accounts from previous years as "Pavolo che sta chon ser Angiolo"

Pierantonio Formichi, Messer. Singer, December 1596–November 1601
Monthly payments of L. 15, then L. 4 as "sagrestano e cantore," then "cantore"

Piergiovanni di Donato. Clerk-singer, December 1594–December 1596
Monthly payments of L. 4 as "cherico mezzano e cantore"; of L. 2 as cantore

Piermaria di Tommaso Romano, Ser. Alto singer, October 1576–March 1577
Monthly payments of L. 28, then L. 14

Piero Antonio di Galgano. Clerk-singer, September 1515, March 1516
Monthly payments of L. 1. 10

Piero Baiardi, Ser. Singer, September 1461–June 1462
Monthly payments of L. 8, then L. 10

Piero Ciotti, Ser. Alto singer, May 1570–November 1587
Monthly payments of L. 4, then L. 9, L. 10

Piero de la Piazza (de Platea). Tenorista, May 1482–June 1485
Monthly payments of L. 24. 11. 4

Piero di Domenico d'Asciano (Ser from 1508). Clerk-singer, August 1493–March 1495; substitute *maestro di cappella,* 1509; *maestro di cappella,* mid-January 1512–December 1516, February 1518–February 1520, March–June 1524, November 1526–July 1527, October 1530–September 1539
Paid L. 70 on 28 May 1494, including L. 20 "for having sung the past ten months with the approval of Misser Alberto [Aringhieri]" (vol. 312, fol. 179ʳ)

Substitute *maestro di cappella* during absences of Giovanni di Maestro di Antonio, 1508: "MDVIIII. Ser Pietro di Domenico d'Asciano, prete che chanta in capella de' . . . avere L. vintiotto s. —, sonno per tanti ce ne fa buoni per lui Giovanni di maestro Iachomo piffero, per lo servito suo, chè detto ser Pietro servì a la chapella del chanto per maestro, in luogho d'esso Giovanni; a lui, in questo, fol. 355. L. XXVIII" (vol. 510, fol. 328 left and right)

Paid L. 104. 5 as singer, March 1514. "Ser Piero di Domenico d'Asciano maestro di chapella de dare . . . [fol. 7 right] Ser Piero di Domenico d'Asciano maestro di scuola di chanto de' chantori dirinchontro de' havere fino a questo dì ultimo di marzo 1514 L. centoquatro s. cinque sono per suo salario d'avere cantato in capella in Duomo" (vol. 511, fol. 7 left). Monthly payments of L. 4 are entered on this folio to the end of December 1516.

Paid 4 ducats on 2 April 1512 as maestro of the school of music: "Spectatissimi viri Magnificus Burghesius Petruccius Iohannes Baptista de Guglielmis et Georgius Verius, operarii et commissarii . . . deliberaverunt quod Scriptor Opere aut depositarius pecuniarum dicte Opere dent et solvant ser Piero Dominici de Asciano, presbitero et magistro Scole musice dicte Opere, ducatos quatuor, quos sibi dantur pro suo servitu; et si in aliquo esset debitor dicte Opere pro denariis habitis occasione scole cantus, cancelletur absque aliqua solutione. Et predicta omni modo etc." (vol. 16, fol. 22ʳ)

Gift to confraternity of San Pietro: "MDXIII. Ser Pietro da Sciano cappellano di Sant'Antonio die dare perfino questo dì primo di maggio sopradecto lire quattro e s.—contanti, li quali sponte sua ha offerto dare di paghare a la congreghatione nostra per augmentarla et accrescerla" (ASS, PR, Compagnia di San Pietro nel Duomo di Siena, vol. 1370, *E&U, 1513–24*, fol. 14 1–r)

Paid L. 40 on 29 April 1514; salary to be L. 4 per month: "Spectatissimi viri . . . Et deliberaverunt etiam quod scriptor Opere solvat ser Piero Dominici de Asciano, magistro Scole canti ecclesie cathedralis, libras quatraginta, videlicet L. 40 s. —, pro eius servitu usque in presentem diem. Item ordinaverunt salarium ordinatum dicto ser Piero pro quolibet mense librarum quatuor, videlicet L. 4, et incipiat dictum salarium dictarum librarum IIII pro quolibet mense in kalendis Aprilis presentis [anni] MDXIIII, et interim ad beneplacitum" (vol. 16, fol. 26ʳ)

Monthly payments of L. 8, February 1518–February 1520 (called *cantore,* but sacristans' reports indicate he was master of the chapel); monthly payments of L. 14 as *maestro di cappella,* March–June 1524, November 1526–July 1527, October 1530–September 1539

Piero di Pasqua, Messer. Canon and archdeacon from October 1406 to December 1472; also singer from 1425 to May 1445

Paid L. 40 on 22 Agosto 1437 retrospectively to 1435; a payment in 1436 indicates that this was extra, for singing in choir: "Misser Pietro di Pasqua, arcidiachano, die avere adì XIII d'otobre lire quaranta, e quagli si li dàno per lo canto del coro, oltre ale sue distribuzioni" (vol. 500, fol. 298ʳ; similar payments from 1437 and 1438 are on fol. 314ʳ)

Pietragnolo di Bernardino Maestri. Trombonist, January 1597–July 1601

Monthly payments of L. 5

Pietragnolo di Giovanni Nastagi (Ser in 1586). Tenor singer, June 1584–April 1586; alto singer, June 1586–March 1587

Monthly payments of L. 4

Pietro del Funaio. Clerk-singer, June 1517, August–September 1518

Monthly payments of L. 1. 10, then L. 3

Pietro di Benedetto. Clerk-singer, March 1516

Monthly payments of L. 1. 10

Pietro di Francesco da Perugia. Chaplain and singer, November 1441–April 1442

Hired 4 November 1441 at a salary of Fl. 40 annually: see Doc. 3.4

Pietro di Gano. Clerk-singer, April 1493–June 1494

Monthly payments of L. 1. 10

Pietro di Ghino (Pietricchino). Soprano singer, May–August 1481 (= Pietrequin Bonnel)

Monthly payments of L. 13

Pietro di Luigi, Ser. Laudese, May 1427–April 1428; May 1430–February 1431; May 1433

Monthly payments of s. 10

Pietro di Maestro Antonio. Clerk-singer, April 1551–March 1555

Monthly payments of L. 3

Pietro (Pietrino) di Maestro Bernardo, Ser. November 1529–September 1530, December 1534, September 1539

Monthly payments of L. 9

Pietro di Maestro Lonardo, Ser. Contralto singer, 10 September 1524–1 April 1527

Monthly salary L. 7

Pietro di Mattia. Clerk-singer, May 1487–April 1488

Monthly payments of L. 1. 10

Pietro di Tommasso da Gubbio. Alto singer, mid-December 1542–September 1554

Monthly payments of L. 8, then L. 14

Pietro Domarlla (Domarllo), Francioso. Singer, November 1447–March 1448 (= Pietro Domarto?)

Paid L. 12 monthly (Petrus Domarla; Petrus Domarlo); *see also under* Giovanni Fanti

Pio di Pietro Paoli. Clerk-singer, August–September 1518

Monthly payments of L. 4

Pompilio di Bernardo. Cantorino, November 1545–April 1548

Monthly payments of L. 2

Pompilio di Francesco Rossini. Clerk-singer, April 1595–February 1603

Monthly payments of L. 2, then L. 3, L. 4

Quintino di Martino. Soprano singer, May–August 1482

Monthly payments of L. 12

Quirico di Luphari. Clerk-singer, April–June 1493

Monthly payments of L. 1.10

Raimondo Bianco da Elci, Frate. Singer, August 1447

Paid L. 12

Rasso di Lorenzo. Singer, August–8 September 1448

Paid L. 8. 19. 4 for August, L. 8 for September

Remigio. Singer, August–October 1474 (probably = Remigius Massin)

Monthly payments of L. 5. 12

Riccardo (Gherardo) di Francia. Tenorista, February–May 1431 (probably Gherardo LeFay or Leay)

Paid s. 50 for February 1431, and L. 6. 13. 4 monthly, March–May

Riccardo di Viviano Francioso. Singer, August 1447

Paid s. 20 for singing at Assumption festivities: "17 Agosto Le spese di casa de l'uopera die dare . . . soldi venti, e quagli denari ebe ser Richard di Viviano, francioso e chantore di duomo, per più dì estè per la festa a cantare, ebe per decto di Messer, L. 1" (vol. 583, fol. 17ʳ)

Ruberto (Rubinetto). Singer, October 1481–10 January 1482

Monthly payments of L. 9 to Ruberto altrimenti Robinetto cantore, October–December 1481, and of L. 3 for ten days in January 1482 ("per lo servitto di dì X di giennaio [1482] et domandò licenzia, L. III"; vol. 304, fol. 119ʳ)

Ruberto di Giovanni Francioso. Singer, January–March 1474 (possibly = Robertus de Ligin)

Monthly payments of L. 8

Ruberto Leuder Piccardo. Singer, April–July 1481

Payments of L. 8 and then L. 10. On 9 July paid s. 45 for eight days "chè questo dì domandò licenzia" (vol. 304)

Rubino Francioso. Singer, April–July 1445

Paid L. 4 for April, L. 5 for May–July

Salindio di Ventura. Clerk-singer, November 1550–March 1552

Monthly payments of L. 1

Salvatore d'Essenga da Modena dell'Ordine de' Servi, Fra. *Maestro di cappella,* 1 December 1570–May 1575

Contract as *maestro di cappella,* from 1 December 1570: "Ricordo questo dì 10 di febraro chome fino addì primo di Dicembre prossimo passato il Magnifico Messer Marcello Tegliacci, Rettore dell'Opera nostra, ha condotto per maestro di cappella del canto nella Chiesa Cattedral, per anni tre dal dì della condotta, il quale s'è obligato fare tutte le chose solite farsi per li altri maestri stati in tal luogho, dovendo tenere la detta cappella fornita a suffisienzia di soprani e sia obrigho suo d'insegniare a' fanciulli [e] a' cherici della chiesa, essendovi voci ragionevoli, altrimenti ad altri a chi parrà a llui et al detto Signor Rettore . . . E per il premio e mercè di tutte le sue fatighe, l'Opera nostra li sia tenuta dare per ciascheduno de' detti tre anni schudi quarantadue di moneta, di lire sette per scudo, ogni messe l'errata, sempre finito i mese, cioè lire 24 soldi 10. E se il detto signor Rettore non fa disdetta al detto maestro Salvadore mesi sei avanti finischino detti tre anni overo ch'esso maestro non domandi licenzia, s'intenda seghuire detta condotto e su' offisio altri tre anni, con li medesimi obrighi e salari antedetti. Al quale fra Salvadore fino il dì primo di dicembre si consegniò la chiave della schuola qual'è in chalonica segniata nº III con masarisie dentrovi e molti libri di musiche di più sorte, quali deva adoperare solo per servisio della detta cappella e renderne conto sicondo l'inventario fattoli, chome si vede al libro dell'inventario delle camere, a ffoglio 63. Io fra Salvadore Essenga da Modona affermo quanto di sopra (vol. 629, fol. 25ʳ, dated 10 February 1571)

Monthly payments of L. 24. 10

Sano. *See* Ansano

Scipione Celli. Clerk-singer, May 1593–March 1596

Monthly payments of L. 1. 10

Scipione di Pavolo Jacomini. Clerk-singer, November 1533–September 1539 (also organist)

Monthly salary of L. 1. 10, then L. 3, L. 4

Letter to an administrator, requesting money, 27 July 1551: see Doc. 6.4

Serafino di Santi, Ser. Clerk-singer, 1534; soprano singer, January 1548–September 1551
Monthly salary of L. 2 as choirboy; L. 14 as singer

Serafino di Ser Lonardo. Clerk-singer, February 1543–December 1545
Monthly payments of L. 4

Silvio d'Anghiari, Messer. Singer, June–November 1593
Monthly payments of L. 6

Silvio d'Antonmaria Marzi. Clerk-singer, soprano, May 1593–January 1596, December 1596–May 1598
Monthly payments of L. 1. 10 as "cherico minore e cantore"; of L. 4 as "cherico mezzano e cantore"

Simone di Bartolomeo. Clerk-singer, May–December 1590
Monthly payments of L. 4 as "cherico mezzano e cantore"

Simone di Domenico. Clerk-singer, soprano, January 1588–April 1590
Monthly payments of L. 1. 10, the L. 3. 10 as "cherico piccolo e soprano"

Simone di Mariano. Cleric and laudese, May 1446, April 1447, December 1448–September 1450; tenorista from choir school, November 1450–October 1456
Paid L. 1 s. 13 on 8 May 1446 "per chantare e Vangiegli nela Quaresima passata in sul p[e]rgholo, e le la[u]de in duomo per la semana santa" (vol. 559, fol. 2ʳ); paid L. 1 monthly for singing laudi during Lent and on Sundays
Appointed 11 February 1451 (see Doc. 4.2); confirmed 13 October 1451 (see Doc. 4.3); reappointed 2 May 1453 (see Doc. 4.5), 3 May 1454 (see Doc. 4.6), 30 December 1454 (see Doc. 4.8)
Monthly payments of L. 4, then L. 4. 10

Simone Francioso. Contrabass singer, August 1489
Payment of L. 6. 4

Teodoro di Niccolò Morelli. Clerk-singer, soprano, May 1588–April 1590; May 1591– April 1593; singer, November 1593–March 1597
Monthly payments of L. 1. 10, then L. 3. 15, L. 4 as soprano, then as "cherico mezzano e cantore"; of L. 2. 10 as "cherico mezzano e cantore"

Teofilo di Giovanmaria Bartolini. Clerk-singer, soprano, May 1590–July 1592
Monthly payments of L. 1. 10 as soprano, then as cantore

Teotonicus. Singer, apparently not hired June 1454
Offered contract 3 June 1454 (see Doc. 4.7)

Tiberio Benedetti. Cantorino, December 1542–September 1545
Monthly payments of L. 2

Tiberio di Girolamo Rivolti. Trombonist, January 1574–May 1580, April 1587–January 1588
Monthly payments of L. 8

Tommaso (Masso) di Jacomo di Matteo. Clerk-singer, May 1487–May 1490, April 1493–March 1495
Monthly payments of L. 4

Tullio di Giovanbattista Tommasi. Clerk-singer, January–June 1530
Monthly payments of L. 2

Ugo di Gidio Francioso. Singer, April–July 1481; December 1481–July 1482
Special payment 12 April 1481, "per detto di misser Alberto"; another of L. 8, 23 May 1481; monthly payments of L. 12, December 1481–July 1482; payment of L. 11 for unspecified month in vol. 509, fol. 44ʳ

Ulisse di Girolamo. Clerk-singer, September 1515, March 1516, June, August 1517, August–September 1518
Monthly payments of L. 1. 10

Ulivieri (Vieri) di Jacomo Gerini da Radicondoli, Ser. Chaplain and bass singer, June 1509–February 1526, with occasional absences; *maestro di cappella,* mid-December 1527–May 1530; singer, May 1530–April 1556; *maestro di cappella,* May 1556–November 1557 (also an organist)
Monthly payments of L. 4, then L. 8, then L. 10 as singer; of L. 17, then L. 20 as *maestro di cappella;* of L. 14 from 1548

Retained after dissolution of chapel, 17 November 1556 (see Doc. 7.1)

Will of 30 October 1556: "Venerabilis vir ser Oliverius Iacobi de Gerinis, presbiter et magister cappellanie cantus figurati ecclesie cathedralis Senarum . . . volens de rebus et bonis suis aquisitis sua industria, videlicet permanendo . . . per annos 47 in circa pro cantore, tum etiam pro magistro cappellanie cantus musice, cum salario . . . scutorum trium auri, aliquando vero scutorum trium cum dimidio et ad presens scutorum duorum . . . , ac etiam docendo et scolam tenendo cantus musice, ad sonandum organa et alia genera instrumentorum . . ." (ASS, Notarile antecosimiano, 2770 No. 146)

Ventura di Giovanni da Castello, Ser. Alto singer, March–April 1580

Monthly payments of L. 21

Verio Veri. Clerk-singer, tenor, May 1582–April 1584

Monthly payments of L. 6 as "cherico grande e tenore"; as "cherico grande," with no indication that he sang, May 1580–April 1582, May 1584–April 1586

Vincentio. Singer, April 1448

Mentioned only upon his departure, 3 May 1448: "Maggio, adì tre del detto mese, si partì Iacomo, Giovanni, Vincentio cantori, con nostra licentia" (vol. 1079, unnumbered folio)

Vincentio di Mattia (Ser from 1523). Clerk-singer, August–September 1518, April 1521–August 1526

Monthly payments of L. 1. 10 as choirboy; of L. 3. 10 from April 1521

Vincenzo Carli da San Casciano, Ser. Singer, May 1590–November 1596

Monthly payments of L. 5, then L. 6, L. 8, L. 10, L. 28, L. 10 as "cantore," as "cappellano cantore," and again as "cantore"

Vito da Polonia. Singer, son of Giovanni, May–December 1449, January 1450–February 1451

Paid 4 lire for May 1449; thereafter the four Polish singers paid 34 lire as a group (*see under* Andrea da Polonia). For contract of 21 January 1450 see Doc. 4.1

II. CATHEDRAL ORGANISTS AND ORGAN BUILDERS

Agostino Agazzari. Organist, January 1597–February 1602

Agostino di Pietro, Don. Organist and chaplain, July 1404–summer 1424 (absent May 1414 through April 1415)

Paid Fl. 16 per year as organist: "1405. Dono Aghustino di Pietro sonatore deli orghani di duomo de' avere adì [gap] Fl. trentadue d'oro e quali deba avere per tenpo di II anni, comi[n]ciò i' suo salaro adì primo di luiglio 1404 e deba finire a dì prima di luiglio 1406 che sono II anni, finendo questo tenpo che noi siamo adì primo d'aprile che ci sono tre messi e questi tre messi deba finire, Fl. XXXIII . . . e die servire infino a primo di lulglio 1406" (vol. 233, fol. 124^r)

An undated entry in an account after April 1424 says that Don Agostino was fired because he was derelict in his duties and that he left cathedral service without official permission: "Don Aghostino di Piero che suona gli organi die avere L. tre s. quindici d. due, come apare al'escita di me Bartholomeo, fo. 92, L. III s. XV d. 2. [below] No' die avere i detti denari perché aveva perduti più suoni che no' metano i denari, e però llo chas[sa]i, e partìssi senza licie[n]za" (vol. 499, fol. 253^r)

Alessandro de' Servi (Coppini), Fra. Organist and composer, organ tester, 1511

Antonio, Ser. Organist, August 1502–March 1503

Monthly payments of L. 8

Antonio di Galgano, Ser. Chaplain and organist, July 1527–May 1530

Monthly salary of L. 8 as chaplain and L. 7 as organist

Antonio Diligente, Ser. Substitute organist, 4 December 1518–December 1519 (also a singer)

Monthly salary of L. 21. In a set of payments to him, one for his services as organist it says "cominciati a dì 4 di dicembre 1518, finiti a dì 4 d'agosto 1519" (vol. 511, fol. 489 right)

Antonio Moneta, Ser. Substitute organist, January 1537

Paid L. 21

Arcangelo da Reggio, Fra. Organist, June 1565–May 1568 (then *maestro di cappella*)
Letter from General of Servite Order giving him permission to become organist, 19 February 1565: see Doc. 7.5; contract, 22 February 1565: see Doc. 7.6
Monthly payments of L. 15

Bartolomeo di Monna Betta. Organist, December 1523, February–March 1524
Monthly payments of L. 1

Bartolomeo di Ser Laio, Don. Chaplain and organist, October 1380–December 1383, 1 November 1385–April 1392, August 1396–August 1398, October 1400–April 1401
The earliest records divide his payments between expenses (Fl. 5 monthly) and salary (Fl. 25 annually): "A don Bartalomeio che suona gli orghani . . . per sete mesi ch'è stato in duomo, a ragione di cinque fl. mese pe' la spesa e vintecinque fl. l'ano di salaro, L. LII s. VIII d. 5" (vol. 1231, fol. 16ʳ, 1380–81). Later payments are at the rate of L. 5 a month
From 1385 his annual salary was 8 gold florins, though he was regularly gone for months and even years at a time. In 1389, when his salary was L. 85, he was exempted from Matins: "Don Bartalomeo di ser Laio nostro chappellano el quale suona gli organi die avere per suo salaro e vita a ragione d'ottanta e cinque L. l'anno, venne a servire la chasa dì primo di magio ano sopradetto ed è asente de' Mattini. E die aver per provisione che gli fecero e chonseglieri ed io per lo tempo fortunoso del charo cinque L. à servito infino adì ultimo d'aprile che uno anno tochagli fra per suo salaro e vita ottanta e cinque Lire" (vol. 522, fol. 28)
Some payments specify when he played: "Lunedì a dì xvii espesi, che dèi a don Bartalomeo per fare sonare gli orghani la sera a Vesparo, Vi soldi. . . . Martedì a dì XVIII espesi, che dèi a don Bartalomeo per sonare gli orghani la not[te] e ma[tu]tino, e la matina a la messa, e la sera a Vesparo, XVIIII soldi" (vol. 1254, fol. 2ʳ, October 1383); "per fare sonare gli orghani el dì di Sancto Frediano e Sancto Bastiano, IIII soldi" (fol. 3ʳ, December)

Payments to bellows workers indicate his duties more specifically: "1385. Tomasso di Pietro e due chompagni volitori della ruota delli orghani dieno avere a dì primo di giugno in giovedì, e fu la pasqua del Chorpo di Christo, in prima per lo Vesparo de la vilia, per soldi II per uno, S. VI; e per la compieta e matino d. 12 per uno, S. III; E per la messa a soldi II per uno, S. VI; e per lo Vesparo de la sera per esso modo, S. VI; E per la chonpieta, soldi III, S. III; per tutto, L. 1. s. IV. . . . La Domenicha seguente fu dì 4, per la messa e per lo Vesparo per d. 16 per uno per la messa e Vesparo, per tutti, S. 8; E dieno avere a dì 11, fu domenica, per essa ragione, S. 8; E dieno avere a dì 18, fu domenica, per essa ragione, S. 8; E dieno avere Sabato dì 24 per San Giovanni per la messa e Vesparo a S. 2 per uno, per tutto, S. 12; E dieno avere la domenica a dì 28 per essa ragione di d. 16 per uno, per tutto, S. 8; E dieno avere il giovedì 29, fu San Pietro e San Pavolo, per la messa e il Vesparo soldi 12, S. 12. Soma L. 4 per tutto giugno" (vol. 1222, fol. 5ᵛ)
AOMS, vol. 225, fol. 80 left: "1396. Donno Bartalomeo di ser Laio chapelano di duomo e sonatore degli organi del duomo adì deto [3 agosto] Fl. sete s. trentoto d. sei e quagli denari sono per lo suo salario che eso à servito el duomo a ufficiare e sonare, cioè di tre mesi, cioè da chalende magio prossimo passato adì ultimo di luglio a ragione di Fl. trenta d'oro l'anno." Additional payments to him in the same volume are on fols. 89 left, 90 left, 91 left, 92 left. A final payment to him is in AOMS, vol. 1224, fol. 14ᵛ: "Don Bartalomeio di ser Laio, monacho di San Vigilio . . . adì ultimo d'aghosto [1398] prese licenzia e non è più nostro chappelllano . . . De' avere per salaro di quatro mesi fiorini X d'oro, L. XXXVIII"
AOMS, vol. 1226, fol. 32ᵛ: "Don Bartalomeio di ser Laio, sonatore delgli orghani venne a servire in duomo a sonare gl'orghani e a dire la messa ongni mattina sichome fanno gl'altri chappellani, e de' avere per suo salaro a ragione di Fl. trenta d'oro l'anno per quello tempo servirà, chon quelle chondizioni che altra volta ebbe nel tempo l'aloghò Fran-

ciescho di Vannuccio, allora operaio. . . .
Chominciò a servire domenicha adì XXIIII
d'ottobre, anno detto [1400]. . . . De'avere
per suo salaro di mesi VI e dì VIII, a ragione
di Fl. XXX l'anno, Fl. XV s. LII"

Bartolomeo Toscani da Venezia, Messer.
Organist, September 1568–January 1573
Monthly salary of L. 15

Benedetto de' Servi, Fra. Organ builder and
tester, 1373

Benedetto di Jacomo da Firenze. Organist,
September 1375–April 1376
Monthly salary of L. 2. 11. 4
Payment for a horse to fetch him from Florence, September 1375: "A lLotto d'Andreia
cherico per ispesa che rimenò uno ronzino
a Fiorenza; fu per Benedetto che suona gli orghani, quando ci vene, vinti s., L. 7" (vol.
207, fol. 56ᵛ)

Bennardo di Salso da Parma, Messer. Organist, May–August 1568
Monthly salary of L. 15

Colo da Pisa, Frate. Organist, January 1394–
April 1396, February 1399–July 1400
Annual salary of Fl. 24. He is called "dei frati di
S. Maria del Carmine" or "de' frati Man-
tellini"

**Cristoforo di Vivaldo da Modena, Mae-
stro.** Organist, July 1515–April 1527
Hired 1 July 1515 at salary of 30 gold ducats:
"Spectatissimi viri . . . operarii . . . servatis
servandis, habita notitia de sufficientia magistri Cristofori de Modana, pulsatore organi, deliberaverunt ipsum magistrum Cristo-
forum conducere et conduxerunt ad
pulsandum organum in ecclesia cathedrali
civitatis Senarum cum illis condicionibus,
modis et obligationibus quibus obligatus erat
frater Laurentius ordinis Minoroum et non
aliter. Et hoc pro tempore duorum annorum
proximorum, incipiendorum die prima presentis mensis Julii et ad beneplacitum postea
dictorum operariorum, pro pretio et mercede ducatorum triginta auri largorum pro
quolibet anno" (vol. 16, fol. 29ʳ, dated 4 July
1515)
Paid L. 56 for purchasing a harpsichord, 30
April 1526: "A maestro Cristofano di Vivaldo, orghanista, il dì L. cinquantasei s. 0,

per lui e suo ordine a missere Raffaello di
Cristofano da Monte Alcino, dise erano per
uno arpicordo li aveva comperato per lui,
conttanti, L. LVI" (vol. 322, fol. 48 left)

Domenico degli Ermini, Frate. Organ
builder, 1372

**Domenico di Lorenzo degli Organi da
Lucca, Maestro.** Organ builder, 1508–21
Awarded contract to build organ in cathedral,
26 September 1508: see Doc. 1.2

Francesco di Guido, called Petruccio. Organist, organ builder, and repairman, later
teacher in the cathedral school, January
1481–July 1500
Monthly payments of L. 8 and additional for repairing the organs (e.g. "Francesco di Guido
detto Petrucio sonatore degli organi de'
avere per achonciare gli orghani e la distribu-
zione del mese di genaio, L. XIII s. VI d.
VIII" (vol. 303, fol. 80).
Monthly payments of L. 14 as singer and organist from 1487; in 1493–95 paid L. 13
monthly as "maestro di chanto e suona[tore]
d'orghani"
Tax declaration in 1491: "Dinanzi da voi Spettabili Cittadini a ffare la nuova lira, Francesco di Guido di Pietro dicie avere li detti
beni: Una chasetta nel populo di Santo Salvadore per la mia habitatione; Una vingnuolo
di staia IIIᵒ in circa posta nel chomune di
Munistero senza chasa e senza ulivo e senza
albori nessuno e di pocho frutto, Fl. 60; Una
chasetta nel populo di Santo Andrea de la
quale ne pagho l'anno al Misericordia L.
tredici e s. dieci di perpetuo; Truovomi una
citola grande da marito. Una orto drieto a
casa mia . . . vale Fl. 10" (ASS, Lira, vol.
224, Terzo di Città, 1491, fol. 111ʳ)

Francesco di Mattia, Ser. Chaplain since
April 1476; organist, May 1479–December
1480
Monthly payments of L. 8 as chaplain; of L. 4
additional for playing organ, May 1479–
March 1480; monthly payments of L. 8,
May–August 1480

Francesco di Nanni, Ser. Chaplain and organist, 15 October 1424–September 1470 (also
a singer)

Reappointed 27 May 1452 at salary of L. 60 per annum (see Doc. 4.4), 2 May 1453 (see Doc. 4.5), 3 May 1454 (see Doc. 4.6), 30 December 1454 (see Doc. 4.8)

Paid L. 5. 10 as organist, L. 15 for training singers in 1454; salary L. 15. 34 in December 1457

Reappointed 11 August 1457: "Item conduxerunt ser Franciscum [gap] in sonatorem organorum, pro uno anno et interim ad beneplacitum, cum salario consueto" (vol. 14, fol. 40ʳ); in 1457 also named as chaplain of S. Crescenzio

Francesco di Piero Bianciardi, Messer. Organist, September 1591–December 1596 (also *maestro di cappella*)

Appointment as organist, 1590: "Ricordo come il signor Rettore messer Giugurta Tomasi l'à condotto per orghanista del duomo a sonare due orghani con obligho che devi sonare tutti i giorni consueti sonarsi egli [*sic*] orghani in detta chiesa a honore di Dio e del divino culto, e di più in quelle giornate strasordinarie che infra l'anno ochorisse. La qual condotta intese e volse esser fatta per uno anno, il quale cominciò il dì primo di genaio prosimo passato che fornirà [*sic*] l'ultimo di dicembre 1591, com [*sic*] patto che volendo e' detto retore licenziarlo e detto messer Francesco partirsi, devi farsi la disdetta da l'una parte a l'a[l]tra e da l'a[l]tra a l'una in modo che il patto sia reciproco, almeno due mesi innanzi; e non si facendo tal disdetta, si intenda sempre seguire uno anno di più, e questo in perpetuo. E per il suo stipendio, à dichiarato il detto signor Rettore doverseli da l'Opera nostra, e per lei da' Kamarlingo di essa, contare fiorini quaranta l'ano, di lire quatro l'uno di muneta sanese, da pagarsene ogni mese la rata, a pagha servita" (vol. 629, fol. 235ʳ) (he was paid as organist only after September 1591)

Monthly salary of L. 16 as organist: "Messer Francesco Bianciardi, già organista et hora modernamente criato maestro della cappella del duomo, deve havere adì primo di genaro [1596/97] lire sedici per il suo ordinato salario d'un mese di detto servitio dell'organo, secondo la lista del sagresta Formica,

L. 16 . . . Gennaro, nel qual principio di mese cominciò a servire per maestro di cappella, come per la lista del sagrestano Formica, L. 32" (vol. 1083, fol. 77ʳ)

Francesco di Tommaso tessitore, Ser. Chaplain and organist, May 1503–May 1508 (also a singer)

Monthly payments of L. 8

Francesco di Vanni da Cortona, Messer. Organist, 14 October 1379–October 1380

Hired 14 October 1379 as organist (paid Fl. 30 per annum) and to officiate in choir, but exempt from singing Mass and being at Matins: "1379. Misser Franciescho di Vanni da Chortona e chalonacho di Chortona venne a stare in duomo adì 14 d'otobre 1379 per sonare gli orghani per tempo d'uno anno ed oficiare in choro e dire messa segiendo [*recte* legiendo] e non chantarla e non esser obrighato d'essere al matino" (vol. 498, fol. 59ʳ)

Francesco Landi, Ser. Organ builder, offered to restore cathedral organ, 1456

Giovannandrea d'Alessandro. Organist, January–March 1524

Two payments, totaling L. 40

Giovanni di Francesco da Valenzia, Frate. Organist, 29 April 1467–June 1479

First payment 29 April 1467: "Frate Giovanni di Francesco, sonatore degli organi in duomo, a dì detto, L. 16 S. 16, ebe contanti in sua mano" (vol. 290, fol. 41ᵛ)

Recommended by Cardinal Francesco Piccolomini, 15 January 1480: see Doc. 5.4

Guasparre, Maestro. Organist, November 1500–June 1502

Monthly salary of L. 8

Jacomo da Modena. Organist, May 1520 (possibly = Jacomo Fogliano)

Paid L. 10. 5

Jacomo da Palermo. Organist, September 1530–March 1531

Paid L. 148 in 1530

Jacomo Panichi. Organist, April 1602–November 1606 (also a singer)

Lazaro di Jacomo, Ser. Chaplain and organist, December 1458–April 1467

Hired 5 December 1458: "Domini operarius et consiliarii . . . decreverunt conducere et conduxerunt ser Lazarum [gap] in cappellanum Opere catredalis [*sic*] ecclesie, cum salario ordinato et consueto, et in sonatorem organorum pro illo salario quo videbitur domino operario non excedendo summam florenorum 16 in anno pro officio organorum. Que conducta sit ad beneplacitum operarii et consiliariorum" (vol. 14, fol. 53ʳ)

Rehired at Fl. 50 per annum, April 1465: "Item deliberarono che per lo presente anno nel quale ser Lazaro serve a sonare, habbi esso ser Lazaro per suo salario ad ragione d'anno per lo tempo servito fiorini 48. Et intendasi essere conducto ffino da mo' per cinque anni proximi advenire per salario di fiorini 50 per ciaschuno anno, ad L. 4 per ciascuno fiorino, per ogni miglior modo etc. Cominciando la sua conducta in Kalendi di luglio proximo che verrà" (vol. 15, fol. XVᵛ)

A tax report from 1465–66 shows that Lazaro and his brother Giovanni owned a house, valued at Fl. 100, in the Via di Salicotto of Terzo San Martino, an area where many of the pifferi later resided. A loan of Fl. 20 on the house was still outstanding. Apparently, Lazaro had no need of cathedral lodgings and was living in the house with his brother, his brother's wife, his mother, and a young clerk "who is is necessary for us to have, although we don't have him at present." ASS, Lira, Terzo di San Martino, 1465–66: "Dinanzi a voi S[ignori] alliratori. Qui di sotto saranno scritti tutti e beni di noi ser Lazaro di Jacomo preste, sonatore degli orghani in Duomo, et di Giovanni suo fratello, et prima: Una casetta nel terzo di Sancto Martino nella campagna di Salicotto di sotto di valuta di [gap] fiorini ciento sopra la quale n'abbiamo debito fiorini XX che non gl'abbiamo anco pagati. Siamo in casa V. boche: 2 utili, cioè noi due, et tre disutigli, cioè la donna di me, Giovanni, et la madre et uno chericho che ci bisogna tenere benché al presente non l'abbiamo. Raccomandianci alle S[ignorie] V[ost]re, le quali Dio in felicità conservi."

Lodovico di Milano called Zoppino, Don (Lodovico Milanese) Auditioned as organist, August 1512; expenses for bringing him

to Siena from Lucca: "Spectatissimi . . . operarii . . . deliberaverunt quod Alexander Galgani de Bichis et socii campsores et depositarii pecuniarum Opere predicte, de denariis dicte Opere solvat ser Paulo Augustini notario Senensi ducatos duos auri pro totidem quod ipse ser Paulus erogavit pro uno numptio cum duobus equis missis ad civitaten Lucensem pro Zoppino, sonatore organorum, et pro expensis factis in conducendum dictum Zoppinum in civitatem Senarum" (vol. 16, fol. 19ʳ, dated 17 August 1512)

Paid 2 gold ducats against his salary, 31 August 1512: "Spectatissimi viri . . . operarii opere predicte, deliberaverunt quod Alexander de Bichis et socii campsores ut depositarii Opere solvant domino Ludovico de Mediolano, alias Zoppino, pulsatori organi, ducatos duos auri, et totidem ponant ad computum sue conducte. Et predicta omni modo etc." (ibid.)

L. 5 paid for a horse to return him to Lucca, 4 September 1512: "Spectatissimi . . . operarii . . . deliberaverunt quod fiat apotissam Iohanni Baptiste Dominici, alias Rosso, scriptori Opere, quod fiat apotissam Bartolino de Mantua, caballario Comunis Senarum, librarum quinque pro mercede unius equi missi per dictum Bartalinum ad civitatem Lucensem pro domino Ludovico de Mediolano, alias Zoppino, et totidem mitatur ad computum dicti domini Ludovici" (ibid., fol. 19ᵛ)

Lorenzo di Jacopo da Prato. Organ builder, 1459

Awarded contract to build organ in cathedral, 20 July 1459: see Doc. 1.1

Lorenzo di Niccolò di Magnio, Fra. Organist, June 1508–March 1515

Contract offered 5 June 1508: "Spectatissimi Pandolfus Petruccius, Iohannes Baptista Francisci et Paulus Vannocii, Operarii et comissarii Opere cathedralis ecclesie civitatis Senarum convocati . . . servatis servandis . . . deliberaverunt . . . conducere et conduxerunt fratrem Laurentium [gap] ordinis Minorum Sancti Francisci, ad pulsandum organum in ecclesia cathedrali predicta, cum obligationibus, salario et modis consuetis et

ad beneplacitum dictorum Operariorum, incipiendo tempus dicte conducte die XI Iunii
MDVIII et ut sequitur, ad beneplacitum tamen dictorum operariorum. Et predicta
omni modo etc." (vol. 16, fol. 11ᵛ)
Monthly payments of L. 10

Mariano di Girolamo Pelori. Organist, May
1563–April 1565, February 1573–December
1590
Contract, 30 April 1563; see Doc. 7.4; monthly
payments of L. 12, then L. 14, L. 16

Matteo di Antonio, Don. Substitute organist,
March 1415
Loan of L. 5 on 26 March 1415 to "dono Ma-
teio d'Antonio delle monache della Badia a
Sancto Donato, suona gli organi in duomo"
(vol. 533, fol. 20ᵛ)

Matteo di Martino, Maestro. Organist,
offered contract in January 1376
Travel expenses to and from Lucca and entertainment, January 1376: "A Matteio sonatore
d'orghani due fiorini d'oro, per la resa del venire a Siena e de' ritornare a Lucha, chome
gli fu promesso per nostra lettara, e per fargli
onore più volte in vino e in fruta, quindici
soldi, VIII L., VIIII s." (vol. 207, fol. 63ʳ)

Matteo di San Giorgio, Messer. Organist,
September through mid–October 1379
Paid L. 5

Monte di Lillo. Organist, 15 September 1376–
September 1379
Contract of 15 September 1376, renewed 20
September 1377: see Docs. 3.2, 3.3

Michelino di Nanni, Ser. Chaplain and organist, June 1392–August 1393, 22 December
1401–spring 1404
Annual salary of L. 100

Nanni di Jacomo, Maestro. Substitute organist, 5 May 1414–4 April 1415
Five payments totaling L. 24. 16. 0

Pavolo di Giovanni, Ser. Chaplain and organist, May 1384–23 October 1385
Paid L. 30 annually for playing organ in 1384,
L. 85 as chaplain and L. 8 for playing organ
in 1395

**Piero di Guasparre Guiducci da Pisa, Mae-
stro.** Organist, July 1458–
Auditioned in February 1458: "Et omnes viso

quod ex Pisis venit sonator ad sonandum
dicta organa et stit hic pluribus diebus, et
bene et dulciter sonavit: volentes in eum uti
liberalitate et cum discretione ei providere,
concorditer deliberaverunt dare ac donare
eidem sonatori et donaverunt ducatos quatuor auri" (vol. 14, fol. 45ʳ, dated 3 February
1457/58)
Contract offered 9 February 1458 with salary of
Fl. 38; began on 1 July: "Domini operarius
et consiliarii . . . deliberaverunt conducere et
conduxerunt magistrum Petrum Ghuasparis
Guiducii de Pisi in sonatorem et pro sonatore organorum catredalis [*sic*] ecclesie Senarum, pro uno anno incipiendo in festo Virginis gloriose, XXV mensis Martii proxime
future et ut sequitur fin[i]endo, cum salario
florenorum triginta otto, de libris quatuor denariorum Senensium pro quolibet floreno
pro dicto anno. Qui magister Petrus sonare
debeat secundum consuetudinem et tempora
solita in dicta ecclesia, et secundum quod de-
clarabitur per dictos dominum operarium,
consiliarios et camerarium. Presente dicto
magistro Petro et predicta acceptante et iu-
rante etc. Die primus Iuliis 1458 incepit
facere officium suum" (ibid., fol. 45ᵛ)

Pietro di Bartolomeo Corradini, Maestro.
Organist, 10 September 1531–10 April 1541
Monthly payments of Duc. 4, 10 September
1531–10 September 1536; yearly salary of
Duc. 52, 10 September 1536–10 April 1538;
monthly salary of L. 30. 6. 8, 10 April–10
April 1541

Pietro Scotto. Hungarian organ builder,
1457–58
Contracted to restore organ in cathedral, 2 April
1457

Scipione di Pavolo Jacomini, Messer. Organist, June 1541–April 1563 (also a singer)
Monthly payments of L. 14 as organist from
June 1541; of L. 17. 10 from November
1545, of L. 28 from May 1551, reduced to
L. 21 on 17 November 1556 ("Deliberorno
anco ridurre e così ridusseno el salario del'organista di duomo a lire vintuna el mese, e
più per l'advenire haver non possa"; vol. 32,
fol. 11ᵛ)

Ugolino de' frati di Camporegi, Frate. Substitute organist, April 1415

Paid L. 4. 4 on 6 April 1415 "per più dì servì a sonare gli orghani" (vol. 242, fol. 51ᵛ)

Ulivieri di Jacomo Gerini. Second organist, April 1541–January 1543 (also a singer)

Paid L. 7 as organist

III. PALACE TRUMPETERS AND SHAWM PLAYERS, TOWN CRIERS, DRUMMERS, AND SINGERS

Agostino di Bindo. Trumpeter, 1343–44

Agostino di Giovanni da Pavia. Trumpeter, 1435–50

Given a month's leave, 7 May 1446: "Concesserunt licentiam Augustini [gap] tubicine palatii, se absentandi ab civitate Senarum per tempus unius mensis, sine amissione salarii et reservato eius loco" (Concistoro, vol. 482, fol. 9ʳ)

Given eight days' leave, 26 March 1450: "Et licentiam concesserunt Augustino Iohannis de Papia, tubicini Comunis Senarum, posse se absentare a civitate Senarum pro tempore otto dierum . . . sine aliqua amissione sui salarii" (vol. 505, fol. 22ʳ)

Alberto di Covaruccio. Trumpeter, 1425–45

Alessandro. Trumpeter, 1544–49

Altovese Arnolfini. Trumpeter and town crier, 1230, 1246, 1249–51

Ambrogio di Duccio. Trumpeter, 1357–65, 1372–79

Andrea. Trumpeter, 1230

Andrea di Antonio da Urbino. Trumpeter, 1444–45, 1447–49

Andrea di Giovanni. Trumpeter, 1490–1526

Tax declaration, 1509: "Al nome di dio adì 18 d'agosto 1509. Dinanzi da voi . . . dicesi per me Andrea di Giovanni tronbetto dei nostri magnifici signori, chome mi truovo: Una casella per la mia abitazione posto in San Salvadore la quale stimato che sono Fl. 60. Trovomi sollo chon la dona e 3 filgliuoli picholi e non ò altro che 'l salario mi danno V. S." (ASS, Lira, vol. 234, 1509, Terzo di Città, fasc. 4, fol. [81]ʳ)

Angelo d'Arrigo da Alamania detto Imperadore. Trumpeter, 1407–42 (also a piffero, 1408–10)

Monthly salary Fl. 3, reduced to Fl. 2 in 1408: see Doc. 9.1

Angelo di Biagio (brother of Chimenti). Trumpeter, 1413–16, 1419–35

Substitutes for Severino called Mancio, 21 February 1413 (Concistoro, vol. 282, fol. 53ᵛ)

Angelo di Vanni. Nakers player, 1407–27

Monthly salary Fl. 3, reduced to Fl. 2 in 1408: see Doc. 9.1

Annibale di Antonio. Trumpeter, 1599–1600

Appointed 5 February 1599: see Doc. 10.19

Annibale dello Spedale. Trumpeter, 1530–34

Salary increased, 17 August 1534: "Et audita et lecta petitione infrascripta . . . Anibalis tubicene, habita super ea matura consideratione et attenta eius bonitate, qualitate et suffitientia, et quod alii tubicine habent plus salarii quam ipse Anibal, et quod propter eius paupertatem non possit commode et recte inservire . . . deliberaverunt salarium dicti Anibalis augere et addere libras 4 denariorum . . . et quod habeat in totum libras quatuordecim denariorum pro quolibet mense, hodie incipiendo . . . Tenor autem dicte petitionis est infrascriptum, videlicet: Dinanzi da Voi, magnifici et eccelsi signori etc. Per il vostro umile e minimo servidore Anibale trombetto si dice e expone come . . . esso non ha altro donde si possa governare se non questo poco salario, et è tanto poco che non può aitarsi et alimentarsi, né ha quanto hanno li altri trombetti delle eccelse Signorie Vostre. Et pertanto humilmente . . . ha preso ardire . . . di pregare strettissimamente le Signorie Vostre eccelse che siano contente deliberare che gli sia concesso al suo poco salario quello più che parrà al vostro eccelso et potente magistrato" (Concistoro 1007, fol. 34ʳ⁻ᵛ)

Annibale di Tommaso (son of Maso detto Briciola). Trumpeter, 1535–36, 1537–

Salary increased 20 November 1537: see Doc. 10.7; salary reduced 2 December 1537: see Doc. 10.6

Ansano di Bartolomeo. Nakers player, 1517–22

Ansano Maria di Geronimo (son of Geronimo di Giovanni). Trumpeter, 1519–20; trombonist, 1521

Antonio di Antonio di Ciuccio. *See* Riccio

Antonio di Ciuccio da Chianciano. Trumpeter and town crier, 1390–1419

Appointed 11 July 1390: "Domini priores . . . eligerunt et nominaverunt infrascriptum in tubatorem et bannitorem Comunis Senarum pro uno anno . . . Antonius Ciucii de Clanciano" (Concistoro, vol. 156, fol. 7ʳ); monthly salary Fl. 3

Accompanies envoys to Milan, August 1391: see Doc. 8.4

Gets half of Tomè di Meio's salary, 1409: see Doc. 9.2

Antonio di Niccolò da Urbino. Trumpeter, 1430

Antonio di Tomè (son of Tomè di Meio). Apprentice trumpeter, 1447; trumpeter, 1448–49, 1456

Assigned next vacant post and permitted in the interim to play with the group and display the commune's arms on his pennant, 19 April 1447: "Magnifici domini . . . informati qualiter Antonius tubicena, filius Tomme tubicene Comunis, est satis intelligens in dicto exercitio tube, eo quo decreverunt quod ipse Antonius possit quandocunque eidem placuerit, exercere se in dicto exercitio tube in palatio dictorum Magnificorum dominorum et ad quascunque festivitates et locha ad qua ipsi Magnifici domini irent, prout eidem Antonio videbitur et de eius processerit voluntate, sine aliquo salario Comunis, portando in tuba pennonem cum armis Comunis prout portant alii tubicene. Insuper eidem Antonio assignaverunt locum primi tubicene vacantis, quem Antonium, vacante alio tubicena, elegerunt in tubicenam Comunis, cum salario et modis consuetis" (Concistoro, vol. 487, fol. 41ʳ)

Hired 17 February 1448: "Et conduxerunt Petrolinum Iohannis et Antonium filium Tome tubicine, in tubicinibus Comunis Senarum, videlicet Antonium predictum loco Clementis hodie defuncti, prout latius constant manu mei [Antonii] Stefani notarii supra et infrascripti" (Concistoro, vol. 492, fol. 37ᵛ)

Suspended for one year for disgraceful remarks, 4 August 1449: "Excelsi et potentes domini . . . informati de pluribus verbis inhonestis

prolatis per Antonium filium Thomme, tubicenam palatii, in verecundiam et dedecus eorumdem magnificorum dominorum, quo pro honestate non dicuntur, concorditer et solemnite decreverunt cassare et cassaverunt dictum Antonium, ita quod de cetero non sit amplius tubicena palatii nec salarium aliquod habeat de cetero, nec aliquid aliud. Et quod infra annum proxime futurum non possit remicti in dicto palatio, nec de eo proponi vel eius remissione" (Concistoro, vol. 501, fol. 25ʳ)

Aquilio di Giovanbattista da Siena. Trumpeter, 1603

Loses competition for post in February 1599: see Doc. 10.19; appointed 13 July 1603: see Doc. 10.22

Arcangelo di Dionisio. Trumpeter, 1584

Austino (Agostino) di Benedetto (son of Benedetto di Domenico, brother of Partenio). Trumpeter, 1544–45

His father petitions to have his post transferred to his brother-in-law Camillo di Marcantonio, 7 August 1542: see Doc. 10.8

Austino di Jacopo del Griccia. Nakers player, 1522–26

Austino di Michelangelo. Trumpeter, 1536–37

Replaces Annibale di Tommaso, 21 March 1536: "Illustrissimi domini . . . visa autoritate concessa . . . super causam Hanibalis Tomasi tubicini, qui vult renunciare locum cuidam Austino Michelangeli tubicini . . . habita matura consideratione et viso quod dictus Hannibal in perpetuum vult relassare locum suum, vive vocis oraculo decreverunt concedere et concesserunt prefato Austino, et commixerunt fieri scripturas in forma et apotissa[m] Camerario Bicherne, quod in loco dicti Hanibalis mictat dictum Austinum etc. cum salario etc" (Concistoro, vol. 1017, fol. 16ᵛ).

Salary reduced 2 December 1537: see Doc. 10.6

Agostino, son of the deceased Michelangelo, "trombettus Magnificorum dominorum," is recorded as having made a pre-marital gift to his wife Bartolomea in a notarial act of 12 April 1537 (ASS, Notarile antecosimiano 1782, no. 401)

Austino di Pietro Pavolo (brother of Giovanni and Mauritio). Trumpeter, 1580–1600
Jailed for violating regulations on outside employment, March 1580: see Doc. 12.19

Balduccio di Angelo. Town crier, 1364–65; trumpeter, 1388, 1390–94

Bartolo di Giovanni. Trumpeter, 1335, 1338

Bartolo di Nicoluccio. Trumpeter, 1356–57, 1365, 1373–81, 1388, 1390, 1392, 1395

Bartolomeo di Crescenzio detto Fanullo. Trumpeter, 1413–15, 1419–24

Bartolomeo di Monaldo (son of Monaldo di Bartolomeo). Trumpeter, 1468; trombonist, 1469

Bartolomeo di Nicoluccio da Castiglione Fiorentino. Trumpeter, 1602
Hired 5 June 1602: see Doc. 10.20; fired 10 July 1602 for not playing in the proper style: see Doc. 10.21

Bartolomeo di Stefano del Griccia. Substitute trumpeter, 1526

Barzalomeo da Pisa. Trumpeter, 1230

Bencivenne. Trumpeter, 1230

Benedetto di Meuccio. Trumpeter, 1357

Bernardino di Monaldo (Monaldi) (son of Monaldo di Bartolomeo). Trumpeter, 1480–81, 1483–1522
Tax declaration 1491: "Dinanzi da voi . . . Exponsi per lo vostro minimo servitore Bernardino di Monaldo trombetto come ha una casa con uno poco di orto di sua habitatione. Altro non ha. Si trova la madre vechia e amalata. Raccomandasi a li V. S. Terzo T. K. di Valderoza" (ASS, Lira, vol. 229, Terzo di Camollia, 1491, fasc. 1, fol. 39ʳ). Bernardino doubtless inherited the house from his father, the former Palace trumpeter Monaldo di Bartolomeo. Also reporting in 1491 was Bernardino's sister Agnese, "daughter of Monaldo trumpeter," who owned half a house next to the church of San Donato in the same contrada. She was apparently a widow with two small children and claimed extreme poverty: "Dinanzi da voi . . . dicesi per me Angniesa figliuola di Monaldo tronbetteo avere una meza chasela posta nela chontrada di Balderozo, terzo di Chamolia e chompagnia di Santo Donato a lato a la chiesa al presente abito; truovomi due figliuoli picholi e non ò

nesuno altro bene . . . che più de la sera ci mancha el pane" (ibid., fol. 1ʳ)
Given a leave of absence, 6 September 1501: see Doc. 10.1

Bernardino di Valerio (son of piffero Valerio di Bartolomeo). Nakers player, 1530, 1544–49

Bertino di Bartolo da Pistoia. Trumpeter, 1391, 1395
Accompanies envoys to Milan, August 1391: see Doc. 8.4

Betto di Giovanni da Prato. Trumpeter, 1399

Biagio di Follo detto Mugnaio. Trumpeter, 1357–65
Payments for playing in two weeks before Assumption: "1359. A Biagio trombatore e compagni vinti soldi chome usanza per loro fadigha quando venghono a trombare XV di inanzi la festa" (AOMS, vol. 340, fol. 42ʳ)

Biagio di Meuccio. Trumpeter, 1373–79, 1388, 1390–95
Payments for playing for feast of the Annunciation, March 1375: "A Biagio tronbatore s. vinti ricievendo per sè e per li chompagni perchè feciero onore di trombare alla capella per Santa Maria di Marzo. L. 1" (AOMS, vol. 204, *E&U della Cappella del Campo, 1374–75,* fol. 68ʳ)

Biagio di Neri. Trumpeter, 1326, 1328, 1335, 1341–43

Bonavita. Trumpeter, 1252

Britio di Sano (son of Sano di Matteo, brother of Domenico). Substitute trumpeter, 1480–84; trumpeter, 1485–1505
Fired for having conversation with his teacher, who spoke with someone who had the plague, 1 September 1486, but reinstated, 3 September: "Attento precepto facto ex parte Dominorum Britio, tubicine eorum Palatii, quod non conversaretur cum Nicolao cecho tubicina, qui conversationem habuit cum quodam amorbato. Et audito responso per eum dato, quod intelligebat et intendit havere conversationem et praticam cum praeceptore suo, in vilipendium Consistorii: servatis servandis decreverunt, ut eius pena aliis servitoribus sit exemplum, ipsum cassare et cassaverunt a servitio Palatii et amplius in futurum non sit tubicina Palatii" (Concistoro, vol. 720, fol. 2ᵛ). "Magnifici domini . . .

habita notitia a fide dignis testibus quod Britius tubicina non protulit verba de quibus supra, deliberaverunt ipsum remunerare . . . et cassaverunt . . . deliberationem suprascriptam contra eum factam" (ibid., fol. 3ʳ)

Camillo di Marcantonio (son-in-law of Benedetto di Domenico). Trumpeter, 1544; 1545–64

His father-in-law petitions to have his son Agostino's post transferred to Camillo, 7 August 1542: see Doc. 10.8

Released from prison, 27 April 1555: "L'Illustrissimi Signori . . . deliberorno, atteso Camillo trombetto essere stato in carcere più giorni, liberarlo da le carcere e così lo liberorno, con precetto che per tutto questo mese non entri in palazzo né anco vadi a sonare in alcuno luogo, escetto [sic] che in accompagnare e sonare quando li Signori escano di palazzo in publico. E mancando, hora per alhora deliberorno darseli due tratti di fune, e così commessero e così li fu significato" (Concistoro, vol. 1127, fol. 19ʳ)

Caprone di Cristoforo. Trumpeter and town crier, 1246–59

Carlo di Piero da Pontremoli. Trumpeter, 1510–26 (absent 1516)

Caroso. Trumpeter, 1252–53

Ceccarello di Birretta. Shawm player, 1357–62

Cecco di Michele. Shawm player, 1364–65, 1372–81

Chimenti di Biagio (brother of Angelo). Trumpeter, 1399–1448; absent 1436–38

Monthly salary Fl. 3, reduced to Fl. 2 in 1408: see Doc. 9.1

Ciecholello Romano. Cantatore, 1414

Paid 15 silver grossi for playing lute and guitar, 26 February 1414: "A Chicholello Romano a dì detto grossi quindici d'ariento, per sua fadigha, però che ven[n]e in Palazo più e più volte a sonare liuto e chiatarlla e dare spasso a' Signiori, per deliberazione de' Signori, roghato ser Niccholò. L. III. s. II d. VI" (Concistoro, vol. 2497, fol. 9ʳ)

Ciereto di Ciereto (brother of Marco and Vanni). Nakers player, 1310

Ciertiere di Guido. Shawm player, 1310, 1316–18, 1326, 1328

Compare di Guido (son of Guido Rossi). Trumpeter, 1251–52

Conte. Trumpeter, 1277

Cornelio di Goro. Trumpeter, 1580–1603

Piero di Domenico detto Ciro renounces his post in favor of Cornelio, 8 May 1581: see Doc. 10.18

Fired 15 June 1602: see Doc. 10.20; reinstated 10 July 1602: see Doc. 10.21; resigns 13 July 1603: see Doc. 10.22

Costantino di Bernardino Monaldi (son of Bernardino). Trumpeter, 1523–26

Receives an expectative to succeed his father, 30 August 1520: see Doc. 10.3

Fired for going to Holy Cross festivities in Lucca without permission, 15 September 1525: see Doc. 10.4

Rehired, 24 January 1526: "Visa et considerata privatione loci tubicinis Constantini Bennardini tubicinis nostri palatii, ipsum Constantinum . . . in pristinum locum imposuerunt, cum salario et emolumentis consuetis, non obstantibus quacunque privatione, concessione de loco suo alteri facta in contrarium disponentibus" (Concistoro, vol. 956, fol. 28ʳ)

Cristoforo di Jacomo (son of Jacomo di Martino). Tabor player, 1341–44, 1347; trumpeter, 1345

Contract of 27 December 1347: see Doc. 8.2

Dionigi di Pavolo. Trumpeter, 1580

Dionisio di Geronimo. Trumpeter, 1522–25

Fired for going to Holy Cross festivities in Lucca without permission, 15 September 1525: see Doc. 10.4

Domenico. Town crier, 1555

Domenico da Brescia detto Voltolina. Trumpeter, 1473–78

Domenico di Biagio. Trumpeter, 1341–42

Domenico di Michele detto Grillo. Trumpeter, 1357–65, 1372–81, 1388, 1390–95

Domenico di Nanni. Town crier, 1364

Domenico di Petruccio. Trumpeter, 1338–40

Domenico di Sano (son of Sano di Matteo, brother of Britio). Substitute trumpeter, 1486–90; trumpeter, 1490–94

Allowed to substitute for his ailing father, 7 November 1486: "Prefati Magnifici et excelsi domini . . . considerata invalitudine Sani tubicene eorum Palatii et quod maxime propter eius senectutem non valet in suo officio servire eorum Dominationibus: attenta etiam ydoneitate ac sufficientia Dominici eius filii qui in huiusmodi exercitio est satis peritus et expertus, servatis servandis etc. concorditer decreverunt ipsum Dominicum deputare et deputaverunt loco dicti Sani sui patris" (Concistoro, vol. 721, fol. 3r–v)

Domenico di Vanni. Trumpeter, 1338–45

Domenico di Voglia. Trumpeter, 1310, 1316–18, 1326–28

Donusdeo. Percussionist, 1230

Duccio. Trumpeter, 1326, 1328

Enea di Senzanome. Apprentice trumpeter, 1473–78; trumpeter, 1478–1511

His father petitions for him to be hired, 16 July 1473: see Doc. 9.8

Permitted to go to Naples with the other Palace musicians, 18 August 1477: "Magnifici et excellentissimi domini . . . decreverunt quod Eneas, filius Senzanome, tubicen, vadat Neapolim cum aliis tubicenibus palatii, et quod participet et participare debeat cum aliis de omni dono, emolumento et liberalitate quam et quam [sic] contigerit eis fieri" (Concistoro, vol. 665, fol. 45v)

Appointed in place of Gaddo di Manno, 1 August 1478: "Et habita notitia quod Enea Senzanome, tubicina de Senis, habet expectativam ingrediendi in palatium loco primi vacantis, et viso quod Ghaddus Manni petiit licentiam de discendendi de palatio et non servit . . . decreverunt ipsum Eneam di Senzanome in tubicinam loco ipsius Ghaddi subrogare et deputare et cerni, aliorum tubicinarum palatii ascribere . . . cum modis, conditionibus, emolumentis, salario et aliis consueti" (Concistoro, vol. 671, fol. 29r)

Given permission to go to Florence for ten days, 5 October 1486: "Prefati Magnifici domini licentiam concesserunt Enee tubicine eorum Palatii, per tempus X dierum eundi Florentiam cum oratore, et quod dimittat unum qui suo loco serviat Palatio per tubicina" (Concistoro, vol. 720, fol. 8v)

Allowed table rights in Palace, 18 March 1488: "Et voluerunt Magnifici domini quod Eneas Senzanome canovarii, tubicen, habeat expensas victus in palatio cum aliis de familia" (Concistoro, vol. 729, fol. 7v)

Tax declaration of his granddaughter, 1548: see Doc. 9.9

Feduccio. Trumpeter, 1277

Feo di Giovanni. Shawm player, 1335, 1338–40

Filippo di Ciuccio. Shawm player, 1345

Francesco di Biagio Lucchese. Trumpeter and nakers player, 1326, 1335, 1338, 1339, 1340–45

A silver trumpet is ordered to be made for him, 30 December 1347: see Doc. 8.1

Francesco di Giuliano. Trumpeter, 1584–1600

Francesco di Jacomo. Trumpeter, 1340–45

Francesco di Mariano di Galgano. Trumpeter, 1525–

Hired 11 November 1525: "Et audita petitione facta nomine Francisci Mariani Galgani, petentis locum unius tubicinis vestri palatii, et attento quod Costantinus Be[r]nardini fuit cassum et deletum, deliberaverunt dictum locum concedere et concesserunt dicto Francisco, cum salario emolumentis et oneribus consuetis" (Concistoro 955, fol. 13v)

Francesco di Vanni. Nakers player, 1434–46

Francio di Viva (brother of Giovanni). Nakers player, 1388, 1390, 1391, 1392, 1395, 1399–1407

Monthly salary Fl. 3

Accompanies envoys to Milan, August 1391: see Doc. 8.4

Gabardino. Trumpeter, 1255, 1257

Gabriel di Tomaso. Trumpeter, 1427

Gabriello di Bencivenni. Nakers player, 1388

Gaddo di Manno (brother of Lodovico). Trumpeter, 1475–78, 1480–87

Resumes the post he resigned in favor of his brother Lodovico, 9 February 1487: see Doc. 9.6

Galgano di Marco. Tabor player, 1335

Geronimo di Giovanni da Iesi. Trumpeter, 1480–86; 1521 (also a trombonist in the Palace wind band)

Geronimo di Meio (son of Meio di Maestro Mino, brother of Niccolò). Nakers player, 1498–1516

Geronimo (Girolamo) di Michelangelo (son of Michelangelo, brother of Niccolò). Trumpeter, 1530–59

Salary reduced 2 December 1537: see Doc. 10.6

His brother petitions to allow him to return from exile and be rehired, 14 February 1538: "Audito pluries Niccolao Michaelisangeli tubicena palatii, nomine Hieronimi sui fratris, super eius petitione restitutionis bonorum et ad patriam humiliter se commendante, deliberaverunt restituere et absolvere et ita restituerunt prefatum Hieronimum ad patriam et ab exilio absolverunt, et similiter ipsum reposuerunt in eius locum tubicene magnifici palatii, mandantes etiam quo eidem restituantur omnia eius bona" (Concistoro, vol. 1028, fol. 35ʳ)

Gherardo di Duccio. Nakers player, 1338

Ghezzo Boninsegna (brother of Malfarsetto). Trumpeter, 1277, 1291, 1298

Giovan Domenico di Camillo detto Il Colonello (son of Camillo di Marcantonio). Trumpeter, 1564–

Petitions to replace his father, 14 December 1564: "Et visa supplicatione Iohannis Dominici Camilli vocati il Colonello, tubicine eorum palatii, porrecta Reverentissimo et Excellentissimo Gubernatori et eius rescripto quod eligatur in dicto offitio, loco dicti sui patris . . . elegerunt dictum Iohannem Dominicum in tubicinam eorum palatii, loco dicto olim eius patris, cum salariis et emolumentis solitis et ordinatis, omni meliori modo etc." (Concistoro, vol. 1182, fol. 23ᵛ)

Admonished for having insulted his stepmother, 22 February 1565: "Udito messer Flavio Guglielmi notaio del'offitio de' Pupilli sopra lo insulto fatto da Giovan Domenico di Camillo trombetto a madonna Antognia sua matrigna, per causa del'haver tolto et levato uno fodarone del letto e guasto certa tenda, e sendo egli stato costretto . . . per due giorni . . . deliberorno licentiare . . . il detto Giovan Domenico da tal costretta dando però prima idonea promessa di non offendare né fare offendare la detta madonna Antonio in detto

o in fatto" (Concistoro, vol. 1183, fols. 36ᵛ–37ʳ)

Giovan Francesco detto El Moro. Trumpeter, 1468–March 1511 (absent 1494)

Tax declaration, 1509: "Dina[n]zi da voi, signori aliratori . . . dicesi per me Giovanfrancesco alttreme[n]tti el Moro, tro[m]betto, dicesi tutti i miei benni mobili e imobili E di prima tutte le pocisioni e case e robe che nele dette pocisioni sono delo Spedale di Santa Maria dela Schala comese ed i[n]corporatte, come figliolo di detta casa, rogatto ser Filiziano g[i]à p[i]ù tempo fa. Item una casa è nel piano de' Ma[n]telini, la quale ène del convento f[r]atti di Santa Maria del Carmine, e le robe che vi sono drentto, dopo la vitta mia e dela mia don[n]a, rogatto ser Pietro di Sa[l]vadore g[i]à p[i]ù tempo fa, e c[i]ò che per l'avenire si trovarà, è del detto co[n]ventto detto di sopra, per titolo di donazione etterna. Racomandomi ale vostre Segniore" (ASS, Lira, vol. 236, Terzo di Città, 1509, fol. 23ʳ)

Giovan Maria di Matteo. Trumpeter, 1592–99

Hired in place of Silverio, 30 December 1597: "Visa supplicatione plurium tubicinarum, petentium sibi concedi locum vacatum per mortem Silverii, tubicinae palatii . . . fuit deliberatum quod tale officium concedatur ei qui plura vota habebit, dummodo ille obtentus prius renunciet locum quem habeat . . . Prevaluit per plura vota: Iohannes Maria olim Matthiae, domicellus eorum palatii" (ASS, Concistoro, vol. 1309, fol. 137ʳ⁻ᵛ)

Giovanbattista Volpini (brother or father of Giulio di Giovambattista detto Volpino). Supernumerary trumpeter, 1546

Appointed December 1546: see Doc. 12.5

Giovanni. Trumpeter, 1253–55, 1257

Giovanni Ceccharelli. Cantore, 1354

Paid salary for twenty-one days while on military service, 1 August 1354: "Item Iohanni Ceccharelli cantori misso [ad] Sanctum Chiricum in Osenna cum bombarda Comunis, pro eius salario XXI dierum quibus stetit in servitium Comunis, florenos VI, soldos XIII" (Biccherna, vol. 234, fol. 96ʳ)

Giovanni detto Mangia. Town crier, 1364–65

Giovanni di Alessandro detto El Gallina.
Trumpeter, 1519–58
Salary reduced 2 December 1537: see Doc. 10.6
Petitions to have his son-in-law Gregorio di Savino replace him, 27 June 1559: see Doc. 10.15

Giovanni di Antonio. Trumpeter, 1434–38

Giovanni di Antonio da Bologna. Trumpeter, 1399–1410 (also a piffero, 1410)
Monthly salary Fl. 3, reduced to Fl. 2 in 1408: see Doc. 9.1

Giovanni di Azzolino detto Sodo. Trumpeter, 1344–45, 1357–65, 1381

Giovanni (Nanni) di Domenico. Nakers player, 1357–65, 1373–81, 1388, 1390, 1392, 1395 (shawm player in 1374)
Assumption Day payments 1381: see Doc. 8.3

Giovanni di Lodovico. Trumpeter, 1521

Giovanni di Martino da Pergola. Trumpeter and town crier, 1436–83
Given leave to go to Rome for fifteen days to seek an indulgence, 6 December 1450: "Et concesserunt licentiam Iohanni Nicholai tubicene eundi Romam pro indulgentia, pro XV diebus, sine amissione salarii" (Concistoro, vol. 508, fol. 38ʳ)
Mortally ill in 1483, his position is taken over by the trombonist Bartolomeo di Monaldo: see Doc. 11.15

Giovanni di Meio. Trumpeter, 1356–57

Giovanni di Niccolò da Iesi. Trumpeter, 1449–78
Given expectative on 9 March 1449: "Magnifici domini . . . loco primi tubicinis vacantis eligerunt et nominaverunt Iohannem Nicolai tubicenam de Iesi, habitatorem civitatis Senarum, cum salario, eo modo et oneribus prout serviunt et sunt conducti alii tubicine nostri palatii et consuetis. Qui tamen, donec locum habuerit, teneatur pulsare quando fuerit requisitus ad pulsandum tubettam pro partes Magnificorum dominorum" (Concistoro, vol. 499, fol. 8ʳ)
Appointed 4 August 1449: "Et statim elegerunt in tubicenam dicti palatii Iohannem de Iecio, cum salarium et modis consuetis, cum hoc quod in presentiarum non habeat vestem pro festivitate Sancte Marie medii Augusti" (Concistoro, vol. 501, fol. 25ʳ)

Giovanni di Petrolino detto Barbulia (son of Pietro di Giovanni detto Petrolino). Trumpeter, 1451–63, 1464–66, 1469–78
Ordered to be tortured, whipped, and imprisoned for six months, 6 June 1463: "Magnifici domini . . . deliberaverunt, auditis multis inhonestatibus factis superioribus diebus per Iohannem Petrolini, tubicenem palatii, ipsum mittendum etiam in manibus Potestatis Senarum, qui eum legari faciat ad collam et torturam et verberari de centum staffilatis per famulos ipsius Potestatis, et ita cesum et nudum destinet ad carceres Comunis, ubi deposita divisa palatii stare debeat per sex menses inde proxime secuturos, ipsum ex nunc cassando a conducta sua" (Concistoro, vol. 580, fol. 31ᵛ)

Giovanni di Petruccio. Trumpeter, 1335

Giovanni di Pietro. Trumpeter, 1592–97

Giovanni di Pietro detto El Civile. Trumpeter, 1495–32
Receives clothing and permission to wear commune's emblem, 4 August 1513: "Et audito Civili tubicini palatii, petenti sibi concedi vestem prout aliis tubicinibus, offerenti se portare divisam palatii etc., deliberaverunt concedere . . . dictam vestem, cum hoc quod ipse ferat divisam prout alii tubicene cum effectu, et casu quo non ferat divisam predictam, quod camerarium Bicherne retineat sibi de suo salario usque ad summam librarum 31 s. 4 denariorum, pro dicta veste sibi concessa et data" (Concistoro, vol. 881, fol. 11ʳ)

Giovanni (Giovanbattista) di Pietro Pavolo (brother of Austino and Mauritio). Trumpeter, 1580–1600
Hired in place of Sacripanto, 9 October 1597: "Visis supplicationibus plurium tubicenorum suplicantium pro obtinenda platea sive loco praedefuncti Sacripantis, tubiceni Illustrissimi Palatii . . . fuit obtentum per plures lupinos albos quod Iohannes quondam Petri haberet locum relictum per Sacripantem, cum oneribus et honoribus solitis et consuetis. Fuit postea obtentum per plures lupinos albos quod Petrus quondam Dominici habeat locum tubicenae in Palatio, relictum per suprascriptum Iohannem successorem Sacripantis" (Concistoro, vol. 1309, fol. 137ʳ⁻ᵛ)

Giovanni di Viva (brother of Francio). Nakers
player, 1381
Giuliano di Bartolomeo da Chianciano.
Trumpeter, 1446–72
Appointed 20 December 1446: "Conduxerunt
insuper in tubicinem palatii ad beneplacitum
Consistorii, Iulianum de Clanciano, cum sala-
rio et emolumentis que habent alii tubicines,
quod salarium incipere debeat in calendis Ianuarii proximi, et interim teneatur servire palatio" (Concistoro, vol. 485, fol. 39ʳ)
Giulio di Giovambattista detto Volpino.
Trumpeter, 1548–57, 1567–70
Looses position through absence, 30 October
1548: see Doc. 10.11
Reclaims position and is reinstated, 21 February
1549: see Doc. 10.12
Dismissed and reinstated, 2 September 1550:
"Et audito Iulio Volpino, iam bannito et privato sui offitii tubicene eorum palatii a pre-
cessoribus, et eius humili pe[t]itione et venia
petita sui falli et excessus iam commissi: servatis etc., deliberaverunt . . . ipse ponatur in
publicis carceribus per dies otto ab hodie . . .
et quod intelligatur et sit liber et absolutus ab
huiusmodi banno, et restitutus ad pristinum
eius offitium et locum tubicene quod iam obtinebat" (Concistoro, vol. 1120, fol. 44ʳ)
The priors send for him to fill place vacated, 17
September 1567: "Et deliberorno mandarsi
per Giulio alias il Golpino, trombetto senese,
assente dalla città et dominio, et volendo egli
il luogo e la piazza vacata per la morte di
Giovanbattista, anzi Niccolò zoppo, già trombetto di palazzo, et essendo il preposito che
se li dia tal piazza e luogo, con licentia et
quando piacia ai Supperiori et all'Illustrissimo integro Consistoro" (Concistoro, vol.
1198, fol. 12ᵛ)
From Split he indicates that he wishes to return,
17 October 1567: "Il Signor Fulvio Marretti,
per l'autorità a lui data . . . disse esserli stato
messo per le mani, per nuovo trombetto di
palazzo Giulio alias Golpino, senese quale al
presente si ritrova a Spalato, et haverno di
ciò conferito con lo Illustrissimo Signor Federigo [Montauto], quale ha detto che si con-
tenta che si dia tal luogo al detto Giulio Golpino . . . e di più essarvi lettere del detto

Golpino che desidera havere tal luogo"
(ibid., fol. 24ʳ)
Rehired, 25 October 1567: "Et deliberorno con-
cedarsi et darsi il luogo et piazza vacata del
trombetto a Giulio di Giovambattista, alias
Golpino, senese trombetto . . . con salario,
pesi, honori, incomodi in forma sì come li
altri trombetti" (ibid., fol. 29ʳ; also fols.
32ᵛ–33ʳ, dated 30 October 1567)
A new case is ordered made for his trumpet, 6
November 1567: "Illustrissimi domini . . .
audito Volpino tubicina palatii, petente ar-
cam sive cassam unam, convertendam in
usum suum pro tuba reponenda et salvandam
prout et alii tubicine . . . mandaverunt sibi
construi ac fieri unam cassam novam ad expensas palatii, et eandem sibi dari pro con-
signari in palatio tantum et non alibi tenen-
dam et fruendi" (Concistoro, vol. 1199, fol.
4ᵛ)
Given meal privileges in exchange for teaching
the trumpet, 8 November 1567: "Illustrissimi domini . . . audita petitione Iuliis Volpini tubicinae palatii et aliorum famulorum
palatii, petentium ex gratia victum et expensas concedi de cetero dicto Iulio, ut possit
commode docere illos qui desiderant discere
tuba[m] canere sive sonare absque alio pagamento . . . concesserunt eidem Iulio Vulpino
victum pro eius persona, de pane et vino tantum, durante eorum presenti supremo ma-
gistratu, et eundem in ultimo recommandare
Illustrissimi dominis subcessoribus" (ibid.,
fol. 5ʳ). These privileges were reconfirmed
by decisions reported in Concistoro, vol.
1200, fol. 3ʳ⁻ᵛ, dated 3 January 1568; and in
vol. 1202, fol. 10ʳ⁻ᵛ, dated 28 May 1568
Imprisoned for three days for introducing dishonest women into the Palace, 23 September 1568: "Il Magnifico Capitano . . . havendo Giulio Volpino menate in palazzo
donne infami e disoneste . . . volendo in
parto procedere al debito gastigo acciò non
ne vada al tutto impunito, fattoli prima moni-
tione che più per l'avvenire non ardisca o
presuma fare tal cosa . . . volse sia confinato
e devi stare giorni tre in palazzo e di quella
non uscire né di dì né di notte per giorni tre

con oggi, sotto grave pena del suo arbitrio"
(Concistoro, vol. 1204, fol. 9ᵛ)

Imprisoned again, 7 February 1570: "Li Magnifici et Eccelsi signori . . . mossi da iuste e
ragionevoli considerationi, deliberorno che
Giulio detto il Golpino vada in pregione et
che se gli levi ogni parte che esso ha in
tinello . . . per sino a tanto che per loro
Signori non sarà in contrario deliberato"
(Concistoro, vol. 1212, fol. 11ᵛ)

Released, placed under house arrest, then released, 20 February 1570: "Deliberorno appresso che Giulio detto Golpino sia excarcerato et confinato in casa di sua habitatione
senza participare alcuna parte del loro tinello,
sino a tanto che per loro Signorie non sarà in
contrario deliberato" (ibid., fol. 12ᵛ); "Li
Magnifici et Eccelsi Signori etc., mossi dalla
intercessione delli homini d'arme della città
di Siena per loro Altezze Serenissime et da altre giuste et ragionevoli considerationi, sole-
nemente deliberorno di liberare . . . Giulio
detto il Golpino dal confino datoli in casa di
sua habitatione . . . con questo però che per
tutto il presente mese non possi né li sia
lecito, né di giorno né di notte in modo
alcuno, entrare nel loro palazo, sotto
gravissima pena del loro arbitrio" (ibid., fol.
15ᵛ)

Jailed upon wife's complaint, 19 April 1570:
"Habita querela a domina Emilia uxore Iulii
Volpini tubicena [sic] . . . mandaverunt et
commiserunt ipsum carcerari ubicumque sit
ad invenire posset . . . Ac etiam mandaverunt
precipi dicto Iulio quatenus statim compareat
et non offendat aliquo modo prefatam dominam Emiliam eius uxorem, sub pena indigna-
tionis eorum Consistorii" (vol. 1213, fol.
15ʳ)

Dismissed and banished forever, 9 August 1570:
"Nella causa della inquisitione formata contra di Giulio di Giovanbattista detto Golpino, trombetta di palazzo e della compagnia delli huomini d'arme di questa città;
vista la detta inquisitione, le citationi fatte, la
contumacci di detto Giulio . . . dechiara-
rorno il detto Giulio contumace e come tale
lo poseno in perpetuo bando dall città e stato

di Siena e dominio di Sua Altezza Serenissima, et di ragione punibile per li delitti da
lui commessi . . . e lo privorno del luogo suo
del trombetto, dechiarando quello essere vacante e retornato alla Camera ducale" (vol.
1215, fol. 14ᵛ)

Guido di Angelo. Trumpeter, 1415–18, 1420–
21, 1424–26

Permitted to wear enamel shield of commune,
18 July 1424 (Concistoro, vol. 351, fol. 13ᵛ)

Guido Rosso. Trumpeter and town crier,
1246–57

Ildino. Shawm player, 1277.

Jacomo di Corso. Trumpeter, 1388,
1390–1404

monthly salary Fl. 3

Jacomo di Martino. Nakers player, 1328,
1335, 1338–45, 1347

Contract of 27 December 1347; see Doc. 8.2

Jacomo di Tomasso . Trumpeter, 1338, 1362

Jacomo Nardi. Nakers player, 1364

Jacomo Palmerini detto Cucioletta. Trumpeter, 1356

Jacopo di Giuliano da Pistoia. Trumpeter,
1496–1504

Hired in place of Meciaro, 14 May 1496: "Deliberaverunt etiam quod Iacobinus Iuliani de
Pistorio, tubicen, intelligatur [esse] et sit conductus in palatio, loco ipsius Meciarii, secundum formam spectative eidem concesse a
Spectatissimis officialibus Balie . . . cum salario et modis consuetis etc." (Concistoro, vol.
778, fol. 6ʳ)

Jacopo di Leonardo da Colle. Trumpeter

Offered contract as trumpeter, 6 July 1390: "Domini priores supradicti . . . eligerunt et nominaverunt et conduxerunt et firmaverunt ad
servitia et stipendia Comunis Senarum in tubatorem et pro tubatore Comunis Senarum
pro uno anno, cum salario et modis et conditionibus solitis . . . Iacobum Leonardi de
Colle" (Concistoro, vol. 156, fol. 5ʳ)

Lando da Faenza. Substitute trumpeter for
Altovese, 1249

Leonardo da Pisa. Percussionist, 1230

Leonardo di Taddeo. Substitute trumpeter,
1497

Lo Stiaccia. Trumpeter, 1532
Lodovico di Manno (brother of Gaddo).
  Trumpeter, 1489–92, 1494
Loses the post his brother Gaddo had resigned
  in his favor, but retains his expectative, 9 February 1487: see Doc. 9.6
Hired, 8 August 1489: "Prefati Magnifici domini . . . visa capsatione facta de Mancino
  tubicena palatii et vacatione sui loci, et vis ex-
  pectativa quam habet Ludovicus Manni tubicena ab oportunis consiliis, de succedendo in
  locum tubiceni primi vacantis . . . dictum Lo-
  dovicum conduxerunt in tubicenam palatii
  eorum, loco dicti Mancini, cum salario,
  emolumentis, gravedinibus et honeribus actenus consuetis et debitis ex forma statutorum" (Concistoro, vol. 737, fol. 12^r, dated
  8 August 1489)
Requests release from service 4 November
  1494, and Piergiovanni di Niccolò replaces
  him 6 November 1494: "audito Ludovico
  Manni, tubicena eorum palatii, petente licentiam sibi dari et se admoveri et ab eius loco
  cassari, deliberaverunt eum cassare et deliberantes cassaverunt" (Concistoro, vol. 346,
  fol. 3^r). "Et deliberaverunt conducere et
  conduxerunt in tubicenam et pro tubicena
  palatii eorum, loco Ludovici Manni tubicene
  licentiati et cassi, Pierum Iohannem Nicholai
  ceci, tubicenam, cum officio, salario, emolumentis et modis actenus ordinatis et consuetis" (Concistoro, vol. 769, fol. 4^r)
Lombardino. Trumpeter, 1252
Lorenzo, Maestro. Singer, 1475–82
Lorenzo di Giovanni. Nakers player, 1339
Lottaringo. Town crier, 1230
Luca di Pietro. Trumpeter, 1357–65, 1372–81

Maffeo Guerrieri. Trumpeter and town crier,
  1246–47, 1255, 1259
Magio di Petruccio. Trumpeter, 1341–45; na-
  kers player, 1347
Contract of 27 December 1347; see Doc. 8.2
Malfarsetto Boninsegna (brother of Guido).
  Trumpeter, 1298, 1310, 1316–18
Manente. Trumpeter, 1253, 1255, 1257
Marco. Trumpeter, 1544–49 (1549 "già trom-
  betto")
Marco di Ciereto (brother of Ciereto and
  Vanni). Tabor player, 1310, 1316–18, 1326,
  1328

Mariano detto Mancino. Trumpeter, 1483–
  85, 1487
Martino da Bologna. Cantatore, 1326, 1341
Paid while in service of Florentine army, 10 Oc-
  tober 1341: "In primis Martino cantatori de
  Bononia . . . pro eius salario XLVIIII dierum
  quibus stetit in exercitu florentino in servitio
  Comunis Senarum, cum uno equo, ad ratio-
  nem XX soldorum pro die, ut patet per
  apodixum Dominorum Novem—XLVIII li-
  bras" (Biccherna, vol. 208, fol. 11^v)
Maso (Tommaso) detto Briciola. Trumpeter, 1511–26, abs. 1521–22
Matteo di Cenno. Shawm player, 1345
Matteo di Giovanni da San Gimignano.
  Trumpeter, 1399
Matteo di Palmero. Shawm player, 1341–43
Mauritio di Pietro Pavolo (brother of Austino and Giovanni). Trumpeter, 1585
Meciaro (nickname; identity uncertain). Trumpeter, 1496
Denounced as a thief and price put on his head,
  14 May 1496: "Illustrissimi domini . . .
  atento quod in proximis preteritis mensibus
  fuit furto subtratta quedam schutella argenti,
  ponderis sex unciarum vel circha, unde habita informatione qualiter Meciarus tubicen
  palatii ipsam fusam vendidit cuidam Ghaspari
  Nicolai aurifici . . . in maximum vilipendium palatii, et ut unusquisque a similibus de-
  sistat . . . ipsum Meciarum deliberaverunt
  corrigere et punire et bannum capitis dederunt eidem si stabit aut veniet in civitate et
  districtu Magnifici Comunis Senarum" (Concistoro, vol. 778, fol. 5^v)
Meio di Maestro Mino. Nakers player,
  1460–97
Because of his poverty and large family is con-
  ceded eight measures of wheat, 30 April
  1481: "Animadversa etiam paupertate Mei nacharini palatii et eius familia inutili, presertim
  de pluribus filiabus aptas [sic] nuptui, quas ex
  paupertate nubere non potest, et aliis misera-
  bilibus necessitatibus dicti Mei . . . decreverunt quod camerarius Consistorii presentis
  emat, expensis Comunis Senarum et dicti
  membri, staria octo grani . . . pro sustenta-
  tione sue familie" (Concistoro, vol.
  687)
Michelangelo di Niccolò (son of Niccolò Tu-

rini, brother of Piergiovanni). Trumpeter, 1480–92, 1495–1525

Tax declaration, 1509: "Al nome di dio adì 24 d'agosto 1509. Dinanzi da voi spettatissimi cittadini . . . dicesi per me Michelagnolo di Niccolò tronbetto vostro servidore avere l'infrascriti beni, cioè Una casa nel terzo di città e populo di San Salvadore dove racomandomi a le vostre spettabilità, truovomi la donna chon duo figlioli picini e non ò altro sosidia se no' lire otto le mese da le Signorie vostre" (Lira, vol. 234, 1509, Terzo di Città, fasc. 4, fol. [11]ʳ)

Monaldo di Bartolomeo da Chianciano. Trumpeter and town crier, 1459–74

Hired 7 July 1459: see Doc. 9.3

Nanni di Domenico. *See* Giovanni di Domenico

Neri Fava. Trumpeter, 1291, 1298, 1316–18

Niccolao. Trumpeter, 1365

Niccolò d'Andrea. Trumpeter, 1356–57, 1373

Niccolò d'Arezzo. Cantatore, 1422

Niccolò di Golino. Trumpeter, 1427–29

Niccolò di Meio Naccharini (son of Meio di Maestro Mino, brother of Geronimo). Trumpeter, 1487–92, 1494

Fired on 4 May 1494: "Et decreverunt quod Nicolaus Nacharini, tubicen palatii, intelligatur esse et sit cassus et non currat amplius sibi salarium" (Concistoro, vol. 768, fol. 18ᵛ)

Rehired on 20 April 1495: "Et quod Nicolaus Nacharinus, tubator, restitutus intelligatur in loco suo tubicinorum, cum hoc quod ille qui erat positus in loco ipsius Nicolai Nacharini redeat in sua iura expectative que prius habebat" (Concistoro, vol. 770, fol. 19ᵛ)

Niccolò di Michelangelo (son of Michelangelo di Niccolò). Trumpeter, 1526–67

Salary reduced 2 December 1537: see Doc. 10.6

Tax declaration, 1549: "Al nome di dio adì 22 di ferraio 1548/49. Questa scrita è di me Nicolò di Michelagnolo tronbetto . . . servidore di Vostre Signorie, come mi truovo una chasa posta in Siena nel Terzo di Città e populo di S. Salvadore per nostro abitare . . . mi truovo esare stropiato . . . mi truovo uno figliolo infermo" (ASS, Lira, vol. 243 Terzo di Città, fasc. 3, 1548, San Salvadore, fol. 26ʳ, no. 1708)

Niccolò di Piero da Città di Castello. Trumpeter, 1457

Assumes Antonio di Tomè's post, but must pay his salary to Antonio's father, February 1457: see Doc. 9.7

Niccolò di Vieri. Trumpeter, 1378, 1381

Assumption Day payments 1381: see Doc. 8.3

Niccolò Teutonico (de Alamania). Trumpeter, 1446–47

Niccolò cieco Turini. Substitute trumpeter, 1452–53; trumpeter, 1454–1504 (absent 1494)

Given a suit of clothing, 16 October 1452: "Deliberaverunt quod camerarios Biccherne det Nicolao Cecho, tubiceni, libras XX denariorum convertendas in una veste, quas sibi dari decrevimus amore Dei" (Concistoro, vol. 516, fol. 37ʳ)

Appointed 18 February 1453: "Deliberaverunt quod, viso quod in presenti bimestri Riccius tubicen palatii nunquam serviverit vel pro raro, ut tenetur, et loco sui suppleverit et serviverit Niccolaus orbus: ex nunc intelligantur et sint actribute dicto Niccolao orbo tubiceni libras sex denariorum senensium de salario quod habere debet et tenetur dictus Riccius a Comuni Senarum pro presenti bimestri, sine aliqua exceptione. Item . . . eligerunt ex nunc supradictum Niccolaum orbum tubicenam in tubicenam palatii, loco prius tubicenis vacantis, cum salario consueto et ordinato et prout habent alii tubicene palatii predicti" (vol. 518, fol. 38ᵛ)

Permitted to use his clothing allowance to buy grain for his family, 31 July 1465: "Supradicti Magnifici domini . . . concesserunt Nicolao Torini tubicini quod denarii pro vesti[bu]s quos habere debet pro festivitate gloriosissime Matris Virginis Marie de mense Augusti, possit convertere in grano pro necessitatibus familie sue" (vol. 593, fol. 25ʳ)

Tax declaration, 1488: "Yhesus 1485: Terzo di Città e compagnia del Chastao di Sopra: Dinanzi da voi spettabilissimi citadini preposti a fare la nuova lira sponsi per me Nicolò di Turino trombetto de' Magnifici Signori avere una chasetta per mio abitare e ò quatro figlioli e devene una femina. Racomandomi a le vostre spettabilità" (ASS, vol. 215, Terzo di Città, 1488, fol. 131ʳ)

Released from jail with his son, 26 September 1494: "Et decreverunt quod Nicolaus cecus et eius filius, detenti in carcere per barigellum eo quod crastina [*sic*] die non sonuerunt tubas in elevatione Corporis Domini iuxta deliberationem contra eos factam, extrahantur et liberentur a carcere, et revocaverunt deliberationem contra eos facta" (Concistoro, vol. 768, fol. 9ᵛ)

Nicola di Bencivenne. Trumpeter, 1310, 1316–18

Orazio del Gallina (son of Giovanni di Alessandro). Trumpeter, 1530–37

Salary reduced 2 December 1537: see Doc. 10.6

Pagno di Marino. Trumpeter and town crier, 1259

Paolo di Guccio. Trumpeter, 1344–45

Paoluccio di Duccio. Nakers player, 1362

Partenio (son of Benedetto di Domenico, brother of Agostino). Trumpeter, 1545

Pavolo. Trumpeter, 1600

Pavolo dello Spedale. Trumpeter, 1536

Pavolo di Giovanni Rimombi. Trumpeter, 1536; 1544–82

Requests permission to serve Chiappino Vitelli, 22 June 1555: "Pavolo trombetto sellaio possi et habbi licentia di andare a servire il Signor Chiappino Vitelli, lassando egli per suo sustituto Domenico bannitore" (Concistoro, vol. 1127, fol. 39ʳ)

Asks to have his son Sacripante replace him during illness, 19 July 1582 (*see under* Sacripante)

Pavolo di Niccolò. Trumpeter and town crier, 1532–49

Pericciuolo Salvucci. Trumpeter, 1310, 1316–18

Petruccio di Tino. Trumpeter, 1316–18, 1328

Pier Domenico di Maestro Antonio, detto El Capone (son of Maestro Antonio da Venezia, brother of Giovanni di Maestro Antonio). Trumpeter and town crier, 1505–12; 1519–37

Petitions for an expectative, approved 16 April 1506: "Dinanzi da Voi Magnifici Signori Officiali di Balìa dela città di Siena. Exponsi per lo vostro fedelissimo servidore Antonio di Pierdomenico [*recte* Pierdomenico di Anto-

nio] dicto Capone, donzello di Palazo, come esso sie sperimentato et affaticato più anni ad imparare a ssonare la tromba in modo che al presente può sonare appresso di tutti li altri sonatori, per tanto pregha Vostre Magnifiche Signori Le piacij darli et concedarli una spectatura di trombetto per lo prima che vaca delli trombetti di Vostre Magnifiche Signori . . . [inserted above: con salari et emolumenti consueti] (Concistoro, vol. 2194, *Scritture concistoriali, 1506–11,* busta 1506, insert, unnumbered folio [margin: Aprobata die 16 Aprile 1506])

Tax declaration, 1509: "Dinanzi da voi . . . notificha li beni di me Pietro tronbeto de la Signoria. Una vigna posto di Santo Matteio in luogo deto el borgeto la quale comprai per prezo di fiorini CCCC. Pagane a dì 15 d'aprile passato fiorini ottanta de la prima paga e resto ò debito chon deto Girolamo . . . E più ò debito fiorini 80 quali debo dare a una mia sorella da marito che tengo in casa, la quale è d'anni 17 e stiamo in Sancto Salvadore a pig[i]one e pago di deta casa L. 18 per ano. A le vostre charità mi rachomando" (Lira, vol. 234, Terzo di Città, 1509, fol. [100]ʳ)

Granted official leave of absence, 1512: "Magnifici domini . . . audito Iohanne magistri Antonii piffaro, nomine Petri fratris sui et bannitoris palatii eorum etc., deliberaverunt quod Michelangelus Nicolai tubicena possit et ei liceat bannire et exercere officium bannitoris durante absentia dicti Petri" (Concistoro, vol. 872, fol. 7ᵛ, dated 29 February 1511/12)

Hired as substitute, August 1520: "Magnifici domini . . . deliberaverunt quod Pier Dominicus Antonii tubicena possit et valeat ad suum beneplacitum sonare seu pulsare tubam et servire pro substituto aliorum tubicenarum, prout processerit de voluntate eorum, omni meliori modo" (Concistoro, vol. 923, fol. 17ʳ)

Salary reduced 2 December 1537: see Doc. 10.6

Piergiovanni di Niccolò (son of Niccolò Turini, brother of Michelangelo). Trumpeter, 1494–1526; town crier, 1544–53

Hired 6 November 1494: "Et deliberaverunt conducere et conduxerunt in tubicenam et pro tubicena palatii eorum, loco Ludovici Manni tubicene licentiati et cassi, Pierum Io-

PALACE TRUMPETERS

officio, salario, emolumentis et modis actenus ordinatis et consuetis" (Concistoro,
vol. 769, fol. 4ʳ)

Tax declaration, 1509: "Piergiovanni di Niccolò, trombetto della Signoria . . . una casa"
(Lira, vol. 234, Terzo di Città, 1509, unnumbered folio)

Subsidy for horse removed, 20 November 1537:
see Doc. 10.7

Salary reduced 2 December 1537: see Doc. 10.6

Tax declaration, 1548: "Magnifici Signori aliratori per Piero tronbetto del Magnifico Comune di Siena si dicie e si espone dinanzi a
le medesime come si trova una casetta con
un poco d'orto nel Terzo di Città e populo
di Santo Salvatore . . . e ogni altro suo bene
à dato in dota a una sua figlia oggi defunta e
perso la figlia e la robba e Dio vi salvi e a voi
si rachomanda. Piero di Niccolò tronbetto di
Palazzo" (Lira, vol. 243, Terzo di Città,
1548, fasc. 3, fol. 62ʳ, no. 180)

Piero. Trumpeter, 1253

Piero del Volpino. Trumpeter, 1544–48

Piero di Domenico detto Ciro. Trumpeter,
1579–81

Makes peace with a barber, 25 January 1579:
"Petrus Dominici alias Ciri, tubicina Palatii,
de Senis, per se etc. ex una, et Iohannes Dominici alias Pisanello, barbitonsor de Senis,
ex alia, de comuni concordia etc. remiserunt
et perdonaverunt sibi ad invicem etc. omnes
et singulas iniurias, manumissiones, vulnera
etc. sibi ad invicem . . . fecerunt veram,
puram et integram pacem perpetuo dura-
turam, pacis osculo . . . sub pena librarum
25" (Concistoro, vol. 1266, fol. 9ʳ⁻ᵛ)

Jailed for violating regulations on outside employment, March 1580: see Doc. 12.19

Renounces post in favor of Cornelio di Goro, 8
May 1581: see Doc. 10.18

Piero di Jacopo detto Nibbio. Trumpeter,
1443–46

Fired 12 December 1446: "Attendentes insuper
plures inhonestates et illicita facinora perpe-
trata per Pietrum Iacobi vocatum Nibbio,
tubicinem palatii, in dedecus et verecundiam
ipsius palatii, et monitiones et correctiones
sibi alias facte non iuvant . . . decreverunt
. . . capsare ipsum Petrum et ita capsaverunt

et privaverunt eum quod non sit amplius tubicen Comunis Senarum nec in perpetuum
esse possit tubicen dicti Comuni" (Concistoro, vol. 485, fol. 33ʳ)

**Piero di Lantecca Rintere da Cortona
(Rintera, Lantera, Lantere).** Nakers
player, 1445–59 (also a lutenist)

Pietro Cavallo. Trumpeter, 1511–18

The trombonist Geronimo is to replace him temporarily, 8 January 1511: see Doc. 10.2

Pietro di Antonio. Trumpeter, 1436

Pietro di Giovanni detto Petrolino. Nakers
player, 1427–34; trumpeter, 1434–36, 1439–
44, 1448–78

Jailed for month of June 1457 for having gone
to a nunnery without permission: "Prelibati
Magnifici domini . . . informati quod Petrolinus tubicen palatii ivit ad monasterium
Sancte Clare sine licentia et contra formam
Statutorum Senarum, et volentes dictum corrigere et condemnare ut non audeat amplius
ad monasteria ire, et ut aliis sit in exemplum,
deliberaverunt dictum Petrolinum condemnare et deliberantes ipsum condemnaverunt ad standum in carceribus Comunis Senarum totum presentem mensem Junii"
(Concistoro, vol. 544, fol. 13ᵛ)

Released from jail for Corpus Christi, 13 June
1457: "Dicti Magnifici domini . . . informati
qualiter Petrolinus tubicen palatii est in carceribus Comunis . . . et viso quod cras est festum Corporis Christi, ad quod festum opor-
tet quod Magnifici domini vadant cum
tubicines ad honorandum Christi Corpus,
quare decreverunt liberare dictum Petrolinum a dictis carceribus, et ipsum liberaverunt et sic mandari decreverunt superstiti-
bus dictarum carcerum" (Concistoro, vol.
544, fol. 18ʳ)

Hired 30 June 1459 as trumpeter and town
crier: "Conduxerunt in tubatorem et pre-
conem Comunis Senarum Petrolinum [gap]
. . . cum salario consueto aliis" (Concistoro,
vol. 556, fol. 57ʳ)

Fired as town crier 7 July 1459 because he
doesn't know how to do the job: see Doc.
9.3

Pietro di Nanni. Nakers player, 1373–74

Pietro di Viviano. Palace mace bearer and
cantarino, 1398–

Paid salary while accompanying ambassadors to
  Pisa, 14 August 1409: "A Pietro di Viviano,
  detto Pietro chantarino, lire quaranta soldi
  dieci, e quali denari li diamo per suo salaro
  per dì XVIII ch'esso andò e stiè a Pisa cho'
  l'ambasc[i]adori al papa Alisandro chon uno
  chavallo, a rag[i]one di soldi 45 il dì netti . . .
  L. XL s. X" (Biccherna, vol. 294, fol. 54ᵛ)

Plinio di Leone. Trumpeter, 1570–84

Hired 27 October 1570: "Visto il memoriale di
  Plinio di Leone, portiere del palazzo, et il rescripto in piedi di quello, fatto dallo Illustrissimo Signor Governatore . . . deliberorno di
  dare et concedare . . . al detto Plinio, per
  uno anno proximo et dipoi a beneplacito del
  loro Illustrissimo Consistorio, la piazza del
  trombetto, con il suo solito salario et con li
  oblighi, pesi et gravezze solite et consuete
  . . . Il tenore del memoriale et rescripto detti
  di sopra hè questo, cioè:

Illustrissimo Signore

Plinio di Leone, portiere del Palazzo, humilissimo supplicante et servitore fidelissimo di
  Vostra Signoria Illustrissima, expone come
  ha servito il Palazzo a sonare la tromba già
  anni tre, sicome al presente serve sera et mattina et quando la Signoria esce fuori et tut-
  t'hora che fa di bisogno, come quelli che vi
  hanno il luogo. Et per essere vacata la piazza
  del trombetto di Giulio Golpino et per essere detto supplicante povera persona, supplica la Signoria Vostra Illustrissima che per
  sua solita cortesia et clementia si vogli degnare concedarli detto luogo vacato, con la
  sua solita provisione. . . .

L'Illustrissimo Consistorio conceda il luogo al
  più benemerito, riguardando la età, la qualità
  et servitio fatto fino al presente. Filippo Mal.
  de mandato, 9 Ottobre '70" (Concistoro,
  vol. 1215, fol. 23ʳ⁻ᵛ)

Fined for carrying a dagger, 10 June 1578: "L'Illustrissimi Signori, il Capitano del populo et
  Signori priori governatori della città di Siena
  per Sua Altezza Serenissima . . . nella causa
  dell'inquisitione formata contra Plinio di Leone, portiere e trombetto del lor Palazzo . . .
  trovatolo colpevole e di ragione punibile per
  haver portato il pugnale di notte tempo per
  la città, contra la forma delli bandi di Sua Al-

tezza Serenissima, come appare per la suo
  confessione . . . condennorno il detto Plinio
  in scudi vinticinque d'oro . . . da pagarli fra
  4 giorni, altrimenti . . . gli si dia due tratti
  di fune" (Concistoro, vol. 1262, fols.
  16ᵛ–17ʳ)

Ordered whipped for failing to pay fine, 21
  June 1578: "L'Illustrissimi Signori . . . essendo stato condennato Plinio di Leone,
  trombetto, per lor Signorie Eccelente in
  scudi 25 . . . e non havendo pagato li scudi
  25 detti infra 4 giorni . . . commessero se li
  dia due tratti di fune per li ministri di giustitia, dentro al palazzo del Capitano di Giustitia . . . Il dì 28 di detto fu dato la fune al
  detto Plinio secondo la detta deliberatione"
  (ibid., fol. 21ʳ)

Imprisoned for malfeasance and ordered to serve
  three months, 31 August 1579: "caporale
  Capitanei platee . . . retulit mihi notario
  quod hoc mane . . . ex causa maleficii commissi per Plinium Leonis tubicinem publici
  Palatii . . . conduxisse in secretas carceres huius civitatis . . . detinendum ad instantiam Illustrissimi ac Excelsi Consitorii" (Concistoro, vol. 1269, fols. 12ᵛ–13ʳ); "Habita
  longa discussione super causa criminali pen-
  dente contra Plinium olim Leonis, tubicinem
  publici Palatii . . . ipsum condennaverunt in
  penam confinii . . . per menses tres, in publico Palatio" (ibid., fol. 33ᵛ)

Jailed for violating regulations on outside employment, March 1580: see Doc. 12.19

Resigns his post, 28 September 1582: "Et udito
  Plino di Leone, portiere del Palazzo, il quale
  ha questa mattina renuntiato liberamente et
  espeditamente il suo luogo di trombetto . . .
  Tal renuntia accettorno . . . et volendo nondimeno al detto luogo del trombetto . . . provedere di qualcheduno altro idoneo e soffi-
  ciente trombetto, acciò il Palazzo non patisca
  . . . Vista la domanda fatta . . . da Giovanbattista di Pietro Pavolo, calzolaio Senese, et
  considerato che il medesimo ha servito più
  tempo in tal exercitio del trombetto il Palazzo loro, e la sua sufficientia et idoneità, et
  attese le sue qualità et costumi . . . lo elesseno e deputorno per trombetto con offitii,

salarii, pesi et altri emolumenti soliti et consueti" (Concistoro, vol. 1288, fol. 7ʳ⁻ᵛ)

Pompilio di Simone (son of Simone Brucia,
brother of Severo). Trumpeter, 1575–76

Ordered to vacate a house, 3 January 1575: "Et
udita [gap] moglie del Barbante et esponente
come da Pompilio trombetto li si ritiene una
sua casa, anchora che sia finita la pigione . . .
mandorno farsi precetto che fra tre giorni
devesse . . . relassare . . . la detta casa libera
. . . sotto pena che per li statuti si contiene"
(Concistoro, vol. 1242, fol. 4ʳ)

Petitions to be released from jail, dated 3 August
1576: "L'Illustrissimi et Excelsi Signori . . .
vista la suplica di Pompilio trombetto, come
desiderava scarcerarsi dando idonea promessa
solamente di rapresentarsi tante volte quante
piacerà all'Illustrissimo Concistoro . . . deliberorno scarcerarsi . . . dando però idonea promessa a rapresentarsi totiens quoties ut supra, sotto pena di scudi 25 d'oro"
(Concistoro, vol. 1251, fol. 15ᵛ). Another entry on fol. 16ʳ notes that on the same day
Pompilio's brother, Silverio di Simone, trombetto, said he would personally see to it that
Pompilio maintained his promise.

Riccio. Shawm player, 1343–44, 1347

Contract of 27 December 1347: see Doc. 8.2

**Riccio d'Antonio da Chianciano (Antonio
d'Antonio detto Riccio)** (son of Antonio
di Ciuccio). Apprentice nakers player, 1401;
trumpeter and town crier, 1402–55

Monthly salary of L. 3 as apprentice nakers
player; Fl. 2, then 3 as trumpeter, reduced to
Fl. 2 in 1408: see Doc. 9.1

Permitted to go to baths for eight days, 5 December 1445: "Et concesserunt Riccio Antonii de Clanciano tibicini et preconi Comunis Senarum, licentiam absentandi se a
Civitate Senarum et standi ad balnea per otto
dies a discessu" (Concistoro, vol. 479, fol. 23ʳ)

Permitted to leave Siena for ten days, 18 January
1453: "Et deliberaverunt concedere licentiam et concesserunt Riccio, tubicene palatii,
se absentandi a civitate Senarum per tempus
X dierum, cum hoc quod loco sui ad servitium palatii alterum tubicenam ponat" (Concistoro, vol. 518, fol. 17ᵛ)

Riccio di Palude. Trumpeter, 1253–55, 1257

Romanello. Trumpeter, 1326, 1328

Rusignolo. Trumpeter, 1230

Sacripante di Pavolo Rimbombi (son of Pavolo di Giovanni). Trumpeter and teacher,
1575–97

Demands extra pay for evening service and is imprisoned, 26 October 1575: see Doc. 10.16

Released from prison, 14 November 1575: see
Doc. 10.17

Petitions for a post, offering to teach the trumpet, and is accepted, 22 June 1579: "Item,
udita la supplica porta da Sacripante di Pavolo Rimbombi, trombetto, dell'infrascricto
[*sic*] tenore, et perciò considerato quanto per
l'addrieto sia stato hauto in consideratione il
sonare della tromba et che il numero de'
trombetti fusse di dodici, sicome per li statuti
è provisto, il quale al presente è ridotto al
numero di sei solamente, et che facilmente,
non essendoci chi possi insegnare tale exercitio si può ridurre anco a minore. Però volendo, perquanto possano, a cciò provedere,
hauto piena informatione delle buone qualità
del sopranominato Sacripante et del suo
buon sapere in tale arte . . . deliberorno concedere . . . al detto Sacripante le spese continue in Palazzo, sicome hanno li altri della
famiglia . . . con conditione et obligo d'insegnare tal arte et exercitio del sonare la
tromba a tutti quelli che haranno desiderio
d'imparare, et particolarmente che sia obligato continuamente havere almeno due persone che imparino. . . .

Il tenore della quale è l'infrascricto, cioè

Magnifici et Illustrissimi et Eccelsi Signori. Sa-
criptante di Pavolo Rimbombi, trombetto
delle Signorie Vostre Illustrissime, espone . . .
come è stata sempre usanza et costume in Palazzo delle Vostre Illustrissime Signorie che al-
l'arte et exercitio della tromba ci sia stato
uno maestro per insegnare il detto esercitio,
acciochè il Palazzo non vadi a tale esercitio
manchando . . . però il medesimo Sacripante
. . . s'offerisce . . . a insegnare a tutti quelli
giovani li quali si diletteranno di tale esercitio" (Concistoro, vol. 1268, fols. 15ᵛ–17ʳ)

Jailed for violating regulations on outside employment, March 1580: see Doc. 12.19

Permitted to substitute for his father, 19 July

1582: "Item, havendo inteso alli giorni passati Sacripante trombetto del palazzo, il quale
espose in nome di Pavolo suo padre che il
medesimo Sacripante fusse per gratia costituto in luogo di detto Pavolo durante l'indi-
spositione sua, deliberorno tal gratia conce-
dersegli . . . et detto Sacripante sostituirno il
prefato Pavolo . . . con tutti li salari, emolumenti, rigaglie et pesi soliti et consueti"
(Concistoro, vol. 1287, fol. 9ʳ)

Cited in dispute with nuns of St. Martha, 18
July 1591: "Item mandaverunt, ad instantiam
reverendarum monialium S. Martae, exequi
gravamen . . . pro libris 60 denariorum contra Sacripantem de Rimbonbis, thubinanam
[*sic*] palatii" (Concistoro, vol. 1303, fol. 70ᵛ)

Salvestro (Silvestro) da Asciano. Trumpeter,
1510–17

Replaces Bernardino Monaldi, on leave of absence, 6 September 1501: see Doc. 10.1

Sano di Matteo da Siena. Trumpeter, 1457–
78, 1480–86

Hired 20 July 1457: "Eligerunt insuper . . . Sa-
num [gap] in tubicinam palatii" (Concistoro,
vol. 545, fol. 15ʳ)

Receives part of clothing allowance of Niccolò
di Piero, 21 July 1457: "Deliberaverunt quod
Sanus, novus tubicina, det et dare teneatur
partem vestis sive denarios ipsius, quem recipere debet in festo proxime futuro, Nicolai
Pieri de Civitate Castelli, qui servivit loco
Tomei nuper defuncti" (Concistoro, vol.
545, fol. 15ʳ)

Santi di Paolo da Volterra. Trumpeter,
1455–59; trombonist, 1463–67

Hired 26 August 1455: "Magnifici et potentes
domini . . . conduxerunt Sanctem Pauli de
Vulterris tubicinam . . . in tubicinam et pro
tubicina palatii prefatorum magnificorum
dominorum . . . ad sonandum tubam . . .
cum salario florenorum duorum de soldis 82
pro quolibet floreno et quolibet mense, sive
detemptione alicuius cabelle . . . Et teneatur
. . . habere a Comunis Senarum anno quolibet, in festivitate Assumptionis Virginis Marie de mense augusti, unam vestem sive tu-
nicham . . . extimationis florenorum decem
auri" (Concistoro, vol. 533, fol. 53ʳ)

Replaced by Monaldo di Bartolomeo, 7 July
1459: see Doc. 9.3

Santi di Riccarduccio da Gubbio. Trumpeter, 1437–67

Given permission to be absent twelve days, 2
March 1449: "Et deliberaverunt concedare licentiam et concesserunt Santi de Augubio,
tubicine ipsorum, se absentandi a civitate Senarum per tempus 12 dierum a die discessus
connumerandorum, sine admissione alicuius
salarii" (Concistoro, vol. 499, fol. 3ʳ)

Given permission to go to Rome for fifteen
days, 6 September 1450: "Concesserunt
etiam licentiam Sancti tubicene se absentandi
a civitate Senarum pro eundo Romam pro
XV diebus" (Concistoro, vol. 507, fol. 7ᵛ)

Savino di Vincenzo. Trumpeter, 1525

Petitions to be hired, 17 September 1525:
"Audito Savino Vincenti tubicena, exponente qualiter sub die trigesimo mensis Iulii
anni MDXXII per Magnificos dominos . . .
fuit sibi concessa gratia expectatura vacui loci
tubicene qui primo vacaverit . . . Et cum
nuper vacent duo loca tubicenarum palatii
pro privatione facta per Consistorium de Dionisio, filio olim Bernardini Monaldi . . . et
propterea petente sibi unum de dictis locis vacantibus declarari et adiudicari . . . Decreverunt ipsi Savino . . . adiudicare . . . et . . .
concesserunt et adiudicaverunt unum de
dictis locis ut supra vacantibus, cum salario
honoribus et honeribus consuetis" (Concistoro 954, fol. 20ᵛ)

Severino di Bartolomeo detto Mancio.
Trumpeter, 1403–25

Monthly salary Fl. 3, reduced to Fl. 2 in 1408:
see Doc. 9.1

Severo (Silverio, Silvio) di Simone (son of
Simone Brucia, brother of Pompilio). Trumpeter, 1565–97

Receives expectative, 10 February 1565: "Udito
Severo di Simone trombetto, et vista la sua
petitione e domanda fatta, come che si degnino farli gratia di concedarli il primo luogo
che vacarà del trombetto, et intanto si degnino permettarli che possa servire in luogo
di Simone suo padre ne' tempi che egli sarà
impedito da sue faccende . . . derno et conce-
dorno al detto Severo il primo luogo che vacarà del trombetto del palazzo . . . Quanto
poi di permettare che possa servire in luogo
di Simone suo padre ne' tempi che egli sarà

impedito da sue faccende, ne parli . . . al Magnifico Signor Capitano del Popolo che per li tempi sarà, et con sua licentia servirà come da esso gli sarà sopra a cciò composto" (ASS, Concistoro, vol. 1183, fol. 31ʳ⁻ᵛ)

Jailed for four days for disturbing the teacher by playing the trumpet and distracting the students, 1 December 1567: "Illustrissimi domini . . . attenta insolentia Silverii magistri Simonis, tubicine palatii, qui absque respettu et absque licentia ausus est molestare et perturbare doctorem dum legebat in scola ginnasii, sonando tuba[m], invitando et movendo animos scolarium ad discendendum de scola dum legebatur, occasione ludendi ad pallonem. De qua insolentia et ut aliis de cetero transeat in exemplum, mandaverunt eundem Silverium carcerari . . . Qui statim fuit ductus ad carceres . . . Die quarta Decembris prefati Illustrissimi domini . . . attenta . . . voluntate Illustrissimi domini Federici Gubernatoris . . . ordinaverunt dictum Silverium scarcerari" (Concistoro, vol. 1199, fol. 11ᵛ)

Demands extra pay for evening service and is imprisoned, 26 October 1575: see Doc. 10.16; released from prison, 14 November 1575: see Doc. 10.17

Guarantees his brother's promise to the priors, 3 August 1576 (*see under* Pompilio)

Jailed for violating regulations on outside employment, March 1580: see Doc. 12.19

Silvestro (Salvestro) di Pio. Trumpeter, 1511–17 (absent 1514–15)

Hired 21 August 1511: "Magnifici domini . . . examinata deliberatione facta . . . in favorem Silvestri olim Pii, servitori eorum palatii, cui concessus fuit locus tubicine primi vacantis immediate post Masum de Pontremulo . . . deliberaverunt confirmare et confirmaverunt deliberationem predictam, declarantes—actenta morte Enee Senzanomine—eius locum pertinere et spectare ad dictum Silvestrum quo ad pulsandum tubam, cum oneribus salario et medis consuetis. Et quod camerarium Bicherne in futurum solvat dicto Silvestro debitum salarium, serviendo ut sunt obligati alii tubicines" (Concistoro, vol. 869, fol. 6ʳ)

Ordered to show cause why he should not be removed, 8 April 1516: "Per parte di Cristoforo sia citato Salvestro di Pio trombetto che in-

fra dodici dì comparisca dinanzi da loro ad contradire perchè non li debbi esser tolto el loco del trombetto per non haver già più tempo fa exercitato altrimenti decto termine passato" (Concistoro, vol. 897, unnumbered folio)

Silvio di Antonio. Trumpeter, 1526

Simone. Tabor player, 1364–65

Simone di Cenno. Trumpeter, 1335, 1338–45

Simone di Manno. Trumpeter, 1335, 1338–45, 1357

Simone di Pavolo Brucia. Trumpeter, 1548–65

Appointed in place of Giulio di Giovambattista Volpino, 30 October 1548: see Doc. 10.11; reappointed as new trumpeter, 21 February 1549: see Doc. 10.12

Sufilello. Trumpeter, 1277

Tomè. Cantarino, 1414

Paid s. 55 for singing, 31 December 1414: "A Tomè chantarino, a dì detto, per più volte ci à chantato, per tuto s. 55, per chomandamento de' Signori. L. II s. XV" (Concistoro, vol. 2497, fol. 29ᵛ)

Tomè di Meio. Trumpeter and town crier, 1407–55

Fired 26 July 1409: see Doc. 9.2

Permission to wear enamel shield of commune, 6 July 1423 (Concistoro, vol. 345, fol. 5ʳ)

Rehired after pilgrimage to Santiago de Compostela, 26 July 1445: "Et viso quod Thomas Mei de Senis, tubicen palatii, fuit die XXII martii proxime preteriti ad Sanctum Iacobum de Galitia pro indulgentia, cum bona licentia Magnificorum dominorum tunc residentium, et habuit salarium pro totum mense martii predicti; viso etiam quod rediit Senas die XXII presentis mensis Iulii, et alius tubicen non est remissus loco sui sed reservatus eius locus, deliberaverunt et decreverunt quod dictus Thommas sit et esse intelligatur remissus et conductus pro tubicene ad servitia dicti palatii, et non pro bannitore, cum salario consueto dari tubicenis et non bannitoribus . . . eius salarium incipiat die primo augusti proximi et non antea" (Concistoro, vol. 477, fol. 19ʳ)

Continues to receive his son's salary after the latter dies, February 1457: see Doc. 9.7

Tommaso di Cristoforo da Forlì. Trumpeter, 1449–54

Hired 2 October 1449: "Magnifici domini . . . deliberaverunt conducere et conduxerunt de
eorum comuni concordia Thomassum
Christofori de Forlivio, pro tubicena et in tubicenam ad servitia palatii ipsorum magnificorum dominorum, cum salario, emolumentis et modis consuetis. Cum hac
conditione tamen, videlicet quod ipse teneatur et debeat servire per totum presentem
mensem octobris absque aliquo salario" (Concistoro, vol. 502, fol. 22ʳ)

Fired 23 February 1454: "Et similiter cassaverunt
Tommasium tubicenum Comuni, motis iustis
causis, ita quod de cetero nullum habeat salarium et non sit amplius de tubicenis Comunis" (Concistoro, vol. 524, fol. 55ʳ)

Tommaso di Malfarsetto. Trumpeter,
1343–44

Tortto. Cantatore, 1403

Paid for singing, 29 April 1403: "A Tortto, chantatore, L. 2 s. 2 per più volte ci chanttò . . . L. 2.
2" (Concistoro, vol. 2495, *Proventi, spese e inventari, 1399–1407,* fol. 94ᵛ)

Vanni di Ciereto (brother of Ciereto and
Marco). Nakers player, 1316–18

Vanni Grasso. Trumpeter, 1291, 1298, 1310

Ventura Tomasini. Town crier, 1230, 1246–59

Vergilio di Pier Giovanni (son of Pier Giovanni
di Niccolò). Trumpeter, 1532–37

Awarded a post at half-salary, 2 February 1531:
"Considerantes fidelem et bonam servitutem
in exercitio tubicenarum eorum Magnifici palatii iam Niccolai Ceci tubicene per totum
tempus sue vite, et successive Pieri filii olim
dicti Niccolai, qui similiter se bene semper exercuit et exercet in dicto servitio tubicenarum
et bannitoris. Et attento etiam quod Virgilius
filius dicti Pieri, adolescens bone indolis, ex-
peritur et recte discit sonum tube, visoque defectu tubicinarum palatii et quod adsunt plures
loci vacantes. Moti pluribus aliis iustis et rationabilibus causis . . . et ad hoc ut dictus Virgilius cum maiori diligentia et pron-
titudine sonum tube valeat discere et exercere in publicum servitium . . . concesserunt
et adsignaverunt prefato Virgilio dimidiam
partem unius dictorum locorum tubicinarum
vacantium palatii, durante tempore eius vite,
cum officio salario emolumentis oneribus et

obligationibus solitis et consuetis. Mandantes
pro predictis camerario Bicherne . . . qua-
temus eidem Virgilio solvant de mense in
mensem salario solitum pro dimidia parte
unius loci tubicinarum" (Concistoro, vol.
986, fols. 26ᵛ–27ʳ)

Salary reduced 2 December 1537: see Doc. 10.6

IV. PALACE PIFFERI

Adriano Imperiale di Luzio (Mangoni) (natural son of Luzio di Pavolo). Piffero,
1545–98

His father petitions for an expectative for Adriano, 14 April 1545: see Doc. 12.4; he succeeds his father, 6 June 1554: see Doc. 12.6

Retained in 1556: see Doc. 12.9

To be punished for not playing at the Elevation,
2 November 1559: [margin: contra Adrianum musicum] "Illustrissimi domini etc. attenta quod Adrianus, unus ex musicis eorum
palatii, hac mane distulit se conferre una cum
aliis musicis ad faciendam solitam musicam
in eorum cappella in elevatione eucharistie,
prout solitum est fieri ad honorem dive Virginis, dederunt auctoritatem magnifico domino Capitaneo populi quod ab eo intelligat
causam quare non intervenit ut supra; et quatenus non sit vel dicto domino Capitaneo
non videatur quod sit legitima causa, habeat
auctoritatem ipsum corrigendi et puniendi
eo modo et forma et prout ei visum fuerit
omni modo etc." (Concistoro, vol. 1152,
fol. 10ʳ)

Deprived of meal privileges for disobedience, 22
November 1563: "Et habita notitia de inobedientia Adriani musici palatii, quia [non] intervenit ad sonandum et canendum hora debita ut tenetur, heri sero . . . deliberaverunt
eundem privare et privaverunt per octo dies
eius portionis victus, et tamen teneatur servire ut prius" (Concistoro, vol. 1176, fol.
14ʳ). Adriano was pardoned three days later
(ibid. fol. 15ᵛ)

Sued for not sharing gratuities, January 1565:
see Doc. 12.15; differences resolved, March
1570: see Doc. 12.17

Loses election for head of Palace musicians, November 1575: see Doc. 12.25

Ordered to prison for violating regulations on

outside employment, March 1580: see Doc. 12.19

Agostino di Benedetto (son of Benedetto di Domenico). Supernumerary piffero, 1546

Appointed December 1546: see Doc. 12.5

Order to show cause why he should not be fired, 4 June 1554: "Et audito Benedicto tubone, musico palatii, deliberaverunt et mandaverunt citari ad eius instantiam in valvis palatii Augustinum eius filium quod infra terminum quinque dierum a die citationis personaliter compareat in Consistorio ad respondendum et contradicendum quare non debeat privare eius loco in palatio ob multa eius asserta demerita" (ASS, Concistoro, vol. 1123, fol. 31ʳ)

Fired 30 June 1554: "Et audita petitione Benedicti tubonis et citatione Augustini eius filii ac relatione inde sequuta, actentis plurimis assertis demeritis Augustini eius filii, ac sufficientia et bonis partibus magistri Vincenti magistri Iohannisbaptiste, musici senensis sui generi, coeteris consideratis deliberaverunt concedere et concesserunt" [the remainder of the page is blank] (ibid., fol. 38ᵛ)

Agostino di Piero da Albania. Trombonist, 1451

Hired 12 December 1451: "Prefati Magnifici et potentes domini . . . conduxerunt infrascriptum in trombonum et pro trombono Comunis . . . Cuius talis est nomen, videlicet: Augustinus" (Concistoro, vol. 512, fol. 37ʳ)

Given a month's leave to go to Venice, 25 March 1452: "Magnifici et potentes domini . . . concesserunt licentiam Augustino Pieri de Albania, trombono palatii et qui pulsat trombonum in palatio, inpune et sine aliqua amissione solite sue provisionis, se absentandi a civitate Senarum . . . per tempus unius mensis incohandi a die sui discessus, ut possit ire Venetias . . . Et si staret ultra dictum mensem, pro eo quod staret ultra dictum mensem non habeat salarium, sed incipiat eius salarium a dicto mense ultra, die qua reversus fuerit. Die XXVII decembris dictus Augustinus recessit" (vol. 513, fol. 26ᵛ)

Alberto di Francesco Gregori. Piffero, 1575–1602; 1603–7; leader of Palace musicians

Hired with half-ration of food, October 1575: see Doc. 12.20; appointed supernumerary, February 1578: see Doc. 12.21

His teacher, Tiberio Rivolti, petitions to exchange posts with him, June 1585: see Doc. 12.30

Quarrel with Giovanbattista Formichi on who was to play first bass, 27 August 1585: see Doc. 12.31; see also Doc. 12.33

Petitions for his son Annibale to be hired, 15 April 1599: see Doc. 12.40

Replaces Tiberio Rivolti, February 1601: see Doc. 12.32

Permission granted to retain post of *maestro di cappella* at Santa Maria della Scala, 27 December 1601: [margin: Licentia et gratia concessa magistro Alberto musico] "Item audito magistro Alberto Ghregorii, huius Palatii musico, dicente se fuisse suffectum et subrogatum in locum magistri Capellae S. Mariae de Scala Senarum, quem obtinebat magister Tiberius Rivoltus, musicus huius palatii, praedefunctus, et propterea petente ut sibi huiusmodi magistrum capellae, per eorumdem Illustrissimorum dominorum . . . humanitatem et gratiam profiteri atque exercere liceat. Decreveunt ei obsequi atque morem gerere . . . dantes et concedentes ipsi magistro Alberto licentiam, facultatem et potestatem horis solitis et consueti canendi musicam et sonandi in dicta ecclesia, et ibi musicam ac magistrum capellae profitendi, et in omnibus et per omnia prout et sicut canebat, sonabat, profitebatur et faciebat idem magister Tiberius, et omni meliori modo etc." (Concistoro, vol. 1313, unnumbered folio)

Replaces Giovanfrancesco di Benedetto as head of Palace musicians, April 1603: see Doc. 12.35

Alberto di Jacomo Latini. Substitute piffero, 1580

Ordered to prison for violating regulations on outside employment, March 1580: see Doc. 12.19

Alfonso di Pavolo. Piffero, 1562–67

Permitted to substitute for Fabio di Geronimo, 1562: see Doc. 12.11

A committee is formed to confer with the captain of justice, who has charged Alfonso with a crime, 14 October 1563: "Et hauta notitia che il Magnifico Capitano di Giustitia procede contra Alfonso di Pavolo, musico del Palazzo, lor familiare, per cagione di certo asserto delitto . . . deliberorno dare . . . autorità al Magnifico Signor Capitano del Popolo di potere eleggere . . . quelli che gli parrà del Concistorio . . . con commissione di dovere essere con l'Eccellentissimo Signor Governatore e conferirli il caso successo del detto Alfonso" (Concistoro, vol. 1175, fol. 11ᵛ)

Fined for assaulting a tailor, 29 January 1564: "nella causa . . . contro Alfonzo di Pavolo trombetto, musico del palazo nostro, per causa delle ferite e delitto per lui commesso nella persona di maestro Pietro di Marco Mazzantini sarto . . . declariamo il detto Alfonzo ritrovato colpevole . . . lo condanniamo a pagare lire cento di denari al fischo . . . infra il tempo e termine di giorni 12" (vol. 1177, fols. 15ʳ–17ʳ)

Rehabilitated, 9 March 1564: "Inoltre deliberorno habilitare . . . Alfonso di Pavolo musico di poter sonare in compagnia delli altri musici del loro palazzo, ala tavola di lor Signori et fuori per la città sì come accadrà di sonare. . . . Et tutto deliberorno acciò il medesimo Alfonso si eserciti nel sonare et attendi alle virtù per poter diventare buon musico in servitio del loro palazzo" (vol. 1178, fol. 9ᵛ)

Succeeds to Savino di Francesco's position, December 1564: see Doc. 12.12

Sues colleagues for not sharing gratuities, January 1565: see Doc. 12.15

Suspended 10 June 1567: see Doc. 12.13

Imprisoned for having sung injurious songs, 14 October 1567: "Et venuto a notitia al'Illustrissimo Signor Capitano di popolo . . . qualmente . . . è stato incarcerato Alfonso di maestro Pavolo, musico di palazzo, senza licentia di loro Signorie excelse . . . atteso che un Giorgio Bonelli merciaio s'è querelato del detto Alfonso per haver . . . cantate certe stanze e versi in dispregio del detto Giorgio

. . . deliberorno andare . . . al'Illustrissimo Signor Federigo Montauto, Governatore nostro: alli quali rispose che ordinarebbe fusse scarcerato e dato in le mani et in potere di loro Signorie" (vol. 1198, fols. 21ᵛ–22ʳ)

Permission sought for his release, 22 October 1567: "Et similmente mandorno darsi permesso per Alfonso musico . . . da farseli politia di relasso . . . et fu scarcerato" (vol. 1198, fol. 27ʳ). A decree from 27 November 1567 says that Alfonso was found guilty and that he was restricted to the Palace for ten days: "in causa contra Alfonsum . . . musicum, condennarunt dictum Alfonsum ad constricta[m] in palatio Magnifici domini Capitanei Iustitie civitatis Senarum per diei decem" (vol. 1199, fol. 10ᵛ). It may be that this was further punishment for his offense, but it could also mean that he had another scrape with the authorities within the month.

Andrea. Trombonist, 1463

Andrea di Giovanni. Substitute piffero, 1490

Andrea di Giovanni da Siena. Substitute piffero, 1524

Hired 24 October 1524: "Excellentissimi domini . . . audita petitione Andreae Ioannis de Senis, tibicine eorum palatii, ipsam aprobaverunt in omnibus et per omnia" (Concistoro, vol. 947, fol. 42ʳ)

Angelino. Piffero, 1415–16

Angelo d'Arrigo, detto Imperadore. Piffero, 1408 (also a trumpeter, 1407–42)

Hired temporarily as piffero 17 October 1408: see Doc. 11.3

Annibale di Alberto Gregori Piffero (son of Alberto di Francesco Gregori). Piffero, 1599–1611

Appointed 15 April 1599: see Doc. 12.40

Relinquishes his post to his brother Francesco, August 1611: see Doc. 12.42

Annibale di Girolamo. Supernumerary piffero, 1578

Substitutes for Jacomo Latini, late 1579: see Doc. 12.22

Ansano Maria di Geronimo (son of Geronimo di Giovanni). Trombonist, 1521–32, 1543–46 (also in cathedral, November 1543–January 1546)

Fired 18 February 1546: "Attenta privatione

facta de Ansano Maria [gap] tubone palatii, et habita notitia de moribus, virtutibus
et fide Tulii [gap] musici et de eius sufficientia et idoneitate in exercitio sonandi tubonem . . . ipsum Tulium . . . eligerunt et
deputaverunt in tubonem et pro tubono
palatii, in loco dicti Ansani Marie et cum
eodem salario, emolumentis et obligationibus dicti loci" (Concistoro, vol. 1076, fol.
38ʳ⁻ᵛ)

Antonio di Giovanni da Bologna (son of
Giovanni di Antonio da Bologna). Piffero,
1408

Hired 11 April 1408: see Doc. 11.2; fired 17 October 1408: see Doc. 11.3; monthly salary
Fl. 3

Antonio di Gregorio da Venezia (Maestro in
1491). Piffero, 1460–94

Hired at very advantageous terms, 27 June
1460: see Doc. 11.12

Given one month's leave to go to Venice, 30
September 1460: "Magnifici et potentes domini . . . concesserunt licentiam Antonio
Gregorii piffero palatii, per tempus unius
mensis eundi Vinetie, cum hoc quod non habeat salarium dum non servit etc." (Concistoro, vol. 564, fol. 16ᵛ)

Recommended to Lorenzo de' Medici, 29 January 1469: see Doc. 11.14

Tax declaration, 1488: "Dinanzi da voi spetabili
citadini a fare la nuova lira. Dicesi per me
maestro Antonio di Ghirighoro pifaro de Palazo avere l'i[n]frascritti beni e prima nela
Conpagnia di San Salvadore,

Una chaseta per la mia abitazione di valuta Fl.
100

Una vingnia di staiora 8 nel chomuno di San
Magliano, di valuta Fl. 90

Io mi tru[o]vo vechio e infermo con tre figlioli
picholini, una femina e due maschi. Rachomandomi a le vostre spettabilità" (Lira, vol.
215, 1488, Terzo di Città, unnumbered
folio)

Tax declaration, 1491: "Dinanzi di voi spetabili
citadini . . . dicesi per me maestro Antonio
di Ghiringoro pifaro nela chompagnia di San
Salvadore avere l'infrascriti beni e prima,

Una chaseta per la mia abitazione posta in
det[t]a chompagnia . . .

Una vingnia di . . . staiora 10 . . . posta nel chomuno di Manzindoli et San Pulinaia di valuta estima Fl. 160 . . .

Debito mi truovo chon più persone Fl. dieci, Fl.
10

Trovomi la donna con quatro figlioli, due femine e due maschi e la donna gravida.

Rachomandomi a le vostre spettabilità
(Lira, vol. 224, 1491, Terzo di Città, fol.
116ʳ)

Recommended that he stop playing since he can
do it only in the old-fashioned way, 9 August 1492: see Doc. 11.16

Antonio di Maestro Cristoforo (son of Cristoforo di Brandino, brother of Niccolò).
Piffero, 1538–55

Substituted by Virginio di Pavolo when absent:
see Doc. 12.1

Competes unsuccessfully with Adriano, 6 June
1554: see Doc. 12.6

Owned a house with his brother in 1509; *see under* Cristoforo

Arrigo di Giovanni da Francoforte. Trombonist, 1455–56, 1458–60

Hired 11 August 1455: "Et conduxerunt pro
trumbone et in trumbonem infrascriptum, ad
beneplacitum Consistorii, cum salario librarum sexdecim denariorum Senensium pro
quolibet mense et cum vestibus ordinatis, cuius nomen est: Arrigus Iohannis de Francoforte t[r]ombonus" (Concistoro, vol. 533,
fol. 39ᵛ)

Rehired 29 January 1460: "Insuper . . . conduxerunt Aricum Iohannis in trombonum palatii
. . . et incipiat eius servitium in calendis Februarii proxime futuri" (vol. 560, fol. 24ᵛ)

Condemned 29 April 1460: "Magnifici domini . . . condemnaverunt trombonem,
prout apparet in libro Balzanelle" (vol. 561,
fol. 55ʳ)

Arrigo di Giovanni da Venezia. Piffero,
1451–57

Hired as piffero and tenorista 7 September
1451: "Magnifici domini et Capitaneus Populi . . . conduxerunt in piffarum et pro
piffaro et tenorista palatii . . . Arrigum Iohannis de Venetiis tenoristam, presentem,
cum salario 4 ducatorum largorum pro quoli-

bet mense, nitidorum de cabella, et duarum vestium quolibet anno, videlicet unius vestis quolibet anno in festo S. Marie Augusti, et alie in festo Nativitatis Domini nostri Yesu Christi . . . Cum hoc quod dictum salarium et conducta incipere debeat quando dictus Arrigus conduxerit familiam et uxorem suam in civitatem Senarum et ibi familiariter habitaret" (Concistoro, vol. 511bis, fol. 6ʳ)

Arrives with wife and family, 23 September 1451: "Arrigus Iohannis piffarus . . . acessit ad civitatem Senarum cum uxore et familia sua die externa, de sero, et ideo [h]odie incipit eius salarium 4 ducatorum largorum, ut deliberatum fuit" (ibid., fol. 22ᵛ)

Voted out, 30 July 1455: see Doc. 11.9; reinstated, 4 August 1455: see Doc. 11.10

Ascanio d'Andrea di Lazaro Marri. Supernumerary trombonist, 1546–51; trombonist, 1551–75; leader of Palace musicians, 1566 or earlier (also a singer)

Appointed December 1546: see Doc. 12.5

Replaces Valerio, 31 December 1551: "Ascanio d'Andrea di Lazzaro, trombone e musico del Palazzo, successore nel luogo di Valerio piffaro hoggi morto . . . ordenorno farsi decreto al camarlingo di Biccherna . . . che cancelli il nome di detto Valerio e vi scriva il nome di detto Ascanio e gli corresponda del salario ordinario" (Concistoro, vol. 1111, fol. 37ʳ)

Retained in 1556: see Doc. 12.9

Punished for not playing at table, 29 November 1559: [margin: Contra Ascanium musicum] "Attento quod externa die Ascanius musicus de sero non interfuit una cum aliis musicis ad faciendum in mensa solitam musicam prout tenetur, ipsoque Ascanio audito et eius non legiptima excusatione, mandaverunt in carceribus sub scalis detendi ibidemque retineri usque ad horam quartam noctis presentis diei, qua elapsa, nunc pro tunc mandaverunt ipsum relaxari cum onere quod durante presentis prioris prioratu teneatur qualibet die personaliter comparere in eorum solito Consistorio coram eis ad petendam veniam de predictis, sub pena eorum arbitrii, omni

melioro modo. Et statim fuit carceratus" (Concistoro, vol. 1152, fol. 15ʳ)

Jailed for failing to perform at Mass, 30 June 1561: "Et actento quod Ascanius musicus palatii heri sero sprevit Magnificum dominum Capitaneus Populi et omnes Magnificos dominos palatii eorumdem, obmictendo facere quicquid sibi per eos impositum fuit, ac etiam heri mane obmisit venire ad sonandum ad missam ut tenebatur cum aliis musicis palatii . . . deliberaverunt quod idem Ascanius pro predictis mictatur in carceribus denominatis sotto ala scala, permansurus in eis per decem dies, et pro dicto tempore ipsum privaverunt eius rata et parte sive provisione quam recipit in tinello palatii una cum aliis de familia ipsius palatii" (vol. 1161, fols. 42ᵛ–43ʳ)

Released, 4 July 1561: "L'Illustrissimi Signori, il Capitano di Populo e Signori Priori Governatori . . . vista et odita la supplica con il rescritto in piei di quella, venuto dal Molto Magnifico . . . Governatore, a favore di Ascanio musico del palazzo, carcerato già da 4 giorni dai predecessori loro per disobbedientia da lui fatta, parendo a lor Signori che ormai detto Ascanio a bastanza habbia reportata penitentia del'errore da lui commesso . . . commessero che detto Ascanio stia solamente prigione tutto 'l giorno di domane . . . e dipoi scarcerato . . . e rimesso al luogo suo come prima" (ASS, Concistoro, vol. 1161, fol. 43ʳ⁻ᵛ)

Sued for not sharing gratuities, January 1565: see Doc. 12.15

Sued for not sharing gratuities, February 1570: see Doc. 12.16; differences resolved, March 1570: see Doc. 12.17

Granted permission to become *maestro di cappella* at cathedral, 27 June 1575: [margin; Pro magistro Ascanio musico] "Audito magistro Ascanio quondam Andree de Marris, musico et magistro cappelle eorum Palatii, exponente qualiter ipse fuit et est electus pro musico et magistro Cappelle ecclesie Cathedralis, et non potest neque debet tale officium acceptare absque licentia Illustrissimarum Dominationum ipsarum. Et attento

quod ipse per annos triginta et ultra inser-
vivit pro musico et magistro cappelle Palatii
predicti accurate, fideliter et diligenter prout
ipse potuit; attento etiam quod ipse habet
plures filios et parum in bonis ut eos alere et
gubernare possit, et propterea petente sibi
concedi licentiam ut ipse possit dictum officium acceptare et in eo se exercere eo maxime quod ipse potest et Publico palatio et
dicte Ecclesie satisfacere absque eo quod nunquam aut rare deficiat in eius officio, prout
tenetur et obligatus est. Auditis et consideratis predictis . . . victum et obtentum lupino
16 omnes albos et nemine discrepante,
eidem magistro Ascanio licentiam petitam
concesserunt, ad beneplacitum tamen Illustrissimi et Excelsi Consistorii, et mandaverunt pro predictis fieri decretum in forma
omni meliori modo. Habuit decretum magister Ascanius" (Concistoro, vol. 1244, fols.
31ᵛ–32ʳ)

Baldassare di Maestro Domenico Ponti.
Piffero, 1575–78
Receives part of Ascanio Marri's salary, 1575:
see Doc. 12.20
Two musicians petition to share his salary, Febru-
ary 1578: see Doc. 12.21

Bartolomeo da Castello. Piffero
Turns down contract offered 1 June 1460: see
Doc. 11.11

Bartolomeo di Monaldo (brother of Giovanni). Trombonist, 1469–86 (formerly a Palace trumpeter); also town crier from 1483
Hired 16 April 1469: "Magnifici domini . . .
viso quod locus tromboni palatii vacat ad presens, decreverunt conducere et conduxerunt
in trombonum palatii et ad sonandum trombonum . . . Bartholomeum Monaldi, cum salario librarum XII pro quolibet mense . . . incipiendo in Kalendis Maii proxime venturi
et deinde ad beneplacitum Concistorii"
(Concistoro, vol. 615, fols. 30ᵛ–31ʳ)
Salary raised to L. 14, 5 July 1469: "Magnifici
domini . . . audito quod Bartholomeus Monaldi de Clanciano, tubicina palatii, bene pulsat trombonem, decreverunt quod ipse in futurum, incipiendo in Kalendis Augusti
proxime futuri 1469, habeat pro eius salario

a Comuni Senarum libras XIIII nitidas, quolibet mense" (vol. 617, fol. 6ᵛ); salary is L. 19
in 1470 (vol. 622, fol. 13ᵛ)
Given leave to go to Rome, 6 March 1470:
"Bartholomeo trombono concesserunt licentiam eundi Romam cum domino Francisco
Lutio pro XII diebus a die discessus et sine
admissione salarii, sin autem si non redit in
termino, perdat salarium pro toto tempore
quo stabit absens" (vol. 621, fol. 4ᵛ)
Appointment as town crier, 23 November 1483,
but with partial pension to Giovanni di Martino: see Doc. 11.15

**Bartolomeo di Piero Bochini da Bologna,
Maestro.** Piffero, 1429–46, 1447
Given leave to be absent, 25 April 1446: "Magnifici domini . . . concesserunt licentiam magistro Bartholomeo [blank] phiffaro palatii,
se absentandi a civitate Senarum usque ad totam diem veneris proxime venturam" (Concistoro, vol. 481, fol. 48ʳ)
Fined for failing to perform at a degree ceremony, October 1446: see Doc. 11.4

Benedetto di Domenico. Trombonist,
1532–54
Admonished for being lax in duties, 1538: see
Doc. 12.3
Reported that he earned L. 80 from the sale of a
horse on 30 August 1543 (ASS, Notarile
antecosimiano, 1804, unnumbered folio). He
owned a house near the Sapienza, the seat of
Siena's university (see Doc. 12.7)
Requests a printing privilege, 14 April 1545: see
Doc. 12.7
Complains about his son Agostino, June 1554
and petitions in favor of his son-in-law
Vincenzo di Maestro Giovanbattista (*see un-
der* Agostino di Benedetto)

Bernardino di Matteo Cartolaio. Supernumerary piffero, 1524–49 (also in cathedral)
A monthly provision of L. 8 approved, 31 October 1524: [margin: Pro Bernardo Mattei car-
tario] "Et attenta servitute, virtute ac diligentia in sonando Bernardini Mattei [gap]
librarii, desiderantis evadere bonum ac per-
fectum sonatorem musicorum instrumentorum auxilio magnifici palatii, cum ipse
sit pauper, et sine aliqua provisione non pos-

sit vacare discipline dictorum instrumentorum. Et viso quod ipse est assiduus in
sonando tam in palatio coram excelsis dominis quam foras, ideo servatis servandis etc. deliberaverunt constituere et constituerunt
eidem provisionis libras octo denariorum pro
quolibet mense, solvendas de introitibus publicis per camerarium Bicherne . . . cum obli-
gatione quod ipse teneatur sonare prout alii
sonatores palatii faciunt et tenentur" (ASS,
Concistoro, vol. 947, fol. 51ʳ⁻ᵛ)
Substituted by Virginio di Pavolo when absent,
23 October 1538: see Doc. 12.1

Bernardino di Valerio. Nakers player, 1555
Owed money by Simone di Domenico, 1555
(*see under* Simone)

Corrado da Alamania. Piffero, 1408–10
Hired 17 October 1408 at monthly salary of Fl.
3: see Doc. 11.3; gets a raise, 26 July 1409:
"Et addiderunt Corrado piffero pro eius salario unum florenum auri, eo modo et forma
de quibus patet manu mei" (Concistoro, vol.
261, fol. 23ʳ)

**Cristoforo (Cristofano) di Brandino Lom-
bardo, Maestro** (as of 1490). Piffero,
1472–95
Tax declaration, 1488: "Dinanzi da voi spettabilissimi cittadini . . . Notifichassi per lo vostro
servidore Cristofano di [gap] piffaro del vostro magnifico palazo e servidore come mi
trovo una vigna posta nel comune di Sancto
Giorgio ne la contrata chiamata la volta di
Fighille di staia otto.
Item si trova lui e la sua donna con quatro
figlioli maschi, e 'l maggior non passa dodici
anni E rachoma[n]domi alle vostre Speta-
bilità.
[verso: Cristofano di Brandino pifaro di Palazo
nel terzo di Città e chompagnia di San Salva-
dore]" (Lira, vol. 215, 1488, Terzo di Città,
unnumbered folio)
Tax declaration, 1491: "Dina[n]zi da voi spetabili eletti a fare la nuova l[ira] dicesi per me
Cristofano di Brandino pifaro di palazo avere
gl'i[n]frascritte beni et prima
Una vingnia di staiora VII nel chomuno di San
Giorgio a Papaliano di valuta di Fl. ciento,
Fl. 100

Trovomi 3 figliuo[li] maschi picchioli
Rachomandomi a la vostra spettabilità" (vol.
224, 1491, Terzo di Città, fol. 114ʳ)
Tax declaration of his sons Niccolò and Antonio, 1509: "Diespone per noi Nicholò e Antonio di maestro Christofano piffari . . . avere
li infrascritti beni, cioè
Un pezo di vignia di stai[or]a otto fuore dela
Porta Avilena, chomuno di San Giorgio Pa-
peianny chon un pocha di chasa in detta
vigna . . . la detta vignia è di stimatione
di dugiento fiorini, cioè Fl. 200, in
circha
Ci rachomandiamo a le Signorie Vostre" (Lira,
vol. 234, 1509, Terzo di Città, [fol. 84ʳ])

Dadio di Bartolomeo. Piffero, 1425

Dionigi di Pavolo. Trumpeter, 1580
Ordered to prison for violating regulations on
outside employment, March 1580: see Doc.
12.19

Domenico di Bartolomeo Fei. Supernumerary piffero, 1575–91
Hired with half-ration of food, October 1575:
see Doc. 12.20; appointed supernumerary,
February 1578: see Doc. 12.21
Suspended for fifteen days for carrying arms at
night, 26 January 1585: "Illustrissimi domini
. . . in causa imputationis facte contra Dominicum Bartolomei, unum ex musicis eorum
palatii, ex quo cum armis fuit a familia Capi-
tane iustitie repertus noctis tempore . . . deliberaverunt . . . illum absolvere et absolverunt ab imputatione predicta . . . Et
nichilominus ex quo fuerat dicto Dominico
prohibitum . . . ut non deportaret arma noctis tempore, et fuit inobediens . . . decreverunt eidem fieri preceptum quod per dies
quindecim non recedat de eorum palatio
eidem pro carcere assignato, sine licentia Illustrissimi domini Capitanei populi" (Concistoro, vol. 1297, fol. 7ʳ)
Imprisoned on complaint of Elisabetta di Francesco, 21 October 1588: "Audita querela hoc
mane data in palatio . . . per dominam Elisa-
beth Francisci . . . contra Dominicum Batho-
lomei, musicum Palatii . . . mandaverunt ipsum Dopminicum capi et captum in
carceribus intrudi, ibique retineri ad in-

stantiam eorum Concistori" (vol. 1300, un-numbered folio)

Ordered imprisoned, 17 November 1588: "L'Il-lustrissimo et Excelso Signor Capitano del Popolo, per buone considerationi et buono effecto, ordinò che Domenico di Bartolo-meo, musico, sia carcerato ad suo instantia et sia messo nelle Stinche" (ibid., unnumbered folio)

Released, 22 November 1588: "L'Illustrissimo Signor Capitano del popolo mandò scarerarsi Domenico musicho, carcerato ad sua in-stantia . . . pagando le debite spese" (ibid., unnumbered folio). Another record concern-ing this affair is on an unnumbered folio dated 27 October 1588, of the same volume.

Petitions for review of denial of salary raise, 27 April 1591: see Doc. 12.24

Resigns, 12 August 1591: "viva et nemine con-tradicente, obtinuerunt ad servitium palatii Dominicum Bartolomei musicum, et sibi de propria provisione salarium dari, ac partem victus ad libitum Illustrissimi et excelsi do-mini Capitanei"; fol. 80ᵛ, dated 19 August 1591: "attenta renunciatione sponte facta per Dominicum magistri Bartolomei barbiton-soris, unum ex musicis palatii, sui loci pro electione alterius facenda loco ipsius et cum eisdem honoribus ac oneribus solitis, concur-rentibus omnibus albis votibus [sic] . . . elege-runt et loco ipsius posuerunt Octavium quon-dam Laurentii, bibliopolam, musicum Senensem" (Concistoro, vol. 1303, fol. 76ʳ)

Domenico di Cristoforo (son of Maestro Cri-stoforo di Brandino). Supernumerary piffero, 1488–92; piffero, 1492–1510

Given meal privileges, 17 January 1488: "Et de-creverunt quod Dominicus Christofori piffarus habeat expensas in palatio in futu-rum, sicut ceteri alii piffari" (Concistoro, vol. 728, fol. 9ᵛ)

Recommendation that he be hired, 9 August 1492: see Doc. 11.16

Sent to jail for failing to perform, 17 June 1493: "Magnifici domini . . . attento quod Domini-cus Christofori, tibicina palatii, hieri in hora cene non se presentavit sonatum iri tibicinam ad fenestras palatii, ut tenebatur et obligatus

erat . . . et alio se contulit absque eorum li-centia . . . decreverunt quod prefatum Domi-nicum se recipiat in carceribus publicis Co-munis Senarum et illic remaneat donec solutum et liberatum fuerit ab eisdem Ma-gnificis dominis" (Concistoro, vol. 760, fols. 13ᵛ–14ʳ)

Fabio di Geronimo. Supernumerary piffero, 1561

His petition granted, 19 December 1561: "Et lecta per eorum notario supplicatione Fabii Hieronymi, musici palatii . . . deliberaverunt dare et concedere . . . dicto Fabio totum id quod per ipsum in dicta eius . . . supplicatio-ne petitum est" (Concistoro, vol. 1164, fol. 11ᵛ)

On leave of absence, 1562: see Doc. 12.11

Federico. Trombonist, 1460

His goods are ordered to be restored after he is pardoned, 29 January 1460: "Excellentes do-mini et Capitaneus populi . . . decreverunt quod bona Federici, tromboni palatii, reco-mendata penes Franciscum Mathei Salvi, olim Operarium Camere Comunis Senarum ad petitionem Consistorii, restituantur eidem Federico, viso maxime quod dictus Federicus absolutus fuit de excessu per eum commisso" (Concistoro, vol. 560, fol. 23ʳ)

His safe conduct is renewed for one month, 2 February 1460: "Prorogaverunt etiam salvum conductum concessum per dictum Magnifi-cum Capitaneum populi Federico tromboni palatii, per totum presentem mensem Febru-arii" (ibid., fol. 26ʳ)

Federigo di Lanberto Francioso (possibly brother of Ferrino). Piffero, 1452

Allowed to use clothing allowance to take care of his wife, 27 July 1452: "Simili modo deli-beraverunt quod Federigho Lamberti francio-so, piffaro palatii, solvantur denarii inconti-genti [sic], loco vestis habende in festo Sancte Marie, attento maxime quod ipse Federighus habet plures vestes honoratas et est bene in-dutus, et eum necesse sit habere denarios pro gubernando uxorem suam, infirmam existen-tem" (Concistoro, vol. 515, fol. 34ᵛ)

Ferrino di Lanberto da Francia (possibly brother of Federigo). Piffero, 1446–71

Permitted to go to Rome to seek indulgence, 10 November 1450: see Doc. 11.8

Filippo di Polo da Venezia. Piffero, 1408

Hired 11 April 1408: see Doc. 11.2; fired for dishonesty 17 October 1408: see Doc. 11.3; monthly salary Fl. 3

Flaminio di Maestro Antonio Signorini. Piffero

Expectative on his position awarded to Giovanbattista di Francesco, 22 November 1568: see Doc. 12.14

Francesco di Piero da Bologna. Piffero, 1421–27

Monthly salary Fl. 3

Francesco Gregori Piffero (brother of Annibale). Piffero, 1611

Receives his brother's post, August 1611: see Doc. 12.42

Fulvio di Matteo. Piffero, 1603

Receives part of Giovanfrancesco di Benedetto's meal allowance, October 1603: see Doc. 12.36

Gano (Galgano) d'Enea Piffero (son of the trumpeter Enea). Piffero, 1526–46 (also a singer)

Student of Giovanni di Maestro Antonio, 1522: see Doc. 12.8

Jailed on 5 January because of his failure to report to the Palace during a civic disturbance, and released two days later: "Magnifici domini . . . decreverunt quod Galganus piffarus, pro eius demeritis, attento quod in die tumulti civitatis cum armis ivit ad domum privatorum civium et non currit ad palatium, mittatur in carceribus sub scala" (Concistoro, 986, fol. 5ᵛ); "Magnifici domini decreverunt quod Galganus piffarus extrahatur de carceribus, et per octo dies non possit exire de palatio" (ibid., fol. 6ʳ).

Substituted by Simone di Domenico Nodi, who succeeded to his post in 1546: see Doc. 12.5

Tax declaration filed by his orphaned daughter in 1548: see Doc. 9.9

Garino (Carino, Guerrino) of Avignon, Maestro. Piffero, 1446

Hired at monthly salary of Fl. 4 on 27 June

1446: see Doc. 11.5; fired 22 May 1447 for failing to return from leave: see Doc. 11.6

Germano (Giordano) da Francia. Piffero, 1446, 1447–49

Fired 22 May 1447 for failing to return from leave: see Doc. 11.6; returns 30 June 1447: see Doc. 11.7

Geronimo (Girolamo) di Giovanni (son of Giovanni da Iesi). Trombonist, 1487–1521 (also a Palace trumpeter)

Permitted to serve as substitute, 2 May 1488: "Deliberaverunt quod Ieronimus Iohannis trombonus et Petruccius sacrestanus palatii possint servire per substitutum viginti diebus, quibus volunt ire ad Sanctam Maria Oreti [recte Loreti], sine amissione salarii" (Concistoro, vol. 730, fol. 2ᵛ)

Tax declaration, 1491: "Dinanzi da voi . . . Exponsi per me Girolamo di Giovanni trombone de le Vostre Excelse Signori avere l'infrascripti beni e prima

Una chasa nel terzo di Chamollia chompagnia di Sancto Antonio, la quale ho chomprata quest'anno da Andrea di Sano choiaio cento dieci fiorini

de' quali n'ò tempo anni tre et in questo mezo ne pago la pigione, si che io lo debito

Apresso una vignuola a Terrenzano di staiora quatro in circha, stimola Fl. 50

Truovomi debito chon Galghano di Stefano mio suociaro, Fl. 20

Et chon più persone Fl. 15

Et chon la madre vechia, la donna e due figliuoli

Rachomandomi a le Vostre Spettabilità" (Lira 229, Terzo di Città, 1491, fasc. 3, fol. 16ʳ)

Gherardo. Piffero, 1409–10

Giovanbattista Cocchi (father of cathedral singer Bernardino). Piffero, 1575–1602

Receives part of Ascanio Marri's salary, 1575: see Doc. 12.20

Ordered to prison for violating regulations on outside employment, March 1580: see Doc. 12.19

Bread allotment increased, 28 June 1588: "Custodibus Illustrissimi domini Capitanei . . . et Iohanni Baptistae de Cochis musico eorum palatii, petentibus, concesserunt medietatem

panis pro quolibet, ultra panes duos cum dimidio, et sic in totum panes tres pro quolibet, qualibet die" (ibid., unnumbered folio)

Salary lowered, 1597: see Doc. 12.34

Receives part of Adriano Mangoni's salary, August 1598: see Doc. 12.28

Named as Simone Nodi's substitute, February
1602: see Doc. 12.26

Giovanbattista di Bennardino. Supernumerary piffero, 1567

Named as replacement, 10 June 1567: see Doc.
12.13

**Giovanbattista di Francesco detto Formica
(Formichi).** Piffero, 1568–1596

Granted expectative on position of Flaminio di
Maestro Antonio Signorini, 22 November
1568: see Doc. 12.14

Imprisoned for eight days for refusing to play
for Signor Achielle Donati, 18 January 1570:
"Li Magnifici et Eccelsi Signori . . . hauto
notitia che il Formica musico ha recusato lo
andare insieme colli altri musici a fare musica
in camera del Signor Achille Donati, in vili-
pendio di esso Signor Achille . . . deliberorno che sia carcerato a beneplacito di loro Signoria Illustrissima et che se li levi . . . la sua
provisione del tinello . . . per otto giorni proximi da hoggi. Et in fatto il detto Formica
spontaneamente se n'andò in prigione" (Concistoro, vol. 1212, fol. 8ᵛ)

'Released, 21 January 1570: "Li Magnifici et Eccelsi Signori . . . deliberorno che il Formica
sia excarcerato e si facci politia di rilasso in
forma. Et fu fatta" (ASS, Concistoro, vol.
1212, fol. 9ʳ)

Receives part of Ascanio Marri's salary, 1575:
see Doc. 12.20

Ordered to prison for violating regulations on
outside employment, March 1580: see Doc.
12.19

Fined for hitting a Palace employee, 4 June
1584: "Et viso et audito processa per Illustrissimos dominos praecessores fabricato adver-
sus Iohannem Baptistam de Formichis, musicum eorum Palatii, eo quo alapam dedit
Dominico Pasquini de Campagnatico, Palatii
famulo, visa confessione dicti Iohannis Baptistae . . . ac pace inter eos infra triduum

inita ipsum condennaverunt . . . in libris sex
et soldis undecim et denariis 3" (Concistoro,
vol. 1296, fols. 48ᵛ–49ʳ)

Quarrel with Alberto di Gregorio on who was
to play first bass, 27 August 1585: see Doc.
12.31; see also Doc. 12.33

Permitted to play in cathedral, 25 January 1588:
"Et udito Giovan Battista di Francesco, musico del Palazzo . . . dettono licenza al medesimo di poter servire et andare a sonare,
sendo stato recerco di ciò dal Signor Rettore
dell'Opera, nella cappella del Duomo, non
sendo per questo pregiudizio alla musica del
Palazzo . . . Et ha fatto detto decreto a dì 23
di Marzo '87 [1588]" (vol. 1300, unnumbered folio)

Giovanfrancesco di Benedetto de' Vedi.
Trombonist, 1548–79; 1594–1603; leader of
Palace musicians from 29 October 1602

Retained in 1556: see Doc. 12.9

Permitted to play in cathedral, 3 July 1558:
"L'Illustrissimi Signori . . . derno licentia
viva voce a Giovanfrancesco trombone, del
lor palazzo di posser sonare ali tempi congrui
nella chiesa chatedrale del duomo di Siena,
non ostante alcuna cosa in contrario etc."
(Concistoro, vol. 1144, fol. 3ʳ)

Having overstayed a leave, is condemned to
serve six months without salary, 30 June
1562: "Et actento quod Iohannesfranciscus
ut dicitur trombone, cum ipse tempore debito et determinato sibi concesso per octo
dies, et sit elapso fere unus mensis, non redierit ad civitatem . . . deliberaverunt . . . che
detto Giovanfrancesco trombone s'intendi
ammunito, cioè che tornando alla città devi
servire al suo medesimo offitio dipoi sarà tornato, per sei mesi senza salario et non possa
né devi havere il vitto per detto tempo in tinello. Et non servendo come è detto et non
accettando la presente deliberatione, hora
per allhora s'intendi et sia casso" (vol. 1167,
fol. 25ʳ)

Sued for not sharing gratuities, January 1565:
see Doc. 12.15

Imprisoned, 29 June 1565: "li Magnifici Gonfaloniere et Consiglieri del magnifico Capitano deliberorno che si mandi per Giovan-

francesco trombone et comparso sia messo in prigione sotto la scala . . . et non comparendo per tutto dì d'hoggi, hora per allora et e converso s'intenda essere et sia privo del suo luogo del trombone . . . Et il dì detto fu menato dalli sbirri et messo in prigione sì come fu deliberato" (vol. 1184, unnumbered folio)

Reinstated with usual salary, 14 August 1565: "mossi da giuste cagioni . . . rimessero liberamente Giovanfrancesco trombone al servitio del palazzo per uno de' musici, con il solito salario" (vol. 1185, unnumbered folio)

Sues Ascanio Marri for not sharing gratuities, February 1570: see Doc. 12.16; differences resolved, March 1570: see Doc. 12.17

Granted leave, 20 October 1588: "A Giovanfrancesco musico di Palazzo concesseno buona licentia di partirsi dal servitio suo del Palazzo" (Balìa, vol. 189, fol. 172ʳ); returns, 25 October 1588: "Al Concistoro . . . rimesseno l'auttorità di accettare per musico al servitio del Palazzo Giovanfrancesco, non ostante la deliberatione di sopra fatta, nel modo che serviva prima" (ibid., fol. 174ᵛ)

Decree on duties, 21 January 1595: see Doc. 12.33

Salary raised, February 1597: see Doc. 12.34

Replaced as head of Palace musicians by Alberto di Gregorio, April 1603: see Doc. 12.35

Giovanni da Alamania, Maestro. Trombonist, 1447–56

Fired, 29 September 1449: "Gloriosi et potentes domini . . . cassaverunt et privaverunt magistrum Ians pulsantem trombone, qui non sit amplius ad servitia palatii, propter certas inhonestates" (Concistoro, vol. 502, fol. 20ᵛ)

Rehired, 4 October 1449: "Prefati Magnifici domini . . . deliberaverunt remictere et reconducere ad servitia palatii et rimiserunt et de novo recondxuerunt magistrum Gians pulsantem trombonem, qui diebus elapsis fuit cassus, cum salario, emolumentis et modis ut alias conductus fuit" (ibid., fol. 23ʳ)

Permitted to go to Rome to seek an indulgence, 2 September 1450: see Doc. 11.8

Appointed, 2 May 1452: "Magnifici domini . . . eligerunt magistrum Iohannem [blank] teu-

tonicum in trombonem et pro trombone Comunis Senarum et eorum palatii, ad beneplacitum Consistorii, cum salario et modis cum quibus alias fuit electus et deservivit. Cuius quidem salarium incipiat die qua incipiet servire palazio [sic]" (Concistoro, vol. 514, fol. 4ᵛ)

Giovanni di Antonio da Bologna. Piffero, 1410 (also a trumpeter)

Giovanni di Fruosino Mangoni da Siena. Piffero, 1465–92, 1494–95

Salary increased, 23 July 1466: "Attento quod Iohannes Fruosino piffarus, conductus cum salario octo librarum pro singulo mense, quotidie in doctrina sonandi proficit et bone est indolis et morigeratus: volentes eum reddere promptiorem ad discendum et spe premii ad virtutem allicere, decreverunt quod in futurum dictus Iohannes habeat pro suo salario libra decem denariorum nitidas omni cabella, pro mense quolibet, incohando in Kalendis Augustis proximi. Ac etiam in festo Assumptionis gloriose Virginis habeat pro hoc anno integram quantitatem denariorum pro veste facienda, prout habent et alii piffari, videlicet libras XXXI soldos IIII, convertendas et erogandas in vestimentis pro persona dicti Iohannis" (Concistoro, vol. 599, fol. 23ᵛ)

New contract, 26 January 1468: "Magnifici domini . . . conduxerunt Iohannem Frosini de Senis in piffarum et pro piffaro et ad canendum tibia in eorum palatio, ad beneplacitum Consistorii, pro pretio librarum quindecim quolibet mense" (vol. 608, fol. 24ʳ)

Monthly salary of L. 19 in 1470

Giovanni di Giovanni da Alamania, Maestro. Piffero, 1460, 1463–65

Hired 19 March 1460: "Magnifici domini et Capitaneus populi . . . conduxerunt Iohannes Iohannis de Alamania in piffarum Comunis, cum hoc quod debeat venisse per totum mensem Aprelis [sic], cum salario librarum decem et novem denariorum pro quolibet mense, et cum veste quolibet anno prout aliis" (Concistoro, vol. 561, fol. 17ᵛ)

Giovanni di Giovanni da Alamania, Maestro. Trombonist, 1463

Permitted to sleep in Palace for month of

March, 11 February 1463: "Antedicti Magnifici domini . . . deliberaverunt quod Iohannes Iohannis de Alamannia, tubicen novus, possit stare in palatio ad dormiendum per totum mensem Marzii [*sic*] proxime futuri" (Concistoro, vol. 578, fol. 32ʳ)

Hired, 2 June 1463: "conduxerunt in trombonum palatii Iohannem Iohannis de Alamania, cum salario librarum decem denariorum nitidorum de cabella pro quolibet mense. Que conducta incipere debeat die qua servire incepit, et duret ad beneplacitum Consistorii" (ASS, Concistoro, vol. 580, fol. 25ᵛ); contract retrospective to 1 May: "Declaraverunt etiam quod conducta Iohannis Iohannis de Alamania, tubonis palatii . . . incipiat pro die prima Maii, prima eorum officii, a quo tempore citra certi sunt ipsum sonavisse" (vol. 580, fol. 34ʳ, dated 11 June 1463)

Giovanni di Giovanni da Francia. Piffero, 1449

Hired in place of Germano, 4 September 1449, but resigns 2 October: "Visoque quod magister Germanus de Francia, piffarus palatii ipsorum Magnificorum dominorum, defunctus est et opus est pro honore et debito palatii providere de alio eius loco, deliberaverunt et . . . conduxerunt in piffarum . . . Iohannem Iohannis de Francia . . . cum salario XII librarum . . . pro quolibet mense" (Concistoro, 502, fol. 4ᵛ). A marginal note says: "Nota quod dictus Iohannes piffarus die II Octobris renuntiavit dictam eius conductam et petiit cassari et ideo cassa [est]"

Rehired 23 October 1449: "Ipsi magnifici domini . . . visa renuntiatione facta per Iohannem Iohannis de Francia, piffarum, sub die secunda presentis mensis, et pro honore palatii opus est de uno tenorista, vis[a] etiam quod iam pluribus diebus dictus Iohannes servivit et servit ad pulsandum, decreverunt reconducere et reconduxerunt ipsum pro futuro tempore, cum salario et modis sue prime conducte" (ibid., fol. 35ᵛ)

Giovanni di Maestro Antonio (son of Antonio di Gregorio). Substitute piffero, 1496–99, piffero and organ builder, 1500–26 (also at cathedral, 1509–10)

Teacher of Galgano d'Enea, 1522: see Doc. 12.8

Permitted to substitute, 25 March 1496: "Magnifici domini . . . deliberaverunt quod durante absentia piffarorum qui sunt ad Montem Politianum, Iohannes filius magistri Antonii iam mortui, vigore cuiusdam gratie et privilegii debeat sonare in palatio durante absentia dictorum piffarorum, et sic habere debeat expensas ut alii piffari, omni modo etc." (Concistoro, vol. 777, fol. 6ᵛ)

Given dining privileges and allowed to play with other pifferi, 20 July 1496: "Magnifici ac potentes domini . . . volentes eorum benignitatem estendere erga suos servitores, attenta fidelitate et bonitate magistri Antonii piffari, qui dum vixit fideliter servivit, decreverunt quod Iohannes eius filius habeat expensas prout habent alii servitores qui commedunt in eorum palatio, et ei liceat sonare contraaltum una cum aliis tibicinibus, et quousque sonabit una cum aliis expensas habeat in futurum omni modo etc." (Concistoro, vol. 779, fol. 5ᵛ). Renewed 3 May 1498: "Et deliberaverunt quod Iohannes magistri Antonii piffarus et nepos Matthei francigene habeant expensas in eorum palatio presenti bimestri, attenta eorum fidelitates" (vol. 790, fol. 3ʳ)

Given clothing every August, 29 October 1496: "Et audito Ioannes magistri Andree [*sic*] piffari et atenta et considerata bona, fideli et longa servitute dicti magistri Antonii eius patris, et quanto tempore ipse magister Antonius servivit eorum palatio. Et viso qualiter Magnifici domini predecessores, predictis atentis et consideratis, et considerato quod Senarum res publica semper fuit grata erga suos fideles servitores: deliberaverunt Ioannem predictum eius filium debere sonare contra alto et habere continuas expensas in eorum palatio prout alii tibicines . . . . Et deliberaverunt ipsum Ioannem magistri Antonii tibicenam habere debere vestem a Comuni Senarum de presenti anno prout habuerunt alii tibicines et prout solitus erat habere magister Antonius eius pater . . . Simili modo deliberaverunt ipsum Ioannem predictum de cetero et in futurum habere debere quolibet

anno in festo S. Marie de mense Augusti,
vestem a Comuni Senarum prout et sicut
habent et habere soliti sunt alii tibicines
et servitores eorum palatii" (vol. 780, fol.
19^{r-v})

Tax declaration, 1509: "Dinanzi da voi spettabilissimi cittadini . . . li beni di Giovanni di
maestro Antonio pifaro

In prima una chasa posta in Siena nel Terzo di
Città e populo di Santo Salvador

Item trovomi debito Fl. 70 e quali debo dare a
una mia sorella la quale è da marito, li quali
sonno per suo dota e sonno oblglighati per
mano di notaio" (Lira, vol. 234, 1509, Terzo
di Città, fasc. 3, [fol. 53^r])

Giovanni di Monaldo (brother of Bartolomeo). Substitute trombonist, 1477

Giovanni di Piero da Colonia. Piffero,
1452–57

Retained 30 July 1455: see Doc. 11.9; fired 4
August 1455: see Doc. 11.10

Giulio di Alessandro Muratore. Piffero,
1598–1601

Receives part of Adriano Mangoni's salary, Au-
gust 1598: see Doc. 12.28; receives part of
Tiberio Rivolti's salary, February 1601: see
Doc. 12.32

Condemned to death for numerous crimes, 10
December 1601: [margin: Sententia contra
Iulium musicum] "Nos Capitaneus Populi et
Priore Gubernatores Magnificae civitatis Senarum . . . in causa et causis . . . contra et ad-
versus Iulium magistri Alexandri fabri murarii, nostri Palatii musicum, in et de furto
qualificato et de bacchationibus per civitatem, pulsando ianuas, auferendo bucinellos,
incidendo cordulas, et alia faciendo . . . Visis
constitutis et confessione ipsius Iulii . . . sen-
tentiamus et declaramus dictum Tullium [sic]
. . . culpabilem et de iure punibilem . . . et
esse condemnandum . . . ad penam furcarum
ita et taliter ut anima separetur a corpore"
(ASS, Concistoro, vol. 1313, unnumbered
folio)

Gualfredo. Piffero, 1449

Guglielmo. Piffero, 1448–51

Permitted to go to Rome to seek an indulgence, 2 September 1450: see Doc. 11.8

Jacomo di Antonio Latini. Supernumerary
piffero, 1573–85

Requests that his privileges be retained if he returns to Siena, 16 June 1573: "L'Illustrissimi
Signori . . . vista et udita la supplica porta da
Iacomo d'Antonio Latini musico, supplicante
et domandante come detto Antonio suo padre essendo andato ad habitare . . . a Casole,
et essendo costretto per l'obligo paterno se-
guitarlo, et già per molti anni essendosi obligato andare a servire loro Illustrissime Signorie, non conoscendo con la provisione solo
di pane et di vino potersi sostenare, domandante licentia et conservarli che quando egli
ritornarà ad habitare alla città o per qualche
giorno verrà in Siena, sempre che venga a
servire li sia dato la sua solita provisione . . .
deliberorno concedere al detto Iacomo . . .
quanto da esso di sopra si domanda" (Concistoro, vol. 1232, fols. 18^v–19^r)

Upon intercession of his colleagues, is jailed
rather than whipped, 10 January 1575: "Et
udita la supplica facta da tucto il corpo della
musica in favore di Iacomo Latini, già condennato dalli antecessori di loro Signorie Illustrissime in due tratti di corda et uno mese
di carcere, esponenti come per essare egli del
corpo della musica di palazzo, verrebbono li
membri suoi et la persona . . . a patire, et
così il corpo della musica . . . Onde li detti Illustrissimi Signori deliberorno agratiare il
detto Iacomo della detta fune et permutare il
detto suo confino . . . et agrattiorno dalla
detta pena della fune et per tal pena devi
stare 15 giorni più da hoggi in le Stinche
dove al presente si trova, et dipoi per un
mese per il palazzo di loro Signorie Illustrissime" (vol. 1242, fol. 7^{r-v})

Released, 30 April 1575: "Et deliberonno ex-
carcerarsi Iacomo di Antonio Latini, incarcerato ad instantia di lor Signorie Illustrissime
nelle pubbliche Stinche come uno de' musici
di loro palzzo, et subbito fu scarcerato et li-
berato" (vol. 1243, unnumbered verso, last
folio)

Receives part of Ascanio Marri's salary, October
1575: see Doc. 12.20

Overstays leave to go to Santa Maria del Loreto

and Foligno and is fined, late 1579: see Doc.
12.23

Ordered released from jail for having carried a
dagger, 10 April 1585: [margin: Iacopo Latini musico sia excarcerato] "Li Illustrissimi
Signori . . . hauto notitia come Iacopo Latini, musicho del palazzo di lor Signori, è
stato messo in carcere dali famegli del
bargello per haverlo trovato con il pugnale
. . . mossi da giuste e ragionevoli considerationi commesseno e mandorno il detto
Iacopo scarcerarsi e perciò farsi politia di
relasso al capitano della piazza" (Concistoro, vol. 1297, fol. 30ʳ)

Given permission to serve a Doria prince, August 1585: see Doc. 12.29

Jacopo di Antonio da Bologna (perhaps
brother of the trumpeter Giovanni di Antonio). Piffero, 1413–20

Jacopo di Salvatore. Piffero, 1487–99

Tax declaration, 1491: "Dina[n]ti da voi spettabili cittadini . . . Jacomo di Salvadore piffaro
de' Magnifici signori.

Una chasa la quale ò comprata dalle rede di Simone di Gobbio per mio abitare la quale ò
comprata fiorini dugento di 4 lire il fiorino;
òlla comprata in questo modo, ch'io n'ò
paghato fiorini cinquanta e resto ne pago la
pigione tanto ch'io l'abbi finita di pagare
Rachomandomi a le vostre Magnificentie"
(verso: T[erzo] di C[ittà] nella compagnia di Sancto Salvadore) (Lira, vol. 224, 1491, Terzo di
Città, fol. 1004)

Tax declaration of his widow, 1509: "Christo
adì 16 d'agosto 1509. Si espone per me
Monna Frasia, donna fù già di Iachomo
piffaro, a voi spettabili cittadini eletti a fare la
nuova lira chome mi truovo una chasa nel
terzo di città et contrada di Sancto Salvadore, la quale chonfine d'un lato Tome di
Barnaba detto Mazone, e dall'altro Giovanni
di maestro Antonio piffaro, e dinanzi la via
del Chomuno e drieto lo merchato vechio,
la detta chasa è di stimazione di fiorini cien-
tosessanta, cioè 160, in circha ed è vechia
. . .

Item mi truovo uno pezo di posticcia nel Chomuno di Frontignano, di staia due incircha,

la quale chonfine d'un lato la via del chomuno e dall'altro la chiesa di detto Fronti-
gniano . . .

Item mi truovo vedova e pocho sono chon tre
figliuoli, lo magiore è di anni 15 senza altro
se non a voi mi racomando" (ibid., 1509,
Terzo di Città, fol. [102ʳ])

Lorenzo della Scala. Piffero, 1603–6

Receives part of Giovanfrancesco di Benedetto's
meal allowance, October 1603: see Doc.
12.36

Accorded meal privileges worth L. 6, 1 July
1606: "Laurentio Schalae, musico Palatii ha-
benti salarium in summa librarum trium pro
quolibet mense, cum evaserit meliorem et in
dies crescat, et ut ei et aliis se bene gerendi
detur occasio, auxerint ei et dederint de pecu-
niis plattae usque ad libras sex pro quolibet
mense, viva voce deliberaverunt et ita poni
et describi in tabulella musicorum" (Concī-
storo, vol. 1317, unnumbered folio)

**Lorenzo di Giovanni da Francia (Teuton-
ico).** Piffero, 1447–48

Hired at monthly salary of L. 12, 22 May 1447:
see Doc. 11.6

Fired as unsuitable, 22 April 1448: "Ac etiam cassaverunt Laurentium [blank] theutonicum,
pifferum, tanquam non ydoneum, et quod
habeat salarium solum per totum presentem
mensem" (Concistoro, vol. 493, fol. 34ʳ)

Lorenzo di Ottavio Basili Piffero (son of Ottavio). Piffero, 1611

Succeeds to his father's post, 27 August 1611:
see Doc. 12.43

Luzio di Pavolo Piffero (son of Pavolo di Giovanni, brother of Virginio). Supernumerary
piffero, 1538–45

Substituted by Virginio di Pavolo when absent,
23 October 1538: see Doc. 12.1

Petitions to succeed his late father, Pavolo, and
give expectative to his son Adriano Imperiale, 14 April 1545: see Doc. 12.3

Mariano di Galgano. Supernumerary piffero,
1488–

Given dining privileges in Palace, 13 January
1488: "Habita informatione de bonitate, virtutibus et diligentia et maxima paupertate

Mariani Galgani, eorum palatii piffari, qui se diligentissime et sollicite exercet ad ipsam pifferam et trumbonem pulsando et discendo, propria pietate moti et pro amore Dei, attenta ipsa paupertate et ipsum non habere aliquod emolumentum de quo vivere possit . . . decreverunt quod ipse Marianus in futurum habeat expensas in palatio prout et sicut ceteri alii piffari et trumbones et seu domicelli" (Concistoro, vol. 728, fol. 9ʳ)

Martino di Corrado Teutonico. Piffero, 1458–60

Hired 7 May 1458: "Magnifici domini . . . visa notula eorum precessorum loquenti de materia tenoriste piffarorum, deliberaverunt conducere et deliberantes conduxerunt Martinum Curradi Theotonicum in piffarum et thenorista piffarorum eorum palatii, pro uno anno incietto [*recte* incepto] die prima Maii presentis . . . cum salario librarum otto denariorum Senensium, nitidorum omni cabella, pro quolibet mense, et una veste tempore ordinato, et cum expensis in palatio prout habent alii pifferi palatii. Et deliberaverunt, visa conducta facta per magnificos eorum precessores de Thomasso Pieri francigeno tenorista, quod dictus Thomas sic conductus servat in palatio loco unius domicelli, cum salario librarum trium denariorum in quolibet mense, et una veste tempore ordinato secundum formam stantiamenti sue conducte" (Concistoro, vol. 550, fol. 4ʳ)

Rehired 6 October 1460: "Et decreverunt . . . de novo conducere et conduxerunt ad servitia eorum palatii Martinum Curradi de Alamania, im [*sic*] pifferum et tenoristam pifferorum prout ad presens servit et prout servunt et serviverunt alii pifferi eorum palatii, et hoc ad beneplacitum Consistorii . . . cum salario librarum decem et novem denariorum Senensium pro quolibet mense, et cum uno vestimento quolibet anno . . . incipiendo dictum eius salarium . . . die primo presentis mensis Ottobris" (vol. 564, fol. 20ʳ); another record is dated 30 October 1460: "Magnifici domini . . . decreverunt conducere et conduxerunt Martinum Curradi de Alamania pifferum, pro piffero et te-

norista pifferorum pro tempore sex mensium firmorum proxime sequendorum, et deinde ad beneplacitum Consistori, cum salario, veste et aliis emolumentis et commodis hactenus consuetis et cum quibus in presentiarum servit et conductus est" (ibid., fol. 31ʳ)

Payment after death, 21 February 1462: "Deliberaverunt etiam quod camerarius Bicherne solvat Martino theotonico, olim piffaro Comunis, defuncto, et pro eo Antonio Guelfi pizicaiuolo, libras 13 soldos 0 denariorum, eidem Antonio debitas pro cera per eum data pro sepoltura dicti olim Martini" (vol. 572, fol. 34ᵛ)

Matteo. Piffero, 1450

Permitted to go to Rome to seek an indulgence, 2 September 1450: see Doc. 11.8

Michele di Giovanni da Alamania. Piffero, 1416–19

Niccolò d'Andrea da Bologna. Piffero, 1421–46, 1447

Fined for failing to perform at a degree ceremony, October 1446: see Doc. 11.4

Niccolò di Aurelio Faraoni. Piffero, 1599–1606

Hired 10 November 1599: [margin: Electione Nicolai Farraoni in musicum Palatii] "Postea levati a mensa et ingressi in talamo domini Capitanei ad ignem in numero octo, ad propositum dicti domini Capitanei quod detur et concedatur medium panem vel, ut dicitur, piatto, vacatum ut supra per mortem dicti Petri, un ex dictis petentibus . . . fuit victum et obtentum quod omnes scrutinentur, et ille qui habuerit plura suffragia . . . ei sit et intelligatur concessum supradictum panem vel provisionem, et habeatur in musico dicti Palatii cum omnibus oneribus et honoribus quos idem Petrus habebat. Quibus omnibus scrutinatis, prevaluit Niccolaus Aurelii de Farraonis, et mandaverunt eidem supradictam electionem et concessionem notificari et decretum in forma fieri omni modo etc." (Concistoro, vol. 1311, unnumbered folio)

Receives increase in dining privileges and salary, 24 December 1601: [margin: Gratia concessa Niccolao Farraono musico] "Item auditis precibus Niccolai quondam Aurelii de Farraonibus, musici huius Palatii, petentis ut sibi in gratia concedatur ea provisio victus et illud modicum salarium, quem et quod consequebatur Iulius olim musicus huius loci, stante sua servitute cum dimidia provisione, absque ullo salario . . . Decreverunt eidem Niccolao largiri et concedere . . . dictam provisionem et salarium. Quam et quod mandaverunt eidem dari et solvi, et decretum fieri in forma omni modo etc." (vol. 1313, unnumbered folio)

Receives part of Giovanfrancesco di Benedetto's salary, October 1603: see Doc. 12.36

Concistoro petitions the Captain of Justice to release Niccolò, imprisoned for playing the cornett late at night, 1 December 1606: "Intesosi che Niccolò musico nostro la sera del 28 del passato, avanti le 4 hore di notte, trovato in piazza sonando di cornetto, era stato condotto pregione . . . dalla fameglia del Bargello . . . fu dall'intero Concistoro fatta poliza di relasso et per condescendere al desiderio del Signor Capitano di Giustitia, precetto al musico che sotto pena di scudi dieci non sonasse di notte per le strade senza licenza del Concistoro e beneplacito del medesimo" (ASS, Concistoro, vol. 1317, fol. 85ʳ)

Niccolò di Giorgio da Zara (Giara). Piffero, 1411–25, 1426–28, 1431–45

Niccolò di Giorgio da Venezia. Trombonist, 1460, 1463

Hired at very advantageous terms, 27 June 1460: see Doc. 11.12

Given month's leave to go to Venice, 17 August 1460: "Magnifici domini . . . concesserunt licentiam Nicolao tromboni eundi Venetias et absentandi se a civitate Senarum sine suo preiudicio aut damno, per totum mensem, admictendo tamen salarium" (Concistoro, vol. 563, fol. 14ᵛ)

Rehired 17 July 1463: "Magnifici et potentes domini . . . conduxerunt Nicolaum Georgii de Corsono tubicenem, pro trombono et in trombonum palatii, ad beneplacitum Consistorii, cum salario ducatorum IIII auri, videlicet librarum XXI soldorum IIII denariorum Senensium in mense quolibet, et cum una veste in anno et aliis indumentis consuetis" (vol. 581, fol. 13ʳ)

Niccolò di Maestro Cristoforo Piffero (brother of Domenico). Piffero, 1510–66; called maestro in 1558 (Doc. 10.14)

Excused from playing at night, and Savino permitted to substitute for him, 6 October 1555: "L'Illustrissimi Signori . . . ateso che Niccolò piffaro del palazo per la longha sua età vede male lume a sonare e maxime la sera, e ancora rispetto lo haversene a andar a casa a tre o quattro hore di notte e con pericolo rispetto alle guardie che si fanno per la città. Considerato che il palazo, ancor che lui non venissi non patisce circa il suo sonare, havuto consideratione alla sua longha e buona servitù verso il palazo detto, e per altre giuste consideratione, deliberonno per l'authorità che hanno, che manchando alcuna volta a sonare detto Niccolò per dette cause, possa sonare in loco suo Savino, figlio di Ceccho Bello, non intendendosi però dare al decto Savino cosa alcuna per la presente deliberatione omni meliori modo" (Concistoro, vol. 1129, fol. 2ʳ).

Retained in 1556: see Doc. 12.9

Sued for not sharing gratuities, January 1565: see Doc. 12.15

Niccolò di Niccolò da Strasburgo. Piffero, 1410–14

Hired 23 May 1410: "Conduxerunt Nicolaum Nicolai de Trasburg de Alamania in piffarum Comunis ad beneplacitum Consistorii, cum soldo quod habent alii qui stant pro tubatoribus Comunis. Quod soldus incipiat die primo Maii presentis" (Concistoro, vol. 266, fol. 17ʳ)

Orindio Bartolini. Piffero, 1598–99

Receives part of Adriano Mangoni's salary, August 1598: see Doc. 12.28

Resigns, May 1599: see Doc. 12.37

Ottavio di Lorenzo Basili. Piffero, 1581–1611 (also in cathedral)

Hired 12 November 1585: [margin: Ottavio di Lorenzo musico] "Et visto che la musica del Palazzo loro viene in mancanza di musici et che di già ne sono partiti due, et acciò tal musica si mantenghi in quella maggior riputatione che sia possibile, et per dare animo a quelli che attendono a tal virtù . . . fu delibe-

rato et vinto che si aggregasse sì come aggre-
gorno nel conserto [sic] della detta musica Ottavio di Lorenzo senese. Et acciò possi
servire bene et diligentemente, ordinorno
darseli per il canovaio del palazzo loro due
pani grandi et una mezzetta di vino, per ciascuno giorno, et altre rigaglie, emolumenti,
oblighi, pesi et carichi che hanno et sogliono
havere li altri lor musici. Et così deliberorno
per ogni miglior modo et mandorno descri-
versi alla tavolella che sta in tinello" (Concistoro, vol. 1297, fol. 102ᵛ)

Request for salary granted, 27 June 1588:
"Audita pariter supplicatione facta ab Octavio Laurentii musico, petente aliquod sibi
dari salarium pro mercede eius laboris et servitutis . . . decreverunt sibi dari . . . libram
unam [soldos] 10 pro quolibet mense" (ASS,
Concistoro, vol. 1300, unnumbered folio)

Request for partial meal privileges and increased
salary granted, 28 July 1591: "Audito Octavio . . . eiusque humili petitione, quam be-
nigne amplectando . . . obtinuere, sex con-
currentibus albis votibus nemine discrepante
. . . eidem Octavio . . . dari solitam sibi da-
tam hucusque partem victus . . . necnon singulo mense solidos triginta denariorum"
(Concistoro, vol. 1303, fol. 72ʳ)

Salary increased, 9 September 1595: "Et essendo
informati delle buone qualità e virtù di Ottavio di Lorenzo Basili, musico già 14 anni
del Palazzo loro . . . et cognosciuto che il
cantar suo fiorisce la musica di detto lor palazzo, oltre al sapere sonare molti instrumenti
che suonano li altri musici; et considerato
che il salario di tre carlini che se gli danno
per ciascuno mese gl'è poca recognitione rispetto alli salarii delli altri musici: volendo
dar maggior animo a detto Ottavio di conti-
nare la sua buona servitù . . . viva voce
deliberorno darsi al detto Ottavio tre carlini
di più per ciascuno mese oltre alli altri tre
datigli per il passato" (Concistoro, vol. 1307,
fol. 135ʳ)

Meal privileges revoked, February 1597: see
Doc. 12.34

Receives full meal privileges, 7 May 1597: "Visa
supplicatione facta per Octavium de Basiliis,

musicum Palatii, continente . . . sibi concedi,
ut dicitur, il piatto, prout habe[n]t alii musici
. . . concedatur eidem Octavio, ut dicitur, il
piatto prout habent alii musici" (vol. 1309,
fol. 50ᵛ)

Receives part of Adriano Mangoni's salary, August 1598: see Doc. 12.28; receives Piero di
Girolamo Rivolti's post, November 1599:
see Doc. 12.38; receives part of Tiberio Rivolti's salary, February 1601: see Doc. 12.32;
receives part of Giovanfrancesco di Benedetto's salary, October 1603: see Doc. 12.36

Renounces his post in favor of his son Lorenzo,
27 August 1611: see Doc. 12.43

**Pamfilo di Ansano Maria detto Trombon-
cino** (son of Ansano Maria). Supernumerary
trombonist, 1545–46

Dining privileges confirmed, 28 June 1545:
"Pari modo approbaverunt expensas seu victum prestitum Pamphilio filio Ansani Mariae
alias Tromboncino, musico, in tinello eorum
palatii, et voluerunt quod idem Pamphilus
eas expensas seu victum percipiat in tinello
dicto in futurum sicut in preteritum habuit,
prout alii musici" (ASS, Concistoro, vol.
1072, fol. 58ᵛ)

Partenio di Benedetto (son of Benedetto di
Domenico). Supernumerary piffero, 1546

Appointed December 1546: see Doc. 12.5

Pavolo di Giovanni (son of Giovanni di Fruosino Mangoni). Piffero, 1497–1544

Petitions for his son Virginio to be granted an
expectative to succeed him, 1525: see Doc.
12.2

Though ailing in his later years, he retained his
post, his son Luzio substituting for him.

Petro Tristano da Valenza. Trombonist,
1468–69

Hired 29 February 1468: "Forma predicta eligerunt in trombonum et pro trombone eorum
palatii Petrum Tristanum de Valenza, pro salario librarum octo denariorum Senensium
quolibet mense" (Concistoro, vol. 608, fol.
57ᵛ); his salary was raised to L. 10 on 30
June 1468 (vol. 609, fol. 36ᵛ)

Salary raised to L. 16 on 28 February 1469: "Attenta sufficientia Tristani [gap] tubonis palatii
. . . ordinaverunt in futurum eius salarium li-

brarum sedicim [denariorum] nitidorum cabella, quolibet mense, et hoc pro uno anno
tantum. Cum hac conditione quod dictus
Tristanus teneatur et debeat portare tunicam
seu clamidem ad divisam prout piffari dicti
palatii" (vol. 614, fol. 42ʳ)

Piergiovanni Odorini. Piffero, 1578–1606

Hired in place of Virgilio di Lorenzo Ricci, October 1591: see Doc. 12.39

Receives part of Adriano Mangoni's salary, Au-
gust 1598: see Doc. 12.28; receives part of
Tiberio Rivolti's salary, February 1601: see
Doc. 12.32; receives part of Giovanfrancesco
di Benedetto's salary, October 1603: see
Doc. 12.36

Piero di Girolamo Rivolti (Risquillo)
(brother of Tiberio Rivolti). Piffero,
1578–99

Salary lowered, 1597: see Doc. 12.34

Appointed to succeed Orindio Bartolini, May
1599: see Doc. 12.37

Pietragnolo di Bernardino Maestri. Piffero,
1591–1603

Given part of Domenico Fei's salary, April 1591:
see Doc. 12.24

Given meal privileges, 30 July 1591: "Auditis Pe-
troangelo Bennardini de Magistris et Virgilio
Laurentii de Ricciis, duobus musicis palatio
eorum inservientibus, eorumque petitione
humiliter facta, illis viva voce confirmarunt
provisionem victus sibi traditam a palatio"
(Concistoro, vol. 1303, fol. 75ᵛ)

Salary lowered, 1597: see Doc. 12.34

Receives part of Adriano Mangoni's salary, August 1598: see Doc. 12.28; receives part of
Giovanfrancesco di Benedetto's salary, October 1603: see Doc. 12.36

Renaldo di Michele da Cesena. Piffero,
1408, 1414–15, 1429–30, 1445–46

Hired 11 April 1408: see Doc. 11.2; fired 17 October 1408: see Doc. 11.3; monthly salary Fl.
3

Rehired 28 December 1414: "Prefati camerarius
Biccherne Rinaldo de Cesena piffaro noviter
conducto, florenos tres auri cum bono fidei-
uxore" (Concistoro, vol. 293, fol. 23ᵛ)

Rehired 27 February 1445: "Magnifici domini
. . . conduxerunt Raynaldum Michaelis de

Cesena in piffarum palatii, cum salario et modis prout constat manu mei infrascripti [Ser
Ranieri di Guido] et ad beneplacitum Consistorii etc." (vol. 474, fol. 38ᵛ)

Fined for failing to perform at a degree ceremony, October 1446: see Doc. 11.4

Santi di Pavolo da Volterra. Trombonist,
1463–67 (formerly a Palace trumpeter)

Hired 24 August 1463: "Magnifici domini . . .
conduxerunt Sanctem [gap] in trombonum
et pro trombono palatii, cum salario librarum
19 denariorum senensium pro quolibet
mense et cum veste et aliis emolumentis consuetis, incipiendo dicta conducta die primo
septembris proxime venturi et duret ad beneplacitum Consistorii" (Concistoro, vol.
581, fol. 28ʳ)

Contract renewed 23 February 1464: "Magnifici domini . . . decreverunt conducere et deliberantes conduxerunt Sanctem Pauli de Vo-
later[r]is, tubicenem, in trombonem et pro
trombone palatii Magnificorum dominorum
et ad serviendum in sonando quottidie trombonem ad istarum [*sic*] piffarorum, cum salario librarum decem et novem denariorum
mundadorum omni cabella, ad beneplacitum
Consistorii . . . cuius tempus incipiat die
primo mensis Martii proxime futuri" (vol.
584, fol. 33ᵛ)

Savino di Francesco Belli. Substitute piffero,
1555; supernumerary piffero, 1563–64

Allowed to substitute, 6 October 1555 (*see under*
Niccolò Piffaro)

Pardoned, 29 October 1563: "Deliberorno assolvere . . . Savino, musico di palazzo, dala
condennatione fattali . . . atteso la sua humile
domanda, e mandorno cassarsi in ogni miglio modo etc." (Concistoro, vol. 1175, fol.
19ʳ)

Petition for increase in dining privileges
granted, 30 November 1563: "Et visa et
lecta petitione Savini Francisi musici palatii,
petentis augmentari sibi salarium ex piatto
Dominorum usque in 6 vel 7 libras denariorum, attento quod habet patrem veterem, et
ex eius servitute et opere, quia non habet
nisi libras 7 pro mense, et ultra petentis quod
concedatur sibi locus primus vacans, cum

conditione quod quando obtinuerit locum vacantem sint remisse dicte libre sex in 7 augendo et revertantur ut dicitur al piatto, servatis etc., visa eiusdem Savini fide ac scientia musice ac fidelitate, deliberaverunt eidem augere . . . et accreverunt eidem libras quinque denariorum pro quolibet mense, et hoc augumentum accipiatur de denariis ut dicitur del piatto delli Signori . . . essendovi, et si non adessent, restent dicte libre septem quas habet ad presens. Cum hac tamen conditione, quod quando obtinuerit aliquem locum vacantem, quod non habeat amplius dictum augumentum librarum quinque, sed restent solum dicte libre septem" (vol. 1176, fols. 16ᵛ–17ʳ)

Succeeded by Alfonso di Pavolo, 30 December 1564: see Doc. 12.12

Simone di Domenico Nodi. Piffero, 1546–1602

Provision increased by L. 4, 30 July 1546: "Audito Simone [gap] piffaro et eius expositione et petitione, et attenta eius fidelitate et bona servitute ac sufficientia in exercitio piffari, et aliis iustis causis moti, servatis etc., deliberaverunt eidem Simoni dare et concedere et concesserunt libras quatuor denariorum que supererant de provisione Panfili filii Ansani Mariae . . . et quod dicte libre sint addite eius provisioni, ad hoc ut possit inservire et se exercere" (Concistoro, vol. 1079, fol. 23ʳ)

Authorized to succeed to Galgano d'Enea's post, 17 December 1546: see Doc. 12.5

Ordered to share gratuities, 10 February 1555: "A Simone di Domenico, piffaro, si comandi che fra otto dì devi haver pagato e sodisfatto tutto quello che deve giustamente a' piffari di palazzo e naccarino, altrimenti hora per allora ne commesseno il gravamento reale e personale contra di lui e suoi beni informa. E così li fu significato subbito per me notaio" (Concistoro, vol. 1126, folio 22ᵛ)

Gratuities to be shared, 8 March 1555: [margin: Piffari] "Ali sottoscritti si de' il gravamento contra Simone di Domenico piffaro, per le sottoscritte somme di denari, in virtù de la deliberatione di sopra fatta in foglio 22: mae-

stro Antonio di maestro Cristofano, lire 19. 1; Ascanio d'Andrea, lire 56; Adriano di [blank], lire 13.9; Bennardino di Valerio, naccarino, lire 13. 6. 4" (ibid., fol. 32ᵛ)

Retained in 1556: see Doc. 12.9

Explains why he disobeyed orders to play solo cornett in absence of his colleagues, 13 September 1564: "Audito Simone, musico palatii, se excusante et dicente quod quicquid nudius tertius fecit, etsi non paruit precepto domini Capitanei Scipionis de Vieris sibi imponenti quod cum cornetta solus caneret . . . quia alii sui consocii cum licentia Illustrissimorum dominorum se contulerunt ad civitatem Lucensem . . . non causa precepta spernendi desinit exequi sibi commissa, sed quia solus exercitio suo uti penitus ignorans videbat non valere sibi et Illustrissimis Dominis satisfacere, et sic non animo peccandi sed potius reverentia ductus sibis commissa non fecit. Attendentes qualitate eius delicti . . . declaraverunt quod dictus Simon cras de mane, coram excelso Concistorio Illustrissimis dominis congregatis compareat veniamque sui delicti humiliter petat, in totum se cum maxima reverentia remictendo" (Concistoro, vol. 1181, fols. 6ᵛ–7ʳ)

Absolved, 17 September 1564: "Attenta remissio facta veniaque postulata . . . a Simone musico palatii, de errore per ipsum commisso . . . considerata qualitate delicti et parvitate ipsius . . . deliberaverunt ipsum absolvere et absolverunt . . . Et deliberaverunt etiam eidem Simoni musico restituere . . . suam victus portionem quotidianum soliti percipi in palatio" (ibid., fol. 8ᵛ)

Sued for not sharing gratuities, January 1565: see Doc. 12.15

Schoolroom in Palace, 1565: see Doc. 12.27

Sues Ascanio Marri for not sharing gratuities, February 1570: see Doc. 12.16; differences resolved, March 1570: see Doc. 12.17

Elected head of Palace musicians, 23 November 1575: see Doc. 12.25

Ordered to prison for violating regulations on outside employment, 21–22 March 1580: see Doc. 12.19

Prison sentence increased because of his refusal

to obey, 23 March 1580: "Essendo che maestro Simone Nodi musico, in dispregio del
precetto hauto il 22 stante del'entrare in carcere conforme alla deliberatione che sopra
fattane . . . ha in presentia del'Illustrissimo Signor Capitano et Illustrissimi Signori con audacia detto che non vuol andare in pregione
né obbedire et osservare la deliberatione et
precetto predetto se ben credesse metterci la
robba e la vita, però tali impertinenti parole
. . . fu solennemente deliberato che il detto
maestro Simone si ritenga per un mese continuo in carcere, et per detto tempo se li
tolga il salario e vitto solito darseli dal Palazzo. . . . Il dì detto. L'Illustrissimo Signor
Capitano di Popolo insieme con l'Illustrissimi Signori Priori Governatori viva voce
mandorno tutti li musici e trombetti carcerati che sopra—eccetto maestro Simone
Nodi—scarcerarsi e farseli politia di relasso
in forma, e tutto senza alcun pagamento"
(vol. 1273, fol. 7ᵛ)

Retired on full salary, 24 December 1601: [mar-
gin: Gratia concessa Simeone de Nodis] "Illustrissimi et excelsi domini . . . habita matura consideratione optimi, fidelis, ogni et
continui servitii per sexaginta pene annos
praestati per Simeonem de Nodis, huius almi
Palatii capellae magistri, nec non eiusdem
senectutis, probitatis, coniuncta cum morum
integritate, pietate et aliis innumeris ipsius be-
nemeritis quibus se reddit infrascriptis maxi-
mae dignum . . . Decreverunt et concordi
voto per omnia suffragia deliberaverunt dictum magistrum Simeonem fore et esse exi-
mendum ab onere amplius in posterum, tam
per se quam per alium, inserviendi dicto suo
muneri, et exemerunt, firmis remanentibus
eius solito salario, victu et emolumento. Exceptis tamen die festo Assumptionis Divae
Virginis, die Pascatis, die Nativitatis Domini
Nostri Iesu Christi, die Pentecostes et diebus
festis in honorem Serenissimi Magni Ducis,
quibus diebus teneatur uti prius inservire intra moenia tantum dicti Palatii. Et ita eidem
concesserunt omni meliori modo etc." (vol.
1313, unnumbered folio)

Giovanbattista Cocchi named as his substitute,
February 1602: see Doc. 12.26

**Stefano di Piero Rusignuoli da Francia (da
  Savoia).** Piffero, 1455–59, 1461
Hired 30 July 1455: see Doc. 11.9
Now in Milan, turns down new offer, 1 June
  1460: see Doc. 11.11

Tiberio di Girolamo Rivolti. Trombonist,
  1564–1601; leaves of absence granted 1578,
  1585 (also in cathedral, January 1574–May
  1580, March 1587–January 1588)
Meal privileges revoked, 9 March 1564: "a Tiberio di Girolamo musico non se li deve più
  dare le spese nel tinello di palazzo,
  annullando e revocando il capitolo lassato
  alla notola dalli antecessori loro" (ASS, Concistoro, vol. 1178, fol. 9ʳ)
Meal privileges reinstated, 10 March 1564: "L'Illustrissimi Signori . . . deliberorno che a Tiberio di Girolamo, musico fanciullo di scarsa
  età e di buona aspettatione nell'essercito del
  musico, per gratia speciale di lor Signorie . . .
  li sieno date le spese nel loro tinello di palazzo durante il tempo del magistrato di loro
  Signorie, cioè per li due presenti mesi Marzo
  e Aprile, con obligo che detto Tiberio devi
  et sia tenuto e obligato all'hore solite intervenire con li altri musici a sonare e presentarsi
  a servire secondo l'obligo deli altri musici del
  loro palazzo" (ibid., fol. 10ʳ⁻ᵛ)
Suspended 10 June 1567: see Doc. 12.13
Ordered to jail for writing injurious words on
  the wall and lying to a colleague, 21 May
  1568: "Deliberonno che . . . Tiberio di Girolamo, musico, devi subbito per se stesso andare e stare in carcere . . . per havere a dì passati scritto nel muro del tinello della famiglia
  certe parole di scandolo e hoggi haver dato
  in decto tinello una mentita a Giovambattista
  di Bennardino musico, per parole occorse fra
  di loro" (ASS, Concistoro, vol. 1202, fol.
  8ʳ⁻ᵛ)
Released, 27 May 1568: "Deliberonno scarcerarsi Tiberio di Girolamo musico . . . e così
  fu scarcerato, e fece pace con Giovambattista
  di Bennardino musico, in camera del signore
  Capitano alla presentia di lor Signorie" (ASS,
  Concistoro, vol. 1202, fol. 10ʳ)
Suspended for two weeks, 26 May 1570: "L'Illustrissimo Signor Capitano mandò farsi co-

mandamento a Tibertio di [gap] musico, che
per 15 giorni non ardisca o presuma in
modo alcuno . . . entrare né venire in palazzo, sotto pena del'arbitrio" (vol. 1214, fol.
10ʳ); changed to jail sentence: "Et attesa la relatione . . . hauta da più gentilhomini, di
certe parole dette da Tiberio musico, più
presto in dispregio di lor Signori che altrimenti, parendoli poco il gastigo di già datoli
dal Signor Capitano; per dare esempio agli altri et per altre giuste considerationi deliberorno che 'l detto Tiberio . . . devi andare e
stare nelle carceri publiche chiamate le Stinche, per giorni 15" (ibid. fols. 10ᵛ–11ʳ)
Released because of his poverty, 2 June 1570:
"E atteso che Tiberio musico fece la solita
obbedientia di entrare nelle Stinche subbito
che li fu comandato, esservi stato più che la
metà del tempo ordinato, attesa ancora la sua
povertà, deliberorno che per gratia sabbato
che saremo alli 3 di questo, da sera, sia scarcerato" (ibid., fol. 12ʳ⁻ᵛ)
Loses election for head of Palace musicians, November 1575: see Doc. 12.25
Ordered to prison for violating regulations on
outside employment, March 1580: see Doc.
12.19
Petitions to exchange posts with his student, Alberto di Francesco Gregori, June 1585: see
Doc. 12.30
Given permission to serve a Doria prince, August 1585: see Doc. 12.29
Salary lowered, 1597: see Doc. 12.34
Receives part of Adriano Mangoni's salary, August 1598: see Doc. 12.28
Tommaso di Biagio da Ungaria. Piffero,
1420–21
Hired 1 February 1419/20: "Prefati domini . . .
conduxerunt infrascriptum virum pro piffaro
Comunis, loco Iacobi de Bononia defuncti,
cum stipendio et modis quibus conductus
erat idem Iacobus . . . Thomassus Blaxii de
Ungaria" (Concistoro, vol. 324, fol. 16ʳ)
Tommaso di Pietro Francisena. Piffero,
1458
Hired 26 April 1458: "Magnifici domini . . .
conduxerunt Tomassum Pietri francisenam
in piffarum et tenoristam piffarorum eorum

palatii, pro uno anno incipiendo die primo
maii proxime venturi . . . cum salario librarum trium pro quolibet mense, nitidos
[sic] de cabella, et cum una veste tempore ordinato, et expensis, ut aliis piffaris. Cum hoc
quod ipse habeat pro se piffarem qua utitur
ad presens, pro pretio librarum XII denariorum Senensium, excomputando in eius salario" (Concistoro, vol. 549, fol. 26ᵛ)
Tulio. Supernumerary trombonist, 1546–49
Hired 18 February 1546: "Attenta privatione
facta de Ansano Maria [gap] tubone palatii,
et habita notitia de moribus, virtutibus et
fide Tulii [gap] musici et de eius sufficientia
et idoneitate in exercitio sonandi tubonem
. . . ipsum Tulium . . . eligerunt et deputaverunt in tubonem et pro tubono palatii, in
loco dicti Ansani Marie et cum eodem salario, emolumentis et obligationibus dicti loci"
(Concistoro, vol. 1076, fol. 38ʳ⁻ᵛ)
The Consistoro attempts to retain his services,
14 July 1548: "derno autorità al Magnifico
Capitano di populo di parlare in balìa a
quelli Signori che si contentino rimuovare la
deliberatione fatta per lor signori in quanto a
Tullio sonatore per esser tant'utile alla musica del Palazo, e che per il Concestoro si trovarà modo che rimettendolo non si crescierà
spesa" (ASS, Concistoro, vol. 1091, fol.
18ᵛ)

Valerio di Bartolomeo (Lelio) (son of drummer Meo di Maestro Mino). Piffero,
1500–51
Meal privileges confirmed, 1 January 1534/35:
"Illustrissimi domini . . . deliberaverunt confirmare et confirmaverunt infrascriptos officiales ad infrascripta officia . . . Lelium [gap]
piffarum in expensorem Palatii" (Concistoro,
vol. 1010, fol. 2ʳ)
Vincenzo di Maestro Giovanbattista (son-
in-law of Benedetto di Domenico). Trombonist, 1554
Named in petition by Benedetto di Domenico,
1554 (*see under* Agostino di Benedetto)
Virgilio di Lorenzo Ricci. Piffero, 1591
Given part of Domenico Fei's salary, April 1591:
see Doc. 12.24
Given meal privileges, 30 July 1591: "Auditis Pe-

troangelo Bennardini de Magistris et Virgilio Laurentii de Ricciis, duobus musicis palatio eorum inservientibus, eorumque petitione humiliter facta, illis viva voce confirmarunt provisionem victus sibi traditam a palatio" (ASS, Concistoro, vol. 1303, fol. 75ᵛ)

Fired October 1591: see Doc. 12.39

Virginio di Pavolo Piffero (son of Pavolo di Giovanni, brother of Luzio). Substitute piffero, 1538–45

Promised expectative of his father's place in 1525: see Doc. 12.2

Cornett taken away from him, 5 February 1535 (Concistoro 1010, fol. 31ʳ)

To be paid 1 carlino when substituting, 23 October 1538: see Doc. 12.1

BIBLIOGRAPHY

Alfieri, Edera. *La cappella musicale di Loreto*. Bologna, 1970.

Allegretti, Allegretto. "Ephemerides Senenses ab Anno MCCCL usque ad MCCCXCVI. Italico Sermone scriptae ab Allegretto de Allegrettis." In Muratori, ed., *Rerum italicarum scriptores,* 23:263–860.

"Annales Senensis ab Anno MCCCLXXXV usque ad MCCCCXXII per Anonymum Scriptorem deducti." In Muratori, *Rerum italicarum scriptores,* vol. 19, 383–428.

Antonio da Fabriano. *Terzina di Antonio da Fabriano facta in nome del Populo di Siena per inpetrare gratia de la Vergine Maria loro Protetrice: nel tempo de la peste.* Siena, 1515.

Arnold, Denis. "Brass Instruments in Italian Church Music of the Sixteenth and Early Seventeenth Centuries." *Brass Quarterly* 1 (1957): 81–92.

Arnold, F. T. *The Art of Accompaniment from a Thorough-Bass.* 2 vols. Oxford, 1931; repr. New York, 1965.

Aronow, Gail. "A Description of the Altars in Siena Cathedral in 1420." In Henk van Os, *Sienese Altarpieces 1215–1460,* 2:225–53. Medievalia Groningana, 9. Groningen, 1990.

———. "A Documentary History of the Pavement Decoration in Siena Cathedral, 1362 through 1506." Ph.D. diss., Columbia University, 1985.

Aschieri, Mario. *Siena nel Rinascimento.* Siena, 1985.

Atlas, Allan. "Alexander Agricola and Ferrante I of Naples." *JAMS* 30 (1977): 313–19.

———. "Aragonese Naples and Medicean Florence: Musical Interrelationships and Influence in the Late Fifteenth Century." In *La musica a Firenze al tempo di Lorenzo il Magnifico,* ed. Piero Gargiulo, 15–45. Florence, 1993.

———. *The Cappella Giulia Chansonnier (Rome, Biblioteca Vaticana, MS Cappella Giulia XIII, 27.* 2 vols. Brooklyn, 1975–76.

———. *Music at the Aragonese Court of Naples.* Cambridge, 1985.

Azzopardi, Giovanni. "La cappella musicale della cattedrale di Malta e i suoi rapporti con la Sicilia." In *Musica sacra in Sicilia tra rinascimento e barocco: Atti del convegno di Caltagirone, 10–12 dicembre 1985,* ed. Daniele Ficola, 47–67. Istituto di storia della musica di Palermo, 5. Palermo, 1988.

Bacci, Pèleo. *Fonti e commenti per la storia dell'arte.* Siena, 1944.

Baggiani, Franco. *Monumenti di arte organaria toscana.* Pisa, 1985.

Baldini, Baccio. *Vita di Cosimo Medici, Primo Gran duca di Toscana.* Florence, 1578.

Banchieri, Adriano. *Conclusioni nel suono dell'organo.* 2d ed. Bologna, 1609; repr. Milan, 1934.

———. *Conclusions for Playing the Organ (1609),* trans. Lee R. Garrett. Colorado Springs, 1982.

Baralli, R. "Un frammento inedito di *discantus.*" *Rassegna Gregoriana* 11 (1912), cols. 5–10.

Barbieri, Patrizio. "On a Continuo Organ Part Attributed to Palestrina." *Early Music* 22 (1994): 587–605.

Barblan, Guglielmo. *Musiche della Cappella di S. Barbara in Mantova.* Florence, 1972.

————. "Vita musicale alla corte sforzesca." In *Storia di Milano*. Vol. 9, *L'epoca di Carlo V (1535–1559)*, 787–852. Milan, 1961.

————. "La vita musicale in Milano nella prima metà del Cinquecento." In *Storia di Milano*. Vol. 9, *L'epoca di Carlo V (1535–1559)*, 853–95. Milan, 1961.

Bargagli, Girolamo. *Dialogo de' Giuochi che nelle vegghie sanesi si usono di fare*. Siena, 1572.

Bargagli, Scipione. *Descrizione dell'entrata dell'Illustriss., e Reverendiss. Monsig. Ascanio Piccolomini, alla possessione del suo Arcivescovado in Siena Il dì XXJ di Novembre. 1589*. Siena, 1599.

————. *Le novelle di Scipione Bargagli*, ed. Luciano Banchi. Siena, 1873.

————. *I trattenimenti di Scipion Bargagli; dove da vaghe donne, e da giovani huomini rappresentati sono honesti, e dilettevoli giuochi, narrate novelle; e cantate alcune amorose canzonette*. Venice, 1587.

Bellissima, Giovanbattista. *Scipione Chigi, illustre senese ignorato, musicista, capitano del popolo, gonfaloniere*. Siena, 1922.

Beluze, Étienne. *Stephani Baluzii Tutilensis Miscellanea nova ordine digesta et non paucis ineditis . . . opera ac studio Joannis Dominici Mansi Lucensis*. 4 vols. Lucca, 1761–64.

Bendinelli, Cesare. *Tutta l'arte del trombetto*. Facsimile of the original Italian manuscript. Documenta Musicologica. 2d ser., vol. 5. Kassel, 1975.

————. *The Entire Art of Trumpet Playing, 1614*. English translation with critical commentary by Edward H. Tarr. Nashville, 1975.

Bent, Margaret. "New and Little-Known Fragments of English Medieval Polyphony." *JAMS* 21 (1968): 137–56.

———— and Roger Bowers. "The Saxilby Fragment." *Early Music History* 1 (1981): 1–27.

Benthem, Jaap van. "Was 'Une Mousse de Biscaye' really Appreciated by L'ami Baudichon?" *Muziek & Wetenschap* 1 (1991): 175–94.

Berger, Karol. *Musica Ficta: Theories of Accidental Inflections in Vocal Polyphony from Marchetto of Padova to Gioseffo Zarlino*. Cambridge, 1987.

Bergquist, Peter. "Lanfranco, Giovanni Maria." *New Grove* 10:441.

Berti, Duilio. "La Musica in Siena." In *Atti dell'Accademia del Conservatorio di Musica L. Cherubini di Firenze*, 13–27. Florence, 1931.

Bianciardi, Francesco. *Opera Omnia*, ed. Siro Cisilino and Lodovico Bertazzo. 6 vols. Padua, 1973–78.

Le Biccherne: Tavole, dipinte delle Magistrature Senesi (Secoli XIII–XVII), ed. L. Borgia, E. Carli, M. A. Ceppari, U. Morandi, P. Sinibaldi, and C. Zanetti. Rome, 1984.

Billeter, Bernhard. "Die Vocalkompositionen von Francesco Bianciardi." *Schweizer Beiträge zur Musikwissenschaft*, 3d ser., vol. 1 (1972): 133–41.

Blackburn, Bonnie J. "Music and Festivities at the Court of Leo X: A Venetian View." *Early Music History* 11 (1992): 1–37.

————. "On Compositional Process in the Fifteenth Century." *JAMS* 40 (1987): 210–84.

————, Edward E. Lowinsky, and Clement A. Miller, eds. *A Correspondence of Renaissance Musicians*. Oxford, 1991.

Bloxam, M. Jennifer. "'La Contenance Italienne': The Motets on *Beata es Maria* by Compère, Obrecht and Brumel." *Early Music History* 11 (1992): 39–89.

Blume, Clemens, and Guido M. Dreves, eds. *Analecta Hymnica Medii Aevi*. 55 vols. Leipzig, 1886–1922.

Bonnelli, Luigi. "Musici d'Avignone al servizio della signoria senese." *La Diana* 3 (1928): 229–31.

————. "Notizie intorno ad alcuni 'musici di palazzo' al servizio della signoria senese nel secolo XV." *BSSP* 30 (1923): 231–35.

Bonta, Stephen. "The Use of Instruments in Sacred Music in Italy 1560–1700." *Early Music* 18 (1990): 519–35.

Borghesi, Scipione, and Luciano Banchi. *Nuovi documenti per la storia dell'arte senese.* Siena, 1898; repr. Soest, 1970.

Borghezio, Gino. "La fondazione del Collegio Nuovo 'Puerorum Innocentium' del duomo di Torino." *Note d'archivio* 1 (1924): 200–66.

Bowsky, William M. *A Medieval Italian Commune: Siena under the Nine, 1287–1355.* Berkeley and Los Angeles, 1981.

Braghieri, Raffaella. "Il teatro a Siena nei primi anni del Cinquecento: L'esperienza teatrale dei pre-Rozzi." *BSSP* 18 (1986): 43–159.

Britio Trombetto and Antonio da Fabriano. *Terzina.* Siena: Simone di Niccolò and Giovanni di Alexando Carrai, 1511.

Brobeck, John. "Some 'Liturgical Motets' for the French Royal Court: A Reconsideration of Genre in the Sixteenth-Century Motet." *Musica Disciplina* 47 (1993): 143–80.

Brown, Howard Mayer. "Catalogus. A Corpus of Trecento Pictures with Musical Subject Matter." *Imago Musicae* 1 (1984): 189–243; 2 (1985): 179–281; 3 (1986): 103–87; 5 (1988): 167–241.

———. *A Florentine Chansonnier from the Time of Lorenzo the Magnificent.* 2 vols. Monuments of Renaissance Music 7. Chicago and London, 1983.

———. *Instrumental Music before 1600: A Bibliography.* Cambridge, Mass., 1965.

———. "Psyche's Lament: Some Music for the Medici Wedding in 1565." In *Words and Music: The Scholar's View . . . in Honor of A. Tillman Merritt,* ed. Laurence Berman, 1–27. Cambridge, Mass., 1972.

———. *Sixteenth-Century Instrumentation: The Music for the Florentine Intermedii.* Musicological Studies and Documents 30. American Institute of Musicology, 1973.

Brumana, Biancamaria, and Galliano Ciliberti. *Orvieto: Una cattedrale e la sua musica (1480–1610).* Historiae Musicae Cultores Biblioteca 58. Florence, 1990.

Buch, Laura Ann. "Seconda prattica and the Aesthetic of Meraviglia: The Canzonettas and Madrigals of Tommaso Pecci (1576–1604)." 2 vols. Ph.D. diss., University of Rochester, 1993.

Burkholder, J. Peter. "Johannes Martini and the Imitation Mass of the Late Fifteenth Century." *JAMS* 38 (1985): 470–523.

Caffi, Francesco. *Storia della musica sacra nella già cappella ducale di San Marco in Venezia dal 1318 al 1797.* Venice, 1854; repr. Bologna, 1972.

Camporeale, Salvatore. "Giovanni Caroli e le 'Vitae Fratrum S. M. Novellae.' Umanesimo e crisi religiosa (1460–1480)." *Memorie domenicane,* n.s., 12 (1981): 141–267.

Cantagalli, Roberto. *La Guerra di Siena (1552–1559).* Siena, 1962.

Cantata pastorale, Fatta per Calen di Maggio in Siena: per Rime, & Imprese nuova, e dilettevole. Siena: Luca Bonetti, 1589.

Cantini, Lorenzo. *Vita di Cosimo de' Medici Primo Gran-Duca di Toscana.* Florence, 1805.

Cantoni, Cristoforo. "Frammento di un Diario di Cristoforo Cantoni (Anno 1479–1483)." In Muratori, ed., *Rerum italicarum scriptores,* vol. 15, pt. 6/2.

Cardamone, Donna G. "Venturi, Pompilio." *New Grove* 19:625.

Carli, Enzo. *Il Duomo di Siena.* Siena, 1979.

———. *Scultura lignea senese.* Milan, 1951.

Caroso, Fabritio. *Il Ballarino.* Venice, 1581; repr. New York, 1967.

———. *Nobiltà di Dame.* Venice, 1600, 1605; repr. Bologna, 1970. Ed. Julia Sutton. Oxford, 1986.

Cartwright, Julia. *Beatrice d'Este.* London and New York, 1926.

Casanova, Eugenio. *La donna senese del Quattrocento nella vita privata.* Siena, 1901.

———. "Un anno della vita privata di Pio II." *BSSP* 38 (1931): 19–34.

Casimiri, Raffaele. "Musica e musicisti nella cattedrale di Padova nei sec. XIV, XV, XVI." *Note d'archivio* 18 (1941): 1–31, 101–214.

Catoni, Giuliano. "La faziosa armonia." In Alessandro Falassi, Giuliano Catoni, Giovanni Cecchini, and Pepi Merisio, *Palio,* 225–72. Milan, 1982.

——— and Sonia Fineschi, eds. *L'Archivio Arcivescovile di Siena.* Ministero dell'Interno, Pubblicazioni degli Archivi di Stato 70. Rome, 1970.

——— and Gabriella Piccinni. "Famiglie e redditi nella Lira Senese del 1453." In *Strutture familiari, epidemie, migrazioni nell'Italia medievale,* ed. R. Comba, G. Piccinni, G. Pinto. *Atti del convegno internazionale, Siena, 28–30 Gennaio 1983,* 291–304. Naples, 1984.

Cattin, Giulio. "Le poesie del Savonarola nelle fonti musicali." *Quadrivium* 12 (1971): 259–80.

———. "Rivisitati alcuni maestri e cantori cinquecenteschi della cattedrale di Vicenza." In *Scritti e memorie in onore di Mons. Carlo Fanton Vescovo ausiliare di Vicenza nel Cinquantesimo di Sacerdozio,* 187–200. Vicenza, 1982.

———, Oscar Mischiati, and Agostino Ziino. "Composizioni polifoniche del primo Quattrocento nei libri corali di Guardiagrele." *Rivista italiana di musicologia* 7 (1962): 153–81.

Cecchini, Giovanni. "L'archivio dell'opera del Duomo e il suo riordinamento e inventario." *BSSP* 60 (1953): 67–77.

———. *Il Caleffo Vecchio del Comune di Siena.* 4 vols. Fonti di storia Senese. Siena, 1931–84.

———. "Palio e Contrade nella loro evoluzione storica." In Alessandro Falassi, Giuliano Catoni, Giovanni Cecchini, and Pepi Merisio, *Palio.* Milan, 1982. Originally published in Giovanni Cecchini and Dario Neri, *Il Palio di Siena.* Siena, 1958.

Cellesi, Luigia. "Documenti per la storia musicale di Firenze." *Rivista musicale italiana* 34 (1927): 579–602; 35 (1928): 553–82.

———. "Il lirismo musicale religioso in Siena nel Trecento e quello profano nel Cinquecento." *BSSP* 41 (1934): 93–112.

———. "L'organo della cappella interna del palazzo comunale di Siena." *BSSP* 37 (1930): 498–509.

———. *Storia della più antica banda musicale Senese.* Siena, 1906.

Census-Catalogue of Manuscript Sources of Polyphonic Music, 1400–1550, compiled by the University of Illinois Musicological Archives for Renaissance Manuscript Studies. 5 vols. American Institute of Musicology–Hänssler-Verlag, 1979–88.

Chapman, Catherine Weeks. "Printed Collections of Polyphonic Music Owned by Ferdinand Columbus." *JAMS* 21 (1968): 34–83.

Chiancone Isaacs, Ann Katherine. "Popolo e monti nella Siena del primo Cinquecento." *Rivista storica italiana* 82 (1970): 32–79.

Christiansen, Keith, Laurence B. Kanter, and Carl Brandon Strehlke. *Painting in Renaissance Siena, 1420–1500.* Exhibition catalogue, The Metropolitan Museum. New York, 1988.

Ciampoli, Donatella. *Il Capitano del popolo a Siena nel primo Trecento.* Siena, 1984.

Ciardi Dupré, Maria Grazia. *I corali del duomo di Siena.* Milan, 1972.

Ciconia, Johannes. *The Works of Johannes Ciconia,* ed. Margaret Bent and Anne Hallmark. Polyphonic Music of the Fourteenth Century 24. Monaco, 1985.

Ciliberti, Galliano. "Diffusione e trasmissione del Credo nelle fonti mensurali del tardomedioevo (Nuove evidenze in Italia centrale)." *Musica Disciplina* 44 (1990): 57–97.

Cini, Giovambattista. *Vita del Serenissimo Signor Cosimo de Medici Primo Gran Duca di Toscana.* Florence, 1611.

Cipolla, Carlo M. *Money in Sixteenth-Century Florence.* Berkeley and Los Angeles, 1989.

Cirni Corso, Anton Francesco. *Entrata del Duca et Duchessa di Firenze in Siena.* Rome, 1560.

Cobin, Marian. "The Compilation of the Aosta Manuscript: A Working Hypothesis." In *Papers Read at the Dufay Quincentenary Conference,* ed. Allan Atlas, 76–101. Brooklyn, 1976.

Coelho, Victor. *The Manuscript Sources of Seventeenth-Century Italian Lute Music.* New York and London, 1995.

————. Review of *Tablature de luth italienne, dit Siena Manuscript (ca. 1560–1570).* In *Notes* 46 (1990): 1060–63.

Cohn, Samuel K., Jr. *Death and Property in Siena, 1205–1800.* Baltimore and London, 1988.

Constitutiones Sacri Capituli Metropolitane Senensis Ecclesiae. Siena, 1579.

Corso, Cosimo. "Araldi e canterini nella repubblica senese del Quattrocento." *BSSP* 62 (1955): 140–60.

Corteccia, Francesco. *Collected Sacred Works: Music for the Triduum Sacrum,* ed. Frank A. D'Accone. Music of the Florentine Renaissance 11. American Institute of Musicology, 1985.

Crawford, David Eugene. "Vespers Polyphony at Modena's Cathedral in the First Half of the Sixteenth Century." Ph.D. diss., University of Illinois, 1967.

"Cronaca Senese dei fatti riguardanti la città e il su territorio di autore anonimo del secolo XIV." In Muratori, *Rerum italicarum scriptores,* vol. 15, pt. 6.

Cummings, Anthony M. "Gian Maria Giudeo, Sonatore del Liuto, and the Medici." *Fontes Artis Musicae* 38 (1991): 312–18.

————. *The Politicized Muse: Music for Medici Festivals, 1512–1537.* Princeton, 1992.

————. "Toward an Interpretation of the Sixteenth-Century Motet." *JAMS* 34 (1981): 43–59.

Curtis, Gareth R. K. "Brussels, Bibliothèque Royale MS. 5557, and the Texting of Dufay's 'Ecce ancilla Domini' and 'Ave regina celorum' Masses." *Acta Musicologica* 51 (1979): 73–86.

D'Accone, Frank A. "Alessandro Coppini and Bartolomeo degli Organi—Two Florentine Composers of the Renaissance." *Analecta Musicologica* 4 (1967): 38–76.

————. "Le compagnie dei laudesi in Firenze durante l'Ars Nova." *L'Ars Nova italiana del Trecento* 3 (1970): 253–80.

————. "A Documentary History of Music at the Florentine Cathedral and Baptistry during the Fifteenth Century." Ph.D. diss., Harvard University, 1960.

————. "Heinrich Isaac in Florence: New and Unpublished Documents." *Musical Quarterly* 49 (1983): 464–83.

————. "Instrumental Resonances in a Sienese Vocal Print of 1515." In *Le Concert des voix et des instruments à la Renaissance: Actes du XXXIVe Colloque International d'Études Supérieures de la Renaissance, 1–11 juillet 1991,* ed. Jean-Michel Vaccaro, 333–59. Paris, 1995.

————. "A Late 15th-Century Sienese Repertory: MS K. I. 2 of the Biblioteca Comunale, Siena." *Musica Disciplina* 37 (1983): 121–70.

————. "Lorenzo il Magnifico e la musica." In *La musica a Firenze al tempo di Lorenzo il Magnifico,* ed. Piero Gargiulo, 219–48. Florence, 1993.

————. "Lorenzo the Magnificent and Music." In *Lorenzo il Magnifico e il suo mondo,* ed. Gian Carlo Garfagnini, 259–90. Florence, 1994.

————. "Music and Musicians at Santa Maria del Fiore in the Early Quattrocento." In *Scritti in onore di Luigi Ronga,* 99–126. Milan, 1973.

————. "Music at the Sienese Cathedral in the Later 16th Century." In *Trasmissione e recezione delle forme di cultura musicale,* ed. L. Bianconi, F. A. Gallo, A. Pompilio, and D.

Restani. *Atti del XIV Congresso della Società Internazionale di Musicologia (Bologna, 1987),* 3:729–36. Turin, 1990.

———. "La musica a Siena nel Trecento, Quattrocento e Cinquecento." In *Umanesimo a Siena: Letteratura, Arti Figurative, Musica,* ed. Elisabetta Cioni and Daniela Fausti, 455–80. Siena, 1994.

———. "The Musical Chapels at the Florentine Cathedral and Baptistry during the First Half of the 16th Century." *JAMS* 24 (1971): 3–50.

———. "The Performance of Sacred Music in Italy during Josquin's Time, c. 1475–1525." In *Josquin des Prez,* ed. Edward E. Lowinsky and Bonnie J. Blackburn, 601–18. London, 1976.

———. "The Sienese Rhymed Office for the Feast of Sant'Ansano." *L'Ars Nova italiana del Trecento* 6 (1992): 21–40.

———. "The Singers of San Giovanni in Florence during the Fifteenth Century." *JAMS* 14 (1961): 307–58.

———. "Some Neglected Composers in the Florentine Chapels, ca. 1475–1525." *Viator* 1 (1970): 264–88.

———. "Una nuova fonte dell'Ars Nova italiana: Il codice di San Lorenzo 2211." *Studi musicali* 13 (1984): 3–31.

———, ed. *London, British Library MS Egerton 3665 ("The Tregian Manuscript").* Renaissance Music in Facsimile 7. New York, 1988.

———, ed. *Music of the Florentine Renaissance.* 12 vols. American Institute of Musicology, 1963–95.

———, ed. *Siena, Biblioteca Comunale degli Intronati, MS K. I. 2.* Renaissance Music in Facsimile 18. New York, 1987.

D'Addario, Arnaldo. *Il problema senese nella storia italiana della prima metà del Cinquecento.* Florence, 1958.

D'Alessi, Giovanni. *La cappella musicale del Duomo di Treviso.* Vedelago, 1954.

———. "Maestri e cantori fiamminghi nella Cappella Musicale del Duomo di Treviso, 1411–1561." *Tijdschrift der Vereeniging voor Nederlandsche Muziekgeschiedenis* 15 (1939): 147–65.

D'Ancona, Alessandro. *La poesia popolare italiana.* Livorno, 1906.

Dati, Agostino. *Augustini Dati Senensis Opera.* Siena, 1503.

Del Grasso, Angolo di Tura. "Cronaca senese attribuita ad Agnolo di Tura del Grasso." In Muratori, ed., *Rerum italicarum scriptores,* vol. 15, pt. 6/1.

Di Bacco, Giuliano. "Alcune nuove osservazioni sul Codice di Londra (British Library, MS Additional 29987)." *Studi musicali* 20 (1991): 181–234.

——— and John Nádas. "Verso uno 'stile internazionale' della musica nelle cappelle papali e cardinalizie durante il Grande Scisma (1378–1417): Il caso di Johannes Ciconia da Liège." *Collectanea* 1 (1994): 7–74.

Disertori, Benvenuto. "L'Archivolatira in un quadro del Seicento." *Rivista musicale italiana* 44 (1940): 199–211.

Dixon, Graham. "The Performance of Palestrina: Some Questions, but Fewer Answers." *Early Music* 22 (1994): 667–75.

Dolmetsch, Mabel. *Dances of Spain and Italy from 1400 to 1600.* London, 1954.

Donati, P. P., et al. *L'Organo di Giovanni Piffero, 1519 del Palazzo Pubblico di Siena: Relazione di Restauro, Saggi, Rilievi di P. P. Donati, R. Giorgetti, R. Lorenzini, O. Mischiati, M. Nigi.* Estratto pubblicato in occasione della Tavola Rotonda tenuta il 25 Febbraio 1983 (Comune di Siena).

Downey, Peter. "A Renaissance Correspondence concerning Trumpet Music." *Early Music* 9 (1981): 325–29.

———. "The Trumpet and Its Role in Music of the Renaissance and Early Baroque." Ph.D. diss., Queen's University of Belfast, 1983.

Ducrot, Ariane. "Histoire de la Cappella Giulia au XVIe siècle." In *Mélanges d'Archéologie et d'Histoire de l'École Française de Rome* 75 (1963).

Dufay, Guillaume. *Opera Omnia,* ed. Heinrich Besseler. 6 vols. American Institute of Musicology, 1951–66.

Dunning, Albert. *Die Staatsmotette 1480–1555.* Utrecht, 1970.

Eustachio Romano. *Musica duorum,* ed. Hans T. David, Howard M. Brown, and Edward E. Lowinsky. Monuments of Renaissance Music 6. Chicago and London, 1975.

Fabris, Dinko. Review of *Tablature de luth Italienne dit Siena Manuscrit (ca. 1560–1570). Journal of the Lute Society of America* 20–21 (1987–88): 165–70.

———. "Tre composizioni per liuto di Claudio Saracini e la tradizione del liuto a Siena tra Cinque e Seicento." *Il Flauto Dolce* 16 (1987): 14–25.

Falletti, Clelia. "Le feste per Eleonora d'Aragona da Napoli a Ferrara (1473)." In *Spettacoli conviviali dall'antichità classica alle corti italiane del '400.* Centro di Studi sul Teatro Medioevale e Rinascimentale, Atti del VII Convegno di Studio, Viterbo, 27–30 Maggio 1982, 269–89. Viterbo, 1983.

Falletti-Fossati, Carlo. *Costumi senese nella seconda metà del secolo XIV.* Siena, 1882.

Fallows, David. *Dufay.* New York, 1982; repr. 1987.

Fasano Guarini, Elena. "Le istituzioni di Siena e del suo stato nel ducato Mediceo." In *I Medici e lo stato senese, 1555–1609, storia e territorio,* ed. Leonardo Rombai. Rome, 1980.

Fecini, Tommaso. "Cronaca Senese di Tommaso Fecini." In Muratori, ed., *Rerum italicarum scriptores,* vol. 15, pt. 6/2.

Fellerer, K. G. "Church Music and the Council of Trent." *Musical Quarterly* 39 (1953): 576–94.

Fenlon, Iain. "Essenga, Salvatore." *New Grove* 6:253.

Fétis, François-Joseph. *Biographie universelle des musiciens.* 2d ed. 8 vols. Paris, 1877.

Folgore da San Gimignano. *I Sonetti,* ed. Ferdinando Neri. Turin, 1917.

Frey, Herman-Walter. "Klemens VII und der Prior der päpstlichen Kapelle Nicholo de Pitti." *Musikforschung* 4 (1951): 175–84.

———. "Regesten zur päpstlichen Kapelle unter Leo X. und zu seiner Privatkapelle." *Musikforschung* 8 (1955): 58–73, 178–99, 412–37; 9 (1956): 46–57, 139–44.

Fromson, Michèle. "Themes of Exile in Willaert's Musica Nova." *JAMS* 47 (1994): 442–87.

Fumi, Luigi, and Alessandro Lisini. *L'incontro di Federigo III imperatore con Eleonora di Portogallo sua novella sposa e il loro soggiorno in Siena.* Siena, 1878.

Fusi, Daniele. "Le frottole nell'edizione di Pietro Sambonetto (Siena 1515)." Tesi di laurea, Università degli Studi di Siena, Facoltà di Lettere e Filosofia, Anno Accademico 1976–77.

Gallo, F. Alberto. "Alcune fonti poco note di musica teorica e pratica." *L'Ars Nova italiana del Trecento* 2 (1968): 49–76.

———. "'Cantus planus binatim': Polifonia primitiva in fonti tardivi." *Quadrivium* 7 (1966): 79–89.

———. "La danza negli spettacoli conviviali nel secondo Quattrocento." In *Spettacoli conviviali dall'antichità classica alle corti italiane del '400.* Centro di Studi sul Teatro Medioevale e Rinascimentale, Atti del VII Convegno di Studio, Viterbo, 27–30 Maggio 1982, 261–67. Viterbo, 1983.

―――. "Due trattatelli sulla notazione del primo Trecento." In *Memorie e contributi . . . offerti a Federico Ghisi,* vol. 1, pp. 119–30. Bologna, 1971.

―――. *Musica nel castello.* Bologna, 1992. English translation as *Music in the Castle,* trans. Anna Herklotz and Kathryn Krug. Chicago, 1995.

Gambassi, Osvaldo. *La cappella musicale di S. Petronio: Maestri, organisti, cantori e strumentisti dal 1436 al 1920.* Florence, 1987.

―――. *Il Concerto Palatino della Signoria di Bologna: Cinque secoli di vita musicali a corte (1250–1797).* Florence, 1989.

―――. "Origine, statuti e ordinamenti del Concerto Palatino della Signoria di Bologna, 1250–1600." *Nuova rivista musicale italiana* 18 (1984): 261–83.

Garosi, Gino. *Inventario dei manoscritti della Biblioteca Comunale di Siena.* 3 vols. Florence, 1978–86.

Garrison, Edward B. *Studies in the History of Medieval Italian Painting.* 4 vols. Florence, 1953–62.

―――. "Towards a New History of the Siena Cathedral Madonnas." In *Studies in the History of Medieval Italian Painting,* 4/1:5–22.

―――. "Twelfth-Century Initial Styles of Central Italy: Indices for the Dating of Manuscripts." In *Studies in the History of Medieval Italian Painting,* vols. 1–4.

Getz, Christine. "The Milanese Cathedral Choir under Hermann Matthias Werrecore, Maestro di Cappella 1522–1550." *Musica Disciplina* 46 (1992): 169–207.

Ghisi, Federigo. "Italian *Ars Nova* Music." *Musica Disciplina* 1 (1946): 173–91; musical supplement, 19–20.

―――. "A Second Sienese Fragment of Italian Ars Nova." *Musica Disciplina* 2 (1948): 173–77.

Giani, Archangelo. *Annalium Sacri Ordinis Fratrum Servorum B. Mariae Virginis.* 2 vols. Florence, 1618–22.

Giantempo, Maria, and Lucia Sandri. *L'Italia delle città: Il popolamento urbano tra Medioevo e Rinascimento (secoli XII–XVI).* Florence, 1990.

Giazotto, Remo. *La musica a Genova.* Genoa, 1951.

Giorgetti, Renzo. "Nota biografica su Giovanni Piffero e documenti inediti." In P. P. Donati et al., *L'organo di Giovanni Piffero, 1519, del Palazzo Pubblico di Siena,* 22–24. Siena, 1983.

Giovio, Paolo. *Lettere,* ed. Giuseppe Guido Ferrero. 2 vols. Rome, 1956.

Giusti, Anna Maria. "Libri Corali per il Duomo di Siena." In *Il Gotico a Siena,* 47–58. Florence, 1982.

Goldthwaite, Richard. *The Building of Renaissance Florence.* Baltimore, 1980.

Gonzato, Gemma. "Alcune considerazioni sull'Ordo Officiorum Ecclesiae Senensis." In *Le polifonie primitive in Friuli e in Europa: Atti del congresso internazionale, Cividale del Friuli, 22–24 agosto 1980,* ed. Cesare Corsi and Pierluigi Petrobelli, 247–93. Rome, 1989.

Gozzi, Marco. "Alcune postille sul Codice Add. 29987 della British Library." *Studi musicali* 22 (1993): 249–77.

Graduale secundum morem sancte romane ecclesie . . . Correctum per fratrem Franciscum de Brugis ordinis minorum de observantia. Venice: Antonio Giunta, 1515.

Grande Dizionario della Lingua Italiana. Turin, 1961.

Guerrini, Paolo. "Un martirologo senese del Trecento nella Biblioteca Queriniana di Brescia." *BSSP* 40 (1940): 57–63.

Haar, James. "Comes, Bartholomaeus." *New Grove* 4:589.

―――. "Cosimo Bartoli on Music." *Early Music History* 8 (1988): 37–79.

―――. "Ivo Barry." *New Grove* 9:430.

————. "On Musical Games in the 16th Century." *JAMS* 15 (1962): 22–34.

Haberl, F. X. "Die römische 'schola cantorum' und die päpstlichen Kapellsänger bis zur Mitte des 16. Jahrhunderts." *Bausteine für Musikgeschichte* 3: 189–296. Leipzig, 1888; repr. Hildesheim, 1971.

Haggh, Barbara. "Itinerancy to Residency: Professional Careers and Performance Practices in 15th-Century Sacred Music." *Early Music* 17 (1989): 358–66.

Hamm, Charles. "Musiche del Quattrocento in S. Petronio." *Rivista italiana di musicologia* 3 (1968): 215–32.

———— and Ann Besser Scott. "A Study and Inventory of the Manuscript Modena, Biblioteca Estense, α.X.1.11 (ModB)." *Musica Disciplina* 26 (1972): 101–43.

Harrán, Don. "Contino, Giovanni." *New Grove* 4:684–85.

Hayum, Andrée. *Giovanni Antonio Bazzi— "Il Sodoma"*. New York, 1976.

Heartz, Daniel. "Sources and Forms of the French Instrumental Dance in the Sixteenth Century." Ph.D. diss., Harvard University, 1957.

Hicks, David. "Sienese Society in the Renaissance." *Comparative Studies in Society and History* 2 (1964): 412–20.

————. "The Sienese State in the Renaissance." In *From the Renaissance to the Counter-Reformation: Essays in Honor of Garrett Mattingly*, ed. Charles H. Carter, 75–94. New York, 1965.

Hol, J. C. "Le veglie di Siena di Horatio Vecchi." *Rivista musicale italiana* 43 (1939): 17–34.

Hook, Judith. *Siena: A City and its History*. London, 1979.

————. *Siena: Una città e la sua storia*, Italian trans., with an introductory essay by Roberto Barzanti. Siena, 1988.

Hughes, Andrew. "Chants in the Rhymed Office of St. Thomas of Canterbury." *Early Music* 16 (1988): 185–201.

————. *Medieval Manuscripts for Mass and Office: A Guide to Their Organization and Terminology*. Toronto, 1982.

————. "Modal Order and Disorder in 13th-Century Rhymed Offices." *Musica Disciplina* 38 (1983): 29–51.

———— and Margaret Bent, eds. *The Old Hall Manuscript*. 4 vols. American Institute of Musicology, 1969–73.

Hughes, Dom Anselm. "The Birth of Polyphony." In *The New Oxford History of Music*, vol. 2: *Early Medieval Music up to 1300*, ed. Dom Anselm Hughes, 270–86. London, 1954.

Huglo, Michel. "A propos de la Summa artis musicae attribuée à Guglielmo Roffredi." *Revue de Musicologie* 58 (1972): 90–94.

Hugo. *De Sancti Hugonis actis liturgicis*, ed. M. Bocci. Documenti della Chiesa Volterrana, vol. 1. Florence, 1984.

Ilari, Lorenzo. *La Biblioteca Pubblica di Siena*. 7 vols. Siena, 1844–48.

L'Ingresso Solenne in Siena dell'Imperatore Federigo III e della Principessa Eleonora di Portogallo sua novella sposa, soggetto storico da rappresentarsi nella Piazza di Siena in occasione delle pubbliche feste d'Agosto di quest'anno 1833 onorate dall'augusta presenza delle altezze loro imperiali e reali Leopoldo II, Arciduca d'Austria, Gran Duca di Toscana, Maria Antonia, real Principessa di Napoli Sua Consorte, e Su. I. E. R. Famiglia. Siena, 1833.

Jachet of Mantua. *Opera Omnia*, vol. 1: *The Four Masses of Scotto's Print of 1554*, ed. Philip T. Jackson. American Institute of Musicology, 1971. *Opera Omnia*, vol. 3: *The Masses of the Flower for Five Voices, Book I (1561)*, ed. Philip T. Jackson. American Institute of Musicology, 1976.

Jeppesen, Knud. "Lauda." *MGG* 8, col. 31.

Jungmann, Joseph A. *The Mass of the Roman Rite: Its Origins and Development,* trans. Francis A. Brunner. 2 vols. New York, 1951–54; repr. Westminster, Md., 1986.

Kämper, Dietrich. *La musica strumentale nel Rinascimento.* Turin, 1976.

Kehr, Paul Fridolin. "Le bolle pontifiche che si conservano negli archivi senesi." *BSSP* 6 (1899): 51–102.

———. *Italia Pontificia.* 8 vols. Berlin, 1906–35.

Kirkendale, Warren. *The Court Musicians in Florence during the Principate of the Medici.* Florence, 1993.

Landi, Alfonso. *Racconto di pitture, sculture e architetture eccellenti che si trovano nel Duomo di Siena* (1655) (BCIS, MS C. II. 30).

Lanfranco, Giovanni Maria. *Scintille di musica.* Brescia, 1533.

Lanzoni, Francesco. *Le diocesi d'Italia dalle origine al principio del sec. VII.* 2 vols. Faenza, 1927; repr. 1963.

Lapini, Agostino. *Diario fiorentino di Agostino Lapini dal 292 al 1596,* ed. Giuseppe Odoardo Corazzini. Florence, 1900.

Larson, Keith A. "Condizione sociale dei musicisti e dei loro committenti nella Napoli del Cinque e Seicento." In *Musica e cultura a Napoli dal XV al XIX secolo,* ed. Lorenzo Bianconi and Renato Bossa, 61–77. Florence, 1983.

Lastri, Marco Antonio. *L'Osservatore Fiorentino sugli edifizi della sua patria. Terza edizione eseguita sopra quella del 1797, riordinata e compiuta dall'autore, coll'aggiunta di varie annotazioni del professore Giuseppe del Rosso . . . Tomo primo.* Florence, 1821.

Lederer, Josef-Horst. "Bianciardi, Francesco." *New Grove* 2:677.

Leech-Wilkinson, Daniel. "Il libro di appunti di un suonatore di tromba del quindicesimo secolo." *Rivista italiana di musicologia* 16 (1981): 16–39.

Liberati, Alessandro. "Nuovi documenti artistici dello Spedale di S. Maria della Scala." *BSSP* 33–34 (1926–27): 147–79.

Libri dell'entrata e dell'uscita del Comune di Siena. Registro 30° (1259, secondo semestre). Rome, 1970.

Libri dell'entrata e dell'uscita della Repubblica di Siena. Libro terzo a 1230. Siena, 1915.

Libri dell'entrata e dell'uscita della Repubblica di Siena. Libro quinto (a 1236) e Sesto (1246). Siena, 1929.

Libri dell'entrata e dell'uscita della Repubblica di Siena. Libro settimo a 1246–7. Siena, 1931.

Libri dell'entrata e dell'uscita della Repubblica di Siena. Nono libro a 1249. Florence, 1933.

Libri dell'entrata e dell'uscita della Repubblica di Siena. Decimo libro a 1249–50. Florence, 1933.

Libri dell'entrata e dell'uscita della Repubblica di Siena. Undecimo libro a 1251. Florence, 1935.

Libri dell'entrata e dell'uscita della Repubblica di Siena. Dodicesimo libro a 1251. Florence, 1935.

Libri dell'entrata e dell'uscita della Repubblica di Siena. Tredicesimo libro a 1252. Firenze, 1936.

Libri dell'entrata e dell'uscita della Repubblica di Siena. Quattordicesimo libro a 1253. Siena, 1937.

Libri dell'entrata e dell'uscita della Repubblica di Siena. Quindicesimo libro a 1253–54. Siena, 1939.

Libri dell'entrata e dell'uscita della Repubblica di Siena. Sedicesimo libro a 1255. Siena, 1940.

Libri dell'entrata e dell'uscita della Repubblica di Siena. Libro XXI (1259, primo semestre). Siena, 1970.

Ligi, B. "La cappella musicale del Duomo d'Urbino." *Note d'archivio* 2 (1925).

Lionnet, Jean. "The Borghese Family and Music during the First Half of the Seventeenth Century." *Music and Letters* 74 (1993): 519–22.

———. "Palestrina e la Cappella pontificia." In *Atti del II convegno internazionale di studi palestriniani,* ed. J. Bianchi and G. C. Rostirolla. [Palestrina, 1991].

———. "Performance Practice in the Papal Chapel during the 17th Century." *Early Music* 15 (1987): 4–15.

Lisini, Alessandro. *Il costituto del Comune di Siena volgarizzato nel MCCCIX–MCCCX.* 2 vols. Siena, 1903.

———. *Le feste fatte in Napoli nel 1465 per il matrimonio di Ippolita Sforza Visconti con Alfonso duca di Calabria.* Siena, 1898.

Liuzzi, Ferdinando. *La lauda e i primordi della melodia italiana.* 2 vols. Rome, 1935.

Llorens, J. M. *Capellae Sixtinae Codices musicis notis instructi sive manuscripti sive praelo excussi.* Studi e testi 202. Vatican City, 1960.

Lockwood, Lewis. *The Counter-Reformation and the Masses of Vincenzo Ruffo.* Venice, 1970.

———. "A Dispute on Accidentals in Sixteenth-Century Rome." *Analecta Musicologica* 2 (1965): 24–40.

———. *Music in Renaissance Ferrara 1400–1505: The Creation of a Musical Center in the Fifteenth Century.* Cambridge, Mass., 1984.

———, ed. *Pope Marcellus Mass.* New York, 1975.

Lorenzetti, Stefano. "Musica vis in animum. On the Relationship between Vocal and Instrumental Practice in the Pedagogical Treatises of the XVIth Century." In *Le Concert des voix et des instruments à la Renaissance: Actes du XXXIVe Colloque International d'Études Supérieures de la Renaissance, 1–11 juillet 1991,* ed. Jean-Michel Vaccaro, 39–50. Paris, 1995.

Lowinsky, Edward E. "Humanism in the Music of the Renaissance." In *Medieval and Renaissance Studies,* ed. Frank Tirro, 87–220. Durham, NC, 1982. Also in *Music in the Culture of the Renaissance,* 154–218.

———. *The Medici Codex of 1518: A Choirbook of Motets Dedicated to Lorenzo de' Medici, Duke of Urbino.* Monuments of Renaissance Music 3–5. Chicago, 1968.

———. "Music in the Culture of the Renaissance." *Journal of the History of Ideas* 15 (1954): 509–53. Also in *Music in the Culture of the Renaissance,* 19–39.

———. *Music in the Culture of the Renaissance and Other Essays,* ed. Bonnie J. Blackburn. Chicago, 1989.

Loyan, Richard. "Reson, Johannes." *New Grove* 15:756–57.

Luciani, Sebastiano A. "La musica in Siena." *La Diana* 3 (1928): 161–86.

———. *La musica in Siena* (Siena, 1942).

Luisi, Francesco. *Del cantar a libro . . . o sulla viola: La musica vocale nel Rinascimento.* Turin, 1977.

———. "La frottola nelle rappresentazioni popolaresche coeve." In *Trasmissione e recezione delle forme di cultura musicale,* ed. L. Bianconi, F. A. Gallo, A. Pompilio, and D. Restani. *Atti del XIV Congresso della Società Internazionale di Musicologia, Bologna, 1987,* 232–35. Turin, 1990.

———. "Musica in commedia nel primo Cinquecento." In *Origini della commedia nell'Europa del Cinquecento.* Centro Studi sul teatro medioevale e rinascimentale, XVII Convegno, Roma 30 settembre–3 ottobre 1993, ed. M. Chiabò and Federico Doglio, 261–311. Rome, 1994.

Lusini, Aldo. "Dante e le sue relazioni con Siena." *La Diana* 3 (1928): 81–103.

———. "Una curiosità musicale senese." *La Diana* 3 (1928): 303–5.

Lusini, Vittorio. *Capitolo della Metropolitana di Siena. Note Storiche.* Siena, 1893; repr. Siena, 1979.

———. *Il Duomo di Siena.* 2 vols. Siena 1911, 1939.

Maas, Chris. *The Theory of Music from the Carolingian Era up to 1400,* vol. 2. RISM, B III 2. Munich-Duisberg, 1968.

Macey, Patrick. "*Infiamma il mio cor:* Savonarolan *Laude* by and for Dominican Nuns in Tuscany." In *The Crannied Wall: Women, Religion, and the Arts in Early Modern Europe,* ed. Craig A. Monson, 161–89. Ann Arbor, 1992.

————. "The Lauda and the Cult of Savonarola." *Renaissance Quarterly* 45 (1992): 439–83.

————. "Savonarola and the Sixteenth-Century Motet." *JAMS* 36 (1983): 422–52.

La Magnifica et honorata festa fatta in Siena, per la Madonna d'Agosto, l'anno 1546. Con l'ordine delle livree, & altri giuochi fatti in essa. Siena: Alla Loggia del Papa, 1582.

Malavolti, Orlando. *Dell'Historia di Siena.* Venice, 1594; repr. Bologna, 1982.

Marchetti, Mino. *La chiesa madre e la madre della chiesa.* Siena, 1979.

Marcuse, Sybil. *Musical Instruments: A Comprehensive Dictionary.* New York, 1964.

Martin, William R. "Vecchi, Orazio." *New Grove* 19:584–86.

Mauro dei Servi, Fra. *Dell'una e l'altra musica,* ed. Frank A. D'Accone. Musicological Studies and Documents 44. American Institute of Musicology, 1984.

Mazzeo, Antonio. *Compositori senesi del 500 e del 600.* Siena, 1981.

Mazzi, Curzio. "La casa di maestro Bartolo di Tura." *BSSP* 3 (1896): 142–76; 4 (1897): 107–14, 395–402; 5 (1898): 81–8, 270–77, 436–61; 6 (1899): 139–46, 393–400, 513–19; 7 (1900): 300–24.

————. *La Congrega dei Rozzi di Siena nel secolo XVI.* 2 vols. Florence, 1882.

McGee, Timothy, J. "Dancing Masters and the Medici Court in the 15th Century." *Studi musicali* 17 (1988): 202–24.

Meconi, Honey. "The Manuscript Basevi 2439 and Chanson Transmission in Italy." In *Trasmissione e recezione delle forme di cultura musicale,* ed. L. Bianconi, F. A. Gallo, A. Pompilio, and D. Restani. *Atti del XIV Congresso della Società Internazionale di Musicologia, Bologna, 1987,* 163–74. Turin, 1990.

————, ed. *Basevi Codex. Florence, Biblioteca del Conservatorio, MS 2439.* Peer, 1990.

Meerseman, G. "Note sull'origine delle compagnie dei Laudesi (a Siena, 1267)." *Rivista di storia delle chiese in Italia* 17 (1963): 395–405.

Milanesi, Gaetano. *Documenti per la storia dell'arte senese.* 3 vols. Siena, 1854–56; repr. 1969.

Miscellanea Storica Senese, 5 (1898): 23–24, under "Notizie" signed by LS.

Mischiati, Oscar. "Documenti sull'organaria padana rinascimentale—I: Giovanni Battista Facchetti." *L'Organo* 22 (1984): 23–160.

Mompellio, Federico. "La cappella del Duomo da Matthis Hermann di Vercore a Vicenzo Ruffo." In *Storia di Milano,* 9:749–85.

Mone, F. J., ed. *Hymni Latini.* 3 vols. Freiburg im Breisgau, 1855.

Montauri, Paolo di Tommaso. "Cronaca Senese conosciuta sotto il nome di Paolo di Tommaso Montauri." In Muratori, *Rerum italicarum scriptores,* vol. 15, pt. 6.

Monteath, Kathryn Bosi. "Draghi, Bernardino." *New Grove* 5:606.

Morales, Cristóbal. *Opera Omnia,* ed. Higinio Anglès. Monumentos de la música española, vols. 11, 13, 15, 17, 20, 21, 24, 34. Barcelona, 1952– .

Morandi, Ubaldo, ed. *Le Biccherne Senesi.* Siena, 1964.

————, and Aldo Cairoli. "Dall'inventario del 1900. I libri corali." In *Lo spedale di Santa Maria della Scala,* 168–75. Siena, 1975.

Morrocchi, Rinaldo. *La musica in Siena.* Siena, 1886; repr. Bologna, 1969.

Moscadelli, Stefano. *L'Archivio dell'Opera della Metropolitana di Siena: Inventario.* Die Kirchen von Siena, Beiheft 1. Munich, 1995.

Motta, Emilio. "Musici alla corte degli Sforza: Ricerche e documenti milanesi." *Archivio Storico Lombardo,* 2 ser., 14 (1887): 29–64, 278–340, 514–61. Repr. as *Musici alla corte degli Sforza.* Geneva, 1977.

Muratori, Lodovico Antonio, ed. *Rerum italicarum scriptores . . .* 25 vols. Milan, 1723–51.

————. *Rerum italicarum scriptores. Raccolta degli storici Italiani . . . nuova edizione,* ed. Giosue Carducci, Vittorio Fiorini, and Pietro Fedele. Bologna, 1935– .

Nanni, Luigi. "La canonica della cattedrale Senese nei secoli XI–XII." In *La vita comune del clero nei secoli XI e XII. Atti della Settimana di Studi, Mendola, Settembre 1959,* vol. 2, pp. 253–59. Miscellanea del Centro di Studi Medievali, 3. Milan, 1962.

Nádas, John. "Further Notes on Magister Antonius dictus Zacharias de Teramo." *Studi musicali* 15 (1986): 167–82.

————. "Manuscript San Lorenzo 2211: Some Further Observations." *L'Ars Nova italiana del Trecento* 6 (1992): 145–68.

Nardi, F. D. "Concubinato e adulterio nella Siena post-tridentina." *BSSP* 96 (1989): 9–171.

Negri, Cesare. *Le gratie d'amore.* Milan, 1602.

Nerici, Luigi. *Storia della musica in Lucca.* Lucca, 1879; repr. Bologna, 1969.

Ness, Arthur. "The Siena Lute Book and its Arrangements of Vocal and Instrumental Part-Music." In *Proceedings of the International Lute Symposium, Utrecht 1986,* ed. L. P. Grijp and W. Mook, 30–49. Utrecht, 1988.

————, ed. *Tablature de luth italienne, dit Siena Manuscript (ca. 1560–1570). Facsimilé du Ms. 28 B 39 (ancienne Bibliothèque Scheurleer) La Haye, Gemeentemuseum.* Geneva, 1988.

Nugent, George. "Jacquet of Mantua." *New Grove* 9:456–58.

Obertello, Alberto. *Madrigali italiani in Inghilterra.* Milan, 1949.

Ongaro, Giulio Maria. "The Chapel of St. Mark's at the Time of Adrian Willaert (1527–1562): A Documentary Study." Ph.D. diss., University of North Carolina at Chapel Hill, 1986.

————. "Sixteenth-Century Patronage at St Mark's, Venice." *Early Music History* 8 (1988): 81–115.

Origo, Iris. *The World of San Bernardino.* New York, 1962.

Osthoff, Wolfgang. *Theatergesang und darstellende Musik in der italienischen Renaissance,* 2 vols. Tutzing, 1969.

Owens, Jessie Ann. "Il Cinquecento." In *Storia della musica al Santo di Padova,* 27–92. Padua, 1990.

Palazzo Pubblico di Siena: Vicende costruttive e decorazione, ed. Cesare Brandi. Milan, 1983.

Palestrina, Pierluigi. *Le opere complete,* ed. Rafaelle Casimiri et al. 34 vols. Rome, 1939–87; repr. Huntington Station, N.Y., n.d.

————. *Werke,* ed. Franz X. Haberl et al. 33 vols. Leipzig, 1862–1907; repr. Farnborough, 1968.

Palisca, Claude V. *Humanism in Italian Renaissance Musical Thought.* New Haven and London, 1985.

Paparelli, Gioacchino. *Enea Silvio Piccolomini, Pio II.* Bari, 1950.

Pecci, Giovanni Antonio. *Memorie storico-critiche della città di Siena fino agli anni MDLIX.* 4 vols. Siena, 1755–60.

————. *Storia del vescovado della città di Siena.* Lucca, 1748.

Pellegrini, Antonio. "Per l'arrivo di Cosimo I a Siena (1560)." *BSSP* 10 (1903): 165–82.

Peverada, Enrico. *Vita musicale nella chiesa ferrarese del Quattrocento.* Ferrara, 1991.

Piccolomini, Aeneas Sylvius, Pope Pius II. *I commentarii,* ed. Luigi Totaro. 2 vols. Milan, 1984.

————. *Memoirs of a Renaissance Pope: The Commentaries of Pius II,* trans. Florence A. Gragg, ed. Leona C. Gabel. New York, 1959. Abridgement of the edition in Smith College Studies in History, 22, 25, 30, 35, 43.

————. *Storia di due amanti di Enea Silvio Piccolomini in seguito Papa Pio Secondo, col testo Latino e la traduzione libera di Alessandro Braccio.* Capolago, 1832.

Piccolomini, Alessandro. *L'amor costante. Comedia del S. Stordito Intronato composta per la venuta dell'Imperatore in Siena L'anno del XXXVI.* Venice: Al segno del Pozzo, 1541.

————. *Della institution morale libri XII.* Venice, 1569.

Pirro, André. "Leo X and Music." *Musical Quarterly* 21 (1935): 1–16.

Pirrotta, Nino. *Li due Orfei.* Turin, 1969. English translation by Karen Eales as *Music and Theatre from Poliziano to Monteverdi.* Cambridge, 1975.

————. "Music and Cultural Tendencies in 15th-Century Italy." *JAMS* 19 (1966): 127–61.

————. "Zacharus musicus." *Quadrivium* 12 (1971): 153–75.

Planchart, Alejandro. "The Early Career of Guillaume Du Fay." *JAMS* 46 (1993): 341–68.

————. "Guillaume Du Fay's Benefices and his Relationship to the Court of Burgundy." *Early Music History* 8 (1988): 117–71.

————. "Guillaume Dufay's Masses: A View of the Manuscript Tradition." In *Papers Read at the Dufay Quincentenary Conference,* ed. Allan Atlas, 26–60. New York, 1976.

Ploeg, Kees van der. "Architectural and Liturgical Aspects of Siena Cathedral in the Middle Ages." In Henk van Os, *Sienese Altarpieces, 1215–1460,* 1. Mediaevalia Groningana 2. Groningen, 1984.

————. *Art, Architecture and Liturgy: Siena Cathedral in the Middle Ages.* Mediaevalia Groningana 12. Groningen, 1993.

Poggiali, Gaetano, ed., *Novelle di Autori Senesi.* 2 vols. Milan, 1815.

Polk, Keith. "Augustein Schubinger and the Zink: Innovation in Performance Practice." *Historic Brass Society Journal* 1 (1989): 83–92.

————. "Civic Patronage and Instrumental Ensembles in Renaissance Florence." *Augsburger Jahrbuch für Musikwissenschaft* 3 (1986): 51–68.

————. *German Instrumental Music of the Late Middle Ages.* Cambridge, 1992.

————. "Innovation in Instrumental Music, 1450–1510: The Role of German Performers within European Culture." In *Music in the German Renaissance: Sources, Styles and Contexts,* ed. John Kmetz, 202–14. Cambridge, 1994.

————. "Instrumental Music in the Urban Centres of Renaissance Germany." *Early Music History* 7 (1987): 159–86.

————. "Municipal Wind Music in Flanders in the Late Middle Ages." *Brass and Woodwind Quarterly* 2 (1969): 1–15.

————. Review of Osvaldo Gambassi's *Il Concerto Palatino della Signoria di Bologna: Cinque secoli di vita musicali a corte (1250–1797).* In *JAMS* 44 (1991): 328–32.

————. "The Schubingers of Augsburg: Innovation in Renaissance Instrumental Music." In *Quaestiones in musica: Festschrift für Franz Krautwurst,* 495–503. Tutzing, 1989.

————. "The Trombone, the Slide Trumpet and the Ensemble Tradition of the Early Renaissance." *Early Music* 17 (1989): 389–97.

Porta, Costanzo. *Opera Omnia,* ed. S. Cisilino. 25 vols. Padua, 1964–.

Prizer, William F. "Bernardino Piffaro e i pifferi e tromboni di Mantova: Strumenti a fiato in una corte italiana." *Rivista italiana di musicologia* 16 (1981): 151–84.

————. "The Frottola and the Unwritten Tradition." *Studi musicali* 15 (1986): 8–19.

————. "Lodovico Milanese." *New Grove* 11:306.

————. "Music at the Court of the Sforza: The Birth and Death of a Musical Center." *Musica Disciplina* 43 (1989): 141–93.

Prophylaeum ad Acta Sanctorum, ed. Socii Bollandini, vol. 76: *Martyrologium Romanum.* Brussels, 1940.

Provedi, Agostino. *Relazione delle pubbliche feste date in Siena negli ultimi cinque secoli.* Siena, 1791.

Reaney, Gilbert. "Zacharias." *New Grove* 20:609–10.

————, ed. Early Fifteenth-Century Music. 7 vols. American Institute of Musicology, 1977–83.

Reardon, Colleen. *Agostino Agazzari and Music at Siena Cathedral, 1597–1641.* Oxford, 1993.

——. "Music and Musicians at Santa Maria di Provenzano, Siena, 1595–1640." *Journal of Musicology* 11 (1993): 106–32.

Reese, Gustave. *Music in the Renaissance.* New York, 1954.

Regestum Senense, vol. 1: *Regesta Chartarum Italiae,* ed. Fedor Schneider. Rome, 1911.

Répertoire international des sources musicales. Munich and Kassel, 1960–.

Reynolds, Christopher. "The Counterpoint of Allusion in Fifteenth-Century Masses." *JAMS* 45 (1992): 228–60.

——. "Musical Careers, Ecclesiastical Benefices, and the Example of Johannes Brunet." *JAMS* 37 (1984): 49–97.

——. *Papal Patronage and the Music of St. Peter's, 1380–1513.* Berkeley and Los Angeles, 1995.

——. "Southern Pull or Northern Push?: Motives for Migration in the Renaissance." In *Trasmissione e recezione delle forme di cultura musicale,* ed. L. Bianconi, F. A. Gallo, A. Pompilio, and D. Restani. *Atti del XIV Congresso della Società Internazionale di Musicologia (Bologna, 1987),* 155–61. Turin, 1990.

Ricchioni, Vincenzo. "Le costituzioni del Vescovado Senese di 1336." *Studi Senesi* 30 (seconda serie, 5, 1914): 100–67.

Riccio, C. M. "Alcuni fatti di Alfonso I di Aragona." *Archivio storico per le provincie napoletane* 6 (1881): 411–61.

Rifkin, Joshua. "Pietrequin Bonnel." *New Grove,* 14:73.

Roche, Jerome. *North Italian Church Music in the Age of Monteverdi.* Oxford, 1984.

Roncaglia, Gino. *La cappella musicale del duomo di Modena.* Florence, 1957.

——. "Orazio Vecchi e le 'Veglie di Siena'." In *Musicisti della scuola emiliana,* ed. Adelmo Damerini and Gino Roncaglia, 83–89. Settimana senese XIII. Siena, 1956.

Rossi, A. "Documenti per la storia dell'arte musicale." *Giornale di erudizione artistica* 3 (1874): 161–73.

Rostirolla, G. C. "La Cappella Giulia in San Pietro negli anni del magistero di Giovanni Pierluigi da Palestrina." In *Atti del Convegno di studi palestriniani,* ed. F. Luisi, 99–294. Palestrina, 1977.

Roth, Adalbert. *Studien zum frühen Repertoire der Päpstlichen Kapelle unter dem Pontifikat Sixtus' IV. (1471–1484): Die Chorbücher 14 und 51 des Fondo Cappella Sistina der Biblioteca Apostolica Vaticana.* Capellae Apostolicae Sixtinaeque Collectanea Acta Monumenta 1. Vatican City, 1991.

Sacchetti-Sassetti, A. "La cappella musicale del Duomo di Rieti." *Note d'Archivio* 17 (1940): 121–70; 18 (1941): 49–88.

Sachs, Curt. *Sammlung alter Musikinstrumente bei der Staatlichen Hochschule für Musik zu Berlin.* Berlin, 1922.

Le sale della mostra dell'Archivio di Stato Siena. Rome, 1956.

Saltini, G. E. "Bianca Cappello in Siena." *Miscellanea Storica Senese* 3 (1895): 97–106.

Sanesi, Emilio. "Maestri d'Organo in S. Maria del Fiore (1436–1600)." *Note d'Archivio* 14 (1937): 171–79.

Sani, Bernardina. "Artisti e committenti a Siena nella prima metà del Quattrocento." In *I ceti dirigenti nella Toscana del Quattrocento,* 485–507. Florence, 1987.

Sansedoni, Giulio. *Vita del Beato Ambrogio Sansedoni.* Rome: Mascardi, 1611.

Sanudo, Marin. *La spedizione di Carlo VIII in Italia,* ed. Rinaldo Fulin. Venice, 1873.

Sartori, Antonio. *Documenti per la storia della musica al Santo e nel Veneto,* ed. Elisa Grossato, with an essay by Giulio Cattin. Vicenza, 1982.

Sartori, Claudio. "La cappella del Duomo dalle origini a Franchino Gaffurio." In "La musica nel Duomo e alla corte sino alla seconda metà del '500." In *Storia di Milano*. Vol. 9, *L'epoca di Carlo V (1535–1559)*, 723–49. Milan, 1961.

———. "Josquin des Près, cantore del Duomo di Milano (1459–1472)." *Annales Musicologiques* 4 (1950): 55–83.

———. "Matteo da Perugia e Bertrand Ferragut, i primi due maestri di cappella del Duomo di Milano." *Acta Musicologica* 28 (1956): 12–27.

Schoenberg-Waldenburg, Grazia. "I codici miniati senesi liturgici della Biblioteca Comunale di Siena dalla fine del sec. XIV alla fine del sec. XV." Tesi di laurea, 2 vols., Università degli Studi di Firenze, Facoltà di Lettere e Filosofia, anno academico 1973/74.

Schuler, Manfred. "Die Musik in Konstanz während des Konzils 1414–1418." *Acta Musicologica* 38 (1966): 150–68.

———. "Zur Geschichte der Kapelle Papst Martin V." *Archiv für Musikwissenschaft* 25 (1968): 30–45.

Scott, Ann Besser. "English Music in Modena, Biblioteca Estense, α. X. 1, 11 and other Italian Manuscripts." *Musica Disciplina* 26 (1972): 145–60.

Seay, Albert. "The 15th-Century Cappella at Santa Maria del Fiore in Florence." *JAMS* 11 (1958): 45–55.

Selfridge-Field, Eleanor. *Venetian Instrumental Music from Gabrieli to Vivaldi*. New York, 1975.

Sermini, Gentile. *Novelle,* ed. Giuseppe Vettori. 2 vols. Rome, 1968.

Sherr, Richard. "Competence and Incompetence in the Papal Choir in the Age of Palestrina." *Early Music* 22 (1994): 606–29.

———. "New Archival Data concerning the Chapel of Clement VII." *JAMS* 29 (1976): 472–78.

———. "Notes on Some Papal Documents in Paris." *Studi musicali* 12 (1983): 5–16.

———. "Performance Practice in the Papal Chapel in the 16th Century." *Early Music* 15 (1987): 453–62.

———. "Questions Concerning Instrumental Ensemble Music in Sacred Contexts in the Early Sixteenth Century." In *Le Concert des voix et des instruments à la Renaissance: Actes du XXXIVe Colloque International d'Études Supérieures de la Renaissance, 1–11 juillet 1991,* ed. Jean-Michel Vaccaro, 145–56. Paris, 1995.

Slim, H. Colin. "Fogliano, Giacomo." *New Grove* 6:687–88.

———. "Gian and Gian Maria, Some Fifteenth- and Sixteenth-Century Namesakes." *Musical Quarterly* 57 (1971): 563–68.

———, ed. *A Gift of Madrigals and Motets*. 2 vols. Chicago and London, 1972.

———, ed. *Musica nova*. Monuments of Renaissance Music 1. Chicago and London, 1964.

Smithers, Don L. *The Music and History of the Baroque Trumpet*. 2d ed. Carbondale and Edwardsville, 1988.

Southern, Eileen. "A Prima Ballerina of the Fifteenth Century." In *Music and Context: Essays for John M. Ward,* ed. Anne Dhu Shapiro, 183–97. Cambridge, Mass., 1985.

———, ed. *Anonymous Pieces in the MS El Escorial IV. a 24*. Corpus Mensurabilis Musicae 88. American Institute of Musicology, 1981.

Sozzini, Alessandro. *Diario delle cose avvenute in Siena dai 20 luglio 1550 ai 28 giugno 1555 scelto da Alessandro Sozzini,* ed. Gaetano Milanesi. Florence, 1842.

Sparti, Barbara. "Da Dante a Leonardo: La danza italiana attraverso le fonti storiche." *La Danza Italiana* 3 (1985): 5–37.

———, ed. *Guglielmo Ebreo of Pesaro. De pratica seu arte tripudii / On the Practice or Art of Dancing*. Oxford, 1993.

Staehelin, Martin. "Pierre de la Rue in Italien." *Archiv für Musikwissenschaft* 27 (1970): 128–37.

Stanze cantate al torneo rappresentato in Siena il dì XX. di Giugno. MDLXXVII. Siena: Apresso Luca Bonetti, 1577.

Starr, Pamela. "The Ferrara Connection: A Case Study of Musical Recruitment in the Renaissance." *Studi musicali* 18 (1989): 3–17.

———. "Music and Music Patronage at the Papal Court, 1447–1464." Ph.D. diss., Yale University, 1987.

———. "Rome as the Centre of the Universe: Papal Grace and Musical Patronage." *Early Music History* 11 (1992): 223–62.

Steib, Murray. "Imitation and Elaboration: The Use of Borrowed Material in Masses from the Late Fifteenth and Early Sixteenth Centuries." Ph.D. diss., University of Chicago, 1992.

Strehlke, Carl Brandon. "Art and Culture in Renaissance Siena." In Christiansen, Kanter, and Strehlke, *Painting in Renaissance Siena.*

Strohm, Reinhard. "European Politics and the Distribution of Music in the Early Fifteenth Century." *Early Music History* 1 (1981): 305–23.

———. *Music in Late Medieval Bruges.* Oxford, 1985.

Tagmann, Pierre M. *Archivalische Studien zur Musikpflege am Dom von Mantua (1500–1627).* Bern and Stuttgart, 1967.

Tarr, Edward. *The Trumpet.* Translated from the German by S. E. Plank and Edward Tarr. Portland, Ore., 1988.

Taucci, Rafaele. "Fra Andrea dei Servi organista e compositore del Trecento." *Studi storici sull'Ordine dei Servi di Maria* 2 (1934–35): 73–108.

Terni, Clemente. "Aspetti musicologici dei corali Piccolomini." In Maria Grazia Ciardi Dupré, *I corali del duomo di Siena,* 23–28. Milan, 1972.

Tizio, Sigismondo. *Historiarum Senensium ab initio urbis Senarum usque ad annum MDXXVIII* (FBNC, MS FN II. V. 140).

Torriti, Piero. *La Pinacoteca Nazionale di Siena: I dipinti dal XII al XV secolo.* 2d ed. Genoa, 1980.

Totaro, Luigi. *Pio II nei suoi Commentarii: Un contributo alla lettura della autobiografia di Enea Silvio de Piccolomini.* Bologna, 1978.

Trexler, Richard. *The Libro Cerimoniale of the Florentine Republic.* Geneva, 1978.

———. *Public Life in Renaissance Florence.* Ithaca and London, 1980.

Trombelli, Giovanni Crisostomo, ed. *Ordo Officiorum Ecclesiae Senensis ab Oderico Eiusdem Ecclesiae Canonico Anno MCCXIII Compositus.* Bologna, 1766.

Tyson, Alan. "The Mozart Fragments." *JAMS* 34 (1981): 471–510.

———. "The Problem of Beethoven's 'First' *Leonore* Overture." *JAMS* 28 (1975): 292–334.

Ugurgieri della Berardenga, Curzio. *Pio II Piccolomini, con notizie su Pio III e altri membri della famiglia.* Florence, 1973.

Ugurgieri-Azzolini, Isidoro. *Le pompe senesi o'vero huomini illustri di Siena.* 2 vols. Pistoia, 1649.

L'Università di Siena: 750 Anni di Storia. Siena, 1991.

Vander Straten, Edmond. *La musique aux Pays-Bas avant le XIXe siècle.* 8 vols. Brussels, 1867–88; repr. in 4 vols. New York, 1969.

Varanini, Giorgio, ed. *Cantari religiosi senesi del Trecento: Neri Pagliaresi, Fra Felice Tancredi da Massa, Niccolò Cicerchia.* Bari, 1965.

———, Luigi Banfi, and Anna Ceruti Burgio, eds. *Laude cortonesi dal secolo XIII al XV.* 4 vols. Florence, 1981–85.

Vecchi, Giuseppe. "Tra monodia e polifonia: Appunti da servire alla storia della melica sacra in Italia nel secolo XIII e al principio del XIV." *Collectanea Historiae Musicae* 2 (1956): 447–64.

Victoria, Tomas Luis. *Opera Omnia,* ed. Felipe Pedrell. 8 vols. Leipzig, 1902–13; repr. Ridgewood, N.J., 1965–66.

———. *Opera Omnia,* ed. Higino Anglès. Monumentos de la música española, vols. 25, 26, 30, 31. Madrid, 1965–68.

Vigo, Pietro, ed. *Carlo Quinto in Siena nell'aprile del 1536.* Scelta di curiosità letterarie o rime inedite 199. Bologna, 1884.

Vincenet, Johannes. *The Collected Works of Vincenet,* ed. Bertran E. Davis. Recent Researches in the Music of the Middle Ages and Early Renaissance 9–10. Madison, 1978.

Von Fischer, Kurt. "Una ballata trecentesca sconosciuta: Aggiunti per i frammenti di Siena." *L'Ars Nova italiana del Trecento* 2 (1968): 39–47.

———. "Das Kantorenamt am Dome von Siena zu Beginn des 13. Jahrhunderts." In *Festschrift Karl Gustav Fellerer,* 155–60. Regensburg, 1962.

———. "Die Rolle der Mehrstimmigkeit am Dome von Siena zu Beginn des 13. Jahrhunderts." *Archiv für Musikwissenchaft* 18 (1961): 167–82.

Wainwright, Valerie. "Conflict and Popular Government in Fourteenth-Century Siena: Il Monte dei Dodici, 1335–1368." In *I ceti dirigenti nella toscana tardo comunale. Comitato di studi sulla storia dei ceti dirigenti in Toscana. Atti del III Convegno: Firenze, 5–7 dicembre 1980,* 57–80. Florence, 1983.

Wegman, Rob C. *Born for the Muses: The Life and Masses of Jacob Obrecht.* Oxford, 1994.

———. "Petrus de Domarto's *Missa Spiritus Almus* and the Early History of the Four-Voice Mass in the Fifteenth Century." *Early Music History* 10 (1991): 235–303.

Weissman, Ronald. "Taking Patronage Seriously: Mediterranean Values and Renaissance Society." In *Patronage, Art, and Society in Renaissance Italy,* ed. F. W. Kent and Patricia Simons, 24–45. Oxford, 1987.

Welch, Evelyn S. "Sight, Sound and Ceremony in the Chapel of Galeazzo Maria Sforza." *Early Music History* 12 (1993): 151–90.

Wienandt, Elwyn. "Perino Fiorentino and His Lute Pieces." *JAMS* 8 (1955): 2–13.

Wilson, Blake. *Music and Merchants: The Laudesi Companies of Republican Florence.* Oxford, 1992.

——— and Nello Barbieri, eds. *The Florence Laudario.* Recent Researches in the Music of the Middle Ages and Early Renaissance 29. Madison, 1995.

Wolf, Johannes. *Handbuch der Notationskunde.* 2 vols. Leipzig, 1913.

Wright, Craig. "Dufay's *Nuper rosarum flores,* King Solomon's Temple, and the Veneration of the Virgin." *JAMS* 47 (1994): 395–439.

———. *Music and Ceremony at Notre Dame of Paris, 500–1550.* Cambridge, 1989.

Yonge, Nicholas. *Musica Transalpina.* London, 1588, 1597. Facs. ed. with an introduction by Denis Stevens. Farnborough, 1972.

Young, Karl. *The Drama of the Medieval Church.* 2 vols. Oxford, 1933.

Zdekauer, Lodovico. "L'Entrata di Carlo VIII Re di Francia, in Siena (1494, 2 Dicembre)." *BSSP* 3 (1896): 248–53.

———. "Statuti criminali nel foro ecclesiastico nei secoli XIII–XIV." *BSSP* 7 (1900): 231–64.

———. *Lo studio di Siena nel Rinascimento.* Milan, 1894; repr. Bologna 1977.

———. *La vita privata dei Senesi nel Dugento.* 2 vols. Siena, 1896–97; repr. Bologna, 1973.

———, ed. *Il Constituto del Comune di Siena dell'anno 1262.* Milan, 1897; repr. Bologna, 1983.

Ziino, Agostino. "Appunti su una nuova fonte di musica polifonica intorno al 1500." *Nuova rivista musicale italiana* 10 (1976): 437–41.

———. "Magister Antonius dictus Zacharias de Teramo: Alcune date e molte ipotesi." *Rivista italiana di musicologia* 14 (1979): 311–48.

———. "Polifonia nella cattedrale di Lucca durante il XIII secolo." *Acta Musicologica* 47 (1975): 16–30.

———. "Testi religiosi medioevale in notazione mensurale." *L'Ars Nova italiana del Trecento* 4 (1978): 447–91.

Zippel, Giuseppe. *I suonatori della Signoria di Firenze*. Trent, 1892.

INDEX